Resistance

HALIK KOCHANSKI

Resistance

The Underground War Against Hitler, 1939–1945

LIVERIGHT PUBLISHING COMPANY
A Division of W. W. Norton & Company

INDEPENDENT PUBLISHERS SINCE 1923

First American Edition 2022

First published in Great Britain in 2022 by Allen Lane, an imprint of Penguin Books,
under the title RESISTANCE: The Underground War in Europe, 1939–1945

Printed in the United States of America

Manufacturing by Lakeside Book Company

Library of Congress Cataloging-in-Publication Data

Names: Kochanski, Halik, author.
Title: Resistance : the underground war against Hitler, 1939–1945 / Halik Kochanski.
Other titles: Underground war against Hitler, 1939–1945
Description: First American edition. | New York : Liveright Publishing Corporation,
A Division of W. W. Norton & Company, Independent Publishers Since 1923, 2022. |
Includes bibliographical references and index.
Identifiers: LCCN 2021060824 | ISBN 9781324091653 (hardcover) | ISBN 9781324091660 (epub)
Subjects: LCSH: World War, 1939–1945—Underground movements. | World War, 1939–1945—
Occupied territories. | World War, 1939–1945—Jewish resistance.
Classification: LCC D802.A2 K63 2022 | DDC 940.53/36—dc23/eng/20220118
LC record available at https://lccn.loc.gov/2021060824

Liveright Publishing Corporation
500 Fifth Avenue, New York, N.Y. 10110
www.wwnorton.com

W. W. Norton & Company Ltd.
15 Carlisle Street, London W1D 3BS

1 2 3 4 5 6 7 8 9 0

To my brother Martin

Contents

PART THREE
Resistance in Action

Acknowledgements

I am grateful to the following for allowing me to examine and quote from archival material in their collections: The Trustees of the Imperial War Museum; The National Archives; Yale University, The Avalon Project; The Keeper of Archives, Polish Institute and Sikorski Museum; and St Antony's College Library, Oxford. I also wish to thank the hard-working librarians at The London Library, The British Library, the University College London Library, and the UCL School of Slavonic and East European Studies Library.

I am also grateful to Professor Amedeo Osti Guerrazzi, Andrzej Suchcitz, and Declan O'Reilly for sharing with me the results of their as yet unpublished research. I would also like to thank Marek Stella-Sawicki for allowing me access to a recently discovered and authenticated Polish document.

Many people have helped me in other ways with my research, by offering advice, support, and encouragement. I had the privilege of talking to a former member of the Dutch resistance, Anton Tek, shortly before he died, and he shared some of his memories of that time. My brother Martin, to whom this book is dedicated, read endless drafts of the manuscript; former British Army officers who are now members of the British Commission for Military History shared with me their struggles in understanding the background to the conflicts in the Balkans in the 1990s which they were attempting to resolve, many of which had their roots in the Second World War; and members of the Military History Seminar at the Institute of Historical Research offered much advice and encouragement, especially David French, Philip Blood, and Major General John Sutherell. My agent Robert Dudley has been very supportive throughout the whole process of writing this book; my editor Simon Winder provided many wise, constructive, and pertinent comments; Guillaume Piketty reviewed the entire manuscript and made some useful comments; the eagle eyes of my copy-editor Richard Mason saved me from many minor errors. Any errors that remain are, of course, my own.

1. Europe on the Eve of the Second World War
0
500 km
0
400 miles
North Sea
IRELAND
Dublin
GREAT
BRITAIN
London
Amsterdam
NETHERLANDS
Brussels
BELGIUM
LUX.
ATLANTIC
OCEAN
Paris
FRANCE
Berne
SWITZ.
PORTUGAL
Lisbon
Madrid
SPAIN
Corsica
Sardinia
ALGERIA (FR.)
MOROCCO (FR.)
TUNISIA
(FR.)

N
FINLAND
NORWAY
SWEDEN
Helsinki
Oslo
Stockholm
Tallinn
ESTONIA
Riga
LATVIA
Moscow
DENMARK
Copenhagen
LITHUANIA
SOVIET UNION
Vilna
EAST PRUSSIA
Minsk
Berlin
Warsaw
GERMANY
POLAND
Prague
CZECHOSLOVAKIA
Vienna
Budapest
AUSTRIA
HUNGARY
ROMANIA
Belgrade
Bucharest
YUGOSLAVIA
ITALY
BULGARIA
Sofia
Rome
ALBANIA
Tirana
Ankara
TURKEY
GREECE
Athens
Sicily
Mediterranean Sea
Crete
Cyprus

List of Illustrations

Every effort has been made to contact all copyright holders. The publishers will be pleased to amend in any future editions any errors or omissions brought to their attention.

Introduction

The aim of this book is to present a clear, balanced, and unified picture of the resistance in every country occupied by Germany or Italy during the Second World War. The advantage of looking at Europe as a whole is that it is possible to avoid the pitfalls of nationalism. It is natural for every nation that was occupied to take its own resistance story and retrospectively magnify its achievements: in a sense it was necessary for the post-war restoration of nationhood and self-respect. But this does tend to inflate the genuine heroism of the resistance into an epic myth, as in General Charles de Gaulle's famous speech in August 1944 which spoke of Paris, and indeed France, having been 'liberated by itself'. Moreover, a national perspective leads inevitably to claims that *x* country was the *only* one to do a certain thing, or *y* country was the *first* to do something, and this is what a Europe-wide history is able to correct. There was not, of course, a 'European resistance' as such – this would have been impossible – but there were common themes across the continent, and the balance between them varies from country to country. There were lessons to be learned, but the isolation of the conquered meant that each country or region had to decide how to respond to its occupation on its own, and the lessons it learned often could not be shared and had to be relearned elsewhere afresh. The only country which could really learn widely applicable lessons from the resistance was Germany, through its efforts to crush it.

An advantage of looking at all the occupied countries is that one can identify a very clear east/west divide in what the resistance fought for and especially in how the Germans responded. Even the Germans admitted that the Poles resisted from the first day of the occupation, largely in response to the drastic loss of nationhood inflicted by the dual occupation of the Germans and Soviets. In western Europe, however, there was a high degree of collaboration with native governments and administrations and the occupations were carried out with a much lighter hand. It can be argued that the reasons why the destruction of the villages of Lidice in the German Protectorate of Bohemia and Moravia and of Oradour-sur-Glane in France are held up as examples of German brutality lie in their rarity in countries where there was a high degree of collaboration with the occupiers. In eastern Europe and in the Balkans, such devastation and mass murder were the norm. Arguably, the severe repression which western Europe suffered at the hands of the Germans in early 1944 was not new in itself but merely the application of existing 'eastern' methods across a wider geographical area.

Two areas are often excluded from general histories of resistance: the Jewish resistance, and the German opposition to Hitler. This book covers the Jewish resistance because it is relevant to the themes explored in the text. The horror of the Holocaust affected not just the victims, the Jews, but also the bystanders, the non-Jewish populations who were suddenly exposed to the sight of the full barbarity of Nazi rule, and the apparent impotence of their native governments and administrations to save a portion of their population. The German 'resistance' is another matter and is not covered in this book. Germany was neither invaded nor occupied and in that sense there was nothing to resist. Much of the German opposition to Hitler was not anti-German and it did not want Germany to lose the war. Indeed, the aim of the actual plots against Hitler was to make Germany win, or at least save it from losing. The internal opposition within a conquering nation has nothing in common with the resistance in the countries it has defeated and occupied. Austria has been excluded for the same reason. Austria was termed 'the first victim of Hitler' by the meeting of the Allied foreign ministers in Moscow in 1943. But in 1938 the vast majority of Austrians had greeted the *Anschluss* with Germany with elation, many of them having longed for it for decades, and they fully participated in the furtherance of German war aims.

The book is divided into three parts following a broad chronology. The first part, 'Why Resist?', covers the period from March 1939 with the occupation of Czechoslovakia and Albania to the German invasion of the Soviet Union in June 1941. This is the period during which the Axis conquered most of Europe, quite possibly permanently, and the Allied armies were forced to leave the continent. It quickly became apparent that the level of resistance was dependent partly on the severity of the occupation regime and partly on the previous record of occupation suffered by each country. This is also the time when those who were pondering resistance had to consider how to resist. As one resister later explained:

> To resist, therefore. But how, when and where? There were no laws, no guidelines, no precedents to show the way. It was not like joining a church or a party or even a club. They all had rules and buildings. For resisting there were no rules and not even a skeleton of an organisation . . . [1]

The initial answers included the rescue of trapped Allied servicemen and the provision of intelligence to the Allies. Yet at the same time, others set out on a path of various degrees of collaboration with the occupiers. The majority settled for a policy of accommodation and *attentisme* – wait and see – opting to engage in neither resistance nor collaboration but to hold fire until it became clear who was going to win. As one early SOE agent in France reported, the French were 'still hoping for their [the Allies'] victory and many, many of them are willing to help but they would appreciate seeing something concrete besides retreating'.[2] During this period the clandestine press played a vital role in stressing the deleterious impact of the occupation and encouraging the people to become more resistance-minded. In Britain the Special Operations Executive (SOE) was set up, in Churchill's words, 'to set Europe ablaze', although it was clear that the fire of resistance was already burning.

The second part, 'Growing the Resistance', covers the period from June 1941, when Germany invaded the Soviet Union, to September 1943, when Italy surrendered. During this period new players appeared on the stage because the communists were now freed from the shackles imposed by the 1939 Molotov–Ribbentrop Pact and were encouraged by Moscow to engage in outright resistance to the Soviet Union's former ally, Germany. This is not to argue, as much communist historiography has done, that there was no resistance until the communists became involved. The impact of the German invasion of the Soviet Union also affected German policies in the occupation regimes across Europe, most notably through the imposition of forced labour and the Holocaust of Europe's Jews. Finally, Allied victories at Stalingrad and in the Western Desert made it clear to more people that German domination of their countries was neither permanent nor irresistible. All these factors combined to make resistance a more attractive proposition. It was during this period that the resistance began to grow dramatically. It was also the time when problems which emerged fully in the later stages of the war began to become evident, such as the debates over how to conduct resistance, the matter of command and control, and the question of whether the principal enemy was the occupier or the political opponents within the resistance.

The number of those engaged in overt resistance was still minuscule but the population as a whole was becoming more resistance-minded. This can be illustrated by two examples. In Warsaw, Jan Nowak was outside a building where a meeting with a fellow resister was to take place when he was questioned by a plain-clothed German on where he had just been. He spotted the brass plate of a female dentist on the door beside him and responded that he had just been there. The German rang the dentist's bell to corroborate Nowak's statement: 'The unknown woman, whom I had never seen and never would see, had not hesitated for a second. She understood in an instant that someone's life was at stake', and confirmed that Nowak was her patient.[3] The second example concerns Leesha Bos, a courier in Amsterdam. While carrying a gun, ration card and blank identity cards, she fled from a German street check on a bicycle and was pursued by a German also on a bicycle: 'Like a flash I got an idea and began to whistle the first four notes of Beethoven's Fifth Symphony in C minor. This was a whistle we used in the underground: if there was a friend nearby he would answer with the second part of the phrase: "bum bum bum bum".' There followed a sudden crash of bicycles as total strangers rode into the path of the pursuing German, knocking him off his bicycle and allowing Leesha to escape.[4]

The third part, 'Resistance in Action', covers the period from September 1943 to the end of the war in May 1945. As the Soviets advanced towards Germany and the Allies landed in Italy and France, the resistance could become more open in its activities. Now its effectiveness in supporting the Allies had to be explored. The question of command and control of the resistance came to the fore, and there are many examples of the resistance independently launching actions that had little chance of success in pursuit of the overarching goal, the liberation of their own country by themselves. The question of who was the enemy re-emerges with greater power than before, as the resistance in many countries was divided on political grounds and the threat of civil war proved to be very real in the battle for post-war supremacy. Again, the question asked in the first part, 'Why Resist?', also re-emerges as Hitler's satellites, Hungary, Romania, and Bulgaria, recognizing the imminence of the defeat of Germany, wanted to change sides and hence create a resistance to the Germans; at the same time, however, they faced the uncomfortable reality of the likelihood of liberation at the hands of the Soviets and the prospect of the imposition of a communist system.

This book focuses on the resistance to Axis occupation. Therefore, the resistance to Soviet occupation in eastern Europe, which existed from September 1939 to June 1941 and then again in 1944–45, is excluded. Resistance in those countries did not end with the conclusion of the Second World War, but continued for more than forty years, until the fall of the Soviet-sponsored communist regimes in 1989, and the situation the resisters had to face, both internally and internationally, was very different.

There are many names for those engaged in resistance to occupation, such as partisans, irregulars, franc-tireurs, guerrillas, maquis, resisters. I have adopted the common terms used in the historiography – partisans in eastern Europe and Italy; Partisans for Yugoslavia; maquis for France; and resisters as a general term. The one term avoided, except in quotations, is 'patriots', simply because this is such a highly emotive word, automatically bringing a value-judgement with it. In fact many of those who participated in collaborating movements saw themselves as patriots just as the members of the resistance did, believing that what they were doing was for the good of their country. The Germans used simpler terms – bandits in the east and terrorists in the west.

The society in which the resisters lived was of course very different from that of today. People were used to hardship and were familiar with death: for example, the supply of food was seasonal, child mortality was still high, and people generally died younger. It was a society in which people were used to making do with what they had and repairing things themselves. They would build their own radios and repair their own cars, though many still relied on bicycles and trains for transport. Most freight was transported by rail, making it extremely vulnerable to sabotage during the war. It was a much more localized and rural society in which a strong sense of community and solidarity against adversity existed: few travelled beyond their nearest town except for military service. Conscription and the prevalence of hunting meant that many men were familiar with the use of guns. In urban areas, loyalties and friendships often centred on the factories and other places of work where the same sense of solidarity often existed.

People often belonged to many associations and clubs – religious, sporting, hiking, student – which provided personal ties that could be exploited carefully to identify those others who might be keen to resist. But assumptions that all members would be like-minded could be cruelly overturned. For example, Erik Hazelhoff initially thought that all fellow members of the prestigious student corps at Leiden University would be as similarly outraged by the German invasion and the swift defeat of the Netherlands as he was, only to find that one of his friends and a fellow corps member promptly joined the Dutch SS.[5] When SOE agent Michael Trotobas was setting up the Farmer circuit in Lille he contacted his girlfriend from his time in the area when serving with the British Expeditionary Force in 1939–40, only to have his meeting place betrayed to the authorities by her father: he evaded arrest on that occasion.[6] Interest in politics was generally high. Before the horrors of Stalinism were known and accepted, communism was seen as an attractive alternative to the perceived failure of the capitalist system which was blamed for having caused the Great Depression. The right wing of politics was also strong, for example the extreme La Cagoule group attempted to overthrow the Popular Front government in France in 1937. During the Second World War some members of La

Cagoule would collaborate with the Germans, participate in the Vichy regime, or found their own right-wing parties; others would flee France and subsequently join the Free French in London or would remain in France and work in the resistance.

Pre-war society was still essentially very male-dominated and women often found a new sense of freedom and independence by serving with the resistance during the war. Few actually fired weapons but many proved their worth by undertaking the extremely perilous roles of couriers, carrying messages and contraband materiel from one group of resisters to another, as well as hiding those in danger, and working for the clandestine press. Campaigns for female suffrage had a long history in Europe, with many countries rewarding women for their sacrifices and work during the First World War with the right to vote. Similarly, the Second World War or shortly thereafter led to equal voting rights for women in the remaining countries such as France, Italy, Albania, Yugoslavia, and Greece.

The map of Europe was different at this time. After a post-First World War rebirth during which time Poland fought a succession of brief wars to establish her frontiers, the country was located further east than it is today. Cities mentioned in this book as Polish such as Lwów (Lviv), Vilna (Vilnius), and Nowogródek (Navahrudak) are now, after Poland was shifted westwards following the Second World War, in Ukraine, Lithuania, and Belarus respectively. Some countries no longer exist: the dissolution of the Soviet Union led to two of its former republics which were occupied by the Germans, the Ukraine and Belorussia, becoming independent countries. Under the pressure of the Second World War, two other countries broke up into their ethnic components: Yugoslavia and Czechoslovakia. After the war both were recreated and later again dissolved after the fall of communism.

Some historians and commentators have made efforts to explore who took part in the resistance by attempting to define the resisters by class or occupation. These efforts have been dismissed by many of those who took part in the resistance. For example, Lieutenant Harry Despaigne described those he fought alongside in France in 1944: 'Among my own people, we had communists to start with, we had socialists, royalists, Bonapartists, Right, Left and what have you. We had Jews, Muslims, Protestants, Catholics, unbelievers; we had Russians, French, Yugoslavs, British and Americans. We were really a multinational thing.'[7] Indeed, the most prevalent feeling among those who resisted was the discovery of the sheer variety of people who worked together during the war yet who in peacetime would have had no reason to be in contact with each other. Winston Churchill summed up the situation well in a BBC broadcast from July 1940:

> This is no war of chieftains or of princes, of dynasties or national ambition; it is a war of peoples and of causes. There are vast numbers not only in this island but in every land, who will render faithful service in this war, but whose names will never be known, whose deeds will never be recorded. This is a War of the Unknown Warriors; but let all strive without failing in faith or in duty, and the dark curse of Hitler will be lifted from our age.[8]

Those who took part in the resistance were not supermen and superwomen but were drawn from all walks of life. Some of the most heroic acts of resistance were performed by people who would not have been expected – even by themselves – to be heroes of any kind at all. Relatively few lived a continuous underground existence and the majority participated in normal life while taking part in resistance activities on occasion as and when needed.

The resisters also like to emphasize that their activities in the resistance did not preclude the majority from enjoying a normal life. Jean-Pierre Lévy described their lives:

> We lived in the shadows as soldiers of the night but our lives were not dark and martial. We were young and we were gay. We loved and we made love and we laughed ... There were arrests, torture, and death for so many of our friends and comrades, and tragedy awaited all of us just around the corner. But we did not live in or with tragedy. We were exhilarated by the challenge and rightness of our cause. It was in many ways the worst of times and in just as many ways the best of times, and the best is what we remember today.[9]

There are numerous examples of humour as the resistance loved to mock the Germans. For example, the Polish resistance, the *Armia Krajowa* (AK), was particularly adept at duplicating German posters but with their own message: so on the occasion when the Germans offered a reward of 10 million złoty for information leading to the arrests of the perpetrators of a heist which netted the AK over 100 million złoty, an AK poster appeared offering an identical reward for information enabling them to repeat the operation.[10] Or there is the sheer audacity of youths in Copenhagen who took a gramophone to the top of a high building and played at full volume 'It's a Long Way to Tipperary'.[11] Other events were accompanied by moments of sheer farce, such as when a party of saboteurs found that their positions along the railway line were betrayed in the bright moonlight by groups of curious cows revealing the location of each man. Fortunately, as the agent recalled, none of the Germans appear to have been country folk who would have recognized the reason for the behaviour of the herd. Or again, one can feel pity for the poor radio operator huddled over his set in a hayloft struggling to hear his messages from London because of a cockerel crowing in his ear.[12]

The occasional instances of fun and humour should not distract from the awareness of the horror which was ever-present:

> Danger was always there, one lived with it even if one was not conscious of it. Also muffled or buried was the strain of being the new you, the false you, of living a parallel, a paradoxical existence, of feeling totally free but trapped, of being integrated, true to oneself and yet marginal, disloyal or outcast, helpless yet almighty, of being shattered by the fate of a friend shot in the morning and yet, by evening, having forced him out of your thoughts. Instinctively, pushing death (your own and other people's) out of your mind, for the sake of survival.[13]

The names of the German-run concentration camps such as Auschwitz, Dachau, and Bergen-Belsen are well known, but for the resistance the threat lay in incarceration within their own countries in prisons such as Fresnes, Breendonk, Grini, or Pawiak, or facing execution in places such as Mont-Valérien, Tir National, or Palmiry; names as infamous in their own countries as the German ones. Many were sent under the *Nacht und Nebel* (Night and Fog) decree without judicial process to fester unknown in the concentration camps of Ravensbrück, Buchenwald, and Mauthausen. Many of these did not return home and in some cases their fate has never been ascertained. Most resisters were arrested by the Germans or Italians, but many were betrayed by their fellow countrymen, people who were used by the occupying authorities to infiltrate resistance networks for political reasons or sometimes just for financial gain or to settle a personal score.

One of the most admirable features of the resistance in all its forms – armed, civilian, and passive – rests in the sheer resilience of those who took part. The resisters were determined to thwart the designs of the Germans, to harass them, to deny them the opportunity to ever exert total control over the peoples of Europe. As the Germans broke up networks again and again, the persistence of the resisters in their belief in the righteousness of their cause led them to rebuild the structures each time and continue to develop the membership to renew the fight against occupation so that the flames of resistance could never be extinguished.

PART ONE

Why Resist?

I
The Shock of Defeat

From the perspective of resistance it is essential to begin the narrative before a single shot had been fired in the Second World War, with the German-inspired dismemberment of Czechoslovakia in March 1939 and the Italian invasion of Albania a month later. Both these occupations reveal a great deal about the rationales lying behind the Axis desire for predominance in Europe, how they intended to rule the countries they conquered, and how the native people were likely to respond.

Czechoslovakia was a post-First World War 'successor state', born out of the collapse of the Austro-Hungarian Empire and the defeat of Germany. It was an artificial construct, based around the Czech lands which had formed the kingdom of Bohemia in the fourteenth century but had since then been under the domination of the Austrian Habsburgs, coupled with the Slovaks and Ruthenes who had been part of Hungary since the eleventh century. In addition, the northern part of the country, the Sudetenland, contained a large number of Germans, and the area around Teschen was disputed between the Czechs and the Poles. In the interwar period the country had to face the challenge of drawing together the predominantly industrialized and Protestant Czechs with the dominantly Roman Catholic and largely agricultural Slovaks.[1] A factor in Hitler's popularity in Germany was his determination not just to reverse the territorial losses forced on Germany by the 1919 Treaty of Versailles but to argue that Germany also had the right to include all Germans residing outside the country in an expanded Reich. The Great Powers had raised no objection to the 1938 *Anschluss* with Austria, so Hitler now turned his attention to demanding the incorporation of the Sudetenland within the Reich, and with the Munich Agreement of September 1938 he achieved his aim.

The loss of the Sudetenland was a death blow to Czechoslovak independence since it meant the loss of nearly a third of its territory, all of her modern fortifications, and a portion of her industry. It revealed the impotence of the Great Powers to stand up to Hitler. Only the Soviet Union had appeared ready to defend Czechoslovak territorial integrity and these lessons were not forgotten during the Second World War. The loss of the Sudetenland fundamentally undermined the ability of the rest of Czechoslovakia to remain an independent state. The Germans and Slovaks now combined forces to weaken the country further from the outside and inside. For the Germans, acquiring the rump of Czechoslovakia represented the first stage in achieving their long-term aim, that of expanding German *Lebensraum* – living space – at the expense of the Slavs living in 'Germanic' territory. The Slovak leader and a Roman Catholic priest, Jozef Tiso, met Hitler on 13 March 1939 to discuss the possibility of establishing an independent Slovak state with German support. On the following day, Tiso issued a declaration of Slovak independence. At his trial in March 1947 he argued: 'Without the pressure exercised by Hitler, the Slovak Diet would never have voted in favour of the independence of Slovakia.'[2] Hitler had ordered the chief of the Wehrmacht, Field Marshal Wilhelm Keitel, to prepare the army for invasion of Bohemia and Moravia as early as December 1938: 'on the assumption that no appreciable resistance is to be expected'.[3] He now summoned the Czech president, Emil Hácha, to Berlin and during all-night negotiations effectively bullied him into accepting the German occupation of Bohemia and Moravia in line with Hitler's 'intention of taking the Czech people under the protection of the German Reich and of guaranteeing them an autonomous development of their ethnic life as suited their character'.[4]

German troops crossed into Bohemia and Moravia at 6 a.m. on 15 March. Prague Radio ordered the population not to resist. Peter Wilkinson, a British intelligence officer stationed in Prague, witnessed the German entry into the city:

> It was miserable weather; wet snow was falling and the sky was heavily overcast. The civilians who watched the proceedings on their way to work looked utterly defeated and gazed blankly as the troop carriers went by with the Germans, in smart uniforms and without greatcoats despite the freezing weather, sitting upright with their rifles between their knees. Some of the older people were in tears and the children on their way to school looked on goggle-eyed but there was no sign of any hostile demonstration; everyone seemed completely cowed.[5]

On the evening of 16 March, Hácha broadcast to the nation that the last twenty years of Czechoslovak independence had 'proved to be a short episode in our national history' and urged the people to accept the new state of affairs and their new masters.[6] Unnoticed at the time, the British helped the head of Czech intelligence, Colonel František Moravec, to fly himself and eleven of his most prized colleagues out of the country. From exile the former president, Edvard Beneš, offered a very different perspective: he would fight diplomatically for the restoration of the independence and territorial integrity of Czechoslovakia, and one of his tools would be support for resistance. But this lay in the future and for the time being it was apparent to the Czechs that only a major war could change the status of their country and offer the hope of an end to the German occupation.[7]

Slovakia was now an independent country and was recognized as such by twenty-seven countries, including Britain, France, and the Soviet Union. But in practice Slovakia was effectively a German protectorate, even though it was never described as such. Germans controlled Slovak foreign policy, and German advisers present in every government department served as advisers to the Slovak ministers. A German military mission exercised a degree of control over the Slovak army.[8]

In April 1939 the Czech lands of Bohemia and Moravia were formally turned into a German protectorate with the appointment of Konstantin von Neurath as Reichsprotektor and the Sudeten German Karl Frank as state secretary. Under von Neurath there operated a Czech government with Hácha remaining as president and Alois Eliáš as prime minister. As with Slovakia, Czech independence was illusory, with German control over foreign policy, military affairs, customs, and finance, and German advisers *in situ* in every ministry.[9] The Nazi racial theorist Wilhelm Stuckart defined German policy towards the Protectorate: 'the Czechs should be treated in a conciliatory manner, though with great strictness and relentless consistency . . . The autonomy of the Protectorate should be restricted only if absolutely necessary.'[10] This was the German ideal of an occupation: German control would appear nominal so long as the native government did exactly as it was told. Eliáš was deeply concerned lest the Czechs be viewed as German collaborators. In June 1939 he secretly made contact with the exiled Czechs and informed Beneš that he and his ministers remained in office solely to protect the Czechs from the Germans, but were prepared to resign should Beneš call for it. The call was not made then and Eliáš maintained secret contacts with the Czechs in London, ultimately paying for them with his life.

Hitler was not the only statesman who resented the post-war settlements: so did Mussolini. In the 1915 Treaty of London which had brought Italy into the First World War, the Entente had promised Italy, among other things, the Albanian port of Vlorë and a protectorate over central Albania, but the post-war peace treaties restored an independent Albania under King Zog. Yet Albania was a country with fundamental internal weaknesses. The country was extremely mountainous and contained almost no industry and conducted little trade. The population was largely tribal, split between the Ghegs of the north and the Tosks of the south, and neither tribe owed much allegiance to the central government in Tirana. Moreover, the Albanians coveted the province of Kosovo whose population was largely Albanian but had been given to the new state of Yugoslavia after the First World War.[11] The situation was therefore ripe for exploitation.

Like Hitler, Mussolini wanted more land for the Italians – *spazio vitale* – and ultimately sought to dominate the whole of the Mediterranean. The conquest of Albania was entrusted to his son-in-law and foreign minister, Count Galeazzo Ciano. On 7 April 1939 the Italian Army invaded Albania and met little resistance, except at Durrës, where 3,000 men under the leadership of Abas Kupi held the Italians at bay until tanks were brought up. Abas Kupi would later emerge as a significant leader of the resistance. Meanwhile King Zog, concerned for the safety of his wife Queen Geraldine and his two-day-old son, had first taken refuge in the American consulate before crossing the frontier into exile. Eventually arriving in London, he would be treated there as an honoured guest but *not* as the leader of an occupied country since Britain, along with many other countries, recognized the Italian occupation of Albania as final: they had long held doubts regarding Albania's ability to maintain an independent existence. The Italians set up a collaborationist government under Shefqet Vërlaci but left it few powers. Albanian ministers were appointed by the Italians, and each had an Italian adviser working with him who was directly responsible to the Lieutenant General of Albania, Francesco Jacomoni.[12]

Poland was not a 'successor state' since the country had existed as the Polish-Lithuanian Commonwealth until the eighteenth century when she had been subjected to three successive partitions by her rapacious and powerful neighbours, Russia, Prussia, and Austria, and effectively wiped off the map as an independent state until 1918. Poland suffered a fiery rebirth, fighting six wars with her neighbours until her frontiers were finally settled by an international treaty in 1921. Both Germany and the Soviet Union regarded Poland as 'the bastard of Versailles' and sought to destroy it. But Britain and France, disillusioned with their ability to control Hitler after the invasion of Czechoslovakia, had guaranteed Poland's existence. Therefore, if Germany invaded Poland it would mean a world war. By securing a treaty with the Soviet Union in August 1939, the Molotov–Ribbentrop Pact, Hitler put himself in a position to take the gamble. A secret protocol to the Pact effectively agreed the fourth partition of Poland.

On 1 September 1939 a new form of warfare was born – *Blitzkrieg*, or lightning war – as German armies poured across the Polish frontier from three directions simultaneously; the Luftwaffe bombed cities and towns, columns of soldiers and refugees. Britain and France duly declared war on Germany on 3 September, but did little else. By the end of the first week Polish armies were in full-scale retreat and the first German columns had reached the outskirts of Warsaw. Despite a brave counter-attack the Poles were pushed back further to the east until, on 17 September, the death blow to the Polish Second Republic was delivered when the Soviet Union invaded from the east. The government fled to Romania, where it was interned. The Polish commander-in-chief ordered the remnants of the army and air force to make for neutral Romania and Hungary and on from there to France to re-form. Warsaw fell on 28 September, although the fighting continued in Poland for another few weeks. In France, General Władysław Sikorski headed a new government under a new president, Władysław Raczkiewicz. Poland had a long tradition of resistance to occupation and of launching uprisings, and the flame of resistance was ignited even as Warsaw fell. The Germans granted Warsaw a forty-eight-hour window for the Poles to gather together all their weapons. Young Poles hid these weapons, cleaned, oiled, and wrapped in oilskins, in the graves dug for the victims of the German onslaught. One participant, Alexander Maisner, noted: 'This entire operation was properly organised (i.e. the weapons were all listed as were their hidden whereabouts) by the nascent Polish underground army.'[13] The defender of Warsaw, General Juliusz Rómmel, had entrusted organization of the resistance to General Michał Karaszewicz-Tokarzewski before going into German captivity.[14]

Hitler's settlement of Poland reflected both his desire for *Lebensraum* and his racial policies. The Soviet Union held the eastern half of pre-war Poland and incorporated that territory into the Soviet Union. The Germans, however, split their half of Poland further. The western area, including the cities of Danzig, Poznań, and Łódź, were annexed to the Reich and divided between two new *Reichsgauen*, Danzig-West Prussia and Warthegau, ruled over respectively by two ardent Nazis, Albert Forster and Arthur Greiser. Polish Upper Silesia was added to German Silesia. The Polish populations of these areas were subjected to a racial screening and those deemed not German enough were deported during the winter of 1939–40 into the General Government, the rump of Poland now ruled over by Hans Frank, a leading Nazi lawyer.

The Czechs, although they were Slavs, were largely protected from the full impact of Nazi racial policies because of the importance of Czech war industries to the German war effort. No such protection applied to the Poles, and Poland was to become the playground and training ground of Nazi racial theories. Collaboration by Poland's administrators was neither sought nor wanted except at the lowest level. Heinrich Himmler, Reichsführer of the SS, stated: 'It is essential that the great German people should consider it as its major task to destroy all Poles.' Hans Frank spoke of the Poles as 'the slaves of the Greater German Reich', and that Poland was to become a 'giant reservoir of labour' for the Germans. Jews were considered even lower on the ladder than the Poles, their very existence only tolerated until a more final solution to them could be devised. Education in Poland above primary level was abolished and the Germans also eradicated all symbols of Polish statehood, stealing or destroying Polish works of art. The country was subjected to economic exploitation, and by February 1941 the Germans had taken control of over 85,000 industrial concerns and over 120,000 commercial enterprises from the Poles.[15] For the Poles the answer to the question of why to resist was easy: they had to do so in order to survive.

Hitler had wanted to attack western Europe in the autumn of 1939 in order to knock out both France and Britain before turning his full attention to attack his arch-enemy, the Soviet Union. His army high command, however, persuaded him that the Polish campaign had demonstrated that the Wehrmacht needed further training and preparation before taking on an enemy with an army of the calibre of France's.

The German invasion of Scandinavia was deemed necessary because control over the lengthy Norwegian coastline would blunt Britain's strategy of naval blockade which had so undermined the war effort of the Central Powers during the First World War. Denmark lay on the way to Norway and on 9 April 1940 the Germans advanced into the country. Denmark had been neutral during the First World War and had had a history of good relations with Germany ever since the catastrophic defeat of Danish forces at the hands of the Prussians in 1864. Danish resistance to the German invasion would have been a pointless waste of life since Denmark had a small army and no strategic defence line on the frontier. The settlement with the Germans was ideal from the point of view of both sides. The coalition government under Thorvald Stauning would continue in office and King Christian X would remain on his throne. The German military presence of around 200 men was deliberately kept low-key and the German military commander, General Kurt Lüdtke, took no part in the administration of the country. Indeed, the German soldiers were instructed: 'You are not entering an enemy country but are marching into Denmark to ensure its protection and the safety of its people.' Danish-German relations were maintained through the German foreign office in the form of its ambassador, Cecil von Renthe-Fink. To all appearances, Denmark was not a participant in the war.[16]

The Germans would ideally have liked a similar solution to be applied to Norway when they invaded that country on 9 April, but circumstances dictated otherwise. In the first place the German high command was infuriated by the resistance put up by the small Norwegian forces, especially the sinking of the German heavy cruiser *Blücher* in Oslo fjord on the first day. There is evidence to suggest that the government under Johan Nygaardsvold would have settled for a solution on the same basis as the Danes had it not been for the conduct of one man, Vidkun Quisling. On the evening of 9 April, as the king and his government fled northwards, Quisling broadcast over the radio, claiming that by abandoning Oslo the government had effectively lost its right to rule and that consequently the *Nasjonal Samling* (NS) was taking over: 'By virtue of circumstances and of the national aims of our movement, we are the only people who can do this and thereby save the country from the desperate situation brought upon us by the party politicians.'[17] There is no doubt that this was treachery, and it was this treason that determined King Haakon VII not to negotiate with the Germans so long as the Germans insisted on Quisling being prime minister.[18] Consequently, on 19 April Hitler appointed Josef Terboven as Reichskommissar. An additional complicating factor was the arrival of an Anglo-French-Polish expeditionary force in Norway in the middle of April. This force initially strengthened the Norwegian defences but was ill-equipped to deal any substantial blow to the Germans and began to be withdrawn at the end of the month.

This left Norwegian affairs and indeed the Norwegians themselves in a state of considerable confusion. The Germans could see that rule by Quisling and his NS party would have little popular support. The opportunity of further negotiations directly with the king was ended when he departed for Britain with most of his ministers on 10 June. Three days later Terboven convened the Norwegian parliament to offer a compromise: in return for relieving the king of his duties and dismissing the Nygaardsvold cabinet, Terboven would stand aside and let the Norwegians govern themselves along the lines of the Danish model. King Haakon refused to accept the deal. Further negotiations over the next few months failed, and on 25 September 1940 Terboven announced the formation of a commissarial government, the deposition of the king and the abolition of the powers of the Nygaardsvold government. All political parties other than the NS were abolished, and nine of the thirteen ministers in the new government belonged to the NS. In a broadcast on the following day Quisling announced his plans: 'Our ideas are those which will be a new foundation for the rebuilding of the Norwegian state and society, and that means a new order in the pattern of Norwegian life.' In effect, Quisling and the NS planned to revolutionize Norwegian society on the back of German bayonets.[19] Churchill spoke publicly of how 'a vile race of Quislings – to use the new word, which will carry the scorn of mankind down the centuries – is hired to fawn upon the conqueror, to "collaborate" in his designs and to enforce his rule upon their fellow countrymen while grovelling low themselves'.[20]

The combination of a high German presence and the existence of the NS lowered the prospects of resistance since clandestine activity could come to their notice quickly. The terrain of the country also militated against the build-up of resistance forces since much of it was mountainous and sub-arctic which meant scarce and vulnerable shelter and food supplies had to be secured. Finally, the course of the war suggested that resistance was futile. The lack of fighting prowess demonstrated by the Allies had not impressed the Norwegians. Men did begin to sail to Britain in small boats from the Norwegian west coast but in general, as Otto Kaurin Nielsen recalled: 'We were cautious in the beginning. We had families to take care of. Why the devil should we fight? It was stupid to try to get to England. People were lukewarm. The general concern was: How can we protect our families?'[21]

On 10 May 1940 Hitler launched his most ambitious scheme to date: the invasion of the Netherlands, Belgium, and France. The military plans were worked out in meticulous detail. The attack on the Low Countries drew the British and French armies northwards, thereby exposing the flank through which the main German attack on France, through the thinly defended Belgian Ardennes, took place. The plan worked: the Dutch surrendered after five days, the Belgians after seventeen, and the British Army began its evacuation from Dunkirk on 27 May, which continued until 4 June. Then the final phase of the battle of France began in earnest and on 17 June the new French premier, the saviour of Verdun, Marshal Philippe Pétain, stunned France and Europe by announcing that he was seeking an armistice with Germany and with Italy, which had belatedly entered the fray on 11 June.

The Dutch had not been invaded since the Napoleonic Wars and possessed a tiny army which was armed with antiquated weapons and no tanks. Furthermore the country, largely flat and intersected by waterways, was unsuitable for a sustained defence and no city lay much more than 100 kilometres from the German border. Notwithstanding these disadvantages the Dutch put up a sustained defence. Their army managed to hold off the German airborne attack on The Hague for sufficiently long to allow Queen Wilhelmina and her government under Dirk Jan de Geer to make their escape to Britain on a British destroyer on 13 May. Negotiations were begun for the Dutch capitulation but the relevant orders did not reach the Luftwaffe in time to prevent a major bombing raid on Rotterdam which destroyed the city centre and killed at least 800 civilians. Shortly afterwards the Dutch commander-in-chief, General Henri Winkelman, offered the surrender of the Dutch armed forces.[22]

Hitler appointed Arthur Seyss-Inquart as Reichskommissar on 18 May. This caused great alarm among the Dutch since Seyss-Inquart had been instrumental in establishing the constitutional basis for the *Anschluss* with Austria and had just served as deputy governor of the General Government under Hans Frank. But Seyss-Inquart quickly allayed Dutch fears with his first address on 29 May: 'I intend to maintain Dutch laws as far as possible and to work with the Dutch civil administration, and I guarantee the independence of the judiciary. We have no desire to force a foreign ideology on the Dutch.' He also did not intend to govern through the agency of the Dutch fascist party, the *Nationaal-Socialistische Beweging* (NSB) and its leader Anton Mussert. The governance of the Netherlands was continued through the senior civil servants, known as secretaries-general. This was in accordance with pre-war directives, drawn up to deal with the possibility of invasion and occupation, which allowed them to remain in office and to resign only if the occupier's demands became too great. The German military administration was under the Luftwaffe General Friedrich Christiansen. Therefore, it appeared, on the surface at least, that life could continue as normal and that there was no urgent requirement for resistance.[23]

The case of Belgium was different. Almost all of Belgium had been occupied by the Germans during the First World War. This occupation had been brutal, with over 200,000 Belgian men deported as forced labour to Germany and Belgian industry being stripped. Resistance had sprung up with the creation of escape lines for Entente soldiers to enable them to reach the Netherlands, as well as effective intelligence networks. The country had been united behind its ruler, King Albert. His son, King Léopold III, was a very different man. He had hoped that the strict interwar policy of Belgian neutrality would protect the country. In fact it only led to a quick and total occupation as well as doing a great deal to damage British and French military strategy. As it became obvious that Belgium was completely defeated, the government headed by Hubert Pierlot, along with his foreign minister, Paul-Henri Spaak, left the country, first for France and eventually for Britain. Léopold surrendered his country to prevent further casualties, and then, on the advice of his defeatist military adviser, Robert van Overstraeten, remained in Brussels rather than going into exile. On 25 May Léopold explained his reasons in a letter to King George VI:

> Whatever trials Belgium may have to face in the future, I am convinced that I can help my people better by remaining with them . . . especially with regard to the hardships of foreign occupation, the menace of forced labour or deportation, and the difficulties of food supply . . . my utmost concern will be to prevent my countrymen from being compelled to associate themselves with any action against the countries which have attempted to help Belgium in her plight.[24]

Pierlot and Spaak feared that the Germans would use Léopold to lead a collaborationist government, and both were outspoken in their criticism of the king. The Belgian people, however, seemed to view the king's move with approval, leaving flowers outside the palace and wearing lapel badges with the letter 'L'. A Belgian Red Cross official warned the Belgian government-in-exile at the end of May: 'You must have no illusions, Belgium is entirely behind the king, you are detested – or, to use a rather coarse expression, you are spewed out. They consider that you have acted in an atrocious manner.'[25]

The German occupation of Belgium was characterized by its strategic importance for continuing attacks on Britain. Belgium was placed under a German military governor, General Alexander von Falkenhausen, and a military administrator, Eggert Reeder. Neither man was a committed Nazi. Much to the relief of the exiled Belgian government, Léopold refused to take any further part in government while his country was under German occupation and retired to his palace at Laeken, considering himself a prisoner of war. As in the Netherlands, the administration of Belgium was continued by the secretaries-general. Reeder worked very effectively with these men, managing to give the impression that the Belgians were free to draft civil ordinances, whereas in fact almost all were issued at the request of the Germans: 'by anchoring wartime decrees in Belgian law, the Germans expected to protect the legitimacy of the Secretaries-General and make them and their subordinates more effective tools in carrying out German orders'.[26] The areas of Belgium around Moresnet, Eupen, and Malmédy, which had been awarded to Belgium as reparations in 1920, were reattached to the Reich on 18 May 1940.[27]

No one expected France to fall: indeed, those nations already defeated and under Hitler's heel based their future plans for eventual rebirth on the certainty that France would not fall. On paper at least, the French Army was strong, well equipped and well trained. The army, however, suffered from a defensive mentality, illustrated by the construction of the Maginot Line in the mid-1930s. Furthermore, although France had emerged from the First World War as a victor, the cost had been extremely high: 1.7

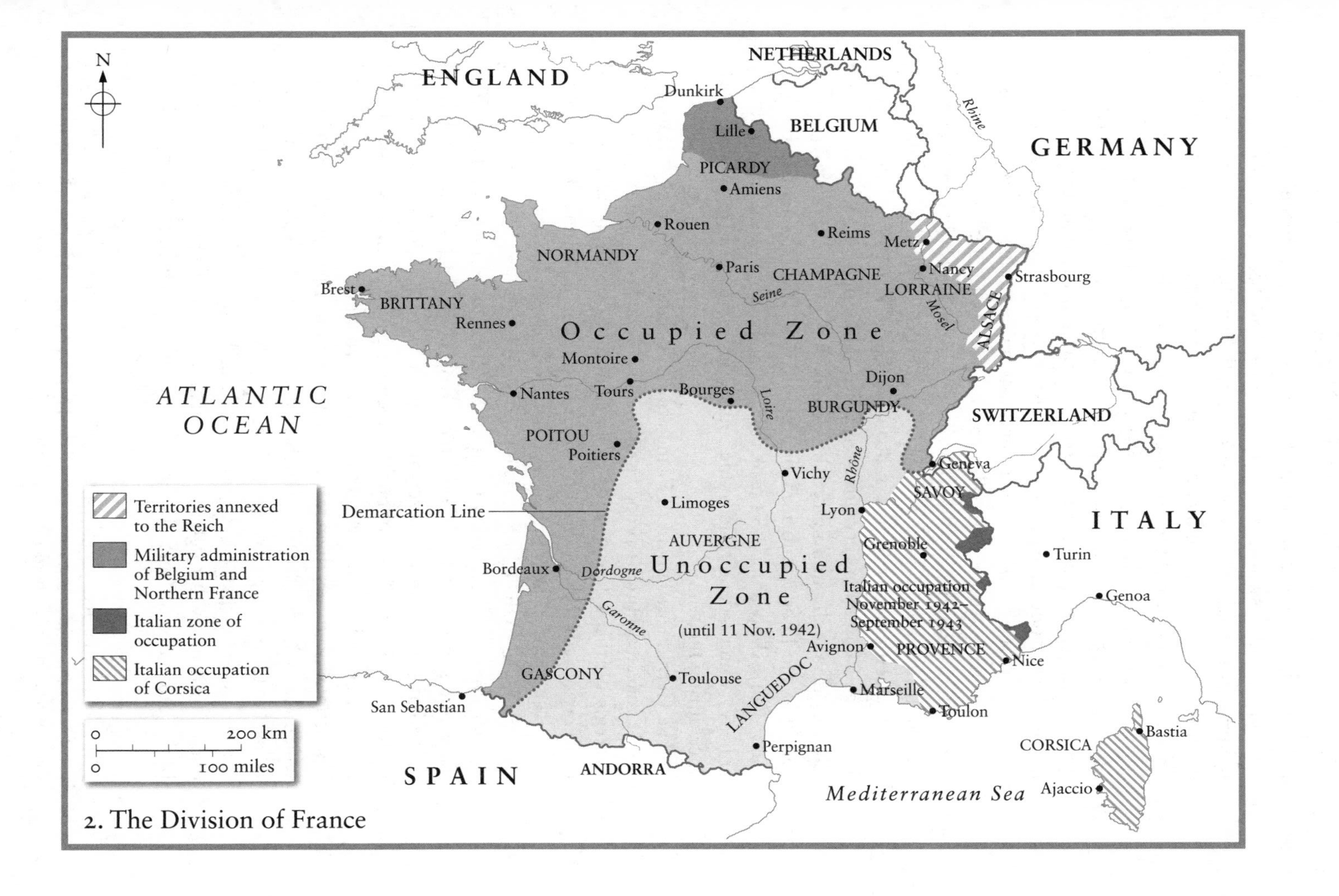

2. The Division of France

million soldiers and civilians had been killed and a further 3.5 million wounded, and a swathe of eastern France had been devastated by the fighting. In 1940 the French Army did not fight well, morale was poor, and communications with high command were frequently patchy. Therefore, on the grounds of military realities it is not surprising that Pétain asked for an armistice. Nevertheless, France could have followed the examples of other defeated nations and formed a government-in-exile. Indeed, she was uniquely well placed to do so since she possessed an empire which included a considerable part of North Africa. Yet Pétain feared a repeat of the events of 1871, when the communists had established a commune in Paris in the power vacuum following France's last defeat at the hands of the Germans. Pétain also did not believe that Britain could continue in the war alone and, by seeking peace now, he hoped to be able to negotiate a tolerable settlement for his countrymen. Largely unnoticed at the time, across the Channel, a very different voice spoke out on 18 June: General Charles de Gaulle announced his leadership of Frenchmen willing to continue the fight. Unnoticed by anyone, the French scientist Frédéric Joliot-Curie slipped out of France, carrying with him France's entire supply of heavy water – deuterium oxide – an action that would grow in importance during the war.

The German settlement of France can only be described as extraordinary. It reflected Hitler's preoccupation with security and economics. The strategic northern departments of Nord and Pas-de-Calais were removed from French control and placed under the military government of Belgium. Alsace and part of Lorraine, long disputed between France and Germany, were annexed to the Reich and administered by the neighbouring *Gaus*. A further zone on the French-German border was termed the Forbidden Zone and subject to close German control. The brief Italian contribution to the battle for France was rewarded with a strip of south-eastern France up to the town of Menton, but not including Nice, which Mussolini had coveted. Overall France was divided into two major zones: Occupied and Unoccupied. Between them ran a demarcation line zigzagging across France which was guarded by the French police with the assistance of the Germans.* In the northern Occupied Zone, the German forces were commanded from Paris by General Otto von Stülpnagel, and civil affairs were conducted principally through the German ambassador to France, Otto Abetz. In the Unoccupied Zone, the French government which had settled in the

* The line ran from the Spanish border to Mont-de-Marsan, then northwards to Bordeaux (occupied) before zigzagging across France on a line from Langon to Dole and finally dropping south to reach the Swiss border near Geneva.

spa town of Vichy theoretically governed the whole of France. The size of the Armistice Army was restricted to 100,000 men, the same figure as the permitted German army after 1919, and France had to pay substantial costs for the German occupation. The existence of the Unoccupied Zone gave the French an illusion of independence and meant that the majority of them were prepared to trust Pétain to save the country from the worst depredations of the Germans. The prospects for resistance in France therefore depended to a great extent on the level of German demands on the population, and on the Vichy regime's ability to limit them.[28]

Hitler had no territorial ambitions towards central Europe and the Balkans. In 1939 Germany concluded an economic agreement with Romania to secure the output of the Ploeşti oilfields. Through the two Vienna Awards of 1938 and 1940 brokered by Germany, the support of Hungary was secured through the restoration of many of Hungary's post-First World War territorial losses.* Germany was drawn more deeply into the Balkans simply as a by-product of Mussolini's disastrous invasion of Greece in October 1940. In November the British government upheld the terms of its treaty of guarantee with Greece and landed British and Commonwealth troops on Crete and despatched RAF units to the Greek mainland thereby bringing the Ploeşti oilfields within their reach. In early March 1941 Allied troops landed on the Greek mainland and deployed to face a German invasion of Greece from Bulgaria. Meanwhile Germany successfully wooed the regent of Yugoslavia, Prince Paul, into joining the Axis on 25 March 1941 and permitting German troops free passage through the country to attack Greece. Two days later, however, a pro-Allied coup deposed Paul and put his eighteen-year-old nephew on the throne as King Peter II. Hitler's immediate reaction was to order the invasion of Yugoslavia and on 6 April its capital Belgrade joined Warsaw and Rotterdam on the list of cities almost completely destroyed by the Luftwaffe. The Yugoslav army was no match for the Germans and the campaign effectively ended on 17 April when King Peter, accompanied by part of his government, fled the country for Egypt, where a government-in-exile was established.

Yugoslavia was a 'successor state' born out of the collapse of the Austro-Hungarian Empire at the end of the First World War. It was built around independent Serbia, and incorporated the republics of Slovenia, Bosnia-Herzegovina, and Montenegro, which had been under Austrian rule, as well as Croatia and part of the Banat which had been Hungarian, and

* The 1938 Vienna Award gave Hungary a common border with Poland. The 1940 award restored northern Transylvania to Hungary from Romania.

included part of Macedonia which had been Bulgarian, and the province of Kosovo, which the Albanians considered belonged to them.[29] This made Yugoslavia a disparate entity. In the first place it had seven frontiers – with Italy, Austria, Hungary, Romania, Bulgaria, Greece, and Albania – all of them countries which had designs on Yugoslav territory. Added to that, the country had three religions – Eastern Orthodox, Roman Catholic, and Muslim – whose mutual loathing served to divide the population. Such divisions were exacerbated by the existence of two alphabets, Latin and Cyrillic.[30] Even within Yugoslavia, land was disputed between the individual republics and the dominance of the Serbs in politics was widely resented by the non-Serb populations. The situation was ripe therefore after Yugoslavia's total collapse for Germany and Italy to carry out a thorough break-up of Yugoslavia. The divisions made then would meet with the approval of some of the population, be disputed by others, and have terrible and unforeseen consequences.

German economic and strategic requirements dominated the process of dismembering Yugoslavia: Hitler needed to safeguard Germany's access to the rich mineral resources of the Balkans, the Danube, and the strategic railway to the Greek coast. He also wanted to reward his allies for their loyalty.

The settlement of Serbia illustrates Hitler's thought processes. The country essentially maintained its pre-1912 borders, but the Banat, through which the Danube flowed, was placed under direct German military administration. Hungary regained the Bačka and Baranja areas, which she had lost after the First World War; Kosovo was given to the Italian-ruled Albanians. The rest of Serbia was ruled over by a collaborationist government headed by Milan Nedić, who offered his services to the German military commander in Serbia, Luftwaffe General Heinrich Dankelmann, on 27 August, an offer which was accepted two days later. Nedić was convinced that Germany had won the war and he wanted to protect the Serbian people, already under threat by events outside Serbia, from total German domination. His government, however, was little more than an administration, tasked with the challenge of keeping the country pacified so that the Germans could exploit it economically, unhindered by the various resistance forces which began to emerge.[31]

Italy had been promised control over territories on the Adriatic coast of what was now Yugoslavia by the Entente in the 1915 Treaty of London, but the 1919 peace settlement had reneged on that promise. Now, in 1941, Hitler promised to deliver what the Entente had failed to do. Slovenia was partitioned: Upper Carniola and Lower Styria, which had been Austrian before 1914 but were now Yugoslav, were placed under a German administration led by Siegfried Uiberreither and Franz Kutschera, with the intention of later formally annexing them to the Reich.[32] The remainder of Slovenia, including the city of Ljubljana, was granted to Italy. Dalmatia was similarly divided, except that in this case a part was awarded to the newly independent country of Croatia, with the majority of the territory, and some of the Adriatic islands, going to Italy.[33]

The settlement of Croatia was very complex. Before the war both the Germans and the Italians had sponsored Croatian separatism. The Italians had supported Ante Pavelić, who led the Ustaše movement which was ideologically akin to fascism; the Germans, on the other hand, supported Vladko Maček, who, as leader of the popular Croatian Peasant Party, appeared to be able to guarantee widespread support for a new regime. But Maček turned out to be a patriot first and foremost and supported the head of the Yugoslav government, General Dušan Simović. Therefore, Hitler made the pragmatic decision to install Pavelić in power on 15 April 1941. Croatia was only nominally independent since both the Germans and Italians retained a large number of troops in the country with a demarcation line between them, the key Germans being General Edmund Glaise von Horstenau and the German ambassador Siegfried Kasche, with the Italians represented by a plenipotentiary general, Giovanni Battista Oxilia. The Duke of Spoleto accepted the crown as King Tomislav II but abdicated in the summer of 1943, having never even visited Croatia.[34] The Ustaše regime was revolutionary, highly nationalistic, and hostile to the presence of non-Croats within its territory. Its actions would divide the population and spark off the growth of the resistance.

After a failed Italian invasion of the country, the German conquest of Greece was concluded rapidly. The invasion began on 6 April 1941 with an advance from Yugoslavia and Bulgaria and within days the Greek and Allied forces were in a headlong retreat, beginning their evacuation from the mainland on 22 April. On 27 April German forces entered Athens and King George II left for Crete and then, after the fall of the island at the end of May, reached Cairo and established a government-in-exile. The Greek commander, General Georgios Tsolakoglou, acknowledged that his forces had been defeated by the Germans and stipulated during the surrender negotiations that the Greeks would surrender to the Germans, not to the Italians, who had not defeated them. General Wilhelm List agreed, but after Mussolini complained to Hitler, Italian officers were present at the surrender ceremony. The territorial settlement of Greece reflected Hitler's needs to reward his allies as well as guard Germany's strategic interests. German direct control was limited to a strip in eastern Thrace on the Turkish border, the port of Piraeus, the southern coast near Athens, and

Salonika in the north, leaving Italy to occupy the remainder of the country, apart from western Thrace and eastern Macedonia, which were returned to Bulgaria, restoring her losses from the Balkan Wars and the First World War. The numerous Greek islands were split between the Italians and Germans, with the Germans maintaining control over the most important ones. After the expulsion of the Allied forces Crete was predominantly under German occupation with an Italian garrison located in the most eastern part of the island. Two Axis plenipotentiaries were appointed, Günther Altenburg and Pellegrino Ghigi, and the military command was similarly split between the commanders of the German 12th Army and the Italian 11th Army.

Even before the Second World War, Greece had been a country with deep political divisions between royalists and republicans, and between the supporters of the Metaxas dictatorship and the opposition. The fall of Greece, the departure of the king, and the formation of a government-in-exile exacerbated those divisions. In Athens a number of Greek politicians were prepared to cooperate or even collaborate with the Germans, but not with the despised Italians. The German solution was to set up a collaborationist government under Tsolakoglou which was 'brought into existence to take the wind out of the sails of the government in exile'. It soon became clear, however, that this Greek government commanded the loyalty of the population of Athens only. Elsewhere royalist groups made preliminary plans for political opposition, if not outright resistance to occupation. Similarly, the considerable number of republicans across the country discussed how they could best exploit the existence of the collaborationist government and the absence of the king to further the prospects for republicanism, but were divided among themselves from the start on political grounds.[35]

The shape of Hitler's 'New Order' in Europe had now been drawn, however the picture remains confused because there was not one system operating throughout the continent, but several. There was the clear desire to permit native governments – in the Czech Protectorate, Slovakia, Norway and Denmark – to continue to run their own affairs to a great extent, though, with the exception of Denmark, subject to close German oversight. In Belgium and the Netherlands the Germans were content to work with the native civil service, which attempted to follow a policy of obeying German decrees while making efforts to protect the population from the full impact of German demands. This has been termed *la politique du moindre mal*, the policy of doing the least harm. In France, however, as will be explained in greater detail in the following chapter, Pétain and the Vichy regime set out to build 'an authoritarian, anti-semitic, corporatist, and clerical regime that would break with the ideals of the French Revolution and the principles of the Republic'.[36]

Nazi racial theory was the principal determinant of how the Germans would treat the conquered peoples. Various nationalities would be wooed on the grounds that they were 'Aryans', such as the Dutch, Norwegians, and Flemings: the French were seen as intermediate, being neither Aryans nor the despised Slavs. The full impact of racial policy fell in the east, where the Slavs and Jews were viewed as *Untermenschen*, people to be fully conquered and then eradicated to make space for Germanic *Lebensraum*. As Seyss-Inquart explained on leaving his post in Poland to serve as Reichskommissar in the Netherlands: 'In the east we have a National Socialist mission; over there in the west we have a function. Therein lies something of a difference!'[37] The Italian approach to *spazio vitale* was different. Whereas for the Germans, the acquisition of *Lebensraum* necessitated the annihilation of the existing population, or at least its transfer out of the area, for the Italians *spazio vitale* was part of a long tradition of imperialism stretching back to the original Roman Empire, which had been refined more recently in the nineteenth century by the British and French empires, whereby 'the occupier of conquered territories transferred its political, social, cultural and economic system to them'.[38]

War and the ensuing redrawing of frontiers caused an immense dislocation of populations. In Poland many people found themselves on the opposite side of the German-Soviet demarcation line from their homes. It was possible to get permission to move between the zones but this took a long time to obtain. Overcrowding in the General Government was worsened by the precipitate arrival of over one million Poles, expelled from their homes in the western provinces now annexed to the Reich. Indeed, such chaos was created that Hans Frank himself called for a halt to the evictions until accommodation could be provided for the incomers.[39]

The invasion of the Low Countries and of France sparked off an exodus of around eight million people fleeing south away from the German armies, and this exodus remained in the memories of all those involved either as refugees or as witnesses:

> It was an unbelievable sight, a long, slow, jostling river of trucks and wagons, sleek cars and jalopies, all piled high with furniture and cherished possessions, from a bird cage to a grandfather clock to a statue of the Virgin Mary. There were stalled cars surrounded by distraught families, cars overturned in ditches. There were soldiers who had thrown away their weapons as they trudged along, grey with fatigue and dust. There was a cyclist with his dog

> bound to his luggage rack like a parcel. A family of peasants from the north lay on the ground in the shade of their wagon, their horses grazing at the side of the road. I remember their children asleep on the road, with their plump rosy cheeks, their flaxen hair in the dust. The sun beat down. We spent as much time stopped as moving.[40]

It is therefore hardly surprising that many greeted Pétain's announcement of his request for an armistice with relief. Jean-Pierre Lévy, later to be active in the resistance but then a reserve artillery lieutenant in the thick of the fighting, recalled: 'It's sad to say, but, alas, it's the truth: around me there was widespread relief at the announcement of the news [armistice]. Soldiers and officers were in favour of ceasing hostilities and did not hide it. Everything happened in a virtually unanimous consensus.'[41]

After the armistice was signed in France, the long-drawn-out process began of trying to get the refugees back to their homes. At the end of June 1940 a decree signed by Pierlot instructed all Belgian government departments and their civil servants to return to Brussels. Pierlot also made plans for the demobilization and repatriation of Belgian troops in France, but Léopold, still smarting from the government's attacks on him, deemed it more politic to allow the International Red Cross to handle the repatriation of Belgian soldiers and civilians.[42] The confused position of the French who were refugees within France was compounded by the division of France into different zones, and not all were allowed to return home. Those who had fled from Paris and the area surrounding the city, or from between the Seine and the Loire, were free to return home. But those whose homes lay between the Seine and the Somme could return home only if they were employed in public services or in agriculture. Those who lived in the areas placed under the military government operating from Brussels – Pas-de-Calais and Nord – were unable to return home under any circumstances.[43] About two-thirds of the 420,000 refugees from Alsace-Lorraine returned home with German encouragement. There they were subjected to an increasing amount of pressure to become Germanized.* In November 1940 about 70,000 Alsatians and Lorrainers who resisted Germanization were expelled and taken by special trains to Lyon.[44] The University of Strasbourg relocated to Clermont-Ferrand, where many of its students and professors would later become involved in the resistance.

Within the German-occupied Yugoslav Slovenian provinces of Upper Carniola and Carinthia an aggressive policy of Germanization was launched and the Slovene language was banned for official use. Those who

* Alsace and Lorraine had been under German control between 1870 and 1918.

were deemed unfit for Germanization were expelled southwards. In June 1941 the Germans reached an agreement with the Croatian government which forced the Croats to accept the majority of those expelled and in return permitted Croatia to expel an equal number of Serbs into Serbia: 'For one week, trains from the region of Gorenjska, filled to capacity with Slovene intellectuals, political leaders, priests, and other influential individuals, including their families, travelled through Ljubljana to unknown destinations in Croatia, Bosnia-Herzegovina, and Serbia.'[45] The Ustaše regime in Croatia could not cope with the massive influx of Serbs and began killing them. It has been estimated that at least 500,000 Serbian men, women, and children were murdered on a variety of pretexts during 1941. Within the Italian-occupied zone in Slovenia and in annexed Dalmatia the Italians launched a massive programme of Italianization and imported fascist organizations into the region.[46] The upheaval caused by the population transfers in the Balkans stimulated the rapid creation of a resistance to the occupiers.

Throughout Europe, there was, of course, a significant portion of the male populations whose return home was considerably delayed, in many cases until the end of the war – the prisoners of war. The Germans took 694,000 Polish officers and soldiers prisoner at the end of the 1939 campaign. The 30,000 officers were sent to POW camps throughout Germany to sit it out until the end of the war. In spring 1940 the rank and file were released from their POW status and became slave workers in Germany, under stringent regulations. The Jews were segregated in the POW camps before being demobilized and returned to Poland, where they were forced into the ghettos being established by the Germans.[47]

In stark contrast, the Danish Army was allowed to continue in existence. Most Norwegian and Dutch POWs were released on parole, subject to recall in case of resistance to German rule in their countries. With regard to the Belgians, the Germans pursued a policy of divide and rule by releasing the Flemish POWs, racially closest to the Germans, first, before allowing a number of French-speaking Walloons to return home at a later date. A similar racial theme was present in the treatment of the Yugoslav Army. Those POWs who came from Croatia, the regions of Slovenia administered by Germany, or from Montenegro were allowed to return to their homes. This meant that of the 181,000 Yugoslav POWs remaining in Germany and the 10,000 in Italy, 90 per cent were Serbs.[48] Two million Frenchmen had been made prisoners of war on the fall of France. Some essential agricultural and industrial workers and First World War veterans were later released, but at least 1.5 million men remained stuck in camps in Germany. These were effectively hostages held by the Germans to ensure the cooperation of the French government; pawns in a complex bargaining game.

The members of the French armed forces who were not in France when the armistice was announced faced the greatest dilemma: should they return home to their families and live under German occupation or the Vichy regime, or should they rally around de Gaulle and remain in exile facing an uncertain future? There were about 18,000 French sailors in Britain in June 1940, and only 50 officers and 200 sailors chose to join de Gaulle while the remainder were repatriated by the British. The ratio was similar in the army.[49] Britain had little concern about the French Army (though de Gaulle of course did) but was principally concerned with the powerful French Navy, which was based in Toulon in France, Alexandria in Egypt, and Mers-el-Kébir in Algeria. Admiral François Darlan had promised the British government that he would not allow the French fleet to fall into German hands. The British did not trust the notoriously anglophobe Darlan, and the risk of allowing the French fleet to fall under German control was so great that Churchill took the difficult decision to order a Royal Navy attack on Mers-el-Kébir on 3 July 1940. The sinking of the French fleet there and the death of so many French sailors deeply shocked the French both on the mainland and in exile, and divided their loyalties. Admiral René Godfrey, who commanded the French squadron at Alexandria, explained the problem he faced in a letter to the British admiral commanding in the Mediterranean:

> For us Frenchmen the fact is that a government still exists in France, a government supported by a parliament established in non-occupied territory and which in consequence cannot be considered as irregular or deposed. The establishment elsewhere of another government, and all support for this other government, would clearly be rebellion.[50]

Godfrey agreed to allow his squadron to be interned. Royal Navy prize crews took over the French ships in British ports in July 1940. The clashes of loyalties among the French were further illustrated by the failure of de Gaulle to rally Senegal to the Free French cause during the ill-fated Dakar expedition in September 1940. Worse still, a joint British-Free French attack on Syria in June and July 1941 led to Frenchmen fighting each other. After the British had secured the country 32,000 French soldiers chose repatriation as opposed to a mere 5,600 who joined the Free French.[51]

These choices are understandable given the situation at the time. In 1940 the evacuation of Britain's small expeditionary force from Dunkirk, the poor performance of her army in all theatres, and the likelihood that Hitler would invade Britain in the near future all combined to counsel against flight to Britain. Arthur Koestler, trapped in France, wrote:

> We did not know that England would carry on the fight alone; nothing in her conduct during the last pre-war decade, nor in the first nine months of actual war, led one to suppose it; and we did not know that, even should she carry on, we would be wanted to help, as was our duty, and be given the shelter, which was our due.[52]

In due course the performance of the RAF in the Battle of Britain lifted the spirits of the people in Europe. It now appeared, as one Norwegian observer wrote, that 'England held on: England could lose battles, but not the war.'[53] But it was equally apparent that the war would be a long one, and in the meantime the peoples of Europe had to find a response to the presence of their occupiers.

2
Choices

The occupation was painfully visible. There was the sheer physical presence of the occupying forces as well as the draping of all public buildings with scarlet banners bearing the swastika. The occupiers took over not just public buildings but private dwellings too, either as billets for the soldiers or, in the case of Warsaw, an entire residential quarter where people were thrown out of their houses at a moment's notice so that only Germans would live there. German street signs and notices appeared everywhere: not only were they in a foreign language but the use of bold gothic script emphasized the alienness of them. A Czech soldier who escaped from the Protectorate after living a year under occupation described what it was like:

> Foreign occupation changes every detail of one's whole life – not only public life, but ordinary, daily, private life. It is not only a question of politics and political activity; even the most simple, unpolitical person is affected. Everything you look at has the hand of occupation upon it. You are ordered about by notices in the street, new notices and new orders, or perhaps just ridiculous and outrageous translations of your own notices continuously hit you in the face. Every time you pass these inscriptions you are forced to realise afresh that you are no longer master of your own country, no longer at home in your own home.[1]

Contact with the occupying powers was unavoidable since papers had to be obtained, ration cards secured, and so on: 'We could not stir an inch, eat or even breathe without becoming the accomplices of our enemy.'[2] Léon Blum, a former prime minister, described the situation in France, which was equally applicable across Europe: 'The country remained silent and inert. It was still suffering the effects of shock, using the word in its pathological sense, in other words from a sort of anaesthesia.'[3] As people began to emerge from this state they faced a number of choices.

Before the war almost every country in Europe had had a fascist party but in the age of democracy none had achieved any significant political following. Now, however, the upheavals caused by military defeat and occupation presented new opportunities for power based on collaboration with the occupiers. The German response varied country by country. In Poland, an approach made by Władysław Studnicki, an advocate of Polish-German cooperation during the First World War, was rejected by the Germans since Poland was to cease to exist and no collaborators were sought. Indeed, Studnicki found himself imprisoned by the Germans.[4] With regard to Denmark, the Germans were content to work with the existing government and saw no reason to encourage the two Danish fascist parties – the Danish National Socialist Party led by Jens Møller or the Danish National Socialist Workers' Party led by Frits Clausen. In fact Clausen himself turned down calls by his party members to join the government, on the grounds that he 'did not want to ride on German bayonets like Quisling'.[5] (Quisling's conduct will be considered below.) Similarly, the Germans felt that in the Protectorate they could work with Hácha and so when the tiny Czech fascist party, the *Vlajka*, attempted to take over the government in August 1940, the German response was to crush the party and send some of its members to concentration camps.[6]

In France too, the Germans rejected the offers of unconditional collaboration which were made by several parties. The two most active parties proposing collaboration were the *Parti Populaire Français* (PPF) led by Jacques Doriot and the *Rassemblement National Populaire* (RNP) led by Marcel Déat. There were also several minor parties equally keen to cultivate the Germans. A new party was even created on 1 October 1940 – the *Mouvement Social Révolutionnaire* (MSR) under Eugène Deloncle. After the war political collaborators such as Georges Albertini, who had been close to Déat, and Jacques Benoist-Méchin of the PPF, justified their collaboration on the grounds that they believed they could limit the damage caused by the occupation to France and raise France 'to an honourable place in the new scheme of things'. The dangers posed by the members of these parties became evident during the war. For example, a May 1941 report by the Vichy minister of the interior noted that 80 per cent of German spies arrested in the Unoccupied Zone since the armistice were Frenchmen. Later research revealed that many of these traitors had strong links to the PPF.[7]

The Germans had no need to rely on these parties at the beginning of the occupation, because there appeared to be every chance that the Vichy regime would do as it was told, as is shown by Pétain's speech following his meeting with Hitler at Montoire in central France on 24 October 1940: 'A collaboration has been envisaged between our two countries. I have accepted the principle of it. The details will be discussed later.'[8] Historians have argued ever since of the exact meaning Pétain ascribed to 'collaboration'. It is clear that Germany held all the cards in any discussions on collaboration. The Vichy regime hoped for an amelioration of the demarcation line, a reduction in the occupation costs and the release of their POWs. But the Germans knew that these were the most powerful weapons in their armoury when it came to dealing with the French. For example, the chief French negotiator on the armistice commission, General Charles Huntziger, was informed by General Otto von Stülpnagel that the demarcation line 'is a bit we have put into the horse's mouth. If France rears, we will tighten the curb, and we will slacken it accordingly as France proves amenable.'[9] German suspicions concerning the sincerity of Vichy's policy of collaboration were confirmed when on 13 December 1940 Pétain removed Pierre Laval from his post as prime minister because Laval was 'guilty of having pursued a policy of voluntary collaboration with excessive zeal and dangerous concessions'.[10] However, after Pierre-Étienne Flandin had briefly followed Laval as prime minister, the position went to Admiral Darlan, who again pursued a policy of collaboration to win over the Germans again. The Paris Protocols of May 1941 marked the high point of Vichy's negotiating strategy with Germany: the Germans accepted the offer of the use of French bases in Syria and North Africa in return for a reduction in the occupation costs and the return home of those POWs who were veterans of the First World War. But the successful Anglo-Free French invasion of Syria in June and July damaged this agreement irrevocably: there was some reduction in the occupation costs and a number of POWs were released, but the Germans no longer trusted the Vichy regime. Pétain concluded that the policy of collaboration was 'an immense labour, which requires on our part as much will as it does patience'.[11] Ultimately, however, French collaboration never worked, because the Germans would not allow it. This in turn damaged Pétain's personal prestige and in due course allowed the resistance to exploit his and Vichy's failures in order to win support.

In the Netherlands and Belgium, the Germans offered a different approach towards the overtures made by the Dutch fascist party, the NSB under Anton Mussert, and the two right-wing parties in Belgium, the Flemish nationalist party, the *Vlaams Nationaal Verbond* (VNV), under Staf de Clercq, and the Walloon Rexist Party (Rex) led by Léon Degrelle. None of these parties was to be projected into government but they could be useful to the Germans in other ways, ways which would make them the principal enemy of the resistance for much of the war. In the Netherlands, members of the NSB were promoted into high positions in local government as being more reliable than the incumbents who owed their loyalty to the queen and the government-in-exile. Seyss-Inquart also gave official approval to the NSB's paramilitary wing, the *Weer Afdeling* (WA), which could be used to crush any future resistance.[12] A similar policy was adopted in Belgium, where the Germans pursued the subtle tactic of ensuring that the VNV and Rex took over the national and local administrations by lowering the retirement age from sixty-five to sixty, thereby at a stroke of the pen removing many senior old-regime stalwarts from office. A key figure here was the minister of the interior, the willing collaborator Gérard Romsée, to whom more and more responsibilities, particularly over the police and gendarmerie, were given. Romsée ensured that the new burgomasters and aldermen appointed came from the ranks of the VNV and Rex. It appears that the Belgians supported a degree of collaboration: the membership of Rex increased to about 15,000–20,000 by the end of 1940; the VNV did even better with an increase from 25,000 in May 1940 to 70,000 on the eve of Operation Barbarossa in June 1941.[13]

The appearance of native collaborators presented a new enemy for the resistance, but one which was more accessible than the occupying forces. The effect has been summarized by the historian Henri Michel:

> Collaboration, as well as occupation, was thus a factor in moulding the character and action of the Resistance. In the first place it meant that both in the order and importance of resistance activities priority had to be given to counter-propaganda – the battle of the mind had to be won before the battle on the ground. Secondly, collaboration meant that a merciless civil war was added to the war between occupiers and occupied.[14]

Most of these battles lay in the future. In the meantime, the people had to learn how to live with the occupier and this led to more subtle forms of collaboration, as described by a Czech journalist, Jan Stránský: 'If we cannot sing with the angels we shall howl with the wolves . . . If the world is to be governed by force rather than by law, let our place be where there is greater force and greater determination. Let us seek – we have no other choice – accommodation with Germany.'[15]

People were forced into economic accommodation because they still needed to work in order to feed their families. Since the Germans soon became the principal source of employment, simply by placing the orders for goods and services, not necessarily by taking over enterprises and running them directly, this meant many people ended up working for the Germans in one way or another. It should be remembered that Europe was just emerging from the Great Depression and unemployment was still at a high level, a situation made worse by the return of demobilized soldiers.

The Germans encouraged workers to come to Germany, exploiting the pre-war tradition of cross-border working. Here again the difference between eastern and western Europe quickly became evident. Before the war, for example, Polish agricultural workers had crossed the frontier to bring in the harvest in Germany, and had been welcomed and treated as equals. Now, however, Nazi racial ideology poisoned what had previously been a peaceful relationship. Not only did the Germans make such extreme demands in terms of the numbers of Polish agricultural workers but once in Germany they were treated as slaves and were subject to strict controls regarding movement and conduct.[16] In contrast, workers from western Europe were welcomed into the factories of the Reich and offered good wages and living accommodation. In the years before the Allied strategic bombing campaign had any significant impact on industry in Germany, work there was an attractive option for the unemployed workers of western Europe. It has been estimated that by August 1941 there were over two million volunteer workers from across Europe working inside the Reich.[17]

Employers faced similar choices. They could either close their factories or go out of business voluntarily, thereby increasing unemployment in their own countries and ruining themselves, or accept contracts to produce war materiel for the Germans. The evidence suggests that the overwhelming number of employers chose to work for the Germans. The French, Czechs, Dutch, and Danes proved particularly adept at securing contracts to produce supplies for the German war industry. The importance of the Czech industries had the welcome effect for the Czechs of abating the impact of the effects of Nazi racial doctrine. The Germans could forget they were dealing with Slavs when they needed the goods they were producing.[18]

Working for the Germans brought benefits over and above simple business survival. For example, after the war, Richard Fiebig, head of the central contract office in the Netherlands, confessed:

> In the war there was the chance to modernise one's own industry, extend firms, gain modern technical procedures at no cost, develop [one's] own ideas further, keep people in employment and, not least, make reasonable profits which enabled the national budget to fulfil its duties through taxation.[19]

For the resistance, the existence of so many factories in their countries producing for the enemy presented opportunities for sabotage. It will be seen later that some employers were prepared to assist the resistance in the sabotage of their own factories, while others were not, arguing that the destruction of their factories would have the unwelcome effect of just providing the Germans with the excuse to draft more workers into the Reich.

There were possibilities open for racial collaboration. Those whom the

Nazi ideologues considered racially pure or valuable, such as the Nordic Danes and Norwegians, the Dutch, and the Belgian Flemings, were to be treated well or indeed cultivated as future partners in the New Order. In the east, however, the situation was more complex. Whereas the Nazis were universally hostile to the Slavs and Jews, they were faced with the problem that in both Poland and Czechoslovakia there had been an intermingling of the Aryans and Slavs and that there was a substantial portion of the population which had some German ancestry. These people could offer themselves willingly for Germanization and in return would receive all the economic and social advantages that such status brought. The only disadvantage was the liability of the Germanized males to be called up for military service in the Wehrmacht.

In the Protectorate, the Sudeten German leader Karl Frank declared in March 1939 that 'A German national is one who himself professes allegiance to the German nation, as long as this conviction is confirmed by certain facts, such as language, education, culture, etc.' By December 1941 the prospect of better employment and higher rations led around 80,000 Czechs to declare themselves voluntarily to be German. This fed into long-standing tensions and grievances between Slavic and Germanic elements in the region. The Czech resistance was shocked by the conduct of these people and issued a stark warning: 'The Germans are opening new German schools where there used to be none. This is your business, women. It is in your hands whether our children grow up to be Czechs or Germanized, patriots or traitors.' The warning was ignored, and the numbers opting to become German increased as the war progressed. After the war it was estimated that one in twenty-five Czechs had registered as German at some time during the conflict.[20]

There were also a substantial number of Polish citizens who had German ancestry. Poles were appalled to discover that some of their neighbours 'suddenly heard the call of their German blood', and became *Volksdeutsche* rather than Polish; some even joined the SS. In contrast to the Protectorate where registration of German nationality was entirely voluntary, though encouraged, in the annexed regions of the former Polish republic the German authorities began the process of systematically categorizing the population according to race in March 1941. The *Volksliste* placed 2.2 million Poles into one of four categories. The first two categories were considered German enough to be immediately eligible for conscription into the Wehrmacht. The third category covered 'persons of German descent' who had 'developed connections with Polish nationality', to whom German citizenship was only granted conditionally. In late 1941 the men from this category were conscripted into the Wehrmacht and served for the most part unwillingly. Later in the war this fact was recognized by the Polish resistance, which helped these men to desert, and by the French resistance, who encouraged them to desert with their weapons and to join the resistance. The final category covered those of German descent who insisted that they were Poles and whom the Germans therefore regarded as renegades.[21]

Political accommodation with the Germans was pursued in both Denmark and the Protectorate. The Danish government went to great lengths to placate the Germans and to fend off the need for a full German occupation with the passage of a number of laws. In July 1940 the Danish parliament passed a law against the publication of anything 'that might be considered harmful to Denmark's relations with foreign countries'. In the first half of 1941 a series of laws made sabotage or giving assistance to the resistance punishable by death.[22] In the Protectorate, the Czech government was increasingly forced to make compromises which drew it closer to outright collaboration. For example, in the spring of 1940 Hácha signed an oath of allegiance to Hitler in response to the German threat to execute students who had been held in German concentration camps since an outbreak of resistance the previous year. Hácha then went further and welcomed prominent and active promoters of collaboration into his government. Foremost among these was the education minister, Emanuel Moravec, who was now given a free hand to nazify the education system.[23] The Germans saw the conduct of these governments as a model of accommodation.

In the Netherlands, talks to establish a collaborationist government in 1940 foundered over Dutch demands for political independence and continued loyalty to the Crown. Nonetheless, there were advocates of a high degree of political accommodation if not outright collaboration. For example, the Dutch prime minister, Dirk Jan de Greer, had accompanied Queen Wilhelmina into exile before concluding that Germany had in effect won the war and returning to the Netherlands.* He produced a pamphlet, endorsed by the Germans, called 'Synthesis in War', which urged the Dutch to collaborate.[24] Similar collaboration was advocated by a former prime minister, Dr Hendrik Colijn, who also wrote a pamphlet advocating if not collaboration then at least accommodation with Germany: 'we will have to accept a German instructor on political, economic and social questions, even if this means that we have to copy him'.[25] The German response was delayed by the emergence of other factors: the start of a mass movement in the

* De Greer was sent from Britain to the East Indies with a diplomatic package but absconded during the scheduled stopover in Lisbon and the Germans repatriated him via Berlin.

Netherlands, mirroring a similar development in the Protectorate, and the attempts at 'national revolutions' being made in Norway and Vichy France.

The collapse into total defeat forced many in the occupied countries to question the validity of liberal democracy. Interwar governments across Europe had often been short-lived and weak, while the sheer number of political parties had led to a focus on government-making rather than government itself. When these weak regimes proved incapable of coping with the Great Depression in the 1930s, the political right and left grew in strength at the expense of the upholders of liberal democracy. On top of this, these weak governments had failed to avert the outbreak of war and then been manifestly incapable of defending their countries against armed aggression. Finally, many of the governments had now gone into exile, leaving a vacuum to be filled back home.

Hácha led the way when, on 21 March 1939, he dissolved the Czech parliament and banned the activities of all political parties. In their place he proposed the establishment of a mass political movement – *Národní Souručenství* – National Solidarity, which would be led by a fifty-member committee. At the committee's first plenary meeting Hácha announced:

> You must keep one aim and one aim only before you. You must prove that the Czech people, which has hitherto been divided into warring groups and conflicting tendencies, will remain for ever a united people with a historical mission and full right to an individual existence.[26]

This mission itself was vague, with references to plans to increase the birth rate, to protect agriculture, to restrict liberalism, to reject socialism and communism, and to exclude Jews from public life. Membership was open to all adult males except Jews. National Solidarity proved to be extremely popular, and by May 1939, 98 per cent of the male population had joined it; by that December there were nearly 9,000 local parties and over 80,000 party officials.[27] But the meaning of National Solidarity was never clear. The American attaché in Prague wrote that the movement had been 'interpreted by the rank and file of the Czechs as an opportunity to demonstrate their numerical strength and their enthusiasm in the face of the German domination'.[28] But enthusiasm for what? It appears that Hácha envisaged the movement as a means of shoring up the authority of his government, and as a way of assuring the Germans that the Czechs were on their side. Indeed, the chairman of the movement told a party meeting in Prague shortly after the fall of France: 'The nation realizes that it is part of the Reich; it wants to be an integral element of the Reich, and it wants to work towards [that end].'[29]

This suggests that National Solidarity was a collaborationist movement. But there is also evidence to indicate that it could have been viewed as a nationalist movement which might undermine the authority of the German Reichsprotektor, von Neurath. Certainly the Germans were aware of the potential threat posed by the movement. Their response was to force Hácha to accept seven overt fascists into the ruling committee; but even so, Karl Frank remained suspicious of National Solidarity and was concerned that 'the Czechs were closely uniting and concentrating'. In spring 1942 von Neurath's replacement as Reichsprotektor, Reinhard Heydrich, ordered the dissolution of the committee. The movement continued in existence but it had lost its impetus and its achievements were negligible.[30]

Defeat and occupation encouraged leading Dutchmen to consider how best to replace the weak political system of the pre-war years, which had been drawn along religious differences and had led to twelve governmental crises. The solution chosen was to create a broad-based political movement, *Nederlandse Unie*, which was established on a number of broad premises, not all of which complemented each other.[31] Colijn participated in the early discussions but the party was actually founded by Professor Jan de Quay of the Catholic Party, the Queen's Commissioner, Johannes Linthorst Homan, and the police chief of Rotterdam, Dr L. Einthoven. The founding proclamation in July 1940 contained the statement that the purpose of the organization was 'to gather all patriots ... in loyal attitudes towards the occupying power', but that it would also uphold Dutch national independence. The new party would overcome the political divisions of the pre-war years and ensure economic strength through a corporative structure. The Dutch people flocked to join the new movement, 250,000 in the first two weeks of recruitment, and by February 1941 the membership of *Nederlandse Unie* stood at 800,000, whereas in contrast the NSB's membership was only 100,000. A new weekly journal, *De Unie*, discussed a wide range of issues facing the Dutch people under German occupation.[32]

The popularity of *Nederlandse Unie* suggests that it was viewed by the Dutch as a nationalist movement, this despite the fact that it had removed references to the popular House of Orange at the request of the Germans. It was also seen as an essential bulwark against the danger of rule by the NSB. Seyss-Inquart, on the other hand, saw the movement differently. Since he recognized the fact that the NSB was too small to be imposed on the Dutch people, Seyss-Inquart welcomed the creation of *Nederlandse Unie* as 'a concentration and revival movement which could win over a large section of the population for "political collaboration" on the basis of an induced free will'. The impossibility of reconciling the differences between nationalism and collaboration led to the decline of the movement. The leadership of *Nederlandse Unie* attempted to make some concessions towards collaboration, for example by banning Jews from full membership and warning members against participation in resistance activities. But the crunch came with the German invasion of the Soviet Union in June 1941. The *Nederlandse Unie* declined German requests to proclaim its support for a crusade against Bolshevism, on the grounds that the Netherlands and the Soviet Union were allies, so the Germans first banned publication of *De Unie* for six weeks and then subjected it to close censorship. The recognition that collaboration came at a price too high to pay led to the leadership of the party choosing to dissolve the party rather than be drawn into further collaboration with the Germans. By the end of 1941 the NSB was the only permitted political party in the Netherlands. Many of the most active members of *Nederlandse Unie* went on to become prominent members of the Dutch resistance.[33]

In Norway, there was a willing and active collaborator ready to work closely with the Germans in the shape of Vidkun Quisling. Reichskommissar Josef Terboven had sidelined Quisling after his precipitate attempt to take over the government on the day of the German invasion. Yet at the same time Terboven also indicated his support for Quisling by banning all political parties other than his *Nasjonal Samling*. Quisling, for his part, retained his ambitions intact, and in a speech on 26 September 1940 set out the programme of the NS: 'Our ideas are those which will be a new foundation for the rebuilding of the Norwegian state and society, and that means a new order in the pattern of Norwegian life.' His early attempts to incorporate industries and professions into single organizations, beginning with agriculture, education, and the law, met with resistance, culminating with the resignations of the members of the Supreme Court in December 1940. This warned Terboven to be cautious in giving too much power to Quisling and the NS.[34] In February 1942, in the changed circumstances of a protracted war, Terboven appointed Quisling head of the government and gave him the freedom to impose his concept of a national revolution on the Norwegian people. The reaction of the population, to be covered later, would prove to be an extraordinary demonstration of civil resistance.

Before Quisling could begin to impose his revolution a crucial decree was enacted: in order to participate in public life, membership of the NS was obligatory. The result was that by 1942 the party had trebled its membership to a peak of around 100,000 people. Because membership of the NS was essential for many people to retain their jobs, it is not clear to what extent this vast increase in membership represented approval of collaboration with the occupying Germans, support for Quisling's programme, or was just a pragmatic move to achieve the means to live. For example, Gunvald Tomstad joined the NS to provide cover for his real work as the radio operator for a key intelligence group in southern Norway. He told his mother: 'No matter what evil you hear spoken of me, no matter what contemptible things you see me do, you and you alone are to know that I am serving my country, and the mean things I do and am, I am and do because someone must pay the price of freedom.'[35]

Of all the defeated peoples in Europe, the French faced the greatest number of choices when considering their response. Philippe de Vomécourt, an early resister, noted the reaction of his friends to the announcement of the armistice:

> There were a dozen or more people in the room at the time, and their reactions to the speech were a reflection of the way in which France was to be divided even to this day. That was the start of it all, although many Frenchmen, who gave their support to Pétain then, were to change their minds later. For some of the people in the room it was enough that Pétain should offer them peace . . .
>
> There were other Frenchmen, including a handful in my home that day we heard Pétain's first message, who could not accept that France should make obeisance to the invaders. Although at the moment their reaction was wholly instinctive, and as yet incapable of translation into any coherent plan for action, they believed that the renaissance of France could be achieved only by resistance to the Germans.[36]

For the latter category, de Gaulle would become their leader, but at that moment he was largely unknown to the French public.

Indeed, one of the principal challenges facing those who opted for resistance from the first hour was how to overcome the cult of personality erected around Pétain, the victor of Verdun:

> Pétain's influence did enormous damage to the Resistance. His hold over the families of prisoners of war was very strong. The trouble was that people's bitterness about the defeat didn't make them want to do something active to change the situation but made them even more submissive to Pétain. They also thought he was playing a double game and was getting ready to defeat the Germans.[37]

Pétain's portrait was displayed everywhere: post offices in the Unoccupied Zone sold over a million copies in two weeks, and a new national hymn,

'*Maréchal, nous voilà!*' replaced the *Marseillaise*.[38] He became 'an idol, a way out, an excuse' for the defeat.[39] This cult of personality was so successful that even early resisters like Henri Frenay would find it hard to shake off their loyalty to Pétain. Furthermore, even as Vichy's policies became more controversial and likely to stir resistance, many people then and indeed after the war continued to distinguish between Pétain, whom they continued to revere, and those who had worked under him, especially Darlan and Laval, whom they blamed.

One of the first steps the Vichy regime took was to end the French Third Republic in July 1940, when all but ninety-seven deputies voted it out of existence.[40] The Third Republic, born after defeat at the hands of the Germans in 1870–71, had been plagued by unstable governments and scandals throughout its existence, and was largely unmourned at its death. The Vichy regime was recognized as the French government by over forty governments, of which six, including the United States, had embassies in Vichy.[41]

Vichy acted swiftly to attempt to counter the threat from de Gaulle, the man Pétain described as 'a viper I clutched to my bosom'.[42] De Gaulle was ordered to return to France the day after his speech on 18 June 1940 calling for Frenchmen to rally round him. Over the next weeks his temporary rank of general was cancelled, then he was compulsorily retired on grounds of discipline, and finally on 28 June de Gaulle received notice to appear at a prison in Toulouse within five days to await trial for inciting mutiny. In his absence the military court sat on 4 July and de Gaulle was found guilty *in absentia* and sentenced to four years' imprisonment and a fine of 100 francs. The regime felt that the sentence was too lenient so a new tribunal met at Clermont-Ferrand and on 2 August condemned de Gaulle to death for desertion and joining the service of a foreign power. Pétain confirmed the sentence, though with the stipulation that it would not be carried out.[43]

There was a widespread desire to find someone to blame for the defeat: 'Ordinary soldiers blamed their officers, the General Staff blamed the politicians, the politicians of the Right blamed those of the Left and vice versa, the government of Pétain blamed the ministers of the Popular Front, they in turn blamed the army, most people blamed the Communists, the Communists blamed the internal Fascists, and the Fascists blamed the Jews.'[44] On 30 July 1940 Pétain empowered the Supreme Court to 'judge whether the former ministers, or their immediate subordinates, had betrayed the duties of their offices by way of acts which contributed to the transition from a state of peace to a state of war before September 1939, and which after that date worsened the consequences of the situation thus created'. The period to be examined lay from 1936 and the start of the Popular

Front government to 1940 and the armistice. The defendants included Léon Blum, Édouard Daladier, the former commander-in-chief, General Maurice Gamelin, and the former minister of air, Guy La Chambre. The opening of the trial in Riom was delayed until February 1942 and was suspended a month later since embarrassing evidence about budgetary cuts made to the armed forces during Pétain's term of office was beginning to emerge. The trial was formally abandoned in February 1943.[45]

One striking feature of French life had been the extent to which substantial elements in the Catholic Church remained antagonistic to the often aggressively secular Third Republic. After the armistice, the archbishop of Toulouse, Jules-Géraud Saliège, preached a sermon in which he asked:

> Have we suffered enough? Have we prayed enough? Have we repented for sixty years of national apostasy, sixty years during which the French spirit has suffered all the perversions of modern ideas ... during which French morality has declined, during which anarchy has strangely developed.[46]

Vichy's solution was to carry out a National Revolution: 'To an extent unique among the occupied nations of Western Europe, France went beyond mere administration during the occupation to carry out a domestic revolution in institutions and values.'[47] It was, in every aspect, a reaction to the defeat, to the weaknesses of the governments of the Third Republic, to the rise of the power of organized labour, to the increase in immigration and arrival of refugees, to the anti-clericalism of the Third Republic, and, in general, to the modern world. It was essentially an attempt to turn back the clock to what was perceived as a happier world: the slogan '*Travail, Famille, Patrie!*' was to replace the revolutionary '*Liberté, Egalité, Fraternité!*' Over a remarkably short period of time Freemasons and Jews were barred from public office and trade unions and employers' associations were banned. The result was the dismissal of over 2,000 civil servants, and 3,000 French Jews were forced out of public office.[48] The anti-clerical laws that had ousted the Catholic Church from state-run schools were repealed, and teachers now had to provide religious instruction. As educators of the next generation, their attitude towards the National Revolution was closely monitored.[49] Vichy's xenophobic attitudes were illustrated by the work of the Commission for Denaturalization which began work in July 1940 and eventually revoked French nationality, and therefore protection, from over 150,000 foreign-born French citizens, many of whom were Jews. Without any prompting by the Germans, Vichy also enacted the first statute against the Jews in October 1940.[50]

The Vichy regime set up a number of organizations to replace those structures it had dismantled and to spread the word about the revolution.

In place of trade unions and employers' associations, a corporative structure was constructed, built around branches of industry or professions.[51] The *Chantiers de Jeunesse* were created to organize the 70,000 twenty-year-olds who could not undertake military service in the much-reduced Armistice Army but needed to be kept occupied in some way. Their main tasks were road-making and forestry and their role was economically helpful to France. However, later in the war the existence of the *Chantiers* organization made it easier for the Vichy regime to attempt to fulfil German demands for French labour, and this sparked opposition.[52] A more controversial organization was created by grouping together various veterans' associations under a new body, the *Légion Française des Combattants*. The government hoped that this organization would help uphold the National Revolution and counter any resistance to it. At its peak the Legion had 1.5 million veterans enrolled in the Unoccupied Zone alone, yet this figure concealed the fact that the majority were veterans from the First World War and not from 1939–40. The Legion became implicated in the more controversial aspects of Vichy, collaboration with the Germans, and especially action against the resistance. The *Service d'Ordre Légionnaire* (SOL) evolved from the Legion and its main purpose was to counter the resistance and other activities damaging to collaboration; out of the SOL grew the political paramilitary organization called the *Milice*, which was arguably the greatest danger the resistance faced.[53]

The National Revolution was French by design and implementation. In no way was it imposed on France by the Germans, nor were the more controversial aspects of it, such as the anti-semitic laws, demanded by the Germans. But the regime at Vichy certainly accepted the dominance of Germany within Europe and, as the only European power to be granted an armistice, desired to reach an understanding with Germany and to secure France's position within the new Europe. This drew the Vichy regime into a policy of collaboration with Germany. Yet it has been noted that 'the question was not whether there should be collaboration but in what direction and to what extent it should be pursued, and the major problem in 1940 was not how to persuade the French people to accept it, but how to persuade the German Government to agree to it'.[54] Hitler did not intend to permit France to become 'a full partner either in the prosecution of the war or in the elaboration of a New European Order'.[55] France was seen as a potential threat to continued German dominance in Europe, and Hitler never forgot that Germany and France had been at war with each other three times over the last century. What Hitler wanted from France was for the French to remain silent while he prepared for war against Britain, and to permit the economic plundering of the country. The development of widespread resistance in the Unoccupied Zone would depend to a great extent on the Vichy regime's ability to mitigate German demands on the country. So long as the majority of the people continued to believe that Pétain was their saviour, then resistance would be slow to develop in the Unoccupied Zone.

Across Europe, the most prevalent attitude was undoubtedly one of *attentisme*, of waiting to see what would happen. There was a general feeling that: 'However you looked at the problem, the match had been played and lost. Without admitting that we were permanently defeated, it was necessary to retire and wait until better days. To stand obstinately against the defeat made no sense. The important thing was to know in what way to retire' or 'to come to terms with yesterday's enemy is not cowardice but wisdom, as well as accepting what is inevitable'.[56] This attitude is entirely understandable since German and Italian forces were in occupation across the continent and the surviving Allied armies had retired in a state of considerable disarray. It was clear that the war, and therefore the occupation, would be lengthy and so overt resistance seemed a pointless response. Nonetheless, there were people who opposed the occupations from the start, from a variety of motives. It was a response broadly defined by a Dutch resister, Erik Hazelhoff: 'In the life of every person there are moments when he says to himself: "Tja, this won't do." And then he does something.'[57] But people needed to know that they were not alone and they needed to know what to do, and one way of solving both problems was through the development of the clandestine press.

3
The Clandestine Press

One of the first actions of the occupying authorities was to seize control of the press, both newspapers and periodicals, in order to control both the news and the climate of opinion. In most countries this control was exerted through the licensing of papers and the imposition of strict censorship over the contents. Some pre-war newspapers continued in publication, such as *Le Soir* in Belgium and *Le Figaro* in France, with articles written by the same journalists. Elsewhere, the Germans might authorize the creation of new newspapers, such as *La Nation Belge*, edited by a former Rexist in Belgium, or *Nowy Kurjer Warszawski* in Poland. A clandestine press developed to contradict the messages carried in the official press. This 'battle of the mind' was waged by the resistance from the start of the war, when tiny numbers of clandestine newspapers were produced under conditions of great difficulty, to grow into, arguably, one of the most important examples of resistance throughout the war.

The clandestine press was complemented by the broadcasts of the BBC from Britain which reached every country. Control of the content of these broadcasts was given to the Political Warfare Executive (PWE), working with a committee which included representatives from the Foreign Office, SOE, the War Office, Admiralty and Air Ministry. Although many of the senior personnel in each country's section were British, émigrés tended to make the actual broadcasts.[1] The effect of the BBC cannot be overestimated:

> The BBC brought people together as well as inspiring action. It acted as a powerful vector and amplifier of the resistance. By the very fact of talking about it, the BBC conferred a national reality on the resistance, giving the impression, however misleading in the early days, of a coherent organisation.[2]

Many of those who listened to the BBC could be termed 'armchair resisters' who undertook no other act of opposition to the occupying forces. Yet listening to the BBC was still important to these people in order to instil the mindset necessary for future action: if not to undertake resistance directly, then to support those who did.[3]

The importance of the clandestine press is demonstrated by the fact that it appeared in every country almost immediately after the occupation had begun. In the case of the Protectorate, the paper *V boj*, the mouthpiece of the resistance group ÚVOD, began publishing in 1939, even before the outbreak of the Second World War. Despite frequent arrests of its editors, it continued publication throughout the war and was joined by the communist *Rudé právo* after the German invasion of the Soviet Union.[4] Less than two weeks after the surrender of Warsaw the first edition of *Polska Żyje* appeared on 10 October 1939, followed on 5 November by the standard-bearer of the underground, *Biuletyn Informacyjny*.[5] In Belgium the secret newspaper *La Libre Belgique*, first published in German-occupied Belgium during the First World War, resumed publication in July 1940 under the editorship of Paul Stuye.[6] In the Netherlands, the first issue of the main underground paper, *Vrij Nederland*, was printed on 31 August 1940, Queen Wilhelmina's birthday.[7] The earliest underground papers in France were *Pantagruel* and *Libre France*, appearing in October 1940 in Paris, and *L'Homme libre*, which later became *La Voix du Nord* that November.[8] In the autumn of 1941 in Yugoslavia, the two resistance leaders, the Četnik Draža Mihailović and the Partisan Josip Tito, started the *Glas Ravne Gore* (Voice of Ravna Gora) and *Borba* (Fight) to promote their movements.[9] Even the Channel Islands, whose size restricted resistance, produced two publications, the Guernsey Active Secret Press (GASP) and the Guernsey Underground News Service (GUNS).[10]

The importance the resistance attributed to the underground press can be demonstrated by the sheer number of publications produced by each country. For example, about 1,200 titles of different newspapers and periodicals can be found in the Polish archives; over 800 in Norway; 500 in Belgium; 1,200 in the Netherlands; 800 in Denmark; and at least 1,000 in France.[11] Many of these were short-lived as the Germans arrested the editors, but some grew to be mass-circulation papers of 300,000 copies per issue, thereby rivalling the official press.*

Even as the first clandestine newspapers were being produced, privately published tracts appeared in several countries advising the population on how to behave towards the occupier. The best known of these is the *Conseils à l'occupé – Advice to the Occupied* – produced in the summer of 1940 by

* A list of some of the major publications in each country can be found under the preceding endnote.

a French journalist, Jean Texcier. Most of the thirty-three items of advice covered the subject of how best to ignore the presence of the occupier, such as avoiding patronizing establishments which welcomed the Germans. But the attitude to take towards the official press was also covered: '14. The reading of newspapers has never been advised as a method of learning to express oneself correctly in French. Still less today, the Paris dailies do not even *think* in French.' *Advice to the Occupied* concluded with:

> 33. It's useless to send your friends to buy this 'Advice to the Occupied' at the bookshop. No doubt you have only one copy and wish to keep it. All right, make some copies and your friends may copy theirs in turn. It's a good occupation for the occupied.[12]

Similar advice was offered by anonymous authors in Norway and Denmark, each with an emphasis suitable for its particular country. The *Ten Commandments for Norwegians* opened with an exhortation to obey King Haakon and to hate Hitler. It counselled the population to denounce traitors and followers of Quisling.[13] The Commandments were directed less at conduct towards the Germans, rather against Quisling and members of his NS party which was determined to take over the country. The *Ten Commandments from a Dane* addressed the challenge faced in Denmark posed by the seemingly benign German occupation. The Germans allowed the Danes more freedom than in any other occupation, anticipating that a quiescent population would continue to work in industries which served the German war machine. Hence three of the Commandments urged the workers to 'do bad work for the Germans'; 'practise working in slow motion for the Germans'; and 'destroy all the tools and machines that could be useful to the Germans'.[14]

It is impossible to know how many people actually saw these tracts at the time, but for those who did it could have an important effect. When Agnès Humbert, involved in the Musée de l'Homme resistance network, which produced an early clandestine newspaper, *Résistance*, came across a copy of the advice, she recorded her reaction in her diary:

> A glimmer of light in the darkness . . . Now we know for certain that we are not alone. There are other people who think like us, who are suffering and organizing the struggle: soon a network will cover the whole of France, and our little group will be just one link in a mighty chain. We are absolutely overjoyed.[15]

This suggests that one of the principal aims of the early clandestine press was to inform people that the resistance existed and to define what it stood for:

> Resistance means above all to act, to be positive, to perform reasonable and useful things. Many of you who have tried are discouraged because you think you are powerless. But some have formed themselves into groups, scattered and weak . . .
>
> Group yourselves in your homes with those whom you know. Choose your leaders. They will find other groups with which to work in common . . . Your immediate task is to organise yourselves so that you can, when you receive the order, take up the fight again. Find resolute men and enrol them with care. Bring comfort and decision to those who doubt or who no longer dare hope.[16]

Above all, the message from the early issues of the newspapers was not to despair, the country might be defeated but the war still continued, and patience was needed before liberation would occur on the occasion of Germany's ultimate defeat.

From east to west, those involved in the clandestine press quite separately came to the same conclusions on the aims of the publications. For example, the editor of the Polish paper *Biuletyn Informacyjny*, Aleksander Kamiński, issued a set of editorial rules, the first of which was largely followed by the clandestine press across Europe:

> 1. Information not agitation; Poles do not need encouragement to resist the Germans or cultivate their patriotism. People deprived of radio sets and the Polish press want to know what is going on in the world and in the country. This information should be provided succinctly and faithfully. The way of presenting facts offers an opportunity which should be exploited wisely (but with moderation) for the purpose of propagating desired behaviours and attitudes.[17]

Lucie Aubrac, involved in *Libération-sud* in France agreed: 'We simply had to tell people what was happening. The Germans gave out much misinformation. On the other hand, there was information the Germans did not want the French to know. They were pillaging and looting our country.'[18] So, while the official press might blame the British blockade for shortages of food and other goods, the clandestine newspapers listed what the Germans had seized and publicized the differences between the rations received by the Germans and those distributed to the natives. On numerous occasions the clandestine press issued advice on specific issues. For example, the Poles were told not to relinquish the warm clothing and boots the Germans demanded in the winter of 1941–42.[19] The Dutch press advised people to hide their silver, bronze, and copper when the Germans ordered the requisition of the metals.[20] During 1942 and 1943 when the Germans began conscripting forced labourers across Europe, the clandestine press made clear calls for evasion of the measure. In a special edition, the Dutch paper *Het Parool* called on the soldiers not to report for re-internment as ordered in spring 1943, pointing out that it would be difficult for the Germans to arrest 300,000 former servicemen.[21]

The clandestine press also served a function in the identification of who was the enemy. For much of the war, the principal targets were the collaborators, and *Défense de la France*, for example, urged direct action against them: 'The assassination of a collaborator is a liquidation, not a murder. In the absence of military courts, spontaneous justice must be meted out to traitors.'[22] The same newspaper warned those women guilty of 'horizontal collaboration' of their future fate after liberation: 'You so-called French women who give your bodies to a German will be shaved, with a notice pinned on your backs *Sold to the enemy*! So will you shameless girls who trip around with the occupiers be shaved and whipped. On all your foreheads a swastika will be branded with hot iron.'[23] In Norway, the Netherlands, Belgium, and Denmark the clandestine press published lists of the names of collaborators along with the documentation to be used in post-war trials.[24] As the clandestine press gained access to better printing presses, it served an essential function in warning the population of particularly active traitors, printing not only physical descriptions and lists of aliases used, but also on many occasions photographs too. At the same time, the clandestine press clearly identified the Allies and the governments-in-exile as the supporters of resistance. News of the progress of the war was severely restricted in the official press, especially as the stream of German victories began to turn into a string of defeats, so the clandestine press filled the gap, publicizing news gleaned from the BBC. Some secret newspapers were little more than a series of BBC bulletins printed up for wider distribution and also included verbatim speeches by Churchill, Roosevelt, and other national leaders.

One important purpose of the clandestine press was to publicize the actual existence of a resistance movement. Indeed, in France in particular, groups came together for the specific purpose of producing a newspaper, and their editors were often the leaders of the resistance group.[25] Henri Frenay, leader of *Combat*, wrote after the war: 'People sometimes forgot the name of our movement but never that of our newspaper.'[26] In general, this link between resistance groups and underground newspapers had a beneficial effect, but there could also be criticism of the sheer number of papers produced. For example, Stefan Korboński, head of the civil resistance in Poland, complained: 'The publication of a newspaper was almost a certificate of importance to even the smallest organisation, for it gave it a position in the underground world.'[27]

The fact that most resistance movements had their own newspaper may suggest that the resistance as a whole was fragmented, but in fact the evidence is that the press could act as a unifying factor. The head of the Polish resistance, the AK, Tadeusz Bór-Komorowski, suggested: 'One of the chief aims of propaganda was to bring about as nearly as possible complete harmony and comradeship between all ranks of our organisation, the members of which originated from very diverse social spheres and professed a multiplicity of political opinions.'[28] The same unity of purpose could apply to those who read the clandestine output. Frenay noted: 'A solidarity of complicity was cemented among all those who received our sheets.'[29] Philippe de Vomécourt noted the value of the papers for the readership:

> They expressed the thoughts that a man might fear to speak aloud; they assured him that, far from being alone, he was one of an already large 'army', which was growing every day. They gave cohesion to the idea of Resistance. They were the cement that bound together the individual units of the Resistance.[30]

Such sentiments could cross international frontiers. Ada Gobetti, a member of the Italian resistance, noted her joy at receiving copies of the French underground papers *Combat* and *Franc-Tireur*: 'It made me emotional to see this tangible sign that they were fighting a battle elsewhere too, with the same spirit as ours.'[31]

The creation, printing, and distribution of the underground press also served as a training ground for the resistance movements. The challenge of operating a printing press in secret necessitated tight security and the formation of small units to guard the premises housing the press. These units developed the sort of discipline essential for the formation of sabotage groups later in the war. Logistics had to be learned: editorial content had to be gathered and delivered to the press; paper and ink obtained without arousing the suspicions of the police or the German authorities; and methods found of warehousing the newspapers once printed, before the distribution network began its work. Betrayal was possible at every point. The nucleus of every group producing a newspaper had to learn how to reach out to strangers who could provide assistance in some element of the process. As Claude Bourdet explained: 'It was the instrument that could measure the sentiments of someone you were hoping to make a sympathizer; it was also the first mode of action and, for many militants, the only likely means of practical action for many long months.'[32] This provided useful practice essential for recruitment of more members and identification of infiltrators. The distribution of the output was of less risk and served as a helpful exercise for novice members of a group. Printing presses could also be used to produce false identity documents. These were first given to the central members of resistance groups, before being extended to other groups under threat, such as evading Allied servicemen, those hiding from forced labour, and the Jews.[33]

During the period of total German domination in Europe the underground press largely avoided calling for direct action against the Germans, but by 1943 as the tide of the war began to turn against the occupying force the tone of the press changed. In Poland, for example, *Biuletyn Informacyjny* provided detailed reports on resistance activity.[34] In March 1944 *Défense de la France* published an editorial, 'A Duty to Kill', which called upon Frenchmen to:

> Kill the German to cleanse our territory, kill him because he kills our own people, kill him to be free. Kill the traitors, kill those who betray, those who aided the enemy. Kill the policeman who has in any way helped arrest patriots. Kill the men of the Milice, exterminate them, because they have chosen to hand over French men and women, because they have embraced betrayal. Shoot them like mad dogs on the street corners. Hang them from the lampposts, following the example of Grenoble. Destroy them like vermin.[35]

That month Albert Camus, writing for *Combat*, warned those French people who thought that the war was no concern of theirs, that the Germans' practice of reprisals involved a slaughter of innocent people: 'There is only one fight, and if you don't join it, your enemy will nevertheless supply you with daily proof that the fight is yours.'[36] After the Normandy invasion of June 1944, the clandestine press in France and the Low Countries printed Allied communiqués, orders from the Allied military authorities, and, in the case of the Netherlands, instructions from the government-in-exile. As liberation approached across Europe, the clandestine press played a vital role in printing so-called 'paroles' or advice on conduct as the Germans either retreated or prepared to lay down their arms, notably in Norway.

The first issue of *Libération-sud* announced in July 1941: 'Tomorrow will be the time for political doctrines. Today our objective must be to escape the wretched condition of a conquered people.'[37] By the next year, however, the clandestine press across Europe was already beginning to consider the future. Throughout Europe there appeared to be a desire to break with the past, including an examination of what had been wrong with the pre-war systems of government and economic management, in order to make plans for a better future. As *Franc-Tireur* stated in March 1944: 'Who would dare to impute to those masses who have risen in

Europe against Nazi rule that they are fighting for a revival of a past whose profound weaknesses and irrevocable collapse they have experienced? Their goal is a new world!'[38] The discussion in the papers was along two broad themes: a new form of internal government; and relations between different nation states.

There was a widespread rejection of the pre-war political systems. In Poland the underground government and therefore its press was run by members of the pre-war opposition parties who strove to develop programmes which would move Poland back towards a liberal democracy and away from the pre-war authoritarian *Sanacja* regime. In this sense, the underground government was in tune with the Polish government-in-exile whose leader, Władysław Sikorski, was also distancing himself from the pre-war regime. Not all governments-in-exile were happy that the resistance was discussing the shape of future government. Radio Free Belgium criticized *La Voix des Belges* for such conduct. In response a clandestine newspaper warned the government:

> When you return, you will find us older and that we have endured much. You have not been able to follow the evolution of the people for four years. You will meet men transformed by four years of fighting, men who have learned to show themselves intransigent . . . you have not suffered under the Nazis nor seen the traitors in action.[39]

Queen Wilhelmina announced that she would consult with the Dutch resistance on the formation of the first post-war cabinet. Reassured by this, the Dutch papers considered whether the cooperation between Protestants and Roman Catholics, notable in the resistance, could continue after the war. This would make a break with a pre-war political and social system divided along religious differences.[40]

The future organization of the economy occupied the minds of underground editors. The communist paper *Franc-Tireur* in its first editorial in December 1941 tried to appeal to a broad swathe of opinion:

> We want to found after the war a new regime, a synthesis between authority and liberty, a true democracy cleansed of the bumblings of political parties and the domination of the trusts and the financial powers. We want neither a military dictatorship, nor a religious dictatorship, nor a proletarian dictatorship, nor a capitalist dictatorship.[41]

The Dutch press devoted much attention to economic matters, with opinions ranging from the communists' desire for the nationalization of all the means of production to the socialist call for the nationalization of only selected industries.[42] The French resistance press also focused on economic matters. Socialism and more worker control and input into management decisions were seen as keys to the future, as a means to achieve a new economic system 'between the last perilous starts of an old moribund capitalism and the youthful excesses of a Marxism still too sectarian and rigid', as *Libération* expressed it. The result of these considerations was a series of *Cahiers*, discussion documents for the establishment of a post-war France. In London, the Free French were producing similar documents.[43]

Appeals to nationalism were vital in triggering resistance to the German occupations, but when considering the shape of the future the underground press urged greater internationalism. In December 1942 *Het Parool* stated the lines along which various clandestine papers were thinking with the greatest clarity:

> This war should be seen as the ultimate crisis of the sovereign state. If the fighting is not to be in vain, the war must result in a European cooperation between states that are ready to cede part of their sovereignty to secure collective sovereignty. A new super-organ must follow – whether a European directorate or a federation – with the power to enforce the collective will and ensure peace. Not a super-organ that dictates all life in Europe from one central point as the Nazis would like to do, but one that leaves the continental national units sufficient autonomy and self-determination.[44]

Just how much power should be taken away from nation states was, however, viewed differently in each country. The Poles appeared to be most keen for post-war federations, whereas the French wanted cooperation restricted to the economic sphere. The inherent weaknesses of the League of Nations were widely recognized and much discussion was centred upon the need to find a place for a future European federation within the framework of a new, more powerful world organization which, unlike the League of Nations, would have the means at its disposal to maintain peace.[45]

Books were also an important output of the clandestine press, with the Dutch and the Poles being particularly active. Whereas the Dutch focused on nationalist literature and a high number of anthologies of poetry, the Poles had to respond to the Germans' complete control of all the means of publishing in Poland, as well as to the closure of libraries and bookshops. The AK set up its own publishing unit in Warsaw and Cracow. These books, manuals, and pamphlets carried the mark KOPR – *Komisja Propagandy BIP w Warszawie* (Propaganda Committee of the Bureau of Information and Propaganda in Warsaw), and a colophon of an open book together with the initials AK. This unit oversaw the production of everything from school textbooks for the underground schools and military manuals for the underground army to literature, poetry, and plays, all vital to maintain the existence of the Polish state, albeit in secret and underground. Whereas the Dutch titles were normally under 100 copies per edition, the Poles were better organized and normal print runs were 2,000–3,000, and occasionally as large as 6,000.[46]

Two books stand out in particular for further analysis. The first is *Le Silence de la mer* (*The Silence of the Sea*) by Vercors in France. The second was not even produced in an occupied country but had an important impact on the resistance nonetheless – John Steinbeck's *The Moon is Down*.

Vercors was the pseudonym of a satirical cartoonist and engraver, Jean Bruller, who had never written a book before. Vercors decided to write the book in 1941 because:

> There were French writers who collaborated. We needed to counter them by urging silence. The idea for my book came from the German Ambassador Otto Abetz, who had drawn up a list of forbidden authors – principally Jews, Communists, and those with a left-wing political orientation.[47]

The story is a political parable about a man and his niece, landed gentry in Brittany, who had a friendly German officer, Werner von Ebrennac, billeted on them. The uncle is the narrator and explains that 'By tacit agreement, my niece and I had decided to make no changes in our life, even in the smallest detail, just as if the officer didn't exist, as if he had been a ghost.'[48] Every evening the young officer tries to make conversation with the French pair, explaining how much he loves France and French literature. He believes in maintaining friendly relations between the French and Germans until a visit to Paris opens his eyes to German intentions as practised in the east. Each night the officer used to retire wishing the pair a good night but, after narrating what he has learned in Paris from his colleagues, the officer withdraws with an *Adieu* and leaves the next morning.

Le Silence de la mer was the first book produced by the underground publishing house Éditions de Minuit. Jean Paulhan was behind the project and received funds from a Paris paediatrician, Robert Debré. The manuscript was initially typed up on thin paper by Dexia, Countess Elisabeth de la Bourdonnaye, and then published as a sixty-page book on thick grey paper with about 300–400 copies. By autumn 1942 a copy had reached London, where it was reprinted and given worldwide distribution. Éditions de Minuit went on to produce a further sixteen books before the liberation.[49]

The American author John Steinbeck wrote *The Moon is Down* as a piece of propaganda at the direct request of the head of OSS, Bill Donovan, in autumn 1941, before the United States was even in the war. It was published in the US in March 1942 just as the country was reeling from the attack on Pearl Harbor the previous December and the defeats in the Pacific. The book tells the story of a small town in occupied Europe, most probably Norway, where a German unit descends on the town to guard the mine and keep it operating. The story shows the challenges posed by invasion and occupation, for both the occupiers and the occupied. The defeat of the town's defending forces came about through the treachery of one of the inhabitants, who is then rejected by the occupying German authorities. The Germans attempt to be friendly to the defeated people and initially establish good relations with the mayor and the local doctor. But then the occupation turns sour when a German is killed by a native miner and the Germans ask the mayor to pass the death sentence. The shock this produces means that a clear line is drawn between occupiers and the occupied, and relations are kept businesslike rather than amicable.

For some of the American critics the portrayal of the Germans as friendly and as human beings was too much, just at the time when the United States was starting military operations. But the book struck a chord with the resistance in the occupied countries, who, after all, had direct experience of the Germans. The book was translated into Norwegian, Danish, Dutch, and French. The Norwegian edition was translated in Sweden and printed there in late 1942 on very thin paper and smuggled into Norway. It proved so popular that a mere five weeks after liberation, a legal edition was published in two printings of 10,000 copies each. The Danish edition was translated at the end of 1942 by two students working with an English dictionary in one hand and a glass of beer in the other. The text was then mimeographed and distributed through a Copenhagen bookseller, Mogens Staffeldt, before proving so popular that other bookshops sold it too as well as large businesses such as shipping companies and banks. The Dutch edition was translated and produced in early 1944 with a print run of over 1,000 copies. The proceeds from the sales went to a resistance group which was supporting actors and actresses who had refused to join the Nazi-sponsored cultural guild and were therefore unemployed. The French edition was published in February 1944 by Éditions de Minuit.[50]

As well as publishing to their own populations the resistance targeted the Germans themselves directly with black propaganda. Much of this material was supplied from Britain, crafted by PWE and distributed by SOE teams. An example of this practice occurred in Norway, where two SOE teams of three men apiece operated in Trondheim and Oslo in 1944. Around 280,000 stickers and 270,000 pamphlets were distributed. The stickers appeared on lamp posts, shop fronts, and on one spectacular occasion, in every tram in Trondheim. A black newspaper pretending to be the official press of the *Deutsche Freiheits Parti* was produced in an attempt to recruit Germans who already believed that the war was lost.[51] The Poles were especially active in the dissemination of black propaganda with around 1,000 people engaged in the scheme, dubbed Operation 'N'. This operation was directly overseen by the underground's Office for Information and Propaganda. It involved the production of journals like *Der Soldat*, *Der Klabautermann*, and *Der Hammer* in German to be distributed to the Wehrmacht and German administration not only in the General Government, but also behind the lines on the Eastern Front and in the annexed western areas of Poland, and even penetrating into the Reich itself. Around 25,000 to 30,000 items of black propaganda were distributed per month.[52] In early 1943 the underground printed a counterfeit edition of the German-sponsored *Nowy Kurjer Warszawski* newspaper. It was identical to the German copy in every respect – format, print, and appearance. Only the contents differed with a statement of the military situation on all fronts, details of underground activity within Poland, a speech by Churchill, and a number of articles derogatory to the Germans. The stunt was repeated on Poland's national day, 3 May 1943, and included an appeal for the day to be treated as a public holiday which was extremely successful.[53]

The Belgians undertook an impressively planned and executed stunt on Armistice Day 1943 – a fake edition of the German-controlled main evening newspaper, *Le Soir*. The operation was overseen by the resistance group *Front de l'Indépendance*. Money was raised for the special printing of about 50,000 copies, and the owner of a large printing press, Ferdinand Wellens, agreed to do the printing. An employee of *Le Soir* and member of the Front, Théo Mullier, stole a mould of the masthead of the paper and provided a list of news kiosks and other distribution points. Distribution was vital for the success of the ruse. The kiosks were used to receiving copies at a set time, so much thought was given to the challenge of delaying the printing of the official *Le Soir* in order to provide a window for the fake *Le Soir* to reach the kiosks first. Sabotage of the printing press was rejected because it would endanger the workers in the plant. Another option was to request the RAF to bomb Brussels that afternoon because as soon as the air-raid sirens were sounded the electricity was cut off in the city, which would stop the presses of *Le Soir*. The RAF agreed to undertake the operation if possible, but in the event arrived twenty-four hours too late. This forced the resistance to adopt its back-up plan of setting fire to some delivery vans and blocking in others to delay the distribution of *Le Soir*. The ruse worked. The fake *Le Soir* arrived at the kiosks only fifteen minutes before the real one, sufficient time for 5,000 copies to have been sold before the Gestapo realized what was happening. A further 45,000 copies were sold throughout Belgium. The Germans hunted down the perpetrators and Ferdinand Wellens and Théo Mullier were both caught by the Germans and died in prison. In total, seventeen of the team of twenty-two involved in the project were killed.[54]

The production of the clandestine press was no easy task since the Germans imposed strict controls over the sale of newsprint and ink. This was followed by a prohibition on the sale of stencils and duplicating machines. Consequently the early output of the underground press was limited in size. For example, in France, Raymond Burgard produced the first two issues of *Valmy* using a child's printing press, and Christian Pineau typed the first issue of *Libération* in December 1940 on his own typewriter.[55] The first issues of most publications were produced with mimeograph machines which required the use of wax stencils and a copious amount of ink. Indeed, Frenay noted of the first machine obtained by *Combat*: 'It was a truly comical contraption. Sometimes it devoured four or five sheets at a time, then it would refuse to take any paper at all. Often – and always at the least expected moment – it would vomit Niagaras of ink.'[56] Frustrating this must have been, but it was also dangerous since the presence of ink on someone's fingers could reveal to the police or Germans that the person was engaged in a surreptitious printing project. The next stage up was the rotary press, which usually used metal plates. These could produce 800 copies before the stencil had to be replaced, a vast improvement on the limit of 100 imposed by the fragile wax stencils. But the rotary presses had disadvantages, namely that a special typewriter was needed to produce the metal stencils and the presses themselves were noisy and large and therefore difficult to conceal.

Large-scale production of newspapers required access to printing presses. The typesetting of the lead would normally be carried out in a separate location from the press itself. The typesetting process was noisy and required regular movements backwards and forwards to insert the lead type and frequent knocking of the type to ensure an even surface. Typesetters tried to minimize the danger by wearing slippers to muffle their movements, and reduce the noise of the knocking by striking at small areas at a time. This of course meant that the production of each newspaper took a long time, one of the many reasons why most of them were only two to eight pages long. Obtaining the lead type was a challenge in itself. In the Netherlands one of the main foundries producing type blocks inadvertently assisted the underground press by deciding to offload its stock of out-of-date gothic typefaces, which were promptly put to use by the underground press.[57] The completed plates then had to be transported clandestinely to the hidden location of the printing press. The plates were heavy and the sight of women and men carrying heavy loads in the street might attract suspicion. One woman in France placed ninety kilos of lead in the pram carrying her sleeping child and she recalled that the lead was so heavy that the pram springs scraped the pavement and made movement extremely difficult. In the Netherlands the clandestine paper *Trouw* used Javanese students to carry the type. Although these men appeared to be of a light build, they were weight-lifters and knew how to carry a heavy suitcase unobtrusively.[58]

The use of mimeograph machines had become widespread before the war and so it was fairly easy to locate one to use in secrecy. For example, the Norwegian underground paper *For Friheten* was produced on the mimeograph at Trondheim High School; *Résistance* was printed on the mimeograph located in the Musée de l'Homme, and *Défense de la France* began production in the cellars of the Sorbonne.[59] One Dutch newspaper was printed on a machine situated in the middle of a helpfully noisy dog pound while another Dutch paper, *Je maintiendrai*, was started in the attic of the Permanent Court of International Justice at The Hague.[60]

The larger the printing enterprise, the more care had to be taken to find a suitable location. By late spring 1943 *Combat* was being printed in a former cement factory outside Lyon which was half underground:

> This covered the noise somewhat and concealed our activities. But we still had to build a wall around the room with the presses. The 'laboratory' had been given a rather vague name: Bureau of Geodesic and Geographic Studies, suggesting a Parisian firm doing research. That way, we could get telephone service and electricity. The shop had two heavy professional presses. One enormous monster [that] Vélin put in working condition weighed five tons; there was also a newer, automated machine.[61]

In Poland, *Biuletyn Informacyjny* was produced in seven printing shops in Warsaw. One was located in the specially excavated cellar of a private house where electricity was taken from the main grid, but the air quality in the cellar was extremely poor.[62] *Défense de la France* housed its powerful Teisch printing press in a factory run by the parents of two of the group's members. The machine was located in the mail room and, when not in use, was concealed by an enormous crate moved using a system of pulleys.[63]

Obtaining ink and paper on the black market was expensive, and raising funds for publishing newspapers could often be the starting point for someone embarking on resistance. For example, in the Netherlands, Herman Friedhoff began his clandestine life by raising funds for *Het Parool*, and found it more difficult than expected: 'I discovered that few people were ready to back sympathetic words with hard cash . . .'[64] In Denmark, Monica Wichfeld was first initiated into the resistance when asked by a lodger on her estate to raise funds for the newspapers *Frit Danmark* and *Land og Folk*.[65] The Polish and Norwegian governments-in-exile and the Czech National Committee all provided funds for the clandestine press. Towards the end of the war, the Dutch government followed suit. Some newspapers refused to accept funds from abroad. In February 1943 *La Voix des Belges* proudly announced: 'Never – we've said it before and we say it again – has our newspaper received from anyone, whether Allies, government, political party, company or private individual, a single centime as a subsidy.' Like many of the French papers, it relied on voluntary contributions or subscriptions from individuals.[66] Newsprint was obtained from a variety of sources, with differing degrees of legality. There were outright thefts from the collaborationist press and hold-ups of lorries carrying paper. Sometimes those working for the official press could be bribed to 'lose' quantities of paper or to manipulate the permitted wastage quota. Some underground movements set up fake companies which could legally purchase paper that was then turned over to the production of the clandestine press.

Distribution of the press from the printing presses to warehouses or other storage facilities required great care and risk. In Warsaw the movement of *Biuletyn Informacyjny* from the printing press to the warehouses was a quasi-military operation:

> Usually, empty beer barrels were used or wooden cases bearing the name of some manufacturer. They had to be so well and tightly closed that it was impossible to see the contents without taking the thing to bits. They were removed on ordinary push-carts, which were then in use in Warsaw for every kind of goods. Near the push-cart, among the passersby, an armed escort would watch over the precious load. If anyone insisted on seeing the contents, a shot was the only way of finishing the argument.[67]

In France, the communist newspaper *Humanité* was distributed via the railway network. In the Netherlands and in Norway, some postal workers proved willing to take the risk of transporting bundles of newspapers.[68]

The distribution of individual copies of newspapers was often used as a test of nerve for novice resisters. For example, Hortense Daman started out as a distributor for *La Libre Belgique* before becoming a courier for the resistance.[69] In Norway *For Friheten* was distributed to subscribers only, with each subscriber being given a unique security number. The newspaper itself would be placed in his mailbox and if the correct number was not written on the paper then he knew it had been planted by the Gestapo and did not collect it.[70] Other distribution methods were more random. In Poland, copies of underground newspapers would be concealed inside an official paper for willing recipients, who would then be told by the seller that 'there was something very interesting inside'.[71] On 14 July 1943 *Défense de la France* undertook a successful and well-organized stunt by sending teams under guard to scatter copies of the newspaper in carriages on the Paris Metro. On another occasion the newspaper was distributed from 'a front-wheel drive cabriolet moving slowly up the Champs-Élysées delivering fistfuls of the paper from the running-board to café terraces'.[72] But not everyone wanted to read the clandestine press. Metod Milać and his brother distributed the first issues of a secret Yugoslav newspaper in Italian-controlled Ljubljana and found that their neighbours secretly returned the newspapers to them but did not betray them to the authorities.[73] Eva Rogers was given copies of *De Frie Danske* to distribute and recorded: 'I feel guilty because I am not sure that I know even that many people who might wish to know the truth, but in the end I decide people must be told, and if they are sensible and don't leave the papers lying around they won't come to any harm.'[74]

The Germans naturally attempted to curtail the activities of the clandestine press by arresting editors and printers. Almost all of the early clandestine newspapers produced in German-occupied France were badly hit by arrests before the end of 1941.[75] The editor of *Voix de Belge*, Camille Joset, was arrested in 1942, but continued to write articles from prison which were smuggled out and printed. In May 1942 the Gestapo happened to stop a van carrying *La Libre Belgique* from Brussels where it had been printed to Lille and found an address book on the driver containing the addresses of about twenty dropping-off points. The Belgian paper *Liberté* was also hit by a number of arrests in June 1942.[76] In the Netherlands *Vrij Nederland* and *Het Parool* were frequently badly affected by arrests of their editorial teams.[77] It is impossible to know for certain the number of people arrested and either imprisoned or executed for activities concerned with the clandestine press. Estimates have been made suggesting that, for example, at least 770 people died because of their work on the secret presses in the Netherlands alone, and over 2,000 people in Belgium.[78]

For all its efforts, the clandestine press could only reach a limited number of people. The broadcasts of the BBC from Britain could, however, reach a far wider audience since radio ownership was widespread in many countries, particularly in western Europe. There are many stories from across Europe narrating how the streets would empty at a certain hour as everyone rushed home to listen to the BBC.* The Germans responded with

* On 1 January 1943 BBC broadcasts to France lasted for 5½ hours; Italy, 4¼ hours; the Netherlands, 2½ hours; Poland, 2 hours and 10 minutes; Czechoslovakia 1¾ hours; and so on down to Albania which was allocated 15 minutes.

widespread bans on listening to foreign radio stations. For example, every owner of a radio in the Protectorate received a gold-coloured plate emblazoned with the words 'Listening to foreign broadcasts is punishable by death'.[79] In France listening to the BBC was banned in the Occupied Zone in October 1940 and in the Unoccupied Zone a year later, yet in the summer of 1942 it was estimated that 75 per cent of the population of Rennes, in the Occupied Zone, were regular listeners.[80] In Denmark, where the population was permitted to listen to foreign broadcasts, a report in October 1941 noted that the engineers in the control room of Copenhagen's electricity supply were seeing a significant spike in consumption at 18.15 as a significant number of people tuned in to the BBC.[81] The possession of radio sets was prohibited in Poland in October 1939 and on the west coast of Norway in September 1941. This led to the birth of 'professional listeners', people who would note down BBC broadcasts in shorthand and then disseminate them either orally or through the clandestine press.[82] The Germans attempted to block the BBC through jamming but met with limited success. In the Netherlands the effect of jamming could be reduced by the use of noise suppressors, although the sound quality remained poor, and the Danes proved particularly adept at sabotaging German jamming operations.[83] The BBC was not the only foreign station listened to by people in the occupied countries. In 1942 Stalin sanctioned the first radio station to broadcast to a foreign country, Radio Free Yugoslavia, operating from Tiflis. This was followed by Radio Kościuszko for Poland and Za slovenskú Slobodu for Slovakia.[84] Swiss radio broadcasts were also popular in southern France.

Black radio stations, pretending to broadcast from the home country but in fact operating in Britain, were also established. Perhaps the most effective of these was Świt, operating into Poland. This was launched in 1942 and each day the underground would radio London with the latest news, which Świt would then beam back to Poland. This gave the impression of such up-to-date news that many assumed that Świt could only be operating within Poland.[85] The Czechs had managed a similar kind of operation for a period in 1940 when a transmitter, Nazdar, transmitted to London and its contents were re-broadcast by the BBC Czech Service to a wider audience.[86] Two transmitters, Christo Bolev and Naroden Glass, gave the impression of broadcasting from within Bulgaria, but in fact were operating from Moscow.[87] Black radio stations also broadcast into France: Radio Catholique to parish priests; Radio Travail to industrial workers and trade union leaders; and Radio Inconnu, which was aimed at the Unoccupied Zone and was overtly hostile to Pétain and the Vichy regime.[88]

The BBC served a vital function in serving as a link between exiled governments and personalities and their home country. For example, Queen Wilhelmina's speeches on Radio Orange committed her government-in-exile to support the home resistance. In Norway: 'The role of the BBC was tremendous. The importance cannot be overestimated of the effect of the King speaking to the people. The role of symbols such as the King, the Flag, and the Constitution was monumental.'[89] Edvard Beneš was an immediate beneficiary since even before his Czech National Committee was recognized as a government-in-exile in 1941, the former president and his allies were given radio time on the Czech BBC programmes. This enabled the Czechs to understand that Beneš was leading the fight for liberation and for the recognition of the integrity of Czechoslovakia. The main Czech resistance organization, ÚVOD, promoted news of the timing of the BBC broadcasts through the underground press and with stickers in phone booths. The effect could be seen when the BBC called for a boycott of the official press during the week of 14 September 1941. Sales of the official newspapers in Prague dropped by 70 per cent, and by between 25 and 50 per cent elsewhere in the Protectorate.[90]

The BBC arguably put de Gaulle on the map as the leader of the Free French. The BBC broadcast two programmes to the French: Maurice Schumann spoke on behalf of the Free French for five minutes a day, followed by the programme *Les Français parlent aux Français*, run by a team led by Michel Saint-Denis, known as Pierre Bourdan. De Gaulle himself gave a total of sixty-seven broadcasts over the BBC. The effect of these broadcasts could be seen when a call made in December 1940 for all French people to remain indoors for a specific hour on 1 January 1941 met with a noticeable response despite the German efforts to tempt the population out with the promise of a delivery of potatoes during that hour. Even more successful were the calls for demonstrations on May Day in 1942. Around 100,000 people gathered in Marseille and in Lyon as well as other smaller demonstrations elsewhere in France. The calls for demonstrations on 14 July 1942 were even more successful with a total of over 1.5 million people taking to the streets in a show of nationalism.[91]

Undoubtedly the most successful visual demonstration of the power and wide reach of the BBC was the success of the 'V' campaign. This was the brainchild of the BBC Belgian editor, who made the suggestion of writing 'Vs' everywhere in a broadcast to Belgium on 14 January 1941.[92] That spring the campaign was extended throughout Europe. The effect was immediate: 'At the moment all over the Protectorate there is a flood of V-symbols, on clothes and ribbons, painted in white on house doors, monuments, on street asphalt in all localities up and down the land, everywhere.' The Czechs adopted the 'V' as the first letter of *vítězství*, meaning victory. They even created a whole sentence made up of Vs: '*Věřit ve vítězství velkého vůdce je velká volovina*' ('To believe in the victory of the great Führer is absolute rubbish').[93] In Denmark and Norway the Vs signified *Vi Vil Vinde* ('We will win'). The Norwegian resistance had a coup when *Vi Vil Vinde* was written in mud on a road, photographed by the RAF and then used on a 20-øre stamp issued by the Norwegian government-in-exile. The Norwegian resistance also sent V stickers to all post offices with a letter, purportedly signed by the local NS organization, which instructed the staff to display the stickers prominently. This was done, even though the staff probably knew that the instruction really came from the resistance. There was no word in Polish suitable for the V to be used but V-signs nonetheless proliferated, often with the addition of 'erloren' to make *Verloren*, meaning 'lost' in German.[94]

Josef Goebbels, the Nazis' propaganda minister, made the error of attempting to take over the V-campaign: 'To respond to English propaganda, the Germans have decreed that V is supposed to be the sign of German Victory. Everywhere they have raised big white flags decorated with a monumental V, and pasted red posters with a black V over the swastika.' Goebbels wanted to suggest that the V stood for the fictitious German pagan god Viktoria or was a reference to Caesar's '*veni, vidi, vici*'.[95] German efforts to eradicate the resistance inscriptions of the V could have an unintentional effect:

> All along the Seine, between the Porte du Carrousel and Place de la Concorde, all the plane trees are displaying a big V around a cross of Lorraine carved deep into their bark . . . The occupying authorities had the inscriptions tarred over, but that makes them still more visible. The black stains attract the eye.[96]

In Louvain, Gaston Vandermeerssche drew a huge V-sign in whitewash on the square in front of the German Kommandantur. The whitewash seeped between the cobblestones, making it impossible for the Germans to eradicate the V-sign entirely and the square was closed to public access until the sign had disappeared.[97] On 27 June 1941 the BBC began using the opening bars of Beethoven's Fifth Symphony as the interval signal for its European service. It had been noticed that the first notes matched the Morse code for the letter V – dot, dot, dot, dash: 'From now on those four notes, those four beats, will be the rallying sign of hope in the prison of Europe . . . A rhythm is contagious in a way that an inscription is not.'[98]

The production of the clandestine press was started by individuals before being taken over by resistance organizations. Its value as the means of disseminating information and opinions was widely recognized and in some countries efforts were made to supervise the underground press to ensure that the newspapers all carried the same message to their readership as liberation approached. The process was begun in France in April 1942 when de Gaulle's official representative in France, Jean Moulin, set up a *Bureau d'Information et de Presse* (BIP) under the control of Georges Bidault. The primary aim of this organization was to link the secret press in both zones and to make the whole process of news production more professional. Later in the war the BIP issued daily bulletins to all the editors of the clandestine press.[99] The Norwegians also established a press secretariat in 1942. One editor sat on the Home Front committee and assumed responsibility for issuing the Home Front's daily orders or paroles to the whole underground press. The secretariat was subjected to several Gestapo raids, notably in November 1943 and February 1944, but replacements were quickly found.[100] In September 1943 Børge Outze, a crime reporter on the official daily newspaper *National Times*, created the Danish Illegal Press Coordinating Committee. This produced a daily bulletin *Information*, which was not only distributed within Denmark but also sent to Sweden, from where it could be sent around the world. Outze himself was captured by the Germans in October 1944 but obtained his release by promising to work for the Germans against the communists, whereupon he promptly departed for Sweden. His replacement Sigvald Kristensen ensured that *Information* was published for the remainder of the war and indeed into peacetime.[101]

The very fact that the clandestine press grew to become the principal medium through which the resistance and government-in-exile could issue orders to the populations on their expected conduct throughout the occupation, and especially on the eve of liberation, shows its very power and success. The resistance in Europe as a whole had its share of successes and failures, but when it came to winning the 'battle of the mind', this must be seen as one of its principal achievements.

4
Escape from Occupied Europe

As much of Europe collapsed into a deep state of despair caused by the rapid German conquests, there still remained a significant number of soldiers and airmen trapped in Europe who wanted to continue the fight. These fell into two categories: evaders who had never fallen into German hands, and escapers, those who had been captured but had then absconded from prisoner-of-war camps or from columns of POWs being marched to Germany. Added to these two categories were those interned, either in still-neutral countries such as Romania and Hungary, or under the terms of the armistice in France. At the beginning the majority of evaders and escapers were soldiers trying to reach Britain to join their national armed forces. Later, however, the majority were airmen, shot down over occupied Europe as the Allied strategic bombing campaign of Germany intensified. Many of these men found people willing to assist them to reach Spain across the Pyrenees as the first step on their journey back to Britain, and so the escape lines were formed.

In December 1939 a section of the War Office called MI9 was created under Major Norman Crockatt. Its remit was wide, encompassing the collection of intelligence regarding the locations of POW camps housing British officers and men and the briefing of servicemen on how to evade capture. This included recommendations on how to pass as a local, which European fauna and flora could be safely eaten, and the provision of escape kits which contained maps printed on silk, a tiny compass, and many other useful pieces of kit. Efforts were also made to smuggle escape material into POW camps, concealed in permitted items.[1] In the summer of 1941 a subsection of MI9 was created, called Room 900 after its War Office address, which was staffed by two men who had first-hand experience of escape lines. One was Jimmy Langley, who had worked in Marseille before being repatriated having lost an arm during the battle for France. The other was Airey Neave, the first British officer to make a successful home run from the supposedly escape-proof POW camp in Colditz Castle in eastern Germany.

It is very difficult to estimate the numbers of people who escaped from France and the Low Countries during the war. The figure of around 3,000 airmen is much quoted but to these must be added the many Allied soldiers who had been left behind in France in 1940 and made their way successfully out of that country to Britain. The escape lines also did not deal exclusively with servicemen. A large number of civilians also utilized them, whether they were Jews fleeing the round-ups, Frenchmen seeking to join the Free French forces, or young men evading conscription for forced labour. This chapter will focus on escapes from the countries which fell to German domination in the period from 1939 to 1941 – Czechoslovakia, Poland, Norway, the Channel Islands, the Netherlands, Belgium, France and Greece. The story of the escapes and evasion of Allied personnel from Italy and Yugoslavia is intricately tied up in the wider story of the progress of the war and will therefore be covered later.

Working on escape lines was not necessarily seen as an act of resistance by the helpers, but often as a humanitarian gesture. For example, a resistance leader in France, Philippe de Vomécourt, suggested that:

> Many of those who organised or aided the escape routes drew a distinction in their own minds between helping people to escape and committing what they considered 'crimes' against the Germans and the spirit of the Armistice. To them, there was a difference in kind between helping troops – French or British prisoners, aircrew, or any other 'active' troops – or political or racial refugees, to escape from the Germans, and the commission of sabotage. The first they considered a duty; either a patriotic duty or a humane one. The escape routes attracted helpers who, by religious conviction or for other sympathetic reasons, could not contemplate the abetting or carrying out of sabotage.[2]

Denys Teare, an RAF evader, identified another possible reason why so many people helped: 'because it was the only contact they had with the opposition to the Germans. Our bombers passing overhead on their way to Germany were a sign of hope for the future, of freedom, and that's what we represented.'[3] After the war Donald Darling estimated that in the Low Countries and France alone about 30,000 people had been involved in working on various escape lines.[4] This figure is, however, far too low because it only covered those lines working to get British and American airmen home and not those who worked on lines helping other nationalities and non-service personnel.

Various features appear in regard to the operation of escape lines which will be evident again and again in the broader resistance narrative. The first is the sheer resilience of those involved. As will be shown below, working on escape lines was an extremely hazardous business and at least 500 people died either through trial and then execution or as a result of the appalling conditions in concentration camps and German prisons. In September 1941 the German commandant in France, General Otto von Stülpnagel, issued a notice that helping Allied aircrew would result in death for the males involved and deportation to concentration camps for the females. He also offered a reward of up to 10,000 francs to anyone who apprehended a downed airman or contributed to his capture.[5] This leads to the second problem, that of traitors. The escape lines were vulnerable to penetration by Germans posing as airmen and steps were taken to lower this risk, but great damage to the escape lines was also caused by several traitors who would then often go on to inflict a similar level of damage on resistance networks. Yet the escape lines continued to operate despite being repeatedly penetrated. Cécile Jouan of the Comet line commented:

> Was it a taste for danger that drove us on? There was plenty of that. But what was at the heart of it? A malicious delight in irritating the occupier. That was part of it too of course, but only a little. Above all it was the joy, the thrill of feeling useful, the camaraderie of battle and the exaltation of this unforeseen conflict, in which all our weapons were born of love.[6]

Arrests ran at such a high level, particularly after the German invasion of southern France in November 1942, that the helpers began to consider how they would respond when they were arrested, not *if* but *when*. The work of the escape lines in France and Belgium only came to an end on the eve of D-Day when the movement of evaders by train became too dangerous as the railways were targeted by both Allied air bombardment and local sabotage.

The Czech and Polish soldiers who left their occupied countries during the bitterly cold winter of 1939–40 to join their new national armies being formed in France may be termed as absconders rather than escapers since they were not in captivity. The Czech armed forces had been disbanded after the German occupation but the servicemen had not been interned. They were therefore free to travel to Hungary, where the Czech underground had established an outpost in Budapest, sharing the same building as the French Embassy, before crossing into still-neutral Yugoslavia and Italy on their way to France. It is not clear how many Czech servicemen chose to take this route.

The Poles, on the other hand, had been interned in Romania and Hungary in large numbers after they had crossed those frontiers at the end of the September 1939 campaign. Yet the cost of maintaining these men was prohibitively expensive and so the authorities turned a blind eye to the 'escapes' of the Polish servicemen. The Polish Embassy in Bucharest was full of 'well informed and enterprising people, scheming, wheeling, dealing, bribing and doing everything they could to get everybody out of Romania before the Germans took over the country'.[7] Around 2,500 soldiers and 1,300 airmen left Romania during October 1939 and the following months. Some headed for the Black Sea ports of Constanța and Balcik and made their way to the Lebanon, where a Polish division was formed. Others travelled overland through Yugoslavia and Italy to France. The Hungarians were notably helpful in facilitating the escape of their Polish guests. The Polish military attaché in Bucharest, Colonel Jan Emisarski-Pindelli, organized the evacuation office and worked in close collaboration with Jozef Antall, an official in the Hungarian Interior Ministry, and with the Hungarian-Polish Committee for the Care of Refugees. Stanisław Maczek, later to command the 1st Polish Armoured Brigade, recalled that 'the Hungarian delegate to the Polish staff, in a confidential face to face conversation with me, promised that the Hungarian authorities would turn a blind eye and will not interfere with the evacuation of brigades to France, so long as it was cautious, quiet, and carried out in small units'.[8]

After the fall of France the Germans had taken prisoner around 1.5 million Frenchmen and about 40,000 British soldiers. Many of these were despatched to POW camps in Poland and the Protectorate and some of them escaped, relying on local people to help them reach the frontiers. The Vichy Embassy in Budapest was prepared to supply passports to escaped French POWs attempting to reach the Lebanon but relied on local guides to get the men across the frontiers. One of these guides, Vera Laska, recalled:

> The borders were heavily patrolled, but the border guards were no match for us, especially those hailing from flat Hungary. They were like fish out of the water in the mountainous terrain that we knew as the palms of our hands from years of camping and skiing. They got easily tired and lost; on skis they made a pretty ridiculous picture.[9]

Many of these guides were women, and this was true for escape lines in general, because women were less likely to be suspected of being engaged in clandestine activity.

In Poland several organizations sprang up to encourage and help British POWs to escape. One, based in Bydgoszcz in the region of Poland annexed to the Reich, smuggled the POWs from the camps in lorries and arranged for them to board ships bound for neutral Sweden. Another, the Anglo-Polish Society, was based in Warsaw and operated an escape line which ran through southern Poland into the Protectorate and finally into Turkey via Romania. In the middle of 1942 the Gestapo penetrated the organization and brought its activities largely to a halt by arresting the main participants. One, however, Mrs Markowska, remained at liberty and continued to shelter escaped British POWs. Some of these went native and became engaged in the Polish underground, the *Armia Krajowa*. Corporal Ronald Jeffery joined an AK intelligence cell and, after that was broken by the Gestapo in May 1943, reached the sanctuary of Sweden. Another, John Ward, stayed with the AK and would go on to provide valuable reports on the Warsaw Uprising during August and September 1944.[10]

The Norwegians had become thoroughly disillusioned with Britain after the poor performance of the British Army during the brief 1940 campaign, but after the Battle of Britain demonstrated that Britain would continue in the war Norwegians made considerable efforts to reach Britain across the North Sea. Oluf Reed Olsen, who would return to Norway as an intelligence agent, noted:

> The plan for the voyage to Britain, however, was to prove rather more complicated than we had at first thought. It was no simple matter to obtain a serviceable boat. The Germans had long ago become alive to the increase in the traffic from the west coast of Norway over to Britain; fishing boats were always disappearing, and the British wireless reported the arrival of many refugees from Norway.[11]

The Germans increased their coastal patrols, and boats needed a special permit to sail outside the harbours. David Howarth, who created a transport service running between the Shetland Islands and Norway, noticed other difficulties: the Germans extinguished the lighthouses and restricted fishing to a zone of fifty miles from the coast which was patrolled by air. Furthermore, collecting escapers in remote locations risked betrayal to the Germans by the local quislings.[12]

The North Sea crossing was very hazardous. In total around 3,300 men, women, and children reached Britain in fishing boats which were not designed to cross such an expanse. Those setting out from the area between Molde in the north and Haugesund in the south headed for the Shetland Islands, while those from the far north sailed to Iceland, and those in the south for Scotland. The men who escaped either joined the Norwegian armed forces or like Reed Olsen and Odd Starheim would join SOE and then return to Norway to carry out resistance. In March 1942 Starheim engineered an audacious hijacking of a coastal steamer, SS *Galtesund*, and reached Aberdeen with important agents aboard. Among them was Einar Skinnarland, who held vital information about the heavy-water plant at

Vemork. The human cost of these voyages was high and 308 people died in their efforts to escape, mostly at sea during storms, or were captured by the Germans. About fifty of those helping the escapers either were executed by the Germans or died in prison. In total, around 10 per cent of those who tried to leave Norway by the sea route died in the attempt.[13]

Many young men from the Channel Islands made their way to Britain after the outbreak of the war in September 1939 to enlist in the armed forces or the merchant navy. They were joined by more after the British government demilitarized the islands in June 1940 and the two British battalions stationed there returned to Britain. Once the Germans had occupied the islands, research has shown that a total of 228 people attempted to escape, of whom sixty-three left Guernsey and thirty-eight left Jersey to make the long dangerous voyage to British shores in the period before the end of September 1940. After this, the Germans mined the coastlines or established prohibited zones. Fishing was restricted to designated harbours, in registered boats, and only during the hours of daylight.

This meant that only around thirty people attempted to leave the heavily fortified islands in the period before D-Day. In November 1940 a Jerseyman, Denis Vibert, rowed to Guernsey as the first stage of his effort to reach Britain. The winds changed and he was unable to progress further, caught influenza and abandoned his escape attempt. A year later he was successful and was picked up by a British destroyer off Portland Bill, having rowed for three days without food after the engines on his dinghy had failed. The escape attempt from Jersey by three teenagers, Peter Hassall, Dennis Audrain, and Maurice Gould, ended in tragedy. Their boat was swamped soon after they started out and Audrain was drowned. Hassall and Gould were caught by the German police on their return to shore and deported to Fresnes prison where Gould died. (Hassall survived the war.) Guernseyman Fred Hockey and his seven companions were spotted by a German plane which dropped a flare:

> Terrified, the men lay flat on the bottom of the boat and held their breath. It was like daylight until the flare burnt out and the men could not understand why they were not seen. They continued on their hazardous journey and at 4 a.m. their engine broke down. This was repaired and on they went. It was foggy which made navigation difficult, but on the credit side the fog was a cloak that hid them from the enemy.

They reached the Devon coast after a nineteen-hour voyage. The Germans carried out reprisals by ordering severe restrictions on fishing, a major step since the islanders relied on the fish for food now that they were cut off from supplies from Britain and France. Furthermore, there was the threat that all men of military age would be deported from the islands. Indeed, in September 1942 deportations of foreign-born men and their families were carried out. These threats meant that the news of successful escapes often met with disapproval from the islanders and their British administrators, who feared the measures the Germans might carry out against them. The sheer isolation of the Channel Islands and the very high German-islander ratio, since the islands formed part of Hitler's Atlantic Wall, made the islanders feel extremely vulnerable and acted as an effective brake in the development of resistance in Guernsey and Jersey. On the other hand, after D-Day the proximity of the liberated coast of France to Jersey acted as an inducement for more escapes.[14]

British servicemen accidentally left behind in Greece and on Crete at the conclusion of the unsuccessful British campaigns in 1941 found people willing to shelter them and prevent them from being sent to POW camps in Germany. MI9's station in Cairo, known as A Force, organized escapes from the Greek mainland and by March 1942 operated five chartered caiques ferrying the escapers across the Aegean to the west coast of Turkey. Lieutenant Commander Noël Rees, the British vice-consul at İzmir, set up a clandestine base near Çesme in Turkey. He was assisted by Commander Vladimir Wolfson, the naval attaché in Istanbul, and by Major General William Arnold, the military attaché in Ankara. Operations were assisted by the fact that the Turks turned a blind eye to the sailings, and the long Greek coastline and numerous offshore islands made it extremely difficult for the Germans to mount sufficient patrols to interdict the caiques.[15]

On 26 July 1941 Commander Francis Pool was landed by submarine to organize the evacuation of British servicemen from Crete. These were being well looked after by the locals because:

> The Cretans deemed it a sacred duty to look after these [Allied] soldiers by whose side they had fought and whom fortune had brought from their far-off country to wage war and to shed their blood on our mountains. We gave them food and clothing so that they could discard their uniforms and move about more freely, and hid them in the most suitable places.[16]

One of these hiding places was the monastery of Preveli, whose abbot agreed to allow it to be used as a gathering place for the escapers. Most reached the monastery after passing through the village of Asi Gonia, at the eastern end of the White Mountains. Two men who would later become involved in British operations to create resistance in Crete, Petro Petrakas and Colonel Andrea Papadakis, were based in or near the village and made their first contacts with the British during these evacuation operations. Francis Pool left Crete by submarine in August having evacuated at least 130 men. One of them, Jack Smith-Hughes, soon returned as the first SOE agent on Crete. Pool's replacement, Monty Woodhouse, arrived in the autumn of 1941 and in the six months before his departure in April 1942 continued to arrange escapes. He found the process deeply frustrating because 'the few boats which called on the south coast usually landed at different points from those I had indicated'. Woodhouse would go on to play an essential role in the resistance on the Greek mainland.[17]

The rapid conquest of the Netherlands, Belgium, and above all France by the Germans left a substantial number of Allied troops stranded on the continent, notwithstanding the evacuation from Dunkirk. Those captured by the Germans were held in makeshift camps in France and Belgium until camps in Germany and occupied Poland had been prepared for them. Many others, British, Polish, French, and Belgian, were never captured and made their way towards the south of France hoping to find shipping to take them to Britain or to make the arduous crossing of the Pyrenees and reach either Lisbon or Gibraltar. Under the terms of the armistice, the Vichy authorities were required to disarm and intern all Allied servicemen in Fort St Jean in Marseille, St Hippolyte du Fort at Nîmes, and La Turbie near Monte Carlo.

The first efforts to assist these escapers and evaders were the result of decisions taken on the spur of the moment, such as picking up a soldier or airman by the side of the road and giving him shelter, or seizing a man out of a column of POWs being marched into captivity. An American woman, Etta Shiber, and a British-born woman, Kitty Bonnefous, were returning to Paris after the armistice when they came upon a British pilot, William Gray, and smuggled him back to Paris in the boot of their car. This led them to use their contacts to smuggle him across the demarcation line. One contact they made was with a priest, Father Christian Ravier, whose church in the Somme district was caring for around 1,000 British servicemen hiding in the woods. By the end of October 1940 this hastily constructed escape line had enabled about 100 men to reach the Unoccupied Zone. Mary Lindell had served with the French Red Cross driving ambulances during the French campaign. After the armistice she made use of the fact that families had become separated to set up a system whereby she would receive German permission to drive a child to the south to be reunited with its parents and would be accompanied by a mechanic, who was actually a British serviceman. She also made contact with farmers in Ruffec whose farms straddled the demarcation line and who were willing to assist evaders in crossing the line. All three women were ultimately arrested in 1941 and sentenced to a few months in prison. Etta Shiber was exchanged for a German spy held in the United States in 1942. Mary Lindell was released in November 1941, reached Britain in July 1942, and returned to France later that year to set up a more formally organized escape line operating under the name Marie-Claire. Kitty Bonnefous survived imprisonment but Father Ravier was sentenced to death: he was rescued from prison by the resistance and resumed his assistance to the escape lines.[18]

Some of the early helpers of evading Allied servicemen later went on to become more deeply involved in the resistance. Germaine Tillion first became involved in resistance when running an escape line in eastern France for escaped French POWs with Colonel Paul Hauet, which helped around 5,000 men reach their homes by the middle of 1941. Another network in eastern France, in German-annexed Alsace, was run by Lucienne Welschinger, and helped several hundred French escapers to reach their homes. Their most famous passenger was General Henri Giraud, who escaped from his POW camp in the castle of Königstein near Dresden in April 1942 and later reported: 'The Alsatians were ready not only to give a prisoner money, but to risk their lives for him. Without knowing a single person there or being helped by any organisation, I passed right through Alsace without problem.' Welschinger was later caught by the Germans and executed in Strasbourg in January 1943. The American former State Department clerk and now correspondent for the *New York Post*, Virginia Hall, had served in France in May 1940 as an ambulance driver before escaping into Spain and reaching Britain where she was recruited by SOE and returned to Lyon in September 1941. Her flat not only became the centre of SOE activity in unoccupied France but she also had contacts with those who were already working on or financing escape lines such as Robert Leprevost and George Whittinghill, the United States vice-consul. British airmen were advised to head for the American consulate in Lyon to make contact with Virginia, who would arrange their onward journey.[19]

The list of the early escape lines is simply too long to enumerate: some focused on certain nationalities while others took servicemen belonging to any Allied nation.[20] What these early lines all had in common was their destination – Marseille:

> Marius, patron saint of all liars, is also the patron saint of this city, which had a reputation for criminal activities second only to Chicago, and like Chicago it was controlled by gangsters. Add to all this a police force whose loyalty to Marshal Pétain and the Government of Free France was doubtful, representatives of the German and Italian Armistice Commissions and a battalion of the Bersaglieri which Mussolini sent to show the flag, and you will have the background of the city which was to be the first operational centre of allied escape and evasion from France.[21]

When Stanisław Maczek and his party of evading Poles from the armoured division reached Marseille in July 1940 he noted that the city was overcrowded with men dressed in civilian clothes whose bearing could not conceal the fact that they were soldiers hoping to get out of France and re-enter the war. Maczek himself reached Britain via Morocco and Lisbon.[22]

The Poles used small wooden sailing ships known as feluccas to extract their countrymen from the Mediterranean coast. The British contacted the Poles and, under Captain Frank Slocum, a successful operation was mounted to collect a party of fifty British evaders from Canet-Plage near Perpignan in July 1942. Two other operations later that year rescued over 100 RAF airmen and commandos who had escaped the debacle of the Dieppe raid that August. The feluccas were also used to land SOE agents in France. When the Germans invaded the south in November 1942 the Polish officer in charge of the feluccas, Lieutenant Jan Buchowski, was forced to write to his superior:

> The French coastline is in all likelihood very strongly guarded by the Germans, so that the idea that a vessel might lie 30–40 miles offshore for the three days needed and remain unnoticed is unthinkable. The French patrolled a coastal strip of about 5 miles; it must be assumed that the current German patrols are covering 100 miles. The vessels used in clandestine work are fishing boats, which are very slow (7 knots). If there has been good observation from the air, a patrol ship can always be sent to check the identity of the vessel. Moreover, the Axis powers will be especially suspicious of a vessel travelling along a north-south route.

Felucca sailings were therefore suspended, but small-scale collections of men continued so that by the end of the war the Polish operation had carried at least 600 men into or out of occupied Europe.[23]

Central to British operations in Marseille was the Seamen's Mission at Rue de Forbin run by the Scotsman Donald Caskie, the minister of the Scots Kirk in Paris, who had joined the exodus south in May 1940. The mission supplied the escapers and evaders with food and shelter. Caskie was assisted by an evader from the Highland Light Infantry, Captain Ian Garrow, who had contacts with the United States consul and with wealthy expatriates. Among these were Louis and Renée Nouveau, who allowed their flat on the Quai Rive Neuve to be used to house Allied servicemen, and Nancy Fiocca, whose husband Henri financed many of the escapes. Nancy would later return to France as Nancy Wake, an SOE agent.[24]

The SOE began smuggling agents back into France in early 1941 by sea, and a misadventure befalling an operation in April 1941 led to the founding of one of the great escape lines – the Pat line. A Belgian doctor, Albert-Marie Guérisse, was forced to swim ashore and was arrested by the French. He claimed that he was a Canadian airman called Patrick O'Leary. He was duly sent to St Hippolyte du Fort, where he made contact with Garrow, who arranged his departure from the fort and into Marseille to help him with the escape line. Caskie described 'O'Leary' as:

> . . . one of the bravest men I have ever known. Gay and fearless, his sense of humour led him to enjoy situations so nerve-racking they might have stopped the stoutest heart. But he was strict, kindly and protective to those under his command: fighting the enemy he was entirely ruthless . . . His efficiency was awe-inspiring. All arrangements for his operations were worked out to the minutest degree. Each man knew his task thoroughly.

The line ran from the north, where Jean de la Olla and his assistants Jacques Wattebled and the Fillerin family gathered together evading airmen. Abbé Pierre Carpentier used his private printing press in Abbeville to supply them with false papers and Madame Arnaud operated from her farm at Les Tuyères to get the evaders across the demarcation line. In the south there were plenty of helpers ready to get the men to Marseille. From there the men would be sent to Toulouse where an elderly Frenchwoman, Françoise Dissart, controlled a group of Pyrenees guides who would take the men into Spain where the British vice-consul Donald Darling would arrange their onward passage.

The operation of the Pat line was so successful that it is unsurprising it attracted the attention of the Vichy police and of the Germans. The first victim was Garrow, whom the French arrested in October 1941 on the charge of supplying intelligence to the British and interned in Mauzac prison, which also housed the early F Section SOE agents caught that year. O'Leary arranged Garrow's escape and escorted him to the Pyrenees where O'Leary bid farewell to Garrow with the words: 'Can this go on much longer?' At the end of April 1942 the French authorities, who had long had their suspicions about the Seamen's Mission, gave Caskie ten days to close the mission. Caskie left for Grenoble and the flats belonging to Louis Nouveau and Dr Georges Rodocanachi took over as shelters for the evaders. The first two radio operators sent to the Pat line were arrested by the French police in the course of 1942. In November 1942 the Germans invaded southern France, creating extremely difficult operating conditions for the escape lines. The Vichy police had arrested only a few evaders and their helpers but the Germans were more determined to stop the radio traffic by using radio-detection vans. In October 1942 a young Australian, Tom Groome, arrived as a radio operator for the Pat line until January

1943 when a German direction-finding team caught him operating his set. He managed to send a signal to Britain warning that he had been arrested (he survived the war) and his courier quickly notified O'Leary.

But the real damage done to the Pat line came through treachery, most notably through one person. A man calling himself Captain Harold Cole, who alleged that he had been left behind after the Dunkirk evacuation, had made contact with the Pat line and offered to escort evaders to the Pyrenees. Enquiries in London revealed that there was no such captain but noted that a Sergeant Cole had absconded from his regiment taking with him the funds of his mess. It later transpired that he was well known to Scotland Yard. Such criminality did not automatically exclude him from being used as a guide, and some of the men who made successful trips into Spain with his help sang his praises. But in the autumn of 1941 suspicions began to grow around Cole's activities. There were unexplained arrests of men as they reached a safe house in Perpignan; Cole had been seen in Marseille when he was supposed to be in the north of France; and, finally, he had not given money to a helper called Duprez in Lille. Caskie had his own suspicions regarding Cole: 'Cole was, I felt, a half man and when the unresolved half was defined he might be a traitor.' In November 1941 Cole was confronted with the evidence against him at a meeting with O'Leary and three helpers on the line, Bruce Dowding, Mario Prassinos, and Duprez at Dr Rodocanachi's flat. Caskie wrote later:

> To my knowledge, O'Leary had decided to kill him that night. Pat and his lieutenants were certain that the case against Cole was complete. His movements in certain areas coincided with betrayals or were close enough to make it likely that he had been more than a possible traitor. All other members of the organisation had been checked. Only Cole remained ambiguous.

During the heated discussion O'Leary beat Cole and threatened to kill him, but Cole escaped from the flat. Efforts were made to warn all who had come into contact with Cole but it was too late. One after another the vital links in the chain were broken in December, starting with Abbé Carpentier and including Dowding and Duprez, and eventually around fifty people were caught by the Germans owing to Cole's treachery. In May 1942 Cole himself and his young French wife Suzanne were arrested by the Vichy police in Lyon. In prison Cole admitted to Suzanne that he was a traitor and, after her release in August, she discovered that he had stolen goods and money from her three aunts in Paris and northern France.[25] Following the German invasion of southern France, Cole worked willingly for SS-Sturmbannführer Hans Josef Kieffer, head of the *Sicherheitsdienst* (SD) in Paris, the director of operations to capture SOE agents, escaped POWs, and resistance fighters. It is alleged that Cole assisted in the capture of around 150 members of the resistance.* O'Leary escaped the net the Germans spread as they followed the contacts supplied by Cole. But treachery on the line did not stop there. In January 1943 Louis Nouveau was approached in Paris by a man calling himself Roger le Neveu, known also as Roger le Légionnaire, who offered to escort airmen south. The first two parties reached the foot of the Pyrenees without trouble but the third, which Nouveau had joined, was suddenly arrested when changing trains at St Pierre des Corps, a suburb of Tours. These arrests were followed by more in Paris. In March, Roger le Légionnaire reached Toulouse and met O'Leary who questioned him about the arrests in Paris. Suddenly O'Leary found himself under arrest by the Gestapo. The arrest of O'Leary effectively meant the end of the Pat line. It had helped around 600 soldiers and airmen reach freedom, and the last travellers along the line were Major Herbert Hasler and Bill Sparks, the two survivors of the Cockleshell raid. At least thirty helpers, including Abbé Carpentier and Dowding, were executed but O'Leary, Nouveau, and Groome survived incarceration in German camps. O'Leary's betrayer, Roger le Légionnaire, would go on to betray many more members of the resistance.[26]

SOE's French Section set up a subsection, DF, led by Leslie Humphreys, to set up escape lines across France for Allied personnel. DF became a separate section of SOE in the spring of 1942. One of its agents, Victor Gerson, established a particularly successful line known as Vic in April 1942, having already served one mission for SOE in France. His Chilean-born wife Giliana Balmaceda had visited France for three weeks in May and June 1941 taking advantage of her Chilean passport to collect a treasure trove of the numerous documents essential for life in Vichy France, thus enabling F Section to equip its agents properly. The Vic line survived until its operations were called to a halt by the proximity of D-Day in the spring of 1944. Its longevity was due largely to the extensive security procedures insisted upon by Gerson and to the fact that his principal assistants George Levin and the Racheline brothers were all Jews, as was Gerson, and were therefore more prepared to pay close attention to security since they were vulnerable to arrest not only as organizers of an escape line but simply as Jews. Furthermore, the Vic line was not a single entity but

* Cole fled Paris as the Allies approached in August 1944. In June 1945 he reappeared in Germany claiming to be a member of a special Allied unit but his fraud was detected and he was sent to prison in Paris from which he escaped in November. In January 1946 the French police found him hiding in a flat above a bar in Paris and he was shot and killed while trying to escape.

three – two lines lay unused and were to come to life only if the first was endangered or cut. Richard Christmann, a notorious Dutch collaborator and traitor whose exploits will appear on several occasions later, attempted to penetrate the Vic line and indeed got as far as Lyon along it before meeting Levin and Gerson, who made their suspicions of him so obvious that Christmann returned to the Netherlands to cause further damage there. Later DF lines included Greyhound/Woodchuck run by George Lovinfosse and Pierre/Jacques under Guido Zembsch-Schreve.[27]

By the spring of 1943 Allied air raids on the German U-boat pens on the French Atlantic coast had resulted in a large number of airmen being forced to bale out, land in Brittany, and hope for a passage out of the country. The Pat line had unsuccessfully tried to set up a branch in Brittany but had made an important contact with the principal leader of the Brittany resistance, François Le Cornec, who lived in the village of Plouha on the north coast, about fifteen miles from the nearest town and rail junction, St Briac, and only two miles from the coast. Plans were made to extract the airmen from the Brittany coast using motor gunboats or MTBs based on the Cornish coast. In February 1943 a White Russian, Vladimir Bouryschkine, 'Val Williams', who had previously worked on the Pat line, and his radio operator, Ray Labrosse, were dropped near Paris to arrange the escape of the evaders in Brittany – Operation Oaktree. The first effort to arrange a seaborne evacuation on 29 May 1943 failed because Labrosse's radio had been damaged during their parachute drop. Bouryschkine then tried to send the party of ninety airmen south but was arrested on 4 June near Pau, in the foothills of the Pyrenees. He was brought back to the prison in Rennes where he realized that the Gestapo had extensive knowledge of his network, probably supplied by Roger le Légionnaire. Bouryschkine escaped from prison, breaking his leg in the process, but reached Paris where the network had not been penetrated. Labrosse escorted the twenty-four airmen trapped in Brittany south to the Pyrenees and crossed the mountains with them. Despite the security of the Paris section of the line, Bouryschkine's successor, a survivor from the Dieppe raid, Lucien Dumais, was instructed not to use any of Bouryschkine's contacts in Paris.[28]

Dumais arrived in France with Labrosse in November 1943 to set up what became known as the Shelburne line.* He made contact with Labrosse who convinced him, against London's warnings, that a member of the Paris network, Paul Campinchi, was trustworthy and was currently caring for a number of airmen in Paris. Dumais then went to meet Le Cornec to explain the plans for sea evacuations from the Brittany coast. Dumais was

* Also known as the Shelburn li72ne.

carrying a briefcase filled with 4 million francs and discussed with Le Cornec how to pay the helpers:

> Seeing all this money, they imagined I was going to dish it out by the fistful. I could not pretend that they were getting paid adequately for the risks they were taking; those were beyond computation. But we did not want anybody working purely for money. We paid a good wage, plus expenses, and to overpay had its own dangers. Some people lose their heads when they get a bit of money, start drinking heavily, and then talking. In addition, if a number of people in a small town suddenly appeared flush, the word would quickly get around and suspicions might be aroused.[29]

Security had to be tight because of rumours that Roger le Légionnaire was active in the region again. The first operation, codenamed Bonaparte, was scheduled for the night of 15 December 1943. A gale meant a postponement for nine nights, during which the nineteen men had to be hidden locally. To reach the beach five miles north of Plouha the men had to slide down a steep 100-foot cliff, a process managed largely on their bottoms. The instructions given were: 'lie on your back, spreadeagle. Dig in your heels. If you hear rocks falling from above, cover your head immediately'. All this had to be accomplished in silence since there were German guard posts nearby. A second operation was undertaken on 26 February 1944 and included one RAF fighter pilot who had been shot down only five days earlier. Three further operations ran in March and one in April before the Germans became aware of what was happening under their noses and laid a wide minefield along the cliff top. Their actions were noted by locals who recorded the precise location of each mine. London then sent over mine detectors and operations continued as normal – each night the mines would be marked with a white cloth which would be removed after all the men had passed through the minefield.

By the end of March 1944 the Shelburne line had sent 118 airmen back to Britain. The operations had not been without difficulties. The pre-D-Day Allied bombardment of the French railway network meant that airmen became trapped in Paris and Dumais 'sometimes wondered whether I wouldn't end up having an air force of my own in France'. On 7 June Dumais was ordered by London to go to Brittany and to stay there until the Allies reached him. With the railways out of operation from Allied bombing and resistance sabotage, Dumais had to cover the 400-mile journey by bicycle. The Shelburne line continued in operation until the end of July, arranging the evacuation of airmen and members of the French SAS parachuted into Brittany after D-Day as well as a French general who was indignant at being collected from his hiding place by a horse and cart.

Dumais and Labrosse joined Le Cornec's maquis and fought with it until liberation in August. In all, the Shelburne line returned 307 people back to Britain.[30]

Not all escape lines were operated under British control. During the First World War a British nurse, Edith Cavell, had helped around 200 Allied soldiers to escape from German-occupied Belgium before she was caught by the Germans and executed in October 1915. Her legend 'was of great significance in the Second World War especially to the Belgians and many young women risked their lives for her example. She was to be an inspiration for those heroes and heroines of the escape lines who felt the humanitarian importance of their work. Of them, it can surely be said, that mere patriotism was not enough.'[31] One of those inspired by her was a young woman, Andrée (Dédée) de Jongh in Brussels, who founded the longest of the escape lines, in terms of both distance and longevity. The Comet line ran from Brussels down to Anglet near Bayonne in the foothills of the western Pyrenees where Elvire de Greef (Tante Go) hid the airmen in St Jean-de-Luz and used a Basque guide, Florentino Goicoechea, to take the evaders into Spain. In August 1941 Dédée arrived at the British consulate in Bilbao accompanied by a British soldier and two Belgian officers who wanted to join the Allies. She promised the bemused officials there that she and her colleagues could organize a regular transit of evaders who had been gathered in Brussels. She was not believed. In one of the ironies of the clandestine war, SIS in London assured the vice-consul Donald Darling of Cole's security but denounced Dédée as an obvious German plant.[32] Dédée may have been small and appeared frail but she was in fact very tough. One of the airmen remembered her as 'tough, intelligent, brave – you'd take orders from her without question. She used to tease the Germans in a way that'd make your blood run cold. We were all in love with her and when we told her, she just scoffed.'[33] Darling believed her and sent his colleague Michael Cresswell to arrange the reception of the arrivals in San Sebastian or Bilbao.

The Brussels end of the line was run by Dédée's father Frédéric until February 1942 when the Gestapo arrived at his flat to arrest him. He was out so they took his other daughter instead and Frédéric fled to Paris. His role was taken over by Baron Jean Greindl who ran a Red Cross canteen financed by the Swedes. He had already been using food from the canteen stores to feed the hidden airmen. In January 1943 Greindl took over leadership of the Comet line after Dédée was arrested at Urrugne while waiting for the weather to improve before crossing the Pyrenees. His leadership did not last long because he was arrested in February. His role was promptly taken over by Baron Jean-François de Nothomb who had already escorted airmen down the entire length of the line and had crossed the Pyrenees.[34] He totally reorganized the line with Jean Serment running operations in Brussels and Frédéric de Jongh and Jacques Le Grelle operating from Paris. The guides became younger and younger as more arrests occurred. Guiding also became a family occupation. For example, Andrée Dumon had become involved in the resistance first by distributing the clandestine newspaper *La Libre Belgique*, before being asked to work as a courier. After she was arrested her role was taken over by her sister Michou. The de Greef family in Bayonne housed airmen before their crossing of the Pyrenees for which their daughter Janine was a guide.

Nothomb travelled to Gibraltar to discuss the operation of the Comet line with the British. Jimmy Langley of MI9's Room 900 noted of the line:

> Comet was unlike any other escape line that came under our jurisdiction – control is too strong a word. The last decision always rested with the men and women in the field, as from the outset Dédée had made it clear that she would brook no interference from the outside. The line was Belgian, would be run by Belgians and any help would be gratefully received; but payment of money was simply reimbursement of expenses and in no way gave us the right to issue orders.[35]

Although Comet accepted payment from MI9 it refused to take on a radio operator. This last point caused problems. Although the Comet leadership rightly identified a radio operator as the most vulnerable link in any resistance organization, the lack of radio contact with the British meant that warnings about possible traitors on the line could not be passed on.

Comet suffered several major disasters. One occurred in Brussels and became known as the Maréchal affair. Georges Maréchal and his wife hid air-force evaders in their house in Brussels and their daughter Elsie would collect the men from their guide Albert Marchal at the steps of St Joseph's Church in the Square Frère Orban. On 19 November 1942 no such arrangement had been made, so Elsie was very disturbed when Marchal arrived at her house with two 'American' airmen dressed as Belgian workmen. She went to consult Greindl and in her absence the Gestapo arrested her mother and later that evening her father too. Greindl sent a helper Victor Michiels to the house to discover what was happening: the Gestapo answered the door and shot and killed Michiels as he fled. One of the French guides, Elvire Morelle, was arrested when she arrived the following morning. In all, 100 people were caught as a result of the Maréchal affair and for a time the Comet line in Belgium was totally out of contact with the Paris branch.

In the spring of 1943 just as the Comet organization in Brussels was rebuilding, disaster struck in Paris. In April, Frédéric de Jongh was approached by a man calling himself Jean Masson (real name Jacques Desoubrie), who claimed to have been working with the resistance in northern France and was now offering his services as a guide. In May he escorted a group of airmen from Brussels to Paris and warned de Jongh that in June he would be bringing a very large party and would need the services of all the helpers in Paris to hide them. On 7 June de Jongh and two helpers waited for Masson at the Gare du Nord when they were suddenly surrounded by German gendarmes and arrested and taken to the Gestapo offices at the Rue des Saussaies where Masson confirmed that he was the traitor. The Paris end of the line was rebuilt by Count Antoine d'Ursel but Masson adopted a new pseudonym, Pierre Boulain, and continued to penetrate the Comet line and cause further arrests. Michou Ugeux, who had escorted 150 men southwards, arrived in Paris and called out to her fellow helpers incarcerated in Fresnes prison who informed her that Masson and Boulain were the same person, and he was a traitor.[36] Another traitor working against the Comet line was a Belgian, Prosper Dezitter.* In January 1944 disaster struck in Paris again when Le Grelle and Nothomb were arrested, but once more the Comet line was rebuilt and one of its leaders was Jean de Blommaert. He made several trips to Britain and in April 1944 returned with orders from MI9 to stop sending airmen south to the Pyrenees. The orders were to establish a camp for the airmen in the Forêt de Fréteval near Châteaudun south-west of Paris to await the arrival of the Allies.[37]

The Comet line delivered its last group of airmen to Spain on 4 June 1944. During its existence it had helped at least 800 airmen to reach freedom and housed a further 100 awaiting rescue in the Forêt de Fréteval. The cost had been high, approximately one person being arrested for each airman who was helped. Eleven people were executed at the Tir National near Brussels in October 1943 as a result of the Maréchal affair. A month earlier Baron Greindl had been killed in his prison cell in Etterbeek by an Allied bomb. Frédéric de Jongh was executed at Mont-Valérien in March 1944. Nothomb, who had been arrested in January 1944, and Dédée and many of the helpers on the Comet line survived incarceration in Fresnes and various German concentration camps.[38]

The escape lines described above focused almost exclusively on the rescue and evacuation of Allied soldiers, especially airmen, although they were sometimes asked to help SOE agents escape from France. The Dutch-Paris

* After the war both Desoubrie and Dezitter were captured in Germany and extradited to their home countries where they were tried, found guilty, and executed.

line, however, was a very different organization. In the early summer of 1942 a wealthy and well-connected Dutch textile businessman in Lyon, Jean Weidner, was contacted by two Dutch Jews who were then in a French internment camp and wanted his help in leaving the country. At this time, deportations of foreign Jews from France to the death camps in the east had just begun. Weidner successfully smuggled them into Switzerland. Dutch-Paris operated partly as a welfare organization, raising the funds necessary for Jewish families in the Netherlands, Belgium, and France to maintain their underground existence. The second strand of its work began in March 1943 when the Germans in the Netherlands introduced the requirement for students to sign a loyalty oath: refusal to sign would lead to conscription for forced labour. Around 85 per cent of students refused to sign the oath. A month later the Germans announced the re-internment of Dutch officers and soldiers who had been demobilized in the summer of 1940. The majority of those under threat of conscription for forced labour opted to go underground in the Netherlands, but around 600 elected to become *Engelandvaarders*, men who wished to travel to Britain via Spain to join the Dutch armed forces in exile. From early 1944 onwards Dutch-Paris extended its operations to assist downed airmen, and soon after also became involved in ferrying microfilmed intelligence between the Dutch resistance and the government-in-exile.

Around 330 men and women worked for Dutch-Paris and they came from all walks of life. The leaders were all businessmen and their motivation was religious. Weidner himself was a Seventh Day Adventist and used his church and business contacts extensively to build up the network. His sister Gabrielle became a vital part of the operation in Paris. Another leader was a Belgian Jew, Edmond Chait, and the third leader was a half-Catholic, half-Jew Dutchman, Jacques Rens. Despite its name Dutch-Paris never had a base in the Netherlands and travellers along the line were not screened until they reached Brussels, which created an obvious security flaw. The Dutch-Belgian frontier crossing at Maastricht was masterminded by a traffic inspector, Jacques Vrij, who used his knowledge of German movements to send men across. The Dutch traitor Christmann succeeded in penetrating the line in late May 1943, leading to some arrests in Paris. The line continued functioning smoothly until February 1944 when Rens visited Paris and passed some food packages for the hidden airmen to a courier, Suzy Kraay. She was arrested soon after by the French police and proved talkative because she naively thought that the French police were on the side of the resistance. She had also committed a major security blunder by carrying on her a notebook listing some of her contacts. The French police did some damage to the line, but this was limited because

Weidner visited Paris two days later and ordered an immediate stoppage on the line until the extent of the betrayals was known. Kraay was passed to the Gestapo and under torture revealed not only the names of the Paris leadership but also the name of the main contact for those passing into Switzerland, Marie Meunier in Annecy, as well as Weidner himself and his main contacts in Lyon. The information Kraay supplied all but broke the line for ever. The leaders all escaped arrest but Weidner's sister Gabrielle was arrested and the infection spread to Brussels where the head of the transport section, David Verloop, was caught along with three of his couriers and the master forger of documents.

The Dutch-Paris line had carried out vital work. It is credited with having saved around 1,000 people, of whom 600 were Dutch, 200 French, 100 Belgian and other nationalities, and 100 Allied aircrew. Among the individuals taken out to safety were Gerrit Jan van Heuven Goedhart, the editor of the clandestine Dutch newspaper *Het Parool*, the two Dutch SOE agents Pieter Dourlein and Ben Ubbink, who returned to Britain to expose the extent of German control over the Dutch resistance, and Bob van der Stok, one of the very few successful escapers involved in the Great Escape from Stalag Luft III.[39]

There was no manual available on how to organize and operate an escape line and the people involved had to think on their feet. Often their involvement began by doing a favour for someone they respected or for a friend. Anne Brusselmans was half English and lived with her husband and two small children in Brussels when she was approached by a local pastor asking for civilian clothes for a British soldier left behind in Belgium. That was the start of her lengthy involvement in the Comet line.[40] Drue Tartière, living outside Paris, was asked by a doctor friend to supply food for the airmen hidden all over Paris.[41] Virginia d'Albert-Lake was contacted by a local baker who needed her to act as an interpreter for three American airmen he was sheltering.[42] Hiding men was extremely dangerous as Darling noted:

> In the Resistance, a saboteur could blow up a railway line or put important factory equipment out of action and then disappear; the man supplying enemy intelligence could if given a few seconds swallow the rice paper on which his notes were made, but the woman, into whose house the Germans might rudely force entry, could not hide one or more evaders under the carpet.[43]

The servicemen could claim the protection of the Geneva Convention but the men and women helping them could not. There are plenty of examples of the Germans shooting the men immediately and arresting the women.

The process began with collecting the evaders: 'At night, people could see a plane crashing in flames and calculate how far distant from the burning wreckage the survivors might be found, taking the wind speed and direction into account.'[44] The Germans unwittingly helped by broadcasting on the radio the number of planes shot down overnight, including the number of airmen killed and captured, leaving the escape line gatherers to do the simple mathematical calculation of how many men they should be searching for. It was commented after the war that almost everyone in Belgium appeared to be connected with Comet in some way or another and airmen would be startled to find someone waiting for them with civilian clothes and sometimes even a bicycle more or less as they landed. Hiding the evaders was extremely hazardous. Anne Brusselmans commented:

> Houses near aerodromes, barracks and railway junctions must be avoided, and it is risky to hide them also where there are children, for children might talk at school. People without children, on the other hand, often don't like to be bothered. There is the jealous husband fearful of competition, the old maid who thinks too much of her reputation, and the young girl who thinks too little of hers. So it does not leave us much choice!

She took the risk of housing the airmen despite having young children, telling them that the visitors were Flemish cousins and spoke English because it was their only language in common. Indeed, her daughter later recorded: 'None of our family knew of my mother's activities in the underground – not even my grandparents. On the front, we were just a normal family going through the daily hardship of enemy occupation, minding our own business. My father went to work; we went to school, and if someone came visiting, the men were hidden in the cellar.'[45]

Children were, however, useful when it came to moving the airmen to their next location because they aroused less suspicion from the Germans and local police. Michèle Agniel began working on the Burgundy line when she was fourteen years old: 'I would wear my blue beret, my school beret, when I met them at the station, and the airmen would know to follow me through the streets. But it was dangerous, particularly with the Americans, who really had no idea at all how to walk like a Frenchman.'[46] Most of the evading airmen were shot down in the Netherlands and Belgium and had to pass across several borders to reach Paris: various secure crossing-points were established. In Paris, however, the trains from Belgium arrived at the Gare du Nord and the evaders then had to be escorted across Paris to the Gare de Lyon for those travelling on to Lyon, Marseille or towards Switzerland, or to the Gare d'Austerlitz for Toulouse and the Pyrenees.

Paris was full of Germans and the conduct of the French police was unpredictable, but Virginia d'Albert-Lake commented:

> Convoying men was thrilling. I never walked the streets with an aviator without pretending to know him well, in order to avoid suspicion. We usually walked arm in arm, engrossed in friendly conversation, being careful to lower our voices when people were within hearing distance . . .
>
> Sometimes, we took the men sightseeing in Paris, which meant rubbing elbows with the Germans, doing the same thing. This was dangerous sport, but sometimes we sensed their vital need of getting out of the house and stretching their legs.[47]

On the trains the evaders would be given German newspapers and magazines to make it less likely that they would be expected to converse. In France, certain seats were reserved for those maimed during the First World War and evaders often occupied them pretending to be deaf and mute or blind.[48]

Most evaders and escapers had to cross the Pyrenees to leave France. There were numerous crossing points between Bayonne on the eastern end to Perpignan on the western end with the middle route near Toulouse being the most arduous. The Vichy police watched the arrivals at the stations in the foothills of the Pyrenees, arresting those without valid passes. The Germans were much more attentive to the escape routes and many individuals who had run hotels sheltering those awaiting the arrival of their mountain guide, or who had supplied food to those about to make the crossing, ended up in German concentration camps. The casualty figures among the guides themselves were also high, which partly explains why they demanded considerable sums of money to continue with their dangerous work whereas many of those working higher up the line did not expect repayment, although MI9 did make strenuous efforts after the war to reimburse them for their expenses.[49]

Most of the evading airmen had a sufficient level of fitness to make the journey without too much difficulty. For them the weather was the greatest problem. Michou Dumon recalled how on one occasion she and her party were caught in a sudden blizzard and she assured the airmen that she knew the way 'but had to ask the men to hold me down to prevent me being blown over'.[50] Civilians were far less prepared:

> Some people while fleeing for their lives would risk their necks, not to mention ours, for material possessions. This to us was incomprehensible. They had been briefed as to physical exertions to be expected and about the

> importance of timing. Yet they would make it harder on themselves and the group burdening themselves with weight that they would discard after the first hour of climbing. As time went on, we learned by experience to carry a lightweight elongated hand shovel to dig deep holes for discarded materials; aspirin to keep the children sleepy; ropes with loops for a handhold; and most of all that one of us had to be last in the line to prevent discarded items from becoming the tell-tale signs of our passing.[51]

The reports of evading airmen and fleeing SOE agents often included references to civilians left behind in the mountains because they simply could not cope with the conditions.

The Germans used the services of traitors such as Roger le Légionnaire and Christmann in their efforts to penetrate the escape lines. The most common effort, however, was to attempt to pass English-speaking Germans posing as downed aircrew down the lines. Those escape lines with radio contact with London, such as the Pat line and Shelburne line, could ask London to verify a man's identity. Dumais recalled how an alleged airman called Olafson had aroused the suspicions of the two Americans sheltering with him in Paris because of his ignorance of flying but had spun a complicated story of how he and his brothers had sailed to Britain and were all working in the armed forces. Checks with London revealed the existence of no such men and orders were sent to execute Olafson, but he escaped and was later revealed as a Dane working for the Germans.[52] The Comet line had to improvise since it lacked radio contact with London and MI9 supplied a list of the locations of pubs and night clubs in London and RAF slang to be used during interrogations since the Germans could not be expected to be up to date on such information.[53] Others adopted the simple method of asking an airman his height and weight which he would know but 'a German would be caught on the hop, trying to convert his weight into stones and pounds'.[54] If the airmen were suspected of being plants then the resistance was as ruthless in dealing with them as the Germans were with helpers on the escape lines: 'After a few days our resistance comrades took them away. They thought they were being moved to another safe house but in fact they were taken to the Seine and shot as suspected Germans. Their bodies were dumped in the river.'[55]

A major point of vulnerability was the conduct of the airmen themselves. There were numerous complaints of airmen bored by hiding until they could be moved on evading their helpers and going out to local restaurants. Evaders had to be taught how to walk like a Frenchman which meant, for example, never putting their hands in their pockets while walking. A briefing document supplied by MI9 warned the evaders of the importance of security:

> One address on a scrap of paper can result in the tracing of many helpers. Never discuss your previous helpers with those with whom you find yourself next . . . There have been cases when evaders and escapers have sent post-cards back to helpers thanking them. The motive may have been good but the supreme stupidity of their actions is almost incredible. Do nothing which can endanger your helpers' lives.

This warning came about after an early RAF evader passed the name and address of a farmer who had helped him near Amiens to a friend who was then shot down over the Western Desert, fell into German hands, whereupon the farmer and his wife were traced and executed. When caught by the Germans servicemen were required only to supply their name, rank, and number but some talked too much. Stan Hope was caught at the same time as Dédée de Jongh and was threatened with torture at the hands of the Gestapo. He was haunted by the consequences: 'I am no hero and I gave in. I gave them the vaguest of names and addresses of people in Brussels. It was now May 1943, five months since I had been there anyway, and I thought and hoped that everyone would have got away. But they hadn't, and the Gestapo picked them up.' The damage to the Comet line was catastrophic. Donald Darling noted the disaster but commented: 'Nevertheless one should remember that in the main the evaders were little more than boys, inexperienced in many ways and only experts at their own various jobs as aircrew. As such they were easy prey for the Gestapo, experienced in questioning and deception and moreover already world-renowned for their brutality.'[56]

Concerns for security also meant that it was deemed inadvisable to mix work on escape lines with other resistance activities. This was easier said than done and was often ignored. Germaine Tillion helped French POWs to escape and also worked for an intelligence circuit. Anne Brusselmans became involved in the Comet line first and then was asked to set up an intelligence cell. Others just ignored London's advice. SOE agent Ben Cowburn explained:

> The official attitude was that we should never risk the security of our circuits by handling escapers. However, no special agent would turn one away. Some of my brother-agents even handled so many that they built up quite a large 'side-line' in this respect. After all, the RAF were our particular friends, our transport and our RASC [Royal Army Service Corps]. When some of the boys in light-blue were in trouble, we felt we were honour bound to help them if we could.

Jimmy Langley acknowledged that often it was easier to put an evader in a spare seat of a Lysander rather than to arrange for his lengthy journey to and across the Pyrenees.[57]

From the Allied perspective, getting a shot-down airman back was an enormous boost to morale in his squadron and also yielded valuable information on German air defences and the results of Allied bomb damage. The people who started out on their clandestine activities as helpers on escape lines would often go on to contribute to other acts of resistance such as the distribution of the underground press or the concealment of other vulnerable people such as Jews or forced labour conscripts. Some of them may have begun their work on purely humanitarian grounds, but the response of the Germans means that escape lines have to be classed as a form of resistance.

5
Resisters of the First Hour

In the early years of the war, overt resistance seemed not only pointless but virtually suicidal. Nonetheless occupation by a foreign power was seen as an affront to nationalism and to the patriotic feelings of the conquered people. The clandestine press urged people to make it clear to the Germans that they were unwelcome, to make them feel 'constantly enveloped by the atmosphere of passive resistance forming a sort of gluey swamp under foot'.[1] Many of the activities described in this chapter can be termed low-risk defiance of the occupiers rather than outright resistance. Yet at the same time those who were inclined to be more open in their hostility to occupation began to seek out those like-minded individuals who were prepared to take the greater risks entailed in resistance and to become organized into numerous groups and movements. During this period, both the nascent resistance and the Germans were learning lessons which would continue to be learned and relearned throughout the war. The resistance was full of people inexperienced in the art of covert activity and consequently suffered high losses until the basic lessons of security had been learned. The resistance also had to decide on the methods to be adopted to hit at the Germans, bearing in mind the consequences of their actions on the general population. For the Germans, there was a clear contrast between east and west over how to treat the resistance. In the east, notably in Poland but also in the Protectorate, no method was deemed too ruthless to launch against those who failed to accept the obliteration of their countries and the relentless German policy of stamping out continuing signs of Polish and Czech nationalism. In the west, however, there was a clear unwillingness by the Germans to resort to 'Polish methods' in crushing the early demonstrations of resistance.

The use of symbols to express opposition to occupation and support for their exiled governments was widespread. For instance, the Dutch used to wear orange blossoms to signify their support for the House of Orange, and on the birthday of the queen's son-in-law, Prince Bernhard, on 29 June

1940, many of them wore a carnation, which was thought to be the prince's favourite flower, on their lapels. In Norway, a paperclip was worn on the lapel to signify support for King Haakon, and a flower on lapels on the king's birthday on 3 August. The sign 'H-7' was daubed on walls as another sign of support for the king. In Prague during the October 1939 demonstrations people wore their National Solidarity badges upside down, so that 'SN' was known to insiders to mean *Smrt Němcům* or 'Death to Germans'.[2] As support for de Gaulle grew, the French began wearing the Cross of Lorraine as badges, key fobs, etc. Even before the launch of the V-campaign by the BBC, graffiti were used to signify opposition to the occupiers. In Poland: 'Everywhere you go there are new indications of resistance: on buildings and signboards you can see the anchor sign *Polska Walcząca* (Fighting Poland). Others are *Polska Zwycięży* (Poland will win); *Deutschland Kaput*; or the sign of a turtle, which is the symbol of a work slowdown.'[3] And in Brussels, embarrassingly for the Germans, in May 1941 the graffiti 'Heil Hess!' appeared as a reaction to the flight of the Deputy Führer Rudolph Hess to Scotland that month.[4]

The German reactions to such demonstrations of nationality were limited. In the Netherlands the commander-in-chief of the Dutch army, General Winkelman, and the mayor of The Hague were arrested after the demonstrations in favour of Prince Bernhard. Elsewhere, graffiti writers and those caught tearing down or vandalizing German propaganda posters were subject to arrest. Only in Poland was such conduct liable to the death penalty. It appears, then, that the Germans saw these demonstrations of nationalism for what they were, a relatively harmless expression of patriotic protest, and not resistance as such but merely defiance. Discontent that dissipated itself in symbolic protests was unlikely to ripen into rebellion. For the nascent resistance, on the other hand, such behaviour by the occupied peoples offered some hope for the future. It suggested an underlying groundswell of opposition to the occupying forces which could, at the appropriate time, be further exploited and lead to an expansion of the organized resistance. Such demonstrations 'gave strength to the amorphous group of people who strongly opposed Hitler's "New Order" but were cut off from all familiar types of political action; and finally they helped to put pressure on hesitant or impressionable souls, and to keep them from hasty attachment to the "new Era"'.[5]

Music was also used to express nationalism, even though the playing of national anthems was banned by the Germans. In the Protectorate, concerts of the nineteenth-century nationalist composer Bedřich Smetana's cycle of symphonic poems *Má Vlast* consistently played to packed houses.[6] An extraordinarily daring piece of resistance through the use of music occurred in Bergen in Norway in January 1941. The first violinist of the Oslo Philharmonic Orchestra, Ernst Glaser, was a Jew, but was permitted to play in Christian Sinding's Violin Concerto. The concert programme, approved by the Germans, also contained the piece by Ole Bull, *Polacca guerriera*, which depicted the 1830 Polish uprising against the Russians. The concert was interrupted by members of the *Hird*, the NS armed guard, who verbally attacked Glaser's Jewishness. Reacting quickly to a volatile situation, the conductor, Harald Heide, switched to the Norwegian national anthem, which brought the *Hird* standing to attention and gave the police time to help Glaser escape.[7]

Public demonstrations were banned by the Germans, but pilgrimages were not. In the Protectorate pilgrimages had always been popular and a major one on St Lawrence's Day in August 1939 was used by the Czechs to demonstrate their resistance to the German occupation. It was celebrated in the Chodsko region in the mountains on the pre-1938 frontier with Germany, a region then split by the Munich Agreement. Specially chartered trains brought over 100,000 Czechs to Chodsko. The climax of the pilgrimage featured speeches by a descendant of the Chod hero Jan Kozina, who had been executed by the Germans during a rebellion against them 244 years earlier, and by the canon of Prague, Monsignor Bohumil Stašek. Stašek outraged the Germans by reading out a national pledge which ended with the words: 'Motherland, we promise that we will be true to thee, that we will love thee truly until the last breath . . . We swear that we will never abandon or betray thee and that we shall love thee until our last heartbeat.' Future pilgrimages were banned and Stašek was sent to Buchenwald concentration camp.[8] In Poland, pilgrimages to the Black Madonna in the Jasna Góra monastery in Częstochowa were forbidden but pilgrims still managed to reach her, among them Karol Wojtyła, the future Pope John Paul II.

The Germans were alive to the possibility that national days of independence, or Armistice Day on 11 November, could be celebrated in ways that might easily turn into overt protestations of opposition to the Germans. Again an east/west split can be seen in their response.

The celebrations of the Czech patron saint, King Wenceslas, passed off peacefully on 28 September 1939, with a Mass, attended by President Hácha and members of his government, celebrated in St Vitus Cathedral in Prague.[9] Therefore, when the Germans became aware that the Czechs were making preparations to celebrate their national day, 28 October, Goebbels advised the Reichsprotektor Konstantin von Neurath 'to make a simple announcement that we have nothing against it'.[10] But the demonstrations turned out to be larger and uglier than the Germans had anticipated: scuffles between the Czechs and Germans broke out, shots were fired, and a student, Jan Opletal, was killed. His funeral was held on 15 November and 3,000 students processed in silence past his coffin. Then the students flooded into the streets and by chance a car carrying Karl Frank's chauffeur was passing by which was attacked by the students; the car was overturned and the passengers beaten up. Frank and von Neurath took the chauffeur to Berlin to see Hitler, who ordered an immediate crack-down on what he perceived as 'a group of Czech intellectuals' that had attempted to disturb the peace and order of the Protectorate.[11]

Karl Frank flew back to Prague to supervise personally the punishment of the students for their temerity. On the night of 16–17 November German police detachments surrounded the five largest student hostels in Prague and two in Brno, and occupied the buildings of Prague University. 'Everywhere occurred scenes of such horror as to be almost indescribable. All the students were dragged out by force one after another, some to be shot there and then, others murdered later for what was called "attempting to escape".'[12] In all, 1,850 students were arrested, of whom 1,200 were sent to Oranienburg concentration camp, and the nine alleged ringleaders were shot without a trial. Ironically, eight of these nine had recently pledged to work for closer Czech-German understanding. Hitler ordered that all Czech universities and institutes of higher education be shut for three years; in the event, they did not reopen until after the war. Factories and businesses in the Protectorate received circulars ordering them not to employ former students, who were now destined to be sent to Germany as forced labourers. The Hácha government revealed its limitations as a broker between the Germans and the Czechs by failing to temper the German reaction. The repression was effective: when the underground called for a demonstration on the birthday of the founder of independent Czechoslovakia, Tomáš Masaryk, on 7 March 1940, there was no response.[13]

Poland's Independence Day fell on 11 November and the Germans proposed drastic measures to quash any sign of nationalism. When Hans Frank was informed by the chief of the Cracow district, Otto Wächter, that posters had appeared on walls of houses marking the day, Frank ordered Wächter to take one man from every house displaying a poster and shoot him. In Warsaw and Cracow prominent people were also taken hostage by the Germans and informed that 'should any riots occur, we would be shot'.[14]

In contrast, there was a more restrained reaction to Norway's Independence Day on 17 May 1940 when crowds gathered in front of the king's palace in Oslo despite the fact that it was occupied by the Germans. In the afternoon a German military band began playing a German march:

> I don't know whether it was to impress us or entertain us. Then they changed the tune to *Wir fahren gegen Engeland*. Probably not malicious, just tactless. But the crowd began to get angry . . . Suddenly a group of people started singing the National Anthem. It caught on like a forest fire. It was wonderful. We all sang as loudly as we could. Thousands and thousands of us. The Germans heard it above the sound of their own playing and realised that the people were singing in slow-march time, not quick-march. So they obligingly altered the timing to keep pace with the singing. It was obvious they had no idea what tune was being sung. If they had known it was the National Anthem, they must have behaved differently.

A German officer did, however, recognize the national anthem and ordered the band to leave the parade ground.[15] The Germans ignored the sight of women walking together dressed so that their apparel represented the national flag. When statues of people representing a patriotic ideal were decorated with national flags or bedecked with flowers, the Germans left it to the local police to remove the decorations.

In Paris, however, there was a strong reaction to the activities of students on Armistice Day, 11 November 1940. The Vichy regime had banned all celebrations of Bastille Day in 1940, instead calling for the day to be one of mourning for the recent defeat of France. Marshal Pétain's instructions were widely obeyed but the situation on Armistice Day was very different. Again the Vichy regime ordered no parades or demonstrations but this time, after Pétain's handshake with Hitler at Montoire, people were less willing to obey these orders blindly.[16] The day began in Paris with the appearance of a large calling card bearing General de Gaulle's name being left by the statue of Georges Clemenceau, the victorious prime minister of the First World War, off the Champs-Élysées. The card had been placed there by two lawyers: André Weil-Curiel, who was one of de Gaulle's first emissaries to France, and Léon Nordmann, a member of the resistance. The card was swiftly removed by the French police.[17]

In the middle of the afternoon hundreds of *lycée* students began to march along the Champs-Élysées towards the Tomb of the Unknown Soldier at the Arc de Triomphe. Two boys were carrying a floral Cross of Lorraine in French colours and managed to leave it briefly by the tomb before a pincer action by the French and German police forced them to run and hide. As the day went on, more students gathered by Clemenceau's statue, some carrying two sticks called *gaules* which they banged together calling out *Deux gaules* or rather 'De Gaulle'. The students then invaded a brasserie used by a French fascist youth group and fighting broke out. German soldiers rushed in to support the French police and the day ended with the arrest of 143 people, largely students. Most were released without charge that evening or over the following days, but the Germans ensured that they received a thorough fright first. Benoîte Groult had a friend who was arrested and held for a week. He told of how he was 'lined up with his comrades against the wall of the Cherché-Midi prison, all night in the rain. They were kicked, hit with rifle butts and spat on by German soldiers. They were told that they would be shot in the morning . . . A kick in the face does more than all propaganda.' The universities and *grandes écoles* were closed temporarily. France then settled back into an uneasy calm. The 11 November demonstration may have been 'one of the first moments of resistance, but it did not set a model for resistance activity throughout France'.[18]

Across Belgium there were also gatherings in all the major cities on 11 November 1940 around monuments to the fallen. Such conduct had been prohibited by the Germans in advance and there were dozens of arrests.[19] Yet arresting and physically assaulting demonstrators was as far as the Germans would go in western Europe; no one was executed.

Students were also active in the Netherlands, but for very different reasons. Uniquely in occupied Europe, the trigger was the dismissal of a respected Jewish academic, Professor Eduard Meijers, from his position at Leiden University. Elsewhere in Europe legislation to oust Jews from public life had met with little reaction. But at Leiden the students were mobilized by a brave professor, Rudolph Cleveringa, appointed to take Meijers's classes, who publicly denounced the German dismissal of Jewish officials as contrary to international law. His speech was published in the clandestine press. Students at Leiden and at the Technical Institute of Delft went on strike, and students elsewhere in the country wrote statements of support. The German authorities were taken by surprise but responded swiftly and effectively. The two institutions were closed for the duration of the war while Cleveringa was arrested and spent the remainder of the war in prison.[20]

Industrial action in the form of strikes is a recognized form of internal economic warfare; when carried out during wartime it can be described as a form of resistance. This is certainly how the Germans viewed strike action. For them, occupied Europe was to be exploited economically and any attempt to undermine their policies was almost bound to lead to a strong reaction. Strikes are also important to the resistance narrative because they illustrate that, given the motives and organization, large numbers of people were prepared to undertake a form of resistance to the German occupation.

What is notable is the contrast between the relatively severe punishments meted out to the strikers in eastern Europe as opposed to those western Europe. In the Protectorate the armament factories were vital to the German war economy. Various attempts at strike action in the factories in Plzeň, Brno, and Moravská Ostrava were met with instant repression.[21] Strikers and strike leaders were executed and the Germans made it known that any future strike action would be met with similarly harsh responses. In Warsaw the tram workers went on strike in December 1940. The Gestapo immediately arrested the leaders and informed the workers that they had ten minutes in which to return to work or the leaders would be executed on the spot. The strike ended immediately.[22]

In Belgium and the Netherlands respectively, neither von Falkenhausen nor Seyss-Inquart wanted to employ 'Polish methods' in crushing strikes which hit the areas under their control. The February 1941 strike in Amsterdam stemmed from a number of causes. The immediate trigger was attacks by the armed wing of the NSB, the *Weer Afdeling* (WA), on Jews and the formation by the Jews of a self-defence organization, *Knokploegen*, to resist the attacks and to retaliate, leading to the death of one WA man. The Germans, who had initially tried to prevent the NSB from provoking the Jews, now stepped in to support the Dutch fascists and on 15 February raided the Jewish quarter and arrested 425 young Jews and deported them to Buchenwald and Mauthausen concentration camps – only one survived the war. Disturbances spread throughout Amsterdam and action became organized with a strike beginning in the shipyards on 17–18 February. The action then escalated so that on 25 February the trams stopped running, the civil servants stayed at home, and the factories closed – in effect a general strike. News of the events in Amsterdam spread across the Netherlands and strikes began in other towns and cities. The German authorities were taken by surprise and reacted immediately and effectively. Martial law was declared throughout the country, over 100 of the strike organizers were arrested, the city of Amsterdam was fined 15 million guilders, and Seyss-Inquart sacked the mayors of Amsterdam, Haarlem, and Zaandam, and replaced them with pro-Germans or NSB men. By 27 February the strikes were over.[23]

The question of what the Amsterdam strike was all about has been debated since. The starting point was essentially the NSB action against the Jews and the German intervention. Although this incident is sometimes highlighted as a unique instance of action in support of the Jews, too much significance should not be placed on this since the Netherlands holds the unenviable position of being the country in western Europe from which the highest percentage of Jews were eventually deported, 75 per cent, a figure which suggests that support for the Jews was very limited. The demands of the Dutch strikers included higher wages and a halt to German plans to deport workers to Germany. Many of the organizers were communists, even though the Molotov–Ribbentrop Pact was still in force, and the communists have since argued that they started the resistance in the Netherlands and dominated it. Such a statement has been challenged. One resister, Herman Friedhoff, felt that the truth was that the communists 'were more disciplined and active [than the bulk of the working population] and hence promoted the strike. But they neither controlled nor initiated it, for the strike was a spontaneous protest of blue- and white-collar and itinerant workers. Whoever suggested the strike first touched a patriotic chord.'[24]

Various lessons were learned from the strike. The Germans realized that their hold over the Netherlands rested on their strength alone since the NSB was obviously too weak and lacked sufficient popular support to take over the government. Nor were the Dutch officials in control of the country: their posters calling for an end to the strike 'If all cooperate, we shall end today's confusion with united efforts' were met with derision.[25] In fact the only people who emerged with any credit were the workers: 'in the strike the working population discovered its own identity in defiance of the occupying power'.[26] The Dutch would employ the strike weapon to real effect at later periods during the war.

On the first anniversary of the German invasion, 10 May 1941, widespread strikes broke out in the industrial basin of Liège, Hainault, Limburg, and across northern France. This area was controlled by the German military government based in Brussels under von Falkenhausen. The strikes were motivated by economic concerns. Among the demands were an increase in pay, since wages had not been raised for a year; better food distribution, especially of potatoes; an increase in the amount of soap provided to workers in often filthy jobs; and the abolition of a tax recently imposed by the Belgian secretaries-general. The strikes involved 70,000 workers in Belgium and 100,000 in northern France. Because of the vital importance of mining, metallurgy, munitions, and engineering to the German war economy, the strikes were bound to lead to a German reaction. Yet the German response was perhaps milder than might have been expected. It is true that 450 ringleaders were arrested, and 244 deported to the Reich as forced labourers, but no one was executed or even threatened with execution. Instead, the German authorities relied on the mine owners themselves to negotiate directly with the strikers. The threat of no wages at all for the second half of May if the strike continued weakened the resolve of the workers and the strike was over by 10 June. But importantly, the strikers did win many of their demands: wages were increased by 8 per cent and the Germans improved the distribution of food and soap. One of the oddities of the war was, of course, that normal tensions between workers and owners continued and it is sometimes difficult to discern where discontent was anti-German or a struggle to improve working conditions.[27]

These strikes were not directly linked to the resistance, but they had implications for the formation of resistance in the region. Such a widespread and lengthy strike demonstrated that the workers had the ability to organize themselves and, indeed, the underground trade union movement, the *Comités de Lutte Syndicale*, developed from the strike. Furthermore, the communists had played an important role in organizing and sustaining the strike, and this implied that if they were not hampered by Comintern orders during the period of the Nazi-Soviet Pact, the communists would be able to establish underground resistance movements in the region; as indeed they did.[28]

Most early efforts at resistance were neither effective nor won popular support. For example, during the German invasion of Norway, a twenty-one-year-old civilian, Oluf Reed Olsen, encountered a British SIS officer who asked him to help the Allied forces by photographing and sketching German installations, in fact to act as a spy. Then Reed Olsen was given some explosives and was asked to blow up the Lysaker Bridge which carried traffic from Oslo to the airport at Fornebu, an important route for German reinforcements. Although Reed Olsen's only previous experience was with blowing up tree stumps, the explosion was successful. As may be expected, Quisling made a radio broadcast criticizing the sabotage, and General Falkenhorst issued warnings of reprisals and summary execution of the perpetrators when caught. But the surprise was the response of the Norwegians: a large group of prominent citizens published a warning to would-be resisters and saboteurs not to endanger the civilian population.[29] This suggested that the first battle of the resistance would have to be to win over the support of the population to their cause.

The importance of the battle for hearts and minds is demonstrated by events elsewhere as the Germans made it clear that they would not permit any sign of resistance and would use a policy of collective responsibility to crush it. For example, in 1939 there were so many cases of sabotage in the vital armaments factories in the Protectorate, especially the Škoda works in Plzeň, that the Germans threatened to decimate the workforce literally, to execute every tenth worker if sabotage continued, whether the worker was guilty of sabotage or not. From the German point of view, this threat finally sank home and the cases of sabotage began to fall as the workers held one another in line.[30]

Another example comes from Poland. Partisan warfare and German anti-partisan warfare are commonly assumed to have begun only after the German invasion of the Soviet Union but in fact the first cases of both occurred in Poland. Major Henryk Dobrzański Hubal had been second-in-command of the 110th Cavalry Regiment during the September 1939 campaign but refused to surrender after Poland's defeat. Instead, he gathered soldiers under him and launched a campaign of partisan warfare in the Kielecczyzna region. In December 1939 Sikorski's government in Paris was informed that the unit was well-armed and consisted of around 250 men. By the spring of 1940 the unit had expanded and in March it destroyed an entire German battalion near the village of Huciska. The German response was to create an anti-partisan unit, formed from SS and Wehrmacht troops as well as Panzers. This unit proceeded to burn numerous villages to the ground and killed over 1,200 people. The villagers, whether guilty of support for Hubal or not, were targeted in order to reduce the food supply available to the partisans. This was the first example of the German practice of anti-partisan warfare: cut off food and punish the villagers for partisan activity in their area. Such a practice would become much more common after the German invasion of the Soviet Union, and, indeed, eventually become codified into a doctrine.

The ruthlessness of the German response led to the villagers becoming hostile to the presence of Hubal's unit. They appealed to the burgeoning local resistance organizations for help. But Hubal refused to accept orders from anyone to disband. This provides an early illustration of a theme that concerns the resistance throughout Europe, that of control. On 15 April 1940 the commander-in-chief of the Polish resistance, General Stefan Rowecki, wrote to his government-in-exile that he was chasing Hubal with the intention of putting him on trial for disobeying orders, before despatching him abroad. In the event, however, the Germans reached Hubal first. On 30 April his unit was ambushed and Hubal was killed. As a show of their strength, the Germans mutilated the body, displayed it in several villages, before finally disposing of it in the town of Tomaszów Mazowiecki.[31]

The first instance of collective responsibility had in fact already occurred in Wawer, near Warsaw, in December 1939. Two German NCOs were killed by local Polish criminals, not resisters. Colonel Max Daume, the acting commander of the *Ordnungspolizei* in Warsaw, ordered an immediate reprisal. From every house in Wawer, one man was rounded up. In houses where more than one man was present, the women had to choose between losing a husband, son, brother, father or other male relative. Every tenth man was shot, a total of 107 men for the deaths of two Germans.[32]

The ferociousness of the German response to signs of resistance was also evident in Crete in 1941. During the German invasion of Crete, civilians from the village of Galatas joined the 6th Greek Regiment and the 18th New Zealand Regiment in attacking and destroying the German 2nd Parachute Battalion. The villagers of Alikianos assisted the 8th Greek Regiment in impeding the German advance, thereby enabling the Allied evacuation to begin. Villagers from Kastelli in western Crete also helped the 1st Greek Regiment.[33] The discovery by the Germans that their soldiers had been butchered with knives and swords led General Kurt Student to issue an order on 31 May 1941:

> It is certain that the civilian population including women and boys have taken part in the fighting, committed sabotage, mutilated and killed wounded soldiers. It is therefore high time to combat all cases of this kind, to undertake reprisals and punitive expeditions which must be carried through with exemplary terror . . .

The reprisals were shootings, fines, total destruction of the villages by burning, and extermination of the male population. From June to September 1941 the Germans carried out ruthless reprisals against the guilty villages, killing at least 1,135 Cretans. Of these, only 224 had even been sentenced by a military tribunal.[34]

In contrast, the German response to resistance activity in western Europe was muted and only those found guilty of sabotage were executed. In France during 1940 there were numerous instances of sabotage, none carried out by organized resistance groups but rather by individuals. A particular target was the extensive network of dedicated military phone lines laid down by the Germans immediately after the defeat of France. A spectacular success on a scale probably not anticipated by the perpetrator, Étienne Achavanne, occurred on 20 June 1940 when he cut the phone lines between the German headquarters and the Luftwaffe airfield at Boos, near Rouen. That night the RAF mounted a bombing raid on the airfield, no warning could be given, and eighteen planes were destroyed on the ground and twenty-two Germans were killed. Achavanne was, however, caught, court-martialled and condemned to death.[35] Throughout the summer of 1940 cables were being repeatedly cut throughout northern France and along the Atlantic coast. Those caught cutting cables were executed and the nearby towns were fined: for example, on one occasion Nantes was fined 2 million francs. Such punishments did not appear to act as a brake to activity and in December 1940 there were 101 cable cuts noted in the Lille area alone.[36]

The principle of collective responsibility was not only applied after the event by the Germans, but was also applied to prevent resistance in the first place. A common practice was to take hostages from among the prominent people in the population in the occupied country, and to hold them in custody in order to prevent opposition. This occurred first in Poland in November 1939, and in February 1940 a German decree in Poland laid down that:

> In the event of subversive action, if the culprit is not found those persons whose names are posted on this list must answer before the law. The penalty for an act of sabotage is imprisonment or death. It is in the interest of the population, and especially the interest of the 'hostages', to keep watch over the public security and to prevent any subversive activity.[37]

In France, the military commander, General Alfred Streccius, set out the principle in the middle of 1940:

> Hostages are local residents who will pay with their lives if the public does not behave flawlessly. Therefore the responsibility for their fate lies in the hands of their fellow countrymen. The population must be publicly warned that hostages will be liable for the hostile acts of individuals.[38]

His successor, Otto von Stülpnagel, endorsed and expanded the regulations. But there was an important difference between the application of the hostage policy in Poland and in France. Von Stülpnagel advised restraint in the application of the hostage policy and was certainly reluctant to execute the hostages if no link could be proved between the perpetrator of an act of resistance and the hostages. In contrast, Hans Frank showed no reluctance in executing any number of Polish hostages. In fact he boasted in a Nazi newspaper, *Völkischer Beobachter*: 'There were large red posters in Prague announcing that today seven Czechs had been shot. I said to myself: if I wanted to hang a poster for every seven Poles that were shot, then all the forests in Poland would not suffice in order to produce the paper necessary for such posters.'[39]

The German response to any form of resistance was undeniably harsh, particularly in eastern Europe, but the question remains: how legal was it? The Hague Convention of 1907 laid out the rules of war to which all the combatants in Europe had subscribed. The most relevant section when considering German conduct is Article 50: 'No general penalty, pecuniary or otherwise, shall be inflicted upon the population on account of the acts of individuals for which they cannot be regarded as jointly or severally responsible.'[40] This rule was open to interpretation, and no international consensus had been reached on exactly how the Article should be applied in practice. British, French, and American military regulations allowed for the seizure of hostages if the population was hostile. Indeed, the French had taken hostages during their occupation of the Ruhr in 1923 in order to crush German resistance.[41] The difference was that during the Second World War, the Germans viewed the seizure and subsequent fate of hostages somewhat differently from the other belligerent nations. Only they were willing to execute the hostages even if no link between an act of resistance and the hostages could be proved. The legality of these executions would be challenged repeatedly after the war. At the Nuremberg trials in 1946 it was established that the executions of hostages had been illegal, but subsequent trials of other defendants overturned this decision, and later convictions took into consideration whether simply an excessive ratio of hostages executed to Germans killed had been applied.[42]

The Hague Convention did not forbid resistance to occupation. Indeed Article 1 of the Hague Convention set out how an army, militia, or volunteer force should be defined. It must fulfil a number of conditions:

> To be commanded by a person responsible for his subordinates; To have a fixed distinctive emblem recognisable at a distance; To carry arms openly; and To conduct their operations in accordance with the laws and customs of war. In countries where militia or volunteer corps constitute the army, or form part of it, they are included under the denomination 'army'.[43]

This article was also open to interpretation, particularly the extent to which it could cover resistance organizations. Resistance activity was by its very nature undercover and secret and therefore many of these conditions could not be fulfilled. Efforts to fulfil the conditions of Article 1 would have implications later in the war, with the formation of secret armies which planned to fight in the open when the time came. The question was: would the Germans recognize the resistance armies as belligerents and therefore subject to the laws of war or not? After all, at the time, with no sign that the Allies would ultimately win the war and a widespread feeling that the Third Reich was permanent, it could be argued that an amoral ferocity was the new permanent reality. Perpetrators and those who authorized their actions felt they were creating new norms which would discourage subsequent defiance. In 1939–41 the prospect of future retribution for their actions would have seemed fantastical.

The Germans took preventative action to limit the formation of resistance movements by arresting those people who might be likely to become leaders. Therefore, on 1 September 1939, as they invaded Poland, the Germans secured their rear by arresting about 2,000 Czech politicians and public leaders.[44] Further arrests followed the demonstrations on the Czech national day, 28 October 1939, and by late November, Goebbels recorded in his diary the success of the measures: 'News from Prague: things have settled down there. One hard blow, and the intelligentsia crawls off into its hole.'[45] Similar measures were taken in Poland soon after the occupation began. On 6 November 1939 the faculty of the Jagiellonian University in Cracow were lured to a meeting, supposedly to discuss a revised curriculum, before 183 were arrested and the majority sent to Sachsenhausen concentration camp. Arrests among the clergy, possible leaders in an intensely Roman Catholic country, also aimed to prevent resistance building up. Yet, whereas the arrests of the intelligentsia in the Protectorate appeared to have the desired consequences and dampened down the resistance, the arrests in Poland only served to raise the Poles' awareness of the harshness of German rule and consequently to increase resistance activity. At the beginning of March 1940 Hans Frank issued a statement to his government: 'Generally we have to take into account the ever-increasing resistance in the circles of the intelligentsia, clergy and former officers. Resistance against our rule in this country has already assumed organised forms.'[46] Frank had orders directly from Hitler to secure peace in Poland because German troops were about to engage in the large enterprise of invading western Europe. He took his task very seriously, and addressed a meeting of his government on 16 May 1940:

> The general war situation forced us to review the internal security situation in the General Government very earnestly. One could deduce from ample indications and acts that resistance movement of the Poles, organized on a large scale, existed in the country and that we were standing on the very brink of considerable and violent events. Thousands of Poles were already enrolled and armed in secret societies and were being incited in the most rebellious manner to commit every kind of outrage.[47]

He later wrote that he and SS-Brigadeführer Bruno Streckenbach had 'worked out a programme of pacification, whereby a possible speedy end will be made with all rebels, resistance politicians and other political suspects in our hands ... I candidly admit that thousands of Poles will pay with their lives and particularly the leaders of the Polish intelligentsia.' The operation was termed Aktion A-B. The Pawiak prison in Warsaw was virtually emptied and the prisoners taken to Palmiry forest and executed; in Cracow prisoners were taken to nearby Krzesławice and shot; those held in Lublin castle met the same fate outside the city; and a sandy area near Częstochowa became the graveyard for groups taken from that town and Radom. In all it has been estimated that about 3,000 members of the Polish intelligentsia were murdered and a further 30,000 were arrested and imprisoned. The former Polish artillery barracks at Oświęcim, in the part of Polish Silesia now incorporated into the Reich, was developed into the first concentration camp on the soil of the pre-war Polish state. It is better known to the world as Auschwitz. The first convoys of Polish political prisoners arrived there in June 1940 just as the Germans were entering Paris.[48]

Throughout the German occupation, active resistance was a minority activity. In the early years the number involved in the resistance was minuscule. One of the early resisters suggested a reason:

> It was an unforeseeable phenomenon, born as much from a challenge to 'common sense' as from a scorn for hollow dogma and calculation of the odds. Isolated and vulnerable, it seemed like an enterprise touched with madness.[49]

Emmanuel d'Astier, founder of *Libération-sud*, suggested that 'to be a resistant, you had to be maladjusted', or to be one of 'nature's rebels waiting for a cause which would transcend the normal and irritating compartmentalisation of actions and beliefs'.[50] Taking part in the resistance meant 'accepting lawlessness on behalf of a higher good and the replacement of routine by a life of relentless improvisation'.[51] Therefore many of the early resisters were people who already felt themselves isolated from the society around them, or, like trade unionists and Jews, they might have been dispossessed by the early actions taken by the Germans and collaborationist governments. A few could claim multiple reasons for joining the resistance. For example, Jean-Pierre Lévy explained: 'I was born in Strasbourg. As an Alsatian, I was, in 1940, fiercely anti-German. Second, you know that I am Jewish, a double reason to hate the Germans. And, of course, I am French, enough reason to hate the traitors and collaborationists of the Vichy regime.'[52] Because of the high risks involved in resistance, many of the early resisters were young people and students who had the least to lose:

> If you were single, and you had some money, it helped: it is always somewhat easier to start to think about these things, than when you have a large family to support, and for most people in an occupied country, the first aim was how to survive. Next, when you could survive, you could think about doing something against the Germans.[53]

Unlike a soldier in a regular army who was usually conscripted to serve his country, each individual resister made a decision to oppose the occupier voluntarily. He or she did this in the full knowledge that this decision was taken against the tide of public opinion, and even in opposition to it.[54] One historian of the resistance in Europe has suggested that: 'Contrary to popular belief, resisters were initially regarded not as heroes or selfless patriots, but as reckless adventurers who at times needlessly endangered the lives of their fellow countrymen for acts of doubtful value.'[55] This was recognized by the early resisters, who realized that the vast majority of their compatriots, even if they were not willing to collaborate, were certainly prepared to follow a policy of accommodation with the occupier. Therefore, 'to stand out against all this and to resist by wanting to go on fighting against the Germans was like being in a foreign country. No one agreed with you and they happily denounced you.'[56] Yet for others like Marie-Madeleine Fourcade resistance was 'a moral obligation to do what you are capable of doing. It was a must. How could you not do it?'[57]

Many of the first resistance movements were founded by army officers who had escaped capture on the fall of their countries as well as pre-war politicians determined to atone for the defeat of their country. The Polish resistance owed its origins to the formal handover of responsibility from General Juliusz Rómmel to General Michał Karaszewicz-Tokarzewski just before Warsaw's surrender. The short-lived organization *Służba Zwycięstwu Polski*, SZP (In Service of Poland's Victory), was replaced in November 1939 by the *Związek Walki Zbrojnej*, ZWZ (Union for Armed Struggle), commanded by Rowecki. In Belgium, army officers formed the *Légion Belge*, in the Netherlands army officers set up the *Orde Dienst* (Order Service), and in Norway *Milorg* was founded by army officers. In France too, army officers were to the fore in establishing early resistance organizations. As France was on the point of defeat, three generals set up a bureau under Colonel Émile Mollard, *Camouflage du Matériel*, to travel around France collecting weapons and ammunition and concealing them from the Germans for use should the Germans invade the Unoccupied Zone. Captain Henri Frenay established the *Mouvement de Libération Nationale*, which later developed into *Combat*.[58]

With the majority of army officers and soldiers in POW camps, the early resistance movements had to become well-organized and have a clear structure and purpose, in order to appeal to the masses who would fill their rank and file. The fulfilment of these aims was not easy to achieve.

In the case of the Protectorate and Poland, the early period needs to be divided into before the fall of France and after it. Indeed, the resistance in the Protectorate should be further divided to cover the period before the outbreak of the Second World War. For the resistance in both countries the fall of France had a cataclysmic effect. Principally it led to the recognition that the war was likely to be a long one and so led to a reappraisal of how best to resist the Germans. The second effect was the immediate rupture of communications between the resistance movements and the Czech National Committee and the Polish government-in-exile, both of which had moved to London when France fell. Prior to the fall of France, couriers had passed through the Balkans on their lengthy way to France carrying messages to and from the central resistance organizations and the governments' representatives outside the homeland. The difficulty in maintaining communications was compounded by the entry of Italy into the war and the German conquests of Greece and Yugoslavia. Thereafter communications had to be conducted primarily by radio.

Czechoslovakia had been denied the opportunity to defend its independence at all and a notable feature of the three resistance organizations that were built up over the summer of 1939 was their focus not on resistance to the Germans, but on planning for the future after the defeat of Germany which they thought was sure to happen once a general war broke out. Two of the groups were created by pre-war politicians. Members of the pre-war political parties formed an organization, *Politické ústředí* (Political Centre), which favoured a return to the pre-war political system with a strong president and a coalition of the five major parties. Left-wing politicians formed a separate body, *Petiční výbor 'Věrni zůstaneme'*, PVVZ (Committee of the Petition 'We Remain Faithful'). The PVVZ believed that the pre-war political system had failed and campaigned for a new kind of democratic socialist state. Czech army officers created the framework of a secret army, *Obrana národa*, ON (Defence of the Nation). The officers favoured a temporary military dictatorship for the period immediately after Germany's defeat. All three groups were hostile to the Protectorate government under Hácha and accepted the authority of Beneš, then in exile. In June 1939 the ON sent its leader, General Sergěj Ingr, to France as its representative, and his role in the homeland was taken over by General Josef Bílý.[59]

Anticipating a short but victorious war, the ON built up a secret army of thirteen 'divisions' covering the whole of the Protectorate, before the outbreak of the Second World War. On 8 September 1939 the ON received a message from London ordering: 'armed resistance and sabotage on a mass scale, to start simultaneously over the entire territory, upon signal by the British radio . . . which will be given shortly'. The rapid defeat of Poland and the inaction of Britain and France led General Ingr to rescind the order on 29 September.[60] Clearly then, the creation of a secret army in this period appeared to be pointless, a fact reinforced by the defeat of France in June 1940. Consequently, the resistance organizations formed a central organ in early 1940 to coordinate strategy, *Ústřední výbor odboje domácího*, ÚVOD (Central Committee of the Home Resistance). For reasons of security, the three groups remained operationally independent.

The Poles had begun preparing for clandestine warfare even before the Second World War broke out. A member of the Polish general staff, Major Edmund Charaskiewicz, planned an organization which would consist of cells of between seven and twenty-five people, formed by those men and women too young or too old for military service, which would carry out partisan and guerrilla warfare utilizing secret caches of weapons and explosives.[61] Charaskiewicz visited Britain and discussed Polish plans and requirements with the War Office there. Although the war broke out before any British supplies, particularly of radios, could be despatched, the visit by Charaskiewicz and others by his colleagues paved the way for fruitful Anglo-Polish cooperation immediately after the fall of France and the creation of SOE.[62]

The principal challenge facing Rowecki when setting up the ZWZ* was uniting under his command the over 100 underground military organizations that had emerged after Poland's defeat. He confided to his deputy Bór-Komorowski:

> I have no means of enforcing such a measure. There are no steps I can take towards it. All I have is the authority of the Polish Government abroad, and this is of necessity a moral authority only, and the future alone can show whether it is sufficiently strong to overcome political differences as well as personal ambitions and unite the whole nation.[63]

The process of creating a single underground military organization was a lengthy one, continuing even after Rowecki's arrest in June 1943 when the leadership was assumed by Bór-Komorowski. The Polish prime minister and commander-in-chief Władysław Sikorski issued a comprehensive set of orders in Instruction No. 1, despatched in December 1939, detailing what the resistance should do. The ZWZ was to concentrate on reconstructing the government and on preparing for an armed uprising to break out behind the German lines when the regular Polish army entered Poland. Before that time, the guidelines were clear:

> In no case does the Polish government permit belligerent actions on the territory of the homeland because at present the political goal of such action seems unclear, and secondly, because in the current beginning stage, a military action would turn out to be weak and could capture only a few points of the country. The result of such an action would most likely be disproportionate to the reprisals they would bring upon the country by giving the occupier an excuse to destroy Poland mercilessly. For now, stay away from diversionary acts and wait for relevant directives from the supreme commander.[64]

Another order was sent in February 1940 which laid out the five key tasks of the resistance: collection and transmission of intelligence; sabotage;

* The ZWZ was renamed the *Armia Krajowa* (AK) in February 1942.

reprisals against Polish spies and traitors and Gestapo agents; diversion; and, in the long term, armed insurrection.[65]

In response, Rowecki created the *Związek Odwetu*, ZO (Union for Retaliation), which undertook sabotage against the railway transports that crossed Poland from the Soviet Union to Germany. Locomotives were disabled by the addition of a specially prepared chemical product to the grease in the greasing box. Practice made perfect and in 1940 the average period of disablement for each locomotive was fourteen hours but was increased to twenty-four hours in later years. (The French resistance undertook similar sabotage in France.) The Poles worked out early on that reprisals could not occur if the Germans had no idea where the sabotage had occurred, so they experimented with the use of timers on bombs placed in oil transports passing through Poland to Germany from the Soviet Union. Once the bomb had gone off, the Germans had no idea whether the bomb had been placed in the Soviet Union, in Poland, or in Germany.[66] After the German invasion of the Soviet Union these attacks on rail transports would escalate considerably on German trains travelling eastwards.

The political resistance began in Poland at the same time as the military organization. Sikorski appointed Cyryl Ratajski as the government delegate in December 1940. His role was to be the secret political leader in Poland and he was tasked with setting up an entire underground state, with departments corresponding to the fifteen pre-war government ministries.[67] The importance of the Polish underground state cannot be underestimated. Unlike elsewhere in Europe at the time, Poland had no collaborationist government, nor did it have a senior civil service, operating as a conduit between the Germans and the population, as in western Europe. The underground state was created to take the place of the civil service. Of the fifteen departments it formed, the three most important dealt with education, justice, and civilian resistance. The Germans had closed all secondary schools and universities shortly after the beginning of the occupation. Himmler had proclaimed the German goal:

> For the non-German population of the East, there must be no higher school than the fourth grade of elementary school. The sole goal of this schooling is to teach them simple arithmetic, nothing above the number 500, writing one's name, and the doctrine that it is divine law to obey the Germans . . . I do not think that reading is desirable.[68]

To counter this determined attempt to reduce the Poles to the level of illiterate slaves, the underground government formed a secret teachers' organization in Warsaw in autumn 1939, which quickly spread across the General Government, eventually setting up almost 2,000 secret secondary schools.[69] One of its leaders, Kazimierz Koźniewski, wrote after the war: 'Underground teaching on all levels of schooling was the most admirable work accomplished by Polish society. Neither tracts, nor violence, nor sabotage were as productive as this last manifestation of the national consciousness.'[70] In November 1939 the Germans had closed all higher educational institutions other than technical schools, but by mid-1940 Warsaw University had begun operating again in secret.[71] The underground state also ran its own legal system, complete with underground courts which could try, condemn, and execute traitors. In April 1941 a directorate for civil resistance was set up under Stefan Korboński.

The fall of France stunned Poland and led to a number of revisions to the strategy of the underground army. Now in London, the Polish general staff prepared grandiose schemes whereby Poland would be liberated by an Allied landing on the Baltic coast after the Allies had achieved air and naval superiority and German forces had been weakened by attacks on several fronts. Such operations, it was envisaged, would be assisted by sabotage and diversionary operations by the underground army, culminating in a general uprising. These plans also anticipated that planes and tanks would be sent to Poland to assist the uprising.[72] The plan, which was shared with the British in May 1941, was of course overtaken by events with the German invasion of the Soviet Union in June. Yet it was important in a number of ways. It demonstrated that the Poles were always thinking on a large scale and assuming that Allied supplies would be available. To build up an underground army capable of seizing sufficient territory from the Germans to enable the Allied planes to land, there would have to be numerous supply drops of instructors, armaments, and radios. It also shows the dominance of the concept of a national uprising within Polish strategic thinking both in Poland itself and in Polish circles in Britain. This, of course, would lead to a great tragedy in 1944.

Poles had flocked to join the resistance from the start and on the eve of the fall of France, the underground had recruited about 40,000 people in the Warsaw region alone, and about 75,000 people in the whole of German-occupied Poland. The fall of France and Sikorski's orders issued on 18 and 20 June 1940 calling for an end to armed resistance, including sabotage, gravely damaged the morale of the Poles. Membership of the underground dropped to 54,000 in the spring of 1941. Some of this drop was intentional: it was impossible to undertake secret activity for a great length of time without the Germans finding out about it, so recruitment was deliberately cut. Security was now a paramount concern. Whereas most senior military officers and prominent politicians went underground early on, others remained at home: 'They argued that if they behaved outwardly in accordance with the stipulations of international law and remained quiet, the Germans could not do this or that.' The executions at Wawer and the seizure of hostages soon disabused them.[73]

The Czechs had also learned the same lesson on security the hard way. The first leaders had 'met almost publicly in such places as coffeehouses, kept files and made up lists of their members, and had far-fetched plans for igniting a mass revolt against the occupiers'.[74] Recruitment was done without the most elementary investigation of the prospective members and on the grounds that 'He's Czech, that's recommendation enough.'[75] Unsurprisingly, the Gestapo found it easy to penetrate the Czech resistance. During summer 1939 and into the winter, the Gestapo virtually wiped out the resistance organizations. Younger members took over but security lapses continued. For example, in March 1940 Beneš received a message: 'Due to the clumsiness of our people, pogrom after pogrom has been directed against us with the result that now we remain merely a handful.'[76] Matters did not improve and Colonel František Moravec, in charge of Czech intelligence in London, recorded the dismal fact that: 'The situation on the home front could be described by a message received at Christmas 1940 and repeated at intervals with only little variations until the autumn of 1941: "Organisation doing more or less well. Moravia was cleaned out again from the top. The conditions there are worst. Many traitors. Will build up again."'[77] Whereas the Poles planned for a great national uprising, the Czechs were more cautious and elected to focus on the provision of intelligence to the Allies, and on upholding the spirit of the Czechoslovak people through the underground press.

According to a participant and historian of the Norwegian resistance, Tore Gjelsvik, it 'came into existence fumblingly, in obscurity and secrecy, in the absence of proper communications, not only between Norway and Britain but between one district and another. Written agreements and reports were banned, and much was done very hastily.'[78] This is particularly true of the military resistance which became known as *Milorg* (Military Organization). *Milorg* was founded in autumn 1940 with the stated intention to 'lie low, go slow' and build up a secret army in the long term. The country was divided into five independent military regions and twenty-two districts. In March 1941 an Anglo-Norwegian commando force made a raid on the Lofoten Islands. The commandos destroyed fish-oil plants and storage tanks, sank 19,000 tons of shipping, and captured 213 Germans and twelve NS members. The prisoners were taken back to Britain, along with 314 Norwegians who wished to join the exiled forces in Britain. Reichskommissar Josef Terboven flew north to take personal control of the reprisals: the property of those who had voluntarily left for Britain was burned, and arrests were made of people identified as having assisted the commandos.[79] The Norwegian government-in-exile was appalled by the German reaction; it was also alarmed by the creation of *Milorg*, of which it knew nothing. The government needed to assert command and control over the situation. Efforts were made to improve communications between the Norwegian government-in-exile and the British high command since the Norwegians had known little of British commando plans. (These will be covered elsewhere.) Contacts between *Milorg* and the Norwegian government were established only in late 1941 when two of its leaders, Professor J. Holst and Captain J. Schive, fled Norway under German pressure and assured the government in London of *Milorg*'s loyalty to the monarchy. *Milorg* was then placed under the Norwegian high command.[80]

The Norwegians faced two enemies: the occupying Germans and the NS under Quisling who were determined to nazify the country. John Rognes founded the Norwegian Front, formed of businessmen, academics, journalists, and trade unionists who opposed Terboven's attempts to form a council of state. This was the start of the civilian resistance, *Sivorg*, which developed and grew in a piecemeal way before becoming united and organized.

The NS attempt to take over sports organizations led to a total sports strike in which sportsmen refused to participate in international, national, or even local matches. Despite the arrests of some leading sportsmen by the summer of 1941, at least 300,000 athletes refused to participate in events organized by the NS minister of sport, Axel Strang. Education was another area which the NS sought to take over and where resistance was evident from the start. On 30 September 1940 a renowned professor, Dr Johan Scharffenberg, addressed students at Oslo University urging them to remain loyal to the king and his government-in-exile. The Gestapo immediately arrested Scharffenberg and dissolved the Students' Union. Then the minister of education, Ragnar Skancke, decided to take this opportunity to promote under-qualified NS cronies to positions in the faculty, which led to an immediate boycott of NS professors by the students and faculty. In response the rector of the university, Dr Seip, was arrested and deported to Germany. Thereafter Oslo University became an ideological and physical battleground between NS students and the others. Skancke's threats to dismiss school teachers if they did not join the NS were no more successful. Bishop Eivind Berggrav drafted a declaration which the teachers' association adopted: 'With reference to the enquiry received, I hereby declare that I will remain true to my teaching vocation and my conscience, and that on that basis I shall, in the future as in the past, carry out the decisions relating to my work which are lawfully given by my superiors.' Skancke backed down on this occasion, but in 1942 he would again attempt to introduce NS values into the educational system and spark off a more serious teachers' revolt.[81]

The legal profession perceived itself as the upholder and protector of international law, a matter of vital importance during the German occupation. In Norway, Terboven had initially promised that the law courts would remain independent, but the NS minister of justice, Sverre Riisnaes, had other ideas. He first authorized himself to appoint and dismiss jurymen, thereby abrogating the independence of the courts, and then set up a new 'People's Court' to judge political cases. The Supreme Court, led by Paal Berg, appealed to Terboven who responded: 'neither the Supreme Court nor any other inferior court was permitted to raise the issue of the validity of decrees issued by him or the commissarial government'. On 12 December 1940 the Supreme Court resigned in protest:

> It is the duty of the courts of justice to examine the constitutionality of decrees and decisions. During a military occupation, courts of justice must be in a position to examine the validity of orders promulgated by the occupying power with respect to international law. We cannot subscribe to the opinions expressed in this area by the Commissioner of the Reich. We therefore find ourselves in the position of no longer being able to maintain our functions.[82]

Berg went on to become one of the leaders of the civilian resistance. In contrast, the Supreme Court in the Netherlands remained in office even when its president, Lodewijk Visser, was dismissed from his position because he was a Jew. No written protest was even made by them and indeed the majority of his fellow judges voted for his removal.[83]

NS activity also led to the chairmen of forty-eight organizations representing business, culture, law, education, labour, and the Church writing a lengthy letter to Terboven on 15 May 1941 appealing to him to intervene on their behalf against the excesses of the NS and its paramilitary wing, the *Hird*:

> ... we wish to call attention to the continued attempts by the NS to usurp powers and privileges to which they are not entitled in our opinion. This cannot possibly be in the interest of the occupier. We refer especially to strong pressures on the state and municipal civil servants to join the *Nasjonal Samling*. They are threatened with dismissal if they do not conform, despite assurances to the contrary, that no one would be forced to become a member of the NS party against his convictions. Several loyal and trusted civil servants were fired or suspended because they were not 'acceptable' to the Party ...'[84]

This letter is open to interpretation. It could simply have been an appeal to Terboven to stop the excesses, suggesting that if he did this, then the German occupation would not be opposed, or it could have been an attempt to put pressure on Terboven by threatening to portray him as acting against the interests of the Germans. But it could also be a less subtle warning: 'control the NS or there will be increased opposition both to the NS and, by implication, to the Germans'. Terboven appears to have chosen to view the letter in this light. He summoned the leaders of the associations to a meeting where he spoke as if he were 'a colonial governor addressing German slaves', and five leaders were arrested. Some organizations were dissolved by decree and others forced to accept nominated leaders. The result was to drive these professional organizations underground, where they provided the early membership of the civilian resistance.[85]

This great groundswell of resistance to the NS by associations and the professions needed organizing, and a Coordinating Committee was established to design and oversee counter-attacks to the NS. At the same time, but independently of the creation of the Coordinating Committee, the *Kretsen* (Circle) was established, led by Berg. The *Kretsen* aimed to establish and maintain contact between the civilian resistance in Norway and the Norwegian government in London. There was an overlap in membership between the Coordinating Committee and the *Kretsen*. This strengthened both organizations, enabling them to work together to issue special instructions or 'paroles' to the Norwegian people instructing them on how to oppose the NS moves, particularly during the worst of Quisling's efforts in 1942.[86]

Resistance to the German occupation began early in the Netherlands. On 15 May 1940, just as the Dutch army was on the point of capitulation, a pamphlet appeared issued under the name of *Geuzenaktie* calling for a continued resistance to the Germans. The *Geuzen* (Beggars) was formed by a local teacher, Bernard IJzerdraat, in the town of Geuzen, near Rotterdam.* The group expanded rapidly and began to sabotage German telephone lines. Poor security enabled the Gestapo to penetrate the group, and in November 1940 over 200 people were arrested. Of these, forty-three were selected to be put on trial in February 1941 and a month later fifteen were condemned to death and shot, alongside the ringleaders of the Amsterdam strike, in the dunes near Scheveningen. A further 157 members of the *Geuzen* were deported to German concentration camps.[87]

The first military resistance group in the Netherlands was the *Orde Dienst*, which was formed by army officers and NCOs, and was organized

* The original *Geuzen* had opposed the Spanish during the Dutch Revolt in the sixteenth century.

along military lines, with a general staff and lower command positions. It had two aims: to undertake sabotage and gather intelligence in the short term, while focusing on slowly building up a secret army to rise up when the Germans were weakened by defeats on other fronts. Some members planned to set up a military government after liberation. Others intended only to maintain law and order until the return of the exile government. In 1941 the *Orde Dienst* was hit hard by a series of arrests among its leaders and members, and thereafter desisted from undertaking much sabotage until later in the occupation. The organization remained active, however, in collecting intelligence.[88] A similar pattern was followed in Belgium where arrests among the first leaders led to a drop in sabotage and an increased focus on intelligence-gathering.

The most notable feature of the early development of the resistance in France was its fragmentary nature. This was not surprising since France was divided geographically into two zones: the north, occupied by the Germans, and the Unoccupied Zone under the Vichy regime. Then there was the thorny question of who the enemy was. In the north the answer was simple: the Germans. But in the south the matter was complicated by the existence of the Vichy regime which some saw as an enemy but many others regarded as a shield against the Germans. The lack of a German presence made it easier for the French in the Unoccupied Zone to ignore the ignominy of their defeat. Henri Frenay wrote despondently in late 1940: 'The general drift of French public opinion was profoundly disappointing. Aside from the few friends whom we recruited, there was not a hint of the spirit of revolt. People had made themselves comfortable in defeat just as they would have done in victory. Their principal and sometimes exclusive worry was food.'[89]

Added to this, there was the question of personalities, since both Pétain and de Gaulle laid claim to the loyalties of the French people. Pétain was seen as the victor of Verdun and therefore as a national hero. For example, the group *Défense de la France*, set up by Sorbonne students in autumn 1940, was divided over support for Pétain.[90] Even Frenay, the founder of *Combat*, wrote in May 1941:

> May Marshal Pétain give us the benefit of his authority and unequalled prestige for a long time. We are totally devoted to the work of the Marshal. We believe De Gaulle's movement is wrong. One defends a country better by staying in it than leaving it. Many undesirable elements are clustered around De Gaulle.[91]

It would be another year before Frenay would break with Pétain. Yet Vichy could be an important shield for resistance activity in the south. Major

Georges Loustaunau-Lacau used his appointment as Pétain's delegate to the *Légion Française des Combattants* to create a network of army officers opposed to the German occupation. Colonel Georges Groussard used his position as the head of Pétain's bodyguard as cover for his resistance activities.[92]

The resistance was equally divided over its level of support for de Gaulle. For Agnès Humbert, involved in the Musée de l'Homme resistance network, de Gaulle was 'a leader of whom we know absolutely nothing, of whom none of us has even seen a photograph' but whose speech as France fell gave the early resisters something very important in their decision to swim against the tide of collaboration and accommodation – hope.[93] But other resisters did not accept the leadership of de Gaulle. Germaine Tillion wrote after the war: 'Among the Resistance in 1940, I knew some who did not become Gaullists until 1942, and others who never became Gaullists. They could not stand the presence of the Germans in France and needed no other motive to act.'[94] Christian Pineau of *Libération-nord* wrote in February 1941 that he approved of de Gaulle as a leader of the military fight against the Germans, but disputed de Gaulle's claim to political leadership.[95] Yet at this early stage in the war de Gaulle himself did not recognize the implications of the resistance in metropolitan France; he was focused on building up the Free French army. Thus when Pierre de Vomécourt went to London to discuss resistance with the Free French, he found little support. His return to France and his organization of networks splitting France into three zones, covered by himself and his two brothers, Jean and Philippe, was overseen by the British.[96]

The French resistance was also fragmented on the question of tactics. Most organizations in the south like *Libération-sud* run by Emmanuel d'Astier and the northern organizations such as *Libération-nord*, *Ceux de la Libération*, *Organisation Civile et Militaire* (OCM), and *Ceux de la Résistance*, all realized that sabotage and armed actions against the Germans would only invite reprisals and focused instead on building up support through the production of clandestine newspapers. These organizations also made tentative moves towards planning for future armed resistance. The greatest moves in this direction were made in the south by Frenay, who envisaged the creation of a secret army, but he too realized the need to focus first on propaganda and the collection of intelligence.[97]

The early stages of the French resistance movements also illustrate another pitfall applicable to other countries – that of trying to do too much. Three employees at the Musée de l'Homme, Boris Vildé, Anatole Lewitzky, and Yvonne Oddon, were determined to oppose the German occupation. The activities of the network they created were extensive, from assisting

French soldiers to escape from POW camps before their transfer to Germany, producing the clandestine newspaper *Résistance*, and collecting intelligence and arranging for it to reach Britain. Such a wide range of activities inevitably involved a large group of people, all of whom knew each other, and they in turn formed links with other small resistance groups. The downfall of the network at the end of December 1940 began when neighbours reported to the French police suspicious activity at a defunct aviation club in a northern suburb of Paris. When they raided the premises, the French police found the mimeograph machine producing copies of *Résistance* and arrested the printers. One of them had a list of the names and addresses of the distributors, who were then also arrested. The Germans had access to the lists of people arrested by the French and so the network began to be unravelled as each member arrested carried the names and addresses of others. The next month plans for voyages to Britain from Brittany were uncovered and over the course of 1941 twenty-three people were arrested. The network's difficulties were compounded when a member, Albert Gaveau, became a traitor.* Lewitzky and Oddon were among the early victims, and in March 1941 Gaveau secured the arrests of two important members. The first was the eighteen-year-old courier René Sénéchal, who was found carrying military intelligence documents as well as numerous names and addresses. His arrest led the Germans to Boris Vildé, the leader of the network. Nineteen of the most important members were put on trial by the Germans together in January 1942 and all were found guilty and condemned to death. Pleas for clemency by the Vichy ambassador to Paris, Fernand de Brinon, were rejected other than that the sentences of the women, including Humbert and Oddon, were commuted to deportation to German concentration camps. The men were executed on 23 February 1942 at Mont-Valérien.[98]

During its short life the Musée de l'Homme network had been highly successful. It had produced five issues of *Résistance*, the last edited by Pierre Brossolette who would go on to play an important role in the French resistance. It had explored routes out of France, both from the Brittany and Mediterranean coasts, which others would exploit more successfully. Finally, intelligence gathered by a member, René Creston, which included the plans of the port of Saint-Nazaire on the Atlantic coast, reached Britain. At the end of March 1942 British forces attacked the port and put its vital dry dock out of commission.

* Gaveau was tried and found guilty of treason after the war and sentenced to life imprisonment.

6

Intelligence Gathering: 1939–41

The provision of accurate and adequate intelligence about the enemy's capabilities to wage war and its future intentions is vital to the successful conduct of war. Intelligence has been defined as:

> . . . the collection, collation and analysis of evidence to enable an effective use of scarce resources. Intelligence is not a form of power, but rather a means to guide its use. Intelligence does not win wars. It does help generals do so. It involves finding true and useful secrets while avoiding false notions, and forcing the opposite on the foe, through security and deception.[1]

Intelligence could be harvested from a great variety of sources: signals intelligence, which for the Allies included breaking the German Enigma codes; air and sea reconnaissance; and human intelligence gathered by people in the occupied countries. The Allies needed intelligence from all these sources so that as complete a picture as possible of the enemy could be created. In countless ways German-occupied Europe was a mystery to the Allies, with everything from the morale of national populations to German plans and troops dispositions almost completely unknown. As a resistance activity, intelligence gathering has the advantage of being of value in any strategic situation; moreover, it is an act of silent resistance in that, unlike sabotage, it is, if successful, completely invisible to the enemy and cannot attract reprisals. Anybody could do it: a passing farm worker on a bicycle might notice unusual security activity or the arrival of a strange piece of machinery. Any degree of commitment was possible: from passing on a single item of information once to coordinating an entire network of agents. Intelligence broadened the range of people who could see themselves as participating in the resistance, and for the resistance itself it provided a way to prove the value of its existence and therefore to be able to demand support from the Allies. As the head of the Free French intelligence agency, the BCRA, explained:

> We constituted a reserve force of men, in many cases courageous men, who, thanks to the chaos produced by the defeat, could return to their own country to observe the enemy, his plan of action, and his movements there. As for the English, they possessed all the indispensable material resources: money, radio sets, false papers, means of transport, correspondents in neutral countries, and so on. Like the blind man and the paralytic, we therefore had to join forces.[2]

For the Allies, the role of the resistance in intelligence gathering was essential after the disaster of the so-called Venlo incident.

The principal agency in Britain for gathering intelligence abroad was the Secret Intelligence Service, SIS, also known as MI6. During peacetime, officers would be attached to British embassies and establish networks to collect intelligence which would then be transmitted to Britain either by secure radio or, in the case of longer reports, by the diplomatic bag. War meant that these embassies were closed and the diplomats expelled, including the representatives of SIS. The SIS office in The Hague under Major Richard Stevens ran agents not only in the Netherlands, but also in much of north-west Europe. In the mid-1930s the Gestapo managed to penetrate the office. The head of SIS, Admiral Hugh Sinclair, suspected this, and instructed one of his deputies, Claude Dansey, to set up a parallel but separate network of agents, known as the Z network, which was run by Sigismund Payne Best. After the German invasion of Poland and the outbreak of the Second World War, SIS in the Netherlands was approached by some German officers who claimed to represent the army's opposition to Hitler. The matter was discussed at cabinet level and SIS was given the go-ahead to open discussions with the Germans. As the historian of SIS has noted: 'SIS was playing for high stakes indeed, and the potential prize was so glittering that critical faculties both in the Netherlands and in London were dangerously blunted.' Several meetings were held between the British and the Germans. The principal German negotiator, Walter Schellenberg, later wrote:

> They accepted me apparently without reservations as the representative of a strong opposition group within the highest spheres of the German Army. I told them that the head of this group was a German general . . . Our aim was the forcible removal of Hitler and the setting up of a new regime.

In fact the entire operation was run by the SD, the SS security service. On 9 November 1939 a meeting was arranged between Stevens, Best, and the German officers at Venlo on the Dutch-German frontier. Shots were exchanged, and the two British officers were bundled into a car and driven across the border into Germany. Himmler, blaming SIS (wrongly) for the recent attempt on Hitler's life in Munich, had personally ordered the arrests. In Germany, the two men, apparently fearing torture, revealed all they knew about SIS's organizations. Their information was compounded by the ultimate security travesty committed by Stevens who was carrying with him a list of Dutch agents run by SIS in the Netherlands when he was arrested. A number of these were also providing information from Germany.[3]

The disaster which befell SIS in northern Europe compounded earlier difficulties caused by the arrest of the head of the SIS station in Vienna after the *Anschluss* of 1938. Indeed, it has been suggested that 'when Germany finally invaded France and the Low Countries in May 1940, SIS was left without a single valuable network in occupied Europe. Apart from Sweden, Switzerland and Portugal, SIS was blind to continental events.'[4] This gap could, however, be partly filled by the governments-in-exile now concentrated in London, and by other representative organizations such as the Czech and French national committees. They could despatch agents from Britain who would recruit agents on the ground from the resistance in the occupied countries.

The Czechs had arrived in London before the outbreak of war. The head of Czech intelligence, František Moravec, had accepted an offer by the British to fly himself and eleven of his most prized colleagues out of the country as the Germans invaded in March 1939. They brought with them access to a vital asset, Paul Thümmel, known as agent A-54. Czech intelligence had recruited Thümmel, an officer in the Abwehr, German military intelligence, in February 1936. He provided the warning that the Germans would invade Bohemia and Moravia and continued to provide valuable and generally reliable intelligence until his arrest in March 1942. Before the outbreak of war, information was smuggled out of the Protectorate into neutral countries. After the outbreak of war, radio contact between the *Obrana národa* (ON) and General Ingr was maintained, with interruptions, until May 1942, when the Gestapo finally tracked down the last remaining radio operators. The importance of the intelligence supplied by Thümmel led the ON to establish a separate cell known as the Three Kings: Colonel Josef Balabán, Colonel Josef Mašín, and Captain Václav Morávek. In spring 1941 Balabán and Mašín were captured and although Morávek escaped, he lost his radio. This meant that the Three Kings were unable to transmit Thümmel's warnings about the imminent German invasion of the Soviet Union. The ON maintained networks of railway and postal workers and employees in armaments industries and these supplied information on the war production of the industries in the Protectorate and the movements of German troops. Edvard Beneš, head of the Czech national committee, saw the contact as vital to restoring the position of Czechoslovakia in the eyes of the Allies, radioing Prague in September 1940: 'Your work has positive results here. The British appreciate us the more when they compare us with the Poles, the Dutch and even the French who have nothing equal to offer. You are contributing greatly to the good name of the whole nation.'[5]

The Polish general staff arrived in London during the summer of 1940 with an already well-established intelligence service, the II Bureau. Colonel Leon Mitkiewicz was appointed to head it but, since he had little experience in intelligence work, he relied largely on his deputy who did, Lieutenant Colonel Stanisław Gano. The British were quick to recognize the benefits of establishing a close relationship with the Poles.[6] The Poles had a reach far beyond that of British intelligence. With radio stations operating in Bucharest, Budapest, Belgrade, and other major cities, the Poles had access to networks of agents who could provide the British with information from the Balkans, a region where SIS was weak. The II Bureau had also ordered the Home Army to set up an intelligence department, with networks to be kept separate from action groups for security. The Poles also had access to Polish communities scattered across Europe, but particularly concentrated in north-western Europe, the very region where the Venlo incident had blinded SIS. The organizational skill, determination to hit back at the Germans, and the possibilities offered by the Poles led to the British giving them a remarkably free hand. The Poles were allowed to utilize their own codes and radio facilities quite independently from the British, on the promise that all intelligence other than that relating to domestic affairs in Poland would be passed to SIS.[7] The arrangement worked very well. Indeed, by the end of the war a British report on intelligence claimed that of the 45,770 intelligence reports from occupied Europe processed by the Allies during the war, nearly half had emanated from Polish sources.[8]

After the fall of France in June 1940 the British desperately needed information from France on German preparations for an invasion of Britain. The Poles were ready to help. Three Polish officers with intelligence experience met in Toulouse, set up an escape line to help Polish soldiers cross the Pyrenees, and established the first Polish network in France, known as F2. The officers were Colonel Wincenty Zarembski, Mieczysław Słowikowski, and Captain Roman Garby-Czerniawski. Słowikowski built a radio transmitter and, remembering the wavelengths and schedules, succeeded in making contact with the Polish Embassy in Madrid. A radio operator there recognized Słowikowski's fist and he was given the means to contact the II Bureau in London directly. The first contact was made on 15 September 1940. By the end of the year F2 had four cells based in Toulouse, Marseille, Lyon, and Paris. Although F2 remained Polish-led throughout its existence, most of its agents were French. Indeed, as early as the middle of 1941, only forty of its 250 agents were Poles. By the end of 1944, F2 controlled over 2,800 agents. These provided vital information on the identity of factories working for the German war industry and their output. F2, under Zarembski, known as 'Tudor', was also especially strong in the provision of naval intelligence.

The Paris cell of F2 was known as *Interallié* and was led by Garby-Czerniawski. It grew to cover the entire Occupied Zone and supplied the Allies with the complete German order of battle in northern France and the location of around 100 German airfields in northern France and Belgium. To begin with, the network lacked a radio of its own and had to send its reports to Toulouse or Marseille for onward radio transmission to Britain. Sleeping-car attendants on the express trains proved to be willing couriers. In July 1941 *Interallié* finally received its own radio and could contact London directly. This, however, led to the network's downfall. In November 1941 *Interallié* was penetrated by the Gestapo and Garby-Czerniawski and his chief of staff, Mathilde Carré, were arrested. Carré was turned by Sergeant Hugo Bleicher and was paid 6,000 francs a month to betray seventy *Interallié* agents, which in turn led to the capture by the Gestapo of all five of *Interallié*'s transmitting stations in the Paris area. The infection spread south and the naval intelligence cell established by Zarembski was particularly badly hit. Zarembski himself was forced to flee to London. *Interallié* was later rebuilt with the assistance of F2 agents. But the turning of Carré also had further consequences. One of SOE's first agents in France, Pierre de Vomécourt, needed access to a radio and Carré persuaded him that Garby-Czerniawski's was safe. Unwittingly, Pierre de Vomécourt gave the Germans an early insight into the workings of SOE, especially its radio communications. Carré then confessed to de Vomécourt that she was a double agent. He should have eliminated her but instead devised a complex plan: Carré would persuade Bleicher to permit her to travel to Britain with de Vomécourt where he hoped to convince her to become a triple agent. Bleicher would believe that she was betraying the secrets of SOE to the Germans whereas in fact SOE would feed the Germans misinformation.[9]

At the same time Garby-Czerniawski allowed himself to be 'turned' by Colonel Oskar Reile of the Abwehr. He agreed to travel to London as a German agent in return for the promise that none of his captured agents would be executed. No sooner had he reached London than he notified his Polish superiors of the deal, and they in turn passed the information on to SIS. Garby-Czerniawski was passed to MI5 and the XX Committee which ran German double agents. He became 'Brutus' and during 1944 supplied the Germans with fake evidence about the Allied plans for the invasion of France and the impact of the V-weapons.[10] Pierre de Vomécourt and Carré arrived in Britain in February 1942. De Vomécourt later returned to France but was arrested and spent the remainder of the war in French prisons and Colditz camp. SOE had no further use for Carré and she spent the remainder of the war in various British prisons before being handed back to the French at the end of the conflict to be tried as a traitor.*

Władysław Sikorski had ambitious plans to mobilize the Polish workers in the mining industries of northern France and Belgium into an army. This army was to be known as *Polska Organizacja Walki o Niepodległość*, POWN, or the Polish Army in France, and was led by Aleksander Kawałkowski. In the long run the purpose of this army was to engage in sabotage, go-slows, and strikes in the workplaces of its members and then, when the Allied invasion was imminent, its armed groups would render assistance to the Allies as they landed. But the time was not ripe for an intensive campaign of sabotage, still less for armed action, so POWN formed an intelligence arm under Jerzy Jankowski. This later grew into the Monika and still later Bardsea networks. Between the middle of June 1940 and 11 November 1942 the network provided II Bureau with about 2,000 reports from northern France and Belgium containing economic and military intelligence.[11]

Within Poland, the resistance, the AK, was hampered in its establishment of an intelligence arm by the departure of most of Poland's trained intelligence officers to Romania and Hungary in September 1939. Nevertheless, an intelligence branch was set up under Major Wacław Berka, who was ordered by Stefan Rowecki, head of the AK, to despatch to London intelligence 'in the most detailed and frequent manner possible: by radio cables at least once a week and written reports once a month, additionally any seized documents'. The AK was not the only organization gathering intelligence: the *Muszkieterzy* (Musketeers) led by Captain Stefan Witkowski also sent intelligence out of the country to the British. The *Muszkieterzy* were loyal to the pre-war *Sanacja* regime rather than Sikorski and stubbornly refused to submit themselves to Rowecki's control. The British ignored the inter-Polish conflict and accepted intelligence from both

* Carré was found guilty and sentenced to death, a sentence then commuted to twenty years in prison. She was freed in 1954 and five years later produced her autobiography *I Was 'The Cat'* after her nickname in the resistance.

groups since the *Muszkieterzy* had formed cells in the Reich, an area the AK had not yet penetrated.[12] Until the Germans overran the Balkans in the spring of 1941 the AK could transmit its reports by radio to various Polish stations operating throughout the Balkans, as well as directly to London by radio from July 1940 onwards. After the German occupation of the Balkans, communications went either directly to London or via the powerful transceiver set up in Cairo with the assistance of the British. Longer reports had to be carried out of the country by couriers crossing the mountains into Hungary and Slovakia and then through the Balkans. One of the best known of these couriers who operated through the harsh winter of 1939–40 was Krystyna Skarbek. When it became clear that Skarbek had fallen under suspicion from the Germans and Hungarians, the British ambassador to Hungary, Sir Owen O'Malley, arranged for her to be smuggled across the Yugoslav border hidden in the boot of a legation car. O'Malley would go on to become the British ambassador to the Polish government-in-exile; Skarbek would later serve in France with SOE as 'Christine Granville'.[13]

Like the Czechs, the Poles also had a means of gathering intelligence directly from the heart of the German decision-making process. Halina Szymańska, the wife of the pre-war Polish military attaché in Berlin, managed to escape to Switzerland after the fall of Poland. While she and her husband had been in Berlin they had come to know Admiral Wilhelm Canaris, the head of the Abwehr. Canaris's loyalty to the Nazi regime has been greatly debated and it is not clear how much he facilitated Szymańska's escape to Switzerland; nor whether he put her directly in contact with the man who would, throughout the war, become a vital contact with the German opposition, Hans Bernd Gisevius, who was then working as the Abwehr representative in Zurich. What is known is that somehow Szymańska became the conduit through which at least twenty-five largely accurate reports were sent from Switzerland to Britain between August 1940 and December 1942 concerning German intentions towards Britain, the Balkans, and the Soviet Union.[14]

Norway occupied a position vital for intelligence gathering. Any German ship leaving its home port in Germany or along the Baltic coast would have to pass along the long Norwegian coastline before reaching the North Atlantic and the vital Allied convoys traversing the ocean. Timely warning of the sailings could assist the Admiralty in preparing for a convoy's defence. The vital importance of gaining timely intelligence from Norway led to a number of errors as semi-trained agents were rushed into Norway and the nascent Norwegian resistance groups were called upon to undertake tasks for which they had had no training at all. At length SIS achieved a satisfactory understanding with the Norwegians for the operation of SIS agents, by which it was agreed that SIS would focus on ship-watching and the Norwegians on the German occupation forces and internal Norwegian affairs.

Norway was a very difficult location in which to operate. The Germans also recognized the importance to the Allies of the coastline and could concentrate their counter-espionage forces in the coastal ports and towns. The Gestapo was also ably assisted by Norwegian collaborators, people against whom the resistance had few defences. For example, the first SIS station, 'Hardware', based in Haugesund, south of Bergen, operated for only eight weeks in the summer of 1940 before a Norwegian collaborator posing as someone who wished to be transported to Britain led the Gestapo to the cell. Ten of its members were sentenced to death, the first such sentences in occupied Norway, although these were later commuted to life imprisonment. In March 1941 the Gestapo all but destroyed the intelligence networks operating in Norway. First they broke into a group based in Oslo. One of the leaders was placed in a prison cell with a friend of his father who gained his confidence. Unfortunately, the man was an informer and this led the Germans to uncover an intelligence group operating from the police headquarters in Ålesund, led by a solicitor, Harald Torsvik. Torsvik and four others were sentenced to death and executed. Inexperience and naivety led to the Germans uncovering further groups in Stavanger and Bergen so that by the middle of 1941 intelligence gathering in Norway was in a state of some disarray.

Yet the picture was not totally bleak. Steps had been taken which would enable the Norwegian resistance to make valuable contributions to intelligence gathering, sabotage, and resistance. Two men in particular came to the fore. One was Odd Starheim who escaped from Norway in August 1940 and was recruited by the Norwegian section of SOE. Returning to Norway by boat in January 1941 he established a cell in the south of Norway, with a radio operator, which proved to be long-lived and provided the Allies with essential information on German naval movements. The other man was professor at the Norwegian Institute of Technology, Leif Tronstad. His network focused on acquiring industrial and economic intelligence. His investigations included the activities of the Norsk Hydro plant at Rjukan which produced heavy water, a vital component in the German nuclear programme. Tronstad's network was hit badly in autumn 1940 when three Norwegian soldiers who had been landed in Bergen to set up an intelligence cell were followed by the Germans and arrested. Information carried by them led to arrests in the Bergen region and also in Trondheim. Tronstad escaped to Britain where he would later become responsible for much of the planning for the Allied attack on the plant at Rjukan.[15]

The relationship between the British and the Belgians was complicated by two factors. In the first place, the Belgian government-in-exile had little standing with the Belgians in occupied Belgium. Secondly, there were two rival Belgian agencies seeking to control resistance activity and intelligence gathering: the *Sûreté*, the security service, and the II Section, the intelligence branch of the Belgian general staff. The head of the *Sûreté*, Fernand Lepage, a former magistrate in Belgium, established a good relationship with SIS. However, Lepage was not content to limit his operations to intelligence gathering and wished to extend his control over the Belgian resistance. It was a cardinal rule of SIS that intelligence should remain completely separate from resistance activity. The II Section was more directly connected to the Belgian resistance but resented any British oversight of its activities and had poor relations with the Belgian section of SOE, T Section. This created the bizarre situation where the *Sûreté* stated that it would only cooperate with T Section if it was informed in advance of every agent's intended role. The II Section then announced that it would only work alongside T Section if the latter had no dealings with the *Sûreté* at all.[16]

Such conduct could only damage the value and process of intelligence gathering within Belgium. This activity was already being hampered by the lack of radio communications since reports had to be taken overland by the lengthy courier route across France and the Pyrenees. But there were many such reports. Walthère Dewé, who had led the Belgian intelligence organization *La Dame Blanche* during the First World War, was now the chief engineer for the Belgian telephone and telegraph network. This placed him in the ideal position to revive his organization, now known as 'Cleveland' and later as 'Service Clarence', using his extensive contacts among engineers, administrators, and businessmen. The organization reported on a wide range of subjects such as the movements of German troops and munitions and the German exploitation of Belgian industry, and supplied drawings of the fortifications constructed around Zeebrugge. At its peak Cleveland/Service Clarence had 1,500 agents. The organization survived Dewé's capture and execution in January 1944. Other networks operated independently: *Zéro*, founded in July 1940 by Fernand Kerkhofs and Jean Moens, gathered military, political, and economic intelligence, while *Luc*, founded by Georges Leclercq and André Cauvin, focused on political intelligence.[17]

The provision of intelligence by the Dutch was bedevilled by internal conflicts within the Dutch government-in-exile. In July 1940 the Dutch set up an intelligence agency, the *Centrale Inlichtingen Dienst*, CID, or Central Intelligence Service. Its first head, François van 't Sant, had formerly been a senior officer in the police in The Hague. During the First World War, despite the neutrality of the Netherlands, he had passed intelligence to SIS. Therefore, it would appear that he was an excellent appointment. But within the government-in-exile the duality of van 't Sant's position as head of intelligence and as the queen's private secretary caused conflict. Therefore, he was replaced in the summer of 1941 by R. P. J. Derksema, who failed to get on with SIS's expert on the Netherlands, Colonel Euan Rabagliati, and was replaced in spring 1942 by Major Jan Somer.[18]

The Netherlands suffered from a huge geographic disadvantage when it came to sending intelligence out of the country because the distance to the Franco-Spanish border was too great. This led to the bizarre early practice of sealing intelligence reports into bottles and dropping them into the river in Rotterdam in the hope that the bottles would be washed ashore in Britain.[19] Remarkably, some were; but this was obviously a totally inadequate solution. Therefore, as early as 28 August 1940 the first CID agent, Lieutenant L. von Hamel, was parachuted into the Netherlands, equipped with a radio. He succeeded in setting up four intelligence groups within a short time, and acquired three radios of Dutch manufacture. Von Hamel was arrested by the Germans in October 1940 and was later executed, but the groups he had set up continued to operate until the Germans crushed them in the course of 1941 and 1942. But importantly, radio communication had been established with the Netherlands and one of the groups set up by von Hamel had established contact with the *Orde Dienst*. By the middle of 1942, however, radio communications and intelligence gathering in the Netherlands had been severely compromised by the *Englandspiel* (to be covered later) and the complete penetration of SOE networks in the Netherlands. The intelligence agents were caught in the same net simply because they had been given the identical contacts in Holland as the SOE agents.[20]

The Danes took the initiative in establishing contacts with the British. They recognized the fact that Denmark occupied a position from which they could report on German naval movements and shipbuilding. In the summer of 1940 the Danish war correspondent on the *Berlingske Tidende*, Ebbe Munck, contacted Danish intelligence officers and suggested a means by which intelligence could be sent to the British. His plan, which was put into practice, was for himself to go to Stockholm as the correspondent of one of the Danish newspapers, and the officers would send him microfilms by courier since travel between Denmark and Sweden was reasonably easy. In Stockholm, Munck established a close relationship with the SOE representative there, Ronald Turnbull. This relationship proved so fruitful that SIS, whose role it should have been to arrange such contacts, agreed to take a background role, and intelligence cooperation was formally confirmed as operating between Danish intelligence and SOE. A second group set up as a private initiative, by a Danish air force lieutenant colonel, Torben Ørum, used demobilized officers, who were working as labourers on German airfields and military installations, to gather intelligence. Ørum himself travelled to Sweden to pass his intelligence on to the British legation in Stockholm. He and his assistant, Lieutenant Jessen, were spotted by the Germans who followed them on their return to Denmark and arrested the two men. Because of the sensitive nature of relations between Germany and Denmark the two men were then handed over for trial in the Danish courts and both received lengthy sentences of imprisonment. After the German takeover of Denmark in August 1943 the German authorities re-examined the case, and Ørum was rescued by the resistance in October just before the Germans were about to ship him to almost certain death in Germany.[21]

France occupied a central position in the intelligence requirements of the Allies in 1940. The British government needed to know with the utmost urgency about German plans to invade Britain. Furthermore, now that Germany controlled the French Atlantic ports, thereby giving her easier access to the vital Atlantic trading routes, the Admiralty needed to know what was going on in those ports. Hence, links between France and Britain were established on several levels and through different channels.

De Gaulle and the Free French recognized the fact that they could gain an immediate standing with their British hosts if they could ensure a regular supply of accurate and useful intelligence. Therefore, when twenty-nine-year-old Captain André Dewavrin, a former lecturer on fortifications at Saint-Cyr military college, was interviewed by de Gaulle after serving with the French expeditionary force in Norway, he was surprised to be appointed head of the Free French intelligence service, the II Bureau. He was given no advice on how to set up such a service and all his knowledge of intelligence work came from spy novels. Dewavrin and his first colleagues took pseudonyms from the Paris Metro map: Dewavrin became known as Passy. Passy was described by one of his most successful agents, Rémy, at their first meeting as 'a seemingly very young officer, prematurely bald, beardless, in riding breeches and white leggings, sitting and reading a document while chewing on his handkerchief'. Passy was brave enough to be parachuted into France on two occasions because he felt it was immoral not to be ready to take the same risks as his agents. It is impressive that from such an unpromising beginning the agency that would become known as *Bureau Central de Renseignement et d'Action* (BCRA) would develop into a highly effective intelligence-gathering arm of the Free French. Relations between the BCRA and SIS were generally good, although the French resented the establishment of independent SIS networks, thereby mirroring their opposition to the existence of SOE's F Section. Nonetheless, Sir Frank Nelson, then head of SOE, recorded that he was 'well-impressed' by Passy, who had been recommended to him by Claude Dansey and SIS.[22]

The BCRA despatched agents to France as early as July 1940. The missions of Jacques Mansion and Hubert Moreau will be dealt with later. Some of these early networks lasted only a short time. For example, the Nimrod network set up by Count Honoré d'Estienne d'Orves in Brittany was betrayed after a few weeks by its radio operator, smarting at being thrown out of the safe house after making unwanted passes at the occupants' maid. The group was rounded up by the Germans and tried in Paris in May 1941. D'Orves became the first Free French agent to be executed by the Germans.[23] Undoubtedly the most successful of the early Free French agents was Gilbert Renault, best known as Rémy, who set up a network called the *Confrérie de Notre-Dame* (CND) operating in all the main ports along the Atlantic coast and in the Paris region. By the end of 1940 he had recruited thirty-two agents, had established safe places to cross the demarcation line, and had contact with Switzerland. Rémy noted that many of his contacts had divided loyalties. For example, his contact in Brest, Lieutenant Commander Jean Philippon, insisted on getting assurance from his superior that providing intelligence to the Allies was not incompatible with loyalty to Pétain. Another example was a man called Vautrin who operated in Paris and sold information for financial reward:

> He contacted true patriots in possession of information which they were anxious to send to London, paid their expenses, and then typed out several copies of the information, two of which he sent to Vichy, and sold the remainder to the highest bidder.

This meant that London often received the same information from different sources. In the beginning Rémy had no radio of his own and was forced to send his despatches to the Unoccupied Zone from which they were taken to Spain. By June 1941 the sheer quantity of reports caused difficulties and a photographic laboratory was set up near Lyon where the reports could be microfilmed and then sent to the French Embassy in Madrid, hidden in a box of pharmaceutical products. When Rémy finally obtained radios the contribution of the CND increased markedly. Indeed, Rémy claimed that 'The business was taking on a regular commercial air ... We were just like a large firm with many branches which kept in touch constantly by telegram' – the head office being of course the headquarters of the Free French in London.[24]

In 1940, SIS established two new sections to produce intelligence on France. One section was led by Commander Kenneth Cohen to cooperate with Passy and the Free French. No formal agreement was ever settled between the two parties since the Free French resented the British control of their communications and the willingness of both SIS and SOE to work with non-Gaullist elements in France. The second section was led by Commander Wilfred Dunderdale. This caused the most offence to the Free French since not only did this section deliberately spurn cooperation with the Free French, but it also cultivated contacts within the Vichy intelligence services.[25]

One of the SIS networks, Jade-Fitzroy, was set up by Claude Lamirault who was parachuted into France in January 1941 with a radio transmitter. His radio operated from the Soeurs-de-Sainte-Agonie convent in Paris with the mother superior and nine nuns acting as radio operators. The network specialized in military intelligence, especially on the aircraft factories in France building planes for the Luftwaffe. Its reach extended across most of Brittany, Normandy, and Châteauroux. By late 1941 the network had four radios in operation.[26]

One of the most extraordinary and highly successful networks which reported to the British was the Alliance network. This was the brainchild of Georges Loustaunau-Lacau. He had been active in right-wing circles before the war and had set up a private intelligence group to investigate the strength of the German armed forces before the outbreak of the war after his dismissal from the French II Bureau. His open criticism of the French high command saw him imprisoned before the war only to be released when the Germans invaded France. He was wounded in action and captured but escaped. His previous service on Pétain's staff enabled Loustaunau-Lacau to gain Pétain's confidence and he was appointed head of the *Légion Française des Combattants*. He used his role to sound out veterans who wished to continue the fight against the Germans and, until such action was feasible, to provide the Allies with intelligence. He divided Unoccupied France into zones for intelligence work and set up communication lines to Spain and Switzerland. He also sent an emissary, Jacques Bridou, to London to meet de Gaulle and the British. The impression Bridou obtained and reported back was that the Free French were not interested in cooperating with Loustaunau-Lacau but that the British certainly were. Loustaunau-Lacau travelled to Portugal where he met Cohen in Lisbon and was supplied with a radio and codes, 5 million francs, and questionnaires on ports, airfields, and troop movements.[27]

Loustaunau-Lacau was arrested in July 1941 in Algiers where he had been planning an anti-Vichy coup, but his organization was re-formed by his assistant, Marie-Madeleine Méric (later Fourcade) who had worked in the same publishing firm as Loustaunau-Lacau before the war. Loustaunau-Lacau described her as having 'the memory of an elephant, the cleverness of a fox, the guile of a serpent, the perseverance of a mule, and the fierceness of a panther'. The animal analogy was carried into the operations of the network. Fourcade later wrote of the network that she would:

> . . . let my companions live again under their underground aliases. Indeed, we rarely knew one another's real names. At the beginning we described ourselves by groups of letters and numbers, by symbols: KSI 42, KIF 141, ASO 43. Later, as the war went on, we adopted the names of animals: Eagle, Humming Bird, Tiger, Ermine . . . The Germans called us Noah's Ark.

The network grew to have about 3,000 agents and it produced much valuable intelligence for the Allies. For example, in summer 1941 the head of the Brittany network, Antoine Hugon, arrived in Pau, in the foothills of the Pyrenees, wearing a huge cloth map of the drawn-to-scale layout of the Saint-Nazaire submarine base and shipyard. The Musée de l'Homme network had also collected intelligence on the shipyard, which was passed to the British. The price paid by Alliance over the course of the war was heavy: around 500 agents died after being arrested by the Germans.[28]

Soon after the armistice was signed the head of the French II Bureau, Colonel Louis Baril, sent a message to SIS promising support and solidarity. The Vichy intelligence services decided that they should cooperate with the British because of:

> . . . a belief that France was alone with numerous enemies including Britain, which had betrayed her, accompanied by the recognition that the number one enemy was Germany, and the liberation of the country was still a priority. With this in mind, one could take advantage of contacts with the British to obtain intelligence about the Germans, even though the British were considered worthy of only very limited trust. The goal was not to work hand in hand with the British, but rather draw the maximum benefits from contacts by giving the British the minimum information required to maintain the link.[29]

But the French intelligence officers were aware of the necessity of concealing their activities both from the Vichy regime – whose ministers with the exception of the war minister General Huntziger, and the air force minister General Bergeret, would certainly not approve of any such contacts – and of course from the Germans, who themselves had plenty of agents operating in Vichy France.

The Vichy French intelligence agencies reinvented themselves as an agricultural association, the *Société d'Entreprises des Travaux Ruraux*, TR, with its headquarters in Marseille. Intelligence about the Germans was passed to Britain by various means: via the Canadian minister at Vichy, the American military attaché, and via the diplomatic pouch to contacts in Berne and Lisbon. By 1941 the TR had about 429 agents reporting mostly from France but with links into the Belgian resistance where the network was headed by a police superintendent, Jeff Dehenin. Dunderdale provided Colonel Georges Ronin, the head of air force intelligence, and Lieutenant Colonel André Perruche, head of army intelligence, with radio sets.[30]

In summer 1940 Maurice Ripoche, a former First World War pilot, founded the *Ceux de la Libération*, an intelligence group to collect information on the Luftwaffe. The intelligence the group gathered was transmitted to the Allies through the SR Air group under Ronin. SR Air had six regional branches in the Unoccupied Zone and two in North Africa to report on air and sea traffic. SR Air also installed monitoring posts along the demarcation line which gathered intelligence sent by radio by the Germans. These messages were decrypted by Gustave Bertrand and the Polish cryptographers who had cracked Enigma and were now operating from the Château des Fouzes in Uzès. The intelligence was then passed to the British by radio or sent across the Spanish border.[31]

Before turning to an examination of what intelligence was supplied, it is worth stressing again the fact that the vast majority of the members of the resistance engaged in gathering intelligence were amateurs who had no training in intelligence work. They often had little idea of what was of importance to the Allies. Advice was sent to the resistance from London. For example, the Polish II Bureau instructed the Home Army intelligence department: 'The general rule underlying good field reports is the proverbial five Ws: *w*ho is doing *w*hat, *w*hen, *w*here, and in *w*hat way'.[32] Similarly, Marie-Madeleine Fourcade of the Alliance network in France was advised:

> Use 'intelligence maps'. As soon as you get a piece of information put it on a map. The questionnaires will undoubtedly arrive one day. Even then we shall probably have to answer only the simplest questions – such as Who? Or What? Where? How? Only precise information is of any value. Report only what has been *seen* and *heard*. It's up to the people using the information to draw the proper conclusions.[33]

Until questionnaires arrived, the resistance was largely working in the dark, gathering information with little knowledge of what was important and what the Allies had not learned from other sources.

Intelligence is made up of numerous small bits of information which in an ideal world would be reconstructed to form a clear picture. Yet the analysis of human intelligence was subject to limitations: there was often too much or too little information, or it was too fragmentary to make sense, or came from a single or an unreliable source. In other words the process of analysing intelligence was as frustrating as the actual gathering of the material. The Vicomtesse de Clarens described this:

> Some of us were told to collect pedestrian facts; others were given specific instructions; others still were asked to keep ears and eyes open for the unusual, the improbable; almost all were working in small, compartmented fields in almost complete isolation . . .
>
> It is not easy to depict the lonesomeness, the chilling fear, the unending waiting, the frustration of not knowing whether the dangerously obtained information would be passed on – or passed on in time – or recognised as vital in the maze of the 'couriers'.[34]

Others, however, enjoyed the work. Rémy wrote:

> In that spring of 1941, our work seemed a kind of game, dangerous perhaps, but still a game. And our few reverses only increased our confidence in our methods. It may seem paradoxical to say so, but the Germans became a sort of myth to us, in spite of the fact that we busied ourselves about night and day, getting as much information as possible on their activities.[35]

The most pressing question facing Allied intelligence during the summer of 1940 was whether the Germans would attempt to invade Britain, and if so, how and when. The challenge was to analyse the vast amount of intelligence that was being received on the issue. It must be stressed that the resistance in western Europe provided only one angle; intelligence was also gleaned from the Ultra decrypts and, above all, through air photographic reconnaissance and naval patrols. Each element provided only a limited snapshot of what the Germans were doing in northern Europe after the fall of France. Much of the intelligence was of poor quality; some of it was extremely fanciful.

The urgent necessity to get agents to report back from France on German preparations for Operation Sealion, the invasion of Britain, provided the Free French with an early opportunity to prove their worth to the Allied war effort. Accordingly, in July 1940, Passy despatched Jacques Mansion and Hubert Moreau. They were briefed to discover all they could on

German dispositions in northern France. Mansion returned in September with maps of the German locations. Moreau recruited two of his school friends and asked them to undertake a reconnaissance by bicycle along the north coast of Brittany; he focused on the area further east in the Saint-Malo area.[36] In Belgium, Dewé's Cleveland network reported on the concentration of German troops in the coastal areas. Reports also came from Norway where an agent warned that:

> . . . considerable quantities of tanks and heavy guns are being collected at Stavanger and Bergen. New aerodromes are being prepared in the neighbourhood of these two towns for the use of giant, troop-carrying machines which are stated to carry 50 men each.

A report from Polish intelligence noted that the Germans had been undertaking trials of amphibious tanks in the Baltic, and also holding exercises on landing from small ships. Another report from Norway notified Allied intelligence of German trials of landing craft capable of carrying tanks.[37]

German preparations could not be easily concealed since it was estimated that at least 260,000 troops would be involved in the opening waves. The requisition of billets and the construction of camps for the soldiers and sailors involved could not be hidden from French or Belgian eyes. Nor could the concentration of the barges needed to transport the troops across the Channel be hidden from photo reconnaissance. At the beginning of September 1940 the German Navy reported that it had 1,910 barges, of which only 800 were motorized, 419 tugs, and 1,600 motorboats, all moored in ports from Rotterdam to Le Havre. These barges had been requisitioned from canals throughout Germany, Belgium, the Netherlands, and northern France. Conversion work necessary for the cross-Channel trip and landing in Britain had been carried out mainly in Germany, but also in shipyards around Amsterdam, Rotterdam, and Antwerp. The resistance were able to report on these concentrations of barges and other shipping, and Allied intelligence could corroborate these reports with evidence gleaned from photo-reconnaissance analysis and naval patrols.[38]

The resistance was considerably less helpful when it came to predicting the date of the invasion. Polish intelligence supplied several reports indicating a start date of between 6 and 8 July or the following week. Extremely exaggerated information was obtained from a debrief of three Dutch army officers who had recently reached Britain from the Netherlands: this suggested the probability of a major airborne landing designed to draw British troops away from the coasts before the seaborne landing. These men stated that the German slogan was 'London on 15th July'. The number of men they claimed the Germans would land was on the same scale as the later

German invasion of the Soviet Union. Even the normally reliable Czech source, Thümmel, was of limited use. On 12 August he reported that there would be no invasion for at least two weeks and in September he stated that it would be delayed until early October. In the middle of October he suggested that the invasion had been postponed until 1941 and repeated this suggestion with another report at the end of the year, when he reported that Field Marshal Wilhelm Keitel, head of the Wehrmacht, had said that Germany would definitely invade Britain in early 1941.[39] We now know that on 17 September 1940 Hitler indefinitely postponed Operation Sealion, and on 19 September Keitel issued the orders to disperse the shipping. By the end of September air reconnaissance revealed a reduction in the number of vessels in the major ports along the north coast of Europe. The Foreign Office then learned that Hitler had told Mussolini at their meeting at the Brenner Pass on 4 October that the invasion of Britain was off.[40]

The Allies were totally in the dark as to what the Germans would do next. The Polish *Interallié* network reported in December 1940 that the Germans were planning to send the Afrika Korps to Tripoli. The report was discounted by British intelligence because it was not backed up by any other source. Yet in January 1941 the Belgian network *Luc* reported that the Wehrmacht had placed orders for thousands of sets of tropical uniforms from the textile factories around Hainault. It had been ascertained that these were not for the Italian Army, then fighting the British in the Western Desert. Thus the resistance had provided the Allies with the intelligence that the Afrika Korps were indeed going to North Africa and it was a failure of intelligence analysis on the part of the British that led to their army being surprised by the appearance of the Germans in the Western Desert in February and March 1941.[41]

Polish intelligence issued a long series of reports from the spring of 1940 concerning the construction of German military installations, fortifications, airfields, and the improvement of the road network all along the east-west axis in Poland, all pointing towards German plans to invade the Soviet Union. After the fall of France the Germans began an accelerated programme of airfield construction between the Vistula and Bug rivers. Thümmel reported in August 1940 that he had learned that the German intelligence branch responsible for the Soviet Union was expanding and that experts on the southern Ukraine, the Crimea, and the Caucasus were being recruited. Yet the British were slow to recognize Hitler's intentions towards the Soviet Union, dismissing the reports of the German concentration of troops in Poland on the grounds that the Germans had to put spare divisions somewhere. In May 1941 the Poles reported that the Germans were planning a series of eight railway troop movements, all named after Polish rivers. The name of one of these was corroborated by Enigma. In the second half of April intelligence was received from the Poles, Czechs, and Yugoslavs of movements of German troops eastwards and the formation of German civilian administrations for the lands to be conquered.[42] Then on 3 June 1941 Stefan Rowecki sent an extremely detailed message warning:

> A German concentration in the east is assuming unusual proportions and just now seems to reach its final phase. Predicted readiness – mid-June. The deployment depth reaches Kraków, Łódź, Płock. Units from the west were arriving until mid-May. Now they report the arrival of elements of 2nd, 6th and 12th armies from Greece and Yugoslavia.[43]

Winston Churchill passed the intelligence evidence of an imminent invasion to Stalin. We know, of course, that Stalin had been receiving reports from his own sources, including the Red Orchestra, his spy network in western Europe, but had discounted them.

An ongoing requirement of Allied intelligence concerned the movements of the German capital ships and U-boats. The resistance undoubtedly made a vital contribution towards the provision of this information, which increased as the war continued. Three broad areas were of the greatest interest. As discussed earlier, any capital ship leaving a German port had to pass along the Norwegian coast on its way to the North Atlantic to intercept the Allied convoys between the United States and Canada and Britain or, after the German invasion of the Soviet Union, the Allied convoys to the Soviet Union through the Arctic Sea. The naval bases along the Atlantic coast of France were rapidly converted to become U-boat bases as well as containing much of the German support shipping for attacks in the Atlantic. The Baltic housed the main shipyards, and intelligence from there was vital in order to predict what the Germans were building and when the ships would be ready.

Germany had a far smaller fleet at the start of the Second World War than in 1914. Nevertheless, the two battleships, *Bismarck* and *Tirpitz*, the battlecruisers *Scharnhorst* and *Gneisenau*, the pocket battleships *Admiral Scheer* and *Lützow* as well as heavy cruisers and light cruisers were all capable of inflicting great damage on the larger but more widely committed Royal Navy and could potentially massacre convoys. The British military attaché in Stockholm, Harry Denham, worked closely with his Norwegian counterpart, Colonel Roscher Lund, to process naval intelligence provided by the Norwegian resistance. However, Denham noted: 'Although we received reports from Norwegian Resistance couriers coming overland to Sweden, owing to the time-lag their operational value was negligible.'[44]

For this reason SIS sent men equipped with radios to Norway as early as September 1940 to establish ship-watching cells. The Admiralty was forced to rely heavily on reports radioed to it from Norway and Sweden because the German Navy maintained radio silence before the ships sailed, rendering signals intelligence impotent, and air reconnaissance could not easily identify individual ships.

The value to the Admiralty of the Norwegian resistance was demonstrated in May 1941. On 18 May *Bismarck* sailed from Gdynia with the heavy cruiser *Prinz Eugen* as its escort. On 20 May *Bismarck* was spotted by a Swedish cruiser sailing through the Kattegat and Stockholm was informed. The close relations between Colonel Petersën, the head of Swedish military intelligence, and the Norwegian and British military attachés paid off and the Admiralty was warned. *Bismarck* was then seen at Christiansand in Norway by a ship's chandler, Viggo Axelsson, who was a member of a resistance group in southern Norway. He informed the radio operator for the group, Gunvald Tomstad, who radioed London. On 25 May the Royal Navy engaged *Bismarck* in the Denmark Strait and shell fire from the *Bismarck* destroyed the British battlecruiser *Hood* and badly damaged the *Prince of Wales*. Information that *Bismarck* was likely to head for Brest for repairs was passed to British intelligence by Rémy. Three days later *Bismarck* itself was sunk by the Royal Navy. That left *Tirpitz*, which left Wilhelmshaven in January 1942 and was spotted by an SIS agent sailing up Trondheim Fjord a few days later with an escort. There were a number of resistance arms dumps in the area and the agent was deeply concerned lest some reckless Norwegian resistance group should attempt to attack the *Tirpitz*. Such an attack would have no chance of success against such a massive target but would bring the Germans into the area and most likely unravel the resistance organizations there. Accordingly, apart from sending a message to London notifying the Admiralty of *Tirpitz*'s location, the details of the ship's vital statistics 'were published at once in the underground newspapers, together with severe warnings to leave the ships alone'. The Norwegian resistance would continue to play a role both in communicating the whereabouts and sailings of *Tirpitz* and in assisting in the complex, long-drawn-out Allied attempts to destroy the ship.[45]

German naval activities in France were watched closely by Free French agents, SIS, and the Polish networks. Intelligence was supplied from northern ports such as Le Havre, right down the coast to Bordeaux. Hubert Moreau made an important contact with the chief engineer at the Lorient naval base who supplied him with a detailed plan of the base, pointing out the new constructions built by the Germans along with the details of the ships and U-boats in the port. Rémy had useful contacts all along the Atlantic coast but especially in Brest. This enabled him to supply the British with complete plans of the harbour defences, including the precise location of the anti-submarine net. His work in Brest was supplemented by the separate 'Johnny' network, which supplied daily reports between March and June 1941 on the seaworthiness after Allied bombing of the battle-cruisers *Scharnhorst* and *Gneisenau*. Various networks operated in the port of Bordeaux supplying intelligence to the Allies. The Free French's agents included two Gironde river pilots who supplied detailed intelligence on the shipping entering or leaving the port. On one occasion the departure of fifteen ships was radioed to London and ten of them were torpedoed soon after leaving the Gironde. The 'Tudor' cell of the Polish F2 network prided itself that no submarine left the ports of Brest, Le Havre, or Bordeaux without London being notified at once. Knowledge of sailings was useful to the Royal Navy but what it really wanted to know was the destination of the U-boats and their patrol areas.[46]

The Baltic ports were very difficult for the British to observe since they were located at the extreme limit of the range of aircraft flying from Britain. This meant that Polish intelligence could plug a vital gap in the Allies' knowledge. Accordingly, at the beginning of June 1941, the Home Army received a telegram from London:

> The surveillance of the German Navy and ports is of utmost significance for our friends [the British] who attach great importance to these issues. It is necessary for our joint effort and winning the war. Therefore, tight surveillance must be organised that would encompass the ports of Gdynia, Hel and Gdansk as well as the ports in eastern Prussia and possibly Szczecin [then Stettin in Germany]. The friends urgently request the quickest possible installation of W/T stations and daily cables to assure continuous information.

This was easier said than done since there was a great shortage of radios in Poland. But during 1941 and especially in 1942 the Poles were able to set up networks in the Polish ports. Gradually their reach extended into the German shipyards too as Polish forced labourers were employed there and could send messages back to Poland for transmission to London. This included the vital information that the Germans were focusing on the construction of submarines and no longer on capital ships.[47]

The outbreak of war severely curtailed the supply of intelligence on the German economy and armaments manufacture. Some information could be gleaned from orders placed in Sweden and Switzerland, but the resistance played its role by supplying what information it could on orders placed by the Germans in factories operating throughout Europe. On the other hand, technical intelligence of new developments proposed by the Germans was far harder to identify. The first major piece of intelligence to reach Britain was the so-called Oslo Report, a seven-page typewritten report and a box which were passed to the British Embassy in Oslo by Hans Ferdinand Mayer, an anti-Nazi German engineer working for Siemens, in November 1939.* The report and the box were sent to London where R. V. Jones, the head of Scientific Intelligence, examined the contents. The report provided information on the development of the Junkers-88 as a dive-bomber, naval construction, the location of a research institute at Peenemünde, various types of remote-controlled explosive devices, fuses, range-finders, and developments of different types of torpedoes. Jones recalled that most ministries would not take the report seriously since they doubted its source but that 'the value of the Oslo report was to become evident as the war proceeded'.[48]

In June 1941 two intrepid Danes, Thomas Sneum and Kjeld Petersen, escaped across the North Sea in an aeroplane that they had built from the airframe of a two-seater sporting plane, a car engine, and various pieces of scrap metal. Their unorthodox means of arrival caused suspicion within the British intelligence community, but they had brought with them some vital information. Sneum had filmed a radar station on the island of Fanø, which showed the aerials turning. MI5, which had been responsible for interrogating the two men, had developed the film and ruined most of it in the process. From the two salvaged frames Jones could identify that Sneum had in fact filmed the Germans' new advanced early-warning radar system Freya in operation.[49]

The near-disaster that befell Sneum's film reveals something of the challenges of getting intelligence to Britain. Mention has been made of the time delay inevitable with the couriering of documents to the nearest neutral country for onward transmission to Britain. This could be partially overcome with an increased use of radios, although, as will be seen in a later chapter, the operation of radios was fraught with difficulty and danger. Longer reports still had to be carried manually by couriers, until the time came when aircraft were able to land to collect the reports. This meant that the resistance had to devise methods to minimize the size of the reports to be carried. Polish intelligence noted as early as April 1940 that there was a problem with undeveloped films being damaged in transit, thereby

* Mayer's action remained undetected during the war and his authorship of the Oslo Report was kept secret from the world at his request until after his and his wife's deaths. It was only revealed in 1989.

wasting the considerable effort that had gone into obtaining the information and collating the reports. As a result clear and detailed instructions were sent to Poland on how best to protect the films. These included details on how to wrap the film and the recommendation that the celluloid layer should be removed first, because then 'the remaining emulsion is a very thin coat that can be easily rolled into the diameter of a match'. Of course, such a small object would be far easier for the courier to conceal than a bulky report, but it could just as easily be lost or destroyed by accident.[50]

By June 1941 the resistance had already proved its value in the collection of intelligence. This would only grow as the war progressed and would indeed prove of priceless value, especially when it came to the supply of information on the development of new armaments such as the V-weapons.

7
The Origins of SOE and OSS

After the withdrawal of the British expeditionary force from Dunkirk, followed soon after by the collapse of France, both strategic planners and politicians began to consider how Britain might be able to continue to prosecute the war against the Axis powers. It was painfully clear that Britain would be in no position to wage war on the European mainland in the foreseeable future because her armies had abandoned their heavy equipment in France and needed to be rebuilt virtually from scratch. This effectively left Britain with economic warfare as the only means through which the Axis powers could be attacked. The strategic option of bombing German industry was viewed in many quarters with alarm because of the fear that German bombers would retaliate against British industry. Furthermore, given the limited range of British bombers and the lack of quality navigational equipment with which to find a target, a large question mark had to be placed over the utility of strategic bombing at this stage of the war, despite the optimism of the staff of Bomber Command. Naval blockade had been effective in the First World War, leading to the so-called 'Turnip Winter' of 1916–17 when Germany faced severe shortages of food, but it would have a limited impact this time around because Germany was in control of the economic resources of much of Europe. Therefore, attention was turned to the possibility of waging economic warfare through sabotage and subversion. Early evidence from Poland and the Protectorate suggested that resistance to occupation was developing but needed help from abroad, particularly in the provision of armaments, in order to expand. It must be stressed, however, that the British planners were operating in the dark and had virtually no idea about conditions in Europe nor about the real prospects for resistance.

In organizational terms Britain was not starting totally from scratch. In 1938 three organizations had been established to examine the questions of economic sabotage and propaganda in the event of war. The first was a department of propaganda, known as Electra House, which was established by the Foreign Office. A section in the War Office, known as MI(R), was set up to research potential targets for sabotage, and Section D of SIS was created to plan attacks on selected targets. Even while the Dunkirk evacuation was in progress, the War Office and SIS began discussions on how best to coordinate their activities and to settle the vital question of which department was to be in control. At the same time the minister of economic warfare, the Labour MP Hugh Dalton, was holding talks with the Chiefs of Staff, the mandarins in Whitehall, and various ministers.[1] These culminated in an important letter from Dalton to the foreign secretary, Lord Halifax, on 14 June 1940, in which Dalton suggested that Britain should follow the examples provided by Sinn Fein, the Chinese guerrillas currently operating against the Japanese, and even the Spanish irregulars who had assisted Wellington, and set up a new organization to coordinate resistance in Europe. He believed, however, that:

> It is quite clear to me that an organization on this scale and of this character is not something which can be handled by the ordinary departmental machinery of either the British Civil Service or the British military machine. What is needed is a new organization to co-ordinate, inspire, control and assist the nationals of the oppressed countries who must themselves be the direct participants. We need absolute secrecy, a certain fanatical enthusiasm, willingness to work with people of different nationalities, complete political reliability. Some of these qualities are certainly to be found in some military officers and, if such men are available, they should undoubtedly be used. But the organization should, in my view, be entirely independent of the War Office machine.[2]

Halifax concurred and the matter was passed to Neville Chamberlain and Churchill, both of whom were immediately enthusiastic. In the last act of his political life, Chamberlain signed SOE's founding charter on 22 July 1940: 'A new organisation shall be established forthwith to coordinate all action, by the way of sabotage and subversion, against the enemy overseas ... This organisation will be known as the Special Operations Executive.'[3] It was to operate under the auspices of the Ministry of Economic Warfare.

Dalton selected Sir Frank Nelson to be the first head of SOE. Nelson had been a merchant in India before serving as a Conservative MP until 1931. Most recently he had been a consul in Berne, which had given him some experience of secret warfare. SOE was initially divided into three branches: SO1 for propaganda, SO2 for active operations, and SO3 for planning, thereby paying tribute to the three organizations set up in 1938. Rex Leeper was appointed to head SO1, which was separated from SOE in August 1941 to become the Political Warfare Executive. SO2 and SO3 were effectively merged.[4] SOE recruited its staff officers from among bankers, lawyers, and businessmen who had international experience. For example, the banker Charles Hambro had extensive contacts in Scandinavia and was therefore appropriately appointed to head the Scandinavian section of SOE; Bickham Sweet-Escott came from Courtaulds and began his SOE career by running the Polish Section; Harry Sporborg came from the City solicitors Slaughter and May and brought with him knowledge of the Low Countries and France. Section heads were normally recruited from among businessmen who had knowledge of the country in question. For instance, Captain Harold Perkins took over the Polish Section from Sweet-Escott. He spoke fluent Polish and had run a small engineering factory in Poland before the war. The first agent sent into Yugoslavia was Bill Hudson, who had run a mine there and spoke fluent Serbo-Croat.

The most important recruit to the management of SOE was Colin Gubbins. He had served on the British military mission to Poland in September 1939 and, after Poland's defeat, had headed the military mission to the Polish and Czech forces being formed in France. In March 1940 he was sent to Norway to form the Independent Companies, which played a minor role during the German invasion. Back in Britain, he was asked to form the Auxiliary Units, the stay-behind parties which would hamper the Germans should they attempt to invade the country. In November 1940 Gubbins was seconded to SOE. As Peter Wilkinson, a close collaborator with Gubbins, later stated:

> Gubbins's arrival really put a professional backbone behind SOE. Without him, in my opinion, or someone like him, it would certainly have gone the way of Section D and disappeared in fantastic dreams and fury among the military establishment in Whitehall.[5]

Gubbins was absolutely the ideal man to put the fledgling organization on its feet, to establish its training requirements, its structure, and to liaise with the War Office. He had also given thought to the conduct of irregular warfare even before the outbreak of war. His short leaflets 'The Art of Guerrilla Warfare', 'Partisan Leader's Handbook', and 'How to use High Explosives', written in May 1939, were to form the first training manuals for SOE.[6] Above all, Gubbins was seen as:

> . . . an inspiring leader, as brave as Wingate and endowed with the additional ability to maintain an atmosphere of friendly respect and loyalty with his subordinates and superiors. He carried, also, the burden of day-to-day

> cooperation with the governments-in-exile. All of these had differing political aims which did not always coincide with the British. None strove harder than he to reconcile these shorter and longer-term legitimate needs, and few had such success.[7]

It was only in 1943, after SOE had faced many battles to secure its continued existence, that Gubbins was appointed head of SOE: but in the meantime he had done much to set up its organization and operational practices. By then his early manuals had been developed into a single SOE publication: *Special Operations Executive Manual: How to be an Agent in Occupied Europe.*

The operational structure of SOE was based on country sections, some of them created at the outset, and others as the need arose. SOE headquarters were at 64 Baker Street and its country sections operated from buildings in the neighbourhood. SOE also established a station in Cairo which would service the missions in Greece, Crete, and Yugoslavia. This was based in Rustum Buildings, known to every Egyptian taxi driver as 'the secret house'. Later in the war, other bases such as Massingham in Algeria or Bari in Italy would be set up as and when needed. Indeed, SOE itself would operate under various guises, depending on location, such as Force 133 or Force 139 (but for reasons of simplicity, it will be referred to as 'SOE' throughout). SOE expanded rapidly and by July 1942 had 2,000 members of staff in Britain and a further 600 in the Middle East.

It was essential that the section heads of SOE should establish a close working relationship with the governments-in-exile, both for operations and especially in the recruitment of agents. In this regard the Polish Section was most fortunate in that both Gubbins and Dalton had a particular interest in Poland. Gubbins, because of his recent service with the Poles, was able to maintain good relations between the two Poles competing for control of the Polish Home Army, General Kazimierz Sosnkowski and the minister of the interior, Stanisław Kot. Dalton himself had a soft spot for the Poles. He learned a little of the language and spent Christmas 1940 with the Polish troops in Scotland.[8] In contrast, the Belgian government-in-exile was viewed as so quarrelsome that T Section of SOE declined to deal with it and demanded the right to operate without informing the Belgian ministers of their activities.[9]

In the summer of 1940 no one knew whether de Gaulle commanded any support in France. Consequently, F Section was created without any reference to him, leading to long-running controversies over agent recruitment and operations.[10] The head of F Section was Maurice Buckmaster. He has been criticized for the many failures which it experienced during the war. One of F Section's early agents, Philippe de Vomécourt, clearly disliked Buckmaster:

> I found him remote in his manner, and remote because he was unable to share, from first-hand experience, the fears and excitements of those who worked in the field. Furthermore, he was not what we French call a *patron*, a boss. He was not firm enough in his orders to us – leaving dangerous doubts in our minds about who was responsible and who was subordinate in the field, and he was not determined enough in fighting his superiors on our behalf.[11]

Another agent, Pearl Witherington, went further, claiming that 'not one agent liked Buckmaster, not one'.[12] Early operations in France revealed that de Gaulle had a sufficient following to justify the creation of a new section, RF, in May 1941, under Captain Eric Piquet-Wicks, specifically to cooperate with the Free French.[13] Wing-Commander Tommy Yeo-Thomas was appointed as the British liaison officer with the Free French.

The recruitment of agents to serve with SOE faced a number of problems. The principal one was that a relatively small number of members of the foreign armed forces had made it to Britain. The natural instinct of the governments-in-exile and national committees was to retain these people to build up their own armed forces. This left a very small number of men who could be recruited to serve with SOE. For example, Richard Laming, the first head of N Section dealing with the Netherlands, found the Dutch government-in-exile unhelpful: few agents were forthcoming, and those who did volunteer often failed to complete their training. A similar problem afflicted T Section and by the end of March 1941 only twenty-eight agents had been recruited, most of whom were shown in training to be unsuitable for service in Belgium.[14] The Danish Section of SOE was slow to get under way because the prospects for resistance in a country treated benignly by the Germans were uncertain. The initial pool of men who could be recruited for SOE were a small number of Danish sailors whose ships had berthed in Britain rather than returning to Denmark at the outbreak of the war. These men were largely unsuitable for SOE, since they appeared to lack leadership qualities and the degree of intelligence required.[15] Even the Poles suffered from a shortage of men coming forward to be trained as *Cichociemni*, the unseen and silent, to be parachuted into Poland. This led Władysław Sikorski to announce: 'I know that in the interest of their own divisions the leaders are reluctant to lose their best officers. Nevertheless they need to understand the need of the Country in this and any other issue must have absolute priority.'[16]

The Free French were outraged that the British felt that they could recruit Frenchmen without reference to them. De Gaulle resented the fact that every foreigner arriving in Britain was sent to the MI5 holding station at the Royal Victoria Patriotic School in Wandsworth, London, for processing on security grounds. De Gaulle complained that SOE and SIS would have first choice of the recent arrivals from France and 'it was only after a series of remonstrances and requests' that Frenchmen could join either the Free French and BCRA or the RF Section of SOE.[17] Buckmaster, on the other hand, claimed that every French person arriving in Britain was sent to de Gaulle and that he was not allowed to recruit them:

> So I was particularly anxious to find anyone British or Canadian who could speak French like a native. This wasn't as easy as it sounds; after all, it isn't every Englishman who can speak French fluently and without an accent and pass for a Frenchman in France. At first we looked for people who weren't French nationals, and it was only in Mauritius that I found some suitable people, with British passports and French as their native tongue ... I had problems with the Canadians as they had such frightful accents, so we had to invent an imaginary background for them, to account for the way they spoke, which wasn't always so easy. They had to learn the backgrounds that had been invented for them until they actually thought they were these imaginary people and not themselves.[18]

There were some agents who, like Pierre de Vomécourt, offered their services to de Gaulle and then were so repelled by the internal politics of the Free French that they joined F Section instead. Others with dual nationality like Yvonne Baseden were sometimes rejected by the Free French as not being French enough and so wound up in F Section. French speakers were also recruited from French-Canadians and Mauritians. But the shortage of fluent French speakers undoubtedly did cause a problem for F Section: George Starr, who turned out to be a highly successful organizer of a network in France, was noted for his poor French, and Harry Rée allegedly spoke French with such a broad Mancunian accent that another agent, Maurice Southgate, refused to work with him.[19]

British agents joined SOE for numerous different reasons. A common reason was disenchantment with regimental life and the fear, after the huge infantry losses during the First World War, that their lives would ultimately just be sacrificed for no good reason. For example, Raymond Basset wanted a job 'where any mistake I made I would suffer from, but I would probably not suffer from the mistake of a superior officer'.[20] Harry Rée was more forthcoming on this reasoning:

> The big difference between choosing to be a civilian parachutist and the other alternatives was that having made your choice it was not an end of

> choosing. A parachutist would continue throughout his war, until arrested or killed, to be faced by various alternative choices, it would be up to him to make repeated decisions immediately affecting his own life, or death.
>
> Here then was the real attraction of the job, an attraction quite as unfamiliar to the chairborne as to the airborne military. To be able to realise that if one were killed or arrested it would not be because of the stupidity of some major or colonel you despised but would quite likely be your own fault. This meant freedom and adult self-responsibility. After a year in the ranks or as a junior officer in the fifth-form atmosphere of the mess, what could be more tempting?[21]

Service behind the lines also appealed to former pacifists. Francis Cammaerts, for example, was registered as a conscientious objector and determined never to kill anyone. However, after the death of his brother in the RAF he began to re-examine his conscience and the turning point was the birth of his first daughter: 'I looked at my daughter and I knew I couldn't not act.'[22]

After the end of the war the British public was surprised to learn that women had been employed as agents by SOE, mostly in France. Both Buckmaster and the chief recruiting officer, Selwyn Jepson, felt it necessary to justify their actions. Buckmaster argued that:

> Women are as brave as and as responsible as men; often more so. They are entitled to a share in the defence of their beliefs no less than are men. The war was not restricted to men. From a purely tactical point of view, women were able to move about without exciting so much suspicion as men and were therefore exceedingly useful to us as couriers. I should have been failing in my duty to the war effort if I had refused to employ them, and I should have been unfair to their abilities if I had considered them unequal to the duties which were imposed upon them.[23]

Jepson went further and claimed that 'in my view, women were very much better than men for the work. Women, as you must know, have a far greater capacity for cool and lonely courage than men. Men usually want a mate with them.'[24] Women were normally recruited from the Women's Auxiliary Air Force (WAAF) or First Aid Nursing Yeomanry (FANY), or were attached to them after recruitment. Again, their motives varied: for example, Violette Szabo wanted revenge after the death of her husband on active service, while Nancy Wake had been repelled by the harsh treatment meted out to the Jews in Vienna after the *Anschluss*.[25]

Because SOE was a secret organization it could not advertise for recruits. Instead, notice was sent out to all branches of the armed services asking for people who spoke foreign languages. This process had been begun before the war, when the War Office had surveyed university dons to see if any had qualifications suitable for use in the event of war. Nicholas Hammond responded that he spoke Greek and some Albanian and had full knowledge of north-western Greece and southern Albania through his participation in archaeological surveys during the 1930s. He later served with SOE in Greece.[26] Roger Landes had no sooner joined the Royal Corps of Signals than he was invited to an interview in London: SOE had discovered that he both spoke fluent French and was a trained wireless operator. He was informed by his interviewer: 'We want you if you will to go to France. You'll be dropped by parachute or motor boat or by fishing boat. You've got a good chance to be arrested, tortured, maybe shot. I give you five minutes to say yes or no.'[27] Many others only discovered the nature of the organization they were joining and their likely tasks during the training. Others, however, were informed bluntly of their work during the initial interview. Xan Fielding, for example, was asked by SOE Cairo: 'Have you any personal objection to committing murder?'[28] As another agent recorded after the war, SOE was looking for people who would be 'gangsters with the knowledge of gangsters but with the behaviour, if possible, of gentlemen'.[29]

This knowledge would be acquired through SOE's training schools housed in so many of Britain's stately homes that the organization gained the acronymic nickname of 'Stately 'omes of England'. For example, F Section was based at Wanborough Manor near Guildford, the Poles at Audley End House near Saffron Walden, and the Norwegians at Fawley Park, near Henley. These served as the preliminary training and selection premises and have been compared by an historian of SOE to 'a set of sieves, each one with a closer mesh than the one before. Recruiting and training intermeshed; one of the objects of the training system was to sieve out the unsuitables before they could wreak havoc abroad'. But the official historian of SOE has also noted that the country sections sent so many unsuitable people onto the first training course that this began to cause a security problem. The first course was focused on physical fitness, elementary map reading, and practice in the use of weapons, but even this course made it clear to the recruits, many of whom had no idea what they had been recruited for, that they were a part of some secret organization. The security problem posed by the need to weed out unsuitable people at any stage of training was solved partly by sending them to a holding station in Scotland, known as 'the Cooler', until their knowledge could no longer endanger operations. Improvements were also made in the selection procedures.[30]

Those recruits who passed the initial course were then sent for commando training in the wilds of Arisaig in Invernesshire. The students were taught a wide variety of skills vital for survival in the field. They learned to shoot with every weapon produced by the British and Americans and were given practice with German and Italian weapons, and were expected to be able to strip, reassemble, and maintain each weapon in the dark as well as by daylight. They were also taught various methods of silent killing from instructors who had formerly served with the Shanghai police. One student recalled: 'By the time we finished our training, I would have willingly enough tackled any man, whatever his strength, size or ability. He taught us to face the possibility of a fight without the slightest tremor of apprehension . . .'[31] The students also learned to live off the land, learning how to poach game and salmon, both abundant in those parts of the Highlands. Since SOE was designed to carry out sabotage abroad an important part of the training was in handling explosives. Lieutenant Robert Ferrier was an instructor at Arisaig and recalled:

> Most of what we taught them on explosives was blowing up railway lines and trains. We took them over to Mallaig, to the terminus there. It was the end of the line from Glasgow via Fort William. By arrangement we were allowed to show the students how to drive a train, how to get underneath it and where to put the explosives if you wanted to blow it up.[32]

The London, Midland, and Scottish Railway proved most helpful in providing rolling stock, and train drivers would cheerfully acknowledge a successful attack, undertaken with dummy explosives.

About a third of any intake would fail the course at Arisaig. Those who passed were then sent to the finishing school at Beaulieu. SOE had taken over a group of houses on the Beaulieu estate where the students were accommodated according to nationality. After the intense physical activity of the Arisaig course the students had to adapt quickly to spending the next two to three weeks largely in the classroom. The courses at Beaulieu focused on conditions abroad, such as the complex plethora of German security agencies and the different types of police likely to be encountered. Training was also given in the use of codes, both encoding and decoding, and how to write reports. Emphasis was placed on security, a subject approached from several angles. Potential agents had to be taught how to recruit sub-agents, how to live their cover convincingly, and how to deal with snap police control points. The students would be woken up in the middle of the night and subjected to mock interrogations by instructors dressed in uniforms of the Axis powers. Instruction was also given in how to throw off a tail. These were normally carried out in Bournemouth, with the department stores of Beales, Bealsons, and Plummers being used to lose the shadowing officer. The final passing-out exercise lasted two to three days and involved being set a task such as placing explosives in a busy railway junction, or establishing a new contact in a town unknown to the student. To make the task more realistic the local police would be alerted that someone was trying something illegal. If caught by the police the students had a phone number of an SOE contact in order to be released.[33]

When the courses began at Beaulieu little was known about the conditions in occupied Europe and this meant that the training was not as useful as it became later. One student said of the training staff:

> I think they felt that they were trying to teach something that they didn't know, they could only guess what sort of things they were instructing us on. They couldn't really tell us how to judge someone you were going to recruit as a colleague in the resistance, that was impossible because they couldn't know.[34]

As more agents returned after a successful mission, the syllabus was continually updated to reflect current conditions. What the SOE instructors were looking for was a certain type of person. John Debenham-Taylor was an instructor at Beaulieu and explained:

> The sort of things that we looked for were indications of how people reacted to surprise situations: whether they were taken aback by them, or whether they managed to treat the whole thing quite calmly and not give any indication of being rattled by them. Secondly, was simply the general intelligence and quickness of people to grasp what you were trying to tell them and to carry it out when they did exercises to show that they'd absorbed the lesson. Thirdly, the question of temperament and readiness to accept instructions and orders. Some people did exactly as they were told and others queried it or tended to be excessively laid back about it, as though it was unimportant. It seemed to me this was an important factor in judging to what extent you know the agent was likely to be obedient to the instructions he got. It was a bit of a hit and miss business assessing an agent, but I feel that if you applied those three maxims, you were getting near an accurate picture.[35]

Personal files were maintained on students right from the initial course to the passing-out exercises. These reveal that the opinions of the instructors could vary widely on the suitability of individuals to serve behind the lines. As will become apparent later, for some country sections urgent requirements led them to overlook reservations voiced by the instructors – sometimes with tragic consequences.

After Beaulieu the agents were sent to Ringway airfield, near Manchester, for parachute training. Then, depending on what their role was to be, they would be sent either to holding centres to await their despatch aboard, or to specialist training centres. Radio operators would be sent to Thame Park where they learned to transmit and receive messages at speeds of up to twenty-five words a minute rather than the usual army radio operators' speed of ten words per minute. This increase in speed was essential to achieve given the enormous danger under which radio operators lived and worked in occupied Europe, under constant threat from detection vehicles. Others were sent to learn the techniques of industrial sabotage in Brickendonbury Manor in Hertfordshire run by Lieutenant Colonel George Rheam, of whom it has been written:

> Anyone trained by him could look at a factory with quite new eyes, spot a few essential machines in it, and understand how to stop them with a few well-placed ounces of explosive; to stop them, moreover, in such a way that some of them could not be restarted promptly by removing undamaged parts from comparable machines nearby.

Training was given in the use of plastic explosive, which could be cut and shaped to fit into small spaces, and in the use of time pencils in which the fuse could be cut to the necessary length to delay the explosion until the sabotage party was clear of the premises.[36]

SOE was established as an independent organization for the very good reason that its work, although in part military, was unorthodox in nature with its focus on sabotage and subversion rather than open fighting, and was also partly political and above all secret. But SOE's independence was under threat throughout its existence. It was widely viewed with distrust by other agencies and government departments. Its independence, moreover, was limited. It needed to cooperate with the War Office in order to secure arms and explosives for the resistance and it had to rely on the RAF or Royal Navy both to get its agents to the European mainland and to furnish the resistance with supplies. As will become apparent throughout this book, the aims of SOE and the resistance it found in Europe could, and often did, bring it into conflict with the Foreign Office. This should not necessarily be surprising since part of the purpose of the Foreign Office was to evaluate British aims and requirements in a given region in the long term while SOE's was to create a resistance that would fight the Axis powers *now*, in the short term.

The most bitter opponent of SOE was SIS, which greatly resented the creation of another secret body with a purpose diametrically opposite to its own. Whereas SOE sought to 'set Europe ablaze' the prospect of bangs and German retribution deeply concerned SIS, whose intelligence-gathering activities, the purpose for which it wanted to utilize the resistance, required peace and a lack of German attention. Hence SIS tried to stifle SOE at the moment of its birth. It 'never fully accepted the SOE–SIS divorce of 1940, and its subsequent behaviour only too often resembled that of an embittered ex-spouse'.[37] It refused to allow SOE to use its training facilities or its instructors. As explained above, SOE successfully established its own training programmes and establishments but, being forced to start from scratch, mistakes were made when the training staff had as little experience of covert activities as the students they were teaching. Two examples suffice to illustrate the SIS–SOE antagonism. Commander Slocum was appointed by SIS to run its agents into Brittany and Gerry Holdsworth was given the same task by SOE: he set up a small navy at a base on the Helford River, near Falmouth in Cornwall. The principal challenge facing both men was the need to beg or borrow ships from the Royal Navy, which proved reluctant to part with them. But above all, Slocum feared that the landing of SOE agents would endanger the work of SIS agents. Hence in early 1942 SIS banned all SOE operations to Brittany. Only over a year later would the two agencies begin to cooperate on naval requirements to northern France.[38]

The second clash had more serious consequences and was focused on SOE's communications with its agents in the field. Under an agreement signed by Stewart Menzies and Sir Frank Nelson on 15 September 1940, SIS retained total control of SOE's communications. All enciphered messages to and from Europe from SOE agents had to pass through SIS and had to be transmitted using SIS's ciphers.[39] As SOE expanded at a rapid rate, SIS communications facilities were overwhelmed with the work. The result was inevitable delays in passing the information on to SOE which in turn affected SOE operations. Worse still, SOE was forced to adopt SIS methods of coding messages. At this time codes were based on a poem, a method which soon proved to be relatively easy for the Germans to break. This topic will be explored more fully in a later chapter but here it is only necessary to note that the blame for those of SOE's early disasters which arose through communications failures should correctly be laid at the door of SIS and not SOE. Only in February 1942 did SOE finally achieve independence from SIS on communications, in terms of facilities, personnel, and codes. At the peak of its operations SOE operated four receiving stations in Britain where it employed around 1,500 operators and cipher clerks.[40] The station in Cairo was smaller and, as it turned out, far too small for the amount of traffic it was required to process when the British military missions in the Balkans were at their most active.

SOE needed the cooperation of the RAF in order to get its agents into occupied Europe. The chief of the air staff, Charles Portal, questioned the morality of SOE operations:

> I think that the dropping of men dressed in civilian clothes for the purpose of attempting to kill members of the opposing forces is not an operation with which the Royal Air Force should be associated. I think you will agree that there is a vast difference, in ethics, between the time-honoured operation of dropping a spy from the air and this entirely new scheme for dropping what one can only call assassins.[41]

Despite Portal's scruples, the RAF did provide aircraft for the dropping of agents. An important reason behind the contrast in numbers of agents despatched to France and those sent to other countries lies in the aircraft needed. The Lysander, which was the mainstay of the flights to France, was by 1940 no longer required for regular RAF operations. It had been designed as a plane for close army-air cooperation and could land on rugged ground and needed only a short runway. Without any major army operations in prospect in Europe, the Lysander could be safely released for service ferrying agents to France.

Aircraft with longer range were in short supply and consequently SOE faced a battle with the RAF to obtain sufficient flights to deliver agents and to supply them in more remote areas. The RAF was focused (many have argued, too exclusively focused) on the strategic bombing of Germany. Portal therefore argued with SOE that:

> . . . your work is a gamble which may give us a valuable dividend or may produce nothing. It is anybody's guess. My bombing offensive is not a gamble. Its dividend is certain; it is a gilt-edged investment. I cannot divert aircraft from a certainty to a gamble which may be a gold-mine or may be completely worthless.[42]

There was also the sheer difficulty of reaching countries such as Poland and the Protectorate. Group Captain Ron Hockey, commanding officer of 138 Special Duties Squadron, explained that flights to both countries had to cover enemy territory for most of the journey. Therefore, flights could only take place during the winter when the nights were long; but then the terrain was often snowbound, making it hard for the reception committee to reach the site.[43]

In September 1940 the Chiefs of Staff undertook the first grand strategic review since the fall of France and among the many points examined was the prospect of resistance in occupied Europe. Its conclusions, however, were depressing. It was felt that the prospects of an armed uprising were only good in Poland and the Protectorate whereas in western Europe the most noticeable feature 'is the spread of apathy and indifference'. Gladwyn

Jebb, Hugh Dalton's assistant, questioned the purpose of hoping that the Germans would be defeated by 'picturesque, mass revolts of apathetic and incidentally unarmed slaves'. Colin Gubbins raised another important point with regard to uprisings:

> A national uprising against the Axis is a card which usually can only be played once . . . It is thus essential not only that these subterranean movements should be supported by us, but also that they should be sufficiently under our control to ensure that they do not explode prematurely.

This suggested that somehow SOE agents on the ground were to assume a degree of command and control over the resistance movements and to ensure that their actions were in line with Allied strategy, an extremely difficult task since the resistance movements had a logic of their own and, as will become apparent, this was not always in line with Allied requirements. In November 1940 the Chiefs of Staff issued a general directive to SOE on 'Subversive Activities in Relation to Strategy', outlining SOE's role in the war. It was clear from this report that the short-term aim was to be attacks on Germany's economic resources and communications across occupied Europe, while the long-term aim was to build up secret armies to foment revolt at the time, potentially years away, when the Allies were about to invade the mainland.[44] It is in the light of this directive that we must view SOE's early operations.

The Balkans was identified as a region which contained economic resources such as oil, metals, and minerals essential to the German war machine. As such, the region became the experimental ground for early SOE operations, which were built on the groundwork established by its predecessors, Section D and MI(R). These operations, in the period preceding the German invasion of the Balkans, illustrate many of the problems that would affect the success of SOE's role there. Of particular impact was the difference between the requirements of the Foreign Office, which was concerned with long-term policy, and SOE, which wanted to prove to its detractors that it could successfully carry out sabotage operations.

SOE's operations in the region were conducted from its office in Belgrade. Among the personnel based there were several men who would later play a much more prominent role in SOE operations in the Balkans, such as Bill Bailey who would enter Yugoslavia in 1942 and join the Četnik resistance leader Draža Mihailović, and Julian Amery who would later serve in Albania. Attention was principally on the oil wells in Romania and the great transit route through the Balkans, the Danube. The Foreign Office, however, looked askance at SOE plans to destroy the Ploeşti oilfields in Romania because it was still a neutral country, albeit one rapidly falling under German influence.

The Foreign Office was similarly appalled by SOE's proposal to blow the Iron Gates, the narrow rapids on the Danube, to block the river for German shipping. A brake was placed on SOE's plans, and the oilfields continued to produce crucial oil for the German war machine until the USAAF began a bombing campaign against them in 1944. Shipping on the Danube and the Iron Gates remained on SOE's target list but could not be attacked until the Yugoslav resistance was mobilized.[45]

SOE played a more prominent role in Albania and learned some vital but painful lessons in the process. Again, the geopolitics of the region served to hinder operations. SOE began, much as it did in Romania, by cultivating potential leaders of the opposition and resistance. Albania was a country full of tribal leaders. Among those identified as willing to undertake operations against the Italians were Gani Bey Kryeziu and his brothers Said and Hasan, who were particularly strong in Kosovo; Muharrem Bajraktari, based around Ljumë; and Abas Kupi, who had resisted the Italian invasion in April 1939. It was hoped that the Albanians would unite around Abas Kupi. The Foreign Office was alarmed by the geopolitical impact of British intervention in Albania. Part of its concern rested on the leaders identified by SOE. The three Kryeziu brothers could raise men in Kosovo, but this would bring up the entire question of the future of Kosovo because both the Albanians and the Yugoslavs laid claim to the area. Similarly, the entire idea of an Albanian revolt alarmed the Greeks, who had territorial claims on a part of Albania and also feared that a revolt there might precipitate an Italian invasion of Greece. Consequently, although many optimistic reports reached Cairo and Istanbul of Albanian attacks on Italian garrisons, reports from Athens played down the importance and impact of the revolt. Even after the Italians invaded Greece in October 1940, the Greeks still did not want the British to interfere in Albania. The head of the southern department at the Foreign Office, Philip Nicholls, wrote: 'This is a matter in which we cannot act contrary to the wishes of the Greek government. It is they who are doing all the hard fighting in Albania.'

SOE nonetheless continued to make preparations to send Colonel Dayrell Oakley-Hill into Albania to stimulate a revolt in the north of the country. On 7 April 1941 Oakley-Hill, accompanied by Abas Kupi, Gani Bey Kryeziu, his brothers, and about 300 Albanians, entered the country from Kosovo. Muharrem Bajraktari mobilized his tribe in support, and as the British-led party advanced, more than 1,000 Muslim tribesmen joined them. They met little Italian resistance until they neared the town of Shkodër. To take this town with its strong Italian garrison, the guerrillas needed an assured supply of weapons, as well as radio communications, none of which were forthcoming. Furthermore, the Catholic tribes surrounding the town refused to join the revolt since the Italians had granted them a privileged position during the occupation. These failures revealed the fundamental weakness of SOE's first foray into stimulating resistance. It had proved relatively easy to encourage rebellion, but far harder to supply it with weapons. Furthermore, SOE needed to clarify its aims better in the future: the inability of the massed bands even to attempt an assault on Shkodër demonstrated that the targets of guerrilla warfare had to be limited to match the manpower and resources available. The revolt began to collapse even before news reached the party that the Germans had successfully invaded Yugoslavia, at which point the Muslims promptly deserted. The guerrilla leaders dispersed into the mountains and the Kryeziu brothers accompanied Oakley-Hill back into Kosovo. They then left for the mountains while Oakley-Hill went to Belgrade and surrendered to the Germans. He spent the next two and a half years as a POW in Germany before being repatriated for medical reasons in late 1943 and joining SOE's operations section.[46]

Historians disagree on the contribution SOE made towards the *coup d'état* in Belgrade in March 1941. It can certainly be argued that SOE played a role by encouraging members of the Serb Peasant Party to put pressure on Prince Paul not to sign a pact with Germany, by threatening to withdraw from the government. The latest analysis of the evidence argues that the vital precipitating factor in stimulating the coup was the contacts between the British air attaché in Belgrade and the Yugoslav air force officers, led by the man who would become prime minister under King Peter, General Simović. Therefore, it can be argued 'that although the action immediately preceding the *coup d'état* may have been directed by others, the necessary preliminary conditions were established largely through the work' of SOE in Belgrade. Nevertheless, 'however close these links and whatever persuasion the British exercised, it is still clear that the initiative came from the Yugoslavs, and only by a stretch of the imagination can the British be said to have planned or directed the *coup d'état*'. The only action that can definitely be attributed to SOE, the provision of wireless transmitters to stay-behind operatives, notably failed since none of them ever came on air.[47]

SOE's plans and operations in Romania and Yugoslavia had been hampered by the opposition of the legations there and the directives emanating from the Foreign Office. The situation was somewhat different in Greece. Ian Pirie first led Section D and then SOE from Athens and established a good working relationship with the British consul-general, Graham Sebastian. This meant that the legation became the first hiding place for small arms, ammunition, grenades, and incendiary bombs smuggled into the capital for use by the resistance should the Axis powers invade Greece. More problematic, however, were the contacts that SOE cultivated. Greece was under the rule of the dictator Ioannis Metaxas, and a large number of opposition Venizelist army officers had been cashiered after the abortive coups of 1933 and 1935. Among these officers were two men who would help both SOE and SIS in its early operations in Greece. The first was Colonel Euripides Bakirdzis, whom SOE chose to lead the first sabotage and resistance organization. He was supplied with a radio and assumed the code name Prometheus. After their arrival in Athens, the Germans soon closed in on Bakirdzis, who fled to Egypt. His place as Prometheus II was taken by Lieutenant Commander Charalambos Koutsogiannopoulos, who despite copies of his codes being sunk when being transported to Crete, succeeded in making contact with SOE in Cairo. One of his reports led ultimately to the arrival of the first British sabotage party into Greece in 1942. SOE also managed to undertake some successful sabotage operations as the Germans invaded. A party led by Peter Fleming set off some demolitions, another SOE officer, David Pawson, destroyed some bridges around Thebes, and explosives supplied by SOE blew up two Bulgarian ships full of munitions in Piraeus harbour.[48]

SOE identified Poland as the country where resistance to the German occupation was most likely to occur on a wide scale, and consequently set about trying to support it. Poland lay at the utmost limit of range for RAF aircraft so initially, while the Balkans were still neutral, armaments were smuggled into Poland from Bucharest and Budapest using Polish-run courier lines. Up to April 1940 this had given the Poles the meagre supplies of four wireless transmitters, 130 revolvers, 1,000lb of high explosives, and 500 incendiary bombs with assorted fuses. Even this pitifully small supply caused problems. The wireless transmitters supplied from SIS stores were incompatible with the Polish electricity supply until adapted, and the revolvers required rimmed ammunition which was not available in central Europe. As Peter Wilkinson, who was much involved in these operations, noted: 'The Poles, amazed at the British failure to supply such simple items, concluded that it was more likely due to unwillingness than inability.'[49]

SOE was more helpful in providing training facilities for the potential *Cichociemni* agents if (and it was a big if) they could be got into Poland. The first agents – Captain Józef Zabielski, Major Stanisław Krzymowski, and Czesław Raczkowski – were briefed by General Sosnkowski before leaving: 'You are flying to Poland as our advance guard. Your task is to prove that we are able to maintain liaison with the home country.' The round trip to Poland was 1,800 miles and would take over eleven hours. The RAF supplied a modified Whitley bomber which flew the men to

Poland on the night of 15 February 1941. The team was dropped around sixty miles from the planned dropping zone, into the Warthegau, the part of Poland annexed to the Reich, instead of into the General Government. Nonetheless, and notwithstanding leg injuries sustained by Zabielski, the three men successfully made their way to their intended location.[50]

The success of the flight had two important consequences. The Germans were aware that a party of parachutists had landed and put up posters enjoining the population to track them down. This had an unintended effect:

> The effectiveness of the grapevine was such that from the moment these posters appeared the whole of German-occupied Poland knew that the men in question were members of the underground army . . . Polish hearts beat faster and hopes rose higher – the Western Allies were at last making their presence felt.[51]

This raises a point regarding the overall effectiveness of SOE's operations: while achievements were few and far between in the early years, the psychological impact of contact between the Allies and the resistance was of inestimable value. Zabielski left Poland in July 1942 with numerous important reports on conditions in Poland and the prospects of resistance for London, which he reached two months later having successfully traversed Germany, Switzerland, France, Spain, and Portugal.[52] But Peter Wilkinson also noted a distressing side effect of the first flight:

> The success of the initial flight to Poland had encouraged the Home Army to think in terms of the liberation of their country by a major airborne invasion as soon as German resistance started to crack. The Polish secret army was at that time SOE's most important asset and Dalton and Gubbins and, for that matter, Perkins, Hazell and I, were so deeply committed to the Polish cause that we funked facing them with the realities of their situation.[53]

This meant that the Polish general staff continued planning on a grand scale for the liberation of their country directly through flights from Britain, and created a Parachute Brigade for the purpose. The reality of the challenge in reaching Poland, however, was immediately evident: it was a year before the second flight took place.

Distance similarly hampered proposed operations to the Protectorate. Despite agreement between Edvard Beneš, General Ingr, and František Moravec with SOE that at least twenty parachutists would be trained for operations there, only one volunteer, Otmar Riedl, had been found and trained by early 1941. Even then the unfortunate agent was accidentally dropped into Austria in April and not the Protectorate, although he succeeded in reaching Prague as the forerunner of SOE operations there. He was followed by another agent in October before the Anthropoid and Silver A and B missions were despatched in December 1941: these will be covered later.[54]

SOE operations in western Europe were hampered by the fact that no one had anticipated the fall of France and no preparations had been made for the eventuality. To give just one example, Douglas Dodds-Parker recalled: 'We had only Michelin road maps which we had managed to collect in secrecy. With no official anticipation of operations except along the 1914/18 Front, only a black and white contour series of maps of the rest of France were to hand which proved useless for planning air drops and navigation by air.'[55] Nor was there any knowledge of local conditions, such as the availability of foodstuffs only on certain days due to rationing, a lack of knowledge which could cost an agent his life. Such information was acquired through the early operations. The first proved abortive and was carried out by French soldiers since F Section had no one trained. It was an attack requested by the RAF on the German pilots operating from Meucon airfield, near Vannes in Brittany. Information had reached Britain that these men travelled to the airfield from Vannes by bus, an ideal target for an ambush. The ambush party arrived on 15 March 1941 and discovered that the pilots now travelled in individual private cars, thereby providing so small a target that the operation was called off. A more successful operation was carried out on the night of 7 June against the Pessac power station near Bordeaux, which supplied electricity to the nearby U-boat base. Incendiary bombs were attached to all eight transformers, six blew up, the attacking party escaped, and the electricity supply to the U-boat facility was limited for a number of weeks. The German response was to fine the Pessac area one million francs and to execute the twelve German sentries for their lapse in security.

SOE was keen to learn the lessons of these first two operations and to project the value of SOE itself to its detractors. Dalton reported to Churchill:

> We may therefore take it as practically certain that three trained men, dropped from one aeroplane, have succeeded in destroying an important industrial target. This strongly suggests that many industrial targets, especially if they cover only a very small area, are more effectively attacked by SOE methods than by air bombardment.

As such, SOE's focus on sabotage was apparently justified. However, the leader of the mission, George Forman, sounded a warning. He noted that the attacking party had been put off the attempt at first because it seemed that the base itself was too heavily guarded. It was only after talking to the gatekeeper that they realized that they could enter the power station. Forman therefore reported: 'It is absolutely vital that other operations of this kind should be prepared by members of the organisation on the spot before the actual team is sent over. One cannot always rely on luck.'[56]

The first F Section agent despatched was Georges Bégué, who was dropped blind in May 1941 into unoccupied France. He was joined a few days later by Pierre de Vomécourt and Roger Cottin. Jacques de Guélis arrived on an independent mission to pave the way for future agents by recruiting local organizers, radio operators, and couriers and to make arrangements for finance. He left France after a successful month-long mission having made numerous important contacts and having gathered a wealth of essential documents, such as ration books and various permits, for copying in London.[57] De Vomécourt recruited his two brothers, Philippe, whose estate near Limoges would be used to receive supply drops, and Jean, who would establish a short-lived circuit in eastern France. Over the course of the summer a total of seventeen F Section agents were dropped into the Unoccupied Zone, chosen because the risk from the Vichy police was deemed lower than from the Germans in the north. The agents were, however, to operate in the Occupied Zone in accordance with a policy dictated to SOE by the government of 'discreet bangs in the Zone Occupée, no bangs without Foreign Office approval in the Zone Non-Occupée'.[58] But SOE had much to learn: all the men were given identity papers in their real names and all were given the same contact address in Marseille, the Villa des Bois. Security lapses meant that the Vichy police arrested several of the first agents, including George Langelaan, who had the address of Philippe Liewer on him, who was also then arrested. Michael Trotobas was caught when visiting one of the 'postboxes', at Fleuret's garage, which was known to all the agents.* Worse followed when Gilbert Turck felt that a conference of the remaining F Section agents might be useful and invited them to meet him at the Villa des Bois where he was hiding and, one after the other, they arrived – only to fall into the hands of the Vichy police. The result was that nearly all the F Section agents sent to France that year had been arrested, including the pathfinder, Bégué. They eventually landed up in Mauzac prison near Bergerac from which they escaped in July 1942. Most, such as Trotobas and Liewer, would return to France again.[59]

Ben Cowburn, who arrived in France in September 1941 on his first mission, concluded that the early agents had achieved virtually nothing: 'I myself had escaped only through the most extraordinary combination of

* Postboxes were dead-letter drops, places where agents could leave messages for other agents without having to meet.

circumstances. I had been unable to blow up any of my targets. The enemy had penetrated us. Our early equipment and means of communication had proved inadequate.'[60] Jean Le Harivel, a radio operator who was among those arrested, concluded later: 'What typified the early days was the fact that we were fumbling. We were really entering into a new kind of war, it was a strange, peculiar type of war and we hadn't any experience of managing that kind of war at all.'[61] But some steps had been taken which would prove invaluable later. Most notably, Bégué had quickly discovered the risks of transmitting by radio and suggested the practice which became adopted widely, that of inserting personal messages into normal BBC broadcasts which could be used to indicate operations or instructions.[62] Nonetheless, SOE's record for 1941 in France was abysmal: in the south by the end of the year only Philippe de Vomécourt, Francis Basin, Georges Duboudin, and Virginia Hall remained at liberty.

Early missions into the Low Countries met with no greater fortune. In September 1941 two agents were dropped into the Netherlands, Aart Albert Homburg and Cornelis Sporre. Homburg was arrested a month later but escaped and returned to Britain where he enlisted in the RAF rather than continue to serve with SOE; Sporre was posted missing presumed drowned when trying to return to Britain by sea in November. The first agent into Belgium, Emile Tromme, was dropped in May 1941 and had the misfortune to land in a POW camp in Germany instead of in Grand Halleux, on the German-Belgian border. The plane also forgot to drop the container containing his clothes and radio. It took Tromme four months to escape from the camp, make his way back into Belgium, and establish contact with T Section. During 1941 a further sixteen agents were sent into Belgium but none achieved much of value.[63]

One of the many dangers inherent in forming SOE's strategy at the beginning of its existence becomes evident when one considers its approach to Norway: SOE simply had no idea of the level of resistance likely in the country. The arrival of Norwegians who had taken to ships to make the risky crossing of the North Sea to Britain suggested that Norway was restless under the German occupation and opposed to the Quislings. Dalton, for example, wrote in early 1941:

> All our reports go to show that, following the winter, Norwegian civilian morale in spite of, or perhaps because of, every kind of oppression and persecution by the Germans and the Norwegian quislings remains at the highest possible level. Our difficulty in fact (which is shared with the Royal Norwegian Government) is not to spur the people on, but to hold them back.[64]

Furthermore, those Norwegians who reached Britain were keen to do something, anything, to wipe the stain of collaborationism that had become attached to the very name Quisling. Consequently, the 'Shetland Bus' was established to transfer agents into Norway by sea.

In March 1941 SOE was asked by the Joint Planning Staff to report on the military implications and logistical requirements of the resistance movements. Colin Gubbins drafted a reply in May 1941 which laid out the potential for sabotage and for the build-up of secret armies in the three most promising countries: Poland, the Protectorate, and France, The logistical requirements were overwhelming and simply impossible to achieve: full implementation of the sabotage plan alone would require the total concentration of 15 per cent of the existing RAF bomber force, and the arming of secret armies would require 40 per cent and necessitate a full-time effort by Bomber Command over six months. The Joint Planning Staff absorbed Gubbins's paper into its review on 'The Distant Future', which it issued on 14 June 1941. The Chiefs of Staff discussed the review on 14 August and rejected it outright. The Chiefs of Staff were sceptical about the value of secret armies and appalled by the logistics required to supply them. They authorized the expansion of the Special Duties flight into a squadron, but otherwise made it clear that in their view SOE was best suited to sabotage and subversion on a scale commensurate with its resources, and the formation of secret armies would just have to wait. The Chiefs of Staff report reflected the completely changed strategic circumstances: Germany had invaded the Soviet Union and the entire nature of the war was about to change.[65]

Imitation may be seen as a form of flattery and so it was with SOE: the Americans established the Office of Strategic Services, OSS, to fulfil much the same role as SOE. Like SOE, the OSS grew out of an earlier agency, the Office of the Coordinator of Information (COI), set up by President Roosevelt in the summer of 1941 while the United States was still a neutral power. It was run by 'Wild Bill' Donovan who was described by a member of his staff:

> Donovan was in his eccentric way a remarkable man, a winning combination of charm, audacity, imagination, optimism and energy – above all energy. He was a disorderly administrator and an impetuous policymaker, racing from here to there with ideas and initiatives and then cheerfully moving on to something else ... He was exasperating but adorable.[66]

As with SOE, the propaganda branch was split off from the COI in summer 1942 to become the Office of War Information, and the remaining branches were renamed OSS with Donovan remaining in charge.

OSS quickly ran into the same problem that SOE had encountered: it was unwanted and unloved. Bill Casey, on Donovan's staff, claimed:

> It is no exaggeration to say that Donovan created the OSS against the fiercest kind of opposition from everybody – the Army, Navy and State Departments, the Joint Chiefs of Staff, regular army brass, the whole Pentagon bureaucracy, and, perhaps most devastatingly, the White House Staff.[67]

Roosevelt was a supporter of OSS, as was Churchill of SOE, and this support ensured the survival of both agencies. Like the Foreign Office, the State Department suspected the OSS of pursuing policies out of line with the foreign policies of the United States and Britain. Suspicions were raised by statements allegedly made by Donovan such as 'I'd put Stalin on the OSS payroll if I thought it would help us defeat Hitler.' The FBI questioned the loyalties of the agents recruited by OSS, many of whom were on the political far left if not actually communists. Yet OSS also recruited the sons of prominent businessmen, for example, both sons of the banker J. P. Morgan served on the staff of OSS.[68] Henry Murray, an OSS agent, concluded that: 'The whole nature of the functions of OSS was particularly inviting to psychopathic characters; it involved sensation, intrigue and the idea of being a mysterious man with secret knowledge.'[69]

OSS had to find a way to work with SOE and the British who made little effort to conceal their contempt for the newcomer; but on the personal level relations were good since both Donovan and the OSS representative in London, David Bruce, were Anglophiles. Donovan received important information on SOE training methods and communications from the representative of British secret service in the United States, William Stephenson. Indeed, the first OSS agents were trained by SOE in secret schools in Canada before the Americans set up their own training programmes. The tension between the two nations centred on the role OSS was to play. In June 1942 the principles of cooperation between SOE and OSS were laid out which emphasized close collaboration between the head offices in London and Washington through liaison officers, and the division of the world into separate zones. This last point caused conflict: in countries such as France and the Low Countries which would be invaded by Allied forces the plan was for a joint SOE–OSS command of the secret forces, but in countries which would not be invaded, there was to be greater independence, though SOE sought to have the upper hand in the Balkans and Middle East. The Balkans in particular would demonstrate the fragility of SOE–OSS relations. Bickham Sweet-Escott noted: 'Our people in Cairo frankly wished to keep any similar American organisation out of the theatre altogether, or if this was not practicable, to keep it under strict control . . .

This attitude was unfortunate because it naturally made the Americans suspicious and eager to conceal their plans from us.'[70]

SOE might have achieved little in its first eighteen months but its representative in Switzerland, Jock McCaffery, felt that the early operations had shown the prospects for resistance in the future:

> The lights were being re-lit, literally across the face of a Nazi-darkened Europe. They were tiny and few at first, but as someone once observed, if you switch off all the floodlights in a crowded stadium, and then in the centre of the pitch, light a single match, its light will pierce the vast surrounding darkness and be seen by all.[71]

The entries of first the Soviet Union and then the United States into the war in June and December 1941 respectively would indeed offer more opportunities for action by clandestine forces.

PART TWO

Growing the Resistance

8
The Early Partisans

On 22 June 1941 Germany launched Operation Barbarossa, the invasion of the Soviet Union. The Germans viewed the invasion as the great opportunity to annihilate their two greatest enemies – the Jews and the Bolsheviks – according to the doctrine of the 'Jewish-Bolshevik conspiracy', which had been part of National Socialism from the very beginning. The commander of the 4th Panzer Army, General Erich Hoepner, explained the historical roots and purpose of the invasion in a deployment order issued on 2 May 1941:

> It is the old struggle of the Germanic people against the Slav world, the desire to prevent European culture from being swamped by ideas from Moscow and Asia, and the rejection of Jewish-Bolshevism. This struggle must have as its goal the destruction of present-day Russia, which is why it must be waged with unprecedented rigour. In its conception and execution, every military action must be guided by the iron will to wipe out the enemy ruthlessly and completely. In particular, this means no quarter should be given to the representatives of the present Russian Bolshevik system.[1]

Accordingly, the war was to be conducted with deliberate extreme brutality to a degree hitherto unknown and to be waged against civilians just as much as against Soviet soldiers. All political commissars found with captured Red Army formations were to be taken away and shot immediately. The racial side of the war was also evident from the outset. Special units, *Einsatzgruppen*, were formed by the SS with the express purpose of exterminating all the Jews in the newly conquered areas. This was rationalized by Arthur Nebe, commander of *Einsatzgruppe* B, on the grounds that: 'Where there are partisans there are Jews, and where there are Jews there are partisans.'[2] This licence to kill was extended to the Wehrmacht by its chief Wilhelm Keitel, who issued a decree on 13 May which stressed that 'guerrilla groups are to be liquidated pitilessly by the troops during combat or during their escape', and 'against localities, from which the Wehrmacht is attacked by ambush or treachery . . . when circumstances do not allow quick identification of the perpetrators, forceful collective measures are to be taken . . .' He exonerated in advance the conduct of the German forces: 'The actions committed by members of the Wehrmacht or its escort against hostile civilians are not to be subjected to any legal proceedings, even when the act in question is a crime or a military crime . . .'[3]

The ultimate purpose of the German invasion of the Soviet Union was to gain coveted *Lebensraum* for the Reich. This led to important differences in strategy. Whereas in Poland, the Poles were viewed as a pool of slave labour to be exploited in the service of the Reich, no such mercy was shown in the German plans for the east. The long-term plan was to depopulate the eastern region of Poland, the Baltic States, Belorussia, and parts of the Ukraine by some 30 million people over a thirty-year period in order to make way for German settlers. The process was to begin immediately, as Professor Dr Franz Alfred Six explained on a visit to the headquarters of Army Group Centre in July 1941:

> Hitler intends to extend the eastern border of the Reich as far as the line Baku-Stalingrad-Moscow-Leningrad. Eastward of this line as far as the Urals, a 'blazing strip' will emerge in which all life is to be erased. It is intended to decimate the around thirty million Russians living in this strip through starvation, by removing all foodstuffs from this enormous territory. All those involved in this operation are to be forbidden on pain of death to give a Russian even a piece of bread. The large cities from Leningrad to Moscow are to be razed to the ground . . .[4]

Exploitation of the captured regions in the east was to be supervised by the East Ministry under the Nazi ideologue Alfred Rosenberg, and by the office of the Four Year Plan run by Hermann Goering; the exploitation of the labour resources of the east was the responsibility of Fritz Sauckel. The Polish territory of East Galicia, which had been taken over by the Soviets, was added to the General Government, and two new regions were created: *Reichskommissariat Ostland* under Hinrich Lohse and *Reichskommissariat Ukraine* under Erich Koch. Behind the front line, the Wehrmacht set up three types of administration: the *Aktionsgebiet* to cover the 15–25 kilometres behind the front line; the Army Rear Area, 20–50 kilometres behind that; and finally, the Army Group Rear Area which extended to a depth of at least 100 kilometres from the front line.[5]

The Germans expected a quick victory of the kind that had occurred elsewhere in Europe. Not expecting a long campaign, the planners had given little thought to the challenges of occupying the areas which straddled their lengthy lines of communication. It was this oversight that would lead to significant errors in German policy towards the local populations, to counter-productive policies and wasted opportunities. The first territory to be occupied by the Germans had been in Soviet hands only since the Second World War had begun and the local populations had little reason to resist the Germans and potentially every reason to welcome them. The Soviet occupation of eastern Poland, and the Baltic States of Lithuania, Estonia, and Latvia had been brutal with widespread imprisonment and murder of political opponents and the deportation of around a million citizens deep into the Soviet interior, and also economically ruinous as the Soviets imposed communism on their new unwilling subjects.[6] The Germans were surprised by the welcome they received. For example, the 2nd SS Cavalry Regiment reported: 'They brought them immediately milk, eggs and other food products which were put at the disposal of the soldiers free of charge and in a spontaneous manner.'[7] As the Germans advanced into the Soviet Ukraine the welcome continued:

> At first they hesitated, but when they saw that we were no beasts, they came closer with great joy and pointed the way to the east, where the Bolsheviks had gone. Then they brought flowers. Women carried their children and showed them to the German soldiers . . . All gave the general large bouquets. Elderly people, who still remembered the time of the tsars, bowed deep and humbly. An old woman, shedding tears and giving thanks, fell to her knees.[8]

The memories of the Soviet man-made famine in the Ukraine in the 1930s, which had killed over 3 million people, meant that many had little or no loyalty to the Soviet system.

The relief that was felt by many of the newly conquered peoples had deeper roots also, in nationalist aspirations which they hoped the Germans would fulfil. On the evening of 30 June 1941 the head of the Ukrainian national assembly in Lwów, Yaroslav Stetsko, issued a proclamation of independence.[9] On 1 July 1941, the day German troops entered Riga, a group of Latvian nationalists under the chairmanship of Colonel Ernests Kreismanis met and appointed a former government minister, Bernhards Einbergs, as the head of its self-proclaimed provisional government of reborn independent Latvia.[10] In Lithuania, the Lithuanian Nationalist Front, which had been sponsored by the Germans during the 1930s, announced the re-establishment of independent Lithuania and the formation of a provisional government. Similarly, by the time the Germans arrived in Tallinn, the Estonians had declared the restoration of the independence of their country.[11] The prospects for peaceful collaboration seemed everywhere favourable; but the Germans did not want the forces of nationalism unleashed, and within a few months they crushed the independence movements. Stepan Bandera and many of his Ukrainian followers were imprisoned in Sachsenhausen. The Lithuanian government was disbanded and all symbols of nationalism were banned. The Latvians and Estonians, seen as more Germanic, fared slightly better. By March 1942, after lengthy discussions and much internal Latvian wrangling, the chief German civilian administrator, Otto Drechsler, permitted the Latvians to form a self-administrative body, though not an independent government: 'In essence the Self-Administration amounted to no more than an administrative organ created to facilitate the German occupation and execute what the Germans wished.' Estonia was also permitted to retain a limited degree of administrative independence under German supervision.[12]

Leaving aside the question of nationalism, the Germans quickly squandered any goodwill that might have greeted their arrival, by the harsh and immediate application of their policies. Jews were rounded up and taken to locations just outside their villages and shot and buried in mass graves. Those not executed by the bullet then and there were herded into hastily constructed and makeshift ghettos for disposal later. Thus what would become the Holocaust began as death by shooting on a massive scale, rather than the industrialized mass gassings which began later in occupied Poland. Most non-Jewish locals were disturbed by the German actions but not to an extent that drove them to resistance. (This subject will be revisited in a later chapter.) But the peasants were immediately and severely affected by the German exploitation of their localities. Hitler envisioned the economic exploitation of the east, particularly the Ukraine, as the means by which to avoid the catastrophic effects the British naval blockade had had on the morale of the civilian population of Germany during the First World War. The instructions issued to the German occupation authorities made this point clear:

> Efforts to save the population from death by starvation by drawing on the surplus of the black earth regions can only be at the expense of the food supply to Europe. They diminish the staying power of Germany in the war and the resistance of Germany and Europe to blockade. There must be absolute clarity about this . . . A claim by the local population on the German administration . . . is rejected right from the start.[13]

The Ukrainians had hoped that the Germans would abolish the detested system of collective farms (kolkhozes) and were appalled to learn that the German authorities retained them on the grounds that it was easier to collect foodstuffs from collective farms than from individual enterprises. Indeed, the agriculture minister, Herbert Backe, stated: 'If the kolkhozes were not introduced by the Soviet authorities they were to be invented by the Germans.'[14]

Nevertheless, the Germans soon realized that the ruthless economic exploitation of the occupied areas was counterproductive. The soldiers were distressed by the sight of starving peasants begging for food from them. In the privacy of his diary, Goebbels wished that a promise of land to the peasants could be made and he praised the decree issued in May 1942 which guaranteed religious tolerance, a measure designed to win over the peasantry and wean them away from the anti-religious Soviet authorities.[15]

The recruitment of civilians to work in the Reich began in November 1941, and the measure was met with an enthusiastic response. For example, in Kharkov nearly 2,000 volunteers signed up in the first five days of recruitment and by mid-January 1942 two trains a week with 1,000 workers per train were leaving Kharkov for the Reich.[16] Once again, however, the Germans squandered their opportunities. They treated these volunteers appallingly, packing them into trains with no access to food or sanitation. Then, in the Reich, the volunteers were housed in closely guarded labour camps and were forced to work longer hours on lower rations than their German counterparts. News of their reception and treatment filtered back and so when, only six months later in summer 1942, Sauckel demanded more labourers from the east, much of the potential workforce fled to the forests and joined the partisans.[17]

By the end of 1941 the Germans had occupied over 850,000 square miles of territory in the east, containing a population of around 70 million people. The newly conquered Poles, Lithuanians, Belorussians, Latvians, Estonians, and Ukrainians found themselves liberated from one oppression into another, raising the question of who was the worst enemy. Memories of the German occupation following the 1917 Treaty of Brest-Litovsk, which had been relatively benign, were quickly wiped out by the harshness of German rule according to Nazi doctrine. As one peasant expressed it, the Germans 'were not Germans at all but merely Russians who had donned other uniforms'.[18] Even the staunchly Nazi Rosenberg was concerned that 'if the population comes to believe that the rule of National Socialism would have even worse effects than Bolshevik policy, the necessary consequence would be the occurrence of acts of sabotage and the formation of partisan bands'.[19]

During 1941 and well into 1942, joining the partisans held little appeal for most of the peasants. At this stage the Germans were still advancing deeper into the Soviet Union and it appeared that collaboration, or at least accommodation, with the occupiers was the safest course to follow. The peasants were also repelled by the conduct of the partisans, who appeared to be no better than bandits who raided their villages at night in search of food. As one village elder expressed the problem: 'We live between the hammer and the anvil. Today we are forced to obey the partisans or they will kill us, tomorrow we will be killed by the Germans for obeying them. The nights belong to the partisans, but during the days we are in no-man's land. Oh, I know the partisans can protect us now, but for how long?'[20] The result was that many early partisan bands were betrayed. For example, a Soviet report from the Kalinin province noted: 'For the first days of activity of the partisan detachment there was no support whatsoever from the remaining civilian population, in fact the opposite. Former kulaks and those repressed by organs of Soviet power, and part of the population under pressure from the Germans assisted them, assisting German units in showing them where the partisans were hiding.'[21]

On 3 July 1941 Stalin issued a call for partisan warfare:

> In the occupied territories partisan units must be formed . . . There must be diversionist groups for fighting enemy units, for spreading the partisan war everywhere, for blowing up and destroying roads and bridges and telephone and telegraph wires; for setting fire to forests, enemy stores and road convoys. In the occupied areas intolerable conditions must be created for the enemy and his accomplices, who must be persecuted and destroyed at every step.[22]

With the exception of the flat treeless steppes of the Ukraine, much of the newly conquered territory was ideal for partisan warfare, with dark dense forests and marshes impassable to large formations.[23] At this time General Gotthard Heinrici wrote home that 'the vast forests are still full of scattered soldiers and fugitives, some of them unarmed, some armed, and they are extremely dangerous. Even when we send divisions through these forests, tens of thousands have managed to avoid capture in this impassable terrain.'[24] The battles of encirclement, for example, around Smolensk, had led to the surrender of over 2 million Soviet soldiers, but a large number evaded capture or escaped from POW columns being marched westward. These soldiers could become dangerous and it was this perception, rather than the reality of partisan warfare, that led the Germans to take extreme measures against their shadowy opponent. Hitler responded to Stalin's appeal with delight: 'The Russians have now ordered partisan warfare behind our front. This partisan warfare has some advantage for us; it enables us to wipe out everyone who opposes us.'[25]

On 16 September 1941 Keitel issued an order which would ultimately have repercussions across the whole of Europe:

1. A communist insurrection movement came into life as early as the military campaign against Soviet Russia in all occupied regions . . .
2. . . . The Führer has ordered to apply everywhere the most severe measures to crush this movement with the shortest possible delay . . .
3. . . . To nip this activity in the bud, it is necessary to take the most severe measures immediately, from the first occurrence, to consolidate the authority of the occupation powers and to prevent the spreading of the movement. It must be kept in mind that human life in the concerned countries often has no value and that dissuasive effects can be obtained only with the help of exceptionally cruel measures . . .

   Only pain of death is the truly effective means of intimidation. Especially in cases of espionage, acts of sabotage . . . the punishment must be death. Illegal possession of arms must also be punished with death.[26]

Broadly speaking, under this decree the vengeance for the loss of one German life was to be between 50 and 100 locals. As partisan warfare intensified, the orders became more extreme: the burning of villages was openly encouraged, along with the seizure of livestock and food stores, and the male and female populations were to be made liable for forced labour.[27]

Part of the reason for the harshness of the German response to any sign of resistance was the sheer weakness of the occupying forces. Fewer than 110,000 men were detailed to control the entire occupied areas in 1941. This was compounded by the poor quality of the men. Most of the officers and men were reservists, too old for front-line action, and had received only a few months' training and were poorly equipped. The scale of the problem is demonstrated by a report in May 1942 when General Max von Schenckendorff judged that of the twenty-five battalions active in the rear area, eleven were totally unbattleworthy. Inevitably, the troops were spread thinly: for example, a single security division protected the main railway across Belorussia which supplied Army Group Centre in its advance on Moscow. The lack of troops forced the Germans to concentrate on holding key points such as bridges, and setting up guard posts along the main roads to enable supply convoys to move freely.[28]

The solution that the Germans adopted unwillingly was to recruit native auxiliaries. Anti-Soviet formations had sprung up in the Baltic States to hasten and harass the Soviet retreat as soon as Operation Barbarossa had been launched. But on 17 July 1941 Hitler declared:

> It must always remain a cast-iron principle that none but Germans shall be allowed to bear arms. Even when . . . it might seem expedient to summon foreign peoples to arm, it would be folly to do so. One day it would be sure

> to prove our absolute and irretrievable undoing. Only the Germans must be permitted to bear arms.[29]

Accordingly, the anti-Soviet nationalist formations were immediately disarmed; but less than a month later, the Germans on the ground changed their minds, and, without asking for Hitler's permission, began enlisting Latvians, Estonians, and Lithuanians into anti-partisan forces. The first actions of these units were the murder of the Jews in their localities.

Recruitment was also opened for locals and Soviet POWs to serve as *Hilfswillige*, volunteer auxiliaries (known as *Hiwis*) throughout the occupied eastern territories. By the spring of 1942 these numbered about 200,000, around 15 per cent of the male working population, and by the summer they were nearly half a million strong and the numbers continued rising. In November 1941 the Germans began arming some of the more reliable elements of these auxiliaries to serve as anti-partisan police forces. These were known as the *Schuma* formations and manned small outposts connecting the main towns.[30] The most notorious anti-partisan formation created from former Soviet soldiers at this time was led by Bronislav Kaminski and was based in the heavily forested region of Bryansk, southwest of Moscow. It started out with a strength of 1,000 men but grew to become a brigade of 20,000 men known as the RONA, the Russian National Liberation Army, which: 'By fighting the Soviet partisans in their own way, they neutralised, if they did not wholly destroy, all the local guerrillas just when the Germans were at full logistic stretch, preparing for the summer drive that was to take them to Stalingrad and into the Caucasus.'[31] The RONA would continue to serve the German cause until the Warsaw Uprising in August 1944. The German practice of arming local collaborators would continue to grow as the war progressed and would ultimately include a number of native SS formations created both from eastern nations and from western Europe.[32]

During the 1920s and early 1930s the Soviets had given serious consideration to the subject of partisan warfare in the event of an invasion. Plans had been drawn up for units to be built around special Communist Party cadres, training programmes had been launched, a chain of bases and arms dumps was being created, and issues such as communications and supply, including by air, were discussed.[33] On the other hand, the prospect of partisan warfare was viewed with suspicion in some political quarters because of bitter memories engendered by the Russian Civil War when some Red partisans had ignored party discipline and others had even defected to the Whites. The Soviet authorities also recognized the fact that partisan

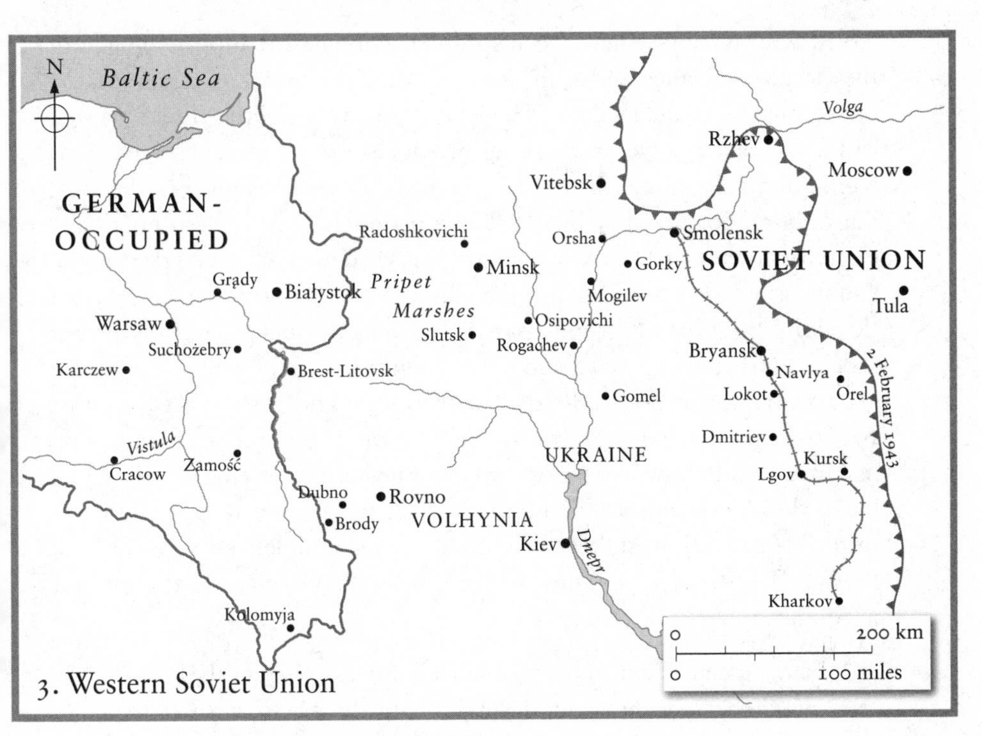

3. Western Soviet Union

warfare would be conducted in regions where the population was least loyal to the Soviet system. In the mid-1930s Soviet doctrine proclaimed the absolute inviolability of the country's frontiers, partisan warfare was deemed unnecessary, and the caches of weapons and supplies were decommissioned and the planning documents destroyed. Many of the planners then lost their lives in Stalin's purge of the officer corps, and of those who survived, most perished in the initial German advance.[34]

All this meant that the Soviets in summer 1941 had to build a new partisan movement in haste, from scratch, and under the extreme pressure of an apparently unstoppable German advance. The Soviet planners had two main ambitions for the partisans: one was political, to proclaim and uphold the Soviet system in the occupied areas; the second was to undertake sabotage and intelligence tasks in the German rear. Above all, the Soviets were determined to have close command and control over the partisan movement from the outset.

The political nature of the partisan movement is apparent from the personnel chosen to lead the first units, NKVD and Komsomol members and senior party figures. The NKVD established Destruction Battalions of between 100 and 200 people, either too young or too old for the Red

Army, who were instructed to institute a scorched-earth policy ahead of the German advance and then, when overrun, to launch partisan attacks on German units and facilities. These failed to undertake the tasks entrusted to them. For example, in the Orel province seventy-five such battalions containing 10,000 men were set up before the Germans reached the area, but only 2,000 stayed to fight.[35] These people may have been politically trustworthy but their lack of military knowledge quickly betrayed them. Commissar Vasily Sergienko in the Ukraine complained about the result: 'Responsibility for infiltrating partisan groups through the enemy's front is often entrusted to people who have absolutely no experience . . . Partisan groups are given contradictory instructions and tasks.' With almost twenty years' unchallenged party domination, the communist leadership had little idea of how to operate covertly. Furthermore, being mostly urban based they were completely unprepared for fighting in the open and as a result elementary mistakes were made. For example, the NKVD's 1st Partisan Regiment was almost wiped out by the Germans near Zhitomir in August 1941:

> We may assume that the 1st Battalion's failure was caused by the following: an unsuitable spot chosen for a halt; lack of necessary reconnaissance and poor security which allowed the Germans to approach unnoticed to within 50 metres; and, finally, possible betrayal of the unit by two partisans who had deserted on the evening before the battle.[36]

The early partisans did fight noticeably better in the Moscow region, where 2,000 operated against the German advance in the autumn. The Soviet authorities eulogized those who made the ultimate sacrifice. For example, the title of 'Hero of the Soviet Union' was awarded to eighteen-year-old Zoya Kosmodemyanskaya who had been captured, tortured, and hanged by Germans despite not having achieved much in terms of resistance.[37]

The Soviet counter-offensive of winter 1941–42 drove the Germans back as much as 100 miles in some places. Behind the front-line troops came the NKVD who investigated the conduct of local leaders and executed those known to have assisted the Germans. The partisans adopted the same policy, and focused their attentions on collaborators rather than on attacking the Germans directly. For example, by the end of January 1942 in the Orel province, the partisans killed over 200 civilians and local officials, and thirty-eight Russian policemen, but only thirty-three Germans.

News of the Soviet successes galvanized the early partisan formations which were now largely formed of Red Army soldiers who had been stranded behind the enemy lines. Sidor Kovpak had served in the Russian

Army during the First World War and the Red Army in the Russian Civil War, and was now destined to become a great partisan leader. He formed a partisan unit first in the Spadshchansky forest and then the Khinelsky forest in the Ukraine in September 1941, mostly from Red Army soldiers but also with a civilian element. His organizational skills, and the news of Red Army advances, transformed the unit between December 1941 and March 1942: 'Then there had been dense, lonely forest, people were living in the woods like badgers in their holes, afraid of the light, but now – there was a big, noisy partisan camp, and around it – an entire Soviet district.'[38] Closer to the front contact between the partisans and the leading Red Army formations had been made which enabled the partisans to receive much-needed supplies. On the Kalinin front in the north-west contact with the partisans was maintained with a corridor through the 'Surazh gate'.[39]

The improvised nature of the early partisans led to high losses and few achievements. In October 1941 the Political Directorate of the North-West Front highlighted the problems:

> The absence of a single centre directing the partisan movement inevitably causes numerous flaws . . . Nobody supplies the partisan movement with radios . . . nobody analyses the experience of partisan struggle, nor do the fronts exchange positive experiences, and, until the present, we have received no instructions from the centre on the organisation of the partisan movement . . . The absence of centralised command also affects the selection of regional commanders. As a rule, these are people picked in an arbitrary fashion, ignorant in military and political matters . . . The leading cadres receive no partisan training; the system of supply and armament of the partisan movement is not developed. All these problems must be urgently solved.[40]

The contact established between the partisans and the Red Army high command during the Soviet winter offensive meant that the Soviet authorities recognized the potential value of the partisans, and the partisans benefited from contact with the men who could supply them both with arms and equipment and with personnel to train the new recruits. In March 1942 Kovpak was forced to move his units to the relative safety of the vast Bryansk forest after the Hungarians had attacked his camp. Further retreats were necessary as the Red Army fell back under the weight of the German spring offensive. The political reliability of the Ukrainians was, however, called into question. On 5 May 1942 Kovpak sent Nikita Khrushchev, Soviet commissar in the Ukraine, a report warning that the peasants 'were demoralised by the retreat of the Red Army and the German reign of terror, while certain strata of the population and a number of Ukrainian villages were happy about the arrival of the occupation troops and hostile towards the partisans and the Soviet regime'.[41]

On 30 May 1942 a Central Staff of the Partisan Movement was set up under Soviet high command, led by the secretary general of the Communist Party in Belorussia, Panteleimon Ponomarenko. The overall purpose of this organization was to create close communication between the partisan staffs and the central staff, to supply the partisans with armaments and radios, and to coordinate partisan actions with the requirements of the Red Army.[42] Every region was divided into 'fronts', each with its own partisan staff. Training centres were established in the Soviet rear to train partisans and saboteurs to provide leadership and expertise for existing partisan units, and by the end of the year every partisan brigade contained some men who had passed through these training schools. Communications were also vastly improved: by the summer of 1942 the partisan headquarters was in radio communication with only 10 per cent of partisan formations, by August 1942 the figure had risen to 42 per cent and by May 1943, when the Red Army was clearly on the offensive, the figure was 87 per cent.[43]

The Central Staff also made service in the partisans compulsory in the occupied territories, both to fill the ranks of a partisan movement decimated by early disastrous operations and the harsh winter, and to deprive the Germans of men for forced labour or service in collaborationist units. For example, a proclamation issued during 1942 made the demands of the partisan staff clear:

> All members of the armed forces who escaped . . . and are at home, also all men in the class of 1925, report to your regular units or join the partisan units. Those who remain in hiding and continue to sit at home in order to save their skins, and those who do not join in the patriotic war to help destroy the German robbers, also those who desert to the Fascist army and help the latter to carry on a robber war against the Soviet people, are traitors to the homeland and will be liquidated by us sooner or later.[44]

The partisans were ordered to build up good relations with the local peasantry and not to terrorize the population through drastic requisitioning of food supplies. Collaborators, on the other hand, were to be executed along with their families as an example. German and partisan reports indicate the scale of these attacks: 917 collaborators and 200 police on the Kalinin front by July 1942.[45] The partisan oath stressed the importance of loyalty to the Soviet regime:

> I, a citizen of the SU, a true son of the heroic Russian people, swear that I will not lay down my weapons until the Fascist serpent in our land has been destroyed . . .
>
> I swear that I would die in terrible battle rather than surrender myself, my family, and the entire Russian people to the Fascist deceivers.
>
> If, out of fear, weakness, or personal depravity, I should fail to uphold this oath and should betray the interests of my people, may I die a dishonourable death at the hands of my own comrades.[46]

A partisan manual was prepared which gave detailed instructions on how to carry out sabotage against the German lines of communication, the roads, railways and bridges, munitions and fuel dumps, and on how to set up ambushes.[47] Alexander Werth, a journalist based in Moscow, noted that in the summer of 1942 a pocket-sized 430-page book *The Partisan's Guide* was for sale: 'The superficial impression the book made on the uninitiated reader was that the Russian Partisan was a sort of glorified boy-scout, and that although it must be difficult to "live in the snow" and not very satisfactory to eat moss and bark in emergencies, the Partisan's life was a wonderful life all the same.'[48]

At the end of August 1942 the most prominent partisan leaders, including Kovpak and Aleksandr Saburov, were invited to a planning conference led in Moscow in the presence of Stalin and Soviet political and military leaders. The decision was taken to spread partisan warfare into areas of the Ukraine where the partisan movement was still weak, and also to make long-distance raids across the Dnepr into Belorussia. The raids were designed to have a maximum political impact by bringing Soviet rule back to the rear areas of the Zhitomir and Kiev provinces, to attack collaborators, increase partisan recruitment, and in general to make a thorough nuisance of themselves by attacking the German lines of communication. The raids were well prepared and well equipped. Weapons and equipment were flown to a secret partisan air strip at Smielizh in southern Russia. Two detachments, 1,408 men under Suborov and 1,075 men under Kovpak, began their march westwards on 26 October 1942. Within a month the brigades had increased in size by 70 per cent and crossed the Dnepr on 10 November, and attacks were made on the railways in the Sarny region. In December 1942 the Germans finally reacted and launched a strong attack on the partisan positions near Glushkevichy and inflicted high casualties on the partisans, who eventually escaped. In 1943 Kovpak would launch raids into the Ukrainian-populated parts of pre-war Poland only to meet a new enemy, the UPA, the Ukrainian nationalist forces.[49]

The partisan command quickly identified communications as the point where the Germans were most vulnerable to attack. The Soviet Union was deficient in the means of modern transport with an estimated 40,000 miles of paved roads, only one of which was of European standards. The passability of these roads was further affected by the weather: dust storms in the summer, ice in the depth of the winter, and deep mud in the seasons in between. There were also only 67,000 miles of railway, of which only 25 per cent was double-tracked. The year 1942 was the one during which the partisans learned how to disrupt the railways and the Germans instituted greater measures to counter the menace. The partisans were advised on how to place explosives on the railways: 'The demolition of railway tracks is most fruitful at those points where maintenance work is particularly difficult, e.g. at bends, in cuttings, or high embankments.' Similarly, roads should be mined at points which could not be easily bypassed, like 'stretches surrounded by woods, in deep cuttings, on high embankments, in localities with deep slopes and declivities, at road crossings . . .'[50] The Germans lacked the troops necessary to guard the entire rail network and were forced to construct strongpoints along the main lines and to post guards on all the main bridges. Locals were recruited or forced to act as mobile guards by the side of the tracks: 'Theirs was an unenviable position, for they and their families were subject to reprisals by the partisans if they did their job well, and to rigorous punishment by the Germans if they did not.'[51] The Germans also cleared the forest on either side of the track for up to nine miles to create a no man's land where the partisans could not conceal themselves. Efforts were made to protect the trains by attaching an empty wagon to run ahead of the locomotive. The partisans responded by using a type of mine which would allow the light empty wagon to pass over unhindered and then explode as the heavier locomotive and laden carriages passed over. The Germans responded by sending wagons full of rocks ahead of the locomotive: the partisans then developed delayed action mines.[52]

The effect of the railway war in 1942 was mixed. The inactivity of the Ukrainian partisans meant that the German spring advance southwards into the Caucasus and towards Stalingrad proceeded without any great hindrance. The northern sector also saw relatively little sabotage. The situation was very different on the central front, where the main railways formed a bottleneck running across Belorussia and through the Bryansk region, a region where the partisans were most numerous, best organized, and prepared to undertake operations. Soviet data suggested that between June and November 1942 the Belorussian partisans derailed some 800 trains, blew up 500 bridges, and destroyed 1,000 enemy vehicles while the Bryansk partisans contributed a further 226 trains and the Smolensk partisans another 300. The Bryansk partisans levelled an important blow by blowing up the double-tracked railway bridge across the Desna river. Within a week the Germans had repaired it so that trains could pass across the bridge, without their heavy locomotives, thereby slowing but not halting rail traffic along the line. The numbers may appear impressive but the percentages reveal a different story: under 10 per cent of trains were sabotaged. For the partisan war on the rails to have any significant impact on German operations the figures would need to rise significantly and to take place across the entire Eastern Front.[53]

The partisans did, however, have an impact in other areas. Hitler had envisaged the Ukraine as a breadbasket for Germany but the Germans had to report that by the end of 1942 partisan activity had severely restricted requisitioning to a level 'calculated as equivalent to the supply of an army of 300,000 men with bread for a year, wheat for three months, potatoes for four months'.[54] The partisans in the deep south had the opportunity to sabotage the oilfields and thereby curtail the supply of fuel to the Germans. The derricks of the vast Kaluga oilfield had been sabotaged by the Red Army and were inactive but there remained huge tanks and pits filled with oil. The oilfield was well guarded by the Germans and lay too close to the front line for the Red Air Force to bomb it. Therefore, the task for the destruction of the fuel stores was entrusted to the partisans. Female partisans carrying baskets of grapes befriended the German guards and after friendships had been established the partisans carried acid bombs into the oilfield, hidden in the grape baskets, and then dropped them into the storage pits. The oilfield burned for three days, totally destroying the stocks of fuel.[55]

Overall the partisan effort in 1942 was more of an irritation than a life-or-death threat to the Germans. But the signs of the partisan build-up in terms both of numbers and of range and scale of activity were alarming omens for the future. Himmler examined the reports of partisan activity and the German attempt to quell it and 'he began to draw the conclusion that eliminating the partisans through extermination was preferable to the army's approach of controlling ground and conducting formal operations'.[56] Accordingly, the Germans launched a series of anti-partisan actions designed to stall and then eliminate the threat. In doing so they irretrievably forced the local population to choose sides, and joining the partisans increasingly became the choice of the peasantry caught in the middle of an ever more vicious war behind the front lines. General Franz Halder was in no doubt concerning the complexity of the partisan sweeps:

> It was our experience that Russian forces, once they were driven into wooded and swampy areas, were extremely difficult to attack by normal means and

> could hardly ever be completely destroyed. On countless occasions, we were confronted with the fact that the Russian was able to move about in these impenetrable forests and treacherous swamps with a certain instinct and sense of security of an animal, whereas any soldier reared and trained in a civilised country of the West was severely restricted in his movements and thereby placed at a disadvantage. There are no effective tactical remedies to compensate for this disadvantage. Even the most thorough training applied to troops from the West cannot replace the natural instinct peculiar to eastern Europeans who were born and raised in a region of forests and swamps.[57]

The German soldiers found the forests and swamps a difficult environment in which to operate. A ditty popular with the security units illustrated their struggle: 'Russians to the front of us, Russians to the rear of us, and in the middle, shooting.'[58]

The German anti-partisan tactics were to encircle the forest or target area and then advance together towards a central point, gradually squeezing the partisans into a limited space in which they could then be annihilated. Major Dr Schaefer described these tactics:

> The elimination and liquidation of these [guerrilla] elements is necessary . . . The aim is not to chase them away, but to annihilate them . . . If a larger area, where the bands are either in control or in which they have infiltrated, can be encircled by surprise movements and can be systematically combed, then success will not be lacking. But this means that the outer ring of encirclement must be so close that an escape or breakthrough of larger units is impossible from the start. Sector by sector and day by day the ring is narrowed, either by a concentrated advance or, according to the situation and territory, by pressing the enemy against a prearranged fortified line, which can be strengthened by utilizing natural obstacles (such as a river). Then it is imperative to press the bandits out of the swampy woods into the open country. On the map the plan for such a major (anti-bandit) action with the various lines of encirclement, which represent the daily objectives aimed at, and the demarcation lines between the various anti-partisan units, look like a spider's web . . . But here as well no blueprint for all situations is possible . . .[59]

Various operations were launched in the Belorussian swamps and forests and against parts of the Bryansk forest throughout the spring, summer, and autumn of 1942, of which the most important were Operations Hanover and Vogelsang, the first in the Yelnya-Dorogobuzh area and the second in the Bryansk forest. Operation Hanover was a large operation utilizing about 40,000 men against about 15,000 partisans of whom about 10,500 were either killed or captured. A Panzer regiment and two infantry regiments, 5,500 men in total, were employed on Operation Vogelsang and resulted in 1,193 partisans killed, 1,400 wounded, and 12,531 people evacuated at small cost to the Germans. In each case such operations had to be repeated time and time again since despite losses of around 1,000 men during most operations, the partisans largely managed to rebuild their forces relatively quickly. It should also be noted that many of the so-called 'partisans' killed were actually local Jews and not partisans, a fact revealed by the paucity of weapons found on the victims. These anti-partisan sweeps did not affect operations at the front. The manpower used, often in large numbers, were drawn principally from rear-area units, security troops, native collaborators, and troops resting and training in the rear areas. Those front-line troops involved in partisan sweeps were used only for short periods of time and usually during pauses in operations at the front.[60]

The apparent inability of the Germans to combat the partisan threat and to cleanse regions for any significant period of time led to the development of rival tactics to mitigate the continuing threat. One line of thinking was to keep the local population cooperative by making a clearer distinction between partisans captured carrying weapons, who could be shot, and innocent villagers caught in the middle, who should be left unharmed. A further variant of this line of thought was to treat partisans, captives, and deserters as prisoners of war in the expectation that news of good treatment would leak out and encourage further desertions. Hitler, however, was adamant that increased ruthlessness was the only way to combat the partisans: 'Only in those instances where the anti-partisan struggle was begun and carried out with ruthless brutality has success not failed to obtain . . . The struggle against the partisans in the entire East is a life-and-death struggle in which one side or the other must be exterminated.'[61] Just the man for this job had already made his presence known. Erich von dem Bach-Zelewski had experienced anti-partisan warfare in his role as SS and Police Leader for the rear area of Army Group Centre, and he approached Himmler with the suggestion that he be appointed to oversee all anti-partisan operations in the east. Himmler agreed, and at the end of October 1942 von dem Bach-Zelewski was duly appointed SS plenipotentiary for anti-partisan warfare. A new level of brutality was thereby inaugurated: the partisans were now to be termed bandits and efforts to counter their activity were to form a new doctrine of *Bandenbekämpfung* – bandit warfare – in which all men, women, and children, armed or unarmed, were to be viewed and treated as the enemy.[62]

In the Balkans, the mobilization of the communist parties was to have enormous implications for the political complexion of the region after the war, when Yugoslavia and Albania would become part of the communist bloc. In 1941, however, the picture was very different since the communist parties in the Balkans were extremely small and insignificant. Under the pressure of occupation, the communists came to dominate the scene and, by doing so, raised the spectre of civil war. This subject will be covered more fully in later chapters: here the intention is to explain the circumstances which led to the rise of the communists, how they became organized, who their opponents were, and what tactics they intended to pursue.

The Balkans were ideal terrain for partisan warfare because the mountains provided refuge for the resistance formations and the few extended and widely spaced lines of communication offered plenty of targets. Resistance in the Balkans could also serve a valuable purpose in the wider war, by drawing off Axis divisions from the Eastern Front. The Germans saw the Balkans as a region full of minerals and metals that needed to be exploited by the German war industry; furthermore, one of the main supply routes for the Afrika Korps ran through the Balkans to the harbour of Piraeus. But strategically they saw it as a sideshow to the main war on the Eastern Front. Therefore, for the Germans the idea was to keep the area quiescent, using ruthless methods if necessary. Part of the reasoning behind the brutality of the reprisals launched against the resistance lay in Austrian memories of the First World War. The commanding general in Serbia, General Franz Böhme, reminded his soldiers that:

> If we do not proceed with all means available and with maximum ruthlessness, our losses will rise to incalculable levels. You will be carrying out your mission in a strip of territory in which, thanks to the treachery of the Serbs, both men and women, rivers of German blood flowed in 1914. You are the avengers of those dead. We must deliver a warning that will make the greatest possible impression on the population.[63]

Böhme was quickly to prove to be an enthusiastic exponent of Keitel's espousal of severe reprisals.

The Yugoslav communists under Tito had not resisted the German occupation in any way until Stalin had made his call for partisan warfare across Europe. The forces Tito created were known as the Partisans and operated throughout Yugoslavia. The communists had experience of underground warfare from the pre-war days, and had support in the towns, and reliable radio communications with Moscow, where Tito was known as 'Walter'. The first resistance had been offered, however, by Draža Mihailović, a royalist officer, in the mountains around Ravna Gora in Serbia, and his forces were known as the Četniks.* Mihailović's principal immediate aim was to preserve the lives of Serbs under terrible threat from the actions of the Croatian Ustaše who had massacred around 100,000 people, mostly Orthodox Serbs, in Croatia and Bosnia-Herzegovina by the end of 1941. His longer-term aim was to build up resistance forces which would go into action when the Allies landed in the Balkans. (Both Mihailović and the Germans expected such a landing since the Allies had sent forces to Salonika during the First World War.) Tito, however, was in a hurry to build up his forces in order to seize political power.

An early example of communist tactics is provided by the rebellion which broke out in Montenegro in mid-July 1941. The rebels were demanding greater autonomy and less Italian interference in the administration. The Italian response was overseen by General Alessandro Pirzio Biroli, who had considerable experience of colonial warfare, and involved the widespread burning of rebel villages and the taking of between 10,000 and 20,000 civilian hostages, including whole families, and their deportation to internment camps. About 67,000 Italian soldiers took part in suppressing the rebellion, which collapsed after a week. After the rebellion had been quelled, Pirzio Biroli ordered a relaxation of the severe methods and many internees were released from custody. The communists had not initiated this rebellion but they did try to take it over. The communist ideologue, Milovan Djilas, attempted to turn Montenegro into a miniature Red republic, but found little popular support. This failure prompted his replacement by Ivan Milutinović. Under orders from Moscow, Tito toned down the language of class war and followed the Moscow line that 'the united Front, not exclusion and subversion of the non-Communists, was to be the watchword of the resistance'.[64]

An uprising that broke out in Serbia in August 1941 began to reveal fundamental differences between Mihailović and Tito. By the end of the month Tito could report to Moscow that the Serbian resistance had reduced the German hold on the country to the larger towns, leaving the countryside to the rebels. The Germans, for their part, were forced to admit that in only ten days the resistance had made 135 attacks on railways, communications, industrial installations and various public offices. The German response was twofold: Milan Aćimović was replaced as prime minister by Milan Nedić, and on 19 September 1941 Böhme was appointed plenipotentiary commanding general in Serbia with a brief to

* Četniks were originally rebels who mounted guerrilla warfare against the Turks during the time of Ottoman rule before the First World War. They were glorified in South Slav folk poetry.

crush the resistance by all means necessary.[65] On the same day, Mihailović and Tito met to discuss the possibilities of cooperation. Mihailović, as a serving officer in the Yugoslav Army, assumed that he should lead all the resistance forces. Tito, however, saw Mihailović as a representative of the 'defeated forces of an alien and reactionary system' with whom only a temporary accommodation might be made, solely in the interests of opposing the Germans. Nevertheless, the united Četnik–Partisan operations that autumn were successful as the resistance captured the towns of Užice, Požega, Gornji Milanovac, and Čačak. This gave the rebels control of the whole of western Serbia as well as the armaments factory at Užice. As a result of the German response, the policy of cooperation proved temporary. In late October 1941 the Germans massacred 1,755 Serbs at Kraljevo and a further 2,300 at Kragujevac a few days later, and the massacres so appalled Mihailović that he called an immediate halt to overt resistance: 'By fragmenting our units into their smallest particles and keeping them temporarily inactive and dispersed across the rugged terrain, we will quickly overcome the present crisis.' Tito, on the other hand, saw the massacres as an opportunity for recruitment to the Partisans, who would offer people protection. He therefore wanted to continue overt resistance whatever the cost.[66]

It can be argued that cooperation between the Četniks and the Partisans would not have lasted in any case, not only because of their differences over the tactics to be adopted in resistance, but primarily because of their opposing political aims. Mihailović was loyal to King Peter while Tito and the Partisans were for him 'fighting against the dynasty, and for the realisation of a social revolution which can never be our aim'.[67] Tito recognized this incompatibility too. On the anniversary of the Soviet October Revolution on 7 November the Partisans celebrated wildly in Užice.[68] When Tito learned of the Soviet success in halting the German advance on Moscow, he issued a statement on 14 December 1941:

> The victory of the Red Army on the Eastern Front establishes a perspective for the rapid defeat of Hitler's tyranny in Europe. Consequently, signs are already showing that the reactionary forces of the imperialistic countries are gathering to disarm the People's Liberation Movement that stems from the depths of the people and unleashes unstoppable revolutionary energy. This action is directed in the first place against the Communists and their ties with the masses . . . [The] reactionary Great Serb centre is dangerous for all the peoples of Yugoslavia. It undoubtedly comprises the main enemy of tomorrow of the liberation struggle of the peoples of Yugoslavia, and today forms the principal bastion of the occupiers.[69]

In other words, civil war against the Četnik forces of Mihailović and his followers was an essential prerequisite to political domination after the end of the war. Tito and his supporters presented the Partisans as a force which viewed all Yugoslavs, not just Serbs, as equals. But first the occupiers had to be beaten and the dominance of the Germans forced both the Četniks and Partisans to abandon Serbia by the end of the year. While Mihailović retreated into the mountains to await future developments in the wider war, the Partisans planned for more immediate resistance, and so on 22 December 1941 the 1st Proletarian Brigade was established from the Serbian and Montenegrin Partisans. The failure of Mihailović to extend his reach into Bosnia-Herzegovina was exploited by Tito with the recruitment of Serbs in those areas, still threatened by the Ustaše, into the ranks of the Partisans.[70]

Whereas Tito was clear about the necessity of destroying what he saw as the reactionary forces of the Četniks as part of the road to power, the Comintern saw things somewhat differently. In August 1942 its head, Georgi Dimitrov, sent an order to Tito:

> Do not call your proletarian brigades proletarian; instead call them shock brigades, we repeat, shock brigades. Understand that this has enormous political significance, both for consolidating people's forces against the occupiers and collaborators within the country and for foreign countries. You are waging a people's liberation war using forces composed of workers, peasants, the people's intelligentsia, and other patriots – you are not waging a proletarian struggle. You must always proceed on this basis. Quit playing into the hands of the enemies of the people, who will always make vicious use of any such lapses on your part.[71]

Tito, however, was in a hurry to place himself in a position to seize power should the Germans be defeated. Thereafter, although in regular communication with Moscow, he began to pursue the independent line that ultimately, after the war, would lead to a break with Stalin.

In June 1941 Albania did not even have a communist party as such, although there were communists such as Enver Hoxha who wanted to create such a party. These appealed to the Yugoslavs for assistance and two emissaries, Miladin Popović and Dušan Mugoša, came to Tirana to advise the communist groups on how to create a party. At the end of July 1942 the communists tested their tactics by calling for a general uprising, and the telegraph and telecommunications network was attacked across Albania. In Tirana successful attacks were mounted on the central telephone exchange and Italian military installations were blown up. In the Kuçovë oilfields the pipelines were destroyed and several petrol dumps blown up. The Italians regained control in Tirana but admitted that they had lost control over much of northern Albania, where the northern bands had risen independently and not as a result of the communist appeal.

In line with Comintern policy, the Albanian communists followed the policy of attempting to create a broad front of resistance. In the middle of September 1942 a large meeting of resistance groups was held in Pezë, eleven miles south-west of Tirana. It was attended by representatives from all the fighting bands and included men of every shade of political opinion. The result was the establishment of the *Levicija Nacional Çlirimtarë*, LNC, which, although dominated by the communists under Hoxha, was to present itself as a National Liberation Front. Not everyone was taken in. A month later a group of largely right-wing republican nationalists in southern Albania set up an alternative organization, the *Balli Kombëtar*, or national front, under the leadership of Midhat Frashëri. The *Balli Kombëtar* hoped to appeal to the political moderates, those who were not taken in by the LNC's presentation of itself as a broad-based national liberation front. Indeed, the *Balli Kombëtar* would be joined by those left-wingers expelled from the LNC for being politically unreliable. The two organizations published superficially common social programmes and had the same organizational structure based on regional committees, but there the similarity ended. As in Yugoslavia, there were divisions over tactics to be used against the occupiers: the *Balli Kombëtar* was more akin to Mihailović's tactics of waiting for the opportune moment for action whereas the LNC, like Tito, pressed for more immediate action.[72]

The German invasion of Greece found the Greek Communist Party in such a weak and divided state that for the whole of 1941 it was totally unable to respond to Stalin's call for partisan warfare. The communists, like the republicans, had been driven underground during the Metaxas dictatorship but, unlike other communist parties which had been forced to operate covertly, the Greek party was extremely divided and lacked a power base or even a clear leadership on which to base its future activities.[73] Yet by the end of the German occupation the Communist Party had grown to such an extent that there was a very real chance it would seize power: and indeed civil war would break out in Greece before and after the liberation. Two major factors facilitated the rise of the Greek resistance: the famine that devastated Greece in 1941–42, and the fact that King George had abandoned Greece without leaving instructions for any resistance, which left the organization of the resistance primarily in the hands of republicans.

Famine swept through Greece as an immediate consequence of the German-sponsored division of the country. Thrace, the main agricultural area, was now under Bulgarian occupation. This left the cities to starve and it is estimated that over 40,000 people died of starvation in Athens and Piraeus in 1941–42.[74] The communists seized the opportunity offered by the extreme situation and in May 1941 set up EA or National Solidarity as an underground relief organization. This was followed by EEAM, the National Workers' Liberation Front in July, and finally by *Ethniko Apeleutherotiko Metopo*, EAM, the National Liberation Front itself on 28 September 1941. EAM attempted to appeal to a broad section of political persuasion but was clearly dominated from the start by the communists under Georgios Siantos. EAM focused initially on building up support and organizational structures in Athens and the major cities. The success of EAM's organization was demonstrated by the strike it led by the Athens and Piraeus postal, telephone, and telegraph workers in April 1942. The strike spread to Salonika. It was a strike for higher wages and those communication workers serving the Italians and Germans were ordered not to join the strike. Like the strikes a year earlier in northern France, the motive behind the strike was economic not resistance and it was recognized as such. The collaborationist government caved in to the strikers' demands and the occupying authorities did not interfere. This success led to an expansion in EAM membership which was estimated at 40,000 by the summer of 1942.

In September 1941 an alternative political grouping *Ethnikos Demokratikos Ellenikos Syndesmos*, EDES, National Republican Greek League, was also founded by pro-democratic Venizelist officers with the aim of bridging the gap between republicans who supported neither the communists nor the royalist political parties. Its nominal leader was General Nikolaos Plastiras, but he was in exile in France, and so the leadership fell to Colonel Napoleon Zervas.[75]

Both groups turned their attention to the possibilities of armed resistance and both identified the mountains of Greece as the best area in which to build up bands of armed men, *andartes*. In April 1942 Siantos instructed Andreas Tsimas to form the first armed groups of EAM in central Greece. He in turn entrusted the formation of the armed wing of EAM, called *Ellenikos Laikos Apeleutherotikos Stratos*, ELAS, to Thanassis Klaras who was known as Aris Velouchiotis. He has been described by Denys Hamson of SOE as:

> ... the most ruthless man I have ever met, the most cold-blooded, the cruellest. He was an ex-schoolmaster, sentenced in Greece for homosexual

> offences and trained in the Moscow School of Communists, an intelligent, able man with no heart, without human pity, an excellent psychologist, a fanatical leader of men.[76]

EDES also established armed units in central Greece. By the summer of 1942 both ELAS and EDES had a number of bands of around 100 men each under arms.

The strategic and economic importance of the Balkans aroused the attention of the British because although the Germans saw the region as something of a sideshow, resistance in the Balkans could serve a valuable purpose in the wider war by drawing off Axis divisions from the Eastern Front. British encouragement of resistance in the region could be used by the British government to demonstrate to Stalin its commitment to the war without the risks of a premature mainland invasion. The arrival of SOE officers and British military missions would, however, add a further level of complexity to the war in the Balkans. Their arrival offered the prospect of arms supplies and consequently more resistance, but the question of who should receive these weapons, what they should and would do with them, was not settled at the outset. This oversight would have extremely serious consequences for the furtherance and conduct of resistance in the region.

9
The Mobilization of the Communists

Before the war the communist parties of western Europe had little political support from the electorate and posed no threat to democratic government. In Poland there was no communist party at all, since Stalin had ordered its disbandment during the 1930s. Where communist parties did exist, notably in France, their attitude before the war was to portray themselves as the principal opponents of fascism and to extol the bravery of their comrades who went to fight in the civil war in Spain. In late August 1939 this policy was completely overturned by the signature of the Molotov–Ribbentrop Pact which 'came crashing down like a paving stone on the heads of the party cadres', and led to scores of communist rank and file deserting the party.[1] The outbreak of the Second World War further confused the situation. On 8 September 1939 the head of the Comintern, Georgi Dimitrov, issued the Comintern's instructions to the communist parties of Europe:

> The war has materially changed the situation. The division of the capitalist states into fascist and democratic [camps] has lost its former significance. Strategy must be altered accordingly. The strategy of Communist parties in all warring lands at this stage of the war is to oppose the war, to expose its imperialist character; where Communist deputies are available, to vote against war credits, to explain to the masses that the war will not bring them anything but adversity and ruin ... Everywhere, Communist parties must undertake a decisive offensive against the treacherous policy of social democracy.[2]

The effect was immediate: in the Protectorate the communist slogan was 'Neither Hácha nor Beneš but the communists', and in France it was 'Neither Churchill nor Hitler'.[3]

After the war began, the French communists, in particular, were widely regarded as traitors, a belief seemingly confirmed when the communist parliamentary leader, Maurice Thorez, deserted his regiment in October 1939 after being called to the colours. He re-emerged in Moscow, and was sentenced *in absentia* by the French courts to five years' imprisonment and stripped of his French citizenship. Immediately after the publication of the Molotov–Ribbentrop Pact, the government of Édouard Daladier banned the publication of the communist newspaper *L'Humanité*. Despite the fact that the communist deputies in the French parliament voted in favour of war credits, before Dimitrov's directive had reached them, the government banned the Communist Party at the end of September 1939. Then in the spring of 1940, fearing that the communists might act as a fifth column, the government ordered direct action against known communists: 2,718 elected communist representatives in local and national governments lost their posts, and around 3,400 communist militants were arrested, along with at least 3,000 foreign communist refugees. They were interned in appalling conditions in camps across southern France.[4]

After the fall of France the communists, now under Jacques Duclos, seemed to confirm the earlier allegations of treachery by openly seeking German assistance to reconnect with their membership. The German authorities were sounded out on the possibility of publishing *L'Humanité* and the initial response from the ambassador to Vichy France, Otto Abetz, was positive and the newspaper went on sale openly. Abetz was equally open to the prospect of reinstating the positions of the communist members of local government who had been fired by the Daladier government. Presumably Abetz was prepared to tolerate the French communists because this was the period when the Germans and Soviets were allies. The French police, however, acting under orders from Vichy, had other ideas, and communists now emerging into the open were arrested. Virtually simultaneously both the Comintern and the German leadership had second thoughts. The Comintern vetoed the plan to republish *L'Humanité*, while Abetz was ordered by Berlin not to permit its publication but to publish *La France au travail* as an alternative newspaper, a step which confused the readership since its articles were very similar to those which *L'Humanité* had been publishing.

Initially, the communists had been as keen to collaborate with the Vichy regime as with the Germans. Two communist leaders, François Billoux and Virgile Barel, offered to testify against their former Popular Front allies, Léon Blum and Daladier, whom the Vichy regime was planning to put on trial. But the sheer extent of the Vichy-inspired arrests of communists dispelled any myths that the communists could now operate throughout France during the German occupation. Once the nature of the Vichy National Revolution became apparent, especially its actions against the trade unions, the communist press made its opposition to Vichy-inspired legislation quite apparent.[5] As one historian has concluded:

> The PCF, then, far from immediately rallying behind the resistance against the occupier, granted priority to the struggle against Vichy, accompanied by a shift in focus to unionist action. Although at first the PCF went easy on the occupier, as the German-Soviet Pact required, it multiplied its attacks in early 1941, then called for the construction of the Front National in May. But it did not throw itself into the armed struggle until after June 22.[6]

Nor was the party any more favourable towards de Gaulle. The sheer difficulty of predicting the war's outcome is perfectly expressed by Pierre Villon, about to head the *Front National*, who wrote in his notebooks: 'As for Gaullism, it will be swept away and it will be useful to us if we give the country freedom, peace and bread (with butter on it) before Britain arrives to do so. And I cannot see Britain capable of managing a landing in France to liberate the country before the Germans rise up in revolt. In that case we shall not wait for de Gaulle to set up soviets.'[7]

Once Germany had invaded the Soviet Union and the countries were no longer allies but enemies, the Comintern directives sent out to the communists in western Europe are a useful indication of how the Soviet authorities believed the resistance could assist in the defence of the Soviet Union: 'In the occupied countries, it is absolutely necessary to combine the political struggle with all possible actions that will disorganise the enemy's rear and hinder the provision and transport of troops and materials. One must do everything in order to rouse the masses to active battle against the occupation.'[8] More specifically: to disrupt 'by any means possible production of arms. Form small detachments for destruction of the war factories, naphtha storage tanks, bridges, railways, roads, telegraphic and telephone communication systems. Prevent by any means transport of troops and arms.'[9] In other words the communists were to begin sabotage operations immediately and to focus on recruitment.

Further directives instructed the communist parties on how to relate to the existing resistance movements. These amounted to a temporary abandonment of all explicit revolutionary aims. For example, in directives sent to the French Communist Party on 25 June 1941 and to the Norwegians and Danes on 6 July, the desired line was clear: 'We insist once again on the absolute necessity of avoiding portraying Germany's war on the Soviet Union in all your agitation as a war between the capitalist system and the socialist system. For the Sov[iet] Union it is a patriotic war against fascist barbarism', and:

> Communists in occupied countries should immediately organise a national unity front, and for this purpose they should make contact with all powers

> fighting against fascist Germany ... The purpose of the national front is to mobilise all classes of society to fight against the German occupation. The movement for the creation of a national front must be formed under the watchword of democracy and national freedom from fascism (Hitler's yoke). Communists do not raise the question of their hegemony in the national front.[10]

Collaboration with non-communist resistance groups was deemed essential by the Soviet authorities because the Soviet Union was too far away to despatch weapons and sabotage materiel to western Europe. There were, however, many matters to be resolved before all the resistance groups could collaborate and launch attacks on the Germans. The non-communist resistance suspected the loyalties of the communists – were they loyal to Moscow or to the government-in-exile? Many of the communists appeared to be hotheads, ready to launch immediate attacks on the Germans without considering the consequent reprisals – so who would control the resistance? Suspicions also were aroused about the long-term aim of the communists – post-war political domination or working within the parliamentary system? Furthermore, should the democratic resistance respond to the communist resistance by becoming more active and, if so, how could they protect innocent civilians from the inevitable German reprisals?

In no country were these questions in more immediate need of answers than in Poland. Poland lay directly across the German lines of communication, and was therefore ideally situated to hamper the despatch of German reinforcements and supplies to the Eastern Front. The Poles also had a well-organized resistance movement in the *Armia Krajowa*, which was capable of undertaking serious sabotage operations in Poland and to provide intelligence from behind German lines. Yet the Polish government-in-exile, the leadership of the AK and Underground Government, and indeed, much of the population had little sympathy for the Soviet Union. Their principal hope and expectation was that the Germans would become embroiled in a lengthy war with the Soviet Union and that both powers would be greatly diminished, allowing Poland to rise again. Bitter memories of the recent Soviet occupation of eastern Poland also made direct collaboration with communists or Soviet partisans on Polish territory less likely. Yet the Polish prime minister Władysław Sikorski needed to tread carefully because he first had to restore diplomatic relations with the Soviet Union. This was achieved by the July 1941 Sikorski–Maisky agreement which also allowed the formation of a Polish army in the Soviet Union manned by those Poles who had been deported to Siberia and Kazakhstan. Yet even then the Soviets were making threatening noises regarding the future frontiers of Poland and its governance. In April 1943 the news broke of the Soviet murder of the Polish officer corps at Katyń in Smolensk, western Russia, in spring 1940, and this led to diplomatic relations being broken off. After this the Polish authorities in London had no influence over Soviet and Polish communist activities in Poland. It was consequently left to the AK and the Underground Government to formulate responses to the rise of the communists and the arrival of Soviet partisans in Poland alone and, at the same time, to demonstrate the value of the AK by increasing the number of acts of sabotage while also attempting to protect the population from German reprisals.

The AK already possessed specialist units, the ZO, trained to undertake sabotage of the railways. These were now sent into action, and it was estimated that in the period from 1 July to 30 November 1941 the Poles destroyed about 400 tanker wagons and sabotaged three oil wells in the Jasło-Krosno basin. In the spring of 1942 further attacks on locomotives and wagons were being reported, and by that summer the Germans had to institute special procedures to protect the railways from sabotage. All railway bridges and viaducts were to be protected by police or military units; special armed trains patrolled key lines; on the most vital lines from Lwów into the Soviet Union military posts were erected every twenty metres.[11] The AK claimed that from June 1942 to January 1943, 1,268 locomotives, 3,318 railway trucks and coaches, and seventy-six railway transports had been set on fire. Its units had also caused twenty-five derailments and ninety interruptions to railway traffic, as well as the destruction of bridges, points, and railway workshops. In one operation on 8 October 1942 the AK stated that it had simultaneously cut six of the seven lines running through Polish territory eastwards. Just how much of this sabotage was actually committed by the AK is open to dispute, since the Belorussian partisans and Soviet partisan units operating in eastern Poland made similar claims.

The Poles also operated further east. In October 1941 a Soviet military delegation arrived in London for staff talks with the British general staff, and it also discussed sabotage with Polish staff officers. The result was the launch of Operation *Wachlarz* whereby Polish sabotage units led by Polish officers parachuted into Poland from Britain, the *Cichociemni*, would operate east of the pre-war Polish–Soviet border. This would avoid reprisals against the Polish population. The whole of the Eastern Front was divided into seven sections with a group allocated to each one. The results were generally disappointing owing to a lack of equipment and the hostility of the local population. The groups in Pinsk and Minsk were either betrayed or discovered by chance before they had undertaken any action, and the group based at Brześć became demoralized and returned to Warsaw.[12]

In spring 1942 the Polish communist radio station, Radio Kościuszko, began broadcasting into Poland from Moscow. Its early broadcasts highlighted the success of the Red Army winter offensive:

> These victories bring the battlefield closer to Poland. Therefore the Polish nation must increase her resistance to the enemy. Polish partisans should operate in thousands, not in small parties. Millions should participate in partisan battles, and the working class should be in the front ranks ... When the resistance reaches its peak, when hundreds of thousands participate in it, then the occupying forces will lose confidence in their secure position in Poland. That would help the Poles get in touch with partisans operating on Polish territory ... [13]

Much to Sikorski's horror and despite his protests, Soviet partisans were beginning to arrive in Poland. After discussion by telegraph with General Rowecki, head of the AK, in November 1942 Sikorski issued the instruction that the resistance organization should make contact with these Soviet partisan groups. The aim was to secure friendly relations between AK partisan units and Soviet partisan units in the disputed territory of eastern Poland. Sikorski emphasized that the ideal solution should be that the two would operate in separate areas. If this was impossible then the Soviet partisans should accept the primacy of the AK command. The initial contacts were not promising: Tadeusz Bór-Komorowski, who later succeeded Rowecki as head of the AK, noted that 'more often than not the Soviet commanders demanded that the local Home Army forces be subordinated to them, although in nearly every case the Polish forces were more numerous than the Russians'.[14] Clashes between the two continued in the forests of eastern Poland throughout 1942 and 1943 before reaching a climax as the Red Army prepared to enter Poland in late 1943.

Sikorski was equally concerned about the build-up of communist forces within Poland. He warned Rowecki that he feared that 'traitors, of the kind of Colonel Berling and Wanda Wasilewska, will tread in the steps of Soviet troops entering Poland, and they will do everything possible in order to bring about disruption of the Polish nation and the undermining of the Polish states'.[15] Sikorski was right to be worried. As early as December 1941 a group of Polish communists led by Marceli Nowotko had been parachuted into Poland with orders not to establish a communist party in name but rather a people's party, the *Polska Partia Robotnicza*, PPR, as 'a National Front to fight for Poland's freedom and independence'. The party would not be a member of the Comintern and, although ideologically aligned to Marxist-Leninist ideology, was to subsume this in favour of a broad approach. Nowotko was to focus on creating partisan units. Recruitment to the communist cause was slow: in June 1942 Nowotko reported to Dimitrov that the party membership had reached 4,000, and the military organization, the *Gwardia Ludowa* (GL), had recruited 3,000 members, though most were unarmed. At the end of November 1942 Nowotko was assassinated by a fellow party member for obscure reasons and the leadership was assumed by Paweł Finder. At the same time radio communication between Poland and Moscow was lost. This had two consequences: the immediate one was that the GL could not request arms supplies from the Soviet Union and Moscow could not send it orders; the second was that the PPR was free to develop its political programme independently of the Union of Polish Patriots which was in the process of being set up by the Polish communists still in the Soviet Union.[16]

The Underground Government closely monitored the communists and sent detailed reports to London. This work was undertaken by the so-called Agency A which in December 1943 was renamed *Antyk*. One particularly detailed report dated 19 October 1942 summarized what the authors perceived as the communist and Soviet aims towards Poland. Apart from the general resistance activities of gathering intelligence, undertaking sabotage, and preparing for a general uprising, it was believed that the communists were also seeking to create a pro-Soviet attitude in the country in the hope of provoking hostility to the AK and Underground Government, which were still loyal to the government-in-exile. The communists, it was thought, also aimed to create a state of anarchy in the country which would enable them to seize power as and when the Red Army approached Poland's border. Further reports indicated that the communist propaganda was becoming more widely accepted, particularly in Warsaw, largely because the communists stressed the level of their own (in fact minor) anti-German activity and portrayed the AK as a mainly passive body.[17]

In Poland, the communists began operations on a small-scale by setting off minor explosions in the Warsaw railway yards, and throwing grenades into restaurants and cafes frequented by the Germans. These actions did little to undermine the German occupation but they did lead to a rise in terror. A few quotations suffice to illustrate the scale of German reprisals:

> For each German killed, ten Poles are shot in the street. They make an announcement on the radio where and at what time the executions will take place, so that people can go and watch; they give the surnames of the poor wretches and their ages. After a few hours they clear the bodies away and

> sprinkle sand on the blood and brains left on the ground. People take flowers and candles to the spot.[18]
>
> People were hunted down in the streets, trapped, put into vans, and driven to a prison. They formed a pool from which at random a hundred or more victims were taken at any one time to their death. Before being delivered to the place of execution, their clothes were changed for paper sacks, their mouths were taped shut to prevent them from shouting 'Long live Poland!' as had happened in the past.[19]

Such a high level of terror meant that 'terror lost its power to terrorise. People simply stopped being afraid because they had nothing much to lose.'[20]

In the course of 1942 the Germans exterminated most of Polish Jewry and by the end of the year were ready to turn their attention towards the rest of the Poles. In late November 1942 a process was initiated to evacuate Poles from over 300 villages in the Zamość region to make way for German colonists.[21] The Poles resisted, and a hospital superintendent in Szczebrzeszyn, Zygmunt Klukowski, noted in his diary in December 1942:

> In the forests around us more and more people are trying to organise fighting units. Some former Polish officers are forming regular units for the AK. Many villagers are forming their own units with only one goal, revenge. They are very well armed. Some try to burn down and completely destroy the evacuated villages before the new owners, mostly German settlers from eastern Europe, take possession of them.[22]

By spring 1943 Hans Frank complained that the newly settled areas were in a state of open rebellion.

The Poles cried out for revenge. There was a danger that if the AK was not being seen to oppose the Germans more openly and actively then impatient people would turn to the communists, not because the communist actions were any more effective, but because they at least publicized their activities.[23] Rowecki and contemporary commentators all noted the danger of the perception of AK inactivity in the face of German terror and the growing desire for revenge. AK attacks consequently began to increase. For example, in March 1943 a prison van carrying newly captured resistance members from the Scout movement to Pawiak prison in Warsaw was ambushed and all the prisoners were released with the loss of three killed in the ambush party and four dead Germans. In reprisal the Germans immediately executed 160 inmates of Pawiak.[24] In January 1943 a new organization, *Kedyw*, was created to supervise sabotage activities undertaken by the AK. In March, Rowecki also ordered the creation of Polish partisan units and these had an immediate effect, notably in the

Krasnobród region and in the forests of eastern Poland. These actions were all reported in the widely read clandestine newspaper *Biuletyn Informacyjny*.[25] By the summer of 1943 resistance throughout Poland had reached such a height that Himmler declared that the entire General Government was to be considered a partisan war zone – no holds were to be barred in crushing the resistance. In Warsaw the process was to be overseen by the appointment of a new Higher SS and Police Leader (HSSPF), SS-Brigadeführer Franz Kutschera.[26]

While the Polish government-in-exile and the Underground Government and AK in Poland made clear their opposition to the communists, the opposite was true with regards to Czechoslovakia. Edvard Beneš believed that the Soviet Union had been the only country willing to come to Czechoslovakia's aid during the Munich crisis of September 1938, and he was therefore keen to establish a close relationship with the Soviet Union as soon as possible. Indeed, his foreign minister, Jan Masaryk, warned his colleagues: 'He now has only Russia on his mind. We must hold him, so that he won't fly off into the sky.'[27] Beneš's overtures were welcomed, and on 18 July the Soviet Union recognized the Czech national committee in London as a government-in-exile. Britain followed suit by granting full recognition *de jure* to the Czechs in London.[28] The Soviet Union was convinced that the Protectorate was ideal terrain for partisan warfare. To further this end, Czech exiles in the Soviet Union were trained near Moscow and on 31 August 1941 the first party was dropped near Warsaw and made its way successfully into the Protectorate. It was joined by a second party which had been dropped around 10 September. Neither party achieved anything of military value but they were good for communist propaganda purposes.[29]

Communists joined the Czech government-in-exile, and Beneš ordered ÚVOD, the principal Czech resistance group, to respond to overtures from the communist underground. In August 1941 ÚVOD was able to report: 'we negotiate with the communists about cooperation . . . We keep regular contacts with them once a week.' Because of post-war political divergences it is now almost impossible to determine the extent of the cooperation between the communists and non-communists. After the war ÚVOD veterans denied the existence of any meaningful cooperation at all, and indeed some non-communist resisters assert that such overtures from the communists were actively resisted, not on political grounds, but from a conviction that the communists had been thoroughly penetrated by the Gestapo. The communists, for their part, argue that in autumn 1941 a central national revolutionary committee of the resistance was established which they came to dominate; while the non-communists deny the existence of any such committee.[30]

Whether sabotage was inspired by the communists or not, the importance of the armaments factories in the Protectorate to the German war economy meant that it could have a significant effect. An early communist leaflet demanded: 'Fascist barbarians out of our fatherland! Carry out all kinds of sabotage! Prepare for a general strike! Everything for the victory of the Red Army and for the freedom of our homeland!' This message was continually driven home by the communist clandestine newspaper *Rudé právo*. Beneš was equally aware of the importance of sabotaging the war industries in the Protectorate, and on 5 September 1941 he sent a message to ÚVOD:

> It is essential to move from theoretical plans and preparations to deeds ... In London and Moscow we have been informed that the destruction or at least a considerable reduction of the weapons industry would have a profound impact on the Germans at this moment ... Our entire position will appear in a permanently unfavourable light if we do not at least keep pace with the others.[31]

The effect of these two calls was immediate: the Germans reported that there had been ten major strikes and twelve walkouts leading to an average fall in industrial production of 18 per cent between 10 August and 10 September 1941. (The resistance claimed the figure was nearer 30 per cent.) In addition, railways were attacked and telephone wires cut, and at one place a fuel depot containing 100,000 litres was set alight. The communists claimed responsibility for all acts of sabotage and *Rudé právo* was published regularly, trumpeting communist underground activity. Observers such as František Moravec, head of Czech intelligence in London, believed that many of these reports were faked, and ÚVOD noted the danger inherent in such publicity: 'The intense, almost public activities of the communist party might in the course of time convince the masses that it is the only capable force which is afraid neither of sacrifice nor of work. It makes an impression on the people and gains their sympathy.'[32]

The consequences of the rise in sabotage were extremely serious. On 22 September 1941 Konstantin von Neurath was recalled to Berlin and relieved of his post as Reichsprotektor, ostensibly on the grounds of ill-health. His replacement, Reinhard Heydrich, arrived in Prague on 27 September, and immediately imposed martial law over the entire Protectorate. Heydrich planned to use the 'carrot and the stick' approach both to quell the resistance and to ensure that it did not rise up again. The stick was applied first. Under martial law, summary courts run by the

Sicherheitsdienst (SD) and *Sicherheitspolizei* (SIPO) passed three sentences: death, concentration camp or, very rarely, release. In only two months 404 death sentences were carried out and about 6,000 arrests were made. The main resistance organization, ÚVOD, was devastated through arrests of most of its membership, including General Bílý who was executed in September. Of the Three Kings, supplying intelligence to the Allies, only Captain Václav Morávek survived. In March 1942, however, his most valuable source, Paul Thümmel, was arrested and was held in Theresienstadt until his execution in early 1945. Future resistance was stymied by the dissolution of an important source of recruits, the sporting association *Sokol*. The government of Emil Hácha was not consulted before the imposition of martial law, nor did it make a protest. The cabinet was divided over whether to resign but, despite the arrest of its prime minister Alois Eliáš, decided to continue in existence. Eliáš was tried in October 1941, pleaded guilty to contacts with the Allies, and was sentenced to death. Hácha appealed to Hitler for clemency and Eliáš was held hostage against the future good behaviour of the population of the Protectorate: the mayor of Prague, Otokar Klapka, was less fortunate and was executed at the beginning of October 1941.

There were two aspects to Heydrich's offer of the carrot to the Protectorate. In the short term, he sought to win over the armament workers and farmers in order to benefit the German war effort. The workers were now to be treated on a par with the German workers and to receive benefits such as increased rations, improved welfare services, free shoes, and a Czech version of the German 'Strength through Joy' movement, which provided entertainment for the workers. Thousands of workers were offered free holidays in resorts. Farmers were wooed with an amnesty to encourage them to correct their former understatement of produce figures. The result brought in large quantities of foodstuffs, especially pigs. These measures were by and large successful. Sabotage all but ceased in the armament factories, and the Protectorate supplied a great amount of winter clothing and skis for the German soldiers on the Eastern Front. In January 1942 martial law was lifted and the students who had been held in concentration camps since the demonstrations in 1939 were released. By January 1942 Goebbels recorded in his diary: 'Heydrich's policy in the Protectorate is truly a model one . . . As a result the Protectorate is now in the best of spirits, quite in contrast to other occupied or annexed areas.'[33]

Heydrich explained his long-term policy in the Protectorate to German officials three days after his arrival: the population was to be divided into three groups: the racially valuable and quiescent group which would be Germanized; the racially inferior and hostile element which would be moved eastwards out of the country; and the third group which was racially valuable but was hostile. The last had to be dealt with immediately:

> These are the most dangerous, because they can form a racially sound stratum of leaders. We can try to relocate some of them into the Reich, put them in a purely German environment, and then Germanise and re-educate them. Should it prove to be impossible, we must put them against the wall.[34]

Martial law and the summary courts dealt effectively with those most hostile elements and Heydrich now turned his attention to the Germanization of those Czechs identified as racially valuable. In this he found a willing collaborator in the education minister, Emanuel Moravec. Special training camps were set up for all non-Jewish Czech children to separate them from their Czech teachers, membership of youth associations, to provide a 'physical, mental and moral education', was made compulsory, and by early 1943 over a million Czech children were being Germanized in these camps.[35]

A feature of the early part of the war in western Europe had been the reluctance of the Germans to introduce harsh measures to suppress every sign of resistance. Resisters caught in the act or betrayed by traitors were not executed without first being tried, and there were no large-scale reprisals against innocent civilians as seen in the east. The rise in resistance in the west occurred partly as a result of the actions of communist resistance groups, but also because the war in the east showed no sign of ending and taking dangerous actions against the Germans therefore no longer seemed futile. To support the war in the east the Germans introduced policies which directly affected more sectors of the population than before and made resistance a more attractive proposition. As resistance increased, the German authorities in the west, Otto von Stülpnagel (France), von Falkenhausen (Belgium), Seyss-Inquart (Holland), and Terboven (Norway), all had to find their own solutions to the rise in resistance. In some cases this meant relying more on the collaborating regimes and administrations.

In France the communists had begun to get organized for resistance even before the Germans invaded the Soviet Union. During autumn 1940 communists had established small groups of no more than six to eight members known as *L'Organisation Spéciale de Combat* (OSC) to protect communist activists against the French police. In August 1941 the *Bataillons de la Jeunesse* (Youth Battalions) were set up, which operated mainly in and around Paris. In addition to these two units, the immigrants of *Main-d'Oeuvre Immigrée* (MOI) formed their own armed groups. In late 1941 the three organizations merged into one new one – *Franc-Tireurs et*

Partisans (FTP) which would eventually become a substantial organization throughout France. During 1942, however, it was still tiny, with only fifty-four activists operating in the Paris region.[36]

The actions of the *Bataillons de la Jeunesse* had an effect completely out of proportion to their numbers. On 13 August 1941 the communists held a demonstration at the Porte Saint-Denis. When the Germans and French police moved in to break it up, two communist agitators, Samuel Tyszelman, known as 'Titi', and Henri Gautherot were arrested, and later executed. In revenge, Pierre Georges, known as Colonel Fabien, and Gilbert Brustlein took the fateful decision to assassinate a German officer. As Brustlein later recalled:

> On the morning of 23 August, Tondu and I had a rendezvous with Fabien inside the metro Barbès at 8 a.m. Fabien was going to do the deed while I provided protection. We spotted a magnificent naval commandant strutting on the platform. Fabien said, 'That one.' The train arrived, the officer got into the first-class carriage and at that moment Fabien fired two shots, turned round, and sprang up the steps leading to the exit shouting, 'Stop him!' I followed him, revolver still in my hand, so that the crowd coming down the other steps thought that the shots had been fired by me. Two men tried to grab me. More supple than strong, I managed to get away and rejoin Fabien.[37]

Far from being a 'magnificent naval commandant', the unfortunate victim was a German naval quartermaster, Alfons Moser, who had the dubious honour of being the first German to be assassinated by the resistance since the start of the occupation.

The German authorities responded swiftly with an announcement that, starting immediately, all Frenchmen arrested by the Germans would be considered hostages and 'in case such an act should happen again, a number of hostages corresponding to the gravity of the crime will be shot'.[38] Further German officers were assassinated in Lille and near the Belgian border in the following days, and hostages were shot on the ratio of ten to every German killed. Overall the German situation reports recorded eighty-two incidents of active resistance in August, rising to 145 in September.[39]

The real turning point, however, came on 20 October 1941 with the assassination, again by Brustlein, of Lieutenant Colonel Karl Hotz, the military commandant of the city of Nantes, followed a day later by the assassination of Hans Gottfried Reimers, legal adviser to the military administration in Bordeaux. Wilhelm Keitel promptly ordered Otto von Stülpnagel to follow his instruction of 16 September 1941, which set a ratio of 50–100 communists to be executed for every German soldier killed by the resistance. Otto von Stülpnagel negotiated with Berlin and then announced:

> Cowardly criminals in the pay of London and Moscow shot the Feldkommandant of Nantes (Loire-Inférieure) on the morning of 20 October 1941. To date the murderers have not been arrested. To expiate this crime I have ordered that fifty hostages will be shot in the first instance. In view of the gravity of the crime, fifty more hostages will be shot if the guilty parties are not arrested before 23 October at midnight. I am offering a reward totalling 15 million francs to inhabitants who contribute to the arrest of the culprits.[40]

The first batch of fifty were shot in Nantes on 22 October, and two days later fifty further hostages were shot in Bordeaux.

The fate of the next fifty hostages slated for execution consumed everyone's minds. The mayor, prefect, and bishop of Nantes went to the German headquarters to plead for clemency. Marshal Pétain allegedly offered to go to the demarcation line and offer himself as a hostage. The Vichy minister of the interior, Pierre Pucheu, attempted to ensure that the hostages to be shot would be selected from the communists held in the Châteaubriand camp. The Germans, however, wanted to set an example in Nantes, and among the hostages shot were non-communist prisoners who were being held in Paris but who came originally from Nantes.[41] Around 5,000 Nantes residents attended the funeral of Hotz, and the prefect reported that most of the population disapproved of the assassination. On 24 October, Otto von Stülpnagel wrote to General Eduard Wagner:

> I have stated my opinion that the great mass of the French population is foreign to these assassinations, which are much more likely to have been carried out by small groups of terrorists in the pay of England. I have clearly come to the view that because of the particular situation in France I am opposed to the mass execution of hostages. This must inevitably provoke increasing bitterness in the population and make future political rapprochement extraordinarily difficult if not impossible . . .
>
> I have myself warned enough against the use of Polish methods in France. I have acted with moderation, and staked my ideas and myself on this. The measures taken in Nantes were imposed on me from above. I was placed under the most intense pressure . . .[42]

From London, de Gaulle broadcast on 23 October 1941 urging the population to keep calm:

> That Germans should be killed by Frenchmen is absolutely normal and absolutely justified. If the Germans did not want to receive death at our

> hands, they had only to stay in their own country. Now at present the watchword I give for the occupied territory is not to kill Germans there. This is for a single but very good reason, which is that for the moment it is too easy for the enemy to reply by the massacring of our fighting men, temporarily disarmed. As soon as we are in a position to move over to the attack, all together, from the outside and at home, you will be given the necessary orders. Until then, patience, preparation, resolution.[43]

On 28 October Hitler agreed to postpone the execution of the second batch of hostages indefinitely.

The institution of mass reprisals for acts of resistance had varied effects for the French. Unlike in Poland, the increase in communist resistance did not inspire the democratic resistance to greater acts. Indeed, Liliane Lévy-Osbert recalled:

> People disapproved of anti-German actions, they did not want to fight, they rejected the idea of rebellion. They were particularly influenced by the fear of reprisals. Fear, timidity and terror faced with the appalling example of so many death sentences terrorised the population. Worse, people turned their anger and their criticisms against the 'adventurers' who threatened the lives of ordinary people. Which was what the Germans wanted. However, I think that, deep down, there may have been some kind of compassion and understanding for those young twenty-year-olds who were sacrificing their future.[44]

One of the leaders of *Combat*, Claude Bourdet, was more expansive:

> On our side, we too found that one could not abstain from an action because of a fear of reprisals against the population, but ... I think that the great majority of the members of our *groupes francs* [the armed units of the non-communist movements of the south] would have had the greatest personal difficulties, as did many communist militants, in gunning down in the street an unknown individual just because he was wearing a German uniform. We [the leaders] did not have the hard, tough courage shown by Fabien in leading by example ... The difference between the communists and us was, then, rather in the order of feelings and sensitivity than of moral attitude: after all, there was scarcely much difference, from this last point of view, between an attack on military vehicles in which enemy soldiers would be killed and shooting a single soldier in the street.[45]

But Colonel Henri Rol-Tanguy, later to lead the 1944 uprising in Paris, was unrepentant: 'Even at the price of this precious blood of hostages, France could not afford to be presented to the world as a passive prostrate country without will to resist and react ... The price had to be paid ...

bitter as it was'.[46] Nonetheless, towards the end of 1941 communist resistance activity largely tailed off apart from minor attacks on German and collaborationist premises in Paris and the surrounding area. The German and French police became more adept at catching the culprits and by the end of the year half the members of the *Bataillons de la Jeunesse* had been arrested.

Not all the Germans were happy with the new policy of mass reprisals and on 15 January 1942 Otto von Stülpnagel wrote to Keitel that it was his intention to respond to assassinations or severe sabotage with 'a *limited* number of executions and will adjust the number to suit the circumstances. At least under present conditions, I can no longer arrange *mass shootings* and answer to history with a clear conscience.'[47] German disapproval of von Stülpnagel's independence of thought and apparent softness led to his resignation on 15 February.[48] His replacement was his cousin, Carl-Heinrich von Stülpnagel, who had served on the Eastern Front. In addition, Hitler appointed Carl Oberg to serve as HSSPF in France on 9 March 1942. Oberg had received his orders directly from Himmler and was to have absolute power in 'all police matters and reprisals against criminals, Jews, and Communists implicated in attacks against the German Reich or the citizens of the Reich'.[49] Yet Carl-Heinrich was no happier with the policy of mass reprisals than his cousin. German action against the resistance in France now relied more on the use of the so-called *Nacht und Nebel* decree which had been issued on 7 December 1941. This decree allowed for the deportation of suspects to Germany where they would disappear into camps: 'To questions from German and foreign authorities concerning these perpetrators, the answer must be that they have been arrested and that investigation proceedings in process do not allow speaking about them . . .'[50] Oberg was responsible for the deportation of at least 6,639 people. The use of this decree resulted in a drop in the number of hostages executed to 254 between June 1942 and December 1943.[51] Oberg, however, initiated the Family Hostage Law under which relatives of those believed to be involved in the resistance would be punished: adult close male relations would be executed, all female relatives sent for forced labour, and their children deposited in institutions for young offenders.[52]

Arguably the principal effect of the new German policies was the increase in collaboration by the Vichy regime: 'the logic of the armistice position thus drew Vichy into trying to do the Germans' dirty work for them'.[53] Vichy instituted its own system of special tribunals to retry prisoners who had already been tried and sentenced for other crimes in order to supply a hostage pool. It was content to see hostages selected from the two most marginalized sections of the community: the communists and the

Jews. Indeed, shortly after the issue of the *Nacht und Nebel* decree the Germans deported a batch of 1,000 Jews and 500 communists to Germany.[54] The Vichy authorities proved ready to assist the Germans with the selection of hostages after the attack in Nantes, and now with Pierre Laval, the arch-collaborator, in power as prime minister, the level of collaboration increased accordingly. This was welcomed by the Germans, and when Heydrich visited Paris in May, he urged Oberg to establish close relations with the French police. Heydrich held the personal belief, drawn from his experience in the Protectorate, that collaboration with native governments paid off. Heydrich was also impressed by his meeting with René Bousquet, the secretary general of French police: 'Heydrich had a sort of penchant for Bousquet who presented himself to him full of goodwill, affirming his desire to collaborate with the German authorities in order to fight against communism. Bousquet professed, at least in words, a great admiration for the courage of the SS.'[55] The Germans also needed French cooperation because of the sheer weakness of the German position in France: the demands of the war in the east meant that the number of German troops tasked with maintaining order in France had dropped from 100,000 in December 1941 to 40,000 in March 1942.[56]

The result was an agreement signed between Oberg and Bousquet on 8 August 1942, under which the full independence of the French police in the Occupied Zone (extended to the former Unoccupied Zone in April 1943 after the German occupation in November 1942) was recognized in all matters of internal order 'against anarchism, terrorism, and communism, and generally against all foreign actions susceptible of troubling order within France'. People charged with these crimes would be tried in French courts. The Germans were limited to the rather loosely termed fight against 'enemies of the Reich'.[57] Although much of the cooperation concerned the deportation of the Jews, overseen by the Germans but undertaken by the French police, it gave the French free rein to attack another common enemy, the communists. For example, in a single operation in Nantes on 27 August 1942 the French police arrested 143 communists, of whom forty-one could be identified as responsible for resistance attacks. By the end of 1942 the French police had arrested around 5,000 communists – a term used very loosely – and 400 other members of the resistance. But the price of such cooperation was high: 'In the end the French police and administration, imagining that they were acting independently, in fact simply did the dirty work of the SS and then found matters taken entirely out of their hands. The French judicial system was totally sidelined.'[58] This development led the French people to question the value of collaboration with the Vichy regime, and it is at this time, for example, that Henri Frenay of *Combat* made an irrevocable break from Pétain. Furthermore, once on the slippery slope of full collaboration, the Vichy regime could not stop, leading eventually to the creation of the *Milice* on 5 January 1943.

In Belgium the communists formed the *Front de l'Indépendance*, partisan groups to launch attacks on the Germans. This raised concerns in the *Légion Belge* regarding the attitude of *Front de l'Indépendance* towards the king and the government-in-exile. Indeed, General Van Overstraeten of the *Légion Belge* asked one of his youthful members François Daman to infiltrate the *Front* to discover whether it harboured any intentions to overthrow the government at the time of liberation. Most resistance activity was directed against the collaborators in the Rexist Party and the *Vlaams Nationaal Verbond* (VNV), some of whom were assassinated. The relatively low level of resistance against the Germans themselves allowed General von Falkenhausen to respond cautiously. His policy was to incarcerate suspects and offenders in a concentration camp on Belgian soil at Breendonk, twenty miles from Antwerp. Executions of communist hostages began in December 1942, but only rose to a significant figure in the first half of 1944.[59]

In the Netherlands, Reichskommissar Seyss-Inquart set out his response to any rise in resistance activity. This would be based on the principle of collective responsibility: fines would be imposed on the local municipalities and a hostage pool would be created. In the summer of 1942 the Germans created a hostage pool of 1,400 prominent Dutch citizens who were held in a Catholic seminary at Beekvliet. On 7 August 1942 the communist resistance attempted to blow up a German troop train in the centre of Rotterdam. An unfortunate Dutch railway worker ran into the explosives and was seriously injured. No Germans were killed or wounded yet the German authorities issued a harsh warning:

> If those guilty of this assault do not report to the police before Friday August 14 or are not identified with the help of citizens, the punishment will be carried out on a number of hostages who stand as the guarantors against such acts of sabotage by order of the Wehrmachtbefehlshaber in the Netherlands. The arrest of the guilty parties is thus in the interest of the whole population, in order to avoid this retaliation against the hostages. A reward of 100,000 florins has been set on prompt reports to an office of the German Wehrmacht or the police leading to the seizure of the perpetrators. All reports will be treated confidentially.

Statements appeared in the newspapers, one signed by forty-two notables who were not collaborators and the other by the combined Protestant

Churches, condemning the attack. No information was received and so, early on the morning of 15 August, five hostages from Beekvliet were shot.

The German authorities were divided on how to evaluate the response of the Dutch population to the execution of the hostages. Naturally the clandestine press condemned the executions in no uncertain terms, but Hanns Rauter, Higher SS and Police Leader, believed that the executions had had a salutary effect on the Dutch and that now 'all of Holland trembles at the thought that somewhere sabotage might be carried out'. The German military authorities under General Christiansen, however, felt that the executions served only to force the Dutch to choose sides and consequently 'an unprecedented rejection, an unknown hatred against Germany is gaining ground in the Netherlands'.[60]

On 29 April 1943 the Dutch were stunned by Christiansen's announcement that, in order to prevent further acts of resistance, all Dutch soldiers who had been released from POW camps in the spring of 1940 would be re-interned and transported to Germany as labourers. The prospect of the re-internment of approximately 300,000 men affected most households in the Netherlands and led to an explosive reaction. Strikes began in the factories in Hengelo in the east of the country and spread to the mines in the south around Limburg and to the Philips factories in Eindhoven: it is estimated that about 500,000 people went on strike. The Germans responded by declaring martial law in five towns, including Hengelo, and opening fire on strikers without warning. In total 175 people were executed or shot dead in the street and 400 were seriously wounded. Thousands of the strikers were arrested and of these 900 were sent to concentration camps in the Netherlands and in Germany. The Germans also took measures to ensure that there would be no repeat of the strikes through purging the local government and dismissing the mayors of towns where the strikes had been most effective. Many of the threatened former soldiers went into hiding or joined the resistance.[61]

In Norway the communists started the war as an insignificant force and, as similarly happened in other countries, they urged immediate action at a time when *Milorg* was still preaching restraint. On 2 August 1941 Reichskommissar Terboven took the initiative against any rise in resistance by announcing that his response would be to institute a state of emergency. Furthermore, he gave the Gestapo the powers to take any step necessary to maintain public order. These included the establishment of special courts martial which could impose long terms of imprisonment or order the executions of those found guilty of anti-German actions. Terboven quickly proved true to his word. On 8 September 1941 the workers in the factories in Oslo were informed that their milk rations had been abolished. They responded by going on strike and the strike spread across Oslo and into the shipyards. Terboven immediately proclaimed a state of emergency, and over 300 Norwegians were arrested, among them the leadership of the resistance organization *Landsorganisasjonen i Norge* (LO) and two communist trade union leaders, Viggo Hansteen and Rolf Wickstrøm. The latter two men were executed. As a resister noted later: 'The Resistance may have wavered before, but after the shots felled Hansteen and Wickstrøm, it never wavered again. In the "second phase", the hidden poison pill was exchanged for a gun. With a gun, a resister might have a chance to get away, and if not, he might take an enemy with him.' The communists might have differed from the democratic resistance on tactics but they were at least as loyal to the king. In November 1941 the communist resistance leaders wrote to the Norwegian government-in-exile expressing its willingness to cooperate with the existing resistance leadership. This was an important move because a united front was essential at a time when Vidkun Quisling, appointed prime minister in February 1942, was about to launch an assault on all aspects of Norwegian society.[62]

The resistance could not, however, control events initiated elsewhere, even when Norwegians became the innocent victims. A case in point centres on the small fishing village of Telavåg on the west coast. This village was used by the 'Shetland Bus' as a transit point between Norway and Britain, bringing SOE and SIS agents into the country and taking out young men who wished to join the Norwegian army. A local informer led the Germans to the village in April 1942 and, after a firefight with two agents, one agent was killed along with two Gestapo men. Terboven immediately declared a local state of emergency and gave the order to raze the village. More than 300 houses were destroyed, fishing vessels were sunk, and the livestock was removed. The entire male population of seventy-six men aged from sixteen to sixty-five was deported to concentration camps in Norway and Germany, while the 260 old people, women, and children were interned. The Germans also took the opportunity to execute eighteen young men who had been captured earlier in Ålesund in transit to Britain.[63]

The reaction to the destruction of Telavåg and the executions was mixed. A German report noted:

> All reports point out that Norwegians stress that they have no war experience and have lived in peace since 1814. At the same time they are very sensitive as regards their national pride and sense of justice. This general sense of justice involves strong individualism and independent thinking. An act is punishable only when guilt is involved. Every average Norwegian

> shares this opinion, not just lawyers. The German procedures on Telavaag are constantly brought up – as reported from Bergen. Burning houses has a wider meaning than just the destruction of material things. It meant the destruction of the result of generations' toil and another fact should also be considered, namely that the Home represents something 'sacred' to Norwegians.[64]

A member of the *Reichskommissariat*, Dr Alfred Huhnhäuser, recognized that Terboven's actions represented a turning point in Norwegian-German relations: 'If he had in the beginning been inclined to treat the Norwegians well because Hitler wished to "win" them, then he changed his methods from the time of the state of emergency and began a reign of terror.'[65] Reports from the resistance suggested a similar conflict and Torolv Solheim wrote in his diary: 'It was sinister how *fear* took hold after the Telavåg terror. People think that they may save their own skin by having nothing to do with those of us who work underground. They don't understand the Germans' plan of repression, but after a while they will realise it.'[66]

The realization came soon. In summer 1942 a British commando force attacked an electricity power plant at Glomfjord and SOE sabotaged the iron-ore mines at Fosdalen. Terboven consequently declared a state of emergency stretching from Majavatn in the north to Røros in the south, including Trondheim, which lasted from 6 to 12 October. During this period thirty-four Norwegians were executed.[67] A Norwegian report at the end of October noted the effect:

> After what happened the mood among those who still remain in the Resistance is very depressed. The disappointment is so great, and the trust so faint that the same active participation from the people as before can no longer be counted on. The best were arrested and those left were reluctant to expose themselves to personal danger any more.[68]

The reprisals further damaged the already delicate relationship between the Norwegian resistance, its government-in-exile, and SOE. It appeared that all resistance, of any political persuasion or inspired by SOE, would have the same deadly consequences for both the perpetrators and the innocent civilians caught in the crossfire.

10

SOE Gets to Work

When SOE was created in July 1940 its primary purpose was to recruit secret armies which would liberate their own countries. During 1941 the entry of the Soviet Union and then the United States into the war offered the long-term prospect that Europe would be liberated by the mass armies of the Allies. Therefore: 'The grandiose theories of the detonator concept, of the secret armies in Europe, of left-wing revolution, of a combined programme of subversive propaganda and action, had all dissolved.'[1] Nevertheless, liberation by the Allied armies remained a distant prospect for much of 1942: the Germans launched a spring offensive which took their armies deep into the Soviet Union as far as Stalingrad; in the Western Desert British and Commonwealth forces were driven back to the border of Egypt; and the United States Army was under 1.5 million men strong in 1941 and faced a period of rapid but long expansion before it could realistically launch offensive operations on a grand scale.

In the interim period before the tide of fortune turned in favour of the Allies the resistance needed a new sense of purpose. In May 1942 a directive issued by the British Chiefs of Staff called upon the resistance to focus on sabotage until the time of the arrival of the Allies, at which point the resistance would supply intelligence on German movements, supply guides to the Allied forces, and protect vital installations from destruction. The role of SOE was to encourage and direct these operations. Unspoken, but with an effect on SOE operations, was the growing realization that both Poland and the Protectorate increasingly lay within the Soviet area of operations and that there was little that the western Allies could do to assist the resistance movements in those countries.

Sabotage, however, carried the risk of inviting reprisals from the Germans against innocent civilians, which might have the undesired effect of dampening resistance to occupation. Consideration had to be given to the moral and utilitarian questions of stoking the fire of resistance too much and too soon by encouraging the resistance to take risky actions while liberation by the Allied armies remained a distant prospect. These questions were raised by Sir Bruce Lockhart, head of the Political Warfare Executive (PWE), in a presentation to the Chiefs of Staff in May 1942.[2] They were expanded on by Peter Wilkinson, a staff officer in SOE, that November. Wilkinson believed that the German threat of severe reprisals had 'substantially weakened the revolutionary capacity of occupied Europe', because 'the people in occupied Europe are reluctant to expedite this seemingly inevitable victory by doing anything which may expose themselves, their families or their friends to death at the hands of the Germans just when liberation is in sight'.[3]

The British policymakers also had to take into account the opinions of the governments-in-exile, which wanted both to encourage resistance but, as a memorandum in April 1943 noted, also feared the consequences:

> In countries where resistance is directed by SOE in conjunction with a refugee government, that government is often reluctant to encourage open resistance for fear of reprisals and the risk of their organisation which they hope to conserve for an eventual rising, and, to a lesser extent, to facilitate their own return home.[4]

Certain governments-in-exile, notably the Poles and Yugoslavs, remained wedded to the concept of secret armies. Others, notably the Norwegians, supported the commitment to sabotage but sought to have stronger control over what operations were carried out. The relationship between SOE and the native resistance groups also had to be taken into consideration. In France and Belgium SOE tended to set up their own circuits which usually consisted of an organizer, a radio operator, and a courier. They recruited their own teams locally and their relationship to the local resistance organizations was largely limited to supplying weapons and training men on their use. Agents within the RF section of SOE agents, however, made direct contact with the French movements such as *Combat*, *Franc-Tireur*, and *Libération-sud*.

By late 1942 the strategic picture had changed greatly. In the east the Germans were besieged in Stalingrad; in the Western Desert the battle of El Alamein had forced the Afrika Korps into retreat; and the Allies had landed in French North Africa. Now the occupied peoples could begin to believe in an ultimate Allied victory. The invasion of southern France by the Germans in November 1942 forced the French people to re-evaluate their attitudes towards the Vichy regime and towards the resistance. As SOE, which now had agents operating in every occupied country, discovered, the changing strategic picture did not necessarily bring forth substantial numbers of recruits to the resistance, but it did make the occupied peoples as a whole more resistance-minded, more willing to help those who were brave enough to be active. In the event, as the following chapters will show, German policies initiated because of the lengthy war against the Soviet Union would prove the main incentive for joining the resistance. The role of SOE was to endeavour to organize, supply, direct, and control the activities of these new recruits.

First of all, the SOE agents had to get to their theatre of operations and learn how to live and work there. The most common method of insertion was by air. Most agents attended the parachute course at Ringway airfield near Manchester or in Haifa in the Middle East. The success of the course is demonstrated by the remarkably few accidents suffered by agents on landing, other than sprained ankles. When accidents did occur they could have serious effects. For example, SOE's first foray into Denmark at the end of December 1941, to establish important contacts with politicians in the country such as Christmas Møller, ended in disaster when SOE agent Carl Johan Bruhn's parachute failed to open and he was killed on impact. His radio operator, Mogens Hammer, went on the run but was unable to contact London since his radio had smashed on landing. Harry Peulevé suffered the misfortune of breaking a leg badly on his arrival in France in July 1942, forcing him to abandon his mission and to hobble painfully over the Pyrenees to safety before returning to France on a later mission. Both Gustave Biéler and Tony Brooks damaged their backs on landing, delaying the start of their work. Other agents were simply unlucky. Bob Sheppard found himself landing on a gendarmerie billet and was arrested even before his feet touched French soil. As he ruefully said later: 'It didn't matter how good a cover story I had, it was quite impossible to explain away my unorthodox method of dropping in.'[5]

The greatest problem facing the pilots was the challenge of navigation, and failures led to agents being dropped well away from where they expected to land. Dropping operations were restricted to the ten- to twelve-day full moon period: 'We needed moonlight to map-read by; we needed moonlight to find our way to the dropping zones for parachuting and to the small fields that served as landing grounds; and we needed moonlight to be able to see the ground clearly enough to make a safe landing.'[6] Flights to France have been the best documented. Lewis Hodges, who flew Whitley bombers, described the approach: 'When we crossed the Channel we came to a low altitude over the sea to avoid detection. Arriving at the coastline we climbed to about 1500 feet to be able to get a clear indication on the coast as to our exact position. Then we would descend to low level again, perhaps 800 or 1000 feet depending on the terrain and weather, all the way to the dropping zone.'[7] Agents suffered immense frustration when the pilot could not locate the reception committee and so aborted the operation. Tommy Yeo-Thomas, an RF agent who undertook several missions to France, lectured to aircrews on the dangers facing reception committees:

> When you do not find the reception committee waiting for you, you think that they have been careless; you do not stop to wonder why they are not there. You fail to understand that a sudden change on the German Order of Battle may make a ground which was safe one day impossible to use the next. While you fly fuming back to your base it does not strike you that the whole reception committee may have been arrested. You complain about the weak lights. Don't you understand that it is difficult to secure batteries in occupied territory? Do you realise that those obtainable are mostly of inferior quality? Do you know that a man may have to bicycle 20 or 30 kilometres in order to obtain one battery?[8]

Indeed, one of the indications that Dutch operations had been completely compromised by the Germans – and something which should have been acknowledged earlier – was the fact that pilots noted the brightness of the torches of the reception committee.* The Lysander and the Hudson were the two planes most commonly used for landing operations. The RAF ran special courses to teach agents the exact requirements for landing grounds, whether for parachutists or actual planes: principally, away from any buildings or German outposts, and with landing, taxi-ing and take-off avenues of a minimum of 600 yards in length with smooth and firm surfaces. The reception committee would form a lit shape of the letter 'L' to indicate to the pilot where to land and turn. Apart from incoming personnel the reception committee would also collect parachuted containers which were hinged all down one side and opened like a pea pod when the catches were unfastened. Inside there were three short, fat, cylindrical canisters which contained the equipment. They were heavy and had two wire handles for carrying: 'Those wire handles are the most horrible finger-cutters in the world!'[9]

Errors in the selection of landing grounds were legendary. For example, Peter Churchill suffered two failures in his efforts to be extracted from France. In the first case he discovered at the last minute that the field selected was unsuitable because it was bisected by a five-foot-high bank and a drainage ditch and so the landing had to be called off. On the second occasion it was noticed, again late in the day, that the Germans had unexpectedly sited an anti-aircraft battery 1,200 yards from the field. Even the

* See Chapter 17.

final and ultimately successful pick-up was not without adventure when it was found that piles of bricks had been strewn all over the field. The reception committee cleared the landing path but failed to consider the return path, forcing the Hudson to slalom between piles of bricks to reach the original landing strip. The plane then got stuck in a bog and two horses had to be found to pull it out. The Hudson eventually took off successfully minus thirty inches off the end of a wing which had got caught in the trees.[10]

Such problems were usually rare since the RAF demanded that once a suitable field had been selected, its location and description should be radioed to London, and the field would only be approved for use once a reconnaissance plane had photographed it and the RAF in London agreed on its suitability. These requirements could lead to difficulties if the agent was operating in an area where suitable landing strips were few and far between and the preparation of a visible one would be equally obvious to a German overflight. Denys Hamson received a message from Cairo while he was in Greece ordering him to find a suitable landing strip 1,400 yards long by 100 yards wide for a Dakota military transport plane to land on. He identified a plateau which was ideal except that it was bisected by a large stream with tributaries and irrigation ditches. Hamson arranged for the streams and ditches to be filled in but quickly realized that the landing ground had become obvious since it 'showed a dull uniform continuous brown against the colours and patterns of the meadows and fields around'. His solution was to cut down firs about three metres high and 'plant' them in the ground at irregular intervals and remove them only when a flight was expected. He was so successful that the RAF in Cairo initially rejected the field because a photograph had shown it to be 'full of hillocks, scrub, small trees and other obstacles'. Only when Hamson explained his system of camouflage and the RAF dropped a bomber pilot to supervise operations was the landing strip passed for use.[11]

Given the high risks involved in low-level flying operations and landing on makeshift landing strips there were remarkably few casualties. In France, for example, thirteen Lysanders were completely written off and six Lysander pilots were killed, but no Hudsons were lost, out of an approximate total of 280 Lysander and 44 Hudson sorties.[12]

Agent insertion by sea was carried out using feluccas, caiques, fishing boats, and submarines. British submarines landed the first agents in Crete and also the first agent in Yugoslavia before Admiral Andrew Cunningham, the commander-in-chief in the Mediterranean, cancelled further such operations on the grounds of risk in mid-1942. Agent landings in Crete were continued by the use of the Greek submarine *Papanikolis* and a fleet of motorboats.[13] Sea operations to the Mediterranean coast of France were severely curtailed after the German invasion of the south. Sea operations were extremely vulnerable to German air and naval patrols, as is demonstrated by the story of the 'Shetland Bus' which ran between Britain and Norway. The winter of 1941–42 proved to be the high point of these clandestine sailings using Norwegian fishing boats. The Germans increased the number of naval patrols and reduced the supply of diesel to the fishing fleets, which forced them to remain in domestic waters whereas previously they had sailed further out to provide cover for the incoming vessels from Shetland. An increasing rate of losses among these vessels in late 1942 and early 1943 led to the conclusion that the days of using fishing vessels were over. Fortunately, in late 1943 OSS supplied SOE with three American submarine chasers. These were faster than fishing boats and being armed meant that they could defend themselves from German attack. This led to a notable increase in the number of operations. Whereas in the 1941–42 and 1942–43 seasons the fishing flotilla had carried out eighty operations, landing sixty-two agents and 165 tons of stores at the cost of the loss of eight boats and nearly fifty lives, the advent of the submarine chasers in the 1943–44 and 1944–45 seasons increased the total to 114 operations which landed 128 agents and 220 tons of stores with no losses.[14]

Once on the ground, an SOE agent had to adapt quickly in order to blend in with the local population, and SOE claimed to prepare its agents thoroughly with the correct clothing and papers. Clothes were collected from refugees who received new ones in return. When this supply dried up, tailors and dressmakers were employed to make clothes in continental styles. Agents, however, reported many errors. Dutch agents noted that the suits they were issued with were unmistakably of an English cut and style, and that they were also given wristwatches which were unobtainable in the Netherlands. Similar errors were reported from Belgium, including the crime of smoking British cigarettes. A member of the *Armia Krajowa* in Poland noted that he had to confiscate Yardley perfumes and British cigarettes from the two agents he received. Agents were supposed to be searched before leaving to check that they were not carrying any evidence of having been in Britain. There were, however, failures which could have cost an agent his life. One agent only realized when preparing his laundry that his pyjamas carried the label 'Harrods – The Man's Shop'. Another agent was already in France when he found an English penny in the turn-ups of his trousers, and yet another found that his washbag was emblazoned with his code name. Tony Brooks was outraged at being greeted by recently arrived radio operator Marcus Bloom with ''Ow are yer, mate?' in English when Brooks had taken pains to conceal his origins. Bloom's conduct was made worse by his appearance, wearing a check suit with plus-four trousers and a pork-pie hat. Brooks refused to work with him. Sources vary on Bloom's efficiency as a radio operator, but when he was caught transmitting by the Germans he at least remained silent under interrogation. Even experienced agents could make errors. Peter Churchill was not subjected to a search before landing in France for his third mission, but after landing by parachute he checked his wallet and to his horror found a ten-shilling note and *The Times* crossword that he had cut out the previous day.[15]

Everyone living in occupied Europe had to carry with them a considerable amount of paperwork consisting of an identity card, ration books, and papers of employment. For male agents it became increasingly important to have paperwork to show that they were exempt from forced labour. Agents leaving an occupied country brought examples of the paperwork with them and SOE proved very successful in replicating these papers. There were some exceptions, however. The Dutch identity card was especially difficult to copy: 'The sophisticated design made use of specially prepared paper, various unusual inks and a complicated, almost foolproof, printing technique.' As the quality of paper deteriorated across Europe SOE faced the challenge of finding suitably poor paper to create identity cards. Gradually the practice was adopted of sending agents with a set of papers to use immediately on arrival plus a photograph so that local forgeries could be made as soon as possible. These photographs had to correspond to the requirements in each country; for example, in Poland the photograph had to show the left ear exposed.[16]

All agents were offered the option of carrying a cyanide pill with them in order to be able to commit suicide rather than face torture. It was very much a personal decision whether or not to carry the pill. Some abhorred the idea of suicide but to others the possession of such a pill was reassuring. Flemming Muus dropped his pill soon after landing in Denmark: 'I searched feverishly for it, and luck was with me: I found it . . . The thought of losing the moral support which one finds in being able to take one's own life was overwhelming. The pill was certainty; it would always be doubtful whether one could reach one's pistol in time.'[17]

Agents adapted in differing degrees to the challenges of operating in occupied Europe. Anne-Marie Walters wrote later: 'It took me nearly three weeks to shake off this form of self-consciousness and to get over the idea that I had "British agent" written all over my face.'[18] Some agents reported feelings of boredom: 'You might spend six weeks hanging about, trying to be inconspicuous, just for the sake of an hour's work which, if it went according to plan, was not very exciting in any case.'[19] Couriers, on the other hand, complained of exhaustion: 'The job of a courier was terribly, terribly, terribly tiring. It was mostly travelling by night. We never wrote and we never phoned. Any messages were taken from A to B and the territory we were working on was really very big, because apart from Paris we had Châteauroux, Montluçon, down to Toulouse, from Toulouse to Tarbes, up to Poitiers. It meant mostly travelling by night and the trains were unheated.'[20]

Spontaneous help for agents in a difficult situation came about more often as the tide of the war began to turn against the Germans and the occupied peoples became more resistance-minded. Wanda Skwirut, a courier in Poland, was travelling by train with a suitcase containing a radio and pistol. A companion offered to put her suitcase on the rack above the seats and noticed that the suitcase was heavier than he had expected. When he left the train at the following station she feared that he was going to inform on her. Far from it, he reappeared carrying a single red rose and advised her to leave the train at the second station before Warsaw because the Germans had set up a control point at the penultimate stop.[21] Rémy, the Free French BCRA intelligence agent, reported that one agent was carrying a radio when he faced a German check at the railway station. He noticed a young boy dragging a heavy suitcase and asked him to swap suitcases to pass the control point. After both had successfully passed through, 'Leon remarked that it was a good thing that they hadn't opened his case because of the radio inside. The boy replied that it was good that they hadn't opened his case because it was full of hand grenades and revolvers.'[22] As liberation approached, agents found that they were warmly welcomed. Francis Cammaerts explained why: 'We were so sheltered by our French friends for whom we were the angel Gabriel. We came with communication with the outside world. We came to help them get over the shame of 1940, nothing more important than that. And so they wouldn't allow us to do anything which put us in danger. They risked everything . . .'[23] Anne-Marie Walters discovered that 'the right to be part of the Resistance and to shelter anything clandestine was an honour to almost everyone I met'.[24]

Agents operating in western Europe and Poland had an enormous advantage over those sent to the Balkans: the terrain, language, and appearance of the locals was familiar to them, while in the Balkans everything was alien. Denys Hamson on the first British mission to Greece recorded his first meeting with a guerrilla:

> They might have stepped out of illustrations of books on the Greek Revolution of 1821. They all wore Greek national dress with the baggy trousers of rough dark material, and one wore a bright red fez on his head. Their hair

> hung down unkempt over their shoulders, their beards nearly to their waists. Their chests were criss-crossed with cartridge belts full of ammunition, and their belts studded with revolvers and old-fashioned daggers.[25]

In Yugoslavia Michael Lees wrote of the first Partisan he encountered:

> He was a short stocky creature dressed in a broadly cut jacket and knicker-bocker breeches of heavy dark cloth; his feet were bare and his body was festooned with cross belts stuffed with ammunition. Three grenades and a murderous looking knife were suspended from his belt, another knife hung under his arm, and he carried an ancient rifle some five feet long slung over one shoulder.[26]

The equipment and armaments of the guerrillas also drew comment. Monty Woodhouse noted that of Colonel Napoleon Zervas's troops: 'Few had any military uniform. Even fewer had boots: leather slippers, strips of goatskin tied round their ankles, slices of rubber tyre fastened with wire, in some cases nothing but threadbare socks.' Some had weapons captured from the Italians but most rifles were of pre-First World War vintage.[27] Lees noted the mixed armament of the Partisans with weapons appropriated from German, Italian, Yugoslav, and Bulgarian sources leading to a logistical nightmare as all those weapons required different calibres of ammunition. The problem of ammunition supply was one reason why the Sten gun, though inaccurate over a distance and prone to jamming, was so widely distributed to the resistance movements everywhere: the Sten fired 9mm Luger ammunition which was easily available.[28]

Some British officers in the Balkans 'turned native'. When Bill Bailey arrived at the headquarters of the Četnik resistance leader Draža Mihailović, he was appalled to find that British officers had adopted the Četnik habit of not shaving. In the Četniks' case the reason was the tradition of not shaving when the country was under foreign occupation, but Bailey felt that the British officers had no excuse for following that particular local tradition and ordered them to shave immediately.[29] George Psychoundakis noted of Xan Fielding that 'in Cretan dress he passed as a Cretan a hundred per cent' whereas when Jack Smith-Hughes wore Cretan dress he was immediately obvious as an Englishman.[30] In Albania, David Smiley wore 'corduroy trousers, Albanian sandals with Alpini studs in the soles, a khaki shirt, a jersey or battledress blouse according to the weather, with a white Albanian fez'. He watched the arrival of the mission under 'Trotsky' Davies with utter amazement: 'We were flabbergasted by the amount of kit they brought, which included a quantity of camp furniture and two containers of stationery; one of the new NCOs was a clerk, complete with typewriter.'

Davies immediately ordered the British officers to dress as British officers and to discard their local apparel.[31]

Few British officers were totally familiar with the language of the country in which they were operating and this predictably had a detrimental effect on establishing working relationships with the guerrillas. Peter Kemp noted that Albanian was a very difficult to language to learn:

> Few of us managed to learn it, which was a great hindrance to our work in the field; unable to converse directly with the inhabitants we were nearly always dependent upon interpreters, whom we could trust neither to render faithfully our own words nor to give us a true picture of local reactions.[32]

Monty Woodhouse endeared himself to the Greeks not only through his ability to speak their language, at first ancient rather than modern Greek, but also because he told them tales of their ancient history they had not known before.[33] OSS agents often had an advantage over their British counterparts in that many were sourced from recent immigrants to the United States. George Musulin made himself popular with the Četniks: 'He occasionally indulged into singing popular songs, and while they were totally unknown to me, some old-timer jumped in excitement, remembering having heard them from his grandmother or great-grandmother.'[34]

Living in the Balkans presented another challenge. Although there were occasions when the British agents had comfortable quarters in towns and villages, many of them lived a troglodytic life in caves. In summer this was not too difficult, leading one man to muse: 'It was curious how quickly you became fond of a cave . . . in fact I felt more sentimentally nostalgic about caves than about former homes.'[35] In winter, however, the existence was miserable since no fire could be lit in case the smoke gave away the position and movement was also difficult since footprints left in the snow would also reveal the location of the cave.[36] For some agents such a lifestyle could become overwhelming. Gerry Field was in charge of the SOE Albania headquarters situated in a cave called Seaview situated at the elbow end of the Karaburun Peninsula. Field hated the Albanians of every political hue and found life in a cave, from which it took six to eight hours of climbing to reach the road, unbearably isolating. He was eventually evacuated to Italy after wounding himself while fishing with grenades.[37]

Working alongside guerrillas, even discounting the political dimension, presented challenges. The maps of Albania, for example, dated from before the Italian occupation and did not include the roads and bridges built by the Italians. Agents such as Peter Kemp soon learned that it was impossible to move around Albania without a guide:

> For although our maps were good enough they did not show the countless tiny tracks which branched in every direction over the mountains; nor, if we left the tracks, could we have moved very far across that savage terrain, even with the best of compasses; on a long journey it might be necessary to change the guide once or twice a day.[38]

'Trotsky' Davies, however, found that the local guides were unreliable. A river crossing failed because the guide he had employed turned out never to have crossed the river although he had lived beside it all his life. Davies then insisted 'that we should lead the column with map and compass. The partisans were as suspicious of the compass as we were of the guides, with the difference that the compass led us correctly.'[39] Nor were the guerrillas themselves any more competent on operations. Stanley Moss recalled that two attempts to ambush the Germans in Greece failed: the first because the *andartes* (resistance fighters) had forgotten to load their guns, and the second because they were having breakfast when the Germans arrived and were out of position.[40] Davies recalled his feelings of frustration at the Albanian habit of firing off prodigious amounts of a limited supply of ammunition at any occasion for celebration: be it a wedding, a circumcision or a funeral.[41]

Yet the appearance of the British mission was welcomed by the guerrillas. As William Deakin wrote of meeting the Partisans in Yugoslavia: 'We represented a symbolic link with the world outside and our physical presence was a token recognition, breaking the isolation, for the first time, of our new companions.'[42] Also in Yugoslavia, Jasper Rootham expanded on this feeling, writing of a supply drop:

> In the flickering light of the fires there darted to and fro the bearded, long-haired figures of the Četniks and there passed us, creaking and groaning on the steep hillside, a wooden cart pulled by two sleepy, docile oxen. It was piled high with containers full of rifles and ammunition. The contrast between this lovely European landscape and the sandy desert I had just left, between the great Liberator roaring overhead and the poor little ox-cart, was so intense that for a moment I hardly believed it was real . . . I felt sentimentally proud that it was a British aeroplane which was disappearing over the crest of the nearby hill. The ox-cart with its rifles seemed a symbol of Serb defiance to the German invader, and the aeroplane a symbol of British power, good faith and Victory.[43]

But Basil Davidson added a word of caution, warning from the outset that the Partisans were fiercely independent and felt bound to no one and to no country just because its agents and aircraft supplied them with weapons.[44]

The quantity of these supplies was a sore point with the agents and the resisters alike. As Lord Ismay told SOE as early as April 1941: 'The COS [Chiefs of Staff] are at present faced with the problem of having to feed many hungry mouths with bread, on which the butter has to be spread very sparingly.'[45] The debates between SOE and the Chiefs of Staff on this issue raged throughout 1942 and 1943, and can be summarized by the July 1943 memo from Charles Portal, chief of the air staff: 'I feel that it would be a serious mistake to divert any more aircraft to supply Resistance Groups in western Europe which will only be of *potential* value next year when these aircraft could be of *immediate and actual* value in accelerating the defeat of Germany by direct attack.' In 1943 SOE had access to only fifty-eight converted bombers, of which thirty-two served in the Balkans, sixteen in western Europe, four in Italy and southern France, and six in Poland and the Protectorate. The situation only improved significantly in the early months of 1944.[46] The inability to obtain sufficient supplies made life difficult for the SOE agents on the ground. For example, in Yugoslavia, Rootham noted the disbelief felt by the Četniks: 'Major, you tell me that the whole of the British Empire can only spare four aeroplanes for this work of supplying the Yugoslav Army in the Fatherland. I am sure that you think you are telling the truth, but you will forgive me if I say that I do not believe you.'[47] Davidson wrote of the Partisans: 'On the issue of supplies they thought in terms of our huge bomber strength and saw our delay in political, not military terms. If we could bombard Germany with five hundred Liberators we could drop them as many tons of machine guns and mortars and boots and battledress – and, if not, then where was the proof of our sincerity?'[48] The Poles too made great efforts to secure more planes for supply missions to Poland, making desperate appeals in both London and Washington.[49] Both the Yugoslav Partisans and the Polish AK were convinced that the lack of supplies was a politically motivated decision and was not due to the actual lack of long-distance aircraft.

The poor supply situation in the Balkans was compounded by outright crassness on the part of SOE in Cairo. Supplies despatched to the Balkans included: atrabin, which was an anti-malarial drug, and anti-snake bite serum, neither of which was needed there; a load of boots just for left feet; a load of boots size 6 suitable only for children; and 30 million Italian occupation lire overprinted with 'Ethiopia'.[50] In Greece, Hamson bitterly noted that when medicine was sent for Brigadier Eddie Myers who had pneumonia, 'there was a large container marked in illiterate Greek, the English counterpart of which would have been "For the seeck Colonello". It seemed incredible to us that, if it *had* to be marked in Greek, our base organisation could not have found somebody to write the language correctly.'[51] The Greek *andartes* 'soon found out that the red container was the one with the comforts in and they went for that first and if you weren't quick they had the red container hidden under the bushes or somewhere and you just didn't get your comforts'.[52] Davies noted that Enver Hoxha was furious at the supplies received in Albania which on one occasion 'delivered mail, lots of explosives and grenades, but no food or ammunition, a few Sten guns and some special winter clothing' for the British party. This at the time when many of the resistance fighters were barefoot and dying for lack of medicine.[53] In France where the supplies were more abundant, there was enough to share with the resisters: 'In among the munitions are some of the all-important comforts: cigarettes, tobacco, slabs of chocolate, a jar of butter, a few tins of food. You hand out a small ration to each and a wonderful human relationship is established between the mysterious HQ in London and the local recruits. They are ready to believe that Winston Churchill himself had the cigarettes put in.'[54]

There were widespread complaints about the inaccuracy of airdrops. In Crete, Sandy Rendel reported that the airdrops were spread over such a wide area that of the thirty-two containers Cairo notified him had been dropped, only sixteen were recovered.[55] Psychoundakis recalled one airdrop landing in the forest and 'when day broke, the whole forest seemed to be garlanded with parachutes, which had settled like great white doves on the tree tops gently beating their wings and making the tall woods look still more beautiful in the light of daybreak'.[56] Fielding was so outraged at the apparent inability of the RAF to drop supplies in the correct place that when on leave in Cairo he took part in one such supply drop. He was soon overcome with admiration at the skills of the RAF:

> To get out of the range of the guns we swooped low beyond the nearest protective ridge, and to me it seemed the surrounding peaks now towered above us. But even at this height I could not distinguish between the separate blazes – shepherd's fires, no doubt – that dotted each slope. It was the captain of the aircraft who picked out on the horizon a glare brighter than the others. We steered towards it, and in less than a minute I could clearly see the bonfires arranged in the pattern which we had been notified to expect.[57]

Silk for parachutes was in extremely short supply, with the RAF and USAAF taking the bulk of the available material. This meant that SOE Algiers began using parachutes made from Egyptian cotton which were prone to failure. A furious Francis Cammaerts radioed back the consequences when one such parachute failure had led to a container landing on the house of a member of the reception committee, breaking the back of his mother.[58] In Yugoslavia experiments were made with free drops – without parachutes – of supplies that would not be damaged by a hard landing. Fitzroy Maclean noted wryly: 'These called for considerable agility on the part of those on the ground: a hundred pairs of ammunition boots whistling through the air at a hundred miles an hour, their fall unbroken by a parachute, were a serious menace to life and limb.'[59]

Waiting for supplies to come was extremely dispiriting: 'I well remember those winter nights, palely lit by the snow that covered everything, when we waited in the intense cold from nine in the evening until five in the morning.'[60] Sometimes enemy action frustrated the RAF's attempts to drop supplies, as when, in Albania, David Smiley was waiting for a Halifax bomber to make a supply drop when an Italian aircraft appeared on the scene:

> I luckily heard it coming and recognised the engine as that of a Caproni and not one of ours. I shouted to the partisans on the dropping ground to clear off and take cover which they did . . . It was really a fantastic sight as the Halifax and the Caproni were taking alternate runs dropping supplies and bombs but they never appeared to see each other.[61]

Those supply drops which failed did so either because the reception committee was unable to get to the field in time or because the pilot failed to see the signals from the committee.

The principal task of the SOE agents was to build up networks, yet the initial reports made depressing reading, from France in particular. Tony Brooks, on his second mission in 1942, struggled to arrange a reception committee for a supply drop: 'I had to use the whole of my first circuit for my first parachute drop because there weren't any bloody volunteers to come and stick their necks out to come and get the containers.'[62] In January 1942 Emmanuel d'Astier ruefully noted that after three months searching for recruits in socialist and trade union circles, 'I had found five disinterested people who were prepared to act without counting the cost and take a deliberate chance rather than resign themselves to the ignominy of a profitable conformity.'[63] Such lack of resistance spirit in the Unoccupied Zone was confirmed in the same month by a report written by the *France Libre* network for the BCRA: 'The people have gone back to their normal activity and very few are considering resisting either the Germans or the government. Proportion of collaborators is quite strong. The majority are counting on the English, and lately the Russians, to chase the Germans from France.'[64] Alfred Newton landed in France in June 1942 expecting 2,000 men waiting impatiently in Marseille for training and weapons, but on reaching the city found only five recruits from among the dockers, of whom only one was any good.[65] Despite these reports and in order to preserve SOE's existence, the new head of SOE, Lord Selborne, wrote up the prospects of a large French resistance army, surreally claiming, for example, that Philippe de Vomécourt had succeeded in building up a network of 20,000 men by February 1942.[66]

Such reports may explain why SOE became so disastrously involved in the so-called Carte affair which took up a disproportionate amount of time in 1942. The real name of Carte was André Girard, a painter living on the Côte d'Azur. He claimed to have extensive contacts within the resistance and especially with the Armistice Army. Carte's list of contacts appeared to offer the prospect of a ready-made secret army in France that could be activated at the opportune moment. In August 1942 Nicolas Bodington was landed in the south to make contact with Carte. Bodington was later described by Cammaerts as 'a rogue ... What he'd done in France had created a lot of death.'[67] Bodington was completely convinced about Carte's sincerity and Peter Churchill was appointed as British liaison officer to Carte in late August. Churchill was delighted with the extent of Carte's contacts but appalled by his utter lack of even the basic elements of security. Carte kept a list of the members of his network in extensive detail – sixty-one paragraphs in total – which covered the names, addresses, telephone numbers, appearance, experience, specialities, capabilities, etc., of everyone he met, all set out on forms. These forms were generally kept in Carte's study, masquerading as a list of clients, but were also carried by some of his supporters. It was this last point that led to the downfall of Carte. In November 1942 André Marsac was carrying a briefcase containing the forms of 200 of the most important members of the network by train from Marseille to Paris. He fell asleep on the train and his briefcase was stolen by an Abwehr agent.

It is not clear precisely whom Marsac informed about his loss but it is clear that it precipitated divisions within the Carte network. Churchill noted that Carte's excessive demands for equipment and armaments sent by radio in lengthy messages created conflict:

> Doubts as to Carte's efficacy as a leader began to form themselves in certain minds, but so great were his zest, his optimism, personality and driving power that ... all such disloyal thoughts and open criticisms amongst themselves simply vanished into thin air under his dynamic presence.[68]

In January 1943 Carte was subjected to a trial of honour, and the movement split between Carte, who still believed that he could build an army, and his former deputy, Henri Frager, who urged more action immediately, particularly in the wake of the November 1942 German invasion of the

Unoccupied Zone. After several abortive attempts Carte was finally extracted from France in March 1943, but on his arrival in Britain neither SOE nor the Free French wanted to have anything more to do with him and he departed for the United States.[69] The Carte episode had achieved nothing of any value, but its failures stemming from the loss of Marsac's briefcase would have an enormously detrimental effect on SOE in the course of 1943.

This was not SOE's only mistake in its search for ready-made secret armies. Georges Duboudin, for example, claimed to have 20,000 men ready to launch a great sabotage campaign once they had received supplies. Virginia Hall failed to convince London that this was a fantasy; she kept her own agents apart from Duboudin's despite his demands to take them over. Peter Churchill also reported Duboudin's unreliability to London. Despite these reports, London preferred to believe Duboudin and sent him both weapons and assistants. One of the latter was Robert Boiteux, who arrived in May 1942. Boiteux had such trouble working with Duboudin that Duboudin was recalled to London in October, and left France without revealing the location of his resistance army to Boiteux, who soon discovered that no such army existed. Indeed, at least 75 per cent of the weapons supplied by SOE to Duboudin ended up in rivers when the Germans invaded the south. Boiteux himself also found recruitment difficult. SOE had given him the name of a contact in Marseille who claimed to have an army of 3,000 men in the city but when questioned about them: 'He got a pencil and paper and started scratching his head, wrote down one name, scratched his head again, wrote down another name. Took him about 20 minutes. He wrote down 14 names. There were no 3,000 men; there was no Maquis.' SOE appeared to have been hoodwinked again. Boiteux then related an amusing story of how the resistance in Marseille was trained:

> Nobody volunteered to give up their house or lodgings. We found a man who wanted to be in the resistance, the manager of the local zoo, and he let us use one of the cages, the bear cage, which was divided in two. Halfway along the bear cage there was a fence, an iron fence, to separate the bears from us and I was doing the training in the bear cage with the bears looking through, very nosy and very interested.[70]

SOE had focused so much attention on the Carte network because of Carte's links with France's Armistice Army. The prospect of a ready-made army of 100,000 trained and armed men naturally appealed to British planners who hoped to use it. Yet when the Germans invaded the Unoccupied Zone in November 1942 as a result of the Anglo-American landings, Operation Torch, in North Africa, the Armistice Army proved a great disappointment: 'The army was disoriented and damaged; it did not move against the enemy.'[71] Only General Jean de Lattre de Tassigny decided to march his forces towards the Pyrenees in the hope of crossing the mountains and continuing the fight from French North Africa. He was caught, later escaped in September 1943, and would eventually lead the French 1st Army back into France in August 1944. The resistance was outraged by the conduct of the Armistice Army: 'It refused to give the arms it had camouflaged to the Resistance, but either threw them into rivers and ponds or surrendered them.'[72] Indeed, Émile Mollard, the officer who had led the movement to conceal the weapons back in 1940, reported:

> At that moment, great fear took hold throughout the southern zone. It was a race to see who could get rid of the weapons and materiel the fastest . . . Even those who didn't dare declare their depots shouted out in cafes: 'I have a depot, and I will not declare it', so that their neighbours would spread the word and discharge them of all responsibility.[73]

In direct contrast, the French Navy efficiently scuttled itself on 27 November when the Germans entered the naval base at Toulon.

The imminent arrival of the Germans meant that Virginia Hall, who had done so much to help SOE become established in France, had to flee the country since the Germans knew too much about her. As the enemy reached Lyon, Virginia had already got to the foot of the Pyrenees and began the climb to freedom across the highest pass. On her way she sent a message to London: 'Cuthbert is being tiresome, but I can cope.' The person who received the message had no idea that Cuthbert was Virginia's false leg and replied: 'If Cuthbert is tiresome, have him eliminated.'[74] Some French prison commandants released captured SOE agents, including Francis Basin and Denis Rake, rather than hand them over to the Germans. SOE and other Allied agents witnessed the arrival of the Germans and Italians in the Unoccupied Zone. On 11 November the Alliance agent Marie-Madeleine Fourcade was driving to Avignon and saw a German car, the vanguard of the occupation force: 'The officer seated by the driver was reading a large map spread across his knees. They were completely unprotected. They were quite at home, like masters.'[75] Boiteux was intensely frustrated:

> Night and day for the next seventy-two hours or so, the streets of Lyon reverberated with the rumble of truck-loads of German soldiers, with their stores and heavy artillery. I found myself in an unenviable spot: without a radio, I could not contact London about my urgent need for more supplies and, particularly, money. Even worse, I could not inform SOE of the location and strength of our newly arrived foreign 'guests'.[76]

George Starr observed the arrival of the Italian Army: 'I remember one morning we woke up and the Italians had landed and marched into Cannes. I watched them through the window. We were on the main road. The Italians were in lorries, playing mandolins.'[77] Peter Churchill was appalled to hear from London that 'On no account are you to impede the Italian occupation.' The reasoning in London was that the Italians were less able to interfere in SOE operations than the Germans.

SOE's main purpose before the Allies were in a position to invade Europe was sabotage. The principal objective of sabotage was to damage the German war economy, and the secondary one was to show people both that a resistance existed and that it was hitting back against the occupiers. The governments-in-exile were concerned about the effect sabotage would have on their countries' infrastructure and this danger was noted by the resistance. A leader of a sabotage group in Belgium, G. Burgers, expressed the dilemma:

> Destruction of a factory should be neither total nor permanent since this would entail deportation of the labour force to the Reich whilst partial but effective destruction kept the workers in the factory; the time required for repairs added to the stoppage of production implied a serious loss to the enemy.[78]

The governments-in-exile were also worried about the German threat of reprisals against the local population as a result of SOE activity. For example, the Norwegian government-in-exile had been horrified by the German reprisals after the commando raids on the Lofoten Islands at the end of 1941 and began to demand a greater say in British actions in Norway. The result was the establishment of the Anglo-Norwegian Collaboration Committee (ANCC) in London in February 1942, with members drawn from SOE and the Norwegian government; SOE's Norway Section was also reorganized and Colonel John Wilson became its head. At that time SOE was under orders to avoid *Milorg* on the ground that *Milorg*'s security was poor. The Norwegians objected to this policy on a number of reasonable grounds, pointing out that in a thinly populated country like Norway it was not feasible to have two separate resistance movements operating at the same time in the same area without one compromising the activities of the other. They pointed out that far from *Milorg* having endangered SOE's operations, the reverse was true. For example, SOE operations in Trøndelag and northern Norway against the Glomfjord power station and the Fosdalen mines had led to the Germans imposing a state of emergency which forced *Milorg* to call a virtual halt to its own activities. By September 1942 SOE was prepared to alter its attitude towards *Milorg*, recognizing the fact that 'Norway had the men, Great Britain had the facilities for training, transport and supply an experience drawn from a wider field; united they stood; divided, they would have fallen.' The benefits of the ANCC and SOE–*Milorg* cooperation would be demonstrated in an operation to be described in the following chapter, against the heavy-water plant at Vemork.[79]

SOE agents were well aware of the necessity of avoiding reprisals against innocent civilians. Peter Kemp expressed the dilemma: 'If we were to do our job properly we were bound to put innocent people in jeopardy; they had to stay and face reprisals while we found safety in flight.'[80] Efforts were made in the Balkans to leave evidence for the Germans showing who was responsible, for example: 'Empty ration boxes were generally left on the site of our sabotage exploits to induce the Germans to put the blame on us instead of wrecking the nearest Albanian homestead or village.'[81] The success of such behaviour generally varied according to the level of repression being waged by the Germans. In France, for example, where the level of repression was far lower than in the east, the Germans were willing to accept that SOE saboteurs were responsible and to leave the local population untouched, or to blame the RAF if there had been an air raid in the locality at the time. But in the east, German repression was untrammelled by any boundaries and life was viewed as cheap.

Both Norway and Yugoslavia contained mines of precious minerals essential to the German war economy. Mines were particularly vulnerable to sabotage since very little equipment was needed in order to cause such severe damage that production would be significantly slowed if not halted totally. Actions against mines in Norway were routinely carried out by Norwegian SOE agents landing by ship or air to sabotage specific targets. The results could be spectacular: the sabotage of the pyrite mines at Orkla cut production by half for six months and the attack on the pyrite mines on Stord, near Bergen, resulted in damage so severe that it was over two years and after the liberation when production even reached 30 per cent of the pre-raid total.[82] In Yugoslavia an attack on the Lissa antimony mine by the Četniks wrecked the 100-metre-long leather belt that propelled the main drive shaft and took the belt. The Germans replaced the belt and increased the number of guards, but further minor sabotage and desertions among the workforce ultimately rendered the mine useless. The raid had the useful side-effect of supplying the Četniks with a lot of much needed leather to repair their boots.[83]

Examples abound in France of operations which halted production in factories for periods of up to six months. In late 1941 Philippe Liewer's Salesman circuit succeeded in damaging the transformers feeding electricity to the Rouen area as well as hitting the electric motors in a steel plant which stopped production for six months. As more circuits were formed and supplies of explosives received, sabotage operations increased in both numbers and effectiveness. In June 1943 the Headmaster circuit led by Sydney Hudson set explosives in the Michelin factory in Clermont-Ferrand which led to a forty-eight-hour-long fire which destroyed 36,000 used tyres. In August two sabotage groups, operating independently from each other, hit the transformers at the Hispano-Suiza factory in Tarbes on the same night. In September, Maurice Southgate's Stationer circuit cut the electricity to the aluminium works at Lannemezan, which led to molten aluminium solidifying in the ovens.[84]

Transport systems were highly vulnerable to sabotage. RF Section circuits were especially active in operations against locks and dams on the French waterways. For example, an attack in August 1943 on the vital lock at La Javacière on the Canal de Briare immobilized 3,400 barges and led to a three-month hold-up of traffic on the canal. The same circuit destroyed two locks on the Marne-au-Rhin canal, blocking traffic for six weeks. Another circuit focused its attention on the dams on the Saône river, where the first operation against the Gigny dam took the Germans three months to repair, whereupon the resistance destroyed it again.[85]

Tony Brooks set up the Pimento circuit in the Unoccupied Zone in the summer of 1942. SOE's ban on causing bangs in the zone was still operative, but Brooks recruited a number of railwaymen and resisters for a large-scale axle-doping programme whereby carborundum powder mixed with grease would damage the bearings and cause the axles to seize up. In November 1942 the ban on bangs was lifted and the railwaymen and resisters were instructed on how to place explosive charges on the rails in order to cause a derailment.[86] In the north, the Farmer circuit of railwaymen under Michael Trotobas was busy disrupting rail traffic through Lille. The circuit's activities included the destruction of seven petrol tankers parked in a siding near Lille, the sabotage of freight trains passing through the area, and explosions in rail workshops.[87] Elsewhere railway water towers were targeted: an attack on one at Ussel limited traffic along the line for six weeks.[88] The Belgian resistance also attacked the railways. For example, operations around Louvain in July 1943 derailed two trains which killed around 250 German officers and men and blocked the lines out of Louvain for eight days.[89]

Attacks on the railway lines were easy to repair and the Germans became very well practised in carrying out these repairs. But what these attacks on the railway lines showed was that they were relatively easy and risk-free to carry out and had good short-term effectiveness. For the SOE planners in London this offered hopes that the railway network in France could genuinely be paralysed by the resistance on the eve of and after D-Day. On that occasion the sabotage would need to be on a very large scale and widespread. The effectiveness of such coordinated attacks was demonstrated by Operation Wieniec launched by the AK in October 1942. The AK aimed for the simultaneous sabotage of all seven railway lines passing through Warsaw carrying reinforcements and supplies to the Eastern Front; the sabotage succeeded in blocking six lines. Thereafter the AK continued the sabotage of the rail system and, for example, over the period from June 1942 to January 1943 they destroyed 1,268 locomotives and 3,318 railway carriages and wagons, derailed trains, and blew up bridges.[90]

The apparent effectiveness of sabotage carried out by SOE circuits has led to the controversial argument that SOE was more successful in putting a factory out of operation than the RAF was by bombing it.[91] This was true to a limited extent in the case of the Fives-Lille locomotive construction and repair works, the second largest in France. The RAF had bombed it four times between October 1942 and January 1943, causing little damage to the works, but casualties among the civilians living nearby. Trotobas was asked to help. He realized that the local workforce might be unwilling to assist him, both because of resentment at the RAF bombing and out of fear that the destruction of their plant would mean the loss of their jobs and therefore deportation to Germany as forced labour. Trotobas therefore put together a specialized team and even persuaded the cousin of one of his assistants to gain employment at the works in order to scout for targets. Trotobas visited the site himself, dressed as a workman. The operation was carried out in June 1943, the central control room and switchboard were set on fire and important transformers and circuit breakers were destroyed, along with 4 million litres of oil. The damage was less than had been hoped for, and post-war investigation revealed that production was never stopped entirely and was back to normal after four days.[92]

The case of the Peugeot works in Montbéliard near Besançon was more clear-cut. On 14 July 1943 the RAF attempted to bomb the factory which was producing tracks and engines for German tanks, but largely missed hitting it while causing heavy damage to the town of Montbéliard and killing a number of French civilians. Two SOE agents witnessed the damage, Henry Rée and Raymond Basset. Rée arranged an appointment with Rodolphe Peugeot and suggested to him that he should assist in the sabotage of his own factories. After establishing Rée's bona fides via the BBC, Peugeot agreed, gave Rée a map of the factory, pointed out the most critical machinery, and put him in contact with a foreman who he knew was a member of the resistance.

At the beginning of November 1943 the first operation was mounted against the transformer building which brought all the electricity into the factory and the assembly hall. Rée later gave details of the operation by the French workmen:

> They put pistols in the pockets of their overalls and they had their explosives, plastic blocks with room for a detonator, in their pockets too. There was a wonderful carelessness about the whole thing. They were playing football with the German guards outside the transformer house – somebody had forgotten to get the key – and in playing football one of them dropped his plastic block of explosive and one of the German guards who was playing football pointed it out to him. 'You've dropped something, sir, I think'. He put it back in his pocket.[93]

The explosives were successfully placed and the power station and assembly hall with its tank parts were destroyed. The furious Germans sent the SS to investigate. Several workers were arrested, but the main sabotage team escaped, although the German hunt was so thorough that Rée had to escape to Switzerland. At Rée's instruction the French carried out further operations against the replacement presses sent from Germany to the factory. One such operation against the barge carrying a press had the useful secondary effect of blocking the Canal du Doubs which the Germans were also using to send midget submarines from the Loire to the Mediterranean.[94]

Few factory owners and managers were so prepared to assist SOE. For example, the owner of the Malin et Fils factory near Bordeaux would only consent to a small explosion:

> At four in the morning a colossal explosion wrecked the place. Turbines were flung hundreds of yards by the force of the blast. The entire shop floor was destroyed. There had never been a bigger explosion in the area.
>
> The owner was absolutely livid. He did not know to whom he should protest; it would scarcely do to tell the Germans that he had never agreed to so large a bang, while the Resistance was not prepared to accept liability.[95]

The factory was out of operation for a year. Other successful operations mounted by SOE in 1943 where the RAF had failed include the Wattelez rubber-recycling factory near Limoges, the Ratier aero factory outside Figeac near Bordeaux, and the Schneider-Creusot armaments factory near Lyon.[96]

Operation Frankton – best known as the Cockleshell raid – is an example of an operation which was undertaken by commandos but would almost certainly have been more successfully conducted by the local resistance. SOE received accurate information on the Bordeaux docks and the German cargo ships from its agent Robert Yves Marie Leroy, who returned to London at the end of May 1942. On 1 September Colin Gubbins attended a meeting of the Combined Operations' Examination Committee where plans were discussed to attack the German blockade runners in Bordeaux, but he failed to mention SOE's presence in the port. In the middle of September 1942 a new SOE organizer, Claude de Baissac, arrived in Bordeaux, and in November he received an explosives expert and a supply drop of 60lb of plastic explosive and fifteen 'clam' mines. De Baissac later reported: 'In spite of the comparative lack of material, [his network] Scientist was well on the way to organising an attack on his shipping targets by the introduction of . . . explosives through the dockers and the paint sealers working on the vessels'. Unknown to de Baissac, preparations for the commando raid under Herbert 'Blondie' Hasler had continued, and a submarine dropped Hasler and his party of Royal Marines to embark on an epic canoe paddle up the Gironde to the port of Bordeaux. On 12 December members of the Scientist network were conducting a reconnaissance of the port 'when they heard some quiet pops below the water and watched as their targets started to settle into the water under their noses'. The epic raid was a failure: the ships were empty and settled only a metre lower in the water, from which they were easily raised: only one ship had to go into a dry dock for repairs. Of the raiding party, six men were killed during the operation, two were murdered later by the Germans, and only Hasler and Bill Sparks succeeded in crossing the Pyrenees into Spain. The raid also meant that Scientist could do nothing further in the docks since the Germans immediately increased the number of guards significantly. Back in London, lessons were learned and greater cooperation between Combined Operations and SOE was instituted.[97]

On the other hand, there were some operations which were best carried out by outsiders and not the local resistance. The coastal area of France was a restricted zone where the locals needed special passes to live and work, and these restrictions naturally curtailed the existence of resistance circuits there. Therefore, the operation against the German radar station at Bruneval in February 1942 to seize equipment and cause damage was best carried out by a group parachuted in from Britain, and SOE's involvement was limited to the provision of some equipment. The operation against the dock gates at Saint-Nazaire was greatly helped by intelligence supplied by the resistance, but only the Royal Navy could bring in the 30 hundredweight of explosive needed to destroy the dock.[98] In late spring 1942 teams from the SAS and SBS were landed in Crete to attack three airfields which were shipping supplies to the Afrika Korps; the role of SOE and the local resistance was limited to acting as guides. The operation was successful in military terms in that twenty-six aircraft and a considerable quantity of supplies, including aviation fuel, were destroyed, but four members of the French SAS were betrayed, leading to the death of one and the others being taken prisoner. Despite these captures of obvious outsiders, the Germans shot fifty Cretan hostages anyway in reprisal.[99]

Sabotage carried out by SOE circuits in 1942 was still on a small scale: 176 attacks on railways and shipyards, and 115 attempts to sabotage factories and public utilities.[100] The official historian of SOE has concluded that it cannot:

> . . . be claimed that anywhere in Europe in the summer of 1942 there existed an organised fighting force taking its directives from Britain. No such force could have been organised in the time and with the means available. But in every country SOE had done something: it had shown that Britain's contribution to the Resistance did not consist solely of inspiring words from the BBC or from one of PWE's Freedom Stations [radio stations broadcasting black propaganda to Europe]. Friends had taken desperate chances to come in person; wireless links had been established; appeals for material help had been answered. All had been done inadequately and sometimes disastrously: but it had been done. It had been proved that Resistance movements could exist, could be fed, could be directed; that the will to resist was there and that the limiting factors were mainly material – more aircraft, better wireless sets, better disguise, more training in the art of conspiracy.[101]

General Gerd von Rundstedt, the German commander-in-chief in the west, reflected that during 1942 'the underground movement in France was still confined within bearable limits'.[102] The situation began to change in the course of 1943 as German policies alienated more sections of the population and greater quantities of supplies arrived from Britain. Major circuits and networks had been established across Europe, and in July 1943 Selborne could inform Churchill that there were 650 SOE agents operating throughout Europe. The Germans had of course noticed the rise in organized resistance and in 1943 were just as active in their efforts to crush it.

11

Three SOE Operations

The three operations covered in this chapter illustrated that SOE could insert a party of agents into an occupied country in order to carry out a specific operation. In all three cases, the success of the operation had controversial and unexpected consequences. Operation Anthropoid was the Czech-inspired plot to assassinate Himmler's deputy, Reinhard Heydrich, the newly appointed Reichsprotektor. The success of this operation led to such savage German reprisals against the Czech population that the attention of the world was drawn to the true nature of German rule in Europe, but it also caused long-lasting damage to resistance in the Protectorate. Operation Harling was the sabotage action against the Gorgopotamos viaduct in Greece. Its logic lay in the need to interdict the supplies reaching Rommel's Afrika Korps through the port of Piraeus during the critical late summer of 1942. It failed in that respect, but the sabotage party then was ordered to remain in place to become the nucleus of the British Military Mission to Greece. In this role SOE became involved in the convoluted politics of the Greek resistance. Operations Grouse/Swallow, Freshman, and Gunnerside targeted the Vemork heavy-water plant near Rjukan in Norway in order to prevent Germany from building an atomic bomb. Moral considerations played a part in Operation Anthropoid and the Norwegian operations. In the first case, the savage reprisals inflicted on the Czech population forced SOE and resistance movements across Europe to assess whether political assassination was an acceptable tool of resistance given the likely consequences. The case of the Norwegian operations was slightly different. The original sabotage operation against the Vemork works was justified by the need to prevent the Germans from developing an atomic bomb. But the secondary operations – the American bombing of Vemork with attendant civilian casualties, and the deliberate sinking of the ferry carrying the remaining stock of heavy water to Germany despite the known presence of civilians – are more controversial. In these cases the authorities ordering the operations had to consider which was the greater evil: innocent deaths or an atomic bomb in German hands.

The genesis of the plan to assassinate Heydrich lay in the poor performance of the Czech resistance when compared to other countries, notably her neighbour Poland. Heydrich himself had taken steps which reduced the effectiveness of what resistance existed, as well as measures to keep the armament workers and farmers relatively content. The result was that the Protectorate had gained a reputation for being peaceful, and the workers were seen as willing collaborators with the German war effort. All this infuriated Edvard Beneš, who was fighting through diplomatic channels for an abrogation of the Munich Agreement, and for a guarantee that after the war Czechoslovakia would be restored to its pre-Munich state.

The sheer violence of the German response to the assassination led those involved in the inception and planning for Operation Anthropoid to deny or downplay their roles and responsibilities later. Many of the records have gone missing, particularly those relating to the decisions made by the Czech committee in London. It is, however, generally accepted that Beneš, his head of intelligence in London, František Moravec, General Ingr, and Rudolph Viest decided to make a grand gesture of resistance, the assassination of an important figure in the Protectorate, preferably to coincide with Czechoslovakia's national independence day, 28 October.[1]

Peter Wilkinson, an SOE staff officer, later recalled that in September 1941 Moravec approached SOE for assistance in getting men and equipment to the Protectorate for a special operation since SOE was already training Czech agents. He suggested that SOE need not know who the target was: 'Our job was merely to arrange for the equipment and for the transport of high-grade assassins from the United Kingdom to Czechoslovakia and who they chose to bump off after they got there was Czech business and not ours.'[2] In fact, on 3 October a meeting was held between Moravec and the head of SOE, Frank Nelson, during which it became clear that the Czechs were formulating a plan to carry out 'a spectacular assassination. Heydrich, if possible.'[3] The Czechs had already been warned by Gubbins that Wilhelm Keitel had recently issued his order for reprisals on the ratio of 100 people for every German killed by the resistance. No one in SOE appears to have considered the implications of its involvement in a political assassination. It has been suggested that SOE sanctioned its role in despatching the two assassins simply because the minister of economic warfare Hugh Dalton felt keenly that SOE had yet to prove its worth and 'I am particularly anxious for a successful operation or two'.[4]

The role of Beneš is less clear. After the assassination of Heydrich he certainly denied any involvement in the scheme and even intimated that he had been opposed to it. Moravec, however, in his memoirs, claimed:

> The cost of Heydrich's life would be high. I said this to Beneš, who listened carefully to my evaluation and then said that, as Supreme Military Commander, he had decided that although the action would admittedly cost lives, it was necessary for the good of the country. He ordered me to carry it out.

Moravec also wrote that Beneš met the two assassins the day before they left for the Protectorate.

The political dimension to the operation affected the selection of the agents – Jozef Gabčik was a Slovak and Karel Svoboda was Czech – to demonstrate that the Czechs and Slovaks were part of one country, Czechoslovakia. After Svoboda was injured in training he was replaced by another Czech, Jan Kubiš. The SOE reports on the two men noted that both were reliable but neither was particularly intelligent.[5] Wilkinson wrote later:

> They were a very typically Czech pair. They were very, very solid citizens. The sort of NCOs who one would have given anything for on active operations: utterly reliable, apparently utterly fearless and absolutely devoted to their cause. I could not have admired them more.[6]

The SOE memorandum on Operation Anthropoid of 22 January 1942 noted that the two agents had been dropped on the night of 28–29 December 1941 to assassinate Heydrich. The method had not yet been decided upon: he might be attacked in Hradčany Castle in Prague, in his office, blown up in his car or armoured train, or killed when attending a public ceremony. SOE had supplied Gabčik and Kubiš with a Sten gun, two pistols, six armour-piercing bombs filled with plastic explosive, two Mills grenades, and assorted other equipment equally useful for sabotage or assassination.[7] The two men were dropped about twenty miles from Prague and not where they expected to land. By good fortune, however, they met a farmer who had contacts in *Sokol*, the Czech sports association, and by the beginning of 1942 the two agents had reached Prague.

Two other parties had been dropped on the same night as Anthropoid: Silver A and Silver B. These aimed at strengthening communications with the Protectorate in the wake of the arrests after Heydrich's arrival, and to carry out their own sabotage activities. Neither party knew of the plan to assassinate Heydrich. Resistance circles in Prague, however, were small, and the same safe houses were used by members of different missions, so it is unsurprising that Silver A, led by Alfred Bartoš, and the Czech resistance soon came to suspect that Gabčik and Kubiš aimed to assassinate Heydrich. They were appalled and felt that the resistance was already suffering enough without the extreme provocation of the assassination of the Reichsprotektor.[8] In May 1942 Bartoš transmitted messages to London warning of the situation in the Protectorate. In the first place, he advised against the despatch of any further agents:

> You are sending us people for whom we have no use. They are a burden on the organisational network which is undesirable in today's critical times. The Czech and German security authorities have so much information and knowledge about us that to repeat these operations would be a waste of people and equipment.[9]

The Czechs in London and SOE both ignored him. Bartoš then transmitted a message from Arnošt Heidrich, a member of ÚVOD:

> This assassination would not be of the least value to the Allies and for our nation it would have unforeseeable consequences. It would threaten not only hostages and political prisoners, but also thousands of other lives. The nation would be the subject of unheard-of reprisals. At the same time it would wipe out the last remainders of any organization. It would then be impossible for the resistance to be useful to the Allies. Therefore we beg you to give the order through SILVER A for the assassination not to take place. Danger in delay, give the order at once. If for reasons of foreign policy the assassination is nevertheless essential, the nation is prepared to offer even the highest sacrifices.[10]

Crucially, however, Bartoš appears to have altered the final sentence to read: 'If for reasons of foreign policy the assassination is nevertheless essential, another target should be chosen.' The Czech resistance favoured the killing of the education minister Emanuel Moravec on the grounds of his extreme collaboration, or of Karl Frank, the Sudeten deputy to Heydrich.[11] This message was transmitted on 12 May and there is considerable difficulty in untangling exactly who saw it and how they reacted, but as one historian has explained: 'Whatever the truth of the matter, one thing is clear – if Beneš did not specifically confirm the assassination order, he certainly never cancelled it.'[12] The head of Czech intelligence in London, František Moravec, replied to the message, stressing the political necessity for the operation to continue.

In April 1942 Heydrich moved his living quarters from Hradčany Castle to the Chateau of Panenské Břežany in the outskirts of Prague. Every day he travelled to his office in his chauffeur-driven car, without an armed escort. The Gestapo later admitted that they had been concerned about

Heydrich's security once they had heard of the arrival of SOE parachutists, but that he had dismissed their fears. Gabčik and Kubiš reconnoitred the route and located the ideal place for an ambush. Just as the car would come down the hill onto V Holešovičkách Street towards the Traja bridge, there was a crossroads on a hairpin bend which would force the car to slow down.[13]

On 27 May, Gabčik and Kubiš, both wearing overcoats, travelled by bicycle to the ambush site and waited for Heydrich to appear. The tram stops gave them cover while waiting. Another parachutist, Josef Valčík, stood further up the hill ready to use a mirror to signal when Heydrich's car was approaching. As the car reached the bend Kubiš stepped out of the shadows and aimed his Sten gun at Heydrich. As used to happen far too frequently, the Sten jammed at the crucial moment. Gabčik immediately threw his bomb which hit the running board of the car and exploded, sending fragments of shrapnel and particles of upholstery into Heydrich's body. Both assassins escaped despite being chased and shot at by the chauffeur and the critically wounded Heydrich. Heydrich was taken to hospital and operated on.[14]

Hitler flew into a rage at the news, and he and Himmler ordered the immediate execution of at least 100 Czechs and the arrest and later execution of up to 10,000 men in reprisal. Karl Frank immediately flew to Berlin and successfully argued that the execution of so many men would be highly counterproductive because it would alienate the workers who were currently working well in the armament factories. Furthermore, the overcoat, Sten gun, and bicycle pointed to the assassins not being members of the local resistance. Hitler backed down but ordered Frank to locate the assassins rapidly.

Before he had left Prague, Frank had imposed martial law on the city: a curfew was imposed from 9 p.m. to 6 a.m.; transport was stopped; and restaurants and places of entertainment were closed. Posters appeared stating: 'For information leading to the arrest of the perpetrators, there will be a reward of 10 million crowns. Whoever shelters these criminals, or helps them or who, having any knowledge of them, does not denounce them, will be shot, along with his entire family.' The Protectorate government offered to double the reward and President Emil Hácha spoke on the radio and denounced Beneš as 'Public Enemy Number One'. The bicycle and coat found at the scene were displayed in a shop window in Wenceslas Square. That night, the acting Reichsprotektor, Kurt Daluege, ordered Prague to be sealed off by the German police and army. The Gestapo, assisted by the SS, Czech gendarmerie, and three Wehrmacht battalions – 12,000 men in all – visited 36,000 homes in search of the assassins, but

Gabčik and Kubiš were not found. They and other parachutists moved gradually to shelter in the Greek Orthodox church of St Cyril and St Methodius. Only Karel Čurda, who had parachuted in on 28 March, remained at large and reached his mother's house outside Prague.

On 4 June, Heydrich died of his wounds. His body was taken to Berlin where he received a state funeral. By then the Gestapo had received at least 1,000 tip-offs, half of them from the Czechs, but still had no positive leads on the whereabouts of Gabčik and Kubiš. One tip-off pointed to the village of Lidice. In the evening of 9 June a squad of security police under SS-Hauptsturmführer Max Rostock cordoned off the village. A total of 199 men were murdered and 195 women were arrested and sent to concentration camps. The ninety-five children were examined to see if they could be Germanized – nine were accepted, and the rest sent to camps. The village itself was burnt and then bulldozed. Emanuel Moravec publicized the massacre and warned of worse to come if the assassins were not found. Karl Frank was appalled by the Lidice massacre and on 13 June suggested a new tactic: a promise of clemency until 18 June to people who knew the whereabouts of the assassins. It worked: on 16 June, Čurda walked into the Gestapo offices in Prague and revealed all he knew. Čurda did not know where the parachutists were hiding but supplied the Gestapo with enough names of people who had assisted them. Torture was used, including presenting the head of his mother in a bucket to one young boy, to pinpoint the location of the church in Prague. Čurda received the reward and moved to Germany where he received Reich citizenship. After the war he was extradited to Czechoslovakia and put on trial. When asked why he had betrayed his colleagues he told the judge: 'I think you would have done the same thing for a million marks, Your Honour.' He was unrepentant even when he was about to be executed.

On 18 June the SS stormed the church and opened battle with three parachutists hiding in the choir loft. When these three had been killed, the SS realized that more were down in the crypt. They threw tear-gas grenades into the crypt to drive the four parachutists out and Prague firemen were ordered to flood the crypt. Čurda was brought to the scene to try to persuade the parachutists to surrender. The trapped agents attempted to dig a tunnel out of the crypt, but after a battle lasting over two hours all the SOE agents had either been killed or had committed suicide after running out of ammunition.

Throughout the rest of the summer reprisals continued across the Protectorate. The village of Ležáky suffered the same fate as Lidice after links between it and the radio operator, Bartoš, who died elsewhere, were found. The former prime minister, Alois Eliáš, was executed and, excluding Lidice and Ležáky, over 3,000 Czechs were arrested, 1,327 sentenced to death, and around 4,000 people with relatives serving abroad were held in concentration camps as hostages. ÚVOD and the communist resistance were virtually wiped out. The Greek Orthodox church was forbidden to operate in the Protectorate and its property was confiscated. Thousands of Czech Jews already in Theresienstadt were sent to their deaths in the extermination camps in occupied Poland.[15]

So was the assassination of Heydrich worth the cost? There is no doubt that Heydrich was an extremely evil man who, through his convening of the Wannsee Conference in January 1942, can be considered one of the main architects of the Final Solution, although at the time of his killing this was unknown to the Allies. It can be argued the German reprisals at Lidice achieved great publicity and reminded the world of the Czech plight. The Germans themselves publicized their actions there to act as a deterrent against future assassinations. The news was picked up by newspapers across the world. The United States Secretary of the Navy, Frank Knox, said: 'If future generations ask us what we were fighting for in this war we shall tell them the story of Lidice.' In the United States, Peru, Brazil, and elsewhere, villages were renamed Lidice. Beneš's response to the massacre was: 'What the Germans are doing is horrible, but from the political point of view they gave us one certainty: under no circumstances can doubts be cast any more upon Czechoslovakia's national integrity and her right to independence.'[16] He was right: on 4 August 1942 the British government repudiated its commitment to the 1938 Munich Agreement and raised the status of the Czech national committee to that of a government-in-exile.[17] From the point of view of the Czech resistance, the reprisals all but destroyed it, and there was almost no further noticeable resistance at all in the Protectorate until the Soviets were about to enter the country. For resistance movements elsewhere, the reprisals demonstrated the dangers of political assassinations. When, for example, the Polish AK were considering the assassination of Franz Kutschera, the senior SS security officer in Warsaw in February 1944, they carefully estimated the number of hostages that would be shot in reprisals before agreeing to the operation, which was successful. In contrast to the bloodbath in the Protectorate, only 300 Poles were shot in reprisal.[18]

Late summer 1942 was the critical point in the war in the Western Desert, with Field Marshal Erwin Rommel's forces poised to strike at Alexandria and Cairo. The British knew, through Enigma interceptions, that Rommel faced a drastic shortage of supplies since the Royal Navy and RAF were sinking his supply ships in the western Mediterranean. These sinkings meant that an estimated 80 per cent of Rommel's supplies were being transported along the single-line standard-gauge railway running along the Greek coast from Salonika to the port of Piraeus in the eastern Mediterranean. This railway had three vulnerable points: the viaducts at Gorgopotamos, Asopos, and Papadia. The strength of the Luftwaffe in Greece meant that the viaducts could not be bombed by the RAF, and consequently plans were drawn up for the insertion of a party of SOE saboteurs to blow up one of the viaducts and close the vital railway to supplies on the eve of the battle of El Alamein – Operation Harling. After the successful conclusion of the operation, the party led by Eddie Myers was to make its way to the coast and be evacuated by submarine. Monty Woodhouse and Themie Marinos were to stay behind and act as liaison officers between the resistance and SOE Cairo.

The British had little reliable intelligence regarding the whereabouts, make-up, and numbers of the resistance bands thought to be operating in the Greek mountains. Woodhouse later wrote of his orders:

> They had nothing to do with the course of events, which we had to improvise as we went along ... It was a highly imaginative document, stitched together out of concealed lacunae. It assigned various guerrilla bands to various locations, all of them fictitious. So were the numbers of men said to compose them.

The problem stemmed in part from the lack of reliable communications with Greece: messages had to be relayed from Cairo to Istanbul, to Prometheus II (Captain Koutsogiannopoulos) in Athens by radio, and then by courier into the mountains.

The consequences affected the entire value of the operation. Woodhouse and his party dropped first on 1 October 1942, expecting to meet but missing a representative of Prometheus II. Woodhouse's radio contact with Cairo failed, and he was forced to send a courier into Athens to use the radio there. Myers and his party landed further north, in the wrong location, anticipating meeting the band led by Napoleon Zervas, the only resistance group in the area SOE Cairo had heard of. A week later Woodhouse and Myers joined forces but it took them over five weeks to locate Zervas. On 30 October the third party finally dropped but they encountered a hitherto unknown resistance force, the communist resistance group ELAS. It was only on his return journey from a reconnaissance of the viaducts that Myers realized that there were two resistance groups, EDES under Zervas and ELAS under Velouchiotis, operating in the area. In what was to become a unique occurrence, both groups agreed to assist the British in their sabotage operation: ELAS supplied about 100 men and EDES fifty.[19]

Myers had carried out a careful reconnaissance of the three viaducts, which were situated within a fifteen-kilometre radius of one another, and rejected attacking the Papadia and Asopos viaducts because the former was too well guarded and the latter offered no easy access or escape. The Gorgopotamos viaduct offered a much better prospect as it:

> ... ran north and south, curving slightly. It consisted of, to the north, five solid masonry piers, and two steel piers to the south. The taller steel pier was about seventy feet high and the spans were all hundred-foot spans. Obviously we wanted to destroy the big steel pier and thus bring down the two contiguous spans as well ... Heavy scrub ... ran to within 300 yards of the southern end of the bridge. Mount Oeta rose steeply half a mile behind us and the first trees were even closer than that.[20]

It was guarded by only eighty Italians, who were thought to be of low quality. Apart from the guards, an additional hazard was the fact that heavily laden and extremely long trains passed along the line every twenty minutes. Therefore, it was decided that the attack should be made by several separate and independent groups against the railway north and south of the viaduct, against the road running nearby, and against the Italian garrisons situated on either side of it. These aimed to prevent rail traffic from interfering with the operation and stop reinforcements reaching the garrisons by road. In the meantime the British demolition parties would make their way down into the valley. A careful reconnaissance was made on 22 November and the *andartes* were divided into groups. The date for the actual operation was set for the night of 25 November.

The operation ran with remarkable smoothness, albeit with a great deal of gunfire. There were seven piers supporting the viaduct, five were of solid masonry and two of steel. Explosives were attached to the steel piers in the anticipation that they would bring down the spans on either side. An immediate hitch encountered and swiftly overcome was that the plans seen in Cairo had called for rectangular charges, but on the ground the demolition parties realized the need for U-shaped charges and a short delay was inevitable while the charges were reshaped.[21] The actual explosion was spectacular, as Woodhouse described it:

> Two spans of the bridge rose a few feet in the air and fell gently into the valley. Simultaneously all the lights in Lamia went out: from what cause, I never knew – it could not have been the force of the explosion. Zervas, Aris and I joined hands and danced on our mound. Being three of us, we sang triumphantly as we danced the klephtic ballad of the *Three Lads of Volos*. It was not very relevant, but it did not have to be.[22]

The viaduct was badly damaged:

> [The pier] stood at a toppling drunken angle. It had jumped up, cut clean through on all four legs, and had come down again in a useless tangle. On the side nearest us, the spaced charges had cut out the section of eight feet on each leg, and it leant alarmingly towards us. The span between it and the first masonry pier had come clean away and lay, badly damaged, half in the river, half on the bank we stood on. The other span which it had supported to the south had also cut away and rested on the rising ground towards the shorter steel column from which it still hung by some bent girders.[23]

All the parties that had taken part reached the rendezvous point in the forest unscathed except for a few minor wounds. About twenty to thirty Italians were reported to have been killed by the covering parties. In reprisals, the Italians seized fourteen civilians from Lamia and shot them at the foot of the destroyed viaduct.

As a tactical operation, Harling was undoubtedly successful. No rail traffic could run along the line for nineteen days after the operation, and it only opened fully on 4 January 1943. On the strategic level, however, it was a total failure. The operation had originally been conceived to assist the Allies during the battle of El Alamein, but that battle had begun a month earlier on 23 October and by the time the Gorgopotamos viaduct was blown up, Rommel's forces were in full retreat and the Torch landings had also taken place. As a demonstration of resistance, on the other hand, it was valuable. The destruction of the viaduct caused fuel shortages and power cuts in Athens which helped to publicize the existence of a Greek resistance. For SOE the operation was extremely worthwhile: 'it showed for the first time in occupied Europe that guerrillas, with the support of Allied officers, could carry out a major tactical operation coordinated with Allied strategic plans'. In Greece the operation is regarded as worthy of commemoration: 25 November is National Resistance Day.[24]

The political impact of Operation Harling was entirely unexpected. The demolition party were to have been withdrawn by submarine from the west coast of Greece, about five miles south of Parga, at the end of December. However, on reaching the embarkation point new orders were received instructing them to stay and form the British Military Mission to Greece. Denys Hamson could not contain his anger at the news:

> I don't think we even looked at each other. There were no words for what we felt . . . We had done our job, and the Navy, the Army and the Air Force had NOT come to fetch us . . . Unanimously, collectively and individually, we said NO. We couldn't get out of Greece for the moment, but, the instant we could, we *would*. We had been badly deceived, and we were not volunteering for anything more. We felt very mutinous.[25]

The party returned to Zervas's headquarters, and on 3 January 1943 a New Zealander, Captain Bill Jordan, arrived with their new orders. Myers was now expected to organize a large-scale guerrilla movement and Woodhouse was to go to Athens to meet the group called the Six Colonels, yet another resistance group. The problem, as would only emerge later, was that SOE Cairo wanted to give assistance to any resistance group, whatever its political complexion, republican or royalist, but had not consulted the Foreign Office, which remained wedded to the Greek king and his government. Nor, at that time, had the strength of the antipathy between the two republican formations, EDES and ELAS, been evident, nor were the political ambitions of ELAS predicted.[26] The stage was therefore set for a whole new chapter in British relations with occupied Greece, and the question that would emerge was the extent to which subsequent guerrilla activity in Greece should be considered as resistance against the occupying powers, or as a civil war over post-war political supremacy.

When Germany conquered Norway in 1940 it also captured Europe's only heavy-water plant, Vemork, near Rjukan, 176 kilometres west of Oslo. It is unnecessary to divert into an in-depth analysis of nuclear physics here other than to note a few important points. Before the war German physicists were leaders in the field but most of them were Jewish and so had fled the country, finding new homes and work in Britain and the United States. Remaining behind by choice was Germany's pre-eminent theoretical physicist, Werner Heisenberg; also in occupied Europe was another important physicist, Niels Bohr, in Copenhagen. Before the war both men had been active in research into the energy-producing properties of uranium. By 1939 it was known that the key to the process was the separation of the isotope uranium-235, the essential element for a chain reaction, from the far more abundant isotope uranium-238. It was widely recognized that the process was immensely inefficient and required vast industrial resources. But the newly discovered artificial element plutonium-239 was at least as good if not better than uranium-235 and could be produced by bombarding uranium-238 with slow neutrons in a nuclear reactor. Key to the creation of plutonium was a moderator to slow down the neutrons, and 'heavy water' (deuterium oxide) was one such moderator. It was originally assumed that several tons of uranium would be necessary to produce a critical mass, but in early 1940 two refugee scientists working at Birmingham University, Otto Frisch and Rudolf Peierls, calculated that the critical mass required could be measured in kilograms. Therefore, it would be perfectly possible to create an atomic bomb. If they could do the calculations, then so too could Heisenberg. This realization effectively set off what was thought to be a race between the Allies and the Germans to produce the world's first atomic bomb.[27]

Heavy water was a by-product of the chemical and fertilizer industry and had no significant use except as a neutron moderator. Therefore, when the British learned from the Norwegian resistance that the Germans had ordered the production of heavy water to be increased from 10 kilograms per month to 100 kilograms, alarm bells began ringing. Britain could do nothing to prevent German access to the only uranium ore mine in Europe at Joachimstahl in Czechoslovakia nor the seizure of Belgian stocks of ore obtained from its uranium mines in the Belgian Congo before the war, but something could and needed to be done to stop the German access to heavy water.

Information on German interest in heavy water came from Leif Tronstad, professor at the Norwegian Institute of Technology, who also oversaw production at Vemork. He attempted to sabotage the production of heavy water by adding cod-liver oil or castor oil. Suspicion fell on him and he was forced to flee Norway in September 1941. On his arrival in Britain he joined the Anglo-Norwegian Collaboration Committee and, with his extensive knowledge of the Vemork plant, was extremely important in planning the operation to destroy it. His successor at Vemork, Jomar Brun, continued to supply intelligence on German plans and also on conversations with visiting German physicists. Another important contact working at the plant was Einar Skinnarland. On 31 December 1941 SOE agent Odd Starheim parachuted back into Norway and made his way to Rjukan to persuade Skinnarland to come to Britain and share his knowledge with the team planning the operation to sabotage Vemork. Skinnarland duly took a period of leave and, in an extraordinarily daring operation, Starheim seized a coastal ship, *Galtesund*, and sailed it to Aberdeen with Skinnarland aboard, reaching their destination on 17 March 1942. After an intensive SOE training course, Skinnarland parachuted back into Norway on 29 March and resumed his duties at the plant. He and Brun would continue to smuggle out photos and blueprints to the resistance for transmission to London.[28]

The town of Rjukan was situated in a very deep, narrow, thickly forested valley accessible by a single road. The sides of the valley rose almost vertically over 3,000 feet to the plateau of Hardangar Vidda. The Vemork plant itself was a seven-storey building situated on a cliff halfway up the mountainside. On one side there were huge pipelines funnelling water from the Møsvatn reservoir into the plant, and at the front there was a 600-foot precipice dropping down to the Mån river in the valley. Access to the plant was over a 75-foot-long suspension bridge across the river. Various options were considered for the destruction of the plant. Bombing was quickly rejected. If the dam was bombed then the inundation from the reservoir would destroy the town of Rjukan. If the plant itself was bombed then the liquid ammonia tanks might be hit, with devastating consequences for the local population. Tronstad was adamant that there was no way the Norwegian government-in-exile would agree to bombing. Sabotage of the heavy-water production was considered but, given that the Germans were already suspicious that this was happening, there was the very real danger that they would carry out reprisals against workers. Therefore, the options narrowed down to the despatch of a party of Norwegian SOE agents to supply intelligence on the defences of the plant to pave the way for the arrival of a Combined Operations team to carry out the actual destruction of the plant – and so Operations Grouse and Freshman were born.[29]

The advance party of Norwegian SOE agents – Operation Grouse – was despatched on 18 October 1942. It was led by Jens Anton Poulsson, and included Knut Haugland, Claus Helberg, and Arne Kjelstrup. Three of the men were natives of Rjukan. They parachuted onto the bleak expanse of the Hardangar Vidda, the uninhabited plateau above Rjukan, landing ten miles away from where they had expected. After finding a suitable summer hut to hide in, they were forced to make several journeys to carry 520lb of equipment from the landing ground to the hut. The journey was made all the harder by the fact that the ground was not yet frozen solid and the snow was knee-deep. Skinnarland had already informed SOE that around 100 Germans were stationed in Rjukan and he and Grouse continued to supply vital information on their dispositions: twelve at the Møsvatn dam guarding the reservoir, twelve at the Vemork plant itself, and forty in Rjukan. Searchlights had been erected on the roof of the plant and three iron hawsers stretched across the valley to prevent attacks by low-flying aircraft. The entrance to the factory was guarded by a hut and the guards there had a machine gun. The bridge had a gate at one end and two guards on patrol, although it appeared that they spent most of their time in the hut. The approach from the rear where the water pipes were located was mined and set with trip wires and booby traps. Back in Britain it was agreed that for Operation Freshman, commandos would attack from the front by killing the guards on the bridge with silenced pistols, cut the telephone wires and fence, and then enter the factory where they would make their way to the basement where the heavy water was stored.[30]

Operation Freshman set off on the evening of 19 November 1942. It consisted of two Halifax bombers towing gliders carrying the commandos. The use of gliders in wartime was still a relatively new concept and had never been tried over such a long distance, let alone at night and in winter. It ended in disaster: one bomber and both gliders crashed 100 miles from

Vemork. The other Halifax had reached the correct landing ground but its Rebecca set, essential to pick up the Eureka signal emitted by a beacon held by the Grouse party, malfunctioned. Grouse heard the aircraft but could not see it. The entire Halifax crew was killed in the crash, as were eight men from the first glider. The survivors from both gliders were captured by the Germans: four seriously wounded men were taken to Stavanger Hospital where the Gestapo, in line with Hitler's 'Commando Order',* murdered them when they realized the men were too injured to be interrogated. The five uninjured survivors from that glider were taken to Grini concentration camp, where they were shot a few months later. The commandos in the second glider gave themselves up to the Germans expecting to be treated as POWs but were executed instead. The Germans found maps in the gliders showing Rjukan and immediately set about improving the defences around Vemork.[31]

The disaster befalling Freshman left the Grouse party out on a limb. Plans were immediately set in train in Britain to despatch a second party – Gunnerside – in December to carry out the attack, but bad weather intervened. As Poulsson later recalled:

> I think we were told the day after the tragedy what had happened, and a couple of days later we were told that a new party would come and join up with us, so we had to stay on. We went further back into the mountains, because the Germans had a large search in the Rjukan valley, and went on to the Vidda. Then we moved to a hut called Svensbu – it belongs to my family actually – and we stayed there and we waited.[32]

What ensued was an enormous feat of endurance as the Grouse party was forced to hide on the bleak plateau throughout the worst of the winter. Helberg later said:

> We soon finished all of our rations apart from a very small amount kept aside for emergencies. We tried to find reindeer but there were none in the area at this time because the migrating herds always head towards the wind and the wind was not blowing in the right direction. We broke into huts to take what we could find, but without much success. During peacetime people left quite a lot of basic supplies like sugar, oats or dried fish, but because of the food shortages of the war, there was very little left in the mountains.[33]

Poulsson recorded: 'Everybody except myself went sick with fever and pains in the stomach. We were short of food and had to eat reindeer moss.'

* In October 1942 the Germans issued an order that all Allied commandos discovered in Europe should be killed immediately without trial, even if in uniform or attempting to surrender.

Just before Christmas he shot a reindeer which provided for 'a happy Christmas celebration'.[34]

Back in Britain the Gunnerside party, led by Joachim Rønneberg and including Knut Haukelid, Kasper Idland, Fredrik Kayser, Hans Storhaug, and Birger Strømsheim, spent the waiting period in extensive training. Mock-up models of the layout of the plant were built. As Rønneberg explained:

> It was very impressive because you had never been there but you knew it exactly, how the buildings were placed compared to each other and where you could get cover and so on. I remember Professor Tronstad told me one day – just more or less by fun, I think – 'If you need a room to lock up the Norwegian watchman, the key for the lavatory is on the left-hand side of the door when you leave the high concentration room.'[35]

Gunnerside were never informed why the destruction of the heavy-water plant was so important, but they were told to focus on destroying the stocks of fluid, the heavy water, in the basement regardless of what other damage they might be able to achieve. Just before they left, Tronstad told the party that the Germans would not take them prisoner but the operation was worth the risk: 'You have no idea how important this mission is, but what you are doing will live in Norway's history for hundreds of years to come.'[36]

Gunnerside made one unsuccessful attempt to locate the designated landing place on 22 January 1943, but on the second attempt on 16 February insisted that the RAF drop them although they had not made contact with Grouse (now renamed Swallow), and all landed safely. None of them knew where they were and Haukelid commented: 'We may be in China for all I know.' They sheltered for five days from a ferocious snowstorm and found a map in the hut which told them that they were about twenty-five kilometres from where they should have landed. On 23 February Gunnerside linked up with Swallow.

Helberg reconnoitred the route to Vemork on 25 February and two days later both parties, dressed in British uniforms, left their hut and made their way towards the plant. Helberg's reconnaissance proved invaluable because he was able to lead the party along a route across the gorge deemed impossible by local guides and across the river where the ice was breaking up.[37] It was hard going:

> When we had to walk downhill the snow was up to our waists, and when we came further down and had to make a shortcut round the houses it even went up to our arms. You had to do a sort of front crawl to get out of the snow and downwards.[38]

The group split into two: the demolition party led by Rønneberg and the covering party led by Haukelid. The demolition party struggled to find a way into the installation and the accuracy of Tronstad's knowledge plaid dividends as they found the cable shaft he had pointed out to them on the plans. Pushing their rucksacks filled with explosives ahead of them, they crawled along the shaft and entered the basement where the heavy water was stored. The Norwegian watchman was shocked to meet heavily armed soldiers, but Kayser showed him his sergeant's stripes and ordered him to tell the Germans that the attackers had been in British uniform.[39] Rønneberg recalled the action:

> We thought it would be very nice to know that we'd succeeded, so we decided to cut the fuses to half a minute, all the two minute fuses. I think it was eight of them, and saw that all of them were burning. We lit one each. And by the time the Germans realised that there was a drain in the flow of the high concentration room, all the heavy water and the half-made, quarter-made and ten per cent made were out in the river.[40]

Outside, the covering party was getting anxious as it watched the guard-house for any sign of German activity: 'We stood there, I dare say, for 20 minutes, but to us it seemed like the whole night . . . At last there was an explosion, but an astonishingly small, insignificant one.'[41]

The fact that the explosion was not louder probably saved the lives of the saboteurs since the only initial German reaction was a brief sweep with a torch outside the guard hut, which missed the hidden Norwegians. But the explosion was totally successful. The chief engineer, Alf Larsen, inspected the damage:

> When I got through the door I could see that all the high-concentration cells had been blown up and the bottom had been knocked out of each individual cell. The whole room was full of spray, which was obviously caused by shrapnel from the explosions having penetrated the water tubes to the plant. It was like standing in a shower. This was a perfect sabotage act.[42]

Both the demolition party and the covering group successfully made their escape back the way they had come and safely reached the hut on the Hardangar Vidda.[43] Haugland radioed back to London on 10 March:

> Operation carried out with 100 per cent success. High Concentration plant completely destroyed. Shots not exchanged since the Germans did not realise anything. The Germans do not appear to know whence they came or whither the party disappeared.[44]

Rønneberg and four of the Gunnerside group successfully made their way to Sweden. Haukelid and Kjelstrup remained on the plateau to observe the aftermath of the operation. Poulsson and Helberg left for Oslo to continue resistance there.

Reichskommissar Josef Terboven visited Rjukan after the raid and ordered the arrest of ten of the town's most prominent citizens, and the local Gestapo chief threatened to shoot them and to arrest fifty workers from Vemork. General Nikolaus von Falkenhorst, commander of German forces in Norway, visited the plant and concluded that the operation had been carried out by saboteurs from outside the area. He blamed the carelessness of the guards and the senior officer, and some of his soldiers were sent to the Eastern Front as punishment. Von Falkenhorst ordered the release of the hostages, declared martial law in the area, and launched a massive manhunt involving an estimated 15,000 men to sweep the area for the saboteurs – unsuccessfully.[45]

In spring 1943 Haukelid reported to London that the Germans had begun to rebuild the heavy-water facility and that his contacts in the plant had made it clear the defences had been strengthened to such a degree as to prevent a repeat of the first sabotage operation.[46] This caused a problem in London because it appeared to suggest that a bombing raid would be necessary to put the plant out of action permanently, regardless of the number of civilian casualties.

At this point, it is necessary to consider what the British knew about the German atomic programme. Much of the information reaching Britain came through Niels Bohr in Copenhagen. In September 1941 he was visited by Heisenberg. The two men have provided conflicting reports about what they discussed at their meeting: Heisenberg is adamant that he tried to convince Bohr that Germany was not building an atomic bomb, but Bohr says he gained exactly the opposite impression. Nor was Bohr any more convinced by a meeting during the summer of 1942 with another German physicist, Hans Jensen, who again tried to convey the message that there was no German bomb programme. Indeed, Jensen repeated this message when visiting Norway. The British knew of these meetings because Bohr was in contact with one of the Princes in Denmark who passed his intelligence on to Sweden. Paul Rosbaud, a physicist and science journalist, also supplied technical information to the British via Switzerland, pointing to the fact that there was in reality no plan for a German atomic bomb. Examination of German scientific journals also suggested that most German physicists were working in their expected university posts, suggesting that no large-scale atomic project was under way. However, an unknown source in Switzerland had sent intelligence to Leo Szilard in the United States which suggested that Germany had, in the middle of 1942, succeeded in getting a chain reaction going which was a major step towards the production of an atomic bomb. If this were true then it would put the Germans ahead in the race since Enrico Fermi had only just achieved the first chain reaction in Chicago on 2 December 1942.[47]

Pressure to bomb Vemork in order to destroy the heavy-water installation came from the head of the Manhattan Project, Colonel Leslie Groves. With such fragmentary and conflicting intelligence regarding German atomic plans, Groves had concluded that it was safest to proceed on the basis that what Germany could do, it would do. SOE was less sure that a bombing raid would be successful, but it was certain that another sabotage raid was impossible. The Norwegian government-in-exile and Tronstad were not informed in advance about the plan to bomb Vemork. On 16 November 1943 the US bombers set out for Vemork, and Haukelid was on the ground to observe the result:

> Three bombs hit the hydro-electric plant's pipelines, but the valves on top in the reservoir stopped the devastating flow of water. Four bombs hit the power station and only two hit the electrolysis plant for heavy water. One bomb hit the suspension bridge across the gorge which collapsed. The high concentration plant underneath – seven stories of concrete in the electrolysis plant – was undamaged. Unfortunately a bomb hit a Norwegian bomb shelter and killed 21 people, mostly women and children, and one man alone was killed far away in the mountains by a stray bomb.[48]

The Norwegians were furious and lodged an official protest with the British government.[49]

The air raid did have the desired effect of putting an end to heavy-water production at Vemork, since the Germans considered the repairs too onerous to be worthwhile. The British committee responsible for considering atomic matters concluded that Germany was no longer attempting to build an atomic bomb and passed this information to Groves. Groves, however, while agreeing with the assessment, replied: 'But we also feel that as long as definite possibilities exist which question the correctness of this opinion in its entirety or in part, we cannot afford to accept it as a final conclusion.'[50] He had doubts because of the information passed to him by Bohr. Bohr had been under pressure by the British and the Danish underground to escape from Denmark but had adamantly refused to do so until it was made clear to him that his life was under threat for a new reason, his Jewish background. Bohr then escaped from Denmark to Sweden, travelled to London and then to the United States, and reached Los Alamos in New Mexico on 31 December 1943. There he showed the physicists a sketch that Heisenberg had given him back in 1941 of what Bohr assumed to be an atomic bomb, but which the scientists in the United States immediately recognized as a nuclear reactor.[51]

The British and Americans remained absolutely determined to prevent the German removal of the remaining heavy-water stocks from the ruined plant at Vemork to Germany. Haukelid was ordered to investigate every possibility for preventing the transfer of the seventy giant drums containing the last 3,600 gallons of heavy water. He reported to London that the railway from Vemork to the ferry terminal on Lake Tinnsjø was too heavily guarded to be attacked, and that the only option was to sink the ferry as it crossed the lake. Despite the fact that civilians used the ferry too, so that innocent lives would inevitably be lost, he was ordered to carry out the operation to sabotage the ferry. Haukelid did all he could to reduce the likely number of civilian deaths by getting his contacts at Vemork to delay the transfer until the morning of 20 February 1944, a Sunday, when there would be fewer passengers. SOE–*Milorg* cooperation proved vital to the success of the operation. Haukelid used *Milorg* men to guard his entrance onto the ferry and to stand guard while he placed the explosives:

> I laid my charges in the bilges, hoping that the hole in the bows would lift up the stern of the ferry and render it immediately un-navigable. I coupled the charges to two separate time-delay mechanisms tied to the stringers on each side. These time-delays I had had specially constructed out of alarm clocks. I reckoned that the charge was big enough to sink the ferry in about 4 or 5 minutes.
>
> I set the time delay for 10.45am the same morning. This was the time which (as I discovered on a previous reconnaissance trip aboard the *Hydro*) would bring the ship to the best place for sinking.[52]

The ferry duly exploded at 11 a.m. and sank immediately. Fourteen Norwegians, one only three years old, were killed along with four Germans. The ferry sank in the deepest part of the lake and recovery of the barrels was impossible. Meanwhile Haukelid and the senior men from Vemork reached the safety of Sweden. The British had made contingency plans for the possible failure of the attack on the ferry: a team of saboteurs would blow up the train south of Lake Tinnsjø or, failing that, the RAF would bomb the ship carrying the barrels as it crossed the Baltic.[53]

In November 1944 the United States Army reached Strasbourg and the Alsos Mission tasked with finding evidence of the German atomic programme entered the offices of the physicist Carl Friedrich von Weizsäcker. His papers revealed that Germany had not succeeded in building a nuclear reactor and that there had never been a serious programme to build an atomic bomb. Further discoveries revealed that German physicists had not even succeeded in creating a self-sustaining chain reaction. It is now known that such efforts as might have been started towards that goal had been stopped in spring 1942 when the new armaments minister, Albert Speer, consulted Heisenberg and other physicists on the timescale and production requirements of an atomic bomb. Speer concluded that such a bomb would take years to build and that Germany's limited industrial resources should instead be directed towards the development of weapons such as the V-1 and V-2, which promised results more quickly. Continuing atomic research would be confined to discovering a way of producing and using nuclear energy.[54] But the Allies did not know this at the time. For the Allies the prospect of an atomic bomb exploding over London was too terrible to contemplate, and so no chances to stall or finally end the prospects of a German bomb were to be missed.

12

The Sauckel Effect

The failure of the Wehrmacht to take Moscow and inflict a final and devastating defeat on Soviet forces by the winter of 1941 meant that German planners now realized that the war would be a long one. Consequently, in early 1942, the Germans began to consider how to put their economy on a full war footing for the first time, freeing manpower to expand the armed forces and replace casualties on the Eastern Front. This process was overseen by two men: Albert Speer, who was appointed minister for armaments and war production in February 1942, and Fritz Sauckel, who was made general plenipotentiary for labour deployment a month later.

The following three chapters consider the effect the new policies applied by the Germans had on the peoples in occupied Europe. Two major new policies were introduced simultaneously: forced labour, which had hitherto applied only in the east, was extended throughout occupied Europe; and the extermination of the Jews was begun.

Hitler's reasoning behind the forced-labour policy was that: 'German soldiers are fighting and shedding their blood. We are therefore entitled to demand that others should work.'[1] Forced labour affected everyone of a working age and made simple co-existence a less viable response to occupation. The working populations faced three choices: comply and go to Germany; hide; or engage in resistance. All but the first were effectively acts of resistance and the increasing failure to cooperate with the occupying authorities was noted by the Germans, who blamed the so-called 'Sauckel effect', the counterproductive effect of the forced-labour policy, for the rise in resistance. As one commentator has written of France – but it is equally true of elsewhere in Europe – by the end of 1943 there was 'a "society in resistance", which is not quite the same as saying that it was a "society of resisters"'.[2] Resistance movements were forced to adapt and improve their organization in order to cater for the large numbers of young people needing their assistance.

This reaction stands in stark contrast to the response of the resistance to the Holocaust, which was to an astonishing extent one largely of indifference. Indeed, in France the term '*déporté*' was applied to people taken by the forced-labour decrees and not to those Jews despatched to the east during the same period.[3] Nevertheless, there were a number of individuals who chose to protect the endangered Jews, and who formed organizations to do so. They may have been acting principally from humanitarian motives, but the danger to themselves meant that their actions must be classified as resistance.

The Germans could not implement the two policies – forced labour and the deportation of the Jews – without substantial assistance from the collaborating regimes and administrations (except in the east, where the Germans had destroyed all governmental structures). Hitherto, the occupied peoples had been able to hope that their native governments and administrations could protect them from the harshest consequences of occupation. Now, however, the collaboration of their so-called 'protectors' with the Germans, and the direct effect it had on the lives of most people, broke the bonds of loyalty. The resistance movements would become the principal beneficiaries, with recruits flooding in. While it is clear that many of the evaders did not plan to take up arms, there was the potential for them to do so, at the appropriate moment, should the armaments, supplies, and leadership be found.

The non-Jewish resistance could afford to wait for the right time to come out into the open and fight. The timeline of the Jewish resistance to the Holocaust was different: the Jews could not afford to wait. At the height of the deportations of the Jews and the first forced labourers, the Germans were still on the offensive on all fronts and by the end of 1943, when most of the Jews who would perish in the Holocaust had been killed, the tide of the war was only starting to turn. There was another reason why inaction was not an option for the Jewish resistance. While obedience to Nazi edicts spelled survival to the non-Jews, the reverse was true in regard to the Jews: 'The more closely they conformed to the law, the less were their chances of surviving. Where they disobeyed the law by changing identity, leaving their homes or their ghettos, or going into hiding, the percentage of losses visibly diminished, sometimes showing a spectacular drop.'[4] Ultimately, Jewish resistance was doomed and the participants knew that. When resistance was discussed by the Jews it became clear that their choice was not that of the general resistance – submit or die – but was rather a choice of how to die: as a passive victim of German policies or as a fighter either within the ghettos and camps or in the forests. Dolek Liebeskind, one of the leaders of the Jewish resistance in Cracow, perhaps best summed up the meaning of Jewish resistance to the Holocaust: 'We are fighting for three lines in the history books to make the world know that the Jewish youth did not go like lambs to the slaughter.'[5]

*

The pre-war tradition of cross-border labour migration – of unemployed skilled workers from western Europe and agricultural seasonal workers from Poland – to seek work in Germany had served the Germans well during the first years of the war. There were noticeable differences between the two groups, with the Poles and Russians treated as little more than slaves. The after-effects of the Depression and the collapse of native industries following the outbreak of the war had led to high unemployment in western Europe. Consequently, skilled workers from France, Belgium, the Netherlands, and Denmark were eager to seek work in the factories in Germany where they were offered high wages. By early 1942, approximately 157,000 French citizens, over 300,000 Belgians, about 200,000 Dutch, and 35,000 Danes were working in German industry voluntarily. Even more worked in their own countries in factories turned over to German war production, directly as servants to the occupying forces or on German defence and building projects. A measure of compulsion operated in the Netherlands, where the secretaries-general decided to withhold unemployment relief from workers who would not go to Germany. In the second half of 1941 this measure also operated in Belgium, again imposed by the Belgian administration but encouraged by the German military government.

In February 1942 German officials estimated that 625,000 workers were required to fuel the war economy immediately and, after his appointment, Sauckel set about obtaining them. In all, Sauckel launched four major drives for workers. The first, running from April to September 1942, was highly successful: 1.6 million workers were called for and found, with a surplus of 40,000. The second, operating from September 1942 to the end of the year, also achieved its target, in this case one million workers. Yet there were ominous signs of a build-up of resistance to the German labour drives. This became evident in the third recruitment drive, in 1943, when there was a shortfall of 200,000 workers from the target of 1.6 million. The German labour recruiting campaign collapsed entirely in the course of 1944 when 4 million workers were demanded but only 1.2 million were sourced.[6]

The first forced-labour decree was issued in Poland in May 1942 and covered both skilled industrial workers and agricultural labourers. By now the pool of unemployed had largely been used up and increasingly brutal methods were used to find workers. In the countryside manhunts were launched which shocked even pro-German Ukrainians who witnessed the process:

> The general nervousness is still more enhanced by the wrong methods of finding labour which have been used more and more frequently in recent

> months. The wild and ruthless manhunt as exercised everywhere in towns and country, in streets, squares, stations, even in churches, at night in houses, has badly shaken the feeling of security of the inhabitants. Everybody is exposed to the danger, to be seized anywhere and at any time by members of the police, suddenly and unexpectedly, and to be brought into an assembly camp. None of his relatives knows what has happened to him, and only months later one or the other gets news of his fate by a postcard.[7]

Polish industry was ordered to comb out excess workers and to reduce the rations of the remaining workforce in order to encourage workers to report to the German labour offices. The directorate of civil resistance under Stefan Korboński was particularly active in urging the employers to protect their workers from the impact of the German demands.[8] In January 1943 Ludwig Fischer, the German commandant in Warsaw, demanded that the mayor of the city, Julian Kulski, should support his demand for Poles to go to Germany. Kulski responded:

> What I demand is that you release Poles from concentration camps, and that you drastically improve working conditions in Germany. Only after this has been done can you expect any change of attitude on the part of the Poles. Signing joint appeal for volunteers will not produce results. The people will know that the signatures were not given freely, and I for one will not sign any such appeal.[9]

He fully expected to be arrested for his resistance but was left in peace.

In March 1943 a small ceremony was held in Cracow to mark the millionth Polish worker sent to Germany. More were called for, and in May and June even thirteen- and fourteen-year-olds were being summoned. The result was that by the middle of June 1943 a further 280,000 workers had been sent to the Reich. This came at a price: on 8 April Sauckel's representative in Warsaw was shot dead in his office by the resistance. His deputy gloomily reported to Berlin:

> It is well known that violent battles occurred just because of these actions. The resistance against the administration established by us is very strong. Quite a number of our men have been exposed to increased dangers, and it was only in the last two or three weeks that some of them were shot dead, e.g., the head of the Labour Office of Warsaw who was shot in his office, and yesterday again, another man. This is how matters stand at present, and the recruiting itself, even if done with the best will, remains extremely difficult unless police reinforcements are at hand.[10]

In September 1943 an audit was carried out of armaments firms in Poland and a quarter were closed down, with the skilled workforce being despatched to Germany.[11]

Further east, the labour round-ups were commonly accompanied by violence. For example, in the town of Oleksandriia in the Ukraine the native police 'beat with butts and shot anybody who tried to run away. There were many wounded and people were shot dead.'[12] Elsewhere the houses of those who refused to report for forced labour were burned down and their families were arrested. Such conduct, along with stringent food requisitioning, the slaughter of the Jews, and a failure to reverse collectivization, fed into the burgeoning Soviet partisan movement. The Wehrmacht commanders were aware of this and warned that 'if we continue with our present attitude, it will be the combat soldier who will pay with his blood for this mistake'. Field Marshal Ewald von Kleist, commander of Army Group A, and General Erich Frederici, commander of Rear Area Army Group South, followed General Count von Schenckendorff's example in Belorussia, and forbade labour recruitment in their areas of responsibility.[13] Sauckel, for his part, strenuously denied any link between his demands and the growth of the partisans. He pointed out that in Kiev his agents had recruited 100,000 workers without opposition, whereas in Belorussia, where there was little forced recruitment, the partisan movement was growing fast.[14] Sauckel had a point: in 1942 there is little evidence to suggest that those men who chose to sleep away from home in the forests to avoid the labour round-ups went on to join the partisans. At this stage of the partisan movement, unarmed men were not welcomed into their ranks.

Yet the Germans continued to make a link between forced-labour decrees and the increase in the numbers of partisans. Goering, in his role as acting director of the Four Year Plan, issued a directive on anti-partisan warfare on 26 October 1942 which included the proviso that 'The entire male and female workforce that may be liable for labour service is to be forcibly recruited and taken to the plenipotentiary for labour, to be used either in the rear areas or in the homeland.'[15] The first example of this policy was Operation Franz in Belorussia in January 1943 when over 1,000 civilians caught in the encirclement were sent to the Reich as forced labourers.[16] But such success depended on the attitude of the German commanders carrying out the partisan sweeps: Operation Hornung, also in Belorussia, in February 1943 saw over 2,000 partisans killed and 10,000 Jews and civilians thought to have aided the partisans executed, but few civilians passed to Sauckel's agents. Operation Cottbus, again in Belorussia, running from the middle of May to the end of June 1943, led to the death of 15,000 partisans either in action or by execution after capture, and only 5,500 civilians were sent for forced labour, all of them women. It seemed that in practice the Germans simply preferred to kill all apparent opposition without filtering out the workers.[17]

By the middle of 1943 the situation on the Eastern Front was rapidly falling out of German control as the Red Army launched its offensives and the partisans became more of a nuisance. On 21 June the whole of the Ukraine was declared a 'bandit area'. On 10 July, Himmler issued a directive: 'The Führer has decided that the whole population has to be evacuated from the partisan-ridden territories of the northern Ukraine and the central Russian sector. All men fit for work and most women to be sent as forced labour.'[18] Anyone who remained in the evacuated or 'dead zones' would be treated as a bandit and shot on sight. Erich von dem Bach-Zelewski, responsible for anti-partisan warfare, issued the relevant orders in September and succeeded in obtaining labourers for Sauckel, but again they were mostly women.[19]

In the Baltic States, Sauckel's search for skilled labour was stymied by Himmler, who wanted the male youth for his SS Legions. In early 1943 all men born between 1919 and 1924 were called upon to register with the authorities, and then be despatched either for labour in the Reich or for service in the SS. In Latvia and Estonia registration was largely successful, although in Latvia there was some resistance from students at Riga University which led to the arrest of twenty of them. The Latvian administration also attempted to hamper Sauckel's agents by finding employment for many of the registrants within Latvia. Similar protests by students were noted in Lithuania, leading to the temporary closure of the universities in Kaunas and Vilna. Again, the Lithuanian administration was less than helpful, linking cooperation with political concessions. The small partisan movements in these countries urged the young men to flee to the forests and to swell their ranks.[20]

High unemployment in Greece and famine in the cities meant that the country should in theory have been a fertile recruiting ground for Sauckel's agents. The prospect of high wages and free return trips home should have made the prospect of work in Germany an attractive proposition, but it did not, and the introduction of compulsion fostered resistance. In 1942 the Germans hoped to attract 30,000 Greek labourers but only 12,000 volunteered. The Germans then discovered that many of these volunteers were too sick to work, and those who did work gained the reputation of being poor workers. Notwithstanding this reputation, on 1 February 1943 the German commander in Greece, General Alexander Löhr, ordered all men aged sixteen to forty-five to register for labour either in Greece or in the Reich. The consequence was a highly effective demonstration of resistance. During February 1943 students in Athens protested against the registration. Their example was soon followed by strikes by bank workers, civil servants, transport workers, and the postal services. In early March the German civil mobilization programme was launched, but *Ethniko Apeleutherotiko Metopo* or EAM (the National Liberation Front) swiftly took control of the ensuing protests and organized a demonstration in Athens of over 7,000 people, including civil servants who did not want to implement the German programme. It was estimated that 65 per cent of government workers joined the protests. Strikes also hit the port of Piraeus. A further large demonstration was held on 25 March, Independence Day. The Germans responded by suspending the labour registration programme until June and replacing the inept prime minister Konstantinos Logothetopoulos with the more pro-German Ioannis Rallis. In late June, when labour registration was resumed, EAM organized a successful general strike in Athens and columns of strikers needed to be dispersed with gunfire from the Germans and collaborating policemen. The success of the resistance is testified by the numbers: 11,977 voluntary workers were recruited in 1942; but in 1943 when compulsion was used, only 2,653 workers came forward.[21]

Fritz Sauckel's most urgent need was for skilled industrial workers. These were hard to find in the east since the Soviet authorities had succeeded in evacuating many factories and their workforces ahead of the German advance. Only a limited supply of skilled workers could be released from the Protectorate, merely 135,000 by the end of 1942, because the native armaments industries already absorbed the majority. In contrast to much of Europe, the number of industrial workers despatched to Germany from the Protectorate fell off sharply during 1943.[22]

As a result of this Sauckel was forced to turn to western Europe to fulfil his requirements. Here the question of forced labour was an extremely sensitive one, especially in Belgium, where the memories of the forced deportation of 120,000 workers in 1916 and 1917 were still strong. The German military government consequently approached the issue with care. Their first decree, in March 1942, gave the military administration the power to assign workers to places of work within Belgium. Employers had to supply the Belgian labour officers with lists of their employees and to seek permission before recruiting more. The Germans could also demand that employers release workers to be placed in factories working for the German war economy in the country, but at this stage going to Germany was still voluntary. The collaboration between the German military administration and the Belgian secretaries-general meant that the process of registering industrial workers ran smoothly, with only few employers refusing to hand over lists of their employees in case they would be used for future compulsory deportations to Germany.[23] In October 1942, however, a degree of coercion was added when all men aged eighteen to fifty, and single women aged between twenty-one and thirty-five, were ordered to register for labour assignments. The emphasis was still on work within Belgium, but the Germans now had the power to demand that workers should go to Germany. A month later short prison sentences were imposed on those refusing to leave for Germany. In the spring of 1943 the Germans began calling up workers by age group and over the next six months more than 100,000 Belgians left for Germany.[24]

Resistance to the 1943 call-up was widespread in Belgium. The clandestine trade unions organized a series of strikes. Resistance groups pressurized employers not to release workers for Germany. The Catholic Church campaigned against the despatch of single women on moral grounds. Even the secretaries- general became less helpful, first by refusing to implement a German demand to withhold ration books from people refusing to work in Germany, and then by refusing to cooperate with the German attempt to introduce a Labour Book for all liable workers. In March 1943 Sauckel stipulated that all students should undertake a year's labour service before beginning their university studies, and that six months' labour should be completed before beginning their second year. School head teachers refused to supply the Germans with lists of graduating pupils. The secretary-general for education ordered the heads of universities not to cooperate, and the head of Liège University and the rector of the Catholic University of Louvain were sent to prison for destroying the lists of students: only Ghent University proved cooperative. About 200,000 young Belgian men and women went into hiding – becoming *réfractaires* or draft dodgers – and the resistance competed for their loyalty. The communist-dominated *Front de l'Indépendance* (FI) was particularly keen to swell its ranks with these people, but faced competition from *Hulp aan Voortvluchtigen*, organized by the Catholic Church, and other groups responsible for hiding workers, such as *L'Aide aux Travailleurs Réfractaires* and *Mission Socrate*. The FI also caused controversy by trying to divert funds sent from London to assist draft evaders, and to use them to help all those being repressed, including its own members. It has been estimated that around 40,000–50,000 evaders received assistance with false papers and money. Nonetheless, ultimately 85 per cent of those called up did travel to Germany.[25]

In the Netherlands, opposition to forced labour followed a similar pattern. As with elsewhere, the process of registering the population for labour went through various stages. In March 1942 a decree made all Dutch citizens liable for work in Germany, but Sauckel's first demand for skilled workers was fulfilled by thinning out the workforce in Dutch factories and closing those factories not geared towards war production.[26] In early December 1942 the heads of universities were required to produce registers of students from which 7,000 individuals would be selected for work in Germany, but only one university rector complied. The others resisted, and at the University of Utrecht the office of the registrar was set alight and the university was closed for the Christmas vacation early. The Free University of Amsterdam, which had witnessed similar protests, was closed down altogether. In early 1943 the involvement of students in the assassination of General Hendrik Seyffardt, commander of the Dutch Waffen-SS, led Hanns Rauter, Higher SS and Police Leader, to launch a raid on universities in Amsterdam, Utrecht, Wageningen, and Delft and to arrest 600 students. The secretary-general for education, Jan van Dam, was keen to avoid the permanent closure of all Dutch universities and sought a compromise solution. In March 1943 he ordered that all students should sign a loyalty pledge:

> This signatory . . . herewith declares solemnly that he will obey existing laws, decrees, and other rules in all honour and conscience. He will refrain from all actions directed against the German Reich, its armed forces, or the Dutch authorities, as well as from actions and utterances that will endanger public order at the universities and technical institutes . . .

After graduation, all students were now required to work in Germany for six months. The universities were split over how to respond, with some advocating compliance and others counselling refusal. The clandestine press called for non-compliance. As a result, only about 15 per cent of students signed the loyalty pledge: the highest rate of compliance was at the Technical Institute in Delft and the lowest at the Catholic University at Nijmegen. The universities were virtually closed down as a result, and all former students were now liable for the labour draft, but only 31 per cent of those reported for the draft, the remainder choosing to go into hiding.[27]

In spring 1943 the working population of the Netherlands was divided into seventeen age cohorts and ordered to register with employment offices, which could then call them up for labour in Germany. The clandestine press called on people not to register and to ignore summonses for work in Germany. The Germans took the Dutch by surprise with an announcement on 29 April 1943 that all former POWs were to be re-interned. The Germans claimed that the measure was necessary because of the resistance activities of former servicemen, but the reason was most probably that the re-internment could yield about 300,000 workers for Germany. The response of the population was immediate: workers abandoned their posts in factories in Hengelo and the strikes spread across the town and into the nearby province of Overijssel. By the next day the strikes had spread to the Philips factory in Eindhoven, the mines in the province of Limburg, and across the country. The clandestine press described the strikes as 'the greatest event since the capitulation . . . For a few moments the fear psychosis was broken and we did not feel like subjects of a terror regime, but like courageous and liberated people suddenly pushed on by an invisible mutual bond.' Even the agricultural community became involved as the farmers in the province of Friesland refused to deliver milk to the dairies. The Germans imposed martial law in five towns and the SS and police were ordered to fire on demonstrators without warning. The strikes petered out by early May but had left ninety-five people shot dead in the street and 400 seriously wounded; eighty strikers were executed and 900 were sent to concentration camps; fifteen mayors of towns where the strikes had been most widespread were removed from office.[28]

The Catholic and Reformed Churches in the Netherlands both issued warnings urging students and former servicemen not to comply with the German demands for labour. Their objections rested on the statement made in the decree that forced labour was required to fight Bolshevism and secure a German victory. The Churches' response was:

> The labour service promised that no one would be prevented from practising religion, but officially it was stated that the labour service can only be National Socialist. This fills us with regret and concern. The views of National Socialism are in direct conflict with Christianity and are the most serious threat to Christian faith and morals. That is why a labour service with Nazi aims is a great danger to youth.[29]

The Churches believed that the best way to oppose Bolshevism was through Christianity. The Dutch government-in-exile, while supporting the strikes, urged caution because the time was not yet ripe for a large-scale uprising. Rather than strike or undertake other visible manifestations of resistance, the government and the underground press urged workers and students to go underground, to become *onderduikers*.

In late 1942 the principal organization that would help *onderduikers*, the *Landelijke Organisatie voor Hulp aan Onderduikers*, LO, was founded by a housewife, Mrs H. Kuipers-Reitberg, and a Calvinist minister forced to resign for anti-Nazi activities, Reverend F. Slomp. The movement spread quickly across the country, uniting both the Catholic and Reformed Church in its activities. The LO also assisted in hiding Jews, but the majority of the people it helped were *onderduikers*. The aim of the organization was to find secure hiding places in the towns and countryside. A related body, the *Landelijke Knokploegen*, LKP, secured new identity papers and ration cards for the *onderduikers*, often by mounting raids on ration offices.[30] Conditions for those living without papers were grim. One young girl, Leesha Bos, a Jew living on false Aryan papers, took supplies to these people:

> I was shocked to see the pitiful condition of most of the people in hiding. The starvation diet of less than five hundred calories a day had left them skinny, weak, and without resistance to sickness. They looked grey and waxen from being shut in and shabby in their old torn clothes, and they smelled unwashed as a result of their lack of soap and laundry detergent.[31]

A major priority of the LKP was to secure papers to allow people to live openly, albeit under false identities. The clandestine press could help in this respect, launching raids on printing presses and producing the false documents. Once armed with these, an *onderduiker* could obtain employment but even that was a strain: 'One learned to live a sort of split existence, half-normal citizen on the job, half-outcast, hunted, endangered, but with the persistent will to survive.'[32] About 200,000 Dutch people became *onderduikers*. In all, almost half a million Dutch people were sent to work in Germany during the war, the majority in the final years of the occupation.

In early June 1942 Sauckel visited Paris and demanded the immediate despatch of 250,000 workers, of whom at least 150,000 must be metalworkers. The demand was accompanied by the threat of compulsory deportations if the French did not cooperate. This was a test for the Vichy regime. Pierre Laval was determined to retain as much French sovereignty as possible but still to prove to the Germans that he was on their side. Therefore, he sought an agreement that allowed the French to retain control of the labour recruitment process, and to persuade the French people that he had achieved a bargain. Thus the concept of the *Relève* was born – one POW would be released for every three workers who went to Germany. However, Laval's speech announcing the scheme, which was delivered on 22 June 1942, the first anniversary of the German invasion of the Soviet Union, caused intense controversy because it contained the pronouncement: 'I desire Germany's victory, because without it, Bolshevism will gain a footing everywhere.' Marshal Pétain tried to add his weight to the scheme by stressing patriotism – the 1.5 million POWs had been in Germany for two years, so it was appropriate that they should be replaced by other men.[33]

Few were taken in. Despite the Vichy regime closing a number of factories on the ostensible ground of shortage of raw materials, thereby forcing the workers either to find alternative employment or to register for the *Relève*, labour-recruiting offices reported only a trickle of registrants. Therefore, on 4 September 1942, Laval announced the compulsory registration of all men aged eighteen to fifty and unmarried women aged twenty-one to thirty-five. The response was explosive: factories across both the Occupied and Unoccupied Zones which were already producing vehicles and weapons for the German war effort came out on strike during October. In Nantes, the situation deteriorated to what the police chief described as a general strike. The local German military authorities entered the SNCASO factory and arrested the workers designated to go to Germany: the mayor resigned in protest. The BBC French Service pointed out that the *Relève* was a poor bargain and launched a campaign *Ne Vas Pas en Allemagne*. The head of the gendarmerie in Clermont-Ferrand reported: 'The *Relève* finds warm supporters only among those who do not risk being sent to Germany.' Recruitment was slow, but even so a total of 240,000 French workers, mostly from the Occupied Zone, eventually left for Germany under the *Relève* scheme.[34] In return around 95,000 POWs were repatriated. It has been noted, however, that many of these returning POWs should or would have been released anyway, sooner or later, since they were either sick or belonged to categories eligible for repatriation, such as being the head of a large family or a First World War veteran.[35] Notwithstanding this fact, the Vichy regime trumpeted the return of the POWs with a great show of publicity. This was somewhat dented by the fact that the first *Relève* train to arrive contained 600 POWs who had consumed the wine rations of the 1,000 expected, and were consequently drunk on arrival back in France.[36]

In early January 1943 Sauckel returned to Paris with a demand for a further 250,000 French workers by the end of March, and the same again by the end of June. Laval again attempted to bargain with Sauckel. He pointed out that: 'I represent a country which has no army, no navy, no empire, and no more gold. I represent a country which still has 1,200,000 prisoners of war in Germany, while 900,000 of its workers, whether in Germany or in France, in the last resort work for Germany.'[37] Laval was under extreme pressure to retain any vestige of a French sovereignty which had been severely compromised by the German military occupation of southern France in November 1942. He hoped that, at the very least, the Germans might release the two northern departments back to French control and remove the demarcation line now that it had become unnecessary. Sauckel refused and instead threatened the Vichy regime with more direct German rule.[38] The result was the publication of the law on *Service du Travail Obligatoire* (STO) under which all men aged eighteen to sixty-five could be called upon to perform compulsory labour, but only those aged between twenty and fifty were liable to do so away from home. In February 1943 the Vichy regime implemented the measure with the call-up of men aged twenty to twenty-two years old. The result was disastrous for Vichy: 'The STO was the single most important factor which demonstrated to the French people the perniciousness of collaboration.'[39]

The implementation of the STO appeared to have run smoothly at the beginning. Jean Guéhenno noted in his diary on 22 February 1943, a week after the call-up was announced:

> The deportation [STO] is continuing, each day more methodical and better organised. They're taking a census of all young men between the ages of twenty and thirty, under the surveillance of the occupying authority. For the past week, they stand in line in the town halls to register as convict labour. With appalling, but henceforth inevitable docility. If there had been a climate of resistance, if every government department had been an accomplice in sabotaging the orders, the Germans would have needed armies of policemen to assemble the trains of convicts. But in the present situation, brave men have almost no means of escape, without papers, identity cards, or ration cards. This whole country is now nothing but a fearful mass of protoplasm.[40]

However, on 13 March 1943, the resistance blew up the railway viaduct over the River Vienne south of Limoges to stop an STO convoy.[41]

The first STO drive was successful, and in April 1943 Sauckel demanded a further 250,000 men. The BBC French Service called for widespread avoidance of the STO by urging the young men to refuse to register, or to gain medical exemption certificates, or at worst, go into hiding; in addition appeals were made to the farming community to provide shelter.[42] French doctors supplied so many exemption certificates that it became necessary for German doctors to be present at medical examinations.[43] The police became increasingly reluctant to arrest the *réfractaires*. A Paris policeman advised his men that he 'would not find a single STO dodger and counted on them to do likewise as good Frenchmen'.[44] Indeed, the Germans in Paris began to notice a change in attitude:

> There is no doubt that the name 'Sauckel' sounds today pretty bad to French ears. The mere announcement in the press of an impending visit of the Gauleiter is sufficient for one to see for days hundreds of young people hurrying to the various Paris stations with their little suitcases.[45]

The increase in resistance was most noticeable in rural France: for example, in the department of Lot, only 12 per cent escaped STO before June 1943, but by August the figure had risen to 95 per cent.[46] Attacks began to be made on the STO offices themselves in order to destroy the registers of STO candidates.[47]

Sauckel believed firmly that foreign workers were most productive working in factories in the Reich. Albert Speer, on the other hand, felt that workers produced more if they were working in their home country. In October 1943 Laval succeeded in driving a bargain with Speer under which 10,000 factories in France were designated so-called 'S-factories' (*Speerbetriebe*) and their workers were exempt from the STO. Other means also existed to keep French workers in France, such as service with the Todt Organization engaged in the construction of the Atlantic Wall, or joining the German forces in France either in the *Kriegsmarine* as fitters and guards, or the NSKK *Motorgruppe* as drivers. By January 1944 over one million French workers had avoided the STO through these means. This statistic suggests that 'most French workers did not mind working *for* Germany as long as they did not have to go *to* Germany' where they would find themselves under the increasing Allied strategic bombing offensive.[48]

For those men who even objected to working *for* Germany there were three main options: to go into hiding at home and hope that the French police and *gardes mobiles* would not detect them; to hide in the countryside and seek employment with farmers and foresters; or to join the maquis. The origin of the term 'maquis' to describe armed groups forming in the countryside is obscure. It has been estimated that only around 15–20 per cent at most of all *réfractaires* became maquisards, meaning that although evading the STO can be perceived as a form of resistance, only a minority actually joined the armed resistance. The figures varied widely according to region. For example, in Doubs in Burgundy only 5 per cent joined the maquis, whereas in Alpes-Maritimes to the south the figure was as high as 20 per cent. But the *réfractaires*, whether in the maquis or not, still had an enormous importance for the French resistance.

The Vichy regime saw the successful implementation of the STO as an important way to emphasize its continuing control over the French, and it adopted a confused attitude towards those young men who rebelled against its authority. In some areas the *gardes mobiles* were under instruction to capture all *réfractaires* and to treat them as outlaws, but at the same time the Vichy authorities recognized the danger that these manhunts would drive the *réfractaires* into the resistance and therefore increase the danger to law and order. Accordingly, in August 1943, the Languedoc gendarmerie was advised to 'treat *réfractaires* as those who have gone astray, not as criminals'. This was followed in October by an amnesty which would allow young men to report for work and to receive ration cards in return for a guarantee of labour in France.[49]

For the resistance, the mass of *réfractaires*, whether destined for the maquis or not, was of enormous importance. The resistance 'was suddenly able to assign its members concrete and accessible goals, while all of a sudden having a mass of volunteers at its disposal'.[50] As early as April 1943 Henri Frenay, founder of *Combat*, distinguished between two categories of *réfractaires*, those who just wanted to hide but needed assistance, and those who wanted to fight and needed organization and training. He created the *Service Nationale Maquis*, run by Michel Brault and Georges Rebattet, to look after the interests of the *réfractaires*. Jean Moulin, de Gaulle's representative in France, also instigated the establishment of the Action Committee against Deportation which focused on producing false papers and work permits. The principal result of these initiatives was to change the mentality of the population. The *réfractaires* inspired widespread sympathy, and the need to hide them drew people into resistance activities they had hitherto avoided. In the summer of 1943 a prefect in the Corrèze in south-western France reported: 'The population in the countryside is living in an atmosphere of fear and has lost all confidence in the police forces. Nevertheless, it is certain that the majority of the bandits known as "Maquis" have the sympathy of the biggest part of the population.' Vichy's sponsorship of the STO also made these helpers suspicious of Vichy's activities and fatally damaged Vichy's role as a shield against the full impact of German occupation. The resistance also benefited, as those wanting to become *réfractaires* came to realize there was a structure in place in the countryside that would care for them.[51]

The first maquis camp was probably established at the end of 1942, but by spring 1943 many more were under development in the Jura, Massif Central, Haute-Savoie, and the Alps. It has been pointed out that the concept of the maquis 'did not exist in January 1943; it was everywhere by June'.[52] Conditions were grim: one maquis leader, Georges Guingouin, recalled the situation of the maquis in the forest of Châteauneuf in Limousin:

> Silver birch branches to sleep on, which for the first few days caused bruises . . . Potatoes and plain water that was their diet at first . . . Unfortunately, they all soon came down with dysentery. The spring from which they drew their drinking water, coming out of the mud in a steep-sided valley that never saw the sun, was polluted.[53]

The resistance worked hard to organize and train the men. Robert Soulage created a national organization for training the new cadres, and schools were established in the Massif de l'Oisans, the Massif de Belledonne, and several in the Basses-Alpes and in Périgord.[54] Lise Lesèvre was involved in the creation of one such school in the Basses-Alpes, near Digne, which serviced young men from Lyon, before working with a camp on the Massif de Belledonne where she would meet the young men at the station and exchange their real identity cards for false ones: 'For all these boys, I think, this exchange of identities was very traumatic, very difficult. I saw some with tears in their eyes when I took their real cards and gave them false ones.' Training generally lasted for around three weeks.[55]

The resistance hoped and expected that the maquis would grow to significant proportions, and these hopes and expectations led to a degree of self-deception on the size of the maquis and what it could achieve. For example, André Pavelet, in charge of the maquis in the Montpellier region, believed that he had 5,000 maquisards, but those operating under him never estimated the numbers as more than a few hundred.[56] This pattern of belief as opposed to reality was played out across France: by autumn 1943 there were probably not more than 15,000 to 20,000 maquisards in total. There were ceaseless discussions about how to keep the maquis movement going and developing. At the end of October 1943 a report concluded:

> One of the best . . . ways of creating cohesion and a team spirit in the camps and of keeping morale high, is action. It trains the *réfractaires*, gives them experience, and helps stop individual actions, most of which are misguided. All those in charge of military action must be fully aware of this necessity: as a result, they must use as many maquis *réfractaires* as possible when they carry out missions. Winter is approaching: we will not keep our men unless they are sufficiently equipped, appropriately fed and unless they have weapons to defend themselves and have the impression that when they act they are useful to our cause. Otherwise we will see the camps dissolve.[57]

Small actions were launched against STO and ration offices. Larger actions were planned for the future and to this end large residential maquis camps were established in the Vercors and Glières in the south-east, which would lead to tragic consequences in 1944.[58] Vichy noted the growth of the maquis with alarm: 'The *guerrilla*, which Pétain and others had feared in 1940 would destroy France, had begun.' The root of the trouble in Sauckel's forced-labour policies was recognized: Laval joked that the AS or *Armée Secrète* had become the *armée Sauckel*.[59]

*

Throughout western Europe the main effect of the forced-labour decrees was that *attentisme* was no longer a viable option. The measure affected so many people across Europe that the choice was now either resistance or collaboration. The collaborating regimes and administrations found that their reputation as protectors of their people against the full impact of German occupation was totally compromised. Public opinion became more polarized as those already calling for collaboration became more strident in their calls to support German measures, while at the same time the resistance movements ultimately benefited from the growing majority of those who opposed the measures imposed by the Germans and sanctioned by their own governmental authorities.

13
The Holocaust: The Christian Response

It is extremely important to place the Christian response to the Holocaust in context. Anti-semitism was widespread in Europe on the eve of the Holocaust, most notably on either side of the continent, in Poland and in France. The largest Jewish population, nearly 3 million, was concentrated in Poland whose territory included part of the Pale of Settlement, the area established by Catherine the Great in 1791 as the only part of the Russian Empire where Jews were permitted permanent residency. Warsaw and Cracow had flourishing Jewish cultures and many of the Jews in those cities were fully assimilated into Polish society and spoke Polish among themselves. In the eastern borderlands, however, where over 1 million Jews lived, 80 per cent were unassimilated and therefore looked different from the Poles: 'the dark, motley crowd, Jews in their traditional garb, with beards and side-locks, in "kaftans", in skull-caps, in black hats'. They also largely communicated in Yiddish.[1] The result was that Poles and Jews each considered non-Poles and non-Jews as 'the other', and both 'distrusted those of their own kind who tried to strike up a relationship with "the others", and there was always that underlying fear of losing substance'.[2]

The Jews in France were emancipated in 1791 during the French Revolution, making France the second country in Europe after Poland to grant equal rights to the Jews. Yet as in Poland, anti-semitism was rife in France, triggering the Dreyfus Affair which split the country in 1894 and reverberated for years afterwards. Opposition to the Popular Front government elected in June 1936 contained anti-semitic overtones in the widespread hatred of the prime minister Léon Blum, who was a Jew.

The Jews in western Europe largely saw themselves as citizens of their country first and Jews second, but not everyone agreed with them. The Netherlands had welcomed refugee Jews from Spain into the country in the seventeenth century, although equal civil rights were not granted until 1796. The majority of Jews settled in Amsterdam, on the surface at least, appeared to be fully assimilated. Yet Dutch society was organized socially and politically along religious lines, with the Protestants, Calvinists, Catholics, and Jews all living parallel but separate lives, maintaining little contact with each other. While there was not much overt anti-semitism in the Netherlands, 'many held social and cultural prejudices against Jews and, if asked, would have agreed that the presence of Jews in the Netherlands was a problem'.[3] The Jewish populations of Belgium, Norway, Denmark, Italy, and Greece were relatively small, but even in those countries anti-semitism was noticeable. For example, in the 1920s a campaign in Norway led to a ban on ritual slaughter, which is essential for kosher meat, and in Greece a law was passed in 1924 stipulating that Sunday was a day of rest with no exceptions made for the Jews, whose Sabbath fell on Saturday.[4]

Latent anti-semitism became more overt in the 1930s as Jews fled from Nazi Germany and, after the *Anschluss*, from Austria. These impoverished and desperate refugees were seen as 'foreign Jews' by the Christian and Jewish communities alike. In Paris, for example, the 90,000 recently arrived Jewish immigrants outnumbered the previously resident Jewish population of 60,000. They were not welcomed by the French Jewish community, and they created their own separate institutions and communicated largely in Yiddish. Belgium and the Netherlands both accepted around 30,000–35,000 Jewish refugees and Denmark around 2,000 in the 1930s, and the vast majority of these did not take Belgian, Dutch, or Danish nationality and therefore remained 'foreign' Jews. In Belgium, France, and the Netherlands camps were opened to house the refugees: of these, Westerbork in the Netherlands would become notorious as the principal Dutch transit camp for the deportations to the extermination camps. Countries such as Poland, Romania, and Italy tried to restrict the flow of refugees by passing laws removing citizenship from anybody who had spent five years outside the country, a measure designed to prevent the return of émigré Polish, Romanian, and Italian Jews from Germany and Austria. Governments also took action to restrict the employment of 'foreign' Jews. For example, the Belgian medical association banned them from practising medicine and the Flemish lawyers' association banned these Jews from membership. Bernard Wasserstein concluded his survey of Jews before the outbreak of the Second World War:

> The Jews of Europe did not react to their predicament passively. They were actors in their own history. They sought by every possible means, individually and collectively, to confront the threats that loomed on every side. They tried emigration, but the exits were blocked. They tried persuasion, but few would listen, and anyway the barking loudspeakers of Nazi propaganda deafened ears. They tried political organisation of every kind, but they were politically

> weightless. A handful, even before the war, tried violent resistance, but their enemies could wreak vengeance a thousandfold – as the Nazis demonstrated on Kristallnacht. Some tried prayer, but their God betrayed them.[5]

After the Second World War broke out the Germans played on the existing anti-semitism in Europe by publishing openly anti-semitic articles in the official press. They also produced propaganda films, notably *Jud Süss* and *Der Ewige Jude*, which circulated around Europe and were viewed by large audiences.

The Germans took numerous steps to isolate all Jews, native and 'foreign', from the Christian populations: some of these steps met with a sympathetic response from Christian communities whereas others had varying degrees of support.

The first step was to identify Jews and effectively to brand them. Jews in the General Government were required to wear white armbands with a blue Star of David, and in the western provinces annexed to Germany, the yellow star. In Warsaw it was observed that: 'At first the Poles tended to express support for the Jews forced to wear the armbands, but in time this feeling cooled, and Poles apparently avoided encounters in the streets with their branded Jewish friends.'[6] When the yellow star was introduced in the Protectorate, the Germans were annoyed that Christian Czechs went out of their way to greet Jews in public places; in one factory in Moravia employees arrived for work with the Star of David attached to their clothing. The official press was ordered to warn the population that Czechs seen fraternizing with Jews would be treated as Jews.[7] The yellow star was only introduced into western Europe in May 1942. A Paris police report at the time noted: 'The implementation of the ordinance, while appearing to have left the public indifferent, nonetheless runs counter to the feelings of a good number of Parisians, who do not see this measure as necessary in terms of the national interest.' Some Jewish sympathizers wore yellow flowers or handkerchiefs to show their support for the branded Jews. About twenty people were arrested for such mockery of German policy and were subjected to a short, sharp period of incarceration in Drancy transit camp to teach them to respect the Germans. Marshal Pétain refused to allow the yellow star to be imposed in the Unoccupied Zone.[8] In most countries the civil services allocated the yellow stars: only in Belgium did the secretaries-general refuse to participate in the German scheme, a rare demonstration of independence.

The Germans next introduced measures to impoverish the Jews by expropriating their properties, businesses, and assets, and depriving them of the means to earn a living. In some places, locals took advantage of German persecution of the Jews and seized Jewish property for their own benefit. Such conduct was criticized in the clandestine press, for example in Poland: 'Cases of mass robbery of former Jewish property bear eloquent witness to the ongoing moral decay', but such criticism and appeals by the government-in-exile not to profit from German policy had little effect. In France, however, the Vichy regime actually encouraged the French people to take over Jewish businesses, arguing that such steps would reduce the threat of a German economic takeover of France. In Belgium the secretaries-general refused to participate in the expropriation of Jewish property, businesses, and assets, thus forcing the Germans to set up their own organization to undertake the process. In the Netherlands, Reichskommissar Seyss-Inquart ordered all civil servants to sign an Aryan Declaration, which led to the dismissal of all Jewish civil servants. The Dutch Supreme Court voted by a majority of twelve to five to dismiss its own Jewish president, Lodewijk Visser. The Dutch secretaries-general made a weak protest to Seyss-Inquart: 'there is no Jewish question in the Netherlands as may possibly be the case in other countries and also no reason to make a distinction between Jews and non-Jews in this country'.[9]

The attitude of the Vichy regime towards Jews stands out for comment. Xavier Vallat was appointed commissioner-general for Jewish Questions and drew up two *Statuts des Juifs*, the first in October 1940 and the second in June 1941. The first statute forced all Jews to register themselves, and forbade them to hold jobs in the civil service, in education, or in the justice system, or to serve in the armed services, or to work in the press or in the entertainment industries. The second statute extended the list of prohibited occupations so that employment was virtually impossible for them. In both cases there were exemptions for Jews whose families had been in France for at least five generations, and for those who had rendered exceptional service to the French state. These statutes were not passed under German orders but were a wholly independent initiative of the Vichy regime. Arguments have raged since regarding the reasons for the French action. The Vichy foreign minister, Paul Baudouin, wrote:

> It is now clear that the only way to stop the application by the Germans in the Occupied Zone of the most drastic anti-semitic measures (we have been warned from Paris that they are imminent) is to announce a number of regulations, which should be much more moderate and framed in a different spirit, applicable to the whole of France.

Vallat himself argued: 'My legislation is not derived at all from the racial anti-semitism of the Nazis. It is derived from a long and continuous anti-Judaism which you will find in complete conformity with the teachings of the Catholic Church.' Indeed, the Vichy regime instructed the French ambassador to the Holy See to investigate whether the Vatican had any objection to the French anti-semitic laws – and received a reply in the negative. Reports from the prefects indicated little public response to the anti-semitic laws or, if anything, suggested that the public appeared in favour of them.[10]

The German policy of forcing Jews to live in certain restricted areas served to isolate them from the wider population. The process of concentrating the Polish Jews into ghettos began in October 1939 with the opening of the first, in Piotrków Trybunalski. This was followed by the creation of at least 400 more in Poland, of which the largest were located in Warsaw, Cracow, and Łódź in 1940. As Raul Hilberg wrote:

> The ghetto was a captive city-state in which territorial confinement was combined with absolute subjugation to German authority. With the creation of the ghettos, the Jewish community of Poland was no longer an integrated whole. Each ghetto was on its own, thrown into sudden isolation, with a multiplicity of internal problems and a reliance on the outside world for basic sustenance.
>
> Fundamental to the very idea of the ghetto was the sheer segregation of its residents. Personal contacts across the boundary were sharply curtailed or severed altogether, leaving in the main only mechanical channels of communication: some telephone lines, banking connections, and post offices for the dispatch and receipt of letters and parcels. Physically the ghetto inhabitant was henceforth incarcerated. Even in a large ghetto he stood never more than a few minutes' walk from a wall or fence. He still had to wear the star, and at night, during curfew hours, he was forced to remain in his apartment house.[11]

The creation of the Warsaw ghetto was a colossal feat of urban reorganization since it forced the relocation of 113,000 Christian Poles from the area to make way for an initial Jewish population of 138,000.[12] By isolating the Jews from the Christian Poles behind a high wall it was only too easy for the latter to become ignorant of the conditions within the ghetto, where starvation stalked the streets. After the German invasion of the Soviet Union, ghettos would be created in every town and city with a substantial Jewish population. Some were tiny, a few streets fenced off with barbed wire, but others, in Lwów, Vilna, and Białystok, were more substantial with larger populations and were better guarded.

In Belgium from August 1941 onwards Jews were permitted to live only in the cities of Brussels, Antwerp, Liège, and Charleroi, where most of the

Jews were already concentrated. After the 1942 strike in Amsterdam in response to attacks on Jews by the *Nationaal-Socialistische Beweging* (NSB), the Jews in the Dutch capital were forced to relocate to certain neighbourhoods in the city. The Jews in Norway were mainly located in Oslo and Trondheim, so no special measures were needed to concentrate them. The Jews in the Protectorate were allowed to live freely until late 1941 when the fortress town of Terezín was turned into the ghetto of Theresienstadt. This ghetto started out as a camp to provide preferential treatment for Czech and German Jews who were either veterans of the First World War or had earned special status by some other means, but from January 1942, Jews from Prague and Brno began to be despatched there, and it was from Theresienstadt that the trains would roll to the death camps.[13]

'Foreign' Jews had already been interned in camps in southern France along with Spanish republicans and communists before the fall of France in 1940. The Vichy regime continued this policy, so that in the summer of 1942, when the deportations eastwards began, there were 20,000 'foreign' Jews interned in the Unoccupied Zone. Parallel to this process, the German and French authorities in the Occupied Zone conducted a series of internments of Jews who were taken by the French police to camps at Pithiviers and Beaune-la-Rolande in the Loiret department of northern France in May 1941. In August 1941 there was a sweep of foreign Jews living in Paris, who were sent to an unfinished housing estate in Drancy in the north-eastern part of the city. An historian of the Holocaust in France has commented: 'The non-Jewish population was not concerned about the first round-ups. No newspaper edited by non-Jews reported the event at the time. It was a matter concerning foreign Jews; the arrests had been made without incident and without being exposed to the view of the people passing by in the street.'[14]

A further factor that served to isolate the Jews from the rest of the population was the creation of Jewish councils to oversee the organization and welfare requirements of the Jews in their country. It was therefore only too easy for the non-Jewish population to assume that the Jews were looking after themselves and needed no assistance from outside: 'If the Jews were handling their own affairs, gentiles told each other, then why interfere to help them?'[15] In the Netherlands the *Joodse Raad* was established in February 1941. It was led by Abraham Asscher, an Amsterdam businessman, and David Cohen, a university professor: 'Both men were essentially humanists and philanthropists who accepted the responsibility of serving as chairmen of the Council in the hope that they might be able to help their people in a time of crisis.'[16] In Belgium, *L'Association des Juifs en Belgique* was established in November 1941 and was led by Salomon Ullman. That month in France, *L'Union Générale des Israélites de France* (UGIF) was set up to bring all Jewish social and philanthropic agencies under one organization. André Baur led the UGIF in the Occupied Zone and Albert Lévy and Raymond-Raoul Lambert worked in the Unoccupied Zone. There was little opposition to the creation of these councils in the Netherlands or in Belgium, but in France the French Jews greatly resented being forced to work with the refugee Jews, whom they viewed as 'foreign'.

Judenräte were established in the ghettos in Poland. The president of the *Judenrat* in Warsaw was Adam Czerniaków, described by the diarist Chaim Kaplan as 'a decent man' while noting that the other members of the *Judenrat* were 'the dregs of humanity'.[17] The head of the *Judenrat* in the Łódź ghetto was Chaim Rumkowski, a failed businessman, of whom it can be argued that power went to his head and led to substantial abuses of that power. After the German invasion of the Soviet Union, more *Judenräte* were established as new ghettos were formed. The role of the leaders of these, Efraim Barasz in Białystok, Henryk Landsberg in Lwów, Jacob Gens in Vilna, Dr Elchanan Elkes in Kovno, Ilya Mushkin in Minsk, as well as the leaders of the Jewish Councils in western Europe, would prove highly controversial once the deportations began.

Long before the Holocaust was launched anti-semitic propaganda had established a link between Jews and communism, and this became another factor in the muted reaction of the Christian population to the anti-Jewish measures instituted by the Germans. Christian Poles in the eastern part of Poland which had been occupied by the Soviets between September 1939 and June 1941 were particularly vulnerable to this kind of anti-semitic propaganda. Some believed that Jews had welcomed the Soviet occupation and had benefited from it, whereas in fact Soviet policy had been just as damaging to the local Jewish communities as to the Christian Poles. The Germans sought to exploit the image of the 'Jewish communist' to encourage the populations in the east to take action against the Jews. Some did, and with German encouragement there were a few notable massacres in places such as Jedwabne, Radziłów, and Łomża. In total it has been estimated that local populations killed at least 12,000 Jews in Poland, 16,000 in Lithuania, and 23,000 in the Ukraine, and that the Belorussians were no less likely to kill their Jewish neighbours. Nonetheless, the Germans were disappointed with the result, as illustrated by a report from Einsatzgruppe B in Belorussia in early August 1941: 'It is true that the population feels hate and fury towards the Jews and approves of the German actions . . . however, it is incapable of taking the initiative into its own hands in dealing with the Jews.'[18]

The Romanians and Hungarians also made a link between communists and Jews. The Romanians believed that Jews had collaborated with the Soviets during the Soviet occupation of the Romanian provinces of Bessarabia and northern Bukovina. Consequently, the prime minister, Ion Antonescu, ordered his army and gendarmerie to kill the Jews in those provinces and between 280,000 and 380,000 Jews were murdered. The Romanian Army would go on to murder the Jews of Odessa. Yet at the same time Antonescu resisted German demands for Jews with Romanian citizenship to be deported to their deaths. During their occupation of Polish East Galicia the Hungarian army expressly warned the Jews of the dangers posed to them by the Germans' murderous policy, and facilitated their departure for the relative sanctuary of Hungary by furnishing them with papers made out with Christian surnames along with false baptismal certificates: these Jews mostly survived the war. However, the Hungarian authorities were ready to expel the Jews from Hungarian-occupied Sub-Carpathian Ruthenia into German-occupied Ukraine, where they perished at Kamianets-Podilskyi.[19]

The spectre of the 'Jewish communist' was not limited to eastern Europe. The Vichy regime made no protest when, on 12 December 1941, the Germans arrested 743 Jews in Paris. The majority of these were French Jews who held prominent positions in society. They were despatched to the internment camp at Compiègne as hostages to be executed in reprisal in the event of attacks on the Germans by the communist resistance. For example, when ninety-five Frenchmen were executed at Mont-Valérien on 15 December as reprisals for resistance attacks, fifty-one of the victims were Jews.[20]

The origins of the decision to exterminate the Jews of Europe are much debated and it is unnecessary to repeat the arguments here, other than to state that, following the Wannsee Conference in January 1942 chaired by Reinhard Heydrich, plans were made to eradicate the Jews everywhere by transporting them by train to specially constructed extermination camps.[21] Bełżec opened in March 1942 and Treblinka and Sobibor began their deadly operations in May: over 1,300,000 Polish Jews died in these camps and only 110 survived to bear witness. Existing gassing operations at Chełmno and Auschwitz were greatly extended to cater for the high number of expected victims: Auschwitz-Birkenau began large-scale gassing operations in March 1942. These sites in occupied Poland were selected because the greatest number of Jews resided in Poland, and it made logistic sense to transport the smaller numbers from the rest of Europe there. It should be stressed that clear evidence of the German genocidal intent against the Jews took time to emerge and even longer to be believed. With the total censorship of newspapers and extremely limited travel in Europe, knowledge of what was happening elsewhere in Europe was hard to come by. It was all too easy for people to dismiss as empty rumours news of actions which, after all, in their depravity had no precedent.

German policy was to ensure the collaboration of native governments and administrations in the process of deporting Jews from their countries. In the case of Slovakia, an agreement was forged between the government of Vojtech Tuka and the German adviser, Dieter Wisliceny, whereby it was agreed that Slovakia would pay the Germans 500 Reichsmarks for every Jew taken and in March 1942 the first batch of 600 Jewish young men left the country, followed soon by family groups, so that between March and August 1942, 56,000 Jews had been deported. The Vatican and the Slovak bishops Ján Vojtaššák and Andrej Škrábik successfully appealed to Jozef Tiso, president of Slovakia, to save the baptized Jews, and around 1,000 exemptions were issued. Pressure from the Vatican and governmental unease at the economic dislocation caused by the deportations led to a halt to the whole process in September 1942. Around 24,000 Jews remained living in camps in Slovakia until they became the principal victims of German reprisals following the 1944 Slovak uprising.[22]

At the end of June 1942 Adolf Eichmann arrived in Paris to start the process of deporting the Jews from France and after his departure his deputy Theo Dannecker remained in charge. On 2 July the Higher SS and Police Leader Carl Oberg and Helmut Knochen met the Vichy chief of police, René Bousquet, and agreed on the initial deportation of 30,000 'foreign' Jews, of whom 20,000 would be taken from the Occupied Zone, principally Paris, and the remainder from the Unoccupied Zone. The original plan envisaged taking the men and women of working age first, leaving their children behind, but Pierre Laval expressly offered to deport the stateless children too, a step seen by the Germans as 'welcome proof that Vichy was prepared to go even further than originally requested'. Laval's attitude was reported to Washington by the United States diplomat Tyler Thompson: Laval 'stated flatly that the foreign Jews had always been a problem in France and that the French government was glad that a change in German attitude to them gave France an opportunity to get rid of them'.[23] By focusing on the 'foreign' Jews, the Vichy regime was also drawing attention away from the fact that the two earlier deportations, in March and May 1942, had included a significant number of prominent French Jews. The Germans recognized that Laval would encounter opposition should they insist too much at this stage on seizing more French Jews. A report by the SS to Berlin in September 1942 noted: 'an attempt was made to arrest Jews of French nationality. The political situation and ... Laval's views on the matter do not permit action ... such an action would have severe consequences ... The Reichsführer SS concurred in this opinion and ordered that no Jews of French nationality are to be arrested for the time being. Large-scale Jewish deportations are therefore impossible.' A possible solution to the problem of fulfilling the quotas lay in revoking the citizenship granted to Jews since 1927. This process was undertaken and it denaturalized 6,307 Jews, including the author Irène Némirovsky.[24]

This distinction between native Jews, who should be protected, and the 'foreign' Jews, who were unwanted, was also shared by the Belgian secretaries-general. Eggert Reeder, the German military administrator of Belgium, reported in September 1942 that: 'Among the Belgian people, the action did not cause much of a stir, as the Jews were relatively unimportant here, and nine-tenths of them were emigrants or other foreigners. Representatives of the Belgian Ministry of Justice and other Belgian offices repeatedly stressed that they would only intervene on behalf of Belgian Jews.' Some 4,000 Belgian Jews were exempted for the time being and were held in the main transit camp at Mechelen.[25]

The principal reason why the Germans held back from insisting on the deportation of native Jews was that they needed the cooperation of the police and local administrations in the countries of western Europe in order to round up and despatch the Jews, since the Germans simply had too few troops and security forces in these countries to carry out the round-ups themselves. For example, on the eve of the great round-up in Paris on 16 July 1942 all police leave was cancelled, and students at the police training academy were mobilized to augment the French police force so that the actual round-up of the foreign Jews was carried out by a total of 4,412 policemen. Childless families and unmarried people were despatched to Drancy and the remainder to the Vélodrome d'Hiver (Vel' d'Hiv) in Paris, where there was little food, water, or shelter and great overcrowding. A total of 12,884 Jews were caught that day. The prefects all reported in the summer of 1942 that public opinion was shocked by the deportations.[26]

In the Netherlands, 11,000 foreign and domestic Jews were taken to Westerbork camp for transport to the east. They were collected from their homes by Dutch policemen, and after the war Wilhelm Lages, the head of the German security police in Amsterdam, alleged: 'The main support of the German forces in the police sector and beyond was the Dutch police. Without it, not 10% of the German occupation tasks would have been fulfilled ... Also it would have been practically impossible to seize even 10% of Dutch Jewry without them.' This cooperation was achieved under threats issued by the Higher SS and Police Leader Hanns Rauter, who promised: 'I will act against any policeman who disobeys an order from the German police to arrest Jews. We will not only dismiss such policemen from the service, irrespective of whether they are state police or municipal police, but there must also be disciplinary proceedings against them.' He was also prepared to order the arrest of policemen who resigned or went underground, as well as their family members. Secretary-General Karel Frederiks protested at the use of the Dutch police, to no avail. To augment the regular Dutch police forces Rauter created a special unit, the Voluntary Auxiliary Police, staffed mainly by NSB members with the express purpose of hunting down fugitive Jews.[27] In Belgium the local police were involved in one raid but otherwise the round-ups were conducted by the Flemish SS and the Rexist security forces.[28] In Norway, the round-ups in Oslo were conducted by the Oslo police, the *Hird*, and other *Nasjonal Samling* (NS) formations, and members of the Norwegian Germanske SS-Norge Division.[29]

Two principal agencies could serve to influence the response of the Christian population to the deportations of the Jews: the Church and the clandestine press. The pre-Vatican II Catholic Church was openly antisemitic: on Good Friday, priests would denounce the 'perfidious Jews' who 'wanted to have the Lord Jesus Christ killed'. Pope Pius XII has been much criticized for remaining largely silent on the fate of the Jews. Evidence suggests that he was much more concerned about communism and believed in the link between Judaism in Europe and communism.[30] Yet senior clergy in several countries were more prepared to voice their concern. In Slovakia, they had in fact succeeded in ending the deportations. In France, the annual assembly of French cardinals and archbishops was meeting in Paris while the Vel' d'Hiv operation took place, and on 22 July Cardinal Suhard took a letter from the assembly to Pétain voicing its distress at the measure. This is the only example of a senior clergyman in the Occupied Zone protesting. On 19 August 1942 Cardinal Gerlier of Lyon sent a letter of protest to Pétain. His example was followed by Cardinal Saliège of Toulouse who read out a pastoral letter on 23 August:

> Jews are men and women. One cannot do just anything to them, to those men, those women, those fathers and mothers. They belong to humankind, they are our brothers, like so many other people. A Christian cannot forget that.

These examples were followed in turn by letters and sermons from other members of the Church hierarchy in the Unoccupied Zone so that by the end of the summer thirty-five Catholic archbishops and bishops had voiced their disquiet. These men had been staunch supporters of the Vichy National Revolution which had sought to undo much of the secularism that had dominated France since the French Revolution. Their appeals can therefore be seen as the first wedge appearing in the previously close relations between the Catholic Church and the Vichy regime. At the beginning of September 1942 Marc Boegner, head of the Protestant Church in France, addressed his fellow pastors on the deportations, and then voiced his displeasure directly to Laval and Bousquet.[31]

It was dangerous for the Church authorities to protest, as is illustrated by events in the Netherlands. On 11 July 1942 all the major Church leaders, Catholic, Protestant, and Calvinist, issued a joint protest to the Germans and obtained an assurance that Christian Jews who had converted before 1 January 1941 would be exempted from the deportations. However, after the protest was read out in the churches on Sunday 26 July, Seyss-Inquart responded by ordering the arrest of 700 Roman Catholic Jews in the country while leaving the Protestant and Calvinist converts untouched in an attempt to divide the united front. This action was duly noted in Belgium where Cardinal Archbishop van Roey made no public protest, while still privately urging his clergy to assist the threatened Jews. In December 1942 the joint Church leadership in Norway issued a letter of protest to Quisling which was also read out from the pulpits. The Germans reported to Berlin that month that: 'The Church more than any other group protested against the *Massnahmen* (measures) against the Jews. Here the deportation had a most negative effect and during church services prayers were sometimes said for the Jews.'[32]

The Polish clergy had been one of the first targets of German terror, and the Roman Catholic Church there was deprived of leadership after Cardinal Hlond precipitately and controversially took flight to Rome in 1939. The Church focused on attempting to save the Jews who had converted to Christianity, yet the Germans insisted that the converts should also be incarcerated in the ghettos. For example, in 1941 there were 1,540 Catholics, 148 Protestants, thirty Orthodox Christians, and forty-three members of other non-Jewish religions in the Warsaw ghetto where three Catholic churches remained within its confines to cater for them. The converts were allowed to leave the ghetto only after death, to be buried in a Catholic cemetery outside the walls. Further east, the Lithuanian Church was notably openly anti-semitic, and the Greek and Russian Orthodox Churches very ambivalent towards the Jews.[33]

The clandestine press voiced concern at the German measures towards the Jews, urging their readership to offer assistance to them. In May 1942, *Het Parool* castigated the Dutch people for their apparent indifference:

> Even now many of our people are undisturbed. They hear nothing, know nothing and would prefer to see nothing. They are blind to the criminal acts by which our Jewish compatriots are being persecuted, by which a part of the Dutch population in our own, hitherto safe, country, is gradually being forced to live like hunted animals, without any protection from the law, fearing for their lives, without knowing what the morrow may hold for them and what new chicanery the satanic Hun will think up.[34]

La Libre Belgique urged the Belgians to show support for the Jews: 'Greet them in passing! Offer them your seat on the tram! Protest against the barbaric measures that are being applied to them. That'll make the Boches furious!'[35] *Le Franc Tireur* called on people to 'expose the horrors of Paris; express your solidarity for all the victims – shelter them, hide them, refuse to allow France to be soiled'. *Combat*, however, linked the suffering of the Jews to the general population: 'All those who suffer at the hands of the Germans, whether Jewish or not, whether communists or not, are our brothers.' In Poland the main underground paper the *Biuletyn Informacyjny* published many articles commenting on the Jewish question. Many of these were sympathetic in part because the editor, Aleksander Kamiński, had been friends before the war with Mordechai Anielewicz, leader of Jewish resistance group ŻOB in the Warsaw ghetto. The writer Zofia Kossak-Szczucka, staunchly Catholic and strongly anti-semitic, issued a leaflet, *Protest!*, with a print run of 5,000 copies, in which she clearly distinguished between attitudes towards the Jews and attitudes towards their persecution. Catholics must do more for the Jews: although 'our feelings towards the Jews have not undergone a change. We have not stopped regarding them as the political, economic and ideological enemies of Poland', nevertheless as dutiful Christians it was essential to obey the commandment to love one's neighbour. She therefore concluded: 'He who does not understand this, who dares to link the proud, free future of Poland to base joy at the misfortune of his neighbour – he is indeed neither a Catholic nor a Pole.'[36]

The deportations were well covered in the clandestine press, especially the Vel' d'Hiv round-up. For example, *Défense de la France*:

> The odious yellow star had already shown that German domination is taking us rapidly back to the darkest days of the barbarism of the Middle Ages ... With the latest measures taken against the Jews, we are sinking even lower. Those who have ordered these measures are for ever condemned in the eyes of all human and divine justice ... We hesitate to use the term bestiality, because a beast does not separate a female from its babies. This is a case of human intelligence entirely in the service of Evil, using all its resources to aid the global triumph of evil, of cruelty, of filth.

Other newspapers followed suit. *Libération-sud* printed 70,000 copies of an issue devoted to the Vel' d'Hiv, and compared the horrors to the 1572 Saint Bartholomew's Day massacre of the French Huguenots. In the Netherlands, *Vrij Nederland* described a round-up in detail in its issue of 10 October 1942, but in general, with the exception of *Het Parool*, other newspapers such as *Trouw* and *De Waarheid* normally ignored the issue, or blamed the Dutch secretaries-general for not doing more, while refraining from encouraging their readership to oppose the German measures.

Disquiet was also voiced at the fact that the round-ups and transport of the Jews were done so openly. For example, SOE agent Ben Cowburn saw a train full of Jews in Lyon station and commented: 'So it was happening here – this vision of Nazi-dominated eastern Europe was in the main station at Lyon in *Unoccupied* France. The miserable Vichy Government had not even thought it necessary to stop the train outside in the marshalling yard.' It is probably true to say the non-Jews of Europe 'were generally more shocked by the manner of the deportation than by the deportation itself, because the story that the Jews were being taken to labour camps in eastern Europe was widely believed'.[37]

The deportations figured in reports from underground leaders to their governments-in-exile and committees in London. For example, from France, Jean Moulin reported in September 1942: 'The arrests of foreign Jews and their handing-over to the Germans and the repulsive measures taken with regard to Jewish children, initially unknown to the general public, are beginning to raise public opposition.'[38] Yet the exiled regimes in London faced a dilemma: if they were outspoken on behalf of the Jews then they could be accused of accepting the religious divisions imposed by the Germans; if, however, they remained silent then they could be accused of complicity in the German crimes. This ambiguity is illustrated by the case of the Dutch government-in-exile. While Pieter Sjoerds Gerbrandy spoke on *Radio Oranje* in September 1942 urging the Dutch to resist the plans to deport all the Dutch Jews and thanking people for the help already given, he nevertheless rejected a suggestion to establish a special commission for Jewish affairs within his government. Queen Wilhelmina's speeches focused on national unity and made very few explicit references to the Jews.

A similar dilemma was evident among the Czechs, who recognized that the resistance in the Protectorate was in part anti-semitic but wanted to encourage the Czechs to help the Jews. The emphasis in broadcasts by the foreign minister, Jan Masaryk, was to stress that the Jews should be considered as true Czechs, and the fact that they largely spoke German should not be viewed as an expression of pro-German sympathies nor of a wider plan to Germanize the Czechs, but had come about largely through the location and history of the Jews in the country.[39]

French anti-semitism also influenced the response from de Gaulle. Early in 1943 Frenay cautioned de Gaulle to be careful not to be seen as 'the man who brings back the Jews. Although it is our duty to eliminate any "racial" distinction, we must in practice take into account the attitude of the population, which has in fact changed in the last two years.' Indeed, de Gaulle's minister of justice, François de Menthon, expressed support for Vichy's naturalization review commission on the grounds that: 'The naturalization of dubious Israelite elements, too numerous in the years preceding the war, has provided a pretext for anti-semitism, which may raise a certain problem on the day of our return.' In October 1943 the resistance received questionnaires from the *Comité Français de Libération Nationale* (CFLN) on the post-war future of France, and one response was: 'The Jews should be kept out of all governmental and public functions . . . if there is some disapproval of the harassment, deportation, etc., to which they have been subjected, no one wants to see them reappear as before the war.'[40]

The muted reaction of the Christian population of Europe, and indeed the wider world, to the fate of the Jews can be explained on the ground that the German lie that the Jews were being sent to work camps in the east was widely believed. After all, the forced-labour policy already showed that the Germans were imposing mass movements on many other populations. Given the difficulty of getting accurate information under occupation, the lie took time to dispel. In August 1941 Radio Moscow reported in Yiddish on the widespread shootings of Jews in eastern Poland and the occupied Soviet Union. In January 1942 Vyacheslav Molotov, the Soviet foreign minister, sent notes to all countries with whom the Soviet Union held diplomatic relations on the 'monstrous villainies, atrocities and outrages committed by the German authorities in the invaded Soviet territories', including the massacre at Babi Yar. The Underground Government in Poland also sent out reports on the German atrocities, many of these gathered by the resister Witold Pilecki, who had deliberately got himself sent to Auschwitz in 1940 and reported on the construction of Auschwitz-Birkenau and the first gassings of Jews there. The Allies themselves had access to independent sources of verification through the Enigma decrypts of transmissions by the SS and German police.

These reports of extermination were widely disbelieved and compared to the stories of German atrocities in Belgium during the First World War, which had largely been shown to have been exaggerated. However, Gerhart

Riegner of the World Jewish Congress in Switzerland then received a report from a German businessman, Eduard Schulte, in August 1942. Riegner telegraphed the contents of the report to prominent American Jews, concluding:

> Received alarming report stating that in Fuehrers headquarters a plan has been discussed and being under consideration according to which total of Jews in countries occupied controlled by Germany numbering three-and-half to four millions should after deportation and concentrated in east be at one blow exterminated in order resolve once for all Jewish question in Europe. Action is reported to be planned for autumn ways of execution still discussed. It has been spoken of prussic acid . . .

This tallied with information smuggled out of Poland by the underground Bund with details about Chełmno and Treblinka.[41]

In October 1942 the Polish resistance courier Jan Karski reached London. He had visited a transit camp that he thought was Bełżec and, most importantly, had been smuggled into the Warsaw ghetto, where he had met Adolf Berman and Leon Feiner and been given an uncompromising message to take out of the country:

> We want you to tell to the Polish government in London and to the Allied governments and leaders that we are completely defenceless in the face of the German criminals. We cannot save ourselves, nor can anyone else in Poland save us. The Polish underground resistance can save a few of us, but not the masses. The Germans do not plan to subordinate us, as they do other nations. We are being systematically exterminated; our community will be totally destroyed . . . Neither a Jewish nor a Polish resistance can do anything to stop the slaughter . . .
>
> We are only too well aware that in the free and civilized world outside, it is not possible to believe all that is happening to us. Let the Jewish people, then, do something that will force the other world to believe us. We are all dying here; let them die too. Let them crowd the offices of Churchill, of all the important English and American leaders and agencies. Let them proclaim a fast before the doors of the mightiest, not retreating until they will believe us, until they will undertake some action to rescue those of our people who are still alive. Let them die a slow death while the world is looking on. This may shake the conscience of the world.[42]

Karski met prominent British politicians and leaders of the Jewish community as well as his own government-in-exile. On 10 December 1942 the Polish foreign ministry issued a statement, *The Mass Extermination of Jews in German Occupied Poland*, in which it announced that the Germans 'aim with systematic deliberation at the total extermination of the Jewish population of Poland'. The information contained in the statement provided the basis for the Allied declaration a week later by eleven governments. German actions were condemned but very little action was actually taken. In January 1943 the RAF dropped more than a million leaflets over Germany condemning the German persecution of the Jews and the Poles.[43]

Still the gulf between knowledge and belief remained. When Karski travelled to the United States he was appalled when the Jewish Supreme Court judge Felix Frankfurter, himself a Jew, told him clearly, 'I am unable to believe you.'[44] In the spring of 1943 more reports were smuggled out of Poland by the resistance to the west: in March 1943 information was given that the new crematorium at Auschwitz-Birkenau was burning 3,000 people per day; in April 1943 Stefan Korboński, leader of the Polish civilian resistance, reported on the discrepancy between the numbers arriving at Auschwitz-Birkenau and the size of the camp population, concluding that 22,000 must have been killed shortly after arrival; in April 1943 a Polish resistance courier, probably Jerzy Salski, provided more information on Auschwitz-Birkenau.[45] Yet when Jan Nowak, another Polish resistance courier, arrived in Britain from Poland in 1943 he was warned by Ignacy Szwarcbart, a Zionist activist on the Polish National Council in London, not to mention the figure of 3 million Polish Jews because no one, not even the Jews, would believe it.[46]

The revelations of the fate of the Jews once they had been transported eastwards received publicity in the clandestine press. For example, the Belgian underground newspaper *Le Flambeau* printed a report by a Belgian businessman who had returned from Warsaw having witnessed the deportations from the ghetto, and in the Netherlands *Het Parool* reported in September that the camps in the east were not labour camps but were designed for extermination.[47]

In the Netherlands, despite its previous experience of the risks of protest, the Church became increasingly outspoken with regard to the German measures. A joint pastoral letter was issued by Johan de Jong, archbishop of Utrecht, and the principal bishops on 17 February 1943 condemning the deportations of Jews and Catholic converts. In her diary, Anne Frank recalled seeing a copy of the episcopal letter and voiced her approval. In his diary, Goebbels decried the 'exceptionally insolent pastoral letter' and was pleased to see that Seyss-Inquart had taken immediate steps against the Church by closing the Calvinist, Catholic, and other denominational universities.[48] Further protests followed the May 1943 German ultimatum to Protestant converts and Jews in mixed marriages, categories hitherto exempt for deportation, to choose sterilization as an alternative to deportation. The Churches reacted strongly: 'Sterilization ... is the logical end result of an anti-Christian doctrine which supports human extermination. It is the result of a boundless self-glorification and an outlook on the world and life which renders a Christian and humane life impossible.' The sterilization procedures were to be carried out by Jewish and Dutch doctors and although suggestions were made to resist the demands by a wholesale resignation of the medical professionals, the population was not yet ready for such a dramatic step towards overt resistance. Over the next thirteen months 1,146 men and 1,416 women opted for sterilization.[49]

Church appeals were largely disregarded by the Germans in their determination to exterminate the Jews of Europe, but the response of the native police forces arguably had a far greater effect in limiting the deportations. It is unclear when collaborating regimes such as Vichy or Quisling actually became aware that deportation meant death, but after the Allied Declaration René Bousquet informed the Germans that French police personnel would not assist in the deportation of French Jews, although the foreign Jews were still subject to deportation. In July 1943 SS-Hauptsturmführer Alois Brunner arrived in France from Salonika, where he had deported the Jewish population, and received the keys to Drancy. Under Brunner the German police sent squads out into the countryside to catch hidden Jews. They were assisted by *La Police aux Questions Juives* and by the *Milice*, whose avowed purpose was to 'combat democracy, Jewish "leprosy", and Gaullist dissent'. The increasing level of non-cooperation by the French police was effective: in 1942, 42,500 Jews had been deported but in 1943 the number fell to 22,000. The numbers fell further as the deportations continued up to August 1944, which leads to the conclusion: 'One can only speculate on how many fewer would have perished if the Nazis had been obliged to identify, arrest, and transport without any French assistance every Jew in France whom they wanted to slaughter.' The Netherlands also witnessed a change of heart among the Dutch police. In the spring of 1943 the Germans reported that 'the Dutch police is unmistakably deteriorating in the fulfilment of its official duties and is demonstrating a passive attitude'. In May the Catholic bishops 'forbade the collaboration of Catholic policemen in the hunting down of Jews, even at the cost of losing their jobs', with the unspoken promise that the Church would finance the policemen and their families if they were forced to go into hiding.[50]

Not everyone was indifferent to the fate of the Jews even before the knowledge of the extermination camps became public. Individuals in every country sheltered or helped Jews in some way, and many paid for their compassion with their lives. In Poland, offering any form of assistance to Jews was punishable by death, as Bruno Probst, a member of German Reserve Battalion 101, confirmed:

> As far as I know, Poles were never arrested and turned over to the competent police authorities on these grounds. From my own observations and from the stories of my comrades, I recall that when the above-mentioned grounds for suspicion were at hand, we always shot Poles on the spot.[51]

The Germans also applied their principle of collective responsibility to those caught hiding Jews. An individual might be prepared to risk his or her own life to hide a Jew, but the German habit of executing entire families, populations of villages, or inhabitants of apartment blocks where a Jew had been found hiding, meant that the risk was extended to strangers: 'to shelter Jews meant risking one's own life and that of one's family, at every moment, over the course of weeks, months, or even years'.[52] Even so, there were Poles willing to take the risks and Yad Vashem has honoured over 5,000 Poles as 'righteous'. The Maximilian Kolbe Foundation has named 2,300 individuals who were executed.[53]

In western Europe the execution of helpers was relatively rare. The most common punishment was a term of imprisonment in the home country or deportation to a German concentration camp. For example, the Dutch people who had hidden the family of Anne Frank either were not arrested at all or were imprisoned in the Netherlands.[54] There were exceptions: when the Gestapo raided a school in Brussels where thirty Jews were hiding, the Jews were deported and their helpers, the Ovart family, were executed.[55]

Before the ultimate fate of the Jews was known, welfare agencies operated to care for Jews trapped in the ghettos in Poland or in internment camps in western Europe. These agencies such as *Rada Główna Opiekuńcza* (Central Welfare Agency), in Poland, and the *Amitié Chrétienne*, CIMADE, and the OSE in France forged important links with the Jews, winning their trust, which was of vital importance when operations began to try to smuggle Jews, especially children, out of the ghettos and camps. In Belgium, the *Comité de Défense des Juifs* (CDJ) was set up to oppose the collaborationism of the official *Association des Juifs en Belgique* and published its own clandestine newspapers and produced forged identity papers.

If, however, the Jews were to survive in any significant numbers, then more needed to be done. One method was to help the Jews escape from their countries. This was particularly necessary when the country in question was itself embarking on the extermination of the Jews. The newly independent state of Croatia targeted the 30,000 Jews in the country as part of the genocidal policy which also saw the murder of 487,000 Orthodox Serbs. Around 20,000–25,000 Jews were either murdered on the spot by squads of Ustaše, or were despatched to the newly established concentration camp in Jasenovac, sixty miles south-east of Zagreb. When the extermination camps opened for business in German-occupied Poland, the Ustaše sent 7,000 Jews to them. In Serbia, 15,000 Jews became victims of the reprisals which followed the 1941 Serbian uprising despite the fact that they had nothing to do with the rebellion. Thereafter the police and gendarmerie of Milan Nedić, the collaborationist prime minister of Serbia, became enthusiastic collaborators in the murder of Jews in Serbia.[56]

The Jews of Yugoslavia found protection from German and native measures from Germany's erstwhile ally, Italy. Numerous Jews fled Croatia for the Italian zone in Dalmatia where the Italian governor, Giuseppe Bastianini, proved sympathetic to their plight. Indeed, when the Germans requested Italian assistance for the round-up of Jews, General Paride Negri rejected the proposal: 'That is totally impossible, because the deportation of Jews goes against the honour of the Italian army.' This sentiment was shared by General Roatta. Indeed, the Italian Army assisted some Jews, for instance helping Ivo Herzer and his family to escape to Fiume by putting them on an Italian troop train. As German pressure on the Italians to cooperate in the Holocaust increased, the Italians sent the 3,500 Croatian Jews they were protecting to the islands of Rab and Korčula off the Dalmatian coast. After Italy's surrender these Jews were rescued by the Partisans, and many of them served with the Partisans as medical personnel for the remainder of the war. In Greece the Italian plenipotentiary refused the German demand to introduce the yellow star for Jews in the Italian zone, and in France it was well known that Jews in the Italian occupation zone of the French Riviera were protected from Vichy and German discriminatory and murderous policies.[57]

In Norway, the clandestine courier routes already used by the resistance were opened up for endangered Jews. The first round-up of the Jews in Trondheim caught everyone by surprise and little could be done to save those victims. At the end of October 1942, however, the resistance received a tip-off that the Jews living in Oslo – around 1,100 of them – were about to be rounded up and transported to Germany and then eastwards. The resistance succeeded in contacting and hiding 930 Jews, whom it then gradually took to Sweden. The border crossers charged the Jews for the journey but not extortionately: the richer Jews were asked to pay the most, and the poor went free of charge. The Norwegian effort was greatly assisted by the attitude of the Swedes. In December 1942 the Swedish minister in Berlin informed the German authorities that his country was ready to accept the Norwegian Jews: the Germans did not respond. The Swedish consulate in Oslo invited Jews with Swedish connections to apply for citizenship. Once across the frontier the Norwegian Jews were well cared for in Sweden. Despite the efforts of the resistance, 600 Norwegian and 120 refugee Jews were transported, and very few of them survived the war.[58]

Escape from mainland Europe was more difficult. The Swiss had become alarmed by the number of Jews seeking sanctuary in their country and had encouraged the Germans to stamp the letter 'J' on the passports of Jews to facilitate their identification. Around 25,000–30,000 Jews were either turned back at the Swiss frontier or detained in Switzerland by the Swiss authorities and returned to the country they had crossed from. In August 1942 the Swiss frontier with France was closed. Jews now had to be smuggled across the border by organizations such as Weidner's Dutch-Paris network. Only the fittest Jews attempted to cross the Pyrenees into Spain, following the same routes as evading Allied aircrew.

The difficulty in escaping from the occupied countries meant that the focus switched to hiding Jews. In the Netherlands the *Landelijke Organisatie voor Hulp aan Onderduikers*, LO, was set up in 1942 to assist anyone who needed to live clandestinely, whether those called up for forced labour or Jews.[59] After the war, one of LO's leaders, Henk van Riessen, explained:

> On work for Jews. Here and there it was linked to the LO, sometimes a [separate] branch, sometimes completely separate, sometimes just a connection to supply ration cards. An *onderduiker* could be dealt with on an assembly line basis. You can understand that, when there were 100 of these men to be dealt with at the exchange, and four were Jews, they never got a look-in. It was essential for the exchange to work quickly and it was very difficult to find places for them. Virtually no one took them. We also knew this and ourselves attempted to deal with the problem of the Jews, who were so much more difficult to hide and who people were so much more afraid [of helping], by using a separate channel or handing it over [to others].[60]

Around 4,000 Jewish adults are estimated to have survived in hiding in the Netherlands. This figure is dwarfed by the work of the *Comité de Défense des Juifs* (CDJ) in Belgium who arranged hiding places for some 12,000 adults, around a quarter of the entire Jewish population in the country. The CDJ was probably more successful than the LO because it was set up earlier and also because it had close links with the resistance group *Front de l'Indépendance*.[61]

In Poland members of the Front for the Rebirth of Poland formed a Council for Aid to the Jews in September 1942, after the great deportations from the Warsaw ghetto. It is best known under its code name *Żegota*. By

December 1942 *Żegota* had been restructured so that most of the main political parties, as well as Leon Feiner for the Bund and Adolf Berman for the Jewish National Congress, were represented on the board, which was led by Julian Grobelny. Whereas rescue efforts in western Europe were the initiative and work of individuals largely without links to resistance organizations, *Żegota* was directly sponsored by the Underground Government:

> In no other country of Europe under the Nazi occupation was a similar council created to attempt to rescue the Jewish population, within which such a wide spectrum of socio-political convictions would be represented, which would be attached to the central underground authorities, whose activities would be financed by the state budget and which would manage to continue for so long.

Żegota's aims were to establish branches in every major city in the General Government and to hide Jews, and to supply them with safe addresses and money for food and clothing. It provided about 500,000 fake sets of documents and directly supported around 4,000 Jews hiding in Warsaw, and a significant number in other cities such as Cracow and Lwów. Special emphasis was placed on the rescue of children and this section was led by Irena Sendler, a social worker who had contacts in the Warsaw ghetto, and successfully placed over 2,500 Jewish children in Christian homes. The Gestapo came for Sendler in October 1943 but before being arrested she just had time to pass the list of children to a co-worker. The list was then buried in glass bottles and after the war was passed to Adolf Berman, who tried to reunite the children with any surviving relatives. Sendler was tortured in Pawiak prison and sentenced to death: her release was obtained through bribery. In Warsaw alone, it has been estimated that around 28,000 Jews survived in hiding until the 1944 uprising and the evacuation of the city: they were assisted by around 70,000–90,000 people.[62]

Across Europe most emphasis was placed on saving Jewish children, largely because it was easier to do so: those under the age of six did not wear the yellow star and did not require papers to travel. In Belgium 4,000 Jewish children were given new identities and homes, leading to a high survival rate.[63] In the Netherlands four networks developed with the specific purpose of helping Jewish children. The Utrecht Children's Committee was founded in July 1942 by university students. They contacted parents who had been ordered to report for transfer to Westerbork and persuaded them to give up their children. The Utrecht students made contact with the separate Amsterdam Students' Group which was working to the same end. The *Naamloze Vennootschap* was a much smaller organization and the final group, based around the clandestine newspaper *Trouw*, only began work in April 1943. One notable source of children was the crèche at the Joodse Schouwburg detention camp. An official on the Jewish Council, Walter Süskind, made contact with the resistance and smuggled out small children and babies in empty milk churns, boxes, and sacks. Süsskind's smuggling operation was facilitated by the conduct of one of the German guards, SS-Unterscharführer Alfons Zündler, who turned a blind eye to the disappearance of children when his fellow guards were drunk or away. In late 1943 he was caught and tried and sentenced to death for helping the Jews, a sentence later commuted to ten years in Dachau, which he survived. Süskind was eventually deported and died in Auschwitz. It has been estimated that these two men saved around 600 babies and children.[64]

In France, the deportation of 'foreign' Jews forced the OSE, CIMADE and the *Amitié Chrétienne* to extend their existing welfare operations in the camps to efforts to remove children from these camps and to find them new homes. Many of these were removed officially with the sanction of the Vichy authorities. The obvious disadvantage of this was that in 1943 when the German demands for Jews to be transported east grew, the Vichy officials knew exactly where these children were to be found. Consequently, the homes run by these organizations began to disperse the children to hidden locations. The OSE had 1,025 children in its care by early 1943 and kept a central registry, matching real and false names, in the safety of Switzerland. The *Union Générale des Israélites de France* (UGIF) ran its own homes and kept lists of the names, numbers, and locations of the children living in them, but the Germans had access to these. This led to tragedy. In February 1943 there was a round-up of children from UGIF homes in Paris as well as the emptying of UGIF old people's homes, and all those caught were sent to Drancy. Such raids led to a spectacular rescue operation when sixty-three children aged between three and eighteen residing in the UGIF home on the Rue Lamarck in Paris were moved in ones or twos by Christian and Jewish women and taken to the Protestant presbytery of L'Oratoire du Louvre, where the pastor, Paul Vergara, arranged new identities and homes for them. Also in February 1943 SS-Hauptsturmführer Klaus Barbie led a raid on the Lyon office of UGIF and seized eighty-four people who were in the office at the time of the raid.[65]

One hiding place in France has become famous – the village of Le Chambon-sur-Lignon on the Plateau Vivarais-Lignon on the eastern side of the Massif Central in the department of Haute-Loire. Its pacifist Protestant pastor, André Trocmé, has become an iconic figure in the historiography of this operation, but it is clear that the entire population of the plateau was involved. The plateau had many advantages as a place for hiding Jews: it was remote and, because it was a successful summer holiday destination, it had sufficient hotels and pensions to house the Jews as well as boarding schools and children's homes. Of greatest importance was the community. The plateau had been a safe haven for the Huguenots when they were persecuted by the kings of France, and it was also home to other Protestant communities such as the Darbyists as well as a small Catholic contingent. The Huguenots explained their willingness to shelter Jews: 'In the past, it was we who were the persecuted; today it is you.' The Vichy prefect for Haute-Loire, Robert Bach, is an enigmatic figure in this story. He was willing to stand up to his regime by, for example, refusing to dismiss a number of his mayors on grounds of political unreliability and instead retaining them because of their competence. When the great round-ups of foreign Jews were ongoing in the Unoccupied Zone, Bach was given a list of 'foreign' Jews to locate and the gendarmerie operations included searching the plateau. But the French police gave plenty of notice of where they were intending to search next, and the thirty-five raids between the middle of August and the middle of September found only one Jew: he was later released on the grounds that he was not Jewish enough to be deported. Indeed, the Haute-Loire department had the lowest rate of deportation in the whole of unoccupied France. In contrast, the prefect of the Haute-Savoie, Édouard Darliac, ordered the gendarmerie to interview passengers at stations and on trains to find out if they were Jews.

Threats to the plateau as a sanctuary grew when the Germans occupied the south of France in November 1942. Trocmé noted:

> These facts about the help being given to refugees in Le Chambon are advertised throughout the south of France: from Nice to Toulouse, from Pau to Macon, from Lyon to Périgueux, passing through Saint-Étienne, it is by tens, by *hundreds* that Jews are being sent to Le Chambon.

The Vichy regime knew exactly what was happening on the plateau since Inspector Praly was stationed in Le Chambon and despatched weekly reports to his superiors. The maquis assassinated him in August 1943 and remarkably there were no reprisals. Under German pressure, the commander of the Haute-Loire gendarmerie, Sébastien Silvani, ordered a raid on the plateau in February 1943 which, since the warning system had failed, led to the capture of eight fugitive Jews with ease and the arrest of fifty-eight out of the eighty-two Jews on the list. The Germans had a convalescent home in Le Chambon for soldiers wounded on the Eastern Front and they must have been aware of the Jews hidden next door but chose to turn a blind eye. The German commander of the garrison at Le Puy, Major Julius Schmähling, is another enigmatic figure in the story. He appears also to have turned a blind eye to the Jews, but he was unable to prevent the raid in June 1943 on the House of the Rocks which led to the arrest of eighteen students of whom only seven were Jews. All these Jews were deported to their deaths but the other students survived. Daniel Trocmé, André's cousin, had been the supervisor of the building and elected to go with his arrested students: he did not survive imprisonment. Schmähling also did nothing to prevent the execution of the doctor from the plateau, Roger Le Forestier, who had given medical aid to the Jews but was caught by the Germans after having given a lift in his car to two maquisards who left weapons in his car. It appears that Schmähling had nothing against the Jews but would fight any signs of armed resistance. The establishment of maquis groups on the plateau served to threaten its status as a sanctuary for Jews and led to more emphasis being placed on smuggling Jews into Switzerland. Estimates regarding the number of Jews saved on the plateau vary widely from 5,000, the most commonly quoted figure, to the more authoritatively researched figure of 1,200. The difference is probably accounted for by the fact that many Jews only stayed for a short time. French Jews who could merge into the population only needed to visit the plateau for a short time to receive new forged identity papers before relocating to a part of France where no one knew their Jewish origins. The 'foreign' Jews whose poor command of French would betray them instantly needed to remain in what was perceived to be a safe place.[66]

Jews living in hiding did not have ration cards, so the financing of their concealment was a major challenge since their food and clothing had to be bought on the black market. In France, the various organizations assisting the Jews were greatly helped by money being smuggled into the country in large quantities by parent organizations in Switzerland. Rich Jews were also asked to donate funds to help the impoverished, often refugee Jews, and this could lead to problems. For example, when Magda Trocmé asked a group of rich Jews sheltering in the village of Le Chambon for assistance she was taken aback by the response: 'These foreigners that you bring to Le Chambon will be the ruin of us. We French Jews are not going to get mixed up with them.'[67] Others were more generous. The work of the Utrecht Children's Committee was largely financed by the sale of Jan Campert's poem 'The Eighteen Dead' (1941) by the clandestine publisher Geert Lubberhuizen.[68] Further finance was obtained from the Churches in the Netherlands, and the Dutch government-in-exile also set up a National Aid Fund and the section, Group J, financed 9,000 Jews in hiding.[69] In Belgium, the queen mother, Elizabeth, encouraged benefactors to fund the concealment of the Jews and the government-in-exile despatched funds with agents parachuted into the country.[70] *Żegota* received finance from the Underground Government, which allocated money received from

Jewish organizations abroad and from the Polish government-in-exile. The money was brought into Poland by couriers travelling through Sweden and by the *Cichociemni* who parachuted in wearing bulky money belts. There was never enough money since the arrival of funds was frequently interrupted and this meant that the grants per Jew constantly dropped.[71]

After the war many of the people who had hidden Jews were asked why they had done so. Few saw themselves as resisters: they had acted purely on humanitarian grounds. Their conduct was rooted in religious conviction, particularly on the commandment to 'Love your neighbour', and the parable of the Good Samaritan. Despite the strong anti-semitism of the Catholic Church, senior and junior clergymen urged their parishioners to help the Jews. In Belgium, the largely Catholic Walloon areas such as around Brussels and Liège had a better record of successful concealment of Jews than the more collaborationist Flemish areas around Antwerp, from which a higher proportion of Jews were deported. Cardinal Archbishop van Roey may not have spoken out publicly to denounce the deportations, but he still ordered his clergy to hide Jews within Catholic institutions, monasteries, convents, and schools.[72] In Poland, 'the Catholic clergy were of invaluable assistance in enabling us to obtain certificates of baptism, for which they provided blank forms, instructions on what to do, and ready-made certificates', as well as concealing Jews in religious institutions.[73] Similar offers of hiding places were available in France where Cardinals Saliège and Théas were especially helpful in passing the names of reliable members of the clergy to Georges Garel whose Circuit B operated to place Jewish children from homes run by the OSE into private households.[74]

Over 6 million Jews died in the Holocaust while only around half a million survived in hiding in the occupied countries, or were still alive when the concentration camps were liberated. These figures suggest that efforts by individuals and the resistance failed to thwart the genocidal policies of the Nazi regime. Nevertheless, the deportations of the Jews and the efforts to resist them had impacts on a wider scale, because the failure of the collaborating authorities to prevent the deportations or to negotiate lower numbers revealed the price of collaboration. The secretaries-general in Belgium and the Netherlands were no longer seen as the protectors of the Belgians and Dutch from German demands. The impact was felt the most in France:

> There developed a dialectical relationship between the evolution of public opinion toward Vichy and the evolution of public opinion toward the Jews. The mass arrests of the summer of 1942 had revealed the moral cost of

> collaboration. The Resistance took on an ethical dimension, while the legitimacy of the Vichy government was seriously shaken: the public's hostility to the German Occupying forces began to spill over on Vichy.[75]

In Poland, the German determination to exterminate all the Jews led to the belief that the Poles, who as Slavs were viewed only marginally more favourably than the Jews by the Germans, would be next. The fate of the Jews might not have led to a significant increase in resistance, but it did serve to make people across Europe more resistance-minded and more determined to take action.

14
The Holocaust: The Jewish Response

The most controversial claims regarding the Jewish response to the Holocaust are that the Jews were passive and made no effort to resist the German efforts to exterminate them. These claims are widespread, and they emerged both at the time as well as in later commentaries. For example, Władysława Chomsowa was active in saving Jews from the Lwów ghetto and noted that 'the greatest difficulty was the passivity of the Jews themselves'.[1] The phrase 'like lambs to the slaughter' first emerged in the New Year's declaration of 1 January 1942 written in the Vilna ghetto by Abba Kovner, and was repeated elsewhere. Emanuel Ringelblum wrote in his *Notes from the Warsaw Ghetto*:

> As long as the deportations were going on ... everyone remained silent. People let themselves be led like sheep to the slaughterhouse ... This can be said about the majority of the men and women who were taken to the Umschlagplatz during the deportations. This will remain a permanent riddle, this passivity of the Jewish population, even towards their own police.[2]

Raul Hilberg has been the most outspoken critic of the apparent passiveness of the Jews:

> The reaction pattern of Jews is characterised by almost complete lack of resistance ... On a European-wide scale the Jews had no resistance organisation, no blueprint for armed action, no plan even for psychological warfare. They were completely unprepared ... The Jews were not oriented towards resistance.[3]

Such thoughts were not confined to the ghettos in the east. In the Netherlands, Reichskommissar Seyss-Inquart commented: 'I could not imagine that Jews capable of labour were working while their relatives were being destroyed. I believed that in that case one could expect nothing else than that every Jew would attack a German and strangle him.'[4]

It is not that Jews were any less likely than Christians to join resistance movements in their own countries. Indeed, it is notable that at a time when few people were active in the resistance anywhere, Jews were often particularly prominent. For example, in the French resistance: Jean-Pierre Lévy, Daniel Mayer, Léo Hamon, Serge Ravanel, Raymond Aubrac, Maurice Kriegel-Valrimont, and Pierre Villon as well as many of the members of the early resistance group, the Musée de l'Homme, were all Jews. Yet these Jews were resisting primarily as Frenchmen, and only secondarily as Jews. They were no more likely than their Christian comrades to take steps to resist the Holocaust of their co-religionists, or to assist the efforts of those Jews who tried to take action.

There were some explicitly Jewish units within the French resistance, notably in the communist groups *Main-d'Oeuvre Immigrée* (MOI) which worked closely with the *Franc-Tireurs et Partisans* (FTP) in Paris. The MOI was composed principally of young Jews from eastern Europe and numbered only a few dozen people, led first by Boris Holban and then by Missak Manouchian. During 1942 and the first half of 1943 the MOI made a series of attacks on German units, soldiers, transport, and premises, culminating in September 1943 in the assassination of Fritz Sauckel's representative in organizing forced labour in Paris, Dr Julius Ritter. Yet these attacks were not mounted to prevent the deportation trains from leaving Paris and thereby to save Jews destined for extermination, but simply as part of a more general campaign to hamper the German occupation.

The relationship between the MOI and FTP is also revealing. During the summer of 1943 the French police unit the *Brigade Spéciale* managed to capture almost the entire MOI leadership following the treachery of the MOI's political commissar, Joseph Davidovitch. Those arrested were sent to Drancy transit camp where three of them organized a resistance within the camp and planned an escape. They asked MOI survivors on the outside to contact the FTP to arrange the smuggling of hand grenades into the camp and to organize an attack on the French guards from the outside. The FTP responded: 'Your plan would require at least five hundred "sporting types". Under present circumstances this is impossible, and we must advise you to count only on your own resources.' In February 1944 Manouchian and twenty-two of his comrades were tried in Paris and executed. MOI survivors contacted the FTP leadership asking to be transferred south, but the Communist Party leadership refused and gradually the MOI in Paris was totally destroyed.[5]

Other Jewish organizations, such as the tiny *Armée Juive* set up by David Knout and Abraham Polonski, had Zionist aims and focused on training young people for life in Palestine and on smuggling them out into Spain from where it was hoped they would reach Britain and join the Jewish Brigade there. Jewish maquis units were also established, growing largely out of the Jewish scout movement. These aimed to fight for the liberation of France and were motivated by the sight of the deportations of their co-religionists. For example, Rabbi Neugewürtz stated: 'I had witnessed scenes of such horror, that joining the maquis was, for me, a deliverance. I went from a state of terror and despondency, to one in which I could engage in armed dialogue with those bringing the evil down upon us.' After D-Day the Jewish armed units combined to form the *Organisation Juive de Combat* (OJC) and fought alongside the mainstream resistance, 'so that we may enjoy freedom and dignity in a liberated France'. The OJC seized documents relating to the persecution and deportation of Jews and arrested people who were associated with the process before handing them over to the post-liberation committees for justice.[6]

There are a few examples of Jewish resisters launching attacks specifically to save Jews under threat of deportation. In October 1943 a raid was mounted on the office of the *Union Générale des Israélites de France* (UGIF) in Marseille and the card index was destroyed. In January 1944 the Lyon office of UGIF was hit. Maurice Haussner recalled:

> We entered the UGIF's headquarters and told all employees to line up against the wall; we told them they were doing nefarious traitors' work in keeping their official files, even if they were providing small stipends to some needy people: by having records of names and addresses, deportations would be greatly facilitated for the Germans. We then removed as many files as we could, and later destroyed them; but the headquarters housed thousands, and many still remained.

The operations were ultimately failures since the Germans held parallel lists of Jews drawn up from the census lists held by the prefectures.[7]

These lists were deadly for the Jews. From 1940 to 1942 the Jews in Europe were forced to register and received identity papers stamped with the letter 'J' to distinguish them from their countrymen. In occupied France around 90 per cent of Jews obeyed the call to register themselves at local police stations. One civil servant in the Seine department, André Tulard, excelled himself by designing a card index which listed all Jews alphabetically, by street, profession, and nationality, thereby facilitating the search for the Jews when the deportations began. The Vichy regime also conducted its own registration process and again most Jews complied. In Norway, the *Nasjonal Samling* (NS) ordered and oversaw the registration of the Jews. In Poland and the Protectorate the process was conducted by the Jews themselves under German orders. One of the leaders of the French Jewish resistance, Louis Gronowski, later wrote:

> In the light of the Holocaust I have wondered if our attitude at the time was right, and if we should not have, from the start, called on the Jewish population to disobey the Vichy ordinances. But it was unimaginable, at that moment, to envisage the idea of thousands of people crossing into illegality overnight. Besides, our minds had not yet taken on board the horrors inflicted on the world by the Nazis.

Indeed, in the Protectorate the Jews were so unaware of the dangers that in 1942 a Jewish newspaper ran a campaign listing unregistered Jews and encouraging readers to turn them in.[8]

The Jews accepted that the Nazis were hostile to them, but it is clear that they did not realize the Germans intended to exterminate all of them. Those outside the camps did have access to radio stations – the BBC, Radio Moscow, and Swiss Radio – which broadcast the news of the extermination camps, but for them the struggle was the same as that facing the Christians, that of belief. The Jews trapped in the ghettos in the east received news of mass shootings and of gassings from couriers who travelled secretly between the ghettos, but for them too it was inconceivable that 'a cultured race like the Germans would have a policy of gassing people and burning them'.[9] Exterminations at Chełmno began in December 1941 and were made public by the clandestine press. The news reached the Warsaw ghetto where it was widely disbelieved, as Marek Edelman later noted:

> The Warsaw ghetto did not believe the news, all those who clung to life could not believe that life could be taken from them in this way, only organized youth movements which were carefully monitoring the rise of German terror accepted these events as probable and real and decided to embark on a large-scale propaganda campaign which would inform the community.[10]

Even when the deportations from the Warsaw ghetto were in full swing and an escaper from a transport to Treblinka, Dawid Nowodworski, returned to the ghetto with the information that Treblinka was nothing more than an extermination camp, few believed him. The same attitude appeared elsewhere. For example, an inmate of the Łódź ghetto, Jakub Poznański, wrote in his diary on 27 September 1943:

> Persistent rumours circulate about the liquidation of the ghettos in various Polish cities. In my opinion, people are exaggerating, as usual. Even if certain excesses have taken place in some cities, that still does not incline one to believe that Jews are being mass-murdered. At least I consider it out of the question.[11]

In France, when UGIF heard of the extermination camps it did not believe the news and did not inform the Jewish population.[12]

It was understandably far easier to believe the German lie that the Jews were being despatched to work camps in the east rather than to their deaths. The Slovakian Jews were explicitly informed that they were being transported to work camps, and they took their tools with them; so did Polish Jews from eastern Poland. When the deportations began from the Warsaw ghetto on 22 July 1942, exemptions were given to members of the *Judenrat*, the Jewish police force, administrators, and those employed in German businesses. This gave rise to the belief that holding a work permit led to exemption from deportation. Suddenly the workshops were flooded by job applicants, and many were accepted onto the workforces despite the lack of work for them. The Germans encouraged such beliefs by removing the unemployed, sick, and starving Jews first, and then in August by issuing 30,000 employment cards which made the Jews believe that those 30,000 were safe from deportation.[13]

The belief that work would save one from deportation was prevalent in other ghettos in the east. For example, the highly controversial leader of the Łódź ghetto, Chaim Rumkowski, was so convinced that working for the German war effort would save the ghetto from being liquidated that on 4 September 1942 he demanded that the aged, sick, and all children aged under ten years old should report for deportation: 'Give into my hands the victims so that we can avoid having further victims, and a population of a hundred thousand Jews can be preserved. So they promised me: if we deliver our victims ourselves, there will be peace.'[14] The head of the *Judenrat* in the Białystok ghetto, Efraim Barasz, thought the same way.

In western Europe, the Germans similarly created the chimera of work in the east as the means of getting the Jewish Councils to collaborate in the process of organizing the transports. On 15 July 1942 the Germans ordered the *L'Association des Juifs en Belgique* (AJB) to set up a labour office and then a week later asked the AJB to distribute 5,000 notices of deportation. The selection of those to be included on the list was the work of Flemish auxiliaries working with the Germans and the notices were issued under the letterhead of General von Falkenhausen. The AJB, however, added its endorsement: 'According to assurances given by the occupation authorities, it [the appeal] is indeed about performing labour and not a measure of deportation', and the pretence was maintained by selecting men and women of working age. The process ran smoothly to begin with, but towards the end of July increasing numbers of people failed to report to the assembly centre at Mechelen and the Germans had to mount raids to fill the quotas. During August, as children and old people began to be included in the deportation lists, the Germans had to undertake more of the work of collecting them themselves.

Once people not of working age began to be taken, the fallacy of being sent east to work camps became evident and so resistance emerged. The member of the AJB responsible for issuing the deportation notices, Robert Holzinger, was assassinated on 29 August 1942, leading to a furious demand by the German officer overseeing the deportations, Kurt Asche: 'If Holzinger's murderers are not found within 24 hours, you'll see what's what! Everything you've known in the past will be child's play in comparison.' The Germans arrested Rabbi Ullman, the head of the Jewish Council, along with five of his colleagues when they refused to carry out the German orders, but they were released from Breendonk concentration camp a week later after protests from the queen mother, Cardinal Archbishop van Roey, and the secretary-general for justice. Despite the reluctance of the AJB to collaborate fully in the deportation process, two-thirds of the Jews who were ultimately deported were despatched to their deaths during that summer before the trains were temporarily halted at the end of October. By then a Jewish resistance had emerged, the *Comité de Défense des Juifs*, focusing on hiding Jews, and working with the *Front de l'Indépendance*.[15]

In the Netherlands the *Joodse Raad* had cooperated with the Germans in the issuing of the yellow star and in the assembly of foreign Jews for deportation in the belief that the Dutch Jews would not be taken. In June 1942 the *Joodse Raad* was informed by the Germans that 800 Jews per day, including Dutch ones, must report for labour service in the Reich. Unlike the AJB, which proved increasingly unhelpful in the deportation process, the leaders of the *Joodse Raad*, Abraham Asscher and David Cohen, agreed to assist in the process if a system of exemptions for employees of the *Joodse Raad* and their families as well as for textile workers and those in the war industries was put in place. 'This suited the German thinking perfectly: they had discovered from experience that as long as one group of Jews thought they were immune they would be willing to help remove another, saving the occupiers a great deal of manpower and effort as well as preserving the appearance of order.' As the numbers failing to report for deportation rose, the Germans seized 700 hostages to be deported if the 4,000 Jews called up did not report. Jacob Presser, a witness to the work of the *Joodse Raad*, wrote:

> A dilemma of the kind that the Jewish Council had been forced to face since the outset had now grown to terrible dimensions; the Council must either resign or else choose between 700, who would probably never return [from concentration camps] and 4,000 who might do so.

The *Joodse Raad* issued two demands for the 4,000 to present themselves for deportation. Many Jews went into hiding and the Germans were forced to hunt for these themselves along with a special battalion of the Amsterdam police.

The members of the *Joodse Raad* thought themselves safe from deportation, but on 21 May 1943 SS-Hauptsturmführer Ferdinand Aus der Fünten told them that the council must provide a list of 7,000 of its employees for deportation. The response was that losing such a number would render the work of the council impossible, whereupon Aus der Fünten threatened to select random letters of the alphabet and deport everyone whose surname began with them. The *Joodse Raad* unanimously agreed to collaborate with the Germans and to produce the lists themselves. There was resistance in some quarters and talk of burning the entire card index, but in the end it was left to individual heads of department to sort out who was to be deported and who was to be saved. It was this collaboration which condemned Asscher and the *Raad* after the war. Pieter Sjoerds Gerbrandy, prime minister of the government-in-exile, told the commission of inquiry:

> We believed that the Jewish Council let itself be used for the liquidation of Dutch Jewry. They collaborated with the Germans by compiling registers [of deportees] and in many other ways, all of which facilitated the final murder of the Jews. I was firmly convinced of this at the time and I still hold this opinion today.

The Germans themselves agreed with this conclusion. When interrogated after the war, Willy Lages, the *Sicherheitsdienst* (SD) chief of Amsterdam at the time of the deportations, stated: 'without the Jewish Council we would not have achieved anything'.[16] Asscher and Cohen survived the war to face a Jewish honour court (see Chapter 32).

In France the UGIF was requested by the Germans to prepare food for the deportees who were about to be collected in the Vel' d'Hiv operation, but did not disseminate the news of the round-ups ahead of time. A clandestine tract written by *Solidarité* did issue a warning, and urged the Jews to hide, but the tract only left the print shop on 10 or 11 July, almost on the eve of the great round-up in Paris on the 16th, and was therefore too late to warn many. Those who did see it were largely the foreign Jews, who were least able to act on the information because they had the least access to hiding places.[17]

The behaviour of the leaders of the *Judenräte* in eastern Europe has led to great controversy. On the one hand, people such as Hannah Arendt and Raul Hilberg have suggested that the leaders were collaborators: 'The Jewish leadership in the Polish ghettos stood at the helm of the compliance movement, and ghetto chiefs were the implementers of surrender. Always they delivered up some Jews to save the other Jews.'[18] On the other hand, Lucy Dawidowicz has argued: 'The officials of the *Judenräte* were coerced by German terror to submit and comply. To say that they "cooperated" or "collaborated' with the Germans is semantic confusion and historical misrepresentation.'[19] Isaiah Trunk has carried out a thorough analysis of the attitudes of the *Judenräte* in the ghettos of eastern Europe, which reveals the immense complexity of the compliance or resistance debate.[20]

On 21 July 1942 the Germans presented the head of the *Judenrat* in Warsaw, Adam Czerniaków, with a demand to furnish 7,000 Jews for deportation on the following day, and 10,000 on the day after that. Czerniaków could not bear the responsibility of what he was being asked to do, and committed suicide rather than comply, leading Chaim Kaplan to comment that Czernaików 'may not have lived his life with honour but he did die with honour'.[21] He was replaced by Marc Lichtenbaum and under his orders the deportation lists were drawn up. The Jews were collected from their homes and moved to the *Umschlagplatz* to board the cattle trucks destined for Treblinka by the ghetto police. The work of these 2,000 Jewish policemen in the Warsaw ghetto has been uniformly condemned by witnesses to their work. One inmate wrote:

> These policemen became *merciless*; they had horse-drawn carts, they'd close a house, everyone had to come down, and they'd go from door to door pulling people out ... They worked because they thought they could save themselves and their families and get some allocation of food. Eventually, when it became more difficult to make up the numbers, they broke doors and dragged people out, pushed them down the stairs and onto the waiting carts.[22]

Abraham Lewin noted in his diary in August 1942: 'The Jewish police have received an order that each one of them must bring five people to be transported. Since there are 2,000 police, they will have to find 10,000 victims. If they do not fulfil their quotas they are liable to the death penalty.'[23] The Jewish policemen became so desperate to keep themselves and their families alive that even those Jews with valid work papers were seized, but on the other hand some policemen could be bribed to let their victims stay alive for longer: 'Jewish policemen distinguished themselves with their fearful corruption and immorality. But they reached the height of viciousness during the resettlement. They said not a single word of protest against this revolting assignment to lead their own brothers to the slaughter.'[24] Some Jewish police refused to cooperate and between twenty and thirty of them paid for their moral courage with their lives.[25] Some of the Jewish police commanders such as Józef Szeryński and Yakov Lejkin were converted Jews, which may have enabled them to distance themselves from their Jewish victims. Their conduct led to the first steps in resistance in the ghetto. Yitzhak Zuckerman wrote later that he regretted that action had not been taken against the policemen sooner since 'there isn't another chapter in Jewish history in which the murderers themselves were basically Jews'.[26] Szeryński committed suicide after a failed attempt to assassinate him. The resistance did, however, succeed in assassinating Lejkin on 29 October 1942 and another prominent collaborator, Alfred Nossig, on 22 February 1943.

Marek Edelman commented eloquently on the dilemma faced by those calling for resistance at the time of the deportations:

> Public opinion was against us. The majority still thought such action provocative and maintained that if the required contingent of Jews could be delivered, the remainder of the Ghetto would be left in peace. The instinct for self-preservation finally drove people into a state of mind permitting them to disregard the safety of others in order to save their own necks. True, nobody as yet believed that the deportation meant death. But the Germans had already succeeded in dividing the Jewish population into two distinct groups – those already condemned to die and those who still hoped to remain alive. Afterwards, step by step, the Germans succeeded in pitting these two groups one against another and occasionally caused some Jews to lead others to certain death in order to save their own skins.[27]

This was in effect the application of the principle of collective responsibility by the Germans to ensure collaboration and cooperation.

Jews planning to resist German demands had to consider carefully the consequences of their action. For example, in the Vilna ghetto, Abba Kovner explained:

> As regards revolt, we cogitated more than anything else over the moral aspect. Were we entitled to do this, and when? Were we entitled to offer people up in flames? Most of them were unarmed – what would happen to all of them? And if in the meantime it turned out that this was not liquidation? We were terribly perplexed as to what right we had to determine their fate.[28]

There is no doubt that the Germans were utterly ruthless. For example, when twenty-one Jews escaped from the Vilna ghetto in July 1943 their families were arrested in reprisal, and, in the case of those with no family, those living in the same room or building were arrested and executed. Work parties leaving the ghettos were made responsible for each other: if one escaped, the other nine in his group would be executed.[29] In Warsaw over

100 Jews perished in reprisal for the assassination of a German soldier in the ghetto, and a further 100 after the body of a Polish policeman killed by smugglers was found outside the ghetto walls.[30] In Westerbork, Etty Hillesum recorded that when one young boy succeeded in escaping from a transport:

> His fellow Jews had to hunt him down – if they didn't find him, scores of others would be put on the transport in his place. He was caught soon enough, hiding in a tent, but 'notwithstanding' . . . all those others had to go on [the] transport anyway, as a deterrent, they said. And so, many good friends were dragged away by that boy. Fifty victims for one moment of insanity.[31]

Her disapproval of the action of this one boy is obvious, and indeed one of the charges against the *Joodse Raad* was that it was too legalist and was more concerned in following German orders than in fostering resistance.

The Wittenberg case in the Vilna ghetto illustrates the terrible dilemma faced by Jews trapped there. In January 1942 the *Fareinigte Partisanen Organisatzie* – the United Partisan Organization, FPO – was set up in the ghetto under the leadership of the communist Itzik Wittenberg, with Abba Kovner and Joseph Glazman as his deputies. The FPO aimed to publicize the fact that deportation meant death and to encourage resistance. The FPO was in contact with the communist resistance in the city of Vilna and with Soviet parachutists who had been dropped into the Skrabouchany forest. In July 1943 the two non-Jewish resistance leaders in Vilna were arrested and Wittenberg's identity was betrayed. The Germans approached the leader of the *Judenrat* and of the ghetto police, Jacob Gens, and demanded that he hand over Wittenberg to them. Gens had an ambivalent attitude towards the FPO. He was convinced that it was work that would save the Jews and frequently publicized the reprisals carried out by the Germans whenever a Jew had escaped or had shown any sign of resistance. On 5 July, Gens ordered Wittenberg's arrest but, as he was being led out of the ghetto to be handed over to the Germans, the FPO attacked and freed him. The Germans threatened to destroy the entire ghetto and its 20,000 inhabitants if Wittenberg did not surrender to them. The FPO was shocked to discover that the public opinion of the ghetto was against them, and after a painful discussion the FPO took the decision to deliver Wittenberg up in order not to have to fight the Jews they were trying to defend. Wittenberg was executed by the Gestapo, and the leadership of the FPO passed to Kovner. Gens reportedly told the FPO:

> You fell into this trap because of your carelessness. You yourselves are to blame for what has happened. Resistance to the Germans is impossible at

> this moment. If we start a battle now, you will be defeated. It is better that you lose one man than you lose all. You must wait for the proper moment, gain time, and at the right moment you can organise a breakout from the ghetto into the forests.

It was all in vain: on 1 September 1943 the ghetto was sealed off and the Germans entered to begin to clear it. There was resistance in several parts of the ghetto until Gens persuaded the Germans to leave the process of conducting the deportations to the *Judenrat*. Over the next four days 8,000 Jews were deported while around 200 FPO members fled to the Rudniki forest. On 15 September a further round of deportations was about to be launched when the Germans cancelled the operation on hearing that the FPO had mobilized to oppose them. The Vilna ghetto was finally liquidated on 23 and 24 September, with the FPO concentrating on sending its fighters to the forests.[32]

The smooth running of the deportation processes and the apparent collaboration of the Jewish authorities should not blind one to the fact that some Jews went willingly to their deaths on religious grounds. Generations of Jews had performed the religious act of Kiddush Hashem, the sanctification of God's name, by deliberately accepting death rather than renounce God, so for them going submissively to their deaths in the gas chambers was a resistance of the spirit not the body.[33] Johtje Vos contacted a man with his wife and a young child in the Amsterdam ghetto, offering to hide them, and received a negative response and the explanation: 'Because I'm a Jew. This has been imposed by God on our people, and I don't think it's right not to accept this burden. There must be a reason for all of this. I have to accept it, and when I am caught and moved to Germany or to a camp, I will accept it without resistance.'[34]

The previous chapter showed that there were Christians who were prepared to help the Jews to hide; this chapter looks at the issue from the Jewish perspective. For a Jew to go into hiding was to accept enormous psychological pressures. In the first place, no one knew for how long a Jew would need to remain hidden, whether days, weeks, months, or, as it turned out, years. Jews often needed to be moved from one hiding place to another, and when one place of concealment was abandoned the shelterers were now safe, but not so the Jew who was still in hiding. Anne Frank's diary demonstrates the pressures of the clandestine life: 'I've asked myself again and again whether it wouldn't have been better of we hadn't gone into hiding, if we were dead now and didn't have to go through this misery, especially so that the others could be spared the burden.'[35]

Hiding in the open, albeit on false papers, required a good knowledge of the local language as well as contacts who could supply hiding places. This option was not available to the majority of refugee Jews in western Europe nor to the eastern European Jews whose first language was Yiddish. For example, Ruth Altbeker, who did leave the Warsaw ghetto, wrote of the fears of her sister-in-law: 'She feared her Polish was not good enough, that her looks were perhaps not sufficiently Aryan, and argued that she might betray herself by her behaviour.'[36] Ringelblum, who was hidden in Warsaw after leaving the ghetto, felt that:

> There are far fewer dangers than the Jew imagines. It is these imaginary perils, this supposed observation by the neighbour, porter, manager or passer-by in the street that constitute the main danger; because the Jew, unaccustomed to life 'on the surface', gives himself away by looking round in every direction to see if anyone is watching him, by the nervous expression on his face, by the frightened look of a hunted animal, smelling danger of some kind everywhere.[37]

One of the major threats facing the Jews was betrayal. Jewish survivors of the Holocaust in Poland remember the ever-present threat of the *szmalcowniki*, blackmailers who were usually youths or young men who, deprived of an opportunity for education and under threat of being deported to the Reich for forced labour, resorted to blackmail in order to make a living. In April 1943 the Underground Government condemned the blackmailing of Jews and, according to Władysław Bartoszewski, began to make stringent efforts to identify the *szmalcowniki*:

> We obtained our information directly from Christian Poles who worked for the security police with the knowledge of, and under orders from, the underground organisations. In this way we managed to unmask several dozen confidence men whose cases were turned over to the special court.[38]

The first death sentences were meted out in September 1943, and in all fifty-nine were executed.[39] In the Netherlands, about 60 per cent of the Jews who went into hiding, most notably Anne Frank and her family, were betrayed by collaborators.[40]

The Germans paid informants for their information but they also employed their own Jewish agents outside the camps and ghettos. In Warsaw they set up the *Żydowska Gwardia Wolności*, the Jewish Militia whose members would trawl the streets of Warsaw searching for Jews. They would drive up behind a person they suspected of being Jewish and calling out in Yiddish or Polish some verses from the Torah in order to gauge the reaction: 'Their eyes were penetrating and the Jews pointed out by them were lost without hope.'[41] In Belgium, the Gestapo employed Icek Glogowski 'Jacques' to search the cities for Jews who had not reported for deportation.[42] Reports of Jewish collaborators operating in France and in the Netherlands have also been made.

Escapes from the transit camps in western Europe presented the final opportunity to save one's life, but it was a step taken by very few people. For example, although escape from Westerbork camp in the Netherlands was relatively easy, only 210 Jews did so.[43] In Belgium there were outstanding efforts made to escape from the transports taking people to the extermination camps. In the middle of January 1943 sixty-four people had escaped from a train leaving the Mechelen camp by taking advantage of the fact that they were being transported in third-class carriages, whose windows opened, and not in closed cattle wagons. This success led to a more audacious plan by the *Comité de Défense des Juifs* (CDJ) to organize a mass escape from the next transport, which was scheduled for the middle of April. Hertz Jospa needed help from the partisans to stop the train and to release the deportees. His contact within the *Front de l'Indépendance*, Jean Terfve, refused to help, arguing that the operation would require at least twenty armed partisans to attack the guard units at both ends of the train. As Henri Neuman explained: 'Given the very limited funds at our disposal for our own actions, and for want of men with experience in handling weapons, we thought it was too difficult, in fact practically impossible, to carry out this action.' Furthermore, the escapers would need to be hidden locally since the FI lacked transport, and this would endanger those hiding from forced-labour call-ups. Jospa was not to be put off the project and he contacted another FI partisan, Youra Livchitz, who recruited two non-Jewish friends, Jean Franklemon and Robert Maistriau, to assist in the operation.

The plan had two parts. The first was carried out within Mechelen where it was known that the April transport would be larger than previous ones, 1,639 people, and they would be transported in between thirty and thirty-five cattle wagons. Jews on work parties outside the camp smuggled in knives, pliers, and saws for breaking out of the wagons, while Jews inside the camp organized the deportation lists so that those ready to fight for their freedom travelled together. The CDJ provided funds so that each escaper would receive 50 francs, the price of a tram ticket. Livchitz and his friends reconnoitred the route of the train and selected an area just after Boortmeerbeek for the attack. This area was uninhabited but was close to means of transport so that the attackers and those who had escaped could reach Brussels, Antwerp, and Charleroi. On 19 April 1943, coincidentally the same day that the Warsaw ghetto uprising began, the transport left Mechelen and the fighters immediately attacked the floorboards so as to be able to escape if Livchitz and his two friends managed to stop the train. One Dutchman lost his nerve and tried to stop the escape, but he was overwhelmed by his fellow deportees. By the track, Livchitz waited armed with a revolver and a lantern covered with red paper. The engine driver obeyed the red signal and halted the train. The German guards did not react immediately, which enabled Maistriau to open the doors of one or two wagons. It has been estimated that 231 people attempted to escape and that twenty-three were killed in the attempt. Some were injured and were sent to a hospital from which Livchitz tried to rescue them. His efforts were thwarted by the fact that one of the men helping him to arrange transport, the Russian Count Pierre Romanovitch, was a traitor and the six injured people were handed straight over to the Germans. Later in the year Romanovitch also betrayed Livchitz and Franklemon who were both arrested and sent to Breendonk, where Livchitz was shot as a hostage in 1944. Maistriau was caught later but survived Buchenwald; Romanovitch was tried and executed after the war. Many of the escapers found refuge in Belgian homes and survived the war. French Jews made similar attempts to escape transports in February and March 1943, but in both cases the escapers were recaptured easily.[44]

In Poland too, desperate Jews jumped from the transports to Treblinka. Zdzisław Rozbicki, a Christian Pole who lived on a farm by the railway leading to Treblinka, was frightened of what might be in the fields near the railway line: 'Some tried to escape by tearing through the barbed wire or smashing holes in the floors of the wagons. Most of these, however, were killed by the machine guns mounted on the train. Many nameless graves were dug on both sides of the track – in our fields, as well.'[45] Some efforts were successful: for example, Ruth Altbeker survived the war having jumped from a transport to Treblinka.

The shock of the mass deportations from the Warsaw ghetto encouraged those Jews who favoured resistance to consider future action but, as Edelman noted: 'To overcome our own terrifying apathy, to force ourselves to the smallest spark of activity, to fight against our own acceptance of the generally prevailing feeling of panic – even these small tasks required truly gigantic effort on our part.'[46] In July 1942 three *Halutz* organizations, *Dror*, *Hashomer Hatzair*, and *Akiba*, joined forces to create *Żydowska Organizacja Bojowa*, ŻOB, the Jewish Combat Organization. In October, after the end of the great deportations, the Bundists and Zionist organizations joined ŻOB under the leadership of Mordechai Anielewicz. He was an experienced youth leader who had not been in the ghetto during the deportations, which gave him the advantage 'that he was free of the reluctance and indecisiveness that had eroded the spirit of the ŻOB members when they realized that their failure to rally the masses to resistance during the deportation was as much a function of their own internal weakness as of the oppressive and paralyzing effect of the German terror operation'. A separate fighting organization, *Żydowski Związek Wojskowy*, ŻZW, was formed by the Revisionists. There are conflicting reports as to why the two organizations remained separate. One theory is that ŻZW contained members of the *Betar* who had undergone military training with the Polish Army before the war and therefore felt that they were best placed to provide military leadership for the resistance, whereas ŻOB insisted on Anielewicz as leader because of his long pedigree in the underground and political acumen. Another theory centred around the difference in tactics in resistance as perceived by both groups: ŻOB intended to fight to the death within the ghetto, whereas ŻZW planned to fight for as long as it was feasible and then to escape through tunnels they had constructed and renew the conflict outside the ghetto.[47]

Similar debates on tactics were held in other ghettos. For example, there was a lengthy meeting in the Białystok ghetto in January 1943 in which 'We had to decide what was more worthwhile, what would cause the Germans more damage – war in the ghetto or in the forest.'[48] The dilemma was well expressed by a participant, Sarah Kopiński:

> If it is a question of honour, we have already long since lost it. In most of the Jewish communities the *Aktionen* were carried out smoothly without a counter-*Aktion*. It is more important to stay alive than to kill five Germans. In a counter-*Aktion* we will without doubt all be killed. In the forest, on the other hand, perhaps 40 or 50% of our people may be saved. That will be our honour and that will be our history. We are still needed, we will yet be of use. As we no longer have honour in any case, let it be our task to remain alive.[49]

The conclusion reached by the leader of the resistance, Mordechai Tenenbaum, was that the resistance should plan to smuggle as many people out of the ghetto as possible, but preparations should be made to fight in the ghetto as soon as the next round of deportations was launched.[50] In the Kovno ghetto the remnants of the FPO concluded: 'There is no longer any hope that battle, which a handful of fighters, limited in number, would initiate, could turn into a mass defence . . . The rebellion, should it break out, would be nothing but an act of individuals alone, of no wide-national value and would not open the door to mass rescue.'[51] In Minsk the underground was entirely in the hands of the communists, who saw the Jewish struggle for life as part of the wider Soviet battle against the German invaders. Hence the emphasis was placed on escapes to join the Soviet partisans in the forests. An activist, Sara Goland, explained: 'In the ghetto, our only option is . . . the struggle of people sentenced to death, and in the forest we can do great things and assist the Red Army to expel the invaders-murderers from our land.'[52]

The great deportations from the Warsaw ghetto had reduced the population to around 60,000 Jews, of whom only a few hundred were members of ŻOB or the ŻZW. Plans were made to resist any future effort by the Germans to reduce the population further. But there were few weapons within the ghetto and contacts had to be forged with the *Armia Krajowa* (AK) and *Gwarda Ludowa/Armia Ludowa* (GL/AL) outside the walls to provide the Jews with the means to withstand the next German onslaught. The tiny and insignificant GL/AL forces lacked weapons to pass to the Jewish resistance but supplied moral encouragement to rise up. The AK, however, was extremely concerned about the pro-Soviet and communist stance of many of the Jewish resisters. The AK commander, Stefan Rowecki, was not convinced that ŻOB would rise up since the great deportations had been conducted with no resistance. Therefore, in December 1942 Rowecki arranged for ten revolvers to be smuggled into the ghetto, informing London on 4 January 1943: 'Jews from a variety of groups, among them communists, have appealed to us at a late date asking for arms, as if our own arsenals were full. As a trial I offered them a few pistols. I have no confidence that they will make use of any of these arms at all.'[53]

Rowecki, and the AK commander in Warsaw, Antoni Chruściel, were extremely concerned that a rising in the ghetto might spread outside the walls. The Jews and the AK were operating on different timelines: the Jews needed to act immediately, whereas the AK needed to wait until German power was clearly about to collapse before launching its own nationwide uprising. At that time the AK arsenal in Warsaw was thought to consist of only 135 heavy machine guns, 190 light machine guns, 6,045 rifles, 1,070 pistols, 7,561 grenades, and seven anti-tank guns.[54] Many of these weapons had been buried in September 1939 as Warsaw surrendered and were now in poor condition. The AK could, however, provide training for ŻOB members who visited an AK base on Marszałkowska street:

> The men from the ghetto were handed various printed instructions on how to use the arms and explosives, studied the techniques of fighting in town, were acquainted on the spot with various anti-tank weapons effective at close range, and were initiated into the manufacture of typical incendiary

> materials, mines and grenades. The ŻOB fighters showed tremendous ardour, lively interest, and a great deal of military ability.[55]

The AK also advised on the construction of mines and manufacture of Molotov cocktails.

On 18 January 1943 the Germans entered the ghetto intending to deport 8,000 Jews. ŻOB was caught by surprise and not all units were able to take part in the fighting. Nonetheless, the Germans were caught totally by surprise by the Jewish resistance shooting at them: 'the moment a revolver appeared, the Jew became a human being who had to be reckoned with, and the Germans' scorn and extravagant self-confidence were instantly deflated'.[56] At the end of the three-day *Aktion* the Germans had managed to deport 5,000 Jews, and had killed a further 1,000 on the streets. German casualty figures from the fighting are unknown, but ŻOB learned important lessons from the January revolt. The first regarded the need to be better organized, as the only female ŻOB fighter, Zivia Lubetkin, explained:

> We learned that it was most important to put the people into a kind of military barracks, to plan the uprising so that all the groups would be ready in their positions, and to make sure that each company commander, each area commander, and each fighter would know what to do, so we would not be surprised when the Germans renewed action.[57]

Edelman noted that 'we realised that street fighting would be too costly for us, since we were not sufficiently prepared for it and lacked proper weapons'.[58] Rifles were needed but these were too difficult to smuggle into the ghetto.

The principal effect of the January rising was psychological: 'The mere fact that because of unexpected resistance, weak as it was, the Germans were forced to interrupt their deportation schedule was of great value.'[59] The clandestine newspaper *Biuletyn Informacyjny* reported on the Jewish resistance with approval: 'The valour of those who have not lost their sense of honour during the saddest moments of Jewish history inspires admiration, and is a glorious chapter in the history of Polish Jewry.'[60] Renewed appeals were made by Anielewicz for more arms from the AK, but contacts between the AK and ŻOB were broken off when ŻOB's chief agent outside the ghetto, Arie Wilner, was arrested on 5 March. There were fears that he would break down under torture, but he held out and was helped to escape from Pawiak prison by a Pole. Wilner's role was taken over by Zuckerman, who continued to press the AK for more weapons: ŻOB received ninety pistols, sixty hand grenades, and fifteen kilograms of explosives.[61] The ŻZW had a separate source of weapons through its contacts with Major Henryk

Iwański, an AK officer, who helped ŻZW smuggle a machine gun and a sub-machine gun into the ghetto through a tunnel built by the ŻZW.[62] Preparations were made to protect the civilian population, as Zuckerman recalled: 'I knew that the whole ghetto was one extensive bunker since, at night, you heard hammers pounding everywhere. We encouraged Jews to set up bunkers, but I didn't get involved in the details.' These bunkers were intended only for the civilians since ŻOB's 'whole strategy was built from the first and with the clear awareness that the fighters had no escape. And the command staff explicitly decided to plan everything on battles in the ghetto we wouldn't survive.'[63] On the eve of the April uprising there were about 750 Jewish fighters in the ghetto, 500 ŻOB, and 250 ŻZW, who were organized in three parts of the ghetto, the centre, the brushmakers' quarter, and the area around the workshops. Every ŻOB fighter had a revolver with ten to fifteen bullets and four to five hand grenades.[64]

In the early hours of 19 April 1943 the ghetto received warnings from outside that 2,100 Germans and Ukrainian auxiliaries with tanks and artillery were massing, and were about to advance into the ghetto to begin the clearing operations under the command of SS and Police Leader Ferdinand von Sammern. The civilian population fled into the bunkers and ŻOB and ŻZW fighters began to prepare for the ghetto's defence. The central ghetto was the first target for the Germans. They marched confidently up the centre of Nalewki Street to set up a bivouac at the intersection of Miła and Zamenhofa Streets when two ŻOB units opened fire on them. Danny Falkner recalled:

> I felt elated that the Jews had fired the first shots; we could see that the Germans were not immune to violence, that violence could be exerted against them as well. Of course we knew it was an impossibility to conquer or resist them completely. We knew that our fate was sealed. But we wanted to bring down as many Germans as possible.[65]

After losing one dead and twenty-four wounded, the Germans retreated from the central ghetto. On 20 April the battle was renewed with an assault on the workshop area, when the Germans attempted to persuade the workers to leave peacefully. Then on 21 April SS-Brigadeführer Jürgen Stroop took over command and ordered a change of tactics: the brushmakers' quarter was deliberately set on fire, forcing the ŻOB fighters to retreat to the central ghetto:

> The flames cling to our clothes, which now start smouldering. The pavement melts under our feet into a block, gooey substance. Broken glass, littering every inch of the streets, is transformed into sticky liquid in which our feet

are caught. Our soles begin to burn from the heat of the stone pavement. One after another we stagger through the conflagration. From house to house, from courtyard to courtyard, with no air to breathe, with a hundred hammers clanging in our heads, with burning rafters continuously falling over us, we finally reach the end of the area under fire.

Fire spread to the central ghetto, driving civilians from their cellar bunkers and hiding places in attics out into the open where the Germans captured them and executed many on the spot.

This effectively marked the end of the active fighting phase. Thereafter the Germans focused on eliminating bunkers one by one, a lengthy process which forced the Jewish fighters on the defensive to protect the civilians. From 25 April onwards incendiary bombs started to be dropped into the ghetto and the Germans also used police dogs, special listening devices, and Jewish informers to locate the bunkers, which were then attacked with chlorine gas. Simha Rotem recalled the desperate state of siege:

> Cannons roar. Machine guns and mortars rumble. Bullets rain down. All of us standing at our positions, and the enemy isn't here. We're in despair, there's nobody to fight against. The Germans have taken up positions outside the walls and put a hail of bullets and grenades down on us. Suddenly, flames surround our house; because of the flames and stifling smoke, we are forced to abandon our positions.[66]

In his post-action report, Stroop estimated that 631 bunkers had needed to be attacked.

For the Jews to hold on they needed help from outside. On 19 April Captain Józef Pszenny led a company of sappers who tried to blow a hole in the ghetto wall to help civilians caught up in the fighting to escape, but the unit was forced to withdraw after two AK members were killed and four were wounded.[67] One of the participants, Zbigniew Młynarski, recalled:

> The street was empty. The Germans were shooting at us from all over. The machine gun on the hospital roof that had been shooting into the Ghetto before was now shooting at us. Behind us, in Krasiński Square, an SS company was stationed, so that when Pszenny exploded that mine that was supposed to collapse the wall – instead it went off in the street and mangled the bodies of our two guys. So we began to withdraw.[68]

On 22 April an AK detachment attacked a unit of Lithuanian auxiliaries near the ghetto walls. On the following day an AK unit under Lieutenant Jerzy Skupieński attacked the gate at Pawia Street, but failed to blow the gate and retreated after killing four SS and police officers.[69] In his post-action report, Stroop complained that his soldiers 'have been repeatedly shot at from outside the Ghetto'.[70] Emanuel Ringelblum noted that the Germans had taken precautions to reduce outside help: the trams were diverted and the Poles 'were forbidden to move freely in the streets bordering the ghetto'.[71] The AK also responded by attempting to smuggle more weapons into the ghetto through the tunnel dug by the ŻZW. Iwański's unit smuggled weapons into the ghetto and some unsubstantiated statements suggest that it might have participated in the fighting within the ghetto.

Thereafter AK efforts were focused on helping Jews to escape from the ghetto. The tunnel at Muranowska Street had been discovered by the Germans, but another, smaller one was still in operation, running from one of the churches to the outside. For example, on 10 May:

> The cast-iron sewer cover at the corner of Prosta and Twarda Streets was pulled off, and a group of Freedom Fighters came out – incredibly, some still carried weapons – in front of astonished passers-by. They were loaded into two waiting trucks of the Underground Army and taken to the woods outside the city.[72]

At this point, the disparity in tactics between ŻOB and ŻZW became evident. During the first two weeks of May as the battle continued to rage in the ghetto, most of the ŻZW contingent escaped from the ghetto. On 12 May, however, they were attacked by the Germans and their leader Paweł Frenkel was killed.[73] Some ŻOB fighters, such as Edelman and Zivia Lubetkin, escaped to fight again in the forests as partisans, but Anielewicz and other ŻOB fighters elected to remain in the ghetto to the end. They retreated to a large smugglers' bunker at 18 Miła Street, which was equipped with electricity and well supplied with food and water. The Germans located and attacked the bunker, whereupon:

> The fighting lasted two hours, and when the Germans convinced themselves that they would be unable to take the bunker by storm, they tossed in a gas-grenade. Whoever survived the German bullets, whoever was not gassed, committed suicide ... Jurek Wilner called upon all partisans to commit suicide together. Lutek Rotblat shot his mother, his sister, and then himself. Ruth fired at herself seven times. Thus 80% of the remaining partisans perished, among them ŻOB Commander, Mordechai Anielewicz.[74]

The final act of the ghetto uprising took place on 16 May when Stroop pressed the button to blow up the Great Synagogue: he then informed his superiors that the uprising was over and that 'the Jewish quarter is no more'. The Germans proceeded to demolish every building in the ghetto, effectively leaving a quarter of Warsaw in a state of total ruin. The area was then used for executions of AK fighters and Jews found in hiding, including the historian of the ghetto, Emanuel Ringelblum. Around 7,000 Jews lay dead, killed in the fighting, and the remaining 30,000 were transported to their deaths at Treblinka.[75]

The ghetto uprising provoked a mixed reaction from the Poles. Some were impressed by the news that the Jews were resisting: 'We are full of admiration for the heroic Jews. Practically defenceless, they took to fighting without the slightest chance of success. They have shown the world how brave they can be and they are perishing like soldiers.'[76] The Underground Government sent a report back to London giving details of the uprising which concluded: 'This war between the Jews and the Germans has awakened feelings of sympathy and admiration on the Aryan side of Warsaw, and shame among the Germans, who feel rightly that the situation that has come about in Warsaw is an uncommon blow to German prestige.'[77] The clandestine press also voiced its approval. Some Poles took advantage of the situation, as described by Ruth Altbeker:

> The scum of society stood by the ghetto walls. Some were tempted by the possibility of looting Jewish property, others lurked for easy prey – a Jew who might try to creep over to the Aryan side through a crevice or chink in the wall. Among the uniformed policemen, manhunters, conmen and all kinds of rascals around the walls, other Poles waited too, looking out for a convenient moment to supply the fighters with arms and ammunition. A girl hungry for thrills would be waiting to convey the needs of the besieged to the Underground Organisation.[78]

For many Poles life went on as usual as they prepared to celebrate Easter on 25 April: 'On Krasiński Square, a merry-go-round, swings, roller coasters have been placed and a loud barrel-organ is blaring. And two steps from there, behind the ghetto walls, sounds of the battle can be heard and the smoke of the burning houses spreads into the streets.'[79] At the same time, the Germans moved to arrest another swathe of the AK to prevent the ghetto uprising from spreading into the rest of Warsaw. The reaction of the government-in-exile was delayed by the crisis engulfing the Poles following the German revelations of the Soviet execution of the Polish officer corps at Katyń. On 4 May, however, Władysław Sikorski did broadcast from London, thanking the population of Warsaw for the assistance it had given to the ghetto fighters and asking them 'to offer all succour and protection to the threatened victims'.[80]

The spark of revolt spread to the Białystok ghetto where Mordechai Tenenbaum was attempting to establish a resistance force like ŻOB. His efforts were hampered by the refusal of the communists to cooperate with the moderate *Dror* movement and by the fact that the *Hashomir Hatzair* was split between the two sides. The leader of the ghetto, Efraim Barasz, was convinced that working for the Germans would save the ghetto, but he was also sympathetic to the resistance and had good relations with Tenenbaum. In February 1943 the Germans launched an *Aktion* to seize 10,000 Jews from the ghetto and take them to be murdered, and Barasz urged Tenenbaum not to resist the *Aktion* other than encourage Jews to hide. There followed a lengthy debate among the three resistance movements regarding the best method to oppose any German effort to liquidate the whole ghetto in the future. These demonstrated sharp divisions over whether to resist in the ghetto or to focus on escaping to the forests and joining the partisan struggle. Communists such as Daniel Moszkowicz and Hela Mendelson were strongly in favour of partisan action, but the majority were in favour of fighting in the ghetto.

In the evening of 15 August 1943 a member of *Hashomir Hatzair* living outside the ghetto, Chasia Bornstein-Bielicka, entered it and warned her colleagues that the city was full of German troops and that an *Aktion* was imminent. She was not believed and Tenenbaum was not informed. At 4 a.m. on 16 August, Barasz issued orders for all the Jews to report for deportation. The resistance was caught unprepared and in any case the 200 fighters only had around 130 firearms and little ammunition. The resisters issued leaflets warning that the destination was Treblinka and urged the population not to report for deportation. The resistance failed to rouse any support in the ghetto and the Jews followed Barasz's instructions to cooperate. The resistance opened fire on the Germans, but by midday the fighters were either dead or had been driven into bunkers. Between 17 and 23 August the Germans sent over 25,000 Jews to Treblinka and Auschwitz. On 20 August, Tenenbaum and Moszkowicz committed suicide.[81]

By the middle of the summer of 1943 the extermination camps of Treblinka and Sobibor had largely finished their lethal work and the small workforces in both camps – 1,000 in Treblinka and 600 in Sobibor – realized that their own end was nearing. The resistance in Treblinka was led by Julian Choronzycki, until he was caught accidentally by the SS guards, whereupon Marceli Galewski took over. The plan was to seize weapons from the SS armoury using a copied key and then to attack the mostly Ukrainian guards and set fire to the camp before escaping to the nearby forests. All the members of the resistance were placed on the afternoon shift of 2 August 1943, when the SS officers Kurt Franz and Kütner Miete would be on leave. The revolt was to start at 4 p.m. with the sound of a gunshot.

In the event, the revolt broke out an hour earlier than planned when a guard became suspicious, and only a few weapons were recovered from the armoury. Nonetheless, the signal was given and fires broke out across the compound as the Jews fled for the fence and across a minefield: 'Our objective was to reach the woods, but the closest patch was five miles away. We ran across swamps, meadows and ditches, with bullets pursuing us fast and furious.' Around 150 to 200 prisoners escaped, but the leaders were killed, and only about sixty survived the ferocious German manhunts. The revolt had focused exclusively on escape from the camp and not on the destruction of the gas chambers: nearly 8,000 Jews from Białystok were murdered there before the camp was finally closed.[82]

Sobibor catered for the Jews from the Netherlands, France, the General Government and, crucially, a contingent of Jewish Soviet POWs from Minsk. The resistance in the camp was led by Leon Feldhendler. He had no military experience and therefore joined forces with one of the Soviet POWs, Aleksandr Pechersky. Their plan was to wait until the senior SS officers, Gustav Wagner and Hubert Gomerski, were out of the camp, and then to lure the other SS officers and NCOs into the workshops, kill them with axes and knives, and steal their weapons. Then, well-armed, they would assemble for the roll call and march on the main gate. The revolt was launched on 14 October 1943 but quickly descended into chaos when the Ukrainian guards noticed that something was amiss and opened fire. Instead of converging on the main gate, the Jews made several breaches in the fence and rushed across the minefield. Around 320 prisoners escaped. Pechersky later recorded:

> Many fell in the open space that was between the camp and the forest. We all agreed that we should not linger in the forest but divide up into small groups and go in different directions. The Polish Jews escaped in the direction of Chełm . . . We, the Soviets, turned east. The Jews who had come from Holland, France and Germany were particularly helpless. In the wide area that surrounded the camp there was none with whom they had a common language.

About 170 prisoners were caught quickly and 100 were discovered in hiding, but around sixty, including Pechersky, reached the partisans and fought with them.[83]

Auschwitz had originally been established as a concentration camp for Polish political prisoners and therefore it is no surprise that a resistance movement was formed by them in the camp. This served two purposes: to ameliorate the conditions of the prisoners by arranging the smuggling of food and medicines into the camp; and to despatch intelligence reports of what was happening in the concentration camp of Auschwitz and the extermination camp at nearby Birkenau to the outside world. In summer 1942 men who would become central to the resistance entered the camp. Witold Pilecki was asked by the AK to join a party of resistance members under arrest who were being sent to Auschwitz, and he entered the camp under the name of Tomasz Serafiński and proceeded to set up the *Związek Organizacji Wojskowej*, ZOW – Union of Military Organization. Two other new arrivals were a socialist, Josef Cyrankiewicz, and a communist, Tadeusz Holij, who formed the Auschwitz *Kampfgruppe*. The *Kampfgruppe* planned an uprising in the camp and made contact with members of *Hashomer Hatzair*, Mordechai Bielanowicz, Rosa Robota, Noah Zabludowicz, and Yakov Kamiński, who had been sent to Auschwitz-Birkenau. The *Kampfgruppe* began plans for an uprising in the camp, but Pilecki felt that such an enterprise was doomed to failure unless substantial help was received from the outside by the AK. Pilecki managed to escape at the end of April 1943 and reached Warsaw where he discovered from the AK command 'that the forces at their disposal were too few and too poorly armed, that the underground organisation inside the camp was almost helpless and the SS garrison too numerous and well-equipped' for an uprising to have any chance of success. The AK also realized that it lacked the resources to care for the estimated 46,000 men and 10,000 women in Auschwitz, all of whom were in poor health.[84]

Inside Auschwitz-Birkenau, plans were being made for an uprising by the *Sonderkommando*, the men forced to operate the crematoria. Two women working in the Union munitions factory, Hadassah Tolman-Zlotnicki and Luisa Ferstenberg, stole and transferred small quantities of gunpowder out of the factory in small matchboxes hidden in special pockets and in the hems of their dresses. Some was given to Cyrankiewicz and the rest to Rosa Robota who worked near Crematorium IV. The gunpowder was used to make small bombs. In September 1944, after the majority of the Jews from Hungary had been exterminated, the SS began to thin out the contingents of the *Sonderkommando* by supposedly sending them to clear bomb damage in the Reich, but in fact executing them in secret. The plan was to start the uprising of the *Sonderkommando* on the evening of 7 October 1944, but the midday conference of the conspirators was interrupted by the sudden appearance of a known SS informer, who was promptly killed. At 1.25 p.m. several SS men entered Crematorium IV, whereupon the *Sonderkommando* 'set up a loud shout, hurled themselves upon the guards with hammers and axes, wounded some of them, the rest they beat with what they could get at . . .' The SS acted swiftly and surrounded Crematorium IV and killed the fighters, but not before the crematorium had been set on fire. The *Sonderkommando* in Crematorium

II thought that this was the signal for the uprising and attacked their guards, made a hole in the fence, and around 100 escaped. Some made it to the small town of Rajsko, a few miles away, before being cornered in a barn by the SS: none of the escapers survived.

During the whole uprising, three SS were killed and a further twelve wounded, while the Jewish losses were between 600 and 700. Crematorium IV was shut down but the others continued working for a further month until Himmler ordered an end to the exterminations at Auschwitz-Birkenau. An inmate of Auschwitz at the time, Israel Gutman, later commented:

> And yet, despite the terrible Jewish losses . . . the day of the uprising of the Sonderkommando became a symbol of revenge and was an inspiration to the prisoners. In the place that had served for years as a field of slaughter for millions of victims, there fell the first Nazis in Auschwitz. And it was the Jews who had done the fighting. In this gigantic camp where tens of thousands of prisoners were confined, a handful of Jews broke free of the pervasive spirit of submission and passive resignation to their cruel fate. The uprising of the Sonderkommando proved to the prisoners of diverse European nationalities that Jews knew how to fight for their lives.

They also knew how to remain silent. A commission was sent from Berlin to investigate how the *Sonderkommando* had been able to get hold of bombs. The women who had smuggled the gunpowder out of the Union factory and Rosa Robota and her assistants were identified and hanged publicly in Auschwitz on 6 January 1945, not long before the complex was evacuated.[85]

The resistance in Minsk ghetto in Belorussia and the Kovno ghetto in Lithuania both focused on facilitating the escape of Jews from the ghettos into the neighbouring forests to join the partisan movement or to set up family camps and defend them. The Kovno ghetto was isolated from the rest of the city, so contacts with the local resistance could not be established. This meant that Jews who escaped had to make their own way to the forests to search for the partisans: only a few hundred were successful.[86] The communist resistance in the Minsk ghetto led by Hersh Smolar was in close contact with the resistance in the city and was covertly supported by the head of the *Judenrat*, Ilya Mushkin. It is estimated that about 10,000 Jews escaped from the Minsk ghetto and of those about 2,500 joined the partisans. When the ghetto was finally liquidated in late October 1943 there were only about 2,000 Jews left in it.[87]

The Jews who fled to the forests did so from two motives: self-defence and revenge. The first group focused on establishing family camps to help

Jews survive the war. The best known of these was run by the Bielski brothers, who had escaped into the Naliboki forest and in the autumn of 1943 set up a family camp which ultimately catered for 1,200 Jews. Most of the people were women and children, old people and the sick and wounded who were defended by a smaller armed unit of around 300 fighters who would take action against informers and cooperated with the local Soviet partisans. Tuvia Bielski cautioned against taking premature offensive action on the grounds: 'Don't rush to fight and die. So few of us are left, we have to save lives. To save a Jew is much more important than to kill Germans.' Another example of a family unit was the one established by Shimon Zorin in the forests near Minsk which cared for 558 people, of whom 137 were fighters who worked in close cooperation with the Soviet partisans.[88]

Other Jews wanted revenge and took an active role in the partisan movement either by working with the numerous existing partisan groups in the forests or by setting up their own Jewish units: 'Most of the Jewish partisans had resigned themselves to the thought that their hope of reaching the day of liberation and salvation was very faint; their desire was to live out the rest of their days as free men, meeting death honourably.'[89] But the Jews found an uncertain welcome in the forests. The AK helped the ŻOB members who had reached the Wyszków forest near Warsaw after the end of the ghetto uprising, but there were clashes between the two, not generally because of anti-semitism, but because the Jews had no money and stole from the local peasants. After discussions between the two parties, the AK and ŻOB settled down to an uneasy but safe relationship.[90] The lack of the means to purchase food led Jews to engage in what the AK commander, Bór-Komorowski, described as banditry in September 1943. He urged the AK to eradicate all banditry, but this order has been seen as specifically targeting the Jews and as evidence of the alleged endemic anti-semitism of the AK. Yet a report to the Bund representative in London from the Bund central committee in Poland also wrote about the Jews who had fled the ghettos for the forests: 'Most of them, in seeking to survive, have come to form wildcat groups which are looting the countryside, and only a few of them have joined partisan groups operating in the respective regions.'[91] Some Jews served with the AK and had no problems with anti-semitism. For example, Dr Julian Alexandrowicz did so because then: 'My life was in my own hands and not any more in the hands of my enemies. I felt that if I perished I would do it only by fighting and not like a helpless creature without any resources nor as those who were forcefully deprived of all freedom.'[92]

The situation further east, in the area that had been part of the 1939–41 Soviet occupation, was however far more complicated. There the AK viewed the Jews as communists and collaborators with the Soviet regime and were therefore generally hostile to Jewish partisans. This belief was only encouraged by the fact that the communist GL/AL had nine units where the Jews were in a large majority and a high number in other units. In 1942 the Soviet partisan movement in Belorussia and the Ukraine was still on a very small scale and was not especially welcoming to Jews either. The leader of the Soviet partisan movement, Panteleimon Ponomarenko, was himself antisemitic, and Jews who reached the Soviet partisans that year reported they were not welcome. For example, Mina Volkowisky reached the Soviet partisans in Belorussia only to have her watch stolen by the commander and to witness the political commissar stealing the possessions of newly arrived Jews. She felt that she only survived because her husband was a doctor and the partisans needed his services. Certainly the most favoured Jews were doctors and skilled workers who could assist the partisans, whereas those who arrived at partisan camps without weapons were frequently turned away. Jews were often encouraged or forced to conceal their identities as Jews in order to stay with the partisans. For example, Abba Kovner was told by the commander of a Lithuanian partisan unit 'to forget who you are'. Indeed, the Soviet partisan leadership wanted everyone – Ukrainian, Lithuanian, Belorussian or Jewish – to consider themselves as Soviet partisans first and foremost. By late 1943 and into 1944 the situation in the forests became even more charged as the Soviet forces advanced westwards and their intention to incorporate the eastern part of Poland that they had occupied earlier into the Soviet Union was fiercely resisted by the AK and the Ukrainian insurgent army, *Ukrains'ka Povstans'ka Armiia* (UPA), who also clashed with each other. Jews who were seen by both the AK and UPA as pro-Soviet sometimes became the unfortunate victims of these clashes.[93]

Jews therefore often chose to maintain their own separate units, and men such as Smolar and Kovner followed this course. They both, however, were finally pressurized into joining the Soviet partisans. The local Soviet partisan leader in the Baranowicze region, General Platon, was initially hostile to the Bielski brothers' independence until he was invited to tour the family camp and gained a favourable impression. He was also struck by the Bielskis' determination to retain the Jewish identity of their unit and ultimately 'the Russians knew the Bielskis were prepared to fight to preserve their unit, to kill Russians if they had to'. The Jews in general proved to be able partisans and Ephraim Bleichman claimed that this made the Germans more cautious about engaging with them because: 'They had their homes, their families. The Jews had nothing.'[94] The story of the Jewish partisans is intricately involved in that of the Soviet partisans in general: their activities during the German retreat will be covered later.

15
Who is the Enemy?

With most of Europe securely under German and Italian occupation, the question of who the enemy was may appear to be a pointless consideration, since the obvious answer should be the occupiers. But this presupposes a population which was content with its pre-war governance, and now, in wartime, was in agreement over the nature of its post-war society and constitution once the Germans had been defeated. Few countries fitted that picture. Consequently, as well as the external enemy, the German occupier, the various resistance forces in each country had internal enemies to deal with. The simplistic spectrum of 'resistance – neutrality or *attentisme* – collaboration' became increasingly twisted and complex and cannot be explained by the simple picture of occupier versus occupied.

The first type of situation was that of Norway and the Netherlands, where the *Nasjonal Samling* (NS) and *Nationaal-Socialistische Beweging in Nederland* (NSB) sought to bring about a national socialist revolution in their countries to actively align them politically with the Third Reich. The efforts to nazify these two countries sparked off a widespread and effective civilian resistance to the proposed measures. As a Norwegian minister in the exiled government wrote later: 'With the administration entirely in the hands of the Germans and the quislings, the battle lines were clear, and the Norwegian resistance movement grew.'[1]

The second type of situation concerns the response of the resistance to the threat posed by collaborators. These collaborators operated from a number of motives. For example, the mobilization of the communist resistance after June 1941 led to the development of forces willing to join the German-sponsored anti-Bolshevik crusade, with the people who joined these formations seeing themselves straightforwardly as patriots. They saw communists as posing a greater threat to their countries than the German occupiers. The resistance, however, sought to attack all collaborators, regardless of their motivations.

The third type of situation arose in eastern Europe where the populations were mixed and consequently viewed the prospect of liberation from the German occupation by Soviet forces differently. Such a liberation from German occupation by the Soviets was welcomed by the Soviet partisans, who were acting as the long arm of Soviet rule, and by the Polish communist resistance. Yet the Polish government-in-exile was determined to reassert rule over eastern Poland, which had been occupied by the Soviets between September 1939 and June 1941 and was now under German occupation. At the same time, the populations of the Baltic States wanted to restore their independence which had existed between 1918 and 1939. Other nationalities, the Ukrainians and Belorussians, sought to assert their right to post-liberation independence, a status not enjoyed before since they had always been part of first the Russian Empire and then the Soviet Union. All these nationalities formed their own armed formations which clashed not only with the German occupying forces, but also with the Poles (in the disputed areas of eastern Poland) and with the Soviets. The result was a complex battle in the forests between the AK and the GL/AL as representatives of Poland, the Soviet partisans, and Ukrainian and other nationalist forces – not forgetting the presence of Jewish partisan units seeking just to survive the war. These formations often fought each other, sometimes made temporary alliances against other groups, and occasionally dealt with the Germans in order to receive weapons with which to fight what they perceived as the principal enemy at that moment.

Vidkun Quisling was widely despised for his premature attempt to take power in April 1940 when the Germans invaded Norway. His early attempts to insert NS influence into professional associations, sports associations, education, the Church, and the law had ended in disaster, and Reichskommissar Terboven had kept Quisling on a tight leash thereafter. In autumn 1941, however, Quisling was convinced that he could persuade the Norwegians to support his initiatives, and told Terboven: 'In hardly any country is it as easy . . . to bring about a national revolution from above as it is in Norway', because the Norwegians were fundamentally a law-abiding people.[2] He had some evidence to support his claim: NS membership was rising, and indeed would not reach its peak until April 1942, at which time it had 42,920 adult and 5,894 youth members.[3] On 1 February 1942 Terboven took a calculated risk by appointing Quisling to the position of Minister-President. The title was largely honorific since most of the real power remained in Terboven's hands. The reaction, however, to Quisling's appointment was both immediate and uniformly hostile. Goebbels confided in his diary on 3 February:

> Quisling's appointment as premier has created a sensation in the countries at war with us and has drawn in its wake great waves of angry commentary. Quisling is hated violently in the entire enemy world and is now the target for vile calumny. He has actually succeeded in becoming a symbol, although he doesn't really deserve it.[4]

But the reaction within Norway itself was far more strident and of greater consequence.

In the Netherlands, Reichskommissar Seyss-Inquart was more cautious in his methods of encouraging the nazification of Dutch society. He elected to keep Anton Mussert, the leader of the NSB, strictly on the sidelines, but encouraged the national socialist initiatives launched by Mussert's colleagues. For example, when a quasi-cabinet was established on 30 January 1943 to challenge the authority of the secretaries-general and, especially, that of the Dutch government-in-exile, Mussert was not even invited to become a member. Unlike in Norway, where Quisling was determined to launch a national socialist revolution regardless of the potential opposition, the nazification process in the Netherlands was much more stealthy, and was implemented by NSB ministers and members of the local administration. Nonetheless, the resistance was just as active in its opposition to these measures.[5]

One of the most striking features of the resistance to nazification was the leadership provided by the Church. In Norway, over 90 per cent of the population belonged to the State Church. In the Netherlands, 84 per cent of the people owed allegiance to the two Protestant denominations or to the Catholic Church. In the Netherlands, social, educational, political, and professional activities were largely stratified along religious lines: for example, each denomination had its own trade union. A feature of the Dutch Churches and their congregations under the German occupation was their willingness to put aside their doctrinal and liturgical differences and to cooperate with each other in the face of the greatest threat of nazification.

The Church in Norway demonstrated its opposition to Quisling's appointment immediately. The service of celebration of the appointment at Trondheim Cathedral in Oslo was boycotted by the Church authorities and their congregations, leading to the dismissal of the cathedral dean, Arne Fjellbu. On 1 March a pastoral letter was read from the pulpits in which the bishops announced that the Church could not support the government under Quisling and now considered itself separate from the state. On Easter Day, 5 April 1942, a new pastoral letter, 'The Church's One Foundation', was read from the pulpits. In it the bishops clarified their opposition to the government and their support for those suffering from the government's measures: 'So long as the conditions named continue and are carried further by new encroachments, the Church must act according to its duty on the Word of God and its confession of faith, accepting whatever may be the consequences . . .'[6] This letter made the separation of Church and state official. The bishops and pastors accepted the loss of their salaries, but insisted on continuing their spiritual responsibilities to their congregations. In all, 645 pastors out of 699 resigned their official positions.

Quisling viewed the Church's response as an act of insurrection and threatened punishment for the rebellious clergy, whereupon fifty pastors withdrew their support for the Church's stance and resumed their official duties. These few pastors found themselves preaching to largely empty churches as the population indicated its support for the Church by filling the churches only when the dissenting pastors were in attendance. Quisling also wanted to charge the Primate of the Norwegian Church, Bishop Berggrav, with high treason, but Berggrav was well connected: prominent German friends of his, such as Helmuth von Moltke and Dietrich Bonhoeffer (members of the German resistance),* travelled to Oslo to speak to Terboven and persuaded him to rein in Quisling. Berggrav was released from prison but was kept under house arrest. Despite Quisling's attempts to appoint new bishops and pastors that spring, Norway in effect had no Established Church from Easter 1942 until the liberation.[7]

In the Netherlands, the Church's resistance to nazification was led by prominent churchmen such as the Catholic Primate in the Netherlands and archbishop of Utrecht, Johannes de Jong, and leading Protestants such as Koeno Gravemeijer and Jan Koopmans. The Churches together proclaimed that membership of the NSB was incompatible with Christian faith and was thereby prohibited. The Catholic Church went so far as to refuse to administer the sacraments to any Catholic 'who was known to support the National Socialist ideal to an important extent', which controversially meant refusing to say a Requiem Mass for Catholic soldiers who were killed in Dutch formations fighting on the Eastern Front. The Churches also issued pastoral letters on certain issues. The first, in 1941, was against the attempt by Seyss-Inquart to disband the separate trade unions and to create a new Labour Front on the German pattern. The next issue, which has been covered already, was the persecution of the Jews. The Churches

* Von Moltke was a founding member of the anti-Nazi opposition group, the Kreisau Circle. He was arrested by the Gestapo in January 1944 and was tried and executed a year later; Bonhoeffer was a Lutheran pastor and theologian who opposed the Nazi policies of euthanasia and the persecution of the Jews. He was arrested by the Gestapo in April 1943 and imprisoned. He was tried and executed in April 1945.

also spoke out against the imposition of forced labour and advised officials in employment offices not to cooperate in the issue of call-up papers, and instructed the police not to hunt down those sought by the Germans such as labour evaders, Jews, and Dutch army officers.[8]

The clandestine press applauded the actions by the Churches, *Vrij Nederland* noting:

> The past years have taught the significance of cooperation and consultation. What no one had believed possible has happened. The Catholic and practically all Protestant Churches have found each other at the decisive moment. Again and again they have drawn up their protests together or issued their messages to the people after previous consultation. This is an important promise for the future. The Churches must get accustomed to this sort of collaboration, locally and nationally.
>
> The time of living apart must irrevocably belong to the past.
>
> The Churches will need a deep insight into their vocation with regard to life itself and to the nation. One of the many miracles of these years is the discovery made by so many: that the Church is the conscience of the Nation.[9]

The Churches paid a high price for their defiance: hundreds of ministers and priests were arrested, while forty-three ministers of the two Protestant denominations and forty-nine Catholic priests were executed.

Although no attempt was made in Belgium to promote nazification, the Catholic Church, representing the majority of the population, made clear its hostility to the *Vlaams Nationaal Verbond* (VNV) and the Rexist Party (Rex). In August 1941 Cardinal Archbishop van Roey declared:

> It is wrong for Catholics to collaborate in the establishment of a tyrannical regime, indeed they are under an obligation to work with those who resist such a regime. They must not cooperate with those seeking to establish such a regime in Belgium.

He repeated his defiance of the German occupation and of the Walloon and Flemish collaborators in later sermons. Under his leadership, permission to use church premises for meetings of Rex and VNV was refused, and sacraments were withheld from members of the Flemish Legion fighting on the Eastern Front.[10]

Two issues serve to illustrate the strength and determination of the civilian resistance to nazification – Quisling's efforts to nazify education in Norway, and the NSB attempt to take control of the medical profession in the Netherlands.

In 1940 Quisling had made his first attempt to promote the NS in education through his demand that all teachers should join the NS or be dismissed if they refused to do so. He was forced to back down in the face of widespread protests. But on 5 February 1942 he tried again, by creating a new NS teachers' union, the *Norges Laerersamband*: membership would be compulsory for all teachers. At the same time it was stipulated that all young people must join the NS youth organization.

The clandestine teachers' union met a few days later to agree a response. In collaboration with Bishop Berggrav, a template letter was drawn up stating: 'I cannot take part in the education of the youth of Norway along the lines stipulated by the *Nasjonal Samling Ungdomsfylking*, as this is against my conscience ... I find it necessary to announce that I cannot consider myself a member of the *Laerersamband*.'[11] Instead of presenting the minister of education, Ragnar Skancke, with one petition on behalf of all the objecting teachers, it was decided that the effect would be greater if each individual teacher copied out the letter, signed it, supplied his address, and sent the letter to the ministry all on the same day, 20 February. Parents were encouraged by the Church to join in the protest. Over two days, the education ministry in Oslo is estimated to have received between 100,000 and 200,000 letters of protest against the attempt to nazify education. Even the children were affected, as one schoolboy in Bergen recorded: 'There was an enormous trust between teachers and students. And everything was either black or white. We hated the Germans, with a red-hot hate ... A Nazi boy in our class would be shown his place: we formed a ring around him. Then we would all turn our backs.'[12] Over half of Norway's teachers submitted their resignations.

On 25 February, Skancke announced that all teachers who did not join the union by 1 March would be dismissed, but in order to make it harder to organize resistance to this step he also ordered all schools to close for a month on the spurious grounds of a shortage of fuel. When the deadline passed only a few teachers had joined the union. Quisling ordered the arrest of over 1,100 of the most vocal protesting teachers, 10 per cent of the total, and their incarceration in Grini concentration camp and in other prisons. The teachers were promised their release only if they would apologize for their conduct and sign a declaration that they would join the new union. After the war, a description was published of the events in one camp:

> The first man to be called to sign the statement of apology was a sickly, rather elderly teacher, who had sole responsibility for a flock of children. The others had to let him know that there would be no reproaches if he signed. He dragged himself up the steps in an obvious state of collapse, which was painful to watch. Two or three minutes passed, and then he came out on to the

> platform at the top of the steps a completely new man. Standing in front of all 600 men, he clenched his fists and shouted: 'I bloody well didn't sign!' Then he went back to his place, and after that it was not easy for anyone else to give way.[13]

Terboven and Quisling then upped the stakes and 500 teachers were put on an old coastal steamer, *Skjerstad*, and sent to Kirkenes in the far north, beyond the Arctic Circle and close to the Finnish border. There they were forced to work on fortifications under appalling conditions alongside Soviet POWs. The bishops protested at this treatment of the teachers, but the teachers themselves held fast. One deportee to Kirkenes smuggled out a letter arguing: 'If things give way here, then everything can give way. If things hold here, then everything will hold. And there is reason to believe that things are holding now.'[14]

On 1 May the schools reopened. Skancke announced that those teachers who returned to work would be considered members of the new union. The teachers, however, undermined this directive by reading out a statement to their classes which had been written by the clandestine union:

> These two things – being a member of the *Norges Laerersamband* and teaching – are incompatible . . . Our task is to give each one of you the necessary knowledge and training to attain fulfilment as a human being, so that you can take your place in society for your own good and that of others. The teacher's vocation is not only to give children knowledge; teachers must also teach their pupils to believe in and uphold truth and justice. Therefore teachers cannot, without betraying their calling, teach anything that violates their consciences . . . That, I promise you, I shall not do.[15]

The teachers' protest was totally successful and is a shining example of the successful mobilization of the civilian resistance. At the end of May 1942 Quisling complained: 'the teachers are responsible for the fact that we have not yet made peace with Germany. You teachers have destroyed everything for me.'[16] Gradually the teachers were released from the prison camps. Terboven concluded that 'in Norway organised resistance to Quisling has started' and accordingly began to keep Quisling on a tighter rein.[17]

Quisling and his NS's attempts to infiltrate the universities proved to be no more successful than with the schools, even though they demonstrated a more conciliatory approach than that shown towards the teachers. In 1940 there had been an unsuccessful attempt to force the professors of Oslo University to accept NS academics into their midst. It had been met by student boycotts of lectures by the NS professors who also found themselves cold-shouldered by their colleagues. In 1942 the NS ordered that students who were members of their party should be admitted to the faculty of medicine ahead of their contemporaries. Again a compromise solution was found: it permitted these NS students to attend some lectures. In 1943, however, the NS attempted to subvert the very independence of the universities. Skancke, with German approval, issued a new set of guidelines regarding admissions. These served to end the right of each faculty to admit its own students and instead gave this responsibility directly to Skancke's department, with the avowed purpose of promoting the interests of NS students. The faculty of Oslo University consulted the Home Front on the response. Such was the determination of the professors to resist the undermining of their independence that Skancke began to back down and agreed to each department setting up its own committee to consider the matter. In October, however, Quisling intervened. He stipulated that Skancke's original ruling should stand and, having consulted Terboven, ordered the arrests of ten of the most outspoken professors and over fifty of their students. Skancke continued his efforts to find a compromise solution but was prevented from achieving his goal by events outside his control. In the early hours of 28 November a resistance group set alight the Aula, the main university hall. The damage was minor but the consequences were extremely serious. Terboven ordered the permanent closure of Oslo University and the arrests of the professors and students. Most were soon released, but 700 students were sent to camps in Germany.[18]

Similar protests against the nazification of higher education were registered in Belgium and the Netherlands. In December 1941 there was a teaching strike at Brussels University in protest against the plan to admit collaborationist professors, and students supported the strike by enrolling at other universities. Brussels University continued to operate clandestinely, with sixty-five professors serving 400 students. In the Netherlands, the entire teaching staff of Leiden University threatened to resign when the NSB under-secretary for education, Jan van Dam, proposed to replace previously dismissed professors with members of the NSB. In May 1942, 80 per cent of the professors actually did carry through their threat to resign when a much-respected professor of constitutional law was dismissed.[19]

In the Netherlands, the NSB launched an underhand assault on the medical profession by sponsoring an NSB Medical Front in November 1940 in an effort to woo doctors away from the dominant medical association. In May 1941, Mussert suggested that a member of the Medical Front should join the board of the principal medical association. This suggestion in itself was innocuous until it became clear that it was only the first step towards bringing Dutch medicine into line with 'the concepts of National Socialist medicine'. At this point most of the 5,700 members of the medical association and the board members chose to resign. In September 1941 a new clandestine medical association, the *Medisch Contact*, was established. Members agreed not to collaborate with the occupiers nor with the NSB, and to refuse to betray Jews or members of the resistance to the police or the Germans. In response the Germans promoted the creation of a new medical union to be controlled by the NSB, the Chamber of Dutch Physicians.

The battle lines were now drawn up. The first step of the *Medisch Contact* was to prepare a letter of protest against the new Chamber which was signed by 4,261 doctors and was delivered on 16 December 1941:

> We physicians are concerned with expressing our conviction that the therapist's function, invested with high moral and spiritual considerations, must remain removed from all political interference ... We have reason to fear that government employees unknown to us ... could interfere with our patients' treatments and make us collaborate more or less directly ... We will never recognise another path than the one recognised by our conscience, our professional duty, and our science.

Doctors were advised by the *Medisch Contact* not to fill out the membership forms for the new Chamber, nor to pay any dues to it.

The Germans responded by arresting and imprisoning a number of doctors. In September 1942 the Chamber made another effort to enforce membership, and again the *Medisch Contact* advised against signature: only about 700 doctors joined the new Chamber. In January 1943 an announcement was made that refusal to sign would be met with a fine of 1,000 florins, with renewed fines as long as the boycott continued. The *Medisch Contact*, relying on funds from the government-in-exile, stated that it would pay the fines of individual doctors. Then the *Medisch Contact* realized that there was a loophole in the law establishing the Chamber which allowed doctors to retire from the profession. On 24 March 1943 around 6,200 doctors, the majority in practice in the Netherlands, simultaneously announced their retirements, removed the plaques giving their title as 'Doctor' from outside their surgeries, but continued to practise medicine. The Germans responded by arresting 360 doctors and imprisoning them. The effect was the paralysis of health provision across the Netherlands as the doctors went underground. Seyss-Inquart was forced to back down and during the summer of 1943 the imprisoned doctors were quietly released from custody.[20]

Other attempts to impose nazification on professional organizations also foundered. The creation of the NSB Netherlands' *Arbeitsfront*, a union designed to incorporate the separate socialist, Catholic, and Protestant trade unions, led to the resignation of between 70 per cent of the socialist and 96 per cent of the Catholic membership of the unions. Artists boycotted the NSB *Kulturkammer* despite this step meaning a prohibition on public performance and a total loss of income.[21]

By early 1943 Norwegians had become highly suspicious of all of Quisling's initiatives. Therefore, when, on 22 February 1943, he announced a new law on a 'common labour effort', which involved the registration of every man aged eighteen to fifty-five and women aged twenty-one to forty, the resistance had to consider its response. The matter was not clear-cut since there had been other labour initiatives previously, such as the voluntary *Arbeidstjenesten* (AT) in 1941 which had put young men to work in forestry, agriculture, and road building, measures that obviously benefited the Norwegian economy. It was the level of compulsion and the fact that Quisling was promoting this law that aroused the suspicions of the resistance and they turned to the government in London for advice. Two days later the response was published in the clandestine press:

> Those who are taken for national labour duty in agriculture, forestry, fisheries and transport shall do their duty to the full for the preservation of the country. All service[s] which . . . imply obligations for the people to take part in military operations against the fatherland *shall be refused*. Service outside the country's frontiers *shall be refused* . . .

The last two sentences are the most important. The law for the common work effort was published in the immediate aftermath of Stalingrad and at the time when Fritz Sauckel was pressing occupied countries to supply more workers for Germany. In fact, Sauckel was ordered to leave Norway alone, and indeed some forced labourers were actually sent to Norway. But the resistance did not know this. The second suspicion that the resistance held was that these labour conscripts would be pressed into service on behalf of the Germans in Norway or into Norwegian armed formations. The head of the clandestine Coordination Committee, Tor Skjønsberg, stated after the war that 'I had no doubt that the drafting for labour service was a camouflaged call-up of Norwegian youth for German military service, and that it must be combated as quickly as possible by every possible means.'

Consequently, although the initial registration proceeded smoothly, by April when the news was received that some draftees at a school for drivers had been put into German uniforms, an instruction was sent out by the Coordinating Committee on 17 April calling for a boycott of registration and refusal to report for work. Three days later the resistance mounted an attack on the labour registration office in Oslo. The Church also came out in opposition to the call-up for labour, leading to the arrest and imprisonment of the two last remaining Church leaders, Ole Hallesby and Ludvig Hope. The result pleased no one: the resistance was disappointed by the fact that registration for the work effort largely proceeded smoothly, although the numbers began dropping noticeably during the summer of 1943, while Quisling was also concerned by the low overall numbers of Norwegians registered and employed.[22]

In August 1943 Quisling resorted to ever more drastic efforts to assert his authority and independence from Terboven, and his actions led to even more divisions within Norwegian society. The first step was an attack on the Norwegian police force. On 9 August a police inspector in Oslo, Gunnar Eilifsen, was arrested after he had repudiated orders to arrest two young women who had refused to report for labour service. This seemingly minor transgression escalated into a cause célèbre. Eilifsen was charged with mutiny under the military code of 1902. Police had not been subject to this code until a new law on 14 August, five days after Eilifsen's arrest, made the police subject to military law. On 15 August, Eilifsen was tried by a special tribunal, found guilty, and condemned to death. This use of a retroactive law was viewed as illegitimate within the country and even among the ranks of the NS, yet Quisling bowed to Terboven's pressure and refused to exercise his power of reprieve. On 16 August, Eilifsen was executed. On the same day the entire police force in Oslo was ordered to assemble in the police barracks where the force was addressed by the police minister, Jonas Lie, and the head of the German security forces, Wilhelm Rediess. The men were ordered up to the rostrum individually and ordered to sign a declaration of loyalty to the Quisling regime. NS members signed readily, but many others refused until threatened with a charge of mutiny and the same fate as Eilifsen. The majority backed down, but by the end of August 500 policemen from all over Norway who had taken a firm stand against Quisling were arrested on German orders and despatched to a 'retraining camp' in Germany.[23]

At the same time as this was going on, Quisling made an attempt to align the entire country on the side of Germany, through proclaiming on 14 August the institution of a Norwegian army to combat an Allied invasion. This army was to be formed from pre-existing military and paramilitary units such as the SS *Norge* and the NS *Hird*, and would swear an oath of loyalty to Quisling and to Hitler. The matter split Quisling's cabinet because the question of whether Norway was in fact at war – and if so, with whom – was never entirely clear. Quisling himself was sure that it was at war with the Allies, and the opening statement of the law establishing the new Norwegian army read:

> A state of war has existed and prevails in Norway because of the aggressive actions of the Soviet Union and its allies against Norwegian territory and Norwegian citizens. Thus these states have acted as, and must in the sense of the law be considered as, enemies of Norway, the great German Reich and its associates as states allied with Norway.

Yet it seems that Quisling was mistaken. On 15 August 1943 Terboven made clear the German belief that Germany considered itself effectively still at war with Norway by ordering the internment of over 1,100 army officers who would now be treated as POWs. Terboven argued for this internment on the grounds that Norwegian officers were suspected of taking part in *Milorg* activities. The resistance was caught completely by surprise: warnings did reach some officers in Oslo and the nearby areas, but elsewhere unsuspecting army officers were caught in their homes, including a number of key men within *Milorg*.[24]

The resistance to attempts to impose the nazification of professional life largely succeeded in Norway and the Netherlands because in both the test cases – education and the medical profession – the teachers and the doctors were ultimately irreplaceable. In areas where the initiatives proposed by the NS could have some benefit to the country, such as the work effort, the resistance was arguably less successful in undermining the measures at this point. In late 1943 and into 1944, however, when it became apparent that the work effort was indeed the first step towards the creation of a new Norwegian army opposed to the Allies, successful resistance to the plans escalated. The steadfastness of the civilian resistance to the nazification of their countries demonstrated to Terboven and Seyss-Inquart the futility of using the agencies of the NS and NSB to govern their countries. In Norway, in particular, Terboven came to realize that Quisling's initiatives had served only to unsettle the country further and thereafter supervised him more closely.

The resisters faced great danger from the enemy within, the collaborators. Oluf Reed Olsen wrote later: 'One was most afraid of one's own people; I think all agents, saboteurs and other "visitors" in Norway will agree this was so.'[25] The potential and actual damage done to the resistance by traitors and collaborators forced the resistance to develop strategies to reduce the threat and, at the same time, to make the internal enemy the principal enemy rather than the German occupiers. This internal war helped to unite the resistance: 'Opposition to the collaborationist minority became a necessary rallying-point for all men of good will and a means for the not entirely united forces of the patriotic majority to express their sense of common purpose.'[26]

Collaboration had many faces. Some traitors acted as individuals, and others formed gangs, but they all worked with the Germans from either financial motives or political belief. One example of an effective gang comes from Norway, where Henry Rinnan was recruited as an informer by the Gestapo in 1940 and formed a gang to assist him. The Rinnan gang did most of its damage during 1942, infiltrating resistance and intelligence groups in the Trøndelag and Trondheim regions, as well as betraying SOE agents. It has been estimated that the activities of the Rinnan group led to the arrest of over 1,000 people, many of whom were then tortured by the gang before being handed over to the Germans who executed at least 100 of these resisters. After the war, Rinnan and forty-one members of his gang were tried and found guilty in 1946: Rinnan and ten of his accomplices were executed for treachery.[27]

The German invasion of the Soviet Union inspired the formation of anti-Bolshevik Legions in many occupied countries.[28] These were promoted by the leaders of the collaborationist parties and, indeed, both Jacques Doriot in France and Léon Degrelle in Belgium even served in their respective Legions, with Degrelle earning the Iron Cross from the Germans. These collaborators hoped that service alongside the Germans would promote their political prospects later. For example, a senior member of the VNV, Reimond Tollenaere, argued: 'If we now prove indeed that we are prepared to take on the common European foe – Communism – we shall have our rightful say later in building a new Europe.'[29] Recruitment to the Legions was always problematic, not least because of the extremely high casualties suffered in the early battles they waged on the Eastern Front. Yet their very existence demonstrated the splits in wartime society, with the anti-Bolshevik crusade proving attractive to some people, as one recruit explained: 'We all believed in a German victory and in our view Bolshevism represented a real threat to freedom in Europe. You just had to go. There was no choice.'[30] Despite their anti-Bolshevik *raison d'être*, the Legions also provided the manpower for collaborationist forces sponsored by the Germans designed to serve in their home countries, guard strategic locations, and take part in German drives against the resistance. Examples of these include the *Gardes Wallonnes*, formed in autumn 1941 from the ranks of Rex in Belgium, and *Vlaamse Wacht*, formed by the VNV. During 1943 further collaborationist police forces were created, such as the notorious Brigade Z in Brussels.[31] Even before the Germans took over direct rule in Denmark at the end of August 1943, a collaborationist force, the Schalburg Corps, had been set up in May with a strength of 600–700 men and a stated purpose of taking the war to the resistance.[32] For these people, communism was seen as a greater enemy than Nazism.

The resistance had a simple approach towards the members of the Legions, shunning them and their families. There are only a few examples of outright resistance to the creation and existence of the Legions such as when, on 27 August 1941, Paul Collette opened fire on Pierre Laval and Marcel Déat when they attended the passing-out parade of the first contingent of the *Légion des Volontaires Français* volunteers in Paris. Both men were seriously wounded and Colette was caught and imprisoned for life. In February 1943 the sponsor of the Netherlands Legion, General Seyffardt, was assassinated by the resistance.[33]

Some attacks on collaborators were acts taken by individual resisters or small units, and others were officially sanctioned by the resistance. This split between arbitrary revenge and organized justice provided a foretaste of what would happen in the immediate post-liberation period.

In Belgium the communists were prominent in advocating the assassinations of members of Rex and the VNV. The few victims in 1941 included Jean Oedekerke in Brussels and Paul Gérard in Tournai. Attacks on collaborators escalated in 1942, so that by April 1943 Rex estimated that around fifty of their supporters, often men in important positions such as *burgomeisters*, had been assassinated. The collaborating parties appealed to the Germans for help, but found that the Germans were unwilling to become embroiled in this quasi-civil war unless Germans were targeted directly. In August 1942 a German report noted: 'numerous attacks on the lodgings and dwellings of Belgians who sympathise with the Germans are the order of the day'. In November 1942, however, General von Falkenhausen sanctioned the execution of eight hostages in Charleroi for attacks on collaborators, and further executions followed over the next two years. In 1943, as attacks on their ranks increased, groups of legionnaires, either on leave or discharged, launched a campaign of assaults against patriots and resisters. For example, a group of former legionnaires led by Jean Pirmolin killed two prominent members of the Liberal Party in Liège in August 1943.[34]

The campaigns against collaborators appear to have been popular with the general population:

> There was little discernible public sympathy for those Rexists who fell victim to the Resistance assaults. Some Belgians did regard such attacks as premature or counter-productive but most seem to have applauded the assassinations. Unlike the anonymous representatives of the Occupying forces, the followers of Degrelle were clearly identifiable targets and the murder of a local Rexist frequently seemed to do more than any distant Allied military victory to raise popular morale.[35]

The clandestine press generally supported and indeed encouraged attacks on collaborators. For example, *Het Parool* saluted the men who had assassinated General Seyffardt, an NSB minister, Hermannus Reydon, and another leading NSB member, Folkert Posthuma, by describing them as 'brave soldiers of the Dutch army' and suggesting 'that those who could not or did not want to follow their example should bear witness that these soldiers on the domestic front have brought victory closer by their own actions'.[36]

There were those who voiced their fears about the civil war against the internal enemy. For example, in Belgium, Cardinal Archbishop van Roey asked:

> Where is all this bloodshed leading? The consequences are clear: insecurity and general turmoil, discord and deadly hatred. The safety of the people must be the supreme principle. In the name of this principle we ask that these bloody actions stop, so that calm and patience may return in the hope of a just peace.[37]

The Belgian government-in-exile attempted to assert control over the quasi-civil war by publishing laws which would be used after the war to try those accused of treachery and collaboration, an example followed by other exiled governments.

The resistance attempted to impose a legal structure to the war on the collaborators. In Poland a system of underground courts was established. Once a collaborator had been identified, he would be followed in order to assess the nature of his crime, and then tried (often *in absentia*) by an underground court. Only when these courts were satisfied that the crime deserved extreme punishment would a sentence of death be passed. An example of this was the Austrian-born actor Igo Sym, who appeared to have considered himself Polish before the war, but now claimed *Volksdeutsche* status and took part in German-sponsored stage productions. He was also known to be a Gestapo informant and this sealed his fate: he was executed at home by two AK soldiers in March 1941. The German reaction to the assassination of collaborators depended to an extent on the position held by the victim. Thus the assassination of the Polish judge Witold Wasilewski in February 1941, on the grounds of collaboration, met with a sharp German response: a curfew in Warsaw and the arrest of thirty hostages. The Underground Government had less control over events outside the cities, and there summary justice was more likely to occur. Those peasants and farmers viewed as too friendly with the Germans might be flogged in punishment. As the German occupation became ever more heavy-handed in the course of 1943 the underground courts cautiously began the practice of identifying and targeting the most dangerous Germans, and assassinations of individual Gestapo and SS officers were authorized. For example, on 7 September 1943, SS-Oberscharführer Franz Burkl, deputy commander of Pawiak prison, was assassinated near his headquarters at Avenue Szucha in Warsaw.[38]

The Dutch also attempted to impose a legal structure on the authorization of assassinations, with the Council of Resistance considering each case. This council, for example, authorized the assassinations of Seyffardt, Reydon, and Posthuma, in February and June 1943. Unsurprisingly perhaps, the collaborators turned to the Germans for protection and revenge. Hanns Rauter, Higher SS and Police Leader, did not want German forces directly implicated in tit-for-tat revenge attacks, but with Himmler's permission he sanctioned the use of Dutchmen from Dutch Germanic SS units, dressed as civilians, to take the battle to the resistance. In September 1943 this anti-resistance unit launched *Aktion Silbertanne*, which accounted for the deaths of fifty-five members of the resistance.[39]

The situation in the Soviet Union was more complex and collaboration was often less voluntary than in the west. Many of those who served in the German-sponsored units did so solely for guaranteed food rations or for security against German reprisals, as the wife of a policeman serving with the Germans explained: 'Better to be in the police than be shot by the Germans.'[40] On 5 September 1942 Stalin stated that a major goal of the partisans was the 'annihilation of the living force of the enemy', the collaborators. The partisans did indeed take the battle to the collaborators and German reports from all across the rear areas testify to the numbers of auxiliaries, policemen, and local government officials assassinated by the partisans. Two months later, however, there was a change of heart among the Soviet officials. The Partisan General Staff now ordered the partisans to begin a policy of actively recruiting Soviets serving with the Germans by offering the possibility 'to atone for their guilt through personal participation in the struggle for the liberation of the motherland from the German-fascist invader'.[41] The partisans launched a leaflet campaign to encourage Soviets to desert from the German formations. The numbers defecting from the *Osttruppen* and *Schuma* formations were small over the winter of 1942–43 but increased in the spring, partly because of the realization that the Soviets were beginning to advance and the Germans to retreat, making each recovered town and village into a potential site of retribution and revenge. This led to the thought process:

> If I stay with the Germans, I shall be shot when the Bolsheviks come; if the Bolsheviks don't come, I shall be shot sooner or later by the Germans. Thus if I stay with the Germans, it means certain death; if I join the partisans, I shall probably save myself.[42]

The German attitude towards the Soviet citizens in their service also helped this line of thought. The poorly armed *Osttruppen* and *Schuma* were placed in precarious positions or forced to guard the German lines of communication which were the principal target of the partisans, leading inevitably to high casualties. The Germans accidentally assisted the defection of the collaborator units by refusing to allow them to operate in more than battalion strength, which allowed for the defection of smaller groups of men rather than of large units, which would have been much harder to arrange.[43]

The rise of the communist resistance had caused great alarm in Poland where the dominant resistance force was the AK, loyal to the government-in-exile. Any possibility of agreement or cooperation between the AK and the armed wing of the communists, the GL/AL, was effectively ended when the Soviet Union broke off diplomatic relations with the Polish government-in-exile at the end of April 1943. Thereafter the AK and GL/AL were implacable enemies. The communists followed a deliberate policy of betraying AK members and arms caches to the Gestapo. Clashes in the countryside led to casualties on both sides.[44]

The AK attempted to counter the threat posed by the communists by providing a united front of as many democratic resistance groups as possible under the command and control of the AK. Success was limited. Support was won from the resistance run by the Socialist Party, and in 1943 the *Bataliony Chłopskie*, the Peasant Battalions, agreed to AK command and control despite viewing the AK as 'the gentlemen's army'. The right-wing resistance groups were more problematic. In November 1942 the *Narodowa Organizacja Wojskowa*, loyal to the National Party, agreed to subordinate itself to the AK command. Some right-wing members, however, formed a splinter formation, the *Narodowe Siły Zbrojne* (NSZ), which remained independent for the remainder of the war. Smaller resistance groups such as Sword and Plough also stayed largely outside AK control.[45]

Before the war the eastern provinces of Poland had contained a very mixed population, divided more or less equally between ethnic Poles, Jews, and members of the ethnic minorities: the Lithuanians, Belorussians, and Ukrainians. The Soviet occupation of the region from September 1939 to June 1941 had upset this balance because Volhynia, Polesie, and East Galicia had been incorporated into the Soviet Union, and Vilna (now Vilnius) had been given to the Lithuanians. Furthermore, a substantial number of ethnic Poles and Jews had been deported by the Soviets to Siberia and Kazakhstan. The German occupation from June 1941 onwards had added a further degree of complexity by exterminating the Jewish population, and sometimes supporting or suppressing the nationalist aspirations of the ethnic minorities.

Consequently, the Poles faced a myriad of challenges to the restoration of the pre-war Polish control over these provinces. The AK at times was forced to fight the Germans, the Lithuanians, Belorussians, and Ukrainians, as well as the increasing number of Soviet partisans who were being parachuted into the area. Stefan Rowecki, head of the AK, and Władysław Sikorski, leader of the government-in-exile, agreed that it was important to take steps immediately, while the German occupation was continuing, to assert Polish control of the area, and they also decided that eastern Poland should be the location where the proposed uprising against the Germans should start:

> It is imperative that we demonstrate to the invading Russians our will to protect our rights and our assets in the eastern areas. This can be achieved by starting open battles against the Germans at a given time and by the immediate restoration of Polish rule of these areas.[46]

AK strategy was to create Polish partisan units, and the first was formed in June 1943 near Stołpce in the province of Nowogródek. It started out with forty-four men but, after successful raids on small German garrisons, a sufficient quantity of weapons was obtained to enable the unit to expand to 650 men.[47]

The Polish partisan units were concentrated in the forests of eastern Poland where they encountered many other similar partisan units, Jewish as well as Soviet. Events in the Naliboki forest, in what is now western Belarus, illustrate the complexity of relations between the various different groups. This dense forest was an ideal hideout, fifty miles long and twenty miles wide intersected by marshy terrain and largely unmapped. In all, it is estimated that the forest was home to between 10,000 and 25,000 partisans all competing for the same limited food resources. Clashes between the various units were commonplace. While some AK units accepted Jews into their ranks, Jewish partisans were often attacked by the far-right *Narodowe Siły Zbrojne* (NSZ) formations which were openly anti-semitic, or even by those of the AK who resented the perceived pro-communist orientation of the Jewish partisans. The Soviet partisans were more welcoming towards the Jews but were unpopular with the local population because they stole food produce, which at least the AK paid for.[48] In May 1943 the Soviet partisans murdered 128 local peasants for their refusal to support them: 'The tension between the local population and the Soviet Partisans grew with every week. The Communists began forcing people to join their units, and dealt ruthlessly with those who refused.'[49]

The AK and the Soviet partisans did sometimes work together against the Germans, such as in June 1943 when the town of Ivyanets near the Naliboki forest was briefly liberated from German control by the combined forces of Polish and Soviet partisan units. Relations between the Polish and Soviet units deteriorated in the summer of 1943 as the April 1943 order from the central committee of the communist parties of Belorussia, Lithuania, and Ukraine was spread: the Soviet partisans should 'combat with every possible means bourgeois-nationalist units and groups', meaning in particular the AK. At the end of August 1943 the impact of this policy was beginning to make itself apparent. The Soviets would invite the Poles for talks on future attacks on the Germans, surround the Poles, disarm them, and liquidate the units. This policy continued right up to the arrival of the Soviet armies.[50]

Minor civil wars were fought in the region as Poles sought to reassert control over the former Polish provinces and encountered the forces of Belorussian and Lithuanian nationalism. The German Reichskommissar, Wilhelm Kube, supported Belorussian nationalism only so far as it promoted conflict with the Poles, but stamped on it if German control was threatened. The Belorussian policy of keeping Poles out of the local administration led the AK to retaliate, for example, massacring about 1,200 Belorussians in the district of Lida. The Lithuanians were pursuing a similar policy of de-polonization in Vilna and the surrounding district. This policy had begun under the Soviet occupation and continued with renewed ferocity in 1942 when the area was still occupied by the Germans. For instance, from the spring and summer of 1942 onwards the Lithuanian police began to arrest and murder local Poles, including the clergy and members of religious orders. The AK retaliated on 15 September 1943 by assassinating a Lithuanian police inspector, Marijonas Podabas. The Germans were alarmed by this breakdown in law and order and in reprisal arrested 100 Poles, of whom ten were immediately executed and the remainder held as hostages.[51]

The ethnic conflict between the Poles and the Belorussians and Lithuanians was nothing, however, in comparison to the war waged by the Ukrainians against the Poles in Volhynia in summer 1943. Ukrainian nationalists had welcomed the German occupation in June 1941 but had found their aspirations for an independent Ukraine frustrated. Now, after Stalingrad and the start of the Soviet advance westwards, the nationalist Ukrainians formed the Ukrainian Insurgent Army – *Ukrains'ka Povstans'ka Armiia* (UPA) – with a strength of about 10,000 to 12,000 men, to assert the right of the Ukrainians to independence. The Ukrainians faced three enemies – the local Poles, the Germans, and the Soviets. A decision was taken to attack the weakest enemy first, the defenceless Polish civilians in Volhynia. What followed was ethnic cleansing of the most brutal kind. Many of the Ukrainians were already experienced killers, having served alongside the Germans in the holocaust of the region's Jews. They fell upon the Polish settlements, murdered the Poles with extreme and terrorizing brutality, razed the villages, and erased every trace of Polishness from the area. It is estimated that around 50,000 Poles were killed in Volhynia that summer. Thousands more fled into Galicia or to the towns still occupied by the Germans. Controversially, some of these refugees then accepted the protection of the Germans by filling the ranks of their auxiliary units, which had been depleted by Ukrainian defections. These armed Poles then joined German actions against the Ukrainians, acting with great ferocity in revenge for the slaughter of their countrymen. During 1943 the Poles killed around 10,000 Ukrainian civilians in revenge for UPA attacks. By August 1943, however, AK demands to desist from collaborating with the Germans, added to the fact that the Soviet front was advancing, encouraged the Poles to abandon their German protectors and reinforce Polish partisan units in the forests, and await the time to rise up against the Germans and establish Polish rule before the arrival of the Soviets.[52]

The Germans proved a more formidable enemy for the Ukrainians. In early April 1943 the Germans, including an SS regiment, attacked UPA formations in Volhynia but withdrew after suffering heavy casualties. Further operations were launched later that spring with high losses on both sides. In April a German report concluded that in Volhynia the Germans held only the main towns and the UPA controlled the entire countryside, some 50,000 square kilometres. In summer 1943 Erich von dem Bach-Zelewski took charge of the German offensive against the UPA. The Germans mustered formidable forces, at least 10,000 men, with ten motorized battalions, artillery, tanks, and aircraft. Losses by the end of September 1943 were 1,237 UPA killed and wounded, and over 3,000 German casualties, but as usual with anti-partisan sweeps, the civilians suffered most, losing at least 5,000 men, women, and children.[53]

The Soviet partisans and the UPA also fought their own war which the Germans joined in. At the end of July 1943 the UPA annihilated the Soviet partisan detachment of 500 to 800 men led by Mykhailov. The following month the UPA inflicted even more damage on Soviet partisans coming from Belorussia. In June 1943 the Soviet partisan leader Sidor Kovpak began a march through the Ukraine and Galicia towards the Carpathians to reassert Soviet control. In Galicia he came up against forces from the

UPA which quickly organized self-defence detachments against his force. The Germans had been largely unaware of Kovpak's activities at the start of his march but began to take notice once his bands reached Galicia. The Luftwaffe assisted greatly in keeping track of Kovpak's movements, inflicting high casualties on his force. There was a brief and very bloody encounter between Kovpak's bands and a company of the 4th SS-Police Regiment. The level of German activity forced Kovpak to retreat to the sanctuary of the Pripet Marshes to await the Soviet approach. This left the UPA in control of the western Ukraine and much of Galicia, fending off the Germans, the Poles, and the Soviets.[54]

It may appear surprising that, despite the rise of nationalist aspirations and the growth in Soviet partisan activity, the Germans could still raise and maintain collaborating forces. These demonstrate the continuing appeal of anti-Bolshevik rhetoric. One early such force was the Russian National People's Army raised by Colonel Sakharov near Orsha in Belorussia, which impressed the Germans with its anti-partisan operations. Yet its very success rested on the fact that it was a national unit and its principal motivation was anti-Soviet rather than pro-German. Therefore, when Günther von Kluge decided to spread its battalions across German units, 300 soldiers from this collaborating army defected to the partisans.[55] Other units were more loyal. Bronislav Kaminski was permitted by the Germans to rule the area around Orel and Kursk as he saw fit, which was effectively a reign of terror. His Russian National Army of Liberation – *Russkaya Osvoboditelnaya Narodnaya Armiia* (RONA) – had 10,000 men and was used by the Germans against the partisans.[56]

Kaminski did at least assist the Germans in their anti-partisan campaign and so was of some immediate benefit to them. But the Germans had very little idea of what to do with another prominent Soviet defector, General Andrey Vlasov. He was taken POW by the Germans in July 1942 and contacted the high command suggesting the formation of a Russian Liberation Army – *Russkaya Osvoboditelnaya Armiia* (ROA). On 27 December 1942 Vlasov was permitted by the Germans to make an appeal:

> Friends and brothers! Bolshevism is the enemy of the Russian people. It has brought countless disasters to our country. Enough blood has been spilled! There has been enough starvation, forced labour and suffering in the Bolshevik torture chambers! Arise and join the struggle for freedom! Long may peace with honour with Germany prevail![57]

Vlasov was apparently an ardent Russian nationalist who had become disenchanted by Soviet communism and had witnessed the relief with which the Ukrainians had greeted the arrival of the German armies in

1941.[58] Yet the Germans were nonplussed since, although they would be grateful for any assistance with manpower, they also were deeply suspicious of Vlasov's nationalism. The Germans finally found a use for Vlasov only in February 1945 when the ROA was sent into action against the Red Army.

Ukrainian collaborators could also still be found. The Germans were desperate to keep Ukrainian youth away from the temptations of the UPA, so the German governor of East Galicia, Otto Wächter, suggested the creation of SS-*Galizien*, which was sanctioned by Himmler in April 1943. Wächter hoped to appeal to all young men resident in East Galicia and not just the Ukrainians, hence the name *Galizien*, and not, as many Ukrainians wanted, 'Ukrainian'. The Ukrainians themselves were split over how to view the formation of this division, and many of the initial 80,000 volunteers for it probably saw the division as a Ukrainian and not a German force. The nationalists too were divided in their response. The UPA was totally hostile to the concept and engaged in propaganda to dissuade Ukrainian youths from joining. On the other hand, the head of the Ukrainian Central Committee, Volodymyr Kubiiovych, made an appeal: 'The long-awaited moment has arrived when the Ukrainian people will again have the opportunity to come out with gun in hand to do battle against its most grievous foe – Bolshevism.' This strand of Ukrainian nationalism therefore perceived the Soviets as the greatest enemy, not the occupying Germans. In contrast, the AK's position was clear: any Pole joining the formation would be regarded as a traitor and suffer the traitor's punishment – death.[59]

16

Divided Loyalties: France 1942–43

An analysis of France in the same timeframe as the previous chapter has to be made separately because of the sheer complexity of the issues under discussion. In the northern Occupied Zone the enemy was clearly the Germans, and the questions and categories of resistance applied there as in other occupied countries. In the southern Unoccupied Zone, however, the existence of the Vichy regime complicated matters. Many French people saw Vichy as the legitimate successor to the Third Republic and some of its policies, especially support for the Church after the strident anti-clericalism of the Third Republic, were popular. Above all, the Vichy regime was seen as the shield and protector of the French against the full weight of German occupation.

Yet there were those in the south who pursued the path of resistance and they, like their compatriots in the north, looked for leadership. De Gaulle was one candidate for the role. Since his speech on 18 June 1940 de Gaulle had been viewed as a *symbol* of resistance and, after the events described in this chapter, by June 1943 he was now widely seen as the *leader* of the resistance. The path had been anything but smooth. In the first place de Gaulle had to discover the resistance, and the resistance in turn had to learn about him, largely through his representative in France, Jean Moulin. In the second place the Allied invasion of North Africa caused immense difficulties. In metropolitan France itself, the invasion led in turn to the German occupation of the Unoccupied Zone on 11 November 1942, thereby calling into question the entire validity of the Vichy regime. Both the southern resistance movements and the Vichy regime had to consider their responses to this invasion, thus dividing loyalties in France even more. If that was not enough, then the American sponsorship of General Henri Giraud as the man to represent France in French North Africa posed an obvious threat to de Gaulle's supremacy over the Free French movement. The resistance in France would make an important contribution to the strengthening of de Gaulle's position in this debate.

*

When de Gaulle issued his famous appeal on 18 June 1940 announcing that France was still in the war, he was thinking along traditional military and political lines. His appeal was directed at the French empire and at those members of the French armed forces who were outside France at the time. It was not aimed at arousing resistance within France itself. Indeed, there is little evidence to suggest that de Gaulle thought much about the possibilities of resistance at the beginning, other than the collection of intelligence, for which he created the BCRA (*Bureau Central de Renseignements et d'Action*) under Colonel Passy. Indeed, his first real statement to the resistance in October 1941 was not the message they expected to hear: it was a call to refrain from killing Germans because of the reprisals the Germans would take against innocent people. Much of de Gaulle's silence on the resistance can be explained by his ignorance of the state of affairs in France and in particular of the growth of the resistance movements.

This situation changed after October 1941 with the arrival in London of Jean Moulin. In 1940, Moulin had been the prefect of Eure-et-Loir who, rather than sign a statement demanded from him by the Germans which would have accused Senegalese troops of committing atrocities against civilians, had cut his own throat. The Germans saved his life but the Vichy regime removed him from his post. Before he left France in September 1941, Moulin assumed various false identities and used his extensive list of contacts to discover all he could about the rumours of resistance. On his arrival in London, Moulin met Passy and de Gaulle. Moulin presented the two men with a 'report on the activity, plans, and needs of the groups formed in France in the aim of national resistance', which he had written while in Lisbon awaiting onward transport to Britain. The information he presented was misleading, though unintentionally so. Moulin thought that he had made contact with all the leaders of the various resistance movements, but in fact he had not met the head of *Libération-sud*, Emmanuel d'Astier. Nor did Moulin realize that there were members of the Vichy regime itself who could potentially be recruited as resisters; nor did he know that the Vichy intelligence service were already in contact with British intelligence. He had formed the impression that the communists were attracting most of the people who wanted a more activist stance, in contrast to the southern resistance movements which were rather more passive and, indeed, some still saw an appeal in loyalty to the Vichy regime. Despite all this, what was clear was the fact that resistance movements existed and were growing, but that they needed direction.[1]

De Gaulle's position in London and his claim to leadership of the Free French had always been weakened by the low calibre of the men surrounding him, but Moulin's arrival transformed this situation since he had been a prefect and was a person of consequence. De Gaulle was enthralled by the knowledge Moulin claimed to have of the resistance. As a result, Moulin was given the title of 'Delegate of the French National Committee' and instructions to return to France and unite the resistance groups in the Unoccupied Zone under the Gaullist flag, and to persuade the movements to unite their military units into one resistance army, the *Armée Secrète* (AS).[2] Moulin was duly parachuted into France on the night of 1–2 January 1942 to begin his mission.

De Gaulle's next important visitor was the leader of *Libération-nord*, Christian Pineau, who arrived in London in March 1942. Pineau had met Henri Frenay, founder of *Combat*, and d'Astier before leaving for London and informed de Gaulle of the resistance concerns regarding de Gaulle's commitment towards democracy. Pineau was appalled by de Gaulle's ignorance about the true state of affairs in France:

> I found de Gaulle's thinking entirely military. When I explained that Pétain had substantial support, and that we were also up against the Communists playing their own game, he was unmoved by the dangers we were running. For him, [it was normal for] every combatant to risk his life whether in a tank in North Africa or posting handbills on walls in France.[3]

De Gaulle did, however, draft a declaration to the resistance movements stating his commitment to democracy, which Pineau took back to France.[4]

Other visitors followed. One was the journalist Pierre Brossolette, who had edited the clandestine newspaper *Résistance* for the Musée de l'Homme group and was also a member of the intelligence network *Confrérie de Notre-Dame* (CND), which operated principally in the Occupied Zone. Brossolette's main concern was the provision of intelligence but he did suggest to de Gaulle and his head of intelligence, Passy, the need for a committee of able men to coordinate the activities of various groups. This was precisely what Moulin had been despatched to France to achieve in the south. Emmanuel d'Astier also reached London in May and filled in the gaps in de Gaulle's knowledge of the southern zone. De Gaulle wrote later that:

> My interviews with these men, for the most [part] young, all of them seething with ardour and tense in their fighting spirit and ambition, helped to show me to what extent the regime under which the French people had been living at the moment of the disaster was discredited in its mind. The resistance was not only the rebound of our self-defence reduced to extremities. It was also arousing the hope of a national revival.[5]

De Gaulle had a complicated attitude towards the politicians and political parties of the Third Republic. On the one hand he blamed them for the disaster of 1940, yet he recognized the fact that if he was to achieve a widespread following in France he needed the support of these people. The first political party to pledge allegiance to de Gaulle was the Socialists. Léon Blum, in prison but fresh from surviving the farce of the Riom trial against him, sent a message of support. In the summer of 1942 the former socialist deputies Félix Gouin, Louis Vallon, and André Philip reached London, and de Gaulle promptly made Philip his interior minister. Messages of support were also received from other politicians of the Third Republic such as Georges Mandel, Paul Reynaud, and Édouard Herriot.[6]

These meetings convinced de Gaulle of the strength of resistance sentiment, if not actual activity, within France. Accordingly, he began to use the BBC French service more frequently to broadcast appeals to the population to make its opposition stance clear. After Pierre Laval returned to power in April 1942, de Gaulle issued the order:

> It is the duty of every Frenchman and Frenchwoman to fight actively, by all means in their power, against the enemy itself and against the agents of Vichy who are the accomplices of the enemy. These people are like the enemy: the French people should hound them, sabotage their plans and hate their leaders. National liberation cannot be separated from national insurrection.[7]

The first manifestation of popular feeling erupted on 1 May 1942, when there were widespread large demonstrations throughout the Unoccupied Zone as well as in Paris and Bordeaux. The success of these demonstrations led Moulin to request de Gaulle to make a new appeal for a celebration of Bastille Day, 14 July 1942. De Gaulle duly broadcast on 13 July:

> Tomorrow, in that part of France they call 'unoccupied', the tricolor shall hang from every house. In every town and village Frenchmen and Frenchwomen shall march to the appointed place, and with a strong voice and tears in their eyes they shall sing the *Marseillaise*.[8]

The call was a great success: the various resistance movements differed in their estimates of the number of demonstrators in Lyon, 100,000 or 200,000, but they agreed on the effect elsewhere, such as 15,000 in Toulouse, and about 5,000 in other, smaller towns, including Saint-Étienne where the *Légion Française des Combattants* attempted to stop the demonstrators and fighting broke out. About 100 people were arrested in Lyon by the French police. The resistance noted that the slogans were evenly split between calls for 'Mort à Laval', and 'Vive de Gaulle'.[9]

Moulin's first mission to France as de Gaulle's representative was a qualified success. He brought with him a letter from de Gaulle to the resistance leaders in the Unoccupied Zone:

> I know the work you are doing, I know your worth. I know your great courage and the immense difficulties you face. Despite everything, you must continue your work and spread your influence. We who are lucky enough to be able to still fight with weapons, we need you now and in the future. Be proud and confident! France will win the war, and she will welcome us in her soil.[10]

This recognition of their work enthralled the resistance leaders in the south: 'The matchbox in which he carried the microfilm of his instructions from de Gaulle had an almost talismanic quality to those resisters starved of contact with the outside world.'[11] But some leaders, particularly Frenay, were concerned about the loss of their independence. Frenay felt that Moulin had brought with him 'extremely precise instructions covering everything down to the tiniest detail of our operation. In fact they were *orders*.'[12] Frenay believed strongly that the resistance movements had to remain independent in order to achieve a broad appeal, and for reasons of security, and that London had fundamentally misunderstood that the movements were engaged in a wide variety of resistance activities, from the clandestine press to armed action, and would not benefit from over-centralization or control by an outsider. The view from London was different. Passy later wrote that, in the Unoccupied Zone, Moulin had found 'an abundance of well-meaning desires, courageous ideas, and exalted theories, which inevitably translated themselves into chaotic and ineffective actions'.[13] Hence what he saw as the need for centralization and rationalization of the different elements of resistance.

Moulin's appeal to the resistance rested on two factors: his contact with de Gaulle and his promise of supplies to the resistance. He achieved some successes in his mission to achieve coordination between the resistance and the Free French. He established a *Bureau d'Information et de Presse* (BIP) under Georges Bidault to act as a conduit for information from the Free French to the clandestine press, and from the clandestine press to the outside world. Moulin also set up a *Comité Général d'Études* formed of administrators and bureaucrats, Paul Bastid, Alexandre Parodi, Robert Lacoste, and François de Menthon, which would plan for the period immediately after the liberation and advise the French National Committee on what the French wanted, thus helping to shape the future government's programme for political, economic, and social reform. Moulin also inspired civil servants to join the *Noyautage des Administrations Publiques*, which aimed at liaison between the administration and the resistance to ensure a smooth transition of power after the liberation. The *Service des Opérations Aériennes et Maritimes* was set up to identify and control landing grounds and drop zones for supplies and the arrival and departure of agents. It was run by three men: Raymond Fassin, Joseph Monjaret, and Paul Schmidt, each representing a different movement in the south.[14]

Moulin's mission was to persuade the three main resistance movements in the south, *Combat*, *Libération-sud*, and *Franc-Tireur*, to merge their movements under one coordinating committee and to separate their political activities from military actions. He faced enormous obstacles. The first stage was relatively straightforward. Moulin met the three leaders individually and in the course of summer 1942 each of them pledged allegiance to de Gaulle.[15] Yet there remained substantial differences between them and in their attitudes towards cooperation. Frenay explained that *Combat* was 'a military force and a revolutionary political expression' at the same time and wanted to retain its independence.[16] D'Astier, head of *Libération-sud*, with his contacts in socialist and trade union circles, was seen as too left-wing by Frenay and, indeed, by many within the Free French in London. Moulin won the greatest support from Jean-Pierre Lévy, leader of *Franc-Tireur*, who often acted as arbiter in disputes between Frenay and D'Astier. Moulin's reports convinced de Gaulle that he needed to meet Frenay and d'Astier in London, and they duly arrived in October 1942. De Gaulle appears to have reassured the two leaders over points of greatest concern to them, and soon after their return to France Moulin achieved one of his main objects, the formation of a loose federation of the three main movements called *Les Mouvements Unis de la Résistance* (MUR).[17] Frenay insisted on a loose structure of command and, since his was the largest movement, Moulin was forced to agree.

The movements proved more reluctant to merge their military units and there was a battle over who would command this new secret army. Frenay wanted the post, although he had only been a captain in the French Army. An historian of the resistance has noted:

> Objectively one must recognize that Frenay was by no means without reason in presenting his candidacy. The official constitution of a Secret Army was the final consummation of an idea that Frenay had been the first to formulate, and it was to rely upon positions that he had secured and to operate under the very name he had chosen. Moreover, considering that the Secret Army was to be composed of already existing irregular outfits, it is incontestable that *Combat* alone contained more men than its two partners combined.[18]

But the two other resistance leaders were categorically opposed to Frenay's candidacy, suspecting him of wanting to become a dictator. D'Astier and Lévy were also suspicious regarding Frenay's contacts with the Vichy authorities, especially Frenay's meeting with the Vichy interior minister,

Pierre Pucheu, in February 1942. Therefore, on Moulin's suggestion, de Gaulle appointed General Charles Delestraint as head of the AS.[19] In February 1943 Moulin and Delestraint left France for London to have further consultations with de Gaulle.

These consultations were essential because everything had been turned upside down by the Allied invasion of French North Africa, then under the rule of the Vichy regime. The challenge facing General Dwight Eisenhower, commander of the Allied forces designated to invade French North Africa at several points along the coasts of Algeria and Morocco, was to ensure as few Allied casualties as possible. Eisenhower recognized the political complications of the operation: 'The Allied invasion of Africa was a most peculiar venture of armed forces into the field of international politics; we were invading a neutral country to create a friend.'[20] Controversially, that 'friend' was Vichy France. Here it is necessary to stray briefly into the attitude of the United States towards the Vichy regime. In 1940 the United States had recognized the Vichy regime under Pétain as the legitimate government of France and Admiral William Leahy, President Roosevelt's close friend, was despatched there as the American ambassador. He was withdrawn in protest at Laval's appointment as prime minister in April 1942, but the embassy remained open with a skeleton staff.[21] Roosevelt also had an intense dislike of de Gaulle, seeing him as a possible dictator on the same lines as Napoleon and General Boulanger. De Gaulle had little influence in French North Africa where the French colonialists were strongly pro-Vichy, anti-British, and supported the Vichy National Revolution with even more enthusiasm than was apparent on the mainland. Therefore, it seemed obvious to the American planners that to ensure few Allied casualties, Vichy France needed to be wooed so that the 140,000-strong French army in North Africa would not resist the landings.

Robert Murphy, the former United States chargé d'affaires to Vichy, was sent to North Africa by the State Department to achieve this aim. He held talks with a number of leading Frenchmen. General Maxime Weygand had been recalled from his command in North Africa by Pétain but still held enormous influence in the area: he, however, was not interested in cooperating, commenting to Murphy that he was too old to become a rebel.[22] Nor did Murphy win any promises from the French commander in Morocco, General Charles Noguès, or the commander in Algiers, General Charles Emmanuel Mast. General Mark Clark, Eisenhower's deputy, was landed in great secrecy by submarine near Algiers to talk to Mast, who suggested that should General Giraud be brought to Algiers from France, he might be the man who could ensure that the landings would be unopposed.[23]

Giraud had been taken prisoner by the Germans in 1940 and incarcerated in the fortress of Königstein, near Dresden, from which he escaped on 17 April 1942. His escape was masterminded by his wife and a repatriated French officer who managed to smuggle lengths of wire cable and civilian clothes to Giraud. French POWs helped Giraud to travel across Germany by train to the Swiss frontier which he then crossed.[24] Giraud arrived in the Unoccupied Zone, creating a furore in the process. Hitler was furious at the audacity and success of the escape and ordered the German ambassador to France, Otto Abetz, to put pressure on Laval to return Giraud to German captivity. The principal German fear was that Giraud would escape to Britain, where they thought he would prove a much more dangerous enemy than de Gaulle, since Giraud greatly outranked de Gaulle, having been made a general while de Gaulle was still only a colonel.[25] Indeed, the foreign secretary Anthony Eden hoped that Giraud would arrive in Britain precisely for that reason: 'We should then have a real leader of the Free French movement, a man whose name and record inspires devotion among all sections of the French Army and people.'[26] The Germans need not have worried. Giraud immediately pledged loyalty to Vichy at a meeting with Pétain on 29 April, and began talks with the Armistice Army. Resistance leaders such as François de Menthon, Claude Bourdet, and Frenay who either met or corresponded with Giraud felt that he could not be trusted. For his part, Giraud privately and confusedly envisaged himself as commander of the resistance throughout Europe and wanted finance and contacts from the British in order to pursue this over-ambitious programme.[27]

Churchill had an extremely complex relationship with de Gaulle and no great liking for Vichy France, but nevertheless he was prepared to do everything possible to ensure the smooth progress of the American landings in North Africa. When Roosevelt wrote to Churchill asking for a free hand in French North Africa, Churchill responded: 'In the whole of Torch, military and political, I consider myself your Lieutenant.'[28] It was a statement he would come to regret. But that lay in the future: in the meantime, the British were able to make an important contribution to the American plans. SIS contacted the Alliance network run by Marie-Madeleine Fourcade and asked her to assist in getting Giraud to the Mediterranean coast in the vicinity of Le Lavandou by 4 November, from where a British submarine, commanded on this sole occasion by an American officer on Giraud's insistence, would collect Giraud and take him to Gibraltar to meet Eisenhower. On the night of 5–6 November Giraud successfully boarded the submarine, commanded by Captain Jerauld Wright of the US Navy. The enterprise was costly to Alliance: the long radio signal needed to make the arrangements led to the arrests of Fourcade herself, three of her deputies, and the radio operator. The second submarine, which collected agents rather than the members of Giraud's staff as planned, brought out the news of the arrests and the BBC broadcast a message: 'Be careful. In the south of France, the animals are ill with the plague.' This was a reference to Alliance's agents being known by animal code names.[29]

Giraud's arrival in Gibraltar on 7 November created a new problem which shocked both Eisenhower and Clark. Eisenhower wrote:

> It was quickly apparent that he had come out of France labouring under the grave misapprehension that he was immediately to assume command of the whole Allied expedition. Upon entering my dungeon, he offered himself to me in that capacity. I could not accept his services in such a role . . . General Giraud was adamant; he believed that the honour of himself and his country was involved and that he could not possibly accept any position in the venture lower than that of complete command.[30]

Furthermore, Giraud wanted the entire invasion force diverted from North Africa to the coast of southern France, where he was convinced that the Armistice Army would assist the Americans. This, of course, was completely out of the question. The landings in North Africa began on the morning of 8 November and the Allies encountered immediate resistance from the French forces at Algiers, Oran, and Casablanca.[31] De Gaulle was furious that he had not been told about, or consulted at all prior to the invasion, commenting to his aide: 'I hope that Vichy's men throw them back into the sea. That is no way to come into France, like a burglar.'[32] He then calmed down and broadcast a message 'to the leaders, soldiers, airmen, officials and French *colons* of North Africa', urging them to join the Allies.[33]

On the morning of 9 November, Clark and Giraud went to Algiers to try to organize a ceasefire. To Giraud's amazement, Eisenhower's shock, and Churchill's concern, Giraud's announcement that he had come to take supreme command of all troops in French North Africa had absolutely no effect. Eisenhower later wrote:

> Without exception every French commander with whom General Clark held exhaustive conversation declined to make any move toward bringing his forces to the side of the Allies unless he could get a legal order to do so. Each of them had sworn an oath of personal fealty to Marshal Pétain.[34]

Pétain ordered resistance by the French forces to continue, and his orders were obeyed. Then Eisenhower learned of the presence in Algiers of the former Vichy prime minister Admiral Darlan, who was there by chance visiting his seriously ill son. Murphy and Clark persuaded Darlan to proclaim a general ceasefire on 10 November, which he did, and it was obeyed.

Pétain reacted with fury and immediately sacked Darlan, whereupon Darlan attempted to rescind his order, but it was too late. French opposition to the Allies in North Africa had ceased and the Germans invaded Vichy France on 11 November. Darlan now pledged his loyalty to the Allies 'in the name of the Marshal' on the grounds that Pétain was no longer at liberty to make his own decisions and that the Germans had violated the terms of the 1940 Armistice. He recognized the strength of his position: 'The Americans must understand that they can have either Giraud without the army or the army without Giraud.'[35] On 13 November, Darlan concluded an armistice with the Americans and assumed supreme command of all French forces in North Africa. Giraud was left in control of the French Army in North Africa and the air force.[36] As late as 19 November Pétain attempted to get this decision reversed, broadcasting to French North Africa:

> Some generals in the service of a foreign power have refused to obey my orders. Generals, officers, NCOs, and soldiers of the Army of Africa, do not obey these unworthy leaders. I repeat to you the order to resist the Anglo-Saxon aggression . . . You have only one duty: to obey.[37]

Pétain bowed to the German demand to station Luftwaffe units in Tunisia.

The American agreement with Darlan sparked a furore in Britain, the United States, and among the resistance groups in France and across Europe. Darlan had blood on his hands: he had been the French premier when the Vichy regime assisted the Germans in the selection of hostages to be executed in reprisal for the assassination of German officers in 1941. As the Labour MP Aneurin Bevan thundered in Parliament:

> Darlan has so many crimes against him now that he can never expunge them. The man who stood on one side and connived at the slaughter of innocent French hostages, friends who gave their lives for us, is not a man with whom we dare cooperate.[38]

Churchill had to call a secret session of Parliament in order to attempt to justify the deal. But he himself had great misgivings, informing Roosevelt on 17 November that the agreement with Darlan must be viewed only as a temporary expedient: 'We must not overlook the serious political injury which may be done to our cause, not only in France but throughout Europe, by the feeling that we are ready to make terms with the local Quislings.'[39] Churchill clearly regretted having given the Americans a free hand to settle political matters in North Africa and appointed Harold Macmillan, then a junior minister in his government, to be British Minister in North Africa.[40]

De Gaulle was prevented from broadcasting his hostile opinion on the deal on the BBC, although Free French radio did broadcast de Gaulle's message of opposition from its stations in the Congo, Cameroon, and Beirut.[41]

Roosevelt bowed to pressure from Churchill and the American press and publicly announced that the deal with Darlan was only temporary. Admiral Leahy later justified the deal in his memoirs on the grounds that 'I advocated that we should indefinitely continue to try to use everybody – good, bad, and indifferent – who promised to be of assistance in reducing the length of our casualty list.'[42] More alarming were the reasons Roosevelt himself gave for agreeing the deal. On 20 November he met de Gaulle's new interior minister, André Philip, and explained his thinking:

> I did the right thing to support Darlan – I saved American lives . . . what's important for me is to get to Berlin. I don't care about anything else. If Darlan gives me Algiers, long live Darlan! If Laval gives me Paris, long live Laval! . . . When we get to France, we will have the power of an occupying force. I cannot recognise de Gaulle, because that would undermine the rights of the French by imposing a government on them . . . By right of occupation, the Americans will remain in France until free elections are organised.[43]

This set out Roosevelt's clear antagonism towards de Gaulle in stark terms. It also raised the question of the attitude the Americans held towards the people in the countries they proposed to liberate.

Resistance movements across Europe bombarded SOE with telegrams voicing their alarm about the Darlan deal. Did the deal, for example, mean that the Americans would make similar arrangements with other men viewed by the resistance as collaborators such as Quisling, Degrelle, and Mussert, solely because such deals might save Allied lives? In France the outrage was the greatest since the Darlan–Clark agreement threatened to undermine much of what the resistance was working towards. The movements in the Unoccupied Zone had worked hard through the clandestine press to shift public opinion away from loyalty to Vichy. In the Occupied Zone, the resistance clearly viewed de Gaulle as its leader. Darlan, and indeed Giraud, as senior military figures were very real threats to the position of de Gaulle and his leadership of the Free French movement. Another factor also was important: the attitude of the communist resistance. Darlan was a noted anti-communist, whereas de Gaulle was trying to get the communists to work together with other resistance movements. If Darlan, and Vichy legislation, continued to rule over French North Africa, it was quite possible that the resistance in France would become increasingly dominated by the communists, who owed their allegiance to Stalin first, with de Gaulle only a poor second, and threaten civil war in the future.[44]

Part of the problem lay in the weakness of Gaullism in French North Africa. On 15 November 1942 Jean Moulin sent a telegram to the Free French headquarters:

> Inform American and British governments in name of resistance movements impossible to explain to French why Algiers landing not immediately accompanied by restoration of republic . . . Why French National Committee not yet installed in Algiers. Why Allied radio friendly to Petain . . . Very bad impression will soon become scandal.[45]

Eisenhower could have supplied the answer to Moulin's question: 'The local antagonism in the French Army and in all echelons of government against de Gaulle was intense.'[46] When Douglas Dodds-Parker arrived in North Africa with the SOE mission, Massingham, on the day after the landings he noted: 'we were not welcome in general, as a Special Service, British, with known Gaullist links'.[47] SOE had been well aware of de Gaulle's unpopularity in North Africa and had instructed the SOE mission to cooperate with OSS in their negotiations with the French authorities by offering the promise that they would not have to serve under de Gaulle.[48] Many of the French leaders in French North Africa viewed the Vichy regime as legitimate and saw de Gaulle as a traitor who had betrayed Pétain. These splits within French society threatened the creation of a unified resistance to the German occupiers.

It can be argued that Darlan was in a very weak position to remain in power for any great length of time: 'Marshal Pétain had disavowed him, the Gaullists were denouncing him, the Giraudists hated him, the British despised him, the Americans publicly described him as a "Temporary Expedient".'[49] Then an event occurred that provided a solution to the problem of Darlan. On 24 December 1942 a young man, Fernand Bonnier de La Chapelle, entered Darlan's quarters in Algiers and assassinated him. He was court-martialled on 26 December, pleaded guilty, but defended his action on the grounds of patriotic duty. He was shot at dawn on the following day. The swiftness of the trial and the execution led to a mystery over why Bonnier had killed Darlan. Certain facts are known: Bonnier was an instructor with SOE and carried out the assassination with a pistol allocated to him by SOE through Abbé Pierre-Marie Cordier. He also had on him about $2,000, which appeared to be payment for carrying out the assassination. Many questions, however, remain unresolved: notably, who precisely ordered Bonnier to kill Darlan. His links with SOE clearly pointed to that organization, but no trace of evidence has been unearthed to suggest that SOE was behind the act. Bonnier was also in contact with the Gaullist resistance through the person of General François d'Astier, and the payment appears to have come out of the funds d'Astier carried with him when he arrived in North Africa in December; but d'Astier had been expelled by Darlan after a very brief stay in the country. Bonnier also had contacts with French royalists through François d'Astier's brother, Henri, and the Comte de Paris, both of whom were in Algiers. There is no evidence that de Gaulle ordered the assassination. Giraud, however, suspected Gaullist influence, and ordered the arrests of large numbers of Gaullists in North Africa in the days after the assassination.[50] While the French factions blamed each other or even posited that the Allies were to blame, one thing at least is certain. As Churchill put it: 'Darlan's murder, however criminal, relieved the Allies of their embarrassment at working with him.'[51]

De Gaulle was not the immediate beneficiary of Darlan's death: Giraud was. In many ways the situation in North Africa looked like 'the substitution of Vichy under American protection for Vichy under German control'.[52] Vichy legislation remained in force, notably the anti-semitic laws, as did Vichy institutions such as the *Service d'Ordre Légionnaire* which had grown out of the *Légion Française des Combattants*. Furthermore, political detainees, including twenty-six communist deputies, were not released. Indeed, Giraud went so far as to appoint the former Vichy interior minister responsible for the first *Statut des Juifs*, Marcel Peyrouton, to the position of governor-general in Algeria.[53]

The American sponsorship of Giraud in North Africa for political and military reasons threatened to cause a split with the British, who had, however unwillingly, pledged support to de Gaulle in 1940 and, despite Churchill's frequent outbursts of frustration against de Gaulle, were not prepared to abandon him so long as he was seen as the symbol of resistance in France. Therefore, it seemed essential for Giraud and de Gaulle to meet and to thrash out an agreement. The scheduled meeting between Roosevelt and Churchill at Casablanca from 14 to 24 January 1943 appeared to present the ideal opportunity for the two French leaders to meet and present a united front which would reassure the resistance in metropolitan France. Both Giraud and de Gaulle appeared to be determined to protect their positions: Giraud viewed de Gaulle as a dissident and a junior officer while de Gaulle hoped that Giraud would be satisfied with an offer of the position of commander-in-chief of the French forces in North Africa and would leave the politics to him.[54] For a long time it was not even clear whether de Gaulle would travel to Casablanca to meet Giraud. It was only when Eden informed de Gaulle on Churchill's orders that British support for the Free French would be cut off if de Gaulle did not go to Casablanca that he arrived at the conference on 22 January.[55] Giraud and de Gaulle reluctantly agreed to be photographed together to give a false impression of unity to the wider public.

There followed months of negotiations between Giraud and de Gaulle, overseen by Murphy and Macmillan, and commented on voluminously in the correspondence between Churchill and Roosevelt.[56] Finally, agreement was reached to establish a central committee, the *Comité Français de Libération Nationale* (CFLN), in Algiers with Giraud and de Gaulle as joint presidents. On 17 May 1943 Giraud formally invited de Gaulle to come to Algiers, which he did on 30 May. Unlike his reluctant arrival at Casablanca in January, de Gaulle was now greeted with a guard of honour and street demonstrations in support of him.[57] This change of attitude towards de Gaulle in North Africa was to a great extent influenced by events in metropolitan France and by de Gaulle's acknowledged position as leader of the French resistance. Indeed, the resistance had urged the formation of such a settlement in January 1943 when the three movements making up the MUR and the four resistance movements in the north had sent an appeal to de Gaulle and Giraud to unite their efforts 'just as the combatants in the interior have united. To de Gaulle, the government he already represents in the eyes of France and abroad – to Giraud, the conduct of military operations.'[58]

The German invasion of southern France on 11 November 1942 effectively ended the *raison d'être* of the Vichy regime. For millions of French men and women it represented the second defeat of France. In 1940 the creation of the Vichy regime meant that it was seen as a shield against the depredations of German occupation, but with the November 1942 invasion that shield had manifestly proved to be an illusion. As de Gaulle later wrote:

> Thus, without Vichy's firing or allowing a single shot to be fired, was dissipated the lying pretence of independence which this regime had claimed to justify its capitulation and to deceive so many well-intentioned Frenchmen. Of the traces of its sovereignty there remained only the fleet at Toulon. It was not to be there for long.[59]

Pierre Laval had been in Berlin when Hitler issued the orders for the occupation, but had not been consulted on the matter: he had merely been informed. The Germans did not, however, impose direct rule over the French in the former Unoccupied Zone: the Vichy regime was still effectively sovereign, and the Armistice Commission remained in existence as the conduit for the transmission of German orders to the French. The activities of the German Embassy under Otto Abetz remained restricted to the north, as did the German military government in France under General

Carl-Heinrich von Stülpnagel. The authority of the SS under Carl Oberg and Helmut Knochen, however, was increased to cover the whole of France, other than the now extended zone of Italian occupation, and SS detachments were attached to regional *préfectures*.* Among the figures arriving in the south was Hauptsturmführer Klaus Barbie, who would soon establish himself as a brutal interrogator in Lyon. German police detachments were despatched to the major cities of Lyon, Marseille, Montpellier, Clermont-Ferrand, Toulouse, and Vichy. The Vichy regime and the authority of the French police remained in place simply because the Germans lacked the manpower necessary to take direct control over the region.

The existence in North Africa of a French administration under Giraud appeared to offer the people in southern France a third way other than collaboration with the Germans as sponsored by the Vichy regime, or joining de Gaulle. The fate of the Armistice Army illustrates the dilemma. As discussed earlier, SOE agents had noted the striking lack of resistance by the Armistice Army to the German invasion. Its soldiers had often disposed of the weapons which had been carefully hidden in 1940 or revealed their whereabouts to the Germans instead of handing over the arms to the resistance. Command of the Armistice Army had been given to General Aubert Frère by Giraud before his departure for Gibraltar: Frère had earlier chaired the court martial that had condemned de Gaulle to death *in absentia* in 1940. The Germans now formally disbanded the Armistice Army. Elements of this army then went underground and formed the *Organisation de Résistance de l'Armée* (ORA), commanded by Frère, assisted by Colonel Henri Zeller, Lieutenant Colonel Pfister, and General Verneau. It pledged allegiance to Giraud and considered itself not 'as the army's resistance but as the army in resistance'. Its declared purpose was to prepare to support the Allied invasion of France. British intelligence warned the heads of Vichy military intelligence, Colonel Rivet and Colonel Ronin, of the danger of their imminent arrest by the Germans and they escaped to Algiers in November. Colonel Paul Paillole, head of the Vichy intelligence group *Travaux Ruraux*, had not received the warning and made his own way to London via Spain and Portugal before being sent to Algiers in January 1943.[60]

The remaining members of the Vichy regime now appeared to consider that the best means of retaining the last vestiges of independence rested on a higher degree of collaboration. The events of January 1943 illustrate this. The city of Marseille, and, in particular, its old port area, was a warren of

* The Italians occupied eight departments east of the Rhône: Drôme, Isère, Hautes-Alpes, Basses-Alpes, Alpes-Maritimes, Savoie, Haute Savoie, and Var.

broken-down houses providing shelter to criminals, Jews, and resisters. The Germans wanted the old port area demolished and its population of 40,000 people evacuated. Laval and Bousquet were appalled at the idea but, in order to preserve a semblance of Vichy independence, Bousquet agreed to cooperate with Kurt Daluege, the German police chief, in the cordoning off of the entire city with 9,100 French police and 2,000 SS troopers on the night of 22 January 1943. The identity cards of 40,000 people were then examined. Some 6,000 suspects were arrested but of these 4,000 were soon released and the remainder despatched to a French military camp in Fréjus. The 782 Jews caught were sent to Compiègne before travelling east to their deaths at Sobibor extermination camp. The resistance had been tipped off in advance by the French police and escaped virtually unscathed. The operation completed, German engineers blew up over 1,400 buildings in the old port area, effectively reducing it to rubble.[61]

Vichy's shift towards greater collaboration is also shown in its creation of two additional police forces to combat the resistance and to capture STO evaders: the *Groupes Mobiles de Réserve* (GMR) and the *Milice*. The *Groupes Mobiles* had been formed in April 1941 as part of the national police but in April 1943 were reorganized and made independent. Each group consisted of 217 well-armed and equipped men distributed around the major towns in southern France. The *Milice* was the brainchild of Joseph Darnand. He had formed the *Service d'Ordre Légionnaire* (SOL) in January 1942 as the most fanatical part of the *Légion Française des Combattants*. On 31 January 1943 the SOL was renamed the *Milice* by Laval, and command remained with Darnand. The *Milice* had a uniform of a khaki shirt, black tie, dark blue trousers and jacket, and a black beret. By autumn 1943 there were 29,000 members of the *Milice*, of both sexes, although only around 10,000 were active. The members swore a twenty-one-point oath condemning 'democracy, individualism, international capitalism, Freemasonry, and Jewish leprosy'. Darnand stated that its aim was to 'establish in France an authoritarian, national socialist regime, enabling France to be an integral part of the Europe of the future'. The *Milice* was unarmed at the beginning, but after its members became targets of the resistance in summer 1943, Darnand made a deal with the Germans under which he agreed to join the French Waffen-SS along with some of his main supporters in return for the Germans supplying arms to 'special units' of the *Milice*, known as the *Franc-Garde*. The *Milice* would become the most feared and despised opponent of the resistance for the remainder of the occupation.[62]

In the north too, collaboration with the Germans continued apace. The section of the French police devoted to countering the resistance, the *Brigades Spéciales*, were ever more active and the head of the *Brigades* met the Gestapo chief in Paris every week.[63] As in Norway, where the Rinnan gang was particularly useful in combating the resistance on behalf of the Germans, so too in France the Germans made use of such gangs. The most notable of these was the Bonny-Lafont gang formed by Henri Lafont (formerly Henri Chamberlin), a career criminal who offered the services of thirty fellow criminals to the Germans in 1940 in return for their release from Fresnes prison, and Pierre Bonny, a former policeman who had been charged with embezzlement. The gang betrayed Jews and penetrated resistance groups. One of its principal successes was the capture of Otto Lambrecht, an important member of the Belgian resistance, and the subsequent capture of some 600 members of his network. Another success was the penetration of the resistance group *Défense de la France*, which led to the rounding up of fifty members of the group in July 1943, including de Gaulle's niece, Geneviève. She was sent to Ravensbrück concentration camp, which she survived.[64] The Germans also had no difficulty in continuing their recruitment of agents. One of the Germans most prominent in the running of these agents was Hugo Bleicher. He explained their motives:

> Some suspected that their comrades had betrayed them and were out for revenge. Some were convinced that the best service they could do for their country was to work with the military forces of the victor to prevent sabotage and so save their fellow countrymen from reprisals. Others thought after Germany had attacked Russia that the war against Bolshevism was more important than anything else. But almost all of them had one main impulse: 'Let's get out of prison, and we'll see later what happens.'[65]

Research has suggested that there were some 32,000 French men and women in the service of the Gestapo.[66]

The resistance movements in the south formed separate special corps to attack the collaborators and, to a lesser extent, the Germans and Italians. These were commanded by Jacques Renouvin for *Combat*, Raymond Aubrac for *Libération-sud*, and Benjamin Roux for *Franc-Tireur*.[67] The clandestine press warned collaborators of their likely fate. For example, *Franc-Tireur* stated: 'To each new murder that they commit, the *milicien* and the PPF must expect immediate and merciless reprisals . . . the French Resistance sends a warning – "For an eye, both eyes; for a tooth, the whole jaw!"'[68] *Libération-sud* published the names of collaborators in its newspaper. *Combat* in the south, and *Défense de la France* and *Libération-nord* in the north, warned French officials that 'their lives depended on their attitude', and that the police should warn resistance members of the danger of imminent arrest and undertake investigations of those arrested slowly.[69] There is indeed some evidence to suggest that the police became notably more reluctant to assist the Germans: SS-Standartenführer Helmut Knochen complained in August 1943 about the increasing unreliability of the Paris police force.

Appeals in the clandestine press may have had some effect, but direct attacks on collaborating personnel undoubtedly had more influence on the people in southern France. In the first nine months of 1943, the Germans recorded 147 resistance attacks on French collaborators, 97 on French policemen, and 281 attacks on German personnel.[70] The first resistance action against the *Milice* was the assassination of the deputy leader of the *Milice* in the Bouches-du-Rhône department in April 1943.[71] Reports sent by the prefect of the Lyon region, Alexandre Angeli, to his superiors in Vichy illustrate the targets of the resistance: members of the *Milice*, the *Légion des Volontaires Français contre le Bolshévisme* (LVF), and the *Légion Française des Combattants*.[72] Law and order was clearly breaking down across southern France. Historians have noted the effect of Vichy's conduct: 'Through its collaboration, Vichy itself was a major factor in bringing some coherence to a fragmented opposition, in provoking Resistance, and providing new motivation across an area where *attentisme* was still the reasoned position of the vast majority.'[73]

The Allied invasion of North Africa affected the resistance in the south in another way too: it offered the possibility of direct American support for the resistance. On his way to take up his position as head of the OSS station in Berne, Allen Dulles and a colleague had met Henri Frenay just before the German occupation of the south. Frenay was offered 37 million francs and a large quantity of arms as well as photographic equipment and other items. OSS was effectively offering to supply the French resistance in the south in return for intelligence material. Frenay was not the only person approached by the Americans: Dulles also reported contacts with the ORA. Frenay was prepared to accept the offer on behalf of his own movement and the MUR since such large sums of money were simply not available from Free French sources – Moulin had given him only 250,000 francs in January 1942 – and there was an increasing amount of work to do which required finance and armaments. Frenay did not see the deal as undermining his allegiance to de Gaulle. To him it was simply a matter of resources: he needed to equip more men in the *Combat* armed formations and also to supply and arm the increasing number of STO (*Service du Travail Obligatoire*) evaders and maquis hiding in the mountains of France. In April 1943 Moulin and de Gaulle learned of the deal and were outraged. The Free French representative in Berne was ordered to approach the

American Embassy in Berne and persuade OSS to break off contact with Frenay in order to forestall an alleged 'American takeover of the French resistance'. Dulles was quick to defend his conduct, arguing that he was well aware of MUR's allegiance to de Gaulle and that 'we do not discuss their political views as our sole objective is to support resistance and build SI [intelligence] channels'. Nonetheless, Dulles broke off contact with the MUR and Frenay, bowing to London's superior knowledge of the state of the French resistance. A furious Frenay turned on Moulin: 'You have tried to strangle us . . . You want to control the resistance without having the means or the stature to do so.'[74]

This left the French resistance entirely dependent on British resources. Yet relations between de Gaulle and the British were frequently strained. De Gaulle resented the activities of F Section of SOE, which was following the policy set out by Colin Gubbins in January 1942:

> It is clear that we cannot build up a proper secret army in France under the aegis or flag of De Gaulle: *that* we must do through our independent French Section until such time as a combination is practical politics . . . I can quite see a solution to the problem if and when De Gaulle is replaced by a man who has the general confidence of the French people in France, but with De Gaulle in the saddle it is difficult to know where our support of the [Free French] plans in France is leading us.[75]

Hence, the increasing numbers of F Section agents sent to France during 1942 and 1943. Yet at the same time, on the political front, things seemed more favourable for de Gaulle when, on 13 July 1942, the British agreed that the Free French could now call themselves 'Fighting France' to symbolize their representation of all French people opposed to Vichy and the occupation.[76] Two major issues still threatened to undermine de Gaulle's relations with the British government. The first was his position vis-à-vis Giraud, which moved towards a solution when Giraud invited de Gaulle to join him in Algiers. The second, the provision of weapons for the resistance, was far harder to solve since SOE resources were stretched so thinly across occupied Europe.

De Gaulle's claim to represent France received various boosts in late 1942 and early 1943. In 1942 he had despatched the BCRA deputy André Manuel to report on the politics of the resistance and on the attitudes of the political parties to the occupation and to the leader of the Free French. Manuel's report suggested that there was a groundswell of members of political parties of the Third Republic who might rally to de Gaulle if they were approached by his representative, Jean Moulin.[77] The only remaining political grouping whose attitude towards de Gaulle remained unclear was the communists, and reports from France suggested that the communists were attracting a large number of members. Therefore, as the historian Henri Michel explained:

> The movements felt a profound need to cooperate with the Communist Party in the Resistance; without it, the common struggle would be missing part of the working-class forces; independent of it, the resistance struggle would suffer from a lack of coordination. But they had contradictory feelings towards the Communist Party: superiority by virtue of anteriority but also admiration combined with fear.[78]

The democratic resistance was also worried about the political activities of the *Front National* led by Pierre Villon, whose manifesto declared:

> The *Front National* collaborates with all the resistance groups in each of the zones and, at the same time, with the national committee in London under General de Gaulle's authority and General Giraud's forces. The *Front National* seeks the union of all the resistance movements, whatever designation they may adopt, into a single large cluster of national liberation forces under a single leadership.[79]

This suggested to many resistance leaders in France that the *Front National* was determined to take them over and then, having done so, take political control of the country on liberation in the service of the communists. In January 1943 the hopes and concerns of the resistance were addressed when the leader of the Communist Party, Fernand Grenier, arrived in London and willingly pledged the allegiance of the communists to de Gaulle.

Given the tangled web that the consequences of Operation Torch and the subsequent German occupation of the south had created, combined with the promise of communist support for de Gaulle, it now became urgent for Moulin to return to France and to unify the resistance movements both in the south and in the north into one united body loyal to de Gaulle.[80] Before Moulin returned to France another mission had taken place which would have an important impact on his work – Brumaire-Arquebuse. Brumaire was the code name given to Pierre Brossolette, whose aim was to form an inventory of all the resistance forces in the Occupied Zone, and to take steps to ensure the 'strictest separation' between the compilation of intelligence from the civilian and military resistance. At the same time Brossolette was to start the process of identifying leaders of the provisional administration who would take over once the Allies had landed in France.[81] Brossolette was landed in France on 26 January 1943. Accompanying him was Tommy Yeo-Thomas of SOE RF Section whom Brossolette had insisted on taking with him because Passy was:

> ... concerned that the statements we would have to make on our return to London could not be disputed or accused of lacking objectivity if, as I supposed, they were to be translated by our Allies at a political level into a fairer appreciation of what General de Gaulle truly represented in France, and translated on a military level into more numerous parachute drops.[82]

He was followed a month later by 'Arquebuse', Colonel Passy, the head of the BCRA, who parachuted into France on 26 February. His mission was to persuade the various movements in the Occupied Zone to rationalize the collection and despatch of intelligence, and to work towards the coordination of military action within the Occupied Zone and contacts and coordination with the Unoccupied Zone.[83]

By the start of April 1943 the Brumaire-Arquebuse mission had borne fruit. Each of the main resistance movements had been visited, and an assessment of their military capabilities and civilian activities had been completed. Although the negotiations had often been bitter, the five main movements had agreed to centralize the gathering of intelligence, and to set up a coordinating committee to plan for the creation of a secret army of 20,000 men to which the movements would contribute forces.[84] Yeo-Thomas issued a word of warning as regards his contact with Georges Beaufils of the FTP (*Franc-Tireurs et Partisans*): 'From my contacts with them I imagine that the rank and file are really patriots and only interested in a free France, whereas the heads have other ideas in mind and are planning well ahead, in fact so far ahead as the period which will follow the "Gouvernement Provisoire".'[85] On 26 March, Brossolette chaired the first meeting, in Neuilly, of the coordinating committee of Colonel Alfred Touny of the OCM (*Organisation Civile et Militaire*), Jacques Lecompte-Boinet of *Ceux de la Résistance*, Roger Coquoin of *Ceux de la Libération*, Jacques Brunschwig-Bordier of *Libération-nord*, and Pierre Villon of the *Front National*. The committee was ready to accept the concept of a resistance council which would be formed of representatives of the resistance movements, but they rejected the inclusion of representatives of the political parties. They also envisaged the council as symbolic rather than as a body with executive powers. It was therefore apparent to Brossolette, and indeed in agreement with his own views, that the resistance movements were determined to retain a certain freedom of action and would reject any plans for centralization and close control.[86]

Moulin returned to France on 20 March 1943 bearing a new set of instructions from de Gaulle:

> Jean Moulin becomes the sole permanent representative of General de Gaulle and the National Committee for the metropolitan territory as a whole. At the earliest possible date there is to be set up a single Council of the Resistance for the whole of the metropolitan territory, presided over by Jean Moulin. This Council of the Resistance will ensure the representation of the resistance movements, the resistant political formations and the resistant workers' union . . . The Council of the Resistance is a national representative body in embryo pending the arrival of General de Gaulle's political council in France.[87]

But Moulin faced opposition from the resistance movements in both zones to his proposals to include the old political parties in the council. From the south, Emmanuel d'Astier warned:

> The movements, which set up the resistance and which are in charge of the executive function, will not abide the creation of a superexecutive body in which the militants of the Resistance would be in the minority, and thanks to which the partisan organizations would retake the levers of power, in order to sate the hunger of the old party cadres for consideration and for future authority.[88]

Brossolette was operating under the misconception that the northern and southern zones were to be kept separate, and was appalled to discover that Moulin's proposed council and leadership of it was to cover the whole of France. He was also strongly opposed to the inclusion of the political parties of the Third Republic. The result was what has been described as an extremely heated meeting on 31 March between Moulin and Brossolette in Paris in a building inhabited by German officers. Colonel Passy recalled:

> It was tragic to think that the Gestapo might be in the room above, next door or below us, and that these verbal fireworks might lead to the capture of two men who had worked so hard for their country. The shouting carried on for a good quarter of an hour. I admit that I wanted only one thing: to leave, as I had the impression I was sitting on a powder keg. Thankfully nothing serious happened and we all left in one piece, although there was no conclusion to the debate.[89]

Further meetings followed between the various resistance movements and between Brossolette, Passy, and Moulin before the Brumaire-Arquebuse mission ended when the two men and Yeo-Thomas left Paris on 14 April to return to London in a Lysander.

The resistance movements across France were also unhappy about the plans for the *Armée Secrète*. Part of their concern rested on the leadership of General Delestraint. Frenay, smarting from the refusal of the other southern movements to accept his leadership of the AS, may have been harsh in his assessment of Delestraint: 'It was clear that Delestraint had not grasped the nature of the organization that had been entrusted to him.'[90] Delestraint thought along traditional military lines with organized formations and a strict command structure. He toured France searching for suitable battlegrounds and one location he identified as suitable for a pitched battle was the Vercors plateau. He made contact with former officers of the Armistice Army and succeeded in establishing a staff structure in both zones. Frenay and the other resistance leaders argued that they had a better understanding of the demands of war in the shadows and objected to many of Delestraint's selections. Moulin was also concerned that Delestraint lacked the necessary understanding of subversive warfare, but he supported him because of his contacts within the former Armistice Army.[91] Delestraint had little concept of security and continued to use his own name.[92] His security failings led to his arrest by the Germans on 9 June 1943, bringing to an end the first stage of the formation of the AS. Delestraint was killed in Dachau concentration camp a few days before the war ended.

Moulin's skill as a negotiator, his extreme determination to have his way and to include the political parties in his council, and, above all, his position as de Gaulle's accredited representative, ultimately led to success. Moulin won the argument with the larger resistance movements who wanted more delegates to the *Conseil National de la Résistance* (CNR) than the smaller groups: Moulin insisted on one delegate per movement or political party.[93] On 27 May 1943 he presided over the first meeting of the new CNR at 48 Rue du Four in Paris. Attending the meeting were representatives of eight resistance movements: *Ceux de la Résistance*, *Ceux de la Libération*, *Front National*, *Libération-nord*, OCM, *Combat*, *Libération-sud*, and *Franc-Tireurs*; and delegates from the political parties: communists, SFIO (*Section Française de l'Internationale Ouvrière*), Radical-Socialists, Popular Democrats, *Alliance Démocratique*, and *Fédération Républicaine*; as well as two union representatives, one each for the CGT (*Confédération Générale du Travail*) and CFTC (*Confédération Française des Travailleurs Chrétiens*).[94] The CNR 'charter' announced that the resistance was determined to remain united after the liberation in order to accomplish a broad programme of political, social, and economic reform.[95] It was a crowning achievement won in the face of bitter arguments and acrimony and possibly was 'more important for what it was than for what it did'.[96] It appeared to represent the unification of the resistance, its allegiance to de Gaulle, and its readiness to ensure a smooth transition from occupation to democratic government after the liberation. Moulin triumphantly reported to de Gaulle: 'I am happy to inform you that all members were present at the meeting, which was conducted in an atmosphere of patriotic and dignified unity.'[97] The apparent unity was, however, short lived. There were two reasons. First, the currents against the alleged 'bureaucratization and sterilization of the resistance' were still strong.[98] Secondly, Moulin himself was arrested by the Germans on 21 June 1943, in circumstances which will be described in the following chapter.

Before his capture Moulin had despatched an important telegram to de Gaulle which strengthened de Gaulle's position in his future discussions with Giraud:

> On the eve of the departure of General de Gaulle for Algiers, all the movements and parties of the Resistance, in the northern and in the southern zones, wish to renew, to him and the National Committee, the assurance of their absolute attachment to the principles which they both embody and must integrally uphold. All the Resistance movements and parties declare that the meeting must take place at the HQ of the Algerian Government General, in the open and among Frenchmen. They also declare:
>
> 1. That political problems must not be excluded from the conversations.
> 2. That the people of France will never agree to General de Gaulle being subordinate to General Giraud, and demand the immediate installation of a provisional government in Algiers under the presidency of General de Gaulle, with General Giraud as military chief.
> 3. That General de Gaulle will remain the sole leader of French Resistance whatever the outcome of negotiations.[99]

This was extremely welcome and important news for de Gaulle. At the beginning of June 1943 the Comité Français de Libération Nationale (CFLN) was created with Giraud and de Gaulle as joint leaders. Over the summer the more politically astute de Gaulle edged out Giraud from political affairs. Giraud was content to limit his authority to the rebirth of a united French army, formed from a merger at the end of July 1943 of the Free French and the Vichy Army of Africa, which would fight alongside the Allies in the liberation of Europe. By the end of the year the CFLN was virtually a provisional government of France under the leadership of de Gaulle.[100]

By the middle of 1943 the future of the French resistance seemed bright; but the Germans were about to strike back.

17
The Germans Hit Back

It is tempting to assume that the development and growth of the resistance movements followed a steady upward curve from the meagre beginnings in 1939–41 to the widespread resistance which was evident across Europe in the summer of 1944. This, however, does not present a true picture: in the summer of 1943 the Germans hit back at the resistance across Europe and effectively brought it to its knees as key leaders were arrested. The German successes came about through a combination of skill, luck, and treachery. The only region in which the Germans failed to achieve their aims was in the Soviet Union, where German anti-partisan warfare proved inadequate to suppress the partisans as they gathered in strength before and after the battle of Kursk.

There is little evidence to support a theory of coordinated action by the Germans in the east and in the west. However, one man, Sturmbannführer Horst Kopkow, in his role in the SS based in Berlin, had gained useful experience in the breaking of networks and in the turning of foreign agents through his destruction of the Soviet spy ring, the Red Orchestra. For example, one agent, Leopold Trepper, was captured in November 1942 and then cooperated with the Gestapo, revealing all he knew about the network until he escaped in September 1943.[1] The lessons learned from the breaking of the Red Orchestra were disseminated to Gestapo offices in western Europe. From summer 1942 onwards the SS was fully operational in both zones of France under the command of Sturmbannführer Karl Boemelburg, who focused on counter-espionage, and Hauptsturmbannführer Hans Kieffer, who concentrated on SOE. After the war Kieffer explained:

> Berlin attached extraordinary importance to the French Section . . . All other matters were pushed into the background, and Berlin showed interest again and again only for French Section matters and we were always obliged to neglect other matters because Berlin considered the French Section particularly dangerous.[2]

Chance played a major role in the Netherlands, where the skills of Hermann Giskes of the Abwehr and Joseph Schreieder of the Gestapo combined to create the *Englandspiel*, the complete control of the Dutch SOE agents by the Germans between March 1942 and December 1943.

The sheer scale of the disasters in western Europe has spurred numerous conspiracy theories. This is especially the case with regard to the arrest of Francis Suttill, 'Prosper', and the collapse of his network in northern France in the summer of 1943. In their memoirs, a number of resisters have suggested that SOE deliberately sacrificed its F Section agents and their French assistants in the service of a deception scheme, and such allegations have been taken up by many thriller writers. The refutation of this theory is complicated by the statements of Maurice Buckmaster, the head of SOE's F Section, in his memoirs. In his 1952 book *Specially Employed* he claimed: 'As early as April 1943, the rumour ran like wildfire that the Allies were about to land in France. The patriotic upsurge of enthusiasm was dangerous. It had to be quelled.' Then in his 1958 book *They Fought Alone*, Buckmaster seems to contradict himself: he now suggests that he had been informed that the Allies were going to invade France in 1943 and therefore encouraged an upsurge in resistance regardless of the risks. It is perhaps useful to note Buckmaster's dedication written in the copy of his books he gave to his assistant Vera Atkins: 'Dedicated to Vera who knows more accurately than I do how, when and why these events occurred.'[3] The conspiracy theories were revived again in 1986 with a *Timewatch* programme and subsequent book by Robert Marshall, *All the King's Men*. A more recent publication, *Shadows in the Fog*, Francis Suttill's carefully researched analysis of his father's life, work, and arrest provides probably the best rebuttal of the conspiracy theorists.

Such conspiracy theories were also present in the Netherlands, where it was widely assumed that the *Englandspiel* was part of a British 'deception scheme so subtle that its purpose has never been revealed'.[4] The conclusion of a Dutch Parliamentary Commission of Inquiry, which examined witnesses for two years between 1948 and 1950 and submitted its very lengthy report in 1956, concluded that the *Englandspiel* was successful for the Germans because of 'errors of judgement'.[5]

Radio communications were always the single greatest point of vulnerability in any resistance network. In the age of modern telecommunications, when a small handheld device can connect one instantly with another person anywhere in the world, it is perhaps difficult to understand the difficulties posed by the state of communications during the Second World War. The radio transceivers available then were bulky, fitted into a small recognizable suitcase, and weighed about 9 kilograms. They operated on shortwave with the frequency determined precisely by a removable crystal which was the shape and size of a two-pin electric light plug. Each operator carried at least two crystals, one for day and one for night work, and these were extremely fragile and easily broken. Communications could be held up for weeks if an operator had lost or been forced to destroy his crystals and had to wait to be resupplied. Indeed, simply asking for new crystals was by definition an extremely difficult process. The radio also required a 70-foot-long aerial which had to be attached to a suitable building, chimney, or tree, and was vulnerable to observation by the opposition. Efforts were made to reduce the size and weight of the radio, and the Type A Mark III suitcase radio supplied to SOE during late 1943 weighed only 4kg. S-phones came into use in 1942 for use on landing grounds to enable the pilot and reception committee to communicate by voice directly: these were secure at a distance but the conversation could be detected at ground level within about 400 metres. Towards the end of the war the chief engineer of Bang & Olufsen in Denmark, Lorens Arne Duus Hansen, developed a version of the radio which was only the size of a telephone directory, weighed just 3lb, and was twice as powerful as British-made radios. These were supplied to SOE agents in Denmark and the Danish resistance but never spread to other countries. By 1945 Hansen had also developed a high-speed Morse transmitter which enabled messages to be transmitted on a perforated tape at high speed to be recorded in Britain on wax disks and played back at a slower, more readable speed.[6]

Radio operators were in short supply, and were at the same time the most vulnerable and most important members of a network. They needed to have a number of safe houses from which they could operate: 'My life as a radio operator was a succession of movements from one house to another. I in no way complained about this as I well knew that it had to be so, but occasionally life could be very monotonous.'[7] But safe houses could be hard to locate. Robert Boiteux noted:

> Somehow it seems strange to say that we could not find houses from which our radio operators could transmit in a town with a population of almost half a million [Lyon], all of whom would call themselves patriotic Frenchmen. Our lack of safe houses cost the lives of many English 'pianists' and ultimately acted as a brake to Resistance work as a whole. Yet one could not help but be intimidated by the Gestapo with their cruelty and the stories one heard of concentration camps. The penalty for anyone caught sheltering 'pianists' was deportation, torture and death.[8]

Security procedures were essential. Women were often used to transfer a radio from one location to another since women carrying suitcases, used generally to transport foodstuffs, aroused far less suspicion than men, who could be stopped at any moment for their papers to be checked in case they were evading a call-up for forced labour. It has to be remembered, of course, that France and Poland particularly were countries where a large number of men were POWs, making those still at liberty more conspicuous. When operating from a house, members of the network needed to guard the location carefully. One of the *Cichociemni* operating in Poland, 'Malina', asked for details about his security and was told that the boy playing with a dog on the balcony of the building opposite him would take off his cap if Germans were spotted; two men digging in a nearby garden were also working as look-outs; and there were men armed with machine guns in the building from which he was transmitting, ready to give him time to escape should the Germans surprise them.[9]

The radios could be powered by mains electricity or by battery, and both methods caused problems. Use of the electricity supply made detection by the Germans easier as they would cut off the power supply to districts where they had detected a radio transmitter in operation, then to certain streets, and then to individual buildings until the precise location of the operator had been identified. Batteries were not vulnerable to this but they needed to be charged. For example, there were three types of pedal-powered generators, and these were often used in Yugoslavia: 'It had a saddle and pedals like a bicycle and made a noise like an enormous egg whisk. Eight or nine hours' pedalling were necessary to charge one battery.' The Partisans hated the hard work involved but eventually realized that no radio meant no supplies, so however unpopular and tiring the method was they pedalled away. In certain districts it was also possible to take batteries to a friendly local garage to be charged.[10]

The Germans put a great deal of effort into radio detection. The first vans they used were easily recognizable because of the roof-mounted rotating aerials, but then the Germans succeeded in fitting all the equipment into the back of a standard commercial van, although the necessary reshaping of the boot still gave them away. Even before the Germans occupied the south of France, radio-detector vans were sent to operate in the Unoccupied Zone and these carried normal number plates. The resistance was assisted by the local prefect who issued forty-five consecutive number plates for these vans and informed the resistance of the first number in the series. The Germans tried to conceal the purpose of their vans by using a number of commercial signs such as 'laundry' or 'bakery'. George Millar noted the German use of 'ambulances' to hide radio-detection equipment:

'But ambulances do not make strange, radio howling and squeaking noises. And ambulances go directly from one point to another instead of stopping at intervals to work at the roadside.' The Germans eventually managed to reduce the size of their radio-detection equipment so that once the broad location of a transmitter had been identified, an operator could wear a more local receiver permanently tuned to the agent's transmitter. This took the form of a 'very light wooden frame, which was strung with wire to serve as an antenna. And then the man, he had a wire through his sleeve, to his ear, with a beret on his head, at an angle, so that nothing was visible, and then he strolled through the area, while he kept turning around until he got to the transmitter', a device strapped to his wrist telling him whether he was getting closer. The resistance team guarding the radio operator learned to keep an eye out for bulky men who constantly turned their heads and looked at their wrist watches. By the beginning of 1943 the radio-detection process in Paris had become virtually automated and in under fifteen minutes the location of a transmitting radio operator could be narrowed down to a 200-metre radius.[11]

As early as 1941, an F Section pioneer, Georges Bégué, had suggested a system of pre-arranged personal messages, and these were then broadcast over the BBC. They could, for example, inform a network over action to be taken or the cancellation of a drop. One method in use by 1943 was to have a series of set questions to which there were equally set answers. In February 1943 Denys Hamson found an obvious flaw in the pre-arranged method with which he received notification from SOE Cairo that an arms delivery was expected that night. He was given a phrase from Gilbert and Sullivan's comic opera *The Mikado*: 'The sun whose rays are all ablaze'. The plane would flash the letter corresponding to the day of the month when over the landing place so, for example, that 'u' would be flashed on the 5th of the month. Hamson radioed back to Cairo that the phrase had only twenty-seven letters and asked what he was supposed to do on the later days. SOE Cairo argued the issue, insisting that the phrase contained twenty-eight letters, but at the same time altered the phrase to read correctly: 'The sun whose rays were all ablaze'.[12]

All SOE radio operators were trained to transmit in the Playfair cipher which had been inherited from SIS. This was a revival of a British Army field cipher dating from the First World War. It had the advantage of being easy to use and the great disadvantage of being just as easy to break. Indeed, even interwar detective novelists understood the code-breaking technique: for example, it was explained in detail in chapters 26–29 of Dorothy L. Sayers's *Have His Carcase* which was published in 1932. Playfair required the sender and receiver to agree on a key word or phrase. The system of both the agent and London having the same copy of a book was quickly discarded in favour of a poem or hymn which the operator could memorize. The key would be one line of that poem or hymn, which would be written out in lines of five letters (I and J counting as one), with duplicate letters omitted; the remainder of the alphabet would fill the rest of the 5 × 5 square. So the first line of the hymn 'I vow to thee, my country' would appear as

IJ	V	O	W	T
H	E	M	Y	C
U	N	R	A	B
D	F	G	K	L
P	Q	S	X	Z

The message to be sent – 'Jacques taken' – is divided into groups of two letters or bigrams, with a random letter used to fill in any gaps. Each of the bigrams is encoded by taking the two opposite corners of the rectangle it forms in the word square: so JA becomes WU. Special rules apply if both letters are in the same line or same column.[13]

In the interests of security SOE adopted additional precautions such as a double transposition system and changing the key for each message, but each increase in complexity made it more likely that the errors would be introduced inadvertently into the whole process. Any message received had to go through a number of stages before it reached the desk of the responsible section officer in Baker Street – encoding by the agent, transmission, reception, teleprinting – thereby increasing the possibilities of errors being inadvertently introduced somewhere along the line. Such errors would make the message indecipherable. Leo Marks, chief coding clerk at SOE's headquarters, was so concerned about the number of indecipherable messages received from agents operating in extreme danger under enormous pressure that he issued a memorandum to the decoders that there should be no such thing as an 'indecipherable', and he suggested methods of attacking an indecipherable message in order to break it. Later the decision was taken to retain each agent's training messages so that typical mistakes made in training could be checked when an indecipherable had been received from that agent.[14]

SOE were well aware of the vulnerabilities of the Playfair code but they had to work with what they had been given. One important concern was to be sure that a message had been sent by the agent and not by an impersonator, and that it had been sent freely and not under duress. Hence the adoption of a system of so-called security checks. Leo Marks made his opinion of the practice very clear in his memoirs:

> SOE's security checks were so insecure that I thought the real ones were being withheld from me. Their function was to tell us whether an agent was coding under duress. To convey this to us without the enemy being aware of it, he was required to insert various dummy letters in the body of each message – and their absence or alteration in any way was supposed to alert us immediately to his capture. As an additional 'precaution' he was instructed to make deliberate spelling mistakes at prearranged spots. The whole concept had all the validity of a child's excuses for staying up late, with none of the imagination. It took no account of the possibility of an agent's code being broken or tortured out of him, when the Gestapo would be in a position to work out the security checks for themselves. Nor did it make any allowances for Morse mutilation, which frequently garbled so much of the text that it was impossible to tell whether the security checks – for what little they were worth – were present.[15]

As will become clear below, the Germans very quickly learned that once they had captured a radio operator, if they could extract his security checks, with or without using torture in the process, they could then 'play back' the agent's radio to London and send whatever message they chose.

From late 1943 the vulnerable poem code began to be replaced by the mathematically unbreakable one-time pad system:

> Small silk handkerchiefs were parachuted in for us, tucked inside ordinary items such as tubes of toothpaste and cigarette packs. These pieces of silk were as fine as they were tough. Each had 120 rows of tiny numbers, and each row of numbers was the key to encoding or decoding one telegram. After using a row, I would take a scissors and snip it off. Then I would burn it . . .[16]

From the security viewpoint this system was infinitely more secure than the poem code but re-adopted the vulnerability of the original book code – the silk handkerchief could be lost. The solution was to possess several silk handkerchiefs and hide them in different places.

Although the blame for the *Englandspiel* has traditionally been placed at the door of SOE, it was errors by SIS agents who were despatched to the Netherlands from August 1941 to March 1942 which enabled the Germans to lay the foundations for the entire edifice. These SIS agents revealed far too much to Giskes and Schreieder: J. J. Zomer had retained copies of around 100 messages between himself and London, and W. J. van der Reyden revealed how the SIS codes worked, although he kept silent about the security checks. Han Jordaan refused to cooperate with the Germans: but when a German radio operator pretended to be him and informed London that he needed to replace Jordaan temporarily, London instructed Jordaan to reveal the use of security checks. Jordaan was so angry at London's crassness that he complied. This revelation proved indispensable to the Germans over the following months.

On 8 November 1941 two agents, Thijs Taconis and his radio operator Huub Lauwers, were dropped into the Netherlands. The radio did not work because of a wiring fault, and Lauwers could not transmit his first message until the beginning of January 1942. The way in which these two men were captured demonstrates the difficulties of operating in a built-up country such as the Netherlands where there were many Dutchmen working for or at least sympathetic to the German cause, and relatively few engaged in the resistance. Taconis approached a friend for assistance to find a lorry to move some stores, and the friend unwittingly put him in contact with George Ridderhof, who was a Dutchman working with the Abwehr. This alerted the Germans to the fact that there were SOE agents at large in the Netherlands. Mischance proved the undoing of Lauwers. On 6 March 1942 he had three messages to send but, when warned of the imminent arrival of a German radio-detection party, he stuffed the three encoded messages into his pocket and tossed his radio out of the window into the snow. Unfortunately, the radio caught on a laundry line and the Germans retrieved it; they also caught Lauwers and his messages.[17]

Here the subtle conduct of Giskes and Schreieder becomes evident. Giskes first of all treated Lauwers with kindness, providing him with cigarettes which Lauwers wanted since he was a heavy smoker. Then the helpfulness of the preceding SIS agents was Lauwers's undoing: he was presented with decoded versions of his three messages. Lauwers then agreed to send his messages to London simply because he hoped that his cooperation would give Taconis more time to hide; but Taconis was arrested three days later. Lauwers also attempted to warn Baker Street that he had been captured by replacing the traditional STOP at the end of each sentence with STIP, STEP or STUP: London did not notice.[18] Lauwers was then appalled to learn from Baker Street that they proposed to send in more agents, not just sabotage materiel. He baulked at being forced to continue sending messages in the German service, but Giskes assured him that none of these agents would be subject to the death penalty and all would be sent to the German prison in Haaren seminary, near Tilburg. With this assurance, Lauwers agreed to continue his cooperation, but at the same time he repeatedly tried to warn Baker Street that he was in German custody. Most radio exchanges ended with the letters QRU for 'I have nothing further for you', which Lauwers replaced with CAU. Similarly, the letters QSY signified that he wanted to change frequencies and Lauwers replaced this with GHT. His subtle deception escaped the notice of the Germans, who watched his transmissions extremely closely; tragically, it escaped London's notice too.[19]

And so the *Englandspiel* was launched. Giskes explained why it was created and continued to operate despite all kinds of scares:

> Messages emanating from an enemy Secret Service and received by a radio set under our control could give us valuable information about enemy intentions. Every task given to agents, every question passed to them and every exchange of messages was a milestone along the road towards the objective of counter-espionage – to penetrate the heart of the enemy Secret Service.[20]

The greatest coup undoubtedly came with the arrival of George Louis Jambroes straight into German hands. He had been despatched by the Dutch government-in-exile at the end of June 1942 to set up contacts with the largest Dutch resistance organization, the *Orde Dienst*, and to instruct them in the principles of and institute recruitment and training for the application of Plan Holland. This plan had been devised through the collaboration of Major Charles Blizard for N Section, SOE, and Colonel de Bruyne for the Dutch government-in-exile. It envisaged the creation of a force of 1,000 saboteurs and a secret army of 5,000 men. Plan Holland was to be launched around the time of D-Day with the broad objectives of severely constricting the German use of the Dutch transport system, especially the railways; preventing the Germans from demolishing facilities of use to the advancing Allies; and ensuring the smooth takeover of the country on the behalf of the Dutch government-in-exile following the departure of the German occupying forces.[21]

Jambroes's arrival posed a test for Giskes and Schreieder because neither man had in fact any idea of the identity of the men of the *Orde Dienst* who had taken over the leadership after a swathe of arrests of the original leaders by the Germans earlier that year. The German tactic was to inform London that Jambroes could not contact the men he had expected to because the *Orde Dienst* had been thoroughly penetrated by the Germans.[22] Giskes wrote later: 'We now proceeded to overwhelm London with a flood of reports about signs of demoralization among the leaders of the [Orde Dienst].' Under German instruction, Jambroes informed London that he was rebuilding the organization from scratch. London gratefully despatched seventeen agents to help him between the end of September and the end of November 1942, and another seventeen in the first three months of 1943 – all falling into German hands.[23] In late September 1942

London asked Jambroes to return to Britain and report on progress. This again posed a dilemma for the Germans. London, however, helpfully provided the contact details of escape lines, mostly from the Vic line in Paris, and Giskes ensured that the line was used successfully by some escaping Allied aircrew to convince London of its effectiveness, while the Germans monitored the entire process and arrested the helpers as and when they wanted. Jambroes, meanwhile, was naturally not permitted to leave and remained in prison, with London continually pressing for his departure. London perceived an apparent necessity for better collaboration with escape lines and on 13 February 1943 despatched Beatrix Terwindt to make the necessary arrangements. Like the other agents being despatched at great regularity at the time, she fell straight into German hands: the only female victim of the *Englandspiel*.[24]

The *Englandspiel* also netted and castrated the leadership of the civilian resistance in the Netherlands. In this the Germans were ably assisted by the Dutch traitor Antonius van der Waals. He had managed to convince the Dutch resistance that he was an agent sent from London, a claim supported by Giskes's supervision of captured agents' traffic, and so gained the confidence of members of the *Orde Dienst*, leading to their arrests. He also was brought into contact with Koos Vorrink, a former socialist prime minister, who was in hiding but creating a National Committee of Resistance. The news of the creation of such a committee was passed to London, who in March 1943 asked Vorrink for the names of the six leaders. Vorrink supplied these to van der Waals and at the beginning of April 1943 all six men, including Vorrink, were arrested by the Germans along with over 100 of their friends and relatives.[25]

But there was one area in which the Germans faced a struggle to demonstrate 'resistance' activity in the Netherlands – sabotage. It was to be expected that as more and more agents were fed into the Netherlands, the level of sabotage would rise accordingly. Acts of sabotage could be independently verified by London through air reconnaissance and in addition there was the real danger for the Germans that some Dutch agents might have been infiltrated into the country through means outside their control and could alert London when a claimed act of sabotage had not really happened. Giskes and Schreieder devised a 'sabotage' campaign. Following orders from London in July 1943 for an attack on the German transmitters at Kootwijk, west of Apeldoorn, which were used by the navy to direct the U-boats operating in the Atlantic, Giskes reported an unsuccessful attack and arranged for newspaper reports to substantiate his story. In August 1943 he similarly used the newspapers to report the alleged explosion of an ammunition train between Breda and Tilburg. This 'explosion' had set off a forest fire which could be seen for miles around. The fire was probably real but the explosion was not. Finally, that month Giskes arranged for the sinking of a barge filled with aircraft scrap in the middle of Rotterdam.[26]

Such measures were necessary because evidence was building up in London that there was something very wrong with operations in the Netherlands. This evidence emanated from three main sources: the air ministry, signals, and human resources.

Flying men and supplies into occupied Europe was a hazardous occupation and planes making such deliveries were shot down all over Europe. Yet the rate of losses for operations to the Netherlands was higher than expected – one in every six planes during the winter of 1942–43 – and, strangely, each was shot down only after having made its delivery. Squadron Leader Frank Griffiths, flying Halifaxes to the Netherlands, explained other concerns:

> People seemed to get a very easy run in and then the aircraft would disappear on the way out. Not all of them, but it was a rough ride out. Also the torches were excellent. Typical Germans. So bloody perfect, you know. Whereas with others there'd be weak batteries or they wouldn't be in a straight line and so on and so forth. But people used to remark, 'God, these Dutch are efficient', and all the time we were dropping to the Germans.[27]

The rate of losses was unsustainable and in late May 1943 all secret flights to the Netherlands were banned: the *Englandspiel* was beginning to unravel.

A breakthrough on the British side, however, came slowly and took a long time to believe. Leo Marks became suspicious about the Dutch traffic but struggled to identify the precise reason for his unease. Then he had a brainwave: 'We had never received an indecipherable from Holland which had been caused by coding mistakes.' He confided in a senior SOE officer: 'I put it to him that indecipherables were a black plague and that there was only one feasible explanation for the Dutch agents' immunity from it. They were operating under duress.' Furthermore, with one exception, 'not a single Dutch WT operator had asked the Home Station to repeat a single message on the grounds that it had been garbled in transmission and couldn't be deciphered'. He analysed all the Dutch communications traffic from 1942 and was appalled by his conclusions:

> Yet despite deaths by drowning, by exploding minefields, by dropping accidents, despite every kind of difficulty, setback and frustration, not a single Dutch agent had been so overwrought that he'd made a mistake in his coding.

> It seemed to me unarguable that the bulk of the messages had been sent by the Germans and that the main question was no longer which agents were caught, but which were free.

Marks tried to play two tricks on Giskes. The first was to send a deliberately undecipherable message to a radio operator knowing that if he was at liberty he would reply immediately that he had been unable to decipher the message: no such reply was made in that operator's next two messages. Finally, a signals officer signed off a message to the Netherlands with the letters HH for Heil Hitler. The German operator masquerading as the SOE agent instinctively responded HH.[28] The game was up.

It was extremely hard for N Section to accept the evidence and take responsibility for the terrible consequences of having sent so many agents straight into German hands. The final piece of the jigsaw needed to come from people leaving the Netherlands. One such piece of evidence was supplied by George Dessing who had been dropped blind and remained uncaptured before escaping to Switzerland where he informed London that he had seen one of the recently arrived SOE agents, Leonard Andringa, in a bar accompanied by the Gestapo.[29] N Section ignored his report. Then Leen Pot, a locally recruited intelligence agent who had no contact with SOE or SIS agents sent from Britain and therefore had not been contaminated by unwitting contact with the Germans, arrived in London in August 1943 and reported that there had in fact been virtually no sabotage in the Netherlands to speak of.[30] This news conflicted with the reports emanating from the German-controlled SOE agents there. Then on 30 August 1943 two SOE agents who had landed straight into the arms of the Germans, Pieter Dourlein and Ben Ubbink, escaped from the prison at Haaren and three months later reached Switzerland, where they informed the Dutch military attaché, General Aleid van Tricht, that they had met many other SOE agents in prison. Van Tricht immediately informed London but N Section dismissed this report too, because Giskes had been extremely clever and sent a warning that Dourlein and Ubbink had been turned by the enemy and anything they said should be ignored. Guido Zembsch-Schreve was sent to Switzerland in November 1943 to interview the two men and was convinced by their stories. He double-checked their news through one of his contacts, Paul Eckmann, who confirmed that the two agents were loyal. This information was passed to London on 1 January 1944. SIS helped Dourlein and Ubbink to reach Spain and both men arrived in London on 1 February 1944 where they were greeted with suspicion and despatched to a holding camp in Guildford under open arrest.[31]

Despite the considerable evidence gathered from various sources that something was very wrong in the Netherlands, N Section was simply unable to believe the unbelievable, that they had been hoodwinked so thoroughly for so long. Then on 1 April 1944 a telegram from ten different radios in the Netherlands was received in London:

> MESSRS BLUNT, BINGHAM AND SUCCS LTD., LONDON.
> IN THE LAST TIME YOU ARE TRYING TO MAKE BUSINESS IN THE NETHERLANDS WITHOUT OUR ASSISTANCE STOP WE THINK THIS RATHER UNFAIR IN VIEW OUR LONG AND SUCCESSFUL COOPERATION AS YOUR SOLE AGENTS STOP BUT NEVER MIND WHENEVER YOU WILL COME TO PAY A VISIT TO THE CONTINENT YOU MAY BE ASSURED THAT YOU WILL BE RECEIVED WITH SAME CARE AND RESULT AS ALL THOSE YOU SENT US BEFORE STOP SO LONG.[32]

Giskes was signing off on the *Englandspiel.*

The *Englandspiel* had netted the Germans 570 containers and 150 parcels containing 15,200kg of explosives, 3,000 Sten guns, 5,000 small arms, 300 Bren guns, 2,000 hand grenades, seventy-five radio transmitters and spare parts, 100 Aldis lamps, torches, and signal apparatus, three Eureka sets (which SOE was very concerned to keep secret), three S-phones, about 500,000 rounds of ammunition, forty bicycles, a large quantity of food and clothing, more than 500,000 guilders, and large sums in pounds, dollars, French and Belgian francs.[33] The *Englandspiel* put an end to the application of Plan Holland, and the effect of this has been disputed. One historian has argued that the failure to carry out the plan during the Allied advance across northern Europe 'brought untold tragedy, hardship and famine upon the Dutch people'; Leen Pot, on the other hand, argued that the plan was deeply flawed and would have been impossible to carry out.[34] Within the Netherlands, the impact of the *Englandspiel* was felt within resistance circles and was seen as 'devastating and continuous, with at least ten if not twenty times the loss of life [of the SOE operations] as well as a poisoning of the atmosphere'.[35] Although the Dutch resistance was rebuilt, as will be described later, any intelligence received from the Netherlands was now viewed with suspicion in London, with tragic consequences for the airborne landings at Arnhem in September 1944.

The impact of the *Englandspiel* was widespread. For example, the Belgian resister Gaston Vandermeerssche was asked to organize a new network in the Netherlands as early as August 1942, without the knowledge of SOE or the Dutch intelligence service. He named it WIM. His success was limited by the fact that the Gestapo got wind of his work under his code name Rinus and in November 1942 spread the rumours that he was a double agent: his bona fides were finally confirmed by the BBC in the middle of January 1943. After his arrest in May 1943 Vandermeerssche was appalled to discover that the Germans had constructed a huge organizational chart of WIM, demonstrating the knowledge gleaned as a result of the damage caused by the *Englandspiel*: after the war he discovered, even more distressingly, that most of the real intelligence his agents had supplied had been ignored by the Dutch intelligence services on the grounds that *all* intelligence from the Netherlands was regarded as suspect.[36]

The Germans were also successful in playing back the radios of captured Belgian agents and it was only towards the end of 1942 that it was accepted that 'what SOE Belgian Section conceived to be its organisation in the field was no more than a mirage created by the Gestapo'.[37]

On 1 December 1943 Air Marshal Norman Bottomley, the vice-chief of the air staff, announced a total suspension of SOE flights across the whole of occupied Europe because of fears that SOE networks in many other countries, in Denmark and Poland in particular, could similarly be in the hands of the Germans.[38] Flemming Muus was in London at the time, and went to the War Office for an intensive, two-hour-long interrogation with thirty senior officers which convinced them that the Danish networks were secure.[39] SOE's actual existence as an independent organization was also threatened. The Joint Intelligence Committee made a thorough analysis of SOE operations which was highly critical of many of them. The head of SOE, Lord Selborne, issued an equally thorough rebuttal, citing in particular a long list of successful sabotage operations carried out by SOE across Europe.[40] Ultimately, however, SOE survived largely because it was too late in the war to construct a new organization to carry out its tasks.

There was no single root cause of the immense damage the Germans managed to inflict on SOE circuits in France and on the French resistance in the summer of 1943. The damage was caused by a fatal series of circumstances: the shortage of radio operators, which forced circuits that should have been operating totally independently to maintain contact with neighbouring circuits; carelessness by a number of agents operating in France, including the need to spend time together to ease the feelings of isolation in a hostile environment, and a naive belief that some Germans were secretly on their side; and crass behaviour by F Section in London, which failed to recognize that agents were operating under duress. This last went on for so long that arrested agents drew the conclusion there was a traitor in London. On top of all this, there actually was a traitor, Henri Déricourt, SOE's chief landing officer for northern France, who was passing information to the Germans at the same time. A final factor was the conduct of the Germans themselves. Instead of the brutality meted out to many captured agents elsewhere in France, a good number of the arrested SOE agents found themselves treated kindly by men such as Hans Kieffer and Dr Goetz, and so were lulled into giving away too much information.

Francis Suttill arrived in France at the beginning of October 1942 to set up the Physician circuit in northern France. This became better known as the Prosper circuit after Suttill's code name. Suttill was accompanied by his radio operator, Gilbert Norman, 'Archambaud', and his courier Andrée Borrel. Suttill was highly successful in organizing resistance in northern France and accordingly he received a high number of arms drops and conducted numerous successful sabotage operations. There was a severe shortage of working radios in northern France and the two Prosper radio operators, Norman and Jack Agazarian, who arrived in December 1942, had to serve the needs of numerous circuits. A few examples will suffice to illustrate the nature of the problem: Michael Trotobas, running the Farmer circuit based in Lille, needed to send messages through Prosper's radio, as did Jean Bouguennec (Francis Garel) and Marcel Rousset of the Butler circuit whose radio had been lost during their drop, Gustave Biéler of Musician, and Émile Garry of Cinema-Phono. Even Ben Cowburn whose Tinker circuit was entirely separate from Prosper, needed to visit Paris to give Prosper new crystals for his radio. All in all, when Jack Agazarian was withdrawn from France in June 1943, he claimed that he had sent messages for twenty-four different agents. Suttill was also in contact with other circuit heads and sub-circuit leaders such as Joseph Antelme, Jean Worms, and George Darling. Worse still, many of these circuit heads and their subordinates socialized together, meeting in black-market restaurants in Paris. This was 'in defiance of such security training as they had received, in defiance of elementary prudence as well, but in response to the desire for companionship with people who could share with them the secret of their identity and their mission'. It has been argued that the Prosper circuit operated with such carelessness in northern France that 'the real wonder is not that Suttill and his friends were caught but that it took so long for the Germans to catch them'.[41] Two of Suttill's contacts, social and professional, proved to be especially dangerous: Henri Frager and Henri Déricourt.

Frager had taken over the northern half of the former Carte network after it was split, setting up Donkeyman, which was based around Auxerre and stretched across a large part of northern France. But Donkeyman was doomed from its inception due to the damage done to Carte when its courier André Marsac had his briefcase, containing a list of 200 members of the network, stolen in December 1942. Frager was in London when the

Germans moved in to arrest the people named on the list. Among these, two of Frager's deputies, Roger Bardet and Jean Kieffer, were taken in by the assurances of Hugo Bleicher, posing as the anti-Nazi Colonel Henri, that he was working secretly against his employers, and they supplied him with contacts in the Annecy region.

The collapse of Carte in southern France had forced those SOE agents who had been working with Carte to flee to the apparent sanctuary of the village of St Jorioz on Lake Annecy. In a total breach of the basic elements of security, too many agents were concentrated in one place. Peter Churchill and Odette Sansom lived in the Hôtel de la Poste, while the Marsacs shared the nearby Villa Tilleuls with Roger Bardet, and across the lake the Fragers lived in another villa. Their radio operator Adolphe Rabinovitch lived up the mountain. The recently arrived Francis Cammaerts viewed the entire arrangement as a nightmare waiting to come true: 'I said to Odette that of course they had the experience and I couldn't go against them but to me it felt like a trap, an impossible fantasy at that stage of the conflict.'[42] He departed to set up his own Jockey network on the French Riviera. Bleicher arrived, vouched for by Bardet, to seek assistance for a flight to London. Rabinovitch informed London of the plan to extract him, only to receive the response to break off all contact with Bleicher immediately. Peter Churchill arrived back on the night of 14–15 April with the same order, and also not to contact Odette until she was no longer in contact with Bleicher. However, although Odette had begun to suspect Bleicher, she nonetheless was in the reception committee which received Peter Churchill, and persuaded him to spend a few nights in St Jorioz. On the following day Bleicher accompanied by some Italian troops arrested both Churchill and Odette. Rabinovitch informed London and then fled to Spain and back to Britain.

Frager remained convinced of the loyalty of his two lieutenants, and believed Bleicher implicitly right up to the time when Bleicher arrested him in the summer of 1944. Suttill was less sure of Frager and tried to keep him away from Prosper operations. Frager for his part was very suspicious of a man whom Suttill trusted implicitly, Déricourt. Déricourt was an extremely complex character whose conduct was disputed both during the war and in several court cases in later years. He was sent to France in January 1943 as the head of the Farrier circuit which was devoted exclusively to the location and management of landing grounds for flights to and from Britain. He was extremely good at his job: Squadron-Leader Hugh Verity was 'pretty confident that Henri Déricourt was one of our best men in France, finding fields for us and laying on our landings', and Cammaerts was received by Déricourt and later commented: 'Déricourt's operation was smooth, quiet, unfussy and absolutely on time. The way he handled his passengers and the way he herded the cattle in the field where the plane was due to land I could only but admire. The operation took place without interference. The security was perfect.'[43] At least forty-three agents passed into France and sixty-seven left for Britain under Déricourt's control.

Frager was informed by Bleicher that Déricourt was a double agent who had struck a deal with Boemelburg and Kieffer by which Déricourt would permit the Germans to inspect all of SOE's outgoing mail and inform the Germans of planned landings. The Germans would then allow these landings to take place unhindered, but members of the Bonny-Lafont gang would then follow the agents from the landing grounds.[44] Suttill refused to believe Frager but suspicions were aroused when other agents also reported rumours of Déricourt's duplicity. Therefore, in February 1944 Déricourt was recalled to London and Verity was sent to collect him: 'We had to kidnap him in France at pistol-point almost and bring him back and tell him that he was accused of being a double agent', to which accusation 'Déricourt's face showed absolutely no trace of emotion of any sort'.[45] Déricourt argued that as a former civil pilot he had made many German friends before the war and naturally encountered some of them in Paris during the war. The evidence was inconclusive but the decision was taken not to permit Déricourt to return to France. Nevertheless, the damage had been done: all agents who had passed through Déricourt's hands were potentially contaminated even though not all had been caught. Déricourt's motives were obscure and can only be guessed at: 'The truth is that his only unswerving loyalty was to himself; he was trapped by circumstances between the upper millstone of loyalty to workmates in SOE and the nether millstone of inextricable entanglements with the Gestapo, and did what he could to serve both sides at once.'[46] He was also paid very well for his treachery.

The final downfall of the Prosper circuit occurred largely through sheer bad luck. On the night of 15–16 June two Canadians, Frank Pickersgill and his radio operator John Macalister, were parachuted into the Cher valley north of Valençay, with orders to establish a new sub-circuit of Prosper, Archdeacon, in the French Ardennes. They were received by a Prosper sub-agent, Pierre Culioli, and a Prosper courier, Yvonne Rudellat. Culioli noticed that the papers of the newly arrived agents were out of date: regulations had recently been changed to stipulate that the papers needed to be attached by rivets, not staples, a fact of which London was unaware. This meant that it was too dangerous for the agents to travel to Paris until they had received new papers. A parachute drop on the night of 10–11 June to Neuvy, in the Sologne, had been disastrous when two of the containers had exploded on landing, alerting the Germans to the fact that SOE was active in the area. Finally, on 21 June when Pickersgill, Macalister, Culioli and Rudellat were travelling by car to catch a train to Paris, they ran into a German roadblock and were arrested. Culioli had with him a briefcase containing papers which revealed details of the Prosper network, among them the addresses of Norman and Borrel. Macalister had not only a new set of crystals for Norman and a list of frequencies to be used, but also his own radio plan, codes, and security checks. Pickersgill and Macalister also had messages marked for Norman and Suttill. On the evening of 23 June the Germans arrested both Norman and Borrel, and on the following day they tracked down Suttill to a small hotel in the Rue de Mazagran in Paris and arrested him.

What happened next has been the subject of much dispute: who talked when, and what did they say? Since none of the main protagonists – Suttill, Norman and Borrel – survived the war, the evidence has come mainly from two Germans, Kieffer and Josef Placke, whose testimonies must be treated with caution since they were both on trial for their lives. Kieffer claimed that an agreement was drawn up whereby Suttill and Norman would provide the Germans with lists of their activities and members of their circuit, the locations of arms caches, and the names and addresses of those guarding them, and that in return the two men would not be executed but would be sent to concentration camps in Germany as ordinary prisoners. In a postwar interview another German who had been present, Ernst Vogt, claimed that neither man made any kind of statement for the first forty-eight hours after their arrests. Then, Kieffer claimed, the two men were shown copies of SOE mail that had been passed through Déricourt, whereupon:

> Prosper did not want to make any statement but Gilbert (Norman), who had not the integrity of Prosper, made a very full statement. Through Norman and through the documentary material available, we received our first insight into the French Section.[47]

Placke, however, contends that Suttill was more helpful than Kieffer suggested and supplied the Germans with the address of George Darling and a letter authorizing the bearer to gather the arms from the cache guarded by Darling. Certainly *someone* had talked because such a letter was produced on 26 June and a lorry was being loaded with arms when Darling arrived on the scene. Sensing a German trap he ran but was wounded and died in hospital on the following day. That summer the Germans succeeded in emptying many of Prosper's arms caches but it is not entirely clear who supplied the information.

The Germans believed that they had sufficient knowledge to play back Norman's radio to London. The first message was sent from it on 7 July informing London of Suttill's arrest. The Germans, however, did not understand the exact working of the security checks. They knew that one set of checks existed and often tortured agents for this information, but until London chided Norman for having forgotten his double security check, they did not know that double checks were in use. This was not an isolated lapse of security by Baker Street. After the war, Maurice Southgate castigated SOE for the messages it sent: 'Time after time, for different men, London sent back messages saying "My dear fellow, you left us only a week ago. On your first messages you go and forget to put in your true check."'[48] Buckmaster defended his section's conduct later on the grounds that: 'We at home had to be flexible and one cannot hide the fact that at times this flexibility led us to give the benefit of the doubt, at least for a while, to an operator who later turned out to be false.'[49] In this particular case London's response had a catastrophic effect on Norman's morale, combined as it was with the revelation that the Germans had been reading SOE's mail. He now cooperated with the Germans to the extent that when Marcel Gouju and others were arrested as a result of the fall of Prosper, Gouju said later: 'I do not think I have known a more painful moment in my life than when . . . Gilbert came towards me and said with the most beautiful poise – You can tell them everything. They are stronger than we are.'[50] Culioli was also convinced to talk both by Norman and by the German assertion that they had an agent in Baker Street. All this information enabled the Germans to make a sweep of the Sologne area, arresting those who guarded the arms caches and emptying the caches. This was very serious for the future of SOE's work in northern France: agents could be and were replaced, but the number of people willing to hide weapons and indeed the number of hiding places was more limited. Many of those helpers never returned from incarceration in German camps.

The interconnection of too many circuits in northern France with the Prosper circuit now led to almost total disaster. The Germans were able to penetrate and carry out many arrests in the Donkeyman, Bricklayer, Chestnut, Butler, Satirist, Cinema-Phono, Orator, Surveyor, and Priest circuits. For those SOE agents at large and for F Section back in London the difficulty was to establish who was arrested and who was at liberty. Ben Cowburn illustrated the nature of the problem:

> As soon as an agent was taken the most extraordinary rumours would immediately begin to circulate. The person who brought the news of the arrest would often give you all the detail of how it had occurred, whose fault it was, where the captive had been taken . . . A few days later someone else would give you an entirely different version on each point.[51]

Claude de Baissac was probably the first man to suspect that Suttill had been arrested, and warnings were sent to Émile Garry of Cinema-Phono and his radio operator Noor Inayat Khan.

Noor Inayat Khan was an Indian princess who had joined the WAAF and been trained as a radio operator. She was recruited for SOE in February 1943. Her SOE personal reports indicate considerable concern by the training staff as to her suitability for work in the field:

> Not overburdened with brains but has worked hard and shown keenness, apart from some dislike of the security side of the course. She has an unstable and temperamental personality and it is very doubtful whether she is really suited to work in the field.[52]

Buckmaster disagreed. He knew that radio operators were in desperately short supply and that the Cinema-Phono circuit needed one urgently, and consequently was prepared to take the risk by sending Noor out to France under the code name of 'Madeleine'. Leo Marks was worried by Noor's weaknesses in learning how to code and her naivety when it came to her deeply held moral conviction as to always telling the truth. She felt that the system of bluff and true checks was against her beliefs, and so Marks suggested an alternative: if a message with a key phrase exactly eighteen letters long was received from her then he would know that she had been caught.[53] Noor's conduct in the field confirmed both Buckmaster's faith in her and her instructors' warnings. As the only radio operator at liberty in Paris, Noor defied London's attempts to bring her home, and continued to serve those agents who had not been arrested, bravely trudging the streets of Paris carrying her radio. Yet, when she was caught on 13 October 1943, the Germans were able to play back her radio successfully because she had left her back messages in her room and the Germans were able to deduce her code from them. This led London to remain totally convinced that she was at liberty well into 1944, despite receiving a message in early October from an unknown agent called Sonja [Sonia Olschanesky] that Noor had been arrested and even despite Marks noticing that a message from Noor had contained the agreed eighteen letters to show she had been captured.

The sheer confusion caused by the arrest of Suttill and the sudden collapse of the Prosper circuit and the sub-circuits led to the despatch of a mission headed by Buckmaster's assistant, Nicholas Bodington, with Agazarian acting as his radio operator. They arrived in France on 22 July 1943. The evidence they discovered proved that the Prosper circuit had been totally blown. But they were still unsure about the fate of Norman until, when a meeting was arranged for Bodington over Norman's radio, Agazarian went in his stead and was arrested by the Germans. Bodington also met Frager in Paris and learned more of the disasters. Frager warned him that the Germans knew that Bodington was in France, that a number of radios were under German control, and that Déricourt was the source of German information on SOE. Bodington, whose judgement had proved flawed when he had enthusiastically endorsed the Carte network, was again at fault. He knew that Suttill had distrusted Frager, since Suttill on his brief visit to London in early 1943 had made it clear that he wanted nothing to do with Frager, and so he dismissed Frager's warnings, which had been issued on information provided by Bleicher. Bodington returned to Britain convinced that all networks in northern France would have to be virtually rebuilt from scratch. The Germans had used 2,000 soldiers to arrest members of the Prosper circuit and related sub-circuits and over 400 resisters who had received and guarded arms caches were arrested. Yet F Section continued to despatch agents into the region, believing for far too long that the radios used to organize these arrivals were being used by operators who had escaped the German round-ups.

The fates of SOE agents and resisters who fell into German hands varied greatly. Some agents were tortured: Brian Rafferty was brought to Dijon prison 'in a lamentable condition, arm broken, unrecognisable, bruised', and Christopher Burney was beaten with an ox-tail whip. John Starr had been shot in the thigh during his arrest and the SS probed the wound with a steel spike.[54] A common practice was water-boarding: 'They drowned me three times. They put my head in the tub and kept it there till I passed out. Before each drowning they beat my shoulders with a club, a special club called *nerf-de-boeuf*, bull's penis. The pain was so bad I couldn't breathe.'[55] Odette Sansom described how she survived the torture inflicted on her in Fresnes prison:

> I could have told them what they wanted to know, just like that . . . I'm not brave or courageous, I just make up my mind about certain things, and when this started, this treatment of me, I thought, 'There must be a breaking point.' Even if in your own mind you don't want to break, physically you're bound to break after a certain time. But I thought, 'If I can survive the next minute without breaking, this is another minute of life, and I can feel that way instead of thinking of what's going to happen in half an hour's time, when having torn out my toenails they're going to start on my fingers.'[56]

Agents sometimes committed suicide rather than submit to further torture; others tried to escape. For example, Noor tried to escape three times and was kept in chains after the last attempt, a punishment that lasted through incarceration in French prisons and then in Pforzheim prison in Germany until her execution at Dachau in September 1944. The courage of those who withstood such treatment and did not talk defies description.

Yet there were those who did talk, and those whose conduct so demoralized others who then talked. It may well be asked why the Germans were so successful in winning the cooperation of the SOE agents who fell into their hands. The answer lies in the careful accumulation of knowledge built up by the Germans through the interrogation of each agent:

> The prisoners who talked produced a cumulative impact: the pile of data in German hands got bigger and bigger ... When the interrogator could describe the colour of the wallpaper in a Beaulieu classroom, and distinguish which of the staff there wore glasses, and which wore moustaches, which smoked cigarettes and which preferred a pipe, it was not easy for a newcomer to resist the belief that 'All was Known'.[57]

In September 1942 all Gestapo and SD offices in western Europe received a memorandum from Berlin listing the schools used for training SOE agents as well as information on the instructors at Beaulieu: all of it was information that had been gleaned from interrogations of SOE agents. During the summer of 1943 the Germans added considerably to their already accumulated bank of knowledge. Gilbert Norman clearly revealed far too much and it is even alleged that he travelled to Bordeaux in the company of German officers to identify other SOE agents.

John Starr's conduct also needs scrutiny. He arrived in Paris in late September 1943 having been tortured in Dijon prison. He had been betrayed by a French traitor, Pierre Martin, whom he had trusted despite Martin being viewed with suspicion by Harry Rée who was operating close by. Vogt introduced him to Norman, who told him that the Germans knew everything about SOE, and he was also shown the SOE correspondence passed to the Germans by Déricourt. Starr noticed that Kieffer had a large map of France with the names and areas of F Section circuits written on it. Since Norman had told him that the Germans knew everything, Starr decided to fill in his own circuit. The Germans were impressed by his penmanship and he was asked to draw a new map for them: Starr complied and also showed his skills as an artist by drawing portraits of Gestapo men. Starr believed, or convinced himself, that he was doing no harm since the Germans already seemed to have so much information on F Section. Indeed, he believed that it was his duty to find out as much as he could about what the Germans knew so that, when he escaped, he could inform London.[58] Yet Starr's presence in relative comfort was extremely demoralizing for recently arrested SOE agents, such as Marcel Rousset, Maurice Southgate, and Harry Peulevé. Starr had his limits, though. The Germans had been playing back Pickersgill's radio, but suspicions had been raised by officials in London who demanded an S-phone conversation with Pickersgill. Pickersgill refused to cooperate so the Germans asked Starr to impersonate him. Starr refused and the guttural tones of the German attempting to impersonate Pickersgill should have revealed to London that the two Canadians had been captured and that the Ardennes circuit was a fake. F Section refused to believe this, on this occasion blaming atmospherics for the distorted voice. Deliveries continued to Archdeacon until the Germans themselves revealed the ruse on D-Day with a radio message similar to that sent to acknowledge the end of the *Englandspiel*.

This *Funkspiel* was not an isolated incident: it has been estimated that between October 1943 and D-Day, 200 operations were flown by the RAF to drop weapons and seventeen agents fell straight into the arms of the Germans. The rebuilding of SOE circuits in northern France was now an even more hazardous operation since no one knew whether the reception committee was organized by the Germans or by SOE.

The Germans were able to inflict substantial damage on the resistance in Bordeaux through the exploitation of one man, André Grandclément. A retired French colonel, Grandclément was the son of an admiral and a former aide-de-camp to the extremely right-wing Colonel François de la Rocque. He was deeply involved in the largest French resistance group, the OCM, and also with F Section's Scientist circuit in Bordeaux run by de Baissac and Roger Landes. Grandclément's knowledge of OCM and SOE activities, personalities, and arms dumps was therefore considerable and his turning by the Germans inflicted enormous damage on both organizations.

In summer 1943 Grandclément was in Paris when the Germans swooped on some of the reception committees in the Bordeaux region and one of the prisoners revealed the address of Grandclément. The Germans raided his home and arrested his wife Lucette. In his office they found a treasure trove of information: Grandclément, like Girard of Carte before him, had maintained lists of members of the resistance thinly disguised as lists of clients, in Grandclément's case in his capacity as an insurance agent. The Germans also took away with them a photograph of Grandclément. This led to his arrest in the middle of September 1943 in Paris and his transfer, in German custody, to Bordeaux.

Grandclément fell into the hands of the skilled Gestapo chief, Friedrich Dohse. Grandclément was offered a deal whereby he, his wife, and the Scientist and OCM members under arrest would all be released if Grandclément revealed the location of the arms dumps. Grandclément felt that this was an acceptable deal. He was released temporarily to consult his colleagues and to win their cooperation. There then followed a stormy meeting between Charles Corbin, a French police inspector and resister, Landes, and Marcel Defence. They were outraged at the deal and Landes later said: 'I wish I had shot him then and I would have done so had there not been two women in the room at the time.' There then ensued a race for the arms dumps, between the Germans guided by Grandclément and Corbin, and Landes and Defence, who tried to warn those guarding the dumps of the Germans' imminent arrival. In all, it appears that the Germans succeeded in collecting around half of the 1,200 containers holding arms, ammunition, and explosives that SOE had dropped to Scientist over the past year and which were located in 132 arms dumps.

Grandclément's treachery did not end there, however, since Dohse played on Grandclément's right-wing beliefs to convince him that the communists were a greater threat to France than the Germans. Dohse suggested a local arrangement by which resistance members would be released from custody if they agreed to form a German-controlled maquis to tackle the FTP units. But as Dohse testified after the war:

> Grandclément went much further than I expected. He suggested that a national agreement could be concluded, by which he and his friends in other parts of France would divulge to the Germans the armament dumps of the Communist-controlled groups. But he said that such an agreement could only be signed by General de Gaulle and Hitler. Grandclément said that he and another leader of his organization would be prepared to go to Algiers and submit the plan to General de Gaulle for his approval.[59]

Dohse had to consult his superiors, who refused to allow Grandclément to travel to Algiers. The Germans did, however, agree to smuggle two representatives into Spain from where they could travel to Algiers. The two men were promptly arrested there on de Gaulle's orders. Grandclément's conduct caused immense confusion in the resistance: men just did not know whether they should remain in the OCM or Scientist, or join Grandclément's German-sponsored *maquis blancs*. Landes had remained at liberty simply because Grandclément did not know his address. Nonetheless, Landes was in considerable danger, so London recalled him and he reached Spain successfully.[60] He would return to Bordeaux in March 1944 to assess the damage caused by Grandclément, and to rebuild the resistance in the city: he would also deal with Grandclément and Lucette.

At the beginning of June 1943 the future of the Gaullist resistance in France appeared bright: Jean Moulin seemingly had achieved the impossible, a high degree of centralization and unification of disparate resistance movements. Yet by the end of the month his plans lay in ruins and Moulin himself was dead. The story is both complex and controversial, and is debated to this day.[61]

Certain facts are known. In March 1943 arrests of resistance members in Lyon led the Germans to uncover a treasure trove of documents relating to the creation and organization of the AS and the locations of 'post-boxes' where resistance members would leave documents for their colleagues. At the beginning of May the Germans' mine of information was increased when a resistance member, Jean Multon, apparently without having been tortured, revealed the locations of more post-boxes and gave up the names of at least 125 resistance members, including Frenay's assistant and lover, Berty Albrecht, who was then arrested. In one of the post-boxes the Germans found a vital message: *Combat* member René Hardy, the man who had created an extensive network of contacts among the railwaymen which would be essential for stopping rail traffic when the Allies invaded, was planning a meeting in Paris with the head of the AS, General Delestraint, to discuss future sabotage plans. The Germans acted swiftly. By sheer misfortune Hardy travelled to Paris on the same train as Multon, who was now working for the Germans, and was recognized. Hardy managed to get a warning out to his *Combat* colleague Pierre Bénouville but was himself arrested before he reached Paris. Delestraint, however, remained ignorant of Hardy's arrest and continued to the meeting place, La Muette metro station in Paris, where the Gestapo arrested him. Delestraint was interrogated and then despatched to Dachau where he was executed in April 1945, days before the camp was liberated. Hardy, on the other hand, was returned to Lyon where he was interrogated by the local head of the Gestapo, Klaus Barbie. Exactly what happened next is a matter of controversy.

Hardy was released a week later and continued his resistance activities: 'he deliberately concealed the truth from all the resistance leaders and resumed his underground activities'.[62] Why Barbie released him is not clear. Hardy later alleged that he made some sort of deal with Barbie because Barbie had found a letter from him to his fiancée, Lydie Bastien, and threatened to arrest Bastien and her family if Hardy did not cooperate. In breach of all basic security procedures, *Combat* did not quarantine Hardy, a process widely adopted by most resistance groups after an arrest to ensure that the person in question had not been turned. Bénouville knew that Hardy had been arrested but just whom he informed is not clear.

Moulin was appalled at the news of Delestraint's arrest, and called a meeting of the paramilitary leaders of the southern resistance movement at the home of Dr Dugoujon in the Lyon suburb of Caluire on 21 June 1943 to settle the choice of Delestraint's successor. Moulin was planning to propose splitting command of the AS between Raymond Aubrac, for the north, and André Lassagne for the south, both members of *Libération-sud*, with Colonel Émile Schwarzfeld of *France d'Abord* in overall command. Frenay, who had just fled to London unaware that his lover Albrecht had just committed suicide in Fresnes prison, had earlier fought an unsuccessful battle with Moulin in an attempt to ensure *Combat*'s dominance of the AS. Now *Combat* scented a new opportunity to seize control and consequently Bénouville encouraged Henri Aubry to take Hardy to the meeting in order to strengthen *Combat*'s position. No other attendee knew that Hardy was to attend, and indeed Moulin was known to distrust Hardy. Security was probably further compromised when Moulin and Aubrac spent thirty minutes waiting for Schwarzfeld to arrive before moving on to the doctor's house. By good fortune Claude Serreulles missed the meeting because he had taken the wrong funicular railway.[63] Minutes after the meeting had begun, the Gestapo led by Barbie burst in. They arrested Aubrac and André Lassagne, Aubry, Schwarzfeld, Bruno Larat of COPA (*Centre d'Opérations de Parachutage et d'Atterrissage*), and Moulin. Hardy was the only person not handcuffed, and he made a run for it. Witnesses reported:

> The road worker told me it was impossible for him not to have been in cahoots with the Gestapo. He shoved past one of the German police and ran zigzagging across the square to get to the path down to the Saône. The police fired a few shots, aiming everywhere except at him. One policeman went after him. How could he have failed to see him in the ditch? The grass there is mostly dried up at this time of year. The other Germans, who were in parked cars, called to him to come back.[64]

Larat, Lassagne, and Aubry were brutally tortured by Barbie and his henchmen, and either one of them or Hardy must have revealed that the man the Germans knew only as 'Max' was Moulin.

Moulin was tortured at length to such an extent that he was barely recognizable by Christian Pineau, under arrest in Lyon prison, who was ordered to shave Moulin:[65]

> One certainty remains, the only one of importance for history: Jean Moulin was one of the very few resistance fighters who did not yield under torture. It is even possible that, immured in his silence, he did not give his true name or acknowledge his role in the resistance. The survival of his fellow fighters, all of whom were left in peace, and the testimony of his tormentor are

proof of that: 'He confessed nothing,' Klaus Barbie would say. For once, he certainly told the truth.[66]

Moulin was sent first to Paris, probably on 28 June, before being transferred to Berlin, probably on 8 July. En route to Berlin, Moulin died of his injuries, taking his secrets to the grave with him.

In the immediate aftermath and in the years that followed the debate has centred around the role of Hardy. Aubrac was convinced that Hardy had betrayed the meeting place and an attempt was made to poison him in prison before he escaped. Hardy did escape prison and made his way to Algiers, where Frenay gave him a job. After the war, Hardy was tried twice, in January 1947 and May 1950, and acquitted on both occasions despite having committed perjury during the first trial. During Barbie's trial in Lyon in 1987 there were high hopes that Barbie would clarify the role of Hardy once and for all, but he gave no useful information on the subject. Of the others arrested: Dr Dugoujon was released in spring 1944; Aubry was released in December 1943 and joined the maquis; Aubrac escaped from prison in October 1943; Schwarzfeld and Larat died in German concentration camps; Lassagne survived the camps and returned to France after the war.[67]

The effects of the German attacks on the resistance in France in 1943 and early 1944 were devastating: 'The leadership had been shattered – Frenay and d'Astier were abroad; Berty Albrecht, Moulin, Manouchian, Brossolette and Médéric were dead; Pineau, Renouvin, Delestraint and Bourdet had all been deported; Jean-Pierre Lévy was in a Parisian jail, his cover still intact.'[68] Yet the groundwork for the organization of the French resistance and its loyalty to de Gaulle had been established. It now remained for new men to take over the reins and rebuild so that the French resistance could play an important role in the liberation of their country.

During 1943 the tempo of the terror waged by the Germans in Poland increased, as did resistance. The Germans set up a special unit led by SS-Hauptsturmführer Alfred Spilker to target the AK leadership. A smaller unit led by SS-Untersturmführer Erich Merten operated under Spilker and controlled a small but lethal number of Polish traitors. These were Ludwik Kalkstein, his brother-in-law Eugeniusz Świerczewski, and Kalkstein's wife, Blanka Kaczorowska. All three had been active in the AK's counter-intelligence unit and had been decorated for a series of successes by the AK. In spring 1942, however, Kalkstein was arrested by the Gestapo and became a traitor. It is a matter of dispute whether he agreed to work for the Germans because he had been tortured, or because of threats made against his family, or because, as it is alleged, he told Merten that he 'felt German'. He was released from Gestapo custody, and recruited Świerczewski and Kaczorowska to work with him. After being quarantined by the AK, in the spring of 1943 the trio were permitted to resume their underground work. But, unknown to the AK, they were now working for the Germans, and their wide network of contacts within the AK made them especially dangerous. Their activities resulted in the arrests of at least 200 AK officers and soldiers, mainly from the intelligence branch.

Of the three traitors, Świerczewski was undoubtedly the most dangerous. He had served under General Rowecki during the Polish-Soviet War in 1920–21 and was trusted implicitly by Rowecki while working in the AK. His motivation for turning traitor may have been family links through Kalkstein but it may also have been from anti-Bolshevik sentiments. It must be remembered that it was in April 1943 that the Germans revealed their discovery of the graves of Polish officers shot by the NKVD in 1940. This news had greatly unsettled the Poles in Poland and the government-in-exile in London. They knew that the Polish officers had not been heard of since spring 1940 and feared, correctly as it turned out, that the Soviets had executed them. Therefore, it is entirely possible that the Germans and Kalkstein may have presented the now advancing Soviet armies as a greater threat to long-term Polish interests than the current brutal German occupation.

Whatever Świerczewski's motivation was, he played a deadly role. By chance he spotted Rowecki in the street in Warsaw, followed him to Spiska Street, and then telephoned Merten to betray Rowecki's location. At around 10 a.m. on 30 June 1943 about sixty cars and trucks containing 200 armed Gestapo men descended on the street, entered all the houses and herded the people into a yard. Świerczewski's role thereafter was to identify which man was Rowecki, and Rowecki was taken to the Gestapo headquarters. A Polish witness whose interrogation was suddenly broken off recalled: 'As he was descending the stairs, the whole building seemed to be in a buzz; officials, agents and even clerks were running down the passages and all seemed very pleased.'[69] He recognized Rowecki as the man under arrest and the news soon reached Rowecki's deputy, Tadeusz Bór-Komorowski.

While the Germans were celebrating their success with champagne, the AK planned to rescue Rowecki. One plan seriously considered was a suicide attack by a volunteer who would drive a German tank, then under repair in a workshop, filled with explosives into the Gestapo headquarters. At the same time a special *Kedyw* group would rush into the building and free Rowecki. The plan was never put into practice since the Germans immediately flew Rowecki to Berlin. There the SS stressed to Rowecki that the real enemy was the communists and that Rowecki should assist them in either forming a Polish anti-Bolshevik unit or at the very least inducing the AK to stop fighting the Germans or even just reduce the scale of its anti-German activities. Rowecki declined to accept any form of deal. He was imprisoned in Sachsenhausen concentration camp until he was executed shortly after the outbreak of the Warsaw Uprising in August 1944.[70]

The loss of Rowecki was a serious blow to the Poles. He was succeeded as head of the AK by his former deputy, Bór-Komorowski, who paid tribute to his predecessor:

> His pseudonym, Grot, was known everywhere. To the public, Grot was a symbol, a mysterious person who, from the Underground, directed the fight of a nation. We, who knew him more intimately and were in immediate contact with him in the work, knew his great value as a leader, a strong personality, and an outstanding brain, directing and linking the complicated Underground machinery.[71]

The AK conducted a thorough investigation into how Rowecki's arrest had come about and identified the traitors. The Polish underground courts sentenced Kalkstein, Świerczewski and Kaczorowska to death. Only Świerczewski was executed, in June 1944. Kalkstein joined the SS, and Kaczorowska was reprieved because she was heavily pregnant at the time. The Germans protected her for the remainder of the occupation.[72]

The Polish government-in-exile attempted to aid Rowecki too. The Polish prime minister, Stanisław Mikołajczyk, wrote to Churchill on 20 July 1943 asking for:

> British intervention either to secure his exchange against a suitable German general, or, if this proves impossible, to assure for General Rowecki the status of a prisoner of war, would be hailed by my compatriots with the deepest gratitude and would contribute to keep up the spirits of the brave men who in Poland defy the invader. British intervention in itself would certainly exert a lasting impression on the minds of these of our men who daily risk their lives for their country, assuring them that they are not forgotten in their lonely struggle but can always look back to a strong supporting hand.[73]

After consulting Eden, Churchill reluctantly responded on 1 August that no such action could be taken by the British government, since after all the British were losing many of their own agents abroad and it was an accepted fact of underground warfare that the resisters were acting outside the normal rules of war and were therefore not covered by the terms of the Geneva Convention.[74]

*

Between the fall of Stalingrad in February 1943 and the battle of Kursk in July–August of that year the strength, role, and activities of the Soviet partisans increased considerably. The partisans were now being supplied by air from the Soviet rear and most bands were in radio contact with partisan command. Indeed, it has been argued that the partisans were better equipped than many of the German rear-area security units. For example, a German Security Regiment reported: 'Many times our railway patrols have come to grips with enemy mine-layers, but on every occasion the bandits have been equipped with machine-pistols and our own troops have not.'[75] Debate still rages as to the actual effectiveness of these better-equipped partisans, centring around the impact they had on the German build-up for the battle of Kursk. Certainly, the Germans were very concerned about the potential if not actual partisan threat, and this period witnessed a change in German tactics in attempting to combat the partisan menace in their rear areas. Unlike the subtlety and considerable success displayed by the German counter-intelligence units in western Europe, the German tactics against the Soviet partisans were marked by increasing levels of violence. The battle of Kursk opened on 5 July and from that date until the Red Army advance units reached the Dnepr river on 22 September 1943 the partisans acted under orders from central command, the *Stavka*, to hamper the German retreat and to prepare the ground for further Red Army offensives.

The role of the partisans was not to wage an open battle with the Germans, hence the German evacuation in March 1943 of the Rzhev salient, north-west of Moscow, an area allegedly full of partisans, was unhindered by partisan intervention, although the partisans did supply Moscow with vital intelligence regarding the German redeployments. The principal activity of the partisans was deemed to be attacks on the German lines of communications. The number of such attacks increased dramatically from 500 in February to 1,460 in July, resulting in the destruction of 1,300 locomotives, 15,000 wagons, numerous water tanks and stations, and seventy-eight railway bridges. The most spectacular attack against the bridges took place in March 1943 when over 1,100 partisans from three units combined their forces to first distract the German security force away from the double-span bridge across the Desna river, before the main partisan force blew up the bridge. This bridge was fifteen miles south-west of Bryansk and on the main supply route for Army Group Centre, carrying between fifteen and twenty trains per day. Its destruction stopped all rail traffic for a week before a temporary structure was constructed which could support entire trains, although without their too-heavy locomotives. The bridge was reopened to rail traffic but the necessity of pushing each train from one side of the bridge to the other obviously slowed the transport of supplies to Army Group Centre. The partisans also hit hard at the rail communications linking Army Group Centre to Army Group North. Supplies to Army Group South, running through more open country unsuitable for partisan activity, continued largely unhampered.

The 'rail war' between the Germans and Soviet partisans demonstrates the flexibility of both forces. The Germans ordered the clearing of the forests from both sides of the tracks so that the partisans could not conceal themselves, and an increase in the number of security patrols with the personnel drawn from the nearby villages who would pay the price in the event of a successful partisan attack. They also placed a flatcar full of rocks ahead of the locomotive to explode the mines. Soldiers travelling on the troop trains were organized as combat units: when the train was attacked, the occupants of the even-numbered carriages would jump out to the left and those in the odd-numbered carriages to the right, to combat the threat. The partisans responded by sending out a force to divert the attention of the patrols or suborning members of them, and by increasing the use of delayed fuses which allowed the flatcar to pass over the mine before exploding under the locomotives. The partisans also increasingly used chain demolitions, a series of mines which would detonate at several points under a train. Some commentators have argued that the partisans were successful in hindering the German preparations for the battle of Kursk by slowing the build-up of reinforcements and materiel. Others have argued the exact opposite, pointing out that the German transport staff operated a flexible schedule which could be altered to move rail traffic away from a particularly hard-hit area, and that the partisans never succeeded in interdicting the main east-west double-track railway to any great degree, notwithstanding their impact on the more common single-track railways. The considerable delays to the launching of the battle of Kursk owed more to Hitler's determination to ensure an ample supply of the latest weapons: the Tiger heavy tank, Ferdinand assault gun, and Panther medium tank. These were all bedevilled by technical and production difficulties, and the delays caused by these were the principal reason for the late start of the German offensive, more than the partisans' attacks on rail communications.[76]

Although partisan successes against German communications may not have been as effective as the Soviet planners had hoped, from the German point of view the partisan threat was still very real. During the course of 1943 the level of brutality evident in the German anti-partisan sweeps became more noticeable. Increasingly, the German mindset came to be that 'the enemy was not to be considered as consisting of partisan groups plus sympathisers, but instead as an entire criminal population minus the collaborators'.[77] A Private Müller recorded later that during one action he took part in 'the order was given that every tenth man in the village was to be shot'. The troops, however, decided to destroy the entire village:

> We filled beer bottles with petrol and put them on the table and, as we were going out, we just threw hand grenades behind it. Immediately everything was burning merrily – all roofs were thatched. The women and children and everyone were shot down; only a few of them were partisans.[78]

Other witness accounts corroborate this behaviour as it became commonplace simply to eradicate a village and its population rather than to make any attempt to identify the partisans. Operation Cottbus, carried out between 3 and 23 June 1943 in the area of Polotsk, Borisov, and Lepel in Belorussia, demonstrates the full brutality of the German tactics: only 492 rifles were taken from the 4,500 dead. The Reichskommissar of the region, Wilhelm Kube, was outraged and argued that 'if the treatment of the native population in the occupied eastern areas is continued in the same manner . . . then in the coming winter we may expect not partisans, but the revolt of the entire country'.[79]

In spring 1943 the Germans conducted numerous operations in Belorussia and the Bryansk sector designed to eradicate or at least contain the partisan threat. As described earlier, the principal tactic employed was the *Grossunternehmen*, a massive encirclement operation, requiring a large number of troops:

> The aim is not to chase them away, but to annihilate them . . . If a larger area, where the bands are either in control or in which they have infiltrated, can be encircled by surprise movements and can be systematically combed, then success will not be lacking. But this means that the outer ring of encirclement must be so close that an escape or breakthrough of larger units is impossible from the start. Sector by sector and day by day the ring is narrowed, either by a concentrated advance or, according to the situation and territory, by pressing the enemy against a prearranged fortified line, which can be strengthened by utilizing natural obstacles (such as a river). Then it is imperative to press the bandits out of the swampy woods into the open country. On the map the plan for such a major (anti-bandit) action with the various lines of encirclement, which represent the daily objectives aimed at, and the demarcation lines between the various anti-partisan units, look like a spider's web.[80]

These sweeps proved of limited effectiveness. In the first place, despite borrowing troops from front-line units in quiet sectors to bolster the strength of the rear troops, there simply were never enough German soldiers to maintain a close cordon, with the result that the partisans could and did escape through gaps in the German lines. Then there was the simple fact that the Germans felt distinctly uncomfortable fighting in the forests and swamps where they could not see their enemy until the last minute: 'The partisans positioned themselves in the bog water, laid reeds and branches to cover their heads and allowed the armoured infantry men, who in any case did not care for this at all, to pass by.'[81] The partisans would then spring up and attack the Germans from behind. The *Grossunternehmen* were successful in that they forced the partisan formations to disperse, but they failed notably to inflict heavy losses on the partisans themselves, and the bulk of the German wrath fell on the innocent local population.[82]

A new German tactic was the formation of *Jagdkommandos*, well-equipped, highly mobile hunter groups, often in civilian clothing, who would take the war to the partisans in the areas where the partisans felt the most comfortable, the forests and swamps. The operating procedures of the *Jagdkommandos* were:

> [The *Jagdkommando*] marches mostly by night and moves into a hidden camp in day-time. March and rest must be protected. Reconnaissance begins when the battle area has been reached. From the footprints of the bands, the band activities are ascertained. In order to avoid treachery, no contact must be made with the population. Again and again the use of stationary reconnaissance troops has been found valuable for *Jagdkommandos*. They observe the routes of approach and paths of the bands in places favourable for attack. Good camouflage, close liaison, and especially patience are the prerequisites of success.[83]

The theory was better than the practice since the Germans simply lacked enough of such highly trained units to maintain pressure on the partisan formations for any length of time.

The battle of Kursk opened on 5 July, but by 12 July the Germans had made only limited gains before being driven back by the Soviet counter-offensive which, by 5 August, allowed the Red Army to recapture Orel and Belgorod before beginning an advance across the whole front, driving the Germans back to the Dnepr river. The Soviet command ordered the partisans to launch large-scale operations to disrupt the German rail communications – the so-called 'Battle of the Rails'. Previous partisan attacks had focused on destroying trains, locomotives, and bridges, but this campaign was designed to destroy the actual railway lines to force the Germans to undertake a programme of constant repair. The battle opened with a strike on the night of 20–21 July by eleven partisan brigades against the railways south of Bryansk supplying Army Groups Centre and South.

The result was that German trains could no longer operate at night and some lines were blocked for two days. During the remainder of July, 1,114 attacks on the rails were noted by the Germans, and various lines had been blocked for a total of 2,688 hours. Partisan activity reached a new height on the night of 3–4 August with an extensive number of rail demolitions, 8,422 separate cuts, throughout Belorussia and on the lines eastwards. The campaign continued for a further month.[84]

The precise number of rails destroyed during the 'Battle of the Rails' is disputed by German and Soviet sources, with the Soviets claiming the higher number, 148,500, as against the German reports of around 32,000. The effectiveness of the campaign is also disputed. A German infantryman, Felix Dresener, claimed the partisans:

> . . . were a constant menace. They slowed our ability to supply the front line and forced us into clearing operations, which took troops away from the front line . . . Our platoon provided protection for several convoys, which kept us from the real battle for over a week. During that time we lost 8 men and goodness knows how many trucks. It was a simple Russian tactic, but effective.[85]

It has also been claimed that the German 6th Air Fleet received only 5,700 tonnes of aviation fuel rather than the 8,600 tonnes it required, and that the German 68th and 125th Infantry Divisions being sent as reinforcements to the front had to disembark from their train some way short of the front and either be transported forward by trucks or march on foot, leading to a week's delay in reaching the front.[86] Nonetheless, during the battle of Kursk, the Germans were still able to send 8,000 trains a month through the apparently partisan-infested areas simply because the Germans rapidly became extremely skilled at repairing the tracks. The 'Battle of the Rails' almost certainly did not affect operations at the front during the battle of Kursk to any great degree, but its continuance throughout September and October probably significantly slowed the retreat of Army Group Centre and made it unable to regroup to counter-attack the Soviet armies.[87]

By late September the Germans were being pushed back to the Dnepr river and during this retreat the partisans served another purpose, the provision of intelligence. Much of this intelligence was provided by children aged eight to fourteen who had received special training to watch the traffic on the roads, not to make notes, but to retain all the information gathered in their heads. One such boy was caught by the Germans and revealed during interrogation that he would cross the Dnepr regularly to report to his superior and be rewarded with bread, sweets, and cigarettes. After his third operation he had been promised a suit.[88] The commander of the

Soviet Central Front, Konstantin Rokossovsky, recorded that he was ordered to advance to and then force the Rivers Desna and Dnepr and move towards Kiev: 'We already had information, confirmed by the Belorussian and Ukrainian partisans, that the Nazis were hastily erecting a strong fortified line along the Rivers Dnepr and Sozh as part of the so-called Eastern Wall.'[89] The battle against this line would take place later in the year.

18

Resistance or Civil War? The Balkans

There is an enormous literature on the wartime conflicts in Yugoslavia during the Second World War, and it is largely split according to the authors' political perspectives. The reunification of Yugoslavia under the victorious Partisans led by Tito, and his dominance of the country until his death in 1980, led to a large body of literature which lauded the Partisans as the only true resistance to the occupiers, and wholeheartedly condemned the Četniks under Draža Mihailović as collaborators; thereby justifying Mihailović's trial and execution in 1946. The split between Tito and Stalin in 1948 has been used to justify the argument that the Partisans were not simply a communist resistance movement, but were the true army of liberation, embracing all Yugoslav nationalities and all political persuasions.

The pro-Partisan bias has been enhanced by the writings of a number of British participants in the wartime conflict in Yugoslavia, most notably by William Deakin who was parachuted into Montenegro in May 1943 to serve alongside the Partisans. Deakin arrived as the Partisans were fleeing from a German attack, Operation Schwarz, and arriving under such circumstances made a deep impression on him: 'The mountain was wreathed in the flames and ashes of villages and settlements. The scattered dead lay, spilt in heaps, as if by a giant hand, across this landscape of the moon.'[1] His early experiences with the Partisans led to his belief that: 'We did not find a group of guerrillas; we found an organized military force.'[2] In fact Deakin never left Tito's headquarters to see the situation for himself, and all his contacts with the Partisans were closely supervised by Vladimir Velebit, a confidant of Tito. Deakin was fed a constant stream of information regarding the alleged high degree of Četnik collaboration with the Italians, with the stress placed on Mihailović's inactivity.[3] Deakin wrote a book, *The Embattled Mountain*, describing the British intervention in Yugoslavia, and contributed articles to many books on the subject in subsequent years as well as conference papers. The result has been what one

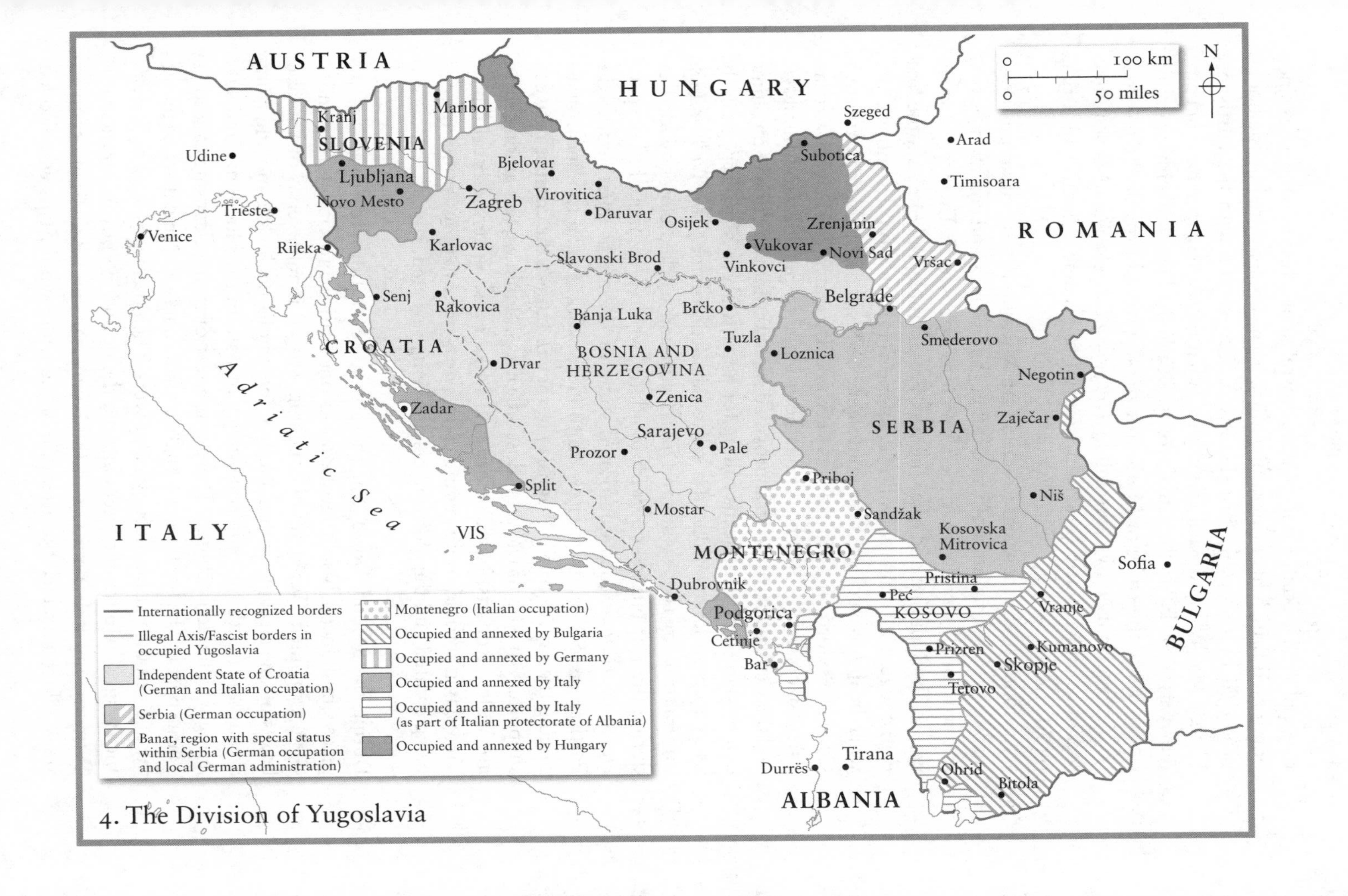

AUSTRIA
HUNGARY
ROMANIA
BULGARIA
ALBANIA
ITALY
SLOVENIA
CROATIA
BOSNIA AND HERZEGOVINA
SERBIA
MONTENEGRO
KOSOVO
Adriatic Sea
VIS
0 100 km
0 50 miles
N
Kranj
Maribor
Ljubljana
Novo Mesto
Udine
Trieste
Venice
Rijeka
Zagreb
Bjelovar
Virovitica
Daruvar
Karlovac
Osijek
Vukovar
Vinkovci
Slavonski Brod
Senj
Rakovica
Banja Luka
Brčko
Tuzla
Drvar
Zenica
Zadar
Sarajevo
Pale
Prozor
Split
Mostar
Szeged
Subotica
Arad
Timisoara
Zrenjanin
Novi Sad
Vršac
Belgrade
Smederovo
Loznica
Negotin
Zaječar
Priboj
Niš
Sandžak
Kosovska Mitrovica
Sofia
Pristina
Peć
Vranje
Dubrovnik
Podgorica
Cetinje
Bar
Prizren
Kumanovo
Skopje
Tetovo
Tirana
Durrës
Ohrid
Bitola
Internationally recognized borders
Illegal Axis/Fascist borders in occupied Yugoslavia
Independent State of Croatia (German and Italian occupation)
Serbia (German occupation)
Banat, region with special status within Serbia (German occupation and local German administration)
Montenegro (Italian occupation)
Occupied and annexed by Bulgaria
Occupied and annexed by Germany
Occupied and annexed by Italy
Occupied and annexed by Italy (as part of Italian protectorate of Albania)
Occupied and annexed by Hungary

4. The Division of Yugoslavia

may call the 'Deakin school' of Yugoslav resistance history which has since dominated British historiography. It has been supplemented by the books produced by two other British officers who served with the Partisans, Fitzroy Maclean and Basil Davidson.[4] What these three men have in common was their skill in the use of words: Deakin had worked with Churchill on his life of the Duke of Marlborough, and would provide the research on Yugoslavia used by Churchill in *The Second World War*; Maclean had served as an MP; and Davidson went on to become a notable historian on Africa.

In contrast, the men sent to serve with Mihailović were either businessmen or professional staff officers, rather than writers and communicators, and it is small wonder that their opinions opposed to Tito were largely ignored both during and after the war. For example, Bill Hudson, the first British agent to reach Mihailović, spoke very rarely on the subject and when he did so, such as at the conference on resistance held at St Antony's College, Oxford, in 1962, he was very poorly treated by the pro-Partisan participants. Still, some effort has been made to rehabilitate Mihailović and the Četniks. David Martin provided a lengthy introduction to a volume commissioned by Americans calling for a fair trial for Mihailović as early as 1946, and later produced a more detailed volume, *The Web of Disinformation*. In 1977 Milovan Djilas, who had worked closely with Tito during the war but fell out with him later, wrote a volume of his experiences, *Wartime*, which questioned some of the myths surrounding the Partisans and Tito. After Tito's death more works began to appear questioning the British role in Yugoslavia: they re-ignited the conflict between supporters of Mihailović and those of Tito. Notable writers among these are Walter Roberts, Nora Beloff, and Mike Lees. Since the break-up of Yugoslavia into separate republics in 1991–92 a new historiography is being created and the old conflicts are being revisited.

During the Second World War there were several different wars taking place simultaneously in Yugoslavia. As one British participant, Alexander Glen, explained: 'What was happening was an infinite series of Chinese boxes of one struggle within another, the whole meanwhile moving from area to area with the only consistency of pattern the blood, fire and suffering which it left behind.'[5] There was a war of ethnic cleansing caused in a large part by the break-up of Yugoslavia into its component states under the aegis of the various occupying powers. Then there was a war of resistance waged by different forces against the occupying powers, principally Germany and Italy with less in the Hungarian- and Bulgarian-occupied areas, which attracted the attention of the wider world. This war also led to two other, simultaneous conflicts: the war waged against collaborators and perceived collaborators which was complicated by temporary accommodations reached between the two main resistance movements, the Četniks under Mihailović and the Partisans under Tito, both with the occupying powers and with their collaborators. At the same time the existence of two resistance movements, each with different tactics and ultimate aims, led to a conflict between them which was effectively a civil war. Into this maelstrom came British missions, hoping to influence the two resistance movements. For various reasons they failed to achieve as much as anticipated and, indeed, may have worsened the situation.

The ethnic conflict launched by the staunchly Catholic Ustaše in Croatia determined to wipe out the Orthodox Serb population of their country, as well as the Jews, dominated the initial response of the Serbs to the break-up of their country triggered by the German and Italian occupation.[6] Mihailović's policy of resistance to the occupiers was tempered by the fear of a repeat of the massacre by the Germans at Kragujevac in 1941. Consequently, his policy was one of little overt resistance, thus avoiding reprisals and conserving his forces until the Allies were ready to invade the Balkans whereupon there would be a general uprising. In the meantime the Četniks were to focus on destroying the internal enemies of the Serbs, principally the Partisans, the Ustaše, and the Muslims.[7] Mihailović was undoubtedly popular in Serbia. British observers noted of the villagers they met: 'They absolutely worshipped him. He was the commanding figure of the Serbian resistance and of their future. He was the Serbian national hero.'[8] Much of this popularity stemmed from Mihailović's contact with the Yugoslav government-in-exile in London and the broadcasts extolling his virtues on the BBC. On 15 November 1941 the BBC had announced that General Simović had appointed Mihailović as commander of the Yugoslav armed forces in the homeland. In January 1942 Mihailović was appointed minister of war *in absentia* in the new Yugoslav government-in-exile under Slobodan Jovanović. In addition, Churchill and his government portrayed Mihailović as the symbol of all resistance to occupation in Europe.[9]

Other Serbs chose different paths in response to the threat of ethnic violence. The government of Milan Nedić sought protection through closer collaboration with the Germans. The head of the official Četnik Association, Kosta Pećanac, had first considered following the route of resistance to the occupiers but soon realized that the twin threats of Ustaše violence and the Partisans made such a task seem hopeless, and put his approximately 8,000-strong force at the disposal of the Nedić government and the Germans.[10] The same course was followed by the Serbian fascist Dimitrije

Ljotić and his followers. Nedić, Pećanac and Ljotić all saw Mihailović as the greatest threat to their leadership of the Serbs. This meant that although Mihailović's forces were known as the Četniks, the Četniks themselves were divided.

The Partisans charged Mihailović at the time with the crime of collaboration with the occupiers, a claim that has been repeated since, and also of being inactive. Apart from the considerations of prudence and strategy outlined above, the lack of resistance by the Mihailović Četniks may not have been a matter of choice in any case since his forces received only two deliveries of supplies from the British, totalling 23 tons, between late December 1942 and the middle of March 1943. This forced Mihailović to seek supplies for his men elsewhere. One source, approved by Mihailović, was for men to join Nedić's forces to gain weapons, clothing, and food, and then to desert when the uprising was imminent.[11] Other Četnik leaders felt less loyalty to Mihailović and were prepared to collaborate with the Italians in return for supplies to be used against the principal enemy, the Partisans. This led to 'live and let live' agreements with the Italians by Četnik leaders such as Momčilo Djujić in Croatia, and Dobroslav Jevdjević in Bosnia-Herzegovina. Others went further in their agreements with the Italians. For example, the Italians supplied the Četniks in Montenegro under Bajo Stanišić, and probably those under Pavle Djurišić, with around 30,000 rifles as well as clothing. Under this agreement the Četniks controlled the countryside and the Italians the towns, and these Četniks participated in the Operations Trio I and II, or the Third Offensive, mounted in spring 1942 against the Partisans in Montenegro.[12] Mihailović was appalled about these agreements but could do little to influence those Četnik commanders. Indeed, the evidence presented at Mihailović's trial suggested that he really had far less control over the Četniks than was commonly ascribed to him at the time.[13]

The Partisan movement under Tito was designed from the outset to be the force that would bring about a revolution in Yugoslavia and overthrow the pre-war ruling system after the occupiers had departed. Implicit in this aim was the reality of civil war: as Djilas explained: 'Those who want to wage wars and revolution must be prepared to kill people, to kill their compatriots – even their friends and relatives.'[14] After the breakdown in negotiations between Tito and Mihailović in autumn 1941 the Četniks were identified as the 'main enemy . . . of the liberation struggle of the peoples of Yugoslavia'. At the same time the Partisans were making hit-and-run attacks on the occupiers in order to provoke reprisals against the local population. The Partisan leader in Slovenia, Edvard Kardelj, explicitly stated:

> We must at all costs push the Croatian as well as the Serb villages into the struggle. Some comrades are afraid of reprisals, and that fear prevents the mobilisation of Croat villages. I consider, the reprisals will have the useful result of throwing Croatian villages on the side of Serb villages. In war, we must not be frightened of the destruction of whole villages. Terror will bring about armed action.[15]

These were the very tactics that Mihailović, striving to preserve the Serb population, was avoiding. But they were desirable from the communist point of view: if the people lost their homes and livelihoods they would have little choice but to join the Partisans in order to survive.

Tito focused on building up an image of the Partisans as a national liberation movement which treated all nationalities equally. Post-war historiography has made much of the fact that only just over half the Partisan formations consisted of Serbs, with 19 per cent Croats, 9 per cent Slovenes, and lower percentages for the other nationalities, thereby suggesting that they had widespread support throughout the country.[16] Much attention has also been paid to the fact that the Četniks were guilty of ethnic cleansing and had conducted large-scale massacres of the Ustaše, Croats, and Muslims in towns such as Goražde, Višegrad, and Srebrenica which they had seized from the Italians. Yet the Partisans were just as guilty of such behaviour. For example, when they entered Borac in April 1942, 'all males more than fourteen years old were killed, the entire surviving population expelled, and all the villages burned down'. The Partisans launched a 'Red terror' in the towns they captured. In Foča, 'their victims were Četnik commanders, organisers and sympathisers, richer peasants, gendarmes, lukewarm communists, Muslims and Croats, people who no longer wanted to fight or who thought differently'.[17] These drastic methods 'greatly contributed to the inherent inhumanity of the civil war. The fact that both sides belonged to one single national element claiming the same national characteristics rendered the conflict all the more barbaric'.[18] Even some Partisans came to see that their tactics were counterproductive, as Djilas noted: 'It became increasingly clear to me that our imprudent, hasty executions, along with hunger and war weariness, were helping to strengthen the Četniks.'[19]

There was also a political dimension to Tito's creation of the Partisans as a national liberation army. On 27 November 1942 the first session of the Anti-Fascist Council for the National Liberation of Yugoslavia (AVNOJ) opened in Bihać in Bosnia. Delegates were appointed from all the regions of Yugoslavia other than Macedonia; the Slovenian and Vojvodinian delegates were unable to attend. A president, two vice-presidents, and an executive council were elected and a civil service established. The choice of personnel for the leading posts reflected Tito's plan to conceal the communist nature of the Partisan movement and his attempt for now to appeal to a broad section of the population. For example, the president was Ivan Ribar, a member of the Democratic Party.[20]

The Partisans adopted two principal strategies for dealing with the Četniks. The first was to crush them militarily. Conflict between the two sides had gone on since late 1941, but a significant defeat was not inflicted on the Četniks until the battle of the Neretva in March 1943, when the Partisans succeeded in expelling them from eastern Bosnia-Herzegovina and then from Montenegro in the following month, forcing the Četniks to retreat back into Serbia.[21] At the same time the Partisans waged a very successful propaganda campaign against the Četniks with the Allies. All Četnik formations were denounced as collaborators, and detailed evidence was supplied to Moscow which was then sent on to London.[22] This propaganda war was important because the Soviet Union had proved unexpectedly incapable of and unwilling to despatch supplies to the Partisans. The telegrams exchanged between Tito and the head of the Comintern, Georgi Dimitrov, at this time show that the Soviet Union was prepared to follow the lead supplied by the British government and the Yugoslav government-in-exile in sponsoring Mihailović as the head of the Yugoslav resistance.

One of the principal charges against Mihailović, as noted, was that of collaboration with the occupiers. Yet the Partisans were equally guilty of collaboration when it suited them. Prisoner exchanges between the occupying forces and guerrilla forces were not unknown. Partisan contacts with the Germans began on this basis in September and November 1942 but grew into something far more important. On 11 or 13 March 1943 a high-level Partisan delegation consisting of Koča Popović, the commander of the 1st Proletarian Division, Djilas and Velebit, met Lieutenant General Benignus Dippold, commander of the 717th Infantry Division at Gornji Vakuf in central Bosnia-Herzegovina. What took place during these negotiations has been confirmed both by captured German documents and by a memorandum signed by the Partisan delegation. The Partisans made an important offer. They saw no reason for fighting the Germans other than in self-defence and said that 'it would be in the interests of both sides if hostilities ceased'. The Partisans made it clear that they considered 'the Četniks as the main enemies'. Even better for the Germans, the Partisans had every intention of fighting the British should they attempt a landing since 'as could still be concluded from their propaganda and official pronouncements – they subverted our power, that is, if they supported the Četnik establishment'. The German minister in Zagreb, Siegfried Kasche, was interested and sent a message to the foreign ministry in Berlin stressing the importance of the possibility 'that Tito and supporters will cease to fight against Germany, Italy and Croatia and retire to the Sandžak region on the Serbian-Montenegrin border in order to settle matters with Mihailović's Četniks'. On 25 March, Djilas and Velebit were brought by plane to the Croatian capital, Zagreb, to continue the negotiations. These, however, were abandoned on foreign minister Joachim von Ribbentrop's orders, although the prisoner exchange did take place.[23]

The news of the Partisan-German negotiations remained hidden at the time from British ears and from Yugoslav history until Walter Roberts revealed them in his 1973 book *Tito, Mihailović and the Allies*. Tito had, however, informed Moscow of these negotiations, and on 1 April 1943 received a furious telegram from Dimitrov:

> What is the meaning of this? The people are waging a fierce war with the occupiers, and suddenly such relations as these arise between you and the Germans. Could this not be connected with the Germans' policy of using our people to incite an internecine struggle among the Yugoslavs themselves and thus hasten the destruction of the People's Liberation Army? Please furnish an explanation in this regard. Furthermore, the fact that displeasure with the English is growing among the entire people is understandable. But do you not think that at the present juncture the interests of the national liberation struggle are best served not by encouraging displeasure with the English, but by stirring up the utmost hatred for the occupiers, first and foremost the Germans? Meanwhile any links with German authorities could undoubtedly abate that popular hatred, which is now so indispensable.[24]

Since the existence of these negotiations was made known, their meaning has been debated. Djilas in 1977 defended the conduct of the Partisans on the grounds that they were seeking a respite from German attacks and that any agreement reached would have broken down quickly anyway because 'the Germans couldn't permit our stabilisation and expansion, and we couldn't permit them to gain strength with the help of pro-German elements and to continue the war in the Balkans'.[25] Nonetheless, it must be noted 'that the Partisans, who labelled Mihailović and the Četniks traitors for their accommodation with the enemy, sent two high-ranking officers to the German general in Zagreb with the purpose of arranging a ceasefire, after having declared in writing that their main enemies were the Četniks and not the occupying Axis forces'.[26]

Mihailović was seen as an important resistance leader by the Germans, who in December 1941 offered a reward of 200,000 dinars for his capture.

The Četniks were taken seriously because they were thought to possess 'the requisite professional officer cadres capable of converting an uprising of loosely organised, irregular forces into a centralised, well-coordinated military organisation' and to appeal to a broader section of the population than the politicized revolutionary Partisans. Therefore, in German eyes the Četniks possessed the potential to mount a substantial resistance to German plans to exploit the economy in Serbia and could also disrupt the railway running through the country to Greece. Yet in the middle of 1942 the Germans were relieved to report that: 'The Mihailović movement in Serbia is completely passive in its attitude to the occupation power, but it continues to engage in military espionage, political propaganda, and its settlement of accounts with the Communists.' Nonetheless, Himmler ordered the German forces to focus on annihilating Mihailović.[27] German policy as expressed by General Löhr in August 1942 was 'all visible enemy groups are, under all circumstances, to be exterminated to the last man'.[28] Minor operations continued against the Četniks in Serbia during 1942 and into 1943 until on 13 May the Germans reached Mihailović's headquarters, which he had only just evacuated after receiving a warning of their approach.[29]

The Partisans exaggerated the size and importance of the German anti-partisan operations mounted against them by terming them 'offensives', numbering them from the first in Serbia in 1941 to the last, the seventh, in May 1944. The use of the word 'offensive' suggests operations on a grand scale complete with major battles. This is manifestly not true when one examines the German aims. From the German point of view the drives against the Partisans were a series of operations like the *Grossunternehmen* mounted in the Soviet Union aimed at either encircling and then exterminating or driving the Partisans out of a certain area and rendering impossible the formation of large, potentially threatening groups. The aim was to mitigate the threat posed by the Partisans and keep them and the Četniks out of Serbia, not to wage open battle with them.[30]

These German operations were almost totally successful. The Second Offensive in January 1942 forced the Partisan staff and 1st Proletarian Brigade to retreat southwards to the town of Foča on the Bosnian-Herzegovinian border with Montenegro having suffered heavy losses.[31] The Third Offensive in April and May 1942 drove the Partisans out of eastern Bosnia-Herzegovina and in June forced the Partisans to begin an organized withdrawal from south-eastern Bosnia-Herzegovina, the so-called 'long march' to strongholds in the north-western region of Bosanska Krajina. The Germans then attacked the Partisans in western Bosnia-Herzegovina forcing them to retreat further south. These operations inflicted far more casualties on the Partisans than were suffered by the Germans. The success of these operations was, however, undermined by the conduct of the Italians and the Croat forces. An agreement had been made between the Italians and the Croat government for a voluntary Italian withdrawal from zone III and part of zone II. The withdrawal of Italian forces occurred so precipitately, before the Ustaše and Croat forces were ready to enter the zones, that the Partisans took full advantage of the voluntary retreat and occupied the towns of Bosanski Petrovac, Drvar, and Glamoč.[32]

Operations Weiss I and II, or the Fourth Offensive, in January 1943 aimed to drive the Partisans out of Croatia and Bosnia-Herzegovina entirely and to put an end to the Partisan threats to the bauxite mines and to the Zagreb–Belgrade railway. Ten Axis divisions totalling 90,000 troops were used, and the first part of the operation against the Partisans in western Bosnia-Herzegovina and Lika was so successful and inflicted such heavy losses on them (estimated at 12,000) that it led to the Partisan initiative in opening negotiations with the Germans. The second part of the operation was directed against Partisan formations in the Drvar and River Neretva area. A feature of these operations was Četnik collaboration with the Italians: the Četniks justified this on the grounds that they shared the same overall aim, to keep the Partisans out of Serbia. The Germans, however, demanded that the Italians should disarm the Četniks immediately. Hitler warned Mussolini that Mihailović 'awaits only the moment when he can turn against us . . . Mihailović seeks to obtain arms and supplies for the execution of these plans by pretending to assist your troops'. In fact, the Četniks were only disarmed after Operation Schwarz, or the Fifth Offensive, in May and June 1943, which was aimed at destroying the Partisans in the Sandžak and Montenegro. In this case the role of the Germans was to drive the Partisans south where the Italians would block their escape. The Partisans dispersed rapidly and retreated into eastern Bosnia-Herzegovina having lost around a third of their force. The largely ineffective Italian and Četnik block in the south led the Germans to disarm the Četniks under Djurišić, who had been operating alongside the Italians.[33]

These German operations were entirely successful in ending the Partisan threat to Serbia. Their success was helped by two main factors. The first was that the Partisans were expending much energy on the civil war, mounting attacks on the Četniks whenever they had a breathing space from Axis operations. The second was that the Germans had limited aims in the whole of Yugoslavia in any case. The Germans did not need to control the whole country but only to keep the resistance, Četnik or Partisan, away from the main mines, the major roads and the railways, and out of the cities, in order to exploit the Yugoslav economy and to retain contact with forces in Greece and elsewhere in the Balkans. From the Partisan perspective, the German offensives made it harder for them to maintain large forces in any one area but did not destroy their ability to recruit replacements for casualties suffered, nor did they threaten to extinguish the Partisan movement as a whole.

Italian military activity against the resistance forces in Croatia was primarily motivated by the requirement to secure the Italian hold over Dalmatia and Slovenia. This region was to be part of Italy's *spazio vitale*, but its rail and road links with Montenegro were extremely vulnerable to interdiction by insurgents. Since the Ustaše and Croatian forces appeared to be manifestly incapable of maintaining law and order in their country, Italian forces occupied parts of Croatia, zones II and III, in September 1941. Yet the Italians were no better at controlling the wild and mountainous territory than the Croatians, and the large, slow-moving Italian convoys were constantly ambushed by the Partisans.

Italy's hold over Slovenia was precarious: attempts at rapid Italianization and the imposition of Fascist institutions unsettled the country, yet, as with elsewhere in Yugoslavia, the resistance was split and an element of civil war was present. The communists quickly dominated the first resistance movement, the *Osvobodilna Fronta*, OF, which was created in April 1941 immediately after the start of the occupation. The OF would become the general staff of Partisan formations in Slovenia. The OF was based in the city of Ljubljana, which Mussolini had set up as an autonomous republic within the kingdom of Italy in May 1941. Unrest in the city, fomented by the communists but by no means limited to their circles, led to an experiment in anti-resistance strategy. Between 23 February and 15 March 1942 the entire city of Ljubljana, with its population of 80,000, was encircled in barbed wire along with a bunker system protected by machine-gun and artillery emplacements. Over 30,000 Slovenes in the city were subjected to interrogation: of these 878 were arrested on suspicion of being Partisans, and a further 936 Slovene suspects were held on other pretexts. Unrest continued in the city so a further round-up was made at the end of June 1942, leading to the arrests of over 17,000 Slovenes and the deportation of over 2,600 to internment camps in Italy. The operation forced the Partisans to relocate the centre of their activities to the countryside.[34]

Once in the countryside, they faced other enemies. The Četniks under Djujić, and Ilija Trifunović, disobeyed Mihailović's orders and openly collaborated with the Italians and received weapons from them. The Četniks were largely unreliable and ineffective at fighting the Partisans, so in July

1942 the Italian commander set up a new anti-Partisan force, the *Milizia Volontaria Anti Comunista* (MVAC). This was created from existing anti-Partisan formations such as the Slovene, Sokol, and National Legions, which had official support and finance from the Yugoslav government-in-exile. Recruitment to them and the MVAC was encouraged by the Slovene Catholic Church. By February 1943 there were forty MVAC detachments totalling over 5,000 men operating alongside the Italian troops throughout Slovenia and the numbers continued to increase, but their existence relied entirely on Italian sponsorship and support. Were this to end then there would be open civil war between the Partisans and these anti-communist units whom the Partisans termed White Guards and considered as implacable enemies.[35]

When General Mario Roatta took over as commander of the Italian 2nd Army in spring 1942 he called for a comprehensive reassessment of Italian tactics. He realized that his army was too weak to hold the entire territory and therefore identified strategic points and key towns to be held at all costs to protect the railways and major roads. On 1 March 1942 Roatta issued the notorious 'Circular 3c', setting out the aims and policies of the Italian occupiers in Slovenia and Croatia. Broadly speaking, the purpose was to identify areas where there was little resistance and where the population was, if not friendly towards the Italians, then at least not overtly hostile, and to distinguish them from the so-called 'abnormal' areas where resistance had already been noted. The tactics to be employed in the 'abnormal' areas were the widespread burning of villages and internment of suspects. Roatta told Mussolini in May that he predicted the need for at least 5,000 internments in Slovenia alone, along with the evacuation of 15,000 people, including women and children, as a preventative measure. By the end of 1942 over 30,000 Slovenians had been interned in camps where the conditions were so poor that even the Vatican complained.

The Italians also mounted a series of anti-Partisan operations in the summer of 1942. The first, in July, aimed at clearing the Partisans from the region of the Fiume–Split railway; the second, in August, was in the mountains south of Split; and the third, in October, was in the triangle formed by the towns of Mostar, Posušje, and Prozor. Like the German operations against the Partisans, those mounted by the Italians yielded the same results: large numbers of Partisan and civilian deaths, low Italian casualties, no firm or long-term control over the area but success in preventing the Partisans from consolidating their positions and strengthening their forces.[36]

By late 1942 the Italian position had been weakened as Roatta was forced to send troops back to Italy to reinforce the garrisons there. Attempts to withdraw forces from Bosnia-Herzegovina in the early months of 1943 were frequently chaotic and allowed the Partisans, and not the Četniks as the Italians had planned, to take over key positions such as Jajce, Banja Luka, and Prozor. Italian participation in German-led operations such as the Fourth and Fifth Offensives had led to significant Italian casualties and the tactics employed appalled many Italian participants. As one Italian officer commented: 'This war is continually degenerating to ever lower depths and we can no longer see it as a war between civilised peoples.'[37]

It is by no means clear the extent to which the British missions which began arriving in Yugoslavia understood the nature of the resistance in the country nor the complexities caused by ethnic cleansing and the conflict between the Četniks and the Partisans.

Bill Hudson arrived in Montenegro in November 1941 by submarine with orders to join Mihailović, who at this stage the British thought was the only resistance leader in Yugoslavia. Hudson had been the manager of a mine in Serbia before the war and spoke the language. There has been some doubt over the exact orders given to him. Hudson himself reported in 1946:

> I was sent into occupied Yugoslavia in September 1941 to despatch by wireless information concerning Axis forces and to report on any Yugoslavian groups that I might find offering resistance. I was furthermore instructed to coordinate the efforts of such groups and to make arrangements for the reception of British military supplies by them.[38]

Two points need to be noted immediately. The first resistance group Hudson encountered were the Partisans, whose existence had previously been unknown to the British. Secondly, Hudson experienced considerable, indeed disastrous, problems with his radio equipment. He had been sent in with two radios: one was the Mark II set, which weighed 55lb and required mains electricity to operate, and the second was a smaller J set, which burned out if operated for more than half an hour and had such a limited range that it could reach Malta from Montenegro but not from Serbia. The first radio was left with the Partisans since it was too cumbersome to carry over the mountains; the second was taken to Ravna Gora in Serbia but proved useless, so Hudson was forced to use Mihailović's radio. When the Četniks were in retreat during the winter of 1941–42 there was no radio contact with Hudson, and the British assumed that he had lost his life. They despatched further missions in early 1942 which all ended in disaster.[39]

These failures in radio communication largely doomed Hudson's mission from the outset since he could neither report regularly on what he had witnessed nor obtain supplies for the Četniks. This was critical at a time when British expectations of the resistance in Yugoslavia were changing. In August 1941 the minister of economic warfare Hugh Dalton outlined the policy to be adopted in a memorandum for Churchill:

> The Yugoslavs, the War Office, and we are all agreed that the guerrilla and sabotage bands now active in Yugoslavia should show sufficient active resistance to cause constant embarrassment to the occupying forces and prevent any reduction in their numbers. But they should keep their main organisation underground and avoid any attempt at large scale risings or ambitious military operations which could only result at present in severe repression and the loss of our key men. They should now do all they can to prepare a widespread underground organisation ready to strike hard later on, when we give the signal.[40]

This is precisely the course of action adopted by Mihailović as regards resistance towards the Axis occupiers and indeed it was in tune with the policies followed by most other non-communist resistance groups elsewhere in Europe. But it did not take into account the challenge posed by the activities of the Partisans.

In September 1942 General Harold Alexander of Middle East Command called for widespread railway sabotage throughout the Balkans to prevent Axis reinforcements and supplies being sent to the Western Desert. This demand led to the despatch of the British mission into Greece to destroy the Gorgopotamos viaduct, as has been described in Chapter 11. Considerable doubt has since been cast on the actual level of German supplies passing through the Balkans, and the weight of evidence now suggests that the bulk of Field Marshal Rommel's supplies reached him from Italy, and were being interdicted by British naval and air power. Nonetheless, in 1942 the British wanted a campaign of railway sabotage in the Balkans, partly to prove to the Soviet Union 'that we are doing everything possible to create the second front in the Balkans which they desire'.[41] From September to November 1941 the Četniks did undertake a campaign of widespread sabotage against the railways running through Serbia, and Mihailović called for a campaign of civil disobedience across Serbia. Mines were damaged and railways subjected to frequent cuts and trains were re-routed to the wrong destinations. Some of this sabotage was witnessed by Hudson personally. The Germans retaliated harshly and at least 1,500 Serbs were executed in reprisal during the autumn of 1942. Since Mihailović was principally concerned to protect Serb lives, these losses caused him to call a halt to the sabotage campaign. Hudson, now using Mihailović's radio, was forced to report that his appeals for further sabotage were being met by an outright refusal by Mihailović who would not 'depart from this standpoint for the sake of any outside interest'. Worse still, Hudson reported that Mihailović and the Četniks were now planning to focus on the threat posed by the Partisans. Hudson considered Mihailović 'perfectly capable of coming to any sound undertaking with either Italians or Germans which he believes might serve his purposes'.[42]

On 25 December 1942 Colonel William Bailey was parachuted in to Mihailović in order to spur him into action and to report on any steps which might be taken to avert the increasing likelihood of civil war in Yugoslavia. The Bailey–Hudson report sent to Cairo for transmission to London was described by its authors as 'something of a counsel of despair' since it was clear to both men that civil war rather than resistance was taking first place in the minds of both the Četniks and the Partisans. They proposed a plan which called for the creation of two operational areas, one for each group, with the demarcation line running from the Yugoslav-Bulgarian border on the Danube in the north-east to the Montenegrin-Albanian border in the south-west. 'Each movement would enjoy full British support in its own area in return for an understanding to eschew all contact with the occupying forces and to abstain from all conflict with, or attempts to penetrate the territory of, the other.' This plan was immediately rejected in London on the grounds that it would aggravate the natural rivalries between the Serbs and Croats and run the serious risk of infecting much of the country with communism which might then spill over into Hungary and Austria.[43]

On 28 February 1943 Mihailović made a speech at a christening party in Gornje Lipovo in Montenegro at which Bailey was present. In it Mihailović castigated the British for placing unrealistic demands on him. He needed to concentrate on eliminating his Yugoslav enemies first before complying with British demands to take the battle to the Axis occupiers. In any case he could not do as the British wished because they had not sent him adequate supplies, forcing him to obtain weapons from the Italians who, unlike the British, at least recognized the danger posed by the Partisans and the blood-letting of the Ustaše.[44] Mihailović was probably just blowing off steam and he did have every reason to be angry with the British since it was true that supplies were not arriving and there was no sign of the anticipated Allied invasion from Salonika, widely expected as a repeat of Allied strategy in the First World War. Despite the unimportance of the occasion Bailey reported the speech to Cairo, from where it was transmitted to London. An historian has commented: 'It is altogether tragic that what was in itself an incident of third-rate importance should have been magnified out of all proportion by misunderstandings and by the intensity of personal feelings. Certainly, the Foreign Office's violent reaction to this report bore no relation to the intentions of the British mission in submitting it or to their own estimate of its importance.' The British were furious and the Yugoslav prime minister of the government-in-exile, Jovanović, was handed a note from Churchill: 'His Majesty's Government cannot ignore this outburst nor accept without explanation and without protest a policy so totally at variance with their own.' Jovanović was strongly advised to bring his minister of war into line with British policy and duly exchanged a series of telegrams with Mihailović.[45]

The British were now in a quandary. It was evident that they were not able to supply Mihailović adequately, nor could they impress on him the need to mount resistance against the Axis, despite having created the public image of Mihailović as the ideal of a resistance leader. At the same time evidence gleaned from Enigma decrypts was increasingly suggesting that the Partisans were posing a major threat to the Axis occupation. This implied that the Partisans should receive British aid to encourage this, while at the same time considerable concern was being voiced at their communist nature.[46] The decision was taken to establish direct contact with the Partisans, but as Eden informed Churchill: 'on a long view . . . we should be wise to go on supporting Mihailović in order to prevent anarchy and Communist chaos after the war'.[47] Churchill was impressed by a paper prepared by SOE Cairo on 30 January 1943 which outlined how they saw the situation in Yugoslavia: Mihailović was successful against the occupiers in Serbia but there was collaboration between Četnik commanders in Montenegro and Bosnia-Herzegovina and the Italians; reports from various sources, including Enigma, suggested that there was considerable resistance activity in Slovenia and Croatia but that 'it is not accurate to adopt the German technique of branding the whole movement in these areas as Communist'. The recommendation from SOE Cairo was to send missions to the Partisans, and a decision to adopt this policy was taken in Cairo on 23 March 1943.[48]

The first missions to the Partisans were sent in April 1943 to Bosnia and Croatia where they were met with considerable suspicion by the Partisans. The next mission was sent into Croatia in the middle of May, led by Major William Jones, who became such an enthusiastic advocate of the Partisans that even they labelled him as 'mad but holy'.[49] The most important mission, however, was led by Deakin, who arrived at Durmitor in Montenegro at the end of May 1943 to join Tito. Deakin was overcome with enthusiasm for Tito and the Partisans and urged the British to send him large quantities of supplies. He was fed a constant stream of information regarding the alleged high degree of Četnik collaboration with the Italians with the stress placed on Mihailović's inactivity.[50] His reports to SOE Cairo were greeted with elation by the two officers there most responsible for interpreting events in Yugoslavia: Basil Davidson and James Klugman. Both were pro-Partisan and increasingly anti-Četnik: Klugman was also a member of the British Communist Party. Both men in their despatches to London enthusiastically endorsed all mentions of Partisan activity and downplayed reports and requests for supplies from William Bailey and the additional British missions which were sent to the Četniks during 1943.[51] Deakin was embarrassed by the contents of the first drop received, on 25 June, seven containers and six packages which contained a spare radio and a small amount of explosives but no urgently needed food or medical equipment, with the result that 'the atmosphere among our party was polite but restrained'.[52]

As the war in North Africa was drawing to a conclusion the Allies began to consider future operations. The Allied target after the surrender of the Axis forces in North Africa on 13 May 1943 was Sicily, and they launched an elaborate deception plan to convince the Germans that they intended to invade the Balkans through Greece in the summer of 1943. Operation Mincemeat, the planting of documents on the body of a dead Royal Marine sent to drift ashore in Spain, was part of this plan, as was the signals activity orchestrated to create the impression of a build-up of troops in Egypt poised for the invasion.[53] SOE was instructed to increase resistance activity across the Balkans to support the deception. At the Foreign Office, Orme Sargent voiced alarm at the possible unintended consequences of the directive:

> It might involve a reversal of the present policy of support for Mihailović which is being followed by the FO, SOE and PWE [*sic*] since Mihailović's playing a long-term game . . . If the scale of guerrilla activity is to be increased in the immediate future it may require that HMG should switch their support from Mihailović to the Partisans . . . But we . . . would probably have to give them promises and assurances which might be very embarrassing politically.[54]

SOE largely appears to have ignored the concerns of the Foreign Office. For SOE, the crux of the matter was to see how the Četniks and Partisans would respond.[55]

For both sides, an important factor in deciding their response was the desire to be in the best position possible to receive and support the Allied invasion which they were certain would occur. Jasper Rootham, serving alongside the Četniks, noted the effect of the Salonika campaign in the First World War: 'It had become a fixed tenet not only that the last war had been won in the Balkans, but that this one would be too, and by the same methods and the same route as before.'[56] Consequently, Mihailović moved his headquarters from Montenegro back into Serbia to prepare for the general rising at the time of the Allied invasion. In order to preserve his troops, he largely ignored British requests for an increase in sabotage attacks on German lines of communication to Greece and against shipping on the Danube. Some sabotage against mines and against the occupation forces in the area between Užice and Ivanjica was carried out, including attacks on German, Italian, and Bulgarian garrisons and troop trains. These were mainly conducted on the initiative of local Četnik commanders, encouraged by the members of the British sub-missions now present in the region. The attacks and sabotage were not on a large scale but they were an irritant, and the Germans were forced to acknowledge that Mihailović was still a dangerous enemy. On 22 July 1943 they placed a large advertisement in various Yugoslav newspapers, with the space equally divided between Mihailović and Tito, offering a reward of 100,000 gold marks for the head of each. The BBC and later historiography ignored the presence of Mihailović on the poster, mentioning only Tito. Two major German attacks on Mihailović's headquarters were later launched on 5 September and 10 October 1943.[57]

The Partisans reacted differently to the prospect of an Allied landing. Indeed, during the Partisan-German negotiations, the Partisan leadership had stated that the Partisans would resist an Allied invasion. They anticipated that any such invasion would be made along the Adriatic coast; and in fact Churchill had toyed with the idea of such a landing and questioned the Chiefs of Staff on the chances of its success.[58] For the Partisans, the apparent likelihood of an Allied invasion made it essential for them to control the coastal regions in order to ensure that they would be treated as the national liberation army and that the Četniks would be completely sidelined. The strategy they adopted formed two broad lines: local actions directed to eliminate Četnik forces working with or without the Italians, and an upsurge in sabotage to prove the value of the Partisan movement to the Allies. The railways spreading out from Sarajevo, the principal city of Bosnia-Herzegovina, were attacked frequently, bringing the rail traffic from the mines to a temporary standstill. Further attacks on the main Zagreb–Belgrade line halted Axis communications with Greece for nearly three days.[59] The BBC only publicized the attacks mounted by the Partisans and even wrongly attributed attacks to the Partisans which had been made by the Četniks.

By July 1943, when the landings on Sicily took place, it was clear to the British that they could not supply both resistance movements in Yugoslavia.

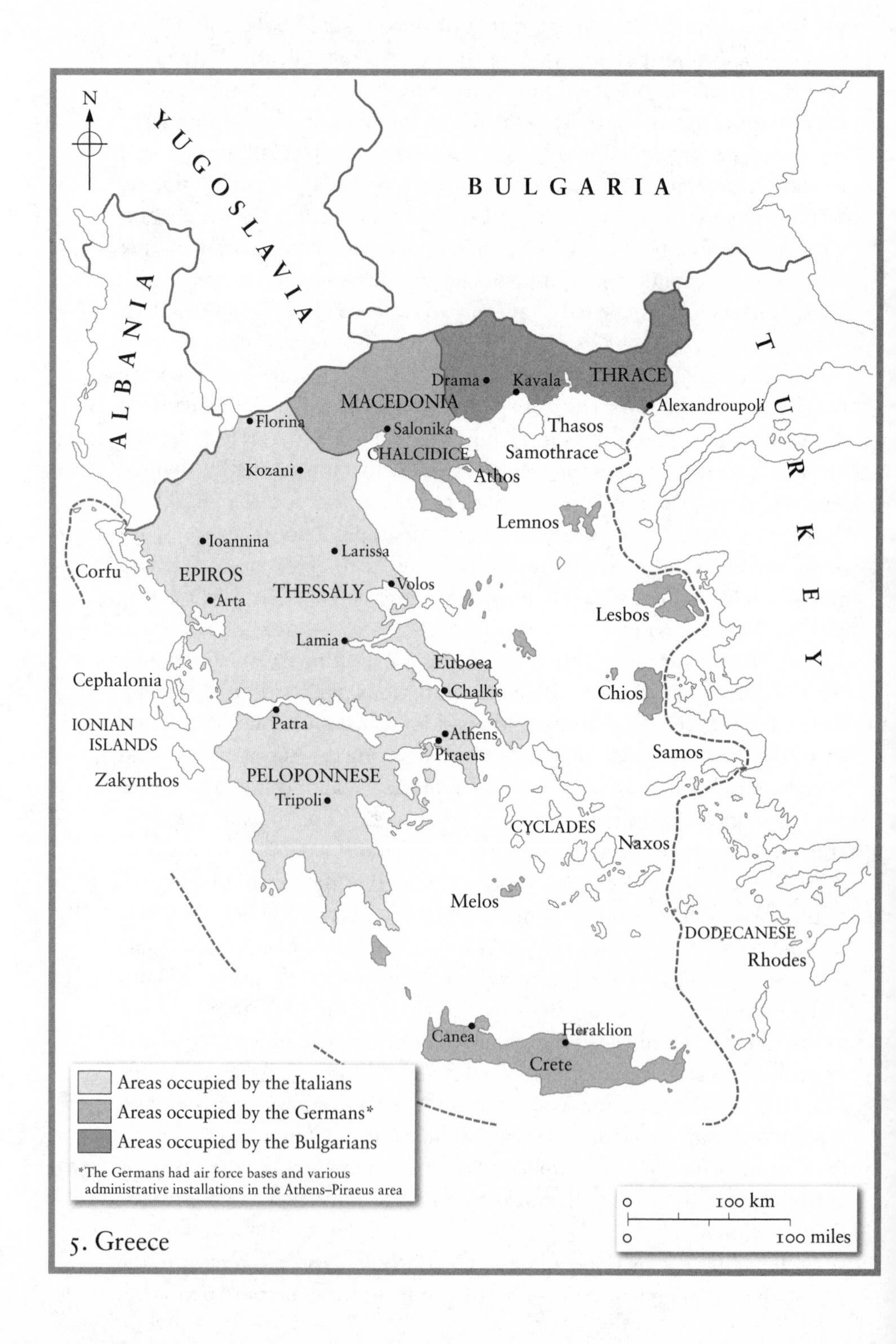
N
YUGOSLAVIA
BULGARIA
ALBANIA
TURKEY
MACEDONIA
THRACE
Drama
Kavala
Alexandroupoli
Florina
Salonika
CHALCIDICE
Thasos
Samothrace
Athos
Kozani
Lemnos
Ioannina
Larissa
Corfu
EPIROS
THESSALY
Volos
Arta
Lesbos
Lamia
Euboea
Cephalonia
Chalkis
Chios
IONIAN
ISLANDS
Patra
Athens
Piraeus
Samos
Zakynthos
PELOPONNESE
Tripoli
CYCLADES
Naxos
Melos
DODECANESE
Rhodes
Canea
Heraklion
Crete
Areas occupied by the Italians
Areas occupied by the Germans*
Areas occupied by the Bulgarians
*The Germans had air force bases and various administrative installations in the Athens–Piraeus area
0
100 km
0
100 miles
5. Greece

The Battle of the Atlantic and the strategic bombing of Germany took priority for the use of the limited number of available long-range aircraft. For example, it was estimated that to service Mihailović alone adequately would require a minimum of twenty-eight sorties per month, whereas the most that could be executed was six. In June 1943 the chief of the air force, Charles Portal, agreed to increase the number of Halifaxes used for operations to Yugoslavia from fourteen to twenty-two. These would be capable of delivering around 150 tons of supplies per month, although the requirement for 500 tons per month was noted.[60] The evidence gleaned from the summer 1943 sabotage campaign was that the Partisans appeared to offer better value for money, but at the same time they were politically suspect. Therefore, in July the decision was taken to send two high-ranking missions into Yugoslavia to report fully on the situation: Brigadier Charles Armstrong to Mihailović, and Brigadier Fitzroy Maclean to Tito.[61] Both men arrived in the country in September 1943, just when the strategic situation had changed completely with the surrender of Italy.

The narrative of the resistance in Greece presents a complex picture of strategic and tactical requirements clashing with political needs. The British government was playing host to King George II and his government-in-exile and the British Foreign Office remained wedded to the idea that the king should be restored to the throne after his country's liberation. Yet George II was unpopular, both as an individual whose ancestry was not pure Greek and whose character was cold and dreary, and because he was blamed for the suspension of the constitution and the imposition of the pre-war dictatorship of Ioannis Metaxas. It was also noted that the men forming the quisling government in Athens were known monarchists.[62] In January 1942 the minister of state in Cairo, Richard Casey, warned the Foreign Office: 'All political parties now in Greece are united in their desire for the establishment of a republic, and except for a few persons attached to the monarchy by personal ties, and certain officers, there is no one who supports the king.'[63] In April 1942 the Greek armed forces in exile, then in the Middle East, staged a mutiny against their royalist officers; a second mutiny in the winter of 1942–43 was organized by left-wing soldiers who arrested the right-wing officers; and a third mutiny occurred in July 1943.[64]

The first task of the newly established British Military Mission in Greece under Eddie Myers and Chris 'Monty' Woodhouse was to resolve the question of the political make-up of the resistance. Myers and Woodhouse very quickly realized that both EDES and ELAS were essentially republican movements both implacably opposed to the return of George II. The

Foreign Office, however, was adamant that the British mission must safeguard the position of the king, which Woodhouse commented, 'could only have been done by ensuring that there was no resistance at all'.[65]

The two principal resistance movements, ELAS and EDES, had been encountered during Operation Harling, when they had assisted in the destruction of the Gorgopotamos viaduct. There were other small bands operating in the mountains against the remote Italian garrisons, but little was known of them. There were also other small groups such as PEAN, operating in the towns, which have been eclipsed in the historiography by the two main movements. In addition, Athens played host to a resistance group known as the Six Colonels, all of whom were royalist officers, and whom the minister of defence in the exiled Greek government, Panagiotis Kanellopoulos, hoped would assume leadership of the resistance throughout Greece. Woodhouse was ordered to go into Athens and meet them. This was a high-risk mission since Woodhouse was over six feet tall and had red hair whereas the majority of Greeks were short and dark-haired.[66] Nonetheless, Woodhouse did manage to meet two of the colonels and later wrote of them:

> They seemed able and patriotic men, but they had no interest in guerrilla warfare. Like many other officers loyal to the monarchy, they feared the consequences of the movement in the mountains, and wished it had never begun. All they wanted to do was to make staff plans for the rapid mobilisation of a new army at the end of the occupation, in order to join in the final defeat of the Germans.[67]

In many ways the Six Colonels appear to be a similar organization to the Princes in wartime Denmark. Both groups thought that the emphasis of their activities should be placed on the acquisition and transmission of intelligence, tasks which both groups carried out extremely well, but both feared the consequences of resistance to the occupation and preferred to plan for widespread action at the moment of Germany's imminent defeat.

The first reports from Myers and Woodhouse caused consternation in Cairo and London, where great hopes had been placed on the Six Colonels.[68] It was clear that the Six Colonels were entirely unsuited to organizing resistance outside the cities, and it was in the mountains that the forces of EDES and ELAS were developing, both of them committed to guerrilla warfare but both republican. The Greek government-in-exile strongly supported the Six Colonels, but British circles in Cairo, both from the Foreign Office and SOE, placed little hope in them. Consequently, the Greek government-in-exile began to be sidelined by the British in Cairo. Instructions from London did not help clarify matters. On 18 March 1943

Churchill ordered the impossible. British policy was to support the king and the Greek government-in-exile strongly, but at the same time:

> In view of the operational importance attached to subversive activities in Greece, there can be no question of SOE refusing to have dealings with a given group merely on the grounds that political sentiments of the group are opposed to the King and Government but subject to special operational necessity SOE should always veer in the direction of groups willing to support the King and Government and furthermore impress on such other groups as may be anti-[monarchy] the fact that the King and Government enjoy the fullest support of HMG. In general nothing should be neglected which might help to promote unity among the resistance groups in Greece and between the latter and the King and Government.[69]

Strategic requirements forced the British mission to encourage the republican resistance forces. As Myers noted: 'A web of Greek politics was already irrevocably woven around our activities; and the political horizon already appeared stormy.'[70]

The first reports from Myers and Woodhouse on EDES and ELAS illustrate the complexities in understanding the resistance in Greece. Both men noted that ELAS was communist-controlled through EAM. Myers felt that this was unimportant and noted the presence of many royalist army officers in the ranks of ELAS. Woodhouse, however, was more aware of the communist influence but agreed with Myers's conclusion that the communist control of EAM was unknown to most members of ELAS, who merely hoped that victory would bring substantial measures of social reform. In February 1943 the solution proposed by Myers and Woodhouse was to strive towards the establishment of national bands which would unite EDES, ELAS, and the smaller EKKA militarily under the orders of the British Middle East Command.

First, however, Myers and Woodhouse needed to assess the relative importance of EDES and ELAS and decide how they should best be supported. EDES was dominated by its leader, Napoleon Zervas, who was an enthusiastic supporter of the British Military Mission, seeing it as a source of weapons for his men. EDES, however, had some fundamental flaws. In the first place it was strong only in Epiros in north-western Greece, although Zervas claimed to have supporters in Thessaly, Macedonia, and the Peloponnese. Secondly, EDES had to a certain degree a cult of leadership centred around Zervas himself and the relationship between the leader and his men has been described as virtually feudal: this was seen as a factor limiting recruitment. Zervas was known to be 'bitterly anti-communist' and a republican; however, he had, at the request of the British in March 1943, made a statement in support of the king. This was clearly insincere since the British mission knew that Zervas was 'not in heart in favour of the King', but he showed that he would desist from making anti-monarchy statements in order not to displease the British. Myers and Woodhouse concluded that Zervas was 'a completely loyal ally and will still do absolutely what we tell him. He is therefore not only our creation but remains an instrument in our hands.'[71] The conclusion was that EDES was useful as a counterweight to ELAS, and as such deserved continued British support.

ELAS held a huge advantage over EDES because it could rely on the support raised throughout much of Greece since the previous year by EAM, particularly in the strategically important area of Thessaly, across much of central Greece, and down into the Peloponnese.[72] From a force numbering only a few thousand in early 1943, ELAS expanded rapidly in the course of the year. ELAS also attracted a growing number of regular army officers, notably Stefanos Sarafis, who went on to become ELAS's principal military commander. Sarafis justified to Myers his decision to join ELAS on the grounds that he believed the existence of several separate resistance organizations weakened the resistance to the Axis occupation as a whole. He was convinced that ELAS was the best organized and therefore, despite its communism, should provide the nucleus around which a single resistance army should be built, 'if we wanted to give better and more speedy help to the Allied struggle, to secure concord and a smooth transition to liberation and political life for the Greek people, to avoid clashes and ultimately a civil war'.[73] Ultimately, Myers decided that British support was essential for ELAS because most of the sabotage targets were in eastern Greece where only ELAS had a significant presence.[74]

Yet some of the activities of ELAS were a cause for concern. From March 1943 onwards it had pursued the policy of absorbing smaller resistance groups operating near its territory, such as PAO, formed from former Greek army officers. Only EKKA under George Kartalis and Colonel Dimitrios Psarros retained its independence from ELAS for a further year.[75] This policy of assimilation enabled the ranks of ELAS to swell to around 12,000 by September 1943.[76] Some ELAS officers felt that the organization was too political. For example, when the commander in Macedonia, Colonel Dimaratos, was ordered to attack EDES, he chose to resign and returned to his village. Other officers who tried to copy his example were shot as deserters.[77]

On 21 February 1943 Myers received a long signal from Cairo outlining the future plans of the Allies: soon after the anticipated surrender of Axis forces in Tunisia, they expected to launch an invasion of Sicily and simultaneously to launch attacks against the Italian-held Dodecanese islands.[78] The Greek resistance was required to step up its attacks, not knowing that this was part of a deception plan to convince the Germans that the Allies were about to launch an invasion of Greece, thus causing the Germans to retain or even augment the number of Axis troops there. The increase in resistance activity ordered for the summer of 1943 was termed Operation Animals. Woodhouse later wrote:

> Myers and I were the only two in Greece who knew that this operation was simply deception. We had to deceive our allies as well as the enemy, in the interests of security. So the guerrilla leaders were also convinced, like the Germans, that the liberation of Greece was planned to take place in 1943. The deception was successful, but the consequences of it were grave.[79]

Here one must question the morality of the use the Allies made of the resistance. Increased resistance would inevitably lead to the deaths of many Greek civilians through reprisals, so by urging the Greek resistance to take more action the Allies were deliberately sacrificing Greek lives in order to preserve the lives of Allied soldiers. This fact was recognized by members of the British missions in Greece.

By spring 1943 there were ten such missions, spread out throughout the country. Myers divided Greece into four areas, each to be supervised by a British lieutenant colonel: Tom Barnes in Epiros, Arthur Edmonds in Roumeli, Rufus Sheppard in Olympus, and Nick Hammond in Macedonia. Their role would be to oversee and direct the efforts of ELAS and EDES in attacks on the Axis communications. It was also the acid test of whether EDES and ELAS would be amenable to following British orders; and whether they could work together, or would oppose each other to the detriment of anti-Axis operations.

The first test came when Myers planned to destroy the Asopos viaduct on the Salonika–Athens railway. Aris Velouchiotis had 900 ELAS *andartes* in the area but declined to help because he considered the viaduct too well guarded. Worse still, it became clear that ELAS headquarters was not prepared to submit to the orders of British Middle East Command. Indeed, Sarafis informed Myers: 'that to avoid delay, he should initially submit his operational plans to us and, if we approved them, we would order their execution. The forces concerned would then discuss the details and equipment needed with the local British liaison officers.' The result was that in June 1943 a British-only force led by Edmonds successfully demolished the viaduct and put the main line down the length of Greece out of action for four critical months: the Germans executed the garrison guard in reprisal. In fact, most of Operation Animals was carried out by the British:

'Through June and into July 1943, the Greek hills and valleys echoed and re-echoed the thunder of explosions, as members of the British Military Mission destroyed bridges, railways, embankments, telephone exchanges, mines and a host of other military targets of use to the Germans.' The roads and railways were cut in the far east of Thessaly by John Mulgan, in Macedonia by Hammond, and in central and western Thessaly by Sheppard and Harker. In Epiros, Barnes destroyed the telephone lines, and in central Greece Edmonds wrecked the mineral mines.[80]

ELAS and EDES did undertake limited operations, mostly mounting ambushes on German and Italian convoys. ELAS, however, scored a major success when an operation against the Kournovo tunnel on the Salonika–Athens railway led to the deaths of around 500 Italian soldiers who had been in a train in the tunnel when the attack took place. In reprisal the Italians took 118 Greeks from Larissa concentration camp and shot them by the tunnel.[81]

The Italian and German reaction to the sudden upsurge in resistance activity was harsh. The Italians burned villages to the ground across Greece and on occasions resorted to aerial bombardment of villages. Neither the Italians nor the Germans made any distinction between resisters and innocent civilians. Epiros became noted as the area where the reprisals were heaviest. This was an Italian-controlled area but in August 1943 a 20,000-strong German force from the 1st Mountain Division arrived to take over anti-partisan action. These men had taken part in actions in the rear of the Eastern Front and brought the brutal methods that had been honed there to Greece. The Germans were issued with guidelines on how to operate:

> All armed men are basically to be shot on the spot. Villages from where shots have been fired, or where armed men have been encountered, are to be destroyed, and the male population of these villages to be shot. Elsewhere all men capable of bearing arms (16 to 60 years old) are to be rounded up and sent to Jannina.

A particularly notorious example of German anti-partisan action took place in the village of Kommeno, south of the town of Arta in Epiros, on 16 August 1943. The Germans from the 98th Regiment of the 1st Mountain Division encircled the village and killed 317 villagers out of a population of just over 600. No guerrillas were identified and there were no German losses. In all, it has been estimated that the 1st Mountain Division destroyed 184 villages and killed nearly 1,300 Greeks and almost 500 Albanians in the course of July and August 1943.[82]

Operation Animals ran officially from 21 June to 14 July and was

1. German troops entering Prague, March 1939.

2. Pétain meets Hitler at Montoire.

3. A selection of clandestine Dutch newspapers.

4. Graffiti in support of the Norwegian King Haakon VII: victory symbol with H7, by the fjord at Kråkevik.

5. Twenty-five year old Belgian woman Mlle Andrée de Jongh, who saved the lives of many British airmen and soldiers, pictured after visiting Buckingham Palace to receive the George Medal in February 1946. From 1941 until her arrest in 1943 she organized the dispatch of Allied Service personnel from Belgium across the Pyrenees into Spain.

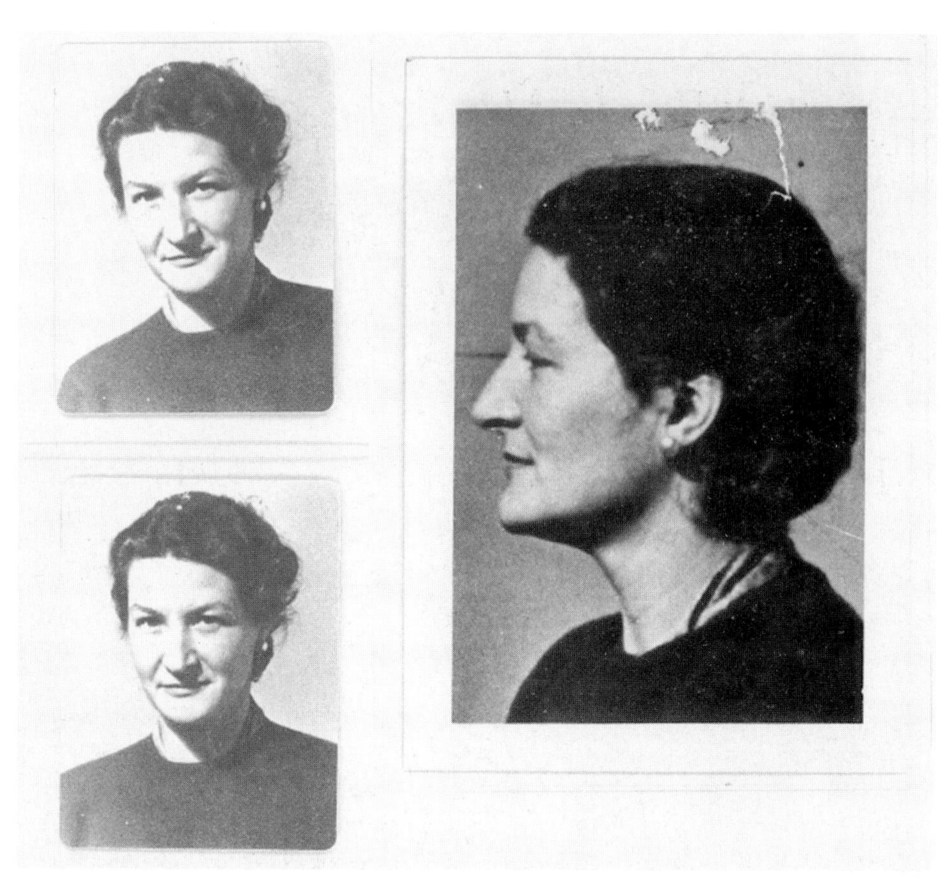

6. Virginia Hall was the first female SOE agent to enter France.

7. German invasion barges in Boulogne harbour, June 1940. The resistance supplied intelligence on German plans to invade Britain.

8. Soviet partisans in the Pinsk region.

9. Captain David Smiley and Major Billy McLean at Bixha, Albania.

10. Hostages executed at Fort de Vincennes near Paris.

11. The scene after the assassination of Reinhard Heydrich, 27 May 1942.

12. A French Maquis encampment.

13. Jewish children hidden in Chambon-sur-Lignon.

14. SS assault troops capture two Jewish resistance fighters during the Warsaw Ghetto Uprising.

15. Vidkun Quisling and General Ludwig Wolff inspecting the Hird.

16. The Milice was the most deadly enemy of the Resistance.

17. Draža Mihailović.

18. An SOE radio, pattern Mk.II (1941).

19. The Ardeatine Caves near Rome, where a massacre of the resistance took place.

20. Sabotage of the Pindstofte Maskinfabrik in Copenhagen, 17 January 1944.

21. Marshal Tito (*on the right*) with his cabinet ministers and Supreme Staff.

22. Members of the 27th division of the Armia Krajowa in the woods in the Volhynia region, 1943.

23. A V2 rocket. The resistance supplied a great deal of information on Germany's V-weapons programme.

24. The maquis collecting supplies dropped in the Haute-Savoie.

25. A train blown up by SOE and the French Resistance.

26. The port of Antwerp, which the resistance saved from destruction.

27. The sewers were used by the AK during the Warsaw Uprising to communicate between sectors and to evacuate troops.

28. The bridge at Arnhem.

29. SOE with EDES in the Greek mountains.

30. The former allies fall out: British paratroopers under fire from ELAS snipers, Athens, December 1944.

31. The partisans parade through Milan.

32. The Resistance never forgot: former SS officer Erich Priebke on trial in 1994.

considered a total success. Hitler was so convinced that the Allies would launch an attack on Greece that he despatched Rommel to take command there, as well as moving four German divisions into the area: the 11th Luftwaffe Division to the Corinth Canal; the 117th Jaeger Division was transferred from Yugoslavia to Greece; the 1st Panzer Division to the Peloponnese; and the 1st Mountain Division to Epiros. Meanwhile the Allies had landed some 160,000 men in Sicily. General Henry Wilson telegraphed Myers on 18 July:

> I wish to convey to all ranks of the guerrilla army of Greece my sincere thanks and congratulations on the recent big successes throughout the whole of Greece . . . General Wilson requests that all operations cease immediately . . . General Wilson now requests that all guerrillas remain quiet and turn their attention to the selection of additional enlistments, to re-equipment and training for future developments the exact dates of which are not yet known.[83]

However, having mobilized the resistance, the British Military Mission now began to lose control of events.

During Operation Animals, ELAS and EDES had largely operated separately. There had been cooperation between the two in early July when they combined to fight the Italians at Rovilista on the Preveza–Ioannina road, but at the same time ELAS objected when EDES forces, supported by the British, entered so-called ELAS territory in Epiros to attack the Ioannina–Kalpaki–Kakavia road. The British had worked alongside ELAS when targeting the railways and roads in eastern and central Greece. But now the Allies had landed in Sicily, should the Allies elect to invade Greece the most likely area would be Epiros, where EDES was strongest. It remained to be seen whether ELAS would be content to let EDES stay in control of the region or whether it would attempt to attack EDES in order to control Epiros from where it would contact the communist resistance in Albania.[84]

The British Military Mission and the authorities in Cairo struggled to define the ultimate aims of ELAS and, if those were thought to be anti-British in the long term, then to devise means to contain ELAS's ambitions. The evidence was contradictory. Myers and Woodhouse were convinced that 'EAM leaders regard English weapons primarily [as] means [to] strengthen their control [of] Greece, only secondarily [to] contribute [to] our war effort insofar as we happen to be fighting their enemy Fascism'. But from Mount Olympus, Rufus Sheppard was presenting a completely different picture: 'there is very little evidence that ELAS is controlled by the Athens EAM and still less that it is controlled by the KKE [Greek Communist Party]'.[85] While the Foreign Office and the British authorities in Cairo, along with SOE Cairo, wrestled with the problem of ELAS, Myers proposed a means to contain ELAS's ambitions: a national bands agreement.

Efforts towards securing such an agreement had begun during the first half of 1943 but only reached fruition when ELAS finally signed the agreement in July. Myers aimed to establish national, non-political guerrilla bands all over the Greek mountains, all of whom would receive arms from the British mission and would be responsible to a joint headquarters of ELAS and EDES established by the British mission. Under the agreement, 'All guerrillas of one organisation recognise the guerrillas of another organisation', and 'Any organisation or persons are free to raise guerrilla bands in any areas so long as they accept the conditions of the agreement and come under the orders of the Joint GHQ.' Bands would operate within defined areas, although a band could operate in neighbouring areas with the permission of, or in cooperation with, the band based there. Although the agreement was only finally signed on 5 July by Myers, Vasilis Samariniotis for EAM and Sarafis and Aris for ELAS, and then by Zervas of EDES on 12 July, the principles were already in operation during Operation Animals. Yet the national bands agreement had unforeseen effects. The existence of numerous small non-communist bands weakened EDES, when the British should perhaps have encouraged them all to join forces with EDES as a counterweight to ELAS. The agreement failed to limit the power and influence of ELAS, which continued to expand its ranks and territorial reach. ELAS attacked the smaller bands in order to incorporate the members into its ranks. The final problem was political: none of these bands, communist or otherwise, had any loyalty to the king.[86]

In August 1943 Myers made a long-overdue visit to Cairo to apprise the authorities there of the situation in the Greek mountains. He proposed to take with him representatives of ELAS, EDES, and EKKA, and to thrash out an agreement between them and the Greek government-in-exile. Myers had three principal concerns. The first was the danger of civil war between different resistance factions now that a halt had been called to open resistance activity; the second concerned civil administration in the mountains; and the third expressed the foreseen dangers inherent in the immediate post-liberation period when the highly politicized resistance would be expected to hand over its powers to the non-representative Greek government-in-exile on its return to Athens. Myers felt that the solution lay in obtaining recognition by the Greek government-in-exile that the resistance was part of the Greek armed forces, and that representatives of this government should be sent into the mountains to maintain political and administrative contact between the two sides.[87]

The visit was an almost total disaster. Myers had planned on taking with him one representative of each of the main resistance groups but at the last minute ELAS demanded that they should have four representatives and forced Myers to take all four – Andreas Tzimas, Petros Roussos, Kostas Despotopoulos, and Ilias Tsirimokos – while EDES had only Komninos Pyromaglou and EKKA George Kartalis. Hugh Dalton wrote in his diary: 'It seems that SOE has been extracting the wrong sort of Greeks from Greece, contrary to the desires of our High Command.'[88] Myers noted that the ELAS delegation went straight to the heart of the political problem as they saw it, overriding the earlier agreed plan of first gaining military recognition for the guerrilla bands. ELAS demanded that the king should not return to Greece until a post-war plebiscite had shown a majority in favour of his return. This demand exposed the separate lines along which SOE's policy and that of the Foreign Office had been travelling. In the eyes of the Foreign Office, as represented by Rex Leeper, the British ambassador to the Greek government-in-exile, British policy was that:

> But for the King it would have been impossible to maintain any Greek Government abroad, and had no Government been ready to enter Athens when the Germans left, there would have been nothing to stop the seizure of power by the Communists.[89]

Churchill was giving his full support to George II and the government-in-exile. Myers, on the other hand, represented the SOE view to the Greek king. Myers warned him that should he remain determined to return to Athens without any evidence of popular support, then ELAS would abandon the national bands agreement, while Zervas and EDES would continue to stand by the king, and civil war would then be inevitable.[90]

The delegation was not treated well in Cairo. Leeper later denied that he had even known it was coming (which was not true), in order to explain why he had not warned the government-in-exile. Although the delegation spent a month in Cairo, little of any value was settled. Myers was sent to London to present his report. There he learned that he and SOE were being widely blamed for the conflict between the resistance and the government-in-exile. As an SOE staff officer, Bickham Sweet-Escott, later commented:

> The Foreign Office would blame SOE for compromising British policy by making undesirable friends. The only reply SOE could make was that the Chiefs of Staff and later on the commanders in the field had told SOE to produce certain results, and supporting these undesirable friends was the only way in which these results could be produced ... SOE thus got the worst of both worlds.[91]

Myers had expected to return to Greece but his place at the head of the British Military Mission was taken by Woodhouse. The delegation itself returned to Greece on the night of 16–17 September. The delegates were absolutely convinced that the British would impose George II on the country regardless of the wishes of the population. Therefore, it seemed to them, as was borne out later, that the battle now was less one of resistance to the occupiers and more of a civil war for power after liberation. Yet their return to Greece coincided with a turning point in the war. Italy had just surrendered, the nature of the occupation in Greece had consequently been altered, and there was much work to be done before liberation – both resistance and civil war concurrently.[92]

The island of Crete is a microcosm of the dilemmas of Greek resistance. Fear of an Allied invasion meant that Crete was held in 1943 by a disproportionately high Axis garrison of 75,000 men controlling a population of only 400,000 Cretans. Crete was in many ways a very suitable terrain for resistance. There was only one main road on the island from Heraklion in the east running through Rethymno to Canea in the west. The south coast was virtually uninhabited, and in between there were several mountain ranges whose network of intersecting valleys enabled the British missions to evade Axis search parties.

British interest in the island had at first focused on the evacuation of Allied soldiers left behind during the withdrawal of June 1941, and then on the collection of intelligence on supplies to the Afrika Korps. An early Cretan resister, Andreas Papadakis, proved to be extremely helpful to the British in achieving both these two aims, but the British, and, in particular his main contact, Xan Fielding, soon tired of him:

> But his gestures of selfless patriotism, his quixotic plans for the freedom of Crete, were largely prompted by a personal ambition so vainglorious that he scarcely bothered to conceal it. He had set himself up as the head of a 'Supreme Liberation Committee', unrecognised by anyone except its four members, all of whom had been elected by himself.

Papadakis was clearly more interested in establishing a position for himself in post-liberation Crete than in organizing resistance against the occupation. This might not have mattered so much had it not been for the fact that Papadakis controlled the first landing grounds for supplies which he then kept for himself. By mid-1942 the British abandoned all efforts to control Papadakis and he was evacuated to Egypt in August.[93]

A far more useful contact was established by Fielding in the person of the sixty-year-old mayor of Canea, Nikolaos Skoulas, on 1 April 1942.

The British found no shortage of Cretans willing to raise armed bands but they needed a respected politician to draw them together and Skoulas was prepared to assist. With British support, Skoulas set up a new nationalist resistance group, EOK, which was effective in uniting all non-communist resistance groups. This step was essential because the tentacles of EAM-ELAS had spread into Crete under the leadership of General Emmanuel Mandakas, who built up his strength in western Crete and around Heraklion and had recruited a major guerrilla leader, Manoli Bandouvas, active in eastern Crete, to his cause. The communists demonstrated their independence by calling a pan-Cretan conference at Karines in April 1943 from which all British officers were excluded. This meeting in fact achieved nothing other than voicing anti-British sentiments. At the same time Mandakas contacted Fielding to demand supplies of weapons and recognition by Middle East Command that he was the official resistance leader on Crete: Fielding refused both demands. The threat posed by the communists was largely offset by the pan-Cretan meeting summoned by EOK at Prines on 15 June 1943. This established a political and military command, a sort of government-in-waiting, across the four main provinces of Crete. Skoulas was soon forced to flee to the mountains as the Germans closed in on him. Nationalist and British interests were, however, served by Major Christos Tsiphakis who succeeded in combining the resistance forces of republicans and monarchists under the EOK umbrella.[94]

The tragedy of the Cretan resistance in this period was that it did not matter. A significant number of British agents were despatched to the island to foster resistance for little purpose and operated in extremely difficult conditions, as reported by Patrick Leigh Fermor in April 1943:

> On looking back, my [first] six months seem to have been one long string of battery troubles, faulty [radio] sets, difficulties about transport, rain, arrests, hide and seek with the Huns, lack of cash, flights at a moment's notice, false alarms, wicked treks over the mountains, laden like a mule, fright among one's collaborators, treachery, and friends getting shot.[95]

There was little purpose in any of this. The British agents on the island supposed in all good faith that the Allies intended to invade Crete at some point, but no such plans were ever made. When Fielding learned this on a visit to Cairo he voiced his opinion: 'This was a bitter disappointment after the dreams I had cherished of a glorious internal uprising supported by a British invasion, for which every patriot in the island was still preparing.'[96] Such was his discomfort at British bad faith that he applied for a transfer to SOE in France. For the British high command, resistance on Crete served two functions: intelligence, and the retention of a large German garrison whose soldiers could not be used elsewhere against the Allies. Little attention was paid to the significant losses suffered by the Cretans as a result of resistance, whether this was organized by the agents on the island or by raids mounted from outside. Leigh Fermor voiced his concerns after British raids on the airfield at Kastelli and a petrol dump at Peza, using Cretans as guides, had led to the mass execution of hostages and the widespread burning of villages: 'I hope the service of this activity to our general strategy has been high, because here it has caused much havoc to morale and caused much anti-British feeling.'[97] These raids led to the Germans replacing the largely conciliatory commander of Crete, General Alexander Andrae, with General Friedrich-Wilhelm Müller, who soon earned the sobriquet of the 'Butcher of Crete'.

On 1 August 1943 the Italian high command reported the following disposition of its forces: 213,000 in Greece and Crete; 55,000 in the Aegean Islands; 108,000 in Albania; 71,000 in Montenegro; and 225,000 in Croatia, Bosnia-Herzegovina, Slovenia, and Dalmatia.[98] On 8 September 1943 it became known that Italy had concluded an armistice with the Allies. The question now was whether the Germans or the resistance forces would fill the gap, and which resistance movements would secure the most weapons from the surrendering Italians.

PART THREE

Resistance in Action

19
The Italian Surrender

On the night of 14 August 1943 a young SOE agent, Dick Mallaby, was parachuted into Lake Como to act as the radio operator for a resistance group in northern Italy. He was dropped by an RAF squadron on its way to bomb industrial targets around Milan but, as the British SOE representative in Switzerland, Jock McCaffery, later wrote:

> It looked a fine cover plan on paper. But first of all there was bright moonlight, and secondly many people living on the shores of the lake had the habit of turning out to see the Milan bombings as if it was a fireworks display. Dick and his parachute therefore floated down to the water before a large and fascinated audience.[1]

Mallaby was captured before his dinghy reached the shore and was thrown into prison. His story would have remained a footnote in the history of SOE had it not been for the intrigues and secrecy surrounding Italy's surrender to the Allies: Mallaby's skills as a radio operator became of vital use in the negotiations between the Italian authorities in Rome and the Allied command in Algiers.[2] It is necessary to go into some detail about the armistice negotiations and the surrender of Italy to the Allies because the fundamental misconceptions held by all parties, and the misunderstandings between them, provide the key to understanding why an Italian resistance became necessary at all, how it was formed, how it operated, and what contribution it made to the Allied campaign in Italy.

Italy had not had a good war. In September 1939 Mussolini had explained to Hitler that Italy was not yet ready to join in the war that her Axis partner had just launched. In June 1940 he took the opportunity offered by the rapid conquest of France by his German ally to declare war on Britain and France. Thereafter Italian forces were overstretched. In October 1940 Mussolini launched the disastrous campaign to conquer Greece; in July 1941 he despatched Italian forces to work alongside the Germans in the invasion of the Soviet Union; Italian forces also suffered a series of mishaps in the Western Desert and struggled to control their area of occupation in the Balkans. At home there were food shortages and the Allies bombed the industrial cities of northern Italy, particularly Turin and Milan. Discontent was becoming more overt, and in March 1943 there was a series of widespread strikes across the cities in Piedmont and Lombardy in northern Italy. Even the Fascist Party, in power for twenty years, recognized the unpopularity of the regime, and it focused its attention on the figure of the Italian dictator, Mussolini.[3]

On 10 July 1943 the Allies invaded Sicily and, after a hard-fought campaign, the first American troops entered the capital, Palermo, on 22 July. Two days later the Fascist Grand Council in Rome met for the first time since September 1939. Count Dino Grandi proposed a motion for a return to a constitutional monarchy and a democratic parliament, and after a long debate the motion was carried by nineteen votes to seven. The common goal of those voting for Grandi's motion was to preserve the Fascist revolution and to safeguard the monarchy. On 25 July, the day after this meeting, King Victor Emmanuel III made the momentous decision to sack Mussolini and have him arrested.* Marshal Pietro Badoglio was appointed the new prime minister of Italy. Mussolini's fall from power was greeted with widespread elation in Italy, and the Italian people were convinced that it meant the end to the war. This was clearly not the case: as Badoglio's first speech as prime minister made clear, the war would go on. Thus began the so-called '45 Days' between the fall of Mussolini and the announcement of the armistice.[4]

The Badoglio government did want to take Italy out of the war, but the overriding question was how it could do so without triggering a German occupation. As General Eisenhower wrote later: 'Then began a series of negotiations, secret communications, clandestine journeys by secret agents, and frequent meetings in hidden places that, if encountered in the fictional world, would have been scorned as incredible melodrama.'[5] This was no exaggeration. The first approach was made by the new Italian counsellor to Lisbon, the Marquis D'Ayeta, to the British ambassador there, Ronald Campbell, on 3 August. This was swiftly followed by another move, this time by an Italian diplomat, Alberto Berio, to the British representative in Tangier. Both these approaches had been authorized by Badoglio. The negotiations only really got going after the arrival in Lisbon of General

* Mussolini was taken to Campo Imperatore in Abruzzo in the Apennines from where he was rescued by a force of German paratroopers led by Otto Skorzeny on 12 September 1943 and taken to Germany.

Giuseppe Castellano, the emissary of General Vittorio Ambrosio, the Italian chief of the general staff, on 12 August. After consultations with Churchill and Roosevelt, two Allied representatives, General Walter Bedell Smith for the Americans, and General Kenneth Strong for the British, were authorized to open negotiations with Castellano, and these began on 19 August. What Castellano stated had not been authorized by his government, but it represented what the Italian general staff wanted: namely that the Italian government sought to transfer to the Allied side and that the Italian Army would then collaborate actively with the Allies against the Germans. If this was deemed acceptable and desirable, then Italy would surrender unconditionally to the Allies. Castellano returned to Rome on 27 August carrying the radio that Mallaby would use to conduct further negotiations.[6]

The Allies were clearly interested in the opportunity to knock Italy out of the war. If Italy pulled out, the Germans would be forced to send more men to the Balkans to replace them. These men would have to come from two fronts: the Eastern Front, where the battle of Kursk was reaching its climax, and northern France, which the Allies planned to invade. Moreover, if German troops were despatched to Italy to occupy the country then this would also serve Allied purposes by further overextending German resources. It also raised the prospect of an Allied campaign in Italy. This was viewed differently by the two western Allies: Churchill saw a campaign in Italy as linked to the prospect of opening up a new front in the Balkans, which would prevent a Soviet takeover of the region; Roosevelt, however, saw (and would continue to see) the campaign in Italy as a sideshow to the invasion of northern France. Both Allies agreed that Italy must surrender unconditionally, a general policy which had been announced by Roosevelt at the Casablanca Conference in January 1943. Consequently, two armistice documents were drawn up to speed up the process: the short one focused solely on the military details of the Italian surrender; the long version contained political, economic, and financial provisions for the proposed Allied occupation of Italy.

The Badoglio government entered into the negotiations with the Allies fearful that at any moment the Germans would get wind of what was going on and occupy their country before the Allies had arrived in force. They had good reason for their fears. On 19 July, Mussolini and Hitler had met at Feltre in northern Italy, and Hitler had been struck by the degree of panic emanating from Mussolini and his entourage following the first Allied bombing that day of the rail yards near Rome. Hitler immediately ordered plans to be drawn up for Operation Achse, the German takeover of Italian positions throughout the Balkans and the despatch of additional

German divisions to parts of Italy, north of Rome. These were to be stationed near Italian formations and to disarm them in case of the Italian surrender. By the middle of August there were at least eight German divisions in Italy and more men were flooding through the Brenner Pass every day. Both the Italians and the Allies were operating under the fundamental misconception that the Germans would withdraw to the Apennines in the north as soon as the Allies landed. But the Germans had no intention of doing so. They might withdraw from southern Italy if the Allies landed in force, but holding central and northern Italy would allow them to establish a Fascist government in the north and to continue to exploit Italy's industrial resources and keep the Allies out of the Balkans.[7]

At the end of August the negotiations between the Badoglio government and the Allies were faltering over the means of achieving the Italian withdrawal from the war. The Italians so feared a German invasion that they wanted to postpone the signature of the armistice until the Allies had landed fifteen divisions north of Rome. The Allies, on the other hand, demanded that the armistice should be signed before the landing, which was scheduled to use fewer divisions than the Italians expected. The Allies also made it clear that the landing would take place in the south. Rome was to be defended by the Italians, assisted by the United States 82nd Airborne Division, which would land on airfields twenty-five miles north-west of Rome. It was the Italians' task to keep those airfields open for this landing, and the Allies believed that the six Italian divisions in the neighbourhood of Rome should be ample to defend the airfields from the two nearby German divisions. Castellano was never given a date when the armistice would be announced, nor the dates of the Allied landings in Italy. The Badoglio government therefore knew in advance that both events were at the discretion of the Allies, but nonetheless authorized Castellano to sign the short armistice on 3 September. That same day two British divisions landed on the Italian mainland at Calabria, across the Messina Straits from Sicily.[8]

Fear of the Germans now totally paralysed the actions of the Italian government and military. Although they later concealed the evidence of their deliberations, it is now known that on 6 September the Italians had reached the decision not to defend Rome against the Germans and had begun making plans for the government and the king to flee the capital. Therefore when, on 7 September, General Maxwell Taylor reached Rome to view the preparations made for the reception of his airborne division, he found that none had been made. Indeed, it appeared that the Italians were withdrawing their troops to the south of Rome to cover the possible evacuation of the king and his government: most notably, General

Giacomo Carboni's motorized troops were moved to Tivoli, thirty kilometres to the east. A furious Taylor ordered that Badoglio should be dragged from his bed to explain the lack of preparation. Badoglio could only plead for the postponement both of the announcement of the armistice and of the airborne landing. Taylor's orders cancelling the airborne landing reached the force shortly before take-off.[9]

Taylor informed Badoglio that the armistice would be announced on 8 September at 6.30 p.m. During the night of 8–9 September the Italian supreme command broadcast a misleading order to its army: 'Consequently, all hostilities against Anglo-American forces by Italian forces, everywhere, must stop. Italian forces, however, will resist any eventual attack coming from any other source.' It was not clear what form this resistance should take if the Germans attacked. On 9 September the main Allied invasion force of eight divisions and two brigades landed at Salerno in the south. That morning the king and his government left Rome for the Adriatic port of Pescara, from where they were taken by ship south to Brindisi, which was behind Allied lines. The Italian failure to defend Rome meant that Field Marshal Albert Kesselring ordered his troops into the city. Rome would remain occupied for the next nine months.[10]

The immediate political consequences of the failure to hold Rome were clear: the Allies would have to continue to deal with the Badoglio government and the king, even if neither Churchill nor Roosevelt was happy with this. Badoglio, in particular, was viewed with deep suspicion because of his record. He had supported General Graziani's atrocities in Libya during the late 1920s, had participated in the Ethiopian campaign in 1935, and was deeply implicated in the Fascist regime. On the other hand he had resigned as chief of the supreme general staff after the disastrous Greek campaign in 1940 and was therefore seen as untainted by later Italian military failures and the brutal occupation of the Balkans.

The Badoglio government immediately disbanded the most obvious Fascist government organs, but the emphasis was placed on ensuring a stable changeover from Mussolini's dictatorship by keeping most of the administration in the same hands. Political party activity remained curtailed, which limited the ability of the anti-Fascists to build up support: no anti-Fascist was invited to join the Badoglio government. Political prisoners were released from prison, with the exception of the communists and anarchists. The Allies may not have liked this situation but felt that it was important to keep the king on his throne, despite his being discredited by his earlier support for Mussolini, in order to give the Italian people someone to rally around, and to lessen the impression that Italy was now totally at the mercy of the Allies and the Germans.[11] No one expected it to take so long to liberate Rome, and the nine-month interregnum before Rome was taken, and a more representative government under Ivanoe Bonomi was installed, created political tensions which would take some time to resolve.

The secrecy preceding the announcement of the armistice caused immense confusion for the Italian armed forces. The air force and navy appear to have received some warning and were consequently able to move most of their resources to Allied bases before the Germans moved in. The situation for the army, however, was disastrous. Directives for opposing the Germans had been drawn up by the army supreme command in the days preceding the announcement of the armistice and despatched to the commands in Italy, but not to those in the Balkans or the Aegean Islands. Yet after 8 September, when army commanders in Italy asked whether the directives should be implemented, there was no one left in Rome to answer their queries.[12]

The consequences in the Balkans will be considered in a later chapter. On the mainland the initiative rested with individual commanders, none of whom appeared to be in charge. An Italian soldier described the situation:

> And then they could not even give us any clear orders. There was a flood of orders, but each one was different or the opposite of the others. Resist the Germans; don't fire on the Germans; don't let the Germans disarm you; kill the Germans; lay down your weapons; don't give up your weapons.[13]

When the Germans tried to disarm the Italian forces, there was some resistance in the north in Milan and in the surrounding area at Como and Varese. There was more resistance in the area close to the north-eastern frontier, where the existing Italian garrisons had been reinforced during 1943 by Alpini soldiers returning from the Soviet Union for reorganization. These Alpini soldiers knew a great deal about German treatment of the people they occupied and were prepared to resist: many formed the first partisan units in the region. Furthermore, Hitler ordered the annexation of the Alto Adige or South Tyrol, and Venezia Giulia, thereby giving the Italian soldiers even more reason to fight back.

Further south, there were isolated examples of resistance to disarmament in the Abruzzi region and in the Marche, the area near Rome. In Rome itself there was serious fighting at Porta San Paolo between the Italian Army, with light tanks, who were joined by civilians, and the incoming German Army. Little action by the Italian Army took place in the southernmost provinces of Campania, Calabria, and Puglia. A notable exception was a successful action mounted by General Nicola Bellomo's forces, which prevented the Germans from destroying the port facilities in Bari and held the port until the arrival of the Canadian Army. Generals Riccardo Pentimalli, Ettore Del Tetto, and Ettore Marino were expected to defend Naples, for which they had sufficient forces and armaments, but they chose instead to abandon the city to the Germans.[14]

Italian soldiers faced three choices: disband and try to get to their homes; accept disarmament at the hands of the Germans and be transported to labour camps in Germany; or form partisan groups to fight the Germans. A tiny minority chose to join the Germans and fight alongside them or join the new forces being raised by Mussolini's RSI regime.* In Turin civilians tried to encourage the soldiers to go home, but found that 'the soldiers were looking at them, tentative and uncertain' and preferred to do nothing but wait on events.[15] Some soldiers made the conscious decision to remain neutral in the face of rapidly changing events: 'I won't fight on their [German] side – nor, since we have been guilty of betrayal, against them, although I think them disgusting.'[16] The Church failed to fill the vacuum left by the army command, as is illustrated by a letter on 25 September from the bishop of Cremona, Giovanni Cazzani, to the archbishop of Milan, Alfredo Schuster, in which Cazzani claimed that he assumed 'no responsibility for advising a definite line of action. I tell them the possible dangers of one or the other path, and that they are to do as they wish'.[17] An estimated 650,000–700,000 Italian soldiers were captured, disarmed and transported to Germany by the Germans; at least 20,000 were killed by the Germans either in combat or after surrendering. The Germans gained almost 10,000 guns of all types, 15,500 vehicles, and 970 tanks and self-propelled guns.[18]

Many Italian soldiers who chose to fight the Germans fled to the hills and mountains and began to form partisan bands. They were joined by the other group which was suffering the consequences of the confusion in the immediate aftermath of the announcement of the armistice: the Allied POWs.

At the time of the armistice there were an estimated 80,000 Allied POWs being held in seventy-two main camps and numerous sub-camps across mainland Italy.[19] Many of these camps had secret radio communication with the Allied organization responsible for POWs, MI9. The initial orders broadcast to the commanding officers in the camps were that: 'In the event of an Allied invasion of Italy, Officers Commanding prison camps will ensure that POWs remain within camp' – that is, that they should not

* Mussolini's *Repubblica Sociale Italiana* (RSI) was set up in Salò in northern Italy under German supervision on 23 September 1943.

attempt mass breakouts which might lead to harsh reprisals. The representative of MI9 in Cairo was Lieutenant Colonel Tony Simonds, and he drew up a different set of orders: 'Senior officers and NCOs are to organise all prisoners into small groups; each group to be self-contained as to rations and where possible with maps and compasses ... All such groups are to make their way to the nearest point of the eastern coast of Italy, and to hide up to await evacuation.' His superior, Norman Crockatt, initially refused to sanction such a risky project, but on 8 September he changed his mind, and some camps received the revised orders; but not all.[20] The confusion surrounding the conduct of the POWs can be partly explained by the initially small size of the staff operating under Simonds: at the time of the armistice it consisted of himself and two other men. By the end of September 1943 there was a headquarters staff of twelve, and seven groups of parachutists were being readied to be dropped to gather and lead escaped POWs to Allied lines.[21]

These conflicting orders unsurprisingly caused chaos in the POW camps. As many as 30,000 POWs stayed put and were promptly caught by the Germans and sent to camps in Germany. Many others escaped in small groups, and by the end of 1943 around 2,000 had reached the safety of Allied lines, mostly without the assistance of MI9. For those rank-and-file POWs who had been in small work camps, escape was relatively easy: they carried on working in the countryside, but now lived with the peasants instead of in the camps and wore civilian clothing. Many of them made no further effort to reach Allied lines but stayed where they were and waited for the Allies to reach them. The peasants were happy to have them since they received free labour in exchange for supplying shelter and sustenance.

The Germans issued proclamations warning of the dire consequences of sheltering escaped POWs. In the middle of October 1943 these were: 'For harbouring or helping escaped prisoners of war: death; For making contacts with them: hard labour for life ...' Leaflets were dropped in November 1943 calling upon the POWs to surrender to the Italian authorities and be re-incarcerated, warning that extreme hunger awaited them if they attempted to continue struggling to survive as winter approached; or even execution if they had joined a partisan band. The Italians were offered 5,000 lire for betraying an Allied escaper, which was raised at the end of November to two months' rations of food and tobacco in addition. The Badoglio government offered a similar reward for sheltering an escaper and keeping him safe. About two-thirds of the escaped POWs were captured by the end of 1943, many having surrendered themselves because they were unable to cope with life as fugitives, others having been betrayed by the peasants for the rewards on offer. In all, between 1,500 and 2,000 escapers were betrayed by Italians for rewards. At least 300 were murdered by the armed forces and militias of Mussolini's RSI and by bounty hunters operating in the Marche.[22]

The Italians set up organizations to assist the POWs. In Milan the *Comitato di Liberazione Nazionale*, CLN (Committee for National Liberation), formed the *Ufficio Assistenza Prigionieri di Guerra Alleati* immediately after the armistice specifically to assist POWs to reach Switzerland. The managing director of the American Standard Electric Corporation factory in Milan, Giuseppe Bacciagaluppi, was tasked by the head of the Milan CLN, Ferruccio Parri, to set up an escape line to Switzerland. This ran up the Cavargna valley to the village of Bogno at the head of the Swiss Val Colla and across the border to Lugano. One young Italian woman agreed to act as a guide on the understanding that her husband would be released from his POW camp in India. Bacciagaluppi was arrested on 3 April 1944 and later escaped and reached Switzerland but he was replaced by Sergio Kasman and Dario Tarantini, neither of whom survived the war. By the time of Bacciagaluppi's arrest, his organization had helped over 1,800 Allied POWs reach Switzerland, where they were interned. They made up just over half the eventual figure of Allied POWs who reached Swiss sanctuary.[23]

MI9 despatched agents across Italy to round up the POWs and to arrange for them to be collected from various fishing ports and harbours. Most notably, three large boatloads of POWs were collected in the Marche region in December 1943, and March and April 1944. Some of these rescues included high-ranking officers. For example, just before Christmas 1943 Generals Richard O'Connor and Philip Neame and Air Vice-Marshal Owen Boyd reached the safety of Allied lines at Termoli. They were followed by a party of five brigadiers and eleven other escapers in the middle of May 1944. Many frustrations dogged MI9's activities: sometimes the Royal Navy failed to arrive at the rendezvous, and frequently the POWs were less than eager to be returned behind Allied lines. Indeed, it has been estimated that the equivalent of two to three divisions of escaped POWs apparently refused the assistance offered by MI9, and preferred to remain working alongside the peasants or to join partisan bands.[24]

One British escaper, Major Sam Derry, reached Rome in November 1943, and found that there was already an organization in the city specifically set up to assist Allied POWs. This Council of Three was formed by Monsignor Hugh O'Flaherty, an Irish priest at the Vatican who had no great love of the British but despised the Germans more after witnessing the round-up of the Roman Jews; Count Sarsfield Salazar, a member of the

Swiss legation; and John May, the butler to Sir D'Arcy Osborne, who was the British minister at the Vatican. Derry lived in Osborne's apartment in the Vatican and was tasked with finding hiding places for POWs reaching Rome and to arrange for supplies to be dropped to those located in the surrounding areas. He was soon joined by two able assistants, Lieutenants John Furman and Bill Simpson. The Vatican denied all knowledge of the organization being run from its precinct, although it did supply the organization with funds. By the time of Rome's liberation there were just under 4,000 Allied escapers, mostly British, in the care of the Rome organization.[25]

Assistance to POWs on the run was often the first act of resistance mounted by the Italian people, just as it had been elsewhere in Europe. Their motivations varied from: 'I did not help them because they were British but because I am a Christian woman and they too are Christians', to definite pro-British sentiments.[26] These could be damaged by events outside Derry's control, notably the bombing of the monastery of Monte Cassino in February 1944. Derry later wrote:

> The raid was a psychological disaster from the point of view of the Rome Organisation. All our Italian helpers were good Catholics, who had always thought of Allied bombing as being directed against specific military objectives, although they appreciated that damage might be done to other property in the process, and they could not understand how a Catholic monastery, still occupied by its monks, could be a military objective.[27]

Derry operated on the principle that it was best to move the escapers out of Rome quickly because of a lack of places to hide them and the extra cost of feeding them just when Rome was suffering from food shortages. One location used for a concentration of escapers was 'a valley nestling in a curve of hills, miles away from the city and trunk roads, admirably suited for air supply drops, well-equipped with farms, where escapers could be billeted, yet with hills providing hiding places in emergency'. Unfortunately, the valley was bisected by a railway viaduct which SOE viewed as a prime target. The successful demolition of the viaduct brought down the wrath of the Germans on the area and in the subsequent round-ups a significant number of former Allied POWs were caught. The dangers to the Rome Organization increased as the Allied front approached and the resistance became more active, leading to a rise in German repressive measures.[28]

Some of the escaped POWs joined the partisan bands that were springing up across northern Italy. Stuart Hood and his party were heading for the Apennines and joined the partisans simply to survive:

> We felt a net of danger tightening round us. We wanted arms to defend ourselves. We guessed that movement would be increasingly difficult now that the snows were spreading. We wanted a secure base for the winter. With luck the partisans would give us both.

He found a band which had few weapons and even less ammunition but possessed the will to continue to fight, and so he remained with the partisans for the remainder of the war.[29] Gordon Lett headed from his prison camp towards the western seaboard of Italy in the hope of reaching Corsica, which was now in French hands, having been captured from the Germans by the Free French at the end of September 1943. He arrived in the Rossano area in the Tuscan-Ligurian Apennines where he found an international medley of escaped POWs and escaped forced labourers. He was asked by the local resistance to form these men into an International Brigade. To start with he was given a few old Italian rifles, some hand grenades, and a supply of flour, tinned meat, and potatoes.[30] The activities of this brigade will be covered later.

When the Germans occupied Rome the city immediately became the centre of the German command: Kesselring was commander-in-chief of all German armed forces in Italy; Karl Wolff headed the SS; General Kurt Mälzer was appointed commandant of Rome; and Ernst von Weizsäcker was the German ambassador to the Holy See. Accompanying the German command and diplomats were the German security forces: Lieutenant Colonel Herbert Kappler commanded the Gestapo in Rome and worked alongside Eugen Dollmann, who was Himmler's personal representative.[31] In October they were joined by Hauptsturmführer Theodor Dannecker with a detachment of crack troops.

The German occupation posed an immediate threat to the Papacy. A precedent had been set during the Napoleonic Wars when French troops had taken Pope Pius VI prisoner in February 1798 and transported him to France where he died. The current Pope, Pius XII, feared that the Germans would invade the Vatican, and much of the Vatican's response to events during the German occupation was tempered by the priority to preserve the liberty of the Pope. The fears were not entirely groundless: Hitler and Wolff did seriously discuss plans to occupy the Vatican and to kidnap the Pope. There was also the question of the extraterritorial status of the many properties owned by the Vatican which were scattered across Rome. The Gestapo and the new Fascist Special Police Unit, known as *Banda Koch* after its commander, the half-German and half-Italian Pietro Koch, tested the waters in December 1943 by launching raids against three properties which were owned by the Vatican but did not possess extraterritorial status: the Seminario Lombardo, the Pontifical Institute of Oriental Studies, and the Russicum Institute. All three were suspected, with good reason, to be harbouring anti-Fascists, military officers, Jews, and Italians hiding from military or labour service call-ups. For the time being properties with actual extraterritorial status, such as the Seminario Romano which harboured most of the leadership of the Rome CLN, including Bonomi, were left alone.[32]

The Jews of Rome were clearly threatened by the German occupation. By now the entire world knew that round-ups led to transport to the east, which in turn led to extermination. The history of the Jews in Rome bears a close resemblance to that of other Jewish communities elsewhere in western Europe. Under Fascism, the Jews had been compulsorily registered and were ruled over by a Jewish organization led by two Jewish former Fascists, Ugo Foà and Dante Almansi, who had been forced to resign their posts in the judiciary and police under the 1938 racial laws. Like the leaders of other Jewish communities they believed that they had nothing to fear from the Germans. The Chief Rabbi in Rome, Israel Zolli, was more sceptical, and he urged the two leaders to order the dispersal of the Jews from Rome. Other prominent Jews such as Renzo Levi and Settimio Sorani, who had contacts with Jewish refugee agencies and the International Red Cross, believed the stories of the Holocaust. They and Zolli all went into hiding.[33]

The first move by the Germans was made by Kappler on 26 September 1943, when he demanded a ransom of 50 kilograms of gold from the Jewish community. This lulled the community leaders into a false sense of security. The amount was raised easily and the Vatican, when approached for a loan, responded favourably.[34] But on 16 October, after Dannecker's arrival, the round-ups of Rome's Jewish community began. The response of the Italians was to hide as many Jews as they could. Kappler reported:

> The behaviour of the Italian people was outright passive resistance which in many individual cases amounted to active resistance . . . German police were breaking into some homes, attempts to hide Jews in nearby apartments were observed, and it is believed in many cases successful. The anti-semitic section of the population was nowhere to be seen . . . only a great mass of people who in some individual cases even tried to cut off the police from the Jews . . .[35]

Many monasteries and convents took in fugitive Jews but others closed their doors to them. The round-ups yielded 1,259 Jews, of whom 1,023 were eventually deported on 18 October, and only fifteen survived the war and returned home. Further Jew-hunts in other northern cities produced a further 3,000 over the next two months. Again, just as elsewhere in

Europe, the refugee Jews proved the most vulnerable, and 25 per cent of them were deported compared to only 8 per cent of the Italian Jews.[36]

During November and December, Dannecker extended his operations to the cities in northern Italy, and various ad hoc rescue groups sprang up to thwart his plans. One of the most active men in this respect was Giovanni Palatucci, the police commissioner for foreigners in Fiume. He first destroyed the files and lists of Italian and non-Italian Jews, and then supplied the Jews with false identity papers. He organized the transport of Jews to the south where his uncles Giuseppe Palatucci, the bishop of Compagna, and Alfonso Palatucci, the Provincial of the Franciscan Order in Puglia, had established havens for Jews behind the Allied lines. His initiative saved an estimated 5,000 Jews before he was arrested in September 1944 and transported to Dachau, where he died. A former camp for British POWs at Servigliano in the province of Ascoli Piceno became a transit camp for the Jews. In early May 1944 the partisans heard that the Jews were about to be moved to camps in the east and radioed the news back to the Allies. The RAF obligingly mounted an air raid which breached the walls of the camp and enabled most of the Jews to escape into the care of the partisans.[37]

It has been argued that the Pope could have done more to save Italian Jews, especially those from Rome who were deported from their homes which lay just outside his windows. He has been castigated for not issuing any kind of statement which specifically referred to the deportation of the Jews. Instead, the Pope confined himself to a very general condemnation of all persecution. Defenders of Pius XII have argued that the Pope did urge Catholic institutions to harbour Jews. The research done in this area suggests, however, that papal leadership was notable by its absence, and the offers of shelter in Vatican extraterritorial institutions to Jews and anti-Fascist politicians were the initiatives and responsibilities of lower-ranked clergy. Around fifty-five monasteries and 100 convents harboured Jews. Some were even housed in the Vatican itself, working in the library and museums or enrolled in the Palatine Guard.[38]

The southern city of Naples had been vital for the supply of Axis troops in North Africa. This fact had led to a high number of German troops being present in the city, and to 120 Allied air raids which had killed 22,000 people. The announcement of the armistice and the Allied landings had taken both the Italians and Germans in Naples by surprise. The first instinct of the German commandant in the city, Colonel Walter Scholl, was to withdraw from Naples, but as soon as it was discovered that the Italians had no intention of defending the city against the Allies, Hitler ordered

Scholl to remain in place. The Italian units withdrew, and the Italian resistance that sprang up in the resultant vacuum immediately launched attacks on the Germans. In reprisal the Germans set fire to the university and began a policy of scorched earth – the destruction of the port facilities, aqueducts, and electrical plants. The Italians successfully resisted the German efforts to blow up the bridge over Via Sanità, a major road artery connecting much of the city to the Capodimonte area.[39] The turning point came on 25 September 1943 when the Germans announced that 30,000 men had to report for compulsory labour service and that 200,000 people living near the port had to leave their homes immediately.

Naples then became the first city in occupied Europe to stage an uprising against the German occupation – the famous 'Four Days'. The revolt was spontaneous and not in any way planned by any resistance organization. It was waged by various sections of the population – disbanded soldiers and sailors who recovered hidden or overlooked weapons, civilians who used every weapon that came to hand, be it an ancient rifle, a broom or a shovel – all assisted by the Italian police, who looked the other way while the street urchins distributed the weapons and messages around the city. The fighting broke out on 28 November when the Germans were prevented from transporting the first forced-labour contingent to Germany. The first armed action took place in Capodimonte where an anti-aircraft battery was used to prevent a column of German Tiger tanks and armoured vehicles from entering the city. By the next day the fighting had spread throughout the city and the barricades erected by the Italians overnight effectively both prevented German reinforcements from reaching the city and also any possible retreat by Scholl's army. Fighting continued into a third day and by the evening Scholl and the Germans had begun to retreat to the suburb of Marano. Humiliatingly, the Germans had been forced to negotiate their retreat with the Italian Colonel Antonino Tarsia, who agreed to allow the Germans free passage in return for the release of hostages seized by them during the uprising. At around 11 a.m. on 1 October the first Allied jeep preceded a column of the King's Dragoon Guards and entered the city.[40]

The uprising in Naples has been rightly identified as a glorious moment in the history of resistance:

> It was David and Goliath in the twentieth century. Granted that the Neapolitans knew the Allies were close at hand, they still did not wait, supine, to be liberated. They fought back. For the first time in the European war, German officers capitulated to a band of civilians.[41]

Unfortunately, the very success of the Naples uprising had disastrous repercussions elsewhere in Europe. It encouraged resistance leaders to think that such uprisings could be successful and would lead to a German withdrawal. But the conditions prevailing in Naples were exceptional. The city and especially its port were of vital use to the Allies who wanted its capture as soon as possible. The Germans were in danger of being cut off by the Allied advance and would have had to withdraw soon in any case. The Neapolitans were also well armed. None of these conditions would exist in subsequent major uprisings across Europe. From the point of view of the Allies, who were still unsure of how the Italians would react to the armistice, the Allied invasion, and the German occupation, the uprising was an indication of favourable Italian sentiments: 'It is very satisfactory to think that several thousands of volunteers have attacked the Germans. A people's insurrection does more than any speech to show the world where their sympathies lie.'[42] The German scorched-earth policy, which began immediately after the announcement of the armistice and continued during the uprising itself despite the insurgents' efforts to stop the demolitions, demonstrated how brutally the Germans would react when forced to withdraw from cities. Thereafter Allied orders to resistance organizations across Europe would be to make anti-scorch preparations a priority: a policy carried out with varying degrees of success.

A feature of the Italian resistance was the speed with which it became organized. On 9 September 1943 a meeting of representatives of the anti-Fascist parties was held in Rome. Ugo La Malfa and Sergio Fenoaltea represented the Action Party, which had been created after Mussolini's fall from power; Pietro Nenni and Giuseppe Romita the Socialists; Count Cesati the Liberals; Alcide De Gasperi the Christian Democrats; Giorgio Amendola and Mauro Scoccimarro the Communists; and Meuccio Ruini on behalf of Badoglio. They passed a motion stating:

> At a time when Nazism tries to restore in Rome and Italy its fascist ally, antifascist parties are creating a National Liberation Committee to call Italians to struggle and resistance, to restore the place that Italy deserves among free nations ... Today, for the sons of Italy, there is only one position: that of defending peace against the Germans and fascist fifth columnists. To arms!

This established the Rome CLN under the presidency of Bonomi to oversee resistance in the capital. The structure of the Rome CLN was replicated throughout Italy. On 11 September representatives of the anti-Fascist parties met in Milan and established the CLNAI, *Comitato di Liberazione Nazionale Alta Italia*, to cover German-occupied northern Italy. The CLNs needed to appeal to the Italian population who faced three demands for their loyalty: to the semi-Fascist Badoglio government; to Mussolini's RSI;

or to the reborn anti-Fascist parties. All this meant that from its inception the Italian resistance was highly politicized.[43]

The Rome CLN anticipated a swift liberation from the German occupation, and its members were concerned primarily with constructing the base of a future democratic Italy. They advocated *attentisme*, saying that 'the Resistance Movement should take no direct military action or political action against the Nazis until such action was fully sanctioned by the Allies and until it became clear that innocent people would not suffer Nazi and Fascist retaliation'.[44] The communists were, however, in tune with the communist resistance elsewhere in Europe in calling for immediate and constant action against the German and Italian fascists. Their activities will be described below.

In the meantime, before Rome was liberated, the resistance in the city was in an ideal position to provide immediate assistance to the Allies through the provision of intelligence. Colonel Giuseppe Montezemolo had remained in Rome when others from the Italian military command had fled. He changed into civilian clothes, went into hiding, and promptly set up two organizations. One, the *Fronte Militare Clandestino*, was designed to coordinate the armaments and military action of the partisan bands developing in the region of Rome. The core of this 9,000-strong force comprised former soldiers and members of the carabinieri who had escaped the round-up of their colleagues by the Germans on 7 October. Around thirty-two partisan bands were kept supplied and they launched a campaign of sabotage against the German lines of communication, blowing up supply depots, cutting telegraph and telephone lines, and attacking German columns. A major achievement was the destruction of the viaduct of Ariccia to hamper the transport of German troops and supplies to the front.[45]

The second organization was the *Centro Militare Clandestino*. From 10 October 1943 to 24 January 1944 Montezemolo was in constant radio contact with Badoglio, and his regular messages, supplemented by reports carried by couriers, 'represent systematic, precise information about what was happening in Rome and in the other occupied zones . . . the size and nature of enemy forces, on the battle array of the divisions, on the movements of the detachments, on where the ammunition was stockpiled'. Montezemolo was not in direct radio contact with the Allies but two of his colleagues were. Unknown to Montezemolo they used different codes when communicating with him and with the Allies, in case he should be captured and tortured to reveal the code.

OSS came of age through its work with the Italian resistance. On 28 October 1943 an OSS agent, Maurizio Giglio, arrived in Rome to serve as liaison between the CLN and Montezemolo, and to operate the OSS radio station, Radio Vittoria. On the night of 21 January 1944 two further OSS agents were landed and made their way to Rome, Peter Tompkins and Captain André Bourgoin: they would become crucial in the provision of intelligence because of the course of events.[46]

On 22 January 1944 the Allies landed a force at Anzio, south of Rome and 100 kilometres behind German lines, under the command of Major General John Lucas. There is considerable controversy over whether this force could have mounted a swift advance across the Alban Hills and into Rome rather than become, as it did, bogged down in a small bridgehead. The Italian resistance certainly thought that the Anzio force could have done more. Messages were sent over the BBC and through clandestine radio communications:

> The hour has arrived for Rome and all Italians to fight in every possible way and with all forces . . . Sabotage the enemy. Block his roads of retreat. Destroy his communications to the last wire. Strike against him everywhere continuing the fight indefatigably, without thought of political questions, until our troops have arrived. Notify all bands and parties.

By the following day these orders were reversed and an immediate halt was called to the sabotage campaign, but the damage had already been done. Because the resistance was anticipating a swift liberation, security had virtually totally collapsed with predictably disastrous consequences: between 22 and 25 January the Germans and their Italian assistants arrested the two most important resistance leaders in Rome, Montezemolo and General Simone Simoni, as well as leaders of the Action Party and many partisans. Montezemolo's arrest meant his radio link with Badoglio was taken off the air, and Tompkins's Radio Vittoria became the only radio link between Rome and the Allies.[47]

Tompkins was able to continue to supply the Allies with vital intelligence because he had linked up with the intelligence service run by Franco Malfatti, which was formed by members of the Socialist Party. Tompkins was therefore able to report that:

> There were Socialist eyes and ears in practically every office, on every street corner, in the farms and villages between Rome and the beachhead, on the carts and trucks that jogged along the country roads; among the labourers who built the military installations for the Germans; among the fisherfolk and sailors – everywhere in fact that human beings lived and worked, and where the Germans had to pass.

All twelve major roads leading out of Rome were under constant watch and intelligence was radioed to the Allies five times a day. Most importantly, on 29 January Tompkins could report on the projected German counter-offensive against the Anzio bridgehead: the attack from the Alban Hills would be a feint and the main assault would be mounted by the German Parachute Corps against the Allied left flank. The warnings reached the Allied forces in time for appropriate defensive dispositions to be made, and for an air raid to be mounted against the headquarters of the Parachute Corps which paralysed its communications. As Bill Donovan, head of OSS, informed Roosevelt and the Chiefs of Staff: 'OSS might well have saved the bridgehead.'[48]

The principal armed and active resistance units in Rome were known as GAP (*Gruppi di Azione Patriottica*, Patriotic Action Groups): they were founded and organized by Antonello Trombadori. Rome was divided into eight zones with sixteen members in each, and each zone into three or four sectors: arms depots were set up along with bomb-making facilities. GAP was probably dominated by the communists but also contained many members of the Action Party and socialists. The first campaign was mounted against the Italian Fascists and lasted to the end of 1943. For example, on a single day, 16 December 1943, GAP killed the leader of the Fascist militia, bombed the Fascist militia headquarters, and attacked a Fascist patrol. Later that month, assaults began on the Germans themselves with attacks on German personnel and the bombing of targets such as the Hotel Flora, a German administrative headquarters, and restaurants and cinemas used by German troops. The assassination of a German lieutenant colonel yielded his briefcase, which contained the details of all German anti-aircraft artillery batteries around Rome. Much use was made of four-pointed nails which successfully pierced the tyres of German vehicles when placed on the main roads out of Rome. The Germans warned the Italians that 'if these acts of sabotage are repeated very grave measures will be taken against those who live along the roads and in the area where such acts are repeated', and advised them to cooperate with the Germans and to report partisan activity in their vicinity.

The rationale behind the GAP campaign was:

> The Wehrmacht had to be made to understand that they were not the masters of Rome, that they had a hostile population on their hands. We had to attack their supply lines, their vehicles whether parked or in transit to the front and their command posts. They could not be allowed to move through the city with impunity.[49]

The Gappists considered the threat of German reprisals very seriously. They were prepared to risk their lives, and the risk was a real one since the Fascists and Gestapo were able to penetrate their organizations. But the

Germans also arrested perfectly innocent Italians, at least 1,000 of them in early 1944, to hold as hostages.[50]

In March 1944 the whole question of GAP tactics and German reprisals came into question and has remained controversial through one single attack. The German habit of marching troops through the streets of Rome singing loudly infuriated the Gappists. One group decided to mount an attack on 23 March 1944, the twenty-fifth anniversary of the founding of Italian Fascism, against troops from the 3rd Battalion of the SS Bozen, a formation recruited from the disputed border region of South Tyrol, who regularly marched along a narrow street, the Via Rasella. Rosario Bentivegna placed a bomb in a street cleaner's cart and on the signal from one of his associates:

> I lifted the cover of the can that was armed with the TNT and put the pipe bowl to the fuse. There was a lot of ash and it took a while to ignite. Then I heard the sizzle, the perfect-catch sound I'd got to know, and then came that smell of acrid smoke. I put down the cover, took off my own cap and put it on the cart – the signal to all the others that the fuse was lit and in fifty seconds the bomb would blow.[51]

Two further groups of Gappists were in place at either end of the street to block the troops' escape. The bomb exploded and the result was described by one of the soldiers, Konrad Sigmund:

> The explosions . . . there wasn't only one. There were several. We all carried five or six hand grenades on our belts, and many exploded, either because they were hit by fragments, or from the heat that grew out of the explosion. This is how many died.[52]

The explosion killed thirty-three of the SS and also ten Italian civilians, among them six children.

General Mälzer and the head of the Italian police, Pietro Caruso, happened to be in the area when the explosion occurred and they immediately rushed to the scene. Both were enraged by what they witnessed, and Mälzer ordered the immediate arrest of 200 civilians from the street, to be followed by their execution. Unusually perhaps, the SS in Rome, whose troops had been targeted, counselled a more moderate response. The Gestapo chief, Kappler, calmed Mälzer and took charge of the scene. Dollmann telephoned his superior, General Wolff, who contacted Himmler, who ordered the deportation of all civilians from Rome. Hitler was informed and demanded the demolition of the entire quarter of Rome where Via Rasella was located. Kesselring, however, believed firmly that such drastic reprisals would serve only to increase resistance in Rome: he suggested that Italians should be executed on the ratio of 50:1 as was common elsewhere in Europe.[53]

Kappler was ordered to draw up the list of reprisal victims. The problem was that there was an insufficient supply of Italians convicted for partisan or resistance activities in German or Italian prisons. Through the night, Kappler struggled to find enough names. SS Hauptsturmführer Erich Priebke later stated:

> So, a further search was made of the records to see if there were any persons who had not been tried, but had been arrested for being . . . concerned in any outrage against German troops or had been found in possession of firearms and explosives or were leaders of 'underground' movements. These names were added to the list.[54]

There was still a shortfall in the numbers, so Jews who had been arrested and not yet deported were added to the list. The execution site selected was the Ardeatine Caves near Rome. From 2 p.m. on 24 March trucks began arriving at the caves. Kappler described the process:

> As each truck arrived at the cave the persons concerned, always five at a time and each accompanied by an SS man, were led to the end of the cave. All persons had their hands tied behind their backs. At the end of the cave five were made to kneel down together, and at the given order they were shot in the back of the head by the accompanying SS officer.[55]

The executions of the 335 victims, of whom the oldest was seventy-four and the youngest fifteen, were over by 8.30 p.m. and the entrance to the caves was blocked off. Among the victims were the two resistance leaders arrested in January, Simoni and Montezemolo.[56]

The executions at the Ardeatine Caves caused a controversy that continues to this day. The Italians generally appear to have blamed the Gappists for the whole outrage, and to have thought that the perpetrators should have owned up. But as Kappler stated in his 1948 trial: 'For the event in via Rasella I made no request to the population, I had no jurisdiction to do so.' The Germans said nothing publicly until the following day, when they issued a statement announcing the names of the victims and ending with the words: 'The execution of these criminals has already been carried out.'[57] Mussolini was appalled by the German response and ordered the release of all political prisoners not charged with murder so that the Germans could not use them as hostages. The Vatican newspaper, *Osservatore Romano*, published an editorial on 26 March deploring both the massacre and the reprisal, but including the remark:

> We call upon the irresponsible elements to respect human life, which they have no right whatsoever to sacrifice, to respect the innocence of those who

> as a consequence are fatally victimised; from the responsible elements we ask for an awareness of their responsibility, towards themselves, towards the lives they wish to safeguard, towards history and civilisation.[58]

It appeared, therefore, that the Vatican considered the partisans guilty for what had occurred. In contrast, a statement issued by the CLN in the middle of April argued: 'Rome will be avenged . . . The blood of our martyrs must not have flowed in vain', and appealed for an increase in resistance.[59] The BBC described those who had carried out the attack as 'Italian patriots'.[60] The population of Rome itself appears to have been badly frightened by the German excesses, and one partisan, Lucia Ottobrini, commented: 'One of our regrets was that we were unable to turn the piercing pain of the people after the massacre of the Fosse Ardeatine into an impulse of rebellion against those who were its real perpetrators.'[61] It was now unclear how the Roman resistance would respond as the Allies drew closer to the city.

The first partisan bands were ad hoc formations of former Italian soldiers and escaped POWs who, with few weapons, could do little. A feature of the Italian partisan movement as a whole is the speed with which it became organized, and the politicization of the movement. It appeared that every non-Fascist political party sponsored its own partisans: the communists had the Garibaldi formations, the *Giustizia e Libertà* (Justice and Liberty) were loyal to the Action Party, and the socialists fostered the *Brigate Matteotti*. Other bands such as the *Brigate Fiamme Verdi* (Green Flames) were known for their staunch Catholicism. The communist *Bandiera Rossa* specialized in sabotage. It should be noted that none of these groupings catered exclusively for people of a certain political opinion. They contained members of all political persuasions, while the leadership itself tended to be more politicized. In addition, there were also the so-called 'autonomous' bands who had no political loyalties and were determined simply to maintain their independence. One partisan, Eugenio Artom, suggested: 'We are what we are; a complex group of individuals: in part disinterested and sincere and in part political opportunists; in part disoriented soldiers fearful of deportation to Germany and in part motivated by a desire of adventure and loot.'[62] Gordon Lett, who formed the International Brigade in the Rossano valley at the request of the Genoa CLN, noted the effect of politics on the partisan movement. A representative of the Action Party approached him with an offer of much-needed weapons in return for political allegiance: Lett turned him down. Then the Garibaldi bands attempted to penetrate the valley: this did not affect Lett directly, but he observed that the Garibaldi and *Giustizia e Libertà* formations were at loggerheads.[63]

The partisans' urgent requirement for weapons gave the Italian and Allied authorities an opportunity to impose command and control over the Italian partisan movement from the start, had they been ready to do so. Badoglio immediately recognized the potential importance of the partisan bands and from October 1943 to May 1944 his government despatched twenty-six missions northwards, twenty-two to investigate the requirements of the partisans, and two to undertake sabotage campaigns.[64] SOE, however, was caught unprepared and there was a confused state of affairs that left no one in overall command. SOE's J Section was run from London by Cecil Roseberry, but agents were despatched from SOE's Massingham base in Algeria under the command of Douglas Dodds-Parker until the end of September 1943 when a substation was established at Monopoli on the Adriatic coast. In November 1943 a much-needed reorganization took place and subversive operations came under the command of the operations group of 15th Army Group north of the La Spezia–Ravenna line, with operations further south run by Massingham and Allied Force Headquarters.[65]

SOE had met with little success in its efforts to penetrate Italy prior to the surrender in September 1943 because of the efficiency of the Italian state security service, the OVRA, and military intelligence department, SIM. Both SOE and OSS struggled to find suitable Italian recruits for their early operations. SOE scoured the Italian internees in Britain and the Italians in POW camps with little success. It appeared that few Italians had the desire to risk their lives in the cause of their country's liberation.[66] The United States contained a large Italian immigrant population, but OSS discovered that the recruits who came forward had entirely unrealistic expectations of what could be achieved.[67] Jock McCaffery was under the impression that he had recruited a number of agents who had formed resistance cells across northern Italy. It was only after the armistice that he learned to his embarrassment that all of his so-called agents had in fact been run by SIM.[68] Allen Dulles, OSS's representative in Berne, had more luck in establishing contacts with politicians. These paid dividends when, soon after the armistice, Parri of the CLNAI sent a representative, Alberto Damiani, to Switzerland where he met Dulles and McCaffery. Parri himself visited Switzerland in October for discussions, but a difference in strategies rapidly became apparent: he appeared to want to raise an army, whereas OSS and SOE preferred the creation of small sabotage groups to be controlled by Allied officers. Parri then agreed to follow the latter course, since that appeared to hold out the prospect of more immediate supplies of arms. Yet, in December 1943, a list of desired weapons and equipment received from the commander of the Green Flames, General Luigi Masini, was so lengthy that 'as someone remarked at the time, the only thing missing from the list was Montgomery!'[69]

By the end of October 1943 six SOE missions had gone into Italy and during the next six months they were followed by a further eighteen. A training centre for agents had been established in Monopoli, but agents about to be dropped into Italy noted the poor quality of their briefings: 'The staff there knew virtually nothing about the area we were going to go and work in ... They had dreadful maps and sort of pre-war picture postcards of the attractive areas but nothing much else.'[70] OSS under Max Corvo had better fortune since in early November 1943 an agreement was reached with Colonel Pompeo Agrifoglio, the head of SIM, to launch a number of combined missions. This was an extremely valuable agreement: SIM had been responsible for crushing the anti-Fascist resistance prior to the armistice and therefore knew where recruits were most likely to be found.[71]

Poor weather and a shortage of aircraft meant that the first supply drop to the partisans took place only in December 1943 and consisted of equipment for only thirty men. That winter a total of 200–300 tons of armaments and equipment were dropped by air and an equivalent amount landed by sea.[72] By the end of 1943 it was estimated that around 10,000 partisans were formed into bands across occupied Italy, but most remained unarmed. These numbers began to increase significantly during the spring and summer of 1944 because the Germans launched a forced-labour programme, demanding workers to work either in Germany or for the Todt Organization building defences in Italy. Mussolini also conscripted men into the various armed formations of the RSI. As a result, men fled their homes for the hills and mountains to evade conscription and labour service, swelling the ranks of the partisans to around 80,000 men in the middle of the summer of 1944.[73] In May 1944 a report from General Alexander's headquarters commented:

> Assistance to the partisans has paid a good dividend. The toll of bridges blown, locomotives derailed, odd Germans eliminated, factories demolished, mounts week by week, and the German nerves are so strained, their unenviable administrative situation taxed so much further, that large bodies of German and Italian Republican troops are constantly tied down in an effort to curtail partisan activity. Occasionally pitched battles have been fought, with losses to the enemy comparable with those they might suffer in a full-scale Allied attack ...[74]

After the liberation of Rome, OSS and SOE agreed to divide northern Italy into zones of operation. OSS focused on the area around Siena and Florence, and SOE around Ancona and La Spezia, and in Piedmont; both would operate in Lombardy and Venice.[75]

The Germans were now aware that they had a potentially very dangerous enemy in their midst and in May 1944 dropped leaflets warning the population:

> Whoever knows the place where a band of rebels is hiding and does not immediately inform the German Army, will be shot. Whoever gives food or shelter to a band or to individual rebels, will be shot. Every house in which rebels are found, or in which a rebel has stayed, will be blown up. So will every house from which anyone has fired on the German forces. In all such cases, all stores of food, wheat, and straw will be burned, the cattle will be taken away, and the inhabitants will be shot.[76]

German and RSI anti-partisan operations – *rastrellamenti* – were brutal and effective. In spring 1944 enormous damage was inflicted on the partisans operating near Genoa, and partisan activity was virtually halted in Piedmont and Venetia by a series of devastating *rastrellamenti*. Reprisals were harsh: for example, in retaliation for a battle south of Rome between a strong partisan band and two German battalions in April 1944, the entire population of the village of Monteangelo was massacred.[77]

The Allied breakout on the Cassino and Anzio fronts began on the night of 11 May 1944. A week later the Polish flag was raised over the ruins of the monastery at Monte Cassino, the Gustav line was broken, and Allied armies began the rush towards Rome, spearheaded by the United States 5th Army under General Mark Clark. The resistance in Rome had been muted since the shock of the massacre at the Ardeatine Caves, and the Germans had succeeded in penetrating more resistance groups, such as the *Bandiera Rossa*. Furthermore, one of the Gappists had turned traitor after his arrest, and now escorted the *Banda Koch* around Rome identifying his former colleagues. In this way Koch was able to carry out over 400 arrests in the months leading up to the liberation.[78] Outside Rome, however, the partisans attacked the retreating Germans in the Alban Hills. The call for a general strike in Rome on 3 May had met with a very limited response, partly because the Germans had inflicted great damage on the resistance, and partly because various forces of moderation were urging no action in order to prevent Rome from becoming a battleground. The Pope feared the prospect of an uprising on the model of Naples, along with a repeat of German scorched-earth tactics. Kesselring sought and obtained permission from Hitler at the start of June to abandon Rome uncontested, but no one knew this. Therefore, on 4 June the Allies dropped leaflets carrying a message which was repeated over the radio from General Alexander calling on the Romans to take steps to prevent the Germans from destroying the city: 'Rome is yours! Your job is to save the city, ours is to destroy the enemy.' The Vatican then informed the CLN that the Germans planned to leave peacefully, and consequently no orders for an insurrection were ever issued.[79]

On 4 June the first American troops entered Rome. A journalist, Eric Sevareid, witnessed the scene:

> Everyone was out on the streets, thousands upon thousands from the outlying areas walking towards the centre of the city. A vast murmurous sound of human voices flooded everywhere and rose in joyous crescendo at every large avenue we crossed . . . The Piazza di Venezia was jammed with a monstrous crowd, and our jeep proceeded at a snail's pace, while flowers rained upon our heads, men grabbed and kissed our hands, old women burst into tears, and girls and boys wanted to climb up beside us . . .[80]

Rome, the penultimate capital city to be occupied by the Germans, became the first capital to be liberated.

The fall of Rome presented the Italians and the Allies with the long-awaited opportunity to reform the Italian government to include the anti-Fascist parties and to abandon existing links with the Fascists, and brought into question the future of the king. At the end of January 1944 the anti-Fascist parties had held a congress at Bari during which all parties agreed on the need to seek alternatives to Badoglio and the king.[81] In early March the leader of the Communist Party, Palmiro Togliatti, had returned to Italy from Moscow, and he stunned the Italian communists with the orders he had received from Stalin and Molotov: 'At the present stage do not call for the King's immediate abdication; Communists can join the Badoglio government; [our] chief efforts must be concentrated on creating and reinforcing unity in the struggle against the Germans.'[82] These orders enabled the Communist Party to move from the shadows and to join a government of national unity which could be formed once Rome had been liberated.[83] The future of the king remained unclear. The Americans were keen to force his abdication, but Churchill's comment was: 'Why break the handle of the coffee pot at this stage and burn your fingers trying to hold it, why not wait till we get to Rome, and let it cool off.'[84] On 12 April the king bowed to pressure and announced his intention to retire from public life when the Allies reached Rome and to be replaced by his son Prince Umberto, who would be called Lieutenant General of the Realm.

On 8 June, Badoglio flew to Rome fully intending to move his government there. Instead, he met with the total hostility of the Rome CLN and was forced to resign. Bonomi formed a new government from the six anti-Fascist parties – the Communists, Socialists, Action Party, Christian Democrats, Labour Democrats, and Liberals.[85] The Bonomi government purported to possess authority over the whole of Italy but was in effect limited to the liberated southern half of the country. There was a real danger that Italy could split into two, and to prevent this there was an urgent requirement for the establishment of a formal relationship between the Bonomi government and the CLNAI in Milan. This was all the more important since partisan warfare was increasing rapidly in the north: indeed, Kesselring suggested that the date of the fall of Rome 'may be called the birthday of all-out guerrilla warfare'. The CLNAI was quick to seize the initiative and control of the resistance when on 9 June it established the *Corpo Volontari della Libertà* (CVL) as a central military command under the joint leadership of Parri and the communist Luigi Longo. At the end of August an important link between the Rome government and the CLNAI was established when General Raffaele Cadorna was parachuted into the north to act as the CLNAI's military consultant and liaison with the Italian government and with the Allies.[86]

20
Denmark Enters the Fray

Denmark had an ambiguous position in German-occupied Europe. It retained its pre-war democratically elected government and its king, Christian X, remained securely on his throne. The Germans deliberately kept their presence at a low level, only guarding the lines of communication to Denmark's northern neighbour, Norway. The Reich plenipotentiary, Cecil von Renthe-Fink, represented the German occupation but interfered very little in Danish governance. Fritz Sauckel's forced-labour decrees had not been applied in Denmark and its Jewish population had been left in peace. Therefore, there was little reason for the Danes to resist the German presence. Indeed, in some ways the occupation was actually of benefit to Denmark since industrial and agricultural exports to Germany increased enormously. Alone in Europe during the war, Denmark held a free general election in March 1943 which gave the most seats to the Social Democrats and the Conservatives: the communists were banned from the election, and the fascist party gained only a tiny share of the vote.

There were, however, some Danes who were not satisfied with the comfortable position held by their country in the midst of a brutal world war. As early as 1940, vital intelligence links with Britain had been established by Ebbe Munck between the Princes intelligence organization, a clandestine group of army officers, and the SOE office in Stockholm. The Danes also produced a number of clandestine newspapers such as *Frit Danmark*, to encourage people to look upon the Germans as enemies. There were representatives of Free Denmark in London, but they were men of little standing and therefore of little influence. In May 1942 this changed with the arrival of the leader of the Conservative Party, Christmas Møller. He had been so outspoken in his criticism of the Germans that he was forced to resign as a minister in October 1940, and as a member of parliament in January 1941. Invitations were sent to Møller and to the leader of the Social Democrats, Hans Hedtoft, to come to London and support the efforts of Free Denmark. Møller arrived alone, only to find himself immediately ignored by SOE.[1]

Møller was sidelined because SOE had little idea of how to treat Denmark. In December 1941 the first mission to the country had ended in disaster because SOE agent Carl Johan Bruhn was killed when his parachute failed to open, leaving his radio operator Mogens Hammer on the run until a new organizer, Christian Rottbøll, arrived in April 1942. Hammer then fled to Sweden and from there reached Britain, only to hear that Rottbøll had been shot by the Danish police. Hammer bravely volunteered to return to Denmark in October 1942, and he and Eigil Borch Johansen started the first resistance networks. These were designed to carry out sabotage. But SOE was also in touch with the Princes. They submitted their so-called P-Plan, which called for the creation of a secret army drawn from army officers and soldiers which would come out in open support of the Allies when they landed in northern Europe. The Princes urged SOE not to rock the boat by encouraging sabotage, and SOE agreed. Møller had spoken to the Princes before leaving Denmark and was not convinced that they would ever take action: Møller urged SOE to invest in Johansen and his networks instead. Colin Gubbins pressed the Princes to produce a concrete plan of action, but when it arrived the plan was greeted with derision since it called for only a limited uprising in the province of Zealand and the Princes expected the support of 3,000 British paratroopers.[2]

News emerging from Denmark hinted at a growing sense of impending crisis. In September 1942 the king had sent an abrupt message of thanks to Hitler on receiving birthday wishes, and the offended Führer decided to teach the Danes a lesson by replacing the conciliatory Renthe-Fink with SS-Gruppenführer Werner Best in November. Best appointed the pro-German appeaser, Erik Scavenius, to serve as prime minister as well as continuing in his post as foreign minister.[3]

SOE therefore committed itself to promoting sabotage in Denmark, and found the right man to organize and lead such a campaign in Flemming Muus, who was parachuted into Denmark in March 1943. Muus had such a wide circle of friends in Denmark that plastic surgery was needed to alter his appearance before he departed. He immediately met resistance leaders, including the communists, who he noted were willing to launch sabotage operations when instructed. In contrast his contact with the Princes asked: 'Why do you want to force things? If you kept quiet, you could sit comfortably and in reasonable peace in Copenhagen for the rest of the war.' Muus personally however felt that his task was to 'help the Danes to find their lost souls. *That* was what was needed: *that* was the essential thing if the Viking blood was ever to course proudly again.' The level of sabotage increased dramatically from two attacks in 1940, twelve in 1941, and fifty-nine in 1942 to 816 in 1943. Scavenius passed an anti-sabotage law and set up a body of 15,000 factory guards. This was an extremely divisive policy since it would force Danes to kill other Danes, and the BBC and the clandestine press attacked it unremittingly so that by June 1943 recruits for the guards were hard to find. During July a series of strikes broke out across Jutland and Funen, beginning in Odense and spreading rapidly until around 10 per cent of the Danish population was on strike. On 3 August Muus sent a telegram to London warning of the likely consequences of the sabotage campaign: 'If we continue sabotage at present rate Huns repeat Huns will have repeat have to take drastic measures within three or four weeks stop shall we slow down or force the issue.' The response from London was to continue regardless.[4]

On 24 August a team of saboteurs blew up the Forum, a large public hall in Copenhagen. The Germans pressed the Danish government to pass a law imposing the death penalty for acts of sabotage, and to proclaim a state of emergency.[5] This was one step too far, and the government resigned on 28 August. The following day, the German general Hermann von Hanneken issued a proclamation:

> The latest events have shown that the Danish Government is no longer capable of maintaining law and order in Denmark. The disturbances provoked by foreign agents are aimed directly at the Wehrmacht. Therefore, in accordance with articles 42–56 of The Hague Convention of the laws and customs of war on land, I declare a military state of emergency in Denmark.[6]

Early on the morning of 29 August the Germans moved in to take over the Danish fleet, which promptly scuttled itself. This delighted Muus: 'There is no doubt about it: the spirit of 1864, when our people had fought such a ferocious battle against the Germans in Southern Jutland, was reborn that night.'[7] The army's resistance was less notable. Although tanks had to be deployed in Copenhagen, elsewhere in the country officers ordered no resistance to the German invasion of their barracks. In a few places this order was ignored, brief battles took place, and weapons were sabotaged.[8] The Princes were forced to flee to Sweden but their intelligence work was taken over and expanded by Svend Truelsen.

It is not clear whether the Danish government had actually wanted a German takeover. In 1944 one Social Democrat politician admitted: 'We did not want a rupture, but when it came we received it with joy.'[9] Denmark was now a fully German-occupied country and there were no barriers to the conduct of the resistance. Danish governance was now in the hands of the senior civil servants, mirroring the situation in both the Netherlands and Belgium.

*

The story of the escape of Denmark's 8,000 Jews has been widely held up as an example of what a population and its resistance could achieve to thwart German measures. For example: 'It is a sign of the greatness of the Danish people and it will never be forgotten, for it shows what might have been done throughout Europe, had a similar readiness to act been in evidence in other countries.'[10] Yet the circumstances in Denmark were unique in a number of ways, not least in the conduct of the two Germans most involved, Werner Best and Georg Duckwitz.

The events of September and October 1943 can be interpreted as Best's efforts to implement the eradication of Jewry from Denmark in accordance with Nazi policy while simultaneously taking steps to ensure that this did not arouse resistance. He undoubtedly hoped that the state of emergency imposed at the end of August would be only temporary and that if the Danish government could not be persuaded to return to work, then at least the Germans could continue more or less normal relations with the Danes through the civil service. Under such conditions Denmark would continue to supply the Reich with agricultural produce, manufacture weapons for the German war machine, and recruit Danish citizens for the SS and other German armed formations.

Best had reason to hope for collaboration with the Danish authorities over the future of the Jews. Although Scavenius had rejected German overtures to impose anti-Jewish measures on the grounds that there was no 'Jewish question' in Denmark, the government had taken steps before the war to place severe restrictions on the number of refugees allowed to settle in the country: around 5,000 had passed through Denmark but only 1,500 received the right to permanent residence, and the Danish Jewish community had been forbidden to undertake relief work on behalf of the refugees in case it encouraged more to arrive. During the war, the government had expelled twenty-one stateless Jews into Germany, all of whom later died in the death camps.[11]

Best was an ardent Nazi who had been instrumental as Heydrich's deputy in developing the Gestapo into a tool of terror. Between 1940 and 1942 he had served in the German military administration in France and had issued orders for the deportation of foreign Jews from Paris. Therefore, he cannot be considered an ally of the Jews. Best telegraphed Hitler via the German foreign office on 8 September 1943 on the subject of drawing up a 'resolution of the Jewish issue' in Denmark. He argued that: 'The measures that this entails must be taken before the current state of emergency ceases, because at a later stage they will cause a reaction in the country that will lead to new emergencies, probably under less favourable conditions than at present.' Best feared that the resistance would make its opposition known through a general strike, and that the existing state of cooperation with the Danish civil service would be damaged. Best's recommendations were to ignore the preliminary steps introduced elsewhere, such as the yellow star, and to proceed directly to rounding up the Jews in a single swift operation, for which he requested additional manpower and shipping. On 17 September, Hitler signalled his agreement for Best's plans to implement the Final Solution in Denmark by despatching SS-Standartenführer Rudolf Mildner to take charge of the 300 Gestapo operatives who would be responsible for collecting the Jews. The German police would be assisted by Danish members of the SS and by the Schalburg Corps which was formed from Danish collaborators. A German cargo ship was also sent to Denmark to transport the Jews east.[12]

The German authorities in Denmark had an option open to them that was not available elsewhere in German-occupied Europe: the presence of neutral Sweden only around seven miles away across the Øresund. The Swedes had welcomed those Norwegian Jews who had managed to cross their frontier, and this fact raised the possibility that Best could make Denmark *Judenfrei* in accordance with Nazi policy not by deporting the Danish Jews to the death camps in the east, but by encouraging their departure for Sweden. He found a willing ally in the person of Duckwitz, the maritime attaché, who has received all the credit for saving the Danish Jews and is a 'Righteous among the Nations'. Duckwitz had a wide circle of Danish contacts from having worked in Copenhagen before the war and these proved useful now. Best encouraged Duckwitz to travel to Sweden, around 21 September, to make arrangements with the Swedes to receive the Danish Jews. The Swedish welcome was assured, especially since American diplomats had promised to cover the cost of accommodating the Danish Jews in the country. On 28 September, Duckwitz met Hans Hedtoft and warned him that the Germans were about to round up the Jews. Hedtoft then passed the information on to Carl Henriques, chairman of the Jewish board of representatives.[13]

While Duckwitz was making arrangements for the reception of the Danish Jews in Sweden, the Danish permanent secretaries met on 29 September to discuss drawing up their own proposals to be placed before Best. The secretary for the justice department, Eivind Larsen, suggested offering Best a scheme whereby the Danes would intern the Jews themselves. This scheme was supported by Nils Svenningsen of the foreign ministry and by the majority of the permanent secretaries. The director of the Danish Red Cross, Helmer Rosting, went a stage further by approaching Best directly with the proposal that the Jews would be interned by the Danes, and in return the Germans would release those Danish soldiers who had been interned since 29 August. Best was ready to accept such a solution, but in his telegram to Ribbentrop he added a further suggestion, that the Jews would serve as hostages to be deported on a ratio of 50 to 100 Jews for each act of sabotage. Thus, Danish internment would have put the Jews in more danger, not less; but in any case von Ribbentrop rejected Best's ideas and so the Best–Danish civil service plan collapsed.[14]

The Jews were now aware of their impending fate, and even knew that the operation against them was scheduled to start on 1 October. On 29 September, the day before the Jewish New Year, Rabbi Marcus Melchior informed the congregation in Copenhagen's principal synagogue on Krystalgade of the impending round-up. Yet the Jewish community did not develop an organized response, nor did it appeal to the resistance for help. Instead rumours abounded, and those who believed them packed up their belongings and fled for the coast of Zealand hoping to find fishermen willing to transport them across the Øresund to Sweden. The more vulnerable members of the Jewish community, the sick and elderly, were overlooked, and the lack of an official response meant that Jews living in the remote provinces did not receive the warning at all. Before the round-ups began on 1 October, 500 to 600 Jews had already reached Sweden, having paid the extortionate fare of around 2,000 kroner per head. Hotels and boarding houses along the coast were also full of confused and frightened Jews hoping for a passage to safety.[15]

Erling Foss supplied weekly intelligence reports to London and these multiplied in number over the days running up to the round-up. On 29 September he noted the alarming rumours circulating in Copenhagen about the impending arrest of all Jews. On the following day he reported that these rumours had been confirmed, but that the Germans appeared to be half-hearted in their plans. This feeling was repeated in another message on 1 October: 'If they get just a few hundred and the rest disappear, this would satisfy and no more would then have to be done because it would be assumed that Hitler would calm down and forget about the matter.' This proved to be an accurate assessment of the Germans' intentions. Orders were issued for the round-up to begin on the evening of 1 October, but Best had issued orders that no Jewish property was to be broken into. Therefore, if no one answered the door then the Jewish family behind it should remain untouched. Best had no desire to see a repeat of the Vel' d'Hiv round-up in Paris where the sympathies of the French had been aroused by the sight of people being dragged through the streets. The orders effectively limited the numbers rounded up: 850 mostly elderly people in Copenhagen, and some from the provinces who had not received the warning in time. The Jews from Copenhagen were put aboard the cargo ship *Wartheland* before those considered half-Jews were released, leaving 202 to be deported. Those from the provinces were put aboard a train destined for Theresienstadt. Best telegraphed Berlin: 'Starting today, Denmark can be considered cleansed of Jews as no Jew can legally reside or work here anymore.'[16]

Despite all the care Best had taken not to arouse resistance to his measures, protests were immediately registered from the king, who wrote to Best 'to emphasise that special actions taken against a group of people who for more than 100 years have enjoyed full civil rights in Denmark could have the most serious consequences'. Letters of protest were also received from the Supreme Court, the Lawyers' Council, Copenhagen University. and various other associations.[17] The political parties also wrote a joint statement condemning the German measures. On 3 October a letter written by the Lutheran bishop of Copenhagen, Hans Fuglsang-Damgaard, was read out in all Lutheran churches:

> Wherever Jews are persecuted because of their religion or race it is the duty of the Christian Church to protest against such persecution, because it is in conflict with the sense of justice inherent in the Danish people and inseparable from our Danish Christian culture through centuries . . . Our different religious views notwithstanding, we shall fight for the cause that our Jewish brothers and sisters may preserve the same freedom which we ourselves evaluate more highly than life itself. With the leaders of the Danish Church there is a clear understanding of our duty to be law-abiding citizens who will not groundlessly rebel against the authorities, but at the same time our conscience bids us to assert the Law and protest against any violation of the Law. We shall therefore in any given event unequivocally adhere to the concept that we must obey God before we obey man.[18]

This was effectively a call to resistance on behalf of the endangered Jews. Best had attempted to stave off such a protest by issuing a statement on the previous day blaming Jews for the sabotage and resistance that summer that had led to the imposition of the state of emergency, and promised that now the Jews were leaving Denmark he would authorize the release of interned Danish soldiers over the next few days. Indeed, Best did keep his word regarding his link between the Jews and resistance by lifting the state of emergency on 6 October.[19]

The Danish people responded immediately with humanitarian gestures to help the Jews. In Copenhagen, patients in hospital with Jewish names were discharged and readmitted with new names. The Bispebjerg Hospital took in groups of up to 100 Jews, raised over a million kroner to finance their escape, and supplied them with food and money before passing them to resistance contacts. Another collection point for Jews was the Nordisk bookshop in Copenhagen, which also housed the headquarters of the

Holger Danske, the largest sabotage group in Denmark.[20] The main task of the resistance was to transport the Jews to the coast, then find them temporary hiding places while boats were located to take them across the Øresund. Gilbert Lassen described his work:

> We used all means, mostly large trucks with straw and hay, vehicles with herring boxes along the sides, medical cars, and the like, and all the transports went around the town a little and towards the country first, then along secondary roads to Smidstrup. Eight of the largest houses were ready for use, we did not ask the owners, but simply borrowed everything we needed. Food and drink were brought from the grocery store and from the guesthouse.[21]

Most Jews were taken across in fishing boats, but one schooner was hired which transported 140 Jews in a single sailing. A young Jewish boy, Leo Goldberger, described his escape from a beach near Copenhagen:

> It was a bitter cold October night. My youngest brother, barely three years old, had been given a sleeping pill to keep him quiet. My brave and stoic little mother was clutching her bag with socks and stockings to be mended which she had taken along for reasons difficult to fathom rationally. We were anxiously and eagerly waiting for the promised light signal . . . Then finally the lights flashed. We were off! Wading straight into the sea, we walked out some 100 feet through icy water, in water that reached up to my chest. My father carried my two small brothers on his arm. My mother held on to her bag of socks. And I clutched my precious flashlight. My older brother tried valiantly to carry the suitcases but finally had to let them drop in the water. We were hauled aboard the boat, directed in whispers to lie concealed in the cargo area, there to stretch out covered by smelly canvases; in the event the German patrols were to inspect the boat, we would be passed over as fish. There seemed to have been some 20 other Jews aboard.[22]

By the end of October virtually all the Jews in Denmark who had not been caught in the first German dragnet had been successfully evacuated to Sweden. The few arrests which occurred came at the hands of a zealous Gestapo officer, Hans Juhl, who searched the villages of north Zealand and located eighty Jews. There were few betrayals by the Danes.[23]

The rescue of the Jews took the Danes into unknown territory because they had no idea how the Germans would react. Unlike elsewhere in Europe, no legal penalties applied for assisting Jews to escape nor for hiding them. The few Danes who were arrested by the Germans were turned over to the Danish police, who occasionally fined them small amounts but usually discharged them unconditionally. German soldiers travelling by train across Denmark turned a blind eye to the carriages full of Jews travelling to the coast. Nor were there any German or Danish police checks at the main stations. Most importantly, the Danish coastguard vessels, which had been taken over by the Germans on 29 August, suspended their patrols during the crucial period of the evacuation. The German Navy continued its patrols but only to prevent Allied shipping from passing through the Skagerrak and into the Baltic: it ignored all other sailings. Therefore, it is clear that, although Danes may have thought they were resisting the Germans by saving the Jews, in fact they were operating with the full knowledge and acquiescence of the German authorities, notably of Best.[24]

Nevertheless, the steps taken to save the Jews did serve to further the cause of resistance across Denmark. For example, a fishmonger in Copenhagen, Mrs Nielsen, had used her contacts with fishermen to arrange trips to Sweden, and thereafter continued to hide members of the resistance who needed to leave the country until her arrest in December 1944. A group in Elsinore, nicknamed the 'sewing club', extended its activities to smuggling resisters and Allied aircrew into Sweden.[25] The action against the Danish Jews by the Germans had shown the Danes that resistance was possible: it just needed to be better organized.

The first task of the Danish resistance was to create a governing body which could organize and coordinate resistance activities within the country and communicate with agencies, notably SOE, abroad. Therefore, in September 1943 the Freedom Council (*Danmarks Frihedsråd*) was established, which drew together in one body representatives from all resistance groups, men such as Mogens Fog of *Frit Danmark*, Frode Jakobsen of *Ringen*, Arne Sørensen of *Dansk Samling*, Børge Houmann for the communists, and the editors of various clandestine newspapers. Muus attended the meetings as an observer on behalf of SOE. He explained the purpose of the Freedom Council to SOE:

> All subversive activities – including all illegal papers – (there are 23 of them with a total circulation of some 250,000 and each copy is read by at least 4 people) are now controlled by this Council which consists of seven members of whom yours truly is one. This is a great step forward towards a common front against the invaders. All parties are represented in this Council – communists working in great harmony with Conservatives etc. It is hoped that this Council may get the collaboration of London – British as well as Danish circles. The Council does certainly NOT aim at anything like forming a government, and it is very much against a government being formed outside Denmark (unless the King – which is most unlikely – should leave

> his land). The Council is absolutely unpolitical and aims at nothing but aid in collecting all forces now opposing the Huns in Denmark.[26]

The first task was to establish and organize a secret army, and to this end Denmark was divided into six districts, each commanded by a former colonel of the Danish Army.

One of the Princes, Captain Volmer Gyth, was deeply concerned that the communists might not obey the orders of the Freedom Council as liberation approached and might mount a separate bid for power. Gyth's proposed solution was the creation of a Danish Brigade in Sweden which would be rapidly transported to Copenhagen as the Germans withdrew:

> The object of this plan is to seize Copenhagen immediately upon possible collapse and prevent chaos and the communistic conquest of this city. For Denmark, Copenhagen is of such prime importance that he who holds sway over Copenhagen in reality holds sway over the country.

SOE was more concerned with immediate action and not with future planning, so it ignored Gyth's request for a loan of 2–2.5 million Swedish kroner to finance the brigade. Ole Lippmann who was working alongside Truelsen in the supply of military intelligence travelled to Sweden in February 1944 and obtained a loan of 2 million Swedish kroner from the Skandinaviske Bank in Stockholm on the basis of a guarantee of repayment to be signed by the former prime minister, Vilhelm Buhl. Lippmann then learned that Buhl would not sign such a document, so he approached the shipping magnate A. P. Møller, who agreed to finance the deal. Danish resistance members who had been forced to flee to Sweden were directed towards the brigade, and from late summer 1944 onwards Swedish Husqvarna machine guns began arriving in Denmark to bolster the secret army, in addition to supplies reaching the country from Britain through SOE.[27]

Gyth's concerns regarding the possibilities of a communist takeover may be dismissed as the fears of a conservative army officer who dreaded the consequences of overt resistance. However, it is questionable whether the Freedom Council actually had much control over the resistance in the period following the German takeover of Denmark, especially over the dramatic increase in sabotage acts after August 1943. Three main groups were responsible for the bulk of the sabotage: *Holger Danske*, BOPA, and an army group of saboteurs organized by Captain E. C. V. Tiemroth and Professor Mogens Westergaard. The sabotage was directed against factories working for the Germans, harbour installations, shipyards, ships and cranes, German military installations and depots as well as restaurants catering for the Germans. The railways were also attacked, with a notable success being scored in November 1943 when the railway bridge at Langå was destroyed, leading to a brief state of siege in Jutland. On 22 June 1944 the resistance scored a real coup when it sent 125 men dressed as workmen into the Rifle Syndicate, the most important arms factory in Copenhagen, and they stole over 100 machine guns before blowing up key points in the factory. Production was halted for five months and fifteen hostages were executed in reprisal. The resistance also assassinated known Danish collaborators and informers.[28]

The Germans reacted to the upsurge in sabotage in several ways. One was an attempt at persuasion by Best in April 1944 when he informed a meeting of editors of the legal Danish press that he would execute the 100 saboteurs currently held in prison as hostages unless the country quietened down. The response of the Freedom Council was an open letter to Best which concluded: 'You can burn, ravage and murder. You can carry out imprisonment and execution. But you can never break our will and ability to fight the power which had plunged the world into war, and robbed Denmark of her freedom.' The Germans also promoted a form of civil war through its use of the Schalburg Corps. These collaborators carried out German orders and, assisted by Gestapo officers, took the war to the resistance with a campaign of assassinations of prominent anti-Nazis such as Ole Bjørn Kraft, a leading parliamentarian, and the dramatist Pastor Kaj Munk as well as doctors, lawyers, journalists, academics, and artists. In response to a resistance raid on a German arms depot in the port of Copenhagen, the Schalburg Corps and the Germans bombed the Tivoli Gardens and blew up the Royal Porcelain Factory in Copenhagen.[29]

The Gestapo in Denmark was commanded by SS-Sturmbannführer Karl Heinz Hoffmann, who was assisted by SS-General Günther Pancke, and by Otto Bovensiepen who oversaw the German police. The Gestapo in Aarhus was particularly active and achieved a major success when it arrested three SOE agents in the city on 13 December 1943. Among the three arrested was one man, Jacob Jensen, who had contacts with many people in the Danish resistance. These included the Hvidsten group in Jutland, and Monica Wichfeld, whose premises in Lolland were used to receive agents and supplies and to shelter wanted people from the Germans. (Her daughter Varinka acted as Muus's secretary and they married in June 1944.) Jensen was Muus's most trusted and favourite agent but Wichfeld had doubts about him because, although he was meticulous about obeying orders, she doubted whether he would hold up during interrogation by the Gestapo. She was right to be concerned, because Jensen and one of the other arrested agents were tortured and revealed the names of forty-four important contacts, including Monica. She refused to go into hiding and was arrested on

15 January 1944, followed soon by members of the Hvidsten group who were arrested in March. In May 1944 the Germans court-martialled Wichfeld and ten other resisters caught as a result of Jensen's revelations. Three men and Wichfeld were condemned to death, five were given various lengths of prison sentences, and two, including Wichfeld's son Viggo, were acquitted. The Germans used the trial to warn the Danes of the consequences of resistance: 'It depends entirely on how the illegal elements and the public bodies responsible for law and order behave in the near future whether the death sentences are to be carried out or whether conditions in the country will permit their being reprieved.' No woman had been executed in Denmark since the Middle Ages and the Danes were appalled at Wichfeld's sentence. The trade unions threatened a general strike and the clergy appealed publicly for clemency. Best was warned by Rosting that the queen was greatly disturbed by the prospect of Wichfeld's execution, especially since she had been friends with Wichfeld's mother. On 19 May 1944 Best bowed to pressure, and Wichfeld's sentence was reduced to hard labour for life: she was despatched to various German concentration camps before dying of pneumonia in Waldheim Prison in February 1945. Those condemned to death at the same time were not so fortunate, and their sentences were carried out. In May and June 1944 the increasing pace of resistance led to further executions of captured saboteurs.[30]

Sabotage was not the only manifestation of growing Danish resistance to the German occupation. Strikes were viewed as a valuable weapon to be deployed against the Germans since many Danish industries were heavily engaged in production for the German war machine. Strike action had virtually paralysed production in North Schleswig in April 1944, and these strikes were followed by more effective action in June and July in Copenhagen. The impetus for the strikes in Copenhagen came not from the news of the Allied landings in Normandy, though these were greeted with enthusiasm, nor from proclamations by the Freedom Council, but from the grassroots. The quasi-state of civil war reigning in Copenhagen between the resistance and the Schalburg Corps led Best to impose a state of emergency with a curfew in place from 8 p.m. to 5 a.m. The workers at Denmark's largest shipyard, the Burmeister og Wain works in Copenhagen, voted on 26 June to write to Best to inform him that, since the curfew denied them the opportunity to tend their vegetable plots in the evening, henceforth they would cease work at noon. By 29 June the strikes had spread to encompass all factories and businesses, transport systems, telephone services, and the press. Best responded by cutting off all gas, electricity, and water supplies to Copenhagen and placing German police units stationed in Zealand under orders to prepare to move into the capital.

On 30 June the situation turned violent as clashes between the Danes and Germans left sixteen people dead and 227 wounded. At this point the Freedom Council stepped in and issued a proclamation on 1 July which supported the strike but counselled restraint and demanded that the Schalburg Corps be withdrawn from the country and the state of emergency restrictions, especially the curfew, be lifted. A second proclamation on the following day added demands for the immediate restoration of the gas, electricity, and water supplies, and a guarantee of no reprisals for the strikes. The situation was extremely tense as German Panzer units and artillery ringed Copenhagen, stopping all traffic from entering the city, and it appeared that the Germans were prepared to starve out the population of 700,000 civilians. The minister for labour and social welfare in the former Danish government, H. H. Koch, feared the outbreak of open warfare, which would have led to extremely high civilian casualties since the resistance was very poorly armed at the time. He used his brother as a courier to the Freedom Council, imploring them to negotiate with Best. On 3 July the Freedom Council agreed to call an end to the strikes if the Germans restored the electricity supply. On 4 July the strikes were ended and the Germans agreed to lift the curfew and to send the Schalburg Corps out of Copenhagen: all essential utilities were restored in the capital.[31]

The events of early July 1944 demonstrated the enormous progress the cause of resistance had made in Denmark during the course of a single year. As Muus wrote later:

> It was of great importance to our position abroad, largely because it was now made clear that the whole nation was now really fighting the Germans. The strike was inspired neither by the Freedom Council nor by foreign broadcasts, and it expressed the feelings of the ordinary Dane, in this case Copenhageners especially.

The population had challenged the Germans openly and willingly: for example, by burning bonfires across Copenhagen during the hours of curfew in contravention of all blackout requirements. Although the Freedom Council had not initiated the strikes, it had soon taken control of the situation and been acknowledged as the voice of resistance by the civil service, former ministers, and crucially by the Germans. The proclamations issued by the Freedom Council had reached the population through the clandestine press, especially *Information*, edited by Børge Outze, and *Frit Danmark*, which had produced several issues per day during the strike. The messages contained in the clandestine press were echoed by broadcasts over the BBC Danish Service. Denmark could now be considered in a state of resistance.[32]

21

Civil War or Resistance – The Balkans

The surrender of Italy had an enormous impact on the Balkans, where many Italian troops had been stationed. Prior to the surrender the numerous British Liaison Officers (BLOs) in the region had managed to have a degree of control over the various resistance forces, who opposed each other just as much as they did the occupiers, by controlling the flow of supplies. The bounty supplied by the surrender of the Italian Army meant the end of this kind of control, and 'as a result the guerrillas were able to put themselves beyond the reach of the only real sanction we had'.[1] Julian Amery, a BLO in Albania, summarized the problem:

> The classical, rather old-fashioned, theory about guerrilla warfare is that you find a movement which already exists and you send one or two officers to advise and guide them and help them with money and arms. But Wingate . . . said it was awfully difficult to get them – even with money and arms – to do the right thing. They take the money and they take the arms and go off and fight private civil wars of their own.[2]

There was a real danger that civil war would take precedence over resistance to the Germans.

The deteriorating situation in Yugoslavia, Albania, and Greece was not helped by decisions made by the Allies, especially the British. The resistance in the Balkans expected an Allied invasion, as indeed did the Germans. When the BLOs made it clear that no such invasion would take place, it appeared to the various resistance movements that there was little point in taking casualties by fighting the Germans when there were internal enemies to be conquered. From their point of view, the Germans would leave the Balkans anyway once they had lost the war and, in the interim, the battle for political dominance in the post-liberation period needed to be fought. The Allied policy towards the Balkans was expressed succinctly in a minute by the Chiefs of Staff on 4 October 1943: 'We should not relax our efforts to contain as many German divisions as possible in Greece and

Yugoslavia.'[3] This meant that for the Allies the purpose of the resistance was to harass the Germans to a degree sufficient to prevent reinforcements being sent to the main battlefronts.

Consequently, the role of the BLOs was to do their best to direct the martial activities of the resistance movements away from each other and towards the Germans. Unsurprisingly, they met with limited success. In the case of Yugoslavia, matters were complicated by the momentous British decision to abandon support for Draža Mihailović and his Četniks, and to direct all resources towards Tito's Partisans, who were seen as more active against the Germans. In Albania it can be argued that the British mission never achieved any degree of control over the various resistance movements, and that civil war was far more prevalent in the country than resistance. Britain had no long-term interests in either Yugoslavia or Albania and so was less concerned about the political complexion of the principal resistance movements: Greece, however, had closer links to Britain, and so more interest was taken in the country. British policy there caused controversy since the British government continued to support the return of the Greek king, whereas the two main resistance groups were, as the BLOs reported, united only in their republicanism. British policy and the reports of the BLOs did, however, agree on one thing: the need to control the communist ELAS and to prevent the communists from taking over the country. Accordingly, strenuous efforts were made to avert civil war in Greece.

German forces in Yugoslavia anticipated the Italian defection and had begun despatching additional troops to the areas containing vital strategic railways, such as Slovenia and Dalmatia, even before the announcement of Italy's surrender. A student, Metod Milać, noted the events of 8 September 1943 in Ljubljana:

> In the very early hours of the next day the Italian military facilities near our house were already surrounded by small German units strategically placed at each entrance/exit of these facilities. With machine guns pointing at the entrances, they disarmed every military person leaving the place.[4]

The Partisans and the Germans raced each other to take control of formerly Italian-occupied territory along the Dalmatian coast and the Adriatic islands. The rapid advance of the Partisan 1st Proletarian Division, led by General Koča Popović and accompanied by William Deakin, was assisted by weapons received from General Pietro Belletti, the commander of the Bergamo Division in Split. The Partisans held Split for ten days until they were forced to evacuate the city after air bombardment and the arrival of the SS Prinz Eugen Division.[5] By the end of September 1943 the Partisans had won the race to the coast, but a month later the Germans launched Operation Kugelblitz or, in Partisan terminology, the Sixth Offensive, to clear the coast of the Partisan menace. By January 1944 the Germans had secured the coast and inflicted heavy but not long-lasting damage on the Partisans. The Partisans were now restricted to the mountains, while the Germans retained control over the strategic railways along the coast which were essential for maintaining the German presence in Albania and southern Yugoslavia, and the continued extraction of minerals vital to the German war economy.[6]

The interval between the Italian surrender and the arrival of the Germans on the Dalmatian coast gave the Allies a brief opportunity to despatch supplies by sea from the Italian mainland. Royal Navy officer Alexander Glen recalled that the main problem was a shortage of weapons to send across the Adriatic. The solution was found by ignoring the terms of the armistice which allowed the Italians to retain their weapons. Glen and his associates:

> . . . got together some trucks and began a visitation which in its speed would be difficult to fault. To each Italian commanding officer we explained the problem frankly, and the urgency of the opportunity, and without exception this courteous approach brought cooperation. Rifles, automatic weapons, machine guns, mortars poured in, together with ammunition.[7]

The Allies managed to send 600 tons to the Partisans by ship before the Germans seized the whole of the Dalmatian coast. Operations then switched to the island of Vis, which the Partisans held. This had a natural harbour guarded by two forts which had been built by the British during the Napoleonic Wars, and was now garrisoned by 1,000 Partisans and by two companies of Royal Marines. SOE moved its main seat of operations in Yugoslavia from Cairo to Bari, and SOE and OSS oversaw the supplies of arms to the Partisans and the care of wounded Partisans evacuated from the mainland.[8]

The heads of the British missions in Yugoslavia, William Bailey with Mihailović and Deakin with Tito, had not received prior warning of the Italian surrender, but on 8 September both men received a signal from GHQ Middle East: 'Get in touch with Italian commanders in your area. Insist implementation of armistice terms and enlist aid against Germans. If Italians unable to fight Germans take possession of arms, aircraft, other military stores.'[9] This is why Deakin had accompanied the Partisans to Split. It is the events in Montenegro, however, that have excited the most controversy. The Italian Venezia Division under General Giovanni Battista Oxilia was based at Berane in the Lim valley, which was an area where Četniks loyal to Mihailović were particularly strong and the Partisan presence was negligible. The Germans were moving swiftly into the area from Serbia and had already entered the town of Prijepolje, eighty kilometres north of Berane. On 11 and 12 September the Četniks fought a battle with the Germans and inflicted 200 casualties on them and secured a quantity of weapons. Mihailović supplied Bailey with 1,000 Četniks under Major Voja Lukačević and Lieutenant Colonel Rudi Perhinek and sent them to Berane to take the Italian surrender. On arrival in Berane, however, there was a difference of opinion between the Četniks and Bailey. The Četniks expected to disarm the Italians, but Bailey, almost certainly on SOE Cairo's orders, agreed in a private meeting with Oxilia that the Venezia Division would be put at the disposal of the Allies and continue to guard the vital communication route south into Albania and Macedonia and east to the Sandžak. The Četniks were forced to be content with merely taking over the civil administration in Berane and the Lim Valley.

Tito now intervened and sent two of his generals, Peko Dapčević and Koča Popović, to advance on Berane: 'My plan is to concentrate the first corps and your second corps in the Sandžak and Metohija so as to move, at the right moment, towards Serbia and Macedonia.' The Partisans duly launched attacks on the Četniks in Berane and sought to win over Oxilia to their cause. The Partisans were in a stronger position than the Četniks because Bailey had returned to Mihailović's headquarters to receive Brigadier Armstrong, who was to report on the mission to Mihailović. The only British presence in the town was a Major Hunter, who was with the Partisans. He told Oxilia that the Četniks were collaborators and that he should put his division at the disposal of the Partisans. Oxilia did this, but he also ensured that the Četnik force withdrew from Berane unhindered.

This was a major turning point in the history of the resistance in Yugoslavia. The arms from the Venezia Division could have supplied Mihailović with weapons for 10,000–15,000 men, five times what the Allies had supplied, and therefore allowed him to play a greater role in resistance activities than he had hitherto been able to mount. When Armstrong and Bailey complained to SOE Cairo about the orders, SOE Cairo's responses suggested that they viewed Mihailović's opposition to Partisan provocations as 'collaboration' whereas Partisan inroads into Mihailović's territory were 'resistance'. Indeed, Cairo even suggested that Mihailović should move his headquarters away from western Serbia because this was provoking the Partisans. The events at Berane were repeated elsewhere. Bill Hudson for SOE and Captain Walter Mansfield for OSS went to Priboj to take the surrender of the large Italian division there. Again the Četniks who accompanied them were not allowed to disarm the Italians. One of Mihailović's staff officers, Colonel Mladen Žujović, went to Rijeka (Fiume) in Croatia to disarm the Italians but was appalled to learn from the Italian commander that he had received orders from Badoglio to surrender to the Partisans.[10]

The situation by the end of September 1943 was that Mihailović was in control of virtually all of Serbia, all Serbian territory annexed to Albania and Bulgaria, as well as the Sandžak, substantial parts of Montenegro, and parts of Bosnia-Herzegovina. The Partisans were present in Croatia, Slovenia, and the remainder of Bosnia-Herzegovina, but the Germans controlled all the main lines of communication and major cities. The map that SOE Cairo used was totally divorced from the actual position on the ground. It indicated that the Partisans were in control of most of the territory of Yugoslavia, including Serbia. The officers in Cairo knew that their map was inaccurate: it reflected their political leanings rather than the true picture provided by the signals from British officers with Mihailović and with the Partisans. Yet this very map was used for the momentous decision taken by the end of 1943 to abandon support for Mihailović and to focus entirely on Tito and the Partisans. The ground had already been prepared for such a move by the BBC, which incorrectly attributed sabotage – such as the destruction of bridges at Mora Gora and Višegrad in October and the capture from the Ustaše of the town of Rogatica in Bosnia – to the Partisans rather than to Mihailović's Četniks.[11]

Churchill had already been impressed by the evidence supplied by SOE Cairo and by Deakin on the activities and possibilities of the Partisans, so in July the decision was taken to obtain a thorough assessment of the situation on the ground by sending two brigadiers to make reports and recommendations, Fitzroy Maclean to the Partisans and Armstrong to Mihailović. The Foreign Office brief for Maclean stated: 'Our first aim is, therefore, to endeavour to bring about the coordination of the military activities of General Mihailović and Partisans . . . under the direction of the Commander-in-Chief, Middle East.' Maclean arrived at Partisan headquarters near Jacje on 17 September, and almost immediately left for a trip to the coast to investigate the possibility of bringing in supplies by sea. He then returned to Tito's headquarters, where he was briefed by Deakin on the military situation. Maclean never saw any action by the Partisans whereas Deakin had, having landed in the middle of the battle around Mount Durmitor. Deakin had not travelled widely around the country but had instead received all his information from Tito's confidant, Vladimir Velebit, who carefully controlled whom Deakin met and what he learned.

In contrast, Armstrong, who arrived at Mihailović's headquarters on 25 September, immediately witnessed sabotage operations by the Četniks, and he and the British liaison officers with Četnik missions had total freedom of movement and contact. Armstrong quickly realized that SOE Cairo had a totally inaccurate picture of the situation in Serbia and telegraphed them on 9 November:

> Ref your comments our Intelligence Bulletins, we would like to know if Partisan BLO statements are based on eyewitness observations or merely circumstantial reports from local Commands. Here we try to be impartial. Hope BLOs with Partisans do same . . .

It is clear that Maclean and Deakin did not.[12]

Maclean left Tito's headquarters on 5 October and returned to Cairo where he wrote his report dated 6 November, which was rapidly circulated among the decision makers. In contrast, Armstrong's report reached SOE Cairo on 10 November by radio. It was then delayed in the cipher department for a week and left unread on the desk of the minister of state, Richard Casey, before finally being sent by telegram to the Foreign Office. By the time Armstrong's report reached the Foreign Office at the end of November, decisions had already been taken on the basis of Maclean's report alone. The Foreign Office, to its credit, was sceptical of all of the claims made for the Partisans by SOE Cairo, and on 11 November the deputy under-secretary at the Foreign Office, Orme Sargent, had suggested to Ralph Stevenson, the ambassador to the Yugoslav government-in-exile, that Armstrong and Bailey should be invited to Cairo at the same time as Maclean so that the British would have a full picture of the situation inside Yugoslavia. Pro-Partisan opinion in Cairo, however, was by then so dominant that neither Armstrong nor Bailey was ordered to make an appearance in Cairo. This omission was vitally important, as was the timing, because Churchill was in Cairo at the time the Maclean report was being circulated, whereas the Armstrong report missed Eden who had just left London for Cairo on his way to join Churchill at the Teheran Conference.[13]

Maclean's report has been termed a 'blockbuster' because of the influence it had. It did indeed have an enormous impact but it was totally inaccurate. The report claimed that the Partisans had a force of 220,000 men organized into twenty-six divisions. In fact, as German and later BLO reports on Partisan forces indicate, the figure was more likely to have been in the region of 60,000 men. Maclean also exaggerated the Partisans' fighting abilities, claiming that for every Partisan lost, five Germans had been killed. From the territorial point of view, Maclean suggested that there were 30,000 Partisans in Serbia, whereas the reports of BLOs on the spot give a figure of only 1,700, and those only in a small portion of south-eastern Serbia. Churchill was enthusiastic about the prospects of the Partisans tying down a substantial number of German divisions in Yugoslavia. He paid less attention to the political dimensions of the Maclean report. Maclean made it clear that the Partisans had no intention of co-operating with Mihailović and the Četniks and indeed saw them as a major enemy. The inference was that if civil war was to be averted in Yugoslavia then the British would have to abandon Mihailović. When Maclean met Churchill again on his return to Cairo from Teheran, he warned Churchill of Tito's commitment to communism, and Churchill asked him: 'Do you intend to make Yugoslavia your home after the war?' Maclean said no and Churchill continued: 'Nor do I. And, that being so, the less you and I worry about the form of government they set up, the better. That is for them to decide. What interests us [is] which of them is doing the most harm to the Germans?'[14]

The Armstrong report examined Mihailović's suitability as a leader of the resistance and concluded that he was 'a career officer, narrow-minded and stubborn, very pan-Serb, wily and a master of evasion and procrastination'. The report recommended that both Mihailović and Tito should be required to put their movements under the control of the commander-in-chief, Middle East, and ordered to focus on the war against the Germans, for which both parties should receive equal quantities of supplies. Both sides should be encouraged to put political questions to one side until the war was over. This was wishful thinking: Tito had every intention of controlling the country after the war, and Mihailović sought to preserve Serb dominance in liberated Yugoslavia.[15]

At the Teheran Conference, Churchill made claims for the Partisans based entirely on Maclean's inaccurate figures. The Soviets were sceptical about the number of German divisions allegedly being held in Yugoslavia by the Partisans, but indicated that they were ready to send a mission to Tito and a separate one to Mihailović as well. This was an entirely sensible proposal since the path of the Soviet advance through the Balkans was likely to lead to Soviet troops entering Yugoslavia through Serbia, which the Soviets knew (but the British did not accept) was still firmly held by Mihailović. The Foreign Office was consulted and Stevenson reported that Armstrong thought Mihailović would accept a Soviet mission. Stevenson, however, went on to say: 'On the other hand, since we are at present trying to eliminate Mihailović not only from the government, but also from Yugoslavia, this is obviously the wrong moment to take this proposal any further.' This view held sway, and no further Soviet action in support of Mihailović was taken. Roosevelt and the Americans voiced no opinion since they had little evidence despite the despatch of OSS officers to both sides. The information supplied by Major Linn Farish, who had dropped with Maclean, enthusiastically endorsed the Partisan line: he would later change his mind once he had seen more of Yugoslavia. Walter Mansfield and Albert Seitz, who were with Mihailović, found their reports held back by SOE Cairo, which had control over OSS signals from the Balkans. It was only later, in March 1944, when the two men reported in person in Washington, that the US State Department and OSS began to doubt the wisdom of throwing all support behind the Partisans. By then it was too late. Churchill's policy of abandoning Mihailović had won the day.[16]

In December 1943 the British government effectively took the decision to withdraw all support from Mihailović. It now needed to provide evidence to convince all interested parties, especially the Yugoslav government-in-exile in which Mihailović was minister of war, that this decision was grounded in fact, as believed by the British government though not actually reflecting the realities on the ground. There was also the practical problem of extracting the BLOs from Mihailović and from the sub-missions spread across Serbia.

The Partisans had convinced Deakin that the Četniks were collaborating with the Italians, and this claim has been examined in an earlier chapter. The evidence suggested that the Četniks immediately under Mihailović were not collaborating, but that various Četnik commanders were. This is further borne out by events immediately after the surrender of Italy. In Slovenia, Četniks under Major Novak and the collaborating MVAC or White Guards had worked alongside the Italians against the Partisans and now concentrated their forces in Grčarice and Turjak to await the expected Allied invasion. They were attacked by the Partisans: Grčarice was quickly lost and Turjak surrendered after a five-day siege. The Partisans murdered about 1,000 of the defenders. The Germans showed no interest in assuming responsibility for the MVAC or the collaborating Četniks but preferred to disarm them. Of the 6,500 men in the various collaborating units, about 3,000 were captured by the Partisans, about 500 were killed in the fighting, about 1,000 elected to switch sides and join the Partisans, while the remaining 2,000 eventually joined the Slovene National Guard which was sponsored by the Germans.[17]

In November 1943 evidence emerged which suggested that Mihailović was ordering collaboration, not with the Germans, but with the forces of Milan Nedić's government. The source was a telegram from Major Bill Cope, the senior BLO with one of Mihailović's subordinates, Radoslav Djurić:

> Just obtained this information from Djurić. Mihailović has ordered Djurić to cooperate with Nedić Government against the Partisans. This is confirmed by report from Nedić officer recently at this headquarters that this news proclaimed to Nedić's troops in Niš.

Cope did not understand Serbo-Croat, and it seems that he misinterpreted what Mihailović's orders to Djurić actually were. It now appears that Mihailović had ordered Djurić to take action against the Partisans who were attempting to penetrate the Sandžak. At the same time Mihailović also wanted to encourage people to join the Nedić forces, where they would receive food and shelter over the winter, in the expectation that they would desert during the following spring, bringing their weapons with them. This was not an unreasonable order. Mihailović simply did not have the means, since he was bereft of Allied supply drops, to care for these men over the winter. Reports from BLOs make it clear the degree of suffering experienced by Mihailović's Četniks, many of whom were barefoot in the snow. Furthermore, not all of Nedić's men were loyal to him: sabotage officers with the Četniks such as Archie Jack and Michael Lees were often assisted on operations by Nedić officers. Nonetheless, this evidence was used by SOE Cairo to build up the case against Mihailović.[18]

The sheer dishonesty with which the British government and authorities in Cairo dealt with Mihailović is demonstrated clearly by the so-called 'test case'. Stevenson needed more evidence to convince the Yugoslav government-in-exile to abandon its minister of war. He telegraphed the Foreign Office on 3 December that 'it was desirable to strengthen the case against him [Mihailović] by calling upon him to carry out by a given date some specific operations known to be within his power, in the certain knowledge that he would fail to do so'. The operations were to be the destruction of two bridges, one over the Ibar river and the other over the Morava. The signal sent to Armstrong by SOE Cairo on 8 December instructed Armstrong to obtain Mihailović's consent *by* 29 December. This is an important point because claims have been made that the operations had to be carried out *before* 29 December. Armstrong delivered the message to Mihailović on the following day, 9 December, but did not speak to him again till 23 December.

The two bridges had already been reconnoitred by British officers. Archie Jack had planned an attack on the Ibar bridge, but had faced difficulties with the local Četniks under Petrović because of the threat of a Partisan offensive in the area by troops under Peko Dapčević. Eric Greenwood had won the support of the local Četnik commander, Jovanović, but his reconnaissance of the Morava bridge had attracted the attention of the

Germans and the garrison had been strengthened. Consequently, on 23 December, it was not unreasonable for Mihailović to inform Armstrong that he would sanction both operations on the condition that he received heavy weapons to carry out the attack. Armstrong agreed with Mihailović, and signalled Cairo:

> I would strongly advise that if we take the big and long view, it will pay us in the end. Mihailović undoubtedly commands superiority in the areas of vital north and south command. In the months ahead you will not want these constantly under attack. The Partisans will not, repeat not, command sufficient support to be able to do this. Mihailović does and will. At present he is committed to cooperation. If you seize the opportunity and support with sorties, the dividends you gather will be greatly increased. If you hesitate to provide material support and continue propaganda attacks you will relapse to the old spirit of the preservation of Serb blood – the British want all but will give nothing in return. As a result the work of the BLOs out here will be wasted and useless.

That the whole point of the exercise was to have Mihailović refuse to carry out the operations is demonstrated by Cairo's response to this request on 2 January 1944: no more weapons or explosives. On 28 December, Stevenson informed the Foreign Office that Mihailović was refusing to undertake the operations until the first half of January, without explaining the reason for the delay. He counselled the Foreign Office to use this to justify abandoning Mihailović. Armstrong was not told that the operations should be cancelled until 4 February, the day before they were due to be carried out.[19]

The most compelling evidence that the 'test case' was a fake comes from the fact that on 13 December, long before any response was expected from Mihailović, SOE Cairo sent identical messages to all sub-missions in Serbia:

> During the next few days, His Majesty's Government may decide to drop Mihailović which would involve evacuation all British personnel from Mihailović HQ and area. Burn this signal after reading. Only method is evacuation through Partisan territory . . . Be prepared to move 15th if journey to Partisans considered possible.

The signal appalled Armstrong, who, in a series of telegrams on 21, 26, and 30 December, argued the case for retaining support for Mihailović since he and only he was in the position to continue resistance in Serbia, where the Partisan presence was negligible. Cairo ignored him.[20] Most BLOs were too far from the nearest Partisan detachments to follow Cairo's orders, and in any case most were loath to do so. The experience of Hudson, Captain Robert Wade, and Seitz illustrated the problems of being evacuated from Partisan territory. The three men went to Berane, which was under the control of Dapčević, where they then spent three months witnessing no anti-German activity at all and being subjected to a stream of Partisan propaganda. Wade reported this to Cairo whereupon the Partisans attempted to seize his radio to prevent him sending further unauthorized messages. Hudson protested and reported the argument to Cairo, which ordered him to surrender his radio to the Partisans. Hudson angrily replied: 'At least refrain from treachery to your officers in the field. Such conduct is unworthy of prostitutes, let alone SOE staff officers.' Three days after this signal, on 28 March 1944, a plane finally appeared to evacuate the three men to Cairo via Italy. Despite his long service in Yugoslavia, Hudson was never even debriefed in Cairo.[21]

There were difficulties in arranging the evacuation and it was only on 2 March 1944 that all the BLOs received orders to concentrate at Armstrong's mission with Mihailović in Pranjani. Lees recalled that on his long, slow journey from south-east Serbia to Pranjani, accompanied by a column of downed Allied aircrew, there was some anti-German activity but no sight of any Partisans. Harry Hainsworth recalled that there was a fear that Mihailović would not allow the BLOs to be evacuated because they were virtually his only contact with the outside world and their departure would make his abandonment by the British a reality. However, Hainsworth recorded that: 'He was most angry but was very gentlemanly about it. He thanked us for the help we had given him and said he was sorry to see us go.' Lees and Rootham made similar observations: 'he held no rancour against us as individuals. He could not have acted with greater dignity or forbearance. It was a gesture of a true gentleman and soldier . . . We, as representatives of a large nation, were given by representatives of a small nation a lesson in manners and how to conduct oneself with dignity in adversity.' Mihailović ordered his men to assist in the creation of a landing strip for the USAAF Dakotas to use. The final flights took place between 29 and 31 May, evacuating over sixty British officers and men, the last OSS operative, George Musulin, and about forty downed aircrew. Like Hudson, the BLOs with Mihailović were not debriefed. Rootham and Jack visited the map room at SOE Bari and were furious to see that the map showed the Partisans were in control of the areas the BLOs had just left. Rootham was so angry that he swept all the flags from the map. Further outrage was delivered by Major General William Stawell, commanding SOE Bari, who told them: 'Now you must remember, you've got it all wrong. The chaps you've been with aren't really on our side at all. The only people who are,

are the Partisans – and you must really snap out of it.' Officers who had served with the Četniks were thereafter banned from the map room.[22]

Maclean wrote an eloquent summary of the abandonment of Mihailović:

> Thus ended a connection which from the first had been based on a misapprehension. With the help of our own propaganda we had in our imagination built up Mihailović into something that he had never seriously claimed to be. Now we were dropping him because he had failed to fulfil our own expectations.[23]

But many questions remained to be answered, not least of which was that of whether the civil war which was now apparently inevitable would prevent any resistance against the Germans.

The British appeared not to understand the political nature of the Partisan movement, nor appreciate that by abandoning Mihailović they had ensured that Yugoslavia would be communist after the war. Churchill appears to have thought that the debate over the future of King Peter would sort itself out once the king had dismissed Mihailović, whom Churchill described to Eden as 'a millstone tied around the neck of the little King'.[24] Eden and the Foreign Office, however, were concerned that no guarantee of support for the restoration of the king had been obtained from Tito. Indeed, at the end of November 1943 the Partisans had held a conference at Jacje during which the formation of a new National Committee was announced and a number of resolutions on the future governance of Yugoslavia were adopted. One of these, clause 7 (b), specifically stated: 'King Peter II, Kara-Georgevic, is forbidden to return to the country until after the liberation of the entire country, when the problem of the king as well as the question of monarchy can be decided.' In correspondence with Tito, Churchill explored the question of the Partisans' acceptance of the king. Churchill thought that the king would have a moderating effect on Tito's espousal of communism, and the issue of a statement of explicit support for the king would open Serbia, the royalist stronghold, to a Partisan advance. Tito prevaricated on the matter, arguing that his new committee, the *Antifašističko Vijeće Narodnog Oslobodjenja Jugoslavije* (Anti-Fascist Council for the National Liberation of Yugoslavia, AVNOJ), should be recognized by the Allies as the sole government of Yugoslavia, rather than the government-in-exile, which was now in Cairo. Eventually, a temporary, compromise solution was adopted: British pressure forced the king to appoint Ivan Šubašić, a man Tito felt he could deal with, as prime minister on 1 June 1944. Maclean described Šubašić: 'He was a rather flabby-looking man of medium size with his hair *en brosse* and small uneasy eyes.

His yellowish skin hung loosely, as though it was too big for him. He looked every inch a politician.' On 16 June the first agreement between Šubašić and the Partisans was signed, the terms of which demonstrated that the Partisans intended to control the entire process of liberating Yugoslavia. When Šubašić attempted to put his ideas forward, he was sharply reminded: 'You have neither the people, nor army nor territory.'[25]

The Soviets had been unwilling to support the Jacje resolutions when they first learned of them, counselling Tito to moderate his communism in favour of the Soviet position of concealing communism behind the facade of an anti-fascist national front. However, after Churchill had made clear at the Teheran Conference that he totally supported Tito, seemingly without regard to the political consequences, Radio Free Yugoslavia, broadcasting from the Soviet Union, endorsed the Jacje resolutions. Furthermore, on 23 February 1944 the long-requested Soviet mission under Lieutenant General Nikolai Korneyev and Major General Anatoli Gorshkov finally arrived at Partisan headquarters.[26]

Mihailović also attempted to state his political beliefs in a congress held in the village of Ba on 25 January 1944. It was largely a Serb affair, and of the 274 participants all but six were Serbs. Živko Topalović was elected president of the congress which voted that the post-war Yugoslavia would be a democratic monarchy made up of three equally important entities – Serbia, Slovenia, and Croatia. Invitations were sent via the British to Croats and Muslims to join the congress, but the British did not pass the messages on to the intended recipients. The Partisans were aware of the Ba Congress but as Djilas later wrote: 'The Central Committee did not even bother to take a stand regarding that congress' since it saw the Četniks as a spent force. The Germans did, however, take note of the proceedings: 'Alerted in all likelihood by local informers, the occupant's police seized a number of participants as they were returning to the capital.' Some were executed, others held as hostages, and a few sent to concentration camps in Germany. The Germans also demonstrated that they still viewed Mihailović as a dangerous enemy by mounting an operation in February in northern Serbia with the SS and Bulgarian troops which resulted in the deaths of eighty Četniks and the capture of over 900.[27]

Evidence supplied by the reports of three OSS operatives, Mansfield, Farish, and Seitz, who had been with the Četniks from the autumn of 1943 to spring 1944, revealed the increasing prevalence of civil war which was hindering the cause of resistance. Mansfield's report on 1 March 1944 stated that there were no Partisans in Serbia, and that the Četniks in the Sandžak and Bosnia-Herzegovina were being forced to spend all their efforts on fighting the Partisans rather than the Germans.[28] This impression was endorsed by Seitz's report in May 1944, in which he noted that he knew of a sabotage operation, against an antimony mine at Ivanjica in south-west Serbia, which had been abandoned by the Četniks in order to fight the Partisans in the neighbourhood. Furthermore, in January 1944 he had been with a column of Četniks which had engaged and killed a group of Germans before coming under fire from Partisans: the Partisans aimed their firepower at the Allied party and not at the Germans.[29] Farish concluded in his report in June 1944: 'It does not seem to me that the Allies had done well in Yugoslavia', and that he wanted efforts made to stop the civil war since 'it appears to me that there are indications in the last few months that there has been less emphasis placed on the fight against the enemy and more preparation for the political struggle to follow the ending of the war'.[30]

It was virtually inevitable that Tito would win the civil war because of the vast disparity between the quantity of supplies received by the Četniks and the Partisans. In the period between Hudson's arrival in Yugoslavia in June 1941 and the last British supply drop to Mihailović in June 1943, the Četniks had received 23 tons of supplies. This amounted to 1,866 rifles, 136 light machine guns, 217 sub-machine guns, 1,500 pistols, 43 mortars, 104 anti-tank guns, 8,728 grenades, 1 million rounds of ammunition, and over 5,000 pounds of explosive, as well as clothing, footwear, medical supplies, and money.[31] In contrast, during the same period the Partisans had only received 6 tons of supplies. Now, however, supplies flooded in to the Partisans: by January 1944 they had received 4,824 tons of supplies, and by April the Americans alone had sent 11,000 tons. These quantities increased during the course of 1944, supplying the Partisans with over 100,000 rifles, more than 50,000 machine guns and sub-machine guns, and over 975 million rounds of ammunition, as well as vast amounts of equipment, including boots.[32]

The Partisans were not grateful for the help they received. Indeed, Basil Davidson noted that they believed that if the Allies 'could bombard Germany with five hundred Liberators we could drop them as many tons of machine guns and mortars and boots and battledress', and if not then it must be for political reasons. The Partisans were also annoyed that the supplies came from Britain and the United States and not from the Soviet Union, even though a Soviet mission was at their headquarters. In March 1944 Djilas and General Velimir Terzić went to Moscow to appeal for Soviet military aid, a loan of an equivalent to $200,000, and recognition of the AVNOJ as the sole legitimate government of Yugoslavia. The trip was a disappointment: 'we waited and waited – much too long – to be received by anyone at all at the Soviet summit, let alone Molotov or Stalin'.

Eventually they had two meetings with Stalin, but emerged with no promise of supplies. The Soviets were embarrassed by their inability to despatch supplies, and the Soviet deputy foreign minister, Andrey Vyshinsky, asked Robert Murphy whether the Americans could not send some cargo ships to Odessa to transport supplies to Tito. Murphy refused to consider the idea because: 'This would have involved the trans-shipment of Lend-Lease goods which the American Government already had sent free of charge to Russia, and the only purpose in moving such goods again would be to give Moscow credit for helping Tito.'[33]

During the spring of 1944 there was only a limited degree of resistance to the German occupation throughout Yugoslavia. In Serbia, Mihailović had lapsed into inaction. Mansfield reported that 'Mihailović's policy is to hold up operations until "D-Day" when he expects an Allied invasion and states that he will throw all he has into one all-out effort against German communications.' He would not undertake operations earlier unless he received substantial quantities of supplies with which to counter the twin threat of Partisan incursions into Serbia and German reprisals against the Serbs. Mihailović claimed that his was a 'one shot' army which would undertake a national uprising at the appropriate moment. Despite Mihailović's lapse into inactivity, the Germans still viewed him as a dangerous enemy.[34]

The Germans were well aware that the Partisans were receiving enormous quantities of arms from the Allies and were now posing a greater threat. In January 1944 the Germans forced Tito out of Jacje, and he retreated to Drvar in west Bosnia. This was where Tito received the Soviet mission and Churchill's son, Randolph. The Partisans used their Allied supplies to attack the main Zagreb–Belgrade railway line and to damage a significant number of lines in Croatia. The Germans reported: 'It is observed that even the main lines are very poorly guarded and guard duty is carried out very superficially. It is also probable that railway employees cooperate with the Partisans in the demolition of the railway tracks.' The Partisans were, however, focusing on an imminent invasion of south-west Serbia. Their first attempt in March 1944 was beaten back by the Germans, Nedić forces, and Bulgarians as well as the Četniks. The Partisans were forced to retreat back to the Sandžak where they reorganized their forces for a more powerful attempt to be mounted later in the summer. From Slovenia, Peter Wilkinson reported a moderate level of sabotage against the main railways from the Reich into north-east Italy. At the same time, he noted that it was apparent the Partisans were conserving their supplies and forces for future operations which would be directed against southern Austria and north-east Italy for territorial gain.[35]

The Germans mounted a series of operations against the Partisans in Croatia and Bosnia-Herzegovina, keeping them on the run. On 25 May 1944 they launched Operation Rösselsprung, or the Seventh Offensive, against Tito's headquarters at Drvar. This was the brainchild of the new German commander of the 2nd Panzer Army, General Lothar Rendulic. He believed that if Tito was captured or killed then the Partisan movement would collapse. Early that morning the Germans despatched a glider force and parachute troops against Drvar. Tito, his staff, and the British mission were forced to flee, in effect abandoning their troops. A British SIS agent, Owen Reed, was in Croatia and heard reports of the German attack. He immediately radioed Bari which sent nearly 300 medium bombers and 200 fighters against the German positions, with Reed supplying a list of targets over the next few days. This enabled most Partisans to escape the German attack although they were scattered in all directions. Maclean arranged for Tito's evacuation to Italy, which was achieved on 3 June by a Soviet-piloted American plane. Tito wanted to re-enter Partisan territory as soon as possible, fearing that the British might hold him captive, and was transported by a British warship from Bari to Vis on the night of 7–8 June.[36] There he was sheltered by the British and the Partisans. Yet his absence from the Yugoslav mainland and his proximity to Italy now meant that the British had a slim opportunity to influence Tito, in particular, his attitude towards King Peter.

The Albanians were a fiercely independent people whose first loyalty was to their tribe and only secondly to their country as a nation state. They resented the presence of all comers, whether the Italians since 1939 or the Germans after September 1943. There were uninfluential collaborationist governments in power throughout the war, but the majority of the country was engaged in some form of resistance. This resistance, however, was totally disunited: the communist LNC (National Liberation Front) under Enver Hoxha sought to take over the entire country in the name of Stalinism; the *Balli Kombëtar* was formed of nationalists united only in their hatred of communists; Abas Kupi gathered together forces who were loyal to the exiled King Zog; and the northern tribes under Muharrem Bajraktari and Gani Bey Kryeziu were in strength in the area of Kosovo. Kosovo had been part of the kingdom of Yugoslavia but after the German invasion of the country in 1941 it was assigned to Albania. The only unifying factor in the Albanian resistance was their hatred of the other parties. Civil war took precedence over resistance to the occupiers.

Two forces competed over the direction of the resistance in Albania: Tito's roving ambassador, 'Tempo' Vukmanović; and the British, whose first mission to Albania, after the abortive effort of 1941, started in April 1943. Vukmanović advised on the development of the LNC and continued to influence its policies. For example, at the beginning of August 1943 there was a concerted effort by the LNC and *Balli Kombëtar* to end the civil war between them and to set up a joint command to resist the Italians and Germans. The Mukje Agreement was probably the last point at which civil war in Albania could have been avoided. Vukmanović, however, was outraged at the agreement because, at the request of the *Balli Kombëtar*, it promised a post-war plebiscite on the future of Kosovo. According to the Yugoslavs, Kosovo was to be restored to Yugoslavia, and so Vukmanović forced the LNC to repudiate the agreement, and to regard the *Balli Kombëtar* as implacable enemies.

The staunch independence of the Albanians is demonstrated by the reaction to the arrival of the first British mission of Major Neil 'Billy' McLean, Captain David Smiley, and Lieutenant Gavin Duffy in April 1943. They crossed into Albania from Greece and met Bedri Spahiu and his LNC contingent. As Smiley wrote later: 'We had naively assumed that he would welcome officers from a country at war with his enemies, who were prepared to help in fighting the Italian occupiers of his country.'[37] Spahiu suspected that the British might be advocating the Greek policy of absorbing southern Albania, which the Greeks referred to as northern Epiros, and ordered the British party to leave until invited back. At the end of June the mission re-entered Albania and met Hoxha. Hoxha was appalled to learn that the British had no intention of landing in the Balkans but also realized that befriending the British could gain him supplies of weapons.

The disparate nature of the resistance in Albania is illustrated by the dispositions of the next missions. In July 1943 Andrew Hands was sent to the Dibër district to contact the chieftains there, and Anthony Neel went to the area north of Tirana where Abas Kupi was in control. In August 1943 four more missions were dropped, consisting of Majors Harold Tilman, Gerry Field, George Seymour, and Peter Kemp. Tilman went to the south to the Gjirokastër district controlled by the LNC; Field to the south-west to the Vlorë region to work alongside the *Balli Kombëtar*; Seymour to the north of Tirana where Kupi held sway; and Kemp to Kosovo. By October 1943 the British missions were sufficiently numerous and spread out so as to need central direction. To provide this, Brigadier Edmund 'Trotsky' Davies and Lieutenant Colonel Arthur Nicholls were parachuted into the country.[38]

The British missions struggled to influence the conduct of the Albanians and to get them to focus on resistance to the occupiers. A BLO, Major Alan Hare, suggested that one of the problems was that:

> The average Albanian has never travelled outside his small country. It is, therefore, far more difficult for him to understand the British outlook than for us to adapt ourselves to see his. To spend hours trying to make an Albanian see the British point of view is a waste of time; the only possible method is to persuade him that some project desired by you is desirable from his point of view.[39]

The LNC remained permanently suspicious of British intentions in Albania. Hoxha circulated several memoranda to his subordinate commanders warning them against alleged British interference in Albanian internal affairs and reminding them that 'our eyes must be turned towards Moscow'.[40] In the same way that William Deakin was kept under control by Velebit at Tito's headquarters, so the LNC controlled the movements of BLOs working alongside them. Tilman, a veteran mountaineer, made himself unpopular with the LNC 'due to the fact that every morning before breakfast he climbed to the top of his local mountain, Mount Nemercke, a not inconsiderable climb, and the wretched bodyguard had to climb it as well'.[41]

In August 1943 the Italians launched a strong attack against the LNC which forced it to flee from its headquarters at Shtylle together with the main British mission and to set up a new base in a monastery near the village of Bixha near Lake Ohrid. Suddenly the BLOs received orders in early September to take the surrender of the Italians and to attempt to persuade them to switch sides. Accordingly, Seymour contacted General Lorenzo Dalmazzo, commander of Italian forces in Albania, to arrange a meeting, and he entered Tirana wearing an Italian greatcoat over his British uniform. He was shocked to discover that while he was talking to Dalmazzo's chief of intelligence, Dalmazzo himself was in the next room talking to the Germans and trying to arrange his own and his family's departure from Albania. Tilman went to Gijirokaster with the LNC to find that General Ernesto Chiminello was in a complete state of funk. The Germans were approaching rapidly, and the area was full of *Balli Kombëtar* forces, who outnumbered the LNC partisans with Tilman. Chiminello had no orders from Rome and refused point blank to surrender his arms or to fight the Germans. After Tilman cut off the water supply to the garrison, Chimello marched his men to the port of Sarandë where ships repatriated them to Italy.

The Italians tended to destroy their weapons and equipment rather than abandon them to Albanians of any political hue. Nonetheless, the LNC succeeded in gathering together weapons from various isolated Italian garrisons, the *Balli Kombëtar* seized the weapons of the Italian garrison at

Dibër, and the northern tribes obtained supplies from the Italians stationed at Kukës. Around 1,500 Italians from the Firenze Division formed the Gramsci battalion and joined the LNC partisans, where they were treated poorly. Most Italian soldiers were abandoned by their officers, who fled back to Italy: Davies noted that there were around 45,000 miserable Italians on the verge of starvation hiding in the mountains.[42]

On 11 September 1943 Hermann Neubacher, the German minister in the Balkans, flew to Tirana and announced the independence of the country under the protection of the Germans. German policy was proclaimed by General Maximilian von Weichs:

> The occupation of Albania was very necessary. We come to Albania not as enemies but as friends, and therefore there is no reason why you should be afraid. We shall leave Albania as soon as we consider it necessary. We shall leave you free in all your internal affairs and shall not interfere with them. We ask for your obedience, and those who do not obey will be punished.

A new collaborationist provisional government was established and the Germans announced the incorporation of Kosovo within Albania. The apparent reasonableness of the German occupation presented the BLOs with a dilemma: 'As time went on it became more and more obvious that we could offer the Albanians little inducement to take up arms compared with the advantages they could enjoy by remaining passive.'[43]

Indeed, the retention of Kosovo within Albania meant that the *Balli Kombëtar* now had little reason to resist the Germans, and the fulfilment of one of its aims effectively split the movement. On 7 October 1943 the central command of the *Balli Kombëtar* ordered a policy of collaboration with the Germans, largely to secure weapons which could then be turned on the LNC. Not all members of the *Balli Kombëtar* agreed with this policy: for example, Skënder Muço, in the Vlorë area, announced that he would continue the fight against the Germans and their Albanian collaborators. For this, he expected to receive arms from the BLOs. The British, for their part, held out little hope of getting the majority of the *Balli Kombëtar* to resist the Germans, but nonetheless recognized the necessity of maintaining relations with the organization since it controlled the coastal region through which seaborne British supplies to the resistance arrived. British policy was directed towards trying to obtain an agreement whereby the LNC and *Balli Kombëtar* would stop fighting each other and would focus instead on the Germans.[44]

The LNC tried to subvert the British efforts by portraying the *Balli Kombëtar* as out-and-out collaborators, a similar line to that pursued by the

Yugoslav Partisans against the Četniks. In directives issued on 9 September, 1 October, and 3 November 1943 Hoxha stated LNC policy was:

> Through clever denunciation and ceaseless work we should seek to discredit *Balli Kombëtar*; to separate the people from it and to bind the people with our organization; to cause divergences among the *Balli* ranks, and to bring about favourable situations in order to accelerate the loosening process among its ranks; to hit decisively and cleverly its reactionary heads; to present *Balli* to the people as the cause of the fratricide; to bring the people to see that the policy of *Balli Kombëtar* would eventually lead to an armed conflict; to cause the people to revolt against such a thing, so that the historic responsibility for the civil war may fall on *Balli*, as in truth it should.[45]

In early November 1943 Davies obtained a written agreement from the *Balli Kombëtar* leaders that they would cease to fight the LNC and would instead engage in resistance against the Germans, and he promised to have the news of the agreement broadcast by the BBC. When Davies informed Hoxha of the statement and asked him to sign a similar agreement:

> There was dead silence. Enver was completely taken by surprise. He had evidently not expected the *Balli* to give the undertaking, whether they meant it or not. He rose to his feet in a fury, he blamed me for interfering, he said what he thought of the BBC and of the *Balli*. He would not be deterred from his purpose to fight the Germans but he would destroy the *Balli* at the same time.[46]

Davies threatened to cut off supplies from the LNC if Hoxha did not make the required declaration. SOE Cairo, however, ordered Davies to keep supplying all sides and to continue his efforts to foster resistance and to dampen down the flames of civil war. During the winter of 1943–44 the LNC continued to focus its efforts on killing members of the *Balli Kombëtar* and destroying the villages where they had sheltered.

The LNC faced a division in its own ranks when Abas Kupi, with the cooperation of the northern nationalist tribes, set up the National Zogist Party on 19 September 1943. His programme was issued in November and called for resistance against the Germans (as the British wanted); the incorporation of ethnic Kosovo Albanian areas within the borders of Albania (to appeal to the *Balli Kombëtar*); social and agrarian reforms (designed to undermine support for the LNC); and the return of King Zog who remained in exile. The LNC's response came in a strongly worded denunciation of Kupi and the Zogists on 3 November, and his formal expulsion from LNC ranks in December. Kupi never recruited many people to his cause: the maximum number of his armed followers has been estimated at around 8,000 whereas by then the LNC ranks were over 10,000 and growing. The northern tribes could muster only a few thousand men between them. The importance of Kupi rested, however, on the fact that he could be used by the BLOs as a nationalist counterweight to the blatant communism of the LNC and the collaborationist line of the *Balli Kombëtar*. This was a difficult course to follow since Amery aptly described Kupi: 'Here is a fish whom many have hooked but none have ever landed.'[47]

The BLOs were largely hapless observers of the civil war and their reports reflect their frustrations with the resistance in Albania. After the arrival of the Davies mission in September 1943, the first BLOs, McLean and Smiley, left for Brindisi to report to the head of the SOE Albanian desk, Philip Leake. They recommended giving aid to all sides, and working towards supporting anti-German resistance and averting a full-scale civil war. Similar sentiments were voiced in Davies's first report in November 1943, although he warned that he believed there was little support for King Zog. His second report, a month later, reflected a change of heart when he called for exclusive support for the LNC, and the denunciation of the *Balli Kombëtar* and Abas Kupi as collaborators. Leake, however, advised against pursuing this policy, since supporting only the LNC would make civil war a certainty and end all hopes of a nationalist uprising against the Germans in the north of the country where the LNC was very weak.

The policy of supporting all sides was reinstated in the January 1944 report by McLean and Smiley, who urged the British to settle the issue of Kosovo because that was essential in order to stop the northern tribes from prevaricating. This last point was a step too far for the Foreign Office and SOE. Peter Kemp reported from Kosovo that 'the majority of Kosovars preferred a German occupation to a Serb' and urged the British government to promise a post-war plebiscite in the region. The British, however, were clearly committed to supporting Tito and the Partisans, who demanded the return of Kosovo to Yugoslavia. As a result, Kemp received orders at the end of January to break off contact with the Kryeziu brothers. Major John Hibberdine, working in the same area, was ordered to cease sabotage operations against the mines because these operations offended the Partisans. Kemp demanded to be withdrawn after his recommendation of continued relations with Gani Bey Kryeziu, who was resisting the Germans, was rejected. Kemp joined Hudson at Berane in Montenegro to await evacuation.[48]

The BLOs worked hard to convince Abas Kupi to engage in resistance rather than remain on the defensive against the LNC. He prevaricated by demanding a direct order from King Zog to do so. The letter Zog initially wrote reflected his understanding of the resistance/reprisals dilemma faced by all resistance organizations, and he urged Kupi to harbour his forces for the national uprising at an opportune moment. The second draft reflected the pressure of the British government and urged Kupi to take steps to avert civil war and start resistance. The reports of other BLOs in the spring of 1944 reflect their frustrations at the Albanian focus on civil war rather than resistance: Anthony Quayle reported on his failed attempts to get the *Balli Kombëtar* to abandon its policy of collaboration; Tilman's and Smiley's reports held out little prospect of ending the civil war.

Between 24 and 28 May 1944 the LNC held a congress at Përmet which laid the political foundations for the communist takeover of Albania. The Anti-Fascist Council of National Liberation was set up to act as an alternative to the collaborationist Albanian government, and the LNC armed formations were renamed the Albanian Liberation Army. This army was then ordered by Hoxha to launch a general offensive to liberate Albania from the Germans and, at the same time, to eradicate the *Balli Kombëtar* and Abas Kupi's Zogists. Tilman knew of the congress when he wrote his final report at the end of the month while in Bari. Yet he wrote that the LNC:

> . . . are not a collection of feudal or tribal chiefs with a personal following, but an organised party representative of both religious faiths, both Geg and Tosk races, and at least 75 per cent of the people of southern and central Albania. And although the Communist Party of Albania is included in the LNC, they welcome anyone who will fight Nazism or Fascism, and have declared time and again that they are fighting for a free, democratic, independent Albania.

Tilman suggested that only the LNC should receive military support from the British since they were the most active resistance movement. Despite this recommendation, British policy in the summer of 1944 remained unchanged: all movements were to be supported simply because it was essential to retain as many German divisions in the country as possible since the Italian campaign had just entered a new critical phase. At the time there were an estimated seventeen German and eight Bulgarian divisions in the Balkans (although these figures are disputed).[49]

British supplies to the Albanian resistance organizations were on a far more modest scale than those to Tito's Partisans. Over 80 tons were dropped between January and April 1944, mostly to the LNC. These enabled the LNC partisans to survive the German onslaughts and to expand their cohorts. Yet the evidence for actual anti-German activity by any party is limited. Much of it was undertaken on the insistence of the BLOs, and often carried out by themselves with little help from the Albanians and, indeed, sometimes in direct conflict with what the Albanians themselves wanted. For example, in September 1943 Smiley identified the bridge over the Shkumbin river on the road to Elbasan as a useful target and duly blew it up, largely 'for I liked blowing things up'. Hoxha, however, was furious because his forces needed that bridge in order to advance on Tirana and into the northern territories.[50] The BLOs also faced difficulties in persuading Abas Kupi to undertake sabotage operations, and he effectively did nothing over the winter and spring of 1943–44. McLean threatened to withhold further supplies unless Kupi took some action, so on 21 June 1944 Kupi's forces assisted Smiley in blowing up the important bridge at Gjoles on the Tirana–Shkodër road. This was so successful that it took six weeks for the Germans to construct a very basic alternative, and during those weeks all German supplies between the major Albanian towns were forced along a narrow dust track which became impassable whenever it rained heavily. The euphoria over the operation was tainted, however, by the news that the LNC had launched a heavy attack on Kupi's forces and were on the advance northwards.[51]

The relatively low level of outright resistance did not stop the Germans from engaging in anti-partisan sweeps during the winter of 1943–44. These were designed to keep the Albanian resistance out of the major towns and away from the lines of communication, and they were largely successful in achieving their aims. In early January 1944 the Germans scored a coup. Three divisions advanced from three different directions on Kostenje, where the headquarters of the LNC and the main British mission were based:

> They had surrounded a big area, with armoured cars and tanks forming a mobile cordon on the roads, and were driving the area from different directions with cavalry and infantry, covered by a cab-rank patrol of Messerschmitt fighters in the air ready to attack the ground, with Fies[e]ler Storch observation planes spotting.

Hoxha and his partisans retreated rapidly to the south, abandoning the British to their fate. Davies was wounded and ordered his chief of staff, Arthur Nicholls, to take over the mission when it became evident that Davies and the other wounded were about to be made POWs. The fate of Nicholls reflected the dangers faced by all BLOs operating in the Balkans in the depths of the winter. His feet were so frostbitten that:

> His means of progression in the first place was to sit on his overcoat and to be pulled down the snow-covered and rocky mountainside by his escort of two partisans. He later succeeded in obtaining a small mule which, although it carried him, was extremely painful since, owing to his height, his mutilated

feet were continually dragging in the snow. He was unable to get his boots on and his feet were wrapped in roughly cured goat skins. Gangrene had set in . . .

By the time Seymour found him, Nicholls was at death's door and he died on 11 February 1944, probably from septicaemia. Davies fared better, as the Germans treated his wounds and he was later flown to Germany.* His plane took him from Tirana over Abas Kupi territory. Davies was furious to note that German traffic was running freely on the roads because Kupi had made no use of the supplies Davies had obtained for him. Another important victim of the German offensives was Philip Leake, who had entered Albania in May 1944 to judge the prospects of resistance for himself, and on 7 June was killed by a German air attack on his camp shortly before his planned departure.[52]

By June 1944 British supplies had enabled the LNC partisans to withstand the German attacks. But it was clear to all observers that civil war had taken precedence over the resistance. It remained to be seen whether the Albanians would make any useful efforts to hamper the German retreat from the Balkans when that occurred.

The announcement of the Italian surrender in September 1943 had caught their garrisons in Yugoslavia and Albania by surprise, but in eastern Crete, the commander of the Italian Siena Division, General Angelo Carta, suspected that Mussolini's overthrow would lead to an armistice and began to make preparations to safeguard his troops. These preparations involved making contact with British liaison officers on the island, notably Patrick Leigh Fermor, and with the local resistance bands led by Manoli Bandouvas. Leigh Fermor received an invitation to secret talks with General Carta through the general's counter-espionage officer, Lieutenant Franco Tavana. He discovered that the Italians were in a quandary: Carta was clearly frightened of the formidable German commander General Friedrich-Wilhelm Müller, who had already visited him to demand that all arms be surrendered to the Germans, whereas Tavana anticipated an Allied invasion and wanted preparations made with the Cretan resistance for opposition to a German takeover.

When news of the armistice reached Crete, General Müller issued a general order which offered the Italians three options: to fight under German command; be disarmed and serve under the Germans in work parties; or be interned. The order contained a warning: 'Whosoever sells or destroys arms of the Italian forces, or whosoever deserts from his unit, will be

* Davies was sent to Mauthausen concentration camp where the commander refused to accept him because Davies was a regular army officer, so he was then sent to the POW camp at Colditz.

considered a *franc-tireur* and as such shot.' Carta recommended following the orders of the Germans, but Bandouvas had other ideas. He encouraged his 160 men to attack the Germans in the Viannos region and sent messengers to Heraklion to urge resistance there. Leigh Fermor and Tom Dunbabin realized that a massacre was in the making and urged Bandouvas to call off his forces. It was too late: on 12 September nearly 2,000 Germans attacked Bandouvas, forcing the band to scatter, and the Germans then destroyed six villages in the Viannos region and executed around 500 civilians. Leigh Fermor managed to reach Carta and offered to escort him to Egypt, and on 16 September the general and a few of his staff officers began making their way to the coast under British escort. The Germans despatched Fieseler Storchs to search for Carta, and dropped leaflets offering a reward of 30 million drachma for handing him over, dead or alive. The evacuation beach was reached on 23 September, where the Carta party was joined by Dunbabin and Bandouvas, the latter demanding evacuation to Egypt. The weather deteriorated during the evacuation and while Carta was securely secreted aboard, there was no room for Bandouvas, and Leigh Fermor was accidentally and unwillingly forced to remain aboard. Bandouvas was safely evacuated a month later.[53]

On mainland Greece the Italian commander of the 11th Army, General Carlo Vecchiarelli, consulted the Germans in Athens, and on the evening of 8 September broadcast to his commanders and troops:

> The Italian troops of the 11th Army will adopt the following line of conduct. If the Germans do not offer armed violence, Italians will not use their arms against them, nor will they make common cause with the rebels or with any Anglo-American forces who may land. They will, however, meet force with force. Every man will remain at his post and his present task. Exemplary discipline will be enforced by every possible means.

Some Italian commanders, however, had different ideas. General Adolfo Infante commanded the Pinerolo Division in Thessaly and was pro-British. He had fought alongside the British during the First World War and had served as an Italian military attaché in London during the 1930s. He was adamant that he would not surrender to the Germans, nor would he give his weapons to the communist ELAS bands. An Italian liaison officer informed John Mulgan: 'These *andartes*, we spit on them. We would not soil ourselves by disputing with them if they want our arms.' Chris 'Monty' Woodhouse managed to secure a co-belligerency agreement whereby the Pinerolo Division would fight alongside the Greek resistance to prevent the German takeover of the large part of Greece formerly garrisoned by the Italian Army. The results were mixed. On 23 September the Italians did fight the Germans, but later on they refused to take part in a British-inspired attack on a German airfield at Larissa. Woodhouse was aware that Italian morale was hopelessly low with the vast majority of men just wanting to go home. He was also alert to the fact that after the failure of the Cairo negotiations,* ELAS wanted to seize as many weapons as possible for its civil war against Napoleon Zervas and was totally uninterested in the fate of the Italian soldiers. Woodhouse successfully arranged the evacuation of General Infante to Italy, via Albania, but in April 1944 British reports suggested that there were around 10,000 dispirited and disarmed Italians wandering around the Greek mountains on the brink of starvation.[54]

The German takeover of Greece was swift, and among the first victims were the Greek Jews. In 1942 the Germans had rounded up the Jews in Salonika, and in 1943 Alois Brunner and Dieter Wisliceny arrived to supervise the transport of 54,000 of them to Auschwitz and Treblinka. Around 3,000–5,000 Jews in German-occupied Greece had found refuge in the Italian zone. These Jews were now in danger, along with the Jews in Athens. In September 1943 Jürgen Stroop and Wisliceny arrived in Athens and summoned the Grand Rabbi, Elias Barzilai, to meet them. Barzilai was ordered to supply the names and addresses of the Athenian Jews. Since the Jews now knew their fate should they obey German orders, there was a calculated policy of non-compliance. Barzilai was smuggled out of Athens by ELAS and many other Jews joined him in the mountains. Only around 1,200 of the 8,000 Jews in Athens complied with German demands to register. The Greek government offered the Germans no assistance and the round-up of the Jews was entirely an SS-led operation. Across Greece the Orthodox Greeks helped Jews to escape from the Germans and to hide. The result was that under 50 per cent of the Jews in the main cities of Athens, Volos, Trikala, and Larissa ever fell into German hands.[55]

German efforts to secure territory formerly occupied by the Italians were brutal and generally successful. The German sweeps across Thessaly and into Epiros reopened the Metsovo–Janina road which had been closed by the resistance during Operation Animals, as well as the railway to Trikala. Mulgan noted the consequences: 'When December began and brought the first heavy snows, free Greece, partisan, *andarte* Greece, was marked by a boundary of blackened villages, its territory determined by a host of starving refugees.' The *andartes* were forced back into the Pindos mountains. Their resistance had 'consisted so often of a few scattered shots fired from a distance, followed by an inevitable and hurried retreat. The Germans

* See Chapter 18.

went where they wanted to go.' Yet German control over the roads and railways was illusory, as the Germans themselves recognized. General Humbert Lanz, commanding the German troops during Operation Panther in Epiros in October and November 1943, noted later: 'Unfortunately the terrain was altogether too inviting for guerrilla warfare. High mountain ranges followed the road on both sides . . . The partisans and those who assisted them lurked everywhere.'[56]

The German conquest of the Peloponnese was especially brutal, to a degree which drew comment even from the Greek collaborationist government under Rallis. At the end of October, guerrillas had abducted and killed 80 German soldiers from General Karlvon Le Suire's 117th Jaeger Division. In reprisal, Le Suire launched operations which led to the execution of 696 Greeks and to the destruction of 25 villages, including the entire male population of Kalavryta. Le Suire was forced to temper the ferocity of his actions, but by spring 1944 the security situation was deteriorating again and in May 1944 he declared martial law over the Peloponnese. German conduct in Macedonia included the massacre of the entire population of the village of Klisura. Neubacher protested:

> It is utter insanity to murder babies, children, women and old men because heavily-armed Red bandits billeted themselves overnight, by force, in their houses, and because they killed two German soldiers near the village. The political effect of this senseless bloodbath doubtless by far exceeds the effect of all propaganda efforts in our fight against Communism . . .
>
> The wonderful result of this heroic deed is that babies are dead. But the partisans continue to live and they will again find quarters by use of submachine guns in completely defenceless villages.[57]

*

The Greeks had offered little resistance to the German takeover of their country because the two opposing forces of ELAS and EDES had become embroiled in what would be round one of the Greek civil war. ELAS had fought the Germans solely for self-defence, but had focused on going on the offensive against its internal enemies, especially EDES under Zervas. It is almost certain that ELAS were the aggressors when they launched attacks on Zervas during October and November 1943 which succeeded in driving EDES back into Epiros, west of the River Arakhthos. In early January 1944 Zervas counter-attacked and advanced deep into Roumeli. In Macedonia ELAS launched attacks on its rival resistance organization, PAO, and Hammond noted:

> Every morning, shortly after dawn, an ELAS firing squad executed Greek civilians, whose crime, presumably, was to be hostile to ELAS . . . These public executions were intended to terrorise the villagers. They certainly did so, and few adults dared to speak to us.

The British response was to cut off the supply of arms and money to ELAS and, after the death of the BLO Lieutenant Hubbard at the hands of ELAS, to question whether the British missions should be withdrawn from Greece altogether. Woodhouse argued against evacuation, and it is a testament to the fact that the British still retained some influence over the Greek resistance that he managed to get all sides, representatives of ELAS, EDES and EKKA, together in Plaka to sign a truce on 29 February 1944. This agreement effectively ended the first round of the civil war, and 'the organisations of EAM/ELAS and EDES undertake the obligation of fighting the Occupation and its collaborators with all their forces, either independently in their respective areas or in common by pre-arranged agreement'. They would also remain within their existing territories and not engage in a turf war.[58]

Round one of the Greek civil war had many consequences. In April 1943 the Rallis government had set up the Security Battalions to assist the Greek gendarmerie to maintain law and order in the country. Recruitment had been slow until the Italian surrender, and the Germans had initially been reluctant to arm and train the recruits. Fears of an Allied invasion impelled the Germans to train and equip the Security Battalions so that they could fight alongside them in that event: however, many officers in the Security Battalions secretly harboured pro-British sentiments. The Security Battalions were united in their detestation of communism. Indeed, much of the growth in the size of the Security Battalions, which reached a maximum strength of 16,000 in the summer of 1944, lay in the fact that many people saw the Security Battalions rather than EDES or EKKA as the main way to forestall a communist takeover of the country. The British SIS agent Nigel Clive reported from Ioannina on the prevailing strand of Greek thought: 'If the Germans win, we have lost Thrace [to Bulgaria]; but if EAM/ELAS wins, we have lost Greece.' Yet the Security Battalions were unpopular in the areas of southern and central Greece where their security operations were conducted with the same high level of brutality as those of the Germans.[59]

EAM used the breathing space granted to ELAS by the Plaka agreement to make another bid for political power. The communists had returned from Cairo in September 1943 convinced that the Greek government-in-exile and the British ambassador Rex Leeper were totally out of sympathy with the true state of republican sentiments within occupied Greece. This was almost certainly the case: the British Foreign Office had blocked the return of Myers to Greece precisely because he reported in depth on the unpopularity of the king in the country. EAM took steps to broaden its appeal during the winter of 1943–4 by making overtures to men such as Georgios Papandreou, a pre-war Liberal politician, and Colonel Euripides Bakirdzis, a member of the right-wing resistance group EKKA. Papandreou ignored EAM/ELAS and travelled to Cairo which he reached on 26 April 1944 and joined the government-in-exile. Bakirdzis agreed to join the new EAM-sponsored *Politiki Epitropi Ethnikis Apeleutherosis*, PEEA (Political Committee of National Liberation), which was set up on 10 March 1944. On 16 March the Greek prime minister in Cairo, Emmanouil Tsouderos, received a telegram from PEEA announcing that it was in effect setting itself up as a provisional government 'for the administration of the areas in Greece already free or being freed', and appealing to Tsouderos to make his government more representative of opinion within Greece. Tsouderos was totally unable to convince the king that he needed to abdicate, or at least to appoint the archbishop of Athens as regent, and therefore resigned. He was replaced by Sofoklis Venizelos, who lasted less than a month before being replaced by Papandreou.

Hammond described the establishment of the PEEA as 'an extremely clever move by Siantos' because it 'cashed in on a reality, the spirit of resistance within Greece', giving the impression of being a broad-based committee, although neither EDES nor EKKA had any representatives on it, despite the fact that EAM control was clear. EAM dominance was apparent when it called elections within 'free Greece'. It was alleged that 1.5 million people voted and EAM emerged as clear victors. Yet this concealed the reality that most of the candidates on the list were members of EAM, the ballot papers were distributed and collected by EAM and the voter had to sign his name (or her name: women voted for the first time) on the ballot sheet.

PEEA proved a popular alternative to the Greek government-in-exile among the Greek armed forces in exile. At the beginning of April 1944 there was a widespread mutiny among the men of the 1st Greek Brigade which was about to sail from Egypt to Italy, and the mutiny spread to three ships of the Greek Navy. The British led the operation to end the mutiny, opening fire on the mutineers at their camp at Bourg-el-Arab on 23 April, and the mutineers surrendered on the following day. The armed services were thoroughly purged, and around 10,000 Greek officers and men were sent to penal camps in southern Egypt. The politically reliable men formed a new 3rd Brigade which later fought in the battle for Rimini in Italy.[60]

Back on mainland Greece the tenuous ceasefire in the civil war between ELAS and EDES brokered by the British in February held, but ELAS turned to eliminating some of its other opponents. Most notable among these was EKKA. This largely conservative movement under Colonel Demetrios Psarros controlled the region of the Parnassos mountains in central Greece which contained the main route into Athens. EKKA was a weak grouping of probably only 350 men and was politically diverse. Some members, notably Captain Euthemios Dedouses, were very conservative, and were in contact with royalist military officers in Athens who were linked to the royalist resistance group *Strateotike Ierarchia* (Military Hierarchy); others such as Bakirdzis leaned to the left and defected to ELAS. In April 1944 ELAS clashed with EKKA over supplies in the village of Dorida and it became clear to the BLO Nick Hammond, now acting as Woodhouse's deputy in Thessaly, that ELAS wanted to use this incident as an excuse to destroy EKKA. Further attacks ensued, followed by the murder of Psarros himself by ELAS on 17 April. The surviving members of EKKA mostly joined the Security Battalions and continued to oppose ELAS. Indeed, the eradication of EKKA had the major effect of stimulating recruitment for the Security Battalions since these battalions were now viewed as the only bulwark against ELAS given that Zervas was located in far-away Epiros.[61]

In April 1944 Nigel Clive summed up the problems in Greece as the population expected liberation that summer:

> What matters most is what will happen thereafter. There is universal apprehension of the immediate aftermath of liberation when it looks as if the towns will become the battlefields of what is now a mountain civil war. Public clamour is for the following things in this order: food, freedom from the German occupation and a minimum of security so that a semblance of democratic life may begin again. No political movement in free Greece is capable of meeting the last requirement. All armed political mountain parties engender different degrees of mistrust.[62]

There was now a real danger that the civil war between ELAS and EDES would be replaced by one between ELAS and the Security Battalions. Although Papandreou and his colleagues in the government-in-exile viewed the Security Battalions as a form of collaboration, which meant that they should be denounced, no formal denunciation of them was made because the government ministers realized that for many people in Greece the Security Battalions were viewed as the only means of preventing the communist domination of Greece.

A conference was set up in Beirut by the British in May 1944 with the hope that representatives of the different resistance groups and the government-in-exile could thrash out an agreement to form a coalition government, a unified military command, and a clarification on the future of the king. Not all the issues were settled when the Lebanon Charter was signed on 20 May. It is worth quoting the charter at length because the aims contained in it highlight issues which caused problems as Greece moved closer to liberation and, indeed, afterwards:

1. The reorganisation and establishment of discipline in the Greek armed forces in the Middle East.
2. Unification, at the appropriate moment, of all guerrilla forces under the command of the Greek government.
3. Cessation of reign of terror in Greek countryside and firm re-establishment of personal security and political liberty of the people, when and where the invader has been driven out.
4. The despatch of sufficient supplies of food and medicines to Greece.
5. The establishment of freedom and order after the liberation to allow the Greek people to freely choose their political and social regime.
6. Severe punishment of traitors and collaborators.
7. Supply of food relief immediately after liberation.
8. The defence of Greece's national rights.

No mention was made of the future of the king: indeed, when EAM/ELAS raised the issue, Papandreou had refused to discuss it. The EAM/ELAS delegates suspected, probably correctly, that much of the charter was specifically designed to forestall a seizure of power by EAM as soon as the German retreat began.

News of the charter received a stormy reception by the ELAS high command. ELAS appears to have decided that the best solution was to win the civil war before the liberation so as to be in a position to dictate terms to the Papandreou government. Therefore, on 19 June, civil war between ELAS and EDES was resumed. It took considerable efforts by the British diplomats and BLOs to persuade EAM to alter its policy at the end of July 1944 and to join the Papandreou government.[63]

With all the evidence of civil war in Greece it is fair to question whether there was any resistance to the German occupation during this period. The records, ELAS, SOE and the Germans, all agree that ELAS was responsible for most sabotage at the time. Between October 1943 and April 1944 SOE concluded that there had been 16 actions by ELAS, 9 by the Allied military mission of which 8 had received ELAS assistance, and only one action by

EDES, and the German records suggest that this is an accurate picture. ELAS records, as listed exhaustively by Sarafis, suggest that ELAS was in constant action against the Germans, but careful analysis of his list demonstrates that while there were sabotage actions against the railways, most of the action by ELAS was of a defensive nature in response to German probes. Indeed, ELAS put up very little resistance to the German anti-partisan drive in the spring of 1944 when three German divisions swept through the main Pindos range 'leaving little in its trail except more burnt villages and more contempt for ELAS's passivity'. Mulgan suggested that ELAS tended to tell stories of battles, but 'it was the height of bad manners to try and check up on one of these battles'. All records show a relatively low level of German casualties: around 100 in the autumn of 1943 and 1,000 between January and June 1944. The *andartes* suffered far higher casualties. This disparity in losses goes a long way to explain the almost total inactivity of Zervas and EDES, which was husbanding its forces from the dual enemies of ELAS and the Germans.[64]

Various different conclusions have been drawn from the events in Greece during this period. David Wallace was parachuted into Greece in July 1944 and, in a report to Cairo despatched in August 1944 shortly before his death while observing an anti-German action by EDES, he concluded:

> Our effort in Greece, in men and money, has not only been out of all proportion to the results we have achieved against the Germans, but also to the value of the Greek people, who are not capable of being saved from themselves, nor are themselves worth it. This is also the unanimous opinion of all British liaison officers, who have been long in this country.[65]

At this time there were seventy officers with the Allied military mission, mostly British but with a few Americans, and a large number of other ranks. An OSS report by Charles Edson in December 1943 concluded: 'One thing I regard as established and in this every person of any information agrees: the British have tragically mismanaged the Greek situation.' OSS argued for an independent American policy in the Balkans, but the British were determined to keep the Americans out of the region and largely succeeded in doing so.[66] As to the future, Brigadier Karl Barker-Benfield, in charge of Greece in SOE Cairo, produced a memorandum in May 1944 arguing:

> Our immediate policy should be the purely military one of giving support to the guerrilla organisations to enable them to assist in liberating their country and ensuring that Greece continues as a British sphere of influence.

> This should give way to the political policy of no support to EAM as soon as liberation is achieved.
>
> The change-over from one to the other is certain to cause opposition from ELAS and can only be carried out successfully if British troops are sent to Greece at the appropriate time. These troops would have two roles, firstly, that of hitting the Germans where they are weakest, and secondly, that of ensuring a British Military control of the whole country.[67]

The efforts to implement this policy will be covered in a later chapter.

The Allied military mission on the Greek mainland was largely unsuccessful in its attempts to quell the flames of civil war, but on Crete, where the same problems emerged on a smaller scale, the BLOs had greater success. Much of this is down to the sensitive work of Xan Fielding, who set up a meeting between representatives of EAM and EOK in November 1943 which resulted in a non-aggression pact. The SOE agent Sandy Rendel, however, noted ominous developments:

> The political leaders in Crete, and a growing number of fellow-travellers and moderates and a large body of non-political peasants, who merely wished to 'resist', were in fact joining the local leftist organisation, which the communists increasingly controlled.[68]

The communist threat to resistance unity did not emerge yet, but there was increasing evidence of Cretan ambivalence towards British operations on the island: this was most evident in the Viannos district which had seen brutal reprisals in the summer of 1943. Rendel noted: 'But instead of the usual comradely welcome which I had come to expect from Cretan men of all ages, when they learnt that I was British, I could feel a suppressed tension.' Attempts to secure the unconditional support of the Cretans were not helped when the likeable Fielding was replaced at the end of 1943 by Dennis Ciclitira, who made little effort to hide his dislike of the Cretans. The principal act of British-sponsored resistance in this period was the kidnap of General Heinrich von Kreipe. This story can be read as a light-hearted caper or as an operation with serious consequences for the Cretans.[69]

Leigh Fermor parachuted back into Crete on 4 February 1944 with the plan to kidnap General Müller, who had ordered brutal reprisals against the Cretans for resistance. The operation was delayed by the bad weather which caused the postponement of the arrival of the supporting party led by Captain Stanley Moss. In the meantime Leigh Fermor cultivated the friendship of Athanasios Bourdzalis and planned to use his band in the kidnap, and of Miki Akoumianakis, who knew the area around the Villa

Ariadne near Knossos, where the general lived, and had also befriended the general's driver. Plans for the kidnap went ahead despite Müller's replacement by General von Kreipe on 1 March 1944.

An attack on the Villa Ariadne was dismissed since reconnaissance revealed that it was surrounded by barbed wire and that the perimeter was regularly patrolled. Therefore, the party concluded that the attack needed to be made when the general was en route from his headquarters in Canea to the Villa Ariadne, a journey always made after dark and often without an escort. Various factors intervened to complicate the planning. ELAS heard of the plan and threatened to betray it, but Leigh Fermor wrote a letter persuading them to hold off. More seriously, some men from Bourdzalis's band had been spotted by the Germans near the target crossroads. Leigh Fermor sent the majority of the men back into the mountains, and retained a few local men to act as a support group to prevent the unplanned arrival of another vehicle on the road while the kidnapping was taking place.

On 26 April 1944 the perfect moment arrived to put the plan into practice, for word was received that the general's car was coming without an escort:

> Capt. Moss and I put on German police corporal uniforms, and hastened with our party to the road fork. Elias [Athanassakis] was posted near Arkhanes to signal one torch flash at the approach of the car (2 flashes if accompanied) to a scout posted nearer us who was to signal down half a kilometre of flex to an electric bell, next to another scout who was to flash the signal to us. Moss and I took up our positions as traffic MPs in the road, the men ... were hidden in ditches either side of the road fork.

The car stopped, then Moss hit the driver and dragged him out of the car onto the road. The general was handcuffed until he gave his word of honour not to attempt to escape. Moss drove the car past the Villa Ariadne where the sentries saluted, through twenty-two control posts and through Heraklion before the car stopped on the Rethymno road where the party split. Moss took the general deep into the mountains and Leigh Fermor drove the car to the coast where he left a letter for the German authorities:

> Gentlemen, Your Divisional Commander, General Kreipe, was captured a short time ago by a British raiding force under our command. By the time you read this both he and we will be on our way to Cairo.
>
> We would like to point out most emphatically that this operation has been carried out without the help of Cretans or Cretan partisans, and the only guides used were serving soldiers of His Hellenic Majesty's Forces in the Middle East, who came with us.

> Your general is an honourable prisoner of war, and will be treated with all the consideration owing to his rank.
>
> Any reprisals against the local population will be wholly unwarranted and unjust.

Leigh Fermor also left a commando beret and a British greatcoat in the car. The message was supposed to be supported by leaflets dropped by the RAF, but bad weather prevented the flight. Furthermore, it was planned that the BBC should announce the kidnapping and state that the general was already on his way to Cairo. Instead, disastrously, the BBC announced that the general 'was being taken off the island'.

The BBC report meant that the Germans immediately launched a massive manhunt on land and from the air, effectively closing off the southern coast for the evacuation. The Germans dropped leaflets:

> To all Cretans, last night German General Kreipe was abducted by bandits. He is now being concealed in the Cretan mountains, and his whereabouts cannot be unknown to the populace. If the General is not returned within three days all rebel villages in the Heraklion district will be razed to the ground and the severest measures of reprisal will be brought to bear on the civilian population.

On 4 May the Germans bombed and totally destroyed the villages of Saktouria, Margarikari, Lokria, and Kamares, but this was because they were known for their resistance and not in direct reprisal for the kidnap. The evacuation was delayed by radio problems and in the meantime von Kreipe and Leigh Fermor struck up a friendship, quoting a Horace ode together. Despite the evidence of an intense German search, von Kreipe was also impressed by the freedom of movement experienced by the Cretans, commenting to Leigh Fermor: 'I am beginning to wonder who is occupying this island – us or the English.' Finally, on the night of 14 May, the general and the abduction party were successfully evacuated from Crete and arrived in Cairo, where von Kreipe was greeted with full military honours by Barker-Benfield.

Back on Crete there was a mixed reaction to the kidnap. Allegedly, the reaction of von Kreipe's chief of staff was: 'Well, gentlemen, I think this calls for champagne all round.' The general's aide-de-camp and the sentries at the Villa Ariadne were arrested by the Gestapo. Controversy has reigned, however, regarding the German reprisals launched immediately after the operation, especially against the villages in the Amari valley in late August. Research into the German records appears to suggest that these reprisals were designed to reassert German dominance and total lack of tolerance for any acts of resistance and were not connected with the kidnap of the general. Manoussos Manoussakis, who had been in Canea at the time when the news of the kidnap arrived, noted that the Cretans were feeling two centimetres taller the next day: rather than being direct reprisals, the German actions were aimed to cut the Cretans down to size.[70]

22

Challenges and Dilemmas in the East

After the battle of Kursk in the mid-summer of 1943 the Soviets launched major drives westwards with such force that the German armies had little option but to retreat. In August 1943 Bryansk, the scene of so many German anti-partisan actions, was liberated, followed soon after by the major city of Kharkov. Field Marshal Erich von Manstein obtained Hitler's reluctant agreement to order a general retreat to the line of the River Dnepr where a new defence line would be constructed stretching from Smolensk to Kiev and on to the Black Sea. The line failed to hold and on 22 September Soviet spearheads crossed the Dnepr, and by the end of the month Smolensk had been liberated. In the south the Germans were cut off in the Crimea and the Kuban bridgehead in the Caucasus had to be abandoned. During the winter of 1943–44 the Soviets advanced in the north, raising the siege of Leningrad and liberating the city, before reaching the frontiers of the Baltic States. In the centre Kiev was liberated on 6 November, and by the end of the year the Soviet armies had reached the pre-war Polish-Soviet frontier. Further south a very powerful offensive was launched in March 1944 which brought Soviet troops to the line of the Carpathian mountains, into Bukovina, across the River Dnestr into Bessarabia, followed by the establishment of bridgeheads across the River Prut into Romania proper. The only German troops now remaining on Soviet territory belonged to Army Group Centre, which held a large salient north of the Pripet Marshes in Belorussia.

The resistance forces from the Baltic to the Black Sea who lay in the path of the Soviet storm towards Germany faced a number of challenges and dilemmas when considering their response. These were countries who had only achieved their independence after the First World War – Poland, Lithuania, Latvia, Estonia, Czechoslovakia – whose predominant concern was the restoration of that independence. Both Poland and Czechoslovakia had armed resistance movements active against the Germans, but they were unclear how the Soviet armies would respond to them. In the case of the Baltic

States, armed resistance was limited but there was a degree of political resistance. The Ukraine and Belorussia were in a similar situation: although they were part of the Soviet Union, there were elements of the population who wanted independence. For all these countries the question was the same – was the greater enemy the retreating Germans or the advancing Soviets?

The position of Hitler's allies – Romania, Hungary, and Bulgaria – was equally challenging. Romania and Hungary had suffered heavy military losses as a result of taking part in the German campaign in the Soviet Union, whereas Bulgaria had declined to take part but had been content to occupy part of Yugoslavia and Greece on the back of German victories. Now the dilemma for these countries and their potential or actual resistance movements was how to abandon the clearly lost German cause without suffering either a German invasion or a Soviet occupation. A complicating factor was the Allied insistence on unconditional surrender by both Germany and its satellites.

To varying degrees these eastern and central European countries looked towards the western Allies, Britain, and the United States, for protection from the threat to their political independence posed by the imminent arrival of the armies of the third Ally, the Soviet Union. They sought comfort from the Atlantic Charter, which had been issued by Roosevelt and Churchill in August 1941 as a broad statement of Allied war aims. Among the eight points, two were of especial relevance: that all people had a right to self-determination, and that territorial adjustments must be in accord with the wishes of the peoples concerned. Yet as early as Eden's visit to Moscow in December 1941, and confirmed by the negotiations for the Anglo-Soviet Treaty in May 1942, it was clear that the Soviet Union expected to achieve her 1941 frontiers at the end of the war. This meant that the Soviet Union would absorb the Baltic States of Estonia, Latvia, and Lithuania, half of Poland, and the Romanian territories of Bessarabia and northern Bukovina. At that time Churchill and Eden firmly rejected Stalin's demands. But during 1943, as it became clear that these countries would be liberated by the Soviet armies, Churchill changed his attitude, writing to Eden on 16 January 1944:

> Undoubtedly my own feelings have changed in the two years that have passed . . . The tremendous victories of the Russian armies, the deep-seated changes which have taken place in the character of the Russian State and Government, the new confidence which has grown in our hearts towards Stalin – these have all had their effect. Most of all is the fact that the Russians may very soon be in physical possession of these territories, and it is absolutely certain that we should never attempt to turn them out.[1]

Part of Churchill's change of heart was rooted in pure pragmatism: eastern and central Europe would be liberated by the Soviets, and this would save Allied lives. But Churchill and Roosevelt also believed that the nature of Stalinism had changed under the pressure of war: for example, the prohibition on religious worship had been relaxed, and the Comintern had been abolished in May 1943.*

The political leaders in the countries of eastern and central Europe, whether in exile or at home, did not share the optimism of the western Allies. What the British ambassador to the Polish government-in-exile, Owen O'Malley, wrote of the Poles is true of the other countries as well:

> This difference of view between the Poles and their allies was natural, for Poland is situated next door to the jungle where the gorillas and rattlesnakes live, and the Poles thought they knew much more about the nature and behaviour of these animals than Mr Churchill and Mr Roosevelt.[2]

The countries in the path of the Soviet advance suspected, with good reason, that Stalin not only wanted physical control over their territories, but also political control over their governance. The resistance armies had to consider whether to husband some of their forces for the future, when their target would be the occupying Soviets. The Soviets were aware of the danger that those engaged in the resistance against the Germans might continue in existence to oppose them. The suspicions held by the Soviets are illustrated by a conversation between Edvard Beneš, head of the Czechoslovak government-in-exile, and Molotov in Moscow at the end of 1943:

> Beneš: We ask you to help us with armaments, because a revolution, a partisan war, will break out in our country at the end.
> Molotov: Between whom?[3]

*

The Soviet partisan movement reached its peak of strength and effectiveness in late 1943 and the first half of 1944. The partisans now fielded around 35,000–40,000 men and women. The increase in numbers had come about largely through conscription of Soviet citizens in newly liberated areas, but also because former collaborators came over to the Soviet side, often having first killed their German overseers. The partisans were also now far better armed and equipped: between May 1943 and January 1944 they had received 32,867 rifles and carbines, 5,710 pistols and revolvers, 17,357 sub-machine guns, 2,608 machine guns, 590 anti-tank rifles,

* The tasks of the Comintern were in fact just taken over by the International Department of the Central Committee of the Communist Party.

737 mortars, as well as a generous allocation of ammunition and grenades. As the front lines moved closer to the partisan areas, Soviet air power enabled a constant supply of weaponry, as well as the despatch of demolition specialists and the evacuation of wounded partisans. The partisans now controlled areas where rudimentary airfields could be constructed on which small aircraft could land, although most supplies were still received through airdrops. Unlike in the early years, partisan action could be coordinated with Red Army attacks since most partisan units now had radios and could receive regular and relevant orders from above. In contrast, the Germans were fast running out of troops, and the quality of officers and men both in the front line and in the rear areas was declining rapidly.[4]

One purpose of the partisans was to supply intelligence regarding German defences and dispositions, especially along the line of the River Dnepr. This was sometimes seriously inaccurate, as in September 1943 when three Soviet airborne divisions were dropped to the bridgehead at Velikii Burin, south of Kiev, only to discover that partisan and Soviet intelligence had overlooked the presence of two Panzer and three infantry divisions in the area, with the result that the Soviet paratroopers suffered exceedingly heavy casualties. There were, however, notable successes such as detailed intelligence on German defences in the Mogilev region in January 1944, and a detailed map of German Army Group Centre's defensive positions in June 1944 on the eve of Operation Bagration.[5]

The principal contribution of the partisans was to maintain the 'rail war' begun before the battle of Kursk. During the Soviet winter offensive towards Leningrad the German war diaries recorded that both the 8th Jaeger and 12th Panzer Divisions were notably delayed on their way to the front by partisan activity. This was at its highest level in Belorussia, the area behind Army Group Centre. In August 1943, for example, there were 21,300 rail attacks, and between September and November 1943 the Rear Area Army Group Centre noted that 20,505 rails had been destroyed, in effect paralysing railway communications in the area. These partisan attacks were now more effective and long-lasting. The combination of delayed explosions and chain explosions meant that the Germans often had to use the rails from one side of a dual-track railway to rebuild one track and keep it open, effectively reducing the railway capacity by half. German difficulties were exacerbated by other factors, such as the increasing number of acts of sabotage committed by native workers who targeted the locomotives. The 'rail war' tailed off during the winter of 1943–44 because of a shortage of mines and explosives before increasing again in the spring and reaching a high in the weeks leading up to the launching of Bagration.[6]

The nuisance value of the Soviet partisans compelled the Germans, despite the weakness of their forces in the rear areas, to mount a series of anti-partisan operations in Belorussia. Operation Entenjagd in the middle of October 1943 and Operation Heinrich in late October aimed at disrupting the partisans in the Rossano forest region, near Nevel and Polotsk. This area had long been held by the partisans but now that it was close to the front lines, SS-Obergruppenführer Erich von dem Bach-Zelewski wanted the region cleared. The operations failed because the partisans declined to give battle, and because the closeness of the front lines necessitated the withdrawal of participating SS police units to strengthen the German defences.[7] In April and May 1944 the Germans launched two operations, Regenschauer and Frühlingsfest, against the 18,000 partisans operating in the Ushachi region, 100 kilometres behind the front line running near Vitebsk. On this occasion the Germans succeeded in hitting the partisans hard, leaving 7,000 partisans dead and capturing a further 7,000. This reduced the threat posed by the partisans to German supply and communication lines running to the vital railheads of Vitebsk and Orsha. Similar German successes were recorded in the last anti-partisan action to take place on pre-war Soviet territory, Operation Kormoran, launched in late May against the wide area around Lepel, Senno, Borisov, Minsk, and Molodechno. On this occasion the partisan defence was uncoordinated as the command was split between a Red Army general officer and a Communist Party official. The result was that the partisans were forced into ever-decreasing areas of swampy ground and suffered heavy losses: they were saved from total annihilation by the start of Bagration.[8]

In a last-ditch effort to reduce the partisan threat, the chief of the German operations staff General Alfred Jodl issued a new manual on anti-partisan warfare in May 1944. Now POW status was to be granted to captured partisans regardless of whether they were wearing uniforms or were in civilian clothing. If, however, the partisan was wearing a German uniform he was to be interrogated carefully and, if found guilty of having taken part in combat, he was to be shot, but if he had not participated in partisan actions he was to be considered a POW. Jodl also counselled against taking reprisals against the civilian population. These positive steps were virtually countermanded and made meaningless by the more general German policy instituted during their retreat – scorched earth. Apart from burning and destroying all buildings or crops of any possible value to the Soviets, the Germans also denuded the country of its population. All men of fighting age were now regarded as POWs and they, and women aged fourteen to forty-five, were herded westwards on foot in columns containing up to 50,000 people. Also in retreat were the estimated

27,000 collaborators who feared Soviet revenge, and among them were Russian units who would continue to serve the German cause, notably those led by Bronislav Kaminsky and General Vlasov.[9]

As the Soviets advanced and overran partisan strongholds, the strongest and fittest partisans were gradually absorbed into the ranks of the Red Army. For those unsuited to the demands of regular warfare there remained the task of hunting down isolated German groups who had become separated from their units during the retreat. Suspected collaborators were investigated and severely punished for their disloyalty to the Soviet Union.[10]

Belorussia had never been an independent country and before the war it had been split between the Soviet Union and Poland. From September 1939 to June 1941 all Belorussian territory had first been incorporated into the Soviet Union and then come under German occupation. Both occupations had been brutal and had crushed the aspirations of those wanting independence. Ideal terrain for partisan warfare meant that Belorussia saw a high level of partisan activity, and the German anti-partisan sweeps caused heavy casualties among the civilian population. The Soviet partisans scored a major victory on the night of 22 September 1943 when Reichskommissar Wilhelm Kube was killed by a bomb placed under his bed by his maid. Kube was replaced by SS General Curt von Gottberg, who quickly gained a reputation for such a reign of terror that even German officials complained to Berlin that his policies meant that 'strongly anti-Bolshevik people, or at least people sympathetic to the Germans, or neutral' were being executed.

As the Soviets advanced the Germans began to make conciliatory approaches designed to win over the peasants and the political class. The Belorussian peasantry deeply resented the imposition of collective farms by the Soviets and in June 1943 Alfred Rosenberg had issued a decree permitting the private ownership of land. The impact of this measure was all but nullified by stringent conditions surrounding its application. In July 1943 Kube had attempted to win over the support of Belorussian politicians by creating a council *Mužy daveru* (Men of Confidence), but it achieved little. In December 1943 Curt von Gottberg convened the council and issued an amnesty to all partisans who would lay down their arms: thousands did so. Von Gottberg then went further and appealed to Belorussian calls for independence by asking the pro-German Radoslav Astroŭski to form a new council, the *Belaruskaya Tsentral'naya Rada* (BTsR), to take over the civilian administration of the country. The first step taken by the BTsR was the creation of a national defence force – the *Krayovaya Abarona* – which would wear Belorussian national colours and would take action against the Soviet partisans. The *Rada* drafted around 100,000 men, formed into eighty battalions, but the German failure to arm them meant that the majority fled to the partisans. The BCR called for elections to a convention which would represent 'all the peoples in Belorussia irrespective of race and creed', and would reassert the very brief declaration of independence which had been issued in March 1918. The convention met for the first time on 27 June 1944 when Bagration had already been launched. Just as in 1918, Belorussian calls for independence were crushed by the arrival of the Soviets.[11]

In the Ukraine aspirations to independence had been dashed by the Germans in 1941 but were now reborn under the UPA, the Ukrainian nationalist army. The UPA challenged all those who would dispute the Ukrainian right to self-determination, whether they were Germans, Soviets, or the Poles who lived in the western part of the Ukraine which had been part of Poland before the war. In October and November 1943 the UPA fought the Germans forty-seven times, and the Soviet partisans fifty-four times. On 29 February 1944 it ambushed and killed the Soviet General N. F. Vatutin, commander of the 1st Ukrainian Front, and at the end of April 1944 there was a major clash between about 5,000 UPA soldiers and 3,000 NKVD police troops in Hurby in the Kremianets region. The UPA policy of murdering Poles on what they considered to be Ukrainian territory now extended into East Galicia. For example, in January and February 1944, 600 Poles were murdered by the UPA in Tarnopol province, and Poles from East Galicia began to flee westwards.[12]

The Poles were defenceless against the UPA, and also struggled to reassert sovereignty over Vilna and its surrounding territory which had been part of Poland before the war but was now in Lithuania. On 20 June 1944 the *Lietuvos Vietiné Rinktiné*, LVR (Lithuanian Defence Force), massacred thirty-nine Polish villagers in Glinciszki (now Glitiškės) in the Vilna area in retaliation for the murder of four Lithuanian collaborating policemen by the Polish AK. In response the AK killed twenty-seven Lithuanian villagers in Dubingiai.[13] Soviet partisans, especially the column led by Sydir Kovpak, sought to reassert Soviet dominance over the region. Kovpak's column travelled over 6,000 miles through eighteen provinces of the Ukraine, Belorussia, and into the Polish Galician provinces of Tarnopol, Rovno, and Stanisławów towards the Carpathians in pursuit of that goal, fighting Ukrainians, Poles, and Germans on the way.[14] The threat posed to the reassertion of Polish pre-war territorial and political integrity by the UPA, the Lithuanians, and the Soviet partisans led to controversial agreements in December 1943 between a few AK commanders – Captain

Adolf Pilch* in the Nowogródek region, Lieutenant Józef Świda in Lida, and Aleksander Krzyżanowski – and the Germans. These agreements stipulated that the AK would receive arms and supplies from the Germans in return for engaging in anti-partisan warfare: these agreements were totally condemned both by the AK high command and by General Sosnkowski in London.[15]

In Poland the resistance to the German occupation had been active since the start. By the summer of 1943 the situation had deteriorated to the extent that the Germans classed the entire General Government as a 'bandit combat area'. This meant that no trials were deemed necessary before a suspect could be executed: indeed, over 8,000 Poles were shot by the Germans in Warsaw alone between October 1943 and July 1944. The Germans were alarmed by the quantity of weapons and explosives the AK had in its caches. For example, in April 1944 the German chief of the security police, Paul Otto Geibel, informed Hans Frank, head of the General Government, that in recent months over 20,000 infantry weapons had been seized, along with the discovery of 75,000 bombs, 14,500 kilograms of explosive, and other materiel suitable for clandestine warfare.[16]

The AK command had been wary of authorizing the assassinations of Germans after the news reached them of the severe reprisals in the Protectorate following the assassination of Heydrich. The escalating nature of the German repression of the Poles during 1943 caused a change of heart. Now assassinations were permitted, but 'only those Germans are to be eliminated whose death will cause the greatest impression on the enemy, most inconvenience and the greatest tactical discomfiture'.[17] On 7 September 1943 SS-Oberscharführer Franz Bürkl, deputy commander of the Pawiak prison, was killed with some of his Gestapo colleagues in Warsaw. On 2 January 1944 the AK attempted to kill the governor of Warsaw, Ludwig Fischer, on his way back from a hunting trip, but the operation failed because Fischer had switched cars at the last moment and his colleague Ludwig Leist became the unintended victim of the operation. Later that month an attempt was made on the life of Hans Frank when a bomb exploded under his train near Cracow. On 1 February 1944 the AK scored a major success. Their target, the SS and Police Leader for Warsaw, General Franz Kutschera, had been deemed worth the deaths of 200 hostages in

* At the beginning of December 1943 Pilch had met the Soviet partisan commander Major Wasiliewicz expecting to receive weapons from the partisans but instead found his unit surrounded and disarmed.

reprisal. He was a difficult target to reach since he only appeared in the open for the brief 200-metre drive from his home to his office. At 9 a.m. his car was blocked by a twelve-strong AK team when trying to enter the courtyard to his office, and he was killed with shots from a Sten gun. Two of the team, including its leader, Bronisław Pietraszewicz, were mortally wounded in a firefight with the SS sentries. Hitler was outraged and ordered that a quota of hostages should be shot in every town in the General Government. The municipality of Warsaw was fined 100 million złoty. Across Poland, other Gestapo chiefs were successfully targeted, such as Otto Schultz in the Opatów area and Franz Witek in Kielce.[18]

The Polish partisans loyal to the AK were also active in the forests, their strength and purpose aided by the arrival of more *Cichociemni* from Britain. In April 1944, at the express request of London the *Cichociemni* launched Operation Jula, the battle of the rails in Poland. The Berlin–Warsaw express was derailed near the station of Szymanów west of Błonie, causing the death of a German general and injuries to many soldiers. The 150-foot span of the railway bridge over the Wisłoka, in the Przeworsk-Rozwadów sector, was targeted by 'Szyb', who later recalled:

> Two trains were coming, one in each direction. They were going to pass each other on the bridge. One locomotive thundered over the bridge and already a long stream of trucks was following. I waited as long as I could; then as the second locomotive was coming over the bridge, we detonated the charges.[19]

In all, the German records confirmed damage to nearly 7,000 locomotives and over 19,000 railway wagons, 732 derailed trains, and thirty-eight destroyed railway bridges: thirty-four railway routes had been targeted in over 6,000 separate incidents. Lord Selborne wrote to the Polish commander-in-chief, General Sosnkowski, expressing his delight at the success of the operation.[20]

The AK faced challenges to their existence in the forests from the Polish communist GL/AL who would attack them. A senior AL officer admitted after the war: 'I was in an organisation that was to fight against the Germans, but instead we were murdering Poles and Jews. We were told that the struggle against the reactionaries and the NSZ was more important than the struggle against the Germans.' The AK suffered from a severe shortage of weapons since it received little from the few airdrops made to them by flights from Italy. In contrast, the GL/AL was becoming better equipped through Soviet airdrops. These supplies enabled them to expand to eleven brigades during the first few months of 1944, and in April a Polish partisan staff was set up under Aleksander Zawadzki.[21]

The Soviet partisans, however, posed the greatest danger to the AK. At the end of November 1943 the chief of staff of the Soviet partisan command, General Ponomarenko, issued an order calling for the disarmament of all Polish partisan units, meaning the AK, and the execution of those members who resisted. The AK knew nothing of this order. Therefore, when Polish AK partisan leaders were invited to meetings with local Soviet partisan units they went along expecting to discuss collaboration in the battle against the German occupier. On several occasions, however, Polish partisan leaders such as 'Bomba' were then surrounded by machine guns, disarmed, and often later murdered. This state of affairs led to unusual temporary collaborationist agreements. For example, the AK noted that 'sometimes the Germans and Russian-led communists were quite close to each other, each in turn attacking the Home Army partisans while leaving the other alone'.[22]

The Polish government-in-exile and the AK high command had long been considering the response of the AK and the Underground Government to the entry of Soviet armies into Polish territory. Before his death in an air crash in July 1943, Władysław Sikorski had argued that the Soviets should be greeted as allies but, should the 'Russian attitude to us become clearly hostile', then it would be advisable 'to reveal only the civilian administration and to withdraw the AK units into the interior of the country to save them from destruction'. General Rowecki, however, was less sanguine about the prospect of cooperating with the Soviet armies and requested permission to prepare a resistance to them. The matter had not been settled before Sikorski's death and Rowecki's arrest. It had to be revisited by the new prime minister, Stanisław Mikołajczyk, Sosnkowski, and the new commander of the AK, Tadeusz Bór-Komorowski. To make things worse, the lack of diplomatic relations between the Polish government-in-exile and the Soviets meant that no cooperation could be discussed by the interested parties. In August 1943 Bór-Komorowski pressed London for advice and for a decision to be made on the circumstances under which he should call for the long-planned-for general uprising.[23]

The reply from London was received on 26 October 1943. It appalled Bór-Komorowski and the government delegate, Jan Jankowski, for its lack of any sense of reality. Plans were to be prepared for a national uprising, known as Operation Burza, along the lines of several possible scenarios: one was that the Red Army would halt on the border of Poland until the western Allies had landed in northern France; another, that the Soviet forces would penetrate into Poland and fight the Germans. In the latter case the Polish government-in-exile stipulated that if diplomatic relations with the Soviets were restored, then both the AK and Underground Government should come out into the open and begin to administer the liberated areas while the Soviet-German conflict continued. If, however, diplomatic relations were not restored (as seemed more likely), then the AK and Underground Government should remain hidden. Bór-Komorowski believed that these instructions were deeply flawed and had ignored all the evidence he had supplied on the growing impatience for action among the ranks of the AK, and the threat posed by the Soviet partisans and those of the GL/AL. As he wrote after the war, he believed that 'the only chance of gaining anything was a constant demonstration of our will to fight Germany to the last, sparing no effort, in the teeth of every adversary'.[24] This meant that the AK had to come out into the open regardless of the possible consequences.

At the end of November 1943 Bór-Komorowski issued orders for Operation Burza. He informed London:

> As can be seen from the order, I have given all commanders and units instructions to emerge into the open after taking part in operations against the retreating Germans. Their task at that moment will be to give evidence of the existence of the Republic of Poland . . . In the event of a second Soviet occupation, I am preparing a skeleton network of a new organisation which will be at the General's [Sosnkowski's] disposal.[25]

As Jan Nowak, a Polish courier present in London when Bór-Komorowski's order arrived, put it: 'a storm blew up in Polish circles'.[26] The strongly anti-Soviet Sosnkowski was incensed since he wanted the uprising to take place later, when the western Allies were pressing at the German frontiers. He was convinced that the Soviet practice of disarming Polish partisan units would only increase as more AK units revealed themselves. The government-in-exile was more optimistic, and in February 1944 Bór-Komorowski received an amended order giving the terms on which the AK units were to reveal themselves to the Soviets: 'By order of the Government of the Polish Republic, we present ourselves as the representatives of the Polish administration (as commanders of AK units) with proposals to establish collaboration on these territories with the armed forces of the Soviet Union, for mutual action against the common enemy.'[27]

The orders issued for Burza indicate the scale and organization of the proposed uprising:

> Partisan groups were assembled into larger units and directed to districts which lay across the German lines of retreat. In the eastern provinces, which were the first to start Burza operations, all soldiers of the Home Army were

> being mobilised. Regiments, battalions and divisions received names and numbers as in 1939. Arms and ammunition, radio and other equipment, stores, warm clothing (short uniform overcoats, caps and boots), hospital equipment, etc. – all these things manufactured at home in secret workshops – were being gradually smuggled to the forests. The Polish partisan groups in the east grew into substantial regular forces long before the Red Army front reached them.[28]

Every unit received a shortwave radio transmitter to keep Bór-Komorowski informed on the attitude and conduct of the Soviet troops.

On the night of 4–5 January 1944 the Red Army crossed the pre-war Polish frontier at Sarny and advanced into Volhynia towards Łuck and Równe (Rivne). On 5 January, Mikołajczyk broadcast to Poland: 'We should have preferred to meet the Soviet troops not merely as allies of our allies, fighting against the common enemy, but as our own allies as well.'[29] The first AK troops encountered by the Soviet armies belonged to the 27th Volhynian Division. This was a well-equipped division commanded by Major Wojciech Kiwerski, containing 7,300 men divided into eight battalions, two squadrons of cavalry, as well as units of signals, engineers, and military police. It was well armed with 4,500 rifles, 700 pistols, 140 submachine guns, 100 machine guns, and three anti-tank guns.[30] The division had been bloodied in actions against the Germans and Ukrainians in Volhynia and had taken control of the town of Turzysk (Turiysk).

The first contact between Kiwerski and the Soviet commanders, General Sergeyev and Colonel Charytonov, seemed very promising: the Poles would agree to 'complete tactical subordination to the Soviet command', and in return would receive arms and equipment from the Soviets and be recognized as 'a Polish division taking orders from Warsaw and London'. The news reached Bór-Komorowski who promptly radioed it back to London: permission was granted to the 27th Division to agree the terms of cooperation. The strategic railway junction of Kowel (Kovel), which was well defended by German troops under the temporary command of Bach-Zelewski, proved to be the acid test of this policy. During the battle for Kowel the Germans counter-attacked against the Poles and Soviets with four divisions, including SS Panzer Division Wiking, composed of collaborators from Denmark, Norway, Estonia, the Netherlands, and Belgium. Under German pressure the Polish and Soviet troops became separated and the Poles were left to fight alone. As losses mounted, the abandoned Poles destroyed their heavy armaments and freed 900 horses, and then 'we took light automatic weapons, as much ammunition as we could carry, and we set off towards the Pripet marshes'. Two months later, having been hunted by the Germans, the remnants of the division, now under Major Tadeusz Sztumberk-Rychter after Kiwerski had been killed in action, was ordered to retreat westwards across the River Bug.[31]

The first major battle of Operation Burza had demonstrated that the front-line Soviet forces could be considered an ally of the Polish partisans, and this boded well for future cooperation as the Soviets pushed the Germans further back across Poland. But there were ominous portents for the future. During the spring and early summer of 1944 the Soviets gradually pushed the Germans out of parts of the Polish provinces of Wołyń, Stanisławów, and Tarnopol before the front stalled. In the interim the NKVD troops arrived and began forcibly disarming all the AK units they encountered. In April conscription was introduced into the 1st Polish Army, and those who resisted disarmament and conscription were arrested and deported into the Soviet Union: by July over 6,000 AK soldiers had been arrested.[32]

There were ominous developments on the political front too. In December 1943 the Polish communists had set up a National Council for the Homeland – *Krajowa Rada Narodowa* – under the presidency of Bolesław Bierut. Its first manifesto was issued on 31 December and stated that the Polish government-in-exile had no right to represent the Polish people, accepted the Soviet demands on the revision of the eastern frontier, and made it clear that only the Communist Party would rule after the war. The Union of Polish Patriots, still in the Soviet Union and sponsors of the 1st Polish Army fighting under Soviet command, also made a bid for post-war political power. Towards the end of 1943 the Union established the Polish National Committee – *Polski Komitet Narodowy* – specifically designed to establish itself as the provisional government of liberated Poland. The anomaly of two communist claimants for power in Poland was resolved in June 1944 when the Polish communists visited Moscow and, on 22 June, the day that Bagration was launched, announced the establishment of a new organization, the Polish Committee for National Liberation – *Polski Komitet Wyzwolenia Narodowego* – better known as the Lublin Committee. The two communist armies, the underground GL/AL and the 1st Polish Army, were merged under one overall commander, General Michał Rola-Żymierski, with General Zygmunt Berling as commander of the 1st Polish Army.[33]

The Underground Government was well aware of communist manoeuvrings within Poland. It took steps to broaden its political appeal and to strengthen its claim to be the provisional government of Poland in the period before the politicians in London could return to their homeland. On 9 January 1944 it established the Council of National Unity – *Rada Jedności Narodowej* – as a quasi-parliament under the chairmanship of

Kazimierz Pużak. It included members of each of the four largest political parties, and one each from the three smaller ones. In May a cabinet was formed under Jankowski. On 15 March the Council issued its manifesto, *O co walczy naród polski*, 'What the Polish nation is fighting for'. Among its provisions was a defence of Poland's pre-war eastern frontier, the statement that the future governance would be a parliamentary democracy with a strong executive, and radical economic, social, and education programme. In London the government-in-exile was fighting a futile battle for post-war recognition of Poland's pre-1939 frontier: Mikołajczyk was not informed until October 1944 that Churchill and Roosevelt had agreed to Stalin's demand for the 1941 frontier at the Teheran Conference.[34]

Therefore, on both the political and the military fronts the evidence in the summer of 1944 before the launch of Bagration gave the strong impression that the Soviets were advancing into Poland not just to defeat the Germans but also to start a new occupation of the country. The AK, therefore, had to consider how best to combat two enemies at the same time.

The resistance organizations in the Protectorate had been almost totally destroyed first by Heydrich's reign of terror, and then by the widespread arrests following his assassination in 1942. Elements of earlier resistance groups, ÚVOD and PRNC, remained at large and came together to form a new leadership, the Council of Three – *Rada Tří* – consisting of Josef Grňa, Karel Štainer, and Josef Robotka. The Council approached General Vojtěch Luža, who had voluntarily held his distance from the early insecure resistance networks, to provide military leadership for partisan warfare: London endorsed Luža's appointment and suggested that he should move to Slovakia where the prospects of an uprising appeared more promising.

There were many factors hindering the development of resistance in the Protectorate. In the first place, the population in general had a higher standard of living than anywhere else in occupied Europe, so there was little incentive to resist. The German tactics were also more subtle than in countries such as Poland since, far from indiscriminate arrests and executions, the Gestapo was relatively adept at identifying culprits and leaving innocent civilians unharmed. The Czech government-in-exile in London was embarrassed by the notable lack of resistance, and from autumn 1943 onwards radio broadcasts increasingly called for a rise in sabotage in the armaments factories. These factories were assuming a greater role than ever in the German war machine as the Allied strategic bombing campaign against Germany hampered increased production there. Yet there was little sabotage in the factories because the workers could see no point in inviting German reprisals, and were in any case under such close supervision as to make successful sabotage difficult. The most the workers could do was to work more slowly, and to arrive late for work or call in sick more often.[35]

The build-up of the nuclei of new resistance groups was a slow, painful, and highly dangerous process. Luža's son, Radomír, toured a wide area around the city of Brno, recruiting a few men from every village and town in order to start forming cadres for armed resistance. He faced a major challenge from the Germans who were using collaborationist Czechs to form bogus resistance organizations to attract would-be resisters, only to betray them. Indeed, both father and son were appalled to learn, from a voluntary confession, that one of their main couriers and a vital contact was in fact a Gestapo agent.[36]

The communist resistance was arguably the most penetrated by the Germans: 'But by this time the renascent Communist resistance networks had been permeated by Gestapo agents – usually Communists who had been arrested and had turned informers as a condition of their release.' One notable example was the pre-war communist parliamentarian Karel Procházka, who was trained in sabotage and partisan warfare by the Soviets before being parachuted back into the Protectorate in May 1943. He found willing recruits among the miners in the district of Kladno, until they noticed that his contacts were soon arrested by the Gestapo. Indeed, it was revealed at his 1946 trial that Procházka had been in regular contact with two other former communists turned Gestapo informants, Fiala and Nachtman. Procházka was sentenced to prison following his trial but released after the communists came to power in 1948.[37]

After Heydrich's assassination only three further SOE missions were despatched to the Protectorate in 1942. The first, Antimony, landed successfully at the end of October near Roždalovice, while the fate of two other missions reflected the dangers of flights to central Europe when the planes carrying them were both shot down over Munich. In April and May 1944 eight new SOE missions successfully reached the Protectorate but little is known of their activities, other than that one group led by Jan Žižka sabotaged the railway near Lískovec.[38]

Throughout his stay in London, Beneš had worked unceasingly for a British renunciation of the Munich Agreement of September 1938 and for the recognition of the territorial integrity of pre-Munich Czechoslovakia. Having achieved this, he was eager to make approaches to Stalin to ensure the future national independence of Czechoslovakia, and to ensure that Czech communists under Klement Gottwald in Moscow would not undermine his intention to form the post-war government. Beneš held successful talks with Stalin, and on 12 December 1943 a pact of mutual aid was signed by the two leaders. Beneš also believed that he had held fruitful discussions with the Czech communists in Moscow and had won their cooperation for the creation of national committees to administer the liberated regions during the interim period before the government returned from London.[39]

The Allies were delighted by the treaty, but in Czech circles and in the Protectorate the reaction was mixed. Luža noted: 'The treaty was quite popular in the Protectorate, where we were not supposed to know about it.'[40] But Beneš's chief of intelligence, František Moravec, was less content:

> The President's vagueness and ambiguity in explaining the results of his Moscow negotiations had, of course, inevitable repercussions on the Czechoslovak public. At home in Czechoslovakia his equivocation put the democratic elements in an embarrassing situation and on the defensive against the Communists, whose position, already disproportionately powerful in relation to their numbers, it strengthened, encouraging them to increased political agitation.[41]

The Czech president Emil Hácha and six of his ministers placed themselves firmly in the collaborationist camp when they issued a declaration of protest against the treaty and on 19 December 1943 founded the Czech League against Bolshevism.[42] In May 1944 a new Czech-Soviet agreement was signed by the two governments which set up the means by which the Soviet armies would transfer liberated zones to the authority of the Czech national committees. Moravec believed that Beneš was naive to assume that such national committees would not be dominated by the communists, supported by the presence of the Soviets.[43]

It seemed obvious to everyone that the Soviet armies would eventually enter Slovakia through the Carpathian passes. Jozef Tiso and his government had been ardent collaborators during the first half of the war. However, public opinion was changing after heavy Slovak losses on the Eastern Front followed by mass desertions, and the defection of Italy from the Axis was widely celebrated in Slovakia. Indeed, the Germans were so concerned that Slovakia might defect to the Allied cause that serious preparations were made for the occupation of the country. Italy's surrender inspired the resistance in Slovakia to unite. It had hitherto been split between democratic elements, led by Ján Ursíny, Jozef Lettrich, and Matej Josko, and the socialists (which included the communists) under Gustáv Husák, Ladislav Novomeský, and Karol Šmidke. Between September and December 1943 these groups came together for fruitful discussions which resulted in the formation of a clandestine Slovak National Council – *Slovenská Národná Rada* – comprising these six men to supply political leadership to the resistance. The Council issued its programme in the so-called Christmas Agreement: the Slovaks and Czechs would be equal partners in the new Czechoslovakia; the principle of democracy was to be upheld and broadened; and the Council would rule and administer the territory and work alongside the Czechoslovak government in London during the period before that government could return to the homeland.[44]

The danger of a German occupation of Slovakia, and the apparently imminent arrival of the Soviet armies, meant that the Slovak National Council began to organize an uprising which would liberate the country before the arrival of the Soviets. This uprising would be mostly carried out by the army but would include armed civilian groups. In March 1944 Lieutenant Colonel (later General) Ján Golian, chief of staff of the command at Banská Bystrica, was appointed commander of the uprising, and he formed a secret military committee to make detailed plans. His appointment was approved by Beneš. The projected uprising was to take place in the regions of the Hron river valley and the nearby mountain ranges, and in the cities of Banská Bystrica, Zvolen, and Brezno nad Hronom. Golian used his position as chief of staff to transfer units of the Slovak army thought to be in favour of the uprising to these regions. He also made contact with the commanders of Slovak and Soviet partisan groups in the mountains and forests to obtain their assurance that they would not undertake any premature action which might precipitate a German occupation before the appropriate time for the uprising. Efforts in this direction were hampered by the fact that these partisan units had been trained in the Soviet Union and were commanded by a separate partisan staff operating from Kiev. Golian did, however, receive support from London when Major Jaroslav Krátký was parachuted in to provide Golian with direct radio communications with London. Timing the uprising was key: it would start either when the Germans started occupying the country, or best of all, when the Soviet armies reached the Carpathian passes.[45]

The three Baltic States of Estonia, Latvia, and Lithuania had been independent only since 1918 as a result of the collapse of the Russian Empire. With German agreement, the Soviets reoccupied the three countries soon after the start of the Second World War. This Soviet occupation had been just as brutal as that in eastern Poland: deportations of the ruling classes were ongoing in June 1941 as the Germans launched Operation Barbarossa. As a result the entry of the Germans was widely welcomed, and Estonians, Latvians, and Lithuanians became Hitler's willing helpers in the implementation of the Holocaust. The Germans saw the Estonians and Latvians as Germanic enough to be recruited into national legions to fight the Soviets on the Eastern Front. The Lithuanians were, however, seen as too Catholic and too similar to the Poles to be trusted to serve in a Legion; 16,000 Lithuanians were nonetheless recruited for the *Schuma* battalions.[46]

The apparent pro-German attitude was present only on the surface: 'We hate the Germans from the depths of our hearts . . . [but] we must . . . show them a smiling face. They undoubtedly help us keep the Bolsheviks outside of our borders.' Many young men had fled to the forests to avoid the forced-labour decrees promulgated by the Germans, and in the latter part of 1943 they were joined by many more after the Germans introduced conscription for the Legions. As the Soviet armies approached the frontiers of the Baltic States, the politicians in those countries made plans for the future after the Germans had departed. This formed a political resistance to occupation by any foreign power. On 13 August 1943 the *Latvijas Centrālā Padome* (Latvian Central Council) was founded under the leadership of Konstantīns Čakste: it represented the four largest political parties of the pre-war parliament. The Council established contacts with Estonian and Lithuanian political oppositions, and a Latvian-Lithuanian resistance conference was held in January 1944, and two all-Baltic ones that April, in Riga. In Lithuania the two principal political resistance movements, the Catholic-oriented *Lietuvių Frontas* (Lithuanian Front) and the more secular *Laisvės Kovotojų Sąjunga* (Union of Freedom Fighters), united in November 1943 into a single Supreme Committee for the Liberation of Lithuania, under the leadership of Steponas Kairys. In Estonia the acting prime minister, Jüri Uluots, led efforts in March 1944 to establish the National Committee of the Republic of Estonia – *Eesti Vabariigi Rahvuskomitee*. The politicians of the three republics realized that they were too small to defend their own independence against the Soviets and made contacts with the western powers. Couriers travelled to Sweden and the reports which reached London and Washington all spoke of the same demand: 'We are convinced that the western nations who have formed the Atlantic Charter . . . will help us, at the right time, to secure and to defend from National Socialism as well as from Communism that for which we are prepared to sacrifice all.'[47]

The overall goal of the Baltic politicians was to restore their independence, and therefore they followed the same policy of attempting to trade the granting of greater measures of self-administration in return for support for the German-sponsored military units. As the Red Army advanced, the prerequisite was largely abandoned. Instead, efforts were made by the Estonians and Latvians to pressurize the Germans into releasing the Legions from front-line service and bring them back to defend their homelands. In Lithuania, support was forthcoming for a German-sponsored LVR to be used solely for self-defence: the Germans reneged on the deal and took steps to incorporate Lithuanians into auxiliary units of the German armed forces. When this step met resistance, the Germans disbanded the units, shot 100 protesting men, and despatched their officers to Stutthof concentration camp. Furthermore, as the Germans realized that the support of the Baltic politicians for native armed units stemmed not from a desire to strengthen the ranks of the German armed forces but from the desire to create an armed and trained nucleus of national armies, they took steps to thwart these ambitions. In the spring and summer of 1944 the Germans stamped down hard on the various clandestine independence committees, sending leaders such as Čakste to concentration camps.[48]

Soviet sources suggest that there were native partisan movements in all three Baltic republics, but the nationalist literature disputes the claim, arguing that such partisan bands as existed were created by Soviet partisans from soldiers left behind during the 1941 retreat or later infiltrated into the countries from the Soviet Union. The terrain in Latvia and Lithuania was suitable for partisan warfare and both countries had the advantage of being relatively close to the Leningrad and Belorussian partisan movements. Yet even Soviet sources admit that partisan war was limited both in scope and effectiveness. For example, in Latvia there were probably under 3,000 partisans in operation in the summer of 1944. Most of these bands had been formed in the Latgale region in the east of the country, where there was a sizeable ethnic Russian population. Latvian sources point out that these partisans engaged in very little anti-German activity but preyed on the locals for food and shelter. Reprisals also fell on the locals when, for example, in January 1942 the village of Audriņi was burned down and its population of 215 were executed by the Latvian police in retaliation for Soviet partisan activity. Soviet sources argue that the partisans in Latvia undertook a campaign of railway sabotage in the spring of 1944 as the Soviet attack in the north was launched, but German records do not substantiate these claims. Soviet partisans were active in the north-east of Lithuania, where again they appear to have terrorized the local population more than they damaged the German occupation forces. The Germans took reprisals against the locals, for example, burning to death 119 villagers in Pirčiupis in Lithuania in reprisal for a Soviet partisan attack in June 1944.[49]

Bulgaria was in a unique position in the Balkans during the Second World War. It was a member of the Axis, but alone out of the Axis members it refused to participate in the war on the Eastern Front, nor would it deport any Bulgarian Jews to the death camps. It was a country which was politically divided, as its ruler Tsar Boris III* explained: 'My army is pro-German, my wife is Italian, my people are pro-Russian. I'm the only pro-Bulgarian in the country.' His pro-Bulgarian policy reaped dividends. Bulgaria had lost Macedonia, which was split between Yugoslavia and Greece, after the First World War, but Hitler's war on the Soviet Union and conquests of Yugoslavia and Greece meant that Bulgaria was rewarded with Southern Dobruja, Macedonia, and Thrace, the very territories for which it had fought the pre-First World War Balkan Wars. Therefore, for the majority of the population, siding with Germany made sense, and the prospects for resistance and taking Bulgaria, which was at war with the Allies, out of the war seemed slim.

Yet there were anti-German stirrings based around the Fatherland Front – *Otechestven Front*, OF. This was dominated by the communists, but its members included representatives of the Agrarians, the Socialists, and a group of former army officers. Its programme was drawn up by the Bulgarian Georgi Dimitrov, the head of the Comintern in Moscow. It was broadcast in July 1942 and called for a break with Germany, the conversion of the army into a people's army which would fight the Germans under Soviet leadership, and the formation of a people's democratic government. This clearly pro-communist line alienated many nationalists, and the OF struggled to gain a broad and widespread following in Bulgaria proper.

The more fertile territory for anti-government and anti-German action appeared to be the recently occupied areas of Macedonia and Thrace, where most of the Bulgarian Army was stationed and where the occupation was brutal, making resistance difficult, especially in Macedonia. SOE agent Michael Lees was dropped into Macedonia to Mihailović's Četniks in June 1943 and spent the first few months of his mission on the run from Bulgarian forces. All the same, SOE Cairo identified the Yugoslav Partisans as the most useful way of contacting the Bulgarian partisans in Macedonia. SOE acted on the basis of information supplied by 'Tempo' Vukmanović and General Mihajlo Apostolski, who wanted to stimulate a pan-Macedonian pro-communist resistance. Vukmanović convinced the British that if they dropped aid into south-eastern Serbia then he could arm the Bulgarian partisans whom the OF was organizing, and engage in sabotage of German rail communications through the region. It should be noted that simultaneously Lees was begging SOE Cairo for weapons and explosives for Mihailović's Četniks to carry out exactly the same sort of sabotage. While Lees received no arms drops, the British were prepared to support Vukmanović's endeavours.

* Boris died in August 1943.

Therefore, in September 1943 Major Mostyn Davies was dropped into Serbia and travelled to Tservena Voda in Macedonia where he met Vukmanović and a delegate of the Bulgarian partisans, 'Sergei' Balgaranov. Davies reported that he had been told there were about 8,000 partisans in Bulgaria but that they desperately needed weapons. Consequently, he received numerous airdrops of supplies, fifteen by the end of November 1943 and twenty-four in a single night in January 1944. He also explained that the OF had organized itself into a People's Liberation Insurgent Army, which planned to rise up in the towns and to suborn members of the Bulgarian armed forces for a general uprising. This promising evidence led SOE to despatch a committed communist, the poet Frank Thompson, in January 1944 with orders to penetrate Bulgaria and to organize the partisans there. However, on 17 March the Bulgarian Army attacked the British mission, forcing it to flee and abandon most of the equipment. Davies was severely wounded and died from his injuries in a ravine near Ruplje in Serbia six days later.

Thompson escaped, and before moving across the border into Bulgaria proper, his mission was reinforced by the arrival of Kenneth Syers and five men, and by a radio operator, Kenneth Scott. Vukmanović, Thompson, and Syers all had different ideas on resistance. Thompson was convinced of the possibility of stimulating an uprising in Bulgaria, whereas Syers believed that there was little evidence this could work. Vukmanović was keen to keep the British mission in Macedonia in order to strengthen the Partisans' position there, preparatory to the Partisan invasion of Serbia. A compromise was reached whereby Syers returned to Serbia with the Yugoslav Partisans, Vukmanović remained in Macedonia, and Thompson and Scott set off for Bulgaria accompanied by 200 Bulgarian partisans. Near the frontier the partisans were welcomed, but Scott later recalled that as they penetrated deeper into the country on the way towards the capital, Sofia, the partisans were less and less popular and the threat of betrayal grew each day. Efforts to secure airdrops of supplies into Bulgaria failed. Finally, on 31 May, the column of partisans was ambushed by the Bulgarian Army near Eleshina and both Thompson and Scott were captured. Scott was well treated by the Bulgarians and Germans in prison. Thompson, however, openly admitted his communism and was put on trial on 4 June: he was found guilty and sentenced to death, and executed on the following day.

The resistance in Bulgaria continued to develop slowly as Germany's retreat on the Eastern Front began. More partisan units were organized, and attacks against the police and gendarmerie increased. On the political front peace overtures towards Britain and the United States were made through Istanbul, but they came to nothing since no Bulgarian delegate ever arrived in Turkey to discuss surrender. The Soviet Union was more successful and launched a propaganda and diplomatic campaign in an effort to persuade the Bulgarian government to switch sides. At the end of May the pro-German government of Dobri Bozhilov resigned, and a new government was formed under Ivan Bagrianov. Through the summer of 1944 this government attempted to prepare the way for Bulgaria to leave the Axis without stimulating a German invasion or a hostile Soviet occupation, but at the same time it stamped down on the growing partisan movement.[50]

The prospects for resistance in the Axis satellites of Hungary and Romania were severely restricted by political and geographical factors. In the case of Hungary, the country had joined the Axis in 1941 when the Germans were poised to invade Yugoslavia, for the pragmatic reason that if Hungary did not join, then the Germans were likely to occupy the country in any case to safeguard their lines of communication to the south. Other factors too governed Hungary's attitude towards the Germans. The 1920 Treaty of Trianon had punished Hungary severely for having been on the losing side during the First World War, and Hungary suffered enormous territorial losses to her neighbours Romania, Czechoslovakia, and Yugoslavia. These were reversed by the Vienna Awards of 1938 and 1940, which were overseen by Hitler. Furthermore, Hungary had witnessed the full drama of the imposition of Bolshevism during the brief but unsettling period of Béla Kun's Hungarian Soviet Republic in 1919. This had turned Hungarians into committed anti-Bolsheviks, and so they enthusiastically joined Hitler's war on the Soviet Union in 1941. The ill-equipped Hungarian forces suffered a high level of casualties during the Soviet winter offensive of 1942–43, and the Hungarian high command and politicians pressed Hitler to permit the withdrawal of Hungarian forces from the east. Such a total withdrawal was not allowed, but Hungarian forces were moved to the rear of the front line, where they gained a fearsome reputation for brutality during anti-partisan actions.[51]

Hungary's attitude towards the western Allies was much more conciliatory. Britain had declared war on Hungary on 6 December 1941 and later that month, under German and Italian pressure, the Hungarian government declared war on the United States. But that was as far as the war against the western Allies went. No Allied aircraft were fired upon when crossing Hungarian air space, and downed airmen were interned in camps and treated well.[52] The Hungarians also cared for 20,000–25,000 Polish refugees and servicemen. Polish civilians were housed in camps around Lake Balaton, and those servicemen who had not managed to take advantage of Hungarian complicity to 'escape' from internment in 1940 were treated well. Indeed, in November 1943 there were extraordinary meetings between the AK's representative in Hungary, Andrzej Sapieha, and the Hungarian chief of staff, General Ferenc Szombathelyi, and the statesman Count István Bethlen, regarding the possibility of the Hungarians arming around 3,000–4000 Polish soldiers who would then cross into Poland to take part in the resistance there. The Hungarian politicians were prepared to allow secret communications between the AK and the Hungarian Army to continue, but held out little prospect of supplying armaments since they were short of weapons themselves.[53]

From early 1943 onwards various peace feelers were extended by Hungarians at the highest level to the western Allies. In an audience with the Pope in spring 1943 the Hungarian prime minister, Miklós Kállay, voiced his country's dilemma:

> Hungary not only could not conclude peace, she could not even surrender; we were powerless to sue for peace because we were a tiny cog in the machine, and we were unable to surrender because none of our enemies was near enough to be approached.[54]

Mussolini warned Kállay of the impossibility of concluding peace, arguing that it would invite a German occupation and lead to the fascist Arrow Cross party being put in power. Furthermore, as had been stated at Casablanca, the Allies were insisting on unconditional surrender, which meant surrender not just to the western Allies, as the Hungarians wanted, but also to the Soviet Union. Nonetheless, Kállay and his 'surrender party', which included many members of the foreign ministry, continued to make peace overtures. Direct contacts with the British were established through Lisbon, and then Istanbul, where a young member of the foreign ministry, László Veress, was authorized to act as the mouthpiece of the 'surrender party'. The pace of the talks accelerated after Italy's own surrender, but stalled because the western Allies were not prepared to compromise the principle of unconditional surrender just at the time when they were uncertain whether the Soviets would continue to advance against Germany when Soviet territory had been cleared of the Germans. Nor could the western Allies offer any prospects of direct intervention since they realized that it would be far more likely that Hungary would in due course be at least temporarily occupied by the Soviet armies.[55]

The western Allies were, however, keen to promote overt resistance through sabotage, and therefore suggested that the Hungarians should accept and assist SOE and OSS missions. The Hungarians were not prepared to go so far. They accepted the radios brought back from Istanbul by Veress, and used them to keep the Allies informed of German activities such as the whereabouts of German anti-aircraft units which had appeared in the country in late 1943 (against Hungarian wishes), but they were opposed to sabotage because it might lead to a German invasion. In the middle of August 1943 SOE despatched the Decima mission under Major Basil Davidson into northern Yugoslavia with orders to contact any resistance elements in Hungary and in the Hungarian-occupied part of Yugoslavia, the Bačka. The mission was a complete failure, and after ten futile months it was withdrawn. On the night of 15 March 1944 the OSS Sparrow mission under Colonel Florimond Duke was despatched. It was met on the ground by an aide of General István Ujszászy, the head of military intelligence, and was taken to Budapest.[56]

By the time that Sparrow arrived the circumstances had changed. As early as April 1943 von Ribbentrop had complained to Admiral Horthy that Kállay and his colleagues were trying to arrange Hungary's defection from the Axis.[57] By November 1943 Goebbels recorded in his diary that the Germans were now also suspicious of Horthy himself: 'The Regent is trying to create the impression that he is neutral about these efforts. That is, however, not at all the case. I even suspect him of being the mainspring of this development.'[58] By 15 March 1944 there was clear evidence that the Germans were massing troops on Hungary's borders. On 17 March Hitler summoned Horthy to a meeting and asked him to invite German troops into his country. Horthy refused and returned to Budapest where he found the Germans already in control:

> In the early morning hours the German occupying army marched in in full style, bands playing. Budapest had to be shown German bayonets . . . There was no jubilant crowd in the streets to greet the parading Germans: not one hat was tossed into the air; not one handkerchief was waved; not one cheer sounded. A profound silence was the reception the German soldiers got.[59]

Kállay fled to the sanctuary of the Turkish Legation, and Horthy appointed a new but powerless government under Döme Sztójay. The Gestapo rounded up most of the members of the surrender group and the radios brought back from Istanbul were discovered. The Sparrow mission was caught up in the German invasion, and was smuggled by the Hungarians across the border to Belgrade, where its members were handed over to the Germans and spent the remainder of the war in POW camps. Six SOE missions were despatched to Hungary between April and September 1944 but none achieved anything, either being captured soon after arrival or voluntarily withdrawing because of the poor prospects for sabotage or of inspiring Hungarian resistance.[60]

In March 1944 Hungary was home to the largest Jewish community left in Europe, 800,000 people, and these now became the target for Adolf Eichmann. Between March and July over 450,000 Jews were despatched to Auschwitz. An SS officer noted:

> Without resistance and in submission, they marched by the hundreds in long columns to railway stations and piled into the trains. Only very few gendarmes were supervising the operation; it would have been easy to flee. In the Carpatho-Ukraine, which contained numerically the strongest Jewish settlements, the forbidding mountains and forests offered an opportunity for prolonged hiding. But only few removed themselves in this way from their doom.

Horthy was under pressure from the Pope, Roosevelt, and the King of Sweden to call a halt to the deportations, which he did in July. Thereafter the Hungarian Jews were concentrated in a ghetto in Budapest, and many survived: even when the Arrow Cross came to power, they preferred to work the Jews to death slowly in labour camps rather than despatch them to Auschwitz.

A Jewish assistance agency formed by Zionists had been helping Jews in eastern Europe to escape from Europe and now turned its attention to the Hungarian Jews: the vice-president, Rudolf Kastner, made an agreement with Eichmann whereby a ransom was paid for around 1,600 Jews who were then sent by train to Switzerland. SOE was keen to encourage resistance in central Europe, and offered to train Jewish agents to be parachuted into Yugoslavia and then to travel onwards to undertake military operations and rescue Jews: the leaders were Hannah Senesz (Szenes) for Hungary; Haviva Reik for Slovakia; and Sara (Surika) Braverman for Romania. On 14 April, Senesz, Joel Palgi, and Peretz Goldstein were dropped into Croatia and crossed into Hungary on 13 June. A month later they were arrested and imprisoned in Budapest: Senesz was found guilty of espionage and executed in November.[61]

Romania was in an extremely awkward position during the Second World War due to her geography and natural resources. Romania had been on the side of the Entente during the First World War, and had been rewarded by gaining Transylvania from Hungary and Bessarabia and northern Bukovina from the Russian and Austro-Hungarian empires. German interest in the country was high because of the Ploeşti oilfields, which were vital to the German war effort, and Romanian politicians lived in fear of a German occupation. They were powerless to prevent the return of Transylvania to Hungary and the cession of Bessarabia and northern Bukovina to the Soviet

Union in 1940. Internal politics were also unsettled. In September 1940 the pro-German Ion Antonescu mounted a successful coup which forced the abdication of King Carol II and his replacement by his nineteen-year-old son Michael, and brought the fascist Iron Guard into the government. Two months later Romania joined the Axis, but this was not a sign of political allegiance to Germany, as is shown by the crushing of the coup mounted by the Iron Guard in January 1941 and the subsequent exclusion of the Iron Guard from the government. Romania also sent a large army to take part in Operation Barbarossa.

Britain, especially SOE, had unsuccessfully explored the possibilities of sabotage in the oilfields in the early years of the war. These clandestine approaches had brought Britain into contact with the leader of the National Peasants Party and former prime minister, Iuliu Maniu, and also with the Liberal leader, Dinu Brătianu, and the foreign ministry through Grigore Niculescu-Buzești. Maniu had access to a radio from spring 1942 and he also despatched couriers to Istanbul to contact SOE. Maniu was, however, very indecisive, particularly over whether he could serve his country best by leaving Romania and forming an opposition outside, or whether he should stay and organize a coup against Antonescu and take Romania out of the war. Maniu clearly would not act until one important question was settled, as he explained to SOE in September 1943:

> So long as we do not know positively . . . that the allied nations are willing to exclude a Russian invasion of Romania once the German front collapses . . . it is practically impossible for our opposition to come out against the Axis and organise anything with concrete effect.

The Foreign Office's attitude is encapsulated in a minute by the permanent under-secretary, Alexander Cadogan, in December 1942:

> The short-term advantages of cooperating with Maniu (i.e. sabotage, disruption of the army etc.) are too small and too problematic to justify the long-term disadvantage of committing ourselves in advance with regard to the political and territorial future of Romania.

The Soviets were approached by the British on whether they wanted to establish direct contacts with Maniu, but during 1943 the Soviets kept changing their minds, although they were content to see British contacts continuing. By the end of the year the Soviets had another channel open with the Romanians via Romanian diplomats in Stockholm. It was never clear whether or not Soviet policy was to insist on unconditional surrender by the Romanians.

While British contacts were maintained with Maniu, another strand of political resistance began to emerge. After the heavy Romanian losses at

Stalingrad, the staunchly anti-Russian but quietly pro-British Ion Antonescu and his foreign minister, Mihai Antonescu (unrelated), began to send out peace feelers to the Allies through the neutral powers and the Papacy during 1943. The Germans quickly became aware of these soundings and in April 1943 Hitler challenged Ion Antonescu on the matter. He received the response that Romania could be considered loyal, and that all the peace feelers were the work of Maniu: Antonescu could not take action against Maniu because his martyrdom would give him greater importance than he possessed while alive.

All peace efforts by Antonescu and Maniu foundered on the apparent Allied insistence on unconditional surrender and the refusal of the western Allies to guarantee Romania's independence from the Soviet Union. This impasse seemed to make the despatch of SOE missions into Romania pointless. The first mission, Ranji, comprising Captain David Russell and a Romanian radio operator, Nicolae Ţurcanu, was despatched in June 1943 with the purpose of 'opening up W/T communications, effecting contact with Maniu's organisation, and establishing a reception area in the Romanian Carpathians'. The mission dropped into Mihailović-controlled Serbia and local Četniks were ordered to escort the two men across the Romanian frontier. The Četnik leader, Velja, warned Russell that he needed a bodyguard, and offered the services of thirty men if Russell could arm them. Russell ignored the warnings and crossed alone with Ţurcanu. Having established a base in a Romanian forest and made contact with SOE Cairo, Russell was then murdered, probably by a Romanian forester, although the identity of the culprit is not known, and Ţurcanu fled to Bucharest with his radio where he was sheltered by Maniu's supporters.

A second mission, Autonomous, consisting of Alfred de Chastelain, Ivor Porter, and a Romanian sabotage expert, Silviu Meţianu, planned to drop in late summer 1943, but in the event was not sent in until 22 December. By then its purpose had changed from sabotage to primarily political action. The party should have been collected by men from Maniu's network, but the contact failed and within twenty-four hours the three men had been arrested by the Romanian gendarmerie and were taken to Bucharest. De Chastelain stuck to the cover story that he had been sent to contact Antonescu, before finally admitting that his main contact was meant to be Maniu. The Germans demanded that the Autonomous party be sent to Germany, but Churchill intervened personally and asked Antonescu to protect them. Thereafter the three men became observers of the machinations of the Romanian government and of Maniu, and acted as the radio link between Britain and Romania.

As the Soviet armies began to close in on the Romanian borders in early

1944, the growing opposition in Romania began to take on some fantastic notions. For example, in January 1944 the British learned that senior Romanian officers – Generals Nicolescu, Potopeanu, and Sănătescu – were prepared to mount a coup on the condition that 1,000–2,000 British paratroopers were dropped into the country. The Romanians would then surrender to the token British force and not to the Soviets. Not only was that impossible because this number represented the majority of paratroopers then in Italy, but it would also anger the Soviets and quite possibly break the alliance. Peace negotiations in Cairo opened in March 1944 and were conducted at the highest level between Prince Barbu Ştirbey and Constantin Vişoianu for Romania, Lord Moyne for Britain, Ambassador MacVeagh for the United States, and Ambassador V. M. Novikov for the Soviet Union. The armistice terms transmitted to Antonescu and Maniu in April were unacceptable to both men: they called for the Romanians to switch sides and fight the Germans, the payment of reparations to the Soviets, the allocation of Bessarabia and northern Bukovina to the Soviet Union and Transylvania to Hungary.

The Allies upped the stakes by bombing Bucharest in early April, causing over 3,000 casualties. The effect of this raid was a contrast to the efforts by the US air force in August 1943 against the heavily defended Ploeşti oilfields, which had resulted in higher losses among the airmen taking part than among the workers and civilians on the ground and which had failed to damage the oilfields to any significant degree. Now, however, in early April 1944 a new strand of political resistance began to emerge, centred around King Michael, who began to plan a coup against Antonescu. A secret committee was established under Colonel Dumitru Dămăceanu to plan the defence of Bucharest against the Germans. Political steps were also taken to unite the opposition parties, and the small Communist Party was included when Maniu invited the Soviet nominee, Lucreţiu Pătrăşcanu, to join their discussions. The communist military representative Emil Bodnăraş attended meetings on the preparations for the coup. The communists joined the three democratic political parties in forming the National Democratic Bloc on 20 June 1944. The Allied representatives in Cairo were informed of the creation of the NDB but, distracted by events in northern France, there was no response from the western Allies. The timing of the coup now depended largely on the direction and speed of the Soviet summer offensive.[62]

23
Intelligence: 1942–44

In the early years of the war both the collection of intelligence by the resistance, and its analysis in Britain, had been hampered by simple lack of experience. Things improved as the war went on. The Allies gained intelligence from a variety of sources: a greater ability to read Enigma traffic; improvements in the interpretation of data from air photo-reconnaissance flights; and information on the ground supplied by the resistance. Photo-reconnaissance flights also increased in numbers:

> Every corner of the fortress of Europe had to be examined under the magnifying glass, every enemy movement watched, every position evaluated. After which, British air reconnaissance planes went on regular photographic missions. Any changes that appeared on the photographs were analysed and cross-checked.[1]

The resistance could tell the organizers of these flights where to look and what they should be looking for. The despatch of more radios to the resistance meant that the intelligence reports could be received in Britain in time for their contents to be acted upon. These radioed reports were complemented and supplemented by well-organized courier routes which could bring out lengthy reports and technical drawings that could not be transmitted by radio. Much of this material was photographed onto microfilm to reduce its bulk. Intelligence analysis had improved greatly, at least in the fields the analysts understood, such as German dispositions and movements, and naval construction. Intelligence analysis did, however, require some basic knowledge, which led to failings in fields where little was known. The most notable instance of this, in which agents' reports were misinterpreted for a long time, was the development of the V-weapons.

The networks in France outlined in the earlier chapter continued to provide intelligence despite coming under sustained and frequently successful attacks by German counter-intelligence agencies. The most notable among these were: Alliance, which reported to SIS; Colonel Rémy's CND which reported to the BCRA; and the Polish networks F2 and POWN, which reported both to SIS and to the Polish government-in-exile. The amount of intelligence generated increased enormously. For example, during the latter half of 1943 the CND was sending out 200,000 roneoed sheets, 60,000 blueprints of plans, and 10,000 photographs every month: the output of Alliance and F2 was similar.[2] In the summer of 1943 the main part of BCRA under Colonel Passy moved to Algiers to be near de Gaulle; the London office was reduced in size and left in charge of Commandant André Manuel.[3]

Two newcomers entered the field of intelligence in France. The first was the Agir network, set up by Michel Hollard in late 1940. Hollard used his cover as the Paris representative for a Dijon firm making *gazogènes* for cars, Société Gazogène de Dijon, to travel extensively across France. In May 1941 he crossed into Switzerland and made contact with the British military attaché in Berne and, after his bona fides had been established, he was taken on by SIS. Hollard established a network of over 100 agents and, in the interests of security, remained the sole contact for each one. He made a total of ninety-eight crossings of the Franco-Swiss frontier to deliver reports. Two of his agents proved especially valuable. Louis Villette was a lorry driver whose route regularly took him into the forbidden coastal zone of northern France. This enabled him to report the exact locations of coastal batteries, the design of the new submarine base at Boulogne, and the locations of Luftwaffe airfields across the region. Another valuable agent was Simone Boirel who owned the Hôtellerie de Pierrelatte, situated about halfway between Valence and Avignon. This was a favourite stopping place for high-ranking German officers who unwittingly provided information on the location and status of German military units. Hollard was betrayed by a French traitor, Henri Marette (known as the Comte de Kergoat), and was arrested by the Gestapo in Paris in February 1944: he survived various German concentration camps.[4]

The second newcomer was OSS. An OSS office had been set up in London under David Bruce in early 1942, which had begun to plan its operations across Europe, mostly in cooperation with SOE and other British agencies. In February 1943 OSS officer Henry Hyde arrived in Algiers to build a new intelligence operation inside southern France. His first two agents, Jacques and Toto, used their personal contacts in Lyon and Clermont-Ferrand to build a network of 2,500 agents and sub-agents which sent intelligence by radio to Algiers. A smaller OSS operation was run from Spain by Gregory Thomas and this had 1,400 agents in southern France. The value of this intelligence was, however, initially hampered by OSS's lack of radio communications in Spain. Reports had to be carried across the Pyrenees by couriers, a process made far more difficult by the Germans sealing off the Pyrenees in the spring of 1944. That same spring, however, four radio circuits were set up by Thomas's network which reported to Algiers. Alan Dulles, based in Switzerland, also controlled some OSS agents operating in south-east France, and this intelligence was sent to both London and Algiers.[5]

The *Englandspiel* had inflicted enormous damage on Dutch intelligence networks. In November 1942 Dutch intelligence was reorganized and renamed the *Bureau Inlichtingen*. Under its new chief from July 1943, Major J. M. Somer, new agents were trained and sent to the Netherlands. These agents had an immediate effect: from 1940 to May 1943 only sixty-eight messages had been received, but in the second half of 1943 the total increased to 700, and by 1944 it had reached almost 6,000. These radio communications were backed up by reports sent by two main courier routes running to Switzerland, from where the material was sent to Britain either via Spain or by mail to Sweden and then forwarded on to Britain. The value of the remaining neutral states to the Allies was in this context incalculable.[6]

The intelligence network set up in Denmark by Ebbe Munck briefly collapsed after the German takeover of the country in August 1943, when the heads of the intelligence services were forced to flee to Sweden. A young army officer, Svend Truelsen, took over as the chief of intelligence and painstakingly rebuilt the organization. Most reports were still sent to Sweden by courier, but from spring 1944 onwards radio communications with London and Stockholm were set up. It has been estimated that the reorganized Danish intelligence service delivered over 15,000 pages of intelligence reports by the end of the war.[7]

It was only to be expected that the Germans would put great effort into penetrating and demolishing intelligence networks. Yet the knowledge that the information they supplied to the Allies was absolutely vital to the war effort meant that the intelligence networks would succeed in rebuilding themselves time and time again.

By 1942 the Polish intelligence service within Poland was clearly organized into four sections: *Stragan* covered the General Government; *Lombard* operated in the whole of Germany and Austria; *Meerauge* covered eastern Poland and the occupied Soviet Union; and *Witzer* dealt with railway transport. The head of AK intelligence, Ludwik Kalkstein, was arrested by the Gestapo in 1942 and was turned. He inflicted enormous damage on Polish intelligence, especially the *Stragan* section, as well as betraying the head of the AK, Stefan Rowecki. In May 1943 the Germans arrested

Captain Karol Trojanowski, who had taken over as head of one of the sections. He knew everyone and became a traitor, betraying them all. Nonetheless, despite the arrests of several hundred intelligence agents, Polish intelligence built up a new, simplified structure under Lieutenant Colonel Marian Drobik, which continued to supply the Allies with vital intelligence. Drobik was in turn arrested in January 1944, and his role was taken over by Colonel Kazimierz Iranek-Osmecki, who remained in place until the Warsaw Uprising.[8]

The principal Polish intelligence network in France, F2, suffered from a high number of arrests in the south. These began in the summer of 1942 when the Vichy police arrested members of the Marseille naval intelligence section, and in October further arrests were carried out by the Vichy authorities following the tracking down of two radio stations. The work of F2 was severely restricted by the German occupation of southern France and the extension of the Italian zone of occupation, and during the last two months of 1942 many arrests were carried out and the leaders of F2 cells were forced to leave the country. Hugo Bleicher of the Abwehr travelled to the south at the end of 1942 to assist in the interrogation of Poles arrested in Nice. He concluded that 'the arrested men were indeed all Poles who would not have betrayed a thing even if we had roasted them'.[9]

F2 was determined to rebuild but faced great difficulties. The first of these was that the quality of the Polish agents who remained at large was alarmingly poor. As one of the main organizers, Lieutenant Wincenty Jordan-Rozwadowski, reported:

> The Polish element – officers or civilians – left behind in a region drained by evacuation is composed either of blunderers or persons of meagre moral qualities. The majority of both groups either speak French poorly or not at all. Meanwhile, one of the results of the German integral occupation of the country is the special attention paid to the Poles. In other words, only a person capable of being taken for a German or a Frenchman can work *effectively*.

Henceforward, the principal F2 network leaders would be Poles, but the vast majority of the agents were French.[10] The second major difficulty was the German attitude to the Poles in general. On 10 March 1943 the head of the Gestapo in France, Helmut Knochen, prepared a report for Berlin on the Polish intelligence organizations in France. The report did not just cover intelligence activities, but in fact consisted of a long list of Polish associations in France which ranged from political to sporting to theatrical. The report included an extremely long list of Poles and the detail is alarming in its thoroughness: it appeared that the Germans had identified the origin and activity of just about every prominent Pole living in France. Knochen concluded his report with his reasoning:

> After this war there will be a Polish community in France, demanding a free Poland. The same aspirations that existed before 1914 will emerge. The opponents of Germany and, in particular, the Catholic Church, will support such renewed strivings. Therefore, it is necessary to pay attention to the Polish community.
>
> The severest measures should be taken against all movements opposing the Reich. Particular attention should be paid to the Poles, who are reported in large numbers to serve in hostile organisations.[11]

In other words, all Poles living in France should be considered hostile to the German occupation and all prominent Poles should be arrested when possible. Given this attitude, it is little wonder the work of F2 was severely limited in scope from early 1943 onwards – though not in value, as British intelligence reports confirm.[12]

Rémy's CND was attacked by the Germans too through their use of French traitors. Rémy himself was sought under the names of Raymond, Jean-Luc, Rémy, and Morin, but the Germans did not appear to realize that they were looking for a single person. Two traitors were particularly effective. Pierre Cartaud had been used as a guard for radio operators but betrayed everyone he encountered. The damage he inflicted was principally limited to the Bordeaux area since he had little knowledge of networks elsewhere. His toll of 100 arrests was surpassed by another traitor, the Belgian Georges-Henri Delfanne, known as 'Christian Masuy', who led the Abwehr to 800 people. (Delfanne was tried and executed after the war.) Yet Rémy continued to rebuild the CND successfully because on hearing of an arrest 'we would get out the map of the network, where checks marked those who had been taken', and warn those who had been in contact with the arrested person. *Organisation Civile et Militaire* (OCM), the northern resistance movement, was less fortunate: at the end of 1943 its leader Roland Farjon was arrested and turned traitor. The damage he inflicted effectively neutralized the OCM in the Amiens and Paris regions.[13]

Virginia Hall was an SOE agent in Lyon but also collected intelligence from the WOL intelligence circuit in Paris to pass to Switzerland. Abbé Robert Alesch was an Alsatian priest who inflicted damage on the resistance in northern France by pretending to be a recruiter for it but instead betrayed the names of recruits to the Abwehr. Alesch had convinced WOL, run by Jacques Legrand and Gabrielle Picabia, that he could be trusted to take a mass of information on the Atlantic Wall to Lyon for onward transmission to SIS. Instead, the Abwehr doctored the material before it was passed to WOL and arrested Legrand and his associate Germaine Tillion. Tillion was carrying the German plans of the coastal defences of Dieppe.* Alesch travelled to Lyon at the beginning of September and contacted Virginia Hall's associate Dr Rousset at his surgery, asking to see Virginia and claiming to be the new courier for WOL. Virginia was unimpressed by him because he appeared not to know about the arrests of members of WOL and was too curious about her own circuit. London knew nothing of him, but Rousset felt that he could be trusted, especially since the intelligence he brought was so important. By October, Alesch had helped the Abwehr arrest around sixty members of WOL, and all the intelligence he sent to Lyon was useless because it had been supplied by the Germans. (Alesch was later tried and executed in 1949.) Virginia Hall herself narrowly escaped capture when the Germans invaded the Unoccupied Zone in November 1942.[14]

By the end of 1942 the Alliance network had been successfully established all over France, with the exception of eastern France where the Germans had arrested the local commander Gérard Novel. Following the German invasion of southern France, however, the Alliance network in the southern zone was devastated by a series of arrests:

> The Nazis had not blown up everything, but their mines had devastated the southern zone. Except for Grenoble, Vichy and central France, all the sectors had been destroyed. Being independent, our actual intelligence services had been more skilful and eluded the Gestapo's tentacles, but they were disintegrating.[15]

A recruitment drive was launched, and within a short space of time new intelligence units sprang up in Lyon, Nice, Toulon, Vichy, Clermont-Ferrand, and Toulouse, organized by Georges Lamarque. But the Germans were closing in on members of the network, aided in the south by Commandant Verteré who turned traitor after his arrest, and in the north by Jean-Paul Lien who revealed to the Germans the considerable depth of his knowledge of Alliance activities there. During September 1943 the Gestapo succeeded in arresting Marie-Madeleine Fourcade's second-in-command, Léon Faye, as well as many of his staff and four radio operators.† Arrests that month effectively closed down the Alliance networks in Paris, Rennes, Brest, Autun, east Brittany, and Normandy. In all, at least 150 agents in northern France had been caught and radio contact between Alliance and

* Tillion was arrested on 12 August 1942. The Allied raid on Dieppe took place a week later on 19 August and the Germans were well prepared for it.

† Faye attempted to escape from German custody in Paris along with Noor Inayat Khan and John Starr.

Britain ceased from the middle of August to early November 1943. In April 1944 the rebuilt Alliance networks along the Atlantic coast, in Paris, and Normandy were hit by a new wave of arrests, among them the senior figure of Jean Sainteny.[16]

Resistance movements helped the Allies with naval intelligence, providing information both on the movements of German ships and on naval construction and repairs. SIS missions and native intelligence groups covered the eastern Mediterranean from their bases in Crete and Greece. The first SIS mission had arrived in Crete on 9 October 1941, led by Ralph Stockbridge, establishing a large network of Cretans who reported on every ship and its cargo from the ports of Heraklion, Rethymno, and Canea. By 1944 the communications system was so sophisticated and effective that the hour and day of a ship's departure could be radioed to Cairo and a British submarine or plane would be despatched to sink the ship. Similar successes were recorded against Luftwaffe transport planes flying from the island.[17]

Several networks operated on the Greek mainland. Lela Karagianni had established a network using members of her extended family to create an escape line for Allied soldiers, and when this supply dried up she directed the activities of her network to observing the movements of Axis shipping from the island of Salamis. Rigas Rigopoulos established a network first in the port of Piraeus before extending it to other Greek ports. The intelligence he supplied to the British facilitated the sinking of fifty-five Axis ships before his group was compromised after the arrest of one agent and Rigopoulos was forced to flee to Turkey in spring 1943. Panagiotis Lykourezos ran a network called Kodros which operated between late 1942 and October 1944. He had been given a radio by SIS and was able to warn the British of the departure of a convoy carrying German reinforcements to the island of Leros, which had been seized by the British after the surrender of Italy. Ultimately, the British were forced to withdraw their forces from the Dodecanese islands, but that particular German convoy was sunk thanks to the arrival of timely intelligence. Another highly successful network was run by Ioannis Peltekis, known by his code name 'Apollo'. He ran 800 agents who not only supplied intelligence on German naval movements but were also responsible for the sabotage of around 250 Axis ships. The work of this network ended in the late summer of 1944 when Apollo fell foul of the murky Greek politics of the time. He was accused by the Greek government-in-exile of having passed money given to him by SOE to the Greek communists, and was summoned by the British to attend a court of inquiry in Cairo. In his absence the Germans penetrated his organization and arrested over seventy of his agents, fifty-three of whom were then executed. Apollo was exonerated of all charges, and alleged that had he been in Athens at the time he could have saved many of his agents.[18]

During 1942 and 1943 while the Battle of the Atlantic was at its height, intelligence on German naval movements supplied by networks in France was essential. Rémy's CND network had extensive contacts in all the major ports on the French Atlantic coast. For example, one CND agent in Brest was a humble seamstress who repaired Mae West life vests and picked up gossip on U-boat sailings from the sailors who brought them in. CND supplied the British with copies of the original German plans of the U-boat bases at Lorient, Brest, Saint-Nazaire, La Pallice, and Bordeaux, which Rémy himself brought to London on a visit in late February 1942. Alliance was also extensively involved in naval intelligence, with contacts in La Rochelle, Lorient, Brest, and Bordeaux. Examples of intelligence supplied by Alliance include the exact location of the cargo ships in Bordeaux targeted by the Cockleshell raiders, and an accurate report on the departure of five U-boats from the port in August 1943, all of which were sunk by the RAF. Yet intelligence was not always acted upon. In January 1942 Alliance reported that the warships *Scharnhorst* and *Gneisenau* were about to leave Brest. This report was, however, sent to the British Admiralty via a radio belonging to the compromised Polish *Interallié* circuit, and was therefore discounted as false intelligence. The dash through the Channel by the two ships on the night of 11–12 February embarrassed the Admiralty but increased the standing of the Alliance network. In November 1942 Michel Hollard managed to enter Toulon dockyard shortly after the French fleet had scuttled itself. He was able to report which French ships had sunk completely and which the Germans were likely to attempt to salvage.[19]

Intelligence on German naval activities in the Baltic and North Sea was the responsibility of networks from several countries. Polish intelligence supplied detailed information on German naval construction from all the major ports on the Baltic coast, and on repairs to ships, including the *Gneisenau*. Danish intelligence provided news of German naval trials in the Baltic and the details of all ships passing through the Skagerrak and into the North Sea.[20] From there Norwegian intelligence took over the task of watching German naval activities. By June 1943 there were twenty-three networks covering from Kirkenes in the far north down through Tromsø, Trondheim, Bergen, Stavanger, Kristiansand, and Oslo. A highly successful agent was Oluf Reed Olsen who was dropped into Norway in April 1943. He set up a network based on the port of Kristiansand, which was the main German naval base and the location where all German convoys were assembled. He had a radio so that the Admiralty received his intelligence within an hour. An example of what intelligence was requested and supplied is provided by this extremely detailed questionnaire sent to Reed Olsen on the net defences of Kristiansand, asking such questions as:

> Were the nets anti-torpedo, anti-submarine or anti-surface vessel? What sort of buoys used to keep the net up? Length of net in different sections and position of moorings? How were the nets moored and what kind of yielding system was used? What influence had ice or other objects on the net? How thick was the wire between the buoys, and how many strands were used? Depth of net? Size of meshes? Thickness and number of strands in the mesh wire? Anchored to the bottom and if so by what means?

Reed Olsen obtained all the information from contacts within the port and also from pieces of net which had accidentally become entangled in a Swedish ship. London needed the answers urgently because of a proposed attack on *Tirpitz*.[21]

The construction of the battleship *Tirpitz* was completed in early 1941 and after extensive sea trials she sailed for Norway in January 1942. Her presence there posed great danger for British shipping not just in the Battle of the Atlantic but also in Arctic convoys to the Soviet Union. In early 1942 Bomber Command made three unsuccessful attempts to sink *Tirpitz* at her anchorage in Trondheimsfjord. SOE in Norway was asked for assistance in locating a ship which could tow British midget submarines (Chariots) to Trondheim, but in the event the attack was made from the Shetland Islands by a small cutter, *Arthur*, at the end of October 1942. Both Chariots sank in the fjord before they could attach explosives to *Tirpitz*, *Arthur* was scuttled, and the Norwegian resistance helped her crew escape to Sweden. One group reached safety, but the other was captured by the Germans and a wounded man was executed by the Germans under Hitler's Commando Order. In early 1943 SIS inserted an agent, Torstein Raaby, to watch *Tirpitz* at her new berth in Altafjord. The Admiralty ignored some of the information which had been supplied by Reed Olsen about the nets which were protecting *Tirpitz*, with the result that during the attack on *Tirpitz* by midget submarines (X-craft) in September 1943 only three of the five passed through the net to place explosives on the hull, and one was actually caught in the net. Raaby transmitted daily reports on the damage sustained by *Tirpitz* and on the repairs over the next ten months. In spring 1944 he reported that *Tirpitz* was ready to sail and Bomber Command mounted another attack: this inflicted sufficient damage to keep *Tirpitz* out of action for another three months. Raaby was forced to flee to Sweden in July 1944, but when *Tirpitz* was moved to Tromsø in the middle of

October his replacement Max Manus reported the exact location of *Tirpitz*, and the RAF finally sank her on 12 November 1944.[22]

As the Allied strategic bombing offensive against Germany intensified, the resistance in Europe was able to supply the Allies with information on German defences and the damage caused by the bombing. The Germans employed local labourers on their airfields in northern Europe and these provided the resistance with intelligence on the purpose of every airfield taken over by the Luftwaffe and the size of the force deployed there. Local firemen also reported on the damage to the airfields caused by Allied air raids.[23] In summer 1943 the British asked Michel Hollard to investigate the large airfield at Cormeilles-en-Vexin near Paris. This airfield had twenty miles of runways and appeared to be divided into three sections, but photo reconnaissance had been unable to determine the purpose of each section. Hollard sent Joseph Brocard to see what he could discover. Brocard was caught in the act and arrested by the SD. He jumped from the third floor of the building where he was held and broke his back. Hollard escorted him, now encased in plaster from neck to the hips, across the border into Switzerland.[24]

Priceless information on Luftwaffe movements and plans was gleaned by the Vengeance network in Paris during 1941 and 1942. Two members of the network, Dr Victor Dupont and Dr François Wetterwald, rented a house in a Paris suburb adjacent to the main German telecommunications cable. A fault on the line was engineered by a telecommunications engineer, Robert Keller, and the Germans asked Keller to repair it. Unknown to the watching Germans, he installed a wiretap which diverted the signals to the rented house. Suspicious neighbours forced Dupont and Wetterwald to move locations, but they managed to install a second wiretap before Keller was betrayed by the head of the French police, René Bousquet, in December 1942, arrested by the Gestapo, and sent to Bergen-Belsen where he died. The information the network had gathered reached the British through Vichy air force intelligence channels.[25]

Belgium lay across the main route to Germany and so Belgian intelligence played an extremely important role in the mapping of German anti-aircraft artillery placements and radar installations in their country. The Belgians managed to break into the office of the regimental commander of a searchlight unit and steal the map showing all the German searchlight and radar locations in northern Belgium. Churchill duly paid tribute to them in his history of the Second World War: 'It was this map, in conjunction with other information, which enabled our experts to unravel the system of the German air defence. By the end of the year we knew not only how the hostile system worked, but how to cope with it.' Anne Brusselmans, a member of the Comet escape line but also involved in intelligence, learned that a noticeable number of Allied aircrew were being forced to bale out near Aerschot, so she took it upon herself to investigate further. She rented a room in a hotel in Westerloo and observed events when the Allied bomber stream passed overhead. Using a compass, she could accurately map the location of the major anti-aircraft artillery and searchlight position to Oolen, and this information duly reached the RAF, enabling them to avoid the area. Other information reached Britain through the seemingly simple expedient of dropping homing pigeons in a box over Belgium. Attached to a leg was a questionnaire asking the person who found the pigeon the simple question: 'Are there any German radio stations in your neighbourhood with aerials that rotate?' Other questionnaires asked for information on the locations of German troops. Unfortunately, this was a hit-and-miss method because many boxes were not found and the pigeons died. Other pigeons ended up in the pot, but some did return home to Britain with completed questionnaires. The information coming out of Belgium was so thorough that a proposed British raid to discover more about a new radio navigational beam used to guide German night fighters was cancelled because the Belgians could supply the required information.[26]

The Allies wanted to know the extent of the damage caused by their bombing raids. Polish intelligence supplied the answers from Germany, although there was a considerable time-lag in the information being transferred from the Polish forced labourers to Polish intelligence in Poland and thence to Britain.[27] When the RAF bombed the Renault factory in March 1942, a French engineer managed to get into the factory before the Germans forbade access and took photographs of the damage. These reached Britain via the CND network and appeared on the front page of the *Daily Herald* on 14 July 1942.[28]

The Allies bombed the U-boat pens at Saint-Nazaire regularly, and it was known that the town itself had sustained a very high level of damage but the extent of damage to the U-boat pens was unknown. This was an extremely difficult area for French intelligence to reach since Saint-Nazaire was located in the forbidden coastal zone and it was rare for adults living outside the zone to obtain permission to visit it. The medical director of the American Hospital in Paris, Dr Sumner Jackson, and his wife were already involved in the resistance through helping on escape lines. They also had contacts with French intelligence, and their principal contact, Paul Ostoya Kinderfreund, believed that the Jacksons' fifteen-year-old son,

Phillip, might be able to help since children from Paris were allowed to visit the area for holidays. The Jacksons were prepared to take the very high risk of sending Phillip into the area, and the task was made easier by the fact that they had friends living near Saint-Nazaire just outside the forbidden zone. In summer 1943 Phillip was carefully briefed on locations in Saint-Nazaire from where he could photograph the U-boat pens, and given the name of a contact who would provide him with a camera. His hosts were appalled that Phillip was carrying a Kodak camera so close to the forbidden zone and confiscated it. Their daughter, however, was made of sterner stuff. She retrieved the confiscated camera, accompanied Phillip into Saint-Nazaire, and kept watch while he photographed the town and U-boat pens from the church bell tower. The camera was left behind and the film was sent to London.[29]

The resistance supplied the Allies with intelligence on the size and locations of German garrisons and the order of battle. In Belgium contacts within the country's telecommunications network supplied advance teleprinter information of German troop and supply movements across the country by rail.[30] In Norway contacts in the local dairies meant that the size of garrisons could be estimated with a reasonable degree of accuracy since each German soldier received a known ration of milk.[31]

In December 1943 Nigel Clive was dropped into the Epiros region of Greece to report on the German order of battle. He was not briefed on the politics of the resistance, which he had to learn when he joined the British Military Mission in Greece. By the end of December he had recruited his first three agents and taught them how to describe the vehicle signs on German transport. These three men then trained local villagers to help them:

> The whole village took pride in its work and proved the authenticity of their observation by drawing the vehicle signs with sufficient accuracy for me to be able to make them match with those in the handbook I was holding. The keenest and best of the team was virtually illiterate; but this in no way decreased the value of the intelligence they provided.

Over the next eight months reports reached Clive twice a week and in this way all German traffic on the main roads north to south and east to west were under constant observation. As the prospect of a German withdrawal from Greece grew closer in the course of 1944, more Greeks, often former collaborators, were ready to help the British:

> . . . following the ritual haggle over the price, a deal could quickly be clinched by 'payment on results', plus the assurance, 'in the name of the British' (which

> always sounded impressive), that switching sides could lead to atonement for collaboration with the Germans.[32]

Inexperienced agents could, however, also supply misleading information. The Cretans warned Xan Fielding that the Germans appeared to be stationing a high number of parachutists in Canea: further investigation revealed that the Cretans had mistaken the Luftwaffe insignia for the wings of the parachute corps.[33]

Various intelligence networks contributed to the Allies' knowledge of the German coastal defences down the Norwegian coastline and along the entire North Sea, English Channel, and French Atlantic coasts. Locations of gun emplacements, minefields, and other defences were mapped and their appearance described in detail. The difficulties in obtaining and updating intelligence are revealed by an interview with a member of the resistance in Caen, André Heintz. He noted that it was hard to establish which minefields were real and which were fake by mere observation. The accurate information could, however, be obtained from the local tax office which had an up-to-date record of which fields could be used by the farmers and which could not.[34]

Heintz also noted that Allied intelligence made requests that French intelligence was simply incapable of fulfilling, through the lack of specialist knowledge:

> I must confess that there were two types of questions that always puzzled me. When a bunker had been found we could describe what type it was as the number of models was limited, but I am afraid we could not always be very accurate about the calibre of the guns. When the guns were brought in, the area was evacuated. If by any chance a local farmer had seen the guns, it was rare luck.
>
> The other thing that often caused a blank in my answers was the last question – how many men would be necessary to invest a certain defence post or headquarters? It was very difficult for inexperienced people like us to assess the answer to such a question. The only thing it did, in fact, was to make us think it was not fair to ask such questions unless D-Day was getting near. Other questions were perfectly useless, like finding out passwords which were changed every day.

The local resistance could, however, supply accurate intelligence on what troops were in the area by chatting to locals at the bus station or by using contacts in the local laundries to discover the unit numbers.[35]

The inexperience of local intelligence agents on military matters inspired the creation of the 'Sussex' teams. This was a joint operation mounted by

OSS and SIS to despatch fifty two-man teams to northern France. The teams were split equally between the intended theatres of operations of the Americans and the British, and reported on the entire area from Brittany up to the Belgian border. The original plan had been to include Frenchmen, but the BCRA was hostile to the idea and the recruits were found to be of 'low medical category or indifferent morale'. The first Sussex teams were parachuted into France in April 1944 with more following in May, so that by D-Day there were fifteen teams in the field. They proved their worth immediately by radioing back the German order of battle and, vitally, reporting the hitherto unknown presence of the German Panzer Lehr Division in France. This report alone was widely seen as justification for the entire Sussex project.[36]

The Alliance network surpassed itself by producing a 55-foot-long map showing every German gun and beach obstacle as well as the locations of German troops and the roads along the coast from the mouth of the Dives river in Normandy to the Cotentin peninsula. Much of this information had been supplied by Robert Douin, who walked or cycled along the coastline with his fourteen-year-old son. As a sculptor who had worked on many of the local churches, he received permission to go up the church towers, from where he could observe the German fortifications. The map was flown to London on 16 March 1944 well in time for D-Day.[37] Over the next month the Germans arrested twenty of the men who had contributed information to the map, including Douin, and executed them on 7 June 1944. Hugh Verity, who flew secret agents to and from France, paid tribute to them:

> It helps to put our pick-ups into a proper sense of proportion to think that the cost of this one map in human lives was much greater than the cost in aircrew lives of all the RAF pick-up operations in France from 1940 to 1944 . . . It is also interesting to speculate how many hundreds or thousands of Allied lives may have been saved by the information on the 55-foot map when American troops took Cotentin.[38]

The gratitude of the Allies towards agents in France who were taking immense risks to obtain intelligence may have been one reason behind the low-level RAF raid on Amiens prison on 18 February 1944 – Operation Jericho – which is still a mystery. No one is quite sure who ordered the raid or why. After the war it was alleged in some quarters that the French resistance had requested the RAF to undertake the raid on 18 February because 100 of its agents were due to be shot by the Germans the next day. For example, in 1946 the head of the Sosies network, Dominique Ponchardier, confirmed that he had made such a request since many members of his network were held in Amiens. Yet it seems strange that at a time when every prison in France housed arrested members of the resistance the RAF should choose the prison in Amiens in particular. It is known that the Germans had caught two important SIS agents and were holding them there. One possibility is suggested by the archives which have revealed that the head of SIS, Stewart Menzies, wrote a letter to the RAF thanking them for mounting the raid. It may be that the purpose of the raid was either to give the agents the opportunity to escape or to kill them in order to ensure that they could not reveal their knowledge, conceivably of the location of D-Day, under torture to the Germans.

Whatever the reason for the raid, the local resistance was asked to supply essential information on the prison to the British. Photo reconnaissance could show the exterior layout of the prison, but only agents on the ground could discover the internal layout, the routine of the guards, and the construction of the buildings and the walls surrounding the prison, as well as the exact location of anti-aircraft defences in the immediate area. The information supplied by the resistance enabled the RAF to make an accurate model of Amiens prison which was used to brief the Mosquito crews who would mount the daring, high-risk, low-level raid on it. The intention was to do sufficient damage to the prison that the resistance fighters could enter it and rescue their comrades. At the time of the raid the prison held 710 inmates: 520 in the French section for criminals; 190 in the German section for political prisoners. Ponchardier wrote later of the raid itself:

> We were getting more than we had bargained for. The first bomb had made a breach in the surrounding wall, but it was quite impossible for us to get inside the prison, where bombs were still exploding. Finally the planes drew off, and we floundered through the dust and the smoke and the fire. But dozens of civilians were doing the same, and the chaos was indescribable. So much for our fine plans! We couldn't find the prisoners we were helping to escape, and kept running into terrified Boches who were creeping out of their shelters; everyone was firing on everyone else in the confusion.[39]

Over 100 prisoners were killed in the raid and 258 escaped, although many were soon recaptured. The fate of the SIS prisoners is not known, but it is thought that they escaped. The RAF sustained a major loss when the plane with the leader of the raid, Group Captain Charles Pickard,* was shot down.[40]

The Polish intelligence network *Lombard* kept the Allies updated on German weapons manufacture. Among the items of intelligence it supplied

* Pickard had been the star of the 1941 film *Target for Tonight*, in which he played himself.

were the plans for new types of submarines, which were secreted out of a Hamburg dockyard, the penetration of the main Focke-Wulf aircraft factory, and information on the development of the new Panther tank. During 1943, the Allied air offensive against Germany meant that the Germans relocated a number of factories manufacturing aircraft, air engines, and spare parts to Poland. This put them out of reach of Allied bombers, but made it easier for Polish intelligence to report on numbers and types of planes produced.[41]

Analysis in Britain of German armaments capabilities was a relatively straightforward process because the intelligence analysts were dealing with familiar types of weaponry. This was far from the case when reports began arriving on the German rocket programme at the end of 1942 and in early 1943. Rocket science was far more developed in Germany than in Britain, and the few British scientists who understood even some of the concepts of rockets had to make assumptions regarding German plans based on their own limited knowledge. As Harry Hinsley, the historian of British intelligence during this period, has noted:

> The assumptions of the British rocket experts did indeed have unfortunate consequences for the collection and interpretation of the intelligence. This was practically unavoidable in view of the novelty of the V-weapons, the paucity of intelligence about their performance and technical characteristics while they remained at the research and development stage and – not least because these were subjects on which Sigint [signals intelligence] was throwing no light and with which SIS agents had no familiarity – the difficulty of distinguishing what was reliable from what was not in the intelligence that was coming in.[42]

Correct interpretation of the pieces of intelligence reaching Britain was further hampered by a great difference of opinion between two of Britain's leading scientists, Lord Cherwell, who did not believe in the existence or possibility of a rocket, and R. V. Jones, who did. In April 1943 Duncan Sandys was appointed to chair a new intelligence subcommittee to coordinate the assessment of intelligence on the rocket and to suggest countermeasures.

On 18 December 1942 the SIS office in Stockholm forwarded a highly alarming report received from a Danish engineer, Aage Andreasen, who travelled extensively in Germany on business. While in Berlin he had had a conversation with a Professor Forner and an engineer, Stefan Szenassy, during which a rocket was mentioned. This rocket allegedly had a maximum range of 200 kilometres and contained five tons of explosive, making it capable of causing damage over an area ten kilometres square. Further reports from Andreasen followed over the next three months, during which Peenemünde on the island of Usedom near Swinemünde was identified as the location of German research and development. Reports then began coming in from Poles, Frenchmen, and Luxembourgers who were working as forced labourers at Peenemünde. One Polish report included a sketch map of the facility and descriptions of the flying weapons seen, but this report, made in February 1943, caused considerable confusion, because it referred to a weapon with the shape of a pilotless plane which took off from a special launch pad made of steel rails. Furthermore, the reports from Peenemünde suggested that the payload of the weapon was about 250 kilograms, considerably less than that reported by Andreasen. Therefore, British intelligence analysts rejected reports of a so-called pilotless aircraft because they did not fit in with what they already understood by rockets. Further confusion was caused by new reports in June 1943. One was from a disenchanted German working in the German weapons department, who wrote of a winged rocket with remote control launched by a catapult. Reports from Sweden and Denmark referred to both rockets at Peenemünde and to a strange radio apparatus being installed on the Danish island of Bornholm.

Despite dismissing reports of the development of a rocket until a taped conversation between captured German Generals Wilhelm von Thoma and Ludwig Crüwell referred explicitly to one, British intelligence did take action. Photo reconnaissance of Peenemünde was requested in January 1943 since the island of Usedom had not been photographed since May 1942, and the new reconnaissance revealed a variety of unfamiliar structures and weapons. Accordingly, on the night of 17 August 1943, Peenemünde was heavily bombed: the raid killed a number of German scientists and engineers as well as 130 of the 600 forced labourers. It appears that the French and Luxembourger informants must have been among the casualties since no further reports were received from them. The raid caused a delay of at least two months to the rocket programme as the Germans began to dismantle the site at Peenemünde. Development was moved to the Traunsee near Salzburg, assembly transferred to an underground factory built and operated by slave labour in the Harz mountains, and testing moved to a new firing range set up at Blizna, near Dębica in Poland. This last facility was now placed under observation by Polish intelligence, who from November 1943 supplied the Allies with dates, times, and direction of launches but could not get close enough to examine methods of launching.[43]

Attention now turned to northern France where photo-reconnaissance flights were requested to support the orders despatched to agents in France and Belgium to report on any strange constructions near the coast. During August 1943 reports arrived from France which conflicted with what had been photographed and reported from Peenemünde. These caused confusion in the minds of British scientists, leading to 'indecision and acrimonious disagreements'. Michel Hollard is widely and probably correctly identified as the 'man who saved London'. He and his Agir network proved the most efficient in drawing up a list of the locations of strange constructions appearing in northern France. These appeared to be a parallel pair of rails about 150 feet long set at an incline of 15 degrees and pointed very accurately in the direction of London: because they were straight for most of their length but then curved at the far end, these structures became known as 'ski sites'. Hollard recruited agents to map the entire Channel coast of northern France, and he himself visited a site at Auffay, about twenty miles north of Rouen. One of his agents, André Comps, volunteered to work on a site at Bois Carré, about ten miles north-east of Abbeville, and succeeded in making tracings of all of the blueprints of the site. Hollard also visited a factory in Auffay where a contact had informed him that crates containing a strange weapon were stored. In near darkness Hollard investigated a weapon with a cigar-shaped body and two flatter parts, and measured what he could reach. The Alliance network sent London a report on the creation of an anti-aircraft regiment, the 155W under Colonel Max Wachtel, which was going to be deployed in France near Amiens by the end of the year to operate the ski sites.[44]

On 22 August 1943 a 'new rocket-propelled glider bomb' went off course and landed on the island of Bornholm. The Danish police commissioner on the island, Johannes Hansen, contacted Lieutenant Commander Vilhelm Christiansen of the Danish air force, whom he knew to be in contact with Danish intelligence, and the two men rushed to the site of the wreckage. Hansen hurriedly took photographs, developed the negatives, and the not very clear photographs and drawings made reached London via Sweden. Eight copies of the report and photographs were despatched to London via different routes. One was discovered by the Germans, and Christiansen was arrested and interrogated. He replied quite truthfully that he had not photographed the wreckage; the resistance rescued him from prison and he reached the safety of Sweden.[45]

All this intelligence caused confusion in London, and Hinsley concluded: 'Until the end of August 1943 the scattered hints in the intelligence about pilotless aircraft had done more to confuse the attempt to establish the characteristics of the long-range rocket than to prompt the conclusion that the Germans were developing two separate weapons.' It was only when a report was smuggled out of the German weapons agency that the Germans were developing *two* separate weapons, a pilotless aircraft – the V-1 – for the Luftwaffe, and a rocket – the V-2 – for the Wehrmacht, that the apparently conflicting intelligence reports began to make sense. In the later months of 1943 the intelligence received and the results of photo reconnaissance were revisited and it was realized, though not by Cherwell, that there had always been two weapons. Indeed, one of the photographs of Peenemünde taken before the raid had actually shown a V-1. The link between the V-1 and the ski sites was made at the end of November, and from December 1943 onwards a programme of systematically bombing all known ski sites began – Operation Crossbow. In early January 1944 Wachtel wrote in his diary: 'If Allied bombing continues at the present rate for two more weeks, the hope of ever using the original site system operationally will have to be abandoned.' By the end of March 1944 nine ski sites had been completely destroyed, thirty-five severely damaged, and a further forty-nine had lesser degrees of damage. This had little impact, however, as the Germans redesigned the launch system so that around 150 less elaborate structures made of prefabricated parts could be rapidly constructed in locations less visible from the air. French and Polish intelligence networks continued to find them and report their locations to London. They also reported on the stores of V-1 weapons, and it was the bombing of these that probably did the most to limit the effectiveness of the V-1 bombardment of London, which opened on 13 June.[46] The danger posed by the V-1s was not, however, completely eradicated until Allied ground forces overran the entire Channel coast in the months after the D-Day landings.

Even when the separate nature of the V-1 flying bomb had been elucidated, confusion about the German rocket programme continued within the ranks of the British scientific and intelligence communities because the scientists knew too little about rockets and made false assumptions regarding the methods of launching a rocket and the type of fuel used. Photographic and ground reconnaissance had revealed large sites at Wizernes, Mimoyecques, Lottinghen, and Siracourt in northern France whose design did not match what was known of the ski sites, but they did not accord with what the British expected rocket-launching sites to look like. The British thought that a piece of equipment – a 'projector' – was essential to fire the rocket into the air before its engine could be started, but neither the intelligence from France nor that from Blizna pointed to the existence of such a projector. Indeed, reports from Blizna suggested that the rocket took off from a near-vertical position: the sites in France were bombed in any case. A further false assumption regarded the fuel used in the rocket. The British assumed that it would be some form of solid propellant, leading to confusion about its likely range and payload; but reports emanating from Blizna pointed towards liquid fuels, since the Poles had noted tanks covered in ice arriving by rail at Blizna. These were presumed to contain liquid oxygen which has to be kept well below freezing point. A Polish agent, Aleksander Pieńkowski, managed to get hold of a flask containing a liquid used in test flights and put it in his pocket, where it began to leak:

> I was not worried too much about getting burned, but about spoiling the material of the trousers. I took the pocket inside out to get it dry, and I covered the trousers with a rubber coat. After 20 minutes, sitting at the station, as a result of self-ignition the material began to burn with light flames similar to burning powder; the temperature was also high. The skin on my thigh and stomach is charred. What is interesting, the material of the pocket taken inside out did not burn, only crumbled when touched.

The contents of the flask were almost certainly hydrogen peroxide, but this information served only to confuse the British even more, since the hydrogen peroxide was not plausible as fuel for the rocket engine itself.[47]

On 20 May 1944 a V-2 fired from Blizna fell intact near the village of Klimczyce, close to Sarnaki on the banks of the River Bug. Members of the AK 22nd Infantry Regiment managed to recover the V-2 and secrete it in a nearby village despite a lengthy German search. Two Polish scientists, Professors Janusz Groszkowski and Marek Struszyński, travelled from Warsaw to dismantle the V-2, make detailed drawings of the components, and photograph the parts. Reports were compiled by Antoni Kocjan and Stefan Waciórski and despatched to London on 12 June and 3 July. The British realized that these reports referred to a different weapon from the V-1s which had just started landing in Britain, and plans were hatched to send a plane from Italy to Poland to collect parts of the rocket and the full reports and photographs compiled by the Poles. On the night of 25–26 July 1944 a Dakota arrived at a secret landing strip near Wał-Ruda near Tarnów. This operation, known as Wildhorn III, was highly dangerous because a German Fieseler Storch had landed on the airstrip earlier that day and a German detachment was nearby. The Dakota landed safely and the parts of the V-2 were loaded. They were accompanied by Captain Jerzy Chmielewski and Czesław Miciński, who kept close watch over the bags of documents. Also on the flight were two important Poles, Józef Retinger, who had been compiling a report on the Polish underground, and Tomasz Arciszewski, the future prime minister of the Polish government-in-exile. Disaster nearly struck as the heavily laden Dakota became stuck in the mud. The pilot was all for abandoning the flight, especially as dawn was approaching, but AK members and locals stripped a nearby barn of wood to give the wheels the necessary traction. Just as dawn broke, the Dakota took off on the fourth attempt and began the hazardous daytime flight back to Italy. On 28 July the parts and the reports reached London, still accompanied by Chmielewski and Miciński who would not let them out of their sight.[48] Analysis of the recovered V-2 revealed that hydrogen peroxide was used to drive the fuel and oxidizer pumps: the fuel itself was an ethanol/water mixture and the oxidizer was liquid oxygen. The British were still confused as to how the rocket was controlled. The Polish evidence suggested that it could send and receive radio signals but could not be operated by remote control. Wreckage of a V-2 recovered in Sweden, however, pointed to the use of remote radio control. This conflict led the British scientists to waste effort on designing countermeasures to confuse the radio signals. These steps were unnecessary since the Swedish model was an anomaly, fitted with radio equipment for research purposes, while the Polish one was a more typical V-2.[49]

The first V-2 landed in Britain on 8 September 1944. There was no effective defence against a rocket arriving from space. The Danish resistance helped in limiting V-2 production by bombing the Globus radio factory in Copenhagen, which was making components for the V-2.[50] The resistance in France and the Low Countries proved of limited use in identifying V-2 launch sites since, contrary to British expectations, they consisted of little more than a concrete pad, or even a platform of railway sleepers. The most effective Allied countermeasures proved to be the bombing of the railways so that the rockets could not reach their launch sites, but ultimately the actual conquest of the territory from which the rockets were launched was the only sure defence, and the last V-2 fell in Britain in March 1945.

24
Preparing for D-Day

During the summer and autumn of 1943 the Germans inflicted enormous damage on the resistance in France. Jean Moulin was arrested and tortured to death, leaving a vacuum which needed to be filled at the head of the French resistance. The Germans had effectively destroyed SOE in northern France with the arrest of Francis Suttill and the crushing of the Prosper circuit. Elsewhere in France, André Grandclément's treachery caused problems in Bordeaux, and various SOE circuits in the south were badly hit by arrests. Yet a year later, when the Allies invaded Normandy on 6 June 1944, the French resistance was able to make a useful contribution. New leaders had been found and SOE's circuits were fully operational.

The Allied invasion planners paid little attention to what the French resistance might be able to contribute to the liberation of their country. The planners' reasoning can be seen in a minute written in 1943 by General Frederick Morgan, in command of logistics for D-Day, who wrote that the French resistance:

> ... could not be warned in advance of the date and time of the operation. Consequently no assistance from resistance groups can be expected during the initial assault. After the assault has taken place, however, pre-arranged plans could be put into effect for the demolition of railway communications in certain specific areas and for guerrilla activities on the German lines of communication ... The assistance of the groups should therefore be treated as a bonus rather than an essential part of the plan.[1]

De Gaulle and the CFLN, were left totally in the dark. French plans for the contribution of the resistance were being formed by various agencies: the CFLN in Algiers, the BCRA, which was split between London and Algiers, and the resistance itself in France. These plans all aimed at the liberation of France, but they often conflicted on the nature of resistance action and its timing, location, and methods of implementation. SOE also formed its own plans and imposed them on its F and RF Sections. It was only remarkably late in the day that these various plans came together and many questions, especially those of command and control, remained unanswered until after the Allies had actually landed in France.

The surrender of Italy appears to have caught the French resistance completely by surprise. In Italian-occupied France no effort was made to suborn Italian officers or men: for example, to obtain agreements to hand their weapons over to the resistance. The Germans, in contrast, were well prepared to extend their occupation into the Italian zone, and indeed the withdrawal of Italian troops from most of the zone, with the exception of the area surrounding Nice, was settled between the Germans and Italians even before the armistice was announced. The result was that, when the armistice came into effect, the Germans took 52,000 Italian soldiers prisoner without difficulty. One observer viewed the Italian prisoners lined up in Nice on the Promenade des Anglais as 'pitiable, with two or three German soldiers in charge of hundreds of Italians in tattered uniforms'. A few Italian units made a run for the Alps hoping to cross back into Italy. They were caught by the Germans, but at least the French resistance in the mountains managed to secure a quantity of the weapons they had abandoned.[2]

The Italian zone had been a little sanctuary for Jews who had colonized Nice and Cannes: they were now all in extreme danger. The experienced SS officer Alois Brunner arrived on the French Riviera and oversaw the first round-up of Jews from the hotels in Cannes immediately after the announcement of the armistice. There was a major round-up in Nice on 10 September, and the remainder of the Riviera was combed for Jews during the rest of the year. Now that the knowledge of the ultimate fate of the Jews was known, there was resistance to the German measures and the Germans struggled to locate the Jews:

> The arrest of Jews in territories until now occupied by the Italians is encountering great difficulties because of the fact that nearly ninety per cent . . . have false papers and are hidden in the villages and mountains. This is why capturing them is only possible with the assistance of local informers.[3]

The Italians and some French prefects had destroyed the lists of Jews, and in Cannes the local government officials changed the names on ration cards from Jewish-sounding names. The bishop of Nice, Monseigneur Paul Rémond, encouraged the Church authorities to hide the Jews. The Jews themselves organized a resistance, based around the Jewish scout movement. Nonetheless, by the end of 1943 nearly 2,000 Jews had been deported.[4]

On the Italian-occupied French island of Corsica the French resistance did have an impact on events, with important implications for the relationship between de Gaulle and his co-leader in Algiers, Henri Giraud. The course of events also highlighted more general problems concerning command and control over the resistance.

The most active resistance movement on Corsica was the communist-dominated *Front National* under Arthur Giovoni, which claimed to have 3,000 members organized across the island. The *Front National* was in contact with Giraud, but the first man to actually arrive on the island to organize the resistance was a Corsican working for de Gaulle's BCRA, Fred Scamaroni. He was landed on 7 January 1943 from a British submarine, accompanied by a radio operator and a sabotage expert. His radio operator, Hellier, proved to be a disaster. He was a heavy drinker and, when arrested in March, betrayed Scamaroni and all the contacts that had been made over the previous two months. Scamaroni was in turn arrested by the Italian OVRA, but his mission had been a failure even before then because the *Front National* saw no reason to hand over the command of their men to him. SOE now intervened and despatched another Corsican, Captain Paul Colonna d'Istria, in April 1943. As a British agent Colonna was able to stand apart from the de Gaulle–Giraud struggle and in May could report: 'All patriots, approximately 9000, are under single command and organized in "cadres" in towns and villages . . . Chain of command is established and based on administrative division of terrain . . .' SOE duly dropped 250 tons of supplies to the resistance. Colonna also established contact with the Italian commander in Bastia, Colonel Gagnoni, who appeared keen to oppose the Germans should the Italians change sides.

The news of the Italian surrender was announced by Radio Algiers on the evening of 8 September. The *Front National* central committee met and quickly decided to launch a general uprising on the island on the following day. They met little resistance from the Italians and took over the *préfecture* and the municipal offices in Ajaccio in the name of the CFLN. Colonna made an approach towards the Italian commander-in-chief, General Giovanni Magli, and was at least partly successful. Magli agreed to oppose neither the resistance nor the Germans, but he declined to pass Italian weapons to the resistance.

It was German activity which now determined the course of events on Corsica. The Germans had decided to withdraw their 20,000-strong garrison from Sardinia to the Italian mainland, had no plan to add Corsica to their operational overstretch, and sought to evacuate the troops via Bastia on Corsica. It would have been suicidal for the resistance to have attempted to hamper the German evacuation on its own. On 11 September

Giraud ordered Colonna to organize his forces to create a bridgehead at Ajaccio for the arrival of 6,000 Free French troops, the *Bataillon de Choc*, by sea, as well as an SOE mission under Major Jacques de Guélis, head of F Section in Algiers, and Commandant Clipet, representing French military intelligence. Colonna then fell ill and the job of liaison with the resistance fell to Clipet, who had little idea of how to use irregular troops. Clipet tried to incorporate the *Front National* partisans into the *Bataillon de Choc*, but met with opposition from the resistance leaders, whose men saw no need to fight around Bastia and Ajaccio, preferring to engage in hampering and sabotage operations nearer their own homes. By the time the Germans withdrew, voluntarily, on 4 October, the casualty figures were seventy-five French soldiers, 245 Italians, and 1,000 Germans. The resistance lost seventy-six men. The main success of the resistance appears to have been that it secured the landing area of the French troops. Once the main battle with the Germans had been joined, the resistance had little purpose other than to act as guides and to supply intelligence, since its members had neither the training nor the inclination to take part in regular operations. One mitigating factor was that, once the island was liberated, the *Front National* was prepared to hand over the civil administration to the Gaullist prefect, Charles Luizet.[5]

The limited role played by the resistance in Corsica called into question the reliability and effectiveness of resistance forces working alongside regular troops. The implications of this would be discussed by the Allies planning the invasion of France. But the most immediate impact of the Corsican operation was political. Giraud had taken action unilaterally and had not informed de Gaulle of what he was doing until French operations were under way. In his memoirs de Gaulle complained that 'Giraud did not breathe one word to me of the action he was taking in Corsica', nor did he know of Giovoni's visit to Algiers or of the power that this effectively gave the communist-dominated *Front National* on the island.[6] De Gaulle was extremely unwilling to share the leadership of the CFLN with Giraud. He recognized Giraud's abilities as a military commander, as indeed shown by the Corsica operation, but resented his presence when political decisions were being taken. In particular, de Gaulle was concerned that the American support for Giraud over himself could have far-reaching implications for the smooth transition of power once the liberation of France had been effected. There were indeed grounds for concern since Giraud still held a power base within metropolitan France through the officers of the disbanded Armistice Army, some of whom had formed the secret ORA, an underground army quite separate from the Gaullist resistance and its own secret army, the AS. In October 1943 Giraud was presented with a choice between commanding the French forces or holding political responsibilities. He chose to withdraw from political life, and eventually would be eased out of the military command too. The British minister in North Africa, Harold Macmillan, wrote in his diary that 'Giraud has deserved his fate', adding that this was a snub to the Americans and of benefit to the British who had a better relationship with de Gaulle.[7]

Yet de Gaulle was still not completely dominant either in Algiers or in France itself. In Algiers, most government officials were secretly still loyal to Vichy. De Gaulle gradually removed these men from their posts and replaced them with men loyal to him. He did not, however, engage in a wholesale revenge on the Vichyites. He did have three former Vichy ministers, Governor Pierre Boisson, Marcel Peyrouton, and Pierre-Étienne Flandin, arrested, but assured Churchill 'that the men under arrest would come to no harm until they were tried after the liberation of France and that meanwhile they were not being ill-treated'. The exception was the former minister of the interior, Pierre Pucheu, who arrived in Algiers in October 1943, and was arrested and charged with treason. His trial was controversial in that prospective witnesses for the defence were still trapped in occupied France and could not take part. Pucheu was charged with collaboration with the Germans, placing the French police at the service of the Germans, and recruiting men for the *Légion des Volontaires Français contre le Bolchévisme*: his defence made the futile point that things had got worse since Pucheu had left France. He was found guilty and sentenced to death. Giraud made a plea for clemency, but de Gaulle was aware that the resistance in France was watching the trial with great interest and the CFLN's delegate in France, Jacques Bingen, had warned that 'any weakness on the part of the court would, at the time of liberation, lead to individuals settling their own scores'. To the resistance Pucheu was 'a double-dyed traitor' who had shown no mercy towards his victims. He was duly executed by firing squad on 20 March 1944. At the same time, de Gaulle and the CFLN announced that Pétain and other prominent collaborators would be tried after the liberation.[8]

In France itself there was a great polarization of society between those who supported the increasing collaborationism of the Vichy regime and the growing forces of the resistance: the resistance itself was also split into different camps. By the end of 1943 it was clear that the Vichy regime had little control over the country and the German authorities in France, Ambassador Otto Abetz and Cecil von Renthe-Fink, demanded stronger action against the resistance and the promotion of staunch collaborators in the Vichy regime. On 1 January 1944 Joseph Darnand was made the secretary general for the maintenance of order. This move extended his existing powers over the *Milice* and *Gardes Mobiles* to all the French police forces. Philippe Henriot was made the minister of propaganda, and his speeches advocating support for Pétain, the Vichy regime, and the Germans, and denigrating the resistance as terrorists, were every bit as vicious as any speech by Goebbels. In March, Marcel Déat, leader of the fascist RNP party, became the minister responsible for labour, an important and controversial post since the Germans were still demanding more forced labourers from France. There were also several purges of prefects and sub-prefects to place men with unquestioned loyalty to Pétain in positions of power.[9]

The *Milice* were undoubtedly the most dangerous enemy of the resistance. Maurice Buckmaster, head of SOE's F section, wrote that their danger lay in being Frenchmen: as such, they were 'indistinguishable from local people, they were able to permeate our organisation with a confidence impossible to the Gestapo and they had the power, like dry rot, of spreading their corrupting influence, among both the discontented and the timid'. The members of the *Milice* were widely detested by the resistance: SOE agent George Millar described them as: 'Scum of the jails, brutalised of the most brutal, cream of the offal, they worked mostly for money and food for their carnal appetites; they worked for German money.' The clandestine press took up the cry, calling for the death sentence without trial for members of the *Milice*, arguing that 'in signing his enlistment papers, [the member] is ratifying his own death sentence'. The resistance took the war to the *Milice* to the same extent as the *Milice* waged war on the resistance, leading to a virtual civil war in many areas. For example, in November 1943 five *Miliciens* were killed and four wounded by the resistance at a meeting in Nice attended by Darnand and Henriot. In retaliation the *Milice* murdered six members of the FTP in prison in Nice in December, and similar tit-for-tat attacks occurred in Antibes in early 1944. It has been estimated that there were at least 2,500 summary executions of collaborators between autumn 1943 and D-Day.[10]

The polarization of French society can be demonstrated by two events: Oyonnax in November 1943, and the response to the Allied bombing of Paris in spring 1944. The Vichy authorities in Oyonnax, a small town in the Rhône-Alpes, followed the official line of denouncing the maquis as a bunch of terrorists and bandits: for their part, the maquis wanted to prove that they were a disciplined force. The town was chosen for a demonstration because there was no German garrison there. On 11 November 1943 over 200 maquisards led by the local leader, Henri Romans-Petit in the full uniform of the French Air Force officer he had been at the time of the armistice, marched through the town at midday and placed a wreath on the war memorial shaped in the Cross of Lorraine with the inscription: 'To the victors of 1914–18, from the victors of tomorrow', and sang the *Marseillaise*. They then withdrew back to their camps in the hills and mountains. The local AS leaders also attended, again dressed in uniform. The march was filmed by André Jacquelin and photographs of it were reproduced in the clandestine press. There was no immediate reaction from the Germans, and the local French police and gendarmerie were known to be sympathetic to the resistance. In Grenoble, however, on the same day, when over 1,500 people marched towards the war memorial to the *Chasseurs Alpins* they were stopped by the French police and then sandwiched between them and the arriving Germans armed with machine guns. Although the crowd immediately dispersed without shots being fired, over 600 people were arrested, tried, and deported to camps in Germany. The German attack on the town of Nantua in December, when the Germans rounded up and deported over 100 men and arrested and executed the local resistance leader, Doctor Mercier, was widely seen as the German revenge for the maquis 'liberation' of Oyonnax.[11]

To many people in France, Pétain was still viewed as 'the saviour of Verdun' and as a man who was now at the mercy of his more collaborationist ministers such as Laval and Darnand. Although much sentiment in France was pro-Allied, the bombing of Paris in March and April 1944 shocked the population, especially the raid on 20 April which left 651 dead and 461 wounded. Six days later, Pétain went to Paris for the first time since the 1940 Armistice and attended a Requiem Mass for the victims, led by Cardinal Suhard, at Notre-Dame cathedral. Outside, a crowd estimated at one million people greeted him enthusiastically. The Allied bombing of a further ten French cities at the end of May, causing 6,000 deaths, further alarmed the French people. Yet Pétain was not the mere puppet of the collaborationists: he took the active decision to make a speech (probably written for him by Henriot) on 28 April, condemning the resistance totally as being controlled by the communists whose actions were leading to civil war. This speech effectively gave official support to Darnand's demands that the law of 20 January, which established courts-martial to try those caught 'in an act of terrorism', should be extended to anyone found with an armed group.[12]

The death of Jean Moulin meant that de Gaulle needed to take steps immediately to reassert his control over the French resistance. The resistance, on the other hand, saw Moulin's death as an opportunity to reverse the organizational measures he had imposed over the opposition of many of the resistance leaders. The leader of *Combat* after Henri Frenay had left France, Claude Bourdet, summed up the problem:

> In reality, what de Gaulle and his services *absolutely could not abide* was the confirmation of the thesis defended in London by several leaders of the Resistance, and by Frenay in particular, namely, that the Resistance, which had come into being without de Gaulle and had freely attached himself to him, supported him as citizens support their chosen government and not as soldiers obey their unit commander.[13]

Until de Gaulle could appoint a new delegate-general, the man left to pick up the pieces was Claude Bouchinet-Serreulles. He had arrived in France in June 1943 and only missed being caught at Caluire with Moulin because he got lost on the way to the meeting. Serreulles was trusted by de Gaulle but his inexperience in underground life and his lack of familiarity with resistance leaders made him unsuitable as leader of the CNR in the long term. It is to Serreulles's credit that he realized his own limitations. He acknowledged that the CNR 'could only be the true organ of expression of the resistance if its chief was a man from the resistance movements and not a man from London'. He therefore approached the head of the *Bureau d'Information et de Presse*, Georges Bidault, and asked him to take over as president of the CNR. Bidault was surprised by the offer but accepted it and was duly elected president in September 1943.[14]

Serreulles also realized that the differences between the resistance movements in the north and those in the south were so marked that it made sense to have a CNR delegate for each region. He was based in Paris and so took over contacts with the resistance in the north, leaving Jacques Bingen, who arrived in France in August, as the representative in the south. This left the question of who should be the delegate-general with authority over the country as a whole. Pierre Brossolette was extremely keen to become the replacement delegate-general but he had the misfortune of being in London when Moulin was arrested, and away from the centre of events. De Gaulle had every reason to suspect that Brossolette had different ideas on the purpose of the CNR from his own, so, when the two men met in Algiers, de Gaulle authorized a mission by Brossolette to France, but refused to appoint him to the delegate-general post that he coveted. Instead, Brossolette played kingmaker, putting forward the name of the former prefect of Lyon who had been sacked by the Vichy regime, Émile Bollaert. Bollaert knew nothing of the resistance and needed to be briefed on the subject by Serreulles and Bingen, as well as by Brossolette when he arrived with SOE agent 'Tommy' Yeo-Thomas on 19 September. When Brossolette arrived in Paris he was appalled by the poor security procedures of

Serreulles and Bingen: the latter allegedly arrived at one meeting with three men clearly tailing him. Worse came when the Gestapo raided Serreulles's office on 25 September and Yeo-Thomas learned 'that four months' couriers and telegrams in both directions, and lists of names "en clair", had been taken', and that Serreulles had no idea of the seriousness of the situation even when arrests of his close associates began. Bingen later committed suicide in prison after his arrest in May 1944.[15]

Yeo-Thomas held a wide brief to explore all angles of the resistance. Having completed his mission, he returned to London to report and made numerous scathing comments about Serreulles. In the meantime, Brossolette continued to make waves as he sought power. Bollaert believed that if he was to have any influence over the resistance then it was essential to go to Algiers and meet de Gaulle. Brossolette accompanied him, but the two men were arrested in Brittany in February 1944 when their boat ran aground. Brossolette was operating under a false identity and was not immediately recognized by the Germans. He had a tell-tale streak of white hair which he had dyed and it was deemed essential to rescue him from the prison at Rennes before the Germans learned his identity. Accordingly, Yeo-Thomas returned to France at the end of the month. On 21 March he had scheduled a meeting with a contact in Paris to discuss air operations, but he missed his contact. As Yeo-Thomas later admitted, he committed a complete breach of tradecraft:

> I was therefore in two minds as to whether I would wait a few minutes, which was absolutely against my principles of security, or give up the contact, but as I was leaving for Rennes and might possibly be away for a few days, I decided that it was imperative to see 'Antonin' in order to give him instructions to cover the possibility of a longer absence than I anticipated.

Yeo-Thomas was arrested and on arrival at the Gestapo headquarters on Avenue Foch he learned that he had been betrayed by a man of whom he had been already suspicious, André Lemonnier. His mission had been in vain. The Gestapo had recognized Brossolette and transferred him to Paris where he jumped from a fifth-floor window and died of his injuries barely an hour before Yeo-Thomas arrived at the Avenue Foch. Bollaert was sent to concentration camps in Germany but survived. In April his successor was named as Alexandre Parodi.[16]

In parallel with regaining political influence over the resistance, de Gaulle instituted a number of steps to win control over the military wing which had been lost after the arrest of General Delestraint in June 1943. He recognized that this could not be done by one man, and in September 1943 he appointed Louis-Eugène Mangin as senior military delegate in the south and Pierre Marchal in the north: after his subsequent arrest Marchal was replaced by Colonel Paul Ély. In March, de Gaulle named Jacques Chaban-Delmas as the national military delegate. In accordance with demands from some resisters and from the Allies that the French operations should be decentralized, a series of regional military delegates (DMRs) were appointed. The DMRs proved of limited value, as the DMR for the Lyon region, Maurice Bourgès-Maunoury, complained:

> We do not have money, weapons do not seem to come when we order them, our cable connection with you is a very uncertain thread that transports questions and answers that never seem to correspond. We might therefore be reduced to calling for discipline, but our position is very poorly defined. Leaving aside the aura, much disparaged, in which the person arriving from the outside is surrounded, we have nothing to contribute but diplomacy, not to say charm.

Poor security meant that by early 1944 four of the seven DMRs in the north had been arrested. By June, however, the situation had greatly improved and the DMRs were proving better able to dispense money and receive weapons.[17]

Despite these steps, de Gaulle's control over the resistance remained limited. Pascal Copeau suggested that: 'The authority of the delegates would be the object of negotiations, and, for all the delegates, even the military ones, the only way to hold on to their authority would be to become in large part interpreters of the real problems of underground action.'[18] Even the creation of the *Forces Françaises de l'Intérieur* (FFI) under General Koenig in February 1944, effectively the merger of the AS and the FTP into one resistance army, only papered over the cracks and numerous questions remained unanswered.

One of these questions was the position of the communists in the resistance. De Gaulle had been alarmed by the militancy of the *Front National* on Corsica and was concerned about the advocacy of immediate action pursued by the FTP in mainland France. Despite theoretically joining the FFI, the communists retained their separate command and organizational structure. Furthermore, the communists dominated many councils of the resistance, especially COMAC (*Comité Militaire d'Action*), the action committee of the CNR, and the Paris Liberation Committee (CPL). The communists also held positions of leadership in many regions, especially in the Rhône-Alpes, Provence, and the Île-de-France. De Gaulle had, however, succeeded in bringing the communists into the CFLN when, at the beginning of April, two communist ministers, Fernand Grenier and François Billoux, were appointed. This raised hopes that the CFLN, which now also included forty representatives of the resistance, would be widely viewed as a body that could control events in France once the liberation began.[19]

A further step was taken with the appointment of regional commissioners who would act as prefects to secure a smooth transfer of power. The final step was taken on 3 June when the CFLN renamed itself the *Gouvernement Provisoire de la République Française*, the Provisional Government. It remained to be seen, however, whether the Allies would actually grant recognition to it.

As a result of security lapses by SOE agents on the ground, the failure of London to recognize that captured agents' radios were being used by the Germans, and the actions of a few traitors, from September 1943 SOE in effect had little presence in northern France. This was a vital area because it lay directly behind the beachheads for the forthcoming invasion. SOE in London failed to learn from its mistakes and, indeed, further compounded them in the early months of 1944. A post-war report on the circuits in France attempted to justify the actions taken by F Section at this time:

> In the meantime further efforts were being made to build up circuits in the area which the Gestapo believed they had cleared of F Section influence, and which both they and we knew to be crucial in relation to the battle to come. They were encouraged to believe that we were unaware of the extent of their penetration, and deliveries of stores were continued to circuits known to be Gestapo-operated, in order to give time for new circuits to establish themselves.[20]

This argument simply does not stand up to examination.

F Section's established incompetence in recognizing when radio operators were operating under duress continued. At the end of February 1944 Julien Detal and Philippe Duclos, who planned to set up a circuit to cut off Brittany from the rest of France, dropped to a reception committee organized by the Butler circuit and were arrested on arrival. Butler had been operated by the Germans since September 1943 when the Germans had arrested its organizer, Jean Bouguennec (known as Francis Garel), and his radio operator, Marcel Rousset. Rousset had tried to warn London by convincing the Germans that he had to transmit in French for Gustave Biéler's Musician circuit and in English for Garel, whereas the opposite was true. London's response to this signal was to ask him why he had changed language. As a result, at the beginning of March, the experienced agents Octave Simon and his radio operator Marcel Defence were dropped to a reception committee organized by the same blown Butler circuit and were arrested on arrival. At the beginning of February 1944 Roland

Alexandre, Francis Deniset, Jacques Ledoux, and a radio operator loaned from OSS, Robert Byerly, were dropped to a reception committee arranged by the blown Phono circuit and were immediately arrested. Byerly had been given a number of special messages to transmit to show that he was at liberty and none of these were sent. Indeed, when he was asked a test question which should have engendered the response 'Merry Xmas', he responded with 'Happy New Year'. The capture of these agents hindered the build-up of the resistance in the area of Angers, Nantes, and Le Mans. London suspected something was wrong but took no action.

London's failure to accept that SOE agent Noor Inayat Khan's radio, and now Byerly's, were under German control resulted in the loss of a man who could have contributed a great deal to the post-invasion period, Joseph Antelme. On an earlier mission, Antelme had made numerous contacts to arrange for supplies of currency and food for the invading armies in the region north of Paris. He escaped the Prosper disaster and his arrival in London in July 1943 provided F Section with the first thorough report on it. At the end of February 1944 he was parachuted back into France with his courier Madeleine Damerment and a radio operator, Lionel Lee, to a reception organized through Noor's radio. His orders were to investigate the security of the Parson circuit around Rennes organized by François Vallée, which London suspected had been penetrated. It had, and its radio operator, Georges Clément, is alleged to have collaborated with the Germans. At the last moment Antelme was also asked to look into Garel's Butler circuit. Finally, he was to set up his own circuit, Surveyor, just south of Paris. Antelme and his two colleagues were arrested on arrival, but F Section received radio messages from Noor's radio and another radio reporting that Antelme had sustained severe head injuries on landing. By then F Section was convinced that all these radios were under German control. This suspicion was confirmed during the brief first mission of Violette Szabo in April. Finally, on 20 April messages were received that Antelme had died in hospital from his injuries; in fact, he had been in prison all along and was later executed in Gross-Rosen concentration camp.

The German-controlled Archdeacon circuit netted the Germans such agents as David Finlayson, Maurice Lepage, Alphonse Defendini, and Francis Michel. These arrests hampered the organization of resistance in the Meuse department around Verdun, and activity around Valenciennes. Two more victims were the highly experienced radio operators Adolphe Rabinovitch and Roger Sabourin, who were caught when they were dropped to a reception organized by Archdeacon at the beginning of March 1944. Rabinovitch had survived both the penetration of the Carte network and the Prosper disaster, and was furious that London's carelessness had led to his arrest. On 6 June, as Allied soldiers stepped ashore on the Normandy beaches, the Germans transmitted a message to Buckmaster through Rousset's radio: 'We thank you for the large deliveries of arms and ammunition which you have been kind enough to send us. We also appreciate the many tips you have given us regarding your plans and intentions which we have carefully noted ...' The message was signed '*Geheime Staatspolizei*'. A similar message was received from a radio supposedly operated by John Macalister in the Ardennes.

Betrayal and carelessness combined to inflict more damage on SOE in northern France. In September 1943 Marcel Clech, the radio operator for the Inventor circuit, was arrested after the Germans had detected his radio transmissions. The Inventor circuit had already been virtually destroyed after Roger Bardet betrayed its organizer, Sidney Jones, and courier, Vera Leigh. In January 1944 Yolande Beekman, the radio operator for Biéler's Musician circuit, was arrested because she had abandoned the basic security procedure of frequently changing locations for transmissions and had continued to operate from the same residence. The Gestapo followed her as she unwittingly led them to Biéler. The fall of these two circuits effectively reduced F Section's presence in the area immediately north of Paris and around Saint-Quentin. Michael Trotobas had run a very successful circuit, Farmer, around Lille but arrests in his circuit led the Germans to Trotobas, who was killed while resisting arrest on 27 November 1943. His circuit survived and the railwaymen he had trained would prove of great benefit in sabotaging the railways after D-Day. Claude Malraux had arrived in France in April 1943 and built up a very successful sabotage circuit, Salesman, in the Rouen and Le Havre areas. In March 1944, however, Malraux was duped by a German posing as a *réfractaire* and was arrested. He was caught with two suitcases full of documents containing the names of his contacts and a list of sabotage targets. The information from the documents along with names extracted from Malraux under torture led the Germans to arrest over thirty sub-agents including all the leaders of the groups in Le Havre. The circuit was rebuilt by Philippe Liewer and Violette Szabo who dropped into France just after D-Day.

Philippe de Vomécourt had taken part in the large, successful mass escape of resisters from Maison Centrale d'Eysses prison in Villeneuve-sur-Lot in January 1944. His contacts facilitated the construction of Sydney Hudson's Headmaster, George Wilkinson's Historian, and Gerard Dedieu's Permit circuits by D-Day. De Vomécourt himself focused on rebuilding Ventriloquist in the southern Loir-et-Cher, an area of importance for German communications. These circuits were of limited value since the organizers only arrived in France during the immediate run-up to D-Day and therefore had little time to prepare. They also found that the German presence was so strong that many Frenchmen feared to show any sign of resistance. Nevertheless, these men had established the nuclei of circuits in the Le Mans, Orléans, and Chartres–Dreux areas, and after D-Day recruits would flood in, resulting in an impressive rate of activity.

Claude de Baissac, who had done so much to organize the resistance in and around Bordeaux earlier, now returned to France to set up Scientist in the Normandy region. All his targets were set well back from the coast, 'as it was evident that no resistance organisation could long survive in the battle area itself', but since the location of the invasion area was a closely guarded secret de Baissac did not know that he was meant to avoid it and consequently began building his circuit in the coastal area as well. By D-Day he had not only supplied a great deal of intelligence on targets but had also prepared five areas for the reception of paratroopers, although in the event they were never used. De Baissac's achievements were limited partly by the large German presence in the area and partly because a network in Normandy which was supposed to be part of Henri Frager's Donkeyman circuit centred on Paris was in fact being run by the Germans and their French helpers. The high level of German activity also meant that resistance never got off the ground in the area of most value for deception operations, the Pas-de-Calais. The French population of the region had been largely deported from the area, which was now full of German troops manning V-weapons installations and the coastal defences. The area of the Franco-German border was similarly hard to penetrate. Harry Rée's Stockbroker circuit around Besançon was hindered by Rée's absence in Switzerland, itself forced by German pressure, until the Comte de Brouville took over the circuit in April. In May the Sacristan team of André Bouchardon and the OSS operative Ernest Floege were dropped to reinforce Stockbroker. On the eve of D-Day, George Millar was dropped to create a new circuit, Chancellor, north of Besançon and into the French Ardennes.

Grandclément's treachery in Bordeaux had effectively destroyed the original Scientist circuit built up by Claude de Baissac and Roger Landes in the summer of 1943. When Landes returned to Bordeaux in March 1944 he found the damage was still continuing. Grandclément had persuaded many section leaders that he was now the head of the circuit and that they should follow his orders. This not only meant the revealing of the locations of many arms caches to the Germans, ostensibly so that the FTP could not use them, but also put an end to sabotage operations in the region. Landes, however, found that there was still an operational group in the port of Bordeaux, another near the Luftwaffe base at Mérignac, and a maquis group near Arcachon. Landes worked remarkably quickly and stated later: 'Within a week of my return I had managed to make contact with the headquarters in London and had an organisation of about 10 groups, about 500 men, and could organise nearly straight away about 20 dropping zones.' By D-Day these numbers had increased to 4,000 well-armed and well-organized men who were poised to interdict the main rail and road routes out of Bordeaux in all directions, but especially the north.

F Section circuits to the south of Paris, and especially in the former Unoccupied Zone, fared much better despite the increase in the German presence since the occupation of the region in November 1942. The importance of these circuits lay in their location. The Germans sent divisions for refitting in the area, most notably SS Das Reich which arrived in Montauban, north of Toulouse, in April 1944. The Allies were also engaged in making plans to invade southern France in the summer of 1944. The role of the resistance therefore in southern and central France would be to hinder the reinforcement of the Normandy beachheads by German divisions stationed south of Paris. Because the impact of these circuits rests on the reputations built up in the post-invasion period, this section will serve as an introduction to the people whose work will be covered in the following chapters.

The far south-west area was the remit of the Wheelwright circuit under George Starr, the brother of the discredited John. He had inherited the circuit from its original organizer, Maurice Pertschuk, who had been arrested with his radio operator Marcus Bloom in April 1943. These arrests meant that Starr was out of radio contact with London after his arrival, and was forced to send his two assistants, Denise Bloch and Sergeant Dupont, to London via Spain to report in person. In August 1943 his new operator, Yvonne Cormeau, arrived. She recalled a meeting with Starr which illustrates the dangers of working undercover in France: 'as we got near a very small village, cycling, we saw on the shutters of a house, which served both as a schoolroom and the town hall, two identikit-type drawings of ourselves. So we looked at them, looked at each other, we didn't say anything and we split up. I went back north and he went south.' This circuit was well organized and received a high level of supplies and reinforcements of personnel, including a courier, Anne-Marie Walters.

The largest circuit in the south was Stationer run by Maurice Southgate, which stretched from Châteauroux to Tarbes. The structure of the circuit had been built up by Ben Cowburn but it was now too large so it was initially split into two parts: August Chantraine ran the northern portion and Charles Rechenmann the southern. The Germans hit the circuit in the winter of 1943, leading to Chantraine's arrest and Rechenmann being forced to leave France temporarily. Rechenmann returned in March 1944 to focus on plans for sabotage in and around Tarbes but was betrayed by a sub-agent at the beginning of May and arrested. Southgate failed to notice signs of hostile activity when returning to his lodging and was arrested on 1 May. His arrest led to a reorganization of the circuit by his very able radio operator, Amédée Maingard, whom Southgate had planned to make his second-in-command. The circuit was split into smaller portions: Maingard retained control of Vienne, Deux-Sèvres, Charente, and part of the Indre, which became the Shipwright circuit. Southgate's courier, Pearl Witherington, became the organizer of a new circuit, Wrestler, based in the northern Indre, and when Liewer arrived in June he took over the southern part of the Haute-Vienne and part of the Dordogne.

Pearl Witherington's area was of particular importance. Part of her mission was to contact the management of the Michelin tyre factory in Clermont-Ferrand and obtain their consent to destroy it through sabotage, just as Rée had done with Peugeot. Witherington, however, sent a despondent report to London on 11 March:

> 1. I regret to inform you that the proposed sabotage of Michelin has completely fallen thro[ugh] in spite of repeated attacks. The management, after agreeing to the proposed destruction, refused to collaborate and still do so. Villiers's sabotage leader has been arrested: he tried to set fire to the M factory by putting thirty incendiaries in one workshop, he did not take into account the working of the fire safety system.
> 2. I wish to put on record the management's attitude vis à vis the sabotage plans. They refused to believe the RAF will have time to bomb Clermont-Ferrand before an Allied landing: in the meantime they are working, turning out material and making money whereas if the sabotage had taken place when proposed they would be doing none of these today. They are playing for time.

She suggested that the RAF should bomb the factory which would 'give the management a lesson'. On 5 April she reported the outcome of the bombing: complete destruction of the main factory with thirty-six casualties among the French workforce.

Pearl Witherington had also been ordered to contact a Frenchman going by the name of 'Gaspard', who claimed that he had control of several thousand men but required weapons from London. Gaspard's real name was Émile Coulaudon and unlike so many promises made to SOE he really did have 5,000 men waiting for weapons. 'Gaspard' was willing to work with the British but he refused to accept instruction on sabotage techniques from Pearl because she was a woman. The build-up of the resistance in the Stationer/Shipwright/Wrestler area was hampered by internal French politics and by the divisions between the Gaullist AS, whose leader Armand Mardon was arrested at the beginning of June, and the communist FTP, with whom the AS men refused to work. The creation of the FFI made no difference to political wranglings in local areas. Part of the challenge facing the organizers in these areas was to persuade their leaders to overcome their political differences and to focus on the immediate enemy, the Germans.

F Section had wasted much of 1942 by focusing its attention on the alleged army created by the Carte organization, which had proved both largely illusory and beset by an appalling lack of security. The lessons were not learned, and when Jean Vincent, known as 'Colonel Vény', contacted Harry Peulevé, whose Author circuit was based in the Corrèze, for weapons for his *Groupes Vény*, which he alleged consisted of several thousand men, London duly sent men to assist him. Vincent claimed to have built an organization based on the Socialist Party and covering the Marseille, Limoges, Lyon, Toulouse, and Montpellier areas. The AS had made a number of approaches to Vincent, hoping to incorporate the *Groupes Vény*, but all had been rejected by Vincent, ostensibly because of the poor security record of the AS, but most probably from personal ambition. F Section sent in several officers to assist Vincent. In January 1944 George Hiller arrived to form the Footman mission and to act as liaison with Vincent and the *Groupes Vény*. Hiller reported that the Vény organization 'was an organisation in power rather than in being', but that he was in contact with a number of men who could usefully be organized and armed to form a maquis in the Lot. In March 1944 Percy Mayer and his brother were sent to Limoges to start up the Fireman circuit and to contact the *Groupes Vény* there. They also found that the *Groupes* were 'more a theoretical conception than a potential reality'. Furthermore, they discovered that one group which the *Groupes Vény* claimed as its own was in fact purely FTP. Its leaders made it very clear that they wanted weapons but refused to accept any direction from London or Algiers. The situation in the area was only sorted out after D-Day. Vincent's illusions also affected the mission by Robert Boiteux who was sent to organize the *Groupes Vény* in Marseille. His briefing suggested that he would find 3,000 men in Marseille and another 300 in Nice. The true situation was, however, very different: the socialists were not interested in fighting, and only fourteen men appeared to be available immediately. By May 1944 Boiteux managed to organize 800 men into the Gardener circuit.

Elsewhere there were greater successes. Harry Peulevé's arrival in the Corrèze was hindered by Grandclément who tried to prevent him from reaching the area. Nevertheless, Peulevé managed to work alongside the AS and the FTP and to organize several maquis formations in a region ideal for small-unit actions. Peulevé was arrested in March 1944 through pure misfortune. He needed to despatch an urgent message to London and had gone to the house in Brive where his radio operator Louis Bertheau was working. A neighbour had become suspicious of the activities at the house and had reported to the police that Jewish black marketeers were operating from it. The Germans and *Milice* raided the house while Bertheau was on air. He managed to send the message: 'We are taken' before both Peulevé and Bertheau were taken into custody. Unfortunately, the Germans also netted a number of valuable documents. The circuit was then taken over by Peulevé's deputy, Jacques Poirier, who by D-Day had 10,000 men of all political complexions under his control.[21]

Francis Cammaerts had successfully established the large Jockey circuit which covered a vital portion of southern France, stretching from the Mediterranean coast up the Rhône valley. In October 1943 he reported 'If the German order of battle was not substantially changed, and if the resistance was properly armed, then a landing on the Mediterranean coast could get to Grenoble in seven days.' This was disbelieved by the Allied planners but in fact proved to be the case. Cammaerts was also involved in the organization of the maquis in the mountains of south-east France. This area was also the remit of the Marksman circuit under Richard Heslop. The activities of these two circuits would be vital in paving a smooth way for the Allied invasion of southern France.[22]

Richard Heslop was sent into France on a tripartite mission, with an American radio operator, Denis Johnson, and a Frenchman, Jean Rosenthal, 'Cantinier', on 21 September 1943 to undertake a tour of the Ain, Isère, Savoie, Haute-Savoie, and Jura, and to report after forty-eight hours on the state of the maquis in this important area of south-east France. Heslop wrote later:

> The local organisers had arranged a Cooks tour, planned almost to the minute, with cars picking me up at one place, and handing me on to another group. Selected camps were seen, men paraded, and hidden arms produced.

He reported on his return to London that the maquis camps were afflicted by poor morale because these men faced another cold winter in the mountains largely unarmed, poorly fed, and with little idea as to their purpose other than to avoid being sent to Germany as forced labourers. But Heslop reported that the maquis was capable of doing more: the structure of a viable organization existed, having been created by the local maquis leader in the region, Henri Romans-Petit, but it needed weapons urgently and a statement of purpose.[23]

Virginia Hall was deemed too much at risk from arrest for SOE to send her back to France. The Gestapo was well aware of her appearance and of her work in Lyon. She was not to be thwarted, however, and joined OSS instead. On the night of 21–22 March 1944 she stepped ashore in Brittany disguised as an old woman. The OSS expected Virginia to be the assistant to and radio operator for a sixty-two-year-old agent, 'Aramis', and their mission was to gather together the survivors of the Prosper disaster. Virginia identified La Creuse, which was located equidistant between the planned northern and southern landing grounds, as the ideal place in which to build a maquis. 'Aramis' disagreed: he could not cope with the primitive living conditions and returned to Paris. Virginia was tracked down by Élisée Allard, with whom she had worked before in Lyon, and his two companions Marcel Leccia and Pierre Geelen. These three men engaged in a sabotage campaign until they were arrested in May. Through them the Gestapo learned that Virginia was back in France. This forced her to change location and move to the Cher region and to cut off contact with those who knew of her link with the three agents. She would go on to provide the radio contact essential for maquis across three departments in central France to receive supplies in the months before and after D-Day.[24]

Until the Allies landed in France sabotage remained the priority for the circuits run by F Section and RF Section. Examples of sabotage undertaken in the months leading up to D-Day include attacks on factories producing materiel for the German war effort, such as the Ratier plant at Figeac which produced propellers for Heinkel and Focke-Wulf aircraft. The raid successfully destroyed three precision machines and two furnaces, and the damage was so extensive that the factory ceased production for the remainder of the war. The Hispano-Suiza aeroplane engine factory in Tarbes was attacked on 29 March and 13 April 1944. Ball-bearing factories also became targets: Malicet et Blin on 19 May 1944, Timken on 6 April, and SKF on 17 May. In September 1943 a team from RF Section attacked the gunpowder depot at Langres, containing 14,000 tons, while F Section virtually destroyed the National Gunpowder Factory south of Toulouse in March 1944. Neither factory had been bombed by the RAF because such bombing would have caused immense damage and death in the wider locality whereas the SOE's carefully targeted sabotage caused damage to a smaller area. RF Section also sent teams to destroy dams and canal locks.[25]

Both SOE sections and the maquis frequently attacked the railways, derailing trains and destroying locomotives. It has been estimated that 1,822 locomotives were sabotaged in the period from June 1943 to May 1944. Until March most of this destruction had been caused by sabotage on the ground, but from April onwards the railways were also a major target of the Allied air forces, especially in northern France. This widespread destruction of the railways made transport by rail across France extremely hazardous. As a consequence the escape lines decided to halt operations to Spain and a camp was established in the forest of Fontainebleau to await the arrival of the Allied armies. Southgate wryly commented that by the spring of 1944 the only passengers on the trains were either Germans or SOE agents.[26]

Sabotage operations served as a useful way of training members of the FFI, who would work closely with SOE. These operations were also of value to the maquis:

> One of the best . . . ways of creating cohesion and a team spirit in the camps and of keeping morale high, is action. It trains the *réfractaires*, gives them experience, and helps stop individual actions, most of which are misguided. All those in charge of military actions must be fully aware of this necessity: as a result, they must use as many maquis *réfractaires* as possible when they carry out missions.[27]

Activities by SOE and the maquis began to have an impact. Peulevé described the situation in the Corrèze:

> We sabotaged [the Germans'] war effort; we stopped their circulation on the roads of the country they were supposedly dominating. We cut short their simple off-duty pleasures by raining lead on them when they walked out of brothels and bars; we burnt out their vehicles and killed their drivers when they switched on the ignition to start their cars; we poisoned their wines and we threw the trains off the line when they went back to Germany for leave.

But he added a sad footnote: 'Their reply to this treatment was the coward's way out. They took revenge on the women, children, and old men.'[28]

General von Rundstedt admitted later: 'From January 1944 the state of affairs in southern France became so dangerous that all commanders reported a general revolt.'[29] Eastern methods of warfare came to France when in January 1944 the Germans launched a series of large-scale anti-partisan sweeps of southern France which were accompanied by all the cruelties prevalent in the east. These were explicitly permitted in orders issued by von Rundstedt's deputy, Field Marshal Hugo Sperrle, which placed the blame for civilian deaths on the 'terrorists' and demanded the arrest of everyone in the area, whether armed or unarmed, and the burning of nearby villages. The first area hit was the southern Ain, where the maquis and Heslop were kept on the run for several weeks. In March the German operations spread across the whole of southern France, with a notable reprisal operation being mounted against the village of Les Crottes in the

Ardèche where the entire population was massacred. German operations continued into April and May, hitting area after area, keeping the maquis on the run. SOE F Section and RF Section circuit leaders sent frantic messages back to London and Algiers calling for more weapons drops to help the maquis resist the German pressure.[30]

Throughout the autumn of 1943 the CFLN and SOE had been bombarding the Chiefs of Staff for a substantial increase in flights to France to drop arms to the resistance. The chief of the British air staff Charles Portal remained hostile to the whole concept of resistance and argued that the RAF based in Italy was overworked, as it was dropping arms into the Balkans, and that taking planes from Bomber Command in Britain would weaken the strategic air offensive against Germany, which he believed secured better results than action by the resistance in France. A change of heart was forced on Portal through the enthusiasm of Churchill. This in turn was due to the direct approaches made to Churchill by Emmanuel d'Astier, leader of *Libération-sud*, who had several meetings with Churchill in North Africa and in London, and Michel Brault, the leader of the maquis service, both on behalf of the CFLN. Another of Churchill's visitors was Yeo-Thomas, who could report on the conditions in northern France and the urgent need for weapons in that area. Churchill was impressed by what he heard and told Lord Selborne, head of SOE, and the resistance representatives: 'He wished and believed [that it was possible] to bring about a situation in the whole area between the Rhone and the Italian frontier and between the Lake of Geneva and the Mediterranean comparable to the situation in Yugoslavia.' Portal remained hostile but promised sixty sorties a month and this figure included flights by USAAF Liberator bombers. Churchill remained interested in the matter, minuting the Chiefs of Staff and Selborne on 2 February 1944:

> I approve the proposals in your minute of 31 January for arming the maquis, but if through bad weather or any other reason the number of sorties in February looks like dropping below your estimate, I want extra efforts made to improvise additional sorties to the maquis on nights when conditions are favourable. Even if fully successful the February programme is not enough. Pray start at once on a programme for the March moon. Let me see it in plenty of time. I want March deliveries to double those planned for February. I am told that the stocks of ammunition in the maquis are far below what is reasonable, even for the few weapons they possess.

Flights to France duly increased, enabling the maquis to become adequately if not well armed. It was estimated that these arms drops enabled about 125,000 maquis and resisters to be armed by SOE F and RF Sections.

These figures were, however, over-optimistic because they did not allow for weapons seized by the Germans during their sweeps through southern France in early 1944.

Brault complained that the maquis remained desperately short of ammunition: many maquisards had enough for only one day's fighting. Furthermore, as far as weapons were concerned only small arms were dropped and few heavy weapons such as machine guns and anti-tank mortars. For example, the resistance received 104,000 Stens and pistols and 17,000 rifles but only 4,000 heavier weapons in the months leading up to D-Day. This may have been a deliberate policy by the Chiefs of Staff. The Allies were suspicious that the French intended to use the weapons supplied to launch uprisings to liberate portions of France. This, the Allies believed, would be premature, and would waste the resources of the resistance, and would keep German units in France just when the invasion was about to be launched. On the other hand the Allies did want more sabotage. Therefore, in late 1943 at least, there appears to have been a policy to drop explosives to RF Sections rather than weapons. F Section, which could be trusted with weapons, would receive a lower proportion of explosives: 13,000lb of explosives for RF compared to 6,000 for F Section.[31]

The concept of the maquis is an elusive one. Its origins lay in the numbers of young men taking to the mountains to evade the STO forced labour round-ups in 1942 and 1943, and it has already been noted that not all of these *réfractaires* were in fact resisters. Local studies have demonstrated the sheer variety of maquis units. Broadly speaking, those organized by the communist-controlled FTP were activists, seeking to hit the Germans as and when they could. In contrast, the AS maquis were more cautious, husbanding their resources for action as the liberation of France commenced. Nonetheless, some of the AS maquis did also mount attacks on the Germans and undertake sabotage. Most conservative of all were the few maquis groups organized by ORA, which maintained a stance of inaction until after the Allied landings. Louis Mangin wrote to London in September 1943 extolling the virtues of the maquis as 'the only tangible form of military strength from within'. Yeo-Thomas also sent important reports suggesting the potential value of the maquis.

The political complexion of the maquis units is equally difficult to pin down. Because weapons could only be secured from SOE, whether from F Section or RF Section, some communists feared that the Allies would not arm them and so concealed their political persuasions. They may not have needed to do this because in fact most SOE circuit leaders were prepared to arm the FTP maquis regardless of whether those maquis planned to accept

Allied orders or policies before and after D-Day. Nonetheless, some FTP maquisards resented the fact that they were short of arms, arguing after the war: 'The Allies and the BBC encouraged us to resist and take to the maquis, and then they refused to arm us. It was a crime. So many young maquisards died because they hadn't the necessary weapons.' Other maquis leaders, notably Henri Romans-Petit, were deliberately non-political and did all they could to dampen down political arguments in the camps and to reject demands from outside resistance leaders for a statement of politics.

The final unanswerable question regarding the maquis was its size. André Pavelet, the coordinator of the five departments in the Montpellier region, believed that he had around 5,000 men under his control, but later reports suggest that the true figure was in the hundreds. Similarly, SOE circuit leaders such as Heslop and Peulevé reported having between 2,500 and 5,000 maquis in their areas. In contrast, Landes made lower claims for his region, with units numbering a few hundred in some areas and below a hundred in others.[32]

There was great concern within Allied ranks over how the maquis would use the weapons being dropped to them, and especially that they might attempt to liberate portions of the country prematurely. Such concerns were fully justified when considering events which occurred in the months running up to D-Day on Glières and Mont Mouchet.

The Glières plateau is located high in the mountains near Annecy. The maquis on the plateau originally consisted of 450 men under the command of a former French infantry officer who had joined the resistance after the disbandment of the Armistice Army, Théodose (Tom) Morel. These men established camps over the plateau and one veteran recalled later:

> Something amazing happened. We had been outlaws, but on the plateau we felt like free men. You got carried away with enthusiasm. Something different, an atmosphere of solidarity, the birth of a community, a new relation between officers and soldiers.

The plateau was an ideal location for receiving arms drops, and there were three major drops on 14 February, 5 and 11 March 1944. This immediately presented the maquis with a problem. The ideal maquis tactics were those of hit-and-run, but the newly received stores needed to be guarded. As an historian of the Glières recorded, the maquis were turned:

> . . . into the guards of a stock of weapons they could not use, since the maquisards had received only light weapons, automatic rifles, and explosives – no machine guns, mortars, or anti-aircraft devices, nothing that would have allowed them to hold the plateau against a well-organised assault.

In other words, the maquis felt they had to engage in static warfare, to which they were not suited, in a region that was entirely unsuitable for such tactics since there were only two points of entry or exit from the plateau. One survivor from Glières, Julien Helfgott, wrote later that there had never been any intention to create a redoubt on Glières and that the maquis there were caught by surprise and simply did not know how to respond to the arrival of parachute drops of supplies and the concentration of Vichy and German forces in the region determined to annihilate them.[33]

The dilemma facing the maquis on Glières was exacerbated by two events. The first was that the BBC French Service advertised the existence of the Glières in early February and encouraged men and women of the Haute-Savoie to join the maquis there. Maurice Schumann's words in this broadcast were designed to make the French people think that there already existed a piece of liberated France which should be defended at all costs. The second point was that the Vichy regime felt compelled to respond both to Schumann's words and to the British weapons drops. There was an unofficial truce in operation between the maquis and the *Groupes Mobiles Réserve* (GMR) in the region. This was broken on 1 March when Michel Fournier, a medical student aide in the maquis, was arrested by the GMR based in Entremont. In response the maquis descended from the Glières on 9 March led by Tom Morel, who went to the GMR headquarters at the Hotel de France in Entremont to arrest the GMR commander, Captain Lefebvre. In the scuffle, Morel was killed. The leadership of the Glières maquis passed to Captain Maurice Anjot.[34]

Joseph Darnand was sure that his *Milice* and the GMR could defeat the growing maquis on Glières. The Germans were less confident and made their own plans. The maquis on the Glières absorbed the men brought to the plateau by Schumann's words, arranged a defence in depth, and prepared for a siege. On 26 March, General Karl Pflaum's 157th Reserve Division launched an assault on the plateau. The maquis stood and fought: desperate appeals were sent to neighbouring maquis formations. Heslop refused to despatch any men, arguing that the defence of Glières was 'glorious, bloody, but not guerrilla warfare', and that to send men 'would only delay the inevitable'. Heslop did, however, order a few arms drops simply to supply the beleaguered maquis with sufficient weapons to break out. Anjot ordered the men to disperse but there were high losses: 210 men were killed and 169 arrested – that is, nearly half of the Glières maquis. Worse still, the Germans seized most of the weapons that had been dropped in February and March. Heslop later wrote of Glières that 'it was madness, a glorious stupidity, which is still spoken of in France with awe and pride'.

Romans-Petit, who subscribed to the guerrilla concept of constant movement, said: 'Glières was a military defeat, but a victory for our souls.'[35]

Mont Mouchet rises about a kilometre high in the Auvergne in the Massif Central. This was the area dominated by the long-standing maquis commanded by 'Gaspard', Émile Coulaudon. By 20 May he was convinced that the invasion was imminent and, through misleading information gleaned from SOE officers, appears to have thought that the Allies supported the concept of a base of operations in southern France on Mont Mouchet and would airlift troops there. Accordingly, 'Gaspard' issued orders for a concentration of all FFI forces on Mont Mouchet and by the end of May about 10,000 resisters had responded to his call, of whom only about a third were well armed. On 2 June an SS battalion, 800 men strong, launched an attack on Mont Mouchet; but it was fought off. Reinforcements were brought up and on 10 June the Germans mounted a major attack with 12,000 troops supported by armoured cars, heavy artillery, mortar batteries, and aircraft.

The FFI forces on Mont Mouchet were outgunned and outnumbered. Desperate appeals for supplies were sent by the SOE radio operator Denis Rake. At one point he was forced to abandon his radio and codebooks and the circuit's courier, Nancy Wake, undertook a marathon bicycle ride of over 200 kilometres in three days from Aurillac to another circuit in Châteauroux to send a message requesting airdrops. After the war she said: 'When I'm asked what I'm most proud of doing during the war, I say "the bike ride".' On her return to the maquis camp she remembered: 'I couldn't stand up, I couldn't sit down. I couldn't do anything. I just cried.' She needed brandy to treat her saddle sores. Several vital airdrops did take place but the heavy weapons which were dropped, such as bazookas, were largely useless because the FFI forces had not been trained in their use. Inter-Allied teams arrived to assist them but could not stave off disaster. By 20 June the battle was effectively over and the FFI forces retreated in a state of some disarray to fight on, but in smaller formations. The FFI forces suffered relatively low losses, inflicting higher ones on the attacking Germans. The balance of loss shifted significantly, however, after the Germans instituted their policy of indiscriminate reprisals on the surrounding area, burning villages and executing, deporting, or imprisoning anyone suspected of resistance activities.[36]

The premature mobilization of the FFI on Mont Mouchet can be excused as over-enthusiasm by the most active resistance leader in the region. Yet Mont Mouchet also demonstrates the expectations held by the

French: that they had only to liberate a portion of France and the Allies would arrive and help them hold it against the inevitable counter-attack. These French illusions would be most brutally exposed in the battle of Vercors, which will be covered in the following chapter.[37]

The Allies believed that the maquis needed firm leadership in order to force them to focus on the tasks of greatest benefits to the Allies as they landed in France. Colin Gubbins had considered this problem as early as 1942, when the first maquis groups were forming. In a memorandum in July 1942 he wrote:

> A project is under consideration for the dropping behind of enemy lines, in cooperation with an Allied invasion of the Continent, of small parties of officers and men to raise and arm the civilian population to carry out guerrilla activities against the enemy's lines of communication. These men are to be recruited and trained by SOE.

The Jedburgh scheme developed from this idea. The plan was to drop small teams of three uniformed soldiers, preferably, French, British, and American, to supply leadership to maquis formations in critical areas. An Allied staff paper in December 1943 explained:

> It is NOT the intention that Jedburgh teams will necessarily usurp the authority of local leaders, but it is felt that the arrival of Allied soldiers, in uniform, behind enemy lines, will have a marked effect on patriotic morale and that these teams, representing as they do Allied High Command, will act as a focus for local resistance.

In all, 300 volunteers were trained and organized into ninety-three teams, but in the event none were dropped into France before D-Day. OSS also created Operational Groups (OGs), which had a similar role to the Jedburghs but were to be dropped closer to the front line. There were fourteen OGs ready before D-Day, but again none reached France before the invasion was under way. Because both the Jedburghs and the OGs arrived on the scene late they struggled to impose their authority on the maquis groups. It was only when the fighting got under way that they would prove useful in providing guidance on tactics and targets and in securing airdrops of urgently needed supplies.[38]

If the Allies were to assume command and control over the maquis then they needed to provide clear plans setting out what they expected from the resistance when the landings began. SOE and the BCRA set up a committee for this purpose in April 1943, and the plans drawn up were approved by the Allied general staff, and were transmitted to SOE and

BCRA section leaders as well as the FFI and DMRs. There were four plans to be put into operation: Plan *Tortue* was to prevent German formations, especially tank divisions, from reaching the landing area; Plan *Vert* was to cut the railway lines leading north; Plan *Violet* targeted German telephone and telegraph communications; and Plan *Bleu* targeted the electricity supplies to major cities. The BCRA was adamant that the plans should be implemented by area according to the rate of the Allied advance. General Walter Bedell Smith on behalf of Eisenhower, however, ordered that the whole of France should be included from the start. The BCRA feared the consequences of this and argued that there should be 'no general insurrection, nor partial uprising, nor general strike'. Their reasoning was that such activity would strengthen the communists, who were the main proponents of such actions.[39]

This difference of opinion reflected the dangers of the duality of command which existed. In March 1944 the CFLN had appointed General Koenig to command the FFI forces. That month the British and Americans had created a Special Forces Headquarters (SFHQ) which would command all the special services in occupied Europe with the exception of the British intelligence service, SIS. SFHQ was incorporated within SHAEF (Supreme Headquarters Allied Expeditionary Force), Eisenhower's command for operations in Europe. It was only in May that the problem of command was solved when it was agreed that Koenig would receive his directives from SHAEF through the medium of the SFHQ and would command all the special forces in France. Koenig and his chief staff officer, Henri Ziegler, were assisted by General Redman for the British, Colonel Haskell for the Americans, Buckmaster for SOE, and Colonel van der Stricht for SOE. In the south of France, General Gabriel Cochet would have a similar role and position within General Wilson's headquarters. On the eve of the Normandy landings it was estimated that there were 100,000 armed men in France ready to act on Allied orders.[40]

Just when it seemed that the plans for what the resistance should do had been settled, and a clear chain of command established, a new problem erupted to darken the horizon – de Gaulle. Ever since he had set up the Free French Committee in Britain in 1940, and even more after the CFLN was established in Algiers, de Gaulle had consistently argued for the British and Americans to recognize him officially as the future leader of France. Churchill was not prepared to grant him such official status, and Roosevelt was even more hostile to the idea.

De Gaulle and the leaders of governments-in-exile were outraged by the general ban on cipher communications which was imposed by the British in April 1944 on grounds of security. This, they argued, prevented them from conducting their affairs of state at a critical juncture: the Poles were particularly affected because they needed to communicate with the AK and Underground Government regularly just when the Soviets were advancing into Poland; and so were the French, whose operations were split between London and Algiers. The cipher ban also affected travel, so de Gaulle was effectively stuck in Algiers. Even Churchill, who had no great love of de Gaulle, could see the problem, and felt that de Gaulle's presence in London was needed before D-Day. Accordingly, a personal invitation was extended to de Gaulle, who arrived in Britain on 3 June. A row immediately blew up because on that day he had announced that the CFLN was henceforth to be regarded as the provisional government of France, something that the Allies were unwilling to concede. The Americans were only prepared to admit that the CFLN was 'the administrator of those territories which recognise its authority', and Moscow considered that the CFLN represented 'the interests of the state of the French Republic'. The British followed the American line but added that 'the CFLN is the organism qualified to conduct the French war effort'.[41]

On 5 June, the eve of D-Day, relations with de Gaulle deteriorated still further. Eisenhower recalled: 'One of our final visitors was General de Gaulle, with whom some disagreement developed, involving the actual timing and nature of the pronouncements to be made to the French population immediately upon landing.' De Gaulle was insulted that the order of BBC broadcasts to occupied Europe on 6 June was the leaders of governments-in-exile, followed by Eisenhower, and then, lastly, himself. De Gaulle, now considering himself a head of state, felt very strongly that he had to precede Eisenhower, otherwise he would be seen by the French as taking orders from a foreign general. Alexander Cadogan wearily recorded that evening's cabinet meeting in his diary:

> We endured the usual passionate anti-de G harangue from PM. On this subject, we get away from politics and diplomacy and even common sense. It's a girls' school. Roosevelt, PM and – it must be admitted de G – all behave like girls approaching the age of puberty. Nothing to be done. During Cabinet, news came that de G has forbidden his liaison officers to embark. Well, that puts the lid on. We always start by putting ourselves in the wrong, and then de G puts himself *more* in the wrong.

Negotiations continued during the night and it was finally agreed, as the first Allied troops were landing in France, that de Gaulle would speak at his own time and without supervision.[42] On the afternoon of 6 June, de Gaulle broadcast to France:

The supreme battle has begun. It is the battle for France and it is the battle of France. France is going to fight this battle furiously. She is going to conduct it in due order. The clear, the sacred duty of the sons of France, wherever they are and whoever they are, is to fight the enemy with all the means at their disposal.

The orders given by the French government and by the French leaders it has named for that purpose [must be] obeyed exactly. The actions we carry out in the enemy's rear [must be] coordinated as closely as possible with those carried out at the same time by the Allied and French armies . . .[43]

25

Summer 1944: France

At 21.45 on 5 June 1944 the BBC French Service broadcast a lengthy series of over 300 personal messages to all fifty-one SOE networks and all twelve regional FFI commanders warning them that the Allies would be landing in northern France on the following day. The broadcast added the warning: 'In due course instructions of great importance will be given to you through this channel. But it will not always be possible to give these instructions at a previously announced time. Therefore you must get into the habit of listening at all hours.'[1] Jamming by the German and Vichy authorities meant that not all circuit leaders heard their messages: for example, both Amédée Maingard and Tony Brooks learned of their mobilization from their colleagues. In Gascony weapons had not been distributed before D-Day so there was an immediate rush to collect them from their hiding places. This included waking up the beekeeper in Castelnau-sur-l'Auvignon so that he could move his hives to reveal the cache of weapons hidden under them.[2]

The news of the Allied landings was greeted with widespread rejoicing in the ranks of the FFI forces. In Périgueux, for example, the MUR announced:

> The hour of insurrection has come.
>
> Every able man between 20 and 46 inclusive must present themselves immediately (within 24 hours) to the town hall in order to be registered in view of their participation in the liberation of the territory. Every Frenchman who does not conform to this order will be considered a deserter.

Such announcements led to a flood of recruits to the maquis which caused immense problems. The existing maquis was barely adequately armed and simply could not absorb such numbers of untrained and unarmed new recruits. This situation was only partially remedied by the arrival of Jedburgh teams whose purpose it was to train these men and whose radios were used to organize supply drops. Enthusiasm overtook ability and new recruits recalled the results later: Jacques Chapet was given a bazooka and was told 'You put it on your shoulder, you will have a loader with you'; whereas Guy Léger was given a Sten gun when he had not even fired a hunting rifle before. The moral fibre of the late recruits was also suspect. Some simply could not handle harsh living in the open and went back to their homes. Others, especially in the southernmost regions of France, quickly grew disenchanted by the remoteness of the action in Normandy from their locale and by the slow progress of the Allies, and similarly returned home to await a more propitious moment such as an Allied invasion of southern France.[3]

SOE agents were amazed and appalled by the conduct of the so-called '*Naphthalinés*', the 'Mothballed', former officers of the French Army who had hitherto taken no part in the resistance, but who now put on their uniforms, which stank of mothballs, and demanded to be given troops to command. Richard Heslop, for one, rejected these officers and suggested that they form their own units, which they did: he noted that they suffered very high losses simply because they did not understand guerrilla warfare. Roger Landes recorded that he could not accept these French officers, 'as we risked losing the confidence of the FFI troops and of the population which supported us'.[4] Philippe de Vomécourt was approached by gendarmes wanting to switch sides, whom he rejected as fighters but used to supply intelligence on German movements.

On the morning of D-Day the Germans executed eighty-seven members of the resistance held in Caen prison just behind the beachhead.[5] The German high command immediately issued a series of orders on the resistance, whereby all French civilians who resisted German orders would be treated as guerrillas, while armed resistance fighters and maquisards would be executed immediately. The arrival of uniformed Jedburgh and SAS teams in the rear led to the order that 'all troops inserted outside the Normandy combat zone must be destroyed as hostile terrorist troops' or passed to the SD for execution after interrogation.[6] The Germans now found that their double agents were 'melting away like snow under a fierce sun'.[7] Vichy was similarly hostile to the arrival of the Allies and the upsurge in resistance. On D-Day itself the head of the *Milice*, Joseph Darnand, broadcast:

> Consider as enemies of France ... those belonging to resistance groups; attack saboteurs, parachutists and others, track down traitors who try to sap the morale of our units. As from today I mobilise the *Franc-Garde* of the *Milice*. I call on my men to leave their work, assemble their families in places of safety, then join their corps.[8]

The *Milice* proved reliable, and fought hard battles against the resistance, which raised the spectre of civil war in France.

The French planners had envisaged calling out the resistance in stages, just ahead of the Allied advance. SHAEF, however, wanted more. It was extremely aware of the disparity between the number of Allied troops which would be landed in Normandy on D-Day – seven divisions, with a hoped-for rise to twenty by 20 June – and the number of German defenders present in northern France and within reach of the beachheads. There were fifty-eight German divisions in France, a total of 750,000 men. The Allies had engaged in a complex deception plan to convince the Germans the Normandy landings were only a feint and that the main invasion was yet to come over the shortest route to the Pas-de-Calais. This was designed to sow confusion in German ranks and prevent the despatch of all German divisions in northern France to the Normandy beachhead while that beachhead was highly vulnerable to counter-attack. The resistance was not expected to make a contribution here, since the Allied air forces were in a better position to interdict German movements in northern France, but the resistance could take action to slow the movement northwards of German Army Group G under General Johannes Blaskowitz, which was stationed in Toulouse, Bordeaux, and across southern France.[9]

SHAEF therefore mobilized the resistance in the whole of France. The important question immediately arose of who, if anyone, was actually in control of the new situation. General Koenig was the theoretical head of the FFI (*Forces Françaises de l'Intérieur*), and de Gaulle had put in place a system of regional delegates and FFI commanders through which he and Koenig hoped to control the resistance. Yet the members of COMAC, the military committee of the CNR, which was dominated by communists, had other ideas. They were adamant that the FFI should be commanded by COMAC, based in Paris, and not by Koenig, who was in London. The arguments raged over the next two months before Koenig reluctantly delegated his powers of command over the FFI to COMAC in August. No one seemed in total control regarding the resistance in southern France. In theory, General Gabriel Cochet, based in Algiers, was responsible, operating under General Wilson, the supreme Allied commander in the region, but Cochet complained: 'My powers and the means to accomplish my mission are not at the level of my responsibilities.'[10]

The lack of overall control was highlighted by the immediate explosion in activity across the whole of France, and by the news that the communist-dominated FTP was leading the way. Therefore, on 10 June, Koenig attempted to rein in the resistance:

> Put maximum check on guerrilla activity. Impossible now to resupply you with arms and munitions in sufficient quantities. Break contact everywhere

> as much as possible to allow reorganisation. Avoid large assemblies. Form isolated groups.[11]

Koenig had misjudged both the mood in France and the way in which the resistance operated, and his message was widely disbelieved and disregarded. Koenig still thought of operations as a regular soldier would: he would issue orders and the formations would obey them, even if those orders were to do nothing. But the resistance was different: once its cohorts had come out into the open it was impossible for the resisters to slink back into the shadows since their identities had become known to the Germans and to the Vichy forces. Koenig belatedly realized this, and on 17 June issued a new order which permitted the resistance to 'continue elusive guerrilla action to the maximum'. Nonetheless, no one was really in overall control. On 14 July the FFI general staff reported: 'For many regions we are almost totally ignorant of not only the numbers and movements of the enemy, but even the state of our own forces and the operations they have undertaken.'[12]

Marcel Baudot, FFI chief in the department of Eure in Normandy, reported the almost religious fervour with which his men set about their tasks, with the result that the activities of 1,700 men made the Germans think that Allied paratroopers had landed in their midst. The 'Surcouf' maquis in Normandy made good use of the terrain, ambushing German convoys travelling through the forests and along sunken roads where the high hedgerows gave little warning of an ambush ahead.[13] Operations so close to the front were extremely dangerous and the Germans hit hard at any signs of resistance activity. Sydney Hudson and Francisque Bec of the Headmaster circuit created a maquis in the Forest of Charnie near Le Mans. This, however, attracted the notice of the Germans, who captured a group of Frenchmen on their way to join the maquis there, interrogated their leader and discovered the exact location of the camp. A sizeable German force attacked on 16 June and Bec was killed, but Hudson continued to lead the circuit in successful attacks on the Germans until the Americans overran the area in August.[14] In general, much of Normandy was fairly quiet for the simple reason that the high German presence and Allied air attacks made action extremely dangerous.

The most successful element of resistance activity immediately after D-Day was undoubtedly the sabotage of the railway network. On the first night, 5–6 June, 950 of the 1,050 planned cuts to railways were made and by the end of the month the number of cuts had risen to 2,000. In June, 217 locomotives were destroyed and in July a further 253. All SOE circuits and FFI commands took part in the rail sabotage programme. On 9 June an RF circuit led by Bernard Amiot and Philippe Lauzier blew up the track on the Bordeaux–Toulouse line just in front of an armoured train carrying the Hermann Goering Division. The Germans gave chase and killed Amiot and two other members of the sabotage group. Brooks's Pimento circuit contained many French rail workers who could identify the precise locations that could cause the most damage. The effects were clear: no rail traffic at all operated on the main Toulouse–Montauban line, and virtually every train which left Marseille and travelled through the Rhône valley to Lyon was derailed at least once on its journey. The diversion of traffic away from the main lines meant that even more resistance networks could get involved. Further north, rail traffic was hampered in passing through the vital Troyes junction by surviving members of Michael Trotobas's Farmer circuit, now renamed Diplomat. Strikes at rail depots and workshops similarly hindered German troop movements towards the beachhead.[15]

SOE agent Bob Maloubier, working in the Limousin, said later: 'Almost every night I used to blow up a bridge. Even if the Germans were very fast at repairing them it took them two or three days. They came with an armoured train and landed a team of workers and rebuilt the bridge.'[16] George Millar recorded that the French were keen to see bridges blown up because of the improved French morale, which was not achieved by blowing up mere telephone poles and signal boxes.[17] An example of repeated action against the railways is supplied by Philippe Liewer's Salesman circuit: this ensured that no train passed through the Haute-Vienne, which contained the main Paris–Toulouse and Bordeaux-Lyon routes. By the end of June the Germans were so angry that they threatened to shoot hostages if the sabotage continued. Accordingly, Liewer decided to make sabotage unnecessary by blocking some lines permanently, and sent two civilian trains, cleared of their passengers, down the Limoges–Brive line and deliberately crashed them in a deep cutting. By early August the Germans had managed to clear only a single track, and any convoy despatched was attacked immediately by the local maquis.[18] Not all FFI members, however, were prepared to risk their lives on sabotage. While the main line between Nice and Monaco was cut after D-Day, the line between Nice and Marseille was not, because the maquis leader in the area would not risk his men's lives in attempting the destruction of the viaduct at Anthéor since it had already been attacked from the air, and could be again.[19]

A British report in September 1944 concluded that the resistance had destroyed 270 railway bridges and 1,750 locomotives, and had made 4,440 cuts to the railways between June and September 1944. Despite the undoubted high level of railway sabotage, it is questionable how much it succeeded in delaying the movement of German forces to the front. For example, the 17th SS Panzer Grenadier Division and the 276th and 708th Infantry Divisions were able to move from their bases south of the Loire to Normandy without any great difficulty. (Allied air attacks later destroyed all bar one of the bridges crossing the Loire.) On the other hand, the 9th and 10th SS Panzer Divisions took seventeen days to reach Avranches from Redon, and, although the 11th Panzer Division took only a week to reach the Rhine from the Eastern Front, it then took three weeks to reach Caen from Strasbourg. These delays have often been quoted as examples of the effectiveness of resistance action, but they could also be put down to Allied air power and to German confusion as to whether to send the divisions to Normandy or redirect them towards the Pas-de-Calais. After all, those German divisions designated from the start for Normandy, the 12th SS Panzer Division and Panzer Lehr, reached their designated concentration areas without difficulty.[20] Millar, operating north of Besançon, recorded the limited effect of the resistance:

> On the main road that paralleled the valley [near Ronchaux], about a thousand yards from the ridge, I often saw German military traffic. Once a convoy of tanks on transporters passed. There were Panzer men sitting on the tanks, aft of the turrets, lounging in nonchalant healthy postures. Still the monarchs. Not many people around us thought the invasion was going to be a success. The bridgehead seemed to be well contained.[21]

An even more frequently quoted example of delays caused by the resistance involves the SS Das Reich Division. This will be examined below.

Other aspects of resistance activity had varying degrees of success. The implementation of the *Violet* plan against German telegraph and telephone communications, designed to force the Germans to use radios, which the Allies could then intercept, proved disappointing. The military delegate entrusted with the dissemination of the plan only arrived in France on 23 May and was not in contact with the chief of the French communications network, the PTT (*Postes, Télégraphes et Téléphones*), until 5 June. The delay meant that the long-distance cables were only sabotaged and hit by air bombardment from 12 June onwards, too late to be really effective. Nonetheless, the resistance managed to cut the main Paris–Berlin cable on numerous occasions and was particularly effective against the telecommunications hub around Le Mans. Further south, Pearl Witherington's Wrestler circuit and Roger Landes's Actor circuit were notably active against German telecommunications, but their actions had the undesirable effect of drawing German attention to them.[22]

The resistance had greater success in supplying intelligence from the area directly inland of the beachhead. By the beginning of July fourteen Sussex teams had been inserted into northern France, and more followed. These teams succeeded in recruiting French men and women to act as intelligence agents on the railways and German airfields. The information these teams supplied was supplemented by the reports of the long-lived Alliance intelligence network. Marie-Madeleine Fourcade returned to France during the July moon and reached Aix-en-Provence, where she was arrested. She was placed in a cell in the army barracks but discovered that the gap between two bars of the window of her cell was wider than normal. With her dress clasped firmly between her teeth she slithered out of the window stark naked and got dressed in a nearby cemetery. She managed to warn her colleagues that the Germans were looking for them. A Special Forces Headquarters report to SHAEF on 20 June stated:

> Although passing of intelligence is not a normal part of the activity of the FFI, much up-to-date intelligence has been received from resistance groups and passed to the authorities concerned. This intelligence has covered, not only information relating to the enemy's movements and dispositions, but also . . . the indication of targets of value to the Allied Air Forces.

For example, the resistance reported the presence of German aircraft concealed in the Bois de Jouarre, east of Paris, about which nothing had been known. This intelligence led to an Allied bombing raid which destroyed fifteen planes and damaged a further ten.[23]

As covert operations became overt, SOE losses mounted. Violette Szabo was dropped into France on 8 June south-east of Limoges, but on the following day her party was trapped by a German roadblock and she and her companions attempted to fight their way out. A surviving colleague, Jacques Dufour, reported that Szabo had hurt an ankle when landing and could not run:

> She insisted she wanted me to try and get away, that there was no point in my staying with her. So I went on while she kept firing from time to time and I managed to hide under a haystack in the courtyard of a small farm.[24]

Szabo was captured and despatched to Germany, from where she did not return. Robert Benoist, who had already escaped from custody once, was arrested in Paris on 18 June and his courier, Denise Bloch, was located and captured a few days later. George Wilkinson of the Historian circuit was caught near Orléans on 28 June, followed by his radio operator Lilian Rolfe six weeks later. None of them survived the war. The death of Baron de Saint-Geniès was particularly unlucky. He had returned from stowing away the containers dropped by the USAAF on 25 June, and a meal was laid out to celebrate in a cheese factory in Dole. The Germans arrived and found one woman with a table set for eight. The Germans realized that more people must be hiding and so fired into the ceiling. One shot hit de Saint-Geniès in the head and the blood from his wound betrayed the hide-out for the whole team. One piece of unfinished business, however, was completed. SOE agent Roger Landes got his hands on André Grandclément, who had done so much damage to the resistance in the Bordeaux area. In July, Grandclément was lured to a meeting supposedly set up to arrange a flight to Britain for himself and his wife. Instead, he was tried and condemned by the resistance. Plenty of men volunteered to execute Grandclément, but as Landes said later: 'nobody wanted to kill the wife. I said I would do it; I was in charge and didn't feel I could order anyone else to kill a woman. We couldn't let her go, you see, because if we did the whole of our group would probably have been arrested . . . I didn't sleep for a week after that.'[25]

The effectiveness of the maquis has been called into question because there were simply not enough trained and armed men to undertake the tasks they embarked upon. The ideal role of the maquis was guerrilla warfare, the pursuit of hit-and-run tactics to harass the Germans without inviting a response or possible annihilation by offering open battle. Yet the FTP, but other resistance movements too, were eager, perhaps too eager, to embark on efforts to liberate portions of France immediately after D-Day. The results could be catastrophic.

Examples of the consequences of premature action abound. Robert Boiteux went to assist a maquis of 200 men in the Plan d'Aups, about twenty miles from Marseille, and was there when the Germans attacked on 9 June. The resulting battle led to the deaths of thirty-three Germans and eleven maquis, and Boiteux himself was wounded twice during the subsequent withdrawal. Pearl Witherington was with the maquis at the Château des Souches when 7,000 Germans attacked 160 maquis. After a lengthy and costly firefight the maquis withdrew. Her report stated: 'This attack completely disorganised the set-up . . . the farming people were not very helpful, as they had seen the Germans setting fire to neighbouring farms. Several of the maquis returned home, and we had to move to another part of the country.' George Starr's 300-strong maquis unit guarding his headquarters at Castelnau were attacked on 21 June by 1,500 SS soldiers. The ensuing battle lasted six hours and cost the Germans 239 killed and 350 wounded against the losses of 17 maquisards killed and 29 wounded.[26]

A particularly striking example of premature action is supplied by the events in the town of Barcelonnette in the Ubaye valley, which held the keys to the Alpine passes to Italy from where the Germans could despatch reinforcements into France. The resistance there decided to seize the valley and hold it for the receipt of parachute drops of supplies and men. SOE did not have a circuit in the region but the resistance was convinced that Algiers would supply its needs. This idea seems to have been based on the presence of an Allied mission, Michel, which included a British officer, Captain Alastair Hay, who had apparently informed the FFI officers that an Allied landing in the south was imminent. When Francis Cammaerts and Henri Zeller, the FFI chief of south-east France, heard the news of events at Barcelonnette they were appalled because it quickly became clear that 600 FFI men, of whom only 250 were armed, could not hold the valley if they were attacked by the nearby German garrison. The attack duly took place a week after the 'Republic of Ubaye' had been declared and the maquis were forced to scatter. Hay was killed along with 150 FFI soldiers.[27]

In the Ain, two parallel strategies of railway sabotage and liberation were adopted by Henri Romans-Petit and Richard Heslop. Their plans to ensure that no train or German convoy could run through the department were highly successful and after D-Day:

> Every road into the department was blocked and needed a pass from maquis headquarters to move. All trains were halted and two main lines north, through Bourg and Bellegarde, immobilised. For a month no supplies or soldiers reached the north from the sector of south-east France.

On the night of 6–7 June the maquis mounted an attack on the rail depot at Ambérieu, which resulted in the destruction of fifty-one locomotives, and they followed up this operation with a further attack in Bourg where fifteen locomotives and a turntable were destroyed. Romans-Petit attempted to dissuade his men from trying to liberate towns, pointing out with regard to Bourg:

> We can, of course, besiege the city, enter it, take many prisoners. But we will have heavy losses and will probably be unable to hold on there, because what can a few heavy weapons do against armoured tanks? The city will probably be retaken and will face terrible reprisal measures.

He was right, but nonetheless the FFI, with the FTP to the forefront, did attempt to seize and hold the towns of Bellegarde, Nantua, and Oyonnax. At the beginning of July the Germans responded by sending four divisions to drive the FFI out of the towns, forcing the resistance to flee back to its camps in the mountains, and enabling the Germans to reopen the important connection between south-eastern France and the Belfort Gap.[28]

It seemed clear that when the Germans wanted to hit the resistance they could do so with impunity. Yet the resistance made life very uncomfortable for the Germans, as Philippe de Vomécourt later explained:

> Day after day, by relatively small means, we scraped away at the exposed nerves of the Germans, who were facing the mass offensive of the Allies on the one hand, and the hostility of the French people on the other. The more jittery they became, the more easily we could scare them. A wire, tied to a tree, and projecting visibly into the road; a stone in the middle of the road and a wire shining on the bank: these were enough to stop a whole convoy, while an explosives specialist was sent to investigate accompanied by a dozen men with machine guns. They dare not pass a single object that might signal danger.[29]

German reports in early July indicated that they were well aware of the hostility of the French people and that they were rapidly losing control of the country now that the Allies had landed and liberation appeared imminent.

Bastille Day, 14 July, saw a number of highly daring demonstrations of patriotism. In Cannes orders were issued by the French and German police forbidding the placing of a wreath on the war memorial, but the FFI ignored the ban and successfully placed one there. In Nice, however, the French police and detachments of German infantry made their presence felt and so prevented the local maquis from marching towards the war memorial. In Marseille the resistance placed a wreath on the city's war memorial dedicated 'To those who fell before us, comrades of the resistance'. A box marked *Achtung Minen* was attached to the wreath. The Germans cleared the cemetery and fired shots at the box, which upon inspection contained only stones. Thirty hostages were executed in reprisal. No such reprisals occurred in the Massif Central where Tommy Macpherson's teams celebrated Bastille Day by creating a flamboyant display of sparks as they blew up a number of the major electricity pylons crossing the massif.[30] Of greater practical use to the resistance were the large daylight parachute drops made by the USAAF that day.

The men in London and Algiers were well aware that the resistance was poorly armed and poorly trained, and hoped to provide a solution to these problems by sending Jedburgh teams, SAS groups, and a medley of other Allied missions into France to discover the needs of the local FFI forces and train and provide direction to these forces. The results were very mixed. The Jedburgh teams were dropped too late and with too little advance information about the area in which they were to operate and the forces they could expect there. For example, Macpherson dropped into the Massif Central near the town of Aurillac on the eve of D-Day and wrote later:

> The most memorable aspect of our preparation was the almost entire absence of any useful information: we had no specific targets, no knowledge of the region in which we were to land and no idea of the probable movement of German forces through our area.

He found seven men, who were disorganized and suffering from poor morale: this improved as soon as he demonstrated how easy it was to sabotage a railway. Team John was dropped to assist Brooks but in the event could not locate him so worked with George Starr instead. Other teams suffered the same frustrations: they were either not expected or were no longer needed.[31]

The SAS had performed exceedingly well in the Western Desert and in Italy, but it was arguably totally unsuited for operations in France since it consisted of squadrons which were large enough to attract German attention but too small for self-defence. The men were armed only with .45 pistols and their heavy armament consisted of Vickers guns mounted on their jeeps. Captain John Tonkin, who had seen active service, was detailed to drop with an advance team on the eve of D-Day near Poitiers in the Vienne with the instructions:

> You will now concentrate on building up secure bases in the area north east of Château Chire, codename Houndsworth, and west of Châteauroux, codename Bulbasket, from D-Day onwards with a view to strategic operations against the enemy lines of communication from the south of France to the Neptune area.

He was met by Amédée Maingard, the head of the local SOE circuit, Shipwright. The main party of SAS for Bulbasket dropped on the night of 10–11 June. The most immediate problem was keeping these men occupied. Railway demolition teams were despatched and carried out their operations successfully, complementing the activities of the nearby Shipwright and Wrestler circuits. The SAS also pinpointed the location, based on a tip-off by the FFI, of a major German petrol dump at Châtellerault contained in eleven trains, and called in an air strike which eradicated the fuel supplies needed by German forces moving from south-west France northwards. In general, however, Tonkin noted that 'there was a general tendency to relax' and to visit local villages by jeep, thus heralding their presence. Security was further compromised by the difficulty of locating camps in the forests capable of hiding, feeding, and supplying water for

100 men. Consequently, the SAS remained in one location in the forest of Verrières for too long, were spotted by informers, and were attacked by substantial German forces in the early hours of 3 July. At the time of the attack there had been thirty-nine SAS soldiers, fifty maquisards, and one downed American airman in the camp. Tonkin and seven of his colleagues escaped but the Germans captured thirty-one British soldiers and the American airman as well as most of the maquis. The members of the maquis were executed immediately, with the SAS soldiers sharing their fate on 7 July. Tonkin and the other survivors were of no use to Maingard since they lacked the linguistic skills to train the maquis: they were evacuated by air in early August.[32]

The Houndsworth contingent fared much better. It was led by Bill Fraser and dropped in two parties on 6 June and 10–11 June, operating in the Monts du Morvan in the Nièvre department south-west of Dijon. Houndsworth collaborated closely with the French resistance and hit the main Lyon–Paris railway on twenty-two occasions, as well as identifying targets more suitable for attack from the air. The Germans attacked the group on 20 August, but on this occasion the SAS was strong enough to withstand the attack and the Germans vented their anger on the local villages.[33]

On 7 July a party of twelve SAS men were dropped at Noailles near Paris. This was a landing ground which, unknown to the Allies, was controlled by the Germans. The SAS fought back and two men were killed, two escaped, and eight were captured. They were brutally interrogated by the Germans until the head of the Gestapo in Berlin, Heinrich Müller, ordered their execution, which was carried out on 7 August, although one man escaped.[34]

It would be impossible to analyse here all the activities by the FFI after D-Day, so the successes and failures of the resistance will be judged through five case studies: the advance of Das Reich; the battle of Vercors; operations in Brittany; the start of Operation Dragoon; and the breakout from Normandy followed by the advance east and towards Paris.

The delay in the arrival of the SS 2nd Panzer Division, Das Reich, in Normandy from its base in south-west France has often been cited as an example of the successful operation of the resistance. Das Reich was a formidable opponent. Its commander, SS-Brigadeführer Heinz Lammerding, had previously served as chief of staff to General Bach-Zelewski on the Eastern Front, where the division had gained valuable experience of anti-partisan operations. In April 1944 Das Reich had arrived in south-west France to receive reinforcements, and for refitting and rest. Controversially, some of the reinforcements were from Alsace, born

Frenchmen but now serving in the SS. The men of Das Reich had quickly established a reputation for brutality meted out against the resistance in France prior to D-Day. During May they had undertaken a series of raids in the Lot which culminated in the discovery of a resistance arsenal in the town of Figeac and the subsequent execution of forty-one people and the deportation of over 1,000. On 7 June, Field Marshal Gerd von Rundstedt ordered Das Reich to begin to move towards Normandy. It was not to take the fastest route but was to focus first on crushing the resistance in south-western and central France. At dawn on 8 June the division, consisting of around 15,000 men and over 1,400 vehicles, set off and immediately came under hit-and-run attacks by local resistance units.[35]

As soon as the leaders of the FTP in the Corrèze, Jean-Jacques Chapou and Louis Godefroy, heard of the D-Day landings they decided to liberate the main towns in the department. They approached the maquis leader Georges Guingouin with the suggestion that his forces should liberate Limoges, but Guingouin declined, believing that such action was premature. Chapou and Godefroy pressed ahead with their plans to liberate Tulle, the departmental capital, not knowing that it lay in the path of Das Reich. On 8 June the FTP entered Tulle and entered into a firefight with the German garrison which resulted in the deaths of sixty Germans and the surrender of a further sixty men. Out of these, around ten, identified as members of the Gestapo, were executed by the French. That evening, Das Reich entered the town and the maquis withdrew promptly, leaving the civilian population to face the wrath of the Germans. The men of Das Reich were outraged by the execution of their countrymen and determined on revenge. On the morning of 9 June, 3,000 men, the entire male population of Tulle, were herded into the town square and the Germans selected 120 of them for immediate execution by hanging from the balconies in the main street. An eyewitness, Antoine Soulier, recorded:

> A ladder topples, a shot rings out, a being falls into the void. The scene unfolded like a local fête. An accordion played accompanying music. In the Tivoli cafe, under the shade of the plane trees, the German officers refreshed themselves and flirted with a woman well known in Tulle.

A later taped recording of German POWs indicated that the German soldiers were deliberately cruel in Tulle: 'With those 150 partisans, whom we hanged, the knots were tied in front, not behind. If the knot is behind, the spine is broken immediately, but in this way they suffocate slowly. That tortures them.' In fact, ninety-nine men were hanged and a further 311 were taken to Limoges, from which around half were deported to Dachau.[36]

Worse was to come at Oradour-sur-Glane in the Limousin on 10 June, now recognized as the scene of the Germans' worst atrocity in France. Full documentation is provided by a report from the regional prefect of Limoges, Marc Freund-Valade, who visited Oradour on 15 June. His report to the Vichy authorities was also widely disseminated by the resistance. In the middle of 10 June, Das Reich arrived in the village to search for explosives and for a missing officer, Major Helmut Kämpfe. They separated the men from the women and children, shepherded the men into a garage, and then machine-gunned them. The women and children were sent to the church at 2 p.m. and locked in. Three hours later the Germans set fire to the locked church, effectively condemning the inmates to a slow death by fire and suffocation, before entering the church and shooting those who attempted to escape. The sole female survivor from the church, Marguerite Rouffanche, recalled later that, after her daughter had been shot, she 'ran through the flames to get behind a high altar. By luck there was a small ladder there. I climbed up and got out of the church through a small window. I fell to the ground on a heap of brambles.' She was wounded several times but lay bleeding and burned until the Germans left and French people from a neighbouring village arrived and saved her. A total of 642 civilians were killed that day, and all the livestock were slaughtered and the houses burned down before Das Reich moved on.[37]

The resistance was not totally successful in slowing the advance of Das Reich. For example, fifteen trains were loaded with the heavy tanks and armoured equipment belonging to Das Reich in Périgueux on 13 and 14 June and reached Normandy without harassment or delays caused by sabotage. Yet those elements of Das Reich travelling by road had a far more difficult journey. Bridges across rivers were blown up in their path, and, as Macpherson explained, there was controlled tree felling:

> We blew two pretty large trees down close together and fortunately we were able to arrange the charges so that they fell across each other. This was quite a formidable barrier that certainly couldn't be moved by a light vehicle. I left one chap there, about one hundred yards behind it, so that when he briefly made himself known he would have the maximum surprise effect . . . When the Germans came up to the first barrier, at first they thought it was just trees that had fallen across the road. The column was led by an armoured car, followed by a half-track with some troops in the back . . . The armoured car tried to push it out of the way and of course couldn't, it was much too heavy, so this caused a long delay. They had to send messages back for the type of tank that is used for engineering work, with a bulldozer and scoop. With some difficulty, they eventually cleared the trees. The whole thing must have taken well over three hours.

Concealed men armed with Sten guns would open fire on the German troops waiting around for the barrier to be moved. An additional refinement was to place anti-tank mines under the felled trees or to dangle hand grenades from the branches. The resistance harassed Das Reich throughout its journey north, ensuring that, for example, over 200 lorries and tanks had been destroyed by the time the division cleared the Lot. Once the division crossed the River Loire the Allied air forces took over. On 13 June the division limped into Normandy.[38]

The Vercors plateau covers an expanse fifty kilometres long and twenty kilometres wide running from Grenoble in the north to Die in the south and overlooking two major transport corridors of the Route Napoléon* to its east and the Rhône valley to its south-west. There were eight roads leading to the plateau, all of which could be easily defended, although the road through Saint-Nizier in the north-east was a weak point. In 1942 the Vercors maquis was founded by Yves Farge of *Franc-Tireur*, and Pierre Dalloz and Captain Alain Le Ray: the latter two were both experienced mountaineers. Dalloz believed that 'a large force could come into action in coordination with Allied landings and hold off the Germans for a few days, just long enough for the Allies to join up with the maquis'. This was the essence of *Plan Montagnards*, which Moulin and Delestraint approved. SOE agent Cammaerts visited the plateau in August 1943 and concluded that '*Plan Montagnards* had an enormous amount to commend it and I backed it as much as I could . . . The supposition was that after Normandy there would be a sea landing in the south of France very shortly after or an airborne landing where the troops, backed by the resistance', would battle the Germans. In January 1944 the Inter-Allied Union mission arrived led by Henry Thackthwaite of SOE, who reported: 'The Vercors plateau offered the best strategic position on which the maquis could be based. From here they would have the best chance of attacking and hindering the Germans, whether or not the expected invasion of the southern coast of France materialised.' It appears that Thackthwaite was thinking in terms of guerrilla warfare, seeing the Vercors plateau as a base of operations for hit-and-run attacks. Dalloz, however, had arrived in Algiers in November 1943 and discovered that the French were thinking along more ambitious lines, seeing the Vercors plateau as a redoubt, a piece of France to be liberated by an insurrection and then defended at all costs.[39]

The tragedy of the Vercors unfolded due to a series of misunderstandings. The French planned an uprising on the Vercors plateau to coincide

* So-called because that was Napoleon's route to Paris in 1815 after escaping from Elba.

with the Allied landings, but no one had stipulated which landings, the north or the south. Early Allied plans had envisaged simultaneous landings in both areas, but in late 1943 it had become apparent that the slow progress of the Allies in Italy coupled with a shortage of landing craft meant that the southern landing would have to take place at some unknown time after the landing in Normandy. The French planners had not been informed of the date of D-Day, but even so the authorities in Algiers must have known that no landing in the south of France was imminent, since no preparations were under way. This information should have been transmitted to the resistance leaders in the Vercors region: Cammaerts of SOE circuit Jockey; Zeller, the FFI chief of south-east France; Marcel Descour, chief of staff of the FFI in the Rhônes-Alpes region; and François Huet, the newly appointed maquis leader on the Vercors.

These men, however, thought that they were being primed for imminent action. Descour told Huet when appointing him commander of the Vercors maquis:

> The Vercors is the only maquis, in the whole of France, which has been given the mission to set up its own free territory. It will receive the arms, ammunition, and troops which will allow it to be the advance guard of a landing in Provence. It is not impossible that de Gaulle himself will land here to make his first proclamation to the French people.

Descour had gained this impression from Eugène Chavant, AS leader on Vercors, who had visited Algiers and returned convinced from his conversations there, notably with de Gaulle's confidant Jacques Soustelle, that preparations needed to be made on the plateau for the reception of 4,000 paratroopers. Hence, although the message specifically mobilizing the Vercors maquis was not despatched on the eve of D-Day, the leaders assumed this was an oversight and issued orders for mobilization. New recruits from the region flooded onto the plateau, bringing numbers up to 4,000 by the middle of July.

The impression that Allied support for the Vercors was forthcoming seemed to be confirmed by massive daylight supply drops to the resistance made by the USAAF across southern France and to the Vercors on 25 June and 14 July. These airdrops alerted the Germans, and the message despatched to Algiers on 14 July highlighted the problem: 'Received daytime parachute drop 14th. About seventy-two planes. Very successful. Have been machine gunned on the ground ever since departure Allied aircraft. Thanks.' In addition to the receipt of supplies essential to arm the new recruits, the Vercors also received two Allied missions, further reinforcing the belief that the Vercors plateau was in the forefront of the minds of the planners in London and Algiers. The first to arrive, on the night of 26–27 June, was the Eucalyptus mission of Desmond Longe, John Houseman, and André Pecquet. The second, OSS mission Justine, consisting of thirteen men led by Lieutenant Vernon Hoppers, arrived two days later. On 3 July the newly appointed regional commissioner of the republic, Yves Farge, arrived on the plateau and set up the Free Republic of Vercors. Bastille Day was celebrated in style, but the omens for the longevity of this free republic were not good. Already, on 13 June, the Germans had made the first effort to dislocate the Vercors maquis when a force was sent against the village of Saint-Nizier, the most vulnerable gateway to the Vercors in the north overlooking Grenoble. This German force was met by heavy gunfire from the maquis who then dispersed deeper into the plateau while the Germans destroyed the village. The Germans then turned their attention to regaining the territory in the Ain that they had lost to the FFI forces commanded by Romans-Petit and Heslop.

German pressure against the Vercors maquis built up gradually. Reconnaissance planes were constantly overhead mapping out maquis locations and strafing any men found out in the open. Cammaerts and Zeller sent increasingly desperate messages to London and Algiers demanding the Allied bombing of the German airfield at Chabeuil, but they received totally unhelpful replies. Then, on 14 July, Houseman wrote in his diary the ominous news:

> Both London and Algiers had sent telegrams saying that we could expect a major attack at almost any moment, and the local information (the intelligence service was excellent) confirmed this. Three divisions were closing in on us from Valence, Romans-sur-Isère, and Grenoble.

On 15 July the Germans took steps to trap the maquis on the plateau by blowing up the tunnel at Engins on the Grenoble side and the bridge over the Isère near Royans on the western side.

The maquis laboured hard to build an airstrip at Vassieux capable of handling the Dakotas which they expected to bring in supplies and paratroopers. Therefore when, on the morning of 21 July, twenty planes towing gliders were spotted, the maquis were sure that they contained the long-anticipated reinforcements. They were wrong. The gliders carried over 200 SS troops, mounting a raid on the centre of the Vercors in a similar manner to the attack on Tito's headquarters at Drvar two months earlier. The German ground offensive used 10,000 men under General Pflaum who advanced onto the Vercors from every direction, aided by the Luftwaffe. One of the maquisards, Claude Forget, recalled: 'We fired at everything we could see. But the Germans supported their people on the ground with heavy air attacks. It seemed as though a stream of fire was falling unceasingly from the sky. We just couldn't move an inch.' Faced with such a powerful offensive the maquis fought back gallantly but ultimately uselessly until, two days later, Huet issued the order to disperse. Desperate appeals for assistance were sent to Algiers and London, and Chavant stated that if nothing was done then the French authorities would be considered 'criminals and cowards'.

It was every man for himself. Cammaerts and Zeller had left the plateau on 21 July, having berated their superiors for abandoning the men on the Vercors. Cammaerts was particularly outraged since he had been under the impression that the Vercors needed to be held only for three weeks until the Allies reached them, but it had been nearly two months since D-Day and there was still no sign of an Allied landing in the south. The maquis withdrew deeper into the forests on the plateau and attempted to escape the area altogether in small groups. This was extremely difficult, as Hoppers reported:

> The entire Isère valley was guarded by one German every 50 metres . . . For 11 days the section lay in one spot while German patrols scoured the woods and fired into the underbrush trying to scare the maquis into the Isère valley, where many were shot trying to escape and many others drowned trying to swim across the river. For 11 days we ate nothing but raw potatoes and occasionally a little cheese.

During the battle sixty-five Germans were killed and 133 were wounded, while the maquis lost 639 killed. The German reprisals were terrible. The wounded were killed in their hideouts and the civilians murdered with extreme brutality. Houseman wrote from the sanctuary of Switzerland: 'The men, after castration, were beaten to death with rifle butts and the girl disembowelled and left to die with her intestines wound round her neck. I saw the photographs later – they were unrecognisable.' Over 500 houses were burned and a further 650 were severely damaged. Nevertheless, the maquis regrouped after the Germans abandoned the Vercors and were capable of playing a part in the liberation of Grenoble in August.

Bitter recriminations followed on from the Vercors tragedy and lasted for years. One dispute centred around the calling out of the maquis on Vercors at the beginning of June. Nearly all protagonists agreed with the benefit of hindsight that this had been a mistake. Cammaerts, however, observed later: 'The notion that there was any mistake in timing I reject entirely. I think the invasion in Normandy was too delicate and too much in the balance to risk anything and that Eisenhower had to play every card he had and so he told all the French resistance to come out and fight as much as they could.' The next point of dispute was the lack of Allied support once the maquis had been mobilized. Romans-Petit believed that the leaders on Vercors, especially Descour, had been over-optimistic: 'The soldiers of Vercors naively believed they could force the Allies to incorporate the Vercors plan of action into their own by becoming a numerically significant force.' This dispute was aired after the war by Soustelle and by Fernand Grenier, the minister of air. Soustelle blamed Grenier personally for failing to despatch help to the Vercors. Grenier argued in his defence that he had prepared the relevant orders but that de Gaulle had failed to sign them. Indeed, evidence has emerged that de Gaulle himself had abandoned the Vercors project in favour of a massive air landing on the Massif Central which would bring Allied troops, including French forces, into a location where they could liberate major cities.

The next part of the debate centred on the behaviour of leaders on the Vercors once it was clear that the Germans were going to attack. Descour argued that it had never been his intention that the Vercors should be turned into a redoubt capable of self-defence. He blamed Huet for the high losses, suggesting that Huet should have ordered the dispersal of the maquis immediately after the Germans attacked on 21 July. Huet did in fact consider such a course of action on the first day of the offensive but felt that the difficulty of disengaging his forces while under attack and withdrawing in an organized manner was too great, since communications had broken down and the attack was coming from all sides and from the centre. Furthermore, he did not want to expose the civilians to German reprisals.

The final part of the debate was whether the battle of the Vercors had been worth it. Alain Le Ray, one of the designers of the *Plan Montagnards*, denied that the Vercors was a disaster. He pointed out that it tied down a significant number of German forces at a crucial time and stated that the 'Vercors is a page of history of which France can be proud'. Others dispute Le Ray's opinion, pointing out that the German divisions used against the Vercors were reserve divisions, ill-equipped and under-trained for battle on the Normandy beachhead. OSS concluded that 'The fall of Vercors is a major reverse for French resistance which had always aspired towards the conception of liberated areas deep within non-liberated France.' De Gaulle no longer pressed his plan for air landings on the Massif Central and was forced to accept the dominance of the Americans and the British in the liberation of his country.[40]

Resistance operations on the Brittany peninsula have been widely regarded as an example of successful cooperation between the FFI and regular forces. Brittany was an important area for the Allied strategic planners. It contained three major U-boat bases at Brest, Saint-Nazaire, and Lorient, and the German 3rd Parachute Division was stationed in the peninsula. It was widely anticipated that this division would receive orders to move towards the Normandy beachheads as soon as the Allies landed. There was a resistance in Brittany, but its arming and organization had been greatly hampered by the heavy German presence. SOE had designated its Butler circuit to cut off Brittany from the rest of France, but that circuit had been penetrated by the Germans. One of the survivors, André Hue, was extracted to Britain, pushed through a condensed SOE training programme, and despatched back to Brittany on the eve of D-Day to set up a new circuit, Hillbilly. Hue dropped with an advance party of 150 men from the French SAS and two Jedburgh teams, George and Frederick.

Questions have been raised earlier in this chapter regarding the suitability of the SAS for covert warfare at this stage of the war, since its presence raised expectations among the local population of an early liberation, and the SAS was not in practice a powerful enough force to defend itself. The events in Brittany reinforce this argument. The advance parties set up two bases in Brittany, codenamed Samwest near Guingamp in the north, and Dingson near Malestroit in the south. Over the next few nights the SAS received numerous planeloads of weapons for the enthusiastic but unarmed FFI men who had emerged to greet them. They also received reinforcements, including the leader of the French SAS party, Commandant Pierre-Louis Bourgoin, who arrived on 9 June. His parachute landing had to be handled with care since Bourgoin had lost his right arm in the Western Desert. He landed safely, all 90 kilos of him, on the head of an unfortunate maquisard who was knocked unconscious. Bourgoin's task was to 'sever, as far as possible, all communications between Brittany and the rest of France', to keep the 15,000 Germans in Brittany and away from the still extremely vulnerable Normandy bridgehead. Then, on orders from London and at the correct moment, he was to spark a large-scale revolt across the whole of Brittany.

The SAS set to work training the FFI forces and also despatching rail demolition groups to cut the main Quimper–Paris railway. This was carried out effectively, and by 15 June the only functioning railway in Brittany was the north–south route between Rennes and Nantes. Hue and the members of the Jedburgh teams were appalled by the overt conduct of the French SAS and by the fact that newly armed resisters proceeded to show off their weapons to their friends and family. This meant that the *Milice*, which was very active on the peninsula, could inform the Germans of the exact locations of the SAS camps. The Germans attacked Samwest on

12 June forcing the survivors, SAS, Jedburghs, and FFI forces, to flee to Dingson to regroup. The Dingson encampment was based around the farm of La Nouette owned by the Ponchard family near the village of Saint-Marcel. Hue was greatly alarmed by the influx of the men from Samwest, especially as there was evidence that the *Milice* members were clothing themselves in Allied uniforms taken from the prisoners captured at Samwest and infiltrating Dingson. One of the Jedburghs, Major Wise, later recalled that 'I personally witnessed the ill-treatment and execution of five *Milice* and none of us felt the least pity for them'. On 18 June the Germans attacked Dingson and the battle raged all day before the various clandestine forces fled into the forest. The battle cost the Germans nearly 600 dead, and fifty men from the SAS died, and 200 from the FFI. The French losses would have been significantly higher had a radio message not been sent out which brought a squadron of forty American Thunderbolts to fire on the German positions. Alarmingly, around 200 maquisards found the experience of battle too much for them, abandoned their weapons, and went home.

The limitations of the FFI forces and the SAS had been exposed and for the remainder of June and into July the Germans and their troops of renegade Russians, and especially the *Milice*, constantly hampered efforts by the underground forces to regroup. For example, Jedburgh team George travelled to Saffré, about forty miles north-east of Saint-Nazaire, to arm the 200 FFI forces there but were betrayed and forced to scatter on the following day. The bitter French commandant, Bourgoin, found himself unable to exercise command because, as Hue noted: 'He was a fighter, and one of the very best, but with one arm he was too conspicuous, and no matter how much disguise he might have covered himself with he was still an obvious target.' Team Frederick returned to northern Brittany where it received further Jedburgh teams to assist in keeping the German garrison in Brest pinned in.

On 18 July the Americans under General Patton captured the key town of Saint-Lô in Normandy and began preparations for a breakout into the Brittany peninsula. By 30 July the Americans had reached Avranches and prepared to split their forces. The US 8th Corps would advance across north-east Brittany led by an armoured division which would head straight for Brest. Another armoured division was detailed to liberate the southern ports. At this stage it was estimated that the FFI forces in Brittany numbered 30,000, of whom only 13,000 were armed. Late in the day, on 3 August, a new command of the FFI was appointed, headed by Colonel Albert-Marie Eon with Colonel Passy, the long-time head of the BCRA, as his chief of staff. On the night of 3 August, Eon and Passy arrived in

Brittany near Guingamp to direct the all-out revolt. Colonel Eon had never parachuted before and had to ask the advice of the Jedburgh team accompanying him on how to land. This new headquarters had direct communications with Patton's headquarters, with London, and with the five regional FFI chiefs in Brittany. The party actually arrived too late to make much impact on affairs since the resistance had already risen up on receipt of the coded message over the BBC.

The Breton resistance acted immediately and by 5 August the FFI had taken the towns of Vannes in the south and Saint-Brieuc in the north:

> Across the fields and through the woods the enemy was chased and harried relentlessly and mercilessly. Groups were divided and split by those who knew the lie of the fields and forests better than any fleeing soldier.

German prisoners were despatched to a camp at Coëtquidan, which had in the course of the war started out as a French base, then been the main location where the Polish Army was re-formed in France in 1940, before becoming a German camp. The principal purpose of the FFI forces changed as the Americans advanced. The FFI now focused on a policy of counter-scorch, especially the protection of vital railway bridges such as those at Saint-Brieuc and Guingamp, and the Plougastel-Daoulas 1,000-foot-long viaduct near Morlaix. The FFI, aided by the SAS and Jedburgh teams, succeeded in keeping the main routes open for the rapid American advance. Within a week most of Brittany was liberated, leading to the surrender of almost 50,000 Germans: Rennes fell on 4 August, Nantes on the 11th, and Quimper on the 13th. The FFI was then tasked with mopping up small parties of Germans and guarding the remaining German garrisons in the ports of Saint-Malo, Lorient, Saint-Nazaire, and Brest while the Americans turned back on themselves and prepared to attack eastwards towards Germany.[41]

The original plans for Operation Dragoon, drawn up by the 7th Army commanded by the American general Alexander Patch, envisaged the landing of General Lucian Truscott's 6th Corps, consisting of three divisions, on fifteen miles of the Mediterranean coast of France between Cavalaire and Saint-Raphaël. Simultaneously, an airborne task force under Brigadier General Robert Frederick would land inland from the landing beaches around Le Muy by parachute and glider to seize the area which provided access to Toulon and Marseille in the south-west and to the Rhône valley in the north-west. The French Army B of five divisions under General de Lattre would land nearer Toulon. These troops had been withdrawn from the front in Italy earlier that year. The overall direction of attack was to take the ports of Toulon and Marseille first, secure the right flank near Nice against counter-attacks from German-held Italy, and then advance up the Rhône valley towards Lyon and Vichy. In the middle of July the commander of the Mediterranean theatre, General Alexander, was authorized to contact the French resistance and clarify their role in the invasion. The FFI was tasked with gaining control of the roads and railways on both sides of the Rhône as far as Lyon to open the route for the American advance; the west–east routes from Bordeaux in the west to Narbonne on the Mediterranean to prevent the only German armoured division in the region, 11th Panzer, from leaving Toulouse for the landing beaches; and the mountain passes on the Franco-Italian border to stop the Germans sending reinforcements across the Alps. These cautious plans were altered radically as the result of the visit to Algiers of Henri Zeller.

Zeller reported to de Gaulle that the FFI largely controlled the southeast of France and that, although the Germans retained small garrisons spread throughout the region, they were afraid to venture out, although their capability to hit the resistance when they wanted to was still considerable. Zeller promised that the FFI would blow up all the bridges on the main rail and road routes; his brother, the chief engineer in the French Army, pleaded with him not to, since he would have to rebuild them. Zeller was appalled at the slow timetable for the American advance which had been confided to him by de Gaulle who was privy to the Dragoon plans. Zeller pointed out that the FFI was in virtual control of the Route Napoléon and the Allies could with a highly mobile advance force reach Grenoble in a week and Lyon soon after. De Gaulle sent Zeller to plead his case in Naples with General Patch. A key point of Zeller's advice was that the German garrisons consisted of 1,000 men in the major towns and under 100 in most places. The morale of these Germans was poor and Zeller suggested that they would be prepared to surrender to the first Allied soldiers they encountered, but not to the resistance.

The resistance in southern France was ready for action, but it was split between the AS, the ORA, and the FTP, of which the ORA was cautious about taking action whereas the FTP was independent-minded and ready to take risks. In some areas local agreements secured separate areas of operation for the AS and the FTP. For example, in Cannes a line was drawn through the centre of the city with Ange-Marie Miniconi's FTP controlling the eastern portion and the AS the western portion of the city. There were FFI commanders in the region capable of uniting the various resistance forces, but many key men had been arrested during the summer of 1944, including Paul Héraud in the Hautes-Alpes, and Louis Martin-Brett and Robert Rossi. De Gaulle appointed Colonel Jean Constans as

FFI commander in Region 2 in south-east France, but Constans only landed in France on 11 August and he had not been supplied with the date of Dragoon: he encountered considerable difficulties in establishing command and control.

The news that the Germans would be more willing to surrender to Allied troops than to the FFI led to the despatch of around 100 uniformed Allied soldiers in Jedburgh teams and other special missions during the first two weeks of August. These supplemented the Jedburgh teams dropped earlier that summer. There are, however, many questions regarding the usefulness of these late arrivals. Jacques de Guélis, operating in the Corrèze, received a party of thirty French SAS together with Jedburgh team James on the night of 10–11 August, but noted:

> It may be said of all these excellently trained soldiers that they arrived too late and with a complete misapprehension of what remained to be done . . . Both the SAS and Jedburghs thought their primary task was demolitions. Unfortunately for them everything which required demolition had long ago been dealt with.

Pearl Witherington was appalled at the arrival of team Julian on 11 August since she had not been warned of it: 'they arrived far too late to do any work of great importance and were never told of my existence'. A maquisard in the Basses-Alpes, Oxent Miesseroff, wrote later of OG team Ruth which arrived on 4 August: 'As the Americans had nothing to do, everything which was worth blowing up having been destroyed long since, they pitched their tents about 500 metres from us, a little vacation camp.' A similar situation had been encountered by Jedburgh team Chloroform, which had arrived in late June to carry out sabotage in the area between Gap and Valence. On learning that the FFI had already carried out all the necessary sabotage, the team moved to the Hautes-Alpes, where there was plenty of work for them to do arming and training the FFI forces.

SOE had long had a presence in southern France through the Jockey circuit run by Francis Cammaerts, whose extreme concern for security had ensured his liberty and enabled him to run a successful circuit covering a very wide area of southern and south-eastern France. But Cammaerts's luck was about to run out. He had been joined in July by Krystyna Skarbek, operating under the nom de guerre 'Christine Granville', whose job was to suborn the Polish-born Wehrmacht soldiers operating in the region.* In early August, Cammaerts and Skarbek received two more Allied officers:

* These Poles had lived in the parts of western Poland which had been incorporated into the Reich and had been conscripted into the Wehrmacht, usually against their will.

Xan Fielding, hoping for more action after a frustrating experience in Crete, and Christian Sorensen. On 13 August, Cammaerts, Fielding, Sorensen, and Claude Renoir were travelling by car from Digne to Seyne when they were stopped at a German checkpoint. To Fielding's horror they were questioned by a Gestapo man who spoke perfect French whereas Fielding was aware that, 'though that language had once been my mother tongue, after so many years' absence from France I could no longer converse in it with practised ease'. Worse still, his papers were missing the stamp for August and it was discovered that he and Sorensen had wads of banknotes with consecutive numbers. All were arrested and imprisoned in Digne. Skarbek heard of the arrests and went to Digne, where she persuaded an Alsatian gendarme, Albert Schenck, to act as a go-between between herself and the Gestapo agent Max Waem. Her argument was that the Allied invasion of southern France was imminent and that it was time to choose sides; a bribe of one million francs parachuted to her from Algiers acted as an additional incentive. On 17 August the men were released. Fielding noted that he was insignificant but was included in the deal only because of the importance of Cammaerts: 'Indirectly, then, I owe my life to him as much as I do, directly, to her.'

Operation Dragoon was launched on 15 August and was an immediate success. The parachute and glider landing near Le Muy went unhampered by the Germans since an FFI team led by OSS captain Geoffrey Jones had blown up the German radar installation at Fayence on the preceding night, which left the Germans blind to the airborne and seaborne invasion forces. Jones would go on to secure vital intelligence of the German defences in the port of Nice. Five planeloads of paratroopers were dropped too early and landed near Saint-Tropez, met the local FFI forces under Marc Rainaud, and liberated the town on the first day. The seaborne landings proceeded just as smoothly and the troops advanced twenty miles inland also on the first day.

On 18 August, General Patch received a critical piece of intelligence via an Enigma decrypt at the same time as it was received by the German commander of the 19th Army, General Friedrich Wiese. Hitler ordered almost the entire 19th Army to withdraw from southern France with the 11th Panzer Division designated as the rearguard in the Rhône valley. Garrisons were to remain behind to defend the Franco-Italian frontier, and Marseille and Toulon were to be defended 'to the last man'. The 19th Army was ordered to construct a new defensive line further north, running from Sens in north-central France through Dijon to the Swiss frontier. This news led to a rearrangement of the Allied forces: General Jean de Lattre and the French Army were to take Marseille and Toulon; General Lucian Truscott would advance up the Rhône valley; Brigadier General Frederick's airborne force would guard the Alpine passes. In addition, General Patch authorized the mobilization of Task Force Butler – so-named after its commander General Frederick Butler – to advance up the Route Napoléon. This was the highly mobile advance guard Zeller had pressed for in July and consisted of 3,000 troops and 1,000 vehicles. It had tanks and mobile artillery which made it strong enough to attack small German formations but was too weak to operate as independently as an armoured division would. Task Force Butler would require the assistance of the FFI to keep the Germans pinned down in locations where the task force could force them to surrender.

Task Force Butler set off on 18 August and quickly learned the benefit of working closely with the FFI. The FFI had over-enthusiastically blown all the bridges needed to reach the vast Valensole plateau but quickly constructed a ford across the Verdon river which enabled Butler's force to enter the Basses-Alpes department. There, the FFI commander, George Bonnaire, successfully persuaded the Americans to take a detour to help the FFI capture the departmental capital Digne where the German garrison surrendered at 7 p.m. on 19 August. The road north along the Route Napoléon appeared to be open and it was apparent that the FFI could work usefully alongside the well-armed American task force. But Butler was still cautious regarding the utility of the French resistance. He deeply offended Cammaerts when the two men met in Sisteron by disparaging the efforts of so-called 'amateur armies'. Cammaerts received a warmer welcome at Patch's headquarters.[42] Butler's curt dismissal of Cammaerts raises a question which will be explored in a later chapter – who liberated southern France: the Allies or the French resistance?

Hitler's order to General Wiese to withdraw from southern France had been inspired by events taking place far in the north. After breaking out from Normandy, Patton had split his 3rd Army, with part going towards Brittany where it worked alongside the FFI forces who had risen up to greet their liberators. After Brittany had been cleared of all German forces other than those holed up in the Atlantic ports, Patton turned his army eastwards. In late July the British and Canadians finally liberated Caen where the German strongholds had held them up since June. The German 7th Army and 5th Panzer Army were trapped in the Falaise pocket. On 19 August the Americans, British, Canadians, and Poles linked up to trap the Germans there, and by the evening of 21 August many of the 50,000 Germans in the Falaise pocket had surrendered or been killed. A significant number, however, had escaped in some disorder, hotly pursued by the Allies.

The FFI and Jedburgh teams in the north were assigned a number of roles. One was to cut the German communication lines by road, rail, telegraph, and telephone. Another was to mop up pockets of Germans left behind by the now swiftly moving Allied advance. To facilitate the advance, the FFI was tasked with supplying intelligence of the location, strength, and defences of the Germans, and to engage in counter-scorch, especially the prevention of the destruction of bridges needed by the Allies. Finally, as the Allies advanced eastwards they left their right flank exposed to the Germans retreating from southern and central France, and the FFI was expected to harass these troops and to supply their locations so that large formations could be hit by air power.

Jedburgh teams were inserted ahead of the Allied advance to prepare the FFI for action. Team Bruce, which included a future head of the CIA, Bill Colby, was dropped on 14–15 August into the Yonne valley, about sixty miles south-east of Paris. This was the area where Henri Frager's Donkeyman circuit had long been operating. But, unknown to team Bruce, Frager had been betrayed by his deputy, Roger Bardet, and through his contacts with the supposed German turncoat Hugo Bleicher. On 2 July Bleicher revealed his true colours and arrested Frager. Bardet's treachery was unknown and he was now in charge. Team Bruce was alarmed to find that he was not keen to attack the Germans in his department and in any case he had only around 500 men under his command. Further investigation reaped rewards though and team Bruce was able to find active FFI leaders such as Adrien Sadoul, who claimed to have 2,000 men ready and awaiting orders and arms. Elsewhere, the FFI had helped the Americans to liberate Orléans and Chartres by the end of 18 August. On 19 August Patton's forces began crossing the Seine south of Paris. The Allied plan was to go due east towards Germany with the FFI promising to guard the army's right flank along the line of the Loire from Angers to Orléans.[43]

De Gaulle wanted to be acknowledged as the new leader of liberated France but faced numerous challenges to his authority. Soon after D-Day, Pétain made several attempts to contact de Gaulle in order to arrange an orderly transfer of power, but de Gaulle refused to take these overtures seriously, refusing to consider the possibility of 'de Gaulle enthroned by Pétain'. He similarly dismissed Laval's proposal to recall the 1940 French Assembly in Paris to receive de Gaulle and the Allies formally. On 14 June, during his brief visit to recently liberated Bayeux, de Gaulle took the first step towards undermining the American plan to install a military government by leaving behind a commissioner of the republic, François Coulet, to oversee all liberated territory in the name of de Gaulle's provisional government. The Americans continued to threaten de Gaulle's authority.

Although Roosevelt partially recognized de Gaulle's government on 11 July, there was plenty of evidence to suggest that the American military commanders were keen to work alongside people of any political affiliation, Vichyist or Gaullist, in the name of smooth administration. For example, Bayeux 'existed in a strange administrative limbo where the Vichy authorities, the Resistance and the Allies cohabited' until Coulet managed to take control, and as late as 10 August the new commissioner of the republic, Michel Debré, found that the Vichy prefect was prepared to withdraw from Angers but the Americans still preferred to deal with him rather than with Debré.[44]

On 28 June the resistance assassinated the Vichy minister of propaganda, Philippe Henriot, at his home. This assassination divided the French population: Cardinal Suhard presided over Henriot's memorial service in Paris, including the absolution rite, but refused to read out a eulogy; in Lyon, Cardinal Gerlier refused both the absolution rite and a eulogy; whereas in Limoges Monsignor Rastouil was arrested by the *Milice* for refusing to conduct a memorial service at all. Laval went as far as he dared by refusing German demands to try three ministers of the Third Republic, Paul Reynaud, Léon Blum, and Georges Mandel, condemn them to death, and execute them in retaliation for the execution of Pucheu in Algiers and the arrests of other Vichy ministers. On 6 July, Carl Oberg, the Higher SS and Police Leader in France, informed the head of the Paris *Milice*, Max Knipping, that Mandel had just arrived in Paris from Germany and was to be taken into French custody. Knipping wanted orders from Vichy, which failed to come, so he decided to transport Mandel to a prison near Vichy under *Milice* escort. Instead, the *Milice* shot Mandel in the Fontainebleau forest. Finally, the Germans acknowledged the end of the Vichy regime by forcibly taking Pétain to Belfort on 20 August, where he joined Laval who had reached Belfort two days earlier with his family. An SOE RF agent, Michel Couvreur, happened to be in Vichy when Pétain departed and promptly took responsibility for law and order in the town. The ultra-collaborationists Darnand, Déat, Doriot, and Fernand de Brinon visited Hitler at his headquarters in East Prussia on 1 September to gain permission to form a new French government on German soil. On 6 September Pétain was moved from Belfort across the frontier into Germany, where this new French government convened in the castle at Sigmaringen in Württemberg. Pétain strongly protested to Hitler about being 'led into captivity in Germany'.[45]

Pétain's departure from Vichy should have made de Gaulle's position as head of a new French government secure but for one factor – the communists. De Gaulle had been frequently alarmed by reports of the prominence of the communists in the French resistance and their reluctance to take orders from the FFI. News coming out of Paris heightened his fears and raised the spectre of a new Commune. On 12 August the entire Paris transport system ground to a halt as the railway workers went on strike. The guardians of law and order were also suspect, and on 15 August a strike was called of the entire police force in Paris. Therefore, there was a real danger not only of an uprising against the Germans but also of the establishment of communist rule since the military committee of the resistance in Paris was dominated by communists. In order to prevent the Paris uprising turning into more than just the liberation of the capital of France, de Gaulle would need the assistance of the Allies.

26

Summer 1944: Other Fronts

The news of the Allied landings in Normandy on D-Day spread across Europe like wildfire. In Italy there had been great joy across the country at the news of the liberation of Rome on the previous day, 5 June. In Italy a member of the resistance, Ada Gobetti, was initially indifferent to the news of D-Day since she was in Turin and far from the fronts in Rome and Normandy, but she soon realized its impact on the population: 'Everyone with whom I spoke and to whom I delivered the newspapers, as well as the friends I met by chance, had heard the news and were elated about it. I even seemed to discern a sense of satisfaction and relief on the faces of people I did not know in the street and on the tram.'[1] In Norway, Oluf Reed Olsen recalled:

> I shall never forget the faces of people in Kristiansand the day the news came, long before the Germans had pulled themselves together and realised what was happening. People stood in small groups eagerly discussing the news; the Germans who had suddenly had to get busy seemed just shabby little creatures scurrying along. But this impression did not last long; as the days passed and the Allied invasion gained more ground, our *Herrenvolk* became more and more hysterical and their actions more aggressive.[2]

Even in Poland, where the population was most concerned about the Soviet advance, the news of D-Day was broadcast by Radio Świt, which operated from near London but pretended to come from within Poland, and was greeted with elation. For the majority of the people across occupied Europe who lacked radios the news was received by word of mouth and from the clandestine press.

The people in western Europe received leaflets produced by the PWE and dropped by the RAF:

> We produced leaflets in German, French, Belgian, Dutch, Danish and Norwegian to the total of thirty-two million for dropping during the immediate

> invasion period, the Eisenhower statement in all languages supported in the case of Norwegian, Belgian and Dutch by the statements of the governments, the Eisenhower leaflets in French followed as a separate leaflet by the de Gaulle statement; leaflet to transport workers; a warning leaflet to populations in the towns to be bombed; impact leaflets in German for the actual landing zone, backed by a message to Polish soldiers in the German army; German leaflets for the reserve troops moving up. The transport workers' leaflet and the warning to the civil population also went to Belgium.[3]

Everyone knew that the Allied invasion was imminent because the spring of 1944 had seen heavy bombing of railways and bridges in France and Belgium. For example, in Belgium over 6,000 people had been killed by the Allied bombing of the railways, with Louvain being particularly badly hit.[4] On 1 June the Belgian resistance received their coded alert messages and action was launched on 8 June. The leaflets and the radio messages combined to make the Germans reluctant to rush reinforcements from Belgium to the front in case the Belgians rose up in their rear.

The Belgian government-in-exile exercised little command and control over the resistance in their country. Unlike in France, this did not matter. The principal resistance groups such as *Légion Belge* (now the *Armée Secrète*) and the *Front de l'Indépendance* were well disciplined and were prepared to cooperate with each other. Special forces agents were sent from Britain to assist the sabotage groups in their organization and selection of targets and also to arrange for supply drops. For example, in February 1944 Léon Joye parachuted into Belgium to organize three large sabotage groups to cover the three frontiers: one located in the Antwerp area, another on the French border, and the third on the German border. Each group was assigned to certain tasks.[5]

The Belgian resistance was asked to focus on the rail network and the communications links used by the Germans. The Belgian rail network was sabotaged very effectively, with the main Brussels–Paris and Aachen–Liège lines virtually put out of use completely by 1,100 separate rail cuts, eighty derailments, and the destruction of 176 locomotives, seventy-nine rail bridges, thirty-five pumping stations, and twenty-five railway turntables. The railway along the right bank of the Upper Meuse was blocked for weeks by a sabotage-induced petrol fire in the Yvoir tunnel, south of Namur.[6] Herman Bodson's sabotage team operating south of Liège was very active. It was asked by London to locate a train filled with aviation fuel. The location was discovered and sent to London but by the time the

RAF arrived the train had moved on. Then it was learned that the train was moving towards Liège under heavy German guard but that it would be parked for the night in a tunnel north of La Gleize. The resistance decided to hijack another train and crash it into the train carrying aviation fuel in the tunnel. A train carrying iron ore was duly hijacked and the engineer and his assistant were ordered to build up speed on the approach to the tunnel and then jump out. The result was spectacular:

> The train had arrived with the screaming thunder of full speed, the rails and wheels spitting fire from the friction of the curves. It disappeared into the tunnel. The earth shook. From inside the mountain, a muffled explosion was heard and an enormous black cloud appeared at the tunnel entrance. The air filled with the odour of gasoline, an expulsion of smoke, and the sound of great suction as the tunnel replenished itself with air, then another muffled explosion and more black smoke.

The explosions continued for a day and night before the Germans ordered the local civilians to spend a week digging out the tunnel before the track could be restored to running order a week later. The same sabotage group was also involved in the destruction of a rail bridge across the Amblève river as a troop train passed over it. Around 600 German soldiers were killed, and 'the next day, the river ran red with blood from dawn to dusk'.[7] There was also widespread sabotage of the canal network.

The principal telephone cables and telegraph lines from Paris to Cologne and Berlin ran through Belgium and the resistance was tasked with keeping these cut in order to force the Germans to use radios, which the Allies could intercept. The cables were buried to a depth of around 18 inches but some locations had been discovered by the resistance before D-Day. Bodson's group carried out its first piece of cable sabotage with a thermite charge in the early hours of 6 June and then watched the Germans digging a trench along the cable to find the fault: 'We needed to know how long it would take them to make the repairs. Then, and only then, would we ignite the next charge so that they would have to start all over again.' They learned that the thermite charge would melt a foot-long section of cable, and that it would take the Germans on average around sixty hours to locate and repair each cut. Victor Eloy's group in the Ardennes did not have thermite charges but discovered that pouring acid on the cables was more effective than cutting them. Actions against telegraph poles were coordinated with neighbouring resistance sections so that the telegraph lines were always cut somewhere along the line. On Belgian Independence Day, 21 July, a spectacular operation was launched to blow up fifty telegraph poles over a distance of a mile and a half. These poles carried sixteen pairs of lines which were cut and thirty-two insulators that were smashed, keeping the telegraph line cut for over a week.[8]

The virtual civil war already raging between the resistance and the collaborators intensified. Statistics compiled by the Belgian police show that whereas there had been ninety-four attacks on collaborators in May, leading to the deaths of seventy-four people, in June the figure rose sharply to 151 attacks and 110 deaths and increased in July to 286 attacks with 217 deaths. The Rexist collaborators retaliated with reprisal actions in Bouillon and across Wallonia, culminating in a reprisal operation in Charleroi, a centre of resistance and where the resistance was assassinating a collaborator a day during the summer of 1944. On 17 August the Rexist *burgomeister* of Grand Charleroi was assassinated along with his wife and son. The Rexist reprisal action resulted in the deaths of twenty-seven locals, some of whom had no connection with the resistance. German attacks on the resistance also became more brutal, with members of the resistance being shot on the spot if caught in the act and prisoners being executed without trials: those already in prison in Belgium were now moved to camps in Germany.[9]

The deteriorating security situation sounded the death knell for the military administration of Belgium under Alexander von Falkenhausen. Himmler had long been campaigning for a greater SS presence in Belgium but there had been important factors which had kept von Falkenhausen in office and the SS out of Belgium. The fact that the Allied landings had taken place in Normandy and not in Belgium or the Pas-de-Calais removed the *raison d'être* for the military administration. Furthermore, von Falkenhausen's correct relations with King Léopold no longer mattered, because on 6 June Werner Kiewitz, the German liaison officer to the king, received orders to inform the king that he was to be removed to Germany and von Falkenhausen confirmed the authenticity of the orders. King Léopold and his family spent the rest of the war in Germany and Austria. In the middle of July, Joseph Grohé took over as Reichskommissar and retained Eggert Reeder as his deputy. Von Falkenhausen was implicated in the 20 July plot against Hitler when, unknown to him, the conspirators had put his name forward as the future chancellor of Germany. He was innocent but was nevertheless arrested and imprisoned for the rest of the war. General Martin Grase was appointed as his successor, but he was dismissed in early August after Grohé reported that Grase had refused to add his signature to his telegram to Hitler congratulating him on surviving the 20 July assassination attempt. Grase was succeeded as military governor by Gruppenführer Richard Jungclaus, who had just been appointed the Higher SS and Police Leader in Belgium but who had no military experience.[10]

By the end of August the Allies had broken out of the Normandy beachheads, routed the German armies around Falaise, and begun a rapid advance eastwards pursuing the apparently broken German forces. The resistance was ordered to launch a full-scale uprising to prevent the Germans from regrouping. This was a particularly dangerous time for the resistance since the SS were now in control of the country and although the large number of German soldiers retreating through Belgium were disorganized, they would still be capable of mounting actions against the resistance. For example, in the Ardennes a successful attack on a German lorry resulted in the despatch of a force of 600 Germans and a severe firefight followed by reprisals: 'The Germans, infuriated by their own losses and their inability to destroy this small force, burn down five farms and the church at Houdremont.' Nonetheless, the resistance continued to hit German convoys in the Ardennes:

> The German authorities now forbid to their convoys the use of certain roads through the forest. At various places round Alle they set up special signposts, showing the detours that must be made, the roads that are 'dangerous'. During the night we simply go and change the direction of the arrows, and thus ensure that the convoys use the roads selected by us. Really, it is very simple.

The SS patrolled the roads continually, firing into bushes and houses with wanton abandon and little care over the casualties suffered by innocent civilians.[11]

By the end of August as the British, Poles, and Canadians approached the Belgian frontier in the north, and the Americans to the south, no one knew whether the Germans would halt in Belgium and make a stand, in which case the Belgian resistance would prove of great value, or whether they would continue retreating into the Netherlands and back into the Reich.

Norway and Denmark lay outside the regions likely to be liberated in the near future. Consequently, the Allies had to engage in a delicate balancing act in their relations with the resistance movements in the two countries: on the one hand offering no hope of imminent liberation but on the other hand encouraging the resistance to continue with sabotage activities.

In June 1944 SHAEF issued a directive on what it required from the resistance in Norway. The most important point was: 'No Allied military offensive operations are planned for this theatre, therefore no steps must be taken to encourage the Resistance Movement as such to overt acts, since no outside support can be forthcoming.' It was important to make this clear because in 1942 the Norwegians had been encouraged to raise their level of resistance as part of the Allied deception plan for Operation Torch. The result had been increased Norwegian casualties and a consequential dive in morale. The possibility of an Allied invasion of Norway formed part of the Allied deception plan for D-Day as well, but crucially on this occasion the Norwegian resistance was alerted to the fact that these plans had no chance of being implemented. There were then around 350,000 Germans in the country and the Allies were anxious to keep them there but not to sacrifice the Norwegian resistance in pursuit of this aim. In the same SHAEF directive the resistance was given instructions to prepare for the possibility of a sudden German collapse and surrender, as had occurred at the end of the First World War, as well as for a partial or complete evacuation of German forces from Norway. In each of these three cases, known as the Rankin Plans, the role of the military resistance, *Milorg*, was to engage in counter-scorch actions and be prepared to cooperate with the civil Home Front (*Hjemmefrontens Ledelse*) under the leadership of Jens Christian Hauge in the maintenance of law and order. While Allied operations got underway in mainland Europe, the Norwegians were to avoid any major clashes with the Germans but were to maintain a steady level of targeted sabotage operations.[12]

Important steps were taken prior to D-Day to integrate the Danish resistance into SHAEF strategy through the SOE Danish Section. Until D-Day Danish nationals were excluded from the planning discussions on the grounds of security, but soon afterwards two veteran resisters forced to flee Denmark, Flemming Juncker and Svend Truelsen, joined the proceedings. SHAEF's orders to Denmark were issued in a BBC broadcast on 14 June 1944. Denmark was divided into seven regions in which the resistance was to be organized so as to be able to go into action independently from its neighbours on receipt of instructions transmitted by the BBC. The priorities accorded to the resistance were: harassing and sabotage attacks on the railways, German telecommunications systems, harbours, and ports, and the electricity supply system. These were the immediate tasks, but the groundwork was also laid for future operations, either diversionary at the request of SHAEF or in conjunction with SHAEF on Danish soil, or aimed at preventing German scorched-earth actions should their forces withdraw from Denmark. With regard to the Freedom Council, SHAEF was ready to discuss political matters with it, but not military operations.[13]

The low importance given to Denmark and Norway was reflected in the despatch of supplies. In the case of Denmark, in the period prior to D-Day there were only twenty-nine successful drops, which provided the resistance with twenty-three tons of supplies. The majority of these supplies were dropped into Jutland, which was approached over open seas and was sparsely enough populated for the reception parties to be able to gather and hide the arms, but it meant that Zealand and Copenhagen remained woefully short of weapons and explosives. From summer 1944 a new entry route was added when British ships rendezvoused with Danish fishing boats on the Dogger Bank to transfer arms at sea. By September 1944 the weapons received were sufficient to arm only 5,000 men.[14] Norway received 141 tons of supplies through airdrops in the whole of 1944, and the landing of an increased volume of supplies by sea was facilitated by the acquisition of fast-moving US submarine chasers. Nonetheless, *Milorg* remained pitifully short of arms.

The value of Danish sabotage against the railways to thwart the movement of German troops from Norway through Denmark to the front after the Allied breakout of the Normandy beachhead is questionable. A report from Jutland stated that a German division had been withdrawn from Norway and transported through Denmark where it had encountered sabotage en route but that the effect had been 'unfortunately small'. Similar delays of a few days were recorded in the three months from August to October 1944, when the Germans moved eight divisions through Denmark and were subjected to over 300 acts of sabotage of the railways and bridges. Although the effects were minor, the Germans were annoyed enough by the sabotage to institute countermeasures. Captured saboteurs were forced to travel on German troop trains as hostages to be executed when the train was halted due to sabotage. The resistance responded by changing its tactics, for example increasing its use of timed charges which would blow the line after the train carrying hostages had passed over, and also with increased attacks against water towers and points. Danish saboteurs were more successful in their attacks on shipping. They waited until the ship was ready for launching before placing explosives in key points such as the engine room and even attaching limpet mines to the hull in case the planted explosives were discovered. It has been recorded that in October and November there were on average three attacks a week on German shipping in Danish harbours.[15]

The constant sabotage attacks convinced the Germans that the Danish police could no longer be relied upon to maintain law and order. In September SS-Obergruppenführer Günther Pancke arrived in Denmark to take control of all security forces in the country. His first step was to transfer 197 Danish prisoners to German concentration camps in contravention of an earlier agreement to imprison them on Danish soil. His second act was to arrange the occupation of every police station in Denmark by the SS and Wehrmacht on 19 September to oversee the dissolution of the entire Danish police force. Nearly 10,000 police officers were arrested, about half the entire force, and of these just under 2,000, mostly from Copenhagen, were sent to camps in Germany with many others held in internment camps in Denmark. Around 7,000 policemen who had avoided arrest and deportation formed an illegal police corps which operated under the command of the Freedom Council. Pancke then transformed the despised Schalburg Corps into the SS Training Battalion 'Schalburg', and one of its units, called the Hipo Corps, took the war directly to the resistance. Between November 1944 and the end of the war it is estimated that this unit murdered or attempted to murder over fifty Danish resisters. The Freedom Council responded by requesting the civil servants to resign, but neither the civil servants nor the authorities in London were keen on such drastic action since the Allied front had stalled after the debacle at Arnhem in September 1944 and such a step was deemed premature.[16]

The Allies were, however, ready to assist the Danish resistance directly when they could. The Danes' lack of experience of resistance meant that important lessons in security had to be learned the hard way, and the Gestapo found it relatively easy to build up a clear and detailed picture of those involved. For example, Pastor Harald Sandbaek had become involved in the resistance through the clandestine press before moving on to receive Allied airdrops. In the middle of September he and eight of his group were arrested in Jutland and taken to Aarhus prison, where he realized that the Germans knew a great deal about the Danish resistance. Much of this information had been gleaned from members of the Freedom Council who had been arrested at the start of September. These arrests occurred because of an unfortunate security lapse when a resister delivered a revolver to the cloakroom at a station wrapped in papers which had his name and address on them: the Germans arrested him and he talked. By the middle of September the original make-up of the Freedom Council had been changed by circumstances: Mogens Fog and Aage Schoch had been arrested; Børge Houmann was seriously ill; and Arne Sørensen was in Sweden. The Gestapo had built up extensive card indices of the resistance which were housed in three headquarters: the Shell House in Copenhagen; an agricultural college near Odense; and Aarhus University. The latter index was the most complete but the university was too heavily guarded for an attack by the resistance to have much chance of success, so the Danes asked the British for assistance. On 31 October an attack was mounted by a Mosquito squadron commanded by a veteran of the successful attack on Amiens prison, Basil Embry, and this succeeded in destroying the card index and killing around 200 Gestapo agents, including their chief, as well as allowing Sandbaek and most of the other prisoners to escape. He and his wife promptly departed for the safety of Sweden. Flemming Muus also found himself hounded by the Germans to the extent that he could no longer function as an intermediary between the remnants of the Freedom Council and SOE: in November he went underground and on 1 December left Denmark.[17]

Sabotage operations in Norway were carried out primarily by the Oslo Gang led by Max Manus and Gunnar Sønsteby, with the assistance of *Milorg* when required. Their targets were the factories engaged in production for the German war machine, and German stores of war materiel. In June, Sønsteby was invited to a meeting with a small group of industrialists to discuss how to paralyse production in munitions factories. The decision was taken to cut off the supply of concentrated sulphuric acid essential to production by destroying the storage tanks at Lysaker and Hurum. The operations against both targets were successfully completed on 28 June and British equipment was left behind in the hope of avoiding reprisals against innocent Norwegians. The sabotage campaign reached a height in August 1944 with numerous attacks. One of the oil stores at Soon on the Oslofjord destroyed 4,700 tons of oil essential for U-boat operations from the area, and the attacks were repeated over the following two months. Another against the Korsvoll bus depot and workshop in Oslo led to the destruction of a large store of aeroplane parts. *Milorg* was active in sabotaging the locomotives running on the narrow-gauge railway serving the vital pyrite mines at Orkla, and the Oslo Gang was tasked with destroying the locomotives that had been transported to Oslo for repair, and did so on 12 September.[18]

The services of the Oslo Gang were also essential during the campaign mounted by the Home Front against Quisling's plans for compulsory labour service. In 1943 Quisling had attempted to set up a scheme for the registration and draft of labourers to work on projects in Norway through the NS-controlled Labour Service or *Arbeidstjenesten* (AT), but the uptake had been low largely due to the hostility of the civilian resistance. The resistance had suspected that Quisling aimed to use the compulsory call-up of Norwegian youth to form Norwegian units to fight on the Eastern Front, and although Quisling and the NS ministers had denied any such intentions at the time, they had been widely disbelieved. With German losses mounting during the winter of 1943–44 and with the increased demand for workers for German coastal fortifications along the extensive Norwegian coast, the NS renewed its attempt to draft Norwegian youth. In January 1944 the minister of justice, Sverre Riisnaes, wrote a memorandum which proposed the mobilization of five age groups, a total of 75,000 men, who would be sent to Germany for training. During the same month Quisling travelled to Hitler's headquarters at Rastenburg and offered Hitler 50,000 men, a draft of three age groups. Riisnaes's memorandum was copied by his secretary and was passed on to the resistance, which published it in the clandestine newspaper *Bulletinen*. On 26 February the Home Front published its response:

> No Norwegian will allow himself to be fooled into fighting for our oppressors against our allies. We know that, NS knows that, and the Germans know that. Therefore it is likely that a mobilisation will be camouflaged. It can most easily be carried out through the Labour Service, which we now for several years have become used to regarding as a relatively harmless group . . . It is therefore time to eliminate the Labour Service . . . The directive is: Strike against the Labour Service . . . For the country's and your own sake: Follow the directive.[19]

The NS issued the mobilization notices for the 1921–23 classes in May 1944. The Oslo Gang set to work to thwart the process, and its first target was the destruction of the Watson & Company's printing machines which were used to produce the draft cards. This operation was successful but then it was learned that another machine was being used as a replacement. This machine was located on the third floor of an insurance company's building in Oslo and was under heavy guard. It was destroyed on the third attempt, when explosives were successfully infiltrated into the canteen located immediately above it. A further attack was undertaken against the Labour Office building on Akers Street in Oslo on the eve of the registration. The attacks in Oslo largely succeeded in delaying the draft registration, a fact acknowledged by the NS regional leader in Oslo, Rolf Holm, who reported: 'The action against the Work Effort must be considered 100 per cent successful for our opponents.'[20]

The NS responded by seizing young men off the streets, which led to a rush of Norwegian youths into the forests and mountains or deciding to stay away from home with friends or relatives. It was estimated that about 3,000 men took shelter in the woods around Oslo, 1,500 in Lower Telemark, and hundreds more across eastern Norway. About 2,000–3000 men were allowed by the Swedes to cross into Sweden and join the Norwegian police troops there, and by the end of August at least 15,000 had sought sanctuary in Sweden. Local sheriffs were warned by the Home Front not to betray the locations of camps on pain of assassination. Suitable young men were recruited by *Milorg* or joined communist partisan units, but they faced the problem of limited supplies of food, weapons, and equipment.[21]

This weakness gave the NS and Germans an opportunity to hit back against the Home Front. The regulations were altered so that the head of a family could no longer collect the monthly ration cards for all members of the family: now each card had to be claimed by the intended recipient. The Norwegian authorities in London were consulted as to whether fake ration cards could be produced there and parachuted or shipped into Norway, but this plan was thwarted by the inability of the resistance to supply the correct type of paper. The Oslo Gang undertook a daring hijacking of a lorry carrying a ton of ration cards, just under 100,000 of them, from the printing works to the ration offices:

> On the morning of 9 August, as soon as the lorry had left the works in the Old Town, Sønsteby and two other members of the Oslo Gang jumped on it at a crossroads; put pistols into the backs of the drivers and guards, who were driven off in another car; and took the vehicle down into the most tightly packed central district. There it was backed into a yard where another gang was waiting with a second lorry, of which the number plates were covered up; the boxes with the cards were at once transferred; and a new driver emerging by a different gate brought the boxes to safety.

The NS government offered a substantial reward of 200,000 kroner for information leading to the arrests of the perpetrators but found no takers. The Home Front telephoned the NS supply minister and promised that the cards would not be misused and could possibly even be returned providing the order to deny ration cards to evaders of the work effort was rescinded: 'Unless you drop the forced signing up we will not give you back the ration cards – it's too late to have new cards printed.' The NS caved in and rescinded the order whereupon the Home Front returned the cards in batches of 10,000, retaining 15,000 for its own use. The only reprisal was the withdrawal of the tobacco and alcohol rations for the entire population for five days. Quisling's dream of an independent Norwegian armed force remained unfulfilled and even efforts to encourage more members of the *Hird* to enlist in front-line units failed as men preferred to resign from the *Hird* rather than face the dangers of the Eastern Front.[22]

The events in Italy in the summer of 1944 are largely glossed over in the traditional histories of the Second World War: these make a leap from the beginning of June, when Rome was liberated, to September, when the Allied armies arrived at the Gothic Line, the immensely strong and deep line of German fortifications bisecting Italy along the Pisa–Rimini line. This advance was painfully slow since the Germans conducted a fighting retreat, and General Harold Alexander's forces were substantially weakened by the withdrawal of seven divisions, four French and three American, to undertake the Operation Dragoon landings in the south of France.

Such histories do not reflect the events on the ground in Italy in the summer of 1944. Those events are important both in their own right and as presenting pointers to the struggles for the eventual liberation of the whole of the Italian peninsula in the following year and to immediate post-war problems. In the summer of 1944 the Italian resistance reached its peak strength with around 82,000 members. These were mostly concentrated in the north: 25,000 in Piedmont, aiming to liberate Turin; 14,000 in Liguria around Genoa; 5,000 in Lombardy near Milan; 5,600 in the Veneto around Venice; and 16,000 in the disputed region of Venezia Giulia in the hinterland of Trieste. Further south, there were 17,000 in the regions of Tuscany and Emilia-Romagna which contained the cities next on the Allied list of conquests, Florence and Bologna. The Germans still had a formidable army in Italy, and part of the Allied strategy was to keep those divisions in Italy so that they could not be used in France against either the D-Day landings or Operation Dragoon. German conduct against the partisans became ever more brutal and the Germans were assisted by Mussolini's National Republican Guard, whose 90,000 men were divided almost equally between forces assigned to support the Germans directly, and formations such as the *Brigate Nere* aimed specifically at waging war on the partisans.[23]

On 8 June the Italian prime minister, Pietro Badoglio, flew to Rome to prepare to move the government there. However, he encountered immediate opposition from the members of the Rome CLN (*Comitato di Liberazione Nazionale*), who viewed both Badoglio and the king as irrevocably contaminated by collaboration with Mussolini. Consequently, on the following day Badoglio was forced to resign and his government was replaced by a new one consisting of representatives of the six main anti-Fascist parties and led by Ivanoe Bonomi. As previously agreed with the Allies, the king reluctantly abdicated in favour of his son, Crown Prince Umberto. A crucial member of the new government was the communist leader, Palmiro Togliatti. He had startled everyone by announcing on his return from Moscow in March that he intended to cooperate with the democratic forces. His presence in the government was widely viewed at the time as the means of preventing the communists from fomenting a revolution. Such fears lay behind the refusal of the Allies in July to agree to the incorporation of now redundant partisan units south of Rome into the Italian Army. The Allies feared the subversion of the royalist army by the largely republican and left-wing partisans if substantial numbers joined up together. Therefore, individual partisans were permitted to enlist but very few, only 807 by the end of October, chose to serve in a royal army under formerly Fascist officers.[24]

Northern Italy was still far from the Allied front and seemed free to arrange its affairs quite separately from the Bonomi government in Rome. The CLNAI (*Comitato di Liberazione Nazionale Alta Italia*) under Alfredo Pizzoni was dominated by the communists and the majority of partisan formations fell under its remit. On 9 June the CLNAI set up its own central military command, the *Corpo Volontari della Libertà* (CVL), led by Ferruccio Parri and Luigi Longo. The CLNAI also underlined its independent stance by concluding agreements with neighbouring resistance forces. In May an agreement was concluded with the French resistance to share supplies and intelligence and to coordinate plans for action in the Alps, and at the end of October a small Italian mission reached Briançon to discuss joint operations in the Alps with the FFI. They were greeted with suspicion but nonetheless returned to Italy at the end of November laden with weapons supplied by the FFI. Also in May a similar agreement was concluded to the east with the Slovene Partisans to create a joint command.[25]

Such independence posed a challenge to the command-and-control structure necessary to ensure that the partisan strategy was in tune with the requirements of the Allies. The CLNAI recognized this and was ready to receive General Raffaele Cadorna as military commander of all partisan forces in northern Italy: he was parachuted into Val Cavallina on 12 August. Cadorna had no staff or separate channels of communication with Rome, which limited his effectiveness. He warned both the Allies and the government about the political nature of the resistance in the north:

> It appears that the Allies continue to consider the partisan war as a normal military campaign, refusing to recognize its predominant political character. It must be stated very clearly that the resistance movement could not have existed without the political organization and that in this partisan warfare the Communist Party is predominant. The encroachment of political factors do [*sic*] not disappear by ignoring them. It is better to give them due consideration.
>
> The Communist Party, which gives the lead, does not try in the least to hide its intention of seizing the reins and setting up a regime similar to the Russian . . . They declare openly that they wish to lean upon Russia and Tito and will rebel rather than submit to the orders of the Western Allies.

In pursuit of their aim of post-war domination the communists' tactics leaned towards the formation of large partisan forces to liberate areas of Italy by themselves. In contrast Gerry Holdsworth, in charge of SOE operations in Italy, summed up the Allies' plans for the resistance as being 'to harass German lines of communication by sabotage and guerrilla warfare and eventually to impede the withdrawal of German forces from Italy in order that the Allied armies may be able to get at them and destroy them'.[26]

To help keep a semblance of command and control over the resistance during the first six months of 1944 fifty-eight SOE and OSS organizers and thirty-nine sabotage teams had been despatched into northern Italy, along with sixteen radio stations.[27] These missions sought to arrange for arms supplies for the partisans, largely irrespective of their political colour, and to focus the partisans' attention on Allied requirements and not on their own political ends. At the beginning of July the head of SOE Italian Section, Cecil Roseberry, reported:

> Throughout the whole area of unliberated Italy active and open hostility to the Germans and neo-Fascists is revealing itself. There is no important sector which has not been penetrated by SOE and which help and assistance have not reached ... Given favourable weather and sufficient lift, the strategic areas should be in a satisfactory state as regards arms and organisation by the end of July.

The provision of supplies remained problematic, with a total of just 365 tons of supplies having been dropped during the first six months of 1944. Gordon Lett wrote: 'We would have sold our souls to the Devil for just one British machine gun and some gelignite', a statement reflecting the overall inadequacy of supplies for partisans in the north. The situation deteriorated further at the end of August when bad weather prevented airdrops to the most northern areas and priority had been assigned to airdrops from Italy in support of Operation Dragoon and, to a lesser extent, to support the Warsaw Uprising. Indeed, a report by OSS concluded that the situation was so serious that there was a very real danger that 'Piedmont, Liguria and Lombardy would become a military pocket where the patriot forces could expect little help and comfort and it was probable that they would be forced to scatter and disband.'[28]

Parri continued to demand more and more weapons in order to create large formations. This earned him a blistering rebuke by SOE's representative in Switzerland, Jock McCaffery, on 16 August:

> You are not receiving adequate arms? I know. They have never had enough arms also in France, Belgium, Poland, Greece, Yugoslavia, Holland, Denmark, Norway and Czechoslovakia. But in four years I have not had complaints from anyone else but from you ...
>
> A long time ago, I said that the greatest military contribution you could make would be continuous and widespread sabotage on a massive scale. You wanted bands. I supported your request because I recognised its moral worth for Italy. The bands have worked well. But you wanted to make an army. Who asked you to do such a thing? Not us. You did it for political reasons;

> precisely to reintegrate Italy. Nobody blames you for this idea. However do not put our generals in the wrong if they basically work to military criteria; and above all do not try to hold us back with your political objectives.
>
> I do not want to say any more but one last word of advice: You have friends. Do not try to lose them.[29]

The Allies feared that large partisan bands would have the potential to carry out a communist revolution: whether this was their intention was not clear, as reports from Allied representatives on the ground in northern Italy gave conflicting opinions.

Gordon Lett had created an International Battalion in the Rossano valley after his escape from a POW camp, but in the summer of 1944 he found that his authority in the area was being challenged by the communist partisans, who were hostile to him and were more numerous than those belonging to the Action Party with whom he was friendly. The situation was not helped by the arrival of Colonel Mario Fontana, who had been despatched by the La Spezia CLN to set up a unified partisan command. Lett commented on Fontana's first staff conference on 2 August:

> The conference deteriorated into an exciting battle of words. The Colonel, handicapped by his regular army training, endeavoured more and more ineffectually to act as mediator, for he, poor fellow, had not yet had time to appreciate the fact that he was sitting on a dangerously active volcano. Actionists and Communists had decided that a lamb must be slaughtered to mark the occasion, and that lamb was to be the International Battalion . . .

The communists may have wanted Lett to leave Rossano, but he used his contacts with Allied headquarters to organize airdrops of supplies, thus giving him a reason to remain in the valley. In the end the dispute was settled by the Germans, who attacked the Rossano and the neighbouring valley on 3 August and forced the International Battalion and the partisans of every political hue to scatter.[30] The Rossano valley is not the only example: Ada Gobetti noted similar disputes in the Meana area where the two principal partisan leaders refused to cooperate. She advocated the appointment of an outsider, 'a trustworthy person who was composed, not too willing to compromise, new, and therefore a stranger to the quarrels that naturally existed among the local groups'. This man, a reserve captain called Chiapusso, was given the role of coordinator and mediator while military decisions were left in the hands of the two partisan leaders, Martino and Laghi. The effect of political differences still emerged, however, when the Fascists attacked in late August and the battle was waged entirely by Laghi's force, whereas the Garibaldi partisans arrived only when the fighting was over to take a share of the weapons captured.[31]

Others noted that the communists appeared to be preferring to harbour resources for the post-war revolution. This was evident all across northern Italy but most notably in the north-east. This was an area, especially around Osoppo, north-west of the disputed city of Trieste, where the communist Garibaldi formations received political and armed sustenance from proximity to the Slovene Partisans. Major Nicholson was despatched into the area as head of the British mission and was immediately impressed by the ten battalions of the Osoppo brigade created by Don Ascanio De Luca, a Catholic priest, and recommended the despatch of supplies to the area. But in July it was clear that the local Garibaldi formations resented the power of the Osoppo brigade and wanted a share of the supplies. A tentative agreement was brokered between the two sides, overseen by Don Aldo Moretti, who represented the Udine CLN: guard duty over the supplies which arrived on the night of 19 July would be split on alternate nights between the two formations, who would receive an equal quantity of supplies. The Germans attacked on the following night and when the Garibaldi were on guard duty. The supplies were saved, but the Osoppo formation was abandoned by the communists during the battle with the Germans. Thereafter there was little prospect of cooperation between the two sides.[32]

With the Allied front line still remote, it may be wrong to place too much emphasis on the impact of political differences among the partisans in northern Italy during the summer of 1944. Perhaps the wry comment of Sergeant Harry Hargreaves, an SOE radio operator, presents a more accurate picture: 'The difference was that the communists, like true Italians, were always dressed to kill – they're all dandies, the Italians – and wore the red neckerchief. The republicans wore the green, white and red neckerchief.'[33] Fears of a communist revolution seem overstated when analysing the republics established in partisan-liberated areas. A number of these sprang up in Piedmont, Lombardy, Liguria, Emilia-Romagna, and the Veneto during the summer in response to a directive issued by the CLNAI on 14 June for a national uprising. The first republic was established around Montefiorino between Modena and La Spezia in the Apennines on 18 June where partisan units, composed of former Italian soldiers led by Mario Ricci, had successfully expelled the local Fascist formations. A rudimentary democratic government was created which set up a tax system, a relief service for the poor, medical facilities, and stipulated the price of goods. Major Johnston was parachuted into the area and organized a high number of airdrops of supplies for the partisans. This naturally attracted the attention of the Germans, who attacked with 5,000–8,000 men at the end of July. After five days' fighting the partisans scattered into the mountains. They had allegedly inflicted 2,080 casualties on the Germans for a loss of 250 partisans killed in the first major battle between the Germans and the Italian partisans. In revenge, the Germans bombarded the towns of Montefiorino and Piandelagotti. The partisans regrouped in the mountains and returned to set up a second republic in January 1945.[34]

Probably the best-known republic was the Ossola republic established around the town of Domodossola in a valley lying north-west of Milan and Lake Maggiore close to the Swiss border. The region was of vital strategic importance since it was the key to the Simplon Pass linking Italy with Switzerland and the main Milan–Geneva railway. It also contained major hydroelectric power facilities and heavy industry. An OSS agent, Donald Jones, gave the impression that he could and would organize substantial supplies for the republic from the Allies but never informed OSS in Caserta of his plans. He encouraged the partisans of every political hue to engage with the German and Fascist garrisons in the area during August. The partisans swept through the region, capturing the town of Cannobio at the start of September, liberating around twenty kilometres of the west bank of Lake Maggiore and advancing on Domodossola from all directions before taking the town on 9 September. A provisional government representing all democratic parties was set up. The Ossola republic was a failure for many reasons: food supplies ran very short; the anticipated arms drops were never made; and political differences meant that the partisan formations did not cooperate with each other. The end was not long in coming. On 10 October the Germans and Fascists mounted an attack on Domodossola and it fell four days later. The provisional government fled and about 2,000 partisans and around 35,000 civilians crossed into Switzerland. The republic of Carnia, in the mountains north of Venice near the Austrian and Slovene borders, lasted longer. It was set up gradually from August to October 1944 and held democratic elections and organized its own industry and finance. The Carnia republic fell in early December to a multinational Axis force led by the Germans but including Italians loyal to Mussolini, Austrians, Ustaše from Croatia, and Frenchmen still loyal to Vichy. Around 12,000 partisans survived the attack and took refuge high on the Prescola mountain for the winter.[35]

Overall, the balance sheet of partisan action during the summer is hard to assess. William Mackenzie probably summarizes the reasons well:

> There was thus a great volume of guerrilla activity, but once the Germans were back on the short line north of Pisa to Ravenna their communications

> were not highly vulnerable at crucial points to attacks of this kind. The Po Valley was bad territory for Partisans, the mountains of the Swiss frontier had little military significance, and the vital roads and railways to Austria and Yugoslavia were restricted objectives and not difficult to protect. The situation was thus very different to that in France, where the area of operations was much wider; the military value of guerrillas was necessarily limited.[36]

The partisans provided much valuable intelligence to the Allies. Gerry Holdsworth recalled that he received sufficient information to brief Generals Alexander and Harding on a weekly basis: 'We would tell them of movements coming through the tunnels in the north of Italy, down from Germany, troop movements, armament movements, in or out.' The Italian resistance obtained the vitally important plans for the German defences on the Gothic Line from two sources. One came by chance when in early June the partisans attacked a German command car, killed the occupants, and found the plans of the Gothic Line in the briefcase of one of the passengers. The plans reached Switzerland safely. Then in early September, Ennio Tassinari, an OSS agent working in the Bologna area, passed through the front lines with further details on the fortifications.[37]

The partisans also inflicted substantial losses on the Germans. Field Marshal Kesselring estimated that between June and August 1944 he had lost around 5,000 soldiers killed and 7,000–8,000 wounded or missing to partisan action.[38] These losses help explain the ferocity of his orders for anti-partisan action. For example, on 17 June: 'The fight against the bands is to be prosecuted with every available means and with the greatest severity. I will support any commander who in his choice and severity of means goes beyond our customary measure of restraint.' The weapons employed were the same as those on the front line: artillery, tanks, and flame-throwers. On 1 July the partisan war was to be extended to those who provided food and shelter to the partisans, and the burning of villages and seizure of hostages were explicitly endorsed. Similar orders were given to the *Brigate Nere* before the so-called 'march on the Vandée' at the end of July to cleanse partisans from the whole of Piedmont and as far north as the Alps; but this campaign ended in failure. Anti-partisan operations were brutal: for example, in early July a sweep between Parma and Piacenza led to the deaths of 200 partisans and the capture and execution of a further forty-three, and later that month forty-eight partisans were executed near Arezzo. The sweeps were also often inefficient since, as Basil Davidson recalled, they could normally be avoided simply by moving from one part of the mountain to another. Ada Gobetti noted how the Germans conducted a sweep of Meana. They marked houses with a 'K' to symbolize that a house should not be burned and with an 'F' if it should be, yet no house actually belonging to a partisan was torched. She concluded that the action 'had the simple goal of pillage and terrorism'. Lett wrote of the sadness of seeing the effect of German reprisals: 'Below us spreading as far as the horizon of dark mountains that marked the coastline was a myriad of lights – lights that wavered, and changed colour intermittently from bright orange to dull red. Hundreds and hundreds of fires were burning, each of them representing the house of some unfortunate peasant.'[39]

Among the German reprisal actions, three massacres in Tuscany carried out by the 16th SS Panzer Grenadier Division stand out: Civitella della Chiana on 29 June; Sant'Anna di Stazzema on 12 August; and Bardine San Terenzo on 19 August. The Civitella massacre has excited much academic dispute. Its immediate cause appears to have been that on 18 June the partisans killed three German soldiers. On 29 June the SS arrived in the village of 800 people who were at Mass and rounded up the attendees and searched the village for those absent from the service. Over 100 men were selected for execution and a further ninety-seven people, both men and women, were collected from neighbouring villages and executed. Controversy surrounds the massacre. Local memories suggest that the partisans were never popular, and even less so when they drew such savage reprisals on the population; the national memory, on the other hand, views the massacre with a certain pride as a reflection of the strength of resistance to German occupation. The German records point to the relatively high level of partisan activity in the wider region and suggest that Civitella was made an example of in order to break the perceived bonds between partisans and local civilians, although the precise reasons for that particular choice remain obscure. Sant'Anna was probably selected as another example because of its proximity to the Gothic Line and the activities of the 10th Garibaldi Brigade in the area. On this occasion, 560 men and women and at least 107 children were executed and the whole village was burned down. The reprisal against Bardine San Terenzo took place in an area of considerable partisan activity. It lasted for four days and included bringing hostages into the village for execution as well as killing the forty-nine civilians found there. Surrounding villages were also included in the massacre, bringing the casualty figures up to a total of 369 civilians killed and the destruction of 454 houses.[40]

The fact that Florence was full of priceless architecture and works of art was not lost on either the Allies or the Germans, so the concept of a protracted battle for the city that would inevitably cause immense destruction was deemed undesirable by both sides. The Allies received detailed intelligence from the clandestine radio station Radio Cora, which supplied reports on German dispositions and strength in and around the city and made it apparent that the Germans were prepared to defend the River Arno which runs through the city. On 7 June the Germans captured the Radio Cora radio operator, Luis Morandi, while he was transmitting, and his capture led to those of organizers of the radio station, Enrico Bossi and Italo Piccagli. Other intelligence groups filled the gap and the Allies remained well informed of German intentions. The CLN in Florence was also well organized and ready to take over the administration as soon as the Germans and local Fascists departed: a unified military structure had been established under Colonel Nello Niccoli. There were, however, differences concerning tactics since many Florentines were opposed to the idea of an uprising which might damage the city's infrastructure and wanted an agreement with the Germans to withdraw peaceably. The partisans were also constrained in what they could do by a shortage of weapons. An arms drop on 14 February had yielded a small supply of weapons which was largely lost a few days later when an informer notified the local Fascists of the location of the arms dump. The approximately 3,000 male and female partisans had only about 1,000 pistols, 1,000 grenades, 900 shotguns, and fifty automatic rifles. The CLN divided the city into four sections with independent partisan commands and tasks for each. The task of the Florentine partisans was to break down the coordinated German defences sufficiently to enable the partisan units outside the city to enter it. These were split into two forces: 1,600 men in the Garibaldi Arno Division led by Aligi Barducci, and 1,000 men of the Action Party's Rosselli Brigade.

In June the Germans took the first steps to prepare for Florence's defence. The gas supply was cut off on 10 June, and four days later a warning to hoard water was issued. The German forces, which were commanded by Colonel Fuchs, had armoured cars and tanks. But the local Fascists were getting jittery and on 7 July the Fascist hierarchy led by Mario Carità left Florence and the CLN began to take over the administration. Fascist nerves had been shattered by the liberation of Siena, forty-five miles south of Florence, on 5 July, which had been witnessed by Stuart Hood, an escaped British POW:

> One morning, before dawn, there was a scuffling noise of feet in the street. I looked out and saw the German rearguards falling back through the town, deliberate, unhurrying, dragging their light anti-tank guns behind them. For half an hour or more, the town lay in the greying light, silent and empty. Quiet figures in long grey cloaks began to slip along the walls. They were almost indistinguishable from those that had preceded them.

French troops had entered the city, remained long enough to mark the liberation with a parade, before departing towards Florence. There followed a lull before Florence became the centre of attention.

By the end of July the Allies were only ten miles from Florence. The Germans were aware that the Allies needed the bridges across the Arno to reach the centre of the city and on the afternoon of 29 July posters appeared ordering the population south of the river, 150,000 people, to be evacuated. This process was begun on the following day when the electricity and water supplies were also cut off. The bridges were mined and efforts by the partisans to defuse the explosives failed. On the night of 3–4 August the Germans blew up five of the six bridges crossing the Arno: the medieval Ponte Santa Trinita was blown up but the Ponte Vecchio was spared. Florence was now effectively split into two with 780 partisans in the southern section and 2,000 in the city centre north of the Arno. At dawn on 4 August, Allied advance units, British and Canadian, entered the southern suburbs of Florence.

At this point the partisans made a very useful discovery. Communication between the two banks of the Arno was possible by using the secret corridor built by the Medicis above the Ponte Vecchio. This ran from the Palazzo Vecchio on the north bank, which was Fuchs's headquarters, to the Pitti Palace on the south bank. The local partisan commander, Enrico Fischer of the Action Party, managed to enter the heavily guarded Palazzo Vecchio and crawled along the corridor. The bridge had been severely damaged by nearby explosions and it was mined at both sides and under close observation by Fascist snipers. Fischer reached Major Charles Macintosh, the Allied SOE officer with the advance party, and presented him with intelligence on German dispositions on the north bank. The corridor was deemed too weak to permit the passage of troops, but a telephone line was run through it to facilitate communication between the partisans in the city and the Allies to the south. Macintosh in his turn revealed Allied plans for pincer movements on either side of Florence to persuade the Germans to evacuate the city. At the same time the partisans would rise up.

During the night of 10–11 August the Germans withdrew from the city centre. At dawn on the 11th the bells at the Palazzo Vecchio began to toll as the signal for the uprising. For two days the partisans took on the Germans alone. They were bolstered by the arrival of the partisans from outside the city who crossed the Arno at the Santa Rosa fish weir. The partisans suffered heavy casualties and were soon running out of ammunition and being pushed back by the Germans, who advanced back into the city centre as far as Via Cavour near the Duomo. Early on 13 August more Allied units crossed the Arno and drove the Germans back, and for the next two weeks the Allies and partisans fought side by side, under

German bombardment from Fiesole and other hill towns. By 27 August Allied pressure on the German lines led to the retreat of German artillery and by 2 September all fighting in Florence and its suburbs had ceased. The partisans had lost a total of 205 dead and 400 wounded. The partisan contribution was honoured by a ceremony on 7 September in the courtyard of the Fortezza da Basso overseen by the chief of the Allied Military Government (AMG) for the 5th Army, the American General Edgar Hume.

Hume's role became complicated. An OSS Research and Analysis Branch report written a few weeks later outlined the problem:

> When the Allied armies arrived in Florence they encountered, for the first time in a major Italian city, a nearly complete administrative organisation established by determined and purposeful anti-Fascist forces. A provisional system, worked out to the last detail, already was functioning as an unchallenged de facto authority under the auspices of the Tuscan Committee of National Liberation, which regards itself as the legitimate representative of the Italian Government and aspires to Allied recognition as such.

The CLN appointed a socialist, Gaetano Pieraccini, as mayor but the AMG had its own list of appointees. A compromise solution was quickly found whereby Pieraccini would work closely with the Allied-appointed representative for Florence, Colonel R. S. Rolph. The independent stance presented by the Florentine CLN did, however, fuel fears within Allied ranks and in the Italian government in Rome regarding the prospects for controlling the process of liberating northern Italy, especially the major cities of Turin, Milan, and Genoa.[41]

On 25 August the Allies launched their attack on the Gothic Line and simultaneously the partisans attacked the Germans from the rear. The Allies had not coordinated their plans with the partisans, so the partisan leaders were left in the dark as to how best to support them. The Gothic Line was breached but not broken by this offensive. Rimini was liberated on 21 September but then the autumn rains and increased German resistance slowed the pace of the Allied advance. At the end of October the Allies had reached Forlì, nearly halfway between Rimini and Bologna, but it had become increasingly clear that the Allies would have to halt for the winter before renewing the offensive in the spring once the ground had dried out.

Obeying Allied orders had come at a high price for the partisans, most notably in the area of Monte Sole which was a 2,000-feet-high mountain near Marzabotto, about fifteen miles south of Bologna. Monte Sole was home to a 1,000-strong partisan unit, the Stella Rossa Brigade, led by Mario Musolesi ('Lupo') and Gianni Rossi. The brigade had been poorly armed until an OSS agent arrived to arrange airdrops of supplies. In the middle of

August, when the front line had moved northwards and ran along the hills of Pistoia, it was possible to walk from Monte Sole to the front line within a few hours. The extremely high German presence so close to the front line meant, however, that the partisans were in considerable danger. They realized their vulnerability and wanted to move away from the mountain, but they received Allied orders to remain there and to split into small groups of thirty to forty men. On 29 September the partisans' worst fears were realized when, with the Allied front line stalled, the Germans turned their attention to Monte Sole and attacked in force. The partisans dispersed under the concerted attack mounted by the SS. Rossi and a few partisans reached the British lines, where they were treated with suspicion and their priceless intimate knowledge of the terrain was ignored: the Americans proved more welcoming. The partisans lost around two-thirds of their strength during their flight, but the full wrath of the Germans fell on the innocent civilians, with over 700 being killed in the region of Monte Sole and Marzabotto. During September the Germans, assisted by the *Brigate Nere*, attacked partisan units around Bologna, in the Veneto, and on the Isonzo. They were then free to dissolve the republics established in Ossopo and Carnia.[42]

The failure of the Allies to reach Bologna before winter set in presented the partisans with a major problem: 'We will have to face another winter, and the prospect is not a happy one. The partisans cannot remain in the mountains, where the snow makes every movement impossible, and getting provisions becomes more and more difficult.'[43] Decisions would have to be taken by the Allied high command, the Italian government in Rome, the CLNAI in the north, and by the partisans themselves on how best to survive the lull in Allied operations while preparing for the renewed advance and liberation of northern Italy in the spring.

Soviet military operations during the first half of 1944 had forced the German armies in the south and north part of the Eastern Front to withdraw and had resulted in the liberation of the majority of Soviet territory. The exception was the large salient in Belorussia jutting out into Soviet territory, which was held by Army Group Centre. By June 1944 this force consisted of sixty-three divisions and three brigades, a total of 1,200,000 men supported by 800 tanks, 9,500 artillery guns, and over 1,000 aircraft. Operation Bagration was designed by the Soviet military command to destroy this army. The Soviets concentrated 166 divisions and twelve corps, totalling 2,400,000 men, equipped with 5,200 tanks, 36,400 artillery guns and mortars, and over 5,000 aircraft. The partisans worked with the Soviet forces and by the summer of 1944 they numbered around 143,000 men who were organized into 150 brigades and forty-seven detachments. The terrain was eminently suitable for partisan warfare. The swampy Pripet Marshes contained many rivers which needed to be crossed, and the marshes also forced the railways to pass through a few nodal points that could be interdicted by the partisans.[44]

On 8 June the Belorussian partisan command issued orders for the 'rail war' to commence on 19 June. This was three days before the launch of Operation Bagration on 22 June, the third anniversary of the German invasion of the Soviet Union. Soviet accounts of the partisan actions refer to 40,000 separate demolitions of railways; German accounts reduce the figure to around 10,500. Whichever figure is correct the result is indisputable. All dual-track railways were forced to a standstill for at least twenty-four hours, and movement along single-track railways was curtailed for forty-eight hours. The main targets were the railways running to the front lines: from Pinsk to Luninets; Borisov to Orsha; and Molodechno to Polotsk. Furthermore, the lateral lines were hit too, preventing the Germans from rushing reinforcements from one sector of the front to another. The partisans also worked closely with the advance units of the Red Army and they particularly served military operations by seizing river crossings. For example, on 17 June the partisans under A. Scliarenko seized and held a vital crossing over the Berezina river until the arrival of the Soviet 35th Guards Tank Brigade. The Soviet 48th Guards Rifle Division was assisted in crossing the Ptich river south of Glusk and near Berezovka by the partisans seizing and holding the crossings for it. Thereafter the partisans continued to work as guides for the advanced units and also to mop up detached and encircled German units left behind during the German retreat. Army Group Centre had totally collapsed, having lost twenty-eight divisions, a total of 350,000 men.

The role of the Soviet partisans was now at an end and this was duly marked by ceremonies before the official disbandment of partisan units in accordance with a Partisan Central Staff decree of 3 November 1943. On 16 July 1944, for example, a parade of thousands of partisans from thirty units took place in recently liberated Minsk and received tributes from the partisan commander, Panteleimon Ponomarenko, and political representatives. One participant, Hersh Smolar, described the parade: 'None of us had ever seen a parade like this before. Brigade after brigade. Men in part-civilian and part-military clothing, carrying the most diverse kind of weapons, some of them "hand-made" with partisan inventiveness.' Of the demobilized partisans, around 92,000 were despatched to serve in regular Red Army units, and a further 48,000 were appointed to administrative posts in the Soviet administration and party organizations.[45]

The Red Army front now moved into territory where Soviet authority was disputed. The efforts of the UPA (*Ukrains'ka Povstans'ka Armiia*) to obtain independence for the Ukraine against any challengers, Soviet, Polish, or German, have already been detailed in earlier chapters. These efforts continued, and the Red Army was forced to keep one cavalry and two motorcycle regiments in the rear, supported by thousands of NKVD troops, to fight the UPA in a war which continued in the Ukrainian forests until 1947. The Belorussian politicians who had spent years swinging between support for the Germans and support for the Soviets, always with the aim of ensuring Belorussian independence, called together a convention of 1,039 delegates in Minsk on 27 June. The convention unanimously reasserted the declaration of Belorussian independence of 25 March 1918 and declared itself 'the only legitimate representative of the Belorussian nation at the present time'. The thunder of guns from the front could already be heard even as the convention was meeting and two days later those Belorussian politicians desiring independence fled Minsk towards Vilna and on into permanent exile. Some Lithuanian officers refused to flee and formed partisan units in the forests to fight the Soviet occupation. Further north, both the Estonians and Latvians also reasserted demands for the independence of their countries. The Estonian committee formed a provisional government on 18 September. Four days later, the Soviet forces entered the capital Tallinn, and the members of the provisional government fled to Sweden. Latvia was split in two by the Soviet breakthrough to the Baltic near Tukums, only twenty-five miles from Riga, on 30 July. German determination to hold the region meant, however, that Riga was only liberated on 13 October, and German forces were bottled up in the Courland region and only surrendered at the very end of the war in May 1945.[46]

The Poles faced the unenviable dilemma of having to deal with two enemies at the same time. The German occupation had been brutal from the outset and this brutality increased once the German retreat from the east began. On 28 June the Higher SS and Police Leader East issued the following order:

> The security situation in the General Government has deteriorated so much during the recent months that the most radical means and the most severe measures must now be employed against these alien assassins and saboteurs. The Reichsführer SS in agreement with the Governor General, has given the order that in every case of assassination or attempted assassination of Germans, not only the perpetrators shall be shot when caught, but that in addition, all their male relatives shall also be executed, and their female relatives above the age of sixteen put into a concentration camp.[47]

The efforts of the AK to assist the Soviet advance, for example, during the liberation of Kowel, had led to disaster when the Soviets then disarmed and arrested the AK partisans.

Yet the AK in eastern Poland continued to fight the Germans. At the end of June, the Red Army was approaching the city of Vilna, and the AK formation of 10,000 men commanded by Lieutenant Colonel Aleksander Krzyżanowski decided to attack the German garrison first, in the name of the Polish government-in-exile. On 7 July the battle opened with the AK attacking Vilna from four directions and receiving artillery, tank, and air support from the Soviets. On 13 July the German defenders surrendered to the AK and for two days the Polish flag flew in the city. Then, however, General Ivan Tchernyakhovski, commander of the Soviet 3rd Belorussian Front, demanded that the AK should form an infantry battalion and a cavalry brigade from its troops and fight alongside the Soviet forces. The Poles refused and on 17 July the NKVD arrested Krzyżanowski and seventy of his officers and sent them to Siberia.[48]

The pattern was repeated during the liberation of Lwów, the largest city in south-east Poland. On 17 July, as Soviet forces advanced into the suburbs, 3,000 poorly armed AK soldiers commanded by Colonel Władysław Filipkowski attacked the German garrisons, which began to withdraw their men from the city. Filipkowski set up his headquarters in Lwów and sent a message to the Soviet headquarters informing it of the liberation of the city. Filipkowski then received an invitation for talks with General Ivanov, representing General Koniev, the commander of the Soviet 1st Ukrainian Front, and with the NKVD General Gruczko. He was thanked for his cooperation with the Red Army, informed that Lwów was no longer a Polish city, and that his units should be disbanded and incorporated into the 1st Polish Army. Further talks were held on 31 July and Filipkowski and his staff were flown to Zhitomir, ostensibly to discuss the future of the AK units. In fact, they were arrested and imprisoned, never to return to Poland. Back in Lwów, the Soviets acted promptly to counter the reassertion of Polish governance by arresting the local government delegate loyal to the government-in-exile, Professor Adam Ostrowski, together with everyone at the AK headquarters. Tadeusz Bór-Komorowski was appalled by the news from Lwów that 'the prison at Lacki Street is packed full of men from the Home Army'. At the end of July he acknowledged that Operation Burza, the Polish underground's uprising in eastern Poland, had been a military success but a total political failure. He ordered the disbandment of all AK units east of the Bug, specifically ordered the men to join the ranks of the 1st Polish Army, and expressly forbade the formation of any anti-Soviet partisan units.[49] The head of the NKVD, Lavrenti Beria, informed Stalin in mid-July that he had despatched 12,000 NKVD troops to capture the remaining AK partisans in the forests, and by 20 July 6,000 AK partisans, including 650 officers, had been arrested by the Soviets.[50]

The Polish prime minister of the government-in-exile, Stanisław Mikołajczyk, kept Churchill informed of the conduct of the Soviet authorities towards the AK in eastern Poland and asked him to intervene on behalf of the Poles. Churchill, however, dismissed Polish concerns and was convinced that the Soviets would be more favourably disposed towards the Poles once they had crossed the Bug into the undisputed territory of Poland.[51] The first major city in the line of the Soviet advance in Poland west of the Bug was Lublin and this would prove a test case of the Soviet attitude towards the AK and Underground Government. The Germans withdrew from Lublin between 23 and 25 July and the local government delegate, Władysław Cholewa, set up a new administration in the town hall in the name of the Polish government. The AK also opened a recruiting office for a Lublin battalion. The authority of those loyal to the government-in-exile was immediately challenged, not by the Soviets, but by their puppets the PKWN (*Polski Komitet Wyzwolenia Narodowego*, Polish Committee of National Liberation) or Lublin Committee. The PKWN delegation led by Edward Ochab arrived in Lublin, followed by units of the 1st Polish Army, held a parade in the city, and approached Cholewa and the Lublin AK commander, Colonel Kazimierz Tumidajski, for talks. The latter two men denied that the PKWN had any legitimacy but stated that they were ready to talk directly to the Soviets. During the Soviet-Polish talks on 27 July the AK was faced with the same choice as that of its comrades east of the Bug: disband and disarm, join the 1st Polish Army, or be arrested. The same formula was offered elsewhere, and where the AK resisted disbandment, such as in Zamość, Białystok, Przemyśl, and Rzeszów, the officers were despatched to the Soviet Union and their men filled the recently vacated German concentration camps, especially Majdanek. By the beginning of October over 21,000 AK soldiers had been arrested and many more had fled westwards.[52]

By the middle of July it was clear that the German army on the Eastern Front was a broken force. The route of their retreat took them through Warsaw, where the inhabitants noted:

> They were no longer soldiers but moving human tatters: exhausted, horrified, inert, in a state of visible physical and moral decline. Perspiring, emaciated, covered in mud . . . They wore long beards and had dispirited faces and sunken eyes.

On 24 July German civilians were advised to evacuate to Łódź and the *Volksdeutsche* began to sell their belongings to the Poles. The Germans ordered the dismantlement of large factories: the Polish Underground Government issued counter-orders to the Poles to sabotage this process and engage in counter-scorch. Although the German administration was clearly moving out of the city the German mayor, Ludwig Leist, refused to formally hand over the keys to Warsaw to the Polish mayor, Julian Kulski.[53] The Soviet advance had reached the line of the Vistula, with bridgeheads established at Puławy and Magnuszew, south of Warsaw. It appeared that the Soviet forces were ready to advance on the Polish capital. Accordingly, the leadership of the AK met in Warsaw and the principal question in their minds was, should an uprising be launched in the city?

27
Uprisings: Warsaw, Paris, Slovakia

Early in the war, British strategy for the resistance in Europe had been based around encouraging the build-up of secret armies which would rise up at an opportune moment. This strategy changed in 1941 after the Soviet Union and the United States had entered the war against Germany, because the liberation of Europe could now be undertaken better by the mass armies of the Allies. Plans for the resistance as a whole now became more focused on sabotage, while the role of resistance armies was downgraded to assisting the Allies during ground operations in their vicinity. But Allied strategists completely failed to understand the emotions of those in occupied Europe, and the desire for each resistance movement to take a notable part in the liberation of its own country. The government-delegate in Poland, Jan Jankowski, expressed this clearly:

> We wanted to show the world that although we wanted to have an independent Poland, we were not prepared to accept this gift of freedom from anyone if it meant accepting conditions contrary to the interests, traditions and dignity of our nation ... We wanted to be free and to owe this freedom to nobody but ourselves.[1]

This need for autonomous action is most clearly understandable in the case of Poland, a country which had disappeared from the map for over a century before being reborn in 1918, and one which had a long history of uprisings against occupiers. Yet the Parisians felt the same, perhaps because the experiences of the French Revolution and the 1870–71 Paris Commune had shown them too that, given sufficient fervour, a people could take their destiny into their own hands. The case of Slovakia was slightly different. In this case the events of the late summer of 1944 can be characterized as more of a mutiny by a portion of Slovakia's armed forces and less as a general uprising of the Slovak people. The overriding motivation of all the resisters in the three uprisings was the same: the restoration of their country's significance and honour.

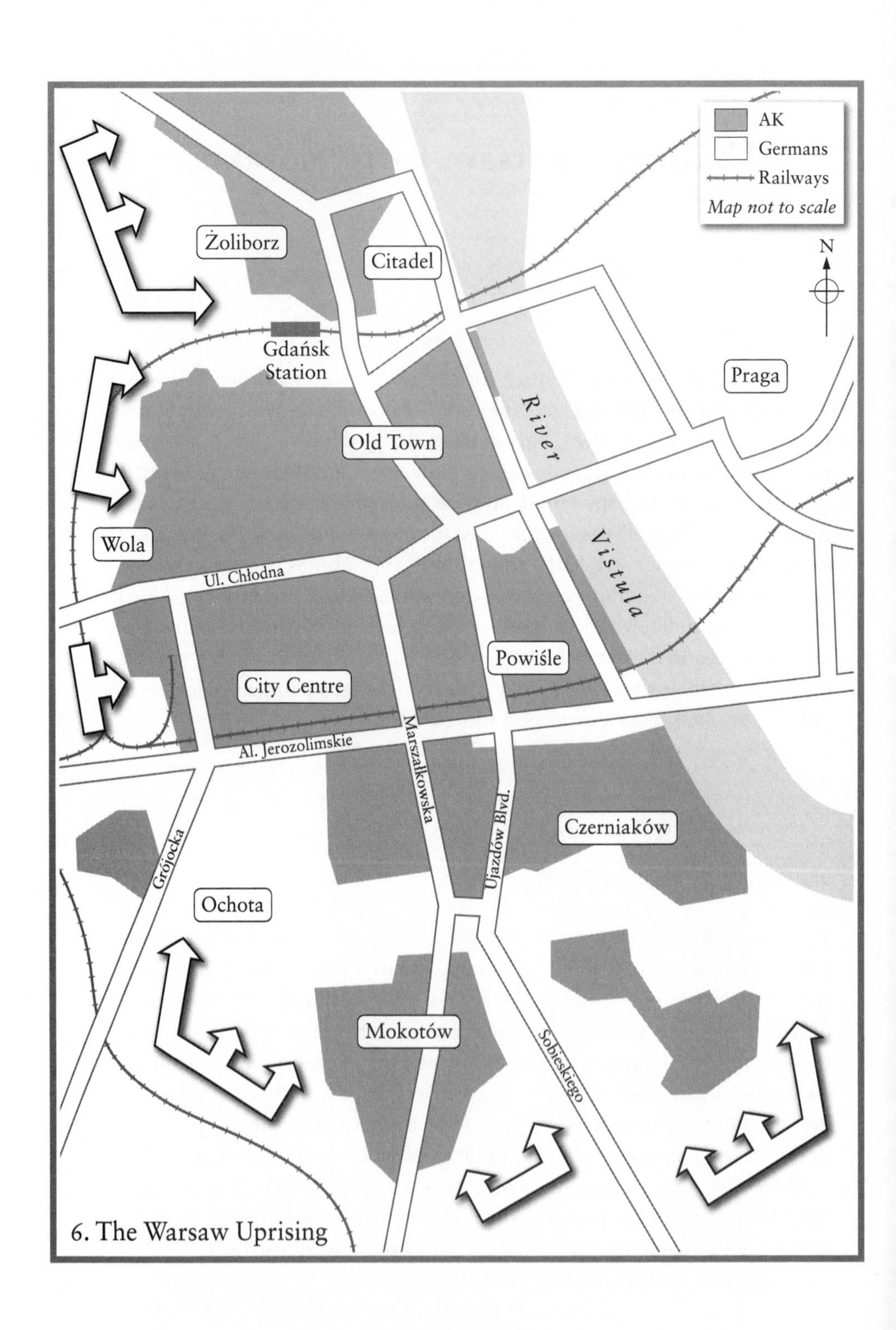

6. The Warsaw Uprising

The importance of the uprisings as part of the struggle for national liberation is demonstrated by the fact that both the Warsaw and the Paris uprisings were caught on film shot at the time by the participants. The Information and Propaganda branch of the AK organized the filming of the Warsaw Uprising and shot 122 reels of film, which then remained hidden in the ruins of Warsaw until 1946. These were assembled into one partial film first shown in 1956. A fuller and more chronologically accurate 85-minute-long version was released as *Powstanie Warszawskie* in 2014. In Paris, the Comité de Libération du Cinéma Français produced a hastily edited film, *La Libération de Paris*, from footage shot during the insurrection. This 32-minute-long film was made public as early as 29 August 1944.

The Warsaw Uprising was launched on 1 August 1944 on the basis of a number of fundamental misconceptions held by its instigator, the AK commander, Tadeusz Bór-Komorowski, and by the man responsible for AK operations in Warsaw, Antoni Chruściel. The first misconception was that the Germans were a beaten force. This impression was gained from the sight of the bedraggled and apparently disorganized German troops retreating through the streets of Warsaw. On 24 July the German governor of Warsaw, Ludwig Fischer, ordered the evacuation of the German civilian administration to Łódź. Two days later he reversed this decision and the Germans returned in strength to Warsaw, but these returning Germans appeared powerless. On 27 July, Fischer issued an order for 100,000 men and women to work on building defences, and the AK issued a counter-order for people to remain at home which was widely obeyed. The very fact that the Germans did not respond to this demonstration of mass disobedience was seen as further evidence that German control was faltering and that an uprising could succeed. The AK lacked knowledge of the heavy fighting taking place around the Soviet bridgeheads on the Vistula at Puławy and Magnuszew. The Germans were rushing reinforcements to the threatened areas but were at the same time encircling Warsaw in a ring of steel. These movements out of the city enhanced the impression of German disorder but they also stalled the Soviet advance. Even if the front-line Germans were to retreat again, the SS and other German-controlled anti-partisan forces were still present in the region in strength, and were prepared to unleash against the Warsaw insurgents a campaign of hitherto unprecedented violence in an urban environment.[2]

Another misconception of the AK leadership was that the insurrection only needed to last for a week before help would be received from outside. This help was expected to come from two sources: the Polish armed forces in Britain, and the Soviets. The government-in-exile had left Bór-Komorowski in the dark regarding the status of the Polish armed forces operating under the command of the western Allies. The Polish Parachute Brigade had been formed under Stanisław Sosabowski with the express purpose of being sent to Poland to assist in the national uprising. The Polish general staff in London had expended much energy in developing plans for transporting the parachute brigade to Poland, but these were totally unrealistic.* After heated negotiations between the Poles and the British from March to May 1944 the Polish Parachute Brigade was put totally at the disposal of the British and was no longer an independent force. The Polish Air Force stationed in Italy was similarly under British command. It was not detailed to focus solely on supplying the AK but also tasked with dropping supplies to partisans in Yugoslavia, Italy, and France. The AK leadership only learned of these facts when Jan Nowak, a courier between Poland and London, returned to Warsaw on 29 July.[3]

The AK also failed to understand the attitude and movements of the Soviets. Operation Burza, the national uprising in eastern Poland launched in November 1943, had shown that the Soviets were hostile to the AK. The situation deteriorated further when the Soviets set up their Polish communist 'Lublin Committee', which purported to be the administrating body of liberated Polish territory. Such threats increased the determination of the AK leadership to liberate the Polish capital in the name of the Polish government-in-exile. Yet not all the members of that government supported this decision. The Polish commander-in-chief, General Sosnkowski, counselled against an uprising, principally on political grounds. For example, on 28 July he telegraphed Bór-Komorowski: 'In present conditions, I am categorically opposed to a general uprising . . . Your appraisal of the situation must be sober and realistic. A mistake would be enormously expensive. It is essential to concentrate all forces, political, moral and physical, to prevent Moscow's annexation designs.'[4] But Sosnkowski did not expressly forbid an uprising in Warsaw. Nor at the crucial time was he available to give orders in light of the rapidly changing circumstances: at the end of July he was visiting the Polish troops in Italy and refusing all calls from his government to return to London.[5]

The AK leadership had no knowledge of whether the Soviets intended to take Warsaw or whether they were planning to bypass the city on either side, leaving the German garrison isolated but besieged. On 29 July they considered an important intelligence report from Janusz Bokszczanin:

* Such an airlift would have required 125 Stirlings or over 200 Halifaxes, or 265 modified Liberators, resources that the Allies simply could not spare without seriously damaging the strategic bombing offensive against Germany.

> Soviet artillery fire is so far only intermittent and light. It does not seem to be an artillery preparation for a general forced crossing of the Vistula and an attack on the city ... Until the Soviet army shows clear intention of attacking the city, we should not start operations. The appearance of some Soviet detachments on the outskirts of Praga does not signify anything. They may simply be reconnaissance patrols.

Further meetings on 31 July revealed splits within the leadership. Both the man who was to command the uprising, Chruściel, and the AK head of intelligence, Kazimierz Iranek-Osmecki, opposed launching the insurrection immediately because of concerns regarding the future path of Soviet operations and the supply situation. Opposing them and strongly in favour of the uprising was General Leopold Okulicki, a former prisoner of the NKVD who had been released under the terms of the Sikorski–Maisky Pact and had parachuted into Poland. His hatred of the Soviets knew no bounds and he was determined to risk all in the assertion of Polish independence. Both Bór-Komorowski and his chief of staff General Tadeusz Pełczyński were undecided. That afternoon, however, Bór-Komorowski and Jankowski came down in favour of launching the uprising. Unanimity was achieved on the receipt of a piece of inaccurate intelligence received by Chruściel in the late afternoon: Soviet tanks had been seen entering Praga, the eastern suburb of Warsaw on the opposite bank of the Vistula. The final decision was taken for the uprising to start at 5 p.m. on 1 August. The starting time was selected because: 'The traffic in the city was at its heaviest, with people returning home from work. It would then be less difficult to conceal units moving to their appointed places in the hurrying crowd of workers coming out of offices and factories.'[6]

The AK did understand that the uprising could only last for a short time because of the dire shortage of weapons and equipment. Between February 1941 and June 1944 the whole of Poland had received only 305 tons of war materiel. (In contrast the Yugoslav Partisans had received over 3,400 tons during the same period.) On 1 August it was estimated that there were 50,700 members of the AK in Warsaw. But on the same day it was also estimated that the weapons at the disposal of the AK consisted of only 1,000 rifles, 300 pistols, sixty light machine guns, seven heavy machine guns, thirty-five special carbines and bazookas, 1,200 revolvers, and 25,000 hand grenades. Ammunition was also in short supply with 190 bullets per rifle, 500 rounds per light machine gun, and 2,300 rounds per heavy machine gun. Therefore, it can be safely assumed that only between one-tenth and one-sixth of the fighters could be armed and none could fight a protracted battle. The AK was dependent on supplies arriving from outside, either from the Soviets who controlled six airfields in Poland, including Dęblin which was 118 kilometres from Warsaw, or the western Allies who would have to fly over 1,312 kilometres from Brindisi in Italy to Warsaw.

The dearth of weapons in Warsaw was due to the fact that the city itself was not included in the plans for the early stages of a national uprising. Indeed, in early July 9,000 sub-machine guns had been sent out of the city to AK units fighting further east. Sheer bad luck had also played a part. In the spring the Germans had located two large arms caches: one had contained 70,000 hand grenades and the other had included 450 flamethrowers. Two major arms caches were situated in Praga and since the uprising failed there, their contents were inaccessible to the AK. There were other arms caches scattered throughout the city and its suburbs but the location of many of these had been lost when the men responsible for them had fallen into German hands, carrying their secrets with them. For example, one arsenal containing 678 Stens and 60,000 rounds of ammunition was 'so jealously guarded by its quartermaster' that he refused to relinquish it to AK fighters who were not known to him: it was only emptied in 1947. Another 'lost' cache was so large that when it was found in 1957 it took two weeks to empty. Thought had been given to securing adequate food supplies for the civilian population during the uprising, but the five food caches created ended up in areas never controlled by the AK. Food supplies in the city were in any event at an all-time low since the Germans had taken everything with them either to the front or further to their rear.[7]

Chruściel's plan of operations for the uprising included the capture of some symbolic targets to demonstrate the resurgence of Polish nationhood in the capital, and also seizing major portions of the city on the west bank: Stare Miasto (the Old Town) and Śródmieście (the city centre); Powiśle; Żoliborz; Wola; Ochota; Mokotów; and Czerniaków, as well as Praga on the east bank, and, in particular, the bridges over the Vistula to pave the way for the Soviet advance. The plan was over-ambitious in the targets selected given the weak, poorly armed forces at Chruściel's disposal.

From the symbolic point of view the uprising was an immediate success. Men and women of the AK flooded to their posts wearing the red and white armband denoting their membership of the AK. Zbigniew Czajkowski felt somewhat bewildered:

> All of a sudden it occurs to me how strange it is to see a Polish soldier on the streets of Warsaw. It feels awkward: here I am, in broad daylight, with a red and white arm band, openly carrying a weapon. The days of Conspiracy are now a distant memory.[8]

A propaganda victory was scored when the Poles occupied the tallest building in Warsaw, belonging to the Prudential Insurance Company, and hung a large Polish flag on it which could be seen across the city. A degree of control was quickly established in most areas with the exception of Praga, where the Germans were concentrated in strength since it lay on the route to the front line against the Soviets.[9]

Various successes and failures were noted across the city by the AK in the first few days. The insurgents had captured a number of buildings such as the Labour Office, the Appellate Court, the former Czech Embassy, and vitally, the power station in Powiśle. The AK had also succeeded in attacking the Waffen-SS supply depots at Stawki, which yielded vast quantities of food, uniforms, and equipment but no weapons.[10] Varying degrees of Polish control had been established in the Old Town, city centre, the areas along the riverbank of Powiśle and Czerników, as well as Ochota and Wola. Units in Żoliborz and Mokotów had been beaten back and forced to retreat, temporarily, to the nearby forests. But the AK had failed to take control of the bridges over the Vistula, and numerous assaults against actual German strongholds across the city failed with heavy losses. Virtually suicidal attacks on Okęcie and Bielany airports failed at high cost. Importantly, German communications continued unhindered as the AK attack on the central telephone exchange in Pius Street was unsuccessful. The AK then besieged the exchange for twenty days before the Germans inside surrendered: 'Disarmed, helmetless, unbuttoned and unbelted they almost looked like civilians. They no longer had their hands up, and they walked normally.'[11] Photographs were taken of the AK fair treatment of German prisoners and given to the Germans both to show them that they could surrender safely and to encourage them to reciprocate in their conduct towards AK prisoners. In the first few days the Poles lost around 10 per cent of their forces, wounded or killed, while the Germans suffered 500 casualties. The Germans had been caught by surprise and the German commander of the Warsaw garrison, Luftwaffe Lieutenant General Reiner Stahel, had been trapped in his headquarters by the fighting for a number of hours.

The ranks of the AK insurgents were bolstered by cooperation with other armed units. The GL/AL, which had about 400 poorly armed men in the city, put itself operationally under the AK command but fought separately. Around 1,000 Jews who had been in hiding in the city also joined in the fight. Two platoons of ŻOB fought, one with the AK and the other with the AL. The AK liberated 348 Jews from a German prison, and of these 130 were strong enough to join in the insurgency. There were various other nationalities also present in Warsaw: Italians who had deserted the Germans; escaped Soviet POWs; Hungarians; Slovaks; and a Frenchman. John Ward, an escaped British POW, had joined the AK and during the uprising would telegraph reports about it to London. Once the Air Ministry had verified his identity, he was invited to submit daily bulletins on the fighting to *The Times*.[12]

The initial response of the civilian population was one of euphoria as the uprising erupted. Polish flags were hung from balconies, patriotic songs were sung everywhere, and precious medicines, blankets, and linen were distributed to the fighters. Czajkowski noted: 'Krasiński Square looks like a carnival. The sun is shining and there are crowds of people wandering about. Somebody has even set up carousels and swings. In the distance you can hear the echoes of gunfire.'[13] Andrew Borowiec wrote that life was quite ordinary in the city centre: 'We still had water, electricity and food. There were soup kitchens and regular distribution of flour, ersatz coffee and other foodstuffs normally controlled by the Germans. There were also outdoor cafes where insurgents could sip their make-believe caffeine while reading the latest *Biuletyn Informacyjny*.'[14] The civilians took part in a scheme of civil defence:

> In case of fire on the roofs or in attics, pails of water and sand were prepared and two voluntary wardens were continuously on duty. Trenches were dug, connecting buildings with one another so that one might walk considerable distances without emerging on the street. Directions, names of streets, and numbers of houses were clearly marked by inscriptions on the cellar walls.[15]

Civilians also helped in the construction of barricades: 'Children, adults, old people all want to help. They carry what they have, paving stones, bricks, tiles, wood, heavy furniture, a child's pram, stone and sandbags.'[16] But the optimism and support of the civilians were transitory, destined to change as a result of the German response to the uprising.

Hitler's first reaction when informed of the uprising was to issue an order to 'raze Warsaw completely' from the air using the Luftwaffe present on the Eastern Front. He was informed that this would cause an enormous number of German casualties because German military units and civilians could not be extracted from the city. Therefore, Himmler and General Heinz Guderian were ordered to smash the uprising and, 'upon stifling the uprising with all available means, Warsaw was to wiped from the face of the earth, all the inhabitants were to be killed, there were to be no prisoners'. No distinction was to be made between AK fighters and unarmed civilians. (In Sachsenhausen concentration camp the former head of the AK, General Rowecki, was executed.) Regular Wehrmacht units were concentrated around the city, guarding it from a Soviet attack and to prevent AK reinforcements from entering Warsaw from other areas. Within the city the Wehrmacht focused on keeping open the main thoroughfares to enable supplies to continue reaching their front line outside Warsaw. This meant that the actual crushing of the uprising was devolved to the SS and German police. A special SS brigade commanded by SS-Obersturmbahnführer Oskar Dirlewanger was rushed from East Prussia to Wola with the order to 'kill anyone you want, according to your desire'. The Dirlewanger brigade was mostly composed of recently released criminals. On the same day Himmler ordered the RONA brigade commanded by SS-General Kaminski to go to Warsaw from Częstochowa.[17] Placed in overall command of the forces to crush the uprising was the experienced anti-partisan commander General Bach-Zelewski.

The first German attack was in the suburb of Wola. This book has already noted a number of massacres carried out by the Germans, and there will be more, but none surpass the sheer scale of the Wola massacre of 40,000 people in just a few days in early August 1944. The operation was overseen by Bach-Zelewski's chief of operations, Gruppenführer Heinz Reinefarth. The Dirlewanger and Kaminski troops advanced street by street murdering every civilian they came across in their homes or driving them along the street towards selected execution sites: the tram depot on Młynarska Street; the macaroni factory at Wolska; the Franciszek and Ursus factories and several foundries; and the railway viaduct at Górczewska. The bodies of the executed were burned in improvised crematoria created in the cellars of buildings: the mausoleum in Sowiński Park in Wola now contains 1,120 kilograms of human ash collected from these crematoria. The Marie Curie Radium Institute was visited several times by the SS soldiers, who raped and murdered the patients and nurses alike, a fate shared by several hospitals in the area.[18]

After the war, Bach-Zelewski claimed that when he arrived in Wola he was sickened by the sight of the slaughter and called a halt to it. He later ordered the Kaminski brigade out of Warsaw at the end of August and the Germans themselves court-martialled Kaminski and executed him on 4 October. However, given his reputation for brutal anti-partisan operations, Bach-Zelewski's order to cease the massacre more probably stemmed from alarm at the 'unbelievable confusion [that] was reigning', since further actions under his orders show that he considered the AK as no different from the Soviet partisans.[19] The Germans began to use civilians, principally women, as living shields:

> With our backs turned to the insurgents we knelt or crouched and the Germans placed themselves on the ground behind us, or knelt on one knee,

> firing over our heads. Including two children there were twenty-three of us, and we were mostly young women. It lasted for two hours. Shots whistled over our heads. The noise of the Germans' rifles so close to our heads nearly deafened us. We were all trying to prepare ourselves to die and saying the Rosary aloud. But as if by some miracle, the incoming bullets only hit our enemy.[20]

Photographs exist showing groups of men and women tied to ladders held horizontally and forced to advance in front of German infantry, and women tied to German tanks. A nurse at an AK nursing station noted: 'The legs of these women were like sieves, full of holes.'[21]

The arrival of traumatized survivors from Wola into the Old Town contributed to a plummeting in civilian morale. Food and water supplies were running very low and the population was forced into a troglodyte existence in cellars. In the skies above, the German Stuka dive bombers flew unmolested by the Soviet aircraft which had been seen over Warsaw earlier in the summer:

> I watch the aeroplanes circling over the rooftops looking for a target. Then, one after another, they climb into the sky before diving onto their chosen objective. Once above a building they release a long bomb, then with a shriek of engines, climb back into the sky . . . The aeroplanes return, having circled around for a while, this time dropping two smaller bombs. Again the ground heaves and more smoke rises above the unfortunate buildings. Even so, that is not enough for those bastards. They circle around for a third time, then they open up with their machine guns.[22]

The air raids came about every forty-five minutes, and artillery bombardments also grew in frequency and intensity. Irena Orska, an AK nurse, was caught in an air raid and forced into a shelter in a cinema where she was appalled to be berated by the crowd, and noted sadly:

> The very people who had hailed the soldiers of the Home Army in the first days of fighting, who had brought to the posts their meagre provisions, their linen, their scanty medicines and their hot tears of wild joy, these same people began to waver at the spectre of loathsome death in their loyalty to the cause they had believed in so fervently.[23]

The AK leadership was well aware of the drop in civilian morale and painfully aware that the uprising which was only supposed to last a week had become disturbingly protracted with no sign of Soviet engagement. If the uprising was to continue then there was an urgent need for supplies to arrive in quantity from outside. In a telegram on 6 August, Bór-Komorowski stated: 'We are not asking for help – we are demanding that it be granted immediately.'[24]

The Allied governments were under no obligation to make airdrops to Warsaw: after all, they had repeatedly warned the Polish government-in-exile that such operations carried impossibly high risks. Nevertheless, as soon as news of the uprising reached London, the Polish ambassador, Edward Raczyński, requested the British government to do all that it could to assist the insurgents. Churchill was in favour of sending support, and requests were sent to the Brindisi air base in Italy to start making airdrops over Warsaw. Air Marshal Sir Jack Slessor, deputy air commander for the Mediterranean area, later explained the difficulties:

> It was one thing to drop supplies to pre-arranged dropping-zones marked by light signals in open country . . . It was quite another to bring a big aircraft down to a thousand feet . . . over a great city, itself the scene of a desperate battle and consequently a mass of fires and flashes from guns and bursting shells . . . and ringed by light AA weapons.

Southern Italy was in the throes of bad weather which prevented all long-distance flights: on 2 and 3 August and between 5 and 8 August no flights could be made to Poland.[25]

The statistics certainly bear out the difficulties faced by the brave air-crews making the hazardous flight to Warsaw. Between 4 August and 21 September a total of 199 aircraft took off from southern Italy, 94 Polish and 105 British and South African, but Warsaw itself only received thirty airdrops and the nearby Kampinos forest another twenty-eight. The difficulties in supplying Warsaw were immense. Flight Lieutenant Roman Chmiel described one sortie:

> Fires were blazing in every district of Warsaw. The dark spots were places occupied by the Jerries. Everything was smothered in smoke through which flickered ruddy, orange flames. I had never believed a big city could burn so. It was terrible: must have been hell for everybody down there.
>
> The German flak was the hottest I have ever been through, so we got down just as low as we could – 70 or a 100 feet above ground; it was really too low, but we had to get out of the line of fire . . . We nearly hit the Poniatowski Bridge as we cracked along the Vistula: the pilot hopped over it by the skin of his teeth . . . We dropped the containers and knew we had made a good job of it.
>
> It was time to clear out. The pilot came down a little lower, keeping an eye for steeples and high buildings. The cabin was full of smoke which got

> into our eyes and made them smart. We could feel the heat from the walls of the burnt-out district.[26]

Jan Nowak and John Ward witnessed a successful airdrop from a Polish plane but then: 'I could not help crying out in anguish at the explosion far away, beyond the city. In the flash when it was hit, for a split second we could see parts of the wings and the fuselage scattering in all directions.'[27] The cost of the Allied airdrops was high, and Slessor later estimated that one bomber was lost for every ton of supplies delivered. No. 1586 (Polish Special Duties) Flight alone lost sixteen crews in flights to Warsaw. The British also lost planes, and one landed on a Soviet-controlled airfield where the crew was interned by the Soviets until the British Embassy in Moscow intervened on their behalf.[28] The AK command sent orders out to the districts to give details concerning the fate of Allied aircrew. These reports would then be radioed back to London so that, ultimately, the British Air Ministry could inform the relatives of the airmen shot down.[29]

The airdrops had, however, provided the AK with 1,344 small arms, 3,855 machine pistols, 380 light machine guns, 237 bazookas, thirteen mortars, 130 rifles, around 14,000 hand grenades, and over 3,000 anti-tank grenades, over 4.5 million rounds of ammunition, eight and a half tons of plastic explosive, and forty-five tons of food. The AK managed to retrieve about 50 per cent of the canisters in the early airdrops but this percentage fell steadily once the Germans had gone on the offensive and the insurgent-held areas shrank.[30] It should also be noted that in addition the Germans needed resupply by air: one lucky AK unit was the recipient of a canister meant for the Germans and found that it contained half a pig, enough to feed the whole unit for a while.[31]

The Soviets were best placed to drop supplies into Warsaw but they refused to do so. Stalin's first argument was to deny that an uprising was taking place at all, and even when he accepted that the uprising was in progress he called it a 'reckless and fearful gamble'. Churchill sent frequent telegrams to Stalin imploring him to send supplies to Warsaw, and in Moscow the chief of staff of the British military mission was making almost daily visits to the Soviet Ministry of Defence to make the same request.[32] Churchill enlisted the support of Roosevelt, which he needed because Churchill wanted the American-Soviet agreement regarding shuttle bombing of Germany, Operation Frantic, to be used to assist Warsaw. On 15 August the deputy Soviet foreign minister Andrey Vyshinsky delivered a firm refusal to allow American bombers to land at the base at Poltava in the Ukraine if they had dropped supplies to Warsaw. Churchill and Roosevelt responded by sending a joint appeal to Stalin on 20 August but received another refusal from the Soviet leader two days later.[33] The deputy chief of the American military mission in Moscow, George Kennan, thought that the Allies should threaten to cut off aid to the Soviet Union if they did not help the Warsaw Uprising with airdrops or at least help the Allies make airdrops.[34]

Under continuing international pressure, Stalin finally relented. On the night of 13–14 September, six weeks after the start of the uprising, the first massive Soviet airdrop of supplies was made to Warsaw by 382 planes carrying a total of 29,000 kilos of food, 18,000 rounds of ammunition, and 1,200 grenades. These flights continued until 29 September. The Soviet airdrops were made from such a low level in order to improve accuracy that many parachutes did not open and the canisters often burst on hitting the ground, destroying their contents. For example, Janusz Zawodny witnessed the descent of a Soviet long-barrelled anti-tank rifle which bent into a pretzel when it hit the ground. Most of the ammunition dropped was of Soviet manufacture and did not fit the Polish weapons or those the Poles had seized from the Germans. It should have been possible for the Soviets to have sent German war materiel which they had captured, but only 350 German carbines were dropped.[35] Stalin also allowed the USAAF to mount one shuttle airdrop, on 18 September, but the USAAF dropped almost 1,300 canisters from such a great height that the parachutes carried them into German-held areas and the AK received only 388 of them.[36]

After the Germans regained control over the suburbs of Wola and Ochota they turned their attention to direct and sustained attacks on the AK positions in the Old Town. This was a six-centuries-old warren of narrow streets which was defended in strength by the AK simply because the Old Town overlooked the Kierbedź road bridge and the northern railway bridge, and holding both bridges would facilitate the Soviet entry into Warsaw. This outcome was precisely what the Germans wanted to avert and so, after probing attacks on 9 and 10 August, their assault began with 8,000 men supported by tanks and artillery. The narrow streets were, however, ideal for defence and the AK could keep the Germans at bay by sniper fire and Molotov cocktails. In response, from 17 to 23 August the Germans resorted to the use of air power to demolish the Old Town street by street: 'A sea of fire and bombs had swallowed up a square kilometre of ancient, dry-rotted buildings, packed with tens of thousands of people.'[37] An estimated 4,000 tons of shells fell on the Old Town that week. The Germans also used Goliaths, remote-controlled miniature tanks filled with explosives, to demolish barricades before their infantry advanced. By 21 August the AK forces in the Old Town had sustained around 2,000 casualties, which represented 30 per cent of their strength at the start of the uprising. Attempts to relieve the Old Town with the help of AK forces in the city centre and Żoliborz failed. On 13 August a booby-trapped German tank exploded in Kiliński Street, killing over 400 people, an incident which the AK fighter Jan Dobraczyński thought 'seemed to presage defeat in the Old Town. From that day there was a considerable increase in the number of victims. More and more graves appeared in the courtyards and on the grass.'[38] Morale plummeted and even the news of the liberation of Paris failed to lift the mood.

It was clear that the Old Town could not hold out against the German onslaught and plans were drawn up to evacuate. Priority was assigned to the AK fighters and the vast majority of civilians and wounded would be abandoned to their fate. Internal radio communications between AK units across the city were non-existent and radio traffic had to be passed through London. Therefore, the AK had, from the start of the uprising, been using the labyrinth of sewers to send messages by courier across the city. The sewers now became the principal evacuation route for the beleaguered fighters in the Old Town and not surprisingly, given the disgusting nature of the journey, the experience has remained in the minds of those who made the trip:

> With the aid of iron grips we slowly descended the narrow pipe of the deep well. The horrible nauseating smell overcame me at once and became worse with every downward step. At last I reached the bottom of the ladder and my feet and legs immediately plunged into the terrifying muddy substance. The stench was incredible . . . The lack of rain in the last few days made the greasy and muddy substance more solid so that wading through it was very tricky and slow. It was like trying to walk through a quagmire . . .[39]

The journey had to be made in silence so as not to attract the attention of the German soldiers above, who would lob grenades into the manholes if they heard anything suspicious. The AK in Powiśle stood by to receive the escapers: 'for three days and nights the sewers continued to spit out the mangled wrecks of men, women and children'.[40] For those who escaped through the sewers the experience of re-emerging into the open was disorienting:

> I'm completely blinded. It's so light! Somebody presses a cup of coffee into my hand. Someone else offers me a cigarette. I look around. Around me all the houses are standing upright! They even have glass in the windows! People are walking around without bothering to take cover behind walls. It feels very strange.[41]

Some people were evacuated to villages outside Warsaw where they were appalled to find that there was no sign of fighting: Warsaw was an isolated case.[42] About 5,000 insurgents were killed in the battle for the Old Town which ended on 2 September, and the Germans also suffered casualties to over half their force.[43] Shortly afterwards the area of Powiśle by the Vistula fell.

The Allies might have been incapable of supplying the AK with the weapons they so urgently needed, but the governments of Britain and the United States did have an important impact on the outcome of the uprising when, on 29 August, they issued separate but identically worded declarations granting combatant rights to the AK: 'The Polish Home Army, which is now mobilised, constitutes a combatant force forming an integral part of the Polish Armed Forces.'[44] On 9 September the British government issued another declaration regarding the civilian population of Warsaw, which effectively extended combatant rights to the civilians.[45]

These statements were of vital importance to Bór-Komorowski and Chruściel since they were aware that the AK was running out of the means to sustain the fight and was being detrimentally impacted by the dramatic fall in civilian morale. As Bór-Komorowski informed London on 6 September: 'The civilian population is undergoing a crisis, which could have a fundamental influence on the fighting units.' He had little idea of the overall progress of the war and asked London: 'Do you think that action in the west will bring about the end of the war within the next few days?'[46] On 6 September he and Jankowski sent a joint communiqué outlining the seriousness of the situation in Warsaw and the options facing the AK. They considered three options: the evacuation of the civilian population of the city with the agreement of the Germans after which the AK would 'fight to the end'; the unconditional surrender of the entire city; or to continue the battle and surrender each district in turn when overwhelmed by the German forces. The two men appeared to favour the last option: 'This solution would gain a little time, but at the same time destroy the whole city.'[47] They hoped that the time gained would enable further supplies to reach them through airdrops and for the Soviet forces to advance to their rescue.

At the same time as this telegram was despatched and before a reply could be received, talks between the Poles and Germans had opened on the possibilities of evacuating civilians from Warsaw. On the three days from 8 to 10 September there were brief ceasefires to allow for evacuations. The clandestine newspaper *Biuletyn Informacyjny* warned that, although the Polish Red Cross would supervise the evacuation, no one knew how the Germans would behave. On 9 September the Underground Government distributed leaflets explaining the events of the previous day and giving news of the evacuation, advising the sick, the old, and mothers with children to leave. It expected all the young men to remain in Warsaw to continue the fight. Estimates on the number of people who left the city at this time vary, but it can be assumed that between 20,000 and 25,000 people left.[48] On 10 September, General Günter Rohr, commanding the German forces in the southern part of Warsaw, invited Bór-Komorowski or his representatives to talks to discuss the terms for surrender. Bór-Komorowski set a number of conditions for a general surrender of Warsaw and informed London of his reasoning. He wished to delay the surrender because: 'Today there was a marked weakening of artillery fire and bombing of the enemy ... Combat aircraft over Warsaw and the sounds of fighting from the direction of Praga. If we hear more gunfire today we will try to continue fighting. Further airdrops daily will allow us to continue resistance.'[49]

When the uprising was launched at the start of August, the Soviet 1st Belorussian Front under General Konstantin Rokossovsky was not in a position to mount an all-out attack to take Warsaw since the bulk of its forces were still heavily engaged at the bridgeheads at Magnuszew and Puławy. Nevertheless, the Soviets could have given both artillery and air support to the insurgents. This opinion was held by a Soviet captain, Konstanty Kalugin, whose reasons for being in Warsaw are obscure and who was not in direct contact with Rokossovsky.* On 8 August, Rokossovsky informed Stalin that he would be in a position to attack Warsaw around 25 August, but Stalin did not respond. It suited his political purposes to allow the Germans to defeat the uprising and destroy the AK, since the AK was loyal to the Polish government-in-exile and was opposed to the 'Lublin Committee' which Stalin was sponsoring. Instead of attacking Warsaw the main Soviet effort was turned southwards towards the Balkans and it appeared that the 1st Belorussian Front was to remain on the defensive outside Warsaw.[50] Rokossovsky was permitted to undertake limited operations to secure the bridgeheads and as a result the momentum of the 1st Belorussian Front and 1st Polish Army carried them into Praga on 11 September. On 13 September the Germans blew the bridges in Warsaw joining the city to the east bank.

After the war, Rokossovsky defended his inaction after Praga had been

* Kalugin's messages were sent by the roundabout route of the AK command to Polish headquarters in London, to the British government, from the Foreign Office to the British Embassy in Moscow, and finally to the Soviet authorities.

reached by citing the lack of communications between AK command and his own headquarters. He denied that the AK attempted to make contact with him, yet AK sources list the liaison officers sent across the Vistula and the instructions on how to open direct telephone contact.[51] For the soldiers in the 1st Polish Army in Praga inactivity was agony as they were forced to watch Warsaw go up in flames, unable to help because the Soviets had taken away the ammunition for their artillery guns: 'Our Soviet officers, under penalty of death, forbade us to come to the aid of the dying city.' On 15 September the Polish commander of the 1st Polish Army, Zygmunt Berling, was authorized to issue orders for an attempt to be made to cross the Vistula towards Czerniaków and Żoliborz, and for operations in the area between the Poniatowski and Kierbedź bridges. The first operation was mounted that night and it was disastrous from the start. According to the artillery commander Colonel Frankowski, many of the Soviet officers were drunk and never took up their commands. The crossing started late, just before dawn, and the boats were spotted by the Germans who used their artillery to destroy them. In the leading company 120 out of 150 were killed.[52] The crossing to Żoliborz took place on the night of 17–18 September but failed to make contact with the AK. A second, more powerful effort to take Czerniaków succeeded in reaching the AK. The Germans counter-attacked in force and in the ensuing fierce eight-day battle the 1st Polish Army suffered the loss of 4,892 men.[53] The withdrawal from the bridgehead took place on the night of 22–23 September.

The collapse of the Czerniaków bridgehead and the evidence that the Soviets were not about to mount a determined assault on Warsaw left the Germans free to concentrate their resources on the reduction of Mokotów and Żoliborz. The AK command faced no option but to surrender on the best terms that could be negotiated. On 28 September a meeting was held between General Bach-Zelewski and Lieutenant Colonel Zygmunt Dobrowolski, representing Bór-Komorowski. Bach-Zelewski made four proposals: the recognition of combatant status for all AK male and female fighters; officers would be allowed to keep their personal arms; the International Red Cross would supervise the surrender; and the civilian population would be evacuated from Warsaw. If the AK wished to continue fighting then the Germans still wanted the evacuation of the civilian population, after which 'the fighting would be carried out with every available means until the town and the army were totally destroyed'.[54] That evening Dobrowolski reported to a meeting of the AK command attended by Bór-Komorowski, Jankowski, Generals Pełczyński, Okulicki, Chruściel, and three other leading members of the underground. After a long discussion it was apparent that opinions on the wisdom of surrender were divided.

Bór-Komorowski concluded that he was in favour of the evacuation of the civilian population but wanted to delay the surrender of the army. He still harboured hopes that the Soviets would advance. The excuse for the delay, given to and accepted by Bach-Zelewski, was that the Poles wanted time to inspect the civilian camp at Pruszków.[55]

Final appeals to the Soviets elicited no response and so, on 1 October, a ceasefire came into operation and on the following day a mass exodus of civilians and AK fighters began. At 9 p.m. on 2 October, Bór-Komorowski signed the capitulation agreement. On 3 October he issued his final order of the day:

> The capitulation of the capital does not signify that we have made peace with the Germans, and Poland, which has fought the Germans during five years of occupation, will not today, even after this brave defeat, being in so unenviable a situation, cease to fight. The demands of Moscow were worse than surrender to the enemy. We would rather die than agree to these conditions. The Soviets wanted to deport us and destroy us in the same way as the 10,000 victims of Katyń.[56]

On 4 October, Bór-Komorowski informed London that he had appointed Okulicki to succeed him as commander of the AK with orders to continue the underground fight. He also told London that he felt morally obliged to march into captivity with the soldiers he had commanded: 'My escape would have been looked upon by the Germans as a breach of the agreement I had signed with them, and would undoubtedly have had repercussions on the fate of both soldiers and civilians.'[57] All civilians were forced to leave Warsaw to be processed at Pruszków before being released to find new homes somewhere in Poland.

On 5 October, 15,378 AK soldiers, including 3,000 women, and 922 officers, marched out in the most orderly formations they could muster: 'We all made one last effort and marched in an even, measured step, as on parade, our rifles on our shoulders. We had to remind the Germans what kind of soldiers they had been fighting during the last two months.'[58] The AK soldiers were forced to lay down their arms: 'I recall the surprise on the faces of the German soldiers on seeing the equipment we were handing over – old revolvers, rifles that had long seen no use, rusty bayonets. It was nothing strange really, most of our functioning weapons had been carefully wrapped and buried: they just might come in handy later.'[59] Some Germans, such as the commander of the Lower Saxony Panzer Division, congratulated the AK on their performance and 'he said he was proud that his division had had the chance to fight against such courageous soldiers'.[60] At Pruszków, German officers noticed an eight-year-old girl with Poland's highest military decoration, the *Virtuti Militari*, pinned to her breast, and saluted her.[61]

The cost of the uprising in terms of human life was stupendous, with total casualty figures for both the AK and civilians varying between 150,000 and 200,000. Most of these victims were civilians, who had been killed in mass executions, died of disease, malnutrition or exhaustion, or were casualties of the fighting, buried in the cellars, blown to bits by shell-fire, or drowned in the sewers trying to escape the fighting. About 40,000 AK soldiers took part in the uprising and the casualty figures give testimony to the determination of their fight: 10,200 killed, 7,000 missing presumed killed, 5,000 seriously wounded, making a casualty rate of over 50 per cent. The 1st Polish Army lost 4,892 killed, wounded or missing. Bach-Zelewski gave the German casualty figures as 10,000 dead, 7,000 missing, and 9,000 wounded.[62]

The population of Paris had experienced a very different kind of occupation compared to the population of Warsaw. In June 1940 Paris had been declared an open city and the Allied bombing of factories had been restricted to the outskirts, with the result that, unlike Warsaw, Paris had suffered very little material damage to her buildings. The Parisians had been appalled by the sight of Jews being dragged from their homes during the Vel' d'Hiv round-up in the summer of 1942, but otherwise had little direct experience of the brutal capabilities of the Germans, particularly as so much of this action had been carried out by the French police. Executions by the Germans in Paris had not taken place in the streets but at the Mont-Valérien execution ground and in the prisons such as Santé and Fresnes.

The resistance leaders and people in Paris were appalled by the news coming out of Warsaw, which was broadcast on the BBC, of the air and artillery bombardment of the city and atrocities committed by the SS. Hitherto, the German response to resistance activities in Paris had been carefully controlled by General von Stülpnagel, but this situation changed in the summer of 1944. Von Stülpnagel had been a member of the 20 July conspiracy against Hitler and, on hearing that Hitler was dead, he had ordered the military commander of Paris, General Hans von Boineburg-Lengsfeld, to arrest all the SS and Gestapo in Paris. His orders were carried out, but the men were released when the news of Hitler's survival reached Paris. Von Stülpnagel was removed from his position, and attempted suicide before being executed in Germany. Boineburg-Lengsfeld remained at liberty in the capital solely to oversee the handover of power to Hitler's new appointee to command in Paris, General Dietrich von Choltitz. The

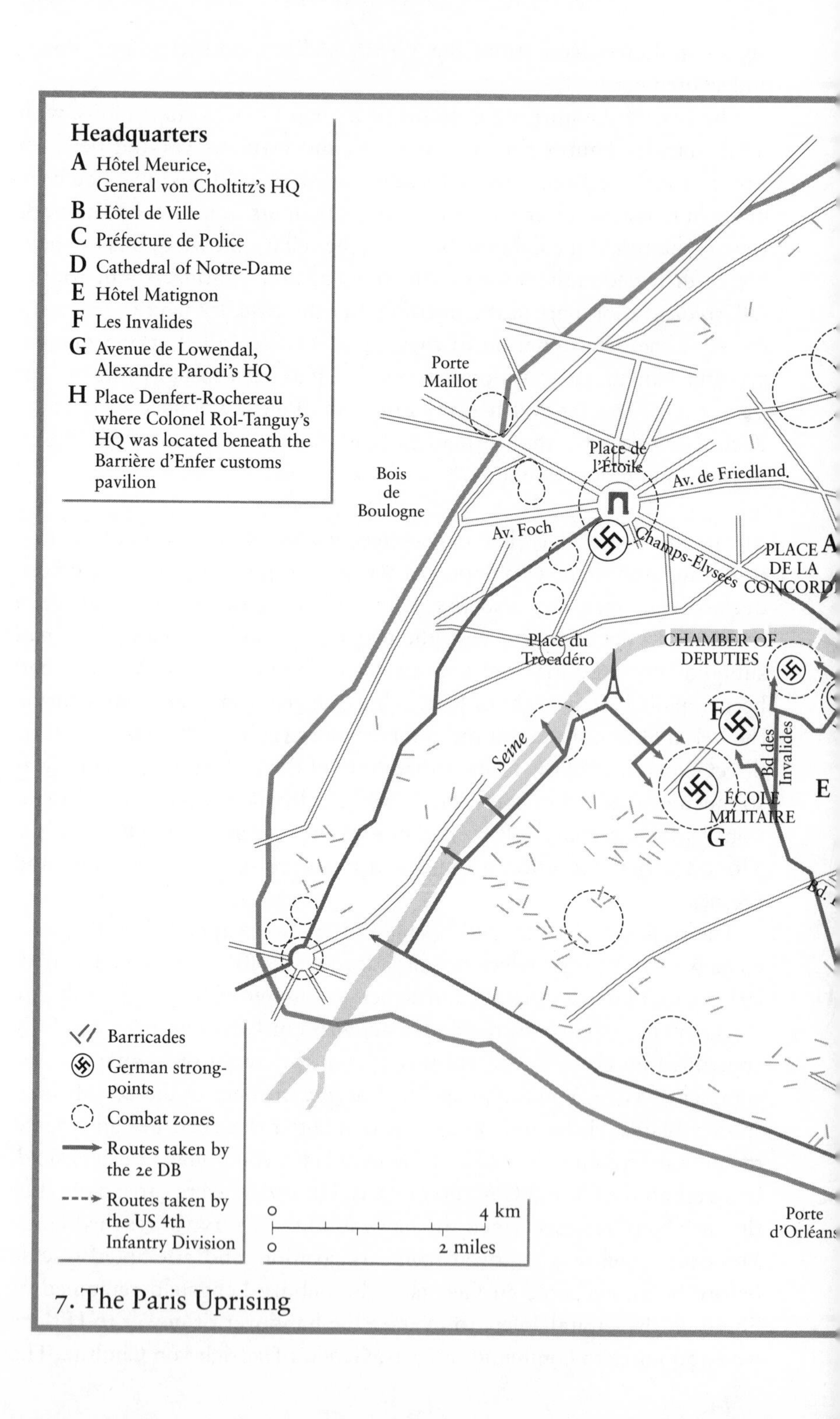
Headquarters
A Hôtel Meurice, General von Choltitz's HQ
B Hôtel de Ville
C Préfecture de Police
D Cathedral of Notre-Dame
E Hôtel Matignon
F Les Invalides
G Avenue de Lowendal, Alexandre Parodi's HQ
H Place Denfert-Rochereau where Colonel Rol-Tanguy's HQ was located beneath the Barrière d'Enfer customs pavilion
Porte Maillot
Bois de Boulogne
Place de l'Étoile
Av. de Friedland.
Av. Foch
Champs-Élysées
PLACE DE LA CONCORDE
A
Place du Trocadéro
CHAMBER OF DEPUTIES
Seine
F
Bd des Invalides
ÉCOLE MILITAIRE
G
E
Barricades
German strong-points
Combat zones
Routes taken by the 2e DB
Routes taken by the US 4th Infantry Division
0
4 km
0
2 miles
Porte d'Orléans

7. The Paris Uprising

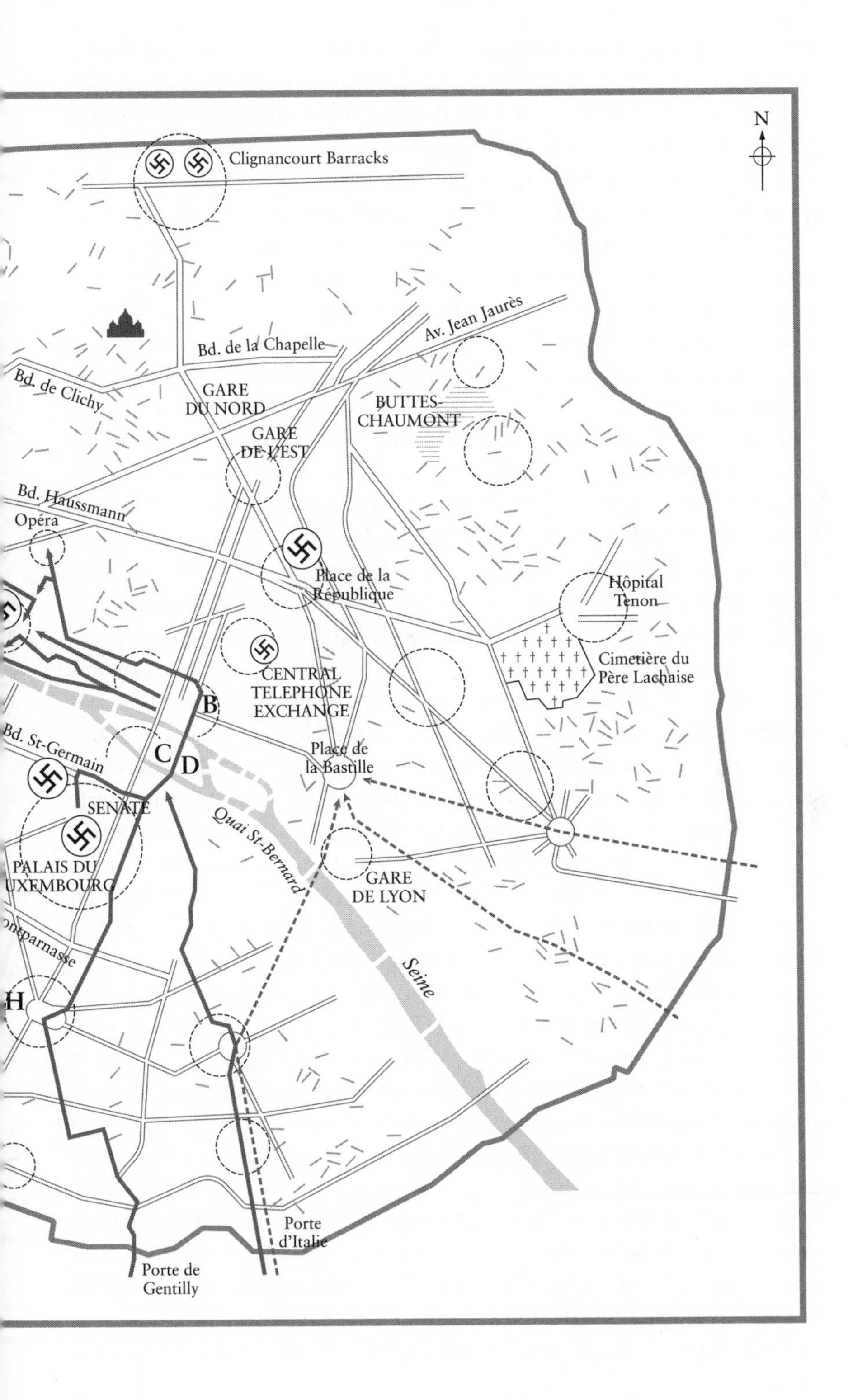

N
Clignancourt Barracks
Av. Jean Jaurès
Bd. de la Chapelle
Bd. de Clichy
GARE
DU NORD
BUTTES-
CHAUMONT
GARE
DE L'EST
Bd. Haussmann
Opéra
Place de la
République
Hôpital
Tenon
CENTRAL
TELEPHONE
EXCHANGE
Cimetière du
Père Lachaise
B
Bd. St-Germain
C
D
Place de
la Bastille
SENATE
Quai St-Bernard
PALAIS DU
UXEMBOURG
GARE
DE LYON
ontparnasse
Seine
H
Porte
d'Italie
Porte de
Gentilly

general had a fearsome reputation: in 1940 he had been present in Rotterdam as the city was bombed and the surrender of the Netherlands secured; later he had served on the Eastern Front and had proved a ruthless commander of forces carrying out the siege of Sebastopol. Therefore, there was every reason to expect that von Choltitz would carry out to the letter his orders from Hitler 'to destroy Paris if the enemy advanced, and defend it from the ruins'. Changes had also been made to the German command on the Western Front with Field Marshal Günter von Kluge being replaced by the more determined and apparently loyal Field Marshal Walter Model. The German command changes took place in the first half of August just as the Allies broke out of Normandy and the German armies were in retreat.[63]

In Warsaw the AK command had clearly been in charge of events surrounding the decision to launch an uprising. In Paris the situation was very different. Everyone of any importance was there, but no single person was in overall control. The national delegate, Alexandre Parodi, had orders from de Gaulle to assert Gaullist control over the administration after wresting it from the Vichy authorities. He was to be assisted by the services of the national military delegate, Jacques Chaban-Delmas, who received orders directly from General Koenig. But, as noted earlier, the CNR and its military committee, COMAC, disputed Koenig's right and ability to control the resistance. The members of COMAC knew the risks, they had shared the danger, and they had every intention of retaining control of events. Two of the three members, Maurice Kriegel-Valrimont and Pierre Villon, were communists, and the other, Count Jean de Vogüé, supported the idea of an insurrection. But then there was also a further committee to be considered, the Paris Liberation Committee (*Comité Parisien de la Libération*, CPL), whose president was the communist André Tollet and whose political head was a communist fellow traveller, Léo Hamon.

Communist domination of the resistance was seemingly confirmed when the communist veteran of the Spanish Civil War, Henri Rol-Tanguy, took over command of the FFI in Paris and its region after the arrest in June of his predecessor, the staunch Gaullist, Pierre Lefaucheux. Fear of communist action and the possibility of civil war dominated the thoughts and actions of de Gaulle and his representatives in Paris, Parodi and Chaban-Delmas. It also influenced the view of the resistance by outside observers. In June, de Gaulle ordered Koenig to stop further arms drops to the Paris region in case they fell into the hands of the communists. Similarly, a later request from the resistance for arms drops was rejected by the British Foreign Office because 'there will always be the temptation to put them to mischievous uses should political passions be inflamed when the war was over'. Yet research has since shown that this threat was in fact exaggerated. Out of the approximately 20,000 FFI forces in and around Paris, only 4,000 were known to be communist. Furthermore, the French Communist Party knew that Stalin did not want a communist revolution in France because it would distract the attention of the Allied armies away from the principal task of defeating the Germans on the battlefront. As events will show, the communists were no more in control than the Gaullists.[64]

As the various resistance bodies met to consider whether, when, and how to launch an insurrection, they had to bear in mind the paucity of their forces and, in particular, the weapons on their side. Figures for the numbers in the Paris resistance vary, but it can safely be assumed that there were around 20,000–25,000 FFI fighters in Paris and a further 60,000 in the surrounding areas who could be mobilized. Yet their armament was pitiful, with only 166 machine guns, 825 revolvers, 562 shotguns and rifles, and 192 grenades. Added to this, the Paris police and gendarmerie were thought to have retained around 20,000 weapons. Against them was ranged the small but still well-equipped German garrison with around 20,000 men and eighty tanks, sixty artillery guns, and thirty armoured vehicles. The number of men on both sides may have been roughly equal but the weight of firepower rested with the Germans should they choose to use it. The Paris garrison was, however, not formed from front-line soldiers. Those capable of active service had been despatched as reinforcements to the battlefront and one German commentator described those who remained as 'dear old daddies'. The Germans were concentrated in six areas: von Choltitz's headquarters in the Hôtel Meurice on the rue de Rivoli; the German administration centre at the Hôtel Majestic near the Arc de Triomphe; the ministry of foreign affairs on the Quai d'Orsay; the parliament building, the Assemblée Nationale in the Palais Bourbon; the Senate and around the Jardin du Luxembourg; and the Prinz Eugen barracks on the Place de la République. There were also further strongpoints with well-constructed bunkers at the École Militaire and Les Invalides.[65]

COMAC and the Gaullist representatives realized that no uprising in Paris could last for long without significant help from outside. The obvious source of assistance would be the Allies, who had just broken out of Normandy. Both at the time and in his memoirs, the supreme Allied commander, Eisenhower, made it clear that there had been no plans for the Allied armies to advance on Paris and take the city. Instead, he had intended to send forces to the north and south of Paris and force the Germans to retreat voluntarily from the French capital.[66] General Omar Bradley, commander of the United States 12th Army Group, was more open on the precise reasons why the Allies did not want to take Paris:

> I feared that the liberation of Paris might cause our supply line to snap. Each ton that went into that city meant one less for the Front, and G-5 [civil-military operations] of Army Group had estimated the Parisians would require an initial 4,000 tons per day. If Paris could pull in its belt and live with the Germans a little longer, each 4,000 tons we saved would mean gasoline enough for three days' motor march toward the German border.[67]

The Free French 2nd Armoured Division under General Philippe Leclerc was operating in Normandy but it was uniformed and equipped by the Americans, under overall American command, and incapable of independent movement towards Paris. Eisenhower warned Leclerc that if he made any attempt at such an operation then his fuel supply would be immediately cut off.

On 11 August, Chaban-Delmas paid a secret visit to London and alerted Koenig to the fact that an uprising was imminent. Koenig, in turn, told Chaban-Delmas that the Allies did not intend to take Paris until early September. On 16 August, Chaban-Delmas reached Paris and informed the resistance leaders of this alarming fact. One feature of the Paris insurrection which was very different from the Warsaw Uprising was that the resistance in Paris was in contact with the Allied forces on the ground. For example, Jean Sainteny of Alliance and Colonel Claude Ollivier of the Jade-Amicol crossed the German lines to keep the Allies up to date on the situation in Paris and the state of German defences. Radio communications between the military and political leaders in Paris, London, and Algiers was less satisfactory. Messages from Paris to Algiers were first sent to London and then transmitted to the CFLN in Algiers, often in batches sent a week apart. Messages to Paris from London and Algiers did, however, reach Paris directly.[68]

Just as Ludwig Fischer's order for 100,000 people from Warsaw to report for the construction of defences contributed to the decision regarding the timing of the launch of the uprising, so in Paris von Choltitz's order for the disarmament of the Paris police to be carried out early on 13 August set events in motion. The Paris police had been drawn into collaboration with the Germans, most notably by rounding up the Jews in 1942 and in hunting down the resistance, but as the tide of war changed in favour of the Allies more policemen became disenchanted with the Vichy regime and the German occupation. Three police resistance groups had been established: the Gaullist *Honneur et Patrie*; the *Police et Patrie*, which was affiliated to *Libération-nord*; and the communist-dominated *Front National de la Police*. The activities of the three groups were coordinated by the Paris head of the *Noyautage de l'Administration Publique*, Yves Bayet, who promised Parodi that the first step to be taken in an uprising would be the installation of a new Gaullist prefect of police, Charles Luizet, in the Préfecture.

Parodi was therefore reassured that a police strike, which Rol-Tanguy was calling for, would not lead to a communist takeover. He accordingly issued joint orders with Rol-Tanguy that the Paris police were to resist disarmament and come out on strike: those who disobeyed the order would be considered as 'traitors and collaborators'. The police strike, by 15,000 men, began on 15 August. Ferdinand Dupuy, a senior administrator at the police station in the 6th arrondissement wrote: 'As one, they suddenly left their posts, threw off their uniforms and disappeared from the streets of the capital as if somebody had waved a magic wand.' Efforts by the Vichy prefect, Amédée Bussière, to get the men back to work with bribes of extra wages and cigarettes failed. So did the release of political prisoners from the prisons at Tourelles and Roquette.[69]

The fears of the consequences of launching a full-scale insurrection preyed on the minds of the members of the CPL, CNR, and COMAC, which each held separate meetings during 17 and 18 August. Alarmingly, opinion was split. At meetings of the CNR, Parodi stressed the weakness of the FFI and the strength of the Germans, whereas Villon wanted immediate action. The CPL was also split with Rol-Tanguy strongly for action and Hamon arguing equally vociferously against what he believed was premature action. Hamon stressed later: 'I knew that an uprising was needed for the honour of Paris. We had to participate in our own liberation. But only in coordination with the Allies, within at most a day of their arrival, not a week or two weeks fighting alone.' COMAC voted for an insurrection to start immediately. On 18 August, Parodi radioed Koenig that the situation in Paris was balanced on a knife edge: there was sporadic shooting all over the city between individual FFI soldiers and the Germans. That evening the FTP seized several town halls in the suburbs. Rumours abounded regarding German movements since the presence of tanks from Panzer Lehr in the north-east suburbs was noted. The regional FFI, however, concluded: 'General impression: the Germans are not thinking of defending Paris so much as protecting the retreat of their troops from Normandy.'[70]

Early in the morning of 19 August the resistance made its first clear strike against the Vichy authorities and the Germans when 3,000 policemen in civilian clothes inspired by Hamon's orders occupied the Paris Préfecture and installed Charles Luizet as prefect: his Vichy predecessor, Bussière, was locked into his apartment. This blow was struck by the Gaullists and not the communists: Rol-Tanguy discovered the occupation by chance when cycling past the building. The apparent ease with which the move had taken place encouraged the CNR and CPL to unite in calling for an uprising to start. The takeover of the Préfecture was also a test case on how the Germans would react, since the resisters inside were very poorly armed. A journalist, Claude Roy, wrote of the scene:

> The courtyard of the Préfecture is full of men and weapons, always on the move. There are German lorries, cars full of ammunition, vans that have been taken from the enemy. The logistics department finds it hard to get the ammunition the fighters need. One man has a French submachine gun, another has a British weapon, another a light machine gun, while yet another has a German gun.

In all, that evening it was estimated that the defenders of the Préfecture had ninety-two automatic weapons, 111 rifles, and nearly 400 handguns, but very little ammunition. If the Germans had chosen to retake the building with infantry supported by armour then they could have done so with ease. Two German tanks did fire at the building and there was infantry support, but the Germans chose not to press home an attack. In the course of 19 August fighting between the FFI and the Germans intensified, especially on the Left Bank and in the suburbs. Around forty Germans were killed and a further seventy were wounded, but the most casualties were suffered by innocent Parisians who were caught in the crossfire: 125 died and nearly 500 were wounded.[71]

There were still deep concerns that the Germans would mount a massive attack on the Préfecture and would redirect the German units who were retreating through Paris from the south towards crushing the uprising. At this point a new important figure entered the scene: the Swedish consul general, Raoul Nordling, who was also a representative of the Swedish ball-bearing manufacturer SKF which had been supplying the Germans. Nordling had already been in contact with the Germans as early as 6 August when he had voiced his concerns regarding the fate of resistance prisoners to a German military judge, and he had followed up his enquiries with two friends in the German administration who were anti-Nazi and may actually have been working for British intelligence, Erich Posch-Pastor and Emil 'Bobby' Bender. Nordling knew that the Germans had executed eighty political prisoners in Caen before leaving the city, and rumours of similar action against the prisoners in Rennes prison had reached Paris. On 15 August the Germans loaded 1,500 men and women prisoners from Fresnes onto transport to take them to Pantin goods station in the north-east suburbs for transport by train to Germany. There they were joined by prisoners from other German-run prisons, Santé, Cherche-Midi,

Romainville, and Compiègne. Their journey to Ravensbrück and Buchenwald, from where the majority did not return, was hampered by Allied bombing of the railway bridges on the way as part of the effort to hamper German reinforcements from reaching France. The difficulty of evacuating the prisoners from Paris raised the threat that the Germans would execute them instead. Indeed, the former military delegate for the northern zone, André Rondenay, had already been removed from the convoy and executed in the forest of Domont. Nordling wanted to broker a deal between the Germans and Parodi whereby the prisoners would be placed under Red Cross protection in return for the unhampered passage out of Paris for the German prison guards. A deal was struck on 17 August just as the final convoy was leaving Compiègne.[72]

The deal was an important move since it gave Nordling the possibility of acting as a neutral intermediary between the Germans and von Choltitz on one side, and the resistance and Parodi on the other. On 19 August Nordling contacted the resisters in the Préfecture, asking them if they would be prepared to settle for a truce with the Germans. Hamon of the CPL, who greatly feared a German counter-attack, was in favour of negotiations; Rol-Tanguy was not consulted. Nordling then approached von Choltitz. The Vichy mayor of Paris, Pierre Taittinger, advised von Choltitz to make a deal on the grounds: 'They are not terrorists. They are the men of Algiers, of the government, French patriots, and if you were a Frenchman you would be with them. I beg you to deal with them.' The agreed truce was to last for thirty-five minutes starting at 9 p.m., ostensibly to enable both sides to recover their wounded, but the prospect of an extension of the truce was evident from the start. Nordling ensured that von Choltitz recognized Parodi as the official representative of the CFLN, and the FFI as regular troops to be treated according to the laws of war. In return the FFI were requested to allow the unhindered retreat of German units through Paris. On 20 August the agreement was pasted onto walls throughout the city and broadcast by loudspeaker cars accompanied by patrols of German soldiers, uniformed police with FFI armbands, and FFI fighters.[73]

The resistance took the opportunity offered by the ceasefire to take over the Hôtel de Ville, 'the building with probably the greatest political symbolism in the city, the building that five times had been the focus of major events – the great revolution of 1789–92, the revolutions of 1830 and 1848, the declaration of the Republic in 1870 and the Paris Commune of 1871'. Importantly, it was taken over by the Gaullists, along with other public ministries, and its takeover marked the death blow to Vichy authority in Paris. At 5.30 p.m. the new Gaullist prefect of the Seine department, Marcel Flouret, entered his new office.

The truce itself caused immense controversy and threatened any unity of purpose between the CNR, COMAC, and the CPL. Villon was against the ceasefire and Rol-Tanguy issued orders for the FFI to ignore it. Parodi was absent from the discussions since he had been stopped by a German patrol and arrested: he was only released on the evening of 20 August by the direct intervention of von Choltitz. The truce was honoured more in the breach than in its effect. Fighting continued on the Left Bank, especially in the Latin Quarter and near the Gare d'Austerlitz and the Jardin des Plantes. Civilians, reassured by the ceasefire, came out of their homes to watch proceedings, as Jean Galtier-Boissière wrote in his diary:

> The public seems to be giving marks to the performances of the resistants and applauding their efforts; they also show a mixture of passionate curiosity and an unbelievable lack of thought, interspersed with sudden bursts of fear. At first, passers-by seem naively to believe that they are in no danger because they are spectators and not actors; all it takes is for a bullet to whizz by or for a man to fall to the ground for them to realise the risks.

During the ceasefire 106 Parisians were killed and 357 wounded, figures only slightly lower than on the preceding day.[74]

On 21 August some form of unity was re-established between the resistance bodies when the CPL voted against an extension of the truce and the CNR bowed to the pressure of events, although Parodi, now at liberty, pushed through a compromise agreement whereby the end of the truce would not be announced until the afternoon of 22 August. The ultimate success of a renewed uprising now depended on the movements of the Allies. On 21 August the British relieved the positions held by Leclerc's 2nd Armoured Division near Argentan, thereby freeing the French troops for a possible advance on Paris. Leclerc promptly ordered one of his officers, Jacques de Guillebon, to take a squadron of light tanks and undertake a detailed reconnaissance of the route towards Versailles. The Americans were not consulted and Leclerc ignored the furious demand by General Leonard Gerow to recall the patrol. On 21 August the Americans advanced further in their encirclement of Paris, taking Rambouillet, halfway between Chartres and Paris, and reaching the Seine south of Paris at Melun, Sens, and Montreau by 22 August. De Gaulle had been at Eisenhower's headquarters since 19 August trying to persuade him to allow Leclerc to advance on Paris. News of the uprising placed further pressure on Eisenhower as Rol-Tanguy's representative, Commandant Roger, and Nordling's brother, Ralph, met Generals Patton and Bradley and pleaded for immediate help. The Americans were by then aware of the weak nature of the German forces between the Allies and Paris.[75]

Such assistance from outside was essential by 22 August as the uprising entered a new stage when the truce ended. Tollet later recalled:

> Barricades were being thrown up with fervour. The science of insurrection had been passed down between the generations. We were very close to the Faubourg Saint-Antoine. I remember an old upholsterer who, as he took tacks from his mouth, was humming Pottier's old song [from the Commune], '*L'insurgé, son vrai nom c'est l'homme.*'

Over 600 barricades were constructed, mostly in the northern and eastern working-class areas, whereas none were built in the wealthy 16th arrondissement. The FFI also stayed away from the areas near the German strongpoints at the Senate, the rue de Rivoli, and the Place de la République. Most public buildings were now in the hands of the resistance and Parodi was able to hold the first meeting of the CFLN secretaries-general at the Hôtel Matignon, the official residence of the prime minister. Jean-Paul Sartre noted the strange state of Paris that day:

> The insurrection is not visible everywhere. On the rue de la Gaîté a blind accordionist is sitting on a stool playing music from *La Traviata*. People are darting towards a bistro for a quick glass of wine. Along the banks of the Seine men and women are swimming or sunbathing in their bathing costumes. And yet the battle is present everywhere.

The clandestine press was distributed openly, and a new resistance radio station, *Radiodiffusion de la Nation Française*, began broadcasting the progress of the insurrection. Sporadic fighting was evident in numerous areas but it was also noticeable that, apart from sending tanks on patrols to demonstrate the continuing German military strength in the city, von Choltitz ordered no assaults on public buildings taken over by the resistance and few German attacks were made against the barricades. It seemed as though both sides were waiting to see what the Allies were going to do.[76]

On the evening of 22 August, Leclerc was informed by Bradley that the French 2nd Armoured Division could begin its advance on Paris and that the Americans would be following behind. As Bradley wrote in his memoirs: 'Any number of American divisions could more easily have spearheaded our march into Paris. But to help the French recapture pride I chose a French force with the tricolour on their Shermans.' The French troops reached Rambouillet on 23 August and began to move towards Paris the following day. A message was dropped by aircraft into the centre of Paris: '*Tenez bon, nous arrivons.*'[77]

The situation inside Paris was extremely volatile. On 23 August, Hitler sent von Choltitz his final orders on the capital, ordering him to destroy the resistance at all costs since the fall of Paris had historically always been followed by the loss of all France, and ending with the demand: 'Paris must not fall into the hands of the enemy, or, if it does, he must find there is nothing but a field of ruins.' Von Choltitz consulted Model's chief of staff, Hans Speidel, on the matter and both men agreed that such destruction would be pointless. German units were passing through Paris on their route to the north-east with little interdiction from the FFI, and the Germans outside Paris were too weak to prevent the Allied advance. While von Choltitz could have dealt a savage blow to the insurgents inside Paris had he chosen to utilize the German tactics that had been adopted in Warsaw, law and order was in fact being maintained by the Free French officials in the city, and the clashes with German soldiers were at a sufficiently low level as to be unimportant. Indeed, the casualty figure of sixty-eight German soldiers killed against 483 civilians dead illustrate the sporadic and unpredictable nature of the uprising.[78]

For reasons that remain obscure a BBC broadcast on 23 August prematurely announced that Paris had been liberated, whereas in fact the Allies only began advancing on the capital on 24 August when Leclerc ordered the 9th Company of the Régiment de Marche du Tchad under Captain Raymond Dronne to make a rapid advance into the city. Dronne's force was composed largely of veterans of the Spanish Civil War and had only fifteen vehicles and three tanks. Nonetheless, at 7.30 p.m. it reached the Porte d'Italie in the south of Paris and travelled north to the Pont d'Austerlitz, reaching the Hôtel de Ville at 9.20 p.m. Dronne introduced himself to the chairman of the CNR, Georges Bidault. The fighting in Paris had been particularly bitter that day as the Germans were driven back to their strongpoints but were still capable of sending out an increased number of armed patrols, which led to mounting casualties on both sides. Dronne's arrival was clearly none too soon.[79] Claire Chevrillon, who had been encoding messages for Parodi throughout the insurrection, recalled:

> There was a clamour outside. I ran onto the balcony. It was growing dark. People were at their windows. They were shouting, they were calling out, they were rushing into the streets. A confused *Marseillaise* was beginning. Was it coming from the radio or from the street? From both.
>
> And then another sound, at first scarcely audible, suddenly swelled and seemed to come from everywhere at once. The bells, all the bells of Paris, were pealing forth together. They had been silent since the beginning of the Occupation. We had forgotten they were there.[80]

At his headquarters in the Hôtel Meurice, von Choltitz phoned Model and Speidel and let them listen to the bells ringing out across Paris. He asked for orders but received no response.[81]

Early on the morning of 25 August, the feast of France's patron saint, Saint Louis, the remainder of Leclerc's force entered Paris followed by the first American troops from the 4th US Infantry. Leclerc set up his headquarters at the Gare Montparnasse, chosen because of its good communications, and was joined there by General Gerow, who wanted to keep a close eye on events.[82] The arrival of the Allies meant that the Paris uprising was effectively over. Now the role of the FFI was to assist the regular Allied troops attain the final liberation of the capital.

The Germans had retreated to their strongholds across Paris. These were formidable defences which would require artillery and tank fire to force them to surrender, tasks suitable only for the regular army but the FFI could still help by supplying intelligence on the location of German bunkers and providing infantry support to the attacking troops. But before any attack took place Colonel Pierre Billotte of the 2nd Armoured Division hoped to persuade von Choltitz that further fighting and bloodshed were pointless. At 11 a.m. he sent von Choltitz an ultimatum, ordering him to formally surrender Paris by 12.15. Von Choltitz declined to consider the matter, arguing that his honour as a German soldier prevented him from surrendering before a real fight. Shortly before 2 p.m. Billotte launched an attack on the Hôtel Meurice, which was protected by at least seven tanks. French infantry under Lieutenant Karcher rushed the building and took von Choltitz prisoner without any great opposition. Lieutenant Colonel Jean de la Horie demanded that von Choltitz must order his men to stop fighting. Von Choltitz agreed, and transport was arranged to take him to the Préfecture to sign the surrender document.[83]

Although the German headquarters at the Hôtel Meurice had fallen with little difficulty, the Germans put up a much fiercer fight elsewhere in the city before von Choltitz formally surrendered. The FFI worked alongside the Free French troops in the attacks on German positions surrounding the foreign ministry on the Quai d'Orsay and around Les Invalides. FFI troops under Colonel Fabien, the man who had assassinated the first German officer in Paris back in 1941, took heavy casualties when working alongside the army against German bunkers and strongpoints surrounding the Luftwaffe headquarters near the Jardin du Luxembourg. The French Army forced the surrender of the German forces at the Hôtel Majestic which housed the German administration, the German-held building near the Opéra, and around the Place de la Concorde. The Germans around the Place de la République had been under attack by the FFI alone since the morning and only surrendered in the afternoon when they learned of von Choltitz's signature of the surrender document. Similarly, the French had been unable to reduce the German positions at the École Militaire and the Senate until the surrender was made known. The German prisoners were marched to collecting points and faced the wrath of the crowd. Lieutenant Dankwart von Arnim recalled the scene when leaving the Hôtel Meurice: 'There was screaming, threats, fists were shaken. The accompanying guards found it difficult to protect us – and themselves. Over and again one of us was knocked down by someone in the crowd and was trampled upon.' By the night of 25 August, 12,000 Germans had surrendered. The uprising, and especially the fighting on 25 August, had cost the Germans 3,200 dead. The French 2nd Armoured Division had, during the advance on Paris and the fighting in the city, lost seventy-one men killed and 225 wounded, which was the hardest fighting that the division had encountered to date. The FFI suffered around 1,000 killed, while the Parisian civilians suffered 582 killed and 2,000 wounded.[84]

When von Choltitz arrived at the Préfecture he was escorted to the billiard room to meet Leclerc, and together they sat down to sign the surrender document, witnessed by the resistance leaders. Von Choltitz was then taken to the Gare de Montparnasse to sign individual documents to be taken to the German strongpoints. Rol-Tanguy also signed the surrender document, placing his signature above that of Leclerc in an attempt to convince everyone that the Germans were surrendering to the FFI. When de Gaulle arrived at the Gare de Montparnasse that evening he was furious at the positioning of Rol-Tanguy's signature but finally agreed that it meant nothing. General Gerow was even more angry since it was his troops that von Choltitz had opposed in Normandy and he believed that he was the military commander in Paris. The surrender document, however, made it clear that von Choltitz had surrendered to those acting as representatives of the CFLN and not as representatives of the Allies.[85]

De Gaulle then went to the Préfecture and met Luizet, Parodi, Bidault and other senior Gaullist representatives. Jacques Lecompte-Boinet wrote of the scene:

> There is a striking contrast between the dishevelled, enthusiastic and heroic FFIs in the courtyard of the Préfecture and the calculated prudence, composure and good manners of those who only have to sit down in the Louis XVI armchairs in order to come into their inheritance.[86]

Luizet and Parodi were eager for de Gaulle to acknowledge the French resistance by meeting the members of the CNR and CPL, the men who had facilitated his path to power. De Gaulle, however, was in a hurry to take over the reins of power before the Americans could dispute his primacy. Consequently, after a brief visit to his former office in the ministry of war, de Gaulle went to the Hôtel de Ville where he gave the speech which established the mythology of the Paris insurrection:

> Why should we hide the feelings that fill us all, we men and women who are here in our own city, in Paris that has risen to free itself and that has succeeded in doing so with its own hands? No! Do not let us hide this deep and sacred emotion. There are moments that go beyond each of our poor little lives. Paris! Paris outraged! Paris broken! Paris martyrised! But Paris liberated! Liberated by itself, liberated by its people with the help of the armies of France, with the support and the help of the whole of France, of France that is fighting, of France alone.[87]

This was virtually the last time that de Gaulle made a statement acknowledging the importance of the resistance. He decried the CNR's desire for him to proclaim the restoration of the republic, arguing that the republic had never ceased to exist. Now his principal objective was to establish undisputed power and restore law and order. By 28 August de Gaulle had disbanded the FFI and had replaced the secretaries-general with ministers from the government in Algiers.[88]

Now it was time to celebrate. De Gaulle organized a victory parade to start at 3 p.m. on 26 August. Gerow sent a signal to Leclerc ordering him not to participate, which Leclerc ignored. The parade gave primacy to the French 2nd Armoured Division and not the FFI whose soldiers lined the route of the parade but did not march alongside their compatriots. De Gaulle took the salute at the Arc de Triomphe and relit the flame at the tomb of the unknown soldier before setting off on foot down the Champs-Élysées towards Notre-Dame:

> A tremendous crowd was jammed together on both sides of the road. Perhaps two million people. The roofs too were black with many more. At every window were crowded other groups waving flags. Human clusters were clinging to ladders, flagpoles and lamp posts. As far as the eye could see, there was nothing but this living tide of humanity in the sunshine, beneath the tricolour.[89]

De Gaulle was followed by his three generals, Leclerc, Koenig, and Alphonse Juin. At first the members of the CNR had not been invited to participate, but they were eventually allowed to march behind de Gaulle and his generals. Shooting by unknown perpetrators broke out at the Place de la Concorde and de Gaulle travelled the remainder of the way to Notre-Dame by car. There, more shots were heard, and again it is not known who fired them. Archbishop Suhard, who had recently greeted Pétain in Paris and presided over the funeral of Philippe Henriot, was absent from the celebration of the Solemn Mass. The wild firing concerned de Gaulle, who requested American help in restoring law and order in Paris. Eisenhower could not spare the troops for any length of time but did permit two American divisions to march through the city as a show of force.[90]

While de Gaulle was taking steps to ensure Gaullist power in France, the Parisians celebrated without abandon. George Langelaan, a former F Section agent, described the scene:

> Paris was expecting us . . . People were clapping, laughing, shouting, or simply staring, much like children stare at wonderful, unattainable toys. Some people were crying, with great tears running down their cheeks as they clapped their hands. The air seemed suddenly loaded with a strange emotional tenseness.
>
> And all the time there was that great, everlasting clamour of cheering and shouting people. Now and again, there were great holes of silence, as though the soundtrack had been cut off in the middle of a film. Then, people would simply look at us and smile, or cry, or both smile and cry, and a second later, like the sound switched on again, the cheering and the shouting seemed louder than ever.
>
> Never shall I forget that frenzy of joy, of joy so great, so absolute, that it becomes pain.[91]

By the summer of 1944 the power of Jozef Tiso's fascist regime in Slovakia was on the wane and the excesses of his Hlinka Guard had alienated many people. A Christmas 1943 agreement between the democrats and the communists gave the impression that the resistance was united in its desire to overthrow the regime, and the clandestine Slovak National Council gave command of the planned uprising to Lieutenant Colonel Ján Golian. As chief of staff of the command at Banská Bystrica in central Slovakia, Golian was in the ideal position to concentrate military forces loyal to him, and disloyal to the regime, in the area. The resistance was also in contact with the minister of defence, General Ferdinand Čatloš, who feared that the Germans were about to occupy Slovakia in order to defend the Carpathian passes against the approaching Soviet front. Golian despatched the two best-equipped Slovak divisions to positions where they could hold open the Carpathian passes to facilitate this Soviet advance. Unlike in the case of the two uprisings described above, the Slovak uprising appears at this stage to have been planned as a mutiny of a portion of the Slovak

8. The Slovak Uprising

armed forces which, since the soldiers were well-armed, appeared to have a good chance of success.

The Slovak National Council sent two representatives, Karol Šmidke who was a communist and Colonel Mikuláš Ferjenčik who was a democrat, behind Soviet lines for consultations. Ferjenčik was interned and ignored but Šmidke was welcomed, especially since he carried a secret message from Čatloš, which offered the prospect of Slovakia changing sides and joining the Soviets in their war against the Germans. A month later the party returned to Slovakia none the wiser regarding Soviet plans.[92]

The truth was that the Soviets did not want the Slovaks to rise up, especially not the military, who might later turn against them. The Soviets had been building up the partisan movement in Slovakia by sending mixed detachments of specially trained Czechoslovak and Soviet partisans, numbering a total of 8,000 men, into the country to play havoc with German communications. These partisan detachments were concentrated in central and northern Slovakia. The Slovak National Council wanted the partisans to subordinate themselves to Golian's secret military command, but Klement Gottwald, the leader of the Czechoslovak Communist Party in Moscow, had agreed with Nikita Khrushchev, the head of the Ukrainian

Communist Party, that the Slovak partisan movement would be directed by the Ukrainian partisan staff based in Kiev. At the end of July 1944 a Soviet paratrooper unit under Lieutenant Pyotr Velichko was sent to Slovakia to take command of the partisans.[93]

It was the activities of these Soviet-sponsored partisans that decided the timing of the Slovak uprising, not Golian. The partisans had spent the summer cutting the strategic railways running through the country: between Bohumin in the Protectorate and Košice in eastern Slovakia; Vrútky near Turčiansky Svätý Martin in the north to Lučenec in the south; and from Žilina in the north to Leopoldov in the west. The partisans had also seized control of towns north of the city of Banská Bystrica. Then on 27 August the partisans attacked a train at Turčiansky Svätý Martin which was carrying the German military mission under General Paul von Otto back to Berlin from Bucharest following the defection of Romania from the Axis. All twenty-eight members of this mission were shot by the partisans. Tiso and Čatloš were so alarmed by the activities of the partisans that, on the evening of 29 August, Čatloš broadcast to the Slovak people that German formations were entering Slovakia to restore law and order and should be welcomed by the Slovak people. German radio reported on 30 August: 'It is officially announced that, at the request of the Slovak Government, German troops have entered Slovakia to take part in the fighting against the partisan menace and to restore peace and order throughout the country.'[94]

Golian and the Slovak National Council now had little option but to announce the start of the uprising, even though the chances of its success against the Germans were almost non-existent. In theory Golian could call on the services of 60,000 Slovak soldiers and expect the 18,000 partisans to work alongside them, but the Germans could put many more men into the field. Immediately after the broadcast by Čatloš, orders were issued by Golian at Banská Bystrica to all Slovak units to resist the Germans and the first armed clash took place that evening near Žilina. Čatloš helped the Germans disarm the Bratislava garrison but then, when it was clear that the Germans were about to arrest him, he went over to the insurgents on 2 September: he was then arrested by Golian, transferred to the partisans and sent to Moscow. On 1 September the Slovak National Council came out into the open under the leadership of Vavro Šrobár and Šmidke and published a declaration that it was 'the supreme organ of the liberation movement at home' and that its stated aim was to overthrow the Tiso regime, and after liberation 'to live together in brotherly unity with the Czech Nation in the new Czechoslovak Republic'. Golian added that 'we do not wish to go over to the Russians . . . above all we wish to take part in the liberation of the Czech lands'.[95]

These calls to rise up divided the Slovaks. On the humanitarian level help flooded in for the insurgents, as the doctor in charge of the main military hospital at Zvolen recorded:

> We could never have managed on our own. Immediately we started cleaning, however, women, children, and men, too, appeared from houses in the vicinity and pitched in with their own buckets, brooms, floor rags and soap. They were soon followed by people from even further afield bringing us their own bed linen, mattresses, and bedside tables. Some of them even brought beds on handcarts, and beds were the most precious gifts of all.[96]

Many Slovaks were disillusioned by Tiso's continued adherence to Hitler, but a significant number still remained in favour of continuing Slovak independence from the Czech lands of Bohemia and Moravia, and therefore were cautious about supporting an uprising which appeared to be in favour of the restoration of Czechoslovakia. Others simply feared the power of the Germans, or felt that the uprising would lead to a communist takeover and Soviet dominance in the country after the war.

Edvard Beneš and the Czech government-in-exile in London had not been consulted regarding the launching of the rising, but they sprang into action as soon as the news of its start reached them. František Moravec claimed that Beneš was less interested in whether the rising succeeded or not than in the political opportunities it offered: 'He wanted the rising to have a *Czechoslovak* appearance – or seem to have. That was important, because it would help to remove from the Slovak nation the stigma of being among the enemies and establish it in the Allied camp.'[97] The Czechs abroad encouraged the Czech resistance to assist their Slovak brothers-in-arms. The deputy Reichsprotektor, Karl Frank, ordered the immediate tightening of the frontier between the Protectorate and Slovakia with the threat of capital punishment for transgressors. This was effective in preventing Czechs crossing the border during the uprising and in halting the retreat of Slovak partisan units towards the end of the uprising. For example, the 300-strong Jan Žižka partisan brigade was annihilated by the Germans when it tried to cross into Moravia.

Golian appears to have lost control of the rising from the start. General Augustín Malár, the commander of the two best-equipped divisions in eastern Slovakia, comprising 24,000 men, believed that the rising had been called prematurely. He ignored Golian's order and flew to the Slovak capital, Bratislava, where he appealed to the army not to rise up. The actions of Golian's deputy, Lieutenant Colonel Viliam Talský, were even more damning: he fled to the Soviet lines, taking with him the bulk of the Slovak air force – thirty-eight planes. These two divisions were therefore left leaderless in the face of German action. The garrisons in Bratislava and in the western towns failed to join the rising in any significant numbers. At the end of August, unknown to the Slovaks, the Soviets had cancelled their planned advance across the Carpathians in favour of operations further south, so the Slovaks were left to fight the Germans alone.[98]

The Germans, commanded by SS-Obergruppenführer Gottlob Berger, converged on Slovakia from all directions – from Austria, the Protectorate, Silesia, and Poland. The German troops consisted of 40,000 men organized into four SS divisions, the Adolf Hitler SS tank division, two Wehrmacht divisions, mountain artillery and infantry, and the Vlasov corps of renegade Russians. The Slovak garrisons in western Slovakia were disarmed with ease. On 31 August the abandoned divisions in the east were surrounded by the Germans and forced to surrender: 2,000 men escaped with their weapons and joined the rebellious army units in central Slovakia. By the middle of September the Germans had recaptured the strategic Bohumín–Košice railway, and the valleys of the Váh and Hornád rivers. The Slovak rebels were now effectively encircled in the region of Banská Bystrica and the Hron valley, and separated from the Soviet lines by a broad swathe of German-held territory. As the insurgent-held area shrank, operations by regular rebellious army units gave way to an increase in partisan warfare and resistance to the Germans stiffened. The slow progress made by Berger towards totally crushing the rising led to his replacement by the more ruthless Hermann Höfle. A Soviet offensive by the 4th Ukrainian Front and 1st Czechoslovak Army Corps against the Dukla pass in the Carpathians was launched on 8 September but failed after heavy casualties on both sides. There now appeared to be little prospect for imminent liberation, and if the rising and partisan warfare were to continue in Slovakia then aid needed to arrive from abroad.[99]

The Czech foreign minister, Ján Masaryk, contacted the Allies in London as soon as the rising began, pleading for arms drops to be made to Slovakia to arm the reserve army units. Neither the British nor the Americans had reliable contacts in Slovakia to inform them independently of the nature of the rising, nor were either of the western Allies interested in action in the region. Indeed, the response of the British Foreign Office and the chiefs of staff was unequivocal: Slovakia lay firmly within the Soviet sphere of action and it was up to the Soviets to provide supplies if they approved of the rising's aims. The western Allies also had a further caveat: they were struggling at the time to supply the Warsaw Uprising and to secure Soviet permission to use air bases in the Ukraine, and so simply lacked the aircraft to supply the Slovaks too. Both the Foreign Office and the State Department did, however, take an important step when, on 7 September, a statement was issued officially recognizing that the Slovak insurgents 'constitute a combat force operating against the Germans' and therefore were entitled to the protection offered by the Geneva Convention.[100]

There were already British and American missions in Slovakia, but none of them were there specifically to assist the rising. On 18 September, Major John Sehmer who had previously served with Draža Mihailović, was dropped as head of Operation Windproof near Banská Bystrica. The purpose of his mission was to cross into Hungary, but shortly after landing he was taken to Golian's headquarters and became a witness to the rising. His report, dated 6 October, noted the close cooperation between the Slovaks and the Soviet officers leading the partisans while at the same time making it clear that 'General Golian is anxious to demonstrate that the country is controlled by the Czechoslovak Government, and not by the partisans.' Sehmer's report reached SOE through Colonel Henry Threlfall, who arrived at Golian's headquarters on 7 October, bringing medical supplies and consulting Golian, before returning to Bari on the same day. He warned Golian 'that the western Allies were not permitted to make any military commitments to the Slovak insurgents, because Slovakia was in the sphere of Soviet military operations and there could be no western interference in this sphere without Soviet permission'. Sehmer remained in Slovakia but he was captured by the Germans on 26 December and executed in Mauthausen a month later. OSS also despatched a mission to Slovakia on 17 September. This mission consisted of six men led by Lieutenant James Holt Green and landed near Banská Bystrica, bringing with it arms and medical supplies. It is unclear whether the principal purpose of the OSS mission was to rescue downed Allied airmen or to assist the Slovak rising. The mission members and the Allied airmen became trapped in the country, joined forces with Sehmer's party, and suffered the same fate after being captured by the Germans and sent to Mauthausen. The Americans did, however, help the insurgents when, on 6 October, American planes collected a three-man delegation of the Slovak National Council – Ján Ursíny, Ladislav Novomeský, and Lieutenant Colonel Miroslav Vesel – who travelled on to London to explain to their government what support the rising needed.[101]

French POWs who had escaped from camps in Hungary and Slovakia formed a detachment under Captain Georges de Lannurien and joined the Slovak insurgent army. The detachment fought its first action at Strečno in northern Slovakia where it suffered heavy casualties. On 11 September Lannurien received a telegram at Golian's headquarters from the Czechoslovak minister of defence in London, General Ingr: 'The French General Staff, informed of the formation of the French group, offers its encouragement in your operations and agrees to your being transferred under

Czechoslovak command.' After the collapse of the rising, the French detachment continued to operate alongside the partisans.[102]

The Soviets were undoubtedly in the best position to send assistance to the Slovak insurgents. Not only could they supply them with much-needed weapons but they also had the manpower ready to serve there. The 2,800-strong 2nd Czechoslovak Parachute Brigade under Colonel Vladimír Přikryl had been formed in the Soviet Union from Slovak deserters or POWs from the Slovak units sent by Tiso to fight on the Eastern Front. Beneš wanted this brigade parachuted into Slovakia to help with the battle against the Germans. The Soviets, however, prevaricated and began inserting units from the brigade into Slovakia only six weeks after the launch of the rising. The brigade never operated as a large formation, nor did it combine forces with the Slovak insurgent army: rather, it was split into smaller groups and sent to reinforce the partisan units. Soviet arms supplies were meagre, consisting of only 150 anti-tank rifles, 350 rifles, a few thousand mines, and some aircraft for which the rebels had no fuel.[103]

By early October the Slovak rising had virtually collapsed, although partisan warfare intensified. General Rudolph Viest arrived from the Soviet Union on 6–7 October to take over command from Golian, who served on as his deputy. Viest faced growing communist efforts to suborn the army and to take over leadership of the rising. On 16 October, Miklós Horthy was overthrown in Hungary and was replaced by the Arrow Cross regime of Ferenc Szálasi. This freed further German forces to move into Slovakia to crush the uprising and on 18 October they launched a determined offensive against the rebels. The rising collapsed rapidly under the onslaught and Banská Bystrica fell on 27 October. On the following day, Viest broadcast his final report over the radio: 'An organized resistance of the army as a whole is no longer possible . . . Accordingly, starting October 29, 1944, the Czechoslovak army units will adapt themselves to the given situation and undertake partisan-type warfare against the Germans.' The Slovak National Council and Viest and Golian retreated to Pohronský Bukovec in the mountains to await the Soviet advance. The two generals were captured by the Germans on 3 December and were later executed at Flossenbürg concentration camp. Partisan warfare continued in Slovakia until the liberation of the country in May 1945.

The Germans responded with great brutality against the partisans and the innocent civilians caught up in the conflict. Incomplete German figures suggest that during the first six weeks after Viest announced the end of the rising, the Germans captured 19,000 people: figures for the later period are unavailable. Around 9,000 Slovaks were sent to camps in Germany, where the vast majority perished. Many of these were Jews who had survived in hiding since the 1942 deportations. After the war, mass graves were uncovered of insurgents and civilians murdered in Slovakia, notably near Turčiansky Svätý Martin and Banská Bystrica. The Hlinka Guard assisted the Germans in their reprisal operations, and indeed the Tiso government utterly condemned the uprising. Shortly after the fall of Banská Bystrica, Tiso attended a Mass in the city during which he spoke of his great sadness regarding 'all the dead that fell victim to this cowardly attack on our state independence'. The ten political leaders of the rising were indicted, and the six members of the Slovak National Council were sentenced to death *in absentia* in early January 1945.[104]

In April 1941 Colin Gubbins of SOE had noted: 'A national uprising against the Axis is a card which usually can only be played once.'[105] In all three cases – Warsaw, Paris, Slovakia – the advance of the Allies, the Soviets towards Warsaw and Slovakia, and the armies of the western Allies towards Paris, inspired the people to rise up with the conviction that they could smooth the path for the rapid liberation of their territories – if the Allies moved swiftly to support them. This last point proved the deciding factor between success and failure: the Soviet armies did not advance to help the insurgents in either Warsaw or Slovakia, and both risings were crushed by the Germans; in France, however, Allied plans were altered to take Paris and the insurrection succeeded in liberating the French capital several weeks earlier than anticipated. In all three cases the Allies knew that the people were about to rise up. The Soviets encouraged the Poles in Warsaw to rise up, then refused to coordinate their movements with the AK, and finally abandoned the insurgents to their fate: all largely on political grounds. Being informed of the intentions of the resistance made no difference to the Soviet response to the uprising in Slovakia: the Soviets just ignored it. Only in the case of Paris did the Allies respond favourably.

There were also differences in how the Germans responded to the uprisings. After the war, von Choltitz claimed that he was the 'saviour of Paris' because, out of love for the city, he had not carried out Hitler's explicit order to destroy it. Yet this claim is open to dispute. Some have argued that von Choltitz was actually incapable of carrying out the orders because of a lack of explosives. In fact, although there were insufficient explosives to create the sea of ruins ordered by Hitler, von Choltitz was still capable of inflicting enormous material damage on Paris. At his first interrogation after capture, he admitted that explosives had been placed in the two central telephone exchanges in the rue des Archives and the rue Saint-Armand, and that there was a 500kg mine under the Pont Saint-Cloud on the outskirts of Paris. There were also substantial quantities of explosives stored in the German strongpoints. Von Choltitz claimed that the explosives had been secured in those locations simply in order to prevent them from falling into the hands of the FFI. Yet, given the architectural importance of certain of these strongpoints, such as the Palais du Luxembourg, the Chambre des Députés, and Les Invalides, it is clear that the Germans could have caused significant material damage to Paris. The reason why von Choltitz did not carry out his orders most probably lies in the knowledge that he was about to become a prisoner of war and that his account of the liberation of Paris might offset some of his actions earlier in the war, notably the liquidation of the Jews in the Crimea: in other words he was trying to save himself from the hangman's noose.[106]

The contrast with Warsaw could not be greater. As the population was marched out of Warsaw the Germans sent in workers to strip the buildings systematically of everything of any value: the museums, libraries, factories, and civilian property:

> All efforts to save as much as possible on the part of the Poles who, with the approval of the underground, worked in the German administration of the city under Burgomeister Leist, remained ineffective; as were all the attempts at intervention with Governor Fischer, who now resided in Sochaczew.[107]

After the looting the special German force began the destruction of the city. Out of Warsaw's 24,724 buildings, 10,455 were completely destroyed. All major public buildings, including St John's Cathedral, the Royal Palace, the Opera and Ballet House and the main library, were blown up.[108] The destruction of Warsaw took three months, and a soldier with the 1st Polish Army, Jan Karniewicz, watched helplessly with his fellow Poles as the Germans burned the city: 'there was an aura over Warsaw in the evening – a red aura, a pink aura'.[109] Maria Ginter was permitted to visit the city on 1 December 1944 and recorded the scene:

> The town looked truly dead. Buildings were burnt out. There was silence everywhere. Some parts of the city were just vast empty spaces. Corpses were still lying on the pavements . . . Nearer to the town's centre houses were still burning. The wiping-out operation progressed methodically. Flame-throwers moved across Warsaw putting finishing touches to the process of annihilation.[110]

When the 1st Polish Army finally liberated Warsaw in January 1945 it entered a dead city.

28

Autumn 1944: Western Europe

On 18 August 1944 Hitler ordered General Wiese, commander of the 19th Army, to withdraw from southern France. There were two lines of retreat, depending on the location of the troops: northwards to the line of the Loire, or north-eastwards towards the Belfort Gap which would take the German troops directly back into the Reich. This order was known to the Americans, and it transformed the situation in the south: the Allies no longer faced the prospect of a pitched battle against an enemy determined to hold its ground, but instead faced a beaten foe on the retreat. This voluntary German withdrawal also altered the role of the resistance. The resistance worked alongside and with the Allies along the German withdrawal routes, harassing the Germans, and supplying the Allies with useful intelligence. Elsewhere, as the Germans withdrew from the cities and towns of southern France the FFI moved in. This led to claims at the time that France liberated itself, claims which were repeated after the war. The truth is more prosaic: where battles were needed then the Allies fought them, and where the Germans had withdrawn voluntarily, the FFI moved in and claimed the honour of liberating parts of France for itself.

The Germans had limited options when selecting the routes of their withdrawal. The Massif Central was believed to be full of FFI troops, so the principal route selected was along the Rhône valley towards Lyon, with the American Task Force Butler in hot pursuit. The most important town on the way was Grenoble, the location of the headquarters of the German 157th Reserve Division under Lieutenant General Pflaum. This division consisted of three infantry regiments and two artillery battalions which were scattered in small garrisons across south-east France. The FFI were strong in the area, particularly in the departments of Isère and Drôme, and they constantly harassed the Germans and supplied Task Force Butler with vital intelligence on the locations of the German defenders. Pflaum received conflicting orders: Wiese demanded that he hold Grenoble until the end of August by which time most of the German army would have passed through the town, but Field Marshal Kesselring for some unknown reason assumed that Pflaum's division was part of his own forces in Italy, and ordered him to hold the Alpine passes. Pflaum himself recognized the weakness of his forces and on 21 August the German garrison in Grenoble burned its records, destroyed various installations, and began to move out of the town. That night the Isère FFI moved in to take over, despite being too weak to withstand a German attack should the Germans return. On the afternoon of 22 August the Americans reached Grenoble and the FFI moved out to guard the north-western road to Lyon.[1]

Directly south of Lyon lay the city of Valence, the prefectural seat of the Drôme department and therefore of political significance to the French. The city, with its bridge over the Rhône, lay on the retreat route of the 11th Panzer Division and was well defended by the Germans. The events that unfolded demonstrate both the weakness of the French claim to have liberated themselves and the danger of over-optimism by the advancing Americans. The FTP launched an attack on the city with 350 men which the Germans repulsed with ease, causing the FTP fifteen casualties and the loss of all its transport. A similarly weak American attack on the night of 24–25 August was also driven back. Indeed, the Germans showed that they were not yet beaten by launching a counter-offensive against the Americans and FFI on 25 August. By the time the Americans had restored the situation on the 27th, and had entered Valence on the 31st, 11th Panzer had passed through the city and was headed towards Lyon where it joined the 19th Army which had withdrawn northwards in good order. The Germans now had 130,000 men with an armoured component with which to defend Lyon.[2]

The liberations of Grenoble and Valence showed that the FFI and Americans could work together well. But there were complaints regarding the use the Americans made of the FFI. For example, Colonel Jean-Pierre de Lassus Saint-Geniès, the FFI chief in the Drôme, complained that 'We are not at the *entire disposition* of the Americans, who have a tendency to engage our troops like the infantry of a regular army.'[3] This was the consequence of Frederick Butler (leader of Task Force Butler) only having one infantry battalion at his disposal. It was also a reflection of conflicting priorities: the FFI wanted to focus on the liberation of towns and French territory, whereas Butler wanted to inflict considerable damage on the retreating German forces. The Americans, for their part, resented having to fight for places such as Valence solely as a consequence of premature action by the FTP.

On the French Riviera, General Truscott was convinced that the Germans would not despatch troops from Italy across the Alpine passes to attack his forces. He therefore left the area to be defended by weak Allied forces, augmented by several special-operations teams. These troops managed to persuade numerous small German garrisons to surrender to them. Yet the FFI needed to be cautious. The town of Briançon guarded the route to the Montgenèvre pass and the FFI entered the town on 23 August but were forced to withdraw five days later under German pressure. The Germans only finally left the town on 5 September when the German high command ordered General Otto Fretter-Pico to withdraw his 148th Division towards the Italian border. This order had been decrypted by the Allies and passed to the regular French Army which was approaching the area. The OSS agent Geoffrey Jones, who was based in Nice, then received a windfall: another copy of Fretter-Pico's order together with the maps to carry it out. Jones translated the order overnight and took it to General Frederick, who ordered him to pass it to General Patch. The order and the plan of withdrawal made it apparent that the liberations of the Riviera towns of Nice and Cannes might be easier than expected.[4]

There was an active resistance in Cannes under Ange-Marie Miniconi. Miniconi took the initiative after he heard that the Germans were planning to blow up all the major buildings in Cannes. He held two clandestine meetings with the German commander, Colonel Erich Schneider. He focused on persuading Schneider not to carry out the demolitions and in return offered him a safe-conduct pass. Schneider took Miniconi to the Hôtel Splendide, in whose cellar lay the central control post for the demolitions, and they watched as the FFI cut the cables. On the night of 23–24 August the bulk of the German garrison along with Schneider withdrew to Nice: Schneider was court-martialled for dereliction of duty and executed. The remnants of the German garrison, who were mostly forcibly conscripted Poles from western Poland, surrendered willingly to the FFI. By the time the American forces arrived on 24 August, Cannes was already totally under French control. Nice had its own committee of liberation but it was very divided between the FTP which was strong in the city and wanted an uprising, and the FFI forces based in the surrounding mountains who wanted an orderly transfer of power. In the event there was little bloodshed because the Germans withdrew voluntarily and resistance activity was confined to anti-scorch actions. The liberation of Nice was celebrated on 28 August by a joint American-FFI parade.[5]

The rearrangement of Allied forces in the middle of August left the liberation of the ports of Toulon and Marseille to the French Army. The resistance in Toulon was dominated by the forces of the ORA under Jacques Lécuyer, and the FFI under Captain Salvatori which was assisted by an OSS team that had arrived in mid-June, and by Mission Gideon under Lieutenant Ménardière. The aim of the resistance was to prevent the

Germans from destroying the port installations and blocking the channels. Their work was hampered by the high German presence but nonetheless they managed to sabotage German efforts to block the principal channel. After Toulon surrendered to the French Army on 24 August, although the port itself held out for a few more days, work was begun to clear the hulks of the French fleet which had been scuttled in November 1942: the port was operating at full capacity by 20 September.[6]

The liberation of Marseille promised to be more of a challenge since its forts and suburbs covered fifteen miles of coastline. The resistance in the city consisted of around 1,000 men who were poorly armed. It was also badly divided following the arrests in July of the regional military delegate, Louis Burdet, and of the regional FFI chief, Robert Rossi. The FTP refused to collaborate with the replacements, Guillaume Widmer and Jean Constans. The SOE circuit leader in the city, Robert Boiteux, could do little to get the various forces to work together. Despite the splits in the resistance a general strike was launched on 20 August, and two days later the city rose up. The Germans took little action since their forces were concentrated outside the city waiting to take on General de Lattre's French army. This enabled the resistance to take over the city and restore French administration under its nominee, Raymond Aubrac, who took over the Préfecture. The French army, guided by the FFI, entered Marseille on 28 August. The resistance might have taken over the administration but it had manifestly failed to prevent German damage to the port, where there was 'an indescribable chaos of twisted ironwork, shattered concrete, and entangled cables'. The Germans had sunk over seventy-five ships in the channels, blown up the basins and quays with 2,000 mines, destroyed over 50,000 square metres of warehouses, and sabotaged 527 cranes. An enormous effort was immediately begun by the Allies to restore the port to working order, and by 30 September one basin was open.[7]

The French continued working their way along the coast towards Montpellier, which was finally liberated on 29 August after the Germans withdrew. Colonel Noel Croft was on hand to witness the liberation, noting that 'the town water supply, electricity and broadcasting station had all developed mysterious faults under the Germans. Suddenly they all started to work again, spare parts appearing like magic from their hiding places.' On 2 September the FFI paraded in front of de Lattre whereupon Croft considered his mission was over, commenting: 'I was thankful to get away from the town since politics had already taken over.'[8]

Nowhere did it seem that politics was more prevalent, controversial, and influential than in the events surrounding the liberation of Toulouse in south-west France. There were numerous resistance groups and their commanders competing for dominance: the chief of the FFI was Serge Ravanel, but the troops under his command were mostly communists; the regional military delegate was Bernard Schlumberger who found it virtually impossible to assert his authority; the 9,000-strong ORA contingent was led by Colonel André Pommiès who refused to bow to Ravanel's authority and who, through a compromise agreement reached in early August, had the right to contact Algiers and London directly. Other minority resistance groups present included a large contingent of Spanish veterans of their civil war and the Jewish 35th FTP–MOI Langer brigade. Adding to the complexity was the presence of George Starr of SOE's Wheelwright circuit. He had arrived in France in November 1942 and the Armagnac battalion he created and led was a thorn in German sides both before and after D-Day. Starr's power in the region is attested by the philosopher A. J. Ayer, then serving in SOE, who arrived in Toulouse in September 1944:

> There is a legend in Toulouse that the Germans, in 1943, already believed [Starr] to be a British General sent in to direct the whole of the resistance in the South West. At the time of the Liberation, the whole of the area was in the hands of a series of feudal lords whose power and influence was strangely similar to that of their fifteenth-century Gascon counterparts. Among these barons [Starr] was, without any question, the most influential.

This obvious disunity in the ranks of the resistance meant that the liberation of the city was more painful than necessary.

The Germans began to withdraw from Toulouse on 19 August in accordance with Hitler's order. The resistance failed to carry out counter-scorch activities and the Germans burned down many major buildings, including the post office, the Cafarelli barracks, Collège Saint-Aubin, and the Magasins Généraux. French firemen were prevented from attempting to extinguish the flames by fire from German machine guns. The Germans even found time to execute some Jews who had emerged from hiding too soon. The resistance did, however, manage to enter Saint-Michel prison and liberate over 400 prisoners, including the resister and author André Malraux. Once the Germans had departed, the various resistance armies moved in to fill the vacuum. Authority should have passed to Jean Cassou, a veteran of the early resistance group, the Musée de l'Homme, who had been appointed commissioner of the republic by de Gaulle. But Cassou was knocked out and left in a coma after a collision with a departing German vehicle: his replacement, Pierre Bertaux, struggled to assert his authority over the resistance. Worse still, communist influences became apparent as workers in the major factories, especially the aeronautical industry, formed soviets and demanded to take over the management of the enterprises. Starr and his men managed to expel the FTP from the Préfecture and handed it over to Bertaux. Law and order completely vanished from the streets of Toulouse as 50,000 armed men took revenge against political opponents as much as against obvious collaborators. As one historian commented: 'Because there were no Allied troops for hundreds of kilometres, Toulouse came to represent the nightmares of those who feared that liberation would turn into revolution.'[9]

The resistance in Bordeaux was similarly deeply divided between the FFI, ORA, and FTP, as well as those men who had remained loyal to André Grandclément. The situation did not descend into the chaos prevalent in Toulouse because of the efforts of two men: Gaston Cusin, the commissioner of the republic, and Roger Landes, the head of the SOE Actor circuit. Cusin confirmed Landes as commander of the FFI units and supported him against all would-be usurpers, with the result that Landes 'refused to recognise any of them, which proved to be a mistake, for he thereby antagonised all of them'. Landes's competitors managed to keep him from making contact with the regional military delegate, Colonel Charles Gaillard, who had arrived in Bordeaux in the middle of July but did not meet Landes until 7 August. The first step taken by Gaillard was to confirm Landes as commander of the FFI: politics could wait until Bordeaux had been liberated.

Bordeaux was a major port with installations stretching along both banks of the Gironde estuary. The Germans planned to mine all the main port and dock facilities in Bordeaux and all the bridges in the region. The laying of the mines was scheduled to begin on 24 August and the demolitions were to be carried out on the night of 26–27 August. But an anti-Nazi German sergeant, Franz Stahlschmidt, got hold of these plans and made contact with the resistance with a proposal to destroy the magazine containing an estimated 400kg of explosives and 4,000 fuses. In return Stahlschmidt wanted nothing more than a guarantee of safe conduct from the FFI. Landes agreed, and, on 22 August, Stahlschmidt entered the magazine and blew it up before reaching an FFI safe house and surviving the war. The Germans were now in no position to destroy the port of Bordeaux and their commander, Lieutenant General Albin Nake, issued a face-saving proclamation on 26 August:

> As supreme commander of German forces in the Bordeaux region, I declare that no destruction will take place in greater Bordeaux, and that the harbour and bridges which are mined will not be destroyed, if the population refrains from all acts of sabotage in greater Bordeaux until the withdrawal from Bordeaux of all German forces.

Landes, in his report to Colonel Buckmaster, suggested that he and Cusin had made an agreement with the Germans to prevent the destruction and largely wrote Stahlschmidt out of the story. The Germans abandoned Bordeaux without difficulty on 28 August. However, they withdrew only as far as their strongpoints at Royan and Pointe de Grave and retained control over the Gironde estuary, where they remained until spring 1945. The following weeks bore witness to internecine French squabbles for power which were only settled when de Gaulle arrived in mid-September.[10]

News of the problems encountered during the liberations of Toulouse and Bordeaux reached London and Algiers and caused considerable alarm. The Allies were determined that the liberation of Lyon should be carried out in a more orderly fashion. The Germans who had withdrawn from garrisons further south were all concentrated in Lyon and fully prepared to defend the city from all attackers. The resistance was both aided and hampered by the presence of numerous experienced leaders in the area: men such as François Huet, André Pecquet, Alain Le Ray, Marcel Descour, Alban Vistel, Henri Provisor, and Henri Romans-Petit. All of them had different ideas on how to liberate the city. The situation did not descend into total chaos as had occurred in south-western France because of the presence of the Allies, the Americans, and the French, advancing on both sides of the Rhône.

The FTP tried to precipitate events and seize the city itself. On 24 August it launched attacks on two prisons near the railway station. These failed but led to an uprising in the working-class Villeurbanne suburb which the Germans crushed easily and ruthlessly. SOE agent Tony Brooks offered to supply the FTP with urgently needed weapons but his offer was rejected because the FTP wanted the uprising to be its work alone. The uprising and its failure led to a dispute over tactics among the FFI forces outside the city. Although Alban Vistel was the regional FFI chief in the region, his subordinates, Provisor and Descour, needed to be handled with care. Provisor, whose troops were mostly FTP, wanted to attack Lyon immediately in conjunction with the FTP inside the city, which raised the prospect of a revolution. Descour, on the other hand, was in contact with the Americans and preferred to wait until the American and French troops were at hand before entering Lyon to ensure that power would be smoothly transferred to de Gaulle's political commissioner, Yves Farge. One solution to end the political impasse was suggested by General Koenig, who ordered Romans-Petit and Richard Heslop to launch their non-political maquis units to take Lyon. Both men refused the order, arguing that their maquis were not trained for urban fighting: the order was repeated and rejected again.

By the end of August, Lyon was almost entirely encircled by FFI units, the Americans were in the eastern outskirts of the city and French troops were approaching from Saint-Étienne to the south-west. In the late afternoon of 1 September the Germans began an orderly withdrawal northwards towards Bourg-en-Bresse, where the 11th Panzer Division constructed a defensive ring and clashed with the American advance units and the FFI at Meximieux. In the ensuing battle American tanks fought those of 11th Panzer, while the FFI fought as infantry alongside and in the same numbers as the Americans. This provided a tribute to the fighting qualities of the FFI which had been recognized and acknowledged by the Americans after earlier battles on the way to Lyon. On 2 September it appeared that all German forces had left Lyon. Behind them lay a scene of destruction since the resistance inside the city had proved incapable of preventing the Germans from blowing up all but one of the numerous bridges crossing the Rhône and the Saône. Finally, on 3 September the French army and the numerous FFI forces entered Lyon. Farge took over the Préfecture and ensured a smooth transition of power.[11]

As the Germans retreated across central France their troops were constantly and successfully harassed by the FFI. For example, Lieutenant General Otto Ottenbacher struggled to extract all his units from the Massif Central. As the Germans retreated further north, they were forced off the main roads by the threat of bombing from the Allied air forces, whereupon they took to the back roads where the FFI could more readily attack them and mine the roads. For example, an entire twenty-kilometre stretch of road up to Autun, south-west of Dijon, was rendered impassable by RAF attacks. The FFI generally did not attempt to liberate towns by themselves but would wait until the Germans had left. An exception was the town of Limoges where the FFI under Philippe Liewer and Georges Guingouin threatened to assault the German garrison of 1,500 troops, which was augmented with tanks and *Milice* units, while at the same time attempting to negotiate a surrender with the German commander, Major General Walter Gleininger. On 20 August the Swiss chargé d'affaires, Jean d'Albis, tried to persuade Gleininger to surrender, but the German commander refused to surrender to the FFI. On the other hand he appeared willing to surrender to Allied troops so, with an enormous amount of bluff and bravado, a hastily put together Anglo-French-American delegation was put together with Liewer representing Britain, Captain Charles Brown the United States, Captain Viguier the French Army, and Captain Guery for the FFI. An agreement was reached with Gleininger for the surrender; the SS, however, refused to comply with his orders and kidnapped him.

Gleininger shot himself rather than face a court martial. On 22 August even the SS bowed to the inevitable and took off along the road to Lyon allowing the triumphant FFI to enter the town.[12]

A similar reluctance to surrender to the FFI was shown by General Botho Elster whose column of 18,000 men was retreating northwards towards the Loire. At the beginning of September the column was located in the triangle formed by the towns of Châteauroux, Vierzon, and Bourges, and was watched closely by 2,000 FFI fighters with an SAS contingent nearby. French negotiators, including Philippe de Vomécourt, attempted to persuade Elster to surrender, as did Tommy Macpherson of Jedburgh team Quinine. Elster feared the consequences of surrendering to the FFI, so Major General Robert Macon of the US 83rd Infantry Division operating north of the Loire travelled to the south-west of Orléans and on 17 September Elster surrendered his troops to Macon at Issoudun. An historian has noted of this surrender that:

> The defeatism of the German general . . . played at least as important a role as the military action of the resistance in this one and only quantifiable major victory of the FFI. But even during the surrender negotiations General Macon did not concede that the capitulation had been forced by the FFI.

Elster impressed Macon with his fear of retribution by the FFI if his troops were forced to march unarmed and unescorted the sixty miles to the Loire where they were to enter American custody. Macon accordingly agreed to allow the soldiers of the Elster column to retain their small arms. De Vomécourt wrote later:

> I can well understand that the Germans preferred not to surrender to the Resistance. I know also that the Americans may have lacked confidence in the Resistance, and in our ability to handle the surrender in a disciplined way. They were wrong . . . But, even so, we should have been content to receive the surrender, and to allow the Americans to see that what followed was according to the book. I should have had no objection to a few American Jeeps assisting us.[13]

At the time he complained to Lieutenant Colonel Powell who referred the matter to Patton and Eisenhower. The sole result was that the march into captivity of the Elster column was delayed by twenty-four hours. The Germans still retained their weapons.[14]

Evidence regarding the conduct of the FFI towards Germans who had surrendered is mixed. Francis Cammaerts is adamant that the French would approach him for advice on the care of the German POWs as stipulated by the Geneva Convention.[15] Others, however, commented on the brutality of the FFI towards their prisoners. For example, Arthur Clutton of Jedburgh team Julian reported from the area of Pearl Witherington's Wrestler circuit that:

> At the beginning of the conflict, the FFI did take prisoners and treated wounded and unwounded with consideration. As time went on and it became obvious that all FFI captured by the enemy were shot like rabbits and in some cases tortured, their attitude changed. Many Germans were shot in reprisal, and towards the end no prisoners were taken.[16]

There is also evidence to suggest that a few German POWs, both Wehrmacht and SS, were tortured by the FFI.

After evacuating Lyon the German 19th Army was in a headlong retreat for the Belfort Gap. This is a natural fifteen-mile-wide gap between the Vosges mountains to the north and the Jura to the south. The Germans planned to mount a sustained defence in the last major town before the Belfort Gap, Besançon, which lay on the Doubs river. The FFI troops under Heslop and Romans-Petit pursued the Germans from the south where they began to encounter the FFI under George Millar, the head of the SOE Treasurer circuit, and the three Jedburgh teams which had been dropped into the area in the middle of August to assist him. The ranks of the FFI were augmented by a mutiny of Ukrainians who had attacked their German officers and then joined the FFI: 1,300 men equipped with heavy weapons, ammunition, and transport. Appeals by Millar for arms drops to strengthen their ranks were left unanswered. Millar had created a small force which specialized in railway sabotage. On one occasion its work had included sending four locomotives to collide with one another in a cutting on the Besançon–Vesoul line, with the result that 'already crowds were gathering for this fantastic sight. Cycling excursions were setting out from all the villages'. Now, however, Millar found it virtually impossible to act in the Doubs valley because:

> The retreating German Army came pouring into the valley, until in many places saturation point was reached, and there was no small space that did not hold a German . . . All the maquis had to fight to exist. The Germans were so numerous that it was a question of holding some piece of ground, some corner of woodland, and in clear spaces going out to hit him on the road.

The Germans were able to blow the bridges across the Doubs and all FFI efforts to prevent these demolitions led to heavy losses. The town of Besançon was only liberated by American troops at the beginning of September following a three-day battle. After the Americans crossed the Moselle their progress into the Vosges mountains was hampered by stiffening German resistance. The American advance was assisted by extremely thorough intelligence supplied by a newly set-up network of retired French artillery officers who reported to OSS agent Justin Greene. All resistance attacks on the Germans were met with harsh reprisals.[17]

On 11 September patrols from the US 3rd Army advancing from the north made contact with French troops from the south near Dijon. The junction of the two invasion forces meant that the liberation of France was almost complete. It is therefore time now to assess the contribution the French resistance made to the liberation of its country. General Bradley commented after the war: 'I don't know how many divisions the resistance shot up or bottled up. But I can tell you this: The French Resistance was worth a hell of a lot of divisions to us. We needed them, and they were there when needed.'[18] Eisenhower paid a similar tribute to the FFI. The historian Henri Michel concluded with regard to the FFI in the north that:

> Without the Allied invasion, the Resistance would have failed in the end. Without the materiel delivered by the Allies, it would have remained powerless. But without the support from the Resistance, the task of the Allies would have been incomparably more difficult and their success would not have materialised as quickly.[19]

These are all generalizations and the exact contribution has proved harder to quantify. Certainly the FFI had assisted the Allies directly in the provision of intelligence from the moment of the Allied landings and had played a useful role in the rapid liberation of Brittany. But the real contribution of the resistance came with the American swing back towards the east when the FFI mobilized 25,000 men to screen the line of the Loire river and thereby protect the right flank of Patton's army.[20]

Further south, the presence of FFI bands helped to dictate the German line of withdrawal along the Rhône valley. Again the FFI provided essential intelligence to the American and French forces and augmented American infantry formations when necessary. General Truscott acknowledged this contribution: 'The Maquis were well provided with arms and explosives by the Allies, and Allied officers with communications had parachuted in to assist them in coordinating their operations. We expected a good deal of assistance from them and we were not disappointed. Their knowledge of the country, of enemy dispositions and movements, was invaluable, and their fighting ability was extraordinary.'[21]

The FFI had certainly hampered the German retreat from the south and south-west of France, but it should be noted that the retreat of General von Blaskowitz's Army Group G was still orderly, especially in comparison to the rapid, disorganized flight of the German armies in the north after the Allied breakout from Normandy and the closure of the Falaise Gap. Blaskowitz's army was 209,000 men strong when the retreat began, and around 130,000 reached the Loire safely. It had, however, lost nearly 90 per cent of its artillery. In addition, German troops crossing the Seine from garrisons in western and central France numbered around 300,000. Therefore, it can be safely concluded that the German army pouring through the Belfort Gap was still in good order and that as a result Patton's forces and the French Army would face hard battles on the German frontier in the future. Post-war research by Philippe Buton, who surveyed the liberation of 212 cities in France, concluded that of these the majority, some 179, owed their liberation to the Allied forces or the voluntary retreat of the German Army and not to the actions of the FFI.[22] One of the important locations liberated by the FFI alone was Nancy, the capital of Lorraine, which fell to FFI forces under Gilbert Grandval on 15 September.[23]

The number of prisoners taken by the FFI and the number of Germans they killed are hard to estimate. The surrender of the Elster column delivered around 18,000 German troops into American hands, and it is thought that approximately a further 22,000 Germans were taken prisoner by the FFI in the period between D-Day and the beginning of September. The figures of Germans killed by the FFI appear to be impossible to establish with any degree of certainty.

The military contribution of the FFI to the liberation was necessarily limited because of its lack of heavy weaponry and its inability to take on large German formations. It was never conceived that the French resistance should engage in regular warfare, but rather that it should focus on guerrilla tactics to keep the Germans unsettled and disorganized. It is therefore somewhat unfair to focus exclusively on the military contribution of the resistance since its effect was political and moral as much as, if not more than, military. The numbers in the ranks of the FFI grew exponentially during the liberation: from 100,000 men in June 1944 to around half a million by August. Casualties, which are again hard to establish with certainty, were relatively low, with around 24,000 FFI combatants killed in the fighting, although there were further losses caused by capture and deportation to concentration camps.[24]

Although Koenig had been appointed commander of the FFI it was apparent that he had limited control of the liberation forces once the Allied invasions had begun. This lack of control caused great alarm in the ranks of the French provisional government as de Gaulle fought for recognition not only from the Allies but also from the people of France. Above all, de

Gaulle feared the communists. After the war, Charles Tillon denied that the communists had ever had any intention of seizing power in 1944:

> Our aim was purely anti-Fascist. We were fighting to root Fascism out of France – both its German and its French aspects. We had never thought of taking over power. We had a concrete part to play in the French battle, and it was directed only at ridding the country of the occupying forces and the Vichy authorities. Even when we had seen the Allies' distrust of anything that could look like revolutionary attitudes among us, and even when we saw that Vichy's men were often replaced by people with ideas of much the same kind, we never thought of using our weapons against anyone belonging to London or Algiers.[25]

In August and September 1944, however, the picture looked very different. It has already been noted that the FTP had often acted too hastily in attempting the liberation of towns and cities, hoping for political kudos if they succeeded. Furthermore, events in cities such as Toulouse showed that revolutionary forces were at work within the ranks of the FTP and Communist Party members. This revolutionary zeal effectively split the resistance at the moment of its victory. De Vomécourt wrote later:

> As we had expected, the Communists sought immediately to exploit their participation in the Resistance, offering themselves as self-proclaimed heroes, riding to power and popularity on the bandwagon of patriotism. They appointed themselves agents of vengeance, using the opportunity to liquidate potential enemies of Communism, and seeking to smear the reputation of others.[26]

Later historians have noted that the communists not only sought to eradicate all Vichy influences from French society now that Pétain, Laval, and their coterie had been evacuated from France by the Germans and had re-established an overtly collaborationist government at Sigmaringen, but also attacked their non-communist former colleagues, tarring them with the brush of collaboration simply because of political differences.[27]

De Gaulle therefore faced an uphill struggle to gain control over France. He took a number of immediate steps in pursuit of his aim. The first was to disband the FFI and its leadership, COMAC. This was ordered on 28 August, before the liberation of the major cities of southern France, and caused outrage within the ranks of the FFI, with the FTP proving particularly reluctant to surrender their weapons. Ultimately, however, the communists were not prepared to initiate a civil war with de Gaulle and fell into line. The combatants from the FFI and FTP were encouraged to join the regular French Army units. For example, in Paris, veterans of the insurrection, including Colonel Fabien, who was later killed in December while attempting to disable a mine, joined General Leclerc's 2nd Armoured Division during its advance eastwards. In the south-east FFI formations under Commandant Christian Sorensen were amalgamated into seven battalions termed the 'Southern Alpine Group', which was attached to General de Lattre's 1st Army. Due acknowledgement of the resistance was made by the group's commander, a regular French soldier Colonel Louis Lanusse, who made the ORA commander, Jacques Lécuyer, his deputy. Doubts were raised regarding the effectiveness of the FFI soldiers in regular army units, with Leclerc informing de Gaulle that only 10 per cent were suitable for current operations, around 30 per cent would be useful after rest and training, while the remainder were useless and probably dangerous.[28]

On 9 September de Gaulle reorganized his government, making it 'a careful balance of Free French, resisters, former politicians who had not blotted their copybook under Vichy, civil servants and experts'. Two communists joined the government: Charles Tillon as minister for aviation and François Billoux for public health. The CNR had vowed that none of its members would join the government but its chairman Georges Bidault then agreed to become minister of foreign affairs: Pierre Villon, however, turned down the post offered to him by de Gaulle.[29]

Most important of all, de Gaulle embarked on a tour of liberated France to let the people put a face to the voice they had only heard over the radio and to assert his authority. He reached Lyon on 14 September where he found that Yves Farge had the situation well under control. But Lyon also demonstrated an important aspect of de Gaulle's attitude towards the resistance. Heslop and Romans-Petit were visited by a three-man delegation from the FFI who arrested Romans-Petit and had ordered Heslop's immediate departure from France. Heslop believed that Romans-Petit was arrested because: 'Any leading Frenchman who seemed to have too heavy an emotional link with England was automatically excluded by General de Gaulle as a possible future leader in the new France.' On 15 September de Gaulle reached Marseille, where he found 'the atmosphere was ominous' with the communists arresting their political opponents without due legal process. He felt that the new commissioner of the republic, Raymond Aubrac, a veteran resister, 'found it difficult to adopt the psychology of high officialdom'.

De Gaulle's agenda involved not only the restoration of order but also the downplaying of SOE's role in the liberation. In Toulouse he was appalled by the mixture of resistance forces on parade: apart from the FFI forces there were the Spaniards, Russian defectors from the German Army, and above all George Starr's SOE contingent. De Gaulle was introduced to Starr and immediately accused him of being a mercenary and ordered him out of the country. Starr responded: 'I am a British soldier on duty. I have a command to exercise. I will not leave except on the order of my superiors in London. I shit on you. You are the head of a provisional government that the Allies have not recognised.' SOE, however, endorsed de Gaulle's dismissal of Starr and he was back in London within the week. De Gaulle was also rude to the Frenchmen who had fought with SOE. Serge Ravanel commented: 'I have discovered that what mattered above all to him was to bring us to heel. And to draw a line under all that we had learned and all that made up the originality of the Resistance.' On 17 September de Gaulle reached Bordeaux and inspected the troops of the FFI who had been armed and trained by Roger Landes. He approached Landes and informed him bluntly: 'You are English? Your place is not here now.' Far from attending the lunch to which he had been invited by the commissioner of the republic to celebrate, Landes was informed that he should leave France immediately.[30]

De Gaulle's tour was undoubtedly a triumph in that it did lead to the restoration of law and order and thereby denied the communists their brief chance of launching a revolution. It was followed by efforts to gain control over the *épuration*, the identification and punishment of collaborators, which will be covered in a later chapter. The tour also helped to establish the myth that France had liberated itself.

Special Forces Headquarters acknowledged that the role of SOE in France was largely over and ordered all SOE agents out of the country on 21 September, and on 13 October this order was extended to British and American members of Jedburgh teams. A few exceptions were made: OSS agent Geoffrey Jones remained in place in south-eastern France to run his intelligence network until March 1945, and a few Jedburgh teams remained in western France until November to oversee the training and supplies of the French forces investing the Atlantic ports. SOE agents were naturally outraged by their abrupt dismissal. Robert Boiteux voiced their feelings:

> What rankled with me was that in all of the newspapers of that period of heady freedom, in all the speeches reported, in all the stories about the Resistance, from its first days to its last, there was no mention that a few Englishmen had stood at the sides of the *résistants*, nor of where those vital arms and other supplies had come from, nor how they had reached France and found their way into the hands of Frenchmen. In the whole of France during the entire war, the English agents sent out by SOE never reached a number which could have turned the tide alone, but they came when England

> and France had their backs to the wall and when all seemed lost for both countries, and they came at a time when it was almost a suicide mission to do so. They brought arms, instruction and a sense of purpose to hundreds of French patriots; and together they planned, trained and lived for the day which was now being so wildly celebrated.

In the years following the war, French awards were made to a number of SOE agents and their role, still downplayed, was at least acknowledged. In 1991 a memorial monument to the ninety-one men and thirteen women members of SOE who lost their lives during the German occupation of France was unveiled at Valençay.[31]

By the end of August the vast majority of German forces had fled northern France, and the Pas-de-Calais and Nord regions were finally liberated in operations between 1 and 5 September. The German presence in France was now limited to the ports of Le Havre, Boulogne, and Calais, which surrendered later in September, and to the Atlantic ports where they were effectively penned in and their movements were under close watch from the French Army along with members of the now-disbanded FFI. The Germans retreated headlong, chased by the Allies who advanced as fast as there was fuel for their tanks and vehicles. On 3 September the Guards Armoured Division entered the Belgian capital, Brussels, to a rapturous welcome.

The rapidity of the arrival of the Allies meant that there was only a limited role for the Belgian resistance. Its *Armée Secrète* had begun to be mobilized region by region from 31 August, but for most of the men there was little work to be done. The Belgian resistance did increase its level of sabotage as liberation approached, carrying out 415 sabotage operations during August. During September there were a further 600 attacks on the railways and the destruction of over fifty bridges and 140 locomotives.[32] The Belgian resistance lacked the weapons to engage in guerrilla warfare against the Germans, and so its role was largely limited to providing the Allies with intelligence on the locations of German units, acting as guides, mopping up isolated pockets of Germans, and maintaining law and order in areas vacated by the Germans but not yet reached by the Allies and the Belgian administrators. The two notable exceptions, places where the resistance did make a useful contribution, were the Ardennes and the port of Antwerp.

In 1943 the Belgian resistance had begun establishing camps in the heavily wooded Ardennes region, but the paucity of food supplies necessarily limited the numbers gathered there, and those who did live in the camps received very few weapons from SOE. In late August and early September 1944 parties of the Belgian SAS began to arrive in the Ardennes to supply weapons and to train the Belgians in their use. One such party was accompanied by Hugh Fraser, who was parachuted in on 1 September to act as liaison between the special forces and the *Armée Secrète*. He was appalled by the situation on the ground, and telegraphed London on 12 September:

> God rot Gubbins' guts. Has SF [Special Forces] any contact in this region? Blunt [Eddy Blondeel, commander of Belgian SAS unit] met one half-witted SF boy who asked him for orders. Is SF aware of frontier changes and unarmed Belgians in the greater Reich since 1940? Is SF aware of atrocities and German bandits in woods? Is SF aware that the prevention of re-infiltration is a Maquis responsibility? Did SF order total mobilisation here about September first knowing that there were no arms? An act amounting to mass murder.

Fraser's impression is confirmed by a Groupe G saboteur, Herman Bodson. He met the Ardennes commander of the *Armée Secrète* who confidently expected to mobilize 600–800 men in the region, but when Bodson met the unit he found around 100 men armed with a few carbines and shotguns. Fraser arranged a number of drops and 2,000 much-needed weapons arrived. Armed with these weapons and directed by the Belgian SAS, the Belgian resistance was able to destroy pockets of German resistance and allow the Allies unhampered travel along the main roads. By the middle of September the Belgian Ardennes had been largely cleared of German troops. Across all of Belgium the resistance had taken 35,000 prisoners, including two German generals. Resistance casualties had been high, around 1,100 killed in action, and more killed after capture or deportation to Germany.[33]

The Belgian resistance is justifiably proud of the role it played in saving the port of Antwerp from destruction as the Germans retreated. The port area covered around twenty-six miles of docks, locks, water towers, cranes, and storage facilities. The Belgians had recognized the importance of counter-scorch plans well before SOE or any outside agency directed them to look into the matter. Back in 1943 a committee had been set up to investigate how Antwerp port could be saved from destruction and the responsibility for drawing up plans was placed in the hands of a regular Belgian army officer, Lieutenant Urban Reniers. He in turn appointed a merchant marine officer, Eugène Colson, leader of the forces inside the immediate port area. By the time that SOE despatched the Comte de Liedekerke in February 1944 to investigate the defence of Antwerp port the plans were well advanced. Teams were trained to disable German mines, booby traps, and explosives, and at the end of August the Belgians destroyed two cement plants which had been producing the special cylinders needed by the Germans to mine the port. On 3 September, as Brussels was liberated, the action teams were mobilized. By 1 p.m. on 4 September the vital Bonaparte and Kattendÿk locks were safely in the hands of the Belgian resistance, followed that afternoon by three more locks and the Strasbourg bridge. Teams were in place to prevent the Germans from opening valves to allow water from the Scheldt to flow into the Antwerp sewer system, which would have caused a major health hazard in the city.

The second line of action by the resistance was to identify the most suitable route along which the Allies could advance. This became the role of a Belgian Army engineer, Robert Vekemans, who reconnoitred the routes south of Antwerp. He quickly identified the most likely point of difficulty: the crossing of the Willebroek Canal and the Rupel Stream at Boom, ten miles south of Antwerp on the road to Aalst. The Germans had mined the two major bridges across both water crossings and had a good field of fire from their defensive positions. Vekemans, however, discovered that a third bridge, the nineteenth-century Pont van Enschodt, had been carelessly mined, was weakly guarded, and the Germans had a limited field of fire. As the first tanks from the 11th Armoured Division commanded by Major General George Roberts came into view just south of Boom, Vekemans made contact with their commander and explained the situation. The tanks duly crossed the old bridge, outflanked the Germans and advanced on the main bridge. One bridge was saved from destruction but the Germans succeeded in demolishing the other. By the end of 4 September the city of Antwerp and its port were safely in Allied hands and the Germans had retreated across the Albert Canal. The Germans had only been able to cause minor damage to three lock gates, which was easily repaired, so in theory the Allies should have been able to use the port from early September. The Scheldt estuary, however, was still held by the Germans, and the port could not be used for almost three months after much bitter fighting.[34]

On 8 September the government-in-exile of Hubert Pierlot returned to Brussels. In contrast to the rapturous welcome accorded to de Gaulle in Paris, Pierlot and his ministers landed at Evere airfield without anyone greeting them, and travelled into the capital in a lorry and post van. The Pierlot government returned to face numerous problems in need of urgent solutions. One was the position of King Léopold, then in internment in Germany. Léopold was hostile to the Pierlot government because of its attitude towards him in 1940. The government and many Belgians were appalled that the king had contracted a morganatic marriage during the war, and also that he had failed to speak out against unpopular German measures such as conscription for forced labour. The government responded by appointing Léopold's brother Charles as regent until the matter of the king's future could be settled after the war. Belgium was also desperately short of food and coal, a worrying situation as winter approached. The government was also widely viewed as being soft on collaborators. The resistance estimated that there were around 400,000 collaborators, yet in the months following the return of the government only 60,000 had been arrested, and most of these would be released before the end of the year.

The Belgian resistance had expanded from around 30,000 to about 70,000 men during the liberation period. Most of them had been denied the opportunity to fight the Germans by the swiftness of the Allied advance. Nonetheless they demanded recognition. The Pierlot government, however, requested them to hand in their weapons and then either join the Belgian Army or the gendarmerie or return to civilian life. SHAEF noted the reaction: 'The resistance representatives have complained that the Government, instead of being appreciative of the part played by the resistance in the liberation of the country, is only concerned in suppressing and disarming resistance groups. There appears to be some truth in this complaint.' On 2 October 1944 Eisenhower attempted to rectify the situation by writing to all Belgian resistance units that their members:

> ... can be justly proud of having by their devoted heroism contributed so largely to the liberation of their beloved homeland. The rapidity of the advance of the Allied forces which has spared much of your country the horrors of war has been due in no small measure to your help ... Fighting is therefore over for most of you as soldiers of Resistance Groups ... Those of [you] who are no longer engaged in fighting or on guard duties, etc., upon orders of Allied Commanders, can best assist the military effort by handing in their arms ... These arms are urgently needed for other purposes.

The resistance, especially members of the *Front de l'Indépendance* (FI), proved very reluctant to hand over their weapons.

The Belgian government became so worried about the possibility of a breakdown in law and order that SOE duly despatched 18,000 Sten guns to be distributed to the Belgian gendarmerie. The head of the SHAEF mission in Belgium, Major General George Erskine, estimated that before these weapons arrived the armed members of the resistance outnumbered those of the police and gendarmerie by ten to one. In November the government decreed that resisters could join the army as individuals, as had occurred in Italy, and not as partisan units: all weapons must be handed over by the end of the month. The FI response was to hold a demonstration on 25 November. The police and gendarmerie fired on the demonstrators, wounding thirty-four of them. The presence of British armoured units in the streets around the demonstration prevented the violence from escalating. Erskine warned the head of the FI, Fernand Demany, and the leader of the Communist Party, Jean Terfve, that the Allies would not tolerate further disturbances. Indeed, the Belgian demobilization crisis fizzled out quickly. The communist call for a general strike on 28 November was largely ignored, by 8 December 12,000 weapons had been handed in, and by February 1945 11,000 former resisters had joined the army.[35]

Belgium had been liberated, but the country was to suffer more of the ravages of war. Antwerp and Liège were targeted by German V-2 attacks, and the Belgian Ardennes became the focus of the Battle of the Bulge. There then followed one of the most controversial strategic debates at this stage of the war. Antwerp lay at the head of the fifty-four-mile-long and three-mile-wide Scheldt estuary, and until this area was firmly in British hands the port could not be reopened for Allied shipping. The port was essential for the Allied advance because until it was opened supplies had to continue being ferried to the front lines by road from Cherbourg, a distance of over 450 miles. The Scheldt estuary was defended by the 80,000-strong German 15th Army under General Gustav von Zangen. Although large, this army had been broken during its retreat from the Pas-de-Calais and could have been relatively easily overwhelmed had the Allies chosen to advance northwards to capture the estuary. To the amazement of the Belgian resistance the British halted firmly on the line of the Albert Canal, seeming to fail to appreciate the necessity of advancing to hold the estuary. The port of Antwerp would only reopen to Allied shipping on 28 November 1944.

There are several reasons for this strategic failure. The Allies had advanced over 500 kilometres in six days and the belief had grown that the war would be over by Christmas. It seemed that just one more thrust would completely break the Germans in western Europe. Field Marshal Montgomery had his eyes firmly set on crossing the Rhine and advancing into Germany's industrial heartland, the Ruhr, while to the south Patton's armies had reached Metz, and Patton was equally adamant that one more thrust by his armies would drive them into Germany. Both men pressed Eisenhower to divert all the limited resources to their advance. Eisenhower, however, made the decision which has been hotly debated ever since, that the Allies should advance on a broad front and that no one commander should have priority.

Evidence that the German army was broken appeared overwhelming and it seemed that the Netherlands might be liberated soon. On 4 September the Dutch service of the BBC broadcast an erroneous report that the Allies had crossed the frontier and had liberated the cities of Roermond and Breda. On 4 September, Queen Wilhelmina had also broadcast to her compatriots a message which was repeated by Eisenhower in his own broadcast: 'The hour of liberation the Netherlands have awaited so long is now very near.' The Dutch prime minister, Pieter Gerbrandy, added 'Now that the Allied armies, in their irresistible advance, have crossed the Netherlands frontier . . . I want all of you to bid our Allies a hearty welcome to our native soil.' Tuesday, 5 September, has been termed 'Mad Tuesday' because of the headlong retreat of the German troops from Belgium crossing the Netherlands to the safety of the Reich. They were followed by 65,000 Dutch collaborators escaping post-liberation retribution. However, the Netherlands were not being evacuated. Reichskommissar Seyss-Inquart and Anton Mussert, head of the NSB (*Nationaal-Socialistische Beweging*), moved from The Hague to a massive underground bunker at Apeldoorn. Seyss-Inquart declared a state of emergency on 5 September, threatening death sentences for even the most minor sign of opposition.

The resistance in the Netherlands had suffered many setbacks during the war. The *Englandspiel*, the German control of SOE agents parachuted into the country, had caused enormous damage, both by greatly hampering the build-up of the resistance and by fostering a lingering suspicion that Dutch intelligence could not be trusted. Yet by autumn 1944 the situation had been transformed. The Dutch intelligence service, the *Bureau Inlichtingen*, had been completely reorganized and revitalized under Colonel Somer, and by September 1944 was a highly efficient service which the Germans never succeeded in breaking, as even Lieutenant Colonel Hermann Giskes, the architect of the *Englandspiel*, admitted. SOE Dutch Section had also succeeded in inserting a number of agents whose networks would be augmented by the insertion of Jedburgh teams. In September the principal Dutch resistance units, the *Knokploegen*, RVV, and *Orde Dienst*, had been grouped together in the new Dutch forces of the interior, the *Nederlandse Binnenlandse Strijdkrachten* (NBS), under Prince Bernhard, who was based in Brussels.[36]

Dutch intelligence in the Arnhem region was led by Piet Kruijff, and his network included men such as Lieutenant Commander Charles Douw van der Krap, Henri Knap, Albert Horstman, Harry Montfroy, and Johannes Penseel. They were able to communicate with other intelligence cells across the country using a secret method devised by a telecoms engineer, Nicolaas de Bode, which meant that by dialling a special 12–15 digits-long number, local switchboards could be bypassed. The resistance also used a private telephone line connecting Arnhem to Nijmegen which belonged to the PGEM electricity company. The intelligence gathered was overwhelming in showing that the pace of the German retreat was slowing, and that the Germans were beginning to concentrate their forces and were preventing units from crossing into the Reich. The sighting of German tanks to the north and north-east of Arnhem suggested the presence of at least one German Panzer division, and the identity of the II SS Panzer Division which had been badly mauled during the retreat from France was confirmed and passed on. Knap checked personally the information that the Hotel Tafelberg in Oosterbeek was being prepared as the headquarters of a German army group. The hotel duly became Field Marshal Model's new headquarters from which he could direct the reorganization and rebuilding of the broken German army. The evidence of the slowing down of the German retreat was confirmed by events on the ground as the Germans launched minor counter-attacks against British positions along the Albert Canal. Furthermore, Enigma decrypts revealed other German movements, and on 15 September, two days before the airborne landings, photo reconnaissance confirmed the presence of German armour in the Arnhem area.

On 17 September, Operation Market Garden was launched and it almost immediately ran into trouble. Only one battalion of the Parachute Regiment, under Colonel John Frost, reached the bridge at Arnhem. The Arnhem underground immediately contacted the British troops to offer assistance, but it was politely turned down. Penseel planned to take over the local radio station and broadcast the liberation of Arnhem but was persuaded not to do so by news from the British airborne landings around Oosterbeek, which suggested that the operations there were not going well, and that the Germans were successfully preventing British airborne troops from reaching Arnhem from that direction. Toon van Daalen and Gysbert Numan, two of Kruijff's trusted associates, reached the British headquarters at the Hotel Hartenstein in Oosterbeek only to find that their offers of help were dismissed because, Numan believed: 'I got the impression that they were in dread of provocateurs and simply did not trust us.' On 18 September Nicolaas de Bode noted the arrival of German tanks on the eastern side of Arnhem and telephoned the British headquarters to warn them, only to find that he was thanked and told that 'the captain is doubtful about the report. After all, he's heard a lot of fairy tales.' The tragedy was that all this could have been avoided. Lieutenant Colonel Hillary Barlow had been nominated as Arnhem's town major and military government chief for the post-battle period and was to be assisted by the Dutch liaison officer with the British airborne forces, Lieutenant Commander Arnoldus Wolters. The two men had been given lists of totally trustworthy members of the Dutch underground to contact after the landings. Unfortunately, Barlow was killed early in the battle and Wolters found that the British staff officers never fully trusted him.

The Dutch resistance found a warmer welcome from the British and American commanders along the land route towards Arnhem. For example, the *Knokploegen* seized the telephone exchange in Eindhoven on 17 September, enabling communications with Amsterdam and The Hague. The underground forces also maintained security in Eindhoven and rounded up members of the NSB, thereby freeing Allied troops for the advance. North of Eindhoven, men from the *Partisanen Actie Nederland* joined the American troops at Woensel: 'Everywhere you look you see men in blue overalls with armbands saying "PAN". They carry a gun over their shoulders and charge around on motorcycles and in cars with flags.' Captain Arie Bestebreurtje, the Dutch liaison officer with the US airborne forces, assembled around 600 Dutch resisters and begged the Americans for weapons. General James Gavin warned them of the risk of execution if captured by the Germans but, recognizing their determination to fight, supplied them with weapons and uniforms and asked them to ensure that the Germans did not blow up the bridge at Nijmegen. The British armoured forces were far less willing to give weapons to the Dutch despite the fact that nearly a hundred PAN members assisted the British in driving back the German effort to cut the road at Best. In Nijmegen the resistance erroneously informed the Americans that the plunger to blow up the main bridge was located in the German-held post office. Dutchmen guided the storming force there, but no plunger was found. The bridge at Nijmegen was not blown, and this fact was attributed to the brave conduct of a young Dutchman who was said to have cut the wires leading to the explosives. The story is widely believed in the Netherlands, but cannot be confirmed. In any case, Model himself had ordered the bridge to be kept open for German counter-attacks.

On 20 September, Frost's severely depleted force by the bridge at Arnhem surrendered. A member of the Dutch underground working alongside the British was identified by the Germans and immediately executed. The German main effort now focused on encircling the British airborne forces around Oosterbeek. Wolters had contacted van der Krap with the request to create a company of volunteers from the Dutch resistance. The British could not arm this force so the men obtained their weapons from supplies retrieved from behind German lines. Van der Krap realized that the British position was extremely precarious and that while the Germans would treat the British as prisoners of war, he and his Dutch associates would be executed. He therefore took the decision to disband the newly formed company.

On 25 September the British began withdrawing across the Lower Rhine from Oosterbeek to Driel. On the previous evening Kruijff had hosted a meeting to discuss what the Dutch clandestine forces should do next. The consensus was that continuing to fight was pointless and that operations should be directed towards continuing to provide intelligence for the Allies based in the Betuwe, the area west of Nijmegen, and to care for and conceal the British wounded who could not be evacuated across the Lower Rhine. Similarly, Major John Olmsted, who had parachuted into the Netherlands as part of Jedburgh team Dudley on 11–12 September, concluded that now the Allies were not advancing into the Netherlands the main task of his team would be to organize the collection and transmission of intelligence from their base in the Hengelo–Almelo area north-east of Arnhem.[37]

The Germans took revenge for the open welcome the Dutch people had extended to their Allied liberators. On 23 and 24 September the population of Arnhem, 150,000 people, was forcibly evacuated – on foot since the Germans refused to supply transport – and afterwards the Germans looted the property of the evacuees. Then it was the turn of Oosterbeek, where the column of Dutch evacuees was examined by former German prisoners of war who identified those who had helped the British. The Dutch had been caring for the Allied wounded, and British brigadiers, Gerald Lathbury and John Hackett, were among the British contingent being treated in the St Elisabeth Hospital in Arnhem: they had both been registered there as corporals. The evacuation of Arnhem put them in danger, but the Dutch were determined to protect them. A South African surgeon described how Kruijff and his assistants helped smuggle Hackett out of the hospital:

> At last we got him more or less dressed in a black suit, though he was bent half double due to weakness and because his wound was by no means soundly healed. Piet then went off to bring the Red Cross car to the side entrance. A couple of nuns were on duty in the main ward and I got the Dutch doctor to divert their attention. When everything was set, the Brigadier, half walking, half carried, was bundled along the ward, down the basement corridors, up the stairs and out into the car.

Hackett was taken to a house in Ede, the home of three sisters, Mien, Cor, and Ann De Nooy, and later wrote a touching memoir of the care he received at their hands.

After the British airborne forces had abandoned Oosterbeek and crossed the Lower Rhine, there were still around 500 members of the British armed forces left on the wrong bank. Major Digby Tatham-Warter changed into civilian clothes and made a proposal to SHAEF that, if arms drops were made, then these troops could join the Dutch resistance forces and wage guerrilla warfare against the Germans until the Allies crossed the Rhine. Since the Allies had no immediate plans to advance deeper into the Netherlands no arms drops were made. Instead, Airey Neave of MI9 planned Operation Pegasus to evacuate the soldiers and shot-down aircrew across the Rhine. These men were being kept hidden by the Dutch underground forces organized by Kruijff and Bill Wildeboer in locations in the area bounded by Arnhem, Apeldoorn, and Ede. This area was described by one evader as ideal for concealment since it was 'about 256 square miles threaded with cart tracks, bicycle paths, interspersed with sheep pens, woodsmen huts, isolated farmhouses and small, scrubby sand dunes'. On 21 October the Dutch underground mobilized to move the hidden men in small numbers and bring them to the crossing point at Renkum. The evacuation was a success: 183 Allied servicemen crossed the Rhine on 22 October.

By the time Pegasus II was mounted a month later, the Germans had learned from a careless journalist about the existence of the private PGEM telephone line and had cut it, forcing all communications within the Netherlands to be routed through London. Furthermore, the *News Chronicle* had published Lathbury's detailed account of how he escaped during the first Pegasus operation. Therefore, when Pegasus II took place the Germans were on high alert. The operation was a disaster: only five of the 110 servicemen crossed the Rhine, with the majority of the remainder being taken prisoner. The Germans exacted revenge on the locals and the Ede underground was particularly hard hit by arrests and executions. Nonetheless, a group of men who knew the waters of the Biesbosch marshes around the Merwede river at the western end of the Betuwe decided to form a transport system to bring evaders by canoe from occupied territory to the safety of the Allied lines: their operations continued throughout the winter. On 30 January 1945 Hackett was escorted from Ede on bicycle by Johan Snoek and was then taken by canoe across the marshes to the Canadian forward positions.[38]

At the end of September the Germans ordered the evacuation of the whole north bank of the Lower Rhine. This order dislocated 200,000 people who were then crammed into a very small area, competing for food and shelter with refugees from the forced evacuation of the North Sea coast. The food situation was about to become worse thanks to an action ordered by the Dutch government-in-exile.

On 17 September, at Eisenhower's request, the Dutch government-in-exile contacted the management of the Netherlands Railways via the BBC with the order: 'The government considers that the moment has come to give orders for a general strike of railway personnel in order to interfere as much as possible with enemy traffic and troop concentrations.' The strike effectively began on 18 September and halted not only military traffic but all rail traffic across the country, including vital food supplies. It was anticipated that it would last for only a few weeks before the Allies liberated the country, but the failure of Operation Market Garden had unforeseen consequences and the strike lasted for seven months. In October 1944 and January 1945 the government appealed for the strike to continue, and the Dutch underground endorsed this demand despite the obvious suffering the strike was causing. The Dutch had become experts at assisting those people who needed to go into hiding, the *onderduikers*, and that experience was now extended towards helping the striking railwaymen. The Dutch government also acceded to the workers' demands for full pay, overtime, and Christmas bonuses while on strike and the railwaymen received around 37 million gulden from the government's National Assistance Fund.

The effect of the rail strike on the population of the occupied Netherlands was appalling. On 28 September, just after Operation Market Garden had failed, Gerbrandy wrote to Churchill:

> Many railway strikers and members of the resistance movement have been and are being executed, and the strongest reprisals are being taken against members of their families. Starvation in the big cities – the term is not too strong – is imminent.

The Germans made the situation worse by destroying the port facilities at Rotterdam and Amsterdam. This destruction had been planned for early September but was then delayed to allow Dutch ships to be used to transport Zangen's army across the Scheldt. The Germans also brought in around 5,000 German rail workers to run the Dutch railways, but these were only to move German troops and transport food supplies for them alone. Starvation among the Dutch population became a reality during the winter of 1944–45. It is estimated that 80 per cent of the deaths that winter were directly caused by the famine, with Rotterdam being the worst-affected city. A few Allied relief ships were sent in late January 1945 which helped, but the urgently needed liberation of the whole of the Netherlands would be delayed until the spring of 1945.[39]

29

The German Retreat from the Balkans

Earlier chapters on the Balkans have highlighted the principal question concerning resistance in the region: whether it aimed at resistance to the occupiers, or civil war. By the early summer of 1944 it had become clear to all observers that the answer was civil war, and that the communists in the Balkans were determined to take their countries over after the now inevitable departure of the Germans. It seemed that neither the Allied governments nor their representatives on the spot had any control over the situation. The challenge the policymakers now faced was to attempt to make the best out of a dire state of affairs, and to recognize that the dominant resistance movements were favourably disposed towards the Soviet Union and were increasingly hostile to the British and American efforts to retain any influence in the region. In June a Foreign Office paper noted:

> The Russians are, generally speaking, out for a predominant position in SE Europe and are using Communist-led movements in Yugoslavia, Albania and Greece as a means to an end . . . If anyone is to blame for the present situation in which the Communist-led movements are the most powerful in Yugoslavia and Greece, it is we ourselves. The Russians have merely sat back and watched us doing their work for them. And it is only when we have shown signs of putting a brake on their movement (such as our continued recognition of King Peter and Mihailović, and more recently the strong line taken against EAM . . .) that they have come into the open and shown where their interests lay . . .[1]

Churchill attempted to solve the problem by initiating a correspondence with Stalin during the summer of 1944 regarding the establishment of spheres of influence. The result of this correspondence would be later encapsulated in the so-called 'naughty document', which was drawn up by Churchill and agreed to by Stalin during their conference in Moscow in October 1944. This allocated percentages of influence to five countries in the Balkans: the Soviets would be dominant in Bulgaria, Hungary, and Romania; British influence would predominate in Greece; and Yugoslavia was to be split on a 50-50 basis.[2]

From the British point of view, Greece was undoubtedly seen as the most important country in the region. In August 1944 Anthony Eden presented a memorandum to the war cabinet outlining Foreign Office policy:

> If we are to maintain any political influence in SE Europe and, above all, our strategic position in the Eastern Mediterranean after the war, it is essential that Greece should be ruled by a Government friendly to us . . . I regard it as essential that British influence in Greece and the traditional connection between the two countries should be preserved, but unless British forces can be sent in there is a serious danger that the Greek people, who still look to us for assistance, will lose faith in Great Britain and that a Government will come into power which would bring the country under Soviet domination.[3]

The war cabinet agreed, and plans began to be drawn up for the despatch of a British force under General Ronald Scobie – Operation Manna – to Greece to maintain law and order and prevent a communist coup once the Germans had departed. From Greece, Nigel Clive, who was based in Epiros, forwarded a report written by Lieutenant General Hubert Lanz, the German commander in northern Greece, which outlined German thinking. The Germans did not expect a direct invasion of Greece by the Allies because this would almost certainly just accelerate the 'existing political confusion', and 'even if we are forced to evacuate, Allied troops will probably be held back to await a fait accompli by one side or the other in a civil war which will be fought under the supervision of the British missions to both sides'.[4]

Albania was omitted from the 'percentages agreement'. The British government had given sanctuary to King Zog after the Italian invasion of his country, but, although it remained keen to see the restoration of Albanian independence after the Germans left, there was no commitment to restore Zog to his throne. With regard to the possibility of post-war British influence in Albania, the Foreign Office's outlook was glum. Orme Sargent wrote in a memorandum for Eden on 26 September that it 'seems inevitable that LNC will gain control over the whole of Albania' after the German withdrawal, and that the communist leaders of the LNC would look towards the Soviet Union rather than to Britain for support. Eden concurred with Sargent's opinions, adding in a memorandum to Churchill that the disunity reigning among the nationalists meant that they were 'not likely to render us important military assistance', and they seemed apparently incapable of resisting the advance of the LNC in the country.

This was despite the fact that the main stronghold of the LNC remained in the south while the centre and north of the country were 'much more primitive and less receptive to extreme left-wing social and political views'.[5]

Where Yugoslavia was concerned, Churchill had been the prime mover in the decision to withdraw British support from Draža Mihailović, the Četnik resistance leader, and to place all trust in Tito and his Partisans to unite the Yugoslav resistance against the Germans. In August 1944 Churchill visited British troops in Italy and took the opportunity to meet Tito, who was flown to Italy from the island of Vis where he had been under British protection since a German attack on his headquarters had forced him to flee Yugoslavia in May. This was the first time that the two men had met and it gave each the opportunity to size the other up. Churchill handed Tito a note which made British policy clear:

> 1. The desire of His Majesty's Government is to see a united Yugoslav Government, in which all Yugoslavs resisting the enemy are represented, and a reconciliation between the Serbian people and the National Liberation Movement.
> 2. His Majesty's Government intend to continue, and if possible to increase, the supply of war material to Yugoslav forces now that an agreement has been reached between the Royal Yugoslav Government and the National Liberation Movement. They expect, in return, that Marshal Tito will make a positive contribution to the unification of Yugoslavia by including in the declaration which he has already agreed with the Yugoslav Prime Minister to make, not only a statement regarding his intention not to impose Communism on the country, but also a statement to the effect that he will not use the armed strength of the Movement to influence the free expression of the will of the people on the future regime of the country . . .
> 4. If it should turn out that any large quantities of ammunition sent by his Majesty's Government are used for fratricidal strife other than in self-defence, it would affect the whole question of Allied supplies, because we do not wish to be involved in Yugoslav political differences . . .[6]

Tito promptly assured Churchill that he had no intention of imposing communism on Yugoslavia. This was manifestly untrue since at that very time Tito was planning the Partisan advance into Serbia, the last royalist and nationalist stronghold: once it had been conquered and liberated from the Germans, Tito would be able to set up a government according to his own wishes. As Milovan Djilas, Tito's confidant, later commented, 'there was nothing for Churchill to do but accept a new Yugoslavia or else get entangled in an unpopular and drawn-out conflict'.[7] Churchill himself was well aware of this danger. On 31 August he sent Eden a memo outlining his fears:

> It would be well to remember how great a responsibility will rest upon us after the war ends, with Tito having all the arms and being able to subjugate the rest of the country by weapons supplied by us. During the war we can put pressure on him to fight the Germans instead of his fellow-countrymen by the threat of stopping supplies, but this will have gone when the war is over. He will have the arms and the country [will be] at his mercy.[8]

Two issues remained to be discussed: the future of King Peter and the future of Trieste.

Of these the latter was discussed at the meeting in Naples. Churchill informed Tito that the British intended to seize Trieste as the port vital for supplying the anticipated British zone of occupation in central Europe. Buoyed by the fall of Rome, Churchill was extremely keen that General Alexander's forces should penetrate central Europe through the Ljubljana Gap and advance towards Vienna, and he wanted Tito's acquiescence and assistance in carrying out this plan. As Churchill informed Roosevelt on 28 August when promoting this controversial Allied move: 'Tito's people will be waiting for us at Istria.' The strategic debates concerning the actual practicability of Churchill's plan are irrelevant here: in the event, Allied troops did not breach the Gothic Line that summer and consequently no advance towards the Ljubljana Gap was possible. Tito was, however, alarmed by Churchill's declaration since he had already publicly proclaimed his support for Slovene irredentism and the inclusion of Trieste and Venezia Giulia within the borders of post-war Yugoslavia.

The matter of Trieste was glossed over at the meeting because Tito realized that he needed to remain on good terms with Churchill in order to continue to receive military supplies from Britain. He was still not totally convinced by Churchill's sincerity in breaking with Mihailović because the Americans still had a mission in Serbia. In October 1943 Captain George Musulin of OSS had arrived in Serbia to organize the repatriation of shot-down Allied aircrew from Četnik-held territory. His mission had been withdrawn in February 1944 in accordance with the policy of abandoning Mihailović, but Allied aircrew continued to be cared for by the Četniks and the need to evacuate them remained. On 2 August 1944 Musulin returned to Serbia to arrange for their repatriation. He was accompanied by Colonel Robert McDowell and three Serbo-Croat-speaking OSS officers who were to undertake an intelligence-gathering mission in the Četnik areas of Bosnia and Serbia. While Musulin arranged for planes to come from Italy to collect the 250 Allied aircrew, McDowell and his officers toured the country. They found clear evidence that the Partisans were hampering all efforts by the Četniks to resist the Germans. They attempted to intervene, as Lieutenant Kramer reported:

> I sent a note by courier to the local Partisan commander, asking for a rendezvous with the idea of stopping this local battle between Yugoslavs because, while this battle was going on, large German columns were passing through the Morava Valley from Prizren to Kruševac and from there to Niš and Belgrade. The Partisan commander did not reply but he told the courier that the Americans had no business becoming interested in the civil war in Serbia, and that they had better get out; and, with that, he had the courier beaten up.

Churchill was concerned that the McDowell–Musulin mission would damage his efforts to get King Peter to make a public break with Mihailović, so he pressed Roosevelt at the beginning of September to order the withdrawal of the mission. Roosevelt complied, and the mission finally left Yugoslavia in November.[9]

On his return to London, Churchill put pressure on the Yugoslav government-in-exile to abandon Mihailović and to announce its support for Tito and the Partisans. On 12 September the king broadcast from London a strongly worded statement which proclaimed:

> None . . . who remain deaf to this appeal shall escape the brand of traitor before his people and before history. By this message I strongly condemn the misuse of the name of the King and the authority of the Crown by which an attempt has been made to justify collaboration with the enemy and to provoke discord amongst our fighting people in the very gravest days of their history, thus solely profiting the enemy.[10]

The effect of this announcement in Yugoslavia will be examined below.

Churchill soon had evidence of Tito's duplicity. In September, Tito 'levanted' from Vis and eventually reached Moscow for discussions with Stalin. Tito's visit had two main purposes: military – to obtain Soviet supplies, especially of heavy weapons for an offensive against Belgrade; and political – to obtain Soviet guarantees that Yugoslavia would be reconstructed as one country, that the liberated portions of the territory would be handed over to Tito's national committee to administer, and that Soviet forces would withdraw from Yugoslavia at the conclusion of operations against the Germans. Tito's visit was a total success, especially in regard to the despatch of Soviet supplies. These are estimated as consisting of around 100,000 rifles, 68,000 machine guns, over 800 anti-tank and field guns, 491 aircraft, sixty-five tanks, and equipment for seven field hospitals. These supplies supplemented the vast quantities already being sent by air and sea from Britain and the United States.[11] When Eden was in Moscow in early October he informed Molotov of British displeasure over Tito's secret departure from Vis:

> If he had had the courtesy to tell us that he was going to Moscow we should have wished him bon voyage. But neither he nor the Soviet Government had thought fit to tell us anything about it although it was we who had armed and equipped Marshal Tito and made his military operations possible. As a result, I must repeat that we felt the strongest resentment at what had happened.

In response Molotov put all the blame on Tito. Churchill was particularly upset by Tito's conduct, telling General Wilson: 'My confidence in Tito . . . has been destroyed by his levanting from Vis in all the circumstances which attended his departure.' Fitzroy Maclean warned Tito that he had offended the British government, and received the response: 'We are an independent state; as the President of the National Committee and the Supreme Commander I am not responsible to anybody outside my country for my activity and work which is in the interest of my nations.'[12]

In Albania it was clear that civil war was spreading during the summer of 1944. On 6 July, Major Victor Smith was parachuted into the country with orders from Bari to arrange a truce, but he found Enver Hoxha totally unreceptive to his pleas. A week later Alan Palmer returned to Albania with a note from General Wilson warning Hoxha that all Allied aid to the LNC would be stopped unless Hoxha stopped attacking Abas Kupi. Hoxha's response was to portray Kupi and the *Balli Kombëtar* not just as political opponents but as outright collaborators. In order to further discussions and to bring the LNC into line with Allied strategic policy, Palmer accompanied a three-man LNC delegation to Bari at the end of July for talks with Lieutenant Colonel Lord Harcourt, Air Vice-Marshal William Elliot, and Harry Fultz of OSS. The talks faltered on the LNC's demands: that the Anti-Fascist National Liberation Committee should be recognized as the provisional government of Albania; that an Albanian military delegation should be established at Bari; that the LNC should have sole responsibility for the distribution of supplies; and, the principal stumbling block, the demand that Allied missions to Kupi should be withdrawn, and that Kupi and the *Balli Kombëtar* be denounced as collaborators. The Foreign Office made its position clear in the middle of August: 'At this present juncture it would be most unwise to commit ourselves irrevocably to the National Liberation Movement as against Kupi, and for the moment there must be no question of withdrawing our BLOs [British Liaison Officers] from the latter.'

While discussions were continuing in Bari, the situation on the ground deteriorated. The LNC began to penetrate important Zogist areas, forcing Kupi to retreat. On 11 August two Soviet officers, Major Ivanov and Lieutenant Turin, arrived at Hoxha's headquarters at Helmës with results described by OSS officer Nick Kukich: 'They received an ovation which will never be forgotten by any of the Yanks here. The Ptz [partisans] began to fire every available weapon they had on hand for a period of two hours.' The partisans were, however, disappointed that the Soviets had arrived solely to gather intelligence and had no means or intention of providing supplies. This shortfall was filled by SOE and OSS, which throughout the July–September period increased the tonnage of supplies entering Albania by sea and air with the vast majority going to Hoxha's partisans. These supplies enabled the partisans to mount an offensive against the Germans in Dibër on 10–11 August at the same time as attacking Kupi in the Mati valley. The battle for Dibër lasted until the end of the month as the partisans successfully resisted German counter-attacks, finally forcing the Germans to withdraw from the town and surrounding area.

It was undoubtedly true that the partisans did mount a serious resistance to the Germans. In August a report was sent to Berlin: 'Communist attacks on German vehicles even in the immediate neighbourhood of Tirana. Losses of men and material. There are shootings here every night', and in September, 'Central and Southern Albania completely dominated by Communist groups apart from a few traffic roads . . . Attacks all the time . . . Red bands are fully mobilised.' In contrast, Kupi was far less able or willing to attack the Germans. In order to prove his good intentions during August, he proposed an overly ambitious scheme to capture Durrës, Albania's second largest city. The BLOs David Smiley and Billy McLean were convinced that the Zogist forces were too weak, and suggested that Kupi focus instead on keeping the Tirana–Scutari road blocked. The plan, however wild, did have one useful consequence: on 1 September, Kupi received an urgently needed supply drop. The result was a brief action against the Germans in a garrison near the village of Kurat which was totally successful. The action proved that Kupi and the Zogists could indeed resist the Germans, though not to the extent of the partisans: the Zogist action resulted in the deaths of ten Germans while in contrast the partisan battle for Dibër left around 400 German dead.

The contrast between what the two main resistance forces could achieve was recognized in the military agreement signed in Bari on 24 August, which officially recognized the Albanian Liberation Army as the only army fighting the Germans in Albania and sanctioned the setting up of a permanent LNC military delegation at Bari: a delegation of two LNC officers arrived there in the middle of September. The LNC failed, however, to achieve recognition as the provisional government. Buoyed by the news of this military agreement, Hoxha upped the stakes in his determination to crush Kupi. On 25 August, Hoxha handed Palmer's deputy, Captain Marcus Lyon, an ultimatum demanding the immediate withdrawal of the McLean–Smiley mission within five days, failing which its members would be captured and tried by a partisan military court. When Palmer returned to Hoxha's headquarters at the end of the month he found that Hoxha was willing to withdraw his ultimatum because he feared that it might lead to the abrogation of the military agreement which had just been signed. Hoxha continued to demand the departure of McLean and Smiley, and Palmer felt it would be wise to comply with this demand. Yet the Allies were not yet prepared to abandon Kupi as they had abandoned Mihailović. With the prospect of German retreat on the horizon they wanted the Albanians of every political persuasion to hamper the process.[13]

On 19 September SOE changed its stance and a signal was sent to McLean, Julian Amery, and Smiley with new orders. McLean and Smiley were to leave for Italy immediately, leaving the British mission in the hands of Amery who was now to adopt the stance of a neutral observer and not encourage Kupi to fight the Germans. Smiley was outraged to learn that the order included the proviso that they should be 'escorted' to the coast by the LNC partisans, and he and McLean were adamant that they would reach the coast independently. Their concern rested on events further north when the LNC partisans had surrounded the British mission led by Anthony Simcox to the three Kryeziu brothers based at Dobrejt. Simcox and another British agent, Bill Collins, had all their kit looted and then were treated as prisoners and marched southwards 'under conditions of the most calculated indignity'. Their Albanian assistant, Lazar Fundo, was taken to the commissioner of the 5th LNC Brigade and 'interrogated, stripped, laid out on the ground, and beaten to death'. The Kryeziu brothers were similarly taken prisoner by the LNC, and Gani Bey Kryeziu was handed over to Tito's Partisans who objected to his activities in the disputed territory of Kosovo. The Yugoslavs sentenced him to five years' hard labour.

At the end of October all the British officers who had served with the British mission to Abas Kupi were evacuated from the coast of Albania, having reached their departure point without the intervention of the LNC. Kupi ruefully commented on their departure: 'Perhaps it is only just that they [the LNC] should come to power. We Gegs have exploited the Tosks for 1,000 years, now it is their turn to exploit us.' Both Amery and Smiley were shocked by their reception in Bari. Amery noted: 'For a long time I felt as if we had come to another world, where people used the same words as we did but with wholly different meanings. It was if they had been colour-blind, or had sought to solve an algebraical problem without knowing what any of the symbols stood for.' Smiley added that 'we were politely treated in the SOE office, though we felt an undercurrent of hostility'. McLean was appalled to learn that Bari had forbidden him to evacuate Kupi with the British party. He sent an appeal to Eden arguing that the British were morally obliged to assist Kupi. This message was inexplicably held up in Bari but a second message reached Eden, who immediately sanctioned the rescue of Kupi. Bari still stalled, so McLean and Amery went to speak directly to Macmillan and General Wilson at Caserta. A clandestine rescue operation was then authorized, but in the event it was not needed because Kupi, his two sons, and three personal followers had managed to obtain a boat. Their boat then drifted helplessly southwards in the Adriatic without food and water before being spotted by a Royal Navy minesweeper which towed them into Brindisi. Prominent *Balli Kombëtar* leaders had already reached the sanctuary of the Italian mainland a month earlier. Kupi and other non-communist Albanian resisters settled in exile in the United States and remained engaged in anti-communist politics.

On Crete the large SOE contingent under Tom Dunbabin assisted an SBS (Special Boat Service) raiding party led by Ian Paterson in blowing up all the German petrol dumps on the island simultaneously. The principal dump was on Kastelli airfield and Sandy Rendel and his band of Cretan resisters guided the SBS onto the airfield and guarded them while the explosives were laid: 'Suddenly somewhere on the front slope of the dump close enough to make us feel we were in the thick of it, there was a wild flash and a whole chunk of the hill seemed to explode and hurl itself into the air.' The resulting fire lasted for several days. The attacks on the other dumps were also successful and it was estimated that the Germans were deprived of 165,000 gallons of fuel. The SBS lost two men who were taken prisoner, but these were later liberated by Yugoslav Partisans from the train taking them to Germany.[14]

The Cretan resistance was also active. On 22 August, Mikhali Xylouris and his band attacked a German outpost near Daphnes in the Anoyia region, killing fifteen German soldiers. General Müller had returned to Crete after the kidnap of General Kreipe and oversaw the reprisals. Müller focused on the town of Anoyia as the alleged centre of SOE-inspired resistance on Crete. Stanley Moss heard of the intended reprisal operation and planned an ambush on the road the reprisal force would take from Heraklion to Rethymno where there was a sharp curve in the road bounded on three sides by high ground with a little bridge in the centre. The ambush became an almost farcical operation as the ambush party first had to escort a shepherd and his flock of sheep off the road:

> But this was only the beginning. During the next hour over eighty civilians, several flocks of sheep, donkeys, goats, and mules came stumbling in all innocence upon our emplacement. It transpired that there was a market day being held at a nearby village; but, by the time we had finished hustling each successive batch of arrivals off the road, it was rather we who appeared to be holding most of the market, for the little valley behind us, crammed to the full with bleating, braying livestock, looked like a corral after the most successful of round-ups.

The success of the ambush was limited to the immediate deaths of forty to fifty German soldiers and the taking prisoner of a further twelve whom the Cretans then executed. Most of the town of Anoyia had been voluntarily evacuated before the Germans arrived, but forty-five men who were found in the town and neighbourhood were executed and most of the town was burnt. Reprisals continued across the island regardless of whether there had been any resistance activity, such as the looting and burning of villages in the Kedros valley in late August.

Political differences within the resistance were becoming more marked, and, on 17 August, Dunbabin organized a meeting between EOK and ELAS at Melidoni to try to find some common policy and ensure that as the time for the German withdrawal approached both groups would focus on killing the Germans and not each other. The Cretan ELAS remained hostile, though at that time they were not actually dangerous. Their future attitude would be determined by events on the mainland and the negotiations taking place in Italy between the differing sides.[15]

On the Greek mainland, the Allied military mission continued to be alarmed by the growing evidence of the aggression of ELAS towards other resistance groups and the development of plans for EAM/ELAS to seize power as soon as the Germans departed. On 28 July a Soviet military mission led by Lieutenant Colonel Popov arrived at ELAS headquarters. Chris 'Monty' Woodhouse was worried that the Soviets would inspire ELAS to become even more anti-British, but his fears were quickly allayed by Popov, who was unimpressed by ELAS's focus on politics rather than resistance. In return ELAS was unimpressed by the Soviet mission: 'On the question of the Red Army undertaking our supply they made no promises, as they had no instructions about this, but said they would send word of our needs to Moscow by radio, and Moscow would decide.' Moscow decided not to despatch any supplies to ELAS. Correspondence between Churchill and Stalin on Greece that summer led towards an agreement whereby the Soviets would take the lead in deciding policy in Romania and the British would do the same in Greece. Roosevelt was kept informed of this correspondence by Churchill and expressed a need for assurances that the Balkans were not about to be carved up into spheres of influence. Churchill ignored Roosevelt's concerns: the reality on the ground was that Britain could do little to aid Romania, which was about to defect from the Axis, but was in a position to help Greece.[16]

The British still faced the problem that all the main resistance forces were republican, but the British were honour bound to help King George return to his throne. EAM/ELAS would not join the government-in-exile until the matter had been settled to their satisfaction. The British were not ready to abandon the king, yet at the same time they needed the Greek resistance, especially ELAS, to take an active role in Operation Noah's Ark, the harassment of the German withdrawal from Greece. On 29 July it appeared a major breakthrough was in the offing when EAM/ELAS informed Cairo that it would join the Greek government-in-exile but only if the prime minister Georgios Papandreou stood down. Churchill was outraged by the demand, writing to Eden on 6 August:

> The behaviour of EAM is absolutely intolerable. Obviously they are seeking nothing but the Communisation of Greece during the confusion of war, without allowing the people to decide in any manner understood by democracy . . .
>
> Should matters go downhill and EAM become master we should have to reconsider keeping any of our mission there and put the Greek people bluntly up against Bolshevism. The case seems to me to have reached the following point: either we support Papandreou, if necessary with force as we have agreed, or we disinterest ourselves utterly in Greece.[17]

Fortunately, on 18 August EAM/ELAS gave in to British pressure and five ministers joined the Greek government. In late September there was a conference at Allied headquarters in Caserta in Italy between the Allies and Stefanos Sarafis for ELAS, and Napoleon Zervas for EDES. The Caserta agreement stipulated that all the guerrilla forces in Greece would place themselves under the orders of General Scobie, the British officer assigned the task of commanding the British troops who would be sent to Greece as the Germans withdrew. Zervas was to remain within the territorial boundary laid out in the earlier Plaka agreement, while ELAS would operate everywhere else in Greece except for two provinces: in Attica the troops would be commanded by General Panayiotis Spiliotopoulos, a member of the early resistance group, the Six Colonels Committee, and in the Peloponnese ELAS would work alongside a British military mission. Both sides were called upon to maintain law and order and prevent a civil war.[18]

During the summer of 1944 the Germans took steps to disrupt the build-up of the guerrilla forces. In August they launched a major sweep through the Pindos mountains and the plain of Thessaly which forced ELAS bands to disperse, leaving the villagers to bear the brunt of German reprisals. In central Greece, for example, Corporal Ed Lawson witnessed the burning of Lidoriki: 'I had previously heard of where atrocities had been committed, Greek villagers, men, women and children, locked in churches and set on fire, but here I was witnessing a whole town blazing before my very eyes.' Captain Pat Evans in Macedonia estimated that around 160 villages had been burned and a considerable amount of supplies lost during the German sweep. Many of the atrocities against civilians were carried out by the collaborating Security Battalions and local collaborating forces created in Thessaly and Macedonia.[19]

On 20 August 1944 an offensive was launched by the 2nd Ukrainian Front under General Rodion Malinovsky and the 3rd Ukrainian Front under General Fyodor Tolbukhin to crush the Romanian army and to cut off the oil supplies from the Ploeşti oilfields. The success of these offensives, which would take Romania and Bulgaria out of the Axis, threatened to trap the German armies in Greece, Yugoslavia, and Albania. The German retreat from the Balkans was therefore forced by events further north and not by the activities of the various resistance groups in the region.

In Romania the resistance to the Axis centred around King Michael and his circle of advisers in the National Democratic Bloc, which included the man in contact with Allied intelligence, Iuliu Maniu. These men planned a coup to overthrow the pro-Axis government of Ion Antonescu and to replace him by someone who could negotiate with the Soviets and ensure that the liberation of Romania would not be a straightforward Soviet conquest but would be controlled by the Romanians themselves. It was a matter of timing: too early, and the substantial German garrison in Bucharest would be able to work alongside pro-Antonescu forces and crush the coup; too late, and the Soviets would impose their own solution. The king and the conspirators planned the coup for 26 August, when Colonel Dumitru Dămăceanu would have men ready to seize the radio station and telephone exchange. Lists of ministers for a new government of unity were drawn up. Maniu declined the position of prime minister, arguing that a soldier was needed for negotiations with the Soviets, and General Constantin Sănătescu was selected.

The plan was for Ion Antonescu to be invited to lunch at the palace on 26 August together with Mihai Antonescu, the foreign minister, whereupon the king would call upon the prime minister to resign in favour of someone who would conclude an armistice with the Allies. If the two Antonescus refused to step down then they would be arrested. On 23 August the conspirators learned that Ion Antonescu planned to visit the front on the 26th and would be absent from Bucharest. The date of the coup was accordingly brought forward and Antonescu reluctantly agreed to attend the palace on 23 August. He refused to resign and the king ordered his arrest, telling him: 'You, I know, consider me to be a stupid stammering child; my Romanians will judge that.' Both Antonescus were arrested and later taken into custody by the Soviets after they entered Bucharest. That evening at 10.12 p.m. the king broadcast to his people:

> Romanians, in the difficult hour of our history I have decided, in full understanding with my people, that there is only one way to save the country from total catastrophe, our withdrawal from the alliance with the Axis powers and the immediate cessation of war with the United Nations. A new government of national unity has been formed.

Furthermore, he ordered the Romanians to turn their weapons against the Germans and work alongside the Allies to liberate Transylvania from Hungarian occupation.

The German representative in Bucharest, Manfred von Killinger, drove to the palace to register a protest, which was rejected. A few days later he shot himself rather than explain to Hitler how and why his important ally had defected. The members of the SOE operation Autonomous were released from custody and taken to the palace along with Nicolae Țurcanu, who had been caught after an earlier failed SOE mission. Alfred de Chastelain, the leader of Autonomous, was invited to fly to Istanbul to confer with the western Allies since the Romanians hoped for a British or American presence in the country to forestall a total Soviet takeover. Țurcanu managed to find a working radio set and broadcast the news of the coup to Cairo before de Chastelain's arrival. On 25 August the Allied air forces bombed the German-held airfields at Băneasa and Otopeni, thereby preventing a German occupation of Bucharest. In the capital itself the 14,000-strong Romanian forces captured and disarmed 50,000 Germans, including seven generals, and killed around 5,000 German soldiers who put up opposition. On 31 August the Soviets entered Bucharest.

The armistice agreement between the Allies and Romania was signed in Moscow on 12 September. By then it was clear that the Soviets intended to dominate the country. De Chastelain was refused permission to return, and the British component of the Allied Control Mission was managed by Ivan Porter. By November, Churchill and Eden were alarmed by the conduct of the Soviets and Churchill warned Eden that 'you had better be careful about this or we shall get retaliation in Greece'.[20]

The Romanian Army began operations alongside the Soviet forces, clearing the southern portion of the country and preventing German incursions from across the frontiers. The 2nd Ukrainian Front continued to move westwards towards Hungary, while the 3rd Ukrainian Front advanced on both sides of the Danube towards the Romanian-Bulgarian border.

Ivan Bagrianov had become prime minister of Bulgaria in May 1944 and his government pursued conflicting policies towards the growing partisan movement in the country. As one politician put it: 'One time we forgive them, another time we persecute them, yet another time we persecute even those suspected of aiding them.' For example, in August 1944 the government offered the partisans an amnesty at the same time as it launched an operation to destroy the partisans in the Sredna Gora. What lay behind this confusion was the question of how to address the inevitable prospect of a Soviet invasion of the country. On 2 September the regency council replaced Bagrianov as prime minister with Konstantin Muraviev in the hope that Muraviev would be able to make peace with the western Allies and that they would then use their influence to ward off a Soviet occupation. Muraviev's government, however, had little support in the country since it contained no members of the main political opposition, the Fatherland Front, which was dominated by the communists.

The partisans, whom the Germans estimated that summer to be 12,000 strong, were not powerful enough to seize power unaided in the name of the Fatherland Front. The resistance therefore began to contact officers of the regular Bulgarian Army, but it met with little success. The best prospects seemed to lie with the officers and men of the 1st Infantry Division, which at the beginning of September was based in Sofia. The partisans planned an uprising for 6 September to coincide with the Soviet armies crossing the Bulgarian border and driving towards Varna, Burgas, and Shumen in the east of the country. The government ordered the army to offer no resistance to the invaders and the Fatherland Front urged the population to welcome the Soviet forces as liberators. Muraviev broke off diplomatic relations with Germany on 7 September. This move was ignored by the Soviets and it led only to German units fleeing westwards towards Yugoslavia. Finally, at 4 p.m. on 8 September, Bulgaria declared war on Germany in the hope that this step would encourage the Soviets to accept the Bulgarian government's request for an armistice.

The Fatherland Front feared that the Soviets would work with the Muraviev government, leaving them powerless. Accordingly, they moved to seize power in collaboration with the Zveno Group of anti-German army officers, which was advised by the war minister, General Ivan Marinov. In the early hours of 9 September the 1st Armoured Brigade under Major Kiril Stanchev entered Sofia and took over the war ministry, the telephone exchange, and the national bank. The partisans of the Fatherland Front arrived soon afterwards only to find that the army had done their work for them. A new government was formed from members of the Fatherland Front with Colonel Kimon Georgiev as prime minister, and a ceasefire with the Soviets came into effect at 10 a.m. on 9 September. The new government contained only four communists, but they dominated proceedings and paved the way for a communist takeover of the country. From the Soviet point of view the solution was ideal: their forces entered Sofia unopposed on 15 September and then continued their advance across Bulgaria towards Yugoslavia. The Bulgarian Army was reinforced with partisan detachments and reorganized to form fifteen divisions to fight under Soviet command in central Europe.[21]

The Hungarians under Admiral Horthy might have been shocked by the German occupation of their country in March 1944, but this did not seem to make them resist the occupation. In summer 1944, SOE summarized the situation in Hungary, based in part on the reports by Major Basil Davidson who had tried and failed to infiltrate agents across the border from Yugoslavia:

> None of the prerequisites of resistance existed. Hungary had never been actively engaged in the war. She had suffered no severe casualties, she was not a defeated nation and, above all, there was no suffering among the civilian population. Far from her alliance with Germany leading to a deterioration of condition of life, Hungary in the last four years has derived nothing but benefit from her association with Germany and the standard of living has, if anything, continued to rise.

There was an element of political resistance, however, as demonstrated by the establishment of the Hungarian Front in May 1944. This was a loose group of opposition parties, trade unions, and nationalist organizations. The Hungarian Front faced a dilemma in that it would prefer to deal with the western Allies, but it was the Soviets who were approaching the borders of the country. On 22 September, General István Náday arrived in Italy to pass on Horthy's request for an armistice and to ask the British and Americans to join the Soviets in occupying the country. The British and Americans were open to his overtures, but Andrey Vyshinsky, on behalf of the Soviets, dismissed them with the argument that Náday lacked the authority to negotiate an armistice.

The Germans were aware of Horthy's approaches to the Allies. Hitler briefly despatched Bach-Zelewski to prepare for the defence of Budapest both against any uprising from within and against a Soviet attack from without. On 15 October, Horthy made a radio broadcast in which he announced his intention to request an armistice and break relations with the German occupiers. The German response was swift: Obersturmbannführer Otto Skorzeny arrived in the country, and kidnapped Horthy's son, Nicholas, and held him hostage to persuade Horthy to change his mind. Horthy himself was arrested on 16 October. Also that day the overtly fascist Arrow Cross under Ferenc Szálasi overthrew the government of General Lakatos which had been in power since late August. This government had attempted to mitigate the worst features of the German occupation, namely the persecution of the Jews and the depredations of the Gestapo. Under Szálasi the Germans were left free to pursue their murderous policies.

The resistance grew in size after Szálasi took over the government. The Soviet advance on Budapest began on 29 October, and by 7 November Soviet troops had reached a line twenty kilometres from the city centre. The Hungarian opposition parties making up the Hungarian Front, along with some army officers and clandestine groups of students, police units, and trade unionists, wanted to play a part in the liberation of their capital. On 19 November they joined forces to set up a Liberation Committee to plan a national uprising to be coordinated with the Soviet advance. The uprising, scheduled to start on 1 December, aimed to open Budapest to the Soviet advance and attack the German and Arrow Cross troops stationed around the city. The uprising was all but doomed to failure when on 23 November the Gestapo arrested the entire military staff of the Liberation Committee and thirty army officers who had been working with it. This marked the end of the brief Hungarian resistance in Budapest. On 19 December the Soviets resumed their attack on Budapest. Szálasi had fled the city ten days earlier so the defence of Budapest was left in the hands of the Germans. By the end of the year Budapest was encircled by Soviet forces and a terrible siege was begun. The priority for Hungarians trapped in the city, both soldiers and civilians, was to survive. There was little support for or loyalty towards any of the alternatives: the Szálasi government, the Germans, or the Soviets. The only notable deserter to the Soviets was Béla Miklós, commander of the 1st Hungarian Army, but few of his men followed. Budapest was declared a fortress city by Hitler and would not fall until February 1945.[22]

The Allied military planners identified three main escape routes which the Germans would have to use through the Balkans. The first and most easterly ran north from Salonika through Gevgelija and on to Skopje and Belgrade; the middle route went through Florina in Greek Macedonia and on to Bitola (Monastir), Sarajevo, Banja Luka, and Zagreb, with a possible diversion through Peć to Podgorica and then via Nikšić to Sarajevo; the final path ran from Ioannina to Tirana and northwards through Cetinje or Podgorica.[23] The Allies planned two major operations for which they needed the cooperation of the Partisans in Yugoslavia and the two main resistance movements in Greece, ELAS and EDES. These were Operation Ratweek to destroy the railway network through Yugoslavia, and Operation Noah's Ark to 'disrupt enemy forces withdrawing from Greece so that they cannot reach another theatre of war without large scale reorganisation'. Steps were taken to ensure that the resistance movements would cooperate with the Allies, whether these were Allied ground forces sent to carry out limited objectives, or the numerous Allied military missions spread across the region. The existence of military delegations from the resistance movements at Caserta helped in this process.

There was, however, one major problem with Allied plans for the Balkan resistance. It was widely known that the Germans would retreat from the Balkans regardless of whether the various resistance forces took any action against them or not. Therefore, it was to an extent counter-intuitive of the Allies to expect them to take personal risks in the pursuit of Allied aims. Woodhouse later commented: 'There were obviously a lot of Greeks in the resistance who were tired of the whole business of occupation, not surprisingly, who were only anxious to see the Germans out of their country and who didn't see any good reason why they should delay them going.'[24] Greece had suffered terribly under the Axis occupation, with a famine in Athens earlier in the war and the destruction of hundreds of villages across the country, so the Greeks were only too happy to see the Germans leave. A similar train of thought was evident in Albania where Peter Kemp noted that the Albanians felt the Germans were bound to leave anyway so why risk reprisals in attacking them and, worse still, that the Germans were the only people protecting them from the communists and their departure would lead to an inevitable increase in the tempo of the civil war.[25]

Operation Ratweek as designed by Fitzroy Maclean was a week-long coordinated attack by the Allied air forces and the Partisans directed against the major railways running through Yugoslavia, which the Germans would need to use for their armies retreating from both Greece and Yugoslavia. Destroying these rail links would force the Germans to travel by road, a journey which could be interdicted by the Partisans and by air power. There were four main targets: the Zagreb–Bosanski Brod–Belgrade line and the Belgrade–Niš–Skopje–Athens railways, the bridges over the Danube near Belgrade, and the railways in Slovenia between the River Sava and the Adriatic. Maclean later highlighted the joint attack by Allied air forces and Partisans on the town of Leskovac in southern Serbia as an example of successful cooperation. The railway through this town had long been identified as a suitable target for sabotage, most notably by Michael Lees when he was serving as a BLO with Mihailović's Četniks. Sabotage had been carried out there in 1943, but SOE had given the credit for it to the Partisans who were not even in the area at the time. Now, however, the Partisans were sent against the railway and they carried out successful attacks which effectively closed the Belgrade–Salonika railway for a period. The heaviest damage to Leskovac, where the Germans had concentrated armoured forces and motor transport, was the work of the USAAF which sent in fifty planes to effectively raze the town. The impact of the destruction of Leskovac was as much political as strategic: 'The destruction of this town in support of the Partisans' march northwards, and in the presence of the chief of the British mission, was taken in Serbia . . . as a clear signal that there was now no alternative to a Communist-led Partisan takeover of the whole country.'[26]

In Slovenia the results of Operation Ratweek were more mixed. This was an area containing vital railways running from Vienna to Italy through the Brenner Pass and the Ljubljana Gap. The three railways traversing the Gap came together at the junction of Zidani Most before branching off either towards Italy or south into the Balkans. Franklin Lindsay had arrived in Slovenia as head of the OSS mission in the summer of 1944. During that summer the Partisans had cooperated in cutting the strategic railways on many occasions, most notably shutting the main double-track line from Vienna to Italy for a month from the middle of June. Towards the end of the summer Lindsay noticed that the Partisans were becoming far less willing to take orders from Allied officers, and he 'began to suspect that the Partisan brigades were under orders to attack the rail lines only if they were sure they would have few if any losses, and to avoid major targets that were defended, no matter how important'. Furthermore, the intelligence supplied by the Partisans on German movements was now given unwillingly and was deliberately made virtually meaningless: 'Through a combination of obstruction, intransigence, half-heartedness, incompetence and outright animosity they rendered the task of intelligence gathering virtually impossible.' Lindsay's experiences were shared by other members of the Allied military missions in Slovenia. During Operation Ratweek half-hearted efforts were made to close the main railways from Vienna through Slovenia, but the Germans were always able to repair the damage quickly. It seemed that the orders given to the Slovenian Partisans by Tito had changed: they were now to avoid taking casualties in actions against the Germans, and were to husband their resources for a future advance on Trieste and into the Carinthia region of Austria.[27]

Mihailović knew that the Partisans were preparing a new attack on Serbia, and he was as keen as the Partisans were to link up with the Soviet forces which were about to enter his country. Despite having been abandoned by the Allies and by his king, Mihailović continued to direct his Četniks to attack the Germans in Serbia, and these attacks were witnessed by members of the McDowell mission. The Germans also reacted. Hitler discussed the matter with Maximilian von Weichs and Hermann Neubacher, the two men responsible for the Balkans, in late August and Alfred Jodl concluded: 'A Serbian army must not be allowed to exist. It is better to have some danger from communism.' There are unsubstantiated rumours that Mihailović and Milan Nedić met in late August to discuss the possibility of uniting their forces to resist the Partisans. Although whether such a meeting took place is uncertain, it is a distinct and logical possibility. Mihailović had long been unable to arm and feed the Četniks under his command and had consequently ordered a number of them to enlist in Nedić's army to receive equipment and supplies they needed to survive and then to desert with their weapons when Mihailović announced a general mobilization for a national uprising. Lees certainly believed that such a course of action would have been successful: 'If we had stayed with Mihailović we could have secured the total defection of the Nedić forces in 1944 when the great uprising was called.'[28]

Mihailović's strategy failed on every level. On 1 September he issued orders for a general uprising in Serbia against the Germans. He had explained to McDowell that the plan was first to attack the minor garrison towns in northern and north-eastern Serbia to gain weapons, and then to mount major attacks on key towns such as Kruševac, Čačak, and Kraljevo, before advancing on Belgrade. It is not known exactly how many people responded to the call for an uprising, nor how many appeared and then departed when they realized that Mihailović had no weapons for them. The Germans estimated that there were around 25,000 armed Četniks in Serbia before the mobilization, and that the figure might have risen to between 30,000 and 40,000 after Mihailović ordered the uprising. The morale of the Četniks was, however, very low and was greatly affected by events out of Mihailović's control. The first of these was Tito's offer in the middle of August of a general amnesty to Mihailović's Četniks and men serving in collaborationist forces provided that they joined the Partisans by the middle of September. This announcement proved unpopular with all sides and yielded little response other than create greater uncertainty about the future. It was the broadcast by the king on 12 September that sealed Mihailović's fate. Mihailović had managed to contain the news of his sacking from the Yugoslav cabinet, but the king's broadcast over the BBC reached many people. It led to a total collapse in Četnik morale and a rise in desertions. Soon afterwards the Partisans overran Mihailović's headquarters near Pranjani, capturing many documents, but narrowly missing Mihailović himself, who fled into eastern Bosnia.[29]

Mihailović's last attempt to save Serbia from the Partisans was an overture to the Soviets. He despatched a mission under Lieutenant Colonel Velimir Piletić to the Soviet headquarters in Craiova in Romania. Mihailović wanted the Soviets to mediate with the Partisans and end the civil war so that both forces could fight the Germans. He also hoped that the Allies would supervise free post-war elections. After meeting the Soviets the mission then planned to travel on to Bucharest and make contact with the British and American missions thought to be stationed there. The Soviets, however, were not impressed and the mission was still at Craiova when Piletić's aide denounced his fellow members as British spies, whereupon on 1 October the Soviets arrested the Četniks and flew them to Moscow, where they were imprisoned.[30]

There is no doubt that the Partisan invasion of Serbia was directed against the Četniks and not against the Germans. Tito's orders, issued on 5 September, make this clear: 'Keep in mind that the basic aim of this operation is to liquidate the Četnik forces of Mihailović and the Nedić forces as well as their people and administrative apparatus. Do not allow Mihailović to carry out his mobilization and to take his people with him.' Consequently, when the Četniks under Major Dragutin Keserović attempted to attack the town of Kruševac, which was an important German communications centre, they found themselves embroiled in a battle with the Partisans and not the Germans. The fight was witnessed by OSS agent Lieutenant Ellsworth Kramer who noted that only the Germans benefited from the conflict since they were able to use the roads through the battlefield unhindered by either side. By the end of September, just before the Soviets entered Serbia, the Partisan forces under Koča Popović and Peko Dapčević had conquered much of Serbia and Macedonia. On 3 October Nedić and his government left Belgrade for Austria.[31]

The Soviets entered Serbia during the first week of October and their first contact was with the Četniks. Keserović approached the Soviet advance guard with a proposal that his Četniks could renew the attempt to take the town of Kruševac from the Germans with Soviet help. He duly did so, with few casualties, and handed over 1,500 German prisoners to the Soviets. The Soviets then disarmed the Četniks and arrested Kramer. Keserović himself was later captured by the Partisans and was tried and executed. Despite the willingness of the Četniks to work alongside the Soviet forces in the liberation of Serbia, it became normal practice for the Soviets to hand over Četniks to the Partisans who then executed them.[32]

The members of the Allied military missions with the Partisans realized that Tito was becoming more openly pro-Soviet and anti-British and anti-American in his outlook. Just before the Soviets entered Serbia, Tito's chief of staff, Arso Jovanović, forbade all members of the Allied mission to move away from the area of the Partisan headquarters. The Partisans were, however, to be disappointed by the reaction of the Soviet troops when they met. Captain Basil Irwin witnessed the first encounter between the Partisans and the Soviets:

> It was quite extraordinary because they treated us with no hostility or suspicion but they treated the Partisans like dirt. Partisan officers, wherever they could, had got uniforms and jackets made and put on some gold stripes or something for rank. And it was a shock to the Partisans, who thought here was the welcome they were giving to their brother Slavs and the great Russian Army and so on, to be really treated like dirt by them.[33]

The battle for Belgrade was a joint enterprise between the Soviets and the Partisans. It was not a hard-fought conflict because the Germans recognized that they needed to withdraw, and on 20 October the Yugoslav capital was finally liberated.[34] Fitzroy Maclean stood next to Tito during the victory parade of the Partisans: 'Veterans of Salonika and the Balkan Wars marched next to boys of sixteen and seventeen; here and there a girl strode along with rifle and pack beside the men; some were tall; some were undersized.'[35]

Basil Davidson noted the bad behaviour of the Soviet troops after the liberation of Belgrade:

> During the first few days after their arrival we noted a large number of cases of drunkenness and looting and indiscipline (much to the horror of the Partisans, who had never conceived of anyone but Fascists behaving like this); but as soon as their forward troops had passed through order appeared to be restored at once.[36]

Djilas was considerably alarmed by the dangers posed by this situation:

> The behaviour of the Soviet soldiers became more crucial for our influence and our stabilisation. This was all the more the case as illusions about the Red Army and consequently about the Communists themselves, were being destroyed, while we, still organisationally undeveloped, operated in a fluid, partly hostile, uncontrolled environment.

When he complained to a Soviet general he was angrily accused of being a Trotskyite.[37] The situation calmed down as the Soviets passed through Yugoslavia and into Hungary.

The liberation of Belgrade marked the end of the guerrilla phase of Tito's conquest of Yugoslavia. Because the conquest of Serbia was the principal aim of the Partisans during the German retreat, little was done elsewhere in the country to hamper, harass, or in any way delay the timing and organization of the departure of German forces from Greece and Albania. The result was that the Germans were able to construct a strong defence line on the Srem front in the north, and this led to bitter fighting in the area during the winter of 1944–45. Despite Tito's growing hostility towards the British, the fact that the Partisans lacked both field artillery and the knowledge of how to use it caused him to ask the British to despatch artillery to Yugoslavia in the middle of October. At the end of the month he also permitted the landing near Dubrovnik of a British party under Brigadier Sir Henry Floyd, of about brigade strength, to operate with the Partisans. In early November Floydforce and the Partisans cooperated in attacks on the retreating Germans. A Partisan ambush at a village near Nikšić was preceded by a British artillery barrage after which the Partisans were supposed to advance. The battery commander fired and then:

> . . . waited – and waited. Then he saw through his field glasses a Partisan galloping furiously across the valley on a horse towards his observation post just under the lee of the hill where his battery had been placed. The messenger arrived breathless – and blurted out: 'We so admired your wonderful shelling of the enemy that we forgot to attack. Could you please do it again!'

The Germans had left the village anyway.[38]

At the end of November, Tito wanted the British to depart. He now claimed that he had never given permission for Floydforce to land in Yugoslavia. Operations came to a halt during the winter, partly because the Partisans restricted the personnel of Floydforce to Dubrovnik and forbade operations elsewhere, and partly because the heavy snow meant that the Germans could not use the roads through the mountains in any case. Tito expressly forbade the British to assist the Partisans in the liberation of Mostar in southern Bosnia-Herzegovina, and rejected a British offer of assistance to a Partisan force struggling to liberate Zadar on the Dalmatian coast from the Germans. In the middle of January 1945 Floydforce was finally withdrawn: 'Though Floydforce was only too glad to move on – for there was no further military action required – the manner of our virtual dismissal from the scene of our wholehearted efforts as allies of the Partisans rather rankled.' Djilas explained the reasons behind Tito's conduct: 'Friction with the British over the landing of commandos in Dubrovnik in larger numbers than had been contemplated would not have aroused our mistrust and ideological ire, had it not been for the fact that an American mission was still stationed with Draža Mihailović, and that the British had begun their intervention in Greece against ELAS.'[39] Tito's ambitions with regard to the acquisition of Trieste should also be added to the list.

In Albania the Allies suspected that the LNC wanted to focus on political domination of the country and would prove of little use in hampering the German retreat. Therefore, the British despatched commandos and other special forces units to take certain limited objectives, hoping for support from the partisans, but not necessarily expecting any. The largest of these operations was mounted on the southern port town of Sarandë using 2 Commando with the Raiding Support Regiment (RSR) providing heavy fire support. Sarandë was identified as an objective because it lay directly across the straits from Corfu where there was still a German garrison. The first raid on 22 September was attended by a degree of farce as almost the entire British force was laid low by chronic seasickness and, far from advancing on Sarandë, were laid out 'in serried lines below a low ridge of sand as if for identification and subsequent burial', saved only by the absence of the enemy who could have annihilated the stricken men with ease.[40] The party was temporarily evacuated, and a stronger attack was launched on 9 October. The fighting for the port of Sarandë was intense with assistance being rendered by the Allied Balkan Air Force and the partisans. These partisans also assisted more minor operations in the nearby towns of Delvinë and Gjashtë. The commander of the British force, Brigadier Tom Churchill, duly paid tribute to their efforts.[41] The German garrison on Corfu, cut off from supplies by the guerrillas in Greece and by the loss of Sarandë, surrendered willingly to a small force of the RSR.[42] Independently, a patrol of SBS operated on the Greek-Albanian frontier where Robert Eden was appalled to hear that some 'German' soldiers were shouting to each other in English:

> My feelings were beyond description. Here were my countrymen, fresh from burning children alive in wooden churches, dropping old people down wells for a laugh, and other disgusting crimes, fighting as mercenaries against their own country.[43]

Those soldiers were presumably members of the British Freikorps.*

On 2 October the German commander in Albania, General Ernst von Leyser, received orders to start the retreat, and a week later the Germans began withdrawing their forces northwards. As the Germans departed the LNC moved in, liberating the towns of Gjirokastër, Vlorë, and Korçë. By the middle of October the whole of Albania south of the town of Berat was free and Hoxha moved his headquarters to Berat. It is questionable whether the LNC assisted this rapid departure to any great degree. The Germans suffered few casualties in the retreat and continued to be able to use the Korçë–Struga road to evacuate their garrisons from northern Greece via Florina. Within Albania, the Germans still held the capital, Tirana, and all the towns to the north. The Germans noted with gratitude that their route through northern Albania was held against LNC incursions by elements from the *Balli Kombëtar* as well as some men who had fought with Abas Kupi. For these people, only the Germans now lay between freedom and domination by the LNC.[44]

On 15 October the Germans began to abandon Tirana and move their forces northwards to concentrate in the town of Shkodër near the Yugoslav border. Hoxha ordered his partisan brigades under Mehmet Shehu to launch an assault on the Albanian capital. OSS agents were on the spot to witness the events and an after-action report concluded:

> In the battle of Tirana, the Germans never made a full commitment of forces. At the very beginning, there were about 4000 Germans in the city, but the tactical plan, according to source, appeared to be an emphasis upon retreat northward while maintaining holding forces in the capital whose number varied slightly around the 1000 figure.

Nonetheless, the battle for Tirana was hard-fought and lengthy with few German prisoners taken. The partisans were assisted by the Allied Balkan Air Force which 'came in and bombed and the partisans came in and picked off the Germans'. German efforts to divert troops retreating from Greece to assist the garrison in Tirana were driven back in the Krraba Pass by the combined ground and air resources. On 17 November the last German troops left Tirana for Shkodër, where they remained for only a further two

* The British Freikorps was a unit of the SS made up of volunteer British POWs.

weeks. Activities by the Yugoslav Partisans in Montenegro, assisted by LNC units operating in Kosovo and by a British paratrooper operation near Lake Ohrid, made the German position in Albania untenable and forced the Germans to retreat towards Sarajevo.[45]

On 28 November, Hoxha and his LNC military commanders entered Tirana. The celebrations began with a flight of six Halifaxes which dropped congratulatory leaflets and some food. The OSS observers noted the muted welcome accorded to Hoxha: 'It looked as if the people were stunned. The cheers I heard sounded almost as if forced by the occasion. There was not the wild display of enthusiasm demonstrated in the south.' Hoxha's speech heaped praise on the Soviet Union and Yugoslavia but hardly mentioned the two countries which had actually rendered him assistance, Britain and the United States. There was even less support for the LNC in Shkodër, where the partisans immediately launched a campaign to annihilate all possible political competitors, among them members of religious orders.[46] Liberated Albania began its journey into seclusion and ardent Stalinism which marked its government for the next forty years.

Despite Hitler having designated the island of Crete as a fortress to be held at all costs, the German garrison there under General Müller was acutely aware of its vulnerability: once the Germans had departed from the mainland it would face a struggle for survival against guerrilla forces directed by a strong Allied contingent of officers. At the beginning of September, German nurses and non-essential German personnel were withdrawn from Crete. Across the island small, isolated German garrisons were withdrawn to the main towns of Heraklion, Rethymno, and Canea. To protect their withdrawal, the Germans launched drives around Lasithi in the east, and in the plain of Heraklion:

> We knew later that the Germans planned to intimidate the villages lying around Heraklion, by rounding up the inhabitants, keeping large numbers of them locked up for a day or so in the village school or chapel, taking hostages, and executing anyone suspicious. This was clearly not an immediate reprisal for anything done by the Cretans, but an act of planned policy to terrorise the neighbourhood and protect the German rear from organised resistance before the time – a week or two later – when the evacuation of Heraklion was to begin in earnest.

Numerous villages and small towns were destroyed, and the Germans estimated that they had killed around 500 guerrillas and their helpers: the British estimate was much higher.

On 7–8 September, Tom Dunbabin hosted a conference at the monastery of Arkadi for the eight British officers on the island, as well as two OSS agents, a representative of the PWE, and a Polish officer, Major Stanislaus Lukas. The party discussed the tactics to be adopted during the German withdrawal. There were several aspects to the Allied plan. On the resistance front, the order from Cairo to 'cease sabotage or any act which might bring harm to the civilian population' was disseminated, and the main thrust of Allied activity was directed in two directions: propaganda and counter-scorch. Propaganda was directed to anti-Nazi German soldiers, those Poles impressed into the Wehrmacht, and those Germans in love with Cretan girls. Propaganda efforts were supported by the publication of the *Kreta Post*, which described how a new Germany would arise after the fall of Hitler. Counter-scorch actions were planned to save the three ports on the north coast of Crete from destruction.

As on the mainland, the resistance on Crete was divided along political lines between EOK, the nationalist resistance, and ELAS. The situation around Heraklion illustrated the divisions. The military representative of the Greek government-in-exile, Colonel Andreas Nathenas, found that his authority was recognized only by the Allied military mission and two EOK bands led by Mikhaili Xylouris and Petrakageorgis which were present in the city and on its western side. Nathenas 'held an impressively stamped piece of paper from the Greek Government in Cairo authorizing him to act as military governor of the island, but he had no real means of controlling the different bands'. There were three ELAS groups, under Yanni Bodias, Manoli Bandouvas, and Nikolaos Plevres, operating independently to the south and east of the town. The British believed that ELAS was more determined to seize power after the Germans departed than to contribute anything to the German retreat. The Allied military mission decided not to arm ELAS, but the bands armed themselves with weapons captured from the Germans.

By early October it was clear that the Germans were withdrawing from Heraklion:

> Each day their perimeter round the town shrank. I doubt now if they had a fixed plan for their departure. It depended partly on the number of air transports which left each evening, and which from nightfall onwards we could hear groaning low over the town. The number of aircraft varied nightly, for the aerodromes round Athens to which they went were ... being much bombed at the time.

Unofficial negotiations were begun with the Germans for the surrender of the aerodrome, which they wanted to blow up, and for the harbour, which they apparently promised not to demolish unless the guerrillas attacked them. On 10 October the Germans had withdrawn most of their troops from Heraklion, leaving behind a garrison of 1,000 men with armoured cars, artillery, and mortars. The Allied party led by Sandy Rendel and Bill Royce argued with the various guerrilla leaders that any premature attack on the town would lead to a bloodbath, and the guerrillas agreed to hold back. On 11 October the last German troops began leaving the town and Rendel and Royce rushed in to try to control events, which were very volatile as the Cretans were making no effort to conceal their delight at the German departure at a time when the Germans were still strong enough to turn around and massacre them. The guerrilla bands were gathered along all the main roads leading to the gates of the town, save for the western one through which the last Germans would leave. As the last German armoured car left, Rendel was amused to see Bodias 'sway through the New Gate on a distinctly recalcitrant pony, which was tossing a heavy chain of flowers draped round its neck and understandably objecting to the cheers of the communist claque behind it'. The guerrilla bands had taken no part in the liberation of Heraklion but their role in the resistance was acknowledged by the newly appointed Greek military commander of Crete, Colonel Nikolaos Papadakis. During the celebrations an unfortunate incident occurred which demonstrated the political divisions within the resistance: Bodias was shot in the arm by Athanasios Bourdzalis on the grounds of a personal slight. Despite the fact that Bodias was treated in hospital by a nationalist surgeon, the bands turned on each other and Dunbabin had to devote much effort to restore peace. To avert civil war he also had to sanction the death sentence passed on Bourdzalis by Papadakis.

On 13 October the last Germans left Rethymno for Canea. Again, there was alarming evidence of the political divisions among the guerrillas rushing to enter the town, and there were demonstrations by EOK and ELAS after the Germans had left. There were also frequent parades and torchlight processions. George Psychoundakis, who had loyally served the Allied mission during most of the occupation, took the opportunity to attend the celebrations 'and read out loud some of the poems I had written in the mountains'. The German retreat to Canea was marked by little guerrilla activity, a few Allied air attacks, and a trail of destruction as the Germans wrecked every bridge on the route, including a Venetian bridge which was widely considered to be an architectural masterpiece. The 11,000-strong German garrison was now contained within a perimeter seventy kilometres in length stretching from the town of Georgioupolis, halfway between Canea and Rethymno, and including the whole of the Gulf of Canea. The Germans, now commanded by Major General Georg Benthack, settled into an uneasy coexistence with the 3,200-strong guerrilla bands who watched their every move. Overtures for the surrender of the Germans were rebuffed, but preparations were made for that eventuality when the Greek government's military representative, Colonel Andreas Nathenas, was replaced by Papadakis and Brigadier Barker-Benfield, head of the Greek desk at SOE Cairo, arrived to take charge of Creteforce.[47]

Barker-Benfield travelled to Greece in August 1944 to explain the requirements of Operation Noah's Ark to the Allied military mission, then seventy-men strong and commanded by Nicky Hammond while Woodhouse was absent in Italy. Barker-Benfield shocked Hammond with his strong faith in ELAS and belief that they would carry out all the necessary harassment actions during the German retreat. Hammond agreed with Woodhouse's estimation of the true situation on the ground: ELAS was more eager to destroy its political rivals, especially EDES, than to take on the Germans. Furthermore, Barker-Benfield seemed naive in how he anticipated operations being conducted:

> He put up some suggestions about details, which showed that he had very little conception of our terrain and of our limitations, which was natural enough in one who seemed to me to be thinking only in terms of regular warfare and orthodox situations . . . He dismissed my past experience and my arguments in a summary manner; he knew the answers both on policy and on military operations.

Moreover, Barker-Benfield intended to exert tight control over events from Cairo, ignoring the fact that terrain and frequent radio problems placed a severe constraint on communications. Hammond was so upset about Barker-Benfield's plans that he tendered his resignation, left Greece at the end of August, and handed over command of the mission to Arthur Edmonds.[48]

It can be argued that the dominant role given to ELAS was only a reflection of the reality on the ground in much of Greece. But the situation in the two areas through which the German retreating forces would have to pass on their way to Albania and Yugoslavia was far more complex. The main road to Albania ran from Arta to Ioannina, precisely the part of Epiros in which ELAS and EDES had been waging a long-standing civil war. At the beginning of September, Lieutenant General Lanz's staff began to make preparations for their retreat. Papers were burned at the headquarters in Ioannina and orders received to surrender only to regular troops and not to either EDES or ELAS. A German drive was launched against the resistance to keep open the Ioannina–Preveza road and secure the Germans' unimpeded withdrawal into Albania. Neither EDES nor ELAS took any significant steps to hamper the Germans. Barker-Benfield ordered Zervas to launch an all-out assault on Ioannina but the British liaison officer, Tom Barnes, refused the order on the grounds that a frontal assault on a defended town was beyond the capacity of the guerrillas. Lanz led the final German convoy out of Ioannina on 15 October.[49]

The situation in Macedonia was even more complex. Western Macedonia had been Greek only since 1913 after the Second Balkan War, and the majority of the inhabitants of the area around the town of Florina spoke a Slavic language as their mother tongue and resented the ban on speaking their own language in public which had been imposed by Metaxas before the war. Rival political groups competed for the loyalty of the population. The Bulgarians, with the support of the Italians and Germans, had set up the Axis-Macedonian Bulgarian committee to encourage separatism and the promise of an independent Macedonia, and its armed militia, the *Komitadji*, patrolled the area between the towns of Florina and Kastoria. ELAS, on the other hand, stood firmly for the retention of western Macedonia within Greek borders. This line was opposed by Tito's Partisans who visited the area in April 1944 to offer the prospect of a communist Macedonia in federation with Yugoslavia. The Partisans claimed that 'ELAS are fascists out for Greek territorial integrity and will oppress you. We are Communists and will liberate you.' These political controversies hampered the build-up of forces available for Noah's Ark. The departure of the local ELAS detachment in May meant that the officer on the spot, Pat Evans, had only about twenty potential saboteurs at his disposal, and the presence of sections of the Allied Raiding Support Regiment, there to provide heavy-weapon support for guerrilla attacks, became essential. During Noah's Ark this small force carried out numerous attacks against the main railway line running through the Kleidi Pass on the route to Yugoslavia and mounted attacks on the road between Vigla and Florina. Evans's signals to Cairo demonstrate that ELAS contributed little to the operations, running away from a weak German force on foot in the Kleidi Pass and allowing columns of Germans with their vehicles and artillery to reach Florina without harassment. Stanley Moss had similar experiences in eastern Macedonia, the fiefdom of the ELAS 'general' Melas. Moss told the story of a planned ambush of a German column which failed on the first attempt because the ELAS *andartes* had forgotten to load their guns, and on the second attempt because the guerrillas were having breakfast. In Eastern Thrace, Captain J. McElroy 'came to the conclusion that 99.99% of all *andartes* were a patriotic crowd of useless "old women"'.[50]

The results of Operation Noah's Ark were disappointing. As Major Ken

Scott concluded: 'What in effect happened in the end was that we, the British, blew a few bridges, organised the ambushing of convoys, but without much Greek support.' Myers summarized the results as being around 100 locomotives destroyed, 500 vehicles destroyed or captured, and around 5,000 Germans killed. He concluded: 'It cannot be denied that, even at high cost, the Germans fulfilled their principal intention of extricating the bulk of their forces intact, leaving only the outlying garrisons of a few islands to keep allied forces busy, and to delay rehabilitation until the final surrender of Germany.' Lanz agreed with this assessment.[51]

The commander of ELAS, Sarafis, claimed that ELAS did undertake numerous operations against the departing Germans but were held back by the members of the Allied military mission:

> The whole attitude of the Allied Mission in Greece made us doubt whether HQ Middle East had any real desire that the Germans who were in Greece should be cut off and prevented from fighting further north. On the contrary, we received the impression that, for political reasons, they wanted to ensure that they took over Greece themselves and that they would allow the Germans to leave the country almost without hindrance so that the German troops in Yugoslavia would be reinforced and Tito and the Red Army would have difficulty in advancing northwards.[52]

Sarafis made this argument simply because he was angry that the Allies had not given ELAS all the weapons they had demanded. The reason why the Allies failed him in this regard is simple: politics. Nigel Clive, in his reports to Cairo, put the case clearly: 'It is strikingly obvious that EAM is an organisation designed to obtain absolute political power in the aftermath of Allied liberation by any means deemed necessary in the circumstances. Any more polite and especially more "liberal" way of putting the case castrates the truth.' Barker-Benfield may have been convinced that 'EAM and ELAS would behave like gentlemen', but Churchill and the Foreign Office were, rightly, less certain.[53]

The British struggled to find enough men to fill Scobie's force which had been initially set at 4,000 men. Consequently, the Germans withdrew from the Peloponnese in early September before British troops were on hand to take over. The result was an extremely brutal civil war as ELAS units led by the most ardent communist, Aris Velouchiotis, effectively massacred members of the now abandoned Greek Security Battalions. Aris demanded total acquiescence from the British mission, which was powerless to prevent the terrible campaign being waged by ELAS against all political opponents.[54] News of events on the Peloponnese raised fears of what would happen in Athens once the Germans withdrew if Scobie's force did not arrive in time. It is undoubtedly true that EAM/ELAS could have seized power in the capital had they decided to, and the reasons why they did not are still disputed. Arguably, the most important factor was that EAM learned that Stalin had been informed of the intended despatch of British troops in late September and had raised no objection. Therefore, EAM/ELAS may have realized that they would have no support from the Soviet Union should they clash with British troops.[55]

On 12 August, Lieutenant Colonel Rufus Sheppard, a veteran of SOE's campaign in Greece, was briefed on what tasks he and his small mission should undertake in German-occupied Athens. His principal role was to 'report and comment' on the plans being made by the Greek military commandant of Athens, Spiliotopoulos, for maintaining law and order should the Germans either withdraw or surrender. Sheppard was also asked to report on ELAS's intentions and on what countermeasures should be taken to prevent a seizure of power without utilizing the Security Battalions, who were seen as collaborators by all Greek resistance groups and the Greek government-in-exile. Sheppard was not explicitly ordered to open negotiations with the Germans on the prospect of their surrender but was required to consult general headquarters for instructions should such offers be made. In fact, as Harry Hainsworth, a member of the mission, recorded, Sheppard did negotiate with the Germans, through the good offices of the Swedish Red Cross. At one time Sheppard was housed on one floor of a building with the Swedes directly above him and the German representatives on the floor above them. It was also feared that the Germans would engage in a scorched-earth campaign, and 'would destroy the many antiquities in Athens and district, blow up the harbour of Piraeus and demolish or pollute the Marathon Dam which was the source of the main water supply to the city'.[56]

On 12 October the last German units left Athens: 'True to their word they had not destroyed any of the antiquities, or interfered with the Marathon Dam and had left the harbour of Piraeus undamaged. The harbour had not been booby-trapped in any way and there was not even any graffiti which might have been expected.' Later that morning the first British troops entered Athens to an ecstatic welcome. The Greek government was due to enter Athens on Tuesday, 17 October, but as Rex Leeper, the British ambassador to the Greek government-in-exile, recalled: 'Consternation reigned. It was on a Tuesday that Constantinople fell in 1453 to the final Turkish assault, and it had become a firmly held and widely respected tradition that nothing of any importance should be initiated on a Tuesday.' The small British fleet carrying the Greek government and British representatives therefore dallied in Piraeus harbour for a day. Woodhouse joined Scobie on board the cruiser *Orion* for the entry into Athens:

> I found Macmillan [the British minister in the Mediterranean], Leeper and Scobie. They did not seem to have anything for me to do, but Scobie's ADC offered me a place in one of the cars which were to take part in the victory parade through Athens the next day. I asked where the guerrilla leaders would be placed, because I would rather be with them. 'The guerrilla leaders?' he asked in astonishment. 'What has it got to do with them?'

Woodhouse consequently declined his place in the parade. The arrival of the Greek Mountain Brigade was particularly welcomed by the Athenians, many of whom regarded it as their only protection against ELAS.[57]

Notwithstanding the joy surrounding the departure of the Germans from Athens, the entry of British troops and the return of the Greek government, the situation in Athens was only momentarily calm. The tasks facing Papandreou's government were formidable: rampant inflation, no proper law enforcement, a need to reconstruct the army, police, and gendarmerie, and the outstanding question of the future of King George II. Above all, there was the urgent need to demobilize the guerrillas, both EDES and ELAS. Of these ELAS, with around 70,000 armed men across the country, continued to pose the greatest threat and one to which some observers felt Scobie's headquarters seemed blind: 'The formal – almost lackadaisical – attitude of the British GHQ to the looming menace was to avoid close consultation with those who had the real answers. As a result, a heavy penalty was exacted for this grave error in intelligent military appreciation and action.'[58] The crisis would erupt in late November and would last through the winter.

30
Nearing the End: Winter 1944–45

By early November 1944 General Alexander realized that his armies in Italy were highly unlikely to break through into the Po valley and on to the city of Bologna before the spring. He therefore called for a reduction in activities at the front. Alexander knew that the Italian partisans had suffered high losses during the autumn, both from operations and through German reprisals, and sought to preserve their strength over the winter by calling a halt to their activities in an order issued on 13 November:

> Patriots! The summer campaign is over and the winter campaign has begun. The coming of the rain and of mud necessitates a slowing down of the rhythm of the battle. Therefore your orders are as follows: 1. Cease for the present operations organized on a large scale. 2. Keep your arms and have them ready for new orders. 3. Listen as often as possible to the programme 'Italy is fighting' transmitted from this General Headquarters, so as to be aware of new orders and changes in the situation.[1]

Alexander was in effect making the same mistake as General Koenig had done in France in June 1944: he assumed that the partisans could and would obey orders just like regular troops.

Alexander had not consulted Special Forces Headquarters before issuing his order, and 'did not consider in detail the psychological effects of the declaration'. The internal history of SOE recorded: 'Despair and confusion filled the minds of the partisans and our Liaison Missions were hard put to control them and re-orientate them to this new policy. Many formations broke up and there were numerous desertions of partisans to the Republican forces in order to ensure food and clothing for the winter.' Enigma decrypts suggested that over 70,000 partisans surrendered that winter.[2] Ada Gobetti recorded in her diary the impracticality of the order:

> As if, surrounded, harassed, and pursued as we are, we can wait without doing anything. I very well understand how, in the general and immense

> picture of the war, the battle of the Italian partisans might be but an episode, but for those like us who are involved, the message has been quite a hard blow. Moreover, we are now without that sense of support – perhaps more imagined than real – that the proximity of the Allies gave us. We know that they are still nearby, but as long as the winter lasts, they have completely lost interest in us, and we should not expect anything from them. Never mind! We will fend for ourselves. I am more and more convinced that we must not rely on foreign help, but on our own forces. Yet we feel a certain bitterness.[3]

Alexander may have thought that the Allies would be unable to supply the partisans over the winter, but Max Corvo has pointed out that the supply situation was not as bad as Alexander feared. With the Germans in full retreat from Greece and Albania, the Allied air forces no longer had to despatch flights to those countries, thereby freeing aircraft to serve the requirements of the Italian partisans. Furthermore, Bill Donovan secured a fleet of thirty American planes to increase the number of flights for OSS missions. Supply drops were able to continue throughout the winter because, completely unpredictably, the weather was unusually mild in northern Italy.[4]

The CVL (*Corpo Volontari della Libertà*) issued the response of the Italian resistance to the order on 2 December. First, it stated categorically that the partisan war was not 'a mere whim, an idle caprice to be refrained from at will' but was a fight for freedom and the right to live. The statement then effectively countermanded Alexander's proclamation:

> The war must go on. There must be no relaxation, no weakening. On the contrary, the struggle must be intensified, the armed forces engaged in it greatly increased. We cannot, indeed, we must not, consider any suggestion calculated to deflect us from our purpose: that of widening the sphere of our activities, bringing still larger numbers into the field, and fighting on with an ever-growing resolution and will to win.[5]

The evident gap between what Allied headquarters thought it could order the partisans to do and the war that the Italian resistance believed it was fighting encouraged the CLNAI (*Comitato di Liberazione Nazionale Alta Italia*) to despatch a mission south, despite the extreme risks, to discuss outstanding issues and future plans with the Allied high command.

Overall, it appears that most Italian partisans did remain inactive over the winter, but there were some notable exceptions. Gordon Lett, for example, reported continued actions by the International Brigade and the partisans in the Rossano valley against the German lines of communication in western Italy. These were intensified after the arrival of a party of SAS under Captain Bob Walker Brown on 27 December. The partisans largely acted as guides as the SAS launched attacks on the Via Aurelia, the only land route for the Germans from Genoa to La Spezia: 'There was keen competition among the partisans to take part in operations side by side with the SAS, and they excelled themselves in individual action.' In the middle of January, Lett and Walker Brown learned that the Germans planned a major offensive against the partisans. The partisan leader, Colonel Fontana, decided to order attacks to be launched against the German columns before they could start their offensive, and requested the support of the International Brigade and the SAS. On 19 January 1945 the partisans went into action but 'when dusk fell, it was clear that the partisan offensive had failed dismally, and that the enemy was fast establishing himself in all the main villages'. The German sweep lasted for four days and succeeded in scattering the partisan formations. However, the Germans then withdrew, which allowed the partisans to return to the Rossano valley 'much shrunken in numbers' and renew attacks on the Via Aurelia alongside the SAS until the SAS departed at the end of February and 'life became colourless', while the partisans and Germans recovered from their losses and awaited the Allied offensive in the spring.[6]

The partisans in Emilia-Romagna remained active during the winter under the command of Ilio Barontini. British liaison officers in the region reported the results at the end of February 1945: seventy-three sizeable bridges destroyed; the mining of the main roads from Modena and Reggio, which had resulted in an average of twelve vehicles a week being destroyed, with further losses caused by ambushes; and 2,530 German casualties. At the end of February, Field Marshal Kesselring reported that the partisans in the western Apennines, especially around Modena, Reggio, and Parma, were becoming a real nuisance and worse still:

> The execution of partisan operations shows considerably more commanding leadership. Up to now it has been possible for us, with a few exceptions, to keep our vital rear lines of communication open by means of slight protective forces, but the situation threatens to change considerably for the worse in the immediate future. Speedy and radical countermeasures must anticipate this development.

SS-General Karl Wolff commanded a mixed force of Wehrmacht, SS, and German police units augmented by Italian Republican troops for a series of operations over the following weeks. A Wehrmacht communiqué stated that the partisans had lost several thousand dead and that over 80,000 had surrendered, concluding: 'This action has cleared the greatest part of Northern Italy from the terrorism of armed bands.'[7]

On the Adriatic coast and close to the Allied front line, the commander of the 28th Garibaldi Brigade in Ravenna hatched a plot with the Allies for the liberation of the city. The plan was for one Allied column to liberate Ravenna itself and advance north-westward to Argenta which lay directly east of Bologna. The second Allied column would assist by advancing from Faenza in a north-easterly direction. Simultaneously, 12,000 partisans would attack the Germans north of Ravenna and cut off their retreat. The operation began on 1 December and succeeded in liberating Ravenna that day, but because, for unknown reasons, the second Allied column did not advance, the partisans were left to fight the Germans north of the city alone, with heavy losses and the break-up of formations.[8]

Operations in north-eastern Italy, the Friuli-Venezia Giulia region, were overseen by missions led by two veteran commanders of resistance forces: Tommy Macpherson, last seen in France, and Harold Tilman, who had operated in Albania. These missions reported the sabotage of major railways leading to Venice and Trieste along which the Germans needed to send reinforcements. There were few derailments of locomotives since the mountainous terrain made it difficult to reach the tracks in suitable places. The partisans focused instead on destroying the electricity pylons, an effective course of action since the trains were electric and the Germans had few steam locomotives in the region. Information on concentrations of troop trains was radioed back to headquarters. This could sometimes yield rapid results, as Tom Roworth noted: 'Within an hour of me sending that message, I was watching the whole of these coaches in Udine being fire bombed by our people. It caused tremendous damage.' Allied officers noted that politics hampered the effectiveness of the resistance. For example, when Macpherson arrived at the beginning of November he found that two sabotage squads had already been trained by British instructors already on the ground, and commented: 'One was of the Garibaldi GAP, which was active but not under control, and one was Osoppo under control but not active.' Worse was to come in early February 1945 as 'the Slovenes and Slovene-controlled Garibaldi attacked two Osoppo detachments, totalling 20 men, all but 2 of whom they killed at the time or later. This eliminated an important link in the Mission's command, intelligence, and communications chain and further problems had to be overcome.' Peter Wilkinson, in his final report on the Clowder mission which had failed to penetrate Austria, reported that the contacts made between the Slovenes and the Italian resistance in Friuli-Venezia Giulia could lead to greater results in the future. He believed that the presence of British officers operating in uniform in this heavily German-occupied area would encourage the partisans to remain active. Their level of activity would, however, depend on events in Yugoslavia just as much as on the efforts of the Allied missions in Italy.[9]

*

After the fall of Belgrade in October 1944 the Germans had two objectives in Yugoslavia. The first was to consolidate a front in Srem in eastern Slovenia to hold open the railways to Italy. The second was to keep open the main Sarajevo–Bosanski Brod–Zagreb road as well as the lateral communications westwards towards Bihać, Banja Luka, and Mostar, to protect the withdrawal of their forces from Greece and Albania. Numerous forces were present in Yugoslavia that could hamper the German retreat: the Partisans; Mihailović's Četniks; Četniks of various loyalties under Dimitrije Ljotić and Pavle Djurišić; and Allied ground and air forces.

It quickly became clear that Tito and the Partisans were more interested in consolidating their power over Yugoslavia than in harassing the German retreat. The Partisans were certainly capable of taking on the Germans. They had received ample supplies from all three Allies, including heavy weaponry supplied by the Soviets, and the introduction of conscription meant that by the end of 1944 Partisan forces numbered around 200,000 troops. However, Tito began to complain about Allied intervention against the Germans in Yugoslavia. For example, in October he objected to Maclean's list of towns in Serbia to be bombed, on the grounds that the Partisans would soon take them. In December, Tito and Churchill corresponded on the subject of Tito's complaints regarding the landing of British troops on the Adriatic coast. Churchill made his position clear: 'we shall land anywhere we like, whatever we like and as much of it as we choose'. Tito's response was to issue orders to set up coastal guns and signals communications along the entire Adriatic coast, to forbid mine-sweeping in the bay of Kotor, and to demand prior permission before any British soldier landed in Yugoslavia. The only exception was permission to build temporary airfields near Zadar. Even then, Tito made his opinion clear in regard to cooperation with the British: 'The airports are ours, they are using them.' When Alexander visited Belgrade in February 1945, his offer to land Allied troops to accelerate the German retreat was rejected out of hand by Tito.[10]

The Partisans drove Mihailović and his dwindling band of supporters out of Serbia and Mihailović took refuge in the Sandžak. This was not a suitable location in which to survive the winter since the Sandžak was a food-deficient area, but Mihailović felt that the move was necessary so as to be in a position to meet the Allied forces that he expected would land on the Dalmatian and Montenegrin coasts. He was convinced that the Allies would soon see that Tito intended to make Yugoslavia a communist country, and that once they had done so they would turn to Mihailović to support their plans for overthrowing Tito. Mihailović maintained contact by radio with his agents in Italy, Topalović and Vuković, awaiting news of Allied intentions. The radio in Italy was operated by Poles who, as survivors of Stalin's Gulag, were staunch anti-communists: the British found out and stopped the communications. Mihailović's offer of 50,000 Četniks to assist the Allied high command went unanswered in October and November, and the Allies failed to respond to reports that the Partisans were rounding up the Četniks and putting them into concentration camps. Mihailović's last message was received at the end of the year:

> The Partisans have instituted a ruthless terror in which the best among the leaders of the community and the heads of the old established families are being indiscriminately killed. Concentration camps are being set up and filled with the flower of the Serbian people. In the hopes of bare survival, people are fleeing to the mountains like animals. There they are exposed to cold and hunger. We entreat you to send a delegation to the country to inform the Allies of our tragic situation. Our appeal is urgent for tomorrow may be too late. Help us find a way out of this hell!

Since the Allies would not help them, Mihailović's Četniks began turning more and more to the only people who could, the Germans; and agreements were concluded for the Četniks to guard the German retreat route between Sarajevo and Bosanski Brod.[11]

In November, Djurišić's force of 15,000 men in Montenegro had a narrow escape from the Partisans who had encircled Cetinje and then took it. Since the Germans had left Montenegro and the Partisans were growing in strength and the civil war there was becoming more vicious, Djurišić took his force north to link up with Mihailović. Djurišić aimed to join Ljotić's Četniks in Slovenia but Mihailović expressly forbade him to do so. Djurišić decided that Mihailović was a spent force and made futile overtures towards the Germans and Ustaše for help to reach Slovenia. Over the winter many of Djurišić's Četniks deserted, and in the spring their path northwards was blocked by strong Ustaše forces. In April the Ustaše destroyed the Četniks and captured and killed Djurišić and around thirty of his followers.[12]

In Slovenia various anti-communist political parties joined together to form the Slovene National Council in October 1944. The Council and its armed force, the Slovene National Guard of around 12,000 troops, were pro-Allies but perfectly prepared to collaborate with the Germans because they saw the Partisans as their principal enemy. The main task assigned to the Slovene National Guard and the Četniks under Ljotić, Jevdjević, and Djujić was to guard the principal railways running through the region. The Germans suspected that in the event of an Allied landing in Istria these forces would turn against their German overseers and work alongside the Allies, and therefore exercised close supervision over them. British liaison officers noted the presence of the collaborators and reported to Allied high command that 'their existence deprives the Partisans of much needed manpower and immeasurably eases the task of the Germans'.

During November the Germans in Slovenia attacked the Partisan strongholds in Semič, Črnomelj, and Metlika, forcing the Partisans to retreat. The Partisans attempted to attack one of the main German garrisons at Kočevje, south-east of Ljubljana, with the assistance of Allied air strikes, but found the Germans too strong. Thereafter the Partisans remained on the defensive, though subject to periodic attacks by the Germans. The strongly pro-Partisan Basil Davidson described the scene that winter:

> In that desolation it required more than mere bravery, or any longing for revenge, if those who survived were to stay sane and stand firm. It required a belief that resistance, and only resistance, could make life possible again. The shooting of prisoners, of women and children along with the men, was only one enemy proof among many. In Srem that winter the ruins of a score of villages were still clothed with the stink of fired houses, a stench that no one will forget who has ever breathed it; and tank tracks stiff in the mud were reminders of as many massacres.

Tito sent reinforcements to the area but the Partisans who had been recently conscripted in Serbia were despatched to the front without proper training or equipment and over the winter many thousands died in clashes with the Germans. The key communication routes remained open, and the German strength in Slovenia continued to mount as their troops successfully concluded a largely unharassed retreat from the Balkans, only leaving Mostar in Croatia on 22 February 1945.[13]

Far to the north the Soviets had been advancing north of Leningrad into Finland since the siege had been lifted in January 1944. German troops and their Finnish allies were driven back and by late August it was clear that Finland could not remain in the war. The peace terms offered by the Soviets to the Finnish government were harsh, a reflection of Finland's successes in stalling the Soviet invasion during the winter of 1939–40 and her role as a German ally in the June 1941 invasion of the Soviet Union. These peace terms included the loss of territory such as Finnish Karelia and large reparations. The armistice between Finland and the Soviet Union was signed on 19 September. The Finns were also ordered to expel the Germans from the country. Initially, Finland and Germany made an informal agreement for an organized withdrawal of German troops from northern Finland, Lapland, into Norway, but then the Soviets ordered the Finns to take a more aggressive stance which led to a brief war between the Finns and the Germans during which the Germans carried out a brutal scorched-earth policy as they retreated from Lapland. The Germans entering Norway formed a new defensive line at Lyngenfjord, just north of Tromsø. In October the Soviets launched a major offensive, and by the 25th had reached the Norwegian fortress town of Kirkenes, which had been heavily garrisoned by the Germans as a vital base from which to attack the Allied Arctic convoys carrying supplies to the Soviet Union. By 13 November the Soviets had advanced a short distance to the line of the Tana river where they halted for the winter.

Northern Norway was defended by the German 20th Mountain Army. This consisted mostly of Austrian soldiers under the command of General Lothar Rendulic, a veteran of the Balkans. The Germans had carried out a scorched-earth policy as they had retreated through Finland, though Kirkenes had been spared since much of the town already lay in ruins after heavy Soviet bombing. Hitler demanded that the scorched-earth policy should now apply in northern Norway and the population be evacuated southwards. On 28 October, Alfred Jodl issued an order to Rendulic:

> Because of the unwillingness of the north Norwegian population to voluntarily evacuate, the Führer has agreed to the proposals of the commissioner for the occupied Norwegian territories and has ordered that the entire Norwegian population east of the fjord of Lyngen be evacuated by force in the interest of their own security and that all homes are to be burned down or destroyed.

This evacuation was deemed necessary to prevent the population from assisting the Soviets with their knowledge of the terrain, and the orders ended with the statement: 'This is not the place for sympathy for the civilian population.' Rendulic issued his own orders on the following day, which signalled his willingness to follow Jodl's orders to the letter and to evacuate forcibly 60,000 civilians from Finnmark.

The Quisling government was appalled by the German plans. It had encouraged a voluntary evacuation, overseen by NS ministers Jonas Lie and Johan Lippestad, but the first ship leaving Kirkenes had carried only twenty-two people out of the war zone, almost all of them NS members. The resistance was equally shocked at the prospect of the forced evacuation, and on 18 November the Home Front issued a directive:

> Where there is any chance of getting away from the Germans and maintaining life until the liberators arrive, there they cling firmly to the spot. Neither must we support the Germans in their military plans. We must not make ourselves participants in the worst war crime which has yet been committed

> in our country. We must not help the Nazi authorities and the Nazi organisations with the deportation.

Ten days later the Home Front leadership realized the full extent of the devastation being brought to Finnmark and urged the population to give every form of assistance to the evacuees now arriving in the south. They also wanted to ensure that neither the NS nor the Germans could gain credit for the care of the deportees.

The devastation of Finnmark was thorough: in two months the German Army destroyed: 11,000 houses, 6,000 farms, 4,700 barns, 27 churches, 140 buildings owned by religious organizations, 53 hotels and inns, 21 hospitals and clinics, 420 shops, 306 fish factories, 106 schools, 60 local government buildings, 230 factories, 108 lighthouses, 350 bridges, 350 motor boats and thousands of rowing boats, and countless numbers of telephone poles. A German report at the end of November, issued while the evacuation was still ongoing, stated that 29,000 people had been moved south to reception centres at Narvik, Mosjøen, and Harstad, 3,500 had moved to the Lofoten Islands, 10,000 remained in eastern Finnmark away from the battlefront, and at least 200 had evaded capture.

Trygve Lie, the foreign minister in the Norwegian government-in-exile, was very concerned that the British planned only to occupy southern Norway to assist in the country's liberation. This meant that there were no safeguards against the Soviets advancing further south and remaining in permanent occupation of northern Norway. The British Foreign Office and Allied high command did not share his fears and offered him no help. Lie took the initiative and opened discussions with the Soviet ambassador to the Norwegian government-in-exile, Victor Lebedev. These bore fruit in May 1944 when the Soviets accepted Lie's offer of Norwegian troops, then being trained in Britain, to assist in their operations. In October and November, Churchill and Stalin corresponded on the subject and agreed on the despatch and reception of 230 Norwegian troops, commanded by Colonel Arne Dahl, who would then operate under the Soviet commander, General Shcherbakov. Operations had halted by the time Dahl and his troops arrived, and their main purpose became one of supplying relief to the Norwegians who had obeyed the first resistance directive and had gone into hiding rather than be evacuated. These people had taken refuge along the coastline in caves, under upturned boats covered with turf and in mountain crevices. By Christmas 1944 the Norwegian troops had located and moved nearly 900 evaders to the safety of liberated eastern Finnmark. In the middle of February 1945 a British destroyer rescued a further 1,000 people who had hidden on the island of Sørøya off Hammerfest and took them to Scotland. The Norwegian troops also assisted in the infiltration of agents from Sweden to carry out the sabotage of the German Army bunkers on the Lyngen Line and to supply intelligence on the strength and dispositions of the German 20th Mountain Army.[14]

Meanwhile, further south, sabotage operations continued as normal. In late 1944 SOE learned that the Germans were planning to move all stocks of ball bearings, a critical component in many armaments, back to the Reich and asked the resistance to intervene. The Oslo Gang, with *Milorg*'s assistance, successfully carried out three attacks which destroyed all sixty tons of ball bearings held by the SKF works. Further attacks were mounted on the German war machine with the destruction of 184 torpedo heads and fifty-three tons of charges in the Horten torpedo store in January, and various attacks were carried out on shipping in Oslo harbour which sank or damaged 50,000 tons of shipping as well as the only crane in Norway capable of handling tanks and heavy artillery. Bases for guerrilla units consisting of up to 2,000 men were established in the mountains: at Bjorn West in the Nordhordland mountains north of Bergen; Bjorn East in the Voss–Hardanger area; Elg in the Buskerud north-west of Oslo; and Varg in the Vest-Agder south-east of Stavanger. Conditions were extremely tough, so that in the event the units never numbered more than a few hundred.[15]

The Germans carried out a high number of arrests of resisters during the late autumn and winter of 1944 which, in many cases, severely limited the functioning of the resistance. Terboven issued a warning that these captured saboteurs were now held as hostages to be executed in case of further sabotage attacks. In February 1945 Quisling invited seven prominent industrialists to a meeting, which five attended, and warned them that the Germans were so angry about the level of sabotage that there was a serious risk that prominent industrialists and other personages would be shot if they did not bring influence to bear on the Home Front to end the sabotage campaign and cease attacking members of the NS. The Home Front seriously considered calling a general strike but after some debate felt that this was premature and settled instead for an intensified propaganda campaign against the NS.

Attacks against the NS and especially its paramilitary wing, the *Hird*, increased. In January 1945 special units of around 3,000 *Hird* men each were created by Quisling and were armed by the Germans to take the battle to the resistance. On 8 February the resistance responded by assassinating the head of the state police and the *Hird*, Major General Karl Marthinsen, on his way to his office. Terboven ordered the execution of seventy-five prisoners and hostages in reprisal: of these fifty would be shot by the Germans and the remainder by the NS. Quisling was outraged by the assassination but felt that the German reprisals were too severe. He negotiated the figure down to thirty-two, of whom five were reprieved. In February 1945 Quisling publicized his plans to conscript all NS party members into the *Hird*. The measure was unpopular with both the *Hird* and the resistance. Many NS members chose to resign their membership of the party, or declined to report for duty, and some actually began to assist the resistance. The Home Front issued a stark warning to the parents of the potential recruits: 'You have a son in the *Hird*. Take care that you do not, in a few weeks' time, have a son in the churchyard.' This warning was reinforced by announcements that members of the *Hird* would be subject to the death penalty, as would NS sheriffs who took any action against the Home Front or *Milorg*. In the event Quisling's plans came to nothing because Himmler was reluctant to allow Quisling control over a Norwegian armed force which would include Norwegian members of the SS. The new commander of German forces in Norway, General Franz Böhme, noted the unpopularity of the NS and urged his soldiers to offer *Hird* members moral support but not more weapons.[16]

By the time operations ceased for the winter in north-western Europe all of Belgium had been liberated along with half of the Netherlands where the line was held by British and Canadian troops. Further south the American and French armies had reached the Vosges mountains on the Franco-German border. Luxembourg and the parts of Belgium around Malmedy which had been annexed to the Reich had been liberated in September, and on 21 October the first German city to be captured, Aachen, had fallen to the Allies.

On 16 December 1944 the Germans launched Operation Herbstnebel, known to the Allies as the Battle of the Bulge, in the Belgian Ardennes. The offensive took the Allies totally by surprise. Most of the German preparations for the attack had taken place on the German side of the frontier, where only a few Allied intelligence agents operated. Reports of German activity were gathered by some OSS agents but the American commanders tended to ignore them, and Colonel Benjamin Dickson of the US 1st Army had even banished the OSS detachment from his headquarters.

Once the battle began there are a few examples of the Belgian resistance assisting the Allies. For example, local resistance fighters guided the American forces through Ettelbrück and Grosbous. Further north, the former leader of the Belgian resistance in the area, Baron Jacques de Villenfagne, rode his motorcycle around the area and reported the positions of the 2nd Panzer Army advancing towards the British Royal Tank Regiment. Local civilians had greeted their Allied liberators with joy and were now made to pay the price as the Germans retook their villages and towns. War crimes were committed by the SS troops under the command of a veteran of anti-partisan warfare on the Eastern Front, Joachim Peiper, whose orders to his subordinate commanders included the phrase: 'Armed civilians will be treated as partisans', meaning that they would be executed. Local Belgians were forced by the Germans to act as their guides and were then killed when they were no longer considered useful. Peiper's troops were especially brutal towards the unarmed civilians in the town of Stavelot, where the Germans were convinced that the civilians had assisted the Americans in delaying the German advance and took their revenge after the Americans had departed: 138 innocent civilians were murdered by the SS. Civilians in Bourcy and Noville suffered a similar fate as the Germans took revenge against those they thought had welcomed the arrival of the Americans: in Noville seven men, including the local priest and the schoolmaster, were murdered by the SS.[17]

The stiffening German defence on the north-western front had an impact on other fronts. It led to a change in orders for the Norwegian resistance even before the Battle of the Bulge began. On 5 December, SHAEF reversed its orders regarding the desirability of railway sabotage. The earlier order had requested *Milorg* to hold back on such attacks since the Allies wanted the Germans to depart from Norway for the mainland European front lines in the belief that they could be destroyed in battle there. Now, however, *Milorg* was called upon to carry out 'maximum railway and road sabotage consistent with the maintenance of Norwegian Resistance at sufficient strength for its primary military role'. *Milorg* obliged, but German records show that seven German divisions were successfully withdrawn from Norway in the first few months of 1945. The sabotage was unpopular in Norway itself: 'Around a month after New Year 1945 even die-hard resisters and declared enemies of the Germans started to condemn sabotage since supplies of food and necessities did not reach Norwegian civilians but were stopped en route by constant train derailing.'[18]

The Danish resistance was also asked to increase its rate of railway sabotage. In November, Paul Brandenborg was parachuted in to organize sabotage parties and led at least fifty such attacks against the railways and war factories before being caught and later executed in February 1945. Field Marshal Montgomery duly praised the efforts of the resistance in delaying the arrival of further German units on the Bulge front. The high level of railway sabotage continued into the New Year, and in January the Randers goods yard was attacked which held up the passage of German troop trains for twenty-four hours. In one week in February the German 233rd Reserve Panzer Division and the 166th Infantry Division began to move out of Denmark and the Danish saboteurs succeeded in delaying over half of the forty-four trains involved in the redeployment, derailing six of them. At the end of February the resistance learned that the commander of all German forces in Denmark, General Lindemann, was to travel by train through Jutland and an attack was mounted: substantial damage was inflicted on the train but Lindemann emerged unhurt.[19]

The Battle of the Bulge delayed Allied plans to liberate the whole of the Netherlands, thereby leaving the Dutch to their fate. German actions were becoming more brutal as they felt more vulnerable. In October 1944 the resistance attacked a Wehrmacht vehicle near the town of Putten, killing several officers. In revenge, the German police evacuated and burned the town and despatched the male inhabitants to German concentration camps, where the majority of them died. At the end of October the Germans decided to arrest and deport all males aged between seventeen and forty from Rotterdam, The Hague, and Amsterdam. The first round-up took place in Rotterdam on 10 November. It caught the Dutch by surprise and netted about 50,000 men for the German war effort. The resistance issued general warnings for all men in the cities to go into hiding, and these were heeded: the second round-up, in The Hague, caught only 13,000 men at home. Walter Maass described the situation in The Hague that November:

> German soldiers and green police patrolled the streets. Younger men stayed in their houses, for nobody knew if the *razzia* would be repeated. The lack of food was already apparent; endless lines formed in front of grocery stores and public kitchens. From time to time, the thunder of the V-2 rocket rose over the city. At night, the giant flying torpedoes, with their fiery tails, were a spectacular sight.

The limited numbers caught in The Hague meant that the Germans abandoned efforts to carry out round-ups in Amsterdam.

The main feature of life in the occupied Netherlands was starvation as the railway strike called for by the government-in-exile, and supported by the resistance, meant that food supplies reached only the Germans. At the beginning of October 1944 the official food ration was 1,400 calories but by January 1945 it had dropped to 500 calories. M. Dekker described the 'Hunger Winter':

> Decrepit dogs scavenged among the heaps of waste; their spindly bodies showed protruding ribs like steel rings on a motor block. But greedy fingers had already plucked anything edible from the heaps. Children with swollen bellies walked barefoot on shrivelled legs and death stared out of their hollow

> eyes. The women had lost all their grace and attraction, they were tired, ugly, and dirty. The girls looked waning, the men weak and exhausted. This whole generation seemed never to have been young, to be born in a half dying state. They were only shadows of the living, creatures made of mist, mildew, and microbes.

Shortly before Christmas the Germans ordered a registration of all Dutch males aged between sixteen and forty for work in the Reich. The draftees were promised good food and decent treatment. The resistance opposed the German order but starvation drove 50,000 to register, out of the 650,000 eligible men.

The Dutch government-in-exile put pressure on the Allies to assist in the humanitarian disaster unfolding in the Netherlands and in late January 1945 the first food-relief ships docked in Dutch ports. Montgomery was accused of delaying his advance further into the Netherlands, and on 20 February he angrily wrote to Eisenhower:

> The issue is quite clear. I have no troops available for attacking the Germans in West Holland. If the Germans withdraw from West Holland, I must go east and fight them. I cannot go east and fight the Germans and also go into West Holland with my present resources. I can do one of these two alternatives, not both . . .

The population of the Netherlands would just have to wait until either the Germans collapsed and sued for peace or the Allied offensive was renewed in the spring.[20]

The failure of the Warsaw Uprising had virtually destroyed the AK, and its commander, Tadeusz Bór-Komorowski, had taken the decision to follow his soldiers into German POW camps. He named his successor as Leopold Okulicki, a man with experience of resistance and impeccable anti-Soviet sentiments, having been sent to a Soviet Gulag in 1940 and released a year later when a Polish army was formed in the Soviet Union. The government-in-exile had not been consulted about the appointment and did not confirm it until 21 December 1944. Okulicki had left Warsaw hidden among the civilian population and travelled via Kielce to Częstochowa where he made an assessment of the state of the AK. The news was not good. In eastern Poland the Soviets had arrested those members of the AK who had participated in Operation Burza, and this policy of arresting AK members loyal to the government-in-exile was extended into areas of Poland east of Warsaw now administered by the Lublin Committee under the supervision of the Soviets.

The Kampinos Group of around 2,400 men operated in the vast forest to the west of Warsaw. It had been trained to operate as a partisan unit and not in urban warfare and so had taken little part in the Warsaw Uprising other than to carry supplies dropped into the forest into the capital. On 27 September 1944 the Germans launched Operation Sternschnuppe to destroy the group. Within two days the forest had been combed, the AK commander killed, and the group had scattered into small parties in order to pass through the German lines. The destruction of this unit was mirrored by events elsewhere. On 9 December 1944 Okulicki reported on the state of the AK:

> Many provincial units, and in particular those which were operating in the Kampinos Forest, have been destroyed, while the soldiers of these units have taken shelter in the area on their own or in small groups. In the desperate situation in which these people find themselves, there lies the danger of the transformation of these small groups into common plundering bands or of their defection to the People's Army, which serves Russia. To sum up: as a result of the loss of the Battle of Warsaw, grave signs of demoralization have appeared in the ranks of the Home Army in the provinces. New attitudes have arisen as well in society, as has a new reality, which must be taken into account.[21]

The AK was still active in the area around Kielce and near Łódź and the situation was most promising in the Radom district where the AK still had two infantry divisions of 7,000 soldiers.

If the AK was to rebuild its strength then it urgently needed supplies but the prospects of receiving them seemed slim. The Allied flight route from Italy to Poland either ran across Romania, where aircraft risked being shot down by the Soviets, or had to face the heavy German air defences between Vienna and Cracow. From Italy, Air Marshal John Slessor informed Charles Portal, chief of the air staff, on 20 November:

> To continue to ask our crews to run the gauntlet of German night fighter defences in the Vienna-Cracow area where they could reach their targets just as easily while flying in safety behind Russian lines is a grave reflection on the status of the Russians as Allies.[22]

The Air Ministry attempted to obtain Soviet permission for operations to Poland to cross Soviet-occupied territory, but the Soviets refused. Portal wrote to Churchill: 'If it is politically necessary to continue to supply the Poles by air, I suggest that we ought to try to get this absurd decision reversed', but Churchill refused to intervene personally in the matter.[23]

The principal problem facing the AK that winter was less a shortage of supplies than a lack of overall purpose. The AK had been extremely disappointed that the Polish government-in-exile had failed to press the Allies for more supply flights during the Warsaw Uprising, and in general felt that this government failed to understand the situation on the ground where the AK was under extreme pressure from both the Germans and the Soviets. In October both the AK and the prime minister, Stanisław Mikołajczyk, had been appalled to learn of the decision taken by the Allied leaders at the Teheran Conference a year earlier to award eastern Poland to the Soviet Union. Mikołajczyk had argued the matter directly with Stalin in Moscow and after the talks failed he resigned. He was replaced as prime minister by Tomasz Arciszewski, who had been smuggled out of Poland earlier that year, and whose government became known as the 'Government of National Protest'. Churchill disowned it and refused to have contact with its members; on the other hand, he also refused to acknowledge the Lublin Committee as the Provisional Government of Poland as Stalin did at the beginning of 1945. The British government had demanded and achieved the resignation of the Polish commander-in-chief, Kazimierz Sosnkowski, on the grounds of his ardent anti-Soviet sentiments. They now made things even more difficult for the government-in-exile by taking the decision to censor all communications between the Poles in London and their representatives in Poland, and to forbid communications with the Poles in Soviet-occupied Poland altogether.[24]

Mikołajczyk believed that the British would show more support for the Poles if they received independent confirmation of what the Poles in Poland were reporting with regard to Soviet conduct. From February 1944 onwards Mikołajczyk pressed the British to despatch a mission of British observers. Churchill and SOE were keen to send such a mission but the Foreign Office objected on the grounds that it could be viewed as a hostile act by the Soviets. In April, Churchill replied to Mikołajczyk that no mission would be sent. The Soviet failure to support the Warsaw Uprising in August greatly disturbed Churchill, and the continued Polish appeals for a mission began to bear fruit. In October the members of the mission were nominated, their purpose decided, and they were despatched to Italy to await an opportune moment for insertion into Poland. On 2 November 1944 Archibald Clark Kerr, the British ambassador in Moscow, informed Molotov that the British were sending liaison officers to Poland to obtain 'direct trustworthy information about events in Poland'. This was to be Operation Freston.[25]

The Freston mission was led by Colonel Bill Hudson, the veteran of British liaison with Mihailović, and the members were: Major Peter Kemp who had operated with the Albanian resistance, Sergeant Major Donald

Galbraith, Major Peter Solly-Flood, and Major Alun Morgan. The interpreter was a Polish lieutenant, Antoni Pospieszalski, using the *nom de guerre* Captain Tony Currie. Adverse weather conditions and British vacillations on the desirability of the mission after Mikołajczyk's resignation caused further delays. Eventually on the night of 26–27 December 1944 the mission parachuted into Poland, landing near Włoszczowa Końskie in the district of Radom. The British soldiers kept on the move, escorted by the AK, but lost their radio equipment after a brief skirmish with the Germans. The mission met Okulicki and was briefed on the state of the AK in Poland and the attitude of the Red Army. On 26 December 1944 the Freston mission wrote a lengthy report on what it had learned, which praised the organization and tactics adopted by the AK. The report made frequent comparisons between the resistance in Poland and that in Yugoslavia, including the observation:

> When one reads in Moscow newspapers that Tito having engaged 600,000 [German] troops in Yugoslavia is partly responsible for Allied success in Italy, one wonders what could have been said with a little goodwill of Polish resistance – which at least was not occupied in cutting its own throat – in helping some stages of the Russian advance.[26]

This comment was about to become especially relevant to the British mission because on 13 January 1945 the Soviets broke out of the bridgeheads on the Vistula and began the vast offensive that would drive the Germans out of Poland and back to the line of the Oder.

On the night of 13 January the sound of Soviet artillery was heard and the mission managed to send a message back to London asking for confirmation of their orders to hand themselves over to the Soviets. They received this confirmation, and Peter Kemp recalled that London reassured them that 'our names and location and the nature of our mission had been communicated to the Russian political and military authorities'. This appeared not to be the case. On 15 January the British mission presented themselves to the nearest Soviet unit and were taken to the Soviet Army Corps headquarters at Żytno and interrogated by an NKVD general who asked them: 'Why have you been spying on the Red Army? Allied soldiers would not be found living with bandits, collaborators, war criminals and enemies of the Red Army.' They were all arrested, and in the middle of February arrived in Moscow before being repatriated via Cairo.[27]

Within two days the Soviet armies had advanced sixty miles further into Poland. Polish cities fell one after the other: Radom, Częstochowa, and Kielce on 16 January, the deserted capital Warsaw on the 17th, the same day that Hans Frank abandoned Cracow, which the Soviets reached two days later. On 27 January the Soviets advanced into Upper Silesia and liberated Auschwitz where they found 7,600 emaciated survivors, the remaining prisoners having been marched westwards in the depth of the winter. The Soviet drive continued westwards to take the fortress city of Poznań, and one Soviet army containing the Polish formations then advanced towards the Baltic coast. The AK took no part in assisting Soviet operations.

Now that the Soviets occupied the whole of Poland there was no reason for the AK to continue in existence. Therefore, on 19 January 1945 Okulicki, with the assent of the Polish government-in-exile, issued his final order to the AK which formally disbanded it:

> Conduct your future work and activity in the spirit of the recovery of the full independence of the state and defence of the Polish population from annihilation. Try to be the nation's guides and creators of an independent Polish state. In this activity each of us must be his own commander. In the conviction that you will obey this order, that you will remain loyal only to Poland, as well as to make your future work easier, on the authorisation of the President of the Polish Republic, I release you from your oath and dissolve the ranks of the AK.[28]

The Underground Government remained in being and in secret, hoping that its members would be invited to take positions in the future government of Poland.[29]

Although it lies outside the compass of this book it is worth saying a little of the Polish reaction to the Soviet occupation. In the aftermath of the Warsaw Uprising, General Emil Fieldorf was ordered to set up a new conspiratorial underground organization from the ranks of the AK. This became known as *Niepodleglość* (NIE) – Independence.* NIE aimed at the infiltration and undermining of the organs of the new Polish Provisional Government where possible and the boycotting of government decrees. Okulicki took over command after disbanding the AK, but NIE had little chance of success given the widespread terror perpetrated by the NKVD and the Provisional Government, and it withered away when Okulicki himself was arrested in March.[30] In place of NIE, as the war in Europe ended, Colonel Jan Rzepecki established the *Delegatura Sił Zbrojnych* – Delegation of the Armed Forces – which aimed to bring some organization to the resistance, necessary because many AK units were refusing to give up the fight. This *Delegatura* was in turn replaced by *Wolność i Niezawisłość*

* NIE is also 'No' in Polish, which is effectively what the resistance was saying to the Soviet occupation.

(WiN) – Freedom and Independence – aimed at organizing the resistance for political ends rather than military activities and to give some sense of purpose to those former AK soldiers who refused to accept the abandonment of Poland to the communists.[31]

As the end of the war grew nearer, Allied policymakers, both military and political, faced the need to take important decisions in order to ensure a smooth transfer of power from the German occupation to the restoration of native governments. Events in Greece demonstrated what could go wrong if the existence and feelings of the resistance were not taken sufficiently into account.

The Papandreou government returned to Athens to great acclamation on 18 October, but this euphoria soon gave way to conflict since the government 'represented an elaborate compromise and a balance of forces whose intricacy defies simple analysis'. It had been created under British pressure and was threatened in Greece by the republicanism of the resistance, and especially the political and military menace of EAM/ELAS. The departure of the German Army and the pro-German government of Ioannis Rallis left a power vacuum that the Papandreou government struggled to fill. The forces of law and order, the police and gendarmerie, were seen by EAM/ELAS as full of collaborators who needed to be purged. The government was keen to start this purge, but slowly and with care so that law and order did not totally collapse. At the same time the government strived to create a new National Guard to replace the gendarmerie, which would then mean that EAM's Civil Guard could be disbanded. With British support, the government ordered the call-up of the first class to form the National Guard on 20 November, to be followed a week later by the disbandment of EAM's Civil Guard. This would be followed by the demobilization of all guerrilla armies, ELAS and EDES, on 1 December. Finally, on 10 December four classes would be conscripted to form a new Greek Army centred on the Greek Mountain Brigade. This brigade reached Athens on 9 November.

General Scobie met the leaders of ELAS and EDES, Stefanos Sarafis and Napoleon Zervas respectively, in Athens on 22 November to discuss the process of demobilization. Zervas signalled his willingness to disband EDES, but Sarafis demanded the receipt of an order signed by all members of Papandreou's government, including the communist ministers, before agreeing to demobilization. Over the next few days EAM/ELAS's stance hardened to a total refusal to disband ELAS until the police and gendarmerie had been purged of collaborators, and the Mountain Brigade, which was formed of officers and men loyal to the king, had been demobilized.

The British government, especially Churchill, encouraged the Greek government to demand the prior disbandment of ELAS in order to prevent a seizure of power by EAM while there were no organized forces of law and order. Effectively 'each side was convinced of the evil intentions of the other; each side believed that it enjoyed popular sympathy and support in its cause. Working at cross purposes they made compromise impossible'. EAM ministers even rejected their own compromise proposal when it was discussed in the full cabinet. A deadline of 10 December was set for demobilization.[32]

On 2 December the EAM ministers resigned from the government, following which EAM called for a mass demonstration in Constitution Square in Athens set for 11 a.m. on 3 December. This would be followed by a general strike in order to force Papandreou either to accept EAM's conditions for demobilization or to resign. The government banned the demonstration and blocked off all the principal roads leading to the square with cordons manned by the demoralized and weak Athens police force. EAM organized a shuttle service to bring crowds into Athens for the demonstration and mobilized its units in Attica, who remained outside the city limits. The streets around Constitution Square were packed with demonstrators, and when a cordon broke and several hundred people ran into the square, an unidentified man in military clothes ordered the police to fire into the crowd: twelve demonstrators were left dead or seriously wounded. When another mob rushed into the square the police fled back into their headquarters. Order was restored in the early afternoon when a company of British paratroopers arrived and, without opposition, cleared the demonstrators out of Constitution Square.[33]

On 4 December, Papandreou planned to resign and suggested Themistoklis Sofoulis should be appointed as his successor. Although this step was seen as necessary by Rex Leeper and the US ambassador, Lincoln MacVeagh, Churchill was implacably opposed. Churchill then issued two orders which, combined with the deaths on Constitution Square and the civil war waged by EAM/ELAS against police stations in the suburbs, effectively plunged Greece into round two of the civil war. On 5 December, Churchill ordered Leeper to insist on Papandreou remaining in office: 'You must force Papandreou to stand to his duty and assure him he will be supported by all our forces if he does so. Should he resign, he should be locked up till he comes to his senses, when the fighting will probably be over.'[34] Churchill's order to Scobie, also on 5 December, was totally uncompromising:

> You are responsible for maintaining order in Athens and for neutralising or destroying all EAM-ELAS bands approaching the city. You may make any

> regulations you like for the strict control of the streets or for the rounding up of any number of truculent persons. Naturally ELAS will try to put women and children in the van where shooting may occur. You must be clever about this and avoid mistakes. But do not hesitate to fire at any armed male in Athens who assails the British authority or Greek authority with which we are working. It would be well of course if your commands were reinforced by the authority of some Greek Government, and Papandreou is being told by Leeper to stop and help. *Do not however hesitate to act as if you were in a conquered city where a local rebellion is in progress.*
>
> With regard to ELAS bands approaching from the outside, you should surely be able with your armour to give some of these a lesson which will make others unlikely to try. You may count upon my support in all reasonable and sensible action taken on this basis. *We have to hold and dominate Athens. It would be a great thing for you to succeed in this without bloodshed if possible, but also with bloodshed if necessary.*[35]

Unfortunately, Scobie was probably not the man for the job. He has been described as: 'a stiff, abrasive and taciturn military man with no natural finesse for the subtleties of politics: his was not the type of personality capable of identifying, let alone defusing, the lively suspicions of the ELAS officers he had to work with.'[36]

Scobie gave ELAS the deadline of midnight on 6–7 December to withdraw its forces from the Athens-Piraeus area, but ELAS, strengthened by the arrival of a 2,000-strong brigade from the Peloponnese, desisted. ELAS continued to attack government buildings and police stations in Athens, although they were careful to avoid attacking British troops who guarded many of these buildings. Churchill informed Scobie that the British government's policy was the complete defeat of EAM and not just an end to the fighting. Reinforcements were rushed from Italy, bringing Scobie's force up from the 5,000 men originally despatched to Athens to 40,000, a figure that would be doubled by the end of December as the situation became more precarious. On 11 December, Macmillan and Alexander visited Athens, and Macmillan summarized the situation faced by the British troops: Piraeus had been lost and no port was in British hands, although the beaches at Phaleron Bay were still under British control; the airfield at Tatoi had been lost and the British airmen there were under siege, and the airfield at Kalamaki was under threat. Questions were asked in Parliament about the conduct of the British forces in Greece when the RAF began to bomb ELAS formations approaching Athens and serious clashes between ELAS and British troops were reported. As Churchill's private secretary, Jock Colville, noted in his diary: 'The general public have no idea of the true nature of ELAS, which they believe to be a heroic left-wing resistance movement', although the communism of EAM was now more apparent.[37]

EAM/ELAS was effectively fighting a war on three fronts. One was against its political opponents in Athens, as described by Major Tobler:

> One awful aspect of civil war is that there is no 'front', as in field warfare, and the enemy is all around one. Twice, while out on the streets, I would pass, or be passed by, an ordinary Greek going about his business. Suddenly a shot was fired close at hand and the unfortunate man dropped dead, a few feet away.[38]

It was estimated that when ELAS finally withdrew from the Athens-Piraeus region it had carried out mass executions of its opponents and taken around 30,000 civilian hostages from Attica.[39] The second aspect of the war was the ELAS offensive against EDES in Epiros launched on 18 December. Zervas was in the process of demobilizing his 8,000 troops when he was attacked by 12,000 men belonging to ELAS commanded by Sarafis. The diversion of these troops to crush EDES almost certainly assisted the British in regaining control in Athens but it spelled the end of EDES and Zervas. 'Monty' Woodhouse was on hand to observe events as EDES was gradually driven back towards the port of Preveza. ELAS took Arta on 22 December and Ioannina on the following day. Woodhouse requested British assistance to evacuate Zervas and most of his troops, and the Royal Navy responded, transporting most of the EDES troops, hundreds of civilians, and Zervas himself to Corfu at the end of the month.[40]

The final front was against the British troops. ELAS realized that it could not ultimately defeat the British since the arrival of reinforcements from Italy meant that British firepower was so much greater. Indeed, the situation around Athens was quickly regularized and ELAS began to retreat from Attica. Nonetheless, the British also faced a major problem. Even if Athens could be made safe, ELAS was still the dominant force in the rest of Greece. The troops landed from Italy could remain in Greece only for a short time while the Italian front was at a standstill but would be required back in Italy in the early months of the New Year in order to prepare for the spring offensive. It was simply inconceivable to consider the possibility of opening, during a world war, a new front against former allies of the British. Alexander telegraphed from Athens on 21 December: 'I earnestly hope that you will be able to find a political solution to the Greek problem, as I am convinced that further military action after we have cleared the Athens-Piraeus area is beyond our strength.'[41]

The principal block against an immediate solution to the political crisis was the uncertain position of King George. In 1943 the king had reluctantly agreed not to return to Greece until he was called for, and now he was expecting that call to come. But quite apart from the republicanism of the two principal resistance forces, there were many Greeks who had not forgiven the king for supporting the Metaxas dictatorship. Eden, Macmillan, and Leeper all agreed that the most likely solution was for the king to stand down and for Archbishop Damaskinos to be appointed as regent. The king, his government, and Churchill strongly opposed this proposal. Churchill decided to visit Athens himself to learn more about the situation. Between 26 and 28 December a conference was held in Athens attended by Churchill, Eden, Macmillan, Alexander, the American and French ambassadors, and Colonel Popov representing the Soviet Union. The archbishop presented his proposals for a settlement which were centred around his immediate appointment as regent, whereupon he would form a new government which would exclude EAM and Papandreou. Churchill's role was to persuade the king of the need for these steps, and, once back in London, Churchill and his ministers put intense pressure on King George to accept. It was only when the British government threatened to switch its support totally from the king to the regent that King George backed down. On 30 December he announced his decision to stand down and designated Damaskinos as regent. On 4 January 1945 General Nikolaos Plastiras, a staunch republican who had spent much of the war outside Greece, was appointed prime minister and formed a government of political moderates.[42]

On 3 January the British offensive against ELAS was renewed with vigour. British airpower bombed ELAS's artillery positions around Athens and drove ELAS forces away from the city. ELAS had sought a truce twice during December, but its conditions regarding the demobilization of the Mountain Brigade had remained unchanged and so the ELAS advances had been rejected. On 10 January, however, ELAS recognized its inability to withstand British attacks and consequently approached Scobie for a truce without attaching the previous conditions. The truce was granted, to come into effect on 15 January. Scobie was vigorously criticized for not having stipulated that ELAS should first release the hostages taken from Athens, and some 4,000 of them were to die in ELAS's hands: Scobie claimed he feared that ELAS would continue the fighting rather than comply. The brief war between ELAS and British forces had cost ELAS around 5,000 men dead and the British 110 killed and 1,190 wounded.[43]

Round two of the civil war was formally ended by the Varkiza Peace Agreement signed near Athens by the Greek government and EAM on 12

February. The provisions called for a plebiscite that year on the constitutional question, to be followed by elections to a new parliament. ELAS was to demobilize immediately and be disarmed, and a new national army would be raised through conscription. An amnesty was granted for 'political crimes' committed. ELAS was given until 15 March 1945 to surrender their weapons and release the civilian hostages. In return, the government promised to purge the security forces and the civil service as soon as possible. On 16 February, Sarafis issued a farewell order to his troops and on 28 February ELAS formally ceased to exist. ELAS surrendered 49,000 rifles and pistols, 1,412 sub-machine guns, 713 automatic rifles, 419 machine guns, 100 artillery pieces, and many light mortars, anti-tank rifles and radios. Some ELAS diehards refused to surrender and moved to the mountains of northern Greece. Among them was the most ardent communist ELAS leader, Aris Velouchiotis, who committed suicide when ambushed by government troops; they then displayed his head in the marketplace of Trikala.[44] The Greek government remained unstable and underwent many changes in composition during 1945. A far more lengthy and damaging civil war broke out in March 1946 and lasted until October 1949.

A temporary solution was found to the Greece crisis largely because neither Tito nor Stalin intervened to complicate matters. Tito allowed ELAS formations to rest in and move through Yugoslav territory but offered no further support. Stalin made it clear at the Yalta Conference that he was content to sit back and watch events unfold in Greece and merely wished to be kept informed but would make no comment. This state of affairs was possible partly because of Churchill's 'percentages' agreement with Stalin in October 1944, and partly because Churchill and Stalin were working closely with Tito to find a political solution in Yugoslavia regarding the future position of King Peter.

At the end of October 1944 Ivan Šubašić, prime minister of the government-in-exile, arrived in Belgrade for discussions with Tito on the formation of a new Yugoslav government. The Tito–Šubašić agreement signed at the beginning of November agreed that Tito's anti-fascist council (AVNOJ) would be the supreme legislative body, and a united government would be formed, made up of twelve members of Tito's committee and six from the royal government. The monarchy would be retained for the time being but King Peter was to remain abroad. In his stead three regents would be appointed until a plebiscite was held on the future of the monarchy. Churchill was initially hostile to the appointment of regents but then changed his mind. King Peter was implacably opposed and accused Šubašić of exceeding his authority. Šubašić visited Moscow for talks with Stalin in November, and thereafter British and Soviet policy remained along the line of forcing the king to accept the Tito–Šubašić agreement. On 11 January 1945 Churchill summed up the position in a letter to Stalin:

> Mr Eden and I tried our best on several occasions with King Peter. He is a spirited young man and feels that the Tito-Šubašić agreement is virtual abdication. He has now put out his own declaration without consultation with us and indeed against our advice. He thinks that if he keeps himself free of all that is going to happen in Yugoslavia in the next few years a day will dawn for him . . .
>
> I now suggest that we make the Tito-Šubašić agreement valid and simply bypass King Peter II. His statement was delivered without advice from any Prime Minister, and as he presents himself as a constitutional sovereign it cannot be regarded as an act of state. This means that we favour the idea of recognising the government of Marshal Tito set up under the Regency of the Royal Yugoslav Government and sending an Ambassador to Belgrade and receiving one here . . .

Stalin agreed, and Roosevelt was kept informed. King Peter refused to back down and was described by the permanent under-secretary Alexander Cadogan as 'a twig defying an avalanche, and a rather rotten twig too'. At the end of January 1945 King Peter dismissed his government and Churchill and Stalin agreed to bypass the king. This policy was encapsulated in a communique issued in Yalta on 11 February 1945:

> We have agreed to recommend to Marshal Tito and Dr Šubašić that the Agreement between them should be put into effect immediately, and that a new Government should be formed on the basis of that Agreement.
>
> We also recommend that as soon as the new Government has been formed, it should declare that:
>
> (i) The Anti-Fascist Assembly of National Liberation (AVNOJ) should be extended to include members of the last Yugoslav Parliament (Skupschina) who have not compromised themselves by collaboration with the enemy, thus forming a body to be known as a temporary Parliament; and
>
> (ii) legislative acts passed by the Anti-Fascist Assembly of National Liberation . . . will be subject to subsequent ratification by a Constituent Assembly.

Tito accepted these proposals and the king continued to argue until he finally appointed regents who were sworn in on 3 March 1945. The regents represented the three most important areas of Yugoslavia: Srdjan Budisavljević was a Serb, Ante Mandić a Croat, and Dušan Sernec a Slovene.[45]

These regents entrusted Tito with the formation of a new government to be made up of twenty-two ministers from within Yugoslavia and six from the Šubašić government in London. Of the latter, three were known to be pro-Partisan and the other three had little power and soon resigned from the government. British and American diplomatic representatives arrived in Belgrade but found that they were subject to severe limitations on their activities and movements. While the war was still raging, Tito did not want to break formally with the western powers, especially since he needed their wealth to rebuild his ravaged country. However, he demonstrated his true political allegiances when he went to Moscow in April 1945 and signed a twenty-year treaty of friendship with the Soviet Union.[46]

The threat of a communist coup in Greece and the conduct of ELAS during the demobilization crisis seriously worried the Allied policymakers in Italy. They knew from the reports of the Allied military missions in northern Italy that the communist partisans were dominant, and also that the Alexander directive in November 1944 had alienated the resistance in the north by signalling its apparent abandonment by the Allies over the winter. General Cadorna's representative, Captain Pieri, visited Switzerland in November and warned Allen Dulles, director of the OSS there, 'that [the] partisan movement [is] now undergoing [a] serious crisis and I gather that much reorganization, and particularly coordination with our military authorities, [is] urgently required', especially the provision of more money and weapons.[47] It was also in the interests of the Allies and the Italian government to confer with representatives of the CLNAI in order to ensure that the latter, through its military committee, the CVL, was ready to obey Allied orders in the spring when the advance would be resumed, and also to clarify the relationship between the Italian government and the CLNAI.

In November a high-level delegation from the CLNAI, formed of Alfredo Pizzoni, Ferruccio Parri, Giancarlo Pajetta, and Eddy Sogno, travelled south for lengthy and often heated discussions with the government of Ivanoe Bonomi and the Allied high command in Rome and Caserta. On 7 December the so-called 'Protocols of Rome' were signed by General Wilson, Bonomi, and the CLNAI delegation. The Rome government recognized the CLNAI as the clandestine provisional government in German-occupied northern Italy subject to certain stipulations. Of these the most important was clause 4:

> When the enemy withdraws from territory occupied by them the CLNAI will exercise its best endeavours to maintain law and order and to continue

> the safeguarding of the economic resources of the country until such time as Allied Military Government is established. Immediately upon the establishment of Allied Military Government, CLNAI will recognise Allied Military Government and will hand over to that Government all authority and powers of local government and administration previously assumed. As the enemy withdraws, all components of the General Command of the Volunteers of Liberty [CVL] in liberated territory will come under direct command of the Commander-in-Chief, AAI [Allied Armies in Italy], acting under the authority of the Supreme Allied Commander, and will obey any order issued by him or by Allied Military Government on his behalf, including such orders to disband and surrender their arms, when required to do so.

This aimed to ensure that the partisans were fighting for the Allies and not for their own political aims, and to ensure that the liberation and demobilization process would not be accompanied by the threat of civil war or present the prospect of the Allies fighting the partisans, as was occurring in Greece at the time. The CLNAI as a whole questioned the benefit of the protocols. Parri later wrote in his defence: 'Let it be enough to say that at a certain moment we asked ourselves if it suited us to sign. But we signed. What we had obtained was too great, too important, to be jeopardised by other considerations.' From the CLNAI viewpoint it had gained recognition for the partisans to be treated as military equals and a commitment to receive 160 million lire a month to finance the partisans and the promise of further supplies of military materiel.[48]

Parri was caught by the Germans on 31 December 1944 as he was returning to Milan from the discussions in the south. He was not executed but held in prison as a hostage to be used during the later discussions between Dulles and the SS commander in northern Italy, General Wolff.[49] His arrest, however, meant that the Allies were deeply concerned that the absence of his restraining influence would allow the communists to gain the upper hand in the CLNAI and CVL. Reports continued reaching Special Forces Headquarters and Allied high command from missions in the north, pointing to the continued threat of the communists. For example, OSS agent Major William White reported: 'The partisans I was working with were 20 per cent for liberation and 80 per cent for Russia. We soon found they were burying arms to save them for use after the war was over and the Americans had pulled out.'[50] Other reports pointed to the danger of civil war, claiming that the Garibaldi formations were fighting 'not for patriotic motives, but for the eradication of all traces of Fascism', which implied everyone who was not communist. More alarmingly, 'Those who are not communists are inspired by patriotic motives, which include the destruction of Fascism; but, latterly, we have evidence that they regard their formations as potential adversaries to the growing communist power.' Orme Sargent warned:

> The picture in northern Italy is reminiscent in the strongest degree of Greece, and we may be helping to build up not only a rival to the Italian Government in Rome but also a rival to the Italian army now fighting on the Allied front, thus creating the essential elements for a civil war in which British troops would inevitably be involved.

Macmillan similarly argued that 'It was vital to neglect no method which could prevent violent action by the communists.' At the beginning of February steps were taken to avert this threat when the Allied command and Special Forces Headquarters threatened to cut off supplies to the north until they were sure that these supplies would be used against the Germans and not for civil war.[51]

More SOE and OSS missions were dropped across northern Italy over the winter. For example, six major British missions were established behind the lines in the Apennines, each covering a separate area, and one near Bologna was in contact with the partisans within the city. Similarly, OSS dropped missions into the same areas, especially the strategically important Belluno region north of Venice. These missions directed the partisans to focus on supplying intelligence to the Allies, sabotaging the German communications, and counter-scorch activities to prevent the Germans from destroying bridges and dykes and flooding the Paduan plain. Plans were also drawn up to parachute units near the major cities such as Turin to ensure that the partisans did not seize power but handed over control to the Allied Military Government as agreed in the Rome Protocols. In return for the collaboration promised in these protocols the partisans received greater quantities of supplies as the weather cleared in late January 1945. Many of these supplies went to the Venezia Giulia region, but orders were issued that none should reach the Garibaldi 'Natisone' Division which was fighting under the 9th Yugoslav Partisan Corps. The Italian communist leader Palmiro Togliatti signalled that he was in favour of Tito's forces occupying Venezia Giulia, but the British opposed this plan. Alexander's discussions with Tito on the subject in Belgrade in February were unsatisfactory: Alexander maintained that he intended to establish the AMG in Venezia Giulia after liberation, while Tito asserted he intended to make a formal claim for the area around Trieste, but he would respect Allied requirements for lines of communication through the region to Austria which the British were expecting to occupy.[52]

*

In north-west Europe the Allies had a far easier time in asserting command and control over the resistance. In Denmark the Allies ensured that men they trusted were in charge of the resistance and that they would facilitate a smooth transfer of power after the Germans had surrendered. General Ebbe Gørtz was appointed commander of the secret army and would operate under the direct orders of SHAEF. Flemming Muus was forced into hiding in November 1944 by the Gestapo, who were determined to find him. Muus was evacuated by the resistance to Sweden and finally reached London in early January. He was replaced by Ole Lippmann, who paid tribute to the work done by Muus:

> I would like to record that the value of Muus's work is appreciated by everyone here and there is no question that he has performed an extremely fine balancing act. In that respect, I cannot match his diplomatic skills and, if one is looking for a measure of his contribution, one need look no further than the way things have gone since he let go of the reins. Intrigues, rumours, innuendo and drivel, directed against everyone and everything. We have lost a lot of ground and we no longer have the renown that we enjoyed in the good old days.

Lippmann oversaw the decentralization of the resistance to give local areas more independence.[53] The Allies substantially increased the number of airdrops to Denmark over the winter, and in January 1945 three motorboats arrived from Sweden carrying about 100 rifles and 1,000 Sten guns. Plans were made to transfer the Danish Police Force, who were in fact regular troops based in Sweden, to Denmark by sea at the time when the Germans either evacuated Denmark or surrendered.[54]

In Norway plans were made by the Allies and the Norwegian government-in-exile to clarify the role to be played by *Milorg* and the Home Front as liberation approached, and for an Allied presence in Norway during the transition phase between the German withdrawal or surrender and the return of the Norwegian government-in-exile. This Allied presence might also serve to reduce Norwegian concerns over the presence of Soviet troops in the far north.

Milorg received considerably more supplies by air and more SOE instructors arrived to train the men in the use of the weapons. These weapons were mostly small arms and machine guns, and no anti-tank weapons or anti-aircraft artillery was sent. *Milorg*'s strength increased to around 40,000 men. The German garrison in Norway was then estimated to be around 365,000 men, so *Milorg* was not expected to fight the Germans openly but was to focus on sabotage and especially on counter-scorch activities. Six anti-scorch schemes were drawn up: three to protect factories, and others to save the harbours and hydroelectric stations, and to keep open the road and rail communications from Sweden to facilitate the arrival of the Norwegian police battalions. The plans for the protection of the hydroelectric plants had been drawn up by Leif Tronstad, who arrived in Norway in October 1944 to take personal control of the plans in the Kongsberg and Upper Telemark area. He was killed in battle with the NS on 11 March 1945.[55]

Earlier in the war the Allies had worked hard to suggest the possibility of an imminent Allied invasion of Norway to ensure the largest possible diversion of German resources there, leading the Germans to maintain around 300,000 troops in the country for an invasion that would never occur. In the winter of 1944–45, however, the Allies became concerned that the large German garrison, commanded from January 1945 by General Böhme after von Falkenhorst retired, would attempt to create a *Festung Norwegen* – Fortress Norway – which would hold out even after the Germans had surrendered in mainland Europe. To avert this SHAEF appointed General Andrew Thorne as Commander, Allied Land Forces, Norway. Thorne planned an initial landing of a SAS regiment and a Norwegian company to take control of the ports of Stavanger and Kristiansand as well as Sola airfield before moving on to Oslo where the Allied party would be joined by a larger number of British troops. Arrangements were also being made with the Swedes to allow the passage of Norwegian troops as fast as possible.[56]

Close cooperation between the Norwegian government-in-exile and the Home Front leadership on the transfer of the civil administration was established in November 1944 when the Norwegian foreign minister, Trygve Lie, and the minister of justice, Terje Wold, stopped off in Stockholm on their way to the Soviet Union. It was agreed that the Home Front leadership would appoint provisional executives to all the ministries apart from foreign affairs, defence, and shipping. Plans were made for the Crown Prince and five ministers to reach Oslo as soon as possible after the German surrender, to be followed shortly by the king and the rest of his government.[57] The Home Front leadership wanted to use the clandestine press to publish its *paroles* or instructions on how the population should behave. Tore Gjelsvik recalled:

> We presumptuously arranged a 'press conference' with the editors of the illegal newspapers. We had been promised masks for this large assembly . . . but there was a hitch and no masks were forthcoming. However, we were never short of good ideas in those days, and we hurriedly got hold of 10-kilo flour bags, in which we cut needful holes for eyes, nose and mouth. The paper

> bags were not exactly made to measure, and when several participants stuck their pipes through the nose or eye holes it was somewhat hard to preserve the seriousness which the situation otherwise required.[58]

These *paroles* were designed to ensure law and order and to encourage the population to assist in the most urgent requirement of the returning government, the expunging of the NS from all aspects of society.

31
To the Bitter End: Spring 1945

By March 1945 the mass armies of the Allies were poised on the frontiers of Germany ready for the final thrust. The Soviets were concentrating their forces on the Seelow Heights for the advance on Berlin. To the west the Allies had recovered from the Battle of the Bulge and were preparing to advance eastwards into the Reich, and north-eastwards to liberate the half of the Netherlands still under German occupation, and then on towards Denmark. On 7 March 1945 the US forces had the good fortune to find that the bridge over the Rhine at Remagen, between Bonn and Koblenz, had not been blown up by the retreating Germans, and they seized the opportunity for a relatively easy crossing of the Rhine. The British set-piece crossing of the Rhine at Wesel, north-west of Essen, followed on 24 March and was observed by Churchill.

The role of the resistance was changing, according to the country involved. In Norway and Denmark, for example, the resistance was called upon to prevent German reinforcements from being withdrawn from those countries and reaching the main battle fronts. On 14 March, Operation Cement-Mixer, a massive coordinated attack on the railways all over southern Norway, was launched by at least 1,000 *Milorg* men. This resulted in more than 1,000 cuts to the principal railways running from Kristiansand to Kongsberg, Eikanger to Drammen, Tinnoset to Brevik, and Kornsjø to Oslo. Additional chaos was caused by an attack on the headquarters of the Norwegian state railway by the Oslo Gang, which severely reduced the Germans' ability to re-route trains around the damaged lines. On 24 March a sixteen-man team of OSS agents led by Major William Colby, who had gained experience in northern France, arrived near Trondheim and destroyed a major railway bridge in the vicinity. Reichskommissar Josef Terboven was furious at the widespread sabotage but his response was strangely muted and only fourteen hostages were executed. These proved to be the last reprisals because the Home Front warned Terboven that a stronger response in future would lead to a general strike and greater disorder. The Norwegian attacks on the railways were mirrored by similar levels of sabotage in Denmark. It was later estimated that these campaigns against the railways delayed the arrival of around 200,000 Germans on the main battle fronts in the Reich.[1]

The Germans attempted to use shipping to transfer their troops from Denmark and Norway, but these sailings were interdicted by Allied air attacks. They were also hampered by an audacious sabotage action in Copenhagen. In March the south harbour in Copenhagen contained over forty large Danish merchant ships which it was thought the Germans would commandeer to move units from Norway. The Langebro lifting bridge, which connected the island of Amager with Copenhagen proper, lay between the south harbour and the sea. The leaders of BOPA (*Borgerlige Partisaner*) met harbour officials in the offices of the transport ministry to discuss how to sabotage this bridge. The challenge was to devise a method by which the bridge would be sufficiently damaged so that it could not be raised to permit the departure of the ships, but not so much as to prevent its use by Danish commuters or its easy repair after the war. A decision was reached that a lorry packed with 200 kilos of explosive should 'break down' outside the engine room on the bridge which housed the hoisting mechanism. The first attempt on the morning of 27 March failed because the twenty German guards helped the driver push the truck off the bridge. A second attempt was mounted in the late afternoon when BOPA railwaymen loaded explosives into the last wagon of a train about to pass over the bridge, and also despatched units to stop the commuter traffic on the bridge so that the detonation could take place without civilian casualties. This attack was a success, but the Germans considered that the repairs would not be difficult. The Danes thwarted German plans to reopen the harbour by sinking two ships at the entrance and sailing most of the tugs to Sweden.[2]

The continued dangers of resistance were illustrated by an event in the Netherlands where half the country was still in the throes of the 'Hunger Winter'. Four members of the resistance decided to rob a meat convoy bound for Germany. They needed a truck to carry out the attack so on the night of 6–7 March they mounted an ambush at Woeste Hoeve on the road from Apeldoorn to Arnhem. To their horror and surprise instead of capturing a truck they found themselves face to face with the most dangerous enemy of the resistance in the Netherlands, the German security head, Hanns Rauter, who was travelling by car. Shots were exchanged, and the resistance thought that all occupants of the car had been killed. Rauter, however, though wounded, survived the night and was found the next morning by a German security patrol and taken to hospital. Himmler was outraged and ordered the immediate execution of 500 hostages. Rauter's deputy, Karl Schöngarth, took charge of the reprisals: 146 hostages were executed in German prisons across the Netherlands and a further 117 men were taken to Woeste Hoeve and executed there.[3]

The Allies were prepared to help the resistance where they could. Many members of the Danish Freedom Council who had been arrested in September 1944 were being held in cells on the top floor of the Gestapo headquarters in the Shell House in Copenhagen. In December the Danish resistance asked the RAF to consider a repeat of the successful low-level air attack on the Gestapo premises in Aarhus by mounting an attack on the Shell House. The resistance was asked to provide details to help the RAF plan such a raid. Svend Truelsen, the former head of intelligence in Denmark but now in London, paid tribute to the work done by agents in Copenhagen: 'We knew the purpose for which the Gestapo used every single room in Shellhaus and every detail of the building's construction. We knew the exact locations and strength of the German anti-aircraft batteries in Copenhagen and throughout Denmark . . .' At one point the RAF planners requested a photograph taken of the Shell House from the bridge over St Jørgen's Lake and were stunned to receive one eight days later. The Shell House was located in a built-up area so Ole Lippmann, the leader of the Danish SOE units, was asked to assess whether the Danes would accept the high risk of civilian casualties should the raid be mounted. Lippmann later recorded that the final decision was left to him, and that taking this decision was made easier by the fact that in late February the Gestapo swept up virtually the entire military leadership of the resistance in Copenhagen. These arrests threatened to halt all resistance activity in the capital at a critical time, so, on 10 March, Lippmann sent a message to London:

> Military leaders arrested and plans in German hands. Situation never before so desperate. Remaining leaders known by Hun. We are regrouping but need help. Bombing of SD Copenhagen will give us breathing space. If any importance attached at all to Danish resistance you must help us irrespective of cost. We shall never forget RAF and you, if you come.

On 21 March eighteen Mosquito bombers escorted by twenty-eight Mustang fighters set off to bomb the Shell House. The plan was to aim the bombs at the base of the building to destroy three of the four staircases, leaving one free for the prisoners to escape. At 11.14 a.m. the first bombs hit the Shell House. Police inspector C. Lyst Hansen managed to escape from his cell. He took the keys from a dazed German guard and released the other thirty-one prisoners: 'We plunged through thick clouds of smoke and dust out into the street. Not a soul was in sight. The Germans had been killed or had bolted.' Almost all the prisoners escaped safely but at least six (some sources say eight) died in the raid. Over 100 Germans were killed, a lower number than anticipated because many were attending the funeral of one of their colleagues. Ambulances arrived on the scene quickly, but the Danish fire brigade deliberately delayed its response. When the firemen did arrive they claimed that the Shell House could not be saved and focused their attention on extinguishing the fires in the nearby buildings. Two days after the raid, the resistance group *Holger Danske* searched the ruins and located five safes, one of which contained a list of Danish Nazis. Tragedy accompanied the raid when Wing Commander Kilboe's windscreen was so salted up by the low-level flight across the North Sea that it impaired his vision. His plane crashed into a pylon near the Frederiksberg goods station, and the fire from the crash confused the third wave of Mosquitos into thinking that this was the target. The bombs dropped by these planes hit the nearby Jeanne d'Arc school, killing eighteen adults, mostly nuns, and eighty-six children. The total RAF losses were four Mosquitos and two Mustangs.[4]

In the spring of 1945 the German presence in Yugoslavia had been reduced to four locations: Sarajevo, the capital of Bosnia-Herzegovina; Zagreb, the capital of Croatia; Ljubljana, the capital of Slovenia; and the Srem front in Slovenia. The German withdrawal from the Balkans had been carried out in an orderly fashion with little interference from the Partisans. This situation changed on 20 March 1945 when the Partisans launched an offensive with four armies. Two armies under Peko Dapčević and Koča Popović advanced towards Zagreb, while a third under Kosta Nadj aimed for the Slovenian-Austrian frontier, and the fourth under Petar Drapšin raced the Allies towards Trieste. The aim of the offensive was to establish a Partisan presence in the disputed areas of Venezia Giulia and Carinthia before the Allies reached those areas from Italy. For the most part the Partisans avoided direct battle with the Germans. The exception was on the Srem front where SIS agent Owen Reed reported:

> The Partisans are now doing tremendous things with tanks and guns which we have presented to them and which we've trained them to use. Side by side with the crack British-trained spearhead are black masses of old-fashioned guerrilla types who come swarming down from the mountains to join the fun. The result is one of the oddest armies ever seen ... halfway between the old-fashioned free-for-all Partisan of a year ago who fights with his teeth if need be, and a well-equipped, well-dressed modern army, with black berets with stars on, Spitfires roaring overhead.

The breakthrough on the Srem front was achieved on 12 April and was described by Milovan Djilas as 'the greatest and bloodiest battle our army ever fought'. Elsewhere the Partisans found it easier, entering Sarajevo on 6 April and Zagreb on 8 May only after the last Germans had departed, which has led one historian to conclude that 'on the whole the final act of liberation was little more than a route march in the wake of a rapidly retreating and vanquished enemy'.[5]

Behind the lines the civil war was reaching a peak. On 13 April Mihailović began a march from northern Bosnia towards Serbia. He was accompanied by around 8,000–12,000 Četnik followers whom he hoped would be the nucleus around which a new anti-communist force could be built. On 10 May, Mihailović's Četniks clashed with a superior Partisan force near the Jezerica tributary of the Neretva. Most of the Četniks were killed either in battle or after capture. Mihailović and a dwindling band of followers escaped to remain on the run in the mountains until he himself was caught in March 1946.[6]

In Croatia the Ustaše leadership under Ante Pavelić were not consulted by the Germans nor warned of their retreat from the Balkans. In the summer of 1944 the Ustaše sent emissaries to General Alexander pleading for Allied protection for an independent Croatian state. The Allied response was firm: the Ustaše should abandon all pretensions to independence and join the Partisans in the effort to expel the German occupiers from the country. Throughout the autumn and winter of 1944 Ustaše soldiers abandoned the cause and made accommodations with the Partisans. At the same time Archbishop Stepinac negotiated with the Germans, promising no Ustaše resistance to the departure of the Germans if they agreed not to carry out a policy of scorched earth or blow up the electricity plant or the bridges over the Sava. In early May, as the time for the German departure approached, and as the Partisans were closing in, the Croatian leadership including Pavelić and the stalwart Ustaše fled Zagreb. General Löhr was prepared to hand over power to responsible Croatian leaders, but he found that Stepinac refused to become a regent, and that the leader of the Peasant Party, Vladimir Maček, who had spent much of the war under house arrest, had also fled Zagreb for Austria. Therefore, he had no choice other than to abandon the Croats to their fate at the hands of the Partisans.[7]

Reed noted that fear was the dominant emotion in Zagreb as the Partisans entered the city:

> These people haven't had a war at all. The place has never been bombed or starving or hit by anything at all. To see the populace in fashioned stockings and Paris summer models watching the dusty sweating Partisans march

> around is a picture. Their faces are the most baffled study in snobbery, guilt, incredulity, resentment and pride that you could possibly imagine. None of them know what's coming to them in the next few days. You couldn't live here without collaborating to a certain extent, and you could [not] collaborate without someone else knowing it, so everyone's waiting to see if everyone else has told on them or not.

The Partisan revenge against their internal opponents would be ferocious. Plans had been agreed by the communist security forces in Belgrade at the end of 1944 to destroy all domestic enemies of communism: 'Politically, it was one of the most important decisions of the entire war period, and it cost a great deal of blood.'[8] A similar state of panic and fear was evident in Ljubljana as the Germans refused to hand over power to the Slovenian Home Guard which was attempting to link up with the Četnik formations under Dimitrije Ljotić. However, there was a general realization that the anti-communist forces could not hold out against the superior Partisan forces advancing towards them and that the Allies were unlikely to arrive in time to save them, so many Slovene units and the Četniks fled into Austria in early May.[9]

The priority for the Partisans in Slovenia was territorial aggrandizement. The Austrian province of Carinthia was a linguistically mixed area in which the Slovene population accounted for only 18 per cent of the population of the province as a whole, but 69 per cent in the Klagenfurt basin. After the First World War a plebiscite had awarded Carinthia to Austria, but now the Yugoslavs laid claim to it. In March 1945 an OSS agent, Franklin Lindsay, was in Belgrade and radioed to Allied headquarters that he had asked Vladimir Velebit whether the Partisans intended to move on Klagenfurt and Villach, and had received the response: 'Certainly we shall occupy them, they belong to us. But in addition we want to occupy a portion of enemy territory.' SOE agent Peter Wilkinson had been frustrated during the previous year when the Partisans failed to support his Clowder mission which had sought to contact the Austrian resistance in the Carinthia area: now he understood why. Wilkinson reached Klagenfurt shortly before the first Allied units arrived, and only hours before the Yugoslav Partisans turned up. The Partisans only in fact remained in Carinthia for a short time since Moscow made it clear that there was no support for their territorial claims in the area. The situation was, however, very different in Venezia Giulia and Trieste where the Allies would also meet the Partisans.[10]

With the Allies closing in on the Reich from all directions there is some doubt whether the spring offensive in Italy was necessary. On strictly military grounds the mere presence of the Allied armies was sufficient to force the Germans to retain divisions there even though they were urgently needed elsewhere. Indeed, there were highly secret negotiations taking place between Karl Wolff, the SS commander in Italy, and Allen Dulles and OSS in Switzerland on the surrender of the German armies in Italy. The story of these negotiations is a complex one and lies outside the scope of this book. From the beginning the Americans were far more convinced of the sincerity of Wolff's overture than Churchill was, and then when Churchill finally began to believe Wolff he insisted on involving Stalin, which complicated matters. The negotiations were also disrupted by the changes of personnel on the German side. Field Marshal Kesselring broadly accepted the necessity for the talks, but on 9 March he was recalled from Italy and was appointed commander-in-chief in the west. His replacement and former subordinate, Heinrich von Vietinghoff, only arrived back in Italy two weeks later.

Mussolini was implacably opposed to the peace negotiations. He had learned of them through the accidental agency of Dick Mallaby, who had crossed into Italy from Switzerland and had been arrested by the *Brigate Nere* in February. Mallaby invented a story claiming that he was the bearer of a message from General Alexander to the most senior Italian army officer still loyal to Mussolini, General Graziani, and so he was imprisoned and not executed. Mallaby was taken to meet Wolff, but he did not take any part in the Wolff negotiations, unlike the important role he had played during the negotiations for the armistice in September 1943. The peace negotiations were ultimately unsuccessful, but one side benefit of them was that Ferruccio Parri was released from imprisonment and could resume his position as a calming influence in the CLNAI.[11]

The principal argument in favour of an Allied spring offensive was not so much military as political. Even after the CLNAI had signed the Rome Protocols in December 1944, both the Allies and the Italian government harboured fears that it planned to set up a separate government in northern Italy. Furthermore, events in Greece had demonstrated the need for Allied representatives to be on hand to ensure a peaceful transfer from war to peace as the Germans departed. Dulles attempted to calm such fears, arguing that Parri would keep the hotheads under control. Nonetheless the Allies acted to ensure the cooperation of the CLNAI and the CVL. Max Salvadori was despatched to serve as the Allied liaison officer with the CLNAI, and he was given a seven-point programme to follow: to coordinate as far as possible the activities of the partisans and GAPs with the operations of the Allied army; to see that supplies in sufficient quantities reach the CVL, irrespective of political colour; to encourage the CLNAI to set up an organization in each province able to take over all the functions of public administration during an interim period; to notify the CLNAI and the CVL that the local committees and bands must take the necessary steps to protect industrial plants and power stations; to prevent individuals and groups affiliated to the CLNAI and CVL from making any kind of agreement with the Germans; to keep informed of the situation on both eastern and western fronts so as to prevent Yugoslav or French infiltration; and to do everything possible to maintain harmony among the parties of the CLNAI. Colonel Peter McMullen and Colonel John Stevens were sent in to oversee the surrenders of Genoa and Turin. Both men had previous experience of working with partisans. At the end of March the CVL command issued a directive to the partisans to cooperate with and protect the members of the Allied military missions in their areas. General Cadorna and Parri were informed by the Allies that the German commanders would be called upon to surrender only to the regular army forces and not to the partisans.[12]

The Allies were determined to maintain command and control over the partisans because of the threat of civil war, either between the partisans and the Fascists or between the communists and everyone else. An order issued by Luigi Longo to the communist partisans on 10 April, the day after the Allied offensive had been launched, caused particular concern:

> In the cities the GAP and SAP units must attack and unsparingly destroy as many Fascist *gerarchi* as they can get to; all those agents and collaborators and Nazi-Fascists who continue to betray the *patria* (*questori*, commissars, high state and municipal officials, industrialists and technical managers of production subservient to the Germans); all Nazi-Fascists and 'republicans' who remain deaf to the *patria*'s injunction to surrender or perish.

This order could have led to the extremely dangerous situation whereby the communists might have classed and then killed anyone as a 'collaborator' simply on the grounds that the person was not a communist. The CLNAI undermined the threat by using the communist directive as the basis for its own official order for a national uprising. This order was signed by Luigi Longo and Emilio Sereni for the communists, along with Parri and Leo Valiani for the Action Party; Achille Marazza and Augusto De Gasperi for the Christian Democrat Party; Giustino Arpesani and Filippo Jacini for the Liberal Party; and Sandro Pertini and Rodolfo Morandi for the Socialist Party, thereby signifying political unity.[13]

The Allied offensive opened on 9 April but the partisans had already begun action. In the Rossano valley Gordon Lett was approached by the bishop of Pontremoli who wanted to prevent an Allied bombing of his town and who also offered to arrange a prisoner exchange between the Germans and the partisans. Lett demanded a detailed breakdown of German billets and positions in Pontremoli in return. The bishop was reluctant to supply this information but eventually passed Lett a bulky envelope containing the required details which he said had been 'found under a tree'. The town was saved from bombing, and instead the German positions were strafed by machine-gun fire from Spitfires. Lett was frustrated by his lack of knowledge of Allied plans and left the valley in the middle of March, eventually reaching Florence.

Nearby a veteran of the war in Yugoslavia, Michael Lees, was training the partisans for an assault on German lines close to the Gothic Line. In early March he was joined by an SAS squadron commanded by Roy Farran. Farran had been given a strict order not to drop with his troops but was hungry for action: 'I persuaded the American aircrew to say that I accidentally fell from the aircraft while dispatching the advance party. It was a thin story that hardly accounted for my good fortune to be wearing a parachute.' The SAS trained the local partisans and succeeded in mounting attacks on a German corps headquarters in Albinea in the Po valley. In general, Farran and Lees found the partisans rather ineffective and clearly reluctant to risk casualties when the more powerfully armed Allies were so close.[14]

On 17 April the Allies broke through the German lines at Argenta and found that the partisans had already liberated much of the Apennine-Liguria area unaided. The partisans were now prepared to take greater risks since the Allies were on hand to help them should the Germans put up a resistance. Lett was sent towards La Spezia to coordinate partisan attacks with elements of the approaching US 5th Army. The Americans halted on the outskirts after a heavy German bombardment and Lett and his partisans entered the city after the Germans had departed but while the situation was still very fluid: 'I hardly expected to find myself within a few hours the uneasy possessor of one of Italy's most important naval bases, complete with its unarmed population.' The Americans soon arrived and the administration was handed over smoothly to the Allied Military Government of Occupied Territories (AMG).

On 24 April the partisans marched through La Spezia, and Lett inspected them for the last time before disbanding them, which he found 'a bitter experience'. Further east, Farran joined forces with the Modena partisans and their Allied liaison officer, Major Jim Davies, to coordinate the partisans' advance on Modena. Davies and Farran both noted the reluctance of the partisans to cooperate: 'I could see that the commanders were temporising. They feared to risk casualties and reprisals. Possibly too they did not really believe the breakthrough was happening . . . It was clear that they would not move.' The news that the Germans had abandoned nearby Reggio resulted in a change of attitude, as Farran noted:

> As we drove north again, we overtook deliriously happy bands of partisans marching on Modena. The word was out everywhere – the Germans were defeated.
>
> These partisans strode along the road, completely without caution, roaring resistance songs at the tops of their voices, waving red flags or Italian flags that flapped back in their faces, as triumphant as men could be.

Harold Macmillan happened to be in Modena on 23 April and witnessed a battle in which the partisans and Allies fought the German and Fascist snipers: 'Of course a lot of partisans fired off their pieces quite aimlessly and threw grenades just for fun. Indeed these gentlemen and their curious assortment of rifles, grenades, tommy-guns, etc., caused me more alarm than our opponents.' The partisans in Bologna were braver. On 19 April they responded to an order received from the BBC Italian service to rise up, and in the fighting they accounted for 300 German dead and 1,000 taken prisoner. The utilities were saved from the threat of demolition, and by the time the Polish Army arrived in Bologna on 21 April, just ahead of the Americans, the city was functioning normally.[15]

The Allies proceeded to chase the Germans along the line of the Alps towards south-east Germany and Austria. The CLNAI issued an order for general uprisings to be launched in the great Italian industrial centres of Genoa, Milan, and Turin.

The prospects of an uprising succeeding in Genoa were slim. General Gunther Meinhold had around 15,000 troops in Genoa itself, and a further 15,000 in the surrounding hills manning the heavy artillery trained on the city. In contrast, the local CLN controlled only around 3,000 men in the city, who were mostly armed with pistols and hand grenades, and there were a further 4,500 partisans hiding in the hills awaiting the order to come into the city. The Allies were still 100 miles away in La Spezia and there were many mountains between them and Genoa. The SOE agent on the spot was Basil Davidson and he was advised to focus the attention of the partisans on counter-scorch activities rather than an uprising. It was known that the Germans intended to blow up the port installations and that permanent demolition squads were stationed in the dockyard. The Germans also intended to block the harbour by scuttling the aircraft carrier *Aquila*. The partisans managed to use corrosive acid to destroy the detonators of the mines in the port and also damaged the *Aquila* so badly that the Germans were unable to scuttle her.

Meinhold realized that his troops were in danger of being cut off by the Allied advance and received orders from von Vietinghoff to start a withdrawal along the Po valley to the Veneto. Meinhold attempted to negotiate a smooth withdrawal of his men from the city with the CLN, using Archbishop Siri as an intermediary. On 23 April, Meinhold requested four days in which to evacuate the German garrison from Genoa unmolested by partisan activity, and in return he promised that no demolitions would take place. The CLN did not trust Meinhold since the first German convoy leaving Genoa that day had also taken twenty-five political prisoners with it as hostages. Therefore, on the evening of 23 April the CLN ordered attacks on the Fascist headquarters. The surrender of the headquarters was achieved with ease and supplied the partisans with weapons which they used to attack isolated German garrison posts and to sabotage the main railway. On the morning of 24 April, Meinhold threatened to bombard the city if these attacks did not cease. The CLN responded that as soon as the first shell fell it would order the execution of the 1,000 German prisoners held by the partisans. After further and intensified partisan attacks during the day, the Germans began leaving the city. Around 7,000 Germans, SS troops among them, retreated to the port area, and during the day fierce battles were waged between the Germans and the partisans for control. Most of Genoa itself was now in partisan hands as units from outside the city marched down from the hills and took control of the roads leading out of the city. On the evening of 25 April, Meinhold entered the archbishop's palace and signed a surrender document with the president of the CLN, Remo Scappini: this was to come into effect on 26 April. Diehard Germans continued to battle the partisans in the port area for a further day before surrendering. The German naval captain had attempted to negotiate with Davidson, arguing in vain that he was only prepared to surrender to the Americans. The partisans had achieved a great victory with the surrender of 9,000 Germans along with their tanks and armoured cars. The port and the important utilities had been saved so that when the Allies arrived in Genoa on 27 April they found all the public services functioning normally.[16]

News of the uprising in Genoa did not reach Milan until 24 April. Milan was not only an industrial city but also the seat of the CLNAI, which was convening in a seminary guarded by the priests. On the morning of 25 April it met to discuss the launch of a general uprising:

> In the large, bare, shuttered room whose approaches were watched by silent black-cassocked figures, there were seven of us. Our hearts were heavy with emotion and a burden had been lifted from our spirits. We knew that this

> was no ordinary day. The end was at hand; the end of the war, for all men; the end of what we had been fighting against for twenty long years, for us. April 25th meant much more to the Italian nation than the *coup d'état* of July 25th, 1943, the result of palace intrigues.[17]

The order to rise up was issued, and the response was immediate. Throughout the city public buildings were taken over by partisans of all political persuasions, the workers in the Pirelli factory turned against their German overseers, and by the evening the main radio stations, printing presses, and military barracks were all in partisan hands. Outside the city the Garibaldi formations advanced and took out isolated German and Fascist garrisons on their way but only reached Milan on 27 April.

This largely unopposed liberation came about because the German garrison in Milan itself did not oppose the partisans. The power of the CLNAI was evident when it came to dealing with Mussolini. On 25 April he met members of the CLNAI at the palace of Cardinal Alfredo Schuster to negotiate his surrender on favourable terms. He was offered only unconditional surrender, and chose to flee Milan with his mistress Claretta Petacci in a German convoy. On 27 April, Umberto Lazzaro, a member of a Garibaldi brigade, was checking a column of retreating German and SS troops at Dongo near the Swiss border when he recognized Mussolini, who was disguised as a common German soldier, and promptly arrested him. The news of Mussolini's capture was sent to Milan that evening. On 25 April the CLNAI had passed the death sentence on all Fascists who had not surrendered. At the same time the Allied headquarters had sent a telegram to the CLNAI: 'Allied command immediately wants presumed location of Mussolini . . . it is ordered that he is held for immediate handover to Allied command.' The telegram did not, however, specify in what condition. Cadorna later said: 'In no case would I voluntarily have proceeded to bring Mussolini into the hands of the Allied forces for him to be tried and executed by foreigners.'[18] On 28 April the partisans executed Mussolini and his mistress and took their bodies back to Milan where they were dumped in the Piazzale Loreto in the early hours of 29 April. The CLNAI then issued a statement:

> The execution of Mussolini and his accomplices is the necessary conclusion of an historical period which leaves our country covered in rubble . . . Only by making this clean break from a shameful and criminal past can the Italian people be sure that the CLNAI has decided to firmly embark upon the road of the country's democratic renewal.

The bodies were hung upside down from the roof of a petrol station and crowds came to view them.[19]

In Turin the situation was highly volatile. The Germans under General Hans Schlemmer had two divisions in and around the city, 35,000 men, and they and the Fascists were fortifying their positions. This suggested that the Germans had no intention of withdrawing while the Allies were still some distance away. Yet the Germans were not in control of the city. On the night of 18–19 April the Turin CLN had ordered a general strike. This had successfully shut the factories and stopped the trains and trams, and encouraged the resistance to think that the Germans were resigned to their defeat: 'The very extent of the strike had averted the danger of reprisals. The Germans certainly cannot arrest half a million people. In reality, the few that we see about have the appearance of beaten dogs.' The CLN was still debating the merits of launching an uprising when it became the victim of misinformation. The Allied liaison officer, Colonel Stevens, told them that the Allies were advancing rapidly, so the CLN issued the order for an uprising to start at 1 a.m. on 26 April: 'Aldo says 26 for one.' On 26 April the workers occupied the Fiat Mirafiori factory and fought fierce battles with the Germans. They desperately needed the support of the partisans from outside the city. These partisans did not advance to support their compatriots because Stevens had realized that he had made a serious error and the Allies were still too far away to help the insurgents. He issued the order to the partisans outside Turin: 'Do not proceed to your objectives in the city without a specific order from high command.' The CLN in the city was not informed of Stevens's order, and so for two days the partisans in the city fought the Germans and the Fascists alone. The partisans from outside the city began arriving on 28 April and helped the local partisans pen the Germans and the Fascists in the area around the German headquarters. By that evening the situation in Turin was electric: 'Parades of partisans, enormous amount of traffic, incredible enthusiasm, newspapers are already being published, the local CLN is in control. Meanwhile the Allies are still far from us.' On 30 April, Schlemmer began to withdraw his forces from the city, heading for the Val d'Aosta, and the Allies entered Turin on 2 May to find the CLN in total control. Schlemmer surrendered his forces to the Allies on the following day.[20]

Elsewhere in Italy uprisings also liberated cities in the Veneto before the Allies arrived. On 27 April the partisans in Padua rose up. They encountered fierce resistance from the Germans and Fascists, who bombarded the city: the partisans killed over 500 Germans and took 20,000 prisoners for the loss of 224 men. On 28 April it was the turn of the people of Venice to rise up and save their historic city from destruction. The partisans succeeded in thwarting German efforts to blow up the Tesina and Bacchiglione bridges and also saved the port. When the Allies arrived on 29 April they found that the partisans had taken 10,000 prisoners and had killed 700 Germans for the loss of around 300 fighters. The route of the German retreat took the fleeing soldiers through the mountainous areas of the Veneto, where the partisans fought hard to hamper the retreat. The partisans liberated the towns of Vicenza, Treviso, Bellumo, and Vittorio Veneto. The fighting was extremely hard and was marked by the German massacre of the population of the village of Pedescala and by the murder of two partisan delegates who had come to discuss the terms of the German surrender.[21] The fighting then moved on into the disputed area of Venezia Giulia.

After the major cities had been liberated it was time to disarm the partisans. The experience of disarming the resistance in Belgium and Greece had shown the Allies that this process had to be handled with delicacy. General Alexander's priority was to ensure a smooth transfer of power to the AMG, and he issued an order for the partisans to hand over their weapons by 19 May. First of all, steps were taken to show the gratitude of the Allies towards the partisans. In Bologna, Macmillan noted:

> They are all to be paraded, and marched past General Clark. They will hand in their rifles and get a sort of certificate from Field Marshal Alexander. (This has already worked in some places further south ...) They are given the choice of joining the Italian Army (if of the right age) or going into special centres where we shall try to feed them and look after them until they can be employed by the Allies or returned to normal civil employment.[22]

Regardless of their political loyalties, the experience of disarmament was an emotional one, as described by Claudio Pavone:

> Disarmament at the barracks took place with great pomp, great eulogies and declarations of gratitude that were never to be forgotten. The partisan was laying down his machine gun, his Sten, his rifle, and with his weapon he was prostrating his soul. For months his weapon had been his faithful daytime and night-time companion ... The moral shock was very violent and found expression in forms of distrust of democracy, of disorientation and often of useless rebellion.[23]

Most partisans obeyed the order to disarm, but a significant number, especially the communist Garibaldi formations, hid their weapons ready for a revolution should a future Italian government not deliver on their demands for social and political reforms. Suspicions regarding Allied intentions were apparently well founded. In Lombardy all public meetings had to be authorized by the AMG, and in the middle of May the Allied police refused to allow either the communist leader Palmiro Togliatti or the socialist leader Pietro Nenni to address a meeting of his party despite the fact that both men were members of the Italian government.[24]

The disarmament of the partisans north of Turin was deliberately delayed by the Allies in response to the conduct of de Gaulle. Before the Allied spring offensive there had been cooperation between the FFI and the Italian partisans. For example, Ada Gobetti had been a member of a mission from Italy which had spent the winter of 1944–45 in France securing a supply of weapons and promises of cooperation against the Germans. But in the spring of 1945 the French attitude changed, and French units penetrated the Val d'Aosta, a French-speaking area of Italy. Initially, the Allies were not concerned, believing that the French presence could control the political threat posed by the Italian partisans and contribute to forcing the Germans to maintain a good mountain division in the area which might otherwise be deployed further east. As soon as the Germans left the Val d'Aosta the French moved in, with the apparent intention of advancing as far as Turin. De Gaulle seemed to be avenging the Italian invasion of France of 1940. Alexander sent American troops to secure the region and to challenge the French directly. The tense situation was resolved at the beginning of June when President Harry Truman* threatened to cut off American supplies to the French forces: an agreement was signed at Caserta which led to the withdrawal of French forces from the Val d'Aosta.[25]

The problem of Trieste would prove far more difficult to resolve. The city had been the principal port of the Austro-Hungarian Empire, but after the First World War Italy had received Trieste and the whole of Venezia Giulia, including the Istrian peninsula with the town of Pola (Pula) at its tip. Trieste itself was filled with a largely Italian-speaking population but the hinterland was principally Slovenian and Croatian. Allied officers on the ground, Owen Reed in Slovenia and Tommy Macpherson in Venezia Giulia, repeatedly warned Allied headquarters in Italy that both the Italian and Slovene partisans were laying claims to Trieste and its hinterland, and that there was collaboration between the Garibaldi Natisone division and the Slovene Partisans to prepare the ground for a Yugoslav takeover of the whole of Venezia Giulia. This collaboration involved eliminating their political opponents in the area: on the Italian side this meant civil war with the Osoppo partisans, and in Slovenia action against the Slovene White Guards. In both cases the communists accused their opponents of collaboration with the Germans, which in the case of the Osoppo was manifestly untrue. Macpherson dejectedly reported that 'Since the beginning of December 1944 neither Slavs nor Garibaldini of the Garibaldi Natisone Division have undertaken

* Roosevelt had died on 12 April 1945.

any action against the enemy west of the Isonzo* except to defend themselves against surprise German attack.' Worse still there was evidence that the Garibaldi units were sending their weapons and food stocks east of the Isonzo in readiness to fight the approaching Allies.

The future of Trieste had been discussed at the Yalta Conference as part of the arrangements for the Allied occupation of Austria. Trieste was designated as the port through which the British troops of occupation in Austria would receive their supplies, and to guard the lines of communication between Austria and Trieste the Allies needed control over the Slovene-populated hinterland. Tito, however, demanded control over the whole of Venezia Giulia, including Trieste. The result was a race for Trieste between Tito's Partisans, who prioritized the acquisition of Trieste over the expulsion of the Germans from Zagreb and Ljubljana, and Lieutenant General Freyberg's New Zealanders. On 30 April the Italian Trieste CLN launched an uprising and the pro-Italian partisans were assisted by pro-communist Italian and Slovene partisans. On 1 May the Yugoslavs entered Trieste, twenty-four hours before the first Allied troops. The Germans had withdrawn to a few strongholds and surrendered to the Allies and not to the Partisans.

There followed a lengthy period of unease. General Alexander was determined to control Trieste and the whole of Venezia Giulia, but was concerned that a battle with the Yugoslavs would 'have the moral backing at least of the Russians', and could lead to a new major war. He was also concerned about the reliability of his troops, who admired the Partisans. The latter point was quickly resolved because the Allied soldiers were appalled by the treatment meted out by the Partisans to non-communist Italians and Slovenes. Eventually, a demarcation line was drawn up which gave Trieste and a strip of land up to the Tarvisio Pass into Austria to the Allies. Finally, an agreement in 1954 between the Yugoslav and Italian governments would result in Italy retaining Trieste, and Yugoslavia gaining the Istrian peninsula.[26]

The last days of the war in Italy were messy. Wolff was still attempting to negotiate the surrender of German troops in Italy but found that his authority, as well as that of von Vietinghoff, was being constantly undermined by contradictory orders from Germany, especially from Kesselring whose authority now extended to Italy as well as western Europe. Alexander and the senior officers gathered at Caserta were frustrated by the German vacillations, which continued even after the news of Hitler's

* The Isonzo was the frontier of Italy and the Austro-Hungarian Empire before 1914. During the First World War it was the site of ten battles. Between the wars the Isonzo was within Italian frontiers but after 1945 it reverted more or less to marking the frontier between Italy and Yugoslavia.

suicide on 30 April had been released. Finally, at 6.30 p.m. on 2 May, Alexander announced the surrender of all German forces in Italy and ordered an immediate ceasefire. That day was, however, marred by the last German reprisals against the partisans in the Carnia region of north-east Italy, where the partisans had attacked the retreating Germans: in the village of Avanzis fifty-one civilians were killed and in Ovaro a further twenty-five. In the latter case the villagers placed the blame firmly on the communist partisans.[27]

In northern Europe there was a contrast between what the resistance and the governments-in-exile feared might happen as liberation approached, and what actually did occur. In the Netherlands the resistance feared that the Germans, now retreating as the Canadians and Poles renewed their advance at the beginning of April, might open the dykes and inundate a significant portion of the country with sea water. Reichskommissar Seyss-Inquart had threatened to do so, and the resistance was helpless in the face of this threat. They could undertake counter-scorch activities against limited targets such as ports and electrical installations, but there were simply too many dykes to be guarded to have any chance of success. In the case of Denmark the danger came less from the German forces still in Denmark than from the general strategic picture, the race for Germany's Baltic ports between the Soviets and the western Allies. No one knew on which side of the east–west line Denmark would fall and which country's forces would liberate it. In Norway the German garrison was estimated at around 300,000 men and could potentially be supported by the *Hird* to make a final stand even after the German troops had surrendered on mainland Europe. Furthermore, Quisling and Terboven were unlikely to relinquish power without a fight.

In the event these fears were largely unrealized. On 15 April the Canadians liberated Arnhem, the scene of bitter fighting the previous September, and moved on towards Apeldoorn. The Canadian troops were accompanied by the Dutch Army, and one of its soldiers was Guido Zembsch-Schreve who had operated as an SOE agent under the name of Pierre Lalande. He was the first Dutch officer to enter Apeldoorn on 17 April:

> And then a little girl with long golden hair tugged her father's hand and cried, 'Look, Papa, a Dutch lion!' She had spotted the emblem of the Netherlands Army. The father peered at me more closely, then threw up his hands and shouted, 'A Dutch officer!' The crowd surged round us. I was dragged from the driver's seat and borne along shoulder-high. Everyone wanted to touch me – to satisfy themselves that I was real. As the first Dutch officer to enter

> Apeldoorn on liberation day, I shall never forget that scene of unalloyed happiness or the delight on the face of that little, fair-headed girl. For the first time I truly sensed the joy that was coursing through the breasts of those who had regained their freedom after so many years. I also felt the quiet satisfaction of one who knows he had done his duty.[28]

The Germans were now effectively trapped in the western portion of the country and still occupying the cities of Amsterdam, Rotterdam, and The Hague. In the liberated parts, the previously appointed 'Representatives of the Government' smoothly took over the role of local administration.

In early April, Seyss-Inquart had realized that the war was lost and had initiated highly secret talks with the Dutch. These seemed promising and the Dutch government-in-exile despatched two veteran resisters, J. van der Gaag and L. Neher, to discuss terms with him. Seyss-Inquart's offer was that if the Allies halted on the Grebbe Line then he would open the port of Rotterdam for food supplies and would not open the dykes. The two Dutchmen travelled back to London to inform their government of the offer. Churchill and Eisenhower were consulted, and they recommended acceptance since military operations could not be guaranteed to clear the country of the Germans without the Netherlands sustaining severe and long-term economic damage. On 28 April, Montgomery's chief of staff, Major General Freddie de Guingand, and senior Canadian officers met German representatives near Amersfoort and agreed to halt military and bombing operations if the Germans allowed supply flights. Operation Manna, the dropping of food into the occupied areas, commenced on 29 April. Walter Maass was in the village of Waardenburg, three miles from German lines: 'Hundreds of planes passed very low above our heads. The whole population stood on the streets waving and shouting. Many were crying. And one excited exclamation was heard again and again: "Now we shall soon be free!"' On 4 May the German forces in the north-west surrendered at Lüneburg Heath, and, on 5 May, Eisenhower and his chief of staff Bedell Smith met Seyss-Inquart to arrange the surrender of the German forces in the Netherlands. The lightly armed resistance played little part in the final actions of the war, but nonetheless General Crerar, the Canadian commander-in-chief, formally thanked them for their role in the liberation of their country: 'Your reports were accurate, prompt and an important factor in the final defeat of the enemy forces in the Netherlands.'[29]

The perceived Soviet threat to Denmark was acknowledged by the Allies after Ole Lippmann had contacted London in early March for assurances that Denmark would be liberated by the western Allies and not by the

Soviets. These assurances had been given: Jedburgh teams were readied to be dropped into Denmark to report on any signs of Soviet infiltration, but were not in fact used. Nonetheless the Danes took steps of their own, and at the beginning of May the Swedes were requested to despatch Danforce, the Danish brigade trained on Swedish soil, to Denmark. On 5 May Danforce landed at Elsinore and proceeded to Copenhagen, where the SOE liaison officer, Major John Ray, became the first Allied officer to enter liberated Copenhagen. Danforce did not have to fight its way to Copenhagen because that afternoon an Allied mission led by General Richard Dewing and Ralph Hollingworth, the head of SOE's Danish Section, had arrived by air at Kastrup airfield accompanied by men of the 13th Airborne Brigade to a reception committee led by Lippmann and containing representatives of various resistance groups. On 7 May more paratroopers arrived and were strengthened by ground troops crossing into Denmark from Germany. The resistance helped the Allied force of 1,800 men disarm around 170,000 Germans. Dewing and Hollingworth drove through the streets of Copenhagen which were lined with armed men belonging to the resistance and soon afterwards Hollingworth toured the country thanking the resistance for their role in the conflict. The transfer of power was smooth since the resistance did not object to demobilization. This process was probably assisted by the fact that the first post-war Danish cabinet contained an equal number of Danish pre-war politicians and resistance leaders.

The Soviet threat may be thought to have been exaggerated but it was in fact very real. As the population of Copenhagen was celebrating the liberation of the country the Soviets announced their intention to bomb the Danish island of Bornholm off the Swedish coast to force the surrender of the German garrison there. The German commander on the island, naval captain Gerhard von Kamptz, refused to surrender to the Soviets since his orders were to do so only to the western Allies. The resistance was appalled by the prospect of being bombed and arranged the movement of the entire 13,000 population of Bornholm's principal town, Rønne, to the countryside for safety. On 9 May a Soviet force landed on Bornholm and accepted the German surrender. The Soviets then refused to leave, and for a year the Danes lived in uncomfortable proximity to 7,000 Soviet occupiers before the Soviets finally departed in April 1946.[30]

Plans for the liberation of Norway had been discussed in Britain between the British and the Norwegian government-in-exile since October 1943. General Andrew Thorne had been appointed Commander, Allied Land Forces, Norway, and King Haakon's son, Crown Prince Olav, was appointed supreme commander of the Norwegian forces. The problem was that the numbers that could be mustered by the Allies were pitifully small: around 14,000 men under training in Sweden; 4,000 Norwegians trained in Scotland; around 15,000 British and American troops earmarked for Norway; and finally, about 40,000 members of the Norwegian resistance, not all of whom were armed and trained. Therefore, the resistance in Norway proceeded with caution: at the end of March all key personnel in *Milorg* and the Home Front were ordered to go into hiding, in April *Milorg* units were mobilized and sent to the forests to await further orders, and in the middle of April all sabotage actions were halted. The exception was a raid mounted by the Oslo Gang to seize two tons of files from the police department and a further half a ton from the department of justice, which supplied the resistance with all the records of NS activities: these were used to great effect in the post-war trials of the collaborators.

At the end of April, news of Himmler's talks with Count Bernadotte regarding a surrender of German forces to the western Allies 'spread like bushfire through Oslo and other towns and brought people out on to the streets, cheering and demonstrating'. The Home Front issued instructions calling for calm. Kate Rieber recalled: 'The effect was tremendous: the first order in public that I've seen *from our own*. More and more it seems like childbirth. An unbearable excitement. The emotions force themselves on us. It is like standing alone against a flood . . . it is as if the flags are slowly creeping up the flagpoles . . . but we are still waiting, keeping calm.' On 30 April, Hitler committed suicide in his bunker in Berlin and the news reached Norway on the evening of 1 May. Hitler's replacement, Admiral Karl Dönitz, summoned Terboven and Böhme to Flensburg. They returned to Norway on 4 May but Terboven was reluctant to impart details to Quisling of what had transpired. On the evening of 5 May, Quisling made his last radio speech, in which he announced that his government was legal and that it would not surrender to the Home Front, which he claimed was dominated by the communists. The Home Front did not bother to reply to Quisling since on that day it had received official credentials from the government-in-exile:

> In the case of German capitulation in Norway, the Home Front leadership is hereby authorised on behalf of the Government to take the necessary steps for the maintenance of order and the establishment of Norwegian administration, based on Norwegian laws and regulations, until members of the Government arrive in Oslo . . .

On 7 May, *Milorg* was mobilized and units began moving into position to take over power from the Germans and the NS.

The liberation was an anticlimax. On 7 May, General Böhme announced over the radio the surrender of all German forces in Norway, and next day Brigadier R. Hilton, Thorne's chief of staff, arrived in Oslo to formally accept the surrender. The SS chief Wilhelm Rediess shot himself rather than surrender, and Terboven blew himself up with dynamite. The head of the Gestapo, Heinrich Fehlis, gave orders to open the gates of Grini prison and release the prisoners, mostly members of the resistance. The NS police minister, Jonas Lie, and the head of the state police, Henrik Rogstad, hid in a farm in Baerum and shot themselves when the farm was surrounded by the resistance. Sverre Riisnaes was also at the farm but he surrendered and then claimed to be mad: he was later certified insane and escaped trial. On 9 May, Quisling, who had declined a German offer of an escape flight to Spain (whereupon his place was taken by the Rexist leader Léon Degrelle who had fled to Norway from Belgium), handed himself in at the police headquarters in Oslo. That day the first Allied units also arrived in Oslo to oversee the disarmament of the German forces, while the Home Front and *Milorg* focused on arresting members of the NS and known collaborators. As Tore Gjelsvik noted:

> The transfer of power went like a dream: instead of shots and cannon fire, we heard church bells all over the country ringing in the peace. Both the German forces and our own behaved with exemplary discipline; and so did the huge crowds in Oslo and the population everywhere. None of us had expected such a painless liberation.

On 15 May the Crown Prince arrived in Oslo with a government delegation and was welcomed by the leaders of the Home Front. Max Manus of the Oslo Gang was in the Crown Prince's car as it drove through Oslo, and he found it a very emotional occasion:

> The people wept floods and shouted hurrah; but we could hear just one roar, like that of a stormy sea beating against the cliffs. It had taken many years, but now we were there. I thought of my comrades who had given their lives, and of the whole people who had been so brave and faithful. I had long since stopped trying to hold back my tears; no Norwegian had the strength to do that today.

On 16 May the Home Front leadership met the Crown Prince at the palace and formally handed over power. On 7 June, King Haakon returned and was greeted by an honour guard of the Linge Company. *Milorg* was demobilized on 15 July and received the formal thanks of the government for its service.[31]

*

Two isolated German garrisons remained, both on islands – Crete and the Channel Islands. Since autumn 1944 the German garrison on Crete had been penned up in Canea after the rest of the island had been effectively liberated. The British were in control of the rest of the island. Brigadier Barker-Benfield arrived to take charge of Creteforce and to oversee the German surrender, the RAF took over the airfield at Kastelli Pediados, and the Royal Navy began a shuttle service bringing supplies to Crete and evacuating German prisoners. The Germans ventured out of Canea on one occasion in December 1944 when they attacked the British headquarters but withdrew after suffering a few casualties. In January 1945 the head of the SOE mission, Dennis Ciclitira, negotiated a prisoner exchange with the Germans, which took place in March when thirty-six Germans were exchanged for ten Cretans. Mainland politics threatened to intrude into Cretan affairs in January when ELAS bands took up positions around Rethymno and closed the main Canea–Heraklion road to anybody suspected of supporting their political opponents, EOK. The EOK commander in Rethymno, Lieutenant Colonel Pavlos Gyparis, attacked ELAS after they had refused to withdraw, and drove them away from the road. Further clashes between ELAS, EOK, and the guerrilla leader Manoli Bandouvas were reported later in the month, and two British soldiers were caught in the crossfire and killed.

On 8 May 1945 Ciclitira was ordered to contact the German commander, General Benthack, to arrange the formal surrender of the German forces on Crete, and the two men met later that day. The next day Benthack was flown from Maleme to Heraklion and taken to the former German headquarters at the Villa Ariadne where he surrendered formally to Major General Colin Callander who had flown to Crete for the occasion. In Canea a somewhat surreal party took place when Ciclitira and his fellow SOE officers celebrated their victory in the same cafe where German officers, some of whom had hunted down the resistance, were waiting to be taken prisoner. Both groups were entertained by a German jazz band. The *andartes*, both ELAS and EOK, entered Canea, without fighting each other, to celebrate: 'There were arches of leaves everywhere, and flowers and placards and signs wishing us welcome by the thousand, and slogans supporting EAM or EOK here or the National Army or ELAS there, and all you could wish for.'[32]

The Channel Islands had been left undefended by the British in May 1940 and had been occupied by the Germans. There was little resistance since the ratio between occupied and occupiers precluded it, and the small size of the islands meant that would-be resisters had no place to hide. In September 1942 British-born men and their families had been deported to internment camps in Germany, and in early 1943 there was a second deportation, this time of retired army officers, in reprisal for the commando raid on Sark. After D-Day the Channel Islands were cut off from France and the German garrison under General Rudolf von Schmettow was subjected to an intense British propaganda campaign exhorting the Germans to surrender. The Germans held out, but being cut off from France meant that no food supplies reached the islands, posing the threat of starvation on the same level as suffered by the Netherlands that winter. The Germans proved willing to negotiate a settlement with the British using a Swiss intermediary. The Germans favoured the evacuation to Britain of a substantial portion of the population, but the British preferred to despatch food supplies to the islands, under Red Cross supervision. The first ship, carrying food parcels for every civilian, docked at St Peter Port and St Helier on 27 December: there were further supply trips during that winter. On 8 May 1945 an advance British force under Brigadier Alfred Snow, accompanied by two British destroyers, arrived in St Peter Port to accept the German surrender of Guernsey: Jersey was formally liberated on the following day.[33]

Even after the formal end of the Second World War, fighting continued in the Protectorate. The level of resistance there had been low for most of the war but in the spring of 1945 there were signs that the Czechs were growing restless and wanted to play a role in the liberation of their country. Goebbels noted in his diary on 9 March: 'The Czechs are now becoming somewhat refractory. This is noticeable in an increase of sabotage activity. The reason is that no one among the Czech people believes in a German victory anymore and the opposition elements are trying to provide themselves with an alibi for the future . . .', and ten days later:

> The Czechs are becoming increasingly impudent. They now regard themselves in the role of freedom fighters. They want to join the whole hostile world now raising its head against us. They have not yet plucked up courage, however, to make an open declaration of war; as we all know, the Czechs are too easy-going and too cowardly for that.[34]

By the spring of 1945 there were around 120 partisan groups in the Protectorate with a total of 7,500 fighters as well as a number of small Soviet partisan units. The arrival of agents parachuted in from Italy meant that the partisan groups had communication with London, and in April the groups received twelve arms drops; but as Radomír Luža, the leader of one partisan group, noted: 'Since the weapons we received were somewhat different from those we had ordered, we weren't quite sure how to use them.' Plastic explosive for sabotage was received instead of the rifles and anti-tank weapons that were needed.[35]

These weapons reflected the role envisaged for the Czech resistance by the Allies. The partisans were expected to engage in sabotage and to ambush small isolated German convoys, not to launch attacks in which they would be outgunned and outnumbered. A high level of military activity by the partisans was deemed unnecessary because the German troops in the Protectorate were about to become trapped in a pincer movement as the Soviets advanced from Slovakia and the 3rd United States Army under General Patton advanced from the west. On 25 March the 2nd Ukrainian Front launched its Bratislava–Brno operation, and by 11 April it had crossed into the Protectorate. Bratislava, the Slovak capital, fell on 4 April and Jozef Tiso and his government fled to Kremsmünster in Austria, where Tiso signed a formal surrender to the US Army on 8 May. On 21 April the Americans entered the Protectorate, reached Aš, and were poised to advance on Plzeň (Pilsen). Five days later the Red Army liberated Brno. Churchill appealed to Truman to encourage the Americans to advance to take Prague:

> In our view, the liberation of Prague and as much as possible of the territory of western Czechoslovakia by US troops might make the whole difference to the post-war situation in Czechoslovakia, and might well influence that in nearby countries.[36]

Patton was keen to continue his advance since his troops were encountering little opposition from the German soldiers, who appeared eager and grateful to surrender to the Americans rather than the vengeful Soviets. Yet Eisenhower was concerned about what Stalin would say, and ordered Patton to halt at Plzeň.[37]

While Churchill was doing his best to ensure political freedom for the Czechs after the war, it can be argued that Edvard Beneš was doing the opposite. When Beneš had signed a treaty of friendship with Stalin in late 1943 he had felt assured that he could control the political destiny of his country. He did not realize the determination of the communists to dominate matters until far too late. In April, Beneš and the Czech communists travelled to the recently liberated Slovak town of Košice, established a provisional government, and issued a programme which opened with the statement:

> After more than six years of foreign subjugation the time has arrived when our humble country has seen the light of freedom's sun . . . Thus it is thanks to our great ally the Soviet Union . . . [that] a new Czechoslovak government can be created.

This was an extraordinary statement since Britain had hosted Beneš and his ministers, and had despatched supplies and agents to the Protectorate throughout the war, but it reflected his hope of collaboration with the communists. To this end Beneš, before going to Moscow on his way to Košice, had sacked his long-time assistants General Ingr and František Moravec because of communist opposition to them. In Košice he accepted a communist sympathizer, Zdeněk Fierlinger, as his prime minister, gave the principal ministries to communists, and appointed General Ludvík Svoboda, the commander of Czech troops raised in the Soviet Union and a communist, as commander of the new Czechoslovak army.[38]

Meanwhile in the Protectorate a Czech national council had been formed, led by Professor Albert Pražák, which united the democratic resistance, the *Rada Tří*, with the communists. This council hoped to exert control over the military who were planning an uprising in Prague: General Karel Kutlvašr was appointed to command the insurgents in Prague, and General František Slunečko to command those in the suburbs.[39] Whereas Beneš was prepared to show gratitude towards the Soviet Union, the resistance in Prague wanted to liberate the Czech capital themselves. The Czechs were growing restless. On 1 May there had been an uprising near Olomouc which had been brutally suppressed by the SS, with the deaths of thirty-one Czechs and the arrests of twenty-one more. Similar unrest was evident in Přerov, Nymburk, Jičín, and Rakovník.

On 5 May the war came to Prague when the Germans bombed the city. The Czechs rose up and were swiftly reinforced by partisans, policemen, and gendarmes arriving from nearby towns. Civil disobedience was evident everywhere as Czechoslovak flags appeared, the main radio station began broadcasting in the banned Czechoslovak languages, tram conductors refused to accept Reichsmarks, and German signs were torn down. German soldiers surrendered willingly to the Czechs: 'On Charles Square a squad of German soldiers arrived, and, full of smiles, handed over their guns to the Czechs. Everyone slapped them on the shoulders and let them go their way.' By the end of 5 May the Prague resistance had seized most of the city east of the river and held the radio station, telephone exchange, and ten of the twelve bridges. Overnight 1,600 barricades were built in the streets.

The Czechs were, however, largely untrained and had few weapons, so that if the Germans chose to counter-attack the insurgents would be massacred. Field Marshal Ferdinand Schörner, the commander of German forces in Bohemia, was rushed from the Soviet front to Prague with an SS force equipped with tanks and armoured vehicles. At this critical point the Czechs gained an unexpected ally – the ROA (Russian Liberation Army) under General Vlasov. These renegade Russians were now terrified of falling into Soviet hands, which would mean execution as traitors, and sought redemption for their anti-partisan activities in Slovakia and Moravia by changing sides and helping the Czechs against the SS. In the early hours of 7 May the German forces in Europe signed a provisional unconditional surrender. Schörner argued that this unconditional surrender did not apply to German forces fighting the Soviets nor to the Czech rebels. The Czech resistance leadership, on the other hand, thought that the unconditional surrender did apply in Prague and so ordered an immediate ceasefire. This caused considerable confusion in the city, and by the end of the day the Czechs had lost much of the ground they had captured previously and only held a salient in the Vinohrady–Strašnice area. The prospects of withstanding the German counter-attack were made much worse by the departure of most ROA units, who rushed westwards to surrender to the Americans who they now knew were not advancing on Prague.

On 8 May, as most of the world was celebrating the end of the Second World War in Europe, the Czech insurgents faced their fiercest battle yet as the Germans launched an air and artillery bombardment of Prague and the SS attacked the Czechs holding the Masaryk railway station. The station fell briefly to the SS, who then murdered about fifty people – both fighters and innocent travellers. The Germans, however, were in terror of falling into the hands of the advancing Soviets and so were willing to negotiate a surrender with the Czech national council. An agreement was concluded in the early hours of 9 May which allowed the Germans to retreat westwards through Prague on condition that they left behind their weapons. At 4 a.m. the first elements of the Soviet forces entered Prague where they quickly overcame the last German defenders and reached the city centre at 8 a.m. Around 2,000 Prague insurgents had been killed in the fighting. Prague, the first capital city to be occupied, was the last to be liberated.[40]

32
The Aftermath

The end of the Second World War in Europe held different meanings for resisters in western and eastern Europe. In the west, liberation meant just that, freedom from occupation and an end to fear. These were concepts that some found hard to grasp:

> Was it really possible to tell people one's real name after suppressing it for years? Was it really possible to believe it was the postman knocking on one's door and not the Gestapo? How many months would it take to get rid of the virus of the occupation?[1]

In eastern Europe, however, a new reality dawned on the resistance movements as they were forced to confront their failure:

> As the smoke cleared from the battlefield it began to emerge that we had suffered a huge national defeat, yet we did not want to, or were simply unable to, believe this. We clutched at the last illusory straws of hope. We had yet to adapt to the new situation, and now faced an enemy within.[2]

The Germans had been defeated but the age of Soviet domination, a new occupation by Soviet troops and governance by Soviet-sponsored governments, had begun. Those countries behind what would soon be called the Iron Curtain would have to wait a further fifty years for true liberation. The situation in the Balkans was somewhere in between. In both Yugoslavia and Greece, civil war had been as important as resistance to the occupiers during the war. In Yugoslavia peace brought the total victory of one of the resistance movements, the Partisans, whereas in Greece the determination of the western powers to ensure that democracy returned to the country led to the eclipse of the resistance credentials of the communist-dominated ELAS and its ultimate return to the political shadows.

Anger was the most visible emotion displayed in the immediate aftermath of liberation. This anger was first directed towards those who had willingly consorted with the enemy, the women who had personal relations with German soldiers. These women were easy targets to locate and punish since local inhabitants knew precisely who they were. Sergeant Jim Chambers, a Jedburgh, witnessed what happened in the Langres area of France:

> They rounded up these ladies who'd associated with the German troops and put them on a chair on the truck, shaved all their hair off, and then – they had these brands in the fire – they branded them on both cheeks with a swastika. There were a lot of cheers and jeering and pushing and prodding. It was quite a happy occasion for those that were watching. The hairdresser made quite a show of it, dancing round and snipping bits off here and there, until he eventually shaved the whole lot off.[3]

Although head shaving has been most notably recorded in France it also occurred in Belgium and the Netherlands. In all three countries the attacks on the women were carried out by local villagers, people who had known these women all their lives. In Norway the attackers in Kirkenes were Norwegian soldiers who had spent the war training in Scotland and were indignant that Norwegian women should have consorted with German soldiers, failing to understand the mixture of temptation and threat in a town where there was one German soldier for every Norwegian citizen.[4]

Governments-in-exile had anticipated that anger would be directed towards the collaborators and had made public promises that judicial processes would be set in place to try them. But in the interim period between the return of these governments and the establishment of the special courts, the population took matters into their own hands in what was termed in France the *épuration sauvage*, a period of wild justice, torture, and secret executions. The victims were known collaborators, especially members of the despised collaborationist police and militia forces such as the *Milice*. SOE agent Bill Jordan overheard the FFI torturing a member of the *Milice*:

> The usual method of inducing the victims to talk with the aid of hot irons was to poke one iron into the stomach, while another interrogator standing behind the victim placed a hot iron hard against his back, giving him the impression that the iron pressed in his stomach had penetrated right through his body.[5]

The collaborator would then be executed. SOE agent George Starr faced an investigation on his return from France after his courier, Anne-Marie Walters, had alleged that he had sanctioned the torture of members of the *Milice* by the men under his command. The case was dismissed for lack of evidence and by the suspicion that the personality clash which had seen

Starr send Walters back to Britain early had spilled over into her post-action report.[6] It has been estimated that in France between 4,500 and 10,000 summary executions occurred during the *épuration sauvage*.[7]

Lynch justice also occurred in Italy where it was officially sanctioned, or at least open to amnesty, if the summary killing took place before the formal end of the war on 8 May, a deadline which was later extended to 31 July 1945. Gordon Lett witnessed one such attack in La Spezia:

> An angry roar began and grew louder and louder as a crowd converged on the Piazza Verdi from all directions, surrounding a man in civilian clothing whom they had recognised as a member of the *Brigate Nere* . . . The miserable wretch screamed as the crowd closed on him, and then disappeared under their feet. As suddenly as it had begun, the yelling ceased. The crowd melted away, as if ashamed of what they had done, dazed by the fact that, after twenty years of despotism, they had the power to do it. A gory mess of human flesh lay in the square, bathed in the bright spring sunshine, and I turned away from the window duly sobered by my first taste of mob violence.

The most murderous region was the so-called 'Red Triangle', an area centred on Bologna but including Reggio Emilia, Modena, and Ferrara, where non-judicial murders continued for three years after the end of the war. There was also a spate of killings in the northern industrial cities of Turin, Milan, and Genoa. It has been estimated that around 9,000 Fascists were killed in the immediate post-liberation period.[8]

As the war ended it seemed at times as if half the population of Europe was on the move. As the Soviets advanced towards the Reich the Germans had formed lengthy columns of Jews and POWs, driving them westwards. In August 1944 the prisons in France had been emptied of the resisters and trainloads of them were despatched to locations unknown to the Allies deep inside the Reich. The end of the war brought additional columns of refugees, Germans expelled from Poland and Czechoslovakia moving westwards and forced labourers from the east trying to make their way home. Somewhere in this mass of humanity were those resisters who had been deported to the prisons and concentration camps. Most had been termed *Nacht und Nebel*, which meant that they disappeared into the fog of war, their fate often unrecorded.

Some of these resisters had already been saved by the intervention of the vice-president of the Swedish Red Cross, Count Folke Bernadotte. In spring 1945 he had opened negotiations with the Germans to arrange for the release of over 15,000 prisoners, mostly Norwegian and Danish, from various concentration camps and prisons, as well as 423 Danish Jews from

Theresienstadt. The so-called White Buses toured the camps for the last two months of the war, and the mission continued after the war. This move undoubtedly saved many of these Norwegian and Danish resisters from execution, but some did not live long enough to be rescued: for example, Monica Wichfeld died from disease and malnutrition shortly before the rescue mission reached her.[9] Others were saved from execution by the intervention of prison and camp commandants. Gaston Vandermeerssche was in the prison in Lüttringhausen when the commandant received orders on 7 May 1945 to execute all eighty *Nacht und Nebel* prisoners. He was aware that the Allies were nearby so he ignored his orders and, in case the SS checked, executed eighty common criminals instead.[10] Odette Sansom had not been executed in Ravensbrück (unlike her fellow F Section agents, Violette Szabo, Lilian Rolfe, and Denise Bloch) because Peter Churchill had claimed she was his wife, and he himself was protected because the Germans thought he was related to the British prime minister. As the Allies approached Ravensbrück, Sansom was taken by Fritz Suhren, the camp commandant, towards the American lines. Suhren hoped to trade her life for immunity from prosecution: Sansom survived and later married Churchill in 1947, although they divorced nine years later; Suhren was tried and executed in 1950.[11]

The governments-in-exile had made plans for the repatriation of their POWs, forced labourers, and prisoners. In France the process was overseen by the veteran resister Henri Frenay. The repatriation of the POWs and forced labourers went smoothly in France and Belgium, but in the Netherlands it was hampered by internal political rivalries. The repatriation of the resisters returning from the concentration camps and prisons was more challenging, and all those involved in receiving and processing them recall their horror at the sight of the emaciated and clearly traumatized wraiths who emerged from the trains and lorries.[12] These survivors clearly needed urgent medical and psychological assistance to overcome their ordeal. Yet few of them were strong enough to ask for this help:

> We wanted to talk and to be understood at last. We had just come back with our experiences still alive and burning within us; we had a frantic desire to tell our friends exactly what we had lived through. But we couldn't. What we had to say was already becoming *unimaginable*, even to ourselves.[13]

In every country the resisters formed associations for members of the resistance so that they could meet and talk with those who would understand. Few spoke or wrote extensively of their experiences. Exceptions were SOE agent Christopher Burney who wrote a short book on Buchenwald, *The Dungeon Democracy* (published in 1946), and a French resister,

Germaine Tillion, who eventually produced, in 1973 an account of her time in Ravensbrück.

Soon after the liberation of Paris, Vera Atkins of F Section SOE set up an office in the city to which surviving agents could report, and where she could closely question each agent about others they might have seen. This was essential information to glean because F Section simply did not know whether silence from an agent meant that he or she had been killed, had gone into hiding, or had been arrested. Marcel Rousset proved extremely valuable in this respect, and he supplied a list of agents he had seen at the Gestapo headquarters in Avenue Foch, in Fresnes prison, and in Ravitsch prison, from which he had escaped. More information arrived when:

> After 8 May people started streaming back from concentration camps. You'd get their stories and it was from them that you'd hear what had happened to those who'd not returned. When a person was arrested, you did not know what happened to them subsequently! – therefore the information brought by the returning agents was more than interesting and more than harrowing.[14]

At the end of the war over 100 F Section agents were still missing, among them sixteen women, and Atkins set out to discover their fate. Information supplied by Brian Stonehouse and Pat O'Leary (Albert-Marie Guérisse) revealed that three women had been spotted arriving at Natzweiler, and further investigation revealed their identities: they were Andrée Borrel, Diana Rowden, and Sonia Olschanesky, all of whom were executed on 6 July 1944. A search of the records at Ravensbrück revealed further executions. Four women remained missing – Noor Inayat Khan, Madeleine Damerment, Éliane Plewman, and Yolande Beekman – and it took a long time to piece together the story of their fate: they had all been taken to Dachau and executed on 13 September 1944.[15]

It slowly emerged that most male SOE agents had been executed in the camps to which they had been sent, principally Flossenbürg and Gross-Rosen, although Francis Suttill was killed in Sachsenhausen. Evidence also appeared of promises broken. For example, Hermann Giskes had promised the victims of the *Englandspiel* that they would be held prisoner in the Netherlands and would not be handed over to the SS. In April 1944, however, orders from Berlin meant that fifty-one of these captured agents were moved to Ravitsch prison in Silesia: only Huub Lauwers and Han Jordaan were spared the move. In September 1944 the group was joined by one American and seven British agents and the entire party was transported to Mauthausen and sent to a bunker where they spent the night. The post-war report on Mauthausen recorded that:

> The morning after their arrival, the forty-seven men were seen to emerge from the bunker barefooted and in their underclothing. Their numbers were written across their chests, which was exceptional. This was usually done only after death for the sake of records before cremation.

The prisoners were taken to the quarry where the steps were lined with SS and each man was given a slab of stone weighing around 60lb to carry up the steps. The process was repeated until the men collapsed, whereupon they were executed: Marcus Bloom was the first to fall. In the middle of the afternoon half the men were executed, and the rest shared their fate on the following day.[16]

On 8 August 1944 thirty-seven men, many but not all from SOE F Section, were loaded onto a train in Paris which then headed into the Reich. On 16 August the train reached Buchenwald where the thirty-seven agents joined others such as Maurice Pertschuk, Christopher Burney, and the Newton brothers, Alfred and Henry, who had been inmates for some time. On the afternoon of 9 September 1944 the inmates were surprised when the usual roll call was ended with an order for sixteen SOE agents to report to the main gate. Initially no one was too concerned about this step, but two days later they learned that the sixteen men had been taken to the basement of the crematorium where they had suffered a slow death after being hanged on meat hooks before their bodies were cremated. The remaining agents realized that they were highly likely to share the same fate in the near future. Tommy Yeo-Thomas and Harry Peulevé came up with a desperate plan that would involve them switching identities with patients in the SS-run medical institute which was experimenting with typhus vaccines. This risky proposition meant that the agents would have to be deliberately infected with typhus and hope to survive the disease as an alternative to being executed. A deal was struck with the SS which meant that Yeo-Thomas and two other men would be saved, but the remaining twenty-one would be abandoned to their fate. Yeo-Thomas selected Peulevé, possibly because he had helped Yeo-Thomas encode secret reports on the camp, and also Stéphane Hessel, a BCRA agent he had known in London. The three men were duly injected with typhus and their identities switched with three dying patients. Maurice Southgate managed to enter the hospital independently of this plot, and Burney successfully hid his identity. The remaining agents were summoned to the main gate on 4 October and were executed on the following day. Yeo-Thomas, Peulevé, and Hessel recovered from typhus and were sent on work commandos until they were liberated.[17]

Precise figures on the number of people who were deported into the

Reich and died there are hard to obtain. Each resistance movement drew up its own list of the missing, which led to duplications as some people had worked for more than one of them. Marie-Madeleine Fourcade was especially thorough in investigating the fate of 450 missing Alliance agents. Soon after the cessation of hostilities she and a fellow agent who had escaped imprisonment, Ferdinand Rodriguez, began a tour of prisons in the British and American sectors of Germany. At the end of the tour Fourcade was forced to conclude that 438 Alliance agents, including her deputy and lover, Léon Faye, had been executed without trial. The Soviets would not allow her to search their zone, but she received reliable intelligence that Faye had been executed in Sonnenburg prison in January 1945 just before the Soviets arrived.[18]

In 1946 the Allies put the major German war criminals on trial at Nuremberg, and this trial was followed by others for lesser war criminals also held there. Field Marshal Kesselring and Generals Mälzer and von Mackensen were tried by the Allies in Venice for their conduct towards the partisans, especially the Ardeatine Caves massacre. All three were sentenced to death which was then commuted to life imprisonment. In his memoirs Kesselring complained: 'Von Mackensen, Mälzer and I were sentenced to death through the failure of our attempts to circumvent one of Hitler's orders, for which we were in no way to blame, as we had in the matter of reprisals been deprived of authority.'[19] Such a defence was typical for the German defendants, but was rejected by those prosecuting them. Hans Kieffer was sentenced to death and executed by the British for the murder of captured SAS soldiers on orders from Berlin, and not for his conduct towards SOE agents in France. Indeed, John Starr spoke out at Kieffer's trial of the good treatment he had received from him at Avenue Foch. Kieffer's superior, Helmut Knochen, was also sentenced to death for the same crime but his sentence was commuted to life imprisonment.[20]

Other German war criminals were extradited to the country where they had committed their crimes. France, for example, tried Otto Abetz, Carl Oberg, and Knochen, and all three men were sentenced to periods in prison. Abetz was released in 1954, and Oberg and Knochen were released as part of a general pardon issued by de Gaulle in 1962. Otto von Stülpnagel committed suicide in prison rather than face a trial in France: his cousin Carl-Heinrich was already dead, having been executed by the SS after the failure of the 20 July 1944 plot against Hitler. In the Netherlands various trials were held of senior German officials but only Hanns Rauter was executed; Belgium and Denmark also sentenced Germans tried there to imprisonment rather than execution. Friedrich-Wilhelm Müller was tried in Athens in 1946 for his conduct in Crete and was executed a year later.

The Allies were notably reluctant to extradite wanted Germans to countries behind the Iron Curtain. Poland was seen as an exception because of the enormity of German crimes there, but even so only about 1,800 Germans from a Polish list of 12,000–15,000 individuals were extradited. The vast majority of German war crimes trials in Poland concerned those responsible for the Holocaust such as Rudolf Höss, the commandant of Auschwitz, and Jürgen Stroop, who had suppressed the Warsaw ghetto uprising, but administrators such as Ludwig Fischer and Erich Koch were also tried: Fischer was executed and Koch died in prison.[21] The Czechs also tried German war criminals and executed Kurt Daluege and Dieter Wisliceny. The Allies were reluctant to extradite Germans to Yugoslavia while the future of Trieste was still under discussion. Nonetheless Alexander Löhr and Siegfried Kasche were tried in Belgrade and both were sentenced to death, and Hermann Neubacher was sentenced to twenty years in prison; Franz Böhme committed suicide rather than be tried by the Yugoslavs.

A number of notable enemies of the resistance got away with their war crimes. The architect of anti-partisan warfare, Bach-Zelewski, appeared at the Nuremberg trials as a witness for the prosecution, and at the later Eichmann trial in Israel as a witness for the defence. He appears to have been protected from prosecution for war crimes by the Allies because they wanted to utilize his knowledge of anti-partisan warfare and of Eastern Europe at the time when it appeared that a third world war might break out with the Soviet Union. He was later tried in several West German courts for murders committed before the war and died in prison in Munich in 1972.[22] Similar protection and later use by intelligence services was extended to Horst Kopkow, the man in Berlin who had ordered the executions of SOE agents and those caught in the *Englandspiel*, and who was thought to have knowledge of Soviet intelligence methods because of his breaking of the Red Orchestra. Kopkow was never prosecuted for his crimes and died in 1996.[23]

As soon as the war ended, the trials of the collaborators opened. De Gaulle explained the need for them: 'The Government's duty was to keep a cool head, but to pass the sponge over so many crimes and abuses would have meant leaving a monstrous abscess to infect the country for ever. Justice must be done.'[24] In April 1945 Marshal Pétain moved from Germany to Switzerland and then into France where he was met by General Koenig.

Pétain's trial took place between 23 July and 15 August 1945, and his opening statement reflected the tenor of his defence:

> Can you understand the difficulty of governing under such conditions? Every day, with a knife at my throat, I struggled against the enemy demands. History will tell all that I saved you from, when my adversaries only thought of reproaching me for the inevitable . . . The occupation obliged me, against my wishes, to make statements and accomplish certain acts for which I have suffered more than you, but in face of enemy demands I abandoned nothing which was essential to the country's existence. On the contrary, for four years, by my actions, I maintained France, I assured life and bread to Frenchmen, I assured our prisoners of the nation's support.

Pétain neglected to mention the steps taken towards collaboration and his belief in the ultimate victory of Germany. His judges were not convinced by his defence and he was sentenced to death. At the same time the court hoped that there would be no execution, and de Gaulle agreed. Pétain was granted a reprieve and lived out his remaining years in seclusion on the Île d'Yeu off the coast of western France.[25]

Pétain was protected from execution largely because he was widely regarded in France as the saviour of Verdun during the First World War. Such protection was not applicable to other French defendants. Pierre Laval, in particular, was singled out to shoulder most of the guilt of collaboration. At the end of his brief trial in October 1945 he was found guilty and sentenced to death. Laval tried to cheat his executioners by taking poison on the day before his scheduled execution, but he was taken to hospital and recovered sufficiently to meet his death by firing squad as planned. Joseph Darnand's trial was also brief and his guilt was obvious. After he had been sentenced to death he wrote to de Gaulle: 'It is not [for] my own pardon that I am asking, but that of my comrades in the *Milice*.' He claimed that the *Milice* had acted as they had out of patriotism: de Gaulle did not reply. Other Vichy ministers were also tried, and while some were sentenced to death which was then commuted to varying lengths of imprisonment, Fernand de Brinon was sentenced to death and executed. Of the leaders of the collaborationist parties, Jacques Doriot had been killed by a low-level air attack in Germany in February 1945, and Marcel Déat had escaped into Italy, where he would remain in hiding until his death in 1955: he was sentenced to death *in absentia*.[26]

Elsewhere other major collaborators were also put on trial. Quisling's trial in Oslo opened on 20 August 1945 and lasted until 7 September when he was condemned to death. Quisling was unapologetic, and in his final speech to the court stated: 'If my activities have been treasonable – as they have been said to be – then I would pray to God that for the sake of Norway a large number of Norway's sons will become such traitors as I, but that they will not be thrown into jail.' Quisling was executed on 24 October.[27] In the Netherlands, Anton Mussert was tried in November 1945 and found guilty and was executed in May 1946. The Belgian collaborator Léon Degrelle had fled first to Norway and then to Spain as the war came to a close. Spain refused efforts to extradite him and Belgian attempts to kidnap him failed: Degrelle was sentenced to death *in absentia*.[28] The Danish Nazi Frits Clausen died in prison in 1947 awaiting trial. In Greece twenty-four former ministers of the Greek collaborationist governments were put on trial. The changing political climate affected the results of these trials. The second round of the civil war and the violence of the communists raised questions as to whose behaviour was worse for Greece: the collaborationists or the communists? The result was that the former prime minister Giorgios Tsolakoglou was sentenced to death but his sentence was commuted, and Ioannis Rallis faced life imprisonment but died in prison in 1946.[29]

The majority of traitors, the internal enemies of the resistance who had done great damage, were located, tried, and executed. An exception was the Dutch traitor Richard Christmann, who convinced the Allies that he had contacts which would be of use to them in a future conflict with the Soviet Union, was protected from prosecution, and ended up working for West German intelligence. In most cases the guilt of the traitors was indisputable, but with two men their guilt could not be assumed. Henri Déricourt had served SOE well as the air-landings officer in France, but he was blamed for the disasters that befell the Prosper circuit. Suspicion had fallen on him during the war and he had been withdrawn from service. Vera Atkins managed to interview Hans Kieffer in 1947 and Kieffer confirmed that Déricourt had been working for the Germans. However, when Déricourt's trial opened in 1948 Kieffer had been executed and no one from SOE gave evidence against Déricourt. Indeed, Nicholas Bodington, who had known Déricourt well, appeared for the defence and his evidence was seen as instrumental to securing Déricourt's acquittal. Déricourt went on to work as a drug and gold smuggler in Laos until he was killed in an air crash in 1962.[30] René Hardy was accused of having betrayed the whereabouts of Jean Moulin to the Germans in June 1943, a betrayal which had led to Moulin's torture and death. Hardy was arrested in 1945 and put on trial in 1947. He denied ever having been arrested by the Germans on the train at Chalon, the point at which he was suspected of having become a traitor, and was acquitted. His fiancée, Lydie Bastien, then produced the evidence of Hardy's presence on that train and Hardy was rearrested. His second trial began in 1950. One witness gave evidence which illustrates the dilemmas surrounding the treatment of suspected traitors: 'In wartime the slightest suspicion must be resolved *against* the suspect; in peacetime, if there is the slightest doubt, it must be resolved *in favour* of the suspect.' Hardy was acquitted and died in 1987. Suspicions of his treachery never abated and the much later trial of Klaus Barbie did nothing to settle the matter.[31]

The Dutch solicitor-general, Professor Langemeyer, summed up the dilemma facing those responsible for trying collaborators: 'It has been one of the great experiences of these courts of Justice, that a person can have fought on the side of the enemy, and yet can be, all in all, more a good man than a bad, and also not a fool.'[32] This realization, added to the recognition that normal life should be restored as soon as possible, determined the nature of the purge of collaborators. In France special courts tried 124,750 people, of whom 767 were executed, and over 38,000 sentenced to some length of prison term or the withdrawal of civil rights. As may be expected after the shame of occupation, the trials proved highly contentious, but at the same time there was also a feeling in favour of reconciliation. In 1947 an amnesty removed the stain of national degradation from minor collaborators, and successive amnesties led to the early release from prison of those found guilty so that by 1964 no collaborator remained in prison.[33] The Dutch government feared a repetition of the *épuration sauvage* which had occurred in France and so, by October 1945, 96,000 alleged collaborators were being held in preventive custody. Special courts tried the Dutch collaborators and around 64,000 men and women received prison sentences or the withdrawal of civil rights: 135 were sentenced to death but only forty were executed.[34] The Belgians arrested about 100,000 people but tried only 87,000, of whom 10,000 were acquitted. Death sentences were passed in 4,170 cases but only 230 were carried out, and about 16,000 collaborators received long prison sentences. The Danes executed forty-six collaborators, sentenced sixty-two to life imprisonment, and around 14,000 received short prison sentences.[35]

Two countries faced unusual difficulties when considering how to purge and punish collaborators: Norway and Italy. In Norway membership of the NS had been essential for many people to retain their jobs, and therefore membership of the collaborationist organization did not necessarily mean that the member was a collaborator. This problem was recognized by the Norwegian courts. Everyone who had been affiliated to the NS during the war, about 93,000 people, was investigated and about half either did not face trial or were acquitted. The great majority of those found guilty, mostly passive NS members, received fines and some also were deprived of their civil rights for a limited period. Of the 18,000 who were imprisoned, including Quisling's ministers (apart from Albert Hagelin and Ragnar Skancke, who had both been executed), successive amnesties, as in France, reduced the length of their sentences so that all collaborators had been released from prison by the end of 1957.[36]

In Italy the recommendations to the government by the CLNAI and CLN were that an attempt should be made to grade the Fascists according to their crime. Mussolini had come to power in 1922 and so to condemn all Fascists to death or imprisonment would have wrecked all chances of rebuilding the country. Accordingly, the forces of retribution were directed against those who had continued to be Fascists after the armistice or had served in the RSI's armed forces such as the *Brigate Nere* and the *Decima Mas*. In 1946 there were around 40,000 Fascists in prison. Prominent Fascists who had preyed on the resistance, such as Pietro Caruso and Pietro Koch, were tried, condemned to death and executed. Those Italians who had served in the Italian zones of occupation in Yugoslavia were never extradited to Yugoslavia. However, General Roatta, whose harsh policies in Yugoslavia had resulted in the deaths of many innocent civilians, faced charges in Italy: he fled to Spain and was sentenced to life imprisonment *in absentia*. This sentence was overturned by a court of appeal in 1948 and Roatta returned to Rome a free man in 1966.

The post-war trials could reveal uncomfortable truths such as when, in January 1953, twenty-one members of SS Das Reich were put on trial for the Oradour massacre. The court discovered that fourteen of the defendants were in fact Frenchmen from Alsace who claimed that they had been forcibly conscripted into the SS and had taken part in the massacre solely from fear of German retribution against their families still residing in German-controlled Alsace. The court accepted their defence and sentenced the men to a period of forced labour. The sentences led to an outcry in Alsace and the French Alsatians were released in February, whereupon there was an uproar from the general public and representations by the deputies for Oradour-Limousin. The trial led to the preservation of Oradour-sur-Glane as a shrine to the brutality of the German occupation.[37] Heinz Lammerding, the German officer responsible for the Oradour massacre, was never extradited from Germany but was tried and sentenced to death *in absentia* by a court in France. He died in 1971 and his funeral featured a large reunion of former SS colleagues.

The major crimes committed during the Second World War were neither forgotten nor forgiven with the passage of time. Klaus Barbie, the former Gestapo chief in Lyon, was protected from immediate post-war retribution by the Americans and settled in Bolivia and then Peru. A French court sentenced him to death *in absentia* but it was not until 1971 that his hiding place was located by the Nazi-hunters Serge and Beate Klarsfeld. In 1984 Barbie was charged with war crimes and was extradited to France where his trial began in May 1987 and led to life imprisonment. His trial reopened old wounds in France and in particular the case of Paul Touvier who had been the *Milice* head of intelligence in Lyon. Touvier had been sentenced to death *in absentia* twice by French courts but had successfully eluded capture. The statute of limitations took effect in 1967, which meant that Touvier was now a free man, though forbidden to reside in the twelve south-eastern departments of France, and he received a presidential pardon in 1971 from Georges Pompidou. Barbie's trial reopened the question of Touvier's pardon because both men were guilty of similar charges. Touvier was arrested in 1989 and charged with crimes against humanity by former resisters and deportees. He was tried in 1993 and sentenced to life imprisonment. The former Vichy police chief, René Bousquet, had been sentenced in 1949 to five years' loss of civil rights. His lenient sentence had been the result of late resistance activity which was seen as offsetting his former collaboration. In 1991 he was charged in the French courts for his conduct leading to the Vel' d'Hiv round-up of Jews but was assassinated in 1993 before his case came to court.[38]

In 1994 Erich Priebke, who had been a senior Gestapo officer in occupied Rome and had escaped to Argentina after the war, described his involvement in the Ardeatine Caves massacre to a reporter from the United States ABC news network, feeling that it was at last safe to do so. He was wrong, and he was extradited to Italy and put on trial. Unexpectedly, however, the judges concluded that Priebke had merely been following orders and that his case fell under the thirty-year statute of limitations and so acquitted him. The ensuing storm of protest from relatives of the victims of the massacre and former resisters led to a new trial and a fifteen-year sentence which was raised to life imprisonment on appeal. Priebke was never imprisoned but was held under house arrest until his death in 2013. Even then the controversy did not end: the Vatican banned the holding of his funeral in any Catholic church in Italy; Argentina refused to accept the return of his coffin so that he could be buried next to his wife; and the German town of his birth refused to take him. Priebke was buried anonymously and secretly by the Italian authorities.[39]

As the enormity of the Holocaust became known the conduct of Jewish leaders during the period was examined. During the war the leaders of the French UGIF (*Union Générale des Israélites de France*) and the Belgian AJB (*L'Association des Juifs en Belgique*) had been condemned as collaborators by the Jewish clandestine press, and after the war Jews pressed for the men to be tried by Jewish honour courts. Little was done in France and Belgium, but in the Netherlands the joint leaders of the *Joodse Raad*, David Cohen and Abraham Asscher, were arrested by order of the public prosecutor in November 1947. The Dutch proved unwilling to prosecute the two men for collaboration, so a Jewish honour court took over the process. This court condemned both men for 'reprehensible' conduct during the occupation, especially with regard to the drawing up of the deportation lists. The court found Asscher and Cohen guilty, recommended the exclusion of both men from honorary and stipendiary offices within the Jewish community, and barred them from attending synagogue services. Appeals led to the verdict being set aside, although official inquiries by the Dutch authorities continued until July 1950 when the case was dropped. By then Asscher had died; Cohen continued to defend his reputation for the rest of his life.[40]

The Jews who had survived the concentration camps found that the knowledge of the Holocaust had done nothing to diminish anti-semitism in western Europe. Of the approximately 107,000 Jews deported from the Netherlands, only about 5,000 survived the concentration camps and returned home. These then struggled to recover their houses, businesses, and possessions, and in the immediate post-war years many chose to emigrate to the United States or to the newly formed country of Israel. In addition, the Dutch had their own narrative of resistance and were not prepared to acknowledge the Jewish story of suffering as in any way distinct from their own. For example, Otto Frank struggled to find a Dutch publisher for his daughter Anne's diary. It was only after an English translation was published in the United States, followed by a play and a film, that the story of Anne Frank became an international symbol and the Anne Frank House museum was established in Amsterdam in 1960.[41] The Danes rightly remembered their role in saving the Danish Jews from extermination but also made it hard for those who had reached the sanctuary of Sweden to return home. In both the Netherlands and Denmark the stateless Jews who had arrived as refugees were often served with deportation orders at short notice. In Paris in June 1945 there was a brief demonstration and riot involving 2,500–3,000 people shouting 'France for the French' when someone in the 4th arrondissement occupying an apartment owned by a Jew was evicted by the owner on his return from the camps.[42]

The Jews in eastern Europe faced a difficult future after the war. Poland was seen as a vast Jewish graveyard after the Holocaust, and some Poles proved hostile to the Jewish survivors, seeing them as communists. On 4 July 1946 there was a pogrom in Kielce in which forty Jews were killed.[43]

Many Jews then chose to leave the country, including survivors of the Warsaw ghetto uprising such as Yitzhak Zuckerman, Zivia Lubetkin, and Simha Rotem, and survivors of the ghettos further east such as Abba Kovner. Marek Edelman, however, chose to remain in Poland, where he was active in post-war politics.

Most countries acknowledged the importance of the resistance. Plaques appeared on street walls marking where resisters had been executed, and resistance medals or crosses were widely issued. In Italy, for example, 25 April, the day the northern cities had risen up, is now commemorated as Liberation Day. In France plans were made for a special service honouring the heroes of the Second World War on Armistice Day, 11 November 1945, at which the coffins representing fifteen remains of French citizens would be brought to a service at Les Invalides. The candidates were chosen by ballot to reflect the breadth of France's experience of the war: two who had fought in the resistance, one male and one female; one man and one woman who had been deported but not on racial grounds; two members of the FFI; and nine soldiers from various branches of the service. The coffins were then taken by military escort to the Arc de Triomphe where de Gaulle delivered a brief address acknowledging them as 'symbolic of the many others who chose the path of glory with the same humbleness'.[44] Plans were begun to erect a monument to the resistance at the execution ground of Mont-Valérien. Elsewhere in Europe similar monuments were erected, and museums opened to pass down the story of the resistance to future generations.

Awards were also made to members of the resistance. In 1946 de Gaulle caused some controversy when he personally chose the first recipients of the *Ordre des Compagnons de la Libération* which he had created in 1940. Most of the 1,036 people listed were members of the Free French forces, but only 107 were intelligence agents and 157 members of the internal resistance. Only six were women and Marie-Madeleine Fourcade was a notable absentee, probably because she had worked for SIS and not the BCRA. There was also a strong political bias to the awards: the communist and left wing of the resistance was barely recognized at all and it was apparent that a significant number of names were noted wartime Gaullists, thirty-eight of whom would go on to serve de Gaulle during the Fifth Republic.[45]

SOE secured military or civil awards for many of its agents. Three female agents, Noor Inayat Khan, Violette Szabo, and Odette Sansom, received George Crosses, the highest British civilian award. A significant number of agents received the DSO, the second highest military honour, including Yeo-Thomas and the participants in the Rjukan raid. Some French awards were made as well, and the French were generous in their awards of the Croix de Guerre. Pearl Witherington was indignant to be offered the CBE on the civil side, and rejected it because 'there was nothing civil about what I did'. John Starr was investigated over his conduct in captivity but was not court-martialled, because of the lack of clear evidence against him. Vera Atkins however concluded: 'We feel he let the side down. And he was the only one who did.' John Starr received no British decoration while his brother George received a DSO.[46]

The British showed their gratitude towards those who had worked in the resistance. At the end of September 1944 Maurice Buckmaster led the Judex mission on a seven-month tour of France to meet and thank the people involved in the resistance. The mission travelled through Normandy to Paris and on to Lille and northern France, to Nancy and the east, before covering the Alps, south, central, and south-west France. Buckmaster was accompanied by various SOE agents such as Tony Brooks, George Starr, Yvonne Cormeau, and Claude de Baissac, all of whom wanted him to meet the people they had worked with. Buckmaster recorded:

> As Judex made its way from north to south, the character of its reception became more and more light-hearted and gay. It was evident that the southerners had not borne the same devastating weight of oppression as their compatriots north of the Loire.

Buckmaster helped collect the names of resisters so that they would receive rewards and pensions. He also arranged for the collection of equipment, especially radio sets, which had been parachuted into France during the war and was now needed in the Far East.[47] Tony Brooks later returned to France for a long mission with Robert Bourne-Patterson which assessed the results of the French resistance. MI9 also set up its own awards bureaux in Belgium, the Netherlands, France, and Italy. These bureaux gave helpers on the escape lines certificates to prove their service, and also offered financial compensation for the hardships they had incurred. The financial reward was often rejected, either because the sum offered was too small to compensate for the risks taken, or because the intended recipients thought it unnecessary because they felt that they had only done what they had to and had not acted in the hope of compensation. Donald Darling worked in the awards bureau in Paris and calculated that at least 30,000 civilians had been involved in working on escape lines. In Italy the figure was higher and 75,000 certificates were issued.[48]

The vast majority of resisters and SOE agents returned to civilian life and back to the obscurity from which they had emerged to carry out their great deeds. Some wrote their memoirs, some recorded their experiences for posterity, but most rarely or never spoke of what they had done during the war. Others had acquired a taste for clandestine warfare and continued in the secret services of their countries: Nigel Clive, Tony Brooks, and André Hue all worked for SIS after the war; Virginia Hall, George Musulin, and William Colby joined the CIA; Robert Maloubier joined the French intelligence services. Others got a taste for adventure, such as Stanley Moss who joined another former SOE agent in the search for the missing Reichsbank gold reserves; Billy McLean who joined an organization plotting the overthrow of Enver Hoxha; and Monty Woodhouse who participated in Operation Boot, an Anglo-American plot to overthrow the prime minister of Iran, Mohammad Mossadegh, in the 1950s.

The end of the Second World War meant that there appeared to be little requirement for the secret agencies – SOE and OSS – which had been born from necessity during the war. In autumn 1944 Roosevelt asked Bill Donovan to outline the future of American intelligence services. Donovan argued: 'When our enemies are defeated the demand will be equally pressing for information that will aid us in solving the problems of peace.' He suggested that OSS should become a 'central intelligence service'. Donovan's memorandum was leaked and there was a storm of disapproval in the press. While Roosevelt had been broadly in favour of an intelligence service, Truman was totally hostile to the idea, and OSS was formally disbanded on 20 September 1945. Three years later Truman recognized that the nature of the new world required an intelligence agency after all, and the CIA was founded. In Britain, SOE seemed similarly unnecessary in the post-war world and was under immediate threat of being taken over by SIS at the end of the war. In May 1945 the head of SOE, Lord Selborne, counselled Churchill against such a step:

> In view of the Russian menace, the situation in Italy, Central Europe and the Balkans, and the smouldering volcanoes in the Middle East, I think it would be madness to allow SOE to be stifled at this juncture. In handing it over to the Foreign Office I cannot help feeling that to ask Sir Orme Sargent to supervise SOE is like inviting an abbess to supervise a brothel.

The new Labour government under Clement Attlee felt differently, and on 15 January 1946 SOE was wound up. Its records were transferred to the Foreign Office – and many were destroyed in a fire soon afterwards.[49]

There was an overwhelming desire in western Europe for life to return to normal, for restoration and renewal. In general, the resistance had little impact either on the restoration of democracy or on post-war politics as the political parties resumed business as normal. Post-war elections showed a shift to the left but no great upsurge in support for the communists. The first post-war Danish cabinet acknowledged the importance of the resistance: of the eighteen ministers, nine had worked in the resistance, of whom four had served on the Freedom Council.[50] In France many of the resistance leaders and members of the CNR went on to have illustrious post-war political careers, including Emmanuel d'Astier, Georges Bidault, Jacques Chaban-Delmas, and Christian Pineau. A new, Fourth Republic was created in 1946 which was little different from its predecessor. Frenay commented on the relationship between the resistance and politics: 'All our disappointed nation ever received was a pathetic caricature of the Third Republic. Politically we had failed.'[51] In Italy the challenges of undoing the years of Fascism and the damage of war proved too much for Ferruccio Parri who had succeeded Ivanoe Bonomi as prime minister in June 1945, and he was replaced by Alcide De Gasperi in December. The Action Party, which Parri had helped to found during the war, did not survive the transition to peace, and its membership split between the socialist and republican parties. A few people such as Luigi Longo and Raffaele Cadorna who had come to prominence through the resistance continued in politics. In June 1946 the Italians voted by a 54 to 46 per cent majority to abolish the monarchy.[52] The monarchy similarly struggled to survive in Belgium. Léopold III had made himself unpopular in the country by failing to protest against German policies in Belgium and by concluding an 'unfortunate marriage'. At the end of the war Léopold was in Austria and the prospect of his return led to a government crisis and the political eclipse of the Catholic royalists: he remained outside Belgium and his brother Charles served as regent. In 1950 the new Catholic–Liberal coalition government held a referendum on the return of Léopold, which led to a narrow majority in favour of it. The king arrived back in Brussels in July 1950, but after a week of violent riots he resigned the throne in favour of his son Baudouin.[53]

In Greece, in contrast, the resistance continued to exert an enormous influence over post-war politics. The conflict of right against left, royalists against republicans, led a series of short-lived Greek governments. The former *andartes* of ELAS found themselves viewed as the enemy, especially by their wartime adversary, Napoleon Zervas, who served as minister for public order in 1947 and ordered the mass arrests of communists. Members of ELAS were not allowed to join the new National Guard even though former members of the collaborationist Security Battalions were welcomed. Stefanos Sarafis bitterly commented about the claim that ELAS:

> . . . did nothing but kill Greeks and cause ruin [which] is the answer given by many former collaborators who ought now to be in jail and by those of bad faith who want to justify their own attitude and inactivity during the occupation and who, since *they* did not do their duty, now seek to present those who did as having caused nothing but harm.

A referendum on the future of the monarchy in September 1946 led to a majority of 68 per cent in favour of the king's return, though Allied overseers reported widespread fraud by the monarchists. George II returned to Greece at the end of September 1946 and reigned until his death in April 1947, when he was succeeded by his son: the monarchy was abolished in Greece in 1973. The irreconcilable split between left and right, evident during the war, led to a much bloodier civil war between March 1946 and October 1949.[54]

In eastern Europe the population could not be split clearly between those who had resisted the German occupation and those who had collaborated with it. In this region there were shades of collaboration – for example, there were those who had collaborated with the Germans at times simply because they saw the communists as the greater enemy. There were also others, notably in the countries of central Europe which had started the war on the side of the Axis but had then switched sides, whose initial collaboration might have been offset by their later resistance, though this was more often political than military. Still others, especially in Poland, had resisted the Germans throughout the occupation but now found themselves labelled as 'collaborators' by the occupying Soviet authorities and the new communist-dominated provisional government. Indeed, politics threw a deep shadow over the resistance narrative in eastern Europe as the new communist-dominated regimes sought to redefine wartime resistance by exaggerating and extolling the efforts of the insignificant number of wartime communist resisters and downplaying or ignoring the much greater efforts of those in the democratic resistance. For the latter the end of the war and the events of the ensuing years marked their defeat. At the end of the war in May 1945 the only assured communist regime was Tito's in Yugoslavia. Elsewhere the communists dominated but cooperated with the democratic parties. But by the end of 1948 communism had taken over totally, forcing the democratic politicians who had sponsored the wartime resistance such as Stanisław Mikołajczyk and Edvard Beneš, and many participants in that resistance such as Stefan Korboński and Radomír Luža, to flee into exile or face imprisonment in their home countries.

The collaboration of some leaders was indisputable. The Croatian leader

Ante Pavelić managed to elude justice and left Austria for Argentina, but the Serb leader Milan Nedić was handed over by the British to the Yugoslav authorities in January 1946 and allegedly committed suicide in prison a month later. In Hungary members of the fascist Arrow Cross were tried as collaborators and their guilt was obvious: for example, Ferenc Szálasi was returned to Hungary by the Americans, then tried, sentenced to death, and executed in 1946. Of the other Hungarian wartime leaders, Admiral Horthy was held under house arrest by the Americans in Germany before being allowed to move to Portugal in 1950, and Miklós Kállay went into exile in the United States. In Romania both Ion and Mihai Antonescu were tried by a People's Tribunal, sentenced to death, and executed in June 1946.

In the newly re-formed Czechoslovakia there were many wartime collaborators and the most notable of them were put on trial. The former president Emil Hácha died in prison awaiting trial, and the former propaganda minister Emanuel Moravec committed suicide, but the Sudeten leader Karl Frank was tried, found guilty, and executed. Over 30,000 people were charged and tried in the higher courts, and of these 700 were executed. Lower courts tried 135,000 cases of 'offences against national honour', people who had voluntarily elected to be considered German rather than Czech, sentencing those found guilty to prison. At the same time transports were 'cleansing' the country of its substantial German population.[55]

The new Czechoslovak constitution granted equality to the Czech lands and to Slovakia in an attempt to heal the wounds caused by the wartime partition. This meant that Beneš had to take care when it came to putting the wartime Slovak leader, Jozef Tiso, on trial. Beneš determined that Tiso should be tried in Bratislava by the Slovaks and most of the prosecuting team and judges were veterans of the 1944 Slovak uprising. After a trial lasting four months Tiso was found guilty of collaboration and was sentenced to death. Pleas for clemency fell on deaf ears and he was executed on 18 April 1947: 'With his execution, Tiso was transformed into competing symbols of the Slovak wartime experience: war criminal and Slovak martyr.' As communism took over in Czechoslovakia, Tiso was seen more favourably in Slovakia as a martyr to Bolshevism and as a national hero. After the amicable split between the Czech Republic and Slovakia in 1993 more apologists have emerged extolling Tiso's virtues.[56]

Those who had participated in the coups in Bulgaria and Romania which took their countries out of the Axis and onto the Soviet side faced persecution by the incoming communist regimes. In Bulgaria the new government under the leadership of the former head of the Comintern, Georgi Dimitrov, put the last two wartime prime ministers on trial. Ivan Bagrianov was convicted of war crimes by a tribunal and was executed, and Konstantin Muraviev was briefly imprisoned and then retired from politics. The monarchy was abolished in 1946 after a referendum, and the last King of Bulgaria, Simeon II, who had been a minor during the war, went into exile in Spain. King Michael of Romania refused to sign communist decrees and was forced to abdicate in December 1947 and went into exile in Switzerland. His fellow wartime conspirators, Dinu Brătianu and Dumitru Dămăceanu, also faced trial and imprisonment at the hands of the communists. The hope of the western Allies during the war, Iuliu Maniu, was persecuted and eventually sent to prison, where he died.

The fate of those who collaborated with the Germans because they saw the Soviets as the greater enemy is still controversial. General Vlasov had created the ROA, the Russian Liberation Army, from renegade Russians who despised the Soviet system. Vlasov was caught by Slovak partisans and sent to Moscow where he was tried and executed in 1946. The men serving under him were also returned to the Soviet Union where they were sent to the Gulag. The western Allies handed over 34,000 Cossacks to the Soviet Union. These men were undoubtedly collaborators in that they had served willingly under the command of the Germans and had been notably violent in their application of anti-partisan warfare in both eastern and western Europe. Yet many of them were not and had never been Soviet citizens, having left Russia during the civil war. Most of the Cossack officers were executed by the Soviets and their men sent to the Gulag.[57] Various anti-communist formations had been sponsored by the Germans in the Baltic States. Most of the Latvian Legion had reached American lines and were disarmed and permitted to enter camps for displaced persons. However, around 5,000–6,000 refugees from the Baltic States had reached the sanctuary of Sweden by the end of the war. Some of them had served in German formations and the Soviets put pressure on Sweden to return them. In January 1946, 151 Latvian soldiers, seven Estonians, and nine Lithuanians were forcibly turned over to the Soviets who despatched them to the Gulag.[58]

A civil war had raged in Yugoslavia between the Partisans and all non-Partisan formations during much of the Axis occupation, and some of the non-Partisans had sought weapons from the Germans in order to save themselves from the Partisans. At the end of the wars, both the civil war in Yugoslavia and the world war in Europe, there was a flood of non-communist Yugoslav refugees entering Austria into the British zone of occupation. The British were uncertain how to deal with these refugees. Hidden among them were undoubtedly some Ustaše who were guilty of war crimes, and some Četniks who had collaborated with the Axis forces, but the majority were just people who despised the communism of the Partisans. The refugees were met in Austria by the Welsh Guards whose task was to assign them to different camps according to nationality and political affiliation, as well as to disarm them all. The British then decided to repatriate the Serbs and Četniks. The first transport left on 24 May 1945, and the first transport of Slovenes took place three days later. Three Serb officers returned to the camps in Austria and informed those in charge that the men had been handed over to the Partisans and then been taken into the woods and executed: 'An indescribable sorrow and agony came over those still in the camp after the full truth of the British betrayal became known.' The Canadian officer in charge of the camp containing Slovene refugees informed the British command in Klagenfurt, and the transports were halted. By then around 18,500 Croats, Serbs, and Slovenes had been forcibly repatriated by the British and then executed by the Partisans. After the transports were halted the remaining refugees were allowed to go to refugee camps in Italy or in Germany.[59]

At the end of the war in Europe it was soon clear that Tito and the Partisans had completely taken over Yugoslavia. In May 1945 the British and American missions were withdrawn, but they had already witnessed the excesses perpetrated by the Partisans and the new secret police, the OZNA (*Odjeljenje za zaštitu naroda*, Department for People's Protection), against their political opponents. Ivan Šubašić resigned as prime minister in March 1945 and in the elections that followed in November the Popular Front swept to power. It promptly declared Yugoslavia a republic and King Peter II never returned to the country. He chose to settle in exile in the United States, where he died in 1970; in 2013 his remains were re-interred in Serbia. Following the war, civil rights were curtailed, the inviolability of private property ignored, and only the Communist Party was allowed to exist. In the 1950s, after Tito had split with Stalin, his close wartime associate Milovan Djilas began to criticize the one-party state and thereafter served various prison terms for his views. Tito died in 1980, and the united federal state of Yugoslavia that he had created began to fall apart before descending into a series of vicious civil wars in the 1990s, which led to the break-up of the country into independent constituent republics.[60]

It was against this backdrop of total communist domination and the actions of the OZNA that one must consider the fate of the Četnik resistance leader Draža Mihailović, who was captured on 12 March 1946 and taken to Belgrade to be tried for treason. Mihailović had been extolled by the Allies as the first major leader of a resistance movement in 1941 and then abandoned by them at the end of 1943. These Allies, Britain and the

United States, now realized that Tito and the Partisans were not the people they had thought: they were communists first and foremost and they had not resisted the Germans to anything like the extent expected. On 9 April 1946 Churchill wrote to the foreign secretary Ernest Bevin asking for the British government to intervene to secure a fair trial for Mihailović. Five of the BLOs (British Liaison Officers) who had served with Mihailović submitted a joint deposition in his defence through the Foreign Office. In the United States a committee for a fair trial for Mihailović established a commission of inquiry which cross-examined the American airmen who had been shot down over Serbia and had been sheltered by Mihailović's forces. The report produced stated: 'On the surface there appears to be a direct and irreconcilable contradiction between the facts testified to by these many Americans and the documents that have been published in several volumes in Belgrade and the United States.'[61]

There was little doubt that Mihailović would not receive a fair trial. A mass of documents had been accumulated by the prosecution, but he was given little time to examine them. The proceedings of the trial reveal that Mihailović had remarkably little control over the bands of men who called themselves Četniks. He was, in fact, one of many Četnik leaders, some of whom had collaborated closely with the occupying forces, and others who had done so temporarily in order to obtain weapons. In his closing statement Mihailović reflected on the helplessness that he had felt during the war:

> I found myself in a whirl of events and intrigues. I found myself in a whirl of events and stirrings . . . Destiny was merciless towards me when it threw me into the most difficult whirlwind. I wanted much, I began much, but the whirlwind, the world whirlwind, carried me and my work away.

The trial of Mihailović opened on 10 June 1946. On 15 July he was found guilty and sentenced to death, and he was executed two days later.[62] The search for his grave still continues.

In Poland the process of branding the members of the AK as collaborators had begun during the war when the incoming Soviet armies and the NKVD began rounding up AK partisans and despatching them to Siberia. In March 1945 fifteen senior members of the AK and the Underground Government were invited for talks with the Soviets, whereupon they were arrested, transported to Moscow, and put on trial in June 1945. They all received prison sentences: Leopold Okulicki and Jan Jankowski received the longest terms and both died in prison. The new provisional Polish government was dominated by communists and was recognized by the

Soviet Union in January 1945 and by Britain and the United States in July, thus abandoning the wartime government-in-exile. A former wartime prime minister of the Polish government-in-exile, Stanisław Mikołajczyk, returned to Poland where his Peasant Party shared power with the communists until a referendum in 1946 and fraudulent elections in 1947 brought the communists to total power.[63]

The new communist government intensified the process of hounding down the AK, and its work was assisted by the new Polish secret police force, the *Urząd Bezpieczeństwa*. Members of the *Cichociemni* were arrested and imprisoned, treated as collaborators. Adam Benrad reported: 'In the same cell where I was, there were four parachutists from London', and Stanisław Kujawiński reported that he received two death sentences, one for belonging to the AK, and the other for not joining the Polish communist army, as well as five years for possessing a radio. Members of the AK often shared prison cells with senior Nazis. For example, Kazimierz Moczarski was incarcerated with the destroyer of the Warsaw ghetto uprising, Jürgen Stroop; Emil Fieldorf shared a cell with the SS and Police Leader of the Lublin district, Jakob Sporrenberg; and Władysław Bartoszewski was with SS-Hauptsturmführer Erich Engels. Indeed, the communist authorities were keener to prosecute the AK than the senior Nazis they had captured. The only crime of these Poles was that they were not communists, and no evidence of any collaboration with the Germans ever emerged.[64]

The Polish forces in exile tried to obtain information about what was going on in their country. Witold Pilecki had joined the Polish II Corps in Italy after his release from a German POW camp at the end of the war. While in Italy he wrote his Auschwitz report, a collection of the evidence he had gathered while a prisoner there before his escape and later participation in the Warsaw Uprising. In December 1945 Pilecki returned to Poland to organize an intelligence network to report on events in Poland for the Polish II Corps. He was arrested by the Polish authorities in May 1947 and was repeatedly tortured before being put on trial in March 1948. Pilecki denied planning the assassination of officials of the ministry of public security, but admitted the other charges, including that of passing information to the II Corps. He defended himself by stating that as an officer of that corps he was not breaking any laws. He was sentenced to death in May and was executed.[65]

Across eastern and central Europe and in Yugoslavia the new communist regimes stole the history of the resistance. In Warsaw, speeches at the 20th anniversary commemoration of the Warsaw Uprising spoke of the 'lunacy and political diversion' of the AK leadership, while at the same time praising the efforts of the common AK soldiers and the people of Warsaw. Across the countries behind the Iron Curtain the communist line was that 'the democratic resistance had not been important, that it was the communists in the underground who had waged the significant resistance struggle'.[66] This was manifestly untrue in every country except Yugoslavia. However, even there it has to be argued that the Partisans showed greater energy and intent on destroying their internal enemies than in resisting or waging warfare against the Germans.

'It was only just worth it.' That was the conclusion that Major Dick Barry, a staff officer with SOE, reached when summarizing the value of SOE during the war. It is, however, an equally valuable comment when considering the purpose of resistance as a whole throughout Europe. This book has considered the question in three sections: 'Why Resist?'; 'Growing the Resistance'; and 'Resistance in Action'. Running throughout the book were two major themes: who was the enemy? and the problem of command and control. These themes will now be considered in reverse order in an attempt to reach some sort of conclusion on the value and purpose of the resistance in Europe during the Second World War.

It is all too easy to dismiss the military value of the resistance since no resistance movement actually liberated its own country. Yet the resistance's role in assisting the Allies who did liberate those countries was still of some importance. The resistance in both western and eastern Europe hampered German operations by slowing the arrival of reinforcements at the front, although these activities were valuable only when the Allies were nearby. When Basil Liddell Hart interviewed a number of German generals after the war, none of them said that the resistance had had any effect whatsoever on the conduct of German military operations: 'They rarely became more than a nuisance unless they coincided with the fact, or imminent threat, of a powerful offensive that absorbed the enemy's main attention.'[67] Where resistance initiatives were concerned, such as the uprisings in Warsaw and Slovakia, the liberation of the Vercors in France, and areas of northern Italy, the resistance was too weak to withstand the German reaction. Sabotage operations were also more of a nuisance than a war-changing activity (with the possible exception of the destruction of the heavy-water plant at Rjukan), and the real value of sabotage and small-scale attacks by the resistance lay in their frequency, making the Germans aware of the vulnerability of their control of the occupied territories. There was, however, one field in which the role of the resistance was vital – the provision of intelligence. The sheer number of agents on the ground reporting what they had seen and where they had seen it helped the Allies to deploy air power to investigate further, or even, as in the case of Peenemünde, to bomb an installation of strategic significance. This continued even after the Allies had landed in Europe, and information supplied by the resistance was extremely helpful in pinpointing the location of German units, and in providing information on the likely obstacles to be faced or the German plan of attack.

Resistance was a minority activity throughout the war, even towards the end of it, but as the war progressed it became an increasingly more attractive option than collaboration (also the choice of a minority) and the more prevailing *attentisme*. The principal motivators for the increase in resistance were the Germans themselves. In the first part of the war, before the invasion of the Soviet Union in June 1941, the population of western Europe was left largely unaffected by the German occupation. In occupied Poland it was different, as the application of German racial ideology and the destruction not just of Poland but of Polishness meant that resistance was an attractive option from the start. The failure of the Germans to take Moscow before the winter of 1941–42 meant that the war would be a long one. The result was a severe shortage of German manpower and the consequent introduction of two polices which affected the whole of Europe – the Holocaust and forced labour. The response of the non-Jewish resistance to the Holocaust was limited. The forced-labour decrees, on the other hand, affected most families in Europe, and avoidance of the decrees implied a fall into criminality, whether by passive evasion or active resistance. Thus it was that German actions led to the creation of nations 'united in resistance', a valid concept despite its exaggeration and over-emphasis by post-war politicians. The numbers engaged in active resistance still remained small, but they now began to receive more support from the wider population. This process of creating wider support for the resistance had been one of the purposes of the clandestine press which developed in every occupied country, to publicize the misdeeds of the Germans and the achievements of the resistance, as well as to maintain the morale of the population.

One frequently overlooked aspect of the resistance was the battle against the internal enemy. In Norway and the Netherlands the passive resistance of the population to efforts by the fascist NS and NSB to nazify their countries was totally successful.

The role of SOE in creating the resistance has been exaggerated. On the other hand, notwithstanding its detractors' criticism of its actions as being ineffective or disastrous or having led to unexpected and undesirable consequences, SOE was important simply because it existed. As its official historian, William Mackenzie, concluded:

> While SOE was at work no European politician could be under the illusion that the British were uninterested or deaf; he might have reason to believe that they were incompetent or sinister, but he was bound to take account of them. The young men whom SOE turned loose on the continent, and the department which backed them, had to be reckoned with seriously by Germany, by Russia, by every political organisation in Europe. They were an important part of history.[68]

The fact that SOE had agents on the ground in every country, as 'a sort of living presence', proved to the native resistance that they had not been abandoned to their fate by the Allies.[69]

Despite the ubiquity of SOE, neither it nor the Allied politicians and planners ever achieved total command and control over the resistance. For example, in the Balkans they were unable to prevent the descent of Yugoslavia, Greece, and Albania into civil war, and indeed the provision of weapons by the Allies to the resistance movements facilitated and encouraged the communists' focus on their internal enemies rather than the Germans. Elsewhere, the Allies were helpless in preventing uprisings or the liberation of portions of territory by the resistance. These actions overextended the limited resources of the resistance and led to a series of disasters. Where uprisings succeeded, such as in Paris, and the northern cities of Italy, they did so because the Allies were close at hand, able and willing to assist, and the Germans had already accepted the need to abandon those areas.

It is hard to pin down why certain people chose the path of resistance, and the resisters themselves often give unsatisfactory responses: 'one had to do something' or 'one just did what one could'. Overall, one can conclude that resistance was 'a spontaneous reaction to oppression, of the soul even more than of the body'.[70] Resistance was a completely unknown way of life, as Jean Cassou, a resistance leader in Toulouse, tried to explain:

> It stays in our memories as a unique period, quite unlike any other experience, something impossible to relate to or explain, almost a dream. We see ourselves there utterly free and naked, an unknown and unknowable version of ourselves, the kind of people no one can ever find again, who existed only in relation to unique and terrible conditions, to things that have since disappeared, to ghosts, or to the dead.[71]

Indeed, the memory of resistance has proved to be more important to the concept of the nation state in the post-war years than the resistance itself was strategically during the time of war. National memories and mythologies demanded a narrative of a united 'nation in resistance', and the uncomfortable truths of divided loyalties had to be overlooked. These distorted memories and myths are necessary because few actually took part in the resistance. Ultimately, the real value of resistance was, as Roger Stéphane wrote:

> This refusal [to accept German victory] allowed us to look at a Russian, British or American soldier without blushing . . . Never have so many men consciously run so many risks for such a small thing; a desire to bear witness. Perhaps it is absurd, but it was by such absurdities that we restored our dignity as men.[72]

Notes

ABBREVIATIONS

AK Documents: H. Czarnocka et al., *Armia Krajowa w dokumentach 1939–1945*
APHC: T. Stirling, D. Nałęcz, and T. Dubicki (eds), *Intelligence Co-operation between Poland and Great Britain during World War II*, vol. I: *The Report of the Anglo-Polish Historical Committee*; vol. II: *Documents*
DGFP: *Documents on German Foreign Policy*
DPSR: Sikorski Institute, *Documents on Polish-Soviet Relations*
FRUS: *Foreign Relations of the United States*
IWM: Imperial War Museum, London
PISM: Polish Institute and Sikorski Museum, London
Stalin Correspondence: *Correspondence between the Chairman of the Council of Ministers of the USSR and the Presidents of the USA and the Prime Ministers of Great Britain during the Great Patriotic War of 1941–1945*
TNA: The National Archives, Kew

INTRODUCTION

1 H. Friedhoff, *Requiem for the Resistance*, 31
2 S. Purnell, *A Woman of No Importance*, 102
3 J. Nowak, *Courier from Warsaw*, 169
4 V. Laska (ed.), *Women in the Resistance and in the Holocaust*, 93
5 E. Hazelhoff, *Soldier of Orange*, 15
6 S. Kent and N. Nicholas, *Agent Michael Trotobas and SOE in Northern France*, 79–80
7 H. Despaigne, IWM 9925
8 'War of the Unknown Warriors', 14 July 1940, BBC Sound Archives
9 D. Schoenbrun, *Soldiers of the Night*, 489
10 H. Michel, *The Shadow War*, 220–21
11 R. Bennett, *Under the Shadow of the Swastika*, 173
12 G. Millar, *Maquis*, 239; J. Doneux, *They Arrived by Moonlight*, 102–3
13 M. Adamson, IWM, 12687.

1. THE SHOCK OF DEFEAT

1 M. Macmillan, *Peacemakers*, 242–53
2 J. Mace Ward, *Priest, Politician, Collaborator*, 181–2; J. Lettrich, *History of Modern Slovakia*, 133
3 *DGFP*, D, IV, 186
4 Ibid., D, IV, 270

5 P. Wilkinson, *Foreign Fields*, 58
6 V. Mastny, *The Czechs under Nazi Rule*, 58
7 Consul General Linnell to chargé in Berlin, 14 April 1939, in G. Kennan, *From Prague after Munich*, 117–18
8 Lettrich, *History of Modern Slovakia*, 139; Ward, *Priest, Politician, Collaborator*, 195; M. Mazower, *Hitler's Empire*, 61
9 G. Rhode, 'The Protectorate of Bohemia and Moravia, 1939–1945', in V. Mamatey and R. Luža (eds), *A History of the Czechoslovak Republic, 1918–1948*, 296–321
10 Mastny, *The Czechs under Nazi Rule*, 53
11 Macmillan, *Peacemakers*, 292, 368, 374
12 B. Fischer, *Albania at War, 1939–1945*, 43
13 A. Maisner, IWM 916
14 *AK Documents*, vol. I, 2
15 H. Kochanski, *The Eagle Unbowed*, 96–100
16 D. Littlejohn, *The Patriotic Traitors*, 56–7; W. Rings, *Life with the Enemy*, 27–8; N. A. Sørensen, 'Narrating the Second World War in Denmark since 1945', *Contemporary European History*, 14:3 (2005), 295–315
17 P. Hayes, *Quisling*, 216–17
18 O. Hoidal, *Quisling*, 379
19 Hayes, *Quisling*, 257, 265–7; *DGFP*, D, IX, 161; T. Gjelsvik, *Norwegian Resistance*, 9
20 H. Dahl, *Quisling*, 186
21 G.S. Gordon, *The Norwegian Resistance during the German Occupation, 1940–1945*, 12
22 J. Dewulf, *Spirit of Resistance*, 149; M. R. D. Foot, *SOE in the Low Countries*, 18–19; L. De Jong, 'The Dutch Resistance Movement and the Allies 1940–1945', in *European Resistance Movements, 1939–1945: Second International Conference on the History of the Resistance Movements*, 340–65
23 W. Warmbrunn, *The Dutch under German Occupation*, 121–2; Littlejohn, *Patriotic Traitors*, 91–2
24 R. Allen, *Churchill's Guests*, 13
25 W. Warmbrunn, *The German Occupation of Belgium*, 48–9; R. Keyes, *Outrageous Fortune*, 359, 382–3
26 J. Geller, 'The Role of Military Administration in German-Occupied Belgium, 1940–1944', *Journal of Military History*, 63:1 (1999), 99–125; Warmbrunn, *The German Occupation of Belgium*, 72, 105
27 Foot, *SOE in the Low Countries*, 240
28 N. Rich, *Hitler's War Aims*, II, 200; J. Jackson, *France: The Dark Years*, 126–9
29 Macmillan, *Peacemakers*, 133
30 W. Roberts, *Tito, Mihailović and the Allies*, 5
31 M. Deroc, *British Special Operations Explored*, 157–9; J. Tomasevich, *Occupation and Collaboration*, 182; Rich, *Hitler's War Aims*, II, 289
32 Tomasevich, *Occupation and Collaboration*, 61–3
33 Ibid., 61–3, 83; T. Kirk, 'Limits of Germandom: Resistance to the Nazi Annexation of Slovenia', *Slavonic and East European Review*, 69:4 (1991), 646–67
34 Diary entry, 26 May 1939, in M. Muggeridge (ed.), *The Ciano Diaries*, 93; Tomasevich, *Occupation and Collaboration*, 50, 60–3; Mazower, *Hitler's Empire*, 346
35 M. Mazower, *Inside Hitler's Greece*, 20–2; A. Gerolymatos, *Guerrilla Warfare and Espionage in Greece*, 169; Rich, *Hitler's War Aims*, II, 304; D. Rodogno, *Fascism's European Empire*, 203
36 O. Wieviorka, *The Resistance in Western Europe, 1940–1945*, 20
37 Rich, *Hitler's War Aims*, I, 151
38 Rodogno, *Fascism's European Empire*, 70
39 Kochanski, *The Eagle Unbowed*, 105
40 C. Chevrillon, *Codename Christiane Clouet*, 11
41 J.-P. Lévy, *Mémoires d'un franc-tireur*, 35
42 Keyes, *Outrageous Fortune*, 420–22

43 R. Gildea, *Marianne in Chains*, 90
44 D. Boyd, *Voices from the Dark Years*, 50, 100
45 M. Milač, *Resistance, Imprisonment, and Forced Labour*, 34; Mazower, *Hitler's Empire*, 203–4; Tomasevich, *Occupation and Collaboration*, 87, 91–2
46 F. P. Verna, 'Notes on Italian Rule in Dalmatia under Bastianini, 1941–1943', *International History Review*, 12:3 (1990), 441–60; D. Martin (ed.), *Patriot or Traitor*, 42
47 Kochanski, *The Eagle Unbowed*, 102–3
48 S. Pavlowitch, *Hitler's New Disorder*, 21
49 R. Paxton, *Vichy France*, 44
50 M. Hastings, *All Hell Let Loose*, 125
51 Boyd, *Voices from the Dark Years*, 55–6; Hastings, *All Hell Let Loose*, 128
52 A. Koestler, *Scum of the Earth*, 184
53 Otto Kaurin Nielsen quoted in Gordon, *The Norwegian Resistance*, 13.

2. CHOICES

1 S. Grant Duff, *A German Protectorate*, 242
2 J.-P. Sartre quoted in Bennett, *Under the Shadow of the Swastika*, ix
3 Michel, *The Shadow War*, 71
4 K. Kunicki, 'Unwanted Collaborators: Leon Kozłowski, Władysław Studnicki and the Problems of Collaboration among Polish Conservative Politicians in World War II', *European Review of History*, 8 (2001), 203–20
5 Dahl, *Quisling*, 187
6 Mastny, *The Czechs under Nazi Rule*, 159
7 Littlejohn, *The Patriotic Traitors*, 189–211; D. Pryce-Jones, *Paris in the Third Reich*, 221–2; B. Gordon, 'The Condottieri of the Collaboration: *Mouvement Social Révolutionnaire*', *Journal of Contemporary History*, 10:2 (1975), 261–82; S. Kitson, *The Hunt for Nazi Spies*, 31–2
8 R. Griffiths, *Marshal Pétain*, 270
9 Diary entry, 13 July 1940, P. Baudouin, *The Private Diaries (March 1940 to January 1941)*, 167
10 S. Hoffmann, 'Collaboration in France during World War II', *Journal of Modern History*, 40:3 (1968), 375–95; Griffiths, *Marshal Pétain*, 276
11 Pétain speech, 12 August 1941, quoted in P. Davies, *Dangerous Liaisons*, 82
12 Littlejohn, *The Patriotic Traitors*, 87–9, 102
13 Warmbrunn, *The German Occupation of Belgium*, 32–3, 110–2; Geller, 'The Role of Military Administration in German-Occupied Belgium'; Littlejohn, *The Patriotic Traitors*, 149–50; Rings, *Life with the Enemy*, 99–100; M. Conway, *Collaboration in Belgium*, 45–6, 76
14 Michel, *The Shadow War*, 39
15 Jan Stránský quoted in Mastny, *The Czechs under Nazi Rule*, 21
16 Kochanski, *The Eagle Unbowed*, 101–2
17 Rings, *Life with the Enemy*, 80
18 R. Gildea, D. Luyten, and J. Fürst, 'To Work or Not to Work?', in R. Gildea, O. Wieviorka, and A. Warring (eds), *Surviving Hitler and Mussolini*, 42–87; C. Bryant, *Prague in Black*, 85; Gildea, *Marianne in Chains*, 83–4; Rings, *Life with the Enemy*, 76–7; P. Giltner, 'The Success of Collaboration: Denmark's Self-Assessment of its Economic Position after Five Years of Nazi Occupation', *Journal of Contemporary History*, 36:3 (2001), 485–506
19 G. Hirschfeld, *Nazi Rule and Dutch Collaboration*, 191
20 Mazower, *Hitler's Empire*, 188; C. Bryant, 'Either German or Czech: Fixing Nationality in Bohemia and Moravia, 1939–1946', *Slavic Review*, 61:4 (2002), 683–706
21 Kochanski, *The Eagle Unbowed*, 103–4
22 Littlejohn, *The Patriotic Traitors*, 58, 62

23 Bryant, *Prague in Black*, 87
24 W.B. Maass, *The Netherlands at War*, 89
25 Hirschfeld, *Nazi Rule*, 60–61; G. Hirschfeld, 'Collaboration and Attentisme in the Netherlands 1940–41', *Journal of Contemporary History*, 16:3 (1981), 467–86
26 Grant Duff, *A German Protectorate*, 173
27 Rhode, 'The Protectorate of Bohemia and Moravia'; Grant Duff, *A German Protectorate*, 176; Rings, *Life with the Enemy*, 109–10
28 Letter from Linnel, 11 May 1939, in Kennan, *From Prague after Munich*, 157
29 Bryant, *Prague in Black*, 86
30 Mastny, *The Czechs under Nazi Rule*, 62–3; Rhode, 'The Protectorate of Bohemia and Moravia'
31 Hirschfeld, *Nazi Rule*, 61–3
32 Warmbrunn, *The Dutch under German Occupation*, 133–4; Hirschfeld, *Nazi Rule*, 71–2; M. L. Smith, 'Neither Resistance nor Collaboration: Historians and the Problem of the *Nederlandse Unie*', *History*, 72: 235 (1987), 251–78
33 Hirschfeld, 'Collaboration and Attentisme in the Netherlands'; Warmbrunn, *The Dutch under German Occupation*, 136; Hirschfeld, *Nazi Rule*, 79–81
34 Hayes, *Quisling*, 267–74
35 R. Hewins, *Quisling*, 206; Hoidal, *Quisling*, 472; P. Hansson, *The Greatest Gamble*, 50
36 P. de Vomécourt, *Who Lived to See the Day*, 23
37 Le Cure Alvitre quoted in H. Kedward, *Resistance in Vichy France*, 256
38 Boyd, *Voices from the Dark Years*, 44
39 Rémy, *The Silent Company*, 336
40 O. Wieviorka, *The French Resistance*, 332
41 R. Vinen, *The Unfree French*, 51
42 R. Murphy, *Diplomat among Warriors*, 82
43 J. Lacouture, *De Gaulle*, 243–4
44 Kedward, *Resistance in Vichy France*, 11
45 Jackson, *France*, 185
46 Ibid., 233
47 R. Paxton, *Vichy France*, 20
48 Boyd, *Voices from the Dark Years*, 68; Rings, *Life with the Enemy*, 45
49 M. Dank, *The French against the French*, 89; R. Austin, 'Political Surveillance and Ideological Control', in H. Kedward and R. Austin (eds), *Vichy France and the Resistance*, 13–35
50 Boyd, *Voices from the Dark Years*, 91
51 Paxton, *Vichy France*, 210–11
52 Boyd, *Voices from the Dark Years*, 36–8; Paxton, *Vichy France*, 164; J. Sweets, *Choices in Vichy France*, 61
53 Sweets, *Choices in Vichy France*, 64–73
54 H. Kedward, *Occupied France*, 32; Paxton, *Vichy France*, 51
55 Sweets, *Choices in Vichy France*, 174
56 Quoted in Kedward, *Resistance in Vichy France*, 16; André Gide quoted in G. Hirschfeld, 'Collaboration in Nazi-Occupied France', in G. Hirschfeld and P. Marsh (eds), *Collaboration in France*, 1–14
57 Hazelhoff, *Soldier of Orange*, Preface.

3. THE CLANDESTINE PRESS

1 Michel, *The Shadow War*, 90–91
2 P. Mangold, *Britain and the Defeated French*, 116
3 Kedward, *Occupied France*, 54

4 Bryant, *Prague in Black*, 39; J. Hronek, *Volcano under Hitler*, 110
5 J. Garliński, 'The Polish Underground State 1939–45', *Journal of Contemporary History*, 10 (1975), 219–59
6 Michel, *The Shadow War*, 95
7 Warmbrunn, *The Dutch under German Occupation*, 226
8 Jackson, *France*, 403
9 H. Stone, *Writing in the Shadow*, 63
10 P. Sanders, "Radio Days", in G. Carr et al. (eds), *Protest, Defiance and Resistance in the Channel Islands*, 65–96
11 Rings, *Life with the Enemy*, 168; Stone, *Writing in the Shadow*, 183–4. Examples include: Poland – *Biuletyn Informacyjny*; *Wiadomości Polski*; *zołnierz Polski*; *Insurekcja*; Belgium – *La Libre Belgique*; *Liberté*; *Voix de la Belge*; Netherlands – *Vrij Nederland*; *Je maintiendrai*; *Het Parool*; *De Waarheid*; *Trouw*; Denmark – *Frit Danmark*; *De Frie Danske*; *Information*; *Land og Folk*; France – *Combat*; *Libération*; *Franc-Tireur*; *Résistance*; *Défense de la France*; *L'Humanité*; Norway – *Norgesposten*; *Alt for Norge*; *For Friheiten*
12 H. Noguères et al., *Histoire de la Résistance en France*, I, 468
13 Mazower, *Hitler's Empire*, 475–6
14 J. Semelin, *Unarmed against Hitler*, 37
15 Diary entry, 18 June 1940, A. Humbert, *Resistance*, 14
16 *Résistance*, 15 December 1940, quoted in M. Blumenson, *The Vildé Affair*, 117–18
17 M. Ney-Krwawicz, *The Polish Home Army*, 88
18 Quoted in M. Collins Weitz, *Sisters in the Resistance*, 72
19 D. Williamson, *The Polish Underground*, 85
20 Dewulf, *Spirit of Resistance*, 69
21 Warmbrunn, *The Dutch under German Occupation*, 250
22 J. Haestrup, *Europe Ablaze*, 453
23 Boyd, *Voices from the Dark Years*, 146
24 Stone, *Writing in the Shadow*, 74–6
25 W. Lipgens, 'European Federation in the Political Thought of Resistance Movements during World War II', *Central European History*, 1:1 (1968), 5–19
26 H. Frenay, *The Night Will End*, 56
27 S. Korboński, *Fighting Warsaw*, 169
28 T. Bór-Komorowski, *The Secret Army*, 166
29 Frenay, *The Night Will End*, 56
30 De Vomécourt, *Who Lived to See the Day*, 102–3
31 Diary entry, 13 July 1944, A. Gobetti, *Partisan Diary*, 136–7
32 C. Bourdet, *L'Aventure incertaine*, 99–100
33 Sweets, *Choices in Vichy France*, 203; Wieviorka, *The French Resistance*, 64–5
34 For example, Diary entry, 11 March 1943, quoting *Biuletyn Informacyjny*, 4 March 1943, Z. Klukowski, *Diary from the Years of Occupation*, 246
35 Quoted in M. Cobb, *The Resistance*, 224
36 *Combat*, March 1944, J. Lévi-Valensi (ed.), *Camus at Combat*, 1–3
37 Jackson, *France*, 515
38 Lipgens, 'European Federation'
39 Quoted in Stone, *Writing in the Shadow*, 181
40 Warmbrunn, *The Dutch under German Occupation*, 254–5
41 Quoted in Schoenbrun, *Soldiers of the Night*, 159
42 Warmbrunn, *The Dutch under German Occupation*, 255
43 A. Shennan, *Rethinking France*, 47, and passim; Jackson, *France*, 515
44 Quoted in Friedhoff, *Requiem for the Resistance*, 116–17
45 Lipgens, 'European Federation'
46 Dewulf, *Spirit of Resistance*, 88; Stone, *Writing in the Shadow*, 79–80; Garliński, 'The Polish Underground State'

47 Quoted in Weitz, *Sisters in the Resistance*, 74
48 Vercors, *Le Silence de la mer*, 6
49 Gildea, *Marianne in Chains*, 65–7; Weitz, *Sisters in the Resistance*, 75; Jackson, *France*, 441, 501
50 Introduction to J. Steinbeck, *The Moon is Down* (2000), by Donald Coers, vii–xxiv
51 C. Cruickshank, *SOE in Scandinavia*, 213–14
52 Garliński, 'The Polish Underground State'; Williamson, *The Polish Underground*, 85
53 Bór-Komorowski, *The Secret Army*, 168
54 G. Watt, *The Comet Connection*, 142–4; Doneux, *They Arrived by Moonlight*, 90–92; P. Lagrou, 'Belgium', in B. Moore (ed.), *Resistance in Western Europe*, 27–63
55 Wieviorka, *The French Resistance*, 58–9
56 Frenay, *The Night Will End*, 55
57 Stone, *Writing in the Shadow*, 98, 100
58 Weitz, *Sisters in the Resistance*, 73; Dewulf, *Spirit of Resistance*, 90
59 Cruickshank, *SOE in Scandinavia*, 216; Diary entry, 22 September 1940, Humbert, *Resistance*, 17
60 Rings, *Life with the Enemy*, 169
61 Weitz, *Sisters in the Resistance*, 3
62 Bór-Komorowski, *The Secret Army*, 165
63 Wieviorka, *The French Resistance*, 228
64 Friedhoff, *Requiem for the Resistance*, 111–12
65 C. Sutherland, *Monica*, 119–20
66 Stone, *Writing in the Shadow*, 108
67 Bór-Komorowski, *The Secret Army*, 166
68 Stone, *Writing in the Shadow*, 107
69 M. Bles, *Child at War*, 43
70 Cruickshank, *SOE in Scandinavia*, 215
71 Kochanski, *The Eagle Unbowed*, 272
72 R. Gildea, *Fighters in the Shadows*, 177
73 Milač, *Resistance, Imprisonment, and Forced Labour*, 36–7
74 E. Rogers, IWM 16766
75 Jackson, *France*, 411
76 Stone, *Writing in the Shadow*, 83–4; A. Mayer, *Gaston's War*, 101–2
77 Warmbrunn, *The Dutch under German Occupation*, 227–9
78 Dewulf, *Spirit of Resistance*, 2; Lagrou, 'Belgium',
79 Bryant, *Prague in Black*, 94
80 Gildea, *Fighters in the Shadows*, 63; Mangold, *Britain and the Defeated French*, 113
81 J. Bennett, *British Broadcasting and the Danish Resistance Movement 1940–1945*, 4, 51
82 O. Riste and B. Nökleby, *Norway, 1940–45*, 35; A. Morriss, 'The BBC Polish Service during World War II', Unpublished PhD thesis, University of London (2016)
83 Dewulf, *Spirit of Resistance*, 69; Bennett, *British Broadcasting and the Danish Resistance Movement*, 4
84 Michel, *The Shadow War*, 92–3
85 Korboński, *Fighting Warsaw*, 200–206, 212–13
86 Hronek, *Volcano under Hitler*, 122
87 Michel, *The Shadow War*, 93
88 Mangold, *Britain and the Defeated French*, 106
89 M. Stenton, *Radio London and Resistance in Occupied Europe*, 50, 53; Gordon, *The Norwegian Resistance*, 26
90 Stenton, *Radio London*, 55; Bryant, *Prague in Black*, 94–5, 132
91 Gildea, *Fighters in the Shadows*, 63; Mangold, *Britain and the Defeated French*, 114–15
92 Stenton, *Radio London*, 99
93 Bryant, *Prague in Black*, 131–2

94 Bennett, *British Broadcasting and the Danish Resistance Movement*, 42; Cruickshank, *SOE in Scandinavia*, 213–14; Diary entry, 3 September 1941, Klukowski, *Diary from the Years of Occupation*, 170
95 Bryant, *Prague in Black*, 131; Diary entry, 25 July 1941, J. Guéhenno, *Diary of the Dark Years, 1940–1944*, 102
96 Diary entry, 20 April 1942, Guéhenno, *Diary of the Dark Years*, 152
97 Mayer, *Gaston's War*, 54
98 Diary entry, 30 June 1941, Guéhenno, *Diary of the Dark Years*, 96
99 Kedward, *Resistance in Vichy France*, 244
100 Stone, *Writing in the Shadow*, 85
101 Ibid., 174–6; D. Lampe, *The Savage Canary*, 6–10.

4. ESCAPE FROM OCCUPIED EUROPE

1 M. R. D. Foot and J. Langley, *MI9*, 34–5
2 De Vomécourt, *Who Lived to See the Day*, 52–3
3 J. Nichol and T. Rennell, *Home Run*, 453
4 D. Darling, *Secret Sunday*, 166
5 R. Lyman, *The Jail Busters*, 68
6 Quoted in E. Stourton, *Cruel Crossing*, 128
7 F. Kornicki, IWM 8131; S. Baluk, *Silent and Unseen*, 47
8 S. Maczek, *Od Podwody do Czotga*, 97–9
9 Laska (ed.), *Women in the Resistance*, 51
10 Williamson, *The Polish Underground*, 81–3; T. Firth, *Prisoner of the Gestapo*, 60, 81
11 O. Reed Olsen, *Two Eggs on My Plate*, 47–8
12 D. Howarth, *The Shetland Bus*, 9, 75–6
13 Gordon, *The Norwegian Resistance*, 225–6; E. Hauge, *Salt-Water Thief*, 72–112
14 L. Willmot, 'Sabotage, Intelligence-Gathering and Escape', in Carr et al. (eds), *Protest, Defiance and Resistance*, 213–42; B. Turner, *Outpost of Occupation*, 160–2
15 N. Rankin, *Ian Fleming's Commandos*, 208; I. Dear, *Escape and Evasion*, 148–51
16 G. Psychoundakis, *The Cretan Runner*, 46
17 A. Beevor, *Crete*, 241–2; C. Woodhouse, *Something Ventured*, 18
18 E. Shiber, *Paris Underground*, passim; B. Wynne, *No Drums*, 36–100
19 Blumenson, *The Vildé Affair*, 92–3, 136; Cobb, *The Resistance*, 51; Boyd, *Voices from the Dark Years*, 151; Purnell, *A Woman of No Importance*, 69–71
20 Edward Stourton has gathered together a long list. Stourton, *Cruel Crossing*, 209–10
21 J. Langley, *Fight another Day*, 100
22 Maczek, *Od Podwody do Czotga*, 123
23 Dear, *Escape and Evasion*, 42–5; B. Richards, *Secret Flotillas*, 500, 578–9, 656–9
24 Foot and Langley, *MI9*, 66–7
25 D. Caskie, *The Tartan Pimpernel*, 90–108; M. Halls, *Escaping Hitler*, 63; A. Neave, *Saturday at M.I.9*, 83–4; G. Young, *In Trust and Treason*, passim
26 Foot and Langley, *MI9*, 140; Dear, *Escape and Evasion*, 48–9
27 M. R. D. Foot, *Six Faces of Courage*, 81–7; M. R. D. Foot, *SOE in France*, 90–91, 143, 170; Dear, *Escape and Evasion*, 59
28 Foot and Langley, *MI9*, 211–12; Neave, *Saturday at M.I.9*, 217, 221–5
29 Nichol and Rennell, *Home Run*, 228
30 L. Dumais, *The Man Who Went Back*, passim; R. Hemingway-Douglas, *The Shelburne Escape Line*, passim; Foot and Langley, *MI9*, 213
31 Neave, *Saturday at M.I.9*, 69
32 Foot and Langley, *MI9*, 79–81
33 Halls, *Escaping Hitler*, 40
34 A. Neave, *Little Cyclone*, passim
35 Langley, *Fight another Day*, 168

36 Neave, *Little Cyclone*, 142–9
37 H. Bodson, *Downed Allied Airmen and Evasion of Capture*, 130–31
38 C. Jouan, *Comète*, passim
39 M. Koreman, *The Escape Line*, passim
40 Brusselmans, IWM 4795
41 D. Leyton, *The House near Paris*, 131–6
42 Report from Philippe d'Albert-Lake in J. Barrett Litoff (ed.), *An American Heroine in the French Resistance*, 90
43 Darling, *Secret Sunday*, 74
44 Ibid., 135
45 A. Brusselmans, *Rendez-vous 127*, 128; Brusselmans, IWM 4795
46 Halls, *Escaping Hitler*, 97
47 Litoff (ed.), *An American Heroine in the French Resistance*, 96
48 Darling, *Secret Sunday*, 77
49 Stourton, *Cruel Crossing*, passim
50 Darling, *Secret Sunday*, 99
51 Laska (ed.), *Women in the Resistance*, 53
52 Dumais, *The Man Who Went Back*, 157–8
53 Neave, *Saturday at M.I.9*, 146
54 De Vomécourt, *Who Lived to See the Day*, 54
55 Nichol and Rennell, *Home Run*, 172
56 Foot and Langley, *MI9*, 84; Nichol and Rennell, *Home Run*, xxiii, 170; Darling, *Secret Sunday*, 101–2
57 Cobb, *The Resistance*, 51; Brusselmans, *Rendez-vous 127*, passim; B. Cowburn, *No Cloak, No Dagger*, 161; Langley, *Fight another Day*, 198.

5. RESISTERS OF THE FIRST HOUR

1 Swedish newspaper quoted in Grant Duff, *A German Protectorate*, 246
2 Mastny, *The Czechs under Nazi Rule*, 113; H. Paape, 'How Dutch Resistance was Organised', in M. R. D. Foot (ed.), *Holland at War against Hitler*, 68–92; Michel, *The Shadow War*, 83; Semelin, *Unarmed against Hitler*, 74
3 Diary entry, 12 May 1940, in J. Kulski, *Dying, We Live*, 46
4 Mazower, *Hitler's Empire*, 476
5 O. Wieviorka and J. Tebinka, 'Resisters: From Everyday Life to Counter-State', in Gildea et al. (eds), *Surviving Hitler and Mussolini*, 153–76; M. Skodvin, 'Norwegian Non-Violent Resistance during the German Occupation', in A. Roberts (ed.), *The Strategy of Civilian Defence*, 136–53
6 Bryant, *Prague in Black*, 36
7 Gordon, *The Norwegian Resistance*, 247. Glaser escaped to Sweden in 1942
8 Hronek, *Volcano under Hitler*, 105–7
9 Bryant, *Prague in Black*, 59
10 Diary entry, 27 October 1939, in F. Taylor (ed.), *The Goebbels Diaries*, 31–2
11 Rings, *Life with the Enemy*, 36; Bryant, *Prague in Black*, 60; R. Luža, *The Hitler Kiss*, 28
12 Hronek, *Volcano under Hitler*, 58
13 Rhode, 'The Protectorate of Bohemia and Moravia'; Mastny, *The Czechs under Nazi Rule*, 116–17; Bryant, *Prague in Black*, 60–61
14 Kochanski, *The Eagle Unbowed*, 112
15 Quoted in D. Baden-Powell, *Operation Jupiter*, 54
16 Kedward, *Occupied France*, 46
17 Blumenson, *The Vildé Affair*, 102
18 Cobb, *The Resistance*, 44–7; Gildea, *Fighters in the Shadows*, 62–3; Kedward, *Occupied France*, 46
19 Lagrou, 'Belgium'

20 Warmbrunn, *The Dutch under German Occupation*, 148
21 Bryant, *Prague in Black*, 85–6
22 Wieviorka and Tebinka, 'Resisters: From Everyday Life to Counter-State'
23 Paape, 'How Dutch Resistance was Organised'; Haestrup, *Europe Ablaze*, 102–3; Warmbrunn, *The Dutch under German Occupation*, 110
24 Friedhoff, *Requiem for the Resistance*, 86–7
25 Maass, *The Netherlands at War*, 66–7
26 Warmbrunn, *The Dutch under German Occupation*, 111
27 Semelin, *Unarmed against Hitler*, 81–2
28 Wieviorka and Tebinka, 'Resisters: From Everyday Life to Counter-State'
29 Reed Olsen, *Two Eggs on My Plate*, 11–18; Riste and Nökleby, *Norway*, 15
30 Hronek, *Volcano under Hitler*, 83–4
31 G. van Frijtag Drabbe Künzel, 'Resistance, Reprisals, Reactions', in Gildea et al., *Surviving Hitler and Mussolini*, 177–205; TNA, HS 4/163; Williamson, *The Polish Underground*, 8–9, 35
32 Kochanski, *The Eagle Unbowed*, 98
33 G.C. Kiriakopoulos, *The Nazi Occupation of Crete*, 19
34 Kiriakopolous, *The Nazi Occupation of Crete*, 10–34; Beevor, *Crete*, 137–8, 236
35 Schoenbrun, *Soldiers of the Night*, 52
36 Cobb, *The Resistance*, 36–7; Michel, *The Shadow War*, 85
37 Central Commission for the Investigation of German Crimes in Poland, *German Crimes in Poland*, 92
38 T. Laub, *After the Fall*, 103
39 Ibid., 105; S. Piotrowski, *Hans Frank's Diary*, 226
40 1907 Hague Convention, Yale Avalon Project
41 Laub, *After the Fall*, 102–3
42 S. Neitzel and H. Welzer, *Soldaten*, 78
43 1907 Hague Convention, Yale Avalon Project
44 C. Vella, 'The Czech Lands', in P. Cooke and B. Shepherd (eds), *European Resistance*, 52–76
45 Diary entry, 21 November 1939, in Taylor (ed.), *The Goebbels Diaries*, 53
46 Central Commission, *German Crimes in Poland*, 22–3
47 Piotrowski, *Hans Frank's Diary*, 236
48 Kochanski, *The Eagle Unbowed*, 99, 112–15
49 A. Vistel, *Nuit sans ombre*, 13
50 E. d'Astier in *The Sorrow and the Pity*; J. King, 'Emmanuel d'Astier and the Nature of the French Resistance', *Journal of Contemporary History*, 8:4 (1973), 25–45
51 Paxton, *Vichy France*, 292
52 Quoted in Schoenbrun, *Soldiers of the Night*, 157
53 Leen Pot quoted in Foot (ed.), *Holland at War against Hitler*, 139–43
54 H. Michel, 'The Psychology of the French Resister', *Journal of Contemporary History*, 5:3 (1970), 159–75
55 Bennett, *Under the Shadow of the Swastika*, 5
56 Madeleine Baudoin quoted in Kedward, *Resistance in Vichy France*, 277
57 L. Olson, *Madame Fourcade's Secret War*, xxiv
58 Garliński, 'The Polish Underground State'; E. Verhoeyen, *La Belgique occupée*, 344; Wieviorka, *The Resistance in Western Europe*, 112–13, 116
59 Bryant, *Prague in Black*, 89, R. Luža, 'The Czech Resistance Movement', in Mamatey and Luža (eds), *A History of the Czechoslovak Republic*, 343–61
60 Mastny, *The Czechs under Nazi Rule*, 147–8
61 Williamson, *The Polish Underground*, 3–4
62 The author is grateful to Andrzej Suchcitz for his assistance on this
63 Bór-Komorowski, *The Secret Army*, 29
64 W. Borodziej, *The Warsaw Uprising of 1944*, 37
65 P. Latawski, 'Poland', in Cooke and Shepherd (eds), *European Resistance*, 150–70

66 Bór-Komorowski, *The Secret Army*, 39–40
67 Garliński, 'The Polish Underground State'
68 S. Milton, 'Non-Jewish Children in the Camps', in M. Berenbaum (ed.), *A Mosaic of Victims*, 150–60
69 Garliński, 'The Polish Underground State'
70 Quoted in Semelin, *Unarmed against Hitler*, 80
71 Bór-Komorowski, *The Secret Army*, 18–19
72 Williamson, *The Polish Underground*, 51–2
73 T. Charman, 'Hugh Dalton, Poland and SOE, 1940–42', in M. Seaman (ed.), *Special Operations Executive*, 61–70; Korboński, *Fighting Warsaw*, 14
74 Luža, *The Hitler Kiss*, 26
75 F. Moravec, *Master of Spies*, 180
76 Mastny, *The Czechs under Nazi Rule*, 147
77 Moravec, *Master of Spies*, 180
78 Gjelsvik, *Norwegian Resistance*, viii
79 Hoidal, *Quisling*, 522; C. Mann, *British Policy and Strategy towards Norway*, 44–6
80 C. Mann, 'Scandinavia', in Cooke and Shepherd (eds), *European Resistance*, 171–87; Rings, *Life with the Enemy*, 206; Gjelsvik, *Norwegian Resistance*, 74
81 Hayes, *Quisling*, 270, 276; Gjelsvik, *Norwegian Resistance*, 33
82 Gjelsvik, *Norwegian Resistance*, 26; Hayes, *Quisling*, 270
83 Maass, *The Netherlands at War*, 59
84 Gordon, *The Norwegian Resistance*, 573–5
85 Skodvin, 'Norwegian Non-Violent Resistance'; Hayes, *Quisling*, 276; Hoidal, *Quisling*, 506
86 Hoidal, *Quisling*, 517–18
87 Paape, 'How Dutch Resistance was Organised'; M. Schwegman, 'The Netherlands', in Cooke and Shepherd (eds), *European Resistance*, 134–49
88 Warmbrunn, *The Dutch under German Occupation*, 186
89 Frenay, *The Night Will End*, 21
90 Gildea, *Fighters in the Shadows*, 70–71
91 Quoted in Boyd, *Voices from the Dark Years*, 113
92 Dank, *The French against the French*, 72–3
93 Diary entries, 20 June and 20 October 1940, Humbert, *Resistance*, 7 and 19–21
94 Dank, *The French against the French*, 123
95 Cobb, *The Resistance*, 66
96 De Vomécourt, *Who Lived to See the Day*, 25, 39
97 Frenay, *The Night Will End*, 47–9; King, 'Emmanuel d'Astier'; Kedward, *Occupied France*, 49
98 Blumenson, *The Vildé Affair*, passim; R. Pike, *Defying Vichy*, 58–9.

6. INTELLIGENCE GATHERING: 1939–41

1 J. Ferris, 'Intelligence' in J. Ferris and E. Mawdsley (eds), *The Cambridge History of the Second World War*, I, 637–63
2 Passy, *II Bureau*, 54–5
3 F. H. Hinsley et al., *British Intelligence in the Second World War*, 57; W. Schellenberg, *The Schellenberg Memoirs*, 85–98; Foot, *SOE in the Low Countries*, 14–16; K. Jeffery, *MI6*, 383–5; S. Payne Best, *The Venlo Incident*, passim
4 R. Bennett, *Behind the Battle*, 290
5 Moravec, *Master of Spies*, 148–9; C. MacDonald, *The Killing of Obergruppenführer Reinhard Heydrich*, 75, 90; P. Winter, 'Penetrating Hitler's High Command: Anglo-Polish HUMINT, 1939–1945', *War in History*, 18 (2011), 85–108; Luža, 'The Czech Resistance Movement'

6 A. Pepłonski and A. Suchcitz, 'Organisation and Operations of the II Bureau of the Polish General Staff', in T. Stirling et al. (eds), *Intelligence Co-operation between Poland and Great Britain during World War II*, I, 81–107
7 Hinsley et al., *British Intelligence in the Second World War*, 276–7
8 G. Bennett, 'Polish-British Intelligence Cooperation', in Stirling et al. (eds), *Intelligence Co-operation*, I, 159–68
9 G. Bennett, 'France and North Africa', and R. Wnuk, 'Polish Intelligence in France', both in Stirling et al. (eds), *Intelligence Cooperation*, I, 220–28, 229–47; Purnell, *A Woman of No Importance*, 95–9
10 Wnuk, 'Polish Intelligence in France'; B. McIntyre, *Double Cross*, passim
11 Wnuk, 'Polish Intelligence in France'
12 A. Pepłoński, 'Cooperation between the II Bureau and SIS', in Stirling et al. (eds), *Intelligence Co-operation*, I, 181–97
13 A. Chmielarz, 'Intelligence Activities of the Home Army General Headquarters', in Stirling et al. (eds), *Intelligence Co-operation*, I, 393–412; Garliński, 'The Polish Underground State'; Williamson, *The Polish Underground*, 53; C. Mulley, *The Spy Who Loved*, 32–101; O. O'Malley, *The Phantom Caravan*, 208–10
14 Jeffery, *MI6*, 380–81
15 R. Ulstein, 'Norwegian Intelligence in the Second World War', in P. Salmon (ed.), *Britain and Norway in the Second World War*, 129–39; Gjelsvik, *Norwegian Resistance*, 10–12; Hauge, *Salt-Water Thief*, 56
16 Haestrup, *Europe Ablaze*, 162–3; Foot, *SOE in the Low Countries*, 231–2
17 Jeffery, *MI6*, 388; Haestrup, *Europe Ablaze*, 161; Verhoeyen, *La Belgique occupée*, 369–70
18 Foot, *SOE in the Low Countries*, 78–80; Hazelhoff, *Soldier of Orange*, 73–109
19 De Jong, 'The Dutch Resistance and the Allies'
20 Warmbrunn, *The Dutch under German Occupation*, 208–10
21 R. Reilly, *The Sixth Floor*, 20; Lampe, *The Savage Canary*, 49
22 Passy, *II Bureau*, 15, 54–5, 138; Jackson, *France*, 115; M. Seaman, *Bravest of the Brave*, 51
23 Gildea, *Fighters in the Shadows*, 113–14
24 Rémy, *The Silent Company*, 108–9, 151–2, 156, 193; Pike, *Defying Vichy*, 40–41
25 Wieviorka, *French Resistance*, 23; Richards, *Secret Flotillas*, 24
26 Wieviorka, *French Resistance*, 20–21
27 Foot, *Six Faces of Courage*, 46–8
28 M.-M. Fourcade, *Noah's Ark*, 16, 28, 31, 55; Olson, *Madame Fourcade's Secret War*, 39, 83
29 Kitson, *The Hunt for Nazi Spies*, 82–3
30 A. L. Funk, 'Contacts with the Resistance in France, 1940–1943', *Military Affairs*, 34:1 (1970), 15–21; Kedward, *Resistance in Vichy France*, 40–41; P. Paillole, *Fighting the Nazis*, 197, 205
31 Wieviorka, *French Resistance*, 68, 80; Kochanski, *The Eagle Unbowed*, 208
32 Chmielarz, 'Intelligence Activities of the Home Army General Headquarters'
33 Fourcade, *Noah's Ark*, 33
34 Foreword to R. V. Jones, *Most Secret War*, 13–14
35 Rémy, *The Silent Company*, 155
36 Richards, *Secret Flotillas*, 57; Wieviorka, *French Resistance*, 17
37 L. McKinstry, *Operation Sealion*, 105, 319–20; Report by Polish General Staff, II Bureau, on German Preparations to Attack England, 15 August 1940, in Stirling et al. (eds), *Intelligence Co-operation*, II, 453–4
38 McKinstry, *Operation Sealion*, 2, 305; P. Schenk, *Invasion of England 1940*, 158
39 McKinstry, *Operation Sealion*, 106, 191–2; Moravec, *Master of Spies*, 196; Hinsley et al., *British Intelligence in the Second World War*, I, 189, 262
40 Hinsley et al., *British Intelligence in the Second World War*, I, 189; McKinstry, *Operation Sealion*, 405, 417
41 Wnuk, 'Polish Intelligence in France'; Haestrup, *Europe Ablaze*, 161

42 Hinsley et al., *British Intelligence in the Second World War*, 435–62; A. Peplonski, 'Intelligence behind the Eastern Front', in Stirling et al. (eds), *Intelligence Co-operation*, I, 413–29

43 Rowecki to Polish General Staff, 3 June 1941, in Stirling et al. (eds), *Intelligence Co-operation*, II, 754

44 H. Denham, *Inside the Nazi Ring*, 99

45 Mann, *British Policy and Strategy towards Norway*, 13–14; Hansson, *The Greatest Gamble*, 31; Baden-Powell, *Operation Jupiter*, 152–3

46 Richards, *Secret Flotillas*, 60; Rémy, *The Silent Company*, 108–9, 153–4; P. Ashdown, *A Brilliant Little Operation*, 15; Wnuk, 'Polish Intelligence in France'; Cobb, *French Resistance*, 54

47 A. Peplonski, T. Dubicki and R. Majzner, 'Naval Intelligence: Movements of Ships, Surveillance of Ports and Shipyards', in Stirling et al. (eds), *Intelligence Co-operation*, I, 490–500

48 Hinsley et al., *British Intelligence in the Second World War*, 508–12; Jones, *Most Secret War*, 105–7

49 Reilly, *The Sixth Floor*, 26; Jones, *Most Secret War*, 262–4

50 Demel to stations in Budapest and Bucharest, 19 April 1940, in Stirling et al. (eds), *Intelligence Co-operation*, II, 640–41.

7. THE ORIGINS OF SOE AND OSS

1 D. Stafford, 'The Detonator Concept: British Strategy, SOE and European Resistance after the Fall of France', *Journal of Contemporary History*, 10:2 (1975), 185–217

2 M. R. D. Foot, 'Was SOE Any Good?', *Journal of Contemporary History*, 16:1 (1981), 167–81

3 W. Mackenzie, *The Secret History of SOE*, 753–5

4 M.R.D. Foot, *SOE*, 23

5 P. Wilkinson, IWM 13289, 12751

6 Mackenzie, *The Secret History of SOE*, 39

7 D. Dodds-Parker, *Setting Europe Ablaze*, 76–7

8 Charman, 'Hugh Dalton, Poland and SOE, 1940–42'; E. Harrison, 'The British Special Operations Executive and Poland', *Historical Journal*, 43 (2000), 1,071–91

9 Foot, *SOE in the Low Countries*, 231

10 Foot, *SOE in France*, xxxi

11 De Vomécourt, *Who Lived to See the Day*, 177

12 C. Seymour-Jones, *She Landed by Moonlight*, 132

13 Seaman, *Bravest of the Brave*, 46

14 Foot, *SOE in the Low Countries*, 99, 243

15 K. Jespersen, *No Small Achievement*, 48–9

16 J. Tucholski, *Cichociemni*, 62

17 C. de Gaulle, *War Memoirs*, I, 157

18 M. Ruby, *F Section, SOE*, 14

19 De Vomécourt, *Who Lived to See the Day*, 25; D. Stafford, *Secret Agent*, 20; A.-M. Walters, *Moondrop to Gascony*, 7; R. Jenkins, *A Pacifist at War*, 37

20 H. Raymond, 'Experiences of an SOE Agent in France', in M. Elliott-Bateman (ed.), *The Fourth Dimension of Warfare*, 111–26

21 H. Rée, IWM 8720

22 Jenkins, *A Pacifist at War*, 47

23 M. Buckmaster, *They Fought Alone*, 213

24 S. Jepson, IWM 31587

25 N. Wake, *The Autobiography of the Woman the Gestapo called the White Mouse*, 4

26 N. Hammond, *Venture into Greece*, 13

27 Stafford, *Secret Agent*, 19

28 X. Fielding, *Hide and Seek*, 11
29 R. Sheppard, IWM 10445
30 Foot, *SOE*, 79–80; D. Rigden, *SOE Syllabus*, 4
31 G. Langelaan, *Knights of the Floating Silk*, 68
32 R. Ferrier, IWM 18559
33 C. Cunningham, *Beaulieu*, 92–7; Rigden, *SOE Syllabus*, 5
34 Cammaerts quoted in Stafford, *Secret Agent*, 45
35 Stafford, *Secret Agent*, 34–5
36 Cunningham, *Beaulieu*, 105; Foot, *SOE*, 91; Rigden, *SOE Syllabus*, 9
37 D. Stafford, *Britain and European Resistance*, 209
38 Richards, *Secret Flotillas*, 142
39 Jeffery, *MI6*, 353
40 Stafford, *Secret Agent*, 123
41 Foot, *SOE in France*, 140
42 Ibid., 15
43 M. Seaman, '"The Most Difficult Country": Some Practical Considerations on British Support for Clandestine Operations in Czechoslovakia during the Second World War', in V. Smetana and K. Geaney (eds), *Exile in London*, 122–32
44 Stafford, *Britain and European Resistance*, 219–24; Wieviorka, *The Resistance in Western Europe*, 33–4
45 Stafford, *Britain and European Resistance*, 54
46 R. Bailey, 'SOE in Albania', in Seaman (ed.), *Special Operations Executive*, 179–92; O. Pearson, *Albania in Occupation and War*, 5, 15–20, 92–9, 139–42; Fischer, *Albania at War*, 102–5
47 N. Wylie, 'Ungentlemanly Warriors or Unreliable Diplomats?', in N. Wylie (ed.), *The Politics and Strategy of Clandestine War*, 109–29; E. Barker, *British Policy in South-East Europe*, 151; D. Stafford, 'SOE and British Involvement in the Belgrade Coup d'État of March 1941', *Slavic Review*, 36:3 (1977), 399–41
48 R. Clogg, 'The Special Operations Executive in Greece', and J. Hondros, 'The Greek Resistance, 1941–1944: A Re-Evaluation', both in J. Iatrides (ed.), *Greece in the 1940s*, 102–18, 37–47; Gerolymatos, *Guerrilla Warfare and Espionage in Greece*, 134
49 Harrison, 'The British Special Operations Executive and Poland'; P. Wilkinson and J. Bright Astley, *Gubbins and SOE*, 47
50 Charman, 'Hugh Dalton, Poland and SOE, 1940–42'; K. Śledziński, *Cichociemni*, 58–61
51 Garliński, 'The Polish Underground State'
52 J. Zbik (Zabielski), *First to Return*, passim
53 Wilkinson, *Foreign Fields*, 124
54 Wilkinson and Bright Astley, *Gubbins and SOE*, 83
55 Dodds-Parker, *Setting Europe Ablaze*, 92
56 Mackenzie, *The Secret History of SOE*, 246–7; Foot, *SOE in France*, 140–41, 144–5
57 D. Isaaman, *Jacques de Guélis*, 66–8
58 Mackenzie, *The Secret History of SOE*, 226
59 Foot, *SOE in France*, 148–9; De Vomécourt, *Who Lived to See the Day*, 39; Pike, *Defying Vichy*, 65–9; Purnell, *A Woman of No Importance*, 53–9; Kent and Nicholas, *Agent Michael Trotobas*, 38–47
60 Cowburn, *No Cloak, No Dagger*, 99
61 Quoted in R. Miller, *Behind the Lines*, 34
62 Foot, *SOE in France*, 148–9
63 Foot, *SOE in the Low Countries*, 103–5, 246; Verhoeyen, *La Belgique occupée*, 447
64 Cruickshank, *SOE in Scandinavia*, 56
65 Stafford, *Britain and European Resistance*, 234–9; Wilkinson, *Foreign Fields*, 88; Stafford, 'The Detonator Concept'
66 M. Hastings, *The Secret War*, 304
67 W. Casey, *The Secret War against Hitler*, 5

68 R. Harris Smith, *OSS*, 10–26
69 Quoted in Miller, *Behind the Lines*, 57
70 Harris Smith, *OSS*, 33; Mackenzie, *The Secret History of SOE*, 391–2; B. Sweet-Escott, *Baker Street Irregular*, 129
71 J. McCaffery, IWM 14093.

8. THE EARLY PARTISANS

1 H. Winkler, *The Age of Catastrophe*, 710–11
2 Mazower, *Hitler's Empire*, 171
3 W. Kosyk, *The Third Reich and the Ukrainian Question*, 498
4 A. Kay, 'The Radicalisation of German Food Policy in Early 1941', in A. Kay, J. Rutherford and D. Stahel (eds), *Nazi Policy on the Eastern Front*, 102–29
5 A. Hill, *The War behind the Eastern Front*, 41
6 Kochanski, *The Eagle Unbowed*, 119–35
7 Kosyk, *The Third Reich and the Ukrainian Question*, 523
8 K. Berkhoff, *Harvest of Despair*, 20
9 Kosyk, *The Third Reich and the Ukrainian Question*, 46–7
10 V. Lumans, *Latvia in World War II*, 161
11 C. Bellamy, *Absolute War*, 194, 198
12 I. Kamenetsky, *Hitler's Occupation of the Ukraine*, 55; T. Remeikis (ed.), *Lithuania under German Occupation*, 8; Lumans, *Latvia in World War II*, 180–83
13 A. Tooze, *The Wages of Destruction*, 480
14 Kamenetsky, *Hitler's Occupation of the Ukraine*, 49; J. Steinberg, 'The Third Reich Reflected: German Civil Administration in the Occupied Soviet Union, 1941–4', *English Historical Review*, 110:437 (1995), 620–51
15 For example, diary entries on 11 February, 2 and 22 May 1942, in L. Lochner (ed.), *The Goebbels Diaries*, 40, 149, 168–9
16 E. Homze, *Foreign Labor in Nazi Germany*, 84–5
17 A. Dallin, *German Rule in Russia*, 430
18 T. Mulligan, *The Politics of Illusion and Empire*, 79
19 Dallin, *German Rule in Russia*, 139
20 K. Slepyan, 'Partisans, Civilians and the Soviet State: An Overview', in B. Shepherd and J. Pattinson (eds), *War in a Twilight World*, 35–57
21 Hill, *The War behind the Eastern Front*, 63
22 A. Werth, *Russia at War*, 164
23 M. Cooper, *The Phantom War*, 17, 28
24 B. Shepherd, *War in the Wild East*, 146
25 G. Reitlinger, *The House Built on Sand*, 232
26 Kosyk, *The Third Reich and the Ukrainian Question*, 536
27 Shepherd, *War in the Wild East*, 366
28 Cooper, *The Phantom War*, 45; J. Armstrong, 'Introduction', in J. Armstrong (ed.), *Soviet Partisans in World War II*, 3–70; Shepherd, *War in the Wild East*, 48–51, 114
29 Lumans, *Latvia in World War II*, 263
30 P. Blood, *Hitler's Bandit Hunters*, 55; J. Enstad, *Soviet Russians under German Occupation*, 198
31 Rings, *Life with the Enemy*, 83; Reitlinger, *The House Built on Sand*, 309–10; Littlejohn, *The Patriotic Traitors*, 298–9, 301; K. Macksey, *The Partisans of Europe*, 78–9
32 J. Armstrong, 'Collaborationism in World War II: The Integral Nationalist Variant in Eastern Europe', *Journal of Modern History*, 40 (1968), 396–412
33 J. Erickson, *The Road to Stalingrad*, 27–8
34 K. Slepyan, *Stalin's Guerrillas*, 2; Hill, *The War behind the Eastern Front*, 38
35 Cooper, *The Phantom War*, 15
36 Hastings, *The Secret War*, 317, 319

37 Cooper, *The Phantom War*, 16; K. Cottam, *Women in War and Resistance*, passim
38 S. Kovpak, *Our Partisan Course*, 12
39 Slepyan, *Stalin's Guerrillas*, 36, 80; N. Vakar, *Belorussia*, 200; Bellamy, *Absolute War*, 336; Erickson, *The Road to Stalingrad*, 323
40 A. Statiev, 'The Soviet Union', in Cooke and Shepherd (eds), *European Resistance in the Second World War*, 188–212
41 Kovpak, *Our Partisan Course*, 52; Hastings, *The Secret War*, 318; Anon., *We are Guerrillas: An Account of the Work of Soviet Guerrillas beyond Nazi Lines*, passim
42 Haestrup, *Europe Ablaze*, 254–5
43 L. Grenkevich, *The Soviet Partisan Movement*, 194; Armstrong, 'Introduction'
44 Cooper, *The Phantom War*, 71
45 Slepyan, *Stalin's Guerrillas*, 80
46 Cooper, *The Phantom War*, 10
47 Ibid., 187–93
48 Werth, *Russia at War*, 711
49 Kovpak, *Our Partisan Course*, 78–93; Kosyk, *The Third Reich and the Ukrainian Question*, 239; Statiev, 'Soviet Union'; Berkhoff, *Harvest of Despair*, 276
50 C. Dixon and O. Heilbrunn, *Communist Guerrilla Warfare*, 73–4
51 Cooper, *The Phantom War*, 131
52 P. Ignatov, *Partisans of the Kuban*, 176–7; Cooper, *The Phantom War*, 131
53 Cooper, *The Phantom War*, 133–4; Grenkevich, *The Soviet Partisan Movement*, 221; Hill, *The War behind the Eastern Front*, 132
54 Shepherd, *War in the Wild East*, 127
55 Ignatov, *Partisans of the Kuban*, 149–50
56 Blood, *Hitler's Bandit Hunters*, 71
57 Cooper, *The Phantom War*, 89
58 T. Schulte, *German Army and Nazi Policies in Occupied Russia*, 260
59 Dixon and Heilbrunn, *Communist Guerrilla Warfare*, 145–6
60 Cooper, *The Phantom War*, 152–61; A. Munoz and O. Romanko, *Hitler's White Russians*, 198–227; Blood, *Hitler's Bandit Hunters*, 70–86
61 Dallin, *German Rule in Russia*, 210
62 Mulligan, *The Politics of Illusion and Empire*, 139–40; Blood, *Hitler's Bandit Hunters*, 78–9
63 W. Manoschek, '"Coming Along to Shoot Some Jews?": The Destruction of the Jews in Serbia', in H. Heer and K. Naumann (eds), *War of Extermination*, 39–51
64 Deroc, *British Special Operations Explored*, 170; H. Burgwyn, *Empire on the Adriatic*, 91–2; Pavlowitch, *Hitler's New Disorder*, 75–6
65 Haestrup, *Europe Ablaze*, 49–50; B. Shepherd, *Terror in the Balkans*, 97
66 W. Deakin, *The Embattled Mountain*, 75; Shepherd, *Terror in the Balkans*, 120; D. Martin, *The Web of Disinformation*, 37–40; Z. Vučković, *A Balkan Tragedy*, 130
67 M. A. Jareb, 'Allies or Foes? Mihailovic's Chetniks during the Second World War', in S. Ramet and O. Listhaug (eds), *Serbia and the Serbs in World War Two*, 155–74
68 Deroc, *British Special Operations Explored*, 182
69 M. A. Hoare, *Genocide and Resistance in Hitler's Bosnia*, 163
70 Martin, *Web of Disinformation*, 49
71 Dimitrov to Tito, 10 August 1942, in I. Banac (ed.), *The Diary of Georgi Dimitrov*, 234
72 Pearson, *Albania in Occupation and War*, 158–9, 164–5, 196–7, 204–10; Fischer, *Albania at War*, 129, 132–4
73 J. Hondros, *Occupation and Resistance*, 108–110
74 P. Voglis, 'Surviving Hunger: Life in the Cities and the Countryside during the Occupation', in Gildea et al. (eds), *Surviving Hitler and Mussolini*, 16–41
75 Mazower, *Inside Hitler's Greece*, 100–106; Gerolymatos, *Guerrilla Warfare and Espionage in Greece*, 209–10; Hondros, 'The Greek Resistance; P. Papastratis, *British Policy towards Greece in the Second World War*, 123
76 D. Hamson, *We Fell among Greeks*, 98.

9. THE MOBILIZATION OF THE COMMUNISTS

1 D. Drake, *Paris at War*, 11
2 Banac (ed.), *The Diary of Georgi Dimitrov*, 117
3 H. G. Skilling, 'The Czechoslovak Struggle for National Liberation in World War II', *Slavonic and East European Review*, 39:92 (1960), 174–97; Dank, *The French against the French*, 106
4 Wieviorka, *The French Resistance*, 34–5; Noguères et al., *Histoire de la Résistance*, I, 143; Koestler, *Scum of the Earth*, passim
5 Drake, *Paris at War*, 93–4; D. W. Pike, 'Between the Junes: The French Communists from the Collapse of France to the Invasion of Russia', *Journal of Contemporary History*, 28 (1993), 465–85; Kedward, *Resistance in Vichy France*, 64, 94; Jackson, *France: The Dark Years*, 420–1
6 Wieviorka, *The French Resistance*, 43
7 P. Villon, *Résistant de la première heure*, 182–3
8 Instructions sent to Norwegians and Danes, 6 July 1941, Banac (ed.), *The Diary of Georgi Dimitrov*, 175
9 Wieviorka, *The French Resistance*, 123
10 Comintern directives, 25 June and 6 July 1941, Banac (ed.), *The Diary of Georgi Dimitrov*, 168–9, 175
11 Williamson, *The Polish Underground*, 70–71
12 E. Maresch, 'SOE and Polish Aspirations', in Stirling et al. (eds), *Intelligence Co-operation*, 198–155; Williamson, *The Polish Underground*, 72
13 Report by Counsellor Weese, 5 March 1942, *DPSR*, I, 287–8
14 Bór-Komorowski, *The Secret Army*, 118–21
15 Sikorski to Grot-Rowecki, 28 November 1942, *DPSR*, I, 457–8
16 A. Prażmowska, *Civil War in Poland 1942–1948*, 41–2; Banac (ed.), *The Diary of Georgi Dimitrov*, 232, 245–6; Kochanski, *The Eagle Unbowed*, 369–71
17 TNA, HS4/138; Prażmowska, *Civil War in Poland*, 43–5
18 K. Stankiewicz, IWM 4158
19 Wanda Jordan quoted in R. Lukas, *Out of the Inferno*, 80
20 Nowak, *Courier from Warsaw*, 105
21 Mazower, *Hitler's Empire*, 214
22 Diary entry, 7 December 1942, Klukowski, *Diary from the Years of Occupation*, 229
23 Borodziej, *The Warsaw Uprising*, 40
24 A. Borowiec, *Destroy Warsaw!*, 140–41
25 Diary entries, 6 February and 11 March 1943, Klukowski, *Diary from the Years of Occupation*, 242–3, 246
26 Mazower, *Hitler's Empire*, 495
27 Bryant, *Prague in Black*, 129
28 Skilling, 'The Czechoslovak Struggle'
29 MacDonald, *The Killing of SS Obergruppenführer Reinhard Heydrich*, 98
30 Bryant, *Prague in Black*, 130–31; Mastny, *The Czechs under Nazi Rule*, 172–3; Luža, *The Hitler Kiss*, 110
31 R. Gerwarth, *Hitler's Hangman*, 3
32 R. Luža, 'The Communist Party of Czechoslovakia and the Czech Resistance, 1939–1945', *Slavic Review*, 28:4 (1969), 561–76; Moravec, *Master of Spies*, 238; Mastny, *The Czechs under Nazi Rule*, 204–5
33 MacDonald, *The Killing of SS Obergruppenführer Reinhard Heydrich*, 108–10; Bryant, *Prague in Black*, 143–4; Gerwarth, *Hitler's Hangman*, 227–40; Mastny, *The Czechs under Nazi Rule*, 191–5; Diary entry, 21 January 1942, Lochner (ed.), *The Goebbels Diaries*, 3
34 Memorial church of St Cyril and St Methodius, Prague
35 Rich, *Hitler's War Aims*, I, 47
36 L. Taylor, 'The Parti Communiste Français and the French Resistance in the Second World War', in T. Judt (ed.), *Resistance and Revolution in Mediterranean Europe*,

53–79; Dank, *The French against the French*, 108–9; Wieviorka, *The French Resistance*, 125–6

37 Quoted in Gildea, *Fighters in the Shadows*, 89–90
38 Dank, *The French against the French*, 110
39 C. Neumaier, 'The Escalation of German Reprisal Policy in Occupied France, 1941–42', *Journal of Contemporary History*, 41:1 (2006), 113–31
40 Gildea, *Marianne in Chains*, 248
41 Gildea, *Fighters in the Shadows*, 90; Künzel, 'Resistance, Reprisals, Reactions'; Dank, *The French against the French*, 136–43
42 Gildea, *Marianne in Chains*, 254–5
43 Lacouture, *De Gaulle*, 376
44 Cobb, *The French Resistance*, 83
45 Stenton, *Radio London*, 184
46 Bennett, *Under the Shadow of the Swastika*, 133
47 T. Laub, 'The Development of German Policy in Occupied France, 1941, against the Backdrop of the War in the East', in Kay et al. (eds), *Nazi Policy on the Eastern Front*, 289–313
48 Dank, *The French against the French*, 161–6
49 Ibid., 130–31
50 Kosyk, *The Third Reich and the Ukrainian Question*, 560–61
51 Laub, *After the Fall*, 188, 191; Neumaier, 'The Escalation of German Reprisal Policy'
52 Drake, *Paris at War*, 271
53 Paxton, *Vichy France*, 227
54 Dank, *The French against the French*, 158
55 De Brinon quoted in D. Pryce-Jones, 'Paris during the German Occupation', in Hirschfeld and Marsh (eds), *Collaboration in France*, 15–31
56 Vinen, *The Unfree French*, 109
57 Paxton, *Vichy France*, 296
58 H. Boog et al., *Germany and the Second World War*, 167; Gildea, *Marianne in Chains*, 269
59 Warmbrunn, *The German Occupation of Belgium*, 145–9; Bles, *Child at War*, 71
60 Künzel, 'Resistance, Reprisals, Reactions'
61 Paape, 'How Dutch Resistance was Organised'; Schwegman, 'The Netherlands'
62 Hayes, *Quisling*, 275–6; Hoidal, *Quisling*, 508–10; Gordon, *The Norwegian Resistance*, 8
63 Riste and Nökleby, *Norway*, 52; Gjelsvik, *Norwegian Resistance*, 78–9
64 Gordon, *The Norwegian Resistance*, 323
65 Hoidal, *Quisling*, 533
66 Gordon, *The Norwegian Resistance*, 296
67 Riste and Nökleby, *Norway*, 54
68 Gordon, *The Norwegian Resistance*, 327.

10. SOE GETS TO WORK

1 Stafford, *Britain and European Resistance*, 78
2 Diary entry, 29 May 1942, in K. Young (ed.), *The Diaries of Sir Robert Bruce Lockhart*, II, 168–71
3 P. Wilkinson, IWM 13289, 12751
4 TNA, CAB 80/69
5 R. Heslop, *Xavier*, 27
6 H. Verity, *We Landed by Moonlight*, 6
7 Stafford, *Secret Agent*, 135
8 B. Marshall, *The White Rabbit*, 83–4
9 Cowburn, *No Cloak, No Dagger*, 128–9
10 P. Churchill, *Duel of Wits*, 192–4, 223, 239–45

11 Hamson, *We Fell among Greeks*, 199–206
12 Verity, *We Landed by Moonlight*, 191
13 Beevor, *Crete*, 253–4
14 Gordon, *The Norwegian Resistance*, 224; Howarth, *The Shetland Bus*, passim; Cruickshank, *SOE in Scandinavia*, 91–7; B. Richards, 'Britain and Norwegian Resistance: Clandestine Sea Transport', in Salmon (ed.), *Britain and Norway in the Second World War*, 161–74
15 Stafford, *Secret Agent*, 55; P. Dourlein, *Inside North Pole*, 90–91; De Jong, 'The Dutch Resistance Movement and the Allies'; Cowburn, *No Cloak, No Dagger*, 112; B. O'Connor, *Churchill's Angels*, 127; W. Sagajllo, *The Man in the Middle*, 79; Churchill, *Duel of Wits*, 93–4; Mayer, *Gaston's War*, 106; M. Seaman, *Saboteur*, 135–7
16 Friedhoff, *Requiem for the Resistance*, 147; Tucholski, *Cichociemni*, 78
17 F. Muus, *The Spark and the Flame*, 137
18 Walters, *Moondrop to Gascony*, 36
19 J. Goldsmith, *Accidental Agent*, 78
20 R. Bailey (ed.), *Forgotten Voices of the Secret War*, 183
21 I. Valentine, *Station 43*, 160
22 Rémy, *Courage and Fear*, 187
23 F. Cammaerts, IWM 16759, 11238
24 Walters, *Moondrop to Gascony*, 30
25 Hamson, *We Fell among Greeks*, 41
26 M. Lees, *Special Operations Executed in Serbia and Italy*, 42–3
27 Woodhouse, *Something Ventured*, 42
28 Lees, *Special Operations*, 54
29 S. Bailey, 'British Policy towards General Draža Mihailović', in P. Auty and R. Clogg (eds), *British Policy towards Wartime Resistance in Yugoslavia and Greece*, 59–90
30 Psychoundakis, *The Cretan Runner*, 75, 69
31 D. Smiley, *Albanian Assignment*, 83–4, 86
32 P. Kemp, *No Colours or Crest*, 76
33 Dodds-Parker, *Setting Europe Ablaze*, 190
34 Vučković, *A Balkan Tragedy*, 232
35 A. Rendel, *Appointment in Crete*, 118
36 Psychoundakis, *The Cretan Runner*, 15
37 P. Lucas, *The OSS in World War II Albania*, 15, 22
38 Kemp, *No Colours or Crest*, 105
39 E. Davies, *Illyrian Adventure*, 117, 138
40 W. S. Moss, *A War of Shadows*, 87–90
41 Davies, *Illyrian Adventure*, 114
42 Deakin, *The Embattled Mountain*, 9
43 J. Rootham, *Miss Fire*, 20
44 B. Davidson, *Partisan Picture*, 12
45 Mackenzie, *The Secret History of SOE*, 250
46 Wilkinson and Bright Astley, *Gubbins and SOE*, 124–7; Wieviorka, *The Resistance in Western Europe*, 180–82
47 Rootham, *Miss Fire*, 49
48 Davidson, *Partisan Picture*, 20
49 Kochanski, *The Eagle Unbowed*, 335
50 Deakin, *The Embattled Mountain*, 81; Smiley, *Albanian Assignment*, 49; Bailey, 'British Policy towards General Draža Mihailović'
51 Hamson, *We Fell among Greeks*, 146
52 B. Kereven, IWM 9723
53 Davies, *Illyrian Adventure*, 125
54 Cowburn, *No Cloak, No Dagger*, 130
55 Rendel, *Appointment in Crete*, 112
56 Psychoundakis, *The Cretan Runner*, 213

57 Fielding, *Hide and Seek*, 72
58 Jenkins, *A Pacifist at War*, 121
59 F. Maclean, *Eastern Approaches*, 428
60 V. Eloy, *The Fight in the Forest*, 42
61 R. Bailey, *The Wildest Province*, 69
62 Brooks, IWM, 9550
63 E. D'Astier, *Seven Times Seven Days*, 32–3
64 Pike, *Defying Vichy*, 78
65 Foot, *SOE in France*, 192
66 Gildea, *Fighters in the Shadows*, 163
67 F. Cammaerts, IWM 16759, 11238
68 Churchill, *Duel of Wits*, 131
69 Foot, *SOE in France*, 184, 188; Churchill, *Duel of Wits*, passim; Stenton, *Radio London*, 222–3
70 R. Boiteux, IWM 9851
71 Paillole, *Fighting the Nazis*, 319
72 Raymond Chauliac in Kedward, *Resistance in Vichy France*, 269
73 Noguères et al., *Histoire de la Résistance*, III, 38
74 Churchill, *Duel of Wits*, 293–4; Purnell, *A Woman of No Importance*, 180–87
75 Fourcade, *Noah's Ark*, 176–7
76 E. Le Chêne, *Watch for Me by Moonlight*, 100
77 G. Starr, IWM 24613
78 Michel, *The Shadow War*, 212
79 A. Moland, 'Milorg and SOE', in Salmon (ed.), *Britain and Norway in the Second World War*, 141–51; S. Kjeldstadli, 'The Resistance Movement in Norway and the Allies 1940–1945', in *Second International Conference*, 324–39; I. Kraglund, 'SOE and Milorg: "Thieves in the Same Market"', in Seaman (ed.), *Special Operations Executive*, 71–82; Cruickshank, *SOE in Scandinavia*, passim; I. Herrington, 'The SIS and SOE in Norway 1940–1945: Conflict or Co-operation?', *War in History*, 9: 1 (2002), 82–110
80 Kemp, *No Colours or Crest*, 121
81 Davies, *Illyrian Adventure*, 56
82 Riste and Nökleby, *Norway*, 61–2; Mackenzie, *The Secret History of SOE*, 655–6
83 Vučković, *A Balkan Tragedy*, 205–6
84 R. Maloubier, IWM 10444; P. McCue, *Behind Enemy Lines with the SAS*, loc. 1, 463–75, 1,583–610; F. Lambert, *Free French Saboteurs*, 105
85 Lambert, *Free French Saboteurs*, 105, 184–5
86 Seaman, *Saboteur*, 126–7, 141
87 Kent and Nicholas, *Agent Michael Trotobas*, 135
88 McCue, *Behind Enemy Lines with the SAS*, loc. 1,463
89 Bles, *Child at War*, 134
90 Maresch, 'SOE and Polish Aspirations'
91 Foot, 'Was SOE Any Good?'
92 Kent and Nicholas, *Agent Michael Trotobas*, 136–7, 141–5
93 H. Rée, IWM 8720
94 Raymond, 'Experiences of an SOE Agent in France'; E. Cookridge, *They Came from the Sky*, 46; Buckmaster, *They Fought Alone*, 158–60
95 Buckmaster, *They Fought Alone*, 177
96 Cobb, *The French Resistance*, 173, 176–7; Casey, *The Secret War against Hitler*, 89
97 Ashdown, *A Brilliant Little Operation*, passim; Foot, *SOE in France*, 248
98 Foot, *SOE in France*, 166
99 Beevor, *Crete*, 261–2
100 Wieviorka, *The Resistance in Western Europe*, 176
101 Mackenzie, *The Secret History of SOE*, 332
102 Foot, *SOE in France*, 201.

11. THREE SOE OPERATIONS

1 Bryant, *Prague in Black*, 167; Moravec, *Master of Spies*, 196; Wilkinson and Bright Astley, *Gubbins and SOE*, 106
2 Wilkinson and Bright Astley, *Gubbins and SOE*, 107–8; Wilkinson, IWM, 13289, 12751
3 TNA, HS 4/79
4 MacDonald, *The Killing of SS Obergruppenführer Reinhard Heydrich*, 123
5 TNA, HS 4/39
6 Wilkinson, IWM, 13289, 12751
7 TNA, HS 4/39
8 Bryant, *Prague in Black*, 167; Gerwarth, *Hitler's Hangman*, 8; Mastny, *The Czechs under Nazi Rule*, 209
9 TNA, HS 4/39
10 Ibid.
11 G. Deschner, *Heydrich: The Pursuit of Total Power*, 262
12 MacDonald, *The Killing of SS Obergruppenführer Reinhard Heydrich*, 157–9
13 Ibid., 161; SOE report, 30 May 1942, TNA, HS 4/39
14 Memorial church of St Cyril and St Methodius, Prague; L. Binet, *HHhH*, passim
15 Gerwarth, *Hitler's Hangman*, 11–12, 284–5; Mastny, *The Czechs under Nazi Rule*, 210–21; MacDonald, *The Killing of SS Obergruppenführer Reinhard Heydrich*, 176–98; Bryant, *Prague in Black*, 169–79; J. Hartman, IWM, 18557; Moravec, *Master of Spies*, 221
16 Mastny, *The Czechs under Nazi Rule*, 217, 261
17 MacDonald, *The Killing of SS Obergruppenführer Reinhard Heydrich*, 200–201
18 Williamson, *The Polish Underground*, 100–101
19 Woodhouse, *Something Ventured*, 24, 30; Gerolymatos, *Guerrilla Warfare and Espionage in Greece*, 277–9; E. Myers, *Greek Entanglement*, 17
20 Hamson, *We Fell among Greeks*, 72–3
21 Myers, *Greek Entanglement*, 72–86
22 Woodhouse, *Something Ventured*, 49
23 Hamson, *We Fell among Greeks*, 115
24 C. Woodhouse, *The Struggle for Greece*, 26; Mazower, *Inside Hitler's Greece*, 113
25 Hamson, *We Fell among Greeks*, 140, 143
26 Clogg, 'The Special Operations Executive in Greece'; Woodhouse, *The Struggle for Greece*, 26–7; Papastratis, *British Policy towards Greece*, 129–30
27 R. Monk, *Inside the Circle*, 291–3 and passim; A. Milward, 'The Economic and Strategic Effectiveness of Resistance', in S. Hawes and R. White (eds), *Resistance in Europe*, 186–203
28 R. Mears, *The Real Heroes of Telemark*, 10, 23–5; Hauge, *Salt-Water Thief*, 75–100
29 Mears, *The Real Heroes of Telemark*, 42–3, 69–70
30 Stafford, *Secret Agent*, 117; Mears, *The Real Heroes of Telemark*, 47–63; Cruickshank, *SOE in Scandinavia*, 198
31 Mann, *British Policy and Strategy towards Norway*, 98–102; Mears, *The Real Heroes of Telemark*, 91–2; Stafford, *Secret Agent*, 111
32 Poulsson, IWM 16625
33 Mears, *The Real Heroes of Telemark*, 101–2
34 Cruickshank, *SOE in Scandinavia*, 199
35 Rønneberg, IWM 27187
36 Mears, *The Real Heroes of Telemark*, 123–4
37 K. Haukelid, *Skis against the Atom*, 107–8
38 Rønneberg, IWM 27187
39 Mears, *The Real Heroes of Telemark*, 159–62
40 Rønneberg, IWM 27187
41 Haukelid, *Skis against the Atom*, 111–12

42 Mears, *The Real Heroes of Telemark*, 169
43 Rønneberg, IWM 27187
44 Mears, *The Real Heroes of Telemark*, 174
45 Haukelid, *Skis against the Atom*, 127, 134–6
46 Ibid., 173–4
47 T. Powers, *Heisenberg's War*, 118–19, 128–9, 157–62; Monk, *Inside the Circle*, 293–7
48 Haukelid, *Skis against the Atom*, 178
49 Mears, *The Real Heroes of Telemark*, 210–11
50 Powers, *Heisenberg's War*, 284–5
51 Ibid., 253
52 TNA, HS 7/181
53 Cruickshank, *SOE in Scandinavia*, 201–2; Bennett, *Under the Shadow of the Swastika*, 251–4
54 Powers, *Heisenberg's War*, 154–5; Monk, *Inside the Circle*, 402.

12. THE SAUCKEL EFFECT

1 Boog et al., *Germany and the Second World War*, 229
2 Jackson, *France*, 480
3 Wieviorka, *The French Resistance*, 206; Jackson, *France*, 376
4 L. Steinberg, *Not as a Lamb*, 6
5 E. Finkel, *Ordinary Jews*, 161
6 Homze, *Foreign Labor in Nazi Germany*, 152
7 Mazower, *Hitler's Empire*, 299
8 Korboński, *Fighting Warsaw*, 118, 223, 225
9 Kulski, *Dying, We Live*, 123–4
10 Mazower, *Hitler's Empire*, 492
11 M. Housden, *Hans Frank*, 196
12 Berkhoff, *Harvest of Despair*, 263
13 Gildea et al., 'To Work or Not to Work?'; Homze, *Foreign Labor in Nazi Germany*, 157
14 Ibid., 163
15 Shepherd, *War in the Wild East*, 127
16 Mazower, *Hitler's Empire*, 493; E. Harvey, 'Last Resort or Key Resource? Women Workers from the Nazi-Occupied Soviet Territories, the Reich Labour Administration and the German War Effort', *Transactions of the Royal Historical Society*, 26 (2016), 149–73
17 Reitlinger, *The House Built on Sand*, 239–42
18 Cooper, *The Phantom War*, 97
19 P. Longerich, *Heinrich Himmler*, 659–60
20 Mulligan, *The Politics of Illusion and Empire*, 85–7; Lumans, *Latvia in World War II*, 197–8; Remeikis (ed.), *Lithuania under German Occupation*, 199
21 Mazower, *Inside Hitler's Greece*, 75–8, 116–20; Hondros, 'The Greek Resistance'; Hondros, *Occupation and Resistance*, 77–8
22 Bryant, *Prague in Black*, 174, 182
23 Warmbrunn, *The German Occupation of Belgium*, 229–30
24 Haestrup, *Europe Ablaze*, 360; Warmbrunn, *The German Occupation of Belgium*, 231
25 Warmbrunn, *The German Occupation of Belgium*, 232–4; Gildea et al., 'To Work or Not to Work?'; Haestrup, *Europe Ablaze*, 360; C. Kesteloot, 'Belgium in Exile: The Experience of the Second World War', in Smetana and Geaney (eds), *Exile in London*, 20–31; Wieviorka, *The Resistance in Western Europe*, 149–52
26 Gildea et al., 'To Work or Not to Work?'
27 Warmbrunn, *The Dutch under German Occupation*, 150–52
28 Paape, 'How Dutch Resistance was Organised'; Warmbrunn, *The Dutch under German Occupation*, 117–18; Haestrup, *Europe Ablaze*, 104–5
29 J. Boas, *Religious Resistance in Holland*, 46, 62; Haestrup, *Europe Ablaze*, 105

30 Warmbrunn, *The Dutch under German Occupation*, 188–94
31 Laska (ed.), *Women in the Resistance*, 89
32 Maass, *The Netherlands at War*, 123
33 Haestrup, *Europe Ablaze*, 118–19
34 Gildea et al., 'To Work or Not to Work?'; Haestrup, *Europe Ablaze*, 118–20; Sweets, *Choices in Vichy France*, 24; Kedward, *Resistance in Vichy France*, 224–6
35 Vinen, *The Unfree French*, 197–8
36 Drake, *Paris at War*, 286; Kedward, *Resistance in Vichy France*, 227
37 Rings, *Life with the Enemy*, 122
38 Homze, *Foreign Labor in Nazi Germany*, 185–6; U. Herbert, *Hitler's Foreign Workers*, passim
39 Gildea, *Marianne in Chains*, 294
40 Diary entry, 22 February 1943, Guéhenno, *Diary of the Dark Years*, 195
41 Cobb, *The French Resistance*, 170
42 Haestrup, *Europe Ablaze*, 122
43 Bennett, *Under the Shadow of the Swastika*, 46
44 Boyd, *Voices from the Dark Years*, 181–2
45 Homze, *Foreign Labor in Nazi Germany*, 189
46 Stenton, *Radio London*, 232
47 Cobb, *The French Resistance*, 197
48 Boog et al., *Germany and the Second World War*, 239; Homze, *Foreign Labor in Nazi Germany*, 193; Boyd, *Voices from the Dark Years*, 181; Drake, *Paris at War*, 307, Hirschfeld, 'Collaboration in Nazi-Occupied France', in Hirschfeld and Marsh (eds), *Collaboration in France*, 1–14
49 H. Kedward, 'The Maquis and the Culture of the Outlaw', in Kedward and Austin (eds), *Vichy France and the Resistance*, 232–51; Mazower, *Hitler's Empire*, 492
50 Wieviorka, *The French Resistance*, 161
51 Frenay, *The Night Will End*, 262; Kedward, 'The Maquis and the Culture of the Outlaw'; Vinen, *The Unfree French*, 257; Pike, *Defying Vichy*, 149
52 H. Kedward, *In Search of the Maquis*, 30–34
53 Wieviorka, *The French Resistance*, 204
54 Frenay, *The Night Will End*, 252
55 Weitz, *Sisters in the Resistance*, 99–101
56 Kedward, *In Search of the Maquis*, 281
57 Cobb, *The French Resistance*, 173
58 Wieviorka, *The French Resistance*, 203, 205; Gildea, *Fighters in the Shadows*, 137
59 Laub, *After the Fall*, 106–10; Paxton, *Vichy France*, 293.

13. THE HOLOCAUST: THE CHRISTIAN RESPONSE

1 R. Lukas, *Forgotten Survivors*, 3
2 Lukas, *Out of the Inferno*, 9
3 I. de Haan, 'An Unresolved Controversy: The Jewish Honor Court in the Netherlands, 1946–1950', in L. Jockusch and G. Finder (eds), *Jewish Honor Courts*, 107–36
4 B. Wasserstein, *On the Eve*, passim; B. Moore, *Victims and Survivors*, 161; B. Moore, *Survivors*, 71
5 Wasserstein, *On the Eve*, 436 and passim.
6 Y. Gutman, *The Jews of Warsaw*, 30
7 J. Láníček, 'Walking on Egg-Shells: The Czechoslovak Exiles and Anti-Semitism in Occupied Europe during the Second World War', in Smetana and Geaney (eds), *Exile in London*, 227–54
8 A. Rayski, *The Choice of Jews under Vichy*, 74; Marrus and Paxton, *Vichy France and the Jews*, 239; Paxton, *Vichy France*, 184–5

9 Dewulf, *Spirit of Resistance*, 125; Hirschfeld, *Nazi Rule*, 145–6; Warmbrunn, *The German Occupation of Belgium*, 154; Gordon, *The Norwegian Resistance*, 489; Hoidal, *Quisling*, 596–7; Mazower, *Hitler's Empire*, 452; Paxton, *Vichy France*, 176–7
10 Marrus and Paxton, *Vichy France and the Jews*, 12, 181–5; L. Allen, 'Resistance and the Catholic Church in France', in Hawes and White (eds), *Resistance in Europe*, 77–93; Boyd, *Voices from the Dark Years*, 98, 119; Baudouin, *The Private Diaries*, 254; D. Cesarani, *Final Solution*, 312
11 R. Hilberg, *The Destruction of the European Jews*, I, 234
12 Kochanski, *The Eagle Unbowed*, 109–11
13 Warmbrunn, *The German Occupation of Belgium*, 155; Dewulf, *Spirit of Resistance*, 67; Rhode, 'The Protectorate of Bohemia and Moravia'
14 Sweets, *Choices in Vichy France*, 124; Rayski, *The Choice of Jews under Vichy*, 49; R. Poznanski, *Jews in France during World War II*, 57
15 Friedhoff, *Requiem for the Resistance*, 140
16 Warmbrunn, *The Dutch under German Occupation*, 64
17 Diary entry, 27 October 1940, A. Katsch (ed.), *Scroll of Agony*, 215–16
18 Kochanski, *The Eagle Unbowed*, 292–3; A. Polonsky, *The Jews in Poland and Russia*, III, 419–22; Quoted in P. Longerich, 'From Mass Murder to the "Final Solution"', in B. Wegner (ed.), *From Peace to War*, 253–75
19 Winkler, *The Age of Catastrophe*, 727; T. Olszański, *Kresy Kresów Stanisławów*, 115; T. Snyder, *Bloodlands*, 199–200
20 Rayski, *The Choice of Jews under Vichy*, 209
21 See the works of David Cesarani and Raul Hilberg
22 Ward, *Priest, Politician, Collaborator*, 8, 229–39; Lettrich, *History of Modern Slovakia*, 181–90; J. Hoensch, 'The Slovak Republic, 1939–1945', in Mamatey and Luža (eds), *A History of the Czechoslovak Republic*, 271–95; Cesarani, *Final Solution*, 525–6
23 Marrus and Paxton, *Vichy France and the Jews*, 278
24 Cesarani, *Final Solution*, 545–6; Rayski, *The Choice of Jews under Vichy*, 80–81; Bennett, *Under the Shadow of the Swastika*, 63; Paxton, *Vichy France*, 171; Thompson to State Department, 7 August 1942, *FRUS* 1942, I, 464; J. Fox, 'How Far Did Vichy France "Sabotage" the Imperatives of Wannsee?', in D. Cesarani (ed.), *The Final Solution*, 194–214
25 M. Schreiber, *Silent Rebels*, 67–8
26 Pryce Jones, 'Paris during the German Occupation'; Dank, *The French against the French*, 243; Jackson, *France*, 216–18; Wieviorka, *The French Resistance*, 216
27 Hirschfeld, *Nazi Rule*, 173–8; J. C. H. Blom, 'The Persecution of the Jews in the Netherlands: A Comparative Western European Perspective', *European History Quarterly*, 19 (1989), 333–51
28 Warmbrunn, *The German Occupation of Belgium*, 152
29 Hilberg, *The Destruction of the European Jews*, 556
30 See especially J. Cornwall, *Hitler's Pope*, passim
31 Jackson, *France*, 375–6; Wieviorka, *The French Resistance*, 216; Poznanski, *Jews in France*, 295–7; Marrus and Paxton, *Vichy France and the Jews*, 270–55
32 Dewulf, *Spirit of Resistance*, 118; Warmbrunn, *The Dutch under German Occupation*, 160–62; Moore, *Victims and Survivors*, 127–8; Moore, *Survivors*, 205–6
33 Polonsky, *The Jews in Poland and Russia*, III, 470–4; Y. Gutman and S. Krakowski, *Unequal Victims*, 185; Lukas, *Out of the Inferno*, 57
34 J. Presser, *Ashes in the Wind*, 325–6
35 Schreiber, *Silent Rebels*, 89
36 N. Tec, *When Light Pierced the Darkness*, 111–12; Polonsky, *The Jews in Poland and Russia*, III, 444–6; W. Bartoszewski, *The Bloodshed Unites Us*, 48
37 Cobb, *The French Resistance*, 136–7; Cesarani, *Final Solution*, 555; Dewulf, *Spirit of Resistance*, 126; Poznanski, *Jews in France*, 298–9; Presser, *Ashes in the Wind*, 162; Cowburn, *No Cloak, No Dagger*, 113; Gildea, *Marianne in Chains*, 276
38 Cesarani, *Final Solution*, 555

39 Boas, *Religious Resistance in Holland*, 47; Dewulf, *Spirit of Resistance*, 126; Láníček, 'Walking on Egg-Shells'
40 Wieviorka, *The French Resistance*, 219; Shennan, *Rethinking France*, 44
41 Rayski, *The Choice of Jews under Vichy*, 54–5; Polonsky, *The Jews in Poland and Russia*, III, 565–6; R. Breitman, *Official Secrets*, 119; Cesarani, *Final Solution*, 491; Mazower, *Hitler's Empire*, 388; J. Fairweather, *The Volunteer*, passim
42 J. Karski, *Story of a Secret State*, 261–77
43 M. Gilbert, *Auschwitz and the Allies*, 103
44 T. Wood and S. Jankowski, *Karski*, 188
45 Breitman, *Official Secrets*, 116–20
46 Nowak, *Courier from Warsaw*, 274–5. There is far more on this subject in Gilbert, *Auschwitz and the Allies*
47 Dewulf, *Spirit of Resistance*, 126; Moore, *Survivors*, 180
48 Boas, *Religious Resistance in Holland*, 58–60; Warmbrunn, *The Dutch under German Occupation*, 160–61; Diary entry, 27 February 1943, Anne Frank in O. Frank and M. Pressler (eds), *The Diary of a Young Girl*, 87; Diary entry, 8 March 1943, in Lochner (ed.), *The Goebbels Diaries*, 211
49 Presser, *Ashes in the Wind*, 196–202; B. Wasserstein, *The Ambiguity of Virtue*, 173; Warmbrunn, *The Dutch under German Occupation*, 162
50 Jackson, *France*, 361; Hilberg, *Destruction of the European Jews*, 656–7; Marrus and Paxton, *Vichy France and the Jews*, 335, 372; Fox, 'How Far Did Vichy France "Sabotage" the Imperatives of Wannsee?'; Hirschfeld, *Nazi Rule*, 179; G. Lewy, *The Catholic Church and Nazi Germany*, 293
51 C. Browning, *Ordinary Men*, 149
52 T. Snyder, *Black Earth*, 316
53 S. Korboński, *The Jews and Poles in World War II*, 67; Tec, *When Light Pierced the Darkness*, 4
54 Frank and Pressler (eds), *The Diary of a Young Girl*, 337–8
55 Steinberg, *Not as a Lamb*, 149
56 J. Steinberg, 'Types of Genocide? Croatians, Serbs and Jews, 1941–5', in Cesarani (ed.), *The Final Solution*, 175–93; Manoschek, '"Coming Along to Shoot Some Jews?"'; Hoare, *Genocide and Resistance in Hitler's Bosnia*, 158–9; Tomasevich, *Occupation and Collaboration*, 605
57 Mazower, *Hitler's Empire*, 399–400; C. Rittner and S. Myers, *The Courage to Care*, 74–7; Burgwyn, *Empire on the Adriatic*, 193; Boyd, *Voices from the Dark Years*, 149
58 Rittner and Myers, *The Courage to Care*, 82–5; Moore, *Survivors*, 76–9
59 Warmbrunn, *The Dutch under German Occupation*, 88–9
60 Moore, *Survivors*, 238
61 Ibid., 178–9
62 T. Prekerowa, 'The Relief Council for Jews in Poland, 1942–1945', in C. Abramsky et al., *The Jews in Poland*, 161–76; Bartoszewski, *The Bloodshed Unites Us*, 87–8, 100–16; J. Zimmerman, *The Polish Underground and the Jews, 1939–1945*, 177, 308, 373; G. Paulsson, *Secret City*, 5; P. Friedman, *Their Brothers' Keepers*, passim.
63 Schreiber, *Silent Rebels*, 102
64 Moore, *Victims and Survivors*, 182–6; Wasserstein, *The Ambiguity of Virtue*, 153; E. Fogelman, *Conscience and Courage*, passim
65 C. Moorehead, *Village of Secrets*, 336, 341–3; L. Lazare, *Rescue as Resistance*, passim
66 Moorehead, *Village of Secrets*, passim; P. Grose, *A Good Place to Hide*, passim; P. Hallie, *Lest Innocent Blood Be Shed*, passim; R. Zaretsky, *Nîmes at War*, 164–5; Rayski, *The Choice of Jews under Vichy*, 184–8; Poznanski, *Jews in France*, 410–4; Rittner and Myers, *The Courage to Care*, 109–15
67 Grose, *A Good Place to Hide*, loc 1402
68 Dewulf, *Spirit of Resistance*, 68
69 Presser, *Ashes in the Wind*, 400

70 Steinberg, *Not as a Lamb*, 148
71 Prekerowa, 'The Relief Council for Jews in Poland'; Bartoszewski, *The Bloodshed Unites Us*, 99
72 Moore, *Survivors*, 192–206
73 K. Iranek-Osmecki, *He Who Saves One Life*, 50
74 Moorehead, *Village of Secrets*, 137–8
75 Poznanski, *Jews in France*, 482.

14. THE HOLOCAUST: THE JEWISH RESPONSE

1 Lukas, *Out of the Inferno*, 11
2 D. Engel, 'Why Punish the Collaborators?', in Jockusch and Finder (eds), *Jewish Honor Courts*, 29–48
3 Hilberg, *Destruction of the European Jews*, III, 1,030
4 Ibid., 539
5 Cobb, *The French Resistance*, 186–8; A. Lissner, 'Diary of a Jewish Partisan in Paris', in Y. Suhl (ed.), *They Fought Back*, 311–27; Rayski, *The Choice of Jews under Vichy*, 137, 234–6; J. Adler, *The Jews of Paris and the Final Solution*, 201
6 Jackson, *France*, 368; Steinberg, *Not as a Lamb*, 111–15; Poznanski, *Jews in France*, 452–5, 460; A. Latour, *The Jewish Resistance in France*, 53; J. Ariel, 'Jewish Self-Defence and Resistance in France during World War II', *Yad Vashem Studies*, VI (1967), 221–50; R. Poznanski, 'Reflections on Jewish Resistance and Jewish Resistants in France', *Jewish Social Studies*, 2:1 (1995), 124–58
7 Poznanski, *Jews in France*, 451; Latour, *The Jewish Resistance in France*, 190
8 Jackson, *France*, 363, 366; Marrus and Paxton, *Vichy France and the Jews*, 243; M. Marrus, 'Jewish Resistance to the Holocaust', *Journal of Contemporary History*, 30:1 (1995), 83–110; Moore, *Victims and Survivors*, 197; Hilberg, *Destruction of the European Jews*, III, 555; Bryant, *Prague in Black*, 151
9 Interview with S. Faull, IWM 18272
10 W. Bartoszewski, 'Polish-Jewish Relations in Occupied Poland, 1939–1945' in Abramsky et al. (eds), *The Jews in Poland*, 147–60
11 M. Gilbert, *The Holocaust*, 608
12 Adler, *The Jews of Paris and the Final Solution*, 46
13 Kochanski, *The Eagle Unbowed*, 304
14 A. Adelson and R. Lapides, *Łódź Ghetto*, 330
15 Warmbrunn, *The German Occupation of Belgium*, 157–8; V. Vanden Daelen and N. Wouters, '"The Lesser Evil" of Jewish Collaboration?', in Jockusch and Finder (eds), *Jewish Honor Courts*, 197–224; Schreiber, *Silent Rebels*, 88; Cesarani, *Final Solution*, 558
16 Cesarani, *Final Solution*, 558–60; Presser, *Ashes in the Wind*, 140–44, 264; Wasserstein, *The Ambiguity of Virtue*, 175, 254; Warmbrunn, *The Dutch under German Occupation*, 66–7
17 Rayski, *The Choice of Jews under Vichy*, 85–6; Jackson, *France*, 364–5
18 Hilberg, *Destruction of the European Jews*, 495
19 L. S. Dawidowicz, *The War against the Jews 1933–1945*, 348
20 I. Trunk, *Judenrat*, passim
21 Katsch (ed.), *Scroll of Agony*, 385
22 Quoted in L. Smith (ed.), *Forgotten Voices of the Holocaust*, 121
23 A. Lewin, *A Cup of Tears*, 179
24 E. Ringelblum, *Notes from the Warsaw Ghetto*, 330
25 Gutman, *The Jews of Warsaw*, 447
26 Y. Zuckerman, *A Surplus of Memory*, 212
27 M. Edelman, *The Ghetto Fights*, 55–6
28 Polonsky, *The Jews in Poland and Russia*, III, 507

29 Gilbert, *Holocaust*, 595; I. Trunk, 'The Attitude of the Judenrats to the Problems of Armed Resistance against the Nazis', in M. Grubsztein (ed.), *Jewish Resistance during the Holocaust*, 202–27
30 Itzhak Cukierman quoted in P. Friedman (ed.), *Martyrs and Fighters*, 205–6
31 E. Hillesum, *Letters from Westerbork*, 125
32 Steinberg, *Not as a Lamb*, 230–38; Polonsky, *The Jews in Poland and Russia*, III, 494, 517; E. Sterling, 'The Ultimate Sacrifice: The Death of Resistance Hero Yitzhak Wittenberg and the Decline of the United Partisan Organization', in R. Rohrlich (ed.), *Resisting the Holocaust*, 59–76
33 M. Dworzecki, 'The Day-to-Day Stand of the Jews', in Grubsztein (ed.), *Jewish Resistance during the Holocaust*, 152–81
34 In the end the child alone was hidden. Rittner and Myers, *The Courage to Care*, 26
35 Diary entry, 26 May 1944, Frank and Pressler (eds), *The Diary of a Young Girl*, 305
36 R. Altbeker Cyprys, *A Jump for Life*, 121
37 E. Ringelblum, *Polish-Jewish Relations*, 100–101
38 Bartoszewski, *The Bloodshed Unites Us*, 87
39 T. Piotrowski, *Poland's Holocaust*, 66; M. Grynberg (ed.), *Words to Outlive Us*, 162, 175; R. Lukas, *Forgotten Holocaust*, 118
40 Maass, *The Netherlands at War*, 121
41 Altbeker Cyprys, *A Jump for Life*, 165
42 Warmbrunn, *The German Occupation of Belgium*, 160
43 Wasserstein, *The Ambiguity of Virtue*, 194
44 Schreiber, *The Silent Rebels*, 1, 623, 173–7, 191–2, 206, 221, 244; Moore, *Survivors*, 180–81; Cobb, *The French Resistance*, 204–7; Poznanski, *Jews in France*, 318
45 Zdzisław Rozbicki quoted in M. Turski, *Polish Witnesses to the Shoah*, 106
46 Edelman, *The Ghetto Fights*, 37
47 Gutman, *The Jews of Warsaw*, 286–7, 294–6
48 Bennett, *Under the Shadow of the Swastika*, 222
49 Y. Arad et al. (eds.), *Documents on the Holocaust*, 161
50 R. Ainsztein, 'The Bialystok Ghetto Revolt', in Suhl (ed.), *They Fought Back*, 158–66
51 J. Glass, *Jewish Resistance during the Holocaust*, 51
52 Finkel, *Ordinary Jews*, 164, 170
53 Rowecki to London, 4 January 1943, *AK Documents*, II, 282
54 *Polskie Siły Zbrojne*, III, 234
55 Quoted in Lukas, *Forgotten Holocaust*, 174
56 Gutman, *The Jews of Warsaw*, 310–11
57 S. Krakowski, *The War of the Doomed*, 182
58 Edelman, *The Ghetto Fights*, 70
59 Ibid., 71
60 Gutman, *The Jews of Warsaw*, 320
61 Lukas, *Forgotten Holocaust*, 175
62 Polonsky, *The Jews in Poland and Russia*, III, 513
63 Zuckerman, *A Surplus of Memory*, 307, 313
64 Gutman, *The Jews of Warsaw*, 365–6; Y. Zuckerman, 'Twenty-Five Years after the Warsaw Ghetto Revolt', in Grubsztein (ed.), *Jewish Resistance during the Holocaust*, 23–34
65 Interview with D. Falkner, IWM 19783
66 S. Rotem, *Memoirs of a Warsaw Ghetto Fighter*, 159
67 Korboński, *The Jews and Poles*, 57–8; Polonsky, *The Jews in Poland and Russia*, III, 515
68 Zimmerman, *The Polish Underground and the Jews*, 215
69 Korboński, *The Jews and the Poles*, 58
70 I. Deák, *Essays on Hitler's Europe*, 73
71 Ringelblum, *Polish-Jewish Relations*, 178–9
72 Kulski, *Dying, We Live*, 146

73 D. Kurzman, *The Bravest Battle*, 283–4
74 Edelman, *The Ghetto Fights*, 41
75 Gilbert, *Holocaust*, 563–5
76 M. Ginter, *Life in Both Hands*, 160
77 Report on the Warsaw Ghetto revolt, 4 May 1943, *AK Documents*, III, 4–6
78 Altbeker Cyprys, *A Jump for Life*, 133
79 J. Iwaszkiewicz, *Notatki 1939–1945*, 84
80 D. Engel, *Facing a Holocaust*, 70–71
81 Finkel, *Ordinary Jews*, 188–9; Steinberg, *Not as a Lamb*, 247–51; Ainsztein, 'Bialystok Ghetto Revolt'; Cesarani, *Final Solution*, 631–2; Polonsky, *The Jews in Poland and Russia*, III, 517–19; R. Hilberg, *Perpetrators, Victims, Bystanders*, 182–3
82 Cesarani, *Final Solution*, 642–3; N. Tec, *Resistance*, 151–2
83 Cesarani, *Final Solution*, 644–6; A. Peczorski [Pechersky], 'The Revolt at the Sobibor Extermination Camp', in Arad et al. (eds), *Documents on the Holocaust*, 356–8
84 J. Garliński, *Fighting Auschwitz*, passim; W. Pilecki, *The Auschwitz Volunteer*, passim; Tec, *Resistance*, 125–30; Fairweather, *The Volunteer*, passim
85 N. Wachsmann, *KL*, 538–40; Tec, *Resistance*, 131–44; Cesarani, *Final Solution*, 746–7
86 N. Eck, 'The Place of Jewish Political Parties in the Countries under Nazi Rule', in Grubsztein (ed.), *Jewish Resistance during the Holocaust*, 132–47; B. Epstein, *The Minsk Ghetto*, 260, 280
87 Epstein, *The Minsk Ghetto*, passim; Finkel, *Ordinary Jews*, 130–31; Polonsky, *The Jews in Poland and Russia*, III, 500
88 N. Tec, *Defiance*, passim; Polonsky, *The Jews in Poland and Russia*, III, 523; Glass, *Jewish Resistance during the Holocaust*, 55; Slepyan, 'Partisans, Civilians and the Soviet State'
89 Z. Bar-On, 'On the Position of the Jewish Partisans in the Soviet Partisan Movement', in *European Resistance Movements, 1939–1945: First International Conference on the History of Resistance Movements*, 215–47
90 Rotem, *Memoirs of a Warsaw Ghetto Fighter*, 93
91 J. Lowell Armstrong, 'The Polish Underground and the Jews: A Reassessment of Home Army Commander Tadeusz Bór-Komorowski's Order 116 against Banditry', *Slavonic and East European Review*, 72 (1994), 259–76; Gutman and Krakowski, *Unequal Victims*, 121–33; R. Ainsztein, *Jewish Resistance in Nazi-Occupied Eastern Europe*, passim
92 Tec, *Resistance*, 106
93 Polonsky, *The Jews in Poland and Russia*, III, 463–9, 520–22, 522–5; Slepyan, *Stalin's Guerrillas*, 56–7, 211–12; Tec, *Defiance*, 151; Tec, *Resistance*, 44
94 Glass, *Jewish Resistance during the Holocaust*, 58; Tec, *Resistance*, 44.

15. WHO IS THE ENEMY?

1 Hoidal, *Quisling*, 515
2 Dahl, *Quisling*, 244
3 Littlejohn, *The Patriotic Traitors*, 20
4 Diary entry, 3 February 1942, in Lochner (ed.), *The Goebbels Diaries*, 30
5 Rings, *Life with the Enemy*, 94–5
6 Gjelsvik, *Norwegian Resistance*, 63–4
7 Semelin, *Unarmed against Hitler*, 67; Hoidal, *Quisling*, 567–8; Dahl, *Quisling*, 260; Rings, *Life with the Enemy*, 160
8 Dewulf, *Spirit of Resistance*, 118; Warmbrunn, *The Dutch under German Occupation*, 163; Boas, *Religious Resistance in Holland*, 11, 25, 31, 46; Haestrup, *Europe Ablaze*, 87; Rings, *Life with the Enemy*, 163
9 Boas, *Religious Resistance in Holland*, 64

10 Haestrup, *Europe Ablaze*, 88; Littlejohn, *The Patriotic Traitors*, 170
11 Skodvin, 'Norwegian Non-Violent Resistance'
12 Gordon, *The Norwegian Resistance*, 211
13 Gjelsvik, *Norwegian Resistance*, 61
14 Hoidal, *Quisling*, 570–71
15 Skodvin, 'Norwegian Non-Violent Resistance'
16 Semelin, *Unarmed against Hitler*, 69
17 Dahl, *Quisling*, 258
18 Hayes, *Quisling*, 276; Gjelsvik, *Norwegian Resistance*, 114–15; Hoidal, *Quisling*, 620–22
19 Rings, *Life with the Enemy*, 166, 176–7
20 Semelin, *Unarmed against Hitler*, 70–72; Rings, *Life with the Enemy*, 158, 175–6; W. Noordhoek Hegt, 'The Resistance of the Medical Profession', *Annals of the American Academy of Political and Social Science*, 245 (1946), 162–8
21 Paape, 'How Dutch Resistance was Organised'
22 Gjelsvik, *Norwegian Resistance*, 93–8; Hoidal, *Quisling*, 610–12
23 Hayes, *Quisling*, 290; Dahl, *Quisling*, 314; Gjelsvik, *Norwegian Resistance*, 108–9
24 J. Andenaes, O. Riste and M. Skodvin, *Norway and the Second World War*, 73–5; Gjelsvik, *Norwegian Resistance*, 110
25 Reed Olsen, *Two Eggs on my Plate*, 234
26 Conway, *Collaboration in Belgium*, 75
27 Gjelsvik, *Norwegian Resistance*, 77–8
28 See Littlejohn, *The Patriotic Traitors*, and Longerich, *Heinrich Himmler*, for further details on the Legions.
29 R.-D. Muller, *The Unknown Eastern Front*, 128
30 Drake, *Paris at War*, 198
31 Conway, *Collaboration in Belgium*, 109, 209–11
32 Littlejohn, *The Patriotic Traitors*, 72–4
33 Ibid., 241; Maass, *The Netherlands at War*, 140
34 Schreiber, *Silent Rebels*, 85; Conway, *Collaboration in Belgium*, 107–8, 154, 166, 186, 216–17
35 Conway, *Collaboration in Belgium*, 155
36 Warmbrunn, *The Dutch under German Occupation*, 208
37 Schreiber, *Silent Rebels*, 139
38 Kochanski, *The Eagle Unbowed*, 276; Williamson, *The Polish Underground*, 58
39 Longerich, *Heinrich Himmler*, 656; Warmbrunn, *The Dutch under German Occupation*, 207; Maass, *The Netherlands at War*, 140–41
40 Slepyan, *Stalin's Guerrillas*, 220
41 Hill, *The War behind the Eastern Front*, 146–7
42 Dallin, *German Rule in Russia*, 219
43 Cooper, *The Phantom War*, 121; Shepherd, *War in the Wild East*, 177
44 Prażmowska, *Civil War in Poland*, 45–59; TNA, HS 4/138; Sagajllo, *The Man in the Middle*, 80
45 Garliński, 'The Polish Underground State'
46 Borodziej, *The Warsaw Uprising*, 44
47 G. Iranek-Osmecki, *The Unseen and Silent*, 144
48 A. Gogun, *Stalin's Commandos*, 257
49 Iranek-Osmecki, *The Unseen and Silent*, 144
50 Kochanski, *The Eagle Unbowed*, 366
51 A. Prusin, *The Lands Between*, 180–87; Piotrowski, *Poland's Holocaust*, 168; C. Łuczak, *Polska i Polacy*, 506
52 Kochanski, *The Eagle Unbowed*, 360–62
53 Kosyk, *The Third Reich and the Ukrainian Question*, 310–11, 341–2, 361–3; B. Krawchenko, 'Soviet Ukraine under Nazi Occupation, 1941–4', in Y. Boshyk (ed.), *Ukraine during World War II*, 15–37

54 Kamenetsky, *Hitler's Occupation of the Ukraine*, 76–7; Reitlinger, *The House Built on Sand*, 246–9; Kovpak, *Our Partisan Course*, passim; Blood, *Hitler's Bandit Hunters*, 190–93
55 Cooper, *The Phantom War*, 121–2
56 R. Overy, *Russia's War*, 128–9
57 Ibid., 125
58 C. Andreyev, *Vlasov and the Russian Liberation Movement*, 19–29, 38–40
59 Kochanski, *The Eagle Unbowed*, 362.

16. DIVIDED LOYALTIES: FRANCE 1942–43

1 Wieviorka, *The French Resistance*, 140–41; Jackson, *France*, 427–9
2 D. Cordier, *Jean Moulin*, 144; Jackson, *France*, 431
3 C. Pineau, *La Simple Vérité*, 158–9
4 Jackson, *France*, 431
5 De Gaulle, *War Memoirs*, I, 277
6 Wieviorka, *The French Resistance*, 173; A. Clinton, *Jean Moulin*, 138
7 Cobb, *The Resistance*, 118
8 Frenay, *The Night Will End*, 184–5
9 Kedward, *Resistance in Vichy France*, 217–18; Wieviorka, *The French Resistance*, 188–9; Clinton, *Jean Moulin*, 135–7
10 Cobb, *The Resistance*, 97; Wieviorka, *The French Resistance*, 166–7
11 Jackson, *France*, 431
12 Frenay, *The Night Will End*, 124–5
13 Colonel Passy, *Souvenirs*, 96
14 Cobb, *The Resistance*, 128–30; Wieviorka, *The French Resistance*, 166–7; De Gaulle, *War Memoirs*, I, 276; Schoenbrun, *Soldiers of the Night*, 238
15 Dank, *The French against the French*, 123–5
16 Cobb, *The Resistance*, 163
17 Boyd, *Voices from the Dark Years*, 188; Frenay, *The Night Will End*, 254–5
18 Noguères et al., *Histoire de la Résistance*, II, 613
19 Dank, *The French against the French*, 133
20 D. Eisenhower, *Crusade in Europe*, 88
21 Paxton, *Vichy France*, 313
22 F. Kersaudy, *Churchill and de Gaulle*, 215
23 Gildea, *Fighters in the Shadows*, 243
24 Alan Brooke, diary entry, 18 January 1943, in A. Danchev and D. Todman (eds), *War Diaries*, 362–3; Boyd, *Voices from the Dark Years*, 151
25 Diary entries, 26 April, 1 and 4 May 1942, in Lochner (ed.), *The Goebbels Diaries*, 136–7, 148, 152; Murphy, *Diplomat among Warriors*, 215
26 Mangold, *Britain and the Defeated French*, 159–60
27 Frenay, *The Night Will End*, 192–3; Mangold, *Britain and the Defeated French*, 160; J. Jackson, *A Certain Idea of France*, 211
28 Roosevelt to Churchill, 2 September 1942, and Churchill to Roosevelt, 14 September 1942, in W. Kimball (ed.), *Churchill and Roosevelt*, I, 589, 594
29 Fourcade, *Noah's Ark*, 156–63; Olson, *Madame Fourcade's Secret War*, 160–69
30 Eisenhower, *Crusade in Europe*, 111
31 Kersaudy, *Churchill and de Gaulle*, 216
32 Gildea, *Fighters in the Shadows*, 241
33 De Gaulle, *War Memoirs*, II, 48
34 Eisenhower, *Crusade in Europe*, 116; W. Churchill, *The Second World War*, IV, 547, 558
35 Jackson, *France*, 224
36 Gildea, *Fighters in the Shadows*, 252; Eisenhower, *Crusade in Europe*, 119; H. Macmillan, *The Blast of War*, 208

37 Dank, *The French against the French*, 201
38 Hansard, vol. 385, 12 November 1942, col. 137
39 Churchill, *The Second World War*, IV, 568
40 G. Maguire, *Anglo-American Policy towards the Free French*, 67
41 De Gaulle, *War Memoirs*, II, 58–9
42 W. Leahy, *I Was There*, 163
43 Cobb, *The Resistance*, 146
44 Mangold, *Britain and the Defeated French*, 164–5
45 Cobb, *The Resistance*, 146
46 Eisenhower, *Crusade in Europe*, 145–6
47 Dodds-Parker, *Setting Europe Ablaze*, 113
48 Wilkinson and Bright Astley, *Gubbins and SOE*, 114
49 Kersaudy, *Churchill and de Gaulle*, 229–30
50 Lacouture, *De Gaulle*, 409–11; Mangold, *Britain and the Defeated French*, 175–7; Maguire, *Anglo-American Policy*, 71–4; Jackson, *A Certain Idea of France*, 250
51 Churchill, *The Second World War*, IV, 578
52 P. Novick, *The Resistance versus Vichy*, 43
53 Wieviorka, *The French Resistance*, 178; Gildea, *Fighters in the Shadows*, 256
54 Jackson, *France*, 448
55 Gildea, *Fighters in the Shadows*, 258
56 Jackson, *France*, 457–60; Gildea *Fighters in the Shadows*, 278–84; Macmillan, *The Blast of War*, 249; Churchill, *The Second World War*, V, 154–64
57 Kersaudy, *Churchill and de Gaulle*, 277
58 Wieviorka, *The French Resistance*, 183
59 De Gaulle, *War Memoirs*, II, 54
60 Wieviorka, *The French Resistance*, 181–2
61 Laub, *After the Fall*, 265–6; Longerich, *Heinrich Himmler*, 651; Mazower, *Hitler's Empire*, 438–40
62 Kedward, *In Search of the Maquis*, 71; Littlejohn, *The Patriotic Traitors*, 230; B. Gordon, *Collaborationism in France during the Second World War*, 180–81; Dank, *The French against the French*, 202–3, 250; Jackson, *France*, 230–31; Drake, *Paris at War*, 313
63 Drake, *Paris at War*, 314; Jackson, *France*, 216
64 Drake, *Paris at War*, 315–17
65 I. Colvin (ed.), *Colonel Henri's Story*, 49–50
66 Dank, *The French against the French*, 222
67 Wieviorka, *The French Resistance*, 231
68 Dank, *The French against the French*, 255
69 H. Lottman, *The People's Anger*, 28–9; Novick, *The Resistance versus Vichy*, 26, 29
70 Rings, *Life with the Enemy*, 199
71 Dank, *The French against the French*, 250
72 Lottman, *The People's Anger*, 23–4
73 Kedward, *Resistance in Vichy France*, 137
74 Maguire, *Anglo-American Policy*, 103; Reports by Dulles, 6 March 1943, 18 May 1943, in N. Petersen (ed.), *From Hitler's Doorstep*, 49, 64–5; Frenay, *The Night Will End*, 263
75 Mackenzie, *The Secret History of SOE*, 285
76 Jackson, *France*, 433–4
77 Schoenbrun, *Soldiers of the Night*, 253–5
78 H. Michel, *Les Courants de pensée de la Résistance*, 272–3
79 Wieviorka, *The French Resistance*, 243
80 Clinton, *Jean Moulin*, 159–60
81 Wieviorka, *The French Resistance*, 254
82 Passy, *Souvenirs: Missions secrètes en France*, 74
83 Ibid., 63
84 Noguères et al., *Histoire de la Résistance*, III, 222–45; Marshall, *The White Rabbit*, 29–35

85 Marshall, *The White Rabbit*, 34
86 Jackson, *France*, 451
87 Lacouture, *De Gaulle*, 437–8
88 Wieviorka, *The French Resistance*, 261
89 Passy, *Souvenirs: Missions secrètes en France*, 181
90 Frenay, *The Night Will End*, 237, 264
91 Clinton, *Jean Moulin*, 141
92 Macksey, *The Partisans of Europe*, 114
93 Dank, *The French against the French*, 137–8
94 Wieviorka, *The French Resistance*, 264–5
95 Novick, *The Resistance versus Vichy*, 36
96 Clinton, *Jean Moulin*, 151
97 Ibid., 174
98 Cordier, *Jean Moulin*, 223–6
99 Kersaudy, *Churchill and de Gaulle*, 276–7
100 Kedward, *Occupied France*, 68; Gildea, *Fighters in the Shadows*, 283.

17. THE GERMANS HIT BACK

1 S. Tyas, *SS-Major Horst Kopkow*, 38–9, 65–9; D. O'Reilly, 'Interrogating the Gestapo: SS-Sturmbannführer Horst Kopkow, the *Rote Kapelle* and Postwar British Intelligence', *Journal of Intelligence History*, forthcoming
2 V. Atkins, IWM 12636, 9551
3 M. Buckmaster, *Specially Employed*, 186–7; Buckmaster, *They Fought Alone*, 207; S. Helm, *A Life in Secrets*, 359
4 See Foot, *SOE in the Low Countries*, 106–206, for details of the agents despatched and of the *Englandspiel* in general.
5 E. Cookridge, *Inside SOE*, 410; N. Kelso, *Errors of Judgement*, 224–5
6 P. Lorain, *Secret Warfare*, 43; F. Boyce and D. Everett, *SOE*, 208–11, 215; Foot, *SOE in France*, 95
7 R. Beauclerk, IWM 14847
8 Le Chêne, *Watch for Me by Moonlight*, 142–3
9 Iranek-Osmecki, *The Unseen and Silent*, 72
10 Boyce, *SOE*, 220–21; Fourcade, *Noah's Ark*, 238–9; Rootham, *Miss Fire*, 55
11 Boyce, *SOE*, 219; Stafford, *Secret Agent*, 147; Le Chêne, *Watch for Me by Moonlight*, 59–60; Millar, *Maquis*, 60; Lorain, *Secret Warfare*, 39
12 Hamson, *We Fell among Greeks*, 183–4
13 Foot, *SOE*, 165
14 Lorain, *Secret Warfare*, 67–8, 71; Foot, *SOE in France*, 99; L. Marks, *Between Silk and Cyanide*, passim.
15 Marks, *Between Silk and Cyanide*, 16
16 Chevrillon, *Codename Christiane Clouet*, 126
17 Foot, *SOE in the Low Countries*, 111–14, 127
18 Lauwers in H. Giskes, *London Calling North Pole*, 184–5
19 Ibid., 75–7, and Lauwers in ibid., 189–90
20 Ibid., 29
21 Kelso, *Errors of Judgement*, 240–55; Cookridge, *Inside SOE*, 429–32; Mackenzie, *Secret History of SOE*, 303
22 Foot, *SOE in the Low Countries*, 134
23 Giskes, *London Calling North Pole*, 105–6
24 Ibid., 110; Foot, *SOE in the Low Countries*, 124
25 P. Ganier-Raymond, *The Tangled Web*, 71–7, 127–39
26 De Jong, Comment, in Foot (ed.), *Holland at War against Hitler*, 147–8; Giskes, *London Calling North Pole*, 109–13

27 F. Griffiths, IWM 12270; Stafford, *Secret Agent*, 141; Foot, *SOE in the Low Countries*, 175
28 Marks, *Between Silk and Cyanide*, 112, 114, 116, 124–5, 205, 215, 348 and passim
29 Foot, *SOE in the Low Countries*, 126
30 Ibid., 178
31 Dourlein, *Inside North Pole*, passim; G. Zembsch-Schreve, *Pierre Lalande*, 107; Marks, *Between Silk and Cyanide*, 430–31, 453, 479
32 Marks, *Between Silk and Cyanide*, 499–500
33 Cookridge, *Inside SOE*, 436
34 Ibid., 487; L. Pot, Comment, in Foot (ed.), *Holland at War against Hitler*, 139–43
35 Friedhoff, *Requiem for the Resistance*, 174
36 Mayer, *Gaston's War*, 121, 129–31, 154, 194
37 Mackenzie, *Secret History of SOE*, 300
38 Stafford, *Britain and European Resistance*, 137–8
39 Muus, *The Spark and the Flame*, 131–3; Haestrup, *Europe Ablaze*, 297–8
40 Stafford, *Britain and European Resistance*, 138–40
41 The following section has relied on a variety of sources, not all of which agree with each other. Particularly useful were: Foot, *SOE in France*; F. Suttill, *Shadows in the Fog*; Helm, *A Life in Secrets*; R. Bourne-Paterson, *SOE in France*; J. Grehan and M. Mace, *Unearthing Churchill's Secret Army*; Seymour-James, *She Landed by Moonlight*, 149; Colvin (ed.), *Colonel Henri's Story*, passim; Mackenzie, *Secret History of SOE*, 568–9; S. Basu, *Spy Princess*, 155–223; C. Glass, *They Fought Alone*, 90–109; J. Rée (ed.), *A Schoolmaster's War*, 38–9, 48; Personal files of SOE agents held in TNA, HS 9 series
42 Jenkins, *A Pacifist at War*, 70–71
43 Ibid., 102
44 Drake, *Paris at War*, 315–17
45 Verity, *We Landed by Moonlight*, 164–5; H. Verity, IWM 9939
46 Foot, *SOE in France*, 259, 266–72
47 Suttill, *Shadows in the Fog*, 153
48 Seymour-Jones, *She Landed by Moonlight*, 229
49 Buckmaster, *They Fought Alone*, 69
50 Suttill, *Shadows in the Fog*, 163
51 Cowburn, *No Cloak, No Dagger*, 118
52 TNA, HS9/836/5
53 Marks, *Between Silk and Cyanide*, 315–20
54 Tyas, *SS-Major Horst Kopkow*, 117; Glass, *They Fought Alone*, 90
55 Watt, *The Comet Connection*, 123; Stafford, *Secret Agent*, 210
56 O. Sansom, IWM 9478
57 Foot, *SOE in the Low Countries*, 167
58 Glass, *They Fought Alone*, 104–9; John Starr was investigated by SOE concerning his conduct in captivity but was not court-martialled since the evidence against him was contradictory
59 Cookridge, *They Came from the Sky*, 196
60 D. Nicolson, *Aristide*, 54–5, 60–3; Foot, *SOE in France*, 249–51; Cookridge, *They Came from the Sky*, 191–9; Bourne-Paterson, *SOE in France*, 65–70; P. Ashdown, *Game of Spies*, passim
61 Cordier, *Jean Moulin*, 430–76; Clinton, *Jean Moulin*, 179–86; Dank, *The French against the French*, 139–57; Cobb, *The Resistance*, 165–9; Wieviorka, *The French Resistance*, 271–6; Jackson, *France*, 461–2
62 Noguères et al., *Histoire de la Résistance*, III, 469
63 Lacouture, *De Gaulle*, 482
64 L. Aubrac, *Outwitting the Gestapo*, 74
65 Pineau, *La Simple Vérité*, 122–4
66 Cordier, *Jean Moulin*, 474

67 Dank, *The French against the French*, 157
68 Cobb, *The Resistance*, 232
69 Bór-Komorowski, *The Secret Army*, 139
70 A summary of the latest research can be found on the website of the Instytut Pamięci Narodowej, ipn.gov.pl; A. Chmielarz and A. K. Kunert, *Spiska 14: Aresztowanie generała 'Grota' – Stefana Roweckiego*, Państwowy Instytut Wydawniczy (Warsaw, 1983); Bór-Komorowski, *The Secret Army*, 139–42
71 Bór-Komorowski, *The Secret Army*, 140
72 Williamson, *The Polish Underground*, 103
73 Mikołajczyk to Churchill, 20 July 1943, *AK Documents*, III, 42–5
74 War Cabinet meeting, 19 July 1943, TNA, CAB 65/35; Churchill to Mikołajczyk, 1 August 1943, *AK Documents*, III, 52
75 Shepherd, *The Wild East*, 170
76 Macksey, *The Partisans of Europe*, 124–32; Cooper, *The Phantom War*, 127–34; Slepyan, *Stalin's Guerrillas*, 89, 93; Grenkevich, *The Soviet Partisan Movement*, 240
77 H. Heer, 'The Logic of the War of Extermination: The Wehrmacht and Anti-Partisan Warfare', in Heer and Naumann (eds), *War of Extermination*, 92–126
78 Private First Class Müller in Neitzel and Welzer, *Soldaten*, 81
79 Mulligan, *The Politics of Illusion and Empire*, 142–3
80 Dixon and Heilbrunn, *Communist Guerrilla Warfare*, 145–6
81 Schulte, *German Army and Nazi Policies in Occupied Russia*, 261
82 Heer, 'The Logic of the War of Extermination'; Macksey, *The Partisans of Europe*, 132–4; K. De Witt and W. Moll, 'The Bryansk Area', in Armstrong (ed.), *Soviet Partisans in World War II*, 465–6; O. Bartov, *The Eastern Front, 1941–1945*, 124; Cooper, *The Phantom War*, 97–100; Blood, *Hitler's Bandit Hunters*, 177–210; Hill, *The War behind the Eastern Front*, 115
83 Grenkevich, *The Soviet Partisan Movement*, 232–3
84 Bellamy, *Absolute War*, 590–91; Cooper, *The Phantom War*, 134–7; Grenkevich, *The Soviet Partisan Movement*, 241–52; Slepyan, *Stalin's Guerrillas*, 98
85 L. Clark, *Kursk*, 311
86 Bellamy, *Absolute War*, 591; Munoz and Romanko, *Hitler's White Russians*, 316
87 Macksey, *The Partisans of Europe*, 208; Hill, *The War behind the Eastern Front*, 132–3
88 Dixon and Heilbrunn, *Communist Guerrilla Warfare*, 50–51
89 K. Rokossovsky, *A Soldier's Duty*, 207.

18. RESISTANCE OR CIVIL WAR? THE BALKANS

1 Deakin, *The Embattled Mountain*, 32
2 Deakin at Conference on Britain and the European Resistance, St Antony's College, Oxford, December 1962
3 H. Williams, *Parachutes, Patriots and Partisans*, 147–9
4 Maclean, *Eastern Approaches*; Davidson, *Partisan Picture*
5 A. Glen, *Footholds against a Whirlwind*, 125
6 E. Greble Balić, 'When Croatia Needed Serbs: Nationalism and Genocide in Sarajevo, 1941–1942', *Slavic Review*, 68:1 (2009), 116–38
7 Hoare, *Genocide and Resistance in Hitler's Bosnia*, 94
8 Major A. Jack, IWM 12697
9 Pavlowitch, *Hitler's New Disorder*, 91
10 J. Tomasevich, *The Chetniks*, 127–8; C. Lawrence, *Irregular Adventure*, 213–14
11 Lawrence, *Irregular Adventure*, 158–9; Pavlowitch, *Hitler's New Disorder*, 105–9
12 Burgwyn, *Empire on the Adriatic*, 220; V. Ivanovic, *LX*, 225; Roberts, *Tito, Mihailović and the Allies*, 68

13 Martin (ed.), *Patriot or Traitor*, 54; Martin, *Web of Disinformation*, 72–6; M. Milazzo, *The Chetnik Movement and the Yugoslav Resistance*, 185; Roberts, *Tito, Mihailović and the Allies*, 68–9; *Trial of Mihailović*, passim
14 M. Djilas, *Wartime*, 75
15 Burgwyn, *Empire on the Adriatic*, 268
16 Hoare, 'The Partisans and the Serbs', in Ramet and Listhaug (eds), *Serbia and the Serbs in World War Two*, 201–21
17 Pavlowitch, *Hitler's New Disorder*, 115
18 Vučković, *A Balkan Tragedy*, 117
19 Djilas, *Wartime*, 148–9
20 Hoare, *Genocide and Resistance in Hitler's Bosnia*, 320–21
21 Hoare, 'The Partisans and the Serbs'
22 Djilas, *Wartime*, 199 and passim.
23 Roberts, *Tito, Mihailović and the Allies*, 108–10; Martin (ed.), *Patriot or Traitor*, 44–5; Tomasevich, *The Chetniks*, 244–6; Djilas, *Wartime*, 242–3; Pavlowitch, *Hitler's New Disorder*, 160–62
24 Dimitrov to Tito, 1 April 1943, in Banac (ed.), *The Diary of Georgi Dimitrov*, 267–8
25 Djilas, *Wartime*, 244
26 Roberts, *Tito, Mihailović and the Allies*, 111
27 Tomasevich, *The Chetniks*, 204; Martin (ed.), *Patriot or Traitor*, 46
28 B. Shepherd, *Hitler's Soldiers*, 313
29 Roberts, *Tito, Mihailović and the Allies*, 103
30 J. Gumz, 'German Counter-Insurgency Policy in Independent Croatia, 1941–1944', *The Historian*, 61 (1998), 22–50; J. Gumz, 'Wehrmacht Perceptions of Mass Violence in Croatia, 1941–1942', *Historical Journal*, 44:4 (2001), 1,015–38; P. Hehn, *The German Struggle against the Yugoslav Guerrillas in World War II: German Counter-Insurgency in Yugoslavia, 1941–1943* (New York, 1979)
31 Hoare, *Genocide and Resistance in Hitler's Bosnia*, 185; Macksey, *The Partisans of Europe*, 138
32 Hoare, *Genocide and Resistance in Hitler's Bosnia*, 272–3; Burgwyn, *Empire on the Adriatic*, 175
33 Hoare, *Genocide and Resistance in Hitler's Bosnia*, 329–33, 339–42; O. Heilbrunn, *Warfare in the Enemy's Rear*, 159; Stenton, *Radio London*, 376; Pavlowitch, *Hitler's New Disorder*, 152–6, 161; Roberts, *Tito, Mihailović and the Allies*, 101–3; N. Beloff, *Tito's Flawed Legacy*, 80
34 D. Rodogno, 'Wartime Occupation by Italy', in R. Bosworth and J. Maiolo (eds), *The Cambridge History of the Second World War*, II, 436–58; Tomasevich, *Occupation and Collaboration*, 103; Burgwyn, *Empire on the Adriatic*, 104–5; A. Osti Guerrazzi, *The Italian Army in Slovenia*, 57–8
35 G. Kranjc, 'Collaboration, Resistance and Liberation in the Balkans, 1941–1945', in Bosworth and Maiolo (eds), *Cambridge History of the Second World War*, 461–4; Tomasevich, *Occupation and Collaboration*, 99–107; Burgwyn, *Empire on the Adriatic*, 108–10, 143, 249; G. Kranjc, *To Walk with the Devil*, passim
36 H. J. Burgwyn, 'General Roatta's War against the Partisans in Yugoslavia: 1942', *Journal of Modern Italian Studies*, 9:3 (2004), 314–29; Burgwyn, *Empire on the Adriatic*, 245; Rodogno, *Fascism's European Empire*, 333–42; Osti Guerrazzi, *The Italian Army in Slovenia*, 59–62; Mazower, *Hitler's Empire*, 350
37 Burgwyn, *Empire on the Adriatic*, 235; S. Trifković, 'Rivalry between Germany and Italy in Croatia, 1942–1943', *Historical Journal*, 36:4 (1993), 879–904
38 S. Trew, *Britain, Mihailović and the Chetniks*, 52
39 M. Kurapovna, *Shadows on the Mountain*, 89–92
40 Dalton to Churchill, 30 August 1941, TNA, PREM 3/510/2
41 Trew, *Britain, Mihailović and the Chetniks*, 72
42 Ibid., 149–56; Vučković, *A Balkan Tragedy*, 131, 177, 221–2; Roberts, *Tito, Mihailović and the Allies*, 70–71; Hudson at Conference on Britain and the European Resistance,

St Antony's College, Oxford, December 1962; Martin (ed.), *Patriot or Traitor*, 49; Pavlowitch, *Hitler's New Disorder*, 98; Williams, *Parachutes, Patriots and Partisans*, 94

43 Bailey, 'British Policy towards General Draža Mihailović'; Deakin, *The Embattled Mountain*, 180

44 *FRUS 1943*, II, 987

45 Bailey, 'British Policy towards General Draža Mihailović'; Roberts, *Tito, Mihailović and the Allies*, 94–7; Martin, *Web of Disinformation*, 77

46 Davidson, *Partisan Picture*, 116–17; Mackenzie, *Secret History of SOE*, 424–5

47 E. Barker, 'Some Factors in British Decision-Making over Yugoslavia 1941–4', in Auty and Clogg (eds), *British Policy towards Wartime Resistance in Yugoslavia and Greece*, 22–58

48 Roberts, *Tito, Mihailović and the Allies*, 90–91

49 Kurapovna, *Shadows on the Mountain*, 95–6

50 Williams, *Parachutes, Patriots and Partisans*, 147–9

51 Martin (ed.), *Patriot or Traitor*, 118–19; Williams, *Parachutes, Patriots and Partisans*, 90, 114–23; R. Bailey, 'Communists in SOE: Explaining James Klugman's Recruitment and Retention', in Wylie (ed.), *The Politics and Strategy of Clandestine War*, 66–89

52 Deakin, *The Embattled Mountain*, 53

53 Hinsley et at., *British Intelligence in the Second World War*, vol. 5 by M. Howard, *Strategic Deception*, 85–91; B. McIntyre, *Operation Mincemeat*, passim

54 Quoted in Stenton, *Radio London*, 373

55 Williams, *Parachutes, Patriots and Partisans*, 123–6, 145–6, is particularly good on this debate.

56 Rootham, *Miss Fire*, 31

57 Bailey, 'British Policy towards General Draža Mihailović'; Martin (ed.), *Patriot or Traitor*, 50, 101; Kurapovna, *Shadows on the Mountain*, 99–100; Lees, *Special Operations*, 99–108

58 W. Deakin, 'The Myth of an Allied Landing in the Balkans during the Second World War', in Auty and Clogg (eds), *British Policy towards Wartime Resistance in Yugoslavia and Greece*, 93–116

59 W. Jones, *Twelve Months with Tito's Partisans*, 45; Deakin, *The Embattled Mountain*, 58–9

60 *RAF and the SOE*, 18–20

61 M. Wheeler, *Britain and the War for Yugoslavia*, 214; Bailey, 'British Policy towards General Draža Mihailović'

62 R. Leeper, *When Greek Meets Greek*, 29

63 Mackenzie, *Secret History of SOE*, 154

64 A. Cooper, *Cairo in the War 1939–1945*, 308–9

65 Woodhouse, *The Struggle for Greece*, 37

66 Myers, *Greek Entanglement*, 106

67 Woodhouse, *Something Ventured*, 58

68 Gerolymatos, *Guerrilla Warfare and Espionage in Greece*, 281–6; Papastratis, *British Policy towards Greece*, 132–3

69 Stafford, *Britain and European Resistance*, 124

70 Myers, *Greek Entanglement*, 109

71 Report by Major David Wallace on his visit to Greece, 14 July–9 August 1943, TNA, FO 371/37213

72 Mazower, *Inside Hitler's Greece*, 109–12

73 S. Sarafis, *ELAS*, 89

74 Myers, *Greek Entanglement*, 108; Mazower, *Inside Hitler's Greece*, 302–4

75 Hondros, 'The Greek Resistance'

76 Gerolymatos, *Guerrilla Warfare and Espionage in Greece*, 291

77 Mazower, *Inside Hitler's Greece*, 303

78 Myers, *Greek Entanglement*, 122–3

79 Woodhouse, *Something Ventured*, 63–4

80 Myers, *Greek Entanglement*, 170–85, 202–5; Sarafis, *ELAS*, 113–14, 122–4; W. Jordan, *Conquest without Victory*, 145–6
81 Sarafis, *ELAS*, 428–9
82 Künzel, 'Resistance, Reprisals, Reactions'; M. Mazower, 'Military Violence and the National Socialist Consensus: The Wehrmacht in Greece, 1941–1944', in Heer and Naumann (eds), *War of Extermination*, 146–74; Shepherd, *Hitler's Soldiers*, 352; Mazower, *Inside Hitler's Greece*, 144–5, 176, 191–7; T. Dyson, 'British Policies toward Axis Reprisals in Occupied Greece: Whitehall vs. SOE', *Contemporary British History*, 16:1 (2002), 11–28
83 Quoted in Sarafis, *ELAS*, 153
84 Sarafis, *ELAS*, 139, 429; Woodhouse, *The Struggle for Greece*, 66
85 C. M. Woodhouse, 'The National Liberation Front and the British Connection', in Iatrides (ed.), *Greece in the 1940s*, 80–101
86 Gerolymatos, *Guerrilla Warfare and Espionage in Greece*, 294–5; Sarafis, *ELAS*, 147–8; Papastratis, *British Policy towards Greece*, 139–43
87 Myers, *Greek Entanglement*, 240
88 Diary entry, 22 September 1943, in B. Pimlott (ed.), *The Second World War Diary of Hugh Dalton*, 643
89 Leeper, *When Greek Meets Greek*, 29
90 Myers, *Greek Entanglement*, 247–53
91 Sweet-Escott, *Baker Street Irregular*, 159
92 Myers, *Greek Entanglement*, 250–62; Gerolymatos, *Guerrilla Warfare and Espionage in Greece*, 300–307; Papastratis, *British Policy towards Greece*, 104
93 Fielding, *Hide and Seek*, 33, 49; Beevor, *Crete*, 243, 264
94 Beevor, *Crete*, 246, 275–7, 282–3; Fielding, *Hide and Seek*, 46, 130–32
95 Report 2, February to April 1943, in P. Leigh Fermor, *Abducting a General*, 117–27
96 Fielding, *Hide and Seek*, 164
97 Report 4, June and July 1943, in Leigh Fermor, *Abducting a General*, 138–9
98 Burgwyn, *Empire on the Adriatic*, 267.

19. THE ITALIAN SURRENDER

1 J. McCaffery, IWM 14093
2 R. Bailey, *Target Italy*, 303, 305; C. Woods, 'SOE in Italy', in Seaman (ed.), *Special Operations Executive*, 91–102
3 Haestrup, *Europe Ablaze*, 110–12
4 E. Agarossi, *A Nation Collapses*, 50–51; P. Morgan, *The Fall of Mussolini*, 37
5 Eisenhower, *Crusade in Europe*, 202–6
6 Churchill, *The Second World War*, V, 88–98; Agarossi, *A Nation Collapses*, 74–80
7 T. Behan, *The Italian Resistance*, 27–8; Agarossi, *A Nation Collapses*, 57; Morgan, *The Fall of Mussolini*, 87
8 Agarossi, *A Nation Collapses*, 77–80
9 Morgan, *The Fall of Mussolini*, 91; Agarossi, *A Nation Collapses*, 84–8
10 Behan, *The Italian Resistance*, 29; Agarossi, *A Nation Collapses*, 96–9; Morgan, *The Fall of Mussolini*, 92–3
11 Murphy, *Diplomat among Warriors*, 246
12 Morgan, *The Fall of Mussolini*, 90, 95
13 Agarossi, *A Nation Collapses*, 105
14 Morgan, *The Fall of Mussolini*, 107–8, 115, 125; Agarossi, *A Nation Collapses*, 105–7
15 Diary entry, 10 September 1943, Gobetti, *Partisan Diary*, 22
16 Hastings, *All Hell Let Loose*, 459
17 C. Pavone, *A Civil War*, 33
18 J. Holland, *Italy's Sorrow*, 59
19 R. Absalom, *A Strange Alliance*, 23

20 R. Lamb, *War in Italy*, 160–62
21 Absalom, *A Strange Alliance*, 25
22 G. Lett, *Rossano*, 26–7; P. Gallo, *For Love and Country*, 107–8; Morgan, *The Fall of Mussolini*, 196–7
23 Absalom, *A Strange Alliance*, 39–43; Lamb, *War in Italy*, 165; Morgan, *The Fall of Mussolini*, 195–6
24 Foot and Langley, *MI9*, 234–40; Lamb, *War in Italy*, 164–7; Behan, *The Italian Resistance*, 208
25 S. Derry, *The Rome Escape Line*, passim; B. Fleming, *The Vatican Pimpernel*, 29; Absalom, *A Strange Alliance*, 283–99; Gallo, *For Love and Country*, 141; J. Gallagher, *Scarlet Pimpernel of the Vatican*, passim; S. Walker, *Hide and Seek*, passim
26 R. Absalom, 'Hiding History: The Allies, the Resistance and the Others in Occupied Italy 1943–1945', *Historical Journal*, 38:1 (1995), 111–31
27 Derry, *The Rome Escape Line*, 167
28 Ibid., 148 and passim
29 S. Hood, *Pebbles from My Skull*, 55–6, 60–61
30 Lett, *Rossano*, 32
31 Gallo, *For Love and Country*, 116
32 R. Katz, *Fatal Silence*, 133; Cornwell, *Hitler's Pope*, 302–17; Lamb, *War in Italy*, 44
33 Katz, *Fatal Silence*, 63–4
34 Cornwell, *Hitler's Pope*, 301–2; Katz, *Fatal Silence*, 74
35 Gallo, *For Love and Country*, 130
36 A. Portelli, *The Order Has Been Carried Out*, 86; Hilberg, *The Destruction of the European Jews*, 669–70; Cesarani, *Final Solution*, 669
37 Gallo, *For Love and Country*, 140; Steinberg, *Not as a Lamb*, 76–7
38 Katz, *Fatal Silence*, 133; Cornwell, *Hitler's Pope*, 302–17; Lamb, *War in Italy*, 44; Fleming, *The Vatican Pimpernel*, 116
39 M. Wilhelm, *The Other Italy*, 53
40 Ibid., 37–56; Behan, *The Italian Resistance*, 32–9; R. Battaglia, *The Story of the Italian Resistance*, 56–7
41 Wilhelm, *The Other Italy*, 36–7
42 M. Salvadori, *The Labour and the Wounds*, 169
43 Behan, *The Italian Resistance*, 52
44 Gallo, *For Love and Country*, 87
45 Ibid., 102–4
46 Ibid., 103, 189
47 Katz, *Fatal Silence*, 146, 157–8
48 Ibid., 166–7; P. Tompkins, *A Spy in Rome*, 90; Gallo, *For Love and Country*, 180
49 Portelli, *The Order Has Been Carried Out*, 153
50 Gallo, *For Love and Country*, 110, 113–15; Portelli, *The Order Has Been Carried Out*, 105–6; Behan, *The Italian Resistance*, 198; Katz, *Fatal Silence*, 88, 125–8; C. Delzell, *Mussolini's Enemies*, 304
51 Behan, *The Italian Resistance*, 224
52 Portelli, *The Order Has Been Carried Out*, 137
53 Gallo, *For Love and Country*, 205–21
54 Behan, *The Italian Resistance*, 238
55 Lamb, *War in Italy*, 59
56 Battaglia, *The Story of the Italian Resistance*, 114; D. Blight, 'Fossilized Lies: A Reflection on Alessandro Portelli's *The Order Has Been Carried Out*', *Oral History Review*, 32:1 (2005), 5–9
57 Portelli, *The Order Has Been Carried Out*, 151; Battaglia, *The Story of the Italian Resistance*, 115
58 Lamb, *War in Italy*, 61; Behan, *The Italian Resistance*, 260
59 Gallo, *For Love and Country*, 242
60 Katz, *Fatal Silence*, 214

61 Portelli, *The Order Has Been Carried Out*, 164
62 Gallo, *For Love and Country*, 111; Behan, *The Italian Resistance*, 67; Morgan, *The Fall of Mussolini*, 179–84; Battaglia, *The Story of the Italian Resistance*, 147; G. Corni, 'Italy', in Moore (ed.), *Resistance in Western Europe*, 157–88
63 Lett, *Rossano*, 58–64
64 P. Badoglio, *Italy in the Second World War*, 192–4
65 Wieviorka, *Resistance in Western Europe*, 260
66 Bailey, *Target Italy*, passim; Dodds-Parker, *Setting Europe Ablaze*, 145–7
67 Salvadori, *The Labour and the Wounds*, 145–8
68 J. McCaffery, IWM 14093; Bailey, *Target Italy*, 190–220 and passim; Woods, 'SOE in Italy'
69 J. McCaffery, IWM 14093; D. Stafford, *Mission Accomplished*, 125–6; Petersen (ed.), *From Hitler's Doorstep*, 127–9; Behan, *The Italian Resistance*, 212–13
70 Captain J. Ross, IWM 27077
71 M. Corvo, *The OSS in Italy*, 124–5
72 Mackenzie, *Secret History of SOE*, 549; Lamb, *War in Italy*, 205
73 Morgan, *The Fall of Mussolini*, 165–6
74 Lamb, *War in Italy*, 207–8
75 Stafford, *Mission Accomplished*, 119
76 Holland, *Italy's Sorrow*, 187
77 Gallo, *For Love and Country*, 241; Delzell, *Mussolini's Enemies*, 376–7
78 Katz, *Fatal Silence*, 280–82, 297; Gallo, *For Love and Country*, 190
79 Behan, *The Italian Resistance*, 201–2; Katz, *Fatal Silence*, 73, 207–8, 312; Gallo, *For Love and Country*, 251
80 Katz, *Fatal Silence*, 320
81 D. Ellwood, *Italy*, 79
82 Diary entry, 4 March 1944, in Banac (ed.), *The Diary of Georgi Dimitrov*, 303
83 D. Travis, 'Communism and Resistance in Italy, 1943–8', in Judt (ed.), *Resistance and Revolution in Mediterranean Europe*, 80–109
84 Alan Brooke, diary entry, 4 February 1944, in Danchev and Todman (eds), *War Diaries*, 518
85 Ellwood, *Italy*, 95
86 Battaglia, *The Story of the Italian Resistance*, 149.

20. DENMARK ENTERS THE FRAY

1 Bennett, *British Broadcasting and the Danish Resistance Movement*, 60–65
2 Jespersen, *No Small Achievement*, 161
3 Boog et al., *Germany and the Second World War*, 18–19
4 Bennett, *British Broadcasting and the Danish Resistance Movement*, 113–14; Wieviorka, *Resistance in Western Europe*, 238; Muus, *The Spark and the Flame*, 87, 102
5 J. Oram Thomas, *The Giant-Killers*, 21–2
6 Reilly, *The Sixth Floor*, 44
7 Muus, *The Spark and the Flame*, 103
8 Rings, *Life with the Enemy*, 134; Thomas, *The Giant-Killers*, 331; J. Nielsen, IWM 13106
9 Gubbins, 'Britain and Denmark', at Conference at St Antony's College, Oxford, December 1962
10 Rittner and Myers, *The Courage to Care*, 130–31
11 V. Örn Vilhjálmsson and B. Blüdnikow, 'Rescue, Expulsion, and Collaboration: Denmark's Difficulties with its World War II Past', *Jewish Political Studies Review*, 18:3/4 (2006), 3–29
12 B. Lidegaard, *Countrymen*, 36, 44–5, 70
13 Cesarani, *The Final Solution*, 689; Lidegaard, *Countrymen*, 66–7, 72

14 Lidegaard, *Countrymen*, 91–2; Vilhjálmsson and Blüdnikow, 'Rescue, Expulsion, and Collaboration'
15 Lidegaard, *Countrymen*, 77
16 Cesarani, *The Final Solution*, 691; Lidegaard, *Countrymen*, 154
17 Cesarani, *The Final Solution*, 691; Lidegaard, *Countrymen*, 131–2
18 M. Goodman, 'Foundations of Resistance in German-Occupied Denmark', in Rohrlich (ed.), *Resisting the Holocaust*, 213–37
19 Lidegaard, *Countrymen*, 158; G. Paulsson, 'The "Bridge over the Øresund": The Historiography on the Expulsion of the Jews from Nazi-Occupied Denmark', *Journal of Contemporary History*, 30 (1995), 431–64
20 Rings, *Life with the Enemy*, 187–8; Thomas, *The Giant-Killers*, 116–29
21 Lidegaard, *Countrymen*, 324
22 Rittner and Myers, *The Courage to Care*, 94–5
23 H. Fein, *Accounting for Genocide*, 148–52
24 Paulsson, 'The "Bridge over the Øresund"'; H. Kirchhoff, 'Denmark: A Light in the Darkness of the Holocaust? A Reply to Gunnar S. Paulsson', *Journal of Contemporary History*, 30 (1995), 465–79
25 Moore, *Survivors*, 94–5
26 Jespersen, *No Small Achievement*, 224
27 Ibid., 274–8; Reilly, *The Sixth Floor*, 60–61
28 Cruickshank, *SOE in Scandinavia*, 229; Thomas, *The Giant-Killers*, 200–201
29 Haestrup, *Europe Ablaze*, 454–5; Rings, *Life with the Enemy*, 199–200; Reilly, *The Sixth Floor*, 93; Lampe, *The Savage Canary*, 98–9
30 Reilly, *The Sixth Floor*, 98; Sutherland, *Monica*, 155–66, 181–93; Muus, *The Spark and the Flame*, 156
31 Lampe, *The Savage Canary*, 99–108; Reilly, *The Sixth Floor*, 70–73; Littlejohn, *The Patriotic Traitors*, 78–9
32 Muus, *The Spark and the Flame*, 159; Thomas, *The Giant-Killers*, 25.

21. CIVIL WAR OR RESISTANCE – THE BALKANS

1 Sweet-Escott, *Baker Street Irregular*, 178
2 J. Amery in Miller, *Behind the Lines*, 176–8
3 Ismay minute, 4 October, TNA, PREM 3/66/2
4 Milač, *Resistance, Imprisonment, and Forced Labour*, 92
5 Pavlowitch, *Hitler's New Disorder*, 99
6 Macksey, *The Partisans of Europe*, 168–9
7 Glen, *Footholds against a Whirlwind*, 145
8 Maclean, *Eastern Approaches*, 386; D. Hamilton-Hill, *SOE Assignment*, 95; V. Dedijer, *The War Diaries of Vladimir Dedijer*, 216–18
9 Williams, *Parachutes, Patriots and Partisans*, 173
10 Martin (ed.), *Patriot or Traitor*, 145–54; Martin, *Web of Disinformation*, 152–4; Tomasevich, *Occupation and Collaboration*, 298; Williams, *Parachutes, Patriots and Partisans*, 174–6, 180–81; M. Lees, *The Rape of Serbia*, 99–103
11 Martin, *Web of Disinformation*, 161–6
12 Bailey, 'British Policy towards Draža Mihailović'; Lees, *The Rape of Serbia*, 93–5, 209
13 Lees, *The Rape of Serbia*, 218–19; Williams, *Parachutes, Patriots and Partisans*, 185
14 Martin, *Web of Disinformation*, 305–14; Williams, *Parachutes, Patriots and Partisans*, 182–3; Lees, *The Rape of Serbia*, 212–13; Beloff, *Tito's Flawed Legacy*, 102; Maclean, *Eastern Approaches*, 402–3
15 Martin, *Web of Disinformation*, 315–25; Lees, *The Rape of Serbia*, 221; Williams, *Parachutes, Patriots and Partisans*, 195
16 Churchill, *The Second World War*, V, 413–14
17 Tomasevich, *Occupation and Collaboration*, 116–19

18 Lees, *The Rape of Serbia*, 184–5
19 Bailey, 'British Policy towards Draža Mihailović'; Martin (ed.), *Patriot or Traitor*, 159; Williams, *Parachutes, Patriots and Partisans*, 198; Beloff, *Tito's Flawed Legacy*, 91–2; Lees, *The Rape of Serbia*, 253–6; Rootham, *Miss Fire*, 193–4
20 Martin (ed.), *Patriot or Traitor*, 160–61
21 Williams, *Parachutes, Patriots and Partisans*, 211; Beloff, *Tito's Flawed Legacy*, 92
22 H. Hainsworth, IWM 12578; Lees, *The Rape of Serbia*, 284–5; Lees, *Special Operations Executed*, 140; Rootham, *Miss Fire*, 203; Roberts, *Tito, Mihailović and the Allies*, 226; Williams, *Parachutes, Patriots and Partisans*, 213; Kurapovna, *Shadows on the Mountain*, 129–30
23 Maclean, *Eastern Approaches*, 438
24 Churchill to Eden, 2 January 1944, Churchill, *The Second World War*, V, 416
25 Jones, *Twelve Months with Tito's Partisans*, 126; Pavlowitch, *Hitler's New Disorder*, 219; Maclean, *Eastern Approaches*, 448; Dedijer, *The War Diaries*, 324–5
26 Barker, 'Some Factors in British Decision-Making over Yugoslavia'
27 Pavlowitch, *Hitler's New Disorder*, 223–6; Vučković, *A Balkan Tragedy*, 257–60; Djilas, *Wartime*, 377
28 Mansfield report, 1 March 1944, Martin, *Web of Disinformation*, 326–62
29 Quoted in Kurapovna, *Shadows on the Mountain*, 127
30 Farish report, 25 June 1944, Martin, *Web of Disinformation*, 371–7
31 Tomasevich, *The Chetniks*, 302
32 Kurapovna, *Shadows on the Mountain*, 137
33 Davidson, *Partisan Picture*, 20–21; Djilas, *Wartime*, 389; Murphy, *Diplomat among Warriors*, 272–3
34 Mansfield report, 1 March 1944; Roberts, *Tito, Mihailović and the Allies*, 153, 225; Rootham, *Miss Fire*, 137–53, 202
35 Tomasevich, *Occupation and Collaboration*, 631–2; Wilkinson reports, 1 and 28 April 1944, IWM 12751; Tomasevich, *The Chetniks*, 407
36 Tomasevich, *Occupation and Collaboration*, 314; Roberts, *Tito, Mihailović and the Allies*, 228; S. Ritchie, *Our Man in Yugoslavia*, 92; Pavlowitch, *Hitler's New Disorder*, 219; Maclean, *Eastern Approaches*, 453
37 Smiley, *Albanian Assignment*, 29
38 Pearson, *Albania in Occupation and War*, 266
39 Hare, TNA, HS 5/139
40 For example, see directives of 16 August and 3 November 1943, Pearson, *Albania in Occupation and War*, 267, 298
41 J. Anderson, *High Mountains and Cold Seas*, 192
42 Fischer, *Albania at War*, 162–5; Kemp, *No Colours or Crest*, 130–31; H. Tilman, *When Men and Mountains Meet*, 125; Anderson, *High Mountains and Cold Seas*, 190–93; Pearson, *Albania in Occupation and War*, 271–2
43 Pearson, *Albania in Occupation and War*, 273–4; P. Kemp, *The Thorns of Memory*, 200
44 Fischer, *Albania at War* 191
45 Hoxha directive, 9 September 1943 in Pearson, *Albania in Occupation and War*, 274
46 Davies, *Illyrian Adventure*, 92
47 Fischer, *Albania at War* 192–3; Hoxha directive, 3 November 1943, in Pearson, *Albania in Occupation and War*, 299–300; J. Amery, *Sons of the Eagle*, 98
48 X. Fielding, *One Man in his Time*, 43; Davies reports, 19 November and 17 December 1943, in Pearson, *Albania in Occupation and War*, 306, 313; Fischer, *Albania at War*, 203–4; Bailey, *The Wildest Province*, 141–2, 172–80; Kemp, *No Colours or Crest*, 217–18; J. G. Hibberdine, IWM 13347
49 McLean and Smiley report, 12 January 1944; Quayle debriefing report, 30 April 1944; Tilman final report, 30 May 1944; Chiefs of Staff committee, 8 June 1944, in Pearson, *Albania in Occupation and War*, 323–4, 343, 348–51, 354
50 Fischer, *Albania at War*, 202; Bailey, *The Wildest Province*, 233; Smiley, *Albanian Assignment*, 78–80; Pearson, *Albania in Occupation and War*, 280

51 Fischer, *Albania at War*, 213; Smiley, *Albanian Assignment*, 121–5; Amery, *Sons of the Eagle*, 182
52 Pearson, *Albania in Occupation and War*, 319–20; Davies, *Illyrian Adventure*, 93–4, 111, 171–2; Bailey, *The Wildest Province*, 123–5
53 Beevor, *Crete*, 288–91; Mazower, *Inside Hitler's Greece*, 292–5; Report no. 6, September 1943, in Leigh Fermor, *Abducting a General*, 145–9
54 Woodhouse, *Something Ventured*, 67–72; Mazower, *Inside Hitler's Greece*, 148–52; J. Mulgan, *Report on Experience*, 131; Sarafis, *ELAS*, 182–6; Lamb, *War in Italy*, 127–8
55 Mazower, *Inside Hitler's Greece*, 244–5, 250–51, 259–61; Cesarani, *Final Solution*, 671
56 Mulgan, *Report on Experience*, 145–6; Mazower, *Inside Hitler's Greece*, 170–72
57 Bennett, *Under the Shadow of the Swastika*, 145–6; Mazower, *Inside Hitler's Greece*, 170–72, 179–81; Sarafis, *ELAS*, 205
58 Woodhouse, *The Struggle for Greece*, 59–60; Sarafis, *ELAS*, 259–60; Gerolymatos, *Guerrilla Warfare and Espionage in Greece*, 313; Papastratis, *British Policy towards Greece during the Second World War*, 152–60
59 Hammond, *Venture into Greece*, 103–6; Mazower, *Inside Hitler's Greece*, 323–7; Myers, *Greek Entanglement*, 267–8; N. Clive, *A Greek Experience 1943–1948*, 102
60 Gerolymatos, *Guerrilla Warfare and Espionage in Greece*, 307–12, 317–21; L. Stavrianos, 'The Mutiny in the Greek Armed Forces, April 1944', *American Slavic & East European Review*, 9 (1950), 302–11; Myers, *Greek Entanglement*, 262; Mazower, *Inside Hitler's Greece*, 291–4; Leeper, *When Greek Meets Greek*, 39–41; Woodhouse, *The Struggle for Greece*, 81; Hammond, *Venture into Greece*, 133; Cooper, *Cairo in the War*, 309–10
61 Hondros, *Occupation and Resistance*, 220–21; Hammond, *Venture into Greece*, 136; Mazower, *Inside Hitler's Greece*, 325
62 Clive, *A Greek Experience*, 85
63 Leeper, *When Greek Meets Greek*, 53–4, 60; Hondros, *Occupation and Resistance*, 219–30
64 Hondros, 'The Greek Resistance'; Sarafis, *ELAS*, 436–45; Hammond, *Venture into Greece*, 146; Mulgan, *Report on Experience*, 149
65 Clive, *A Greek Experience*, 128
66 Charles Edson, OSS Research and Analysis Branch, Cairo, to Robert Wolff, Head of Balkan OSS R and A Branch, Washington, 11 December 1943, in R. Clogg, *Greece, 1940–1949*, 163–6
67 Quoted in L. Baerentzen, 'British Strategy towards Greece in 1944', in W. Deakin et al. (eds), *British Political and Military Strategy in Central, Eastern and Southern Europe in 1944*, 130–50
68 Rendel, *Appointment in Crete*, 155–6
69 Ibid., 154–5; Beevor, *Crete*, 300
70 W. S. Moss, *Ill Met by Moonlight*, passim; Leigh Fermor, *Abducting a General*, passim; Short report, 16 May 1944, in Leigh Fermor, *Abducting a General*, 153–62; Beevor, *Crete*, 303–11; Psychoundakis, *The Cretan Runner*, 271.

22. CHALLENGES AND DILEMMAS IN THE EAST

1 TNA, PREM 3/399/6
2 O'Malley, *Phantom Caravan*, 230
3 W. Deakin, 'Resistance in Occupied Central and South-eastern Europe', in Deakin et al. (eds), *British Political and Military Strategy*, 78–110
4 R. Mavrogordato and E. Ziemke, 'The Polotsk Lowland', in Armstrong (ed.), *Soviet Partisans in World War II*, 517–56; Grenkevich, *The Soviet Partisan Movement*, 241–2; Hill, *The War behind the Eastern Front*, 124–5
5 A. Beevor, *The Second World War*, 507; Grenkevich, *The Soviet Partisan Movement*, 287, 304–6

6 Cooper, *The Phantom War*, 134–9; Bellamy, *Absolute War*, 590–91; Blood, *Hitler's Bandit Hunters*, 101
7 Mavrogordato and Ziemke, 'The Polotsk Lowland'
8 Munoz and Romanko, *Hitler's White Russians*, 366–73, 392–8; Cooper, *The Phantom War*, 156–7; P. Adair, *Hitler's Greatest Defeat*, 76
9 Dixon and Heilbrunn, *Communist Guerrilla Warfare*, 203–23; Reitlinger, *The House Built on Sand*, 344–5
10 Schulte, *German Army and Nazi Policies in Occupied Russia*, 278; Shepherd, *War in the Wild East*, 223–4; J. Jones, '"Every Family Has its Freak": Perceptions of Collaboration in Occupied Soviet Russia, 1943–1948', *Slavic Review*, 64:4 (2005), 747–70; T. Penter, 'Collaboration on Trial: New Source Material on Soviet Postwar Trials against Collaborators', *Slavic Review*, 64:4 (2005), 782–90
11 Dallin, *German Rule in Russia*, 223–3; Vakar, *Belorussia*, 193–4, 202–5
12 Kosyk, *The Third Reich and the Ukrainian Question*, 389; Grenkevich, *The Soviet Partisan Movement*, 134
13 Prusin, *The Lands Between*, 187, 198; Piotrowski, *Poland's Holocaust*, 168–9
14 Kovpak, *Our Partisan Course*, 125
15 Piotrowski, *Poland's Holocaust*, 88
16 Longerich, *Heinrich Himmler*, 659; Housden, *Hans Frank*, 209
17 TNA, HS 8/29
18 Iranek-Osmecki, *The Unseen and Silent*, 101–13; A. Borowiec, *Warsaw Boy*, 149, 158; Williamson, *The Polish Underground*, 100–102; Sagajllo, *The Man in the Middle*, 85–7
19 Iranek-Osmecki, *The Unseen and Silent*, 90
20 Kochanski, *The Eagle Unbowed*, 392; Iranek-Osmecki, *The Unseen and Silent*, 82–90; Selborne to Sosnkowski, 3 May 1944, *AK Documents*, III, no. 610, 431
21 M. Chodakiewicz, *Between Nazis and Soviets*, 197; J. Erickson, *The Road to Berlin*, 258–9
22 Iranek-Osmecki, *The Unseen and Silent*, 152–7; Sagajllo, *The Man in the Middle*, 113
23 Kochanski, *The Eagle Unbowed*, 387; Bór-Komorowski to Sosnkowski, 2 August 1943, *AK Documents*, III, no. 474, 52
24 Polish Government to Bór-Komorowski, 26 October 1943, *AK Documents*, III, no. 496, 182–5; Bór-Komorowski, *The Secret Army*, 182
25 Bór-Komorowski to Sosnkowski, 26 November 1943, *AK Documents*, III, no. 509, 209–13
26 Nowak, *Courier from Warsaw*, 231
27 Sosnkowski to Bór-Komorowski, 17 February 1944, *AK Documents*, III, no. 552, 282–4
28 Bór-Komorowski, *The Secret Army*, 183–4
29 S. Mikołajczyk, *The Rape of Poland*, 305
30 Borowiec, *Destroy Warsaw!*, 73
31 TNA, HS 4/138; Bór-Komorowski, *The Secret Army*, 186–7; Kochanski, *The Eagle Unbowed*, 390; Iranek-Osmecki, *The Unseen and Silent*, 180; Blood, *Hitler's Bandit Hunters*, 225–7
32 Kochanski, *The Eagle Unbowed*, 390–91
33 A. Polonsky and B. Drukier (eds), *The Beginnings of Communist Rule in Poland*, 10–15; K. Kersten, *The Establishment of Communist Rule in Poland, 1943–1948*, 19, 36, 60–64; Prażmowska, *Civil War in Poland*, 74–8
34 J. Hanson, *The Civilian Population and the Warsaw Uprising*, 60; J. Garliński, 'The Polish Underground State'; Declaration by the RJN, 15 March 1944, *AK Documents*, III, no. 573, 361–70
35 Bryant, *Prague in Black*, 184–8
36 Luža, *The Hitler Kiss*, 64, 108, 115–19
37 Ibid., 110; J. Korbel, *The Communist Subversion of Czechoslovakia, 1938–1948*, 62–3

38 Army Museum, Prague
39 Skilling, 'The Czechoslovak Struggle'
40 Luža, *The Hitler Kiss*, 113
41 Moravec, *Master of Spies*, 232
42 Rhode, 'The Protectorate of Bohemia and Moravia'
43 Skilling, 'The Czechoslovak Struggle'; Moravec, *Master of Spies*, 242
44 Lettrich, *History of Modern Slovakia*, 199, 303–5; Hoensch, 'The Slovak Republic'; A. Josko, 'The Slovak Resistance Movement', in Mamatey and Luža (eds), *A History of the Czechoslovak Republic*, 362–83, 271–95
45 Lettrich, *History of Modern Slovakia*, 200–203; Erickson, *The Road to Berlin*, 291–2
46 Longerich, *Heinrich Himmler*, 678
47 Lumans, *Latvia in World War II*, 264; R. Misiunas and R. Taagepera, *The Baltic States*, 63–5; Remeikis (ed.), *Lithuania under German Occupation*, 10; P. Buttar, *Between Giants*, 133–56
48 Lumans, *Latvia in World War II*, 296–7, 365; Misiunas and Taagepera, *The Baltic States*, 56–7, 65; Buttar, *Between Giants*, 157–84
49 Lumans, *Latvia in World War II*, 318; 15 November 1943, Johnson to Secretary of State, in Remeikis (ed.), *Lithuania under German Occupation*, 487
50 M. L. Miller, *Bulgaria during the Second World War*, 1, 117–20, 195–203; Barker, *British Policy in South-East Europe*, 189–215; Banac (ed.), *The Diary of Georgi Dimitrov*, 301–2; Deakin, 'Resistance in Occupied Central and South-Eastern Europe'; D. Elazar, 'Anti-Fascist Resistance in Bulgaria–1944', E. Barker, 'Problems of the Alliance: Misconceptions and Misunderstandings', M. Mackintosh, 'Soviet Policy on the Balkans in 1944: A British View', all in Deakin et al. (eds), *British Political and Military Strategy*, 190–200, 40–53, 235–52; Lees, *Special Operations Executed*, 51–3; S. Johnson, *Agents Extraordinary*, passim
51 Shepherd, *War in the Wild East*, 171–4
52 M. Kállay, *Hungarian Premier*, 63–4
53 Colonel Korkozowicz to AK command, 2 November 1943; A. Sapieha to AK command, 6 and 17 November 1943, all in *AK Documents*, III, 193–4, 201–4
54 Kállay, *Hungarian Premier*, 172
55 Barker, *British Policy in South-East Europe*, 251–6; Deakin, 'Resistance in Occupied Central and South-Eastern Europe'; Kállay, *Hungarian Premier*, 206–12; I. Mócsy, 'Hungary's Failed Strategic Surrender: Secret Wartime Negotiations with Britain', in N. Dreisziger (ed.), *Hungary in the Age of Total War*, 85–106
56 A. Ogden, *Through Hitler's Back Door*, 30–36; T. Meszerics, 'Undermine, or Bring Them Over: SOE and OSS Plans for Hungary in 1943', *Journal of Contemporary History*, 43 (2008), 195–216; Davidson, *Partisan Picture*, 110–13, 158; Petersen (ed.), *From Hitler's Doorstep*, 194
57 Kállay, *Hungarian Premier*, 180–83
58 Diary entry, 10 November 1943, in Lochner (ed.), *The Goebbels Diaries*, 413
59 Kállay, *Hungarian Premier*, 426
60 Deakin, 'Resistance in Occupied Central and South-Eastern Europe'; Ogden, *Through Hitler's Back Door*, 35–6
61 Hilberg, *The Destruction of the European Jews*, 841–3; J. T. Baumel, 'The Parachutists' Mission from a Gender Perspective', in Rohrlich (ed.), *Resisting the Holocaust*, 95–113; Mazower, *Hitler's Empire*, 404–5
62 Barker, *British Policy in South-East Europe*, 223–37; D. Deletant, *Hitler's Forgotten Ally*, 230–32; Barker, 'Problems of the Alliance: Misconceptions and Misunderstandings'; Deakin, 'Resistance in Occupied Central and South-Eastern Europe'; Ogden, *Through Hitler's Back Door*, 230–57; I. Porter, *Operation Autonomous*, passim; D. Deletant, *British Clandestine Activities in Romania during the Second World War*, 15, 18–20, 90–118.

23. INTELLIGENCE: 1942–44

1 Fourcade, *Noah's Ark*, 277
2 Rémy, *Courage and Fear*, 283–4
3 Richards, *Secret Flotillas*, 164
4 G. Martelli, *Agent Extraordinary*, passim
5 N. D. Lankford (ed.), *OSS against the Reich*, 38, 133–4
6 Warmbrunn, *The Dutch under German Occupation*, 209–11; Baron D'Aulnis in Foot (ed.), *Holland at War against Hitler*, 101–7
7 Reilly, *The Sixth Floor*, 55–6; Jespersen, *No Small Achievement*, 229–30
8 Chmielarz, 'Intelligence Activities of the Home Army General Headquarters'
9 Wnuk, 'Polish Intelligence in France'; Colvin (ed.), *Colonel Henri's Story*, 69–70
10 Wnuk, 'Polish Intelligence in France'
11 Report on the Poles in France, Knochen, 10 March 1943. The author thanks Dr Marek Stella-Sawicki for letting her use this recently discovered and authenticated report
12 G. Bennett, 'The Achievements of the Polish Intelligence Service', in Stirling et at. (eds), *Intelligence Co-operation*, I, 433–42
13 Rémy, *The Silent Company*, 220–22; Lyman, *The Jail Busters*, 90–91, 106–7
14 Purnell, *A Woman of No Importance*, 162–71
15 Fourcade, *Noah's Ark*, 214
16 Jeffery, *MI6*, 528; Fourcade, *Noah's Ark*, 196–310; Olson, *Madame Fourcade's War*, 263–6, 276–8
17 Beevor, *Crete*, 243, 259; Psychoundakis, *The Cretan Runner*, 251; Fielding, *Hide and Seek*, 54
18 Gerolymatos, *Guerrilla Warfare and Espionage in Greece*, 232–56; Sweet-Escott, *Baker Street Irregular*, 221–2
19 Rémy, *The Silent Company*, 239; Wieveroka, *The French Resistance*, 133; Schoenbrun, *Soldiers of the Night*, 258; Fourcade, *Noah's Ark*, 106, 216; Foot, *Six Faces of Courage*, 49; Olson, *Madame Fourcade's War*, 184–6; Martelli, *Agent Extraordinary*, 133–5
20 Peplonski, Dubicki and Majzner, 'Naval Intelligence'; Bennett, *British Broadcasting and the Danish Resistance Movement*, 72
21 Olson, *Madame Fourcade's War*, 152, 176–7
22 Mann, *British Policy and Strategy towards Norway*, 25–6; E. Thomas, 'Norway's Role in Britain's Wartime Intelligence', in Salmon (ed.), *Britain and Norway in the Second World War*, 121–8; Denham, *Inside the Nazi Ring*, 104–7
23 Lampe, *The Savage Canary*, 49; Brusselmans, *Rendez-vous 127*, 74; Lyman, *The Jail Busters*, 12
24 Martelli, *Agent Extraordinary*, 140–49
25 Cobb, *The Resistance*, 121–2
26 Churchill, *The Second World War*, IV, 249; Jones, *Most Secret War*, 334–7, 341–3, 355–7; Brusselmans, *Rendez-vous 127*, 86; Eloy, *The Fight in the Forest*, 57
27 R. Wnuk, 'Polish Intelligence and the German "Secret Weapons": V-1 and V-2', in Stirling et at. (eds), *Intelligence Co-operation*, I, 473–82
28 Rémy, *Courage and Fear*, 86–7
29 H. Vaughan, *Doctor in the Resistance*, 64, 71–76
30 Casey, *The Secret War against Hitler*, 45
31 Ulstein, 'Norwegian Intelligence in the Second World War'
32 Clive, *A Greek Experience*, 26–30, 55, 70–74
33 Fielding, *Hide and Seek*, 47
34 A. Heintz in R. Miller, *Nothing Less than Victory*, 223
35 Jeffery, *MI6*, 521–2, 542; Brusselmans, *Rendez-vous 127*, 76–80; Lyman, *The Jail Busters*, 12; Heintz in Miller, *Nothing Less than Victory*, 223
36 Jeffery, *MI6*, 536–8; Casey, *The Secret War against Hitler*, 38, 92–3; Colonel Francis Miller, in Miller, *Behind the Lines*, 59–60

37 Fourcade, *Noah's Ark*, 303; Schoenbrun, *Soldiers of the Night*, 367
38 Verity, *We Landed by Moonlight*, 175
39 Lyman, *The Jail Busters*, 204–5
40 Ibid., passim; Schoenbrun, *Soldiers of the Night*, 431–4; Reilly, *The Sixth Floor*, 84–6
41 Chmielarz, 'Intelligence Activities'; T. Dubicki, R. Majzner and K. Spruch, 'Air Force Intelligence: The Construction of Aeroplanes and Airfields and the Effects of Air Raids', in Stirling et al. (eds), *Intelligence Co-operation*, I, 501–11
42 Hinsley et al., *British Intelligence in the Second World War*, III, 365
43 Ibid., 360–62, 385; Jeffery, *MI6*, 533; Wnuk, 'Polish Intelligence and the German "Secret Weapons"'; Jones, *Most Secret War*, 425, 430–32, 441
44 Martelli, *Agent Extraordinary*, 153–85; Fourcade, *Noah's Ark*, 287
45 Lampe, *The Savage Canary*, 122–8; Thomas, *The Giant-Killers*, 32
46 Hinsley et al., *British Intelligence in the Second World War*, III, 375–6, 385–6, 390–91, 409–13, 423–6; Jones, *Most Secret War*, 540; Martelli, *Agent Extraordinary*, 185–6; Verity, *We Landed by Moonlight*, 175
47 Hinsley et al., *British Intelligence in the Second World War*, III, 371, 435–8; Wnuk, 'Polish Intelligence and the German "Secret Weapons"'; Reports from Polish intelligence, 8 and 20 April 1944, 20 May 1944, 10, 13, 17, 20, and 21 June 1944, in Stirling et al. (eds), *Intelligence Co-operation*, II, 855–904
48 Wnuk, 'Polish Intelligence and the German "Secret Weapons"'; J. Walker, *Poland Alone*, 100–105; Nowak, *Courier from Warsaw*, 320–21; Jones, *Most Secret War*, 599–601
49 Hinsley et al., *British Intelligence in the Second World War*, III, 437–8, 445, 447
50 Lampe, *The Savage Canary*, 43–4; Thomas, *The Giant-Killers*, 191.

24. PREPARING FOR D-DAY

1 Wieviorka, *The French Resistance*, 330
2 Lamb, *War in Italy*, 177; G. Kundahl, *The Riviera at War*, 55–9
3 Rayski, *The Choice of Jews under Vichy*, 203
4 Kundahl, *The Riviera at War*, 91–100
5 Mackenzie, *The Secret History of SOE*, 543–5; Cobb, *The Resistance*, 189–93; Schoenbrunn, *Soldiers of the Night*, 328–9; Richards, *Secret Flotillas*, 629–42; Vinen, *The Unfree French*, 322; Wieviorka, *The French Resistance*, 312–14
6 De Gaulle, *War Memoirs*, II, 145–9
7 Diary entry, 6 April 1944, H. Macmillan, *War Diaries*, 409; Wieviorka, *The French Resistance*, 297
8 Lacouture, *De Gaulle*, 510; Diary entry, 10 March 1944, Macmillan, *War Diaries*, 382; Kersaudy, *Churchill and de Gaulle*, 311; Wieviorka, *The French Resistance*, 297–9
9 Jackson, *France*, 569–70; Dank, *The French against the French*, 253–4; Gordon, *Collaborationism in France*, 289–92
10 Buckmaster, *They Fought Alone*, 85–6; Millar, *Maquis*, 55; Kundahl, *The Riviera at War*, 67–8; Lottman, *The People's Anger*, 33
11 Noguères et al., *Histoire de la Résistance*, IV, 112–18; Boyd, *Voices from the Dark Years*, 200; Cobb, *The Resistance*, 180–81; Kedward, *In Search of the Maquis*, 65–7; Heslop, *Xavier*, 190–91; P. Ashdown, *The Cruel Victory*, 69
12 Jackson, *France*, 553; Cobb, *The Resistance*, 215; H. Kedward, 'The Vichy of the Other Philippe', in Hirschfeld and Marsh (eds), *Collaboration in France*, 32–46; Gordon, *Collaborationism in France*, 293
13 Wieviorka, *The French Resistance*, 286
14 Jackson, *France*, 462–4; Wieviorka, *The French Resistance*, 289–94; Schoenbrun, *Soldiers of the Night*, 310–11
15 Jackson, *A Certain Idea of France*, 295–6; Marshall, *The White Rabbit*, 49–58; Seaman, *Bravest of the Brave*, 91–2, 101
16 Marshall, *The White Rabbit*, 89–99; Seaman, *Bravest of the Brave*, 135

17 Wieviorka, *The French Resistance*, 332–4; S. Albertelli, *Les Services secrets du Général de Gaulle*, 477–83
18 Noguères et al., *Histoire de la Résistance*, III, 509
19 Gildea, *Fighters in the Shadows*, 290–95; Wieviorka, *The French Resistance*, 315–16
20 Bourne-Paterson, *SOE in France*, 16
21 J. Poirier, *The Giraffe Has a Long Neck*, passim
22 Foot, *SOE in France*, 309–38; Bourne-Paterson, *SOE in France*, passim; Grehan and Mace, *Unearthing Churchill's Secret Army*, passim; Marks, *Between Silk and Cyanide*, 522; Helm, *A Life in Secrets*, 53–8; Cookridge, *They Came from the Sky*, 98–105, 209–20; Jenkins, *A Pacifist at War*, 81–9, 108; Seymour-Jones, *She Landed by Moonlight*, 171–94, 243; Millar, *Maquis*, 15–16; Le Chêne, *Watch for Me by Moonlight*, 150–65; Nicolson, *Aristide*, 101–4; Kent and Nicholas, *Agent Michael Trotobas*, 234–5; N. Perrin, *Spirit of Resistance*, 84–117; R. Landes, IWM 8641; C. Watney, IWM 10123, 12698; Y. Cormeau, IWM 7369; F. Cammaerts, IWM 16759, 11238
23 Heslop, *Xavier*, 156–61
24 Purnell, *A Woman of No Importance*, 223–43
25 Cookridge, *They Came from the Sky*, 313; Mackenzie, *The Secret History of SOE*, 599; Heslop, *Xavier*, 198–9; Cobb, *The Resistance*, 176–7; Albertelli, *Les Services secrets*, 453–4; Glass, *They Fought Alone*, 155–6; Lambert, *Free French Saboteurs*, passim
26 Wieviorka, *The Resistance in Western Europe*, 319; McCue, *Behind Enemy Lines with the SAS*, loc. 1,980
27 Cobb, *The Resistance*, 173
28 Perrin, *Spirit of Resistance*, 111
29 Foot, *SOE in France*, 314
30 Laub, *After the Fall*, 267–71; Kedward, *In Search of the Maquis*, 243; Heslop, *Xavier*, 208–25, 238–9; F. Cammaerts, IWM 16759, 11238
31 Noguères et al., *Histoire de la Résistance*, IV, 298–309; Albertelli, *Les Services secrets*, 440–43; Stafford, *Britain and European Resistance*, 147–51; Mackenzie, *The Secret History of SOE*, 602; Foot, *SOE in France*, 311–14; *RAF and the SOE*, 83; Marshall, *The White Rabbit*, 87–9; Wieviorka, *The French Resistance*, 330
32 Kedward, *In Search of the Maquis*, 118–21, 253, 281; Albertelli, *Les Services secrets*, 434; S. Farmer, 'The Communist Resistance in the Haute-Vienne', *French Historical Studies*, 14:1 (1985), 89–116; Cobb, *The Resistance*, 176; Kundahl, *The Riviera at War*, 131; Perrin, *Spirit of Resistance*, 117; Heslop, *Xavier*, 206; F. Cammaerts, IWM 16759, 11238
33 Cobb, *The Resistance*, 240; Barbier quoted in Wieviorka, *The French Resistance*, 325; Albertelli, *Les Services secrets*, 449; Noguères et al., *Histoire de la Résistance*, IV, 425
34 Noguères et al., *Histoire de la Résistance*, IV, 422–30; Wieviorka, *The French Resistance*, 326–7; Kedward, *In Search of the Maquis*, 136–8
35 Kedward, 'The Vichy of the Other Philippe'; Schoenbrun, *Soldiers of the Night*, 350; Wieviorka, *The French Resistance*, 327–8; Heslop, *Xavier*, 230–32; Cobb, *The Resistance*, 241; M. Bird, *The Secret Battalion*, passim
36 Sweets, *Choices in Vichy France*, 221–3; Schoenbrun, *Soldiers of the Night*, 381–2; Kedward, *Occupied France*, 72–3; Cookridge, *They Came from the Sky*, 360–62; Kedward, *In Search of the Maquis*, 164–8; Wake, *The White Mouse*, 135; O'Connor, *Churchill's Angels*, 283
37 Albertelli, *Les Services secrets*, 445–6
38 H. Verlander, *My War in SOE*, 9; Casey, *The Secret War against Hitler*, 75, 93; Mackenzie, *The Secret History of SOE*, 605–6; Wieviorka, *The Resistance in Western Europe*, 284
39 Albertelli, *Les Services secrets*, 464–75; Jackson, *France*, 541
40 Wieviorka, *The French Resistance*, 353–4; Maguire, *Anglo-American Policy*, 110–12; Seaman, *Saboteur*, 243
41 Mangold, *Britain and the Defeated French*, 219–23; Frenay, *The Night Will End*, 294

42 Eisenhower, *Crusade in Europe*, 272; Diary entry, 5 June 1944, in D. Dilks (ed.), *The Diaries of Sir Alexander Cadogan*, 634–5
43 Lacouture, *De Gaulle*, 525–6.

25. SUMMER 1944: FRANCE

1 BBC French Service, 21.45 on 5 June 1944; Wieviorka, *The French Resistance*, 356
2 McCue, *Behind Enemy lines with the SAS*, loc. 1,330; Seaman, *Saboteur*, 248; Glass, *They Fought Alone*, 171
3 Kedward, *In Search of the Maquis*, 187; Pike, *Defying Vichy*, 241–2, 253–4
4 Heslop, *Xavier*, 251; De Vomécourt, *Who Lived to See the Day*, 255; Bourne-Paterson, *SOE in France*, 74
5 A. Beevor, *D-Day*, 146
6 Laub, *After the Fall*, 275
7 Colvin (ed.), *Colonel Henri's Story*, 158
8 Littlejohn, *The Patriotic Traitors*, 274
9 Cookridge, *They Came from the Sky*, 226
10 A. Funk, *Hidden Ally*, 60–62
11 Noguères et al., *Histoire de la Résistance*, V, 147
12 Wieviorka, *The French Resistance*, 371–3; Jackson, *France*, 547–9; Gildea, *Fighters in the Shadows*, 346
13 Noguères et al., *Histoire de la Résistance*, V, 66–7
14 S. Hudson, IWM 16376
15 C. Watney, IWM 10123, 12698; Foot, *SOE in France*, 342
16 R. Maloubier, IWM 10444
17 Millar, *Maquis*, 83–4
18 Bourne-Paterson, *SOE in France*, 159–60
19 Kundahl, *The Riviera at War*, 163
20 Albertelli, *Les Services secrets*, 496–7; Wieviorka, *The French Resistance*, 360; Macksey, *The Partisans of Europe*, 190–91
21 Millar, *Maquis*, 95
22 Albertelli, *Les Services secrets*, 498; Macksey, *The Partisans of Europe*, 192
23 Casey, *The Secret War against Hitler*, 109–10; Olson, *Madame Fourcade's Secret War*, 317–23; Wieviorka, *The Resistance in Western Europe*, 316
24 Grehan and Mace, *Unearthing Churchill's Secret Army*, 181
25 Foot, *SOE in France*, 361; Grehan and Mace, *Unearthing Churchill's Secret Army*, 161; Landes in Miller, *Behind the Lines*, 100–101
26 Le Chêne, *Watch for Me by Moonlight*, 171–85; Seymour-Jones, *She Landed by Moonlight*, 257–65, 274; Glass, *They Fought Alone*, 191–5
27 Funk, *Hidden Ally*, 42–6; Jenkins, *A Pacifist at War*, 141–4; Cookridge, *They Came from the Sky*, 120–24
28 Heslop, *Xavier*, 249–83; Wieviorka, *The Resistance in Western Europe*, 322
29 De Vomécourt, *Who Lived to See the Day*, 225–6
30 P. Leslie, *The Liberation of the Riviera*, 193; Bennett, *Under the Shadow of the Swastika*, 41; De Vomécourt, *Who Lived to See the Day*, 247–8; T. Macpherson, *Behind Enemy Lines*, 146–7
31 Macpherson, *Behind Enemy Lines*, 129–33; Seaman, *Saboteur*, 272–4
32 M. Hastings, *Das Reich*, 212–35; McCue, *Behind Enemy lines with the SAS*, loc. 2,332–514, 2,680–781, 2,871–3,032
33 I. Wellsted, *SAS with the Maquis*, passim
34 Tyas, *SS-Major Horst Kopkow*, 120
35 Noguères et al., *Histoire de la Résistance*, V, 118–21; Hastings, *Das Reich*, 19, 89–99

36 Cobb, *The Resistance*, 248–9; Farmer, 'The Communist Resistance in the Haute-Vienne'; Kedward, *In Search of the Maquis*, 171–2; Gildea, *Fighters in the Shadows*, 347–8; Hastings, *Das Reich*, 116–40
37 Noguères et al., *Histoire de la Résistance*, V, 130–32; Cobb, *The Resistance*, 249–50; Hastings, *Das Reich*, 185–202
38 Pike, *Defying Vichy*, 251; T. Macpherson, IWM, 17912, 13335; C. Watney, IWM 10123, 12698; Macpherson, *Behind Enemy Lines*, 138–9; Beevor, *D-Day*, 166
39 Ashdown, *The Cruel Victory*, 34–5, 89, 94–5; F. Cammaerts, IWM 16759, 11238; M. Adamson, IWM 12687; Schoenbrun, *Soldiers of the Night*, 383–5; Kedward, *In Search of the Maquis*, 48–9
40 Noguères et al., *Histoire de la Résistance*, V, 173–82, 271–5, 336–86; Ashdown, *The Cruel Victory*, passim; M. Pearson, *Tears of Glory*, passim; Kedward, *In Search of the Maquis*, 174–81; J. Houseman, IWM 12083; F. Cammaerts, IWM 16759, 11238; Jenkins, *A Pacifist at War*, 150–82; Foot, *SOE in France*, 345–6; Cookridge, *They Came from the Sky*, 125–37; Wieviorka, *The Resistance in Western Europe*, 321–2
41 Casey, *The Secret War against Hitler*, 122–9; Macksey, *The Partisans of Europe*, 195–7; Foot, *SOE in France*, 357–8; Wieviorka, *The French Resistance*, 362–4, 374; W. Irwin, *The Jedburghs*, loc. 1,606–2,408; A. Hue, *The Next Moon*, passim.
42 Funk, *Hidden Ally*, 57–123; Casey, *The Secret War against Hitler*, 135–42; Irwin, *The Jedburghs*, loc. 3,554–659; Leslie, *The Liberation of the Riviera*, 209–10; Kundahl, *The Riviera at War*, 170; J. de Guélis, IWM 15350; Seymour-Jones, *She Landed by Moonlight*, 311; Cookridge, *They Came from the Sky*, 160–62; Fielding, *Hide and Seek*, 177–8, 185; Mulley, *The Spy Who Loved*, 245–9
43 Irwin, *The Jedburghs*, loc. 2,725–840; Colvin (ed.), *Colonel Henri's Story*, 139; Casey, *The Secret War against Hitler*, 130
44 Lacouture, *De Gaulle*, 555–6; De Gaulle, *War Memoirs*, II, 290–91; Jackson, *France*, 552; Gildea, *Fighters in the Shadows*, 383; Jackson, *A Certain Idea of France*, 315
45 Boyd, *Voices from the Dark Years*, 234; Dank, *The French against the French*, 262–3, 270; Gordon, *Collaborationism in France*, 307; Littlejohn, *The Patriotic Traitors*, 276–7; Lambert, *Free French Saboteurs*, 109.

26. SUMMER 1944: OTHER FRONTS

1 Diary entry, 6 June 1944, Gobetti, *Partisan Diary*, 117
2 Reed Olsen, *Two Eggs on My Plate*, 240
3 Diary entry, 6 June 1944, in Young (ed.), *The Diaries of Sir Bruce Lockhart*, II, 321
4 Bles, *Child at War*, 221
5 Allen, *Churchill's Guests*, 109–10; H. Bodson, *Agent for the Resistance*, 95
6 Mackenzie, *The Secret History of SOE*, 634; Casey, *The Secret War against Hitler*, 157; Foot, *SOE in the Low Countries*, 365
7 Bodson, *Agent for the Resistance*, 140–42, 153
8 Eloy, *The Fight in the Forest*, 140–43; Bodson, *Agent for the Resistance*, 133–5
9 Conway, *Collaboration in Belgium*, 258–63, 272; Warmbrunn, *The German Occupation of Belgium*, 144–6
10 Warmbrunn, *The German Occupation of Belgium*, 101–3, 129; Geller, 'The Role of Military Administration in German-Occupied Belgium, 1940–1944', *Journal of Military History*, 63:1 (1999), 99–125
11 Eloy, *The Fight in the Forest*, 170–78
12 Kjeldstadli, 'The Resistance Movement in Norway and the Allies'
13 Bennett, *British Broadcasting and the Danish Resistance Movement*, 205–7; Mackenzie, *The Secret History of SOE*, 681
14 Jespersen, *No Small Achievement*, 360; Haestrup, *Europe Ablaze*, 292
15 Cruickshank, *SOE in Scandinavia*, 230–32; Lampe, *The Savage Canary*, 169–72

16 Littlejohn, *The Patriotic Traitors*, 79–80; Bennett, *British Broadcasting and the Danish Resistance Movement*, 53; Haestrup, *Europe Ablaze*, 145; Jespersen, *No Small Achievement*, 360, 361–2
17 Lampe, *The Savage Canary*, 140–41, 146–50; Reilly, *The Sixth Floor*, 87–9; Muus, *The Spark and the Flame*, 162–6
18 G. Sonsteby, *Report from No. 24*, 123–5, 132–8; Mackenzie, *The Secret History of SOE*, 670; Cruickshank, *SOE in Scandinavia*, 245–6
19 Hoidal, *Quisling*, 625
20 Sonsteby, *Report from No. 24*, 106–13; Dahl, *Quisling*, 327
21 Gjelsvik, *Norwegian Resistance*, 136–8
22 Ibid., 153–61; Hoidal, *Quisling*, 631–8; Dahl, *Quisling*, 326–43, 344–5; M. Skodvin, 'Norway', at Conference at St Antony's College, Oxford, December 1962
23 Battaglia, *The Story of the Italian Resistance*, 166–7
24 Ellwood, *Italy*, 95; Haestrup, *Europe Ablaze*, 342; G. Quazza, 'The Politics of the Italian Resistance', in S. Woolf (ed.), *The Rebirth of Italy*, 1–29; Lamb, *War in Italy*, 212
25 Battaglia, *The Story of the Italian Resistance*, 149–51; Gobetti, *Partisan Diary*, 221–9
26 Corvo, *The OSS in Italy*, 180; Ellwood, *Italy*, 158
27 Stafford, *Mission Accomplished*, 156–7
28 Lett, *Rossano*, 98; Corvo, *The OSS in Italy*, 196
29 Stafford, *Mission Accomplished*, 172–4; Salvadori, *The Labour and the Wounds*, 204–5
30 Lett, *Rossano*, 93–5, 100–104
31 Diary entries, 19 and 28 August 1944, Gobetti, *Partisan Diary*, 163–4, 169
32 J. Ross, IWM 27077; W. Fowler, *The Secret War in Italy*, 84–5, 92–3; Wilhelm, *The Other Italy*, 188–90
33 H. Hargreaves, IWM 12158
34 Battaglia, *The Story of the Italian Resistance*, 189; Behan, *The Italian Resistance*, 176–8
35 Stafford, *Mission Accomplished*, 209; Corvo, *The OSS in Italy*, 202–4; Behan, *The Italian Resistance*, 176–88
36 Mackenzie, *The Secret History of SOE*, 552–3
37 G. Holdsworth in Bailey (ed.), *Forgotten Voices*, 282; J. Olsen, *Silence on Monte Sole*, 14–15; Corvo, *The OSS in Italy*, 201
38 A. Kesselring, *The Memoirs of Field Marshal Kesselring*, 227
39 Ibid., 302–4; A. Osti Guerazzi, 'Italian Counterinsurgency Operations during the Italian Civil War 1943–5', presented at the Conference at King's College London, 2018. The author thanks Professor Osti Guerazzi for permission to use this paper; Diary entry, 7 August 1944, Gobetti, *Partisan Diary*, 157; Lett, *Rossano*, 111
40 Künzel, 'Resistance, Reprisals, Reactions'; M. Geyer, 'Civitella della Chiana on 29 June 1944: The Reconstruction of a German "Measure"', in Heer and Naumann (eds), *War of Extermination*, 175–207; P. Pezzino, *Memory and Massacre*, passim; Gallo, *For Love and Country*, 259; Lamb, *War in Italy*, 73–5
41 Wilhelm, *The Other Italy*, 130–34, 215–36; Hood, *Pebbles from My Skull*, 139; C. Macintosh, *From Cloak to Dagger*, 52–8, 64–6, 72–82; Behan, *The Italian Resistance*, 86–91
42 Olsen, *Silence on Monte Sole*, 107–8, 113–14, 296; Holland, *Italy's Sorrow*, 385; Battaglia, *The Story of the Italian Resistance*, 201–7
43 Diary entry, 5 October 1944, Gobetti, *Partisan Diary*, 194–5
44 Adair, *Hitler's Greatest Defeat*, 52, 76–8
45 Grenkevich, *The Soviet Partisan Movement*, 257–60; Munoz and Romanko, *Hitler's White Russians*, 401; Slepyan, *Stalin's Guerrillas*, 272–3
46 Armstrong (ed.), *Soviet Partisans in World War II*, 59; Vakar, *Belorussia*, 203–6; Misiunas and Taagepera, *The Baltic States*, 66; Johnson to Secretary of State, 7 August 1944

in Remeikis (ed.), *Lithuania under German Occupation*, 667; Lumans, *Latvia in World War II*, 335
47 Evidence to Nuremberg trial, Hans Frank, The Avalon Project, Yale University
48 Kochanski, *The Eagle Unbowed*, 394
49 Ibid., 395
50 A. Applebaum, *Iron Curtain*, 100–101
51 Memorandum by Mikołajczyk to Churchill; note of conversation between Mikołajczyk, Churchill, and Eden, both on 18 July 1944, *DPSR*, II, 288–91
52 Bór-Komorowski, *The Secret Army*, 198; Kochanski, *The Eagle Unbowed*, 395–6
53 Hanson, *Civilian Population*, 68–9.

27. UPRISINGS: WARSAW, PARIS, SLOVAKIA

1 J. Zawodny, *Nothing but Honour*, 15
2 Kochanski, *The Eagle Unbowed*, 400
3 Walker, *Poland Alone*, 219; Nowak, *Courier from Warsaw*, 333–4; Kochanski, *The Eagle Unbowed*, 486–7
4 Sosnkowski to Bór-Komorowski, 28 July 1944, *AK Documents*, IV, no. 724, 17
5 J. Ciechanowski, *The Warsaw Rising of 1944*, 296
6 Bór-Komorowski, *The Secret Army*, 215
7 Kochanski, *The Eagle Unbowed*, 402–4
8 Z. Czajkowski, *Warsaw 1944*, 29
9 Borodziej, *The Warsaw Uprising*, 75
10 Walker, *Poland Alone*, 219
11 Borowiec, *Warsaw Boy*, 210–11
12 Kochanski, *The Eagle Unbowed*, 404
13 Czajkowski, *Warsaw 1944*, 42
14 Borowiec, *Warsaw Boy*, 195
15 Kochanski, *The Eagle Unbowed*, 405
16 A. Richie, *Warsaw 1944*, 217
17 Kochanski, *The Eagle Unbowed*, 406
18 Richie, *Warsaw 1944*, 255–308
19 Zawodny, *Nothing but Honour*, 63
20 Borowiec, *Warsaw Boy*, 201
21 Irene Barbarska quoted in Lukas, *Out of the Inferno*, 19; B. Hryniewicz, *My Boyhood War*, 91–2
22 Czajkowski, *Warsaw 1944*, 83
23 I. Orska, *Silent is the Vistula*, 127
24 Bór-Komorowski to Sosnkowski, 6 August 1944, *AK Documents*, IV, no. 776, 61
25 Kochanski, *The Eagle Unbowed*, 408
26 Ibid., 410–11
27 Nowak, *Courier from Warsaw*, 358
28 P. Siudak to Korboński, 30 August 1944, *AK Documents*, IV, no. 959, 237
29 Bór-Komorowski to AK commanders, 31 August 1944, *AK Documents*, IV, no. 968, 245
30 Kochanski, *The Eagle Unbowed*, 411
31 Orska, *Silent is the Vistula*, 118
32 Hugh Lunghi quoted in L. Rees, *World War II behind Closed Doors*, 289. Lunghi was the interpreter with the mission
33 Churchill to Stalin, 4 August 1944; Stalin to Churchill, 5 August 1944, *Stalin Correspondence*, I, nos 311 and 313, 251–3; Mikołajczyk to Polish Government, 9 August 1944, *DPSR*, II, no. 89, 336; Harriman to Cordell Hull, 10 August 1944, *FRUS 1944*, III, 1,308–10; Vyshinsky to Harriman, 15 August 1944, TNA, FO 371 1075/8/55; Churchill and Roosevelt to Stalin, 20 August 1944, in F. Loewenheim et al. (eds),

Roosevelt and Churchill, 565; Stalin to Churchill and Roosevelt, 22 August 1944, *Stalin Correspondence*, no. 323, 258. Shuttle bombing began on 2 June 1944 with US bombers flying from bases in Britain, bombing targets such as the marshalling yards at Debrecen in Hungary or against oil installations in Romania, before landing at the Soviet airfield at Poltava in the Ukraine for refuelling

34 C. Bohlen, *Witness to History*, 161
35 Kochanski, *The Eagle Unbowed*, 419; Zawodny, *Nothing but Honour*, 184–5
36 Korboński, *Fighting Warsaw*, 379
37 Ibid., 367; Kochanski, *The Eagle Unbowed*, 411–12
38 Hanson, *Civilian Population*, 107
39 Ginter, *Life in Both Hands*, 216
40 Orska, *Silent is the Vistula*, 151
41 Czajkowski, *Warsaw 1944*, 132
42 Ginter, *Life in Both Hands*, 229
43 Zawodny, *Nothing but Honour*, 149
44 Declaration by the British government, 29 August 1944; declaration by the United States government, 29 August 1944, *AK Documents*, IV, nos 952 and 953, 225–8
45 Declaration by the British government, 9 September 1944, *AK Documents*, IV, no. 1,030, 303
46 Bór-Komorowski to London, 6 September 1944, *AK Documents*, IV, no. 1,007, 284
47 Jankowski and Bór-Komorowski to London, 6 September 1944, *AK Documents*, IV, no. 1,006, 282–4
48 W. Bartoszewski, *Powstanie Warszawskie*, 213–20; Hanson, *Civilian Population*, 156–8
49 Bór-Komorowski to London, 10 September 1944, *AK Documents*, IV, no. 1,034, 306
50 C. Grzelak et al., *Bez Możliwości Wyboru*, 166–75; Zawodny, *Nothing but Honour*, 72–4. The author goes into great detail examining the case of whether the capture of Warsaw was part of the Soviet plans and whether the Soviet armies could have attacked the city; N. Davies, *Rising '44*, 271
51 Zawodny, *Nothing but Honour*, 202. The author lists the attempts to establish communications during September 1944
52 Kochanski, *The Eagle Unbowed*, 418–20; Grzelak et al., *Bez Możliwości Wyboru*, 177–8
53 Zawodny, *Nothing but Honour*, 182; Davies, *Rising '44*, 396
54 Hanson, *Civilian Population*, 194
55 Ibid., 194–6
56 TNA, HS 4/156
57 Bór-Komorowski to London, 1 and 4 October 1944, *AK Documents*, IV, nos 1,201, 1,217, 423, 441; Bór-Komorowski, *The Secret Army*, 372. Bór-Komorowski and his fellow commanders were imprisoned in various camps: Oflag 73 in Langwasser near Nuremberg; Colditz; a civilian camp at Laufen in Czechoslovakia, before being handed over to the Swiss on 4 May 1945
58 Kulski, *Dying, We Live*, 265
59 Baluk, *Silent and Unseen*, 249
60 Kulski, *Dying, We Live*, 269
61 Orska, *Silent is the Vistula*, 258
62 Borowiec, *Destroy Warsaw!*, 179; Zawodny, *Nothing but Honour*, 210–11
63 Beevor, *D-Day*, 483; Drake, *Paris at War*, 376–7
64 Schoenbrun, *Soldiers of the Night*, 426–9; Wieviorka, *The French Resistance*, 376; Jackson, *France*, 565–6; M. Cobb, *Eleven Days in August*, 14, 34; De Gaulle, *War Memoirs*, II, 294
65 Wieviorka, *The French Resistance*, 377; Cobb, *Eleven Days in August*, 14, 62; Pryce-Jones, *Paris in the Third Reich*, 257–9; Beevor, *D-Day*, 484
66 Eisenhower, *Crusade in Europe*, 325
67 O. Bradley, *A Soldier's Story of the Allied Campaign from Tunis to the Elbe*, 386–7

68 Cobb, *Eleven Days in August*, 36; Fourcade, *Noah's Ark*, 347; Maguire, *Anglo-American Policy*, 139
69 Noguères et al., *Histoire de la Résistance*, V, 458; Boyd, *Voices from the Dark Years*, 242; Schoenbrun, *Soldiers of the Night*, 432–4; Drake, *Paris at War*, 380; S. Kitson, 'From Enthusiasm to Disenchantment: The French Police and the Vichy Regime, 1940–1944', *Contemporary European History*, 11:3 (2002), 371–90
70 Schoenbrun, *Soldiers of the Night*, 436–8, 449; Chevrillon, *Codename Christiane Clouet*, 157–8; Noguères et al., *Histoire de la Résistance*, V, 469–72; Cobb, *Eleven Days in August*, 116
71 Noguères et al., *Histoire de la Résistance*, V, 473–4, 478–80; Beevor, *D-Day*, 486; Cobb, *Eleven Days in August*, 144–6, 161–3
72 Cobb, *Eleven Days in August*, 79–91; Noguères et al., *Histoire de la Résistance*, V, 468
73 Cobb, *Eleven Days in August*, 169; Schoenbrun, *Soldiers of the Night*, 454; Jackson, *France*, 563–4
74 Noguères et al., *Histoire de la Résistance*, V, 481–503; Cobb, *Eleven Days in August*, 165; L. Collins and D. Lapierre, *Is Paris Burning?*, 145
75 Cobb, *Eleven Days in August*, 195–203; Noguères et al., *Histoire de la Résistance*, V, 504, 509–12; Beevor, *D-Day*, 488–9
76 Noguères et al., *Histoire de la Résistance*, V, 505–8, 513–15, 519–21, 524–5; Cobb, *Eleven Days in August*, 211, 219–20, 225; Drake, *Paris at War*, 392; Jackson, *France*, 564; Gildea, *Fighters in the Shadows*, 399
77 Beevor, *D-Day*, 493–7; Noguères et al., *Histoire de la Résistance*, V, 539
78 Collins and Lapierre, *Is Paris Burning?*, preface; Cobb, *Eleven Days in August*, 233, 237, 246–7; Noguères et al., *Histoire de la Résistance*, V, 529–31
79 Beevor, *D-Day*, 502–3; Lacouture, *De Gaulle*, 570; Cobb, *Eleven Days in August*, 268–9
80 Chevrillon, *Codename Christiane Clouet*, 166
81 Cobb, *Eleven Days in August*, 275
82 Beevor, *D-Day*, 504–5
83 Cobb, *Eleven Days in August*, 294–7; Beevor, *D-Day*, 508; Noguères et al., *Histoire de la Résistance*, V, 551
84 Noguères et al., *Histoire de la Résistance*, V, 532–7, 549–50; Cobb, *Eleven Days in August*, 283–98, 304, 307; Beevor, *D-Day*, 513
85 Noguères et al., *Histoire de la Résistance*, V, 552–6; Cobb, *Eleven Days in August*, 299–300
86 Gildea, *Fighters in the Shadows*, 403
87 Lacouture, *De Gaulle*, 575
88 De Gaulle, *War Memoirs*, II, 318; Cobb, *Eleven Days in August*, 341–2; Noguères et al., *Histoire de la Résistance*, V, 560
89 De Gaulle, *War Memoirs*, II, 311
90 Noguères et al., *Histoire de la Résistance*, V, 566–9; Beevor, *D-Day*, 514–15
91 Langelaan, *Knights of the Floating Silk*, 316
92 Erickson, *The Road to Berlin*, 291, 295; Korbel, *The Communist Subversion of Czechoslovakia*, 68–9; Hoensch, 'The Slovak Republic'; Josko, 'The Slovak Resistance Movement'
93 Grenkevich, *The Soviet Partisan Movement*, 264; Armstrong (ed.), *Soviet Partisans in World War II*, 63
94 Lettrich, *History of Modern Slovakia*, 203–5; Josko, 'The Slovak Resistance Movement'
95 Lettrich, *History of Modern Slovakia*, 207–8; Skilling, 'The Czechoslovak Struggle'
96 B. Chňoupek, *A Breaking of Seals*, 70–71
97 Moravec, *Master of Spies*, 243; Luža, 'The Czech Resistance Movement'
98 Josko, 'The Slovak Resistance Movement'; Erickson, *The Road to Berlin*, 297–8
99 Lettrich, *History of Modern Slovakia*, 205, 209; Josko, 'The Slovak Resistance Movement'; Erickson, *The Road to Berlin*, 299, 302–3

100 Deakin, 'Resistance in Occupied Central and South-Eastern Europe'; Josko, 'The Slovak Resistance Movement'

101 Korbel, *The Communist Subversion of Czechoslovakia*, 71; Josko, 'The Slovak Resistance Movement'; Deakin, 'Resistance in Occupied Central and South-Eastern Europe'; V. Prečan, 'The 1944 Slovak Rising', in Deakin et al. (eds), *British Political and Military Strategy*, 223–34; Lettrich, *History of Modern Slovakia*, 212–13; P. O'Donnell, *Operatives, Spies, and Saboteurs*, 217–25

102 Chňoupek, *A Breaking of Seals*, passim

103 Josko, 'The Slovak Resistance Movement'; Prečan, 'The 1944 Slovak Rising'; Lettrich, *History of Modern Slovakia*, 211

104 Lettrich, *History of Modern Slovakia*, 213–24; Josko, 'The Slovak Resistance Movement'; Ward, *Priest, Politician, Collaborator*, 253; Erickson, *The Road to Berlin*, 306

105 Wieviorka, *The Resistance in Western Europe*, 34

106 Collins and Lapierre, *Is Paris Burning?*, passim; Schoenbrun, *Soldiers of the Night*, 463; Cobb, *Eleven Days in August*, 300

107 Korboński, *Fighting Warsaw*, 407

108 Kochanski, *The Eagle Unbowed*, 425

109 Quoted in Rees, *World War II*, 297

110 Ginter, *Life in Both Hands*, 429.

28. AUTUMN 1944: WESTERN EUROPE

1 Funk, *Hidden Ally*, 131–3; J. Ludewig, *Rückzug*, 66

2 Funk, *Hidden Ally*, 166–73; M. Adamson, IWM 12687

3 Funk, *Hidden Ally*, 159–60

4 Ibid., 179–97

5 Ibid., 202–4; Leslie, *The Liberation of the Riviera*, 227–33

6 Funk, *Hidden Ally*, 211–12

7 Ibid., 213–15; Schoenbrun, *Soldiers of the Night*, 417; Kundahl, *The Riviera at War*, 226–9; Jackson, *France*, 559

8 N. A. C. Croft, IWM 12850

9 Gildea, *Fighters in the Shadows*, 365–7, 386; Cookridge, *Inside SOE*, 344–5; Foot, *SOE in France*, 369; Cobb, *The Resistance*, 274–5; Glass, *They Fought Alone*, 219–20, 228–9

10 Cookridge, *They Came from the Sky*, 238–50; Boyd, *Voices from the Dark Years*, 252; Landes report in Buckmaster, *They Fought Alone*, 246–56

11 Funk, *Hidden Ally*, 238–52; Noguères et al., *Histoire de la Résistance*, V, 633–45, 657–61, 666–70, 687–9; Cobb, *The Resistance*, 273; Heslop, *Xavier*, 295

12 H. Verneret, *Teenage Resistance Fighter*, 68, 98

13 De Vomécourt, *Who Lived to See the Day*, 273

14 Irwin, *The Jedburghs*, loc. 4,182; Seymour-Jones, *She Landed by Moonlight*, 327–37; T. Macpherson, IWM 17913, 13335; Ludewig, *Rückzug*, 181

15 Kedward, *In Search of the Maquis*, 279

16 Schoenbrun, *Soldiers of the Night*, 323

17 Millar, *Maquis*, 336, 347–9; Irwin, *The Jedburghs*, loc. 3,953, 4,078; Ludewig, *Rückzug*, 243; Casey, *The Secret War against Hitler*, 175

18 Schoenbrun, *Soldiers of the Night*, 374

19 H. Michel, *Histoire de la Résistance*, 118

20 Casey, *The Secret War against Hitler*, 130

21 Funk, *Hidden Ally*, 254

22 Wieviorka, *The French Resistance*, 375–6; Beevor, *D-Day*, 447; Macksey, *The Partisans of Europe*, 203

23 Casey, *The Secret War against Hitler*, 154–5

24 Jackson, *France*, 557

25 Lacouture, *De Gaulle*, 553

26 De Vomécourt, *Who Lived to See the Day*, 279
27 Vinen, *The Unfree French*, 336–8; Littlejohn, *The Patriotic Traitors*, 276–9
28 Cobb, *The Resistance*, 276; Funk, *Hidden Ally*, 208; Cobb, *Eleven Days in August*, 341–2
29 Jackson, *A Certain Idea of France*, 335
30 Cobb, *The Resistance*, 276–7; De Gaulle, *War Memoirs*, III, 17–26; Heslop, *Xavier*, 297–300; Glass, *They Fought Alone*, 229–31; Cookridge, *They Came from the Sky*, 255; Jackson, *A Certain Idea of France*, 337
31 Mangold, *Britain and the Defeated French*, 234; Irwin, *The Jedburghs*, loc. 4,321; Verlander, *My War in SOE*, 127–8, 140, 145–6; Le Chêne, *Watch for Me by Moonlight*, 211
32 Wieviorka, *The Resistance in Western Europe*, 334–5
33 Foot, *SOE in the Low Countries*, 371–83; Bodson, *Agent for the Resistance*, 171–8; Eloy, *The Fight in the Forest*, 185–91; C. de Groote, IWM 12832
34 Casey, *The Secret War against Hitler*, 158–61; Foot, *SOE in the Low Countries*, 380–81; General Bouhon, 'Le Rôle prépondérant de la Résistance dans la Libération du Port D'Anvers', in *First International Conference*, 257–83
35 Allen, *Churchill's Guests*, 155–6; Foot, *SOE in the Low Countries*, 400; Wieviorka, *The Resistance in Western Europe*, 363–7; M. Conway, *The Sorrows of Belgium*, 43, 63, 92–108; Beevor, *D-Day*, 50–51; P. Lagrou, *The Legacy of Nazi Occupation*, 32; G. Warner, 'Allies, Government and Resistance: The Belgian Political Crisis of November 1944', *Transactions of the Royal Historical Society*, 28 (1978), 45–60
36 Casey, *The Secret War against Hitler*, 166; Haestrup, *Europe Ablaze*, 167–8; Mackenzie, *Secret History of SOE*, 641; Giskes, *London Calling North Pole*, 150
37 A. Beevor, *Arnhem*, passim; C. Ryan, *A Bridge Too Far*, passim; J. Olmsted, IWM 12855
38 D. Paul, *Surgeon at Arms*, 112, 124, 153, 132; L. Heaps, *The Grey Goose of Arnhem*, 104–5, 151–60, 183–4, 215–28; Beevor, *Arnhem*, 362–3; J. Hackett, *I Was a Stranger*, passim
39 Paape, 'How Dutch Resistance was Organised'; P. Kamphuis, 'Caught between Hope and Fear: Operation Market Garden and its Effects on the Civilian Population in the Netherlands', in Foot (ed.), *Holland at War against Hitler*, 170–77; Warmbrunn, *The Dutch under German Occupation*, 193–5; Rings, *Life with the Enemy*, 80–81; Mackenzie, *Secret History of SOE*, 643; Haestrup, *Europe Ablaze*, 106–8; Beevor, *Arnhem*, 372–3.

29. THE GERMAN RETREAT FROM THE BALKANS

1 Barker, 'Some Factors in British Decision-Making over Yugoslavia'
2 A. Resis, 'The Churchill-Stalin Secret "Percentages" Agreement on the Balkans, Moscow, October 1944', *American Historical Review*, 83: 2 (1978), 368–87
3 Papastratis, *British Policy towards Greece*, 202
4 Clive, *A Greek Experience*, 120
5 Pearson, *Albania in Occupation and War*, 391–4
6 Churchill, *The Second World War*, VI, 82–3
7 Djilas, *Wartime*, 401
8 Williams, *Parachutes, Patriots and Partisans*, 229
9 Kurapovna, *Shadows on the Mountain*, 46–7, 152; Diary of Lieutenant E. R. Kamer, 17 September, quoted in Miller, *Behind the Lines*, 191–2; Lees, *The Rape of Serbia*, 287; Churchill to Roosevelt, 1 September 1944, Roosevelt to Churchill, 3 September 1944, both in Loewenheim et al. (eds), *Roosevelt and Churchill*, 570–71
10 Roberts, *Tito, Mihailović and the Allies*, 260
11 Erickson, *The Road to Berlin*, 384; Hamilton-Hill, *SOE Assignment*, 182–3; D. Biber, 'The Yugoslav Partisans and the British in 1944', in Deakin (ed.), *British Political and Military Strategy*, 111–29
12 A. Eden, *The Eden Memoirs*, 482; Djilas, *Wartime*, 406; Biber, 'The Yugoslav Partisans and the British in 1944'

13 Pearson, *Albania in Occupation and War*, 366–84; Lucas, *The OSS in World War II Albania*, 113; Fischer, *Albania at War*, 217–18; Bailey, *The Wildest Province*, 285–6; Fielding, *One Man in his Time*, 49–50
14 Rendel, *Appointment in Crete*, 176–85; Beevor, *Crete*, 312–13
15 Moss, *A War of Shadows*, 67; Beevor, *Crete*, 315–17; Psychoundakis, *The Cretan Runner*, 285–6
16 Woodhouse, *Something Ventured*, 86–7; Sarafis, *ELAS*, 354; Churchill to Roosevelt, 31 May 1944, Roosevelt to Churchill, 10 June 1944, and Churchill to Roosevelt, 23 June 1944, all in Loewenheim et al. (eds), *Roosevelt and Churchill*, 502–3, 526–7, 539–41; Churchill to Stalin, 12 July 1944, in *Stalin Correspondence*, 239–40
17 Churchill to Eden, 6 August 1944, in Churchill, *The Second World War*, VI, 97
18 Baerentzen, 'British Strategy towards Greece in 1944'; Papastratis, *British Policy towards Greece*, 200–214, 327; Sarafis, *ELAS*, 387–9; Hammond, *Venture into Greece*, 167–73
19 E. Lawson, IWM 9110; T. Evans, *With SOE in Greece*, 85–6
20 Deletant, *Hitler's Forgotten Ally*, 240–4; Deletant, *British Clandestine Activities in Romania*, 117–18, 132–3; Ogden, *Through Hitler's Back Door*, 260; G. Zaharia, 'The Birth and Growth of Romania's Anti-Fascist Resistance Movement', and I. Porter, 'Some Notes on Operation Autonomous: Romania, 1944', both in Deakin et al. (eds), *British Political and Military Strategy*, 151–61, 162–79; Barker, *British Policy in South-East Europe*, 241–2
21 M. L. Miller, *Bulgaria during the Second World War*, 202–3, 215–16; E. Barker, 'Bulgaria in August 1944: A British View' in Deakin et al. (eds), *British Political and Military Strategy*, 201–11; Macintosh, 'Soviet Policy on the Balkans in 1944'; Erickson, *The Road to Berlin*, 377–8
22 Ogden, *Through Hitler's Back Door*, 43; Barker, *British Policy in South-East Europe*, 262; G. Juhász, 'Problems of the Hungarian Resistance after the German Occupation, 1944', in Deakin et al. (eds), *British Political and Military Strategy*, 180–99; Kállay, *Hungarian Premier*, 454–66; Blood, *Hitler's Bandit Hunters*, 270–71; K. Ungváry, *Battle for Budapest*, passim.
23 Hamilton-Hill, *SOE Assignment*, 167
24 C. M. Woodhouse, IWM, 10139
25 P. Kemp, IWM 12299
26 Maclean, *Eastern Approaches*, 472, 487–9; F. Lindsay, *Beacons in the Night*, 142; Ivanovic, *LX*, 265
27 Lindsay, *Beacons in the Night*, 71, 104, 136–42; Ritchie, *Our Man in Yugoslavia*, 141
28 Martin (ed.), *Patriot or Traitor*, 47; Pavlowitch, *Hitler's New Disorder*, 228; Lees, *The Rape of Serbia*, 78
29 Martin, *Web of Disinformation*, 252–7; Djilas, *Wartime*, 403; Roberts, *Tito, Mihailović and the Allies*, 260–61; Pavlowitch, *Hitler's New Disorder*, 231–2
30 Roberts, *Tito, Mihailović and the Allies*, 390–92
31 Tomasevich, *The Chetniks*, 411–17; Biber, 'The Yugoslav Partisans and the British in 1944'; Martin (ed.), *Patriot or Traitor*, 55
32 Martin (ed.), *Patriot or Traitor*, 56; Roberts, *Tito, Mihailović and the Allies*, 261
33 B. Irwin, IWM 9772
34 Tomasevich, *The Chetniks*, 420
35 Maclean, *Eastern Approaches*, 515
36 Davidson, *Partisan Picture*, 323
37 Djilas, *Wartime*, 420
38 Roberts, *Tito, Mihailović and the Allies*, 285; Hamilton-Hill, *SOE Assignment*, 173; Biber, 'The Yugoslav Partisans and the British in 1944'
39 Hamilton-Hill, *SOE Assignment*, 178–9; Djilas, *Wartime*, 425; Beloff, *Tito's Flawed Legacy*, 121–2
40 W. Jones, *Raiding Support Regiment*, 154
41 Pearson, *Albania in Occupation and War*, 389–98; Bailey, *The Wildest Province*, 300–302

42 Jones, *Raiding Support Regiment*, 180–83
43 R. Eden, IWM 13339
44 Fischer, *Albania at War*, 231–2
45 Pearson, *Albania in Occupation and War*, 403–14; Fischer, *Albania at War*, 234–7; Lucas, *The OSS in World War II Albania*, 149–51; Bailey, *The Wildest Province*, 309–10; R. Bailey, 'OSS-SOE Relations, Albania 1943–44', *Intelligence & National Security*, 15:2 (2000), 20–35
46 Lucas, *The OSS in World War II Albania*, 156–61; Pearson, *Albania in Occupation and War*, 413–14
47 Beevor, *Crete*, 318–30; Rendel, *Appointment in Crete*, 190–98, 208, 217–18, 222–6; Psychoundakis, *The Cretan Runner*, 290–93, 297
48 Hammond, *Venture into Greece*, 170–71; Evans, *With SOE in Greece*, 88
49 Clive, *A Greek Experience*, 130–31; Woodhouse, *Something Ventured*, 91
50 Evans, *With SOE in Greece*, 52–4, 66–7, 89–90; Moss, *A War of Shadows*, 87–90, 97–9; TNA, HS 5/634
51 K. Scott, IWM, 9249; D. Tobler, IWM 12798; Myers, *Greek Entanglement*, 271
52 Sarafis, *ELAS*, 352
53 Clive, *A Greek Experience*, 112; Hammond, *Venture into Greece*, 177
54 L. Baerentzen, 'The Liberation of the Peloponnese, September 1944', in Iatrides (ed.), *Greece in the 1940s*, 131–41
55 Mazower, *Inside Hitler's Greece*, 360; Papastratis, *British Policy towards Greece*, 202
56 H. Hainsworth, IWM 12578
57 Ibid.; Leeper, *When Greek Meets Greek*, 75; Woodhouse, *Something Ventured*, 93; D. Tobler, IWM 12798
58 Woodhouse, *The Struggle for Greece*, 97; Woodhouse, *Something Ventured*, 95; Hamilton-Hill, *SOE Assignment*, 158.

30. NEARING THE END: WINTER 1944–45

1 Haestrup, *Europe Ablaze*, 343
2 Stafford, *Mission Accomplished*, 232, 261; L. Lewis, *Echoes of Resistance*, 76–7; Macintosh, *From Cloak to Dagger*, 117; Ellwood, *Italy*, 164
3 Diary entry, 1 December 1944, Gobetti, *Partisan Diary*, 232
4 Corvo, *The OSS in Italy*, 200
5 Battaglia, *The Story of the Italian Resistance*, 238–9
6 Lett, *Rossano*, 136–78
7 Macintosh, *From Cloak to Dagger*, 140, 146; Stafford, *Mission Accomplished*, 278
8 Battaglia, *The Story of the Italian Resistance*, 233–4
9 Report on Coolant Mission, 30 July 1945, T. Macpherson, IWM 17913, 13335; Lewis, *Echoes of Resistance*, 96; Final Report on the Clowder Mission, Wilkinson, 1 October 1945, IWM 12751
10 Martin, *Web of Disinformation*, 272; Biber, 'The Yugoslav Partisans and the British in 1944'; G. Trifković, 'The Yugoslav Partisans' Lost Victories: Operations in Montenegro and Bosnia-Herzegovina, 1944–1945', *Journal of Military History*, 82:1 (2018), 95–124
11 Tomasevich, *The Chetniks*, 424–30; Pavlowitch, *Hitler's New Disorder*, 254; Roberts, *Tito, Mihailović and the Allies*, 282–4; Beloff, *Tito's Flawed Legacy*, 116
12 Pavlowitch, *Hitler's New Disorder*, 254–6
13 Tomasevich, *Occupation and Collaboration*, 126–8; Pavlowitch, *Hitler's New Disorder*, 249, 256–7; Ritchie, *Our Man in Yugoslavia*, 143
14 V. Hunt, *Fire and Ice*, passim; Mann, *British Policy and Strategy towards Norway*, 177–91; Gjelsvik, *Norwegian Resistance*, 183–6; Hoidal, *Quisling*, 669–71; Dahl, *Quisling*, 348; Churchill to Stalin and Stalin to Churchill, 24 October 1944, Churchill to Stalin, 31 October 1944, Stalin to Churchill, 7 November 1944, all in *Stalin Correspondence*, 268–9, 271

15 Mackenzie, *Secret History of SOE*, 670–71; Sonsteby, *Report from No. 24*, 160; Riste and Nökleby, *Norway*, 78; T. Nielsen, *Inside Fortress Norway*, 40–41
16 Gjelsvik, *Norwegian Resistance*, 191, 196–7, 207–8; Hoidal, *Quisling*, 683–7; Hunt, *Fire and Ice*, 90; Dahl, *Quisling*, 357–8
17 Beevor, *Ardennes 1944*, 227, 257, 259–60; P. Caddick-Adams, *Snow and Steel*, 148, 350, 482, 515, 604, 608–9
18 Mackenzie, *Secret History of SOE*, 671; Hunt, *Fire and Ice*, 81; Gordon, *The Norwegian Resistance*, 385
19 Cruickshank, *SOE in Scandinavia*, 230; Lampe, *The Savage Canary*, 175–6; Stafford, *Britain and European Resistance*, 157
20 Künzel, 'Resistance, Reprisals, Reactions'; Maass, *The Netherlands at War*, 200–203, 211–14; Beevor, *Arnhem*, 375
21 Okulicki to Raczkiewicz, 9 December 1944, *AK Documents*, V, no. 1344, 170–84
22 M. Gilbert, *Winston S. Churchill*, VII, 1,068
23 TNA, PREM 3/352/11
24 Kochanski, *The Eagle Unbowed*, 450–60; Eden to Raczyński, 22 December 1944, *AK Documents*, V, no. 1361, 202–4
25 Mikołajczyk to Churchill, 21 February 1944, Churchill to Mikołajczyk, 7 April 1944; Clark Kerr to Molotov, 2 November 1944, all in *AK Documents*, VI, nos. 1807, 1817 and 1888, on 373, 386 and 437; Walker, *Poland Alone*, 266, 274
26 Report on the British Observer Mission despatched to Occupied Poland 26 December 1944, IWM 13124
27 J. Bines, *Operation Freston*, passim; Kemp, *The Thorns of Memory*, 233–65
28 Okulicki Order, 19 January 1945, *AK Documents*, V, no. 1391, 239
29 Baluk, *Silent and Unseen*, 262
30 Okulicki, 22 January 1945, *AK Documents*, VI, no. 1909, 455
31 Prażmowska, *Civil War in Poland*, 150–51
32 J. Iatrides, *Revolt in Athens*, 157–78; Evans, *With SOE in Greece*, 97–100; Mazower, *Inside Hitler's Greece*, 351–2; G. Alexander, 'The Demobilisation Crisis of November 1944', in Iatrides (ed.), *Greece in the 1940s*, 156–66
33 Iatrides, *Revolt in Athens*, 188–94
34 Evans, *With SOE in Greece*, 101
35 Churchill, *The Second World War*, VI, 289
36 Mazower, *Inside Hitler's Greece*, 364
37 Iatrides, *Revolt in Athens*, 226; Mazower, *Inside Hitler's Greece*, 371–2; Churchill, *The Second World War*, VI, 291; Alan Brooke, diary entries, 3 and 23–30 December 1944, Danchev and Todman (eds), *War Diaries*, 631–2, 638; Diary entry, 11 December 1944, Macmillan, *War Diaries*, 602; Diary entry, 7 December, J. Colville, *The Fringes of Power*, 533
38 D. Tobler, IWM 12798
39 Iatrides, *Revolt in Athens*, 250
40 Woodhouse, *Something Ventured*, 96
41 Diary entry, 21 December 1944, Dilks (ed.), *The Diaries of Sir Alexander Cadogan*, 689
42 Churchill, *The Second World War*, VI, 252–83; Diary entries, 15, 16, 21, 22, and 29 December 1944, Cadogan, Dilks (ed.), *The Diaries of Sir Alexander Cadogan*, 687–91; Iatrides, *Revolt in Athens*, 242–6; Leeper, *When Greek Meets Greek*, 127
43 Macksey, *The Partisans of Europe*, 233–4; Woodhouse, *The Struggle for Greece*, 130–31
44 Iatrides, *Revolt in Athens*, 251–6; Sarafis, *ELAS*, 523–4
45 Roberts, *Tito, Mihailović and the Allies*, 273, 305–6, 312; Churchill to Stalin, 5 November 1944, 11 and 23 January 1945, and Stalin to Churchill, 24 November 1944, 13 and 25 January 1945, *Stalin Correspondence*, 270, 275, 297–8, 289, 302–3; Diary entry, 15 January 1945, Dilks (ed.), *The Diaries of Sir Alexander Cadogan*, 695
46 Pavlowitch, *Hitler's New Disorder*, 253; Roberts, *Tito, Mihailović and the Allies*, 317
47 Dulles to Caserta, 24 November 1944, in Petersen (ed.), *From Hitler's Doorstep*, 401–2

48 Behan, *The Italian Resistance*, 215; Morgan, *The Fall of Mussolini*, 215; Battaglia, *The Story of the Italian Resistance*, 239–40; Wilhelm, *The Other Italy*, 209–10; Stafford, *Mission Accomplished*, 258
49 Wilhelm, *The Other Italy*, 211
50 Miller, *Behind the Lines*, 197; R. Tolson, IWM 13553
51 Ellwood, *Italy*, 176–7; Diary entry, 22 January 1945, Macmillan, *War Diaries*, 657; Lamb, *War in Italy*, 233–4
52 Macintosh, *From Cloak to Dagger*, 132–4; Stafford, *Mission Accomplished*, 263–4; Battaglia, *The Story of the Italian Resistance*, 225–6, 240–41; Corvo, *The OSS in Italy*, 214, 232–5; Behan, *The Italian Resistance*, 211; Ellwood, *Italy*, 181
53 Jespersen, *No Small Achievement*, 443; Mackenzie, *Secret History of SOE*, 684
54 Mackenzie, *Secret History of SOE*, 683
55 J. C. Hauge, *The Liberation of Norway*, 31; Gjelsvik, *Norwegian Resistance*, 199–200; Cruickshank, *SOE in Scandinavia*, 249–50; Mann, *British Policy and Strategy towards Norway*, 190–94
56 Mann, *British Policy and Strategy towards Norway*, 191–2
57 Hauge, *The Liberation of Norway*, 20
58 Gjelsvik, *Norwegian Resistance*, 202.

31. TO THE BITTER END: SPRING 1945

1 Mackenzie, *Secret History of SOE*, 671; Sonsteby, *Report from No. 24*, 169–72; Hunt, *Fire and Ice*, 206; Cruickshank, *SOE in Scandinavia*, 243; Hoidal, *Quisling*, 686; Bennett, *British Broadcasting*, 214–15
2 Thomas, *The Giant-Killers*, 200–205
3 Künzel, 'Resistance, Reprisals, Reactions'; Maass, *The Netherlands at War*, 221–2; Beevor, *Arnhem*, 375
4 Reilly, *The Sixth Floor*, 155–9, 178, 192, 200; Lampe, *The Savage Canary*, 179–97; Thomas, *The Giant-Killers*, 318–23; O. Lippmann, IWM 14723
5 Roberts, *Tito, Mihailović and the Allies*, 319; Ritchie, *Our Man in Yugoslavia*, 158; Pavlowitch, *Hitler's New Disorder*, 259; Martin, *Web of Disinformation*, 272
6 Pavlowitch, *Hitler's New Disorder*, 267; Tomasevich, *Chetniks*, 456
7 Pavlowitch, *Hitler's New Disorder*, 245–62; Tomasevich, *Chetniks*, 438
8 Ritchie, *Our Man in Yugoslavia*, 161; Tomasevich, *Chetniks*, 438
9 Pavlowitch, *Hitler's New Disorder*, 263
10 Lindsay, *Beacons in the Night*, 176; T. Barker, *Social Revolutionaries and Secret Agents*, 60; Kirk, 'Limits of Germandom'
11 Petersen (ed.), *From Hitler's Doorstep*, 465, 467–71, 478–9, 486–9, 495–6; Lamb, *War in Italy*, 284–93; J. McCaffery, IWM 14093
12 Dulles to Caserta, 13 March 1945, in Petersen (ed.), *From Hitler's Doorstep*, 473; Salvadori, *The Labour and the Wounds*, 204–5; Battaglia, *The Story of the Italian Resistance*, 248, 258–9; Beevor, *SOE*, 143
13 Pavone, *A Civil War*, 306; Battaglia, *The Story of the Italian Resistance*, 260–61
14 Lett, *Rossano*, 179–86; R. Farran, *Operation Tombola*, 19, 109–14
15 Battaglia, *The Story of the Italian Resistance*, 244–5, 263–5; Lett, *Rossano*, 192–6; Farran, *Operation Tombola*, 245; Macintosh, *From Cloak to Dagger*, 158; Diary entry, 23 April 1945, Macmillan, *War Diaries*, 743; Fowler, *The Secret War in Italy*, 139; Behan, *The Italian Resistance*, 96
16 Behan, *The Italian Resistance*, 102–5; B. Davidson, *Special Operations Europe*, 265–8; Macintosh, *From Cloak to Dagger*, 165; Battaglia, *The Story of the Italian Resistance*, 256–7, 266–8; Wilhelm, *The Other Italy*, 241–2
17 Salvadori, *The Labour and the Wounds*, 224
18 D. Stafford, *Endgame*, 194

19 Behan, *The Italian Resistance*, 100–12; Battaglia, *The Story of the Italian Resistance*, 269; Corvo, *The OSS in Italy*, 253
20 Battaglia, *The Story of the Italian Resistance*, 255, 275–7; Wilhelm, *The Other Italy*, 85, 243–4; Behan, *The Italian Resistance*, 96–100; Diary entry, 18 and 28 April 1945, Gobetti, *Partisan Diary*, 327, 336–47
21 Battaglia, *The Story of the Italian Resistance*, 278–80; Wilhelm, *The Other Italy*, 244
22 Diary entry, 23 April 1945, Macmillan, *War Diaries*, 743
23 Pavone, *A Civil War*, 525
24 Behan, *The Italian Resistance*, 220–21
25 Gobetti, *Partisan Diary*, 244–305; Diary entry, 20 April 1945, Macmillan, *War Diaries*, 739; Ellwood, *Italy*, 182–3; Morgan, *The Fall of Mussolini*, 207; J. Wildgen, 'The Liberation of the Valle d'Aosta, 1943–1945', *Journal of Modern History*, 42:1 (1970), 21–41
26 T. Macpherson, IWM 17913, 13335; Morgan, *The Fall of Mussolini*, 209–19; Ellwood, *Italy*, 196–8; Ritchie, *Our Man in Yugoslavia*, 93; E. Morris, *Circles of Hell*, 432–3; J.R. Whittam, 'Drawing the Line: Britain and the Emergence of the Trieste Question, January 1941–May 1945', *English Historical Review*, 106 (1991), 346–70
27 Lamb, *War in Italy*, 262–4, 292–5
28 Zembsch-Schreve, *Pierre Lalande*, 181
29 Maass, *The Netherlands at War*, 236–40; Warmbrunn, *The Dutch under German Occupation*, 219–20; Beevor, *Arnhem*, 376; P. Louis D'Aulnis de Bourouill, in Foot (ed.), *Holland at War against Hitler*, 101–7
30 Jespersen, *No Small Achievement*, 474–8; Mackenzie, *Secret History of SOE*, 685; Cruickshank, *SOE in Scandinavia*, 240, 267–8; N. A. C. Croft, IWM 12850, 14820
31 Hauge, *The Liberation of Norway*, passim; Dahl, *Quisling*, 361–73; Gjelsvik, *Norwegian Resistance*, 208–14; Gordon, *The Norwegian Resistance*, 456; Sonsteby, *Report from No. 24*, 180–87; Hoidal, *Quisling*, 707–11; Mann, *British Policy and Strategy towards Norway*, 194–226; Cruickshank, *SOE in Scandinavia*, 268
32 Beevor, *Crete*, 329–39; Psychoundakis, *The Cretan Runner*, 313
33 Turner, *Outpost of Occupation*, 113, 119–24, 185–6, 197–201, 222, 232–3
34 Diary entries, 9 and 19 March 1945, in H. Trevor-Roper (ed.), *The Goebbels Diaries*, 89, 173
35 Mackenzie, *Secret History of SOE*, 530; Bryant, *Prague in Black*, 186; K. Bartošek, *The Prague Uprising*, 101; Luža, *The Hitler Kiss*, 208
36 Gilbert, *Churchill*, VII, 1,322
37 Erickson, *The Road to Berlin*, 625–30; Hoensch, 'The Slovak Republic'
38 Bryant, *Prague in Black*, 231–2; Moravec, *Master of Spies*, 239–42, 243–6
39 Bartošek, *The Prague Uprising*, 34–6
40 Bryant, *Prague in Black*, 232–5; Bartošek, *The Prague Uprising*, passim; Erickson, *The Road to Berlin*, 635–6; Luža, 'The Communist Party of Czechoslovakia and the Czech Resistance'; Luža, 'The Czech Resistance Movement'.

32. THE AFTERMATH

1 Fourcade, *Noah's Ark*, 356
2 Baluk, *Silent and Unseen*, 262
3 J. Chambers, IWM 17983
4 Hunt, *Fire and Ice*, 32
5 Jordan, *Conquest without Victory*, 271
6 Glass, *They Fought Alone*, 232–45
7 Vinen, *The Unfree French*, 340; Paxton, *Vichy France*, 329; Littlejohn, *The Patriotic Traitors*, 289; M. Koreman, *The Expectation of Justice*, passim
8 Morgan, *The Fall of Mussolini*, 216; Lett, *Rossano*, 197; Stafford, *Endgame*, 420–22

9 Vilhjálmsson and Blüdnikow, 'Rescue, Expulsion, and Collaboration'; Stafford, *Endgame*, 197–8; Sutherland, *Monica*, 218–24
10 Mayer, *Gaston's War*, 191
11 Tyas, *SS-Major Horst Kopkow*, 179–82; O'Reilly, 'Interrogating the Gestapo'
12 Lagrou, *The Legacy of Nazi Occupation*, 94–105
13 Chevrillon, *Codename Christiane Clouet*, 167
14 Helm, *A Life in Secrets*, 67–73; V. Atkins, IWM 9551, 12636
15 Helm, *A Life in Secrets*, 190–315
16 Kelso, *Errors of Judgement*, 169–71; E. Le Chêne, *Mauthausen*, 123
17 Perrin, *Spirit of Resistance*, 151–62; D. Hackett (ed.), *The Buchenwald Report*, 80–81
18 Fourcade, *Noah's Ark*, 363–70; Olson, *Madame Fourcade's Secret War*, 356–64
19 Kesselring, *The Memoirs of Field Marshal Kesselring*, 300
20 Glass, *They Fought Alone*, 258
21 G. Finder and A. Prusin, *Justice behind the Iron Curtain*, 5–6, 254, and passim
22 Blood, *Hitler's Bandit Hunters*, 279–94
23 Tyas, *SS-Major Horst Kopkow*, 205–56
24 De Gaulle, *War Memoirs*, III, 108
25 Griffiths, *Marshal Pétain*, 335–7
26 Dank, *The French against the French*, 309, 321–2
27 Hoidal, *Quisling*, 727–8; Andenaes et al., *Norway and the Second World War*, 126–7
28 Littlejohn, *The Patriotic Traitors*, 126–7, 182–3
29 Leeper, *When Greek Meets Greek*, 166
30 Helm, *A Life in Secrets*, 356, 362–4
31 Clinton, *Jean Moulin*, 186; Dank, *The French against the French*, 157
32 H. Mason, *The Purge of the Dutch Quislings*, 25
33 Paxton, *Vichy France*, 329; Vinen, *The Unfree French*, 324–5; Dank, *The French against the French*, 322–3
34 Mason, *The Purge of the Dutch Quislings*, 40–41; Littlejohn, *The Patriotic Traitors*, 127–8
35 Littlejohn, *The Patriotic Traitors*, 182–3, 82; Sørensen, 'Narrating the Second World War in Denmark since 1945'
36 Hoidal, *Quisling*, 773–4
37 Bennett, *Under the Shadow of the Swastika*, 69
38 H. Rousso, *The Vichy Syndrome*, 116–26, 205–11; Weitz, *Sisters in the Resistance*, 13
39 G. Walters, *Hunting Evil*, 575–6
40 De Haan, 'The Unresolved Controversy'; Wasserstein, *The Ambiguity of Virtue*, 229–31; Presser, *Ashes in the Wind*, 270–71
41 Dewulf, *Spirit of Resistance*, 190–93, 210
42 Vilhjálmsson and Blüdnikow, 'Rescue, Expulsion, and Collaboration'; Lagrou, *The Legacy of Nazi Occupation*, 255–6
43 Kochanski, *The Eagle Unbowed*, 549–51
44 Frenay, *The Night Will End*, 434–7; Rousso, *The Vichy Syndrome*, 25
45 Lagrou, *The Legacy of Nazi Occupation*, 39; Olson, *Madame Fourcade's Secret War*, 378
46 Glass, *They Fought Alone*, 250–53; M. Tillotson (ed.), *SOE and the Resistance as Told in* The Times *Obituaries*, passim
47 Buckmaster, *Specially Employed*, 193–9; TNA, HS 7/134
48 Darling, *Secret Sunday*, 166; Fleming, *The Vatican Pimpernel*, 171; Absalom, 'Hiding History'
49 Harris Smith, *OSS*, 363–4; Wilkinson and Bright Astley, *Gubbins and SOE*, 232
50 Reilly, *The Sixth Floor*, 208; Cruickshank, *SOE in Scandinavia*, 267–8
51 Frenay, *The Night Will End*, 448
52 Wilhelm, *The Other Italy*, 257–61
53 Conway, *The Sorrows of Belgium*, 169–75; Lagrou, *The Legacy of Nazi Occupation*, 33
54 Mazower, *Inside Hitler's Greece*, 376; Iatrides, *Revolt in Athens*, 260; Sarafis, *ELAS*, 423
55 Bryant, *Prague in Black*, 247–53
56 Ward, *Priest, Politician, Collaborator*, 9, 257–67

57 N. Tolstoy, *Victims of Yalta*, passim; Stafford, *Endgame*, 428–31
58 Lumans, *Latvia in World War II*, 390
59 Milač, *Resistance, Imprisonment, Forced Labour*, 193–203; Beloff, *Tito's Flawed Legacy*, 123–7
60 Williams, *Parachutes, Patriots and Partisans*, 242; Roberts, *Tito, Mihailović and the Allies*, 323; Ritchie, *Our Man in Yugoslavia*, 163–6; Pavlowitch, *Hitler's New Disorder*, 242
61 Lees, *The Rape of Serbia*, 336; Martin (ed.), *Patriot or Traitor*, 42, 49–50
62 *Proceedings of the Trial of Mihailović*, passim, 499; Tomasevich, *The Chetniks*, 461–2
63 Kochanski, *The Eagle Unbowed*, 529, 535
64 A. Benrad, IWM 8683; S. Kujawiński, IWM 12018; Finder and Prusin, *Justice Behind the Iron Curtain*, 133
65 Fairweather, *The Volunteer*, 368–85
66 Kochanski, *The Eagle Unbowed*, 585; Luža, *The Hitler Kiss*, 236
67 B. Liddell Hart, 'Lessons from Resistance Movements – Guerrilla and Non-Violent', in Roberts (ed.), *The Strategy of Civilian Defence*, 195–211
68 Mackenzie, *The Secret History of SOE*, 746
69 H. Rée, IWM 8720
70 Dodds-Parker, *Setting Europe Ablaze*, 3
71 Stourton, *Cruel Crossing*, 3–4
72 Vinen, *The Unfree French*, 313.

List of Abbreviations

Albania

LNC	*Levicija Nacional Çlirimtarë*

Baltic States

LVR	*Lietuvos Vietinė Rinktinė*

Belgium

AJB	
CDJ	*Comité de Défense des Juifs*
FI	*Front de l'Indépendance*
VNV	

Britain and the United States

AMG	Allied Military Government (of occupied Territories)
BLO	British Liaison Officer
OG	Operational Group
OSS	Office of Strategic Services
PWE	Political Warfare Executive
SAS	Special Air Service
SBS	Special Boat Service
SHAEF	Supreme Headquarters Allied Expeditionary Force
SIS	Secret Intelligence Service
SOE	Special Operations Executive

Czechoslovakia

ON	*Obrana národa*
ÚVOD	*Ústřední výbor odboje domácího*

Denmark

BOPA	*Borgerlige Partisaner*

France

AS	*Armée Secrète*
BCRA	*Bureau Central de Renseignements et d'Action*
BIP	*Bureau d'Information et de Presse*
CFLN	*Comité Français de Libération Nationale*
CND	*Confrérie de Notre-Dame*
CNR	*Conseil National de la Résistance*
COMAC	*Comité Militaire d'Action*
CPL	*Comité Parisien de la Libération*
DMR	*Délégué Militaire Régional*

FFI *Forces Françaises de l'Intérieur*
FN *Front National*
FTP *Franc-Tireurs et Partisans*
GMR *Groupes Mobiles de Réserve*
LVF *Légion des Volontaires Français*
MOI *Main-d'Oeuvre Immigrée*
MUR *Les Mouvements Unis de la Résistance*
OCM *Organisation Civile et Militaire*
OJC *Organisation Juive de Combat*
ORA *Organisation de Résistance de l'Armée*
POWN *Polska Organizacja Walki o Niepodległość*
PPF *Parti Populaire Français*
RNP *Rassemblement National Populaire*
SOL *Service d'Ordre Légionnaire*
STO *Service du Travail Obligatoire*
UGIF *L'Union Générale des Israélites de France*

Greece
EAM *Ethniko Apeleutherotiko Metopo*
EDES *Ethnikos Demokratikos Ellenikos Syndesmos*
EKKA *Ethniki kai Koinoniki Apeleutherosis*
ELAS *Ellenikos Laikos Apeleutherotikos Stratos*
EOK *Ethniki Organosi Kritis*
PEAN *Panellinios Enosis Agonizomenon Neon*
PEEA *Politiki Epitropi Ethnikis Apeleutherosis*

Italy
CLN *Comitato di Liberazione Nazionale*
CLNAI *Comitato di Liberazione Nazionale Alta Italia*
CVL *Corpo Volontari della Libertà*
GAP *Gruppi di Azione Patriottica*
RSI *Reppublica Sociale Italia*

Netherlands
LKP *Landelijke Knokploegen*
LO *Landelijke Organisatie voor Hulp aan Onderduikers*
NBS *Nederlandse Binnenlandse Strijdkrachten*
NSB *Nationaal-Socialistische Beweging*
PAN *Partisanen Actie Nederland*
VNV *Vlaams Nationaal Verbond*
WA *Weer Afdeling*

Norway
ANCC Anglo-Norwegian Collaboration Committee
AT *Arbeidstjenesten*
NS *Nasjonal Samling*

Poland
AK *Armia Krajowa*
FPO *Fareinigte Partisanen Organisatzie*
GL/AL *Gwarda Ludowa/Armia Ludowa*
NSZ *Narodowe Siły Zbrojne*
PKWN *Polski Komitet Wyzwolenia Narodowego*
PPR *Polska Partia Robotnicza*
ZO *Związek Odwetu*

ŻOB	*Żydowska Organizacja Bojowa*
ZOW	*Związek Organizacji Wojskowej*
ZWZ	*Związek Walki Zbrojnej*
ŻZW	*Żydowski Związek Wojskowy*

Soviet Union

BCR	*Belaruskaja Central' Naja Rada*
NKVD	*Naródnyy Komissariát Vnútrennikh Del*
ROA	*Russkaya Osvoboditelnaya Armiia*
RONA	*Russkaya Osvoboditelnaya Narodnaya Armiia*
UPA	*Ukrains'ka Povstans'ka Armiia*

Yugoslavia

AVNOJ	*Antifašističko Vijeće Narodnog Oslobodienja Jugoslavije*
MVAC	*Milizia Volontaria Anti Comunista*
OF	*Osvobodilna Fronta*

Bibliography

All publications are in London unless otherwise stated.

Abramsky, C., Jachimczyk, M., and Polonsky, A. (eds), *The Jews in Poland* (Oxford, 1986)

Absalom, R., *A Strange Alliance: Aspects of Escape and Survival in Italy 1943–45* (Florence, 1991)

—'Hiding History: The Allies, the Resistance and the Others in Occupied Italy 1943–1945', *Historical Journal*, 38:1 (1995), 111–31

Adair, P., *Hitler's Greatest Defeat: The Collapse of Army Group Centre, June 1944* (1994)

Adelson, A. and Lapides, R., *Łódź Ghetto: Inside a Community under Siege* (New York, 1989)

Adler, J., *The Jews of Paris and the Final Solution: Communal Response and Internal Conflicts* (New York, 1987)

Agarossi, E., *A Nation Collapses: The Italian Surrender of September 1943* (Cambridge, 2000)

Ainsztein, R., *Jewish Resistance in Nazi-Occupied Eastern Europe* (1974)

Albertelli, S., *Les Services secrets du Général de Gaulle: Le BCRA 1940–1944* (Paris, 2009)

Allen, R., *Churchill's Guests: Britain and the Belgian Exiles during World War II* (Westport, CT, 2003)

Altbeker Cyprys, R., *A Jump for Life* (1997)

Amery, J., *Sons of the Eagle* (1948)

Andenaes, J., Riste, O., and Skodvin, M., *Norway and the Second World War* (Oslo, 1966)

Anderson, J., *High Mountains and Cold Seas: A Biography of H. W. Tilman* (1980)

Andreyev, C., *Vlasov and the Russian Liberation Movement: Soviet Reality and Émigré Theories* (Cambridge, 1987)

Anon., *We are Guerrillas: An Account of the Work of Soviet Guerrillas beyond Nazi Lines* (1942)

Applebaum, A., *Iron Curtain: The Crushing of Eastern Europe 1944–56* (2012)

Arad, Y., Gutman, Y., and Margaliot, A., (eds), *Documents on the Holocaust: Selected Sources on the Destruction of the Jews of Germany and Austria, Poland, and the Soviet Union* (Jerusalem, 1981)

Ariel, J., 'Jewish Self-Defence and Resistance in France during World War II', *Yad Vashem Studies*, VI (1967), 221–50

Armstrong, J., 'Collaborationism in World War II: The Integral Nationalist Variant in Eastern Europe', *Journal of Modern History*, 40 (1968), 396–412

—(ed.), *Soviet Partisans in World War II* (Madison, WI, 1964)

Ashdown, P., *A Brilliant Little Operation: The Cockleshell Heroes and the Most Courageous Raid of WW2* (2012)

—*The Cruel Victory: The French Resistance, D-Day and the Battle for the Vercors, 1944* (2014)

—*Game of Spies: The Secret Agent, the Traitor and the Nazi, Bordeaux 1942–1944* (2016)

d'Astier, E., *Seven Times Seven Days* (1958)

Aubrac, L., *Outwitting the Gestapo* (Lincoln, NB, 1993)

Auty, P. and Clogg, R. (eds), *British Policy towards Wartime Resistance in Yugoslavia and Greece* (1975)

Baden-Powell, D., *Operation Jupiter: SOE's Secret War in Norway* (1982)

Badoglio, P., *Italy in the Second World War: Memories and Documents* (Westport, CT, 1976)
Bailey, R., *The Wildest Province: SOE in the Land of the Eagle* (2008)
—*Target Italy: The Secret War against Mussolini, 1940–1943* (2014)
—'OSS-SOE Relations, Albania 1943–44', *Intelligence and National Security*, 15:2 (2000), 20–35
—(ed.), *Forgotten Voices of the Secret War: An Inside History of Special Operations during the Second World War* (2008)
Baluk, S., *Silent and Unseen: I Was a Polish WWII Special Ops Commando* (Warsaw, 2009)
Banac, I. (ed.), *The Diary of Georgi Dimitrov, 1933–1949* (New Haven, CT, 2003)
Barker, E., *British Policy in South-East Europe* (1976)
Barker, T., *Social Revolutionaries and Secret Agents: The Carinthian Slovene Partisans and Britain's Special Operations Executive* (Boulder, CO, 1990)
Bartošek, K., *The Prague Uprising* (Prague, 1965)
Bartoszewski, W., *The Bloodshed Unites Us* (Warsaw, 1970)
—*Powstanie Warszawskie* (Warsaw, 2009)
Bartov, O., *The Eastern Front, 1941–1945: German Troops and the Barbarisation of Warfare* (Basingstoke, 1986)
Basu, S., *Spy Princess: The Life of Noor Inayat Khan* (Stroud, 2006)
Battaglia, R., *The Story of the Italian Resistance* (1957)
Baudouin, P., *The Private Diaries (March 1940 to January 1941)* (1948)
Beevor, A., *Crete: The Battle and the Resistance* (2005)
—*D-Day: The Battle for Normandy* (2009)
—*The Second World War* (2012)
—*Ardennes 1944: Hitler's Last Gamble* (2015)
—*Arnhem: The Battle for the Bridges, 1944* (2018)
Beevor, J., *SOE: Recollections and Reflections, 1940–1945* (1981)
Behan, T., *The Italian Resistance: Fascists, Guerrillas and the Allies* (2009)
Bellamy, C., *Absolute War: Soviet Russia in the Second World War* (2008)
Beloff, N., *Tito's Flawed Legacy: Yugoslavia and the West, 1939–84* (1985)
Bennett, J., *British Broadcasting and the Danish Resistance Movement 1940–1945* (Cambridge, 1966)
Bennett, R., *Behind the Battle: Intelligence in the War with Germany 1939–1945* (1994)
—*Under the Shadow of the Swastika: The Moral Dilemmas of Resistance and Collaboration in Hitler's Europe* (1999)
Berenbaum, M. (ed.), *A Mosaic of Victims: Non-Jews Persecuted and Murdered by the Nazis* (New York, 1990)
Berkhoff, K., *Harvest of Despair: Life and Death in the Ukraine under Nazi Rule* (Cambridge, MA, 2004)
Berr, H., *Journal* (2008)
Best, S. Payne, *The Venlo Incident* (1950)
Bines, J., *Operation Freston* (Saffron Walden, 1999)
Binet, L., *HHhH* (2013)
Bird, M., *The Secret Battalion* (1965)
Blackwell, J., 'The Warsaw Uprising: The View from Lublin', *Slavonic and East European Review*, 89:2 (2011), 274–300
Bles, M., *Child at War: The True Story of Hortense Daman* (1989)
Blight, D., 'Fossilized Lies: A Reflection on Alessandro Portelli's *The Order Has Been Carried Out*', *Oral History Review*, 32:1 (2005), 5–9
Blom, J. C. H., 'The Persecution of the Jews in the Netherlands: A Comparative Western European Perspective', *European History Quarterly*, 19 (1989), 333–51
Blood, P., *Hitler's Bandit Hunters: The SS and the Nazi Occupation of Europe* (Washington DC, 2006)
Blumenson, M., *The Vildé Affair: Beginnings of the French Resistance* (1978)
Boas, J., *Religious Resistance in Holland* (1945)
Bodson, H., *Agent for the Resistance: A Belgian Saboteur in World War II* (College Station, 1994)

—*Downed Allied Airmen and Evasion of Capture: The Role of Local Resistance Networks in World War II* (Jefferson, NC, 2005)
Bohlen, C., *Witness to History* (New York, 1973)
Boog, H. et al., *Germany and the Second World War*, 9 vols (Oxford, 1990–2014)
Bór-Komorowski, T., *The Secret Army* (1950)
Borodziej, W., *The Warsaw Uprising* (Madison, WI, 2006)
Borowiec, A., *Destroy Warsaw! Hitler's Punishment, Stalin's Revenge* (Westport, CT, 2001)
—*Warsaw Boy: A Memoir of a Wartime Childhood* (2014)
Boshyk, Y. (ed.), *Ukraine during World War II: History and its Aftermath* (Edmonton, AL, 1986)
Bosworth, R., and Maiolo, J. (eds), *The Cambridge History of the Second World War*, vol. 2 (Cambridge, 2015)
Bourdet, C., *L'Aventure incertaine. De la résistance à la restauration* (Paris, 1975)
Bourne-Paterson, R., *SOE in France 1941–1945: An Official Account of the Special Operations Executive's French Circuits* (Barnsley, 2016)
Boyce, F. and Everett, D., *SOE: The Scientific Secrets* (Stroud, 2003)
Boyd, D., *Voices from the Dark Years: The Truth about Occupied France* (Stroud, 2007)
Braddon, R., *Nancy Wake: The Story of a Very Brave Woman* (1956)
Bradley, O., *A Soldier's Story of the Allied Campaign from Tunis to the Elbe* (1951)
Breitman, R., *Official Secrets: What the Nazis Planned, What the British and Americans Knew* (1999)
Browning, C., *Ordinary Men* (New York, 1992)
Brusselmans, A., *Rendez-vous 127: The Diary of Madame Brusselmans, M.B.E., September 1940–September 1944* (1954)
Bryant, C., *Prague in Black: Nazi Rule and Czech Nationalism* (Cambridge, MA, 2007)
—'Either German or Czech: Fixing Nationality in Bohemia and Moravia, 1939–1946', *Slavic Review*, 61:4 (2002), 683–706
Buckmaster, M., *Specially Employed: The Story of British Aid to French Patriots and the Resistance* (1952)
—*They Fought Alone: The Story of British Agents in France* (1958)
Burgwyn, H. J., *Empire on the Adriatic: Mussolini's Conquest of Yugoslavia, 1941–1943* (New York, 2005)
—'General Roatta's War against the Partisans in Yugoslavia: 1942', *Journal of Modern Italian Studies*, 9:3 (2004), 314–29
Buttar, P., *Between Giants: The Battle for the Baltics in World War II* (Oxford, 2013)
Caddick-Adams, P., *Snow and Steel: The Battle of the Bulge* (2014)
Carr, G., Sanders, P., and Willmot, L. (eds), *Protest, Defiance and Resistance in the Channel Islands: German Occupation, 1940–45* (2014)
Casey, W., *The Secret War against Hitler* (1989)
Caskie, D., *The Tartan Pimpernel* (Birnam 1957)
Catherwood, C., *Churchill and Tito: SOE, Bletchley Park and Supporting the Yugoslav Communists in World War II* (Barnsley, 2019)
Central Commission for the Investigation of German Crimes in Poland, *German Crimes in Poland* (Warsaw, 1946–7)
Cesarani, D., *Final Solution: The Fate of the Jews 1933–49* (2016)
—(ed.), *The Final Solution: Origins and Implementation* (1994)
Chevrillon, C., *Codename Christiane Clouet: A Woman in the French Resistance* (1995)
Chňoupek, B., *A Breaking of Seals: The French Resistance in Slovakia* (Oxford, 1988)
Chodakiewicz, M., *Between Nazis and Soviets: A Case Study of Occupation Politics in Poland 1939–1947* (Lanham, MD, 2004)
Churchill, P., *Duel of Wits* (1953)
Churchill, W., *The Second World War*, 6 vols (1948–54)
Ciechanowski, J., *The Warsaw Rising of 1944* (Cambridge, 1974)
Clark, L., *Kursk: The Greatest Battle, Eastern Front 1943* (2011)
Clinton, A., *Jean Moulin, 1899–1943: The French Resistance and the Republic* (Basingstoke, 2002)

Clive, N., *A Greek Experience 1943–1948* (Salisbury, 1985)
Clogg, R., *Greece, 1940–1949: Occupation, Resistance, Civil War: A Documentary History* (Basingstoke, 2002)
Cobb, M., *The Resistance: The French Fight against the Nazis* (2009)
—*Eleven Days in August: The Liberation of Paris in 1944* (2013)
Collins, L. and Lapierre, D., *Is Paris Burning?* (1965)
Colville, J., *The Fringes of Power* (1985)
Colvin, I. (ed.), *Colonel Henri's Story: The War Memoirs of Hugo Bleicher, Former German Secret Agent* (1954)
Conway, M., *Collaboration in Belgium: Léon Degrelle and the Rexist Movement, 1940–1944* (New Haven, CT, 1994)
—*The Sorrows of Belgium: Liberation and Political Reconstruction 1944–1947* (Oxford, 2012)
Cooke, P. and Shepherd, B. (eds), *European Resistance in the Second World War* (Barnsley, 2013)
Cookridge, E., *They Came from the Sky: The Stories of Lieutenant-Colonel Francis Cammaerts, Major Roger Landes and Captain Harry Rée* (1965)
—*Inside SOE: The Story of Special Operations in Western Europe 1940–45* (1966)
Cooper, A., *Cairo in the War 1939–1945* (2013)
Cooper, M., *The Phantom War: The German Struggle against Soviet Partisans* (1979)
Cordier, D., *Jean Moulin: La République des catacombes* (Paris, 1999)
Cornwall, J., *Hitler's Pope: The Secret History of Pius XII* (1999)
Corvo, M., *The OSS in Italy, 1942–1945: A Personal Memoir* (New York, 1990)
Cottam, K., *Women in War and Resistance: Selected Biographies of Soviet Women Soldiers* (Newburyport, MA, 1998)
Cowburn, B., *No Cloak, No Dagger* (1960)
Cruickshank, C., *SOE in Scandinavia* (Oxford, 1986)
Cunningham, C. *Beaulieu: The Finishing School for Secret Agents* (1998)
Czajkowski, Z., *Warsaw 1944: An Insurgent's Journal of the Uprising* (Barnsley, 2012)
Czarnocka, H. et al., *Armia Krajowa w dokumentach 1939–1945*, 6 vols (1970–89)
Czechoslovak Ministry of Foreign Affairs, *Memorandum of the Czechoslovak Government on the Reign of Terror in Bohemia and Moravia under the Regime of Reinhard Heydrich* (1942)
Dahl, H., *Quisling: A Study in Treachery* (Cambridge, 1999)
Dahlø, R., *A Typical SOE Story: The Unknown Warriors of the Norwegian Resistance* (2017)
Dallin, A., *German Rule in Russia, 1941–1945* (1957)
D'Amelio, D., 'Italian Women in the Resistance, World War II', *Italian Americana*, 19:2 (2001), 127–41
Danchev, A. and Todman, D. (eds), *War Diaries 1939–1945: Field Marshal Lord Alanbrooke* (2001)
Dank, M., *The French against the French: Collaboration and Resistance* (1978)
Darling, D., *Secret Sunday* (1975)
Davidson, B., *Partisan Picture* (Bedford, 1946)
—*Special Operations Europe: Scenes from the Anti-Nazi War* (1980)
Davies, E., *Illyrian Venture: The Story of the British Military Mission to Enemy-Occupied Albania 1943–44* (1952)
Davies, N., *Rising '44* (2003)
Davies, P., *Dangerous Liaisons: Collaboration and World War Two* (2004)
Davis, W., *The Ariadne Objective: Patrick Leigh Fermor and the Underground War to Rescue Crete from the Nazis* (2014)
Dawidowicz, L. S., *The War against the Jews 1933–1945* (1975)
De Gaulle, C., *War Memoirs*, 3 vols (1955–60)
Deák, I., *Essays on Hitler's Europe* (2001)
—Gross, J. and Judt, T. (eds), *The Politics of Retribution in Europe: World War II and its Aftermath* (Princeton, NJ, 2006)
Deakin, W., *The Embattled Mountain* (Oxford, 1971)
—, Barker, E. and Chadwick, J. (eds), *British Political and Military Strategy in Central, Eastern and Southern Europe in 1944* (Basingstoke, 1988)

Dean, M., *Collaboration in the Holocaust: Crimes of the Local Police in Belorussia and Ukraine, 1941–1944* (Basingstoke, 2000)
Dear, I., *Escape and Evasion: Prisoner of War Breakouts and the Routes to Safety in World War Two* (1997)
Debruyne, E., *La Guerre secrète des espions belges, 1940–1944* (Brussels, 2008)
Dedijer, V., *With Tito through the War: Partisan Diary 1941–1944* (1951)
—*The War Diaries of Vladimir Dedijer*, 3 vols (Ann Arbor, MI, 1990)
Deletant, D., *Hitler's Forgotten Ally: Ion Antonescu and his Regime, Romania 1940–1944* (2006)
—*British Clandestine Activities in Romania during the Second World War* (Basingstoke, 2016)
Delzell, C., *Mussolini's Enemies: The Italian Anti-Fascist Resistance* (Princeton, NJ, 1961)
Denham, H., *Inside the Nazi Ring: A Naval Attaché in Sweden* (New York, 1984)
Deroc, M., *British Special Operations Explored: Yugoslavia in Turmoil, 1941–1943 and the British Response* (Boulder, CO, 1988)
Derry, S., *The Rome Escape Line* (1960)
Deschner, G., *Heydrich: The Pursuit of Total Power* (1981)
Dewulf, J., *Spirit of Resistance: Dutch Clandestine Literature during the Nazi Occupation* (Rochester, NY, 2010)
Dilks, D. (ed.), *The Diaries of Sir Alexander Cadogan 1938–1945* (1971)
Dixon, C. and Heilbrunn, O., *Communist Guerrilla Warfare* (1954)
Djilas, M. *Wartime* (1977)
Documents on German Foreign Policy, Series D, Vol. 4
Dodds-Parker, D., *Setting Europe Ablaze: Some Accounts of Ungentlemanly Warfare* (Windlesham, 1983)
Dombrády, L., *Army and Politics in Hungary, 1938–1944* (New York, 2005)
Doneux, J., *They Arrived by Moonlight* (2000)
Dourlein, P., *Inside North Pole: A Secret Agent's Story* (1953)
Drake, D., *Paris at War* (Cambridge, MA, 2015)
Dreisziger, N. (ed.), *Hungary in the Age of Total War* (New York, 1998)
Dumais, L., *The Man Who Went Back* (1975)
Duncan, S. and P., *Anne Brusselmans, M.B.E.* (1959)
Dyson, T., 'British Policies toward Axis Reprisals in Occupied Greece: Whitehall vs. SOE', *Contemporary British History*, 16:1 (2002), 11–28
Edelman, M., *The Ghetto Fights* (1990)
Eden, A., *The Eden Memoirs: The Reckoning* (1965)
Einwohner, E., 'Opportunity, Honor, and Action in the Warsaw Ghetto Uprising of 1943', *American Journal of Sociology*, 109 (2003), 650–75
Eisenhower, D., *Crusade in Europe* (1948)
Elliott-Bateman, M. (ed.), *The Fourth Dimension of Warfare*, vol. 1 (Manchester, 1970)
Ellwood, D., *Italy 1943–1945* (Leicester, 1985)
Eloy, V., *The Fight in the Forest* (1949)
Engel, D., *Facing a Holocaust: The Polish Government-in-Exile and the Jews, 1943–1945* (1993)
Enstad, J. D., *Soviet Russians under Nazi Occupation: Fragile Loyalties in World War II* (Cambridge, 2018)
Epstein, B., *The Minsk Ghetto, 1941–1943: Jewish Resistance and Soviet Internationalism* (Berkeley, CA, 2008)
Erickson, J., *The Road to Stalingrad* (1975)
—*The Road to Berlin* (1983)
European Resistance Movements, 1939–1945: First International Conference on the History of the Resistance Movements (Oxford, 1960)
European Resistance Movements, 1939–1945: Second International Conference on the History of the Resistance Movements (Oxford, 1964)
Evans, R., *The Third Reich at War* (2009)
Evans, T., *With SOE in Greece: The Wartime Experiences of Captain Pat Evans* (Barnsley, 2018)
Fairweather, J., *The Volunteer: The True Story of the Resistance Hero who Infiltrated Auschwitz* (2019)

Farmer, S., 'The Communist Resistance in the Haute-Vienne', *French Historical Studies*, 14:1 (1985), 89–116
Farran, R., *Operation Tombola* (1960)
Fein, H., *Accounting for Genocide: National Responses and Jewish Victimisation during the Holocaust* (Chicago, IL, 1979)
Ferris, J. and Mawdsley, E. (eds), *The Cambridge History of the Second World War*, vol. 1 (Cambridge, 2015)
Fielding, X., *Hide and Seek: The Story of a Wartime Agent* (Philadelphia, PA, 1954, 2013)
—*One Man in his Time: The Life of Lieutenant-Colonel N. L. D. McLean* (1990)
Finder, G. and Prusin, A., *Justice behind the Iron Curtain: Nazis on Trial in Communist Poland* (Toronto, 2018)
Finkel, E., *Ordinary Jews: Choice and Survival during the Holocaust* (Princeton, NJ, 2017)
Firth, T., *Prisoner of the Gestapo* (Barnsley, 2010)
Fischer, B., *Albania at War, 1939–1945* (1999)
Fleming, B., *The Vatican Pimpernel: The Wartime Exploits of Monsignor Hugh O'Flaherty* (Cork, 2008)
Fogelman, E., *Conscience and Courage: Rescuers of Jews during the Holocaust* (1995)
Foot, M. R. D., *Resistance: An Analysis of European Resistance to Nazism, 1940–1945* (1976)
—*Six Faces of Courage* (1978)
—*SOE: The Special Operations Executive 1940–46* (1984)
—*SOE in the Low Countries* (2001)
—*SOE in France* (2004)
—'Was SOE Any Good?', *Journal of Contemporary History*, 16:1 (1981) 167–81
—(ed.), *Holland at War against Hitler: Anglo-Dutch Relations, 1940–1945* (1990)
—and Langley, J., *M19: The British Secret Service that Fostered Escape and Evasion, and its American Counterpart* (1979)
Foray, J., 'The "Clean Wehrmacht" in the German-Occupied Netherlands, 1940–5', *Journal of Contemporary History*, 45 (2010), 768–87
Fourcade, M.-M., *Noah's Ark: The Story of the Alliance Intelligence Network in Occupied France* (1973)
Fowler, W., *The Secret War in Italy* (Hersham, Surrey, 2010)
Frank, O. and Pressler, M. (eds), *The Diary of a Young Girl: The Definitive Edition* (1997)
Frenay, H., *The Night Will End* (1976)
Friedhoff, H., *Requiem for the Resistance: The Civilian Struggle against Nazism in Holland and Germany* (1988)
Friedman, P., *Their Brothers' Keepers* (New York, 1957)
—(ed.), *Martyrs and Fighters: The Epic of the Warsaw Ghetto* (1954)
Funk, A. L., *Hidden Ally: The French Resistance, Special Operations and the Landings in Southern France* (1992)
—'Contacts with the Resistance in France, 1940–1943', *Military Affairs*, 34:1 (1970), 15–21
—'Churchill, Eisenhower, and the French Resistance', *Military Affairs*, 45:1 (1981), 29–34
Gallagher, J., *Scarlet Pimpernel of the Vatican* (1967)
Gallo, P., *For Love and Country: The Italian Resistance* (Lanham, MD, 2003)
Ganier-Raymond, P., *The Tangled Web* (1968)
Garliński, J., *Fighting Auschwitz: The Resistance Movement in the Concentration Camp* (1975)
—*The Survival of Love: Memoirs of a Resistance Officer* (Oxford, 1991)
—'The Polish Underground State 1939–45', *Journal of Contemporary History*, 10 (1975), 219–59
Geller, J., 'The Role of Military Administration in German-Occupied Belgium, 1940–1944', *Journal of Military History*, 63:1 (1999), 99–125
Gerolymatos, A., *Guerrilla Warfare and Espionage in Greece* (New York, 1992)
Gerwarth, R., *Hitler's Hangman: The Life of Heydrich* (New Haven, CT, 2011)
Gilbert, M., *Auschwitz and the Allies* (1981)
—*Winston S. Churchill*, vols 6–8 (1983–8)
—*The Holocaust: The Jewish Tragedy* (1986)

Gildea, R., *Marianne in Chains: In Search of the German Occupation 1940–45* (2002)
—*Fighters in the Shadows: A New History of the French Resistance* (2015)
—'Resistance, Reprisals and Community in Occupied France', *Transactions of the Royal Historical Society*, 13 (2003), 163–85
—, Wieviorka, O., and Warring, A. (eds), *Surviving Hitler and Mussolini: Daily Life in Occupied Europe* (Oxford, 2006)
Giltner, P., 'The Success of Collaboration: Denmark's Self-Assessment of its Economic Position after Five Years of Nazi Occupation', *Journal of Contemporary History*, 36:3 (2001), 485–506
Ginter, M., *Life in Both Hands* (1964)
Giskes, H., *London Calling North Pole* (1953)
Gjelsvik, T., *Norwegian Resistance* (1979)
Glass, C., *They Fought Alone: The True Story of the Starr Brothers* (New York, 2018)
Glass, J., *Jewish Resistance during the Holocaust: Moral Uses of Violence and Will* (Basingstoke, 2004)
Glen, A., *Footholds against a Whirlwind* (1975)
Gobetti, A., *Partisan Diary: A Woman's Life in the Italian Resistance* (Oxford, 2014)
Gogun, A., *Stalin's Commandos: Ukrainian Partisan Forces on the Eastern Front* (New York, 2016)
Goldsmith, J., *Accidental Agent* (1971)
Gordon, B., *Collaborationism in France during the Second World War* (Ithaca, NY, 1980)
—'The Condottieri of the Collaboration: *Mouvement Social Révolutionnaire*', *Journal of Contemporary History*, 10:2 (1975), 261–82
Gordon, G. S., *The Norwegian Resistance during the German Occupation, 1940–1945: Repression, Terror and Resistance: The West Country of Norway* (Ann Arbor, MI, 1984)
Grant Duff, S., *A German Protectorate: The Czechs under Nazi Rule* (1942)
Greble Balić, E., 'When Croatia Needed Serbs: Nationalism and Genocide in Sarajevo, 1941–1942', *Slavic Review*, 68:1 (2009), 116–38
Grehan, J. and Mace, M., *Unearthing Churchill's Secret Army: The Official List of SOE Casualties and their Stories* (Barnsley, 2012)
Grenkevich, L., *The Soviet Partisan Movement 1941–1944* (1999)
Griffiths, R., *Marshal Pétain* (2011)
Grose, P., *A Good Place to Hide: How One French Community Saved Thousands of Lives from the Nazis* (2014)
Grubsztein, M. (ed.), *Jewish Resistance during the Holocaust: Proceedings of Conference* (Jerusalem, 1968)
Grynberg, M. (ed.), *Words to Outlive Us: Eyewitness Accounts from the Warsaw Ghetto* (2003)
Grzelak, C., Stańczyk, H., and Zwoliński, S., *Bez Możliwości Wyboru: Wojsko Polskie na Froncie Wschodnim 1943–1945* (Warsaw, 1993)
Guéhenno, J., *Diary of the Dark Years, 1940–1944* (Oxford, 2014)
Guiet, J.-C., *Dead on Time: The Memoir of an SOE and OSS Agent in Occupied France* (Stroud, 2016)
Gumz, J., 'German Counter-Insurgency Policy in Independent Croatia, 1941–1944', *The Historian*, 61 (1998), 22–50
—'Wehrmacht Perceptions of Mass Violence in Croatia, 1941–1942', *Historical Journal*, 44:4 (2001), 1,015–38
Gutman, Y., *The Jews of Warsaw, 1939–1943: Ghetto, Underground, Revolt* (Bloomington, IN, 1982)
—and Krakowski, S., *Unequal Victims: Poles and Jews during World War II* (New York, 1986)
Hackett, D. (ed.), *The Buchenwald Report* (Boulder, CO, 1995)
Hackett, J., *I Was a Stranger* (1977)
Haestrup, J., *Europe Ablaze: An Analysis of the History of the European Resistance Movements* (Odense, 1978)
Hallie, P., *Lest Innocent Blood Be Shed* (1979)
Halls, M., *Escaping Hitler: Heroic True Stories of Great Escapes in Nazi Europe* (2017)

Hamilton-Hill, D., *SOE Assignment* (1973)
Hammond, N., *Venture into Greece: With the Guerrillas 1943–1944* (1983)
Hamson, D., *We Fell among Greeks* (1946)
Hanson, J., *The Civilian Population and the Warsaw Uprising* (Cambridge, 1982)
Hansson, P., *The Greatest Gamble* (1967)
Harris Smith, R., *OSS: The Secret History of America's First Central Intelligence Agency* (Berkeley, CA, 1972)
Harrison, E., 'The British Special Operations Executive and Poland', *Historical Journal*, 43 (2000), 1,071–91
Harvey, E., 'Last Resort or Key Resource? Women Workers from the Nazi-Occupied Soviet Territories, the Reich Labour Administration and the German War Effort', *Transactions of the Royal Historical Society*, 26 (2016), 149–73
Hastings, M., *Das Reich: The March of the 2nd SS Panzer Division through France, June 1944* (2005)
—*All Hell Let Loose* (2012)
—*The Secret War: Spies, Codes and Guerrillas 1939–1945* (2015)
Hauge, E., *Salt-Water Thief* (1958)
Hauge, J. C., *The Liberation of Norway* (Oslo, 1950, 1995)
Haukelid, K., *Skis against the Atom* (Minot, ND, 1989)
Hawes, S. and White, R. (eds), *Resistance in Europe, 1939–1945* (1975)
Hayes, P., *Quisling: The Career and Political Ideas of Vidkun Quisling 1887–1945* (Newton Abbot, 1971)
Hazelhoff, E., *Soldier of Orange* (1972)
Heaps, L., *The Grey Goose of Arnhem* (1976)
Heer, H. and Naumann, K. (eds), *War of Extermination: The German Military in World War II* (New York, 2000)
Hehn, P., *The German Struggle against the Yugoslav Guerrillas in World War II: German Counter-Insurgency in Yugoslavia, 1941–1943* (New York, 1979)
Heilbrunn, O., *Warfare in the Enemy's Rear* (1963)
Helm, S., *A Life in Secrets: The Story of Vera Atkins and the Lost Agents of SOE* (2006)
Hemingway-Douglas, R., *The Shelburne Escape Line* (Anacortes, WA, 2014)
Herbert, U., *Hitler's Foreign Workers: Enforced Foreign Labour in Germany under the Third Reich* (Cambridge, 1997)
Herrington, I., 'The SIS and SOE in Norway 1940–1945: Conflict or Co-operation?', *War in History*, 9:1 (2002), 82–110
Heslop, R., *Xavier: A British Agent with the French Resistance* (1970)
Hewins, R., *Quisling: Prophet without Honour* (1965)
Hilberg, R., *The Destruction of the European Jews*, 3 vols (New York, 1985)
—*Perpetrators, Victims, Bystanders: The Jewish Catastrophe 1933–1945* (1992)
Hill, A., *The War behind the Eastern Front: The Soviet Partisan Movement in North-West Russia* (2004)
Hillesum, E., *Letters from Westerbork* (1987)
Hinsley, F. H., et al. *British Intelligence in the Second World War*, 5 vols (1979–90)
Hirschfeld , G., *Nazi Rule and Dutch Collaboration: The Netherlands under German Occupation 1940–1945* (Oxford, 1988)
—'Collaboration and Attentisme in the Netherlands 1940–41', *Journal of Contemporary History*, 16:3 (1981), 467–86
—and Marsh, P. (eds), *Collaboration in France* (Oxford, 1989)
Hoare, M. A., *Genocide and Resistance in Hitler's Bosnia: The Partisans and the Chetniks, 1941–1943* (Oxford, 2006)
Hoffmann, S., 'Collaboration in France during World War II', *Journal of Modern History*, 40:3 (1968), 375–95
Hoidal, O., *Quisling: A Study in Treason* (Oslo, 1988)
Holland, J., *Italy's Sorrow: A Year of War, 1944–1945* (2008)
Homze, E., *Foreign Labor in Nazi Germany* (Princeton, NJ, 1967)

Hondros, J., *Occupation and Resistance: The Greek Agony, 1941–1944* (New York, 1983)
Hood, S., *Pebbles from My Skull* (1963)
Hoogstraten, B., *The Resistance Fighters: The Immense Struggle of Holland during World War II* (2008)
Housden, M., *Hans Frank: Lebensraum and Holocaust* (Basingstoke, 2003)
Howarth, D., *The Shetland Bus* (1951)
—*We Die Alone* (1955)
Hronek, J., *Volcano under Hitler: The Underground War in Czechoslovakia* (1941)
Hryniewicz, B., *My Boyhood War: Warsaw 1944* (Stroud, 2015)
Hue, A., *The Next Moon: The Remarkable True Story of a British Agent behind the Lines in Wartime France* (2004)
Humbert, A., *Resistance: Memoirs of Occupied France* (2008)
Hunt, V., *Fire and Ice: The Nazis' Scorched Earth Campaign in Norway* (Stroud, 2014)
Iatrides, J., *Revolt in Athens: The Greek Communist 'Second Round' 1944–45* (Princeton, NJ, 1972)
—(ed.) *Greece in the 1940s: A Nation in Crisis* (Hanover, NH, 1981)
Ignatov, P., *Partisans of the Kuban* (1945)
Iranek-Osmecki, G., *The Unseen and Silent: Adventures from the Underground Movement* (1954)
Iranek-Osmecki, K., *He Who Saves One Life* (New York, 1971)
Irwin, W., *The Jedburghs* (New York, 2005)
Isaaman, D., *Jacques de Guélis: SOE's Genial Giant* (2018)
Ivanovic, V., *LX: Memoirs of a Yugoslav* (1977)
Iwaszkiewicz, J., *Notatki 1939–1945* (Wrocław, 1991)
Jackson, J., *France: The Dark Years, 1940–1944* (Oxford, 2001)
—*A Certain Idea of France: The Life of Charles de Gaulle* (2018)
Jeffery, K., *MI6: The History of the Secret Intelligence Service, 1909–1949* (2010)
Jenkins, R., *A Pacifist at War: The Silence of Francis Cammaerts* (2009)
Jespersen, K., *No Small Achievement: Special Operations Executive and the Danish Resistance* (Odense, 2002)
Jockusch, L. and Finder, G. (eds), *Jewish Honor Courts: Revenge, Retribution, and Reconciliation in Europe and Israel after the Holocaust* (Detroit, MI, 2015)
Johnson, S., *Agents Extraordinary* (1975)
Jones, J., '"Every Family Has Its Freak": Perceptions of Collaboration in Occupied Soviet Russia, 1943–1948', *Slavic Review*, 64:4 (2005), 747–70
Jones, R. V., *Most Secret War* (1979)
Jones, W., *Twelve Months with Tito's Partisans* (Bedford, 1946)
Jones, W. *Raiding Support Regiment: The Diary of a Special Forces Soldier, 1943–1945* (Plymouth, 2011)
Jong, L. de, *The Netherlands and Nazi Germany* (Cambridge, MA, 1990)
Jordan, W., *Conquest without Victory: A New Zealander's Experiences in the Resistance Movements in Greece and France* (1970)
Jouan, C., *Comète: histoire d'une ligne d'évasion* (Brussels, 1948)
Jucker, N., *Curfew in Paris: A Record of the German Occupation* (1960)
Judt, T. (ed.), *Resistance and Revolution in Mediterranean Europe, 1939–1948* (1989)
Kállay, M., *Hungarian Premier: A Personal Account of a Nation's Struggle in the Second World War* (1954)
Kamenetsky, I., *Hitler's Occupation of Ukraine, 1941–1944: A Study of Totalitarian Imperialism* (New York, 1956)
Karski, J., *Story of a Secret State* (1945)
Katsch, A. (ed.), *Scroll of Agony: The Warsaw Diary of Chaim A. Kaplan* (1966)
Katz, R., *Fatal Silence: The Pope, the Resistance and the German Occupation of Rome* (2003)
Kay, A., Rutherford, J., and Stahel, D. (eds), *Nazi Policy on the Eastern Front, 1941: Total War, Genocide, and Radicalization* (Rochester, NY, 2012)
Kedward, H., *Resistance in Vichy France: A Study of Ideas and Motivation in the Southern Zone, 1940–1942* (Oxford, 1978)

—*Occupied France: Collaboration and Resistance* (Oxford, 1985)
—*In Search of the Maquis: Rural Resistance in Southern France* (Oxford, 1993)
—'Resiting the French Resistance', *Transactions of the Royal Historical Society*, 9 (1999), 271–82
—and Austin, R. (eds), *Vichy France and the Resistance: Culture and Ideology* (1985)
Kelso, N., *Errors of Judgement: SOE's Disaster in the Netherlands, 1941–1944* (1944)
Kemp, P., *No Colours or Crest* (1958)
—*The Thorns of Memory* (1990)
Kennan, G., *From Prague after Munich: Diplomatic Papers 1938–1940* (Princeton, NJ, 1968)
Kent, S. and Nicholas, N., *Agent Michael Trotobas and SOE in Northern France* (Barnsley, 2015)
Kersaudy, F., *Churchill and de Gaulle* (New York, 1982)
Kershaw, I., *Hitler: Nemesis 1936–1945* (2000)
Kersten, K., *The Establishment of Communist Rule in Poland, 1943–1948* (Berkeley, CA, 1991)
Kesselring, A., *The Memoirs of Field Marshal Kesselring* (1953)
Keyes, R., *Outrageous Fortune: The Tragedy of Leopold II of the Belgians, 1901–41* (1984)
Kimball, W. (ed.), *Churchill and Roosevelt: The Complete Correspondence*, 3 vols (Princeton, NJ, 1984)
King, J., 'Emmanuel d'Astier and the Nature of the French Resistance', *Journal of Contemporary History*, 8:4 (1973), 25–45
Kirchhoff, H., 'Denmark: A Light in the Darkness of the Holocaust? A Reply to Gunnar S. Paulsson', *Journal of Contemporary History*, 30 (1995), 465–79
Kiriakopoulos, G. C., *The Nazi Occupation of Crete 1941–1945* (Westport, CT, 1995)
Kirk, T., 'Limits of Germandom: Resistance to the Nazi Annexation of Slovenia', *Slavonic and East European Review*, 69:4 (1991), 646–67
Kitchen, M., *Nazi Germany at War* (1995)
Kitson, S., *The Hunt for Nazi Spies: Fighting Espionage in Vichy France* (Chicago, IL, 2007)
—'From Enthusiasm to Disenchantment: The French Police and the Vichy Regime, 1940–1944', *Contemporary European History*, 11:3 (2002), 371–90
Klukowski, Z., *Diary from the Years of Occupation 1939–44* (Urbana, IL, 1993)
Kochanski, H., *The Eagle Unbowed: Poland and the Poles in the Second World War* (2012)
Koestler, A., *Scum of the Earth* (1955)
Korbel, J., *The Communist Subversion of Czechoslovakia, 1938–1948: The Failure of Coexistence* (Princeton, NJ, 1959)
Korboński, S., *Fighting Warsaw: The Story of the Polish Underground State* (New York, 1956)
—*The Jews and Poles in World War II* (New York, 1989)
Koreman, M., *The Expectation of Justice: France, 1944–1946* (Durham, NC, 1999)
—*The Escape Line: How the Ordinary Heroes of Dutch-Paris Resisted the Nazi Occupation of Western Europe* (New York, 2018)
Kosyk, W., *The Third Reich and the Ukrainian Question: Documents 1934–1944* (New York, 1993)
Kovpak, S., *Our Partisan Course* (1947)
Krakowski, S., *The War of the Doomed: Jewish Armed Resistance in Poland* (New York, 1984)
Kranjc, G., *To Walk with the Devil: Slovene Collaboration and Axis Occupation* (Toronto, 2013)
Kulski, J., *Dying, We Live: The Personal Chronicle of a Young Freedom Fighter in Warsaw* (New York, 1979)
Kundahl, G., *The Riviera at War: World War II on the Côte d'Azur* (New York, 2017)
Kunicki, K., 'Unwanted Collaborators: Leon Kozłowski, Władysław Studnicki and the Problems of Collaboration among Polish Conservative Politicians in World War II', *European Review of History*, 8 (2001), 203–20
Kurapovna, M., *Shadows on the Mountain: The Allies, the Resistance, and the Rivalries that Doomed WWII Yugoslavia* (Hoboken, NJ, 2009)
Kurzman, D., *The Bravest Battle: The 28 Days of the Warsaw Ghetto Uprising* (New York, 1993)
Lacouture, J., *De Gaulle: The Rebel, 1890–1944* (1993)
Lagrou, P., *The Legacy of Nazi Occupation: Patriotic Memory and National Recovery in Western Europe 1945–1965* (Cambridge, 1999)

Lamb, R., *War in Italy 1943–1945: A Brutal Story* (1993)
Lambert, F., *Free French Saboteurs* (Paris, 2015)
Lampe, D., *The Savage Canary: The Story of Resistance in Denmark* (1957)
Langelaan, G., *Knights of the Floating Silk* (1959)
Langley, J., *Fight another Day* (1974)
Lankford, N. D. (ed.), *OSS against the Reich: The World War II Diaries of Colonel David K. E. Bruce* (Kent, OH, 1991)
Laska, V. (ed.), *Women in the Resistance and in the Holocaust: The Voices of Eyewitnesses* (Westwood, CT, 1983)
Latour, A., *The Jewish Resistance in France, 1940–1944* (New York, 1981)
Laub, T., *After the Fall: German Policy in Occupied France* (Oxford, 2010)
Lawrence, C., *Irregular Adventure* (1947)
Lazare, L., *Rescue as Resistance: How Jewish Organisations Fought the Holocaust in France* (New York, 1986)
Le Chêne, E., *Mauthausen: The History of a Death Camp* (1971)
—*Watch for Me by Moonlight: A British Agent with the French Resistance* (1973)
Leahy, W., *I Was There* (1950)
Leeper, R., *When Greek Meets Greek* (1950)
Lees, M., *Special Operations Executed in Serbia and Italy* (1986)
—*The Rape of Serbia: The British Role in Tito's Grab for Power, 1943–44* (1990)
Leigh Fermor, P., *Abducting a General: The Kreipe Operation and SOE in Crete* (2014)
Leslie, P., *The Liberation of the Riviera: The Resistance to the Nazis in the South of France and the Story of its Heroic Leader Ange-Marie Miniconi* (1981)
Lett, G., *Rossano: An Adventure of the Italian Resistance* (1955)
Lettrich, J., *History of Modern Slovakia* (1955)
Lévi-Valensi, J. (ed.), *Camus at Combat: Writing 1944–1947* (2006)
Lévy, J.-P., *Mémoires d'un franc-tireur* (Paris, 1998)
Lewin, A., *A Cup of Tears: A Diary of the Warsaw Ghetto* (Oxford, 1998)
Lewis, L., *Echoes of Resistance: British Involvement with the Italian Partisans* (Tunbridge Wells, 1985)
Lewy, G., *The Catholic Church and Nazi Germany* (New York, 1964)
Leyton, D., *The House near Paris: An American Woman's Story of Traffic in Patriots* (1947)
Lidegaard, B., *Countrymen: The Untold Story of How Denmark's Jews Escaped the Nazis* (2015)
Lindsay, F., *Beacons in the Night: With the OSS and Tito's Partisans in Wartime Yugoslavia* (Stanford, CA, 1993)
Lipgens, W., 'European Federation in the Political Thought of Resistance Movements during World War II', *Central European History*, 1:1 (1968), 5–19
Litoff, J. Barrett (ed.), *An American Heroine in the French Resistance: The Diary and Memoir of Virginia d'Albert-Lake* (New York, 2006)
Littlejohn, D., *The Patriotic Traitors: A History of Collaborationism in German-Occupied Europe, 1940–1945* (1972)
Lochner, L. (ed.), *The Goebbels Diaries* (1948)
Loewenheim, F., Langley, H., and Jonas, M. (eds), *Roosevelt and Churchill: Their Secret Wartime Correspondence* (1975)
Longerich, P., *Heinrich Himmler* (Oxford, 2012)
Lorain, P., *Secret Warfare: The Arms and Techniques of the Resistance* (1984)
Lottman, H., *The People's Anger: Justice and Revenge in Post-Liberation France* (1986)
Lowell Armstrong, J., 'The Polish Underground and the Jews: A Reassessment of Home Army Commander Tadeusz Bor-Komorowski's Order 116 against Banditry', *Slavonic and East European Review*, 72 (1994), 259–76
Lucas, P., *The OSS in World War II Albania: Covert Operations and Collaboration with Communist Partisans* (Jefferson, NC, 2007)
Łuczak, C., *Polska i Polacy w drugiej wojnie światowej* (Poznań, 1993)
Ludewig, J., *Rückzug: The German Retreat from France, 1944* (Lexington, KY, 2012)

Lukacs, J., *The Last European War: September 1939–December 1941* (1977)
Lukas, R., *Out of the Inferno: Poles Remember the Holocaust* (Lexington, KY, 1989)
—*Forgotten Holocaust: The Poles under German Occupation, 1939–1944* (New York, 1997)
—*Forgotten Survivors: Polish Christians Remember the Nazi Occupation* (Lawrence, KS, 2004)
Lumans, V., *Latvia in World War II* (New York, 2006)
Luža, R., *The Hitler Kiss: A Memoir of the Czech Resistance* (Baton Rouge, LO, 2002)
—'The Communist Party of Czechoslovakia and the Czech Resistance, 1939–1945', *Slavic Review*, 28:4 (1969), 561–76
Lyman, R., *The Jail Busters: The Secret Story of MI6, the French Resistance and Operation Jericho* (2013)
Maass, W. B., *The Netherlands at War* (1970)
MacDonald, C., *The Killing of SS Obergruppenführer Reinhard Heydrich, 27 May 1942* (1989)
Macintosh, C., *From Cloak to Dagger: An SOE Agent in Italy, 1943–1945* (1982)
Mackenzie, W., *The Secret History of SOE* (2000)
Macksey, K., *The Partisans of Europe in World War II* (1975)
Maclean, F., *Eastern Approaches* (1949)
Macmillan, H., *The Blast of War: 1939–45* (1967)
—*War Diaries: Politics and War in the Mediterranean, January 1943–May 1945* (1984)
Macmillan, M., *Peacemakers* (2001)
Macpherson T., *Behind Enemy Lines: The Autobiography of Britain's Most Decorated War Hero* (Edinburgh, 2010)
Maczek, S., *Od Podwody do Czołga* (Edinburgh, 1961)
Maguire, G., *Anglo-American Policy towards the Free French* (Basingstoke, 1995)
Mamatey, V. and Luža, R. (eds), *A History of the Czechoslovak Republic, 1918–1948* (Princeton, NJ, 1973)
Mangold, P., *Britain and the Defeated French: From Occupation to Liberation, 1940–1944* (2012)
Mann, C., *British Policy and Strategy towards Norway* (Basingstoke, 2012)
Marks, L., *Between Silk and Cyanide: The Story of SOE's Code War* (1998)
Marrus, M., 'Jewish Resistance to the Holocaust', *Journal of Contemporary History*, 30:1 (1995), 83–110
—and Paxton, R., *Vichy France and the Jews* (New York, 1981)
Marshall, B., *The White Rabbit* (1952)
Martelli, G., *Agent Extraordinary: The Story of Michel Hollard* (1960)
Martin, D., *The Web of Disinformation: Churchill's Yugoslav Blunder* (New York, 1990)
—(ed.), *Patriot or Traitor: The Case of General Mihailovich: Proceedings and Report of the Commission of Inquiry of the Committee for a Fair Trial for Draja Mihailovich* (Stanford, CA, 1978)
Mason, H., *The Purge of the Dutch Quislings* (The Hague, 1952)
—'Testing Human Bonds within Nations: Jews in the Occupied Netherlands', *Political Science Quarterly*, 99 (1984), 315–43
Mastny, V., *The Czechs under Nazi Rule: The Failure of National Resistance, 1939–1942* (New York, 1972)
Mayer, A., *Gaston's War: A True Story of a Hero of the Resistance in World War II* (Novato, CA, 1988)
Mazower, M., *Inside Hitler's Greece: The Experience of Occupation, 1941–44* (New Haven, CT, 1993)
—*Hitler's Empire: Nazi Rule in Occupied Europe* (2008)
McCue, P., *Behind Enemy Lines with the SAS: The Story of Amédée Maingard, SOE Agent* (Barnsley, 2019)
McIntyre, B., *Operation Mincemeat: The True Spy Story that Changed the Course of World War II* (2010)
—*Double Cross: The True Story of the D-Day Spies* (2012)
McKinstry, L., *Operation Sealion: How Britain Crushed the German War Machine's Dream of Invasion in 1940* (2014)

McPhail, H., *The Long Silence: Civilian Life under the German Occupation of Northern France, 1914–1918* (1999)
Mears, R., *The Real Heroes of Telemark* (2003)
Meszerics, T., 'Undermine, or Bring Them Over: SOE and OSS Plans for Hungary in 1943', *Journal of Contemporary History*, 43:2 (2008), 195–216
Michel, H., *Les Courants de pensée de la Résistance* (Paris, 1962)
—*The Shadow War: Resistance in Europe, 1939–1945* (1972)
—*Histoire de la Résistance* (Paris, 1984)
—'The Psychology of the French Resister', *Journal of Contemporary History*, 5:3 (1970), 159–75
Mikołajczyk, S., *The Rape of Poland: Pattern of Soviet Aggression* (New York, 1948)
Milač, M., *Resistance, Imprisonment, and Forced Labour: A Slovene Student in World War II* (New York, 2002)
Milazzo, M., *The Chetnik Movement and the Yugoslav Resistance* (Baltimore, MD, 1975)
Millar, G., *Maquis: The French Resistance at War* (Bath, 2006)
Miller, M. L., *Bulgaria during the Second World War* (Stanford, CA, 1975)
Miller, R., *Nothing Less than Victory: An Oral History of D-Day* (1993)
—*Behind the Lines: The Oral History of Special Operations in World War II* (2002)
Milton, G., *The Ministry of Ungentlemanly Warfare: Churchill's Mavericks Plotting Hitler's Defeat* (2016)
Milward, A., *The Fascist Economy in Norway* (Oxford, 1972)
Misiunas, R. and Taagepera, R., *The Baltic States: Years of Dependence 1940–1980* (1983)
Monk, R., *Inside the Circle: The Life of J. Robert Oppenheimer* (2012)
Moore, B., *Victims and Survivors: The Nazi Persecution of the Jews in the Netherlands 1940–1945* (1997)
—*Survivors: Jewish Self-Help and Rescue in Nazi-Occupied Western Europe* (Oxford, 2010)
—'Louis De Jong: Writing the History of Occupied Europe', *Contemporary European History*, 14:3 (2005), 415–17
—(ed.), *Resistance in Western Europe* (Oxford, 2000)
Moorehead, C., *Iris Origo: Marchesa of Val d'Orcia* (2000)
—*Village of Secrets: Defying the Nazis in Vichy France* (2014)
Moravec, F., *Master of Spies: The Memoirs of General Frantisek Moravec* (1975)
Morgan, P., *The Fall of Mussolini: Italy, the Italians and the Second World War* (Oxford, 2007)
Morris, E., *Circles of Hell: The War in Italy, 1943–1945* (1993)
Moss, W. S., *Ill Met by Moonlight* (1950)
—*A War of Shadows* (1952)
Muggeridge, M. (ed.), *The Ciano Diaries 1939–1943* (1947)
Mulgan, J., *Report on Experience* (1947)
Muller, R.-D., *The Unknown Eastern Front: The Wehrmacht and Hitler's Foreign Soldiers* (New York, 2012)
Mulley, C., *The Spy Who Loved: The Secrets and Lives of Christine Granville, Britain's First Female Special Agent of the Second World War* (2012)
Mulligan, T., *The Politics of Illusion and Empire: German Occupation Policy in the Soviet Union, 1942–43* (New York, 1988)
Munoz, A. and Romanko, O., *Hitler's White Russians: Collaboration, Extermination, and Anti-Partisan Warfare in Byelorussia, 1941–1944* (New York, 2003)
Murphy, R., *Diplomat among Warriors* (1964)
Muus, F., *The Spark and the Flame* (1956)
Myers, E., *Greek Entanglement* (Gloucester, 1985)
Neave, A., *Little Cyclone* (1954)
—*Saturday at M.I.9: A History of Underground Escape Lines in North-West Europe in 1940–5* (1969)
Neilsen, T., *Inside Fortress Norway* (2000)
Neitzel, S. (ed.), *Tapping Hitler's Generals: Transcripts of Secret Conversations, 1942–1945* (Barnsley, 2007)

—and Welzer, H., *Soldaten: On Fighting, Killing, and Dying: The Secret World War II Tapes of German POWs* (2012)
Némirovsky, I., *Suite Française* (2007)
Neumaier, C., 'The Escalation of German Reprisal Policy in Occupied France, 1941–42', *Journal of Contemporary History*, 41:1 (2006), 113–31
Ney-Krwawicz, M., *The Polish Home Army 1939–1945* (2001)
Nichol, J. and Rennell, T., *Home Run: Escape from Nazi Europe* (2007)
Nicolson, D., *Aristide: The Story of Roger Landes* (1994)
Nielsen, *Inside Fortress Norway: Bjørn West Norwegian Guerrilla Base, 1944–1945* (Manhattan, KS, 2000)
Noguères, H., Degliame-Fouché, M., and Vigier, J.-L., *Histoire de la Résistance en France de 1940 à 1945*, 5 vols (Paris, 1967–81)
Noordhoek Hegt, W. F., 'The Resistance of the Medical Profession', *Annals of the American Academy of Political and Social Science*, 245 (1946), 162–8
Novick, P., *The Resistance versus Vichy: The Purge of Collaborators in Liberated France* (New York, 1968)
Nowak, J., *Courier from Warsaw* (1982)
O'Connor, B., *Churchill's Angels* (Stroud, 2014)
O'Donnell, P., *Operatives, Spies, and Saboteurs: The Unknown Story of WWII's OSS* (New York, 2004)
Ogden, A., *Through Hitler's Back Door: SOE Operations in Hungary, Slovakia, Romania and Bulgaria* (Barnsley, 2010)
Olsen, J., *Silence on Monte Sole* (1969)
Olson, L., *Madame Fourcade's Secret War* (New York, 2019)
Olszański, T., *Kresy Kresów Stanisławów* (Warsaw, 2008)
O'Malley, O., *The Phantom Caravan* (1954)
O'Reilly, D., 'Interrogating the Gestapo: SS Sturmbannführer Horst Kopkow, the *Rote Kapelle* and Postwar British Intelligence', *Journal of Intelligence History*, forthcoming
Origo, I., *War in Val d'Orcia: A Diary* (1947, 2017)
Orska, I., *Silent is the Vistula* (1946)
Osti Guerrazzi, A., *The Italian Army in Slovenia: Strategies of Antipartisan Repression, 1941–1943* (New York, 2013)
Overy, R., *Russia's War* (1999)
Paillole, P., *Fighting the Nazis: French Military Intelligence and Counterintelligence 1935–1945* (New York, 2003)
Papastratis, P., *British Policy towards Greece during the Second World War, 1941–1945* (Cambridge, 1984)
Passy, Colonel, *Souvenirs*, 3 vols (Monte Carlo, 1947)
Paul, D., *Surgeon at Arms* (1958)
Paulsson, G., *Secret City: The Hidden Jews of Warsaw 1940–1945* (New Haven, CT, 2002)
—'The "Bridge over the Oresund": The Historiography on the Expulsion of the Jews from Nazi-Occupied Denmark', *Journal of Contemporary History*, 30 (1995), 431–64
Pavlowitch, S., *Hitler's New Disorder: The Second World War in Yugoslavia* (2008)
Pavone, C., *A Civil War: A History of the Italian Resistance* (2013)
Paxton, R., *Vichy France* (1972)
Pearson, M., *Tears of Glory: The Betrayal of Vercors* (1978)
Pearson, O., *Albania in Occupation and War: From Fascism to Communism 1940–1945*, vol. 2 (New York, 2005)
Penter, T., 'Collaboration on Trial: New Source Material on Soviet Postwar Trials against Collaborators', *Slavic Review*, 64:4 (2005), 782–90
Perrin, N., *Spirit of Resistance: The Life of SOE Agent Harry Peulevé DSO MC* (2008)
Petersen, N. (ed.), *From Hitler's Doorstep: The Wartime Intelligence Reports of Allen Dulles* (Philadelphia, PA, 1996)
Pezzino, P., *Memory and Massacre: Revisiting Sant'Anna di Stazzema* (New York, 2012)

Pike, D., 'Between the Junes: The French Communists from the Collapse of France to the Invasion of Russia', *Journal of Contemporary History*, 28 (1993), 465–85
Pike, R., *Defying Vichy: Blood, Fear and French Resistance* (Stroud, 2018)
Pilecki, W., *The Auschwitz Volunteer: Beyond Bravery* (Los Angeles, CA, 2012)
Pimlott, B. (ed.), *The Second World War Diary of Hugh Dalton 1940–45* (1986)
Pineau, C., *La Simple Vérité* (Paris, 1960)
Piotrowski, S., *Hans Frank's Diary* (Warsaw, 1961)
Piotrowski, T., *Poland's Holocaust: Ethnic Strife, Collaboration with Occupying Forces and Genocide in the Second Republic 1918–1947* (Jefferson, NC, 2000)
Poirier, J., *The Giraffe Has a Long Neck* (1995)
Polonsky, A., *The Jews in Poland and Russia*, vol. 3: *1914 to 2008* (Portland, OR, 2012)
—and Drukier, B. (eds), *The Beginnings of Communist Rule in Poland: December 1943–June 1945* (1980)
Portelli, A., *The Order Has Been Carried Out: History, Memory, and Meaning of a Nazi Massacre in Rome* (New York, 2003)
Porter, I., *Operation Autonomous* (1989)
Powers, T., *Heisenberg's War: The Secret History of the German Bomb* (1994)
Poznanski, R., *Jews in France during World War II* (Hanover, NH, 2001)
—'Reflections on Jewish Resistance and Jewish Resistants in France', *Jewish Social Studies*, 2:1 (1995), 124–58
Prażmowska, A., *Civil War in Poland 1942–1948* (Basingstoke, 2004)
Presser, J., *Ashes in the Wind: The Destruction of Dutch Jewry* (2010)
Prusin, A., *The Lands Between: Conflict in the East European Borderlands, 1870–1992* (Oxford, 2010)
Pryce-Jones, D., *Paris in the Third Reich: A History of the German Occupation, 1940–1944* (New York, 1981)
Psychoundakis, G., *The Cretan Runner: His Story of the German Occupation* (1998)
Purnell, S., *A Woman of No Importance: The Untold Story of Virginia Hall* (2019)
RAF and the SOE: Special Duty Operations in Europe during WW2. An Official Account (Barnsley, 2016)
Ramet, S. and Listhaug, O. (eds), *Serbia and the Serbs in World War Two* (Basingstoke, 2011)
Rankin, N., *Ian Fleming's Commandos: The Story of 30 Assault Unit in WWII* (2012)
Rayski, A., *The Choice of the Jews under Vichy: Between Submission and Resistance* (Notre Dame, IN, 2005)
Rée, J. (ed.), *A Schoolmaster's War: Harry Rée, British Agent in the French Resistance* (New Haven, CT, 2020)
Reed Olsen, O., *Two Eggs on My Plate* (1952)
Rees, L., *World War II behind Closed Doors* (2008)
Reilly, R., *The Sixth Floor* (1969)
Reitlinger, G., *The House Built on Sand: The Conflicts of German Policy in Russia, 1939–1945* (1960)
Remeikis, T. (ed.), *Lithuania under German Occupation, 1941–1945: Dispatches from the US Legation in Stockholm* (Vilnius, 2005)
Rémy, *The Silent Company* (1948)
—*Courage and Fear* (1950)
Rendel, A., *Appointment in Crete: The Story of a British Agent* (1953)
Resis, A., 'The Churchill-Stalin Secret "Percentages" Agreement on the Balkans, Moscow, October 1944', *American Historical Review*, 83:2 (1978), 368–87
Rich, N., *Hitler's War Aims*, 2 vols (New York, 1974)
Richards, B., *Secret Flotillas: The Clandestine Sea Lines to France and French North Africa, 1940–1944*, 2 vols (1996, 2004)
Richie, A., *Warsaw 1944: Hitler, Himmler and the Warsaw Uprising* (New York, 2013)
Rigden, D., *SOE Syllabus: Lessons in Ungentlemanly Warfare* (2001)

Ringelblum, E., *Notes from the Warsaw Ghetto: The Journal of Emmanuel Ringelblum* (New York, 1958)
—*Polish-Jewish Relations during the Second World War* (Jerusalem, 1974)
Rings, W., *Life with the Enemy: Collaboration and Resistance in Hitler's Europe, 1939–1945* (New York, 1982)
Riste, O. and Nökleby, B., *Norway, 1940–45: The Resistance Movement* (Oslo, 1970)
Ritchie, S., *Our Man in Yugoslavia: The Story of a Secret Service Operative* (2004)
Rittner, C. and Myers, S., *The Courage to Care: Rescuers of Jews during the Holocaust* (New York, 1986)
Roberts, A. (ed.), *The Strategy of Civilian Defence: Non-Violent Resistance to Aggression* (1967)
Roberts, W., *Tito, Mihailović and the Allies* (Durham, NC, 1987)
Robertson, K. G. (ed.), *War, Resistance and Intelligence: Essays in Honour of M. R. D. Foot* (1999)
Rodogno, D., *Fascism's European Empire: Italian Occupation during the Second World War* (Cambridge, 2006)
Rohrlich, R. (ed.), *Resisting the Holocaust* (New York, 1998)
Rokossovsky, K., *A Soldier's Duty* (Moscow, 1985)
Romein, J. M., 'The Spirit of the Dutch People during the Occupation', *Annals of the American Academy of Political and Social Science*, 245 (1946), 169–80
Rootham, J., *Miss Fire: The Chronicle of a British Mission to Mihailovich, 1943–1944* (1946)
Rotem, S., *Memoirs of a Warsaw Ghetto Fighter: The Past within Me* (New Haven, CT, 1994)
Rousso, H., *The Vichy Syndrome* (Cambridge, MA, 1994)
Ruby, M., *F Section, SOE: The Buckmaster Networks* (1988)
Ryan, C., *A Bridge Too Far* (1974)
Sagajllo, W., *The Man in the Middle: A Story of Polish Resistance, 1940–45* (1984)
Salmon, P. (ed.), *Britain and Norway in the Second World War* (1995)
Salvadori, M., *The Labour and the Wounds: A Personal Chronicle of One Man's Fight for Freedom* (1958)
Sarafis, S., *ELAS: Greek Resistance Army* (1980)
Schellenberg, W., *The Schellenberg Memoirs* (1956)
Schenk, P., *Invasion of England 1940: The Planning of Operation Sealion* (1990)
Schoenbrun, D., *Soldiers of the Night: The Story of the French Resistance* (New York, 1980)
Schreiber, M., *Silent Rebels: The True Story of the Raid on the Twentieth Train to Auschwitz* (2003)
Schulte, T., *German Army and Nazi Policies in Occupied Russia* (New York, 1989)
Seaman, M., *Bravest of the Brave: The True Story of Wing Commander 'Tommy' Yeo-Thomas, SOE Secret Agent, Codename 'The White Rabbit'* (1997)
—*Saboteur: The Untold Story of SOE's Youngest Agent at the Heart of the French Resistance* (2018)
—(ed.), *Special Operations Executive: A New Instrument of War* (2006)
Semelin, J., *Unarmed against Hitler: Civilian Resistance in Europe, 1939–1943* (Westport, CT, 1993)
Seymour-Jones, C., *She Landed by Moonlight: The Story of Secret Agent Pearl Witherington* (2014)
Shennan, A., *Rethinking France: Plans for Renewal 1940–1946* (Oxford, 1989)
Shepherd, B., *War in the Wild East: The German Army and Soviet Partisans* (Cambridge, MA, 2004)
—*Terror in the Balkans: German Armies and Partisan Warfare* (Cambridge, MA, 2012)
—*Hitler's Soldiers: The German Army in the Third Reich* (New Haven, CT, 2016)
—and Pattinson, J. (eds), *War in a Twilight World: Partisan and Anti-Partisan Warfare in Eastern Europe, 1939–45* (Basingstoke, 2010)
Shiber, E., *Paris Underground* (1944)
Sikorski Institute, *Documents on Polish-Soviet Relations*, 2 vols (1961–7)
Skilling, H. G., 'The Czechoslovak Struggle for National Liberation in World War II', *Slavonic and East European Review*, 39:92 (1960), 174–97
Slaughter, J., *Women and the Italian Resistance, 1943–1945* (Denver, CO, 1997)

Śledziński, K., *Cichociemni: Elita polskiej dywersji* (Cracow, 2012)
Slepyan, K., *Stalin's Guerrillas: Soviet Partisans in World War Two* (Lawrence, KS, 2006)
Smetana, V. and Geaney, K. (eds), *Exile in London: The Experience of Czechoslovakia and Other Occupied Nations* (Prague, 2017)
Smiley, D., *Albanian Assignment* (1984)
Smith, L. (ed.), *Forgotten Voices of the Holocaust* (2005)
Smith, M. L., 'Neither Resistance nor Collaboration: Historians and the Problem of the *Nederlandse Unie*', *History*, 72:235 (1987), 251–78
Snyder, T., *Bloodlands: Europe between Hitler and Stalin* (2010)
—*Black Earth: The Holocaust as History and Warning* (2015)
Sonsteby, G., *Report from No. 24* (1964)
Sørensen, N. A., 'Narrating the Second World War in Denmark since 1945', *Contemporary European History*, 14:3 (2005), 295–315
Special Operations Executive Manual: How to Be an Agent in Occupied Europe (2014)
Stafford, D., *Britain and European Resistance, 1940–1945: A Survey of the Special Operations Executive, with Documents* (1980)
—*Secret Agent: The True Story of the Special Operations Executive* (2002)
—*Endgame 1945* (2007)
—*Mission Accomplished: SOE and Italy* (2011)
—'The Detonator Concept: British Strategy, SOE and European Resistance after the Fall of France', *Journal of Contemporary History*, 10:2 (1975), 185–217
—'SOE and British Involvement in the Belgrade Coup d'État of March 1941', *Slavic Review*, 36:3 (1977), 399–419
Stargardt, N., *The German War: A Nation under Arms, 1939–1945* (2015)
Stavrianos, L. S., 'The Greek National Liberation Front (EAM): A Study in Resistance Organization and Administration', *Journal of Modern History*, 24:1 (1952), 42–55
Steinbeck, J., *The Moon is Down* (2000)
Steinberg, J., 'The Third Reich Reflected: German Civil Administration in the Occupied Soviet Union, 1941–4', *English Historical Review*, 110:437 (1995), 620–51
Steinberg, L., *Not as a Lamb: The Jews against Hitler* (Farnborough, 1974)
Stenton, M., *Radio London and Resistance in Occupied Europe: British Political Warfare 1939–1943* (Oxford, 2000)
Stirling, T., Nałęcz, D., and Dubicki, T. (eds), *Intelligence Co-operation between Poland and Great Britain during World War II*, vol. I: *The Report of the Anglo-Polish Historical Committee* (2005); vol. II: *Documents* (Warsaw, 2006)
Stone, H., *Writing in the Shadow: Resistance Publications in Occupied Europe* (1996)
Stourton, E., *Cruel Crossing: Escaping Hitler across the Pyrenees* (2013)
Suhl, Y. (ed.), *They Fought Back* (New York, 1968)
Sutherland, C., *Monica: Heroine of the Danish Resistance* (1992)
Suttill, F., *Shadows in the Fog: The True Story of Major Suttill and the Prosper French Resistance Network* (Stroud, 2014)
Sweet-Escott, B., *Baker Street Irregular* (1965)
Sweets, J., *Choices in Vichy France: The French under Nazi Occupation* (Oxford, 1986)
—'Hold That Pendulum! Redefining Fascism, Collaborationism and Resistance in France', *French Historical Studies*, 15:4 (1988), 731–58
Taylor, F. (ed.), *The Goebbels Diaries: 1939–1941* (1982)
Taylor, L. *Between Resistance and Collaboration: Popular Protest in Northern France* (Basingstoke, 2000)
Tec, N., *When Light Pierced the Darkness: Christian Rescue of Jews in Nazi-Occupied Poland* (Oxford, 1986)
—*Defiance: The Bielski Partisans* (New York, 1993)
—*Resistance: How Jews and Christians Fought Back against the Nazis* (Oxford, 2013)
Thomas, J. Oram, *The Giant-Killers: The Story of the Danish Resistance Movement, 1940–1945* (1975)
Tillotson, M. (ed.), *SOE and the Resistance as Told in* The Times *Obituaries* (2011)

Tilman, H., *When Men and Mountains Meet* (Cambridge, 1946)

Tolstoy, N., *Victims of Yalta* (1977)

Tomasevich, J., *War and Revolution in Yugoslavia, 1941–1945: The Chetniks* (Stanford, CA, 1975)

—*War and Revolution in Yugoslavia, 1941–1945: Occupation and Collaboration* (Stanford, CA, 2001)

Tompkins, P., *A Spy in Rome* (1962)

Tooze, A., *The Wages of Destruction* (2007)

Torrie, J., *German Soldiers and the Occupation of France, 1940–1944* (Cambridge, 2018)

Touw, H. C., 'The Resistance of the Netherlands Churches', *Annals of the American Academy of Political and Social Science*, 245 (1946), 149–61

Trevor-Roper, H. (ed.), *The Goebbels Diaries: The Last Days* (1978)

Trew, S., *Britain, Mihailović and the Chetniks, 1941–42* (Basingstoke, 1998)

Trifković, G., 'The Yugoslav Partisans' Lost Victories: Operations in Montenegro and Bosnia-Herzegovina, 1944–1945', *Journal of Military History*, 82:1 (2018), 95–124

Trifković, S., 'Rivalry between Germany and Italy in Croatia, 1942–1943', *Historical Journal*, 36:4 (1993), 879–904

Trunk, I., *Judenrat: The Jewish Councils in Eastern Europe under Nazi Occupation* (New York, 1977)

Tucholski, J., *Cichociemni* (Warsaw, 1984)

Turner, B., *Outpost of Occupation: How the Channel Islands Survived Nazi Rule 1940–45* (2010)

Turner, D., *Kiriakos: A British Partisan in Wartime Greece* (1982)

Turski, M., *Polish Witnesses to the Shoah* (2010)

Tyas, S., *SS-Major Horst Kopkow: From the Gestapo to British Intelligence* (Stroud, 2017)

Ungváry, K., *Battle for Budapest: 100 Days in World War II* (New York, 2011)

Vakar, N., *Belorussia: The Making of a Nation* (Cambridge, MA, 1956)

Valentine, I., *Station 43: Audley End House and SOE's Polish Section* (Stroud, 2004)

Vaughan, H., *Doctor to the Resistance: The Heroic True Story of an American Surgeon and his Family in Occupied Paris* (Lincoln, NB, 2005)

Vercors, *Le Silence de la mer* (Geneva, 1945)

Verhoeyen, E., *La Belgique occupée. De l'an 40 à la Libération* (Brussels, 1994)

Verity, H., *We Landed by Moonlight: Secret RAF Landings in France, 1940–1944* (1998)

Verlander, H., *My War in SOE* (Bromley, 2010)

Verna, F. P., 'Notes on Italian Rule in Dalmatia under Bastianini, 1941–1943', *International History Review*, 12:3 (1990), 441–60

Verneret, H., *Teenage Resistance Fighter: With the Maquisards in Occupied France* (Oxford, 2017)

Vilhjálmsson, V. Örn and Blüdnikow, B., 'Rescue, Expulsion, and Collaboration: Denmark's Difficulties with its World War II Past', *Jewish Political Studies Review*, 18:3/4 (2006), 3–29

Villon, P., *Résistant de la première heure* (Paris, 1983)

Vinen, R., *The Unfree French: Life under the Occupation* (2006)

Vistel, A., *Nuit sans ombre* (Paris, 1970)

Vomécourt, P. de, *Who Lived to See the Day: France in Arms* (1961)

Vučković, Z., *A Balkan Tragedy – Yugoslavia, 1941–1946: Memoirs of a Guerrilla Fighter* (New York, 2004)

Wachsmann, N., *KL: A History of the Nazi Concentration Camps* (2015)

Wake, N., *The Autobiography of the Woman the Gestapo called the White Mouse* (Melbourne, 1985)

Walker, J., *Poland Alone: Britain, SOE and the Collapse of Polish Resistance* (Stroud, 2008)

Walker, S., *Hide and Seek: The Irish Priest in the Vatican who Defied the Nazi Command: A Dramatic True Story of Rivalry and Survival during World War II* (2011)

Walters, A.-M., *Moondrop to Gascony* (1946)

Walters, G., *Hunting Evil* (2009)

Ward, J. Mace, *Priest, Politician, Collaborator: Jozef Tiso and the Making of Fascist Slovakia* (Ithaca, NY, 2013)
Warlimont, W., *Inside Hitler's Headquarters* (1964)
Warmbrunn, W., *The Dutch under German Occupation* (Stanford, CA, 1963)
—*The German Occupation of Belgium* (New York, 1993)
Warner, G., 'Allies, Government and Resistance: The Belgian Political Crisis of November 1944', *Transactions of the Royal Historical Society*, 28 (1978), 45–60
Warrack, G., *Travel by Dark: After Arnhem* (1963)
Wasserstein, B., *On the Eve: The Jews of Europe before the Second World War* (2012)
—*The Ambiguity of Virtue: Gertrude van Tijn and the Fate of the Dutch Jews* (Cambridge, MA, 2014)
Watt, G., *The Comet Connection: Escape from Hitler's Europe* (Lexington, KY, 1990)
Wegner, B. (ed.), *From Peace to War: Germany, Soviet Russia and the West* (Providence, RI, 1997)
Weitz, M. Collins, *Sisters in the Resistance: How Women Fought to Free France, 1940–1945* (New York, 1995)
Wellsted, I., *SAS with the Maquis: In Action with the French Resistance, June–September 1944* (Barnsley, 2016)
Werth, A., *Russia at War* (1964)
Wheeler, M., *Britain and the War for Yugoslavia, 1940–1943* (Boulder, CO, 1980)
Whittam, J. R., 'Drawing the Line: Britain and the Emergence of the Trieste Question, January 1941–May 1945', *English Historical Review*, 106 (1991), 346–70
Wieczynski, J. (ed.), *Operation Barbarossa: The German Attack on the Soviet Union, June 22, 1941* (Salt Lake City, UT, 1993)
Wieviorka, O., *Orphans of the Republic: The Nation's Legislators in Vichy France* (Cambridge, MA, 2009)
—*The French Resistance* (Cambridge, MA, 2016)
—*The Resistance in Western Europe, 1940–1945* (New York, 2019)
Wildgen, J., 'The Liberation of the Valle d'Aosta, 1943–1945', *Journal of Modern History*, 42:1 (1970), 21–41
Wilhelm, M. de Blasio, *The Other Italy: Italian Resistance in World War II* (New York, 1988)
Wilkinson, P., *Foreign Fields: The Story of an SOE Operative* (1997)
—and Bright Astley, J., *Gubbins and SOE* (1993)
Williams, H., *Parachutes, Patriots and Partisans: The Special Operations Executive and Yugoslavia* (2003)
Williamson, D., *The Polish Underground 1939–1947* (Barnsley, 2012)
Winkler, H., *The Age of Catastrophe: A History of the West, 1914–1945* (New Haven, CT, 2015)
Winter, P., 'Penetrating Hitler's High Command: Anglo-Polish HUMINT, 1939–1945', *War in History*, 18 (2011), 85–108
Wood, T. and Jankowski, S., *Karski: How One Man Tried to Stop the Holocaust* (New York, 1994)
Woodhouse, C. M., *The Struggle for Greece, 1941–1949* (1976)
—*Something Ventured* (1982)
Woolf, S. (ed.), *The Rebirth of Italy* (1972)
Wright, G., 'Reflections on the French Resistance (1940–1944)', *Political Science Quarterly*, 23:3 (1962), 336–49
Wylie, N. (ed.), *The Politics and Strategy of Clandestine War: Special Operations Executive 1940–46* (2006)
Wynne, B., *No Drums . . . No Trumpets: The Story of Mary Lindell* (1961)
Young, G., *In Trust and Treason: The Strange Story of Suzanne Warren* (1959)
Young, K. (ed.), *The Diaries of Sir Robert Bruce Lockhart*, vol. 2: *1939–1965* (1980)
Zaretsky, R., *Nîmes at War: Religion, Politics, and Public Opinion in the Gard, 1938–1944* (Philadelphia, PA, 1995)

Zawodny, J., *Nothing but Honour: The Story of the Warsaw Uprising, 1944* (1978)
Zbik, J., *First to Return* (Wrocław, 2017)
Zembsch-Schreve, G., *Pierre Lalande, Special Agent: The Wartime Memoirs of Guido Zembsch-Schreve* (1996)
Zimmerman, J., *The Polish Underground and the Jews, 1939–1945* (New York, 2015)
Zuckerman, Y., *A Surplus of Memory: Chronicle of the Warsaw Ghetto Uprising* (Los Angeles, CA, 1993)

Index